MW01612101

SMALL BUSINESS MANAGEMENT & ENTREPRENEURSHIP

KENT Series in International Dimensions of Business
Series Consulting Editor, David A. Ricks

Adler, *International Dimensions of Organizational Behavior,* Second Edition
AlHashim/Arpan, *International Dimensions of Accounting,* Third Edition
Dowling/Schuler, *International Dimensions of Human Resource Management*
Folks/Aggarwal, *International Dimensions of Financial Management*
Garland/Farmer/Taylor, *International Dimensions of Business Policy and Strategy,* Second Edition
Litka, *International Dimensions of the Legal Environment of Business,* Second Edition
Phatak, *International Dimensions of Management,* Second Edition
Terpstra, *International Dimensions of Marketing,* Second Edition

KENT Series in Human Resource Management
Series Consulting Editor, Richard W. Beatty

Bernardin/Beatty, *Performance Appraisal: Assessing Human Behavior at Work*
Cascio, *Costing Human Resources: The Financial Impact of Behavior in Organizations,* Third Edition
Kavanagh/Gueutal/Tannenbaum, *Human Resource Information Systems: Development and Application*
Ledvinka/Scarpello, *Federal Regulation of Personnel and Human Resource Management,* Second Edition
McCaffery, *Employee Benefit Programs: A Total Compensation Perspective*
Wallace/Fay, *Compensation Theory and Practice,* Second Edition

KENT Series in Management
Carland/Carland, *Small Business Management: Tools for Success*
Davis/Cosenza, *Business Research for Decision Making,* Second Edition
Duncan/Ginter/Swayne, *Strategic Management of Health Care Organizations*
Finley, *Entrepreneurial Strategies: Text and Cases*
Kemper/Yehudai, *Experiencing Operations Management: A Walk-Through*
Lane/DiStefano, *International Management Behavior,* Second Edition
Mendenhall/Oddou, *Readings and Cases in International Human Resource Management*
Mitchell, *Human Resource Management: An Economic Approach*
Nkomo/Fottler/McAfee, *Applications in Personnel/Human Resource Management: Cases, Exercises, and Skill Builders,* Second Edition
Plunkett/Attner, *Introduction to Management,* Fourth Edition
Punnett, *Experiencing International Management*
Punnett/Ricks, *International Business*
Roberts/Hunt, *Organizational Behavior*
Scarpello/Ledvinka, *Personnel/Human Resource Management: Environments and Functions,* Second Edition
Singer, *Human Resource Management*
Stahl/Grigsby, *Strategic Management for Decision Making*
Starling, *The Changing Environment of Business,* Third Edition
Steers/Ungson/Mowday, *Managing Effective Organizations: An Introduction*
Tate/Hoy/Stewart/Cox/Scarpello, *Small Business Management & Entrepreneurship*
Tosi, *Organizational Behavior and Management: A Contingency Approach*

SMALL BUSINESS MANAGEMENT & ENTREPRENEURSHIP

CURTIS E. TATE, JR.
University of Georgia

JAMES F. COX
University of Georgia

FRANK HOY
Georgia State University

VIDA SCARPELLO
University of Florida

W. WOODROW STEWART
Stewart, Melvin & House

PWS-KENT PUBLISHING COMPANY

Boston

PWS–KENT
Publishing Company

20 Park Plaza
Boston, Massachusetts 02116

Copyright © 1992 by PWS-KENT Publishing Company

All rights reserved. No part of this book may be reproduced, stored in a retrieval system, or transcribed, in any form or by an means—electronic, mechanical, photocopying, recording, or otherwise—without the prior written permission of PWS-KENT Publishing Company.

PWS-KENT Publishing Company is a division of Wadsworth, Inc.

Library of Congress Cataloging-in-Publication Data

Small business management/entrepreneurship / Curtis E. Tate, Jr. . . .
  [et al.].
        p. cm.
    Includes index.
    ISBN 0–534–92357–7
    1. Small business—Management. I. Tate, Curtis E.
HD62.7.S594   1992
658.02'2—dc20   91–9751
                                                          CIP

Sponsoring Editor: Rolf A. Janke
Production Coordinator: Robine Andrau
Manufacturing Coordinator: Peter D. Leatherwood
Cover Designer: Julia Gecha
Cover Photo: © 1990 Lightscapes/The Stock Market
Interior Illustrator: George Nichols
Cover Printer: New England Book Components, Inc.
Typesetter: Graphic Composition, Inc.
Printer and Binder: Arcata Graphics/Halliday

Printed in the United States of America
92 93 94 95 96 — 10 9 8 7 6 5 4 3 2 1

BRIEF CONTENTS

CONTENTS

PART FOUR
MARKETING YOUR PRODUCTS AND SERVICES   237

PREFACE

The economic shrinkage found today in the world of large business enterprises creates an opportunity for small businesses to fill a void. The future for small businesses appears bright. It is our perception that small businesses will be the door to our nation's economic future. If that future is to provide us with employment and growing income as well as increased output of goods and services, then this segment of the economy must function dynamically. It is our goal to contribute to that dynamic activity.

This book has been designed for a diverse audience. It is written to address the needs of the individuals who aspire to own and operate their own business as well as those who already own and operate one.

Small Business Management & Entrepreneurship focuses on the total firm. It provides information for today's and tomorrow's managers and owners of small businesses. The comprehensiveness of this text is evident in the titles of its thirty chapters. Taken as a whole, these chapters provide thorough coverage of the problems involved in planning, implementing, and operating a small business. You are led from the origin of an idea for a business to analyzing that idea's feasibility, planning operations, running the business successfully, and, finally, considering the issues involved in selling or retiring from the business.

This text is particularly valuable because it contains many topics not addressed in similar books. Many innovative chapters provide information and advice vital to the success of any manager or owner of a small business. These innovative chapters include the following: Chapter 4, "Comparing New and Old Business Opportunities"; Chapter 5, "Valuation of an Existing Business"; the section of Chapter 7 that discusses franchising your own business; Chapter 8, "Choosing Your Professional Advisers"; Chapter 9, "Negotiation"; Chapter 13; "Your Business and the Tax Laws"; Chapter 14, "Business Agreements You Will Need"; Chapter 20, "Managing Operations"; Chapter 25, "Compensating Your Employees"; Chapter 26, "Staffing Your Business"; Chapter 29, "Managing a Unionized Workforce"; and Chapter 30, "When All Else Fails—Bankruptcy."

In addition to this coverage of important but often overlooked topics, this text has a number of strengths. The writing style is accessible, with the material addressed directly to you, the reader. Experience has shown that such an approach helps the instructor, student, and practitioner comprehend and use the information effectively.

A number of features enhance the effectiveness of this text. Each of the seven main parts of the book begins with an overview of the chapters within that part. These synopses orient the reader to what is to come. As a summary of the chapter content, they also provide a valuable learning instrument if course time is insufficient to allow for the assignment of a particular chapter. Students can still get the gist of that chapter's material by reading this overview.

Another valuable feature is the inclusion of many exhibits. These numerous and diverse supplements to the chapter content provide many real-world examples and models that the budding entrepreneur can use. A number of the exhibits are forms that may be used to collect data needed in planning or implementing a business activity. These forms can help any entrepreneur in the course of developing his or her business.

Each chapter ends with a set of assignments that can be used to reinforce or extend the material. Taking the form of review questions, discussion questions, or activities, these assignments provide instructors and students with an opportunity to assess student comprehension.

Perhaps the most significant addition to this text is its body of thirty-three real-world cases. These cases, field researched and written exclusively for this textbook, offer actual examples of small businesses facing the challenges in startup, operations, finances, personnel, marketing, and continuance that are discussed in the chapters. The businesses, locations, and issues raised by the cases cover a diversity of activities, providing a rich vein of material for analysis and discussion.

Supplementing this text and its cases are two ancillaries: the *Instructor's Manual* and the computerized *Test Bank*.

This book was conceived over a long period of time; as one coauthor puts it, *Small Business Management & Entrepreneurship* is the result of a lifetime of observation of academic and practical experience in the world of small business. The authors have been carefully chosen for reasons of authorship, academic stature, hands-on experience, and area of expertise. As a group, their areas make a comprehensive entrepreneurship package:

- Professor Curtis E. Tate, Jr., a generalist whose expertise covers small business management and case research, writing, and teaching
- Professor James F. Cox, lead professor of the University of Georgia's Production Group, whose specialty is production
- Professor Frank Hoy, Carl R. Zwerner Professor of Family-Owned Businesses at Georgia State University, whose area is the small business
- Professor Vida Scarpello, of the University of Florida, who focuses on human resource management
- W. Woodrow Stewart, a senior partner in Stewart, Melvin, and House, whose specialty is business and tax law

We have a strong appreciation of what it takes to make an enterprise successful. The results of this orientation are evident in the success enjoyed by our students and clients.

We would be remiss if we failed to extend special thanks to Mary Combs Tate, Mary Ann Cox, Patricia Hoy, and Lynda Stewart for their patience and support in this undertaking.

We also wish to express our gratitude for the untiring support that our secretarial staff has provided. We say thanks to Melanie Blakeman, Sharon Cheely, Kristen Crawford, Nancy Fajardo, Mary Moore, Billie Najour, Robin Ricks, and Karen Turner. In addition, we appreciate Laurie Ann Cox for her picture-taking efforts.

A special thanks is given to our many colleagues for their diligent work in researching and writing cases. These efforts resulted in excellent case material appearing in this book, as well as useful case notes that appear in the *Instructor's Manual*.

We also wish to thank Mark Starik for his untiring efforts in the preparation of the *Instructor's Manual*.

Finally, we and the publisher wish to acknowledge the following reviewers for their valuable insights:

- J. Michael Cicero, Highline Community College
- Paula S. Funkhouser, Truckee Meadows Community College
- Otha L. Gray, Virginia State University
- Nicholas Sarantakes, Austin Community College
- Melvin Stanford, Mankato State University

Curtis E. Tate, Jr.
James F. Cox
Frank Hoy
Vida Scarpello
W. Woodrow Stewart

INTRODUCTION

Being an entrepreneur is a unique, challenging, rewarding, and sometimes quite frustrating experience. You can be the owner, manager, designer, buyer, seller, transporter, and collector for the business. Most entrepreneurs wear several of these hats at the same time. Further, you may be the doer also—the worker who produces the good or service. Obviously, you cannot be an expert at each of these activities, but you must know enough about each to judge the impact that actions taken in each of these areas will have on other areas—and more importantly on the company's bottom line. You are on the firing line most of the time in a small business—there is no room for the lazy or the faint-hearted. Good ideas require planning and hard work to implement. This text is designed to provide you with the knowledge to make your business ventures and ideas succeed. The book will carry you step by step from the inception of your business idea to your concluding relationship with the business.

Structure of the Book

The text is divided into thirty chapters that cover topics vital to the small business owner and entrepreneur. While we would like each student to read each chapter and work each assignment, we also know that the time constraints placed on you by other classes, by work, and by family activities make such an outcome unlikely. We have attempted to write everything that we felt was extremely important for the small business student to know. We also wanted to provide enough in-depth coverage so that you could use each tool or technique effectively without requiring additional assistance of several texts. We wanted to create a text that you would not only enjoy during your course but also find indispensable after the course, when you are managing your own small business.

We have structured the thirty chapters into seven parts, each of which begins with a concise overview of each chapter in that part. Thus if your instructor has to eliminate entire chapters to tailor the material to class needs and time constraints, you can read these overviews to gain a broad understanding of the chapter topics.

The seven parts of the text are

- Part One: You and Your Business
- Part Two: Entering a New or Old Business
- Part Three: Getting It All Together

- Part Four: Marketing Your Products and Services
- Part Five: Managing Your Operations
- Part Six: Managing Your Personnel
- Part Seven: The Crisis

Part One is an introduction to the world of small business and entrepreneurship. Chapter 1 describes personal characteristics of successful small business owners or managers. The chapter includes vignettes that illustrate successful small business ventures. Business success or failure generally depends on the owner's ability to plan and control business activities. Chapter 2 explores several characteristics related to poor and successful business owners. Chapter 3 contains several ways of deciding on what business is right or wrong for you. This part provides you an overview of what small businesses are all about and allows you to assess your personal characteristics against those generally viewed as required for successful management of a small business.

Part Two begins in Chapter 4 by exploring the positive and negative factors related to both starting a new business and acquiring an existing business. Chapter 5 helps you determine how much an existing business is worth. This material is must reading for anyone considering the purchase of an existing business. An appendix to the chapter provides a detailed illustration of the valuation process. Chapter 6 helps you determine the feasibility of a business idea. The following chapter offers detailed information on franchising, including discussion of the best and worst franchising opportunities and the risks and opportunities of franchising. While you should know as much as possible about the various technical aspects of your business (financial, legal, accounting, and insurance), it is impossible for you to know everything. You must therefore select and depend on advisers to keep you informed about the risks and opportunities you face. Chapter 8 addresses the subject of your team of advisers. Because you will continually negotiate with your workers, managers, vendors, and customers, you should understand how to be a skillful negotiator. Chapter 9 provides help in developing negotiating skills.

Part Three explores ways to structure your business for success. Its six chapters cover the legal forms your business can take, how to raise capital to organize and support your business activities, how to develop your financial plan to determine your capital needs, understanding the tax laws and your business obligations, how to structure the business agreements you will need, and how to develop a formal business plan. This part provides you with the knowledge to start and maintain your business on a sound legal and financial basis.

Part Four describes how to market your products and services. The theme of these three chapters is that customer satisfaction and profit maximization are two long-range goals of the marketing concept for any business. Chapter 16 discusses how to identify your customers. The next chapter covers developing a marketing strategy based on your business's competitive edges (price, quality, lead time, and so on). Chapter 18 completes the discussion by showing how the business's efforts can be aimed at achieving customer satisfaction.

Part Five focuses on designing and managing your operations and inventories to support your business strategy. The first chapter provides an overview of operations and the significant issues. Chapter 20, on managing operations, describes such new approaches as the just-in-time philosophy and the OPT philosophy. The chapter describes several techniques related to designing a more effective organization, providing examples to assist you in learning how to use these techniques. Chapter 21 addresses methods of managing inventory more effectively. Information systems and computer systems are described in Chapter 22 to provide help in selecting software and hardware. Lastly Chapter 23 looks at controlling your operations so that you know what your performance is and how to improve it; such information management is of critical importance in managing your business.

Part Six, about managing your personnel, consists of six chapters. These chapters explore planning the size and scope of your workforce, compensating them, staffing your business, training your employees, and managing in a unionized and nonunionized environment. The chapters address several laws, policies, and procedures related to hiring, managing, compensating, training, and firing your employees. This information is vital to managing the most valuable asset your business has—your employees.

Part Seven is about bankruptcy. While no one wishes to contemplate filing bankruptcy, you should know what it is, what your options are, and what the procedures and ramifications of filing bankruptcy are.

We have given you a brief overview of the entire book. Each issue addressed in the book presents decision points; the choices you make affect the present and future directions of your business. You may not even realize the full impact of your decision at the time that you make it. In this text we attempt to provide you with enough information on how to make an informed decision, how to examine your options, and how to minimize the risk of undesirable results. As you study this text, you will get an idea of the power of the material presented, but its true value will surface in the future when you face these decision points and must choose the future of your business.

The World of Small Business

Often we have heard people say, "I want to start my own business." Some people make this statement with little thought of it becoming a reality. Perhaps they are dreamers, not implementers. Others say it with serious intent and a commitment to making it come true. As we have observed for years, a requisite for becoming an entrepreneur is to have guts in the tummy and brass on the face. One of our students, after entering his second business, returned to verify this observation. "You are right," he said. "It does take guts in the tummy and brass on the face." Some twenty-five years later, he continues as a successful business owner. Without question, he has always had serious intent and commitment toward his business.

You may find it useful to answer the questions found in the exhibit at the end of this Introduction.

Those who want to start a business can have a number of different reasons:

- To be one's own boss
- To be independent
- To make a lot of money
- To have the prestige of an entrepreneur
- To provide a product or service that one would like to sell
- To have the opportunity for creative expression that one's own business would provide
- To have the power that comes from owning one's own business
- To control the number of hours worked
- To receive the tax benefits that come from owning a business
- To provide for an early retirement
- To live the good life that one's own business can provide

Perhaps there are other items you could add to this list.

Another reason that many pursue a small or independent business is family. Through the years, many of our students have followed into a family business. Such a beginning can become the start to a larger career. Once a student sought the counsel of one of the coauthors. The student had grown up in rural south Georgia, but thought he preferred city life to an agricultural one. His father, however, was pressuring him to return home after graduation. In his discussion with the professor, he indicated that his father and grandfather each had 300 or so acres of fertile farmland. Then he said, "You know, I am the only one available to look after those farms." The coauthor responded, "I don't believe this decision was ever yours to make. It was made for you a long time ago. Just think about the economics of it. You can't afford to do anything but go back—you've got too much at stake." The student did return home. A number of years later, he and the coauthor were talking again. He was asked, "Wasn't it right for you to go back home?" His response was, "I couldn't see it then, but I can now. I am very glad I came back." Today that individual, in addition to his farms, owns a number of small businesses and is president of one of the local banks.

There are probably as many definitions of small business as there are references to it. We are certain that any definition of the term *small or independent business* would be arbitrary. We use the term in the traditional sense to mean a business whose ownership is closely held. As you survey the cases included in this book, you will note that some closely held businesses are hardly small; they may represent substantial capital investment and dollar sales. However, they are businesses that are owned and controlled by a small number of persons.

Historically, American businesses started as small enterprises—for example, General Electric began with Thomas A. Edison's small shop; Ford Motor Company started with Henry Ford's small shop and the "Tin Lizzy"; Rubbermaid grew from James R. Caldwell's creation of a rubber dustpan. There are numerous other examples of small businesses that grew into large-scale enterprises. Many of the products and services that we enjoy could have originated only in the flexible environment of the smaller firm. The computer hardware and software field offers many examples, the most famous of which may be Apple Computer, which was begun in a garage.

Small businesses play an important role in the economy today. From 1970 to 1980, Canadian employment growth occurred in small firms, not in large firms. In fact, the large enterprises in Canadian economy experienced zero employment growth. Tom Peters, in an article in the July 1988 *INC*, indicates the importance of small businesses in the United States. From 1980 to 1988, he notes, the Fortune 500 companies lost 2.8 million jobs. During the same period, however, employment increased by 10 million—the majority of which were created by small, growing companies.

The founders of these small businesses are a varied group. As a coauthor's father often remarked, "Some people have to start their own business in order to have a job and an income." Many new entrepreneurs are immigrants. They are the Asians, the Europeans, the Hispanics, the Middle Easterners, and the Africans. Many small businesses are started today because of language and literacy barriers; many of these people have no other choice but to work for themselves.

Another significant group of new entrepreneurs are those people who have been displaced by the decline in smokestack industries and the growth of foreign competition. The security of large enterprises is fading as benefits deteriorate and early retirements and job losses become more prevalent. Consequently, many of these economically displaced individuals have turned to establishing their own businesses. Exhibit I.1 reveals the growth in the number of discharged executives who start their own business. Today, women outnumber men in starting new businesses, and women own 35 percent of all franchises.

Another group of entrepreneurs are those belonging to the cottage or home industry category. These are persons who work at home. Some industries employing such labor are furniture, musical instruments, quilts, special apparel, woven fabric, wood crafts, china painting, jewelry, pottery, stained glass, and leather goods. In addition, some workers produce services in the home environment, such as processing information with a computer.

Life Cycles and the Small Business

You may view business in the context of a number of life cycles:

1. The life cycle of the owner or owners, with their many decision points
2. The life cycle of the owner's (or owners') heirs, with decision points for themselves, the parent-owner, and the business
3. The life cycle of the business itself
4. The life cycles of all employees
5. The life cycle of the industry
6. The life cycles of suppliers
7. The life cycle of the product or service provided
8. The life cycle of the customers

Exhibit I.1

**PERCENTAGE OF DISCHARGED EXECUTIVES WHO HAVE STARTED
THEIR OWN BUSINESSES**

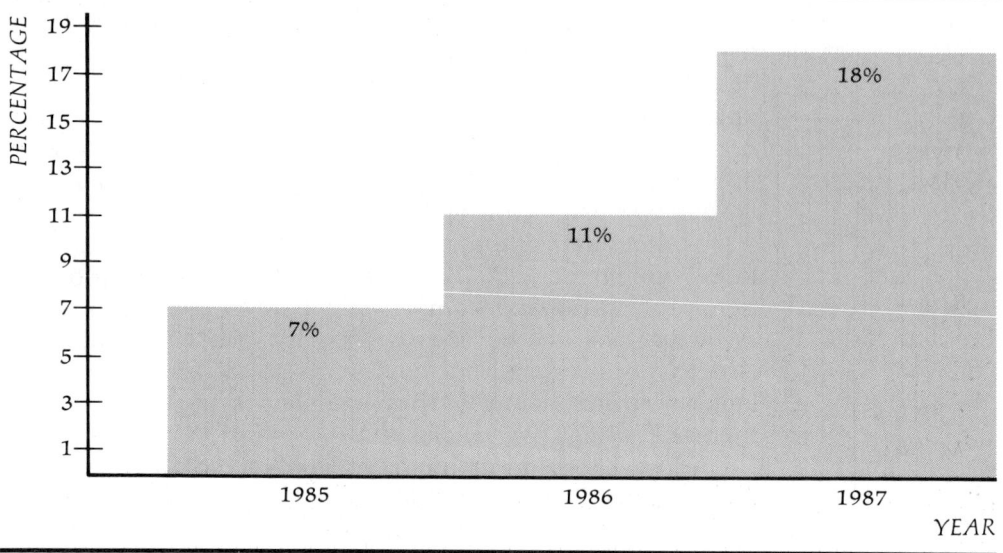

Reprinted with permission, *Inc.* magazine (February 1988). Copyright © 1988 by Goldhirsh Group, Inc., 38 Commercial Wharf, Boston, MA 02110.

Exhibit I.2 shows what each of these life cycles looks like. Each life cycle generates various decision points, each requiring significant decisions. The fact that the small business tends to be a very personal matter affecting the lives of both the business owner and family members makes the life cycle concept a useful context in which to study small business. You will find this concept arise throughout the text.

Where are you in your life cycle? Is your age comparable to that of a traditional student? Have you been out of school for five, ten, or more years? Do you have the know-how to establish and successfully operate a business? Are you able to assume the risk of owning your own business? Do you have the resources necessary for financing your own business? Do you think that you need five or ten years of work experience to provide you with the opportunity to accumulate the capital for starting your business? Whatever the stage of your life, if you are interested in owning your own business, this text will help prepare you to meet the challenges of opening and operating that business.

Exhibit I.2
LIFE CYCLES OF THE SMALL BUSINESS

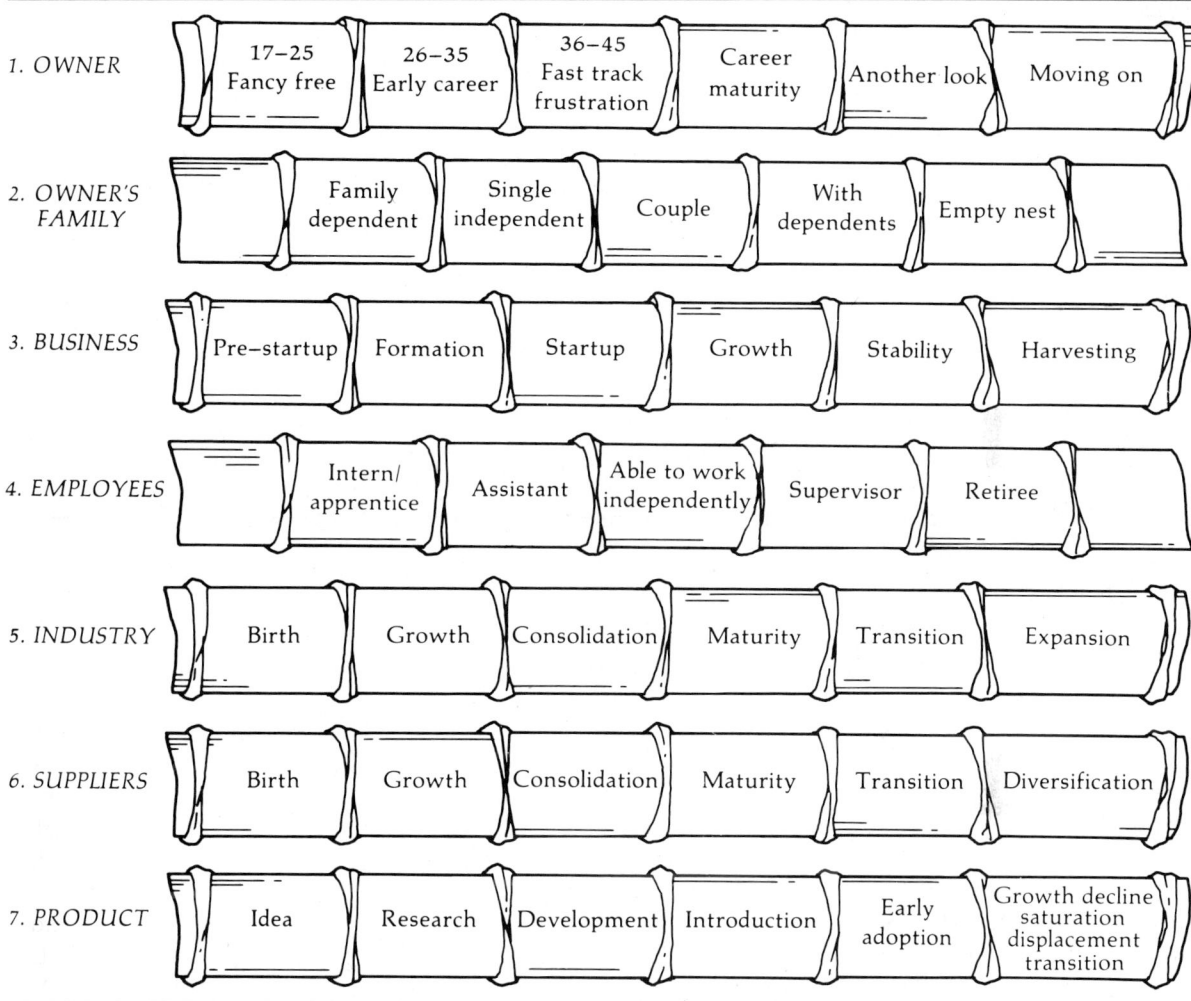

1. OWNER	17–25 Fancy free	26–35 Early career	36–45 Fast track frustration	Career maturity	Another look	Moving on
2. OWNER'S FAMILY	Family dependent	Single independent	Couple	With dependents	Empty nest	
3. BUSINESS	Pre–startup	Formation	Startup	Growth	Stability	Harvesting
4. EMPLOYEES	Intern/ apprentice	Assistant	Able to work independently	Supervisor	Retiree	
5. INDUSTRY	Birth	Growth	Consolidation	Maturity	Transition	Expansion
6. SUPPLIERS	Birth	Growth	Consolidation	Maturity	Transition	Diversification
7. PRODUCT	Idea	Research	Development	Introduction	Early adoption	Growth decline saturation displacement transition

Exhibit I.3
PERFORMING A PERSONAL SELF-ANALYSIS

The purpose of the questionnaire that follows is to aid in the analysis and evaluation of the objectives, responsibilities, abilities, interests, health, and economic status of the businessperson in relation to running a business versus working for someone else.

Please indicate your choice by checking the appropriate space.

1. My objective in life is
   a. To make a lot of money _____
   b. To be my own boss _____

Exhibit I.3
PERFORMING A PERSONAL SELF-ANALYSIS (*continued*)

    c. To have a comfortable living _____

    d. To have a business of my own that will allow me leisure time _____

    e. To work for someone else _____

    f. To avoid accepting responsibility

        (1) For providing employment for others _____

        (2) For providing products or service to others _____

    g. To spend whatever time and effort necessary to achieve success _____

2. My marital status is

    a. Single _____

        Married _____

        Separated or divorced _____

    b. I have children   Yes _____   No _____

        Ages _____

    c. Given these responsibilities, I plan to commit myself to (circle one):   20   40   60   80   hours per week to the business.

3. My education is

    a. Elementary _____

    b. High school

        1 year _____   2 years _____

        3 years _____   4 years _____

    c. Technical school _____

        Type of training _____

    d. College

        1 year _____   2 years _____

        3 years _____   4 years _____

        Kind of degree _____

        Major _____   Minor _____

        Master's degree _____

        Kind _____

        Fields _____

        Other _____

4. My experience is (list in order from latest to earliest)

    a. Last or current job _____

        Employer _____

        Title _____

        Dates of employment _____ to _____

    b. Job _____

       * Employer _____

Title _____

Dates of employment _____ to _____

c. Job _____

Employer _____

Title _____

Dates of employment _____ to _____

Abilities I gained from each employment situation

_____

_____

_____

_____

5. My expertise is (check one)

Type	High	Medium	Low
_____	_____	_____	_____
_____	_____	_____	_____
_____	_____	_____	_____

6. My hobbies are _____

_____

_____

7. I spend my free time doing _____

_____

_____

8. My capabilities are

a. Directing the activities of others _____

b. Planning an activity in a manner that takes the least time, effort, and material _____

c. Serving people in a pleasing manner _____

d. Helping people resolve their personal differences _____

e. Managing money _____

f. Keeping records _____

g. Organizing people, money, machines, and things to produce products or services _____

h. Effectively following instructions and directions of others _____

i. Being my own boss _____

j. Being a self-starter _____

k. Taking initiative _____

l. Making decisions _____

m. Creating new ideas for products and services _____

n. Other _____

9. My inadequacies are

a. I can't make decisions _____

b. I postpone making decisions _____

c. I try to get others to make decisions for me _____

Exhibit I.3
PERFORMING A PERSONAL SELF-ANALYSIS (*continued*)

    d. I dislike assuming responsibility   _____

    e. I avoid responsibility whenever possible   _____

    f. I do not handle money well   _____

    g. I seem unable to keep my checkbook balanced   _____

    h. I am generally insecure without someone to guide and support me   _____

    i. Other   _____

10. Regarding my health

    a. I always feel good   _____

    b. I can work two jobs without ever getting tired   _____

    c. I frequently find it difficult to finish the day   _____

    d. I am absent from work

        (1) One day a week   _____

        (2) One day every two weeks   _____

        (3) One to two days per month   _____

        (4) Four to five days a year   _____

        (5) Rarely   _____

    e. My last complete physical was (date)   _____

    f. I have these known health problems   _____

        _____

    g. I have no known health problems   _____

11. My health permits me to (check one)

    a. Travel a great amount   Yes   _____   No   _____

    b. Engage in a lot of physical work   Yes   _____   No   _____

    c. Work long hours   Yes   _____   No   _____

    d. Function well in tense situations   Yes   _____   No   _____

    e. Use my eyes extensively   Yes   _____   No   _____

12. My health keeps me from   _____

    _____

13. Regarding my present economic status

    a. My net worth is

        (1) Equity value of real estate $ _____

        (2) Cash surrender value of life insurance $ _____

        (3) Marketable securities $ _____

        (4) Savings $ _____

        (5) Other $ _____

    b. My annual income is

        (1) Salary $ _____

        (2) Special income $ _____

  (3) Investment

    (a) Rental income $ _____

    (b) Stocks $ _____

    (c) Bonds $ _____

      Total investment income $ _____

  (4) Interest $ _____

  (5) Annuities $ _____

  (6) Trust $ _____

  (7) Estate $ _____

  (8) Other $ _____

    Total annual income $ _____

 c. My annual financial responsibilities are

  (1) Mortgage payments $ _____

  (2) House insurance $ _____

  (3) Real and personal property taxes $ _____

  (4) Car payments $ _____

  (5) Life insurance $ _____

  (6) Utility bills $ _____

  (7) Other loan repayments $ _____

  (8) Alimony and child support $ _____

  (9) Children's education expense $ _____

  (10) Medical or dental expense $ _____

  (11) Medical insurance $ _____

  (12) Household expense $ _____

  (13) House or lawn maintenance $ _____

  (14) Auto expense $ _____

  (15) Food $ _____

  (16) Business or professional expense $ _____

  (17) Other $ _____

    Total annual personal expense $ _____

14. How much can I afford to risk? $ _____

15. Considering my responsibilities, my interests, my hobbies, my health, and my economic status, I am willing (a) to devote _____ hours per week to the business, and (b) to invest $ _____ in the business.

16. What specific kind of business would I be most happy operating as an owner-manager? _____

_____

_____

_____

_____

17. How would I compensate for my inadequacies? _____

_____

Exhibit I.3
PERFORMING A PERSONAL SELF-ANALYSIS (*continued*)

18. After carefully reviewing the answers I have given to the questions above, being honest and frank with myself, I think that I could accomplish my objectives in life, and achieve a reasonable level of success and happiness by

   a. Having my own independent business   _____

   b. Working for someone else   _____

YOU AND YOUR BUSINESS

Chapter 1
So, You Want to Make a Lot of Money
This chapter explains the role of setting life objectives and planning for your small business. Life objectives play an important part in defining what business you should be involved in or whether owning or managing a small business is for you. Four vignettes in the chapter describe highly successful businesses that started small and achieved wealth for their founders. These vignettes demonstrate that personal characteristics such as a good idea, a willingness to persevere, and patience, tenacity, and stability are fundamental to small business success.

Chapter 2
Small Business Anticipation
Your ability to work hard and think clearly are good predictors of your business success. Success is not an accident; it is based on a well-formulated plan that is properly executed. In contrast, failure is many times the result of poor planning and execution. Success and failure are also based on the business owner's personal knowledge, skills, and characteristics.

Chapter 3
What Business for You?
This chapter provides you with several alternatives for deciding what business is for you. These include an existing business, a specific locale, a target customer group, using new technology or a traditional technology, or basing the business on your talent, expertise, abilities, interests, or hobby. Some entrepreneurs go into a family business.

SO, YOU WANT TO MAKE A LOT OF MONEY

The simple statement, "I want to make a lot of money," is one we have heard many times. Yet in most instances a series of complex activities is required to achieve this objective. Our purpose in this chapter is to aid you in identifying the process that will facilitate your endeavor of making a lot of money.

We will begin by explaining the role of objectives in making a lot of money. We will then place in perspective the role of planning in your business endeavor. You will be given directions on how to plan and what to include in your plan. Next, we stress the importance of the image of your business.

In the process of choosing a business, we emphasize the importance of predetermined objectives and the criteria needed for achieving these objectives.

In keeping with the chapter title, we have included four vignettes describing entrepreneurs who started small and grew to be wealthy. These vignettes are taken from known business situations. They are followed by notes on how to search for a business opportunity. The last section of the chapter deals with the personal attributes essential to success in business: expertise, patience, tenacity, and stability.

After reading this chapter, you will be able to

- Explain the importance of objectives and planning to promoting business success
- Identify the factors that contributed to the success of four entrepreneurs
- List four personal attributes that are essential to success in business

The Role of Your Objectives

Observation has shown us the importance of defining your life's objectives. Until you have identified these objectives, you are unable to know what business is for you. The business you select should be the vehicle to facilitate the achievement of your objectives—for example, are you interested in making a lot of money fast, or are you willing to be patient and make it over a longer time? Which of these objectives you select will determine what business is for you: some businesses produce a lot of money in a hurry while others produce it more slowly. Later in the chapter we discuss how to choose the business that will best serve as the vehicle for achieving your objective.

Planning

In business, as in all endeavors, planning is a key element in the formulation of the activities essential for achieving your objectives. Your planning process should include the what, the how, the where, and the when of your entrepreneurial endeavor. Planning should not be thought of as a one-time event, but rather as a continuous process.

An efficient way to plan is to commit your plans to paper, i.e., to make a formal statement of your plans. Doing so will make your plans available for ready reference and will better serve you in periods of review.

Planning the What

In the *what* process, you will be planning your enterprise. You will want to define its value, its size, its location, and its structure. A crucial question to answer is what it will cost to establish your business. People often start to launch a business without truly dealing with these matters.

There are basic economic elements to consider before launching a business. These factors include identifying an economic base of sufficient strength to support your business. Some of these factors are

- Targeting the site for your business
- Determining the population for your market area, including defining the total population, the population by age segment, the education level of the population, and the population's per-capita income and income range by age segment
- Determining the demographic patterns
- Identifying the status of your potential competition
- Learning the state of the art or current technology for your business

The Business Plan

As you prepare to initiate this business, you will need to collect a lot of factual information in order to prepare a business plan. A business plan is a formal plan that contains all the essential information required to move the business from the idea stage to the opening-door stage. There is a sequence of events that the typical new business founder follows. This sequence involves identifying a series of cost items:

- Location
- Building or facility
- Parking accommodations
- Equipment
- Utilities
- Taxes (business, special, FICA, state and federal income, workers' compensation, and unemployment)

- Communication needs (including local and long-distance telephone, telex, electronic mail, and face-to-face)
- Inventory
- Management and other personnel

After identifying these cost factors, the business founder must prepare projections in the form of the following financial statements:

- An operating budget
- A cash-flow budget
- A capital budget
- A plan for financing your business

These points are covered in more detail at a later point in this text.

Image

If your business objective is to make a lot of money, you will need to be sensitive to the image your business projects. As you will become aware, many of the items listed above will impact on your firm's image. Therefore, as you deal with each of these items, you must implement your actions to support and achieve the image you want.

Choosing a Business

How can you select a business that will make you a lot of money? Your first step should be to see if your idea is one that has appeal to a large number of people. In the past, the entrepreneurs who succeeded were those who selected a product or service that appealed to the mass public—one that the masses would buy at a price the masses would pay. The vignettes that follow are examples of entrepreneurs whose businesses started small and grew larger, resulting in their owners becoming wealthy.[1]

Xavier Roberts of Original Appalachian Artworks

Xavier Roberts organized Original Appalachian Artworks (OAA) in 1978 to make Little People, the forerunners of the Original Cabbage Patch Kids. Since that time, his company has manufactured and sold over 500,000 of the hand-sewn babies at an average price of $135 each. In addition, the company makes and sells Furskin Bears and Bunnybees and receives royalties from over 100 licensees. The major licensee is Coleco, which had sales of approximately $316 million from its small version of Cabbage Patch Kids in 1984, its first year to sell the product. OAA employs approximately 300 people.

Roberts was reared in a small north Georgia community. His father died when he was a young boy, and his mother provided for her children by making quilts and other crafts. While he was a student at a junior college in his home town, Roberts learned the old German technique of soft sculpture, or needle molding.

---

1. These vignettes were field researched and written by Dr. Cynthia D. Heagy of the University of Georgia and Professor Glenda Brock of Christian Brothers University.

After making his first babies, modeled after his newborn nieces and nephews, Roberts displayed them at a state park gift shop where he worked summers to earn money for college expenses. Customers showed a strong interest in the dolls, but Roberts refused to sell them because of his strong attachment to them, based on the many hours he spent to make each one. Finally a persistent customer persuaded him to turn loose of one of the dolls. Still refusing to sell the doll, and without any forethought, Roberts told her she could "adopt" the baby for a fee of $30. This slip of the tongue was the genesis for the adoption concept for Cabbage Patch Kids. As the babies caught on, his mother and brothers and sisters helped make them, and Roberts showed the babies at arts and craft shows as well as the gift shop. When he went back to school that fall, Roberts talked six close friends into quitting school and pooling their resources to incorporate OAA.

The first task of the newly formed company was to renovate a former medical clinic into a showroom, which was renamed BabyLand General Hospital. One member of the group sold her car to raise money for the renovation. Great pains were taken to display the dolls in realistic settings so that people would become involved in the Cabbage Patch Kids fantasy. Also in keeping with the fantasy was the practice of including birth certificates and adoption papers with each baby.

When he started, Roberts had a credit card with an $800 limit. He would buy materials and sell enough dolls to pay off the balance and then charge another $800 of materials. He had no success in securing a loan from a bank. The company was on the verge of closing in 1981 when one of the partners left for a bank in Chattanooga resolving to return with money in his pockets. When he returned with a loan, the television program "Real People" was at BabyLand to film a story about the company. This publicity was a big break for OAA. Soon after, an arrangement was made with Coleco to produce a lower-priced version of the Cabbage Patch Kids. Then Cabbage Patch fever struck in a big way. Christmas 1983 saw near riots in stores as the demand for the babies far exceeded the supply. Employees at OAA were stunned when they returned from the Thanksgiving weekend to hear telephones ringing off the walls (until the lone Cleveland, Georgia, trunk line overloaded) and to see people swarming and helicopters landing. All this activity grew from the news media's attempt to get a story on the Cabbage Patch phenomenon. People began to call employees offering bribes for the dolls.

Roberts, who now owns 85 percent of OAA, works almost daily at the company. His major contribution always has been in the area of creating and stimulating product ideas. He ensures that the company adheres to its original purposes: to make only high-quality products indigenous to the north Georgia culture. While he makes all major decisions, Roberts has depended on former partners and managers to handle the day-to-day financial, managerial, and marketing phases of the company's operation. Team effort and maintaining an open atmosphere conducive to creativity are the philosophy of OAA.

One reward to Roberts is that he has raised himself from a humble background to wealth. He says that he knew without a doubt that he was going to be rich some day, but did not know how he would do it. Although he sincerely believed in his success, he says that he did not dream that he would do as well

Xavier Roberts's crea-
tion—Babyland Gen-
eral Hospital.

as he has. Another reward is the satisfaction of bringing happiness to children, for whom he has deep love. His original purpose was for Cabbage Patch Kids to be toys for children. Ironically, the largest adopters of the hand-sewn Original Cabbage Patch Kids made by OAA are adult collectors.

Roberts claims that he did not take any risks: he started with nothing, so he had nothing to lose. Even the showroom was leased rather than owned. Roberts's advice to other entrepreneurs is to hold on to the dream no matter how tough things get. He is convinced that people can make their dreams come true.

Lee Smith of Trav-L-File

Lee Smith sold insurance, operating out of the trunk of his car. When he was in motel parking lots, he could see that the trunks of other salespeople's cars resembled rat's nests. In rain, moisture would get into the trunk every time it was opened. He realized that instead of a messy cardboard box, salespeople needed a durable, lightweight, waterproof box with a see-through cover to pro- vide easy access. So at age fifty-five, Smith started designing his better mouse- trap. In the third year of business, sales were around $500,000. Eight years later, they grew to $1.5 million. Many nationally known companies use the file box, including R. J. Reynolds, Philip Morris, Eastman Kodak, DuPont, Exxon, General Electric, Johnson & Johnson, Kraft, PPG Industries, Procter & Gamble, RCA, Schering Plough, and the U.S. General Services Administration.

Although manufacturing the file box appeared easy at first, several ob- stacles lay between the idea and the finished product. Smith had to find an appropriate material and processing technique. He tried fiberglass and plastic vacuum molding, but each box came out differently. After much discouragement and persistence, he realized that only one, very costly method would work—injection molding of hard plastic. The cost of obtaining the mold was a monumental $50,000. One-half of that had to be paid up front, and he had to wait six months to get it; in other words, Smith had to await the business to generate sufficient funds to resolve this problem. Meanwhile, other manufacturing problems were tackled. After getting all the glitches out of the manufacturing process, Smith got a product that did not at all resemble what he had envisioned.

Several marketing issues had to be resolved by Smith as well. He knew the dangers of overpricing the product. When he discussed price with potential customers, they would point out that he was trying to sell them a box for $25 that previously had not cost anything. Knowing that using a middleman would increase the cost to the customer, Smith decided to rely on mail and telephone direct sales.

Smith claims that one reward from being an entrepreneur is the ability to produce a product that affords him a comfortable living. Also, he gets a great deal of satisfaction from being able to provide jobs for a lot of people, particularly family and friends. Another obvious reward is that he enjoys his work. He says, "If it never gets better than this, this is great."

In talking about the risks of being an entrepreneur, Smith says that he was apprehensive about going into a business about which he knew very little, leaving behind a profession about which he knew a great deal. He had to take a second mortgage on his home and invest long hours and relentless effort. He viewed the possibility of losing time and money, especially risky for someone who was fifty-five years old. At times he would think that he should be slowing down at his age instead of cluttering his mind with all the problems of a new business. But then he would tell himself that someone else might be successful with the same product if he gave up, and this thought would put him back to work on his idea. The challenge replaced the problems. "If it [the business venture] fails and I'm standing in a soup line at age seventy, I can say I gave it my best shot." Perhaps Smith is as easily motivated by challenge as he is by financial security.

Susan Bowen of Champion Awards

Susan Bowen and her husband realized seventeen years ago that it was difficult for clubs to find trophies to present at competitions. So they took $2,000 from their savings and borrowed $5,000 from a bank to start assembling trophies and awards. Today the company has over $3 million in annual sales, generated from trophies and awards, promotional materials, and T-shirts and other silk-screened apparel. Champion is one of the largest companies of its type in the United States and is the fastest growing corporate fashion house. In the last five years, the company has grown 1,900 percent in sales. Clients include Federal Express, Schering Plough, Auto Shack, Nike, Kroger, Digital Equipment, and Holiday Inn.

Before the Bowens started the business, they conducted some market research. They contacted local saddle clubs to find out if the clubs would buy trophies and awards. After determining that they had a market and after looking into the costs involved, the Bowens operated the business in their home in their spare time. To differentiate their product, they delivered the trophies and awards and set up the place for presentation. A year later, Susan Bowen quit her full-time job to become chief executive officer of Champion. Her husband joined her a few years later. While Marris Bowen's talents are ideas, Susan Bowen's talents are in managment.

She says, "The biggest obstacle was my lack of education. I found that I had to study constantly to learn about accounting, marketing, and management." Her experience with bankers, lawyers, and accountants led her to conclude that they did not have much knowledge about operating a small business. She resolved to learn for herself and not depend on anyone else. "I find it interesting that students can't wait until they finish school—that is when education really begins." Another difficulty faced by Susan Bowen was finding employees who were willing to put in a full day's work and show an interest in what they were doing.

Several strategies have contributed to the company's success. Champion purchased a silk-screen lettering shop. The quality of materials and the techniques in the shop were upgraded. Art and production departments were added to provide faster turnaround and to give customers the ability to work out their design ideas with professionals. With the silk-screening operation, Champion was able to expand into promotional materials for corporate customers. The Bowens have found that corporations are willing to pay more for better quality and service; marketing to corporate customers was a big boost to the company.

Susan Bowen has always engaged in both short- and long-term planning. Her short-term planning consists of budgeting. Her long-term plans go years into the future. She has also implemented a successful incentive plan to reduce costs. A budget is prepared for the next year. If, during the year, employees can reduce the expenses in the budget, the savings are returned to the employees as bonuses. To keep up with customer needs, Bowen keeps in constant contact with the customer and attends many trade shows.

It is apparent that for Bowen the reward is the challenge of successfully implementing an idea. She claims that coming up with an idea is easy; the difficulty is in implementing it. She is proud of her achievements and her self-education. She takes all the blame as well as all the credit for the business. Bowen welcomes growth and the challenges that go with it.

Risks are not a big concern. She says that if you do not try things, you are not going to grow. She does not object to twelve-hour days or six-day weeks because she enjoys her work. She claims to be conservative and advises other entrepreneurs to hold on to the money they have made. Her entrepreneurial spirit is best evidenced by the following statement: "If I were to go bankrupt tomorrow, I would start another business the next day."

Charles Loudermilk of Aaron Rents

Thirty years ago, Charles Loudermilk borrowed $500, got a telephone answering machine, placed an advertisement in the yellow pages, and began a chair and table rental company. Today, Aaron Rents is the largest furniture rental company in the United States, is in the top fifty in furniture sales, and is in the top 10 percent in the manufacture of furniture. The most recent fiscal year showed approximately $110 million in revenues. The company has 170 retail stores from Seattle to San Diego and Boston to Miami, has four manufacturing plants, and employs 1,500 people. Stock in the company is traded over the counter. The stock value of the company is approximately $100 million.

Loudermilk was raised on what he calls the other side of the tracks. His mother worked in a school cafeteria to send him and his brother to college. After earning a business degree from the University of North Carolina, he started the chair and table rental company. He named the company Aaron so that, when people looked in the yellow pages for rentals, they would see his company first. His first order was for 300 chairs for a three-day estate auction. He bought some Army surplus chairs and rented them for fifteen cents each. Tables, china, party supplies, tents, hospital equipment, and television sets were added to his inventory. Ten years after opening, he added home furniture and later office furniture. In between, he sold the hospital and party lines.

The four manufacturing plants supply about 30 percent of the company's furniture needs. Two more plants are being added. When asked why he decided to manufacture his furniture, Loudermilk explained that other manufacturers were not able to deliver furniture when he needed it and of the quality he required at a fair price. Manufacturing the furniture gives him more control over the destiny of the company.

Before going public in 1983, Loudermilk had to borrow to finance the company. He was paying 4 percent over prime when interest rates were 20 percent. At that time, he had $8 million in debt. Until going public, his biggest problem was financing. Now bankers try to do more business with him. Because his business was different, lenders looked at the collateral as being used furniture rather than as being net income. But the numbers started improving five years ago, and lenders understand the furniture rental business better now.

In the early stages of the business, Loudermilk did not prepare any budgets or forecasts. Bankers criticized him, but he thinks that a successful businessperson needs a gut feeling about whether things are going right or wrong. He claims that numbers do not necessarily reflect what is really happening inside a company. However, when he considers buying a company that he is not familiar with, he examines that company's numbers. He has bought over twenty of his competitors. Now he hires people strong in accounting to overcome his weakness in that area.

While Loudermilk is not a numbers person, he enjoys being involved in operations. He gets great pleasure from going into plants to be with his employees and to see merchandise moving and furniture being made.

Loudermilk's philosophy is homespun—an open, honest policy. He pledges to everyone that he will not lie to them, nor will he tolerate employees lying to anyone under them or to customers. This is the personality of his company. He demands 100 percent honesty on the job. No one in his company has to compromise his or her morality, and people find this refreshing. Every store has a sign for employees: "Tell Charlie your problems." Blank paper and stamped envelopes are available nearby to write him. He mostly hears good things, but he does get about one complaint a week. Once a year, Loudermilk sends each employee a note stating that he does not discriminate and that he will not tolerate discrimination.

A few years ago, Loudermilk realized that the bookkeepers in the stores were discontented because, while they were the stabilizing force in the store, there was no position for them to advance to. So he opened a management training program for them. A few took advantage of it; but even those who chose not to were satisfied to know that the opportunity was available.

Customer service is important to Loudermilk. Every customer is sent a questionnaire for rating both the service provided by his employees and the material rented. The store manager calls the customer the day after the rental has been delivered to see if he or she is satisfied. Knowing that they will be rated by the customer gives managers an incentive to provide excellent service.

Loudermilk says that his number one reward is the feeling of success. On paper his net worth is $50 million. "But after the first $1 million, those figures do not have a lot of meaning," he comments. He has no desire to leave a legacy. His reward is taking on a job and feeling that he has been successful with it. He likes to tackle a project, complete it, and go on to another. He considers his work to be his play; there is nothing else he would rather be doing.

Loudermilk never saw any risks, but the problems were certainly there: "If anyone had told me the price I would have to pay, I would never have tried it." Because of the long hours, the headaches, and the difficulty in financing, he asked himself many times what he was doing in the business; he even thought briefly of getting out. He worried about the fact that all his energies were concentrated in a single purpose, often wondering if he was giving enough to his family and country and fulfilling his obligations to the less fortunate. He was constantly occupied with the business—how to make the payroll, what equipment to buy. It was not the physical work and long hours that bothered him, but the mental anguish.

Loudermilk has had time to reflect on his experiences and has the following advice for other entrepreneurs. Having an idea is not as important as being able to implement it. An entrepreneur must have a commitment and be willing to pay the price. A great thing about America is that a small business idea can become profitable. It is not only the super intelligent that are successful; top grades in college are not the criteria for success. The most important quality is the ability to get along with people and to inspire them to do a good job. You make money through other people. An entrepreneur must have the capability to put a team together. Finally, compensation is important: people and services are purchased like any other product. "The difference in success and failure is setting appropriate compensation levels. Employers must be fair but should be guided by the price they would have to pay to get that same job done by someone else. Set the pay level at what it takes to get that job done. Many owners cannot get this in mind. They pay their personnel 20 to 30 percent over the market and then at the end of the year do not have any funds to put back into the company."

Your Choice of a Business

In your search for a business opportunity, you may need to survey the business environment looking for what people want but cannot find to buy. Another approach is to locate a product or service that people want and when they become aware of its existence are intent on purchasing it. It is not always the complex or complicated things that beckon. On occasion, it may be something very simple that affords you an opportunity.

The wife of one of our former students became successful debeaking[2] baby chicks for chicken farmers. She started out at four o'clock each morning in her station wagon with four assistants and five debeaking machines. (These machines trimmed and cauterized the chicks' beaks in a single operation.) By noon she and her assistants would have processed 150,000 baby chicks at the rate of 3 cents per chick—and $4,500 is not a bad day's work.

A McDonald's, Burger King, or Domino Pizza franchise could be another way to go. An income check of one of these franchises might surprise you.

Personal Characteristics

Expertise

An individual's expertise may give him or her a decided advantage in becoming an entrepreneur. Do you have a rare skill that will give you an advantage in establishing a business to make you rich? Some more recent examples are to be found in computer hardware or software, or in Burt Rutan's skill in designing aircraft with unique performance capabilities. Do you have a creative skill? Such an attribute may be utilized to propel you toward your objective.

Patience and Tenacity

During the years we have been involved with small business in the academic environment, as well as in the world of the functioning small business, we have become aware of the significance of patience and tenacity. We have seen people with great plans and with what appeared to be solid ideas for success, lose patience and scuttle the whole idea. Giving up occurs because the individual is unaware of the complexities involved in the formation of a new business or because he or she is unaware of the many hurdles to be cleared to have the business come to fruition.

As small business professors, we frequently experience the disappointments of students not making their business a reality. It has not been the lack of an opportunity afforded by the business idea, but rather the lack of perseverance needed to carry the idea to fruition. For example, a former student came to one of us for assistance in starting a business to remove vegetation from existing public utility right-of-way. The plan was for this student and another to acquire a group of existing right-of-way businesses, aided by a successful right-of-way clearing business operator and another individual associated with a major financial institution. The plan for starting the business called for the two principals to raise $200,000 equity capital and, with the aid of a small regional investment banker, raise an additional $2 million through the sale of limited partnership participations.

2. Debeaking is a procedure used to trim the beaks of three- to five-day-old chicks. If this is not done, the chicks may peck each other to death, resulting in a substantial loss to the poultry farmer.

The planning phase of the business seemed to be progressing well until discussion turned to the preparation of two documents essential to the sale of the limited partnership participations. One of these would be prepared by a lawyer knowledgeable about such matters and the other would be prepared by a CPA. The plan abruptly stopped when the two principals were made aware of the cost of preparing these documents ($40,000 to $50,000 each). Unfortunately for them, they were ill prepared to accept such a cost. One of the sad facts was that one of the businesses they planned to acquire was earning 58 percent net profit on sales.

Patience and tenacity create an expanded time frame—a time frame that goes well beyond the individual's conceptualized time frame. We have seen good projects terminated because the individual lacked the key ingredient of tenacity. Many cannot comprehend that it is not possible to push a button and be in business instantaneously. So plan to be prepared in starting your business—have patience and be tenacious.

Stability

Stability is an area to which many prospective entrepreneurs fail to give credence. Whether you are perceived as a stable or unstable person makes a lot of difference. People respond more positively if you are thought of as a stable person. On the other hand, if people think of you as an unstable person, you may find your transactions more difficult to consummate. You do not want to be thought of as a butterfly chasing from flower to flower. Such a person might be called a "buck chaser"—someone who always seems to be "chasing bucks," but never settles down to a single business. To project an image of stability in your daily activities is important.

Summary

In this chapter, we have led you through the maze of considerations, needs, and characteristics essential to the person forming a successful business. We have used real-life examples of successful endeavors that have resulted in the founders becoming wealthy.

The purpose was to stimulate and motivate you to initiate action that will carry you forward to your objective. We have attempted to make you aware of the many variables involved in starting a new business. There exists no magic potion to ensure success; it is essential that you select the group of elements that have proven successful for a variety of businesses in the past. There exists no single business success formula.

Class Assignments

1. Why would you want to make a lot of money?
2. What in your background will support you in a business whose objective and capacity is to make a lot of money?
3. How will the idea, "I want to make a lot of money," relate to your conceptualization of a business?

SMALL BUSINESS ANTICIPATION

Our experience in working with students has revealed the importance of the student's involvement with many of the business's activities. The small or independent business is an environment in which the owner-manager becomes personally involved with the various facets of the business.

You may encounter an idea or see a business that excites your interest. You think it is a business that you would like to own. It is easy to get caught up in thoughts like these. You are thinking of the benefits that can be derived from such an endeavor:

1. It will make you a lot of money.
2. You can derive some tax benefits.
3. It will enable you to make a contribution to the community.
4. It will give you prestige.
5. It can be a challenge.
6. It will provide an opportunity for creative expression.
7. I will provide an opportunity for achievement.

It is easy to perceive these benefits, but this perception may prove to be a fantasy. There is more to owning and operating a business than paying lip service to goals. Entrepreneurship requires hard work and clear thinking.

In the remainder of this chapter, we will discuss business failure and success. Either may occur by happenstance; however, this is not likely. As a general rule, success is not an accident; it comes from a well-formulated and implemented plan of action. Failure is often the result of poor planning, deficient knowledge, and poor work habits.

After reading this chapter, you will be able to

- Identify factors that result in business failure
- Identify factors that result in business success

Every Business Is a Loser

One coauthor observed early in life a situation that made a lasting impression. The son of a neighbor, with the aid of funds supplied by his mother, decided to start a rolling store business. He would tour the adjoining rural area exchanging his goods for the farm family's eggs and chickens. The fact that he knew nothing of cost and revenue records ultimately resulted in the failure of his business.

Every business is a loser if the owner's behavior results in deficiencies and failure. Losing owners are persons who

1. Neglect to perform an economic feasibility study or develop a business plan
2. Lack business experience, especially concerning their specific business
3. Lack technical and managerial skills
4. Lack the ability to get work done through others
5. Are unable to create a mental concept of how the business will look
6. Are unable to effectively budget their time and economic resources
7. Fail to utilize available resources
8. Fail in their people relationships
9. Lack the perseverance to stay with a task until it is finished
10. Possess a negative or antagonistic personality
11. Lack good judgment
12. Fail to meet the competition
13. Are poor money managers
14. Take too much money out of the business
15. Have a tendency to overextend credit to customers
16. Find it difficult to effectively collect accounts receivable
17. Produce a poor quality product or service
18. Permit their families to interfere with the effective operation of the business
19. Possess bad personal habits that adversely affect the business
20. Permit employees and customers to pilfer merchandise or equipment
21. Select the wrong location for the business
22. Fail to identify their target market

It should not be assumed that all of these factors will occur simultaneously. However, we have observed that any one of a number of these, when experienced for any length of time, may make the business a loser. Our purpose in presenting these items is to sensitize you to the pitfalls that can interfere with the success of your business.

Every Business Is a Winner

By this point, it should be obvious that owning your own business is a very personal matter. It is not unusual for an owner to say, "My business is a part of me. I can't seem to separate it from the other things I do." A comment often heard from business owners is, "I can't separate myself from my business. This occasionally creates difficulties for me as I try to operate my business." You should begin to understand that what you do and what you are like influence the success of your business. As you reflect on the itemized list relating to a business being a loser, you realize that many of those items deal with personal matters.

What makes a business a winner? Your first response may be that the elements of success are the opposite of those elements that characterize a business as a loser. Surely this is true, but there are other differentiating factors. One of paramount importance is whether you are a disciplined person. If you are to be in control of yourself and able to direct your actions toward the achievement of your goals, you must be disciplined.

To make your business a winner, you also need to possess certain key behavioral characteristics. A student who spent his summer vacations being an entrepreneur provided one example of this point. He learned that with a minimal investment he could acquire a snow-cone machine. By obtaining a location in an active strip shopping center, he could be in business shortly with a minimal overhead. As he began his business in early summer, he was able to benefit from the peak summer season. The fact that he had to return to college in the fall concealed the slowdown in sales that fall and winter would bring his business.

The items that follow contribute greatly to business success:

1. Before you invest any money in your business idea, you should perform an economic feasibility study and create a comprehensive business plan (everything needed from the idea to opening the door for business, including costs, budgets, and personnel).
2. You need to have technical knowledge of your businesses activites or at least a good overview of the technical aspects.
3. You must have a managerial concept. Exhibit 2.1 places management and managerial activities in perspective.
4. Prior to entering your business, it is desirable to spend from two to five years working in a comparable business to gain experience.
5. You must be able to get things done through others.
6. You need to conceptualize the complete dimensions of your business.
7. You must be able to manage your time and economic resources.
8. You need to identify all the resources your business requires and to use them in the most efficient way.
9. You must get along with people.
10. You must have the perseverance to always complete a task.
11. You possess neither a negative nor an antagonistic personality.
12. You need good judgment.
13. You must meet your competition successfully.
14. You must not remove too much money from your business.
15. You must control the volume of credit you extend; the overextension of credit has been the downfall of many businesses.
16. You must monitor your accounts receivable and collect them within an appropriate time. Remember, you are not in the banking business.
17. You must produce goods and services of high quality.

Exhibit 2.1
DEFINITION AND FUNCTIONS OF MANAGEMENT

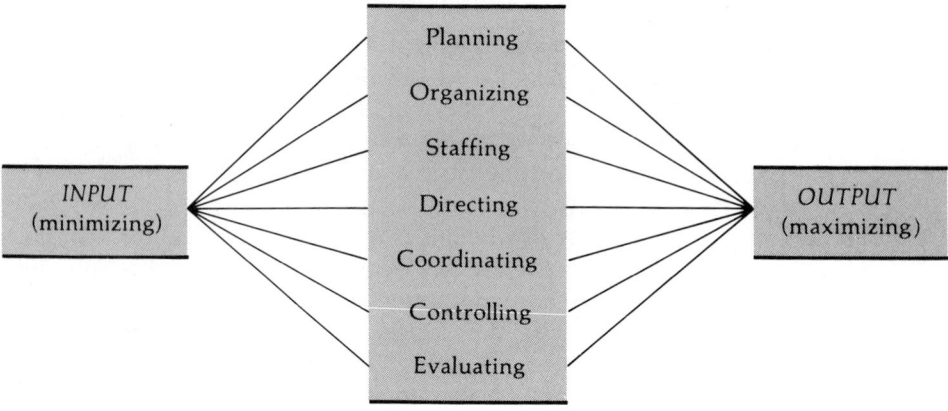

Management is
1. Doing through others
2. Decision making
3. Resource allocation

18. You must be a good money manager.
19. You must not permit members of your family to interfere with the operation of your business.
20. Your personal habits must not have an adverse effect on your business.
21. Your business security system should prevent employees and customers from removing merchandise or equipment from your business.
22. The location for your business must make sense to your customers, employees, and suppliers.
23. You need to know who your market is.
24. Finally, you must do three things:
    a. Exercise initiative.
    b. Be aggressive.
    c. Be prepared to take risks.

In reflecting on these factors, you can tie them back to self-discipline. The successful person is self-disciplined. This trait enables you to govern your behavior in accordance with the requisites imposed by this list of characteristics.

Summary
Businesses that fail have a number of common features. Many of these features stem from failings in the business owner, whose character, ability to plan, and knowledge are crucial to the success of his or her enterprise. Such traits as a lack of technical or managerial skill, poor planning, poor financial control, and the inability to work well with others may doom a business to flounder and perish.

Conversely, the business owner with positive characteristics and the foresight to plan ahead will go far toward ensuring his or her business's success. Knowing the market and the competition; working well with others and being a leader; and above all, formulating a sound business plan and performing an economic feasibility study are all factors that contribute toward business success.

Class Assignments

1. Locate a business that is failing or has failed. Determine which of the items listed as contributing to business failures would relate to this situation.
2. Find a business that appears to be successful. Determine which of the factors associated with creating a business that is a winner are applicable.

WHAT BUSINESS
FOR YOU?

Now that we have identified the factors that help ensure business success, it is time to turn our attention to the question of how an entrepreneur chooses a business. There are, in fact, many alternative approaches to finding a business, ranging from opening a new business to buying an existing one. There are also many different foundations upon which a business can be built, from exploiting new technology to reviving an old technology, from producing goods to providing services. In this chapter, we explore each of the various categories available to identifying the right business for you.

After reading this chapter, you will be able to

- Name twelve categories of business opportunities
- Evaluate the advantages and disadvantages of businesses in each of these categories

Finding a Business

Businesses originate in a variety of ways. Some are the result of a series of chance events, while others emanate from a series of planned events. From our experience we have identified twelve categories of business opportunities:

1. Looking for an existing business
2. Identifying a specific locale
3. Finding a target population group
4. Identifying new technology with a business application
5. Using older technology
6. Searching patent files for expired or unused patents
7. Developing products with a business potential
8. Packaging activities as a new venture
9. Identifying a specific service
10. Building a business based on your talent, expertise, ability, interest, or hobby

11. Inheriting a business
12. Forming a satellite business.

If you are to be objective and deliberate as the owner of a small business, we urge you to give careful consideration and study to each of these categories. Only by doing so will you be able to decide on your business.

Searching for an Existing Business

Every ongoing business is not a promising opportunity. It may be an opportunity, but a very thorough internal and external analysis is needed to determine the true state of the business's affairs. (Such an analysis is described in Chapter 4.) It may be that, due to inept or contrived managerial action, the business has deteriorated. Acquiring such a business is still an option if your analysis of the firm reveals that with revitalization the business can be restored to growth and profitability. On the other hand, the business may be in an environment where the odds are against a reasonable expectation of recovery. The business may be in a deteriorating neighborhood, or it may be located in an area of population transition or changing traffic patterns. These factors tend to have a long-term adverse effect on existing businesses. Therefore, you should avoid a commitment to a business in this kind of environment.

Then there is the prosperous business that may be available due to the owner's ill-health or approaching retirement. While such reasons may make the opportunity seem attractive, you still should perform a thorough analysis in an effort to determine the true economic status of the business.

Some people are in the business of buying and selling businesses. Others make a profession of starting new businesses and then, once the business is established, offering it for sale. In either case, perform a detailed analysis to determine the firm's present and future potential.

Identifying a Specific Locale

Recently, some business publications have carried articles indicating geographic regions that offer a new business opportunity. On occasion, these articles have not only designated areas for opportunity but have indicated the kind of business needed (see Exhibit 3.1).

As you view a geographic area, be sure to determine if an adequate public education system exists. You may find that in some rural smaller towns a major percentage of the population consists of older people. It is not unusual in this environment to find an antagonistic attitude toward public education because of the tax levy it requires. Such communities may offer the opportunity of starting a business to serve an older segment of the population. However, you may find that the long-term prospects in such an area are not favorable. It is essential that the population replenish itself. Other important factors in evaluating a locale are an available supply of labor, an adequate transportation system, and an environment that provides a good quality of life.

Another factor to consider about any geographic area is the value of public

Exhibit 3.1
BUSINESS OPPORTUNITIES IN GEOGRAPHIC REGIONS

BUSINESSES MOST FREQUENTLY STARTED IN REMOTE PLACES

Rank	Type of Industry	Survival Rank	Growth Rank
1	Miscellaneous business services	91	48
2	Eating and drinking places	123	78
3	Miscellaneous shopping goods	119	129
4	Automotive repair shops	63	123
5	Miscellaneous repair shops	52	108
6	Grocery stores	71	77
7	Miscellaneous retail stores	87	116
8	Residential construction	104	100
9	Women's clothing stores	154	112
10	Retail furniture and furnishings	142	105

Many hinterland start-ups try to make it by meeting neighbors' basic needs. (Total field for rankings is 158 businesses.)

BUSINESSES MOST LIKELY TO GROW SIGNIFICANTLY IN REMOTE PLACES

Rank	Type of Industry	Start-up Rank	Survival Rank
1	Commercial savings banks	88	9
2	Miscellaneous plastic products manufacturer	94	127
3	Floor coverings manufacturer	146	152
4	Metalworking machinery manufacturer	111	11
5	Nursing and personal care facilities	85	14
6	Miscellaneous fabricated metals manufacturer	152	47
7	Motor vehicles and parts manufacturer	134	146
8	Miscellaneous wood products manufacturer	124	43
9	Mill work and structural material manufacturer	82	131
10	Ship and boat manufacturer	157	148

Boondocks banking: Commercial banks aren't started very often, but they usually survive—and they almost always grow.

BUSINESSES MOST LIKELY TO SURVIVE IN REMOTE PLACES

Rank	Type of Industry	Survival Rank	Growth Rank
1	Veterinary services	95	137
2	Legal services	103	100
3	Funeral services	105	126
4	Dentist's offices	153	143
5	Public warehousing	129	64
6	Cash grain crops	112	150
7	Fuel and ice retailers	136	97
8	Hotels and motels	11	72
9	Commercial savings banks	88	1
10	Bowling and billiards places	67	123

The lodgings business is among the easiest to enter and most likely to survive, but hotels and motels don't grow much.

RURAL START-UP HOT SPOTS

	Remote Places with Highest Start-up Frequency		Remote Places Where Start-ups Have Greatest Chance of Growth
1	Rural Georgia	1	Vermont
2	Northwestern rural Ohio	2	North Georgia mountains
3	South central Wisconsin	3	Eastern Maryland
4	North central Texas	4	Rural Maine
5	Southern rural Missouri	5	Alaska

The most fertile start-up seedbed is in rural Georgia, but Vermont is where new businesses are most likely to grow.

Source: Reprinted with permission, *Inc.* magazine (February 1988). Copyright © 1988 by Goldhirsh Group, Inc., 38 Commercial Wharf, Boston, MA 02110.

services provided in relation to the taxes collected. When larger firms are searching for a new site, many will not object to a high tax rate so long as the value of government service is equal to or more than the tax bill. You should view the tax-benefit relationship in the same way—what are you receiving for your tax dollar?

Finding a Target Population Group

Most businesses want a location that offers a market for their products or services. As a general rule, this is determined by the age distribution of the population. Some businesses attempt to sell to the general population; others aim for a particular segment of the population; still others are concerned with selected segments of the population. The nature of your business will determine which population categories you address. In the final analysis, it will be your decision, based on your perception of the better opportunity.

Surely, population will be important in the business selection process, but so is income. The amount of income and its distribution within the population will be important in determining the purchasing capacity of the population. A large population segment with little disposable income is not an attractive market.

Identifying a New Technology

You may find that new technology has possibilities for opening a new business. Many new technology items are available for little or no cost. Two major sources for this kind of information are the NASA Technology Utilization Centers in Washington, D.C., and at the Marshall Space Flight Center, in Huntsville, Alabama. Historically, no other program has generated as much new technical information as has NASA's space program. In addition to the NASA source, you will find a number of periodicals in your general library, science library, or engineering library. You may find publications such as *Technology Review* (an MIT publication) and *High Technology Business* to be useful.

Composite materials are creating many new product opportunities, as has the continuing flow of microchip and fiber-optic technology. Prior to performing your technology-related research, you should determine your area of expertise. The combination of your expertise and the right new technology should increase your opportunity for success.

Using an Older Technology

We are not always dependent on new technology to provide a business opportunity. Old technology may give us an equally good opportunity. For instance some years ago Arkla (the Arkansas-Louisiana Gas Company) developed an interest in the production and sale of gaslights for the home. This could be a means of increasing the sale of natural gas. In keeping with the image created by the gaslights, Arkla next became involved with the production and sale of horse-drawn buggies. Later Arkla purchased a buggy company in Illinois.

For another example, Mid-continent Aircraft Company (of Hayti, Missouri) specializes in the restoration and modification of Stearman airplanes, a "two-hole," open-cockpit biplane that was used to train pilots in World War II. An other entrepreneur (in Eastman, Georgia), acquired the rights to the Laker vintage biplane, a pre–World War II product, then began production modifying the aircraft to custom order. Other such ventures include the restoration of antique automobiles or the customization of automobiles.

Your interest and expertise could serve to guide you if this category interests you.

Searching the Patent Files

The patent file is a rich resource that is often ignored. Numerous products with expired patents could once again be in demand if they were to become available. You could have an advantage in this category if you have knowledge of the product and its application. In recent years, we have encountered two such examples, both of which seemed to achieve successful results. They are the reintroduction of the historically popular Parker shotgun and the reintroduction of the popular woodsman Colt handgun. In both instances the principals were knowledgeable about the products and their acceptance in the marketplace.

Developing a New Product

You may be a creative person with the knack for producing a new product—that is, you saw a need and you created something to satisfy the need. One such person was a graduate student who broke his arm and later found it difficult to take a shower because the water always seemed to run down inside his cast. To resolve this problem, he created a cast guard consisting of a plastic tube with one end sealed and the other open but surrounded by a velcro band. The open end could be pulled over the cast, then sealed with the velcro. This guard prevented the water from running inside the cast.

Later, the same student created a plastic tourniquet for use at construction sites or by paramedics and fire fighters. The device was a plastic envelope sealed at each end. A tube with a closing clamp was inserted in the side of the envelope. After placing the envelope around a wounded limb, a rescuer could inflate it to stop the flow of blood.

For another example, a machinist developed a unique plumbing system by using metal pipes with neoprene ring inserts. These inserts sealed more tightly as the pressure within the pipes increased. In this system, pipes were fastened together with unions and elbows held in place by Allen screws. A local machine shop owner developed a machine to produce seamless hosiery. His development completely revolutionized the hosiery industry.

Have you followed Burt Rutan and his aircraft designs, innovative material applications, and aircraft construction wizardry? If you have, you are aware of the genius of his achievements.

Then there is James Caldwell and his rubber dustpan. Seeking something that would not mar the floor, he conceived a rubber dustpan. This was the beginning of what became the multimillion dollar Rubbermaid Company.

These diverse ideas have enabled each developer to become a successful business person.

Selecting Activities

Numerous businesses have been started based on activities that keep people fit and healthy. Look at all the spas, bowling alleys, racketball and tennis clubs, aerobics centers, and so on. Another example can be found in Benton County, Tennessee, in the Kentucy Lake and Birdsong Creek area. There cultured pearl activity is well underway. (See Exhibit 3.2).

You may be able to collect a different group of activities that can be assembled into a viable business. As in previous categories, your personal interest should play a major role in the kind of business that will best meet your needs. By using your hobby or interest, you too may be able to formulate a business based on activities.

Providing a Service

In recent years, because of its rapid growth, service activity has attracted major interest. Once you have identified a new or existing service business opportunity, your next move will be to find a location that needs the service and has the economic resources to support your business.

Some examples of some recently established service business are:

1. *Rent-a-maid.* A business that provides singles or working couples with a temporary maid service on a scheduled or intermittent basis.
2. *A shopping service.* Buying groceries, medicine, or miscellaneous other items and running other errands for the elderly or housebound.
3. *Rent-a-plant.* The business provides plants and containers as well as maintenance of the plants to hotels, motels, shopping malls, restaurants, medical clinics and hospitals, and office buildings.
4. *A lawn care and maintenance service.* These businesses form another rapidly growing area.
5. *Escort service.* The car with the yellow flashing light that precedes tractors pulling mobile homes along highways is such a service.

In many situations, the capital requirements for a service business are much less than for businesses that produce goods. The low capital requirements make service businesses attractive for the prospective entrepreneur.

Building a Business on Your Attributes

Your attributes may be one of the following:

1. Creativity may enable you to initiate a business in such fields as design, advertising, unique food business (cookies, ice cream, sandwiches, or soups), or packaging consultant.
2. Expertise that is in demand by others can be the basis for establishing a

Exhibit 3.2
CAMDEN CULTURE PEARL OPERATION

1. Scuba diver collects live mussel from lake bottom.
2. Mussel shells are cleaned.
3. Mussel is transferred to laboratory where technician pries the shell open with a scalpel, makes an incision, and implants a bead of mussel shell.
4. Mussel is kept for a week in tank with 70° water and fed with rich plankton.
5. Mussel is moved to a net in the lake.
6. Each 90 days, mussel shells are removed from the water and cleaned of algae.
7. Two to five years later, a cultured pearl is ready to be removed from the host mussel.

business. However, make sure that the demand is there prior to committing yourself to the business.

3. Ability may be used in a variety of ways to establish a business. For example, if you are a good organizer or if you are good at managing information and are able to communicate the results, you may establish a consulting business. In another direction, you may be one of those with a knack for recognizing an opportunity when you see it. These kinds of abilities may serve you well in establishing your business.
4. Interest can drive a business, as we have noted earlier. Perhaps this is your niche. Do you have an interest that can evolve into a business?
5. Hobbies can be turned into a business, though this is not true of all hobbies. In part it will depend on your degree of skill. But there are many examples of hobbies that have become successful businesses. A person whose hobby is flowers and plants may be able to develop a greenhouse or florist business. Another example is one coauthor's acquaintance, whose hobby was building model airplanes. Once his expertise became known, he was in demand to create models for movie crash and action scenes. There are those whose hobby was customizing automobiles. Later, when their customizing skills were recognized, they were persuaded to establish a full-time customizing business.

Each of the examples enumerated may serve you as a business. It all depends on the interest, skill, and motivation.

Gaining an Inheritance

You may enter a business by way of an inheritance. You will be in luck if the previous owner has maintained the physical facilities, the equipment has been maintained and upgraded, and the inventory is balanced and current. However, such is not always the case. Instead of having gained an asset, you may have inherited a liability. In such a situation, your first move will be to determine whether the business can be salvaged or if your best choice will be to liquidate the business. In the latter case, you may be able to salvage sufficient assets to begin a new business.

Inheritances do not always come in the form of a business. They may come as real estate, marketable securities, or cash. In such a case, you may wish to shift these inherited assets to a business. Then it becomes your responsibility to find a business that will best meet your needs.

Starting a Satellite Business

A satellite business is one that is organized for the purpose of being a supplier for a major company. In some instances, the business may be established to supply a lesser business. Occasionally the larger firm, in addition to signing a long-term supply contract, makes a capital contribution to the satellite firm. These funds may be used for site preparation, plant construction, and plant equipment. Historically, Sears has had such arrangements with some of its suppliers.

Other examples of this arrangement involve state and government agencies. These agencies often serve as intermediaries in arranging the supply contract. A local governmental agency may furnish the site in a local industrial park. In addition, it may supply some or all of the capital required to prepare the site, construct the plant, and equip the plant. In a recent year, for example, the governor's office of a southern state arranged for the supply contract while the local industrial development authority provided funds for site preparation, plant construction, and equipment. In this instance, the larger company was one of the Big Three automakers.

Sometimes the arrangement is between two lesser companies. In one case a sheet metal company was established to provide a machine shop with its sheet metal requirements. Later, the sheet metal firm became an independent operation producing proprietary products.

If your interest is in this kind of arrangement, be prepared to spend a considerable amount of time in exploratory work to locate a satellite opportunity.

Summary

In this chapter we have defined twelve categories of business opportunities. These opportunities are an existing business, a specific locale, a target population group, a new technology, an older technology, unused patents, producing a product, packaging activities, providing a service, building a business based on your own special attributes, inheriting a business, and starting a satellite business.

We suggest that you probe each category, looking for the right opportunity for the business that you have in mind.

Class Assignments

1. Make a list of businesses that relate to each category. In each case, explain what the relationship is.
2. Evaluate the following research observations:
   a. Entrepreneurs typically open businesses that are related to their prior work experience (the same type of business as a former employer; a former em-

ployer becomes a customer; a new venture based on skills acquired at the last job; and so on).

b. Entrepreneurs typically open businesses in locales where they were most recently working.

c. Entrepreneurs, having started a business, become aware of or exposed to opportunities that they did not see before being business owners; thus, they start subsequent ventures.

ENTERING A NEW OR OLD BUSINESS

Chapter 4
Comparing New and Old Business Opportunities

Chapter 4 aids you in comparing entry into a new business to entry into an established business. In this chapter, we list the advantages and disadvantages of new and established businesses to provide you with an opportunity to make the best decision. The fact that business ownership is a personal matter of necessity makes this decision rest with you given your best frame of reference.

Chapter 5
Valuation of an Existing Business

In considering the purchase of an existing business, a major factor is the determination of the business value. The objective of Chapter 5 is to aid you in making such a determination. In order to accomplish this, you will need to identify all the tangible assets of the business and determine their value. Because the value of intangible assets tends to be elusive, a word of caution is needed here. You should not only be interested in determining the value of assets but also be concerned about the identity of all liability items as well as the dollar amount of these items.

Chapter 6
Conducting an Economic Feasibility Study

Chapter 6 addresses the question, "Is this business feasible?" The significance of this question originated from observing people who entered a business without first determining its economic feasibility. It is too late to make this determination once your resources have been committed. In this chapter you will be guided by a series of field-tested questions that facilitate the collection of appropriate economic data. This array of data, when assembled, should assist you in making the best decision.

Chapter 7
Franchising

The objectives of Chapter 7 are to view franchising from two perspectives—the selection of a franchise business for you to acquire and franchising your own business. Using characteristics observed in successful franchisors, a series of criteria have been identified that will ensure success should you franchise your own business. This success is predicated on integrity and good faith. What are the characteristics you should look for in a franchise that has proven historically successful. Because many franchises have turned out to be fraudulent in nature, it is essential that we alert you to these pitfalls. You should keep in mind that a good franchise will produce a satisfactory income for you. By the same token, the poor franchise will take your money and leave you on the street empty handed.

Chapter 8
Choosing Your Professional Advisers

Chapter 8 delves into a subject that academicians sometimes avoid, the selection of professional advisers. It is not uncommon for the new entrepreneur to be in need of good business counseling. The chapter explores where to turn, whom to trust, and whom you can depend on for this kind of assistance. The author of this chapter has had many years of experience in this role. His advice has aided many in need of this kind assistance to achieve success. In playing the role of adviser, he has developed an appreciation for the contribution advisers are able to make to the individual entrepreneur.

Chapter 9
Negotiation

Chapter 9 launches into a field ripe unto harvest—the role played by negotiation is a vital one. Your ability to negotiate is significant to your success. Each day your time is filled with negotiation activities, whether it be with employers, customers, suppliers, or government personnel. This chapter describes some of the negotiating techniques that will enable you to be successful in your negotiations. Remember, success is often controlled by your ability to negotiate.

C H A P T E R 4

COMPARING NEW AND OLD BUSINESS OPPORTUNITIES

One question that confronts the prospective new entrepreneur is, What business will be right for me? An equally important question is, Should I select a new business, a business that must be started from the beginning, or should I acquire an established business? It is significant for us to approach these questions objectively. In the process of deciding these questions, we should match our experience, education, and personal attributes to the business (see Exhibit 4.1 for an aid in creating that match).

It is essential to ascertain what you have (i.e., what are the attributes that give you an advantage, and what are your strengths). In your self-analysis (see Exhibit 4.1), you should identify these factors and relate them to the business situation that will best benefit from them. In so doing, you help yourself make the best choice of a business for you.

Factors that influence your choice of an existing business or a new business are not all personal. There are external factors, both pro and con, that require your consideration. These are covered in the latter portion of this chapter.

After reading this chapter you will be able to

- Analyze the environment of an existing business
- Assess the advantages and disadvantages of acquiring a specific existing business
- Assess the advantages and disadvantages of starting a new business

Profile of the Economic Environment of a Potential Business

Certain key questions are of paramount importance in your general evaluation of whether an existing business or a new business will provide you the opportunity you seek:

1. How many firms are in this industry?
2. Is there a tendency for firms to be uniform in size, or are there noticeable size variations?

41

3. What kind of geographic distribution do firms in this industry have?
4. Do established relationships exist between the smaller firms in this industry and larger firms in other industries (for example, the relationship between the small auto-parts producer and the major automobile manufacturer)?
5. Does the firm operate only in the domestic market? Does it serve international markets only? Does it serve both domestic and international markets?
6. What is the attitude of local, state, and federal government officials toward this kind of business?
7. What is the attitude of the local community toward this kind of business?

You should carefully research the answers to these questions. By collecting this information in advance, it should help you avoid future problems.

Exhibit 4.1
PERFORMING A PERSONAL SELF-ANALYSIS

The purpose of the questionnaire that follows is to aid in the analysis and evaluation of the objectives, responsibilities, abilities, interests, health, and economic status of the businessperson in relation to running a business versus working for someone else.

Please indicate your choice by checking the appropriate space.

1. My objective in life is
    a. To make a lot of money _____
    b. To be my own boss _____
    c. To have a comfortable living _____
    d. To have a business of my own that will allow me leisure time _____
    e. To work for someone else _____
    f. To avoid accepting responsibility
        (1) For providing employment for others _____
        (2) For providing products or service to others _____
    g. To spend whatever time and effort necessary to achieve success _____
2. My marital status is
    a. Single _____
        Married _____
        Separated or divorced _____
    b. I have children   Yes _____   No _____
        Ages _____

   c. Given these responsibilities, I plan to commit myself to (circle one):   20   40   60   80   hours per week to the business.

3. My education is

   a. Elementary _____

   b. High school

      1 year _____   2 years _____

      3 years _____   4 years _____

   c. Technical school _____

      Type of training _____

   d. College

      1 year _____   2 years _____

      3 years _____   4 years _____

      Kind of degree _____

      Major _____   Minor _____

      Master's degree _____

      Kind _____

      Fields _____

      Other _____

4. My experience is (list in order from latest to earliest):

   a. Last or current job _____

      Employer _____

      Title _____

      Dates of employment _____ to _____

   b. Job _____

      Employer _____

      Title _____

      Dates of employment _____ to _____

   c. Job _____

      Employer _____

      Title _____

      Dates of employment _____ to _____

      Abilities I gained from each employment situation

      _____

      _____

      _____

5. My expertise is (check one)

Type	*High*	*Medium*	*Low*
_____	_____	_____	_____
_____	_____	_____	_____
_____	_____	_____	_____

Exhibit 4.1
PERFORMING A PERSONAL SELF-ANALYSIS (*continued*)

6. My hobbies are _____

_____

_____

7. I spend my free time doing _____

_____

_____

8. My capabilities are
    a. Directing the activities of others _____
    b. Planning an activity in a manner that takes the least time, effort, and material _____
    c. Serving people in a pleasing manner _____
    d. Helping people resolve their personal differences _____
    e. Managing money _____
    f. Keeping records _____
    g. Organizing people, money, machines, and things to produce products or services _____
    h. Effectively following instructions and directions of others _____
    i. Being my own boss _____
    j. Being a self-starter _____
    k. Taking initiative _____
    l. Making decisions _____
    m. Creating new ideas for products and services _____
    n. Other _____

9. My inadequacies are
    a. I can't make decisions _____
    b. I postpone making decisions _____
    c. I try to get others to make decisions for me _____
    d. I dislike assuming responsibility _____
    e. I avoid responsibility whenever possible _____
    f. I do not handle money well _____
    g. I seem unable to keep my checkbook balanced _____
    h. I am generally insecure without someone to guide and support me _____
    i. Other _____

10. Regarding my health
    a. I always feel good _____
    b. I can work two jobs without ever getting tired _____
    c. I frequently find it difficult to finish the day _____
    d. I am absent from work

       (1) One day a week _____

       (2) One day every two weeks _____

       (3) One to two days per month _____

       (4) Four to five days a year _____

       (5) Rarely _____

  e. My last complete physical was (date) _____

  f. I have these known health problems _____

_____

  g. I have no known health problems _____

11. My health permits me to (check one)

  a. Travel a great amount   Yes _____   No _____

  b. Engage in a lot of physical work   Yes _____   No _____

  c. Work long hours   Yes _____   No _____

  d. Function well in tense situations   Yes _____   No _____

  e. Use my eyes extensively   Yes _____   No _____

12. My health keeps me from _____

_____

_____

13. Regarding my present economic status

  a. My net worth is

     (1) Equity value of real estate $ _____

     (2) Cash surrender value of life insurance $ _____

     (3) Marketable securities $ _____

     (4) Savings $ _____

     (5) Other $ _____

  b. My annual income is

     (1) Salary $ _____

     (2) Special income $ _____

     (3) Investment

        (a) Rental income $ _____

        (b) Stocks $ _____

        (c) Bonds $ _____

            Total investment income $ _____

     (4) Interest $ _____

     (5) Annuities $ _____

     (6) Trust $ _____

     (7) Estate $ _____

     (8) Other $ _____

        Total annual income $ _____

Exhibit 4.1
PERFORMING A PERSONAL SELF-ANALYSIS (*continued*)

    c. My annual financial responsibilities are

        (1) Mortgage payments $ _____

        (2) House insurance $ _____

        (3) Real and personal property taxes $ _____

        (4) Car payments $ _____

        (5) Life insurance $ _____

        (6) Utility bills $ _____

        (7) Other loan repayments $ _____

        (8) Alimony and child support $ _____

        (9) Children's education expense $ _____

      (10) Medical or dental expense $ _____

      (11) Medical insurance $ _____

      (12) Household expense $ _____

      (13) House or lawn maintenance $ _____

      (14) Auto expense $ _____

      (15) Food $ _____

      (16) Business or professional expense $ _____

      (17) Other $ _____

                 Total annual personal expense $ _____

14. How much can I afford to risk? $ _____

15. Considering my responsibilities, my interests, my hobbies, my health, and my economic status, I am willing (a) to devote _____ hours per week to the business, and (b) to invest $ _____ in the business.

16. What specific kind of business would I be most happy operating as an owner-manager? _____

_____

_____

_____

_____

17. How would I compensate for my inadequacies? _____

_____

_____

_____

_____

18. After carefully reviewing the answers I have given to the questions above, being honest and frank with myself, I think that I could accomplish my objectives in life, and achieve a reasonable level of success and happiness by

    a. Having my own independent business   _____

    b. Working for someone else   _____

Evaluating an Existing Business

When you are considering the possibility of acquiring an existing business, you should seek answers to the questions described in this chapter. The answers that you obtain should guide you in deciding whether to acquire this business or pass it by for another that seems more favorable to you.

There are a number of sources to aid you in locating existing businesses that are being offered for sale. You may want to check classified ads in the *Wall Street Journal,* your local newspaper, regional or national publications, as well as trade publications. Other sources you may wish to use are your banker, CPA, business broker, or lawyer or a consultant specializing in your area of interest. In recent years there has been a noticeable increase in the number of business brokers; some of these specialize in a particular type of business, but others are generalists.

In your search for an available existing business to purchase, you may find a variety of situations. Some businesses are not available for purchase at any price and others are only available at a high price. Then there are those business owners who are willing to sell anything they own for a price. In other instances, you will find a business owner actively searching for a buyer for his or her business.

General Considerations

As we shall see, there are reasons for selecting an existing business to enter. By the same token, there are factors against choosing an existing business. There are key questions that need to be answered. The answers we derive will provide us with some guidance.

1. What is happening to the neighborhood: is it growing, declining, or deteriorating?
2. What is the status of competition: is it becoming more intense, declining, or maintaining the status quo? Can you explain the present state of the competitive environment?
3. Is there an outbound migration that is draining off the neighborhood's population or is the population growing?
4. Are new technical innovations adversely affecting the business or are innovations providing new opportunities for this business?
5. What is the status of highways and streets? We have seen street and highway construction and maintenance programs prove very disruptive for weeks, months, and even years. Many times the net result is the failure of the affected business.

Positive and Negative Factors for an Existing Business

The advantages of entering an existing business are

1. Facilities—building, equipment, inventory, and people—are in place.
2. An existing product or service is being produced and marketed.

3. An established market exists.
4. Revenue and profits are being produced.
5. The business has an established location.
6. Banks and trade creditors are comfortable with credit.

The disadvantages of entering an existing business are

1. Physical facilities (building and equipment) and the product line may be old and obsolete.
2. Employees may be stagnant with a poor production record.
3. The business may have an antagonistic union.
4. Inventory may contain a lot of dead stock, unsalable at any price.
5. Too large a percentage of the assets may be in overaged accounts receivable.
6. The business location may be bad.
7. The financial status and financial relations with institutions may be poor and deteriorating.
8. Some customers may be draining off the assets of the firm.

Determining Why an Existing Business Is Available

It is essential that you determine why a business is available for purchase. The reason can be a red flag, i.e., a warning that something is wrong. You need to ascertain whether something is wrong and, if so, why the problem exists and what if anything may be done to correct it.

The items that follow are intended to aid you in determining if a particular available business is right for you.

Questions to Ask   The answer to the question, "Why is this business available for purchase?" should aid you in establishing the validity of the owner's stated purpose for selling the business. It may be in accordance with the old adage, "Anything I have is for sale—at a price, that is, for the right price." Some reasons may provide you with a positive opportunity while others may be indicative of a negative opportunity. We suggest that you conduct the following analysis to determine the firm's potential.

Does the Present Owner Have Too Many Irons in the Fire? We have observed many business situations in which one person owns a number of different business entities. In some of these situations, the owner lacks sufficient time to effectively manage all of his or her business's interests.

What Is the Present Condition of the Business? In making this determination, you need comprehensive answers to the questions that follow:

1. Are the physical facilities worn out? If the plant, equipment, tools, and furniture are worn out, it is likely that the maintenance costs of the business will be excessive. Therefore, it is likely that the firm can no longer effectively compete in the marketplace.

2. Does the inventory contain mostly dead stock? The firm's inventory may be unsalable at any price because it is no longer in demand or has deteriorated. We have observed new owners of businesses traumatically shocked when discovering this dilemma.
3. Is the market for the firm's product declining? The demand for a business's products may be declining due to one or more of the following reasons:
   a. Changing neighborhood—either a change in the residents' economic status, a change from one ethnic group to another, a change from one age group to another, or a change in the lifestyle of the inhabitants
   b. Declining population—the outward movement of the population in both urban and agrarian areas has had a devastating economic effect on some firms
   c. Technological change—the advent and installation of new technology may immediately cause the firm to become obsolete
4. Is the business solvent? The business may be insolvent. Sometimes people discover too late that the firm that they purchased possessed fewer assets than liabilities. We suggest that you obtain the services of a reputable accounting firm to make such a determination before purchasing a business. You should avoid purchasing the firm's accounts receivable. Many times it is easier for an old owner to collect these receivables than it is a new owner. You may wish to use the protective measure of an escrow, in which part of the purchase price is placed in safekeeping until all aspects of the sale are complete.

What Are the Present Owner's Future Intentions? Will the present owner remain in competition? Sometimes, due to poor location or old facilities or equipment, an owner decides to dispose of his or her firm and then open another that competes with the purchaser of his old firm. As a matter of protection, you should have an attorney draw up an agreement stating that the present owner will not reenter a similar business in the community or market area for a reasonable time period. These agreements are sometimes difficult to enforce, but most businesspeople do live up to an agreement.[1]

Is the Present Owner in Good Health? If the owner is in poor health, determine whether the cause is physical or economic.

Does the Present Owner Desire to Retire? The owner may have reached an age that he wishes to retire, which is a valid reason for offering the business for sale. Because of taxes, the owner may prefer that you pay for the business over a period of years. In such an arrangement, the owner wants a declining-value life insurance policy on you to protect him or her in the event of your premature death. The request is reasonable under such circumstances. In some situations, the former owner may desire that part of his or her compensation be in

---

1. Recent court decisions have raised questions as to the enforceability of contracts that impose restrictions on the business activity of former owners. In some instances, these decisions have been based on the fact that such contracts serve as a restraint of trade.

the form of a consulting contract covering a period of years. Be aware, however, that the continued presence of the former owner may have an adverse effect on the new owner's business.

Analysis of Accounting Information   The purpose of analyzing the accounting information of the firm is to ascertain the firm's economic health. It is essential that you take a physical inventory of the firm's assets and liabilities. The true economic health of the firm is important to your economic future. You should be specifically interested in these items:

- Cash position
- Ratio analysis
- Volume of debt outstanding
- Validity of firm's financial statements
- Analysis of cash flow
- Adequacy of cost data (important in pricing and profit planning)

Obviously, to obtain this volume of information requires a considerable amount of probing. However, your future economic health demands it.

Appraisal of Operations, Plant, and Equipment   The purpose of this analysis is to ascertain the quality of the total operation.

Management Effectiveness. How effective is the firm's management? In acquiring an ongoing business, you are interested in the quality of existing management. Are they individually or collectively worth keeping?

Plant Efficiency. You need answers to these questions:

1. How effective are personnel?
   a. What is the rate of labor turnover?
   b. What is the percentage of absenteeism?
   c. Is there evidence that some employees commit deliberate acts of sabotage that reflect on the product and company image?
2. What is the amount of waste? (Waste serves as an important key to profit and loss.) If you closely observe operations, you can determine the amount of material and supplies being needlessly wasted.
3. What is the quality of production? The quality of products or services produced by employees should be graded, which can be done by answering questions like these:
   a. What percentage of production is completed without defects?
   b. What percentage of the rejects may be reworked, and what is the cost of the rework process?
   c. What percentage of rejects are not reworkable?
   d. On a cost basis, how many shipments must be reshipped because the original shipment was not of usable quality?
4. What is the physical condition of the plant? Consider present and future demands that will be made on the plant as well as

a. The adequacy of the plant's size and design. Is it of sufficient size and design to meet current and projected requirements?

b. The efficiency of the plant's layout. Optimum results are only attainable if the plant is effectively laid out. In this regard, an important item to be considered is whether the equipment is spaced and laid out in a sequence of productive steps. If it is laid out in such a fashion, only a nominal quantity of work in process will be required. The greater the number of operations that require doubling back and crossing over, the greater will be the inventory requirements.

c. The cost of materials-handling. The more frequently that work-in-process inventory has to be moved, the greater will be the cost of handling it. The manner in which a plant is laid out has a direct relationship with the firm's labor requirements and therefore its labor costs.

Other Considerations   What is the age of the equipment? How does the present equipment compare with the latest technology in terms of operating costs and rate of production? What is the state of repair of the present equipment? Is it well kept or does it appear that as little effort as possible is spent on maintenance?

Answers to these questions are significant in terms of their relationship to future capital requirements and efficiency of operations. Occasionally, old equipment that is well maintained but that has been fully depreciated offers a cost advantage over newer, more modern equipment. On the other hand, the continued use of older equipment may cut into profits by reducing productivity. Sometimes it is necessary to purchase new equipment on an installment basis. The effect of this on cash flow should be carefully analyzed before undertaking the purchase.

Decision: Starting a New Business

If you have decided to start a new business and have decided on what the business is to be, your first step should be to conduct an economic feasibility study (see Chapter 6). The results should indicate to you if the business is economically feasible for you.

Recently we were approached for assistance by a person who had invested $14,500 in a new venture. This investment had been undertaken without performing a feasibility study. That individual now is wringing his hands in desperation because the $14,500 inventory remains unsold.

After many years of consulting with prospective new entrepreneurs, we find that it is essential to develop a formal plan and to work vigorously toward its implementation. The list that follows shows what we perceive to be an appropriate step-by-step plan of action for bringing a new business to fruition:

1. Develop a timetable (from idea to opening the doors)
2. Establish your business objectives
3. Develop your organizational structure

In a span of a few short years, this party balloon plant has grown from nothing to this large facility with a recent addition.

4. Determine your personnel requirements
5. Define your physical plant needs
6. Plan your approach to the market
7. Prepare your budget
8. Locate sources of funds
9. Implement your plans

Positive and Negative Factors for Entering a New Business

As we have looked at the positive and negative factors of beginning a business by acquiring an established business, it is now time to view the positive and negative factors of establishing a new business. The positive aspects of starting a new business are as follows:

1. You are able to define the nature of your business.
2. You can create the type of physical facilities you prefer.
3. You will have the opportunity to take advantage of the latest technology, equipment, and materials.
4. You will be able to use the most recent processes and procedures.
5. You will be able to obtain fresh inventory.
6. You will be free to select, hire, develop, and motivate your employees.
7. You will be able to create your own management information system.
8. You can choose your own market location.
9. You can select your own management style.

The negative factors of starting your own business are as follows:

1. Selecting the right business can be a problem.
2. The business lacks a track record in sales, reliability, service, and profits.
3. Assembling the resources—location, building, equipment, material, people, and customers—can be difficult.
4. Developing a competent workforce can be a problem.
5. The business lacks a product or service line.
6. It is uncertain how you will handle operational problems associated with launching a new business.
7. The business lacks established markets or channels of distribution.
8. Developing a management information system can be difficult.
9. Formulating a control system presents difficulties.

For Me, Which—an Established or New Business?

After you have considered the material previously discussed in this chapter, some additional comparative analysis is suggested. Using Exhibit 4.2 will help you make a comparison between owning a new business and owning an established business. After you have completed this exhibit, you should come to a conclusion as to which type of business is for you.

If you decide to purchase an existing business, Chapter 5 provides guidance in valuing such a business.

Exhibit 4.2
DECIDING WHETHER TO START A NEW BUSINESS OR BUY AN EXISTING ONE

Should I start a new business or buy an existing business? The material that follows in Part A should aid you in making this choice. If your choice is to enter an established business, then the material in Part B should aid you in deciding whether a particular business is one that you should buy.

Part A

Before deciding whether you will establish a new business or purchase an established business, you need to give consideration to the positive and negative features of each. More important, you should rate each point a plus or minus as you perceive the significance of the point and its value to you.

1. Define the nature of the business.

   _____

   _____

2. Favorable points for establishing a new business (plus + or minus −)

   a. Opportunity to create the type of physical facilities I prefer. _____

   b. Ability to take advantage of the latest technology in selecting equipment, materials, and tools. _____

   c. Opportunity to utilize the most recent processes and procedures. _____

Exhibit 4.2
DECIDING WHETHER TO START A NEW BUSINESS OR BUY
AN EXISTING ONE (*continued*)

    d. Opportunity to obtain fresh inventory.   _____

    e. Opportunity to have a free hand in selecting, training, developing, and motivating personnel.   _____

    f. Opportunity to design my own management information system.   _____

    g. Opportunity to select my competitive environment within limits.   _____

3. Favorable points for selecting an established business (plus + or minus −)

    a. Avoiding the difficulty of a business with an unproved performance record in sales, reliability, service, and profits.   _____

    b. Avoiding the problems associated with assembling the composite resources—including location, building, equipment, material, and people.   _____

    c. Avoiding the necessity of selecting and training a new work force.   _____

    d. Avoiding the lack of an established product line.   _____

    e. Avoiding production problems associated with the start-up of a new business.   _____

    f. Avoiding the lack of established market channels of distribution.   _____

    g. Avoiding the problems in establishing a basic accounting and control system.   _____

    h. Avoiding the difficulties in working out the "bugs" that occur in the initial operation.   _____

4. Check back over the points covered in 2 and 3 above. Based on the pluses and minuses, I conclude:

    a. I want to establish a new business.   _____

    b. I prefer to enter an established business.   _____

5. If your answer in 4 is b, then proceed with Part B.

Part B

Considerations for selecting an established business, your responses, those of the present owner, and the facts concerning the status of the established business should guide you to a comfortable decision as to whether this business is for you.

6. Why is the business available for purchase?

_____

_____

7. Are the physical facilities worn out or outdated?   Yes _____   No _____

8. Does the inventory contain mostly "dead stock"?   Yes _____   No _____

9. Is the market for the firm's product or service declining?   Yes _____   No _____

    a. Changing neighborhood?   Yes _____   No _____

    b. Declining population?   Yes _____   No _____

    c. Technological change?   Yes _____   No _____

10. Has the union recently won an election as a bargaining agent for the company's employees?

    Yes _____   No _____

11. Is the business solvent?   Yes _____   No _____

Have you had a reputable CPA appraise the firm's assets and liabilities?   Yes _____
No _____

12.   What are the intentions of the present owner?

_____

_____

13.   Does the present owner plan to establish a new business or to acquire another business that would leave him or her in competition with you?   Yes _____   No _____

14.   Is the present owner in good health?   Yes _____   No _____

15.   Does the present owner wish to retire?   Yes _____   No _____

16.   Does the present owner wish to continue to be associated with the business as a minority owner/consultant?   Yes _____   No _____

17.   Analysis of accounting information
    a.   Cash position
        (1)   Cash on hand $ _____
        (2)   Cash in bank $ _____
              Total cash $ _____
    b.   Current ratio (Current assets/Current liabilities)   _____
    c.   Quick ratio (Current assets − inventories/Current liabilities)   _____
    d.   Debt-to-equity ratio (Debt [current liabilities, notes, bonds]/ Owner's funds [common stock, preferred stock, capital surplus, and retained earnings])   _____
    e.   Ratio of net income to sales (Net income/Net sales)   _____
    f.   Net income to investment ratio (Net income/Investment)   _____
    g.   Amount of debt
        (1)   Notes $_____
        (2)   Bonds $_____
        Terms of debt   _____

        _____

    h.   Validity of financial statements
        Accurate _____   Overstated _____   Understated _____
        Warning: Check to see relationship of book value of fixed assets to replacement costs
        Percentage of total accounts receivable over 90 days _____%
        Nature of accounts receivable prevent aging   Yes _____   No _____
        Dollar amount of bad debts charged off in   Last 6 months $_____
        12 months $_____   36 months $_____
    i.   Adequacy of cost data. Can you accurately determine the cost of producing product or service?
        Yes _____   No _____
    j.   Is there available data to enable you to accurately break down the price of a product or service into costs and profit?   Yes _____   No _____

18.   Appraisal of operations, plant, and equipment
    a.   How effective are the personnel
        (1)   What is the rate of labor turnover? _____%
        (2)   What is the rate of absenteeism? _____%

Exhibit 4.2
DECIDING WHETHER TO START A NEW BUSINESS OR BUY
AN EXISTING ONE (*continued*)

(3) Is there evidence of deliberate acts of employee sabotage?

b. What is the amount of waste

(1) Material? _____% $_____/day

(2) Machine time? _____% $_____/day

(3) Personnel time? _____% $_____/day

c. What is the quality of the production

(1) What proportion of production or service is completed without defects? _____%

(2) What proportion of the rejects may be reworked? _____%

If reworked, how much additional time is involved in this process? _____

(3) What proportion of production results in rejects that cannot be reworked? _____%

d. What is the physical condition of the plant?

(1) Is the plant of sufficient size and design to meet current and projected requirements?

Yes _____   No _____

(2) Does the plant appear to be laid out for the most effective use of people, machines,

and material? Yes _____   No _____

(3) Does the materials handling system seem to be designed and laid out to accomplish a minimum labor demand and a minimum demand for time in transit? Yes _____

No _____

(4) How does the plant equipment compare with the latest available? _____

_____

(5) What is the maintenance status of plant equipment?

Excellent _____   Fair _____   Good _____   Poor _____

Summary

In this chapter, we have presented the considerations involved in choosing whether to select an existing business or initiating a new business. As we indicated earlier, owning your own business is a very personal matter. This means that your decisions relating to starting your own business are made within the context of your personal values.

**Class
Assignments**

1. Use Exhibit 4.2 in preparing an analysis to determine if you should enter an existing business or start a new business.

VALUATION OF AN EXISTING BUSINESS

This chapter is devoted to assisting you in determining the worth of the business that you wish to purchase. This chapter should be studied in conjunction with Chapter 9, on negotiation, since attaining your objective requires knowledge both of how to value a business and how to negotiate with the seller. That objective, of course, is to acquire a business at a fair price. This chapter should also be studied in conjunction with Chapter 12, on developing a financial plan, since you must know how the purchase price will affect the operations and profitability of your business. You may operate the business efficiently after you acquire it, but if you paid too much for it you may nevertheless ultimately fail. If the purchase price is higher than it should be, you may never turn the corner and earn enough to pay off the debt (if the purchase was financed) or you may never obtain a fair return on your invested capital (if you paid cash).

Keep in mind that as a buyer you want to know what return you can expect on your investment. As we will see, another way of saying this is, "What is the value of the future earning power of this business?"

Various methods can be used to compute what the business is worth. There is no set formula that can be used in every case. In this chapter we will explore various methods.

After reading this chapter you will be able to

- Explain the various methods for valuing a business and how to use them
- Calculate the maximum purchase price that can be paid for a business without jeopardizing its long-term success
- Determine which valuation method is most applicable to the business you wish to purchase to identify the range of prices you are willing to offer

Asset Valuation

Businesses are often evaluated by the assets on their balance sheets. In this case, the focus is on the replacement value of the tangible assets or on the liquidation value of the assets. Studying these assets is important, but you must always keep in mind the reason you are buying the business. If you are buying the business to operate it and earn a living from it, the single most important factor to consider is the profit you can expect the business to earn. Assets are only significant to the extent that they enable a business to manufacture goods, sell products, or provide services. In other words, assets are only meaningful to the extent that they allow the business to generate profits. With this in mind, we will analyze various ways to look at assets to see what they can tell us.

Book Value

Book value is set by the balance sheet of the business. Often called the *net worth* of the business, book value is total assets minus total liabilities, adjusted for any intangible assets such as goodwill and deferred financing costs. For example, if the book value is $200,000 and there are $25,000 of intangibles, the net book value is $175,000.

Some businesses simply use the book value reported by the accountant. Sometimes book value is a fair indication of a business's value, but most often it is not. In some instances, a business might sell for less than its book value. For example, if a large part of its assets are represented by specialized equipment, slow-moving inventory, or obsolete inventory, the book value of the business may not represent its true value, especially where the sales volume is down and the net income is 5 percent or less of its net worth. For example, if the book value of a business is $200,000 but the company is only earning $10,000, you might well not want to pay book value for the business. With $10,000 in earnings, you would have to value the business at twenty times earnings to arrive at a value equal to book value.

Another situation in which valuing a business at book value can be dangerous is if earnings have been accumulated over a long period of time (if retained earnings are high). A purchase price equal to book value might be unwise if the earnings in recent years are low and the prospects for increased future earnings are not good.

Nevertheless, you should definitely inspect the balance sheet and the accompanying statement of income and operations for the past three to five years, as well as this same information for the most recent period. Review these documents to get an idea of the business's capital structure, net worth, and trends. This information will give you some indication of the soundness of the business. Bear in mind that some assets—such as real estate, investments, and other nonoperating assets—should be studied separately.

In computing the book value, assets like real estate and other nonoperating assets should be valued on the basis of the current market prices. Then book value should be adjusted to take these changes into account. For example, a piece of real estate that has been on the books for fifteen years at cost, say $25,000, may now be worth $125,000 if it were offered for sale. This $100,000 difference is real value, but it is not shown on the balance sheet. This is called an off–balance sheet adjustment. This adjustment, less any potential capital gains tax liability, should be added to the value determined for the operating assets and business.

It would be pure coincidence if the market value of a going business and the book value were the same. As the court of appeals said in the case of *Ketler* v. *Commissioner*, "It is quite evident that the book value of a stock is a very unreliable basis upon which to determine the fair market value."

Replacement Value

Some small business owners value their companies on the basis of replacement value. Replacement value is the current cost of replacing the assets of the business. The reasoning is as follows: The cost of duplicating the assets of the business will be higher than what is shown on the balance sheet because the balance sheet shows cost less depreciation. Although the book value shown is less than the original cost of the assets, the equipment (or buildings or other assets) do the job now as well as they did when they were new. Also, costs for equipment (or buildings or other assets) have increased. Thus, it would cost more to replace them today than they originally cost. In inflationary times, this is a valid statement.

A disadvantage of replacement value is that it tends to set a high asking price on a business. You may be able to start a new business with less capital than it takes to buy a business if the purchase were based on replacement value. Therefore, be wary of falling into the trap of agreeing with the seller's logic and valuing the business using replacement value.

Liquidation Value

The liquidation value is the amount that would be available to the owners in the event that the business were liquidated. In liquidation, time is always a factor; outside factors (bank, creditors, and so on) often demand cash immediately. As a result, the business may be sold at a substantial discount. In evaluating a business to buy, bear in mind that its liquidation value signals its minimum value. Knowing this floor provides you with useful information: it tells you what you will be able to obtain if, as an owner of the business, you are forced to liquidate it. Knowing whether you will have sufficient proceeds to pay the lenders if the business is not successful is valuable information. This information is also useful in negotiating to buy the business because you know the bottom line figure the owner will take for it. If the price you offer is lower than the liquidation value, the owner would be better off to liquidate the business than to sell it to you.

Capitalized Earnings Value

When you buy a small company, you need to know about that company's ability to earn profits. Past profits will give you data about history; future profits are much more meaningful. Just because a business has made good profits in the past does not guarantee that it will continue to do so. Many factors can change past experience. Increased competition, new technology, and revolutionary changes in the industry are just a few. The capitalized earning approach considers a business as a constantly changing entity that uses its assets to produce the maximum return on investment.

Capitalized earnings is easier to understand if you approach it by using two steps. First, you determine the business's earning power by looking at its past experience and future expectations. Second, you capitalize these earnings at a rate that is reasonable given the risks involved.

Determining a Business's Earnings

Past earnings give you some idea of what you might expect future earnings to be. You should review the income statements of the business for the immediate five-year period in order to get an appreciation for the trends.

You should then adjust the income from the income statement for: (1) extraordinary or nonrecurring gains or losses, which you do not expect to occur again; (2) unusually low salaries, which might have to be raised to get competent employees, or high salaries or bonuses paid to owners, which you would not require; (3) inventory write-offs or write-downs; and (4) unusually excessive bad debts, due to a bankruptcy or other unusual circumstances. You need to find out what accounting procedures the owner has been using. Some owners may expense items that generally accepted accounting principles would indicate should be capitalized. This practice will have the dual effect of depressing earnings and understating retained earnings, and therefore understating the book value. Other owners may amortize the cost of such equipment. If they have elected to amortize, look to see how long they have elected to depreciate these assets. Depreciating equipment over a longer period than its normal useful life will have the effect of increasing earnings and, as a result, overstating book value.

When you adjust for nonrecurring items and for varying accounting practices, you are trying to determine what the future earnings might be under your ownership. Your return on investment will have to come from future earnings. Your pro-forma income statements should be based on what you realistically think you can do with the business. (Refer to Chapter 12 on how to prepare pro-forma statements of income and expense.)

If the business has had fluctuating earnings, you will need to pick the one figure from the five-year period that you feel reflects the true earnings picture of the business. It is preferable not to use a five-year average of earnings. In selecting the year, emphasis should be placed upon the most current earnings. If the business is new but has good potential, future earnings estimates should be done on a conservative basis. In any event, prospective earnings are acknowledged by valuation experts to be the most important factor in valuing operating businesses whose worth is dependent upon continuation as a going concern.

Choosing a Capitalization Rate

The rate at which you capitalize a business's earning power is determined by the risks involved. The greater the risk of generating projected earnings, the lower the capitalization rate. Recall that it is from future earnings that you will realize a return on your purchase price.

One question that arises is whether income taxes should be deducted in determining the earnings to be capitalized. If the business is a corporation or if you will make it a corporation, corporate income taxes should be deducted. If the business is not a corporation, estimate personal federal and state income taxes and deduct those from your earnings. If you are going to incorporate the business but plan to elect S corporation tax treatment (which means that the corporation will be taxed as if it were a sole proprietorship or a partnership, depending upon the number of shareholders), you should estimate your taxes and capitalize the net after-tax earnings.

Capitalizing the earnings means dividing the net earnings by the capitalization rate. For example, if you have net earnings of $25,000 and you are going to use a capitalization rate of 12 percent, you would divide $25,000 by 0.12; the result, $208,333, is the business's value. (You can arrive at the same result by determining the reciprocal of the capitalization rate and multiplying that factor by earnings. That is, the reciprocal of 12 percent is determined by dividing 100 by 12, which is 8.33. Multiplying $25,000 by 8.33 also produces a value of $208,333.)

Arthur S. Dewing wrote a two-volume treatise, *Financial Policy of Corporations,* which appeared in its fifth (and final) edition in 1953. This treatise has been the source most frequently cited by courts and commentators for guidance on the choice of an appropriate multiplier. Due to its age, this work is considered by some to be somewhat outdated.

A more recent effort to refine the process of choosing the multiplier for closely held businesses is set out in "A Rational Approach to Capitalization Rates for Discounting the Future Income Stream of a Closely Held Company" (*The Financial Planner,* January 1982, p. 56). The author begins with the assumption that the capitalization rate should be based upon the current risk-free rate of return (the author suggests using the return on long-term U.S. treasury bonds), plus a premium for the risk associated with the particular income stream. Exhibit 5.1 indicates the risk categories and the appropriate risk premium for each one (in a range of five percentage points, to allow for some flexibility).

The risk premium related to one of these categories would be added to the interest rates on long-term treasury bonds. For example, if you checked with your bank and the current long-term treasury bonds were yielding 8 percent, and you determined from the chart that the risk premium for the business you want to buy is 11 percent, then the capitalization rate would be 19 percent (8 + 11). These capitalization rates are designed to be applied to *pretax income* because of the variation in the effective tax rates among corporations. Suppose that you projected pretax earnings to be $70,000. By applying a capitalization rate of 19 percent, you would arrive at a value of $368,000 ($70,000 divided by 0.19).

This new formulation is useful, but the Dewing treatise and its suggested capitalization rates are still instructive. Under Dewing's theory, it is possible to place businesses into different categories. From these categories you can form

Exhibit 5.1

RISK PREMIUMS FOR DISCOUNTING PROJECTED INCOME STREAM

	CATEGORY	*PREMIUM*
1.	An established business that has a strong trade position, is well financed, has depth in management, has stable past earnings, and has a highly predictable future.	6–10%
2.	An established business in a more competitive industry that is well financed and has depth in management.	11–15%
3.	A business in a highly competitive industry that requires little capital to enter, has no management depth, and has a high element of risk although the past record may be good.	16–20%
4.	A small business that depends upon the special skill of one or two people. Future earnings may be expected to deviate widely from projections.	21–25%
5.	A small one-person business of a personal services nature, where the transferability of the income stream is in question.	26–30%

some estimate of the value of a business by capitalizing its earnings. Dewing's categories are set forth as Exhibit 5.2.

A Three-Step Approach to Valuation

To get a good estimate of the value of a business, we recommend a three-part approach. The data necessary to arrive at this valuation are (1) the net book value of the business, (2) the average net after-tax earnings for the last five years, and (3) the most current year's net after-tax earnings. The five-year average earnings give you the history of earnings, and the most current year's earnings gives you the trend. From Dewing's categories set forth in Exhibit 5.2, you select the appropriate multiplier, or capitalization rate. You then capitalize the five-year average earnings by that rate; the result becomes one part of the three-part formula. You then capitalize the most current year's earnings by the same capitalization rate; this result becomes the second part of the formula. The third part of the formula is net book value.

For example, assume that a business has a net book value of $75,000; average after-tax earnings for the five-year period of $35,000, and current year's earnings of $60,000. Further assume that the business is a well-established firm requiring managerial care. As can be seen from Exhibit 5.2, such a business would call for a capitalization rate of 12.5 percent. The valuation can be worked out as follows:

Five year average earnings	$35,000 × 8 =	$280,000
Most current year's earnings	$60,000 × 8 =	480,000
Net book value		75,000
Total		$835,000

To arrive at the value of the business, the sum of these three parts of the formula is divided by 3, which gives you the average of the three components.

Exhibit 5.2
CATEGORIES OF BUSINESSES USED FOR CAPITALIZING EARNINGS

1. Old established businesses, with large capital assets and excellent goodwill: 10 percent, a value ten times the net earnings. Very few enterprises come within this category.
2. Businesses that are well established, but require considerable managerial care: 12.5 percent, a value eight times net earnings. To this category belongs the great number of old, successful businesses.
3. Businesses that are well established, but involving possible loss due to shifts in economic conditions: 15 percent, a value approximately seven times the net earnings. These are strong, well-established businesses that produce a type of commodity that makes them vulnerable to depressions. They require considerable managerial ability, but little special knowledge on the part of the executives.
4. Businesses requiring average executive ability and comparatively small capital investment: 20 percent, a value approximately five times the net earnings. These businesses are highly competitive, but established goodwill is of distinct importance. This class includes the rank and file of medium-sized, highly competitive industrial enterprises.
5. Small industrial businesses that are highly competitive and require a relatively small capital outlay: 25 percent, a value approximately four times net earnings. These are businesses that anyone, even with little capital, may enter.
6. Industrial businesses, which depend on the special, often unusual skill of one person or a small group of managers: 50 percent, a value approximately two times net earnings. These businesses involve only a small amount of capital; they are highly competitive, and the failure rate is high.
7. Personal service businesses: 100 percent, a value equal approximately to the earnings of a single year. They require no capital, or at the most a desk and a telephone. The manager must have a special skill coupled with an intensive and thorough knowledge of the field. The earnings of the enterprise are the objective reflection of this skill; the owner is not likely to be able to create an organization that can successfully carry on after he or she is gone. The owner can sell the business, including the reputation and the plan of business but cannot sell himself or herself, the only truly valuable part of the enterprise.

In this case $835,000 divided by three yields a proposed valuation of $278,333. This approach is a conservative one, but is useful to arrive at a beginning point for negotiations.

Goodwill

In almost every purchase of a business, the subject of goodwill will arise. Goodwill has been defined as the favorable disposition that customers entertain towards a particular enterprise, which may induce them to continue giving their business to it (*Meredith Broadcasting Company,* 196 Court of Claims 1; 405 F.2d 214 [1968]).

One measure of goodwill is the amount that future earnings potential is in excess of a reasonable return on net tangible assets (see Chapter 12 for the definition of net tangible assets). This excess is called excess earnings (*Charlotte Corporation*, T.C. Memo 1960–97, Rev. Rul. 68–609, 1968 C.B. 327).

Revenue Ruling 68–609 provides a formula for determining the total fair market value of all intangible assets of a business (goodwill being one example of an intangible asset) arising from its excess earnings. This method involves capitalizing the amount of a business's most recent average earnings that are in excess of a fair return on the net tangible assets. In other words, you are expected to obtain a fair return on your net tangible assets. It is only the earnings in excess of a fair return on those assets that are capitalized to determine goodwill.

One piece of information necessary to perform this computation is the industry average rate of return on net worth. That is the figure used to determine what portion of earnings are excess earnings. One source for this information is the Robert Morris Associate's *Annual Statement Studies*. The commercial loan officer at the bank will usually have a copy. Find the industry that includes the business you wish to purchase. Then determine the average rate of return on net worth for that industry.

For example, assume that the average net after-tax income of the business you wish to buy is $35,000. Assume further that the net worth (net book value) of the business is $150,000. To compute the average return of net worth, divide the net income by the net worth; the result is a return on net worth of 23 percent. Assume that the industry average of this return is 20 percent. Thus, the business you want to buy has a rate of return on net worth 3 percent greater than the industry average. Assume that the capitalization rate of the business, using the Dewing chart in Exhibit 5.2, is 12.5 percent. We have determined that 3 percent of the earnings represents excess earnings, which equals $1,050 of excess earnings on net income of $35,000. To arrive at goodwill, you need to capitalize these excess earnings by 12.5 percent. The value of goodwill, then, is $8,400 ($1,050 divided by .0125).

Summary

In summary, the fair market value of a business is the amount at which the business would exchange hands between a willing buyer and a willing seller, neither being under compulsion to buy or sell, each being aware of all relevant facts and circumstances. To arrive at fair market value, several elements must be examined:

1. The nature of the business and the history of the business from its beginning
2. The economic outlook in general and the condition of the specific business in particular
3. The earning capacity of the business
4. The book value of the business and the financial condition of the business
5. Whether or not the business has goodwill

All five of these factors are important in the valuation process. In the final analysis, judgment must be used to assign weights to these various factors. There is no set formula to value a business because every business is different. Valuation is not a science, but an art. The information contained in this chapter will help you analyze the business and determine the range of values within which you can negotiate.

To assist you in pulling all these elements together, an example of a valuation of a closely held business is set forth in the appendix to this chapter. While the valuation is hypothetical, the principles and methodology are instructive.

Class Assignments

1. What is the rational justification for applying a discount to a minority interest in a closely held corporation?
2. Why is the book value of a business seldom equal to its fair market value?

Appendix: A Sample Business Valuation

Heavenly Cylinders, Inc. (HCI), is a closely held corporation with no public market for the trading of its shares. The company was started in January 1978. The owner is an engineer, the former employee of a large car-haul transportation company. He had resigned to start HCI to build hydraulic cylinders for the car-haul industry. The company started with three employees and now employs thirty-five skilled and semiskilled workers. HCI now manufactures 85 percent of all hydraulic cylinders and systems for car-haul manufacturers. In addition to manufacturing hydraulic systems for new car-haul trailers, the company also custom manufactures hydraulics for used car-haul trailers. The company has a modern manufacturing facility with state-of-the-art equipment.

The car-hauling industry is directly related to the automobile and truck manufacturing industry. Industry analysts just published a report that indicated that auto dealers' inventories were on the heavy side, with stocks being equivalent to 75 days of sales. (The 60-day level is considered normal.) Auto sales usually reflect general economic conditions. In periods of high inflation, high interest rates and unemployment will cause auto sales to fall rapidly.

Financial Review

Summary balance sheets for the company for the last five years were reviewed. The company has shown steady growth in its net worth. The company's net book value for the year just ended was $224,800. Summary income statements for the same years show operating profits to have been increasing steadily over the last four years.

Goodwill is based on earning capacity. The presence of goodwill may be associated with the prestige and renown of the business, the trade name, and a record of repeat customers; however, the measure of the value of this intangible asset rests with the company's ability to earn over and above a fair return on invested capital. The company is experiencing such earnings presently and has had a history of above-average returns on net worth.

Methods of Valuation

The value of the company was determined by considering a number of conventional approaches. The most relevant have been selected and weights were assigned to each. Three basic approaches are used to value the company:

1. Net book value approach
2. Return on capital approach
3. Discounted future earnings approach

Net Book Value Approach   Book value is important to the extent that it provides an adequate base for the continuance of the business. HCI's net book value at the end of its fiscal year was $224,800. However, additional adjustments are necessary to properly estimate net book value. They are land and goodwill. The net book value of the land account at the end of the fiscal year was $7,500. A current valuation by a local independent appraiser estimates fair market value at $35,000. Using these findings would result in an increased land value of $27,500.

HCI enjoys a level of profitability in excess of the industry average. The following procedures were used to place a value on goodwill. Using financial statements for the last three years, average net income was determined. Then average return on net worth was computed. Taking the difference between average rate of return on net worth and the industry average rate of return on net worth (using Robert Morris Associate's *Annual Statement Studies*), the excess rate of return being earned by HCI was computed. Applying the excess rate of return to the average of the earnings for the last three years, the amount of earnings attributable to goodwill was calculated. Applying a capitalization rate of 20 percent to the excess earnings, the value for goodwill was found to be $78,052.

Thus the net book value of $224,800 would be increased as follows:

Book value at last year-end	$224,800
Land	27,500
Goodwill	78,052
Adjusted net book value	$330,352

Return on Capital Approach   The return on capital approach assumes that a potential investor has a desired return on invested capital (ROI) that he or she would like to achieve if he or she were to acquire some or all of the business. Return on invested capital is usually expressed as a percentage, which shows the relation of profit to invested capital. The investor can calculate the maximum price to pay by taking the desired ROI and applying it against the recent yearly profits of the business.

The key with the return on capital approach is selecting the appropriate rate at which profits should be capitalized. There are three basic factors involved in this selection: the nature of the business; the risk involved; and the stability or irregularity of profits. A risky business with fluctuating income levels would have a higher capitalization rate (lower multiple of earnings) than a nonrisky business with steady income levels.

Robert Morris Associates, a national association of bank loan and credit officers, publishes *Annual Statement Studies* each year. This periodical is a valuation standard that lists median financial ratios for a large number of businesses. In its last edition, this publication indicates a percentage profit before taxes to tangible net worth of 21.4 percent for HCI's kind of business. This rate is felt to be appropriate for this company.

Once the investor arrives at a capitalization rate, he must determine the appropriate level of net profits to capitalize. We believe that because of the possible fluctuation in income levels that the industry may experience, the investor considering HCI's current and historical performance should put primary emphasis on current performance. By capitalizing HCI's operating profits by this industry average rate of return, the value is $421,900.

Discounted Future Earnings Approach   Another acceptable method of valuing a company, the discounted future earnings approach, is based on the theory that a purchaser of stock is investing today's dollars for a future stream of earnings that the company expects to produce. Under this approach, the value of the company to the investor is equal to the present value of that expected future income stream.

The first step in this approach is to estimate the company's future financial performance. Based on the operating income projections of HCI for the current year, and a 40 percent effective tax rate, an annual growth rate of 10 percent for the next five years is projected. The company is assumed to produce, at the end of five years, a constant stream of earnings that are capitalized at the chosen discount rate.

The second step of this method is to select the appropriate discount rate for capitalizing the remaining earnings and for calculating the present worth of the entire income stream. The discount rate should be the rate of return available on alternative investment opportunities of comparable risk. For the purpose of this valuation, a discount rate of 16 percent is used; this amount is approximately twice the current rate of United States government bonds. This rate will attract a venture capitalist investor.

The final step is to calculate the present worth of the future earnings stream. The calculation is as shown in Exhibit 5.3.

The mechanics of the schedule in Exhibit 5.3 are rather simple. For example, if you had $63,760 on the first day of year 1 and it had earned 16 percent for a full year, you should have $74,745 at the end of year 1. Stating it another way, $63,760 is the present value of $74,745 one year from now.

Determining the Value of HCI   We have discussed the three methods that we believe are appropriate to properly value HCI. An informed purchaser would certainly consider all of these methods, giving weight to those methods that more clearly reflect the current economic and investment rationale. In this case, we give considerably more weight to the return on invested capital approach and the discounted future earnings method than the adjusted net book value

Exhibit 5.3

SAMPLE CALCULATION OF PRESENT WORTH OF FUTURE INCOME

YEAR	PROJECTED NET INCOME	DISCOUNT FACTOR (16%)	PRESENT WORTH
19X4	$74,745	0.853	$63,760
19X5	82,219	0.727	59,773
19X6	90,440	0.620	56,072
19X7	99,484	0.529	52,627
19X8	109,432	0.452	49,463
After 19X8[b]	683,950	0.452	309,145
			$590,837

a. The 19X4 after-tax income was derived using the 19X3 adjusted pretax profit of $113,250 plus 10 percent growth, less 40 percent federal and state income taxes.

b. After five years, we have assumed a constant stream of earnings of $109,432 per year. When capitalized at 16 percent ($109,432 divided by 0.16), these earnings would yield a business value of $683,950.

method because HCI has demonstrated a sound history for the past several years in a specialized market and has attained a 85 percent market share.

Based on this weighting, the fair market value of HCI is as follows:

Adjusting net book value	$330,352 × 1/6	$ 55,058
Discounted future earning	$590,800 × 2/6	196,993
Return on invested capital	$421,900 × 3/6	210,950
Fair market value		$463,001

CONDUCTING AN ECONOMIC FEASIBILITY STUDY

In thinking about the establishment of your own business, you should be aware of the need to perform an economic feasibility study. As soon as possible, you will want to determine if your idea for a business is feasible. It is better to do this study than to spend your money and time on an idea that offers little opportunity for success. Throughout this book we offer suggestions that are based on our observation of proven successful efforts.

Whatever your business, it is essential for you to make the best determination possible to see if your business idea has a reasonable possibility of succeeding.

We think of an economic feasibility study as a collection of data to help forecast whether a venture will survive. This profile of information should lead you to a definitive decision—seeing the idea as either a go or a no-go situation. You may wish to think of the feasibility study as a research project, which it is.

Early in the process of defining your business, you are called upon to define its external and internal environment. This means identifying the internal components (personnel, equipment, capital, and so on) as well as the external factors (competitors, government, society, and so on) that will impact your firm. You also need to consider various factors to make a promising site selection.

After reading this chapter you will be able to

- Analyze the external environment of your business idea
- Choose a viable site for your business
- Assess the internal environment of your business idea
- Perform an economic feasibility study of a new business or existing business

**Defining the Ex-
ternal Environ-
ment**

As you view the business's external environment, you are viewing a number of important factors that can influence the business's success:

1. The nature of the economic environment
2. The nature of the industry's environment
3. The labor environment
4. Local, state, and federal government relations
5. The status of the technology
6. The nature of the population
7. Income distribution among the population
8. The nature of transportation systems
9. The available water supply
10. Available waste facilities
11. Available public utilities (power and gas)
12. The availability and accessibility of sources of supply

As you evaluate the nature of the economic environment, consider the number of similar firms and the competitive situation. In addition, you should estimate total dollar sales figures for these firms and what portion of these sales you may reasonably expect to acquire, that is, what will be your market share.

Another area of interest you should study is the nature of the life cycle of your prospective business's industry. Does it fit in the embryonic, child-hood, adolescent, adult, mature, or waning years stage? Whichever stage you identify will suggest the competitive position of the industry, the state of its technology, and the future opportunity you perceive for your proposed business.

In viewing the labor environment, you are looking at the workforce supply, the age distribution of the population, the fertility rate, the education level, the attitude of the labor force toward unions, the adaptability of the workforce toward change, and, finally, the general culture of the group.

Because of the importance of government attitudes toward business, you should be concerned about the attitude toward your particular kind of business at each level of government. It will not be in your best interest to become involved with a business that will be embroiled in conflict with some arm of government.

The future of any business is closely related to the state of technology involved in its activity. Often the business opportunity will hinge on your knowledge of related technology and your creative ability to make constructive additions to the technology.

You should be interested in the nature of the population for a number of reasons. Not only does the population provide a source for your labor supply, but it also determines the nature of your market potential. The birthrate and age distribution of the population will have a long-run impact on your business as both will influence the future characteristics of the population, which, in turn, relates to your supply of labor and customers. The purchasing power of the population influences the ability of your potential customers to buy the goods or services that your business will offer. Therefore, it is essential for you to ascertain income distribution within the population.

The nature of the transportation system is important for many reasons:

1. In the inbound transportation of goods, equipment, and supplies
2. In the transportation of employees to and from work
3. In the outbound transportation of goods and services

Highway, street, road, railroad, pipelines, and airport facilities may be key elements in the transportation network that your business will employ.

The effects of the transportation network can be seen in some examples. The owner of a baking company chose to keep his plant in a low-income residential neighborhood. By doing so, he was able to attract employees from the surrounding area. They were able to walk to work and go home for lunch. As a result, the company was able to maintain a lower labor cost. The plant was also located near enough to main transportation arteries to have good inbound and outbound transportation, thus enabling the bakery to receive supplies and ship goods. For another example, a Southern wire mill, because of its access to the interstate highway system, has been able to use its trucks to deliver the finished product. On the return trip the truck brings usable scrap. This combination of transportation factors has enabled the company to maintain a price advantage. For a third example, consider the manufacturer of transportation equipment that developed a special trailer. Outbound the trailers were used as car carriers; inbound the car decks were dropped and components trundled in for use in manufacture of the automobiles.

Depending on the nature of your business, the water supply may be an important element. Some businesses in processing industries require large quantities of water. In such an industry, you will want to ascertain if the water supply will meet your requirements.

An important determination that needs to be made early is what your waste disposal requirements will be. The increasing stringency of government regulations concerning the transportation of waste and waste dump sites may make this consideration vital in your planning. This factor is important to gas stations, beauty salons, dry cleaners, and so on, not just to manufacturers.

In today's environment, few people consider the accessibility of utilities to be a problem, but it can be. You will want to ascertain if electric and gas service will be available with sufficient capacity to satisfy your requirements.

It is not unusual for new business owners to fail to determine the availability of suppliers. In some locales, you may find that sources of supply to satisfy your equipment, material, and supply needs are inadequate. If so, you will have to anticipate your requirements for these things further in advance, which means that your investment in inventory will be higher. In addition, the risk of disruption to operations becomes higher because a replacement part may be 50, 100, 500 or more miles away.

Site Selection

Site Selection for Retail Businesses

We have observed that, in developing an economic feasibility study, many prospective small business owners tend to make improper use of traffic flow information. A location with a high traffic flow is not necessarily a good business site. An important consideration is the purpose and destination of those traveling the roadway. It is also important to recognize the relationship between the traffic flow and the appropriate side of the street as a site location. For example, locations that require cars to make a left turn in the face of oncoming traffic are not good sites. Also undesirable is a site on an artery that contains a high density of fast-moving traffic.

Another important consideration is to relate trip types to specific business:

1. A dry cleaner will want to be on the going-to-work side of the street.
2. A convenience store will want to be on the going-home side of the street.
3. A retailer will want a site on the right side of the street approaching the shopping district and adjacent to streets carrying the traffic into, out of, or across town.
4. The retailer choosing a site in a row-store location should seek a site at the beginning or end of the group of stores.
5. When considering a site on the side of the street containing older businesses, there may be a clue as to which is the best site. Check the status of these businesses: are they growing, static, or declining? If the latter, the location is obviously not a good one.
6. People on a pleasure or recreational trip may be in the market for services, such as motels, restaurants, and service stations. The prospects for success will be better if a location is chosen along the side of a well-traveled highway and adjacent to a major entrance into the community.

In selecting a site, remember that a vacant building frequently is a bad omen. Some locations seem to be born losers—places where no one succeeds.

The type of consumer goods—convenience, shopping, or speciality—will impact on the site choice.

Site Selection for Industrial Businesses

In selecting a site for an industrial business, several factors should be considered:

1. Access to transportation facilities (railroads, expressways, interstate highways, and so on)
2. Access to utilities, including
   a. An adequate source of electric power
   b. An adequate quantity of natural gas and any other required petroleum product
   c. An abundant source of water
   d. Facilities for disposition of waste materials
3. A supply of productive and reasonably priced labor
4. An available source of needed materials, equipment, and supplies
5. A favorable attitude toward your type of business by the local community and local, state, and federal government officials

Be sure to find a good location (above) or you may find a spot that is a born loser (right).

Site Selection for Service Businesses

The requisites for a service business are similar to those of other types of business. Some key factors for service businesses are

1. Low cost transportation
2. Close proximity to your markets
3. Accessibility to your customers
4. Good revenue potential
5. Population density sufficient to satisfy revenue requirements
6. A population with adequate purchasing power to support the business
7. A population that can meet labor needs

The Internal Environment

In viewing the internal environment of your business, you are concerned with the physical aspects of the business. This includes the nature of land requirements (lease or buy), parking and building, equipment (production, administrative, storage, and materials handling), and people requirements. Surely, the kind of business you plan to enter will influence the physical needs for your business. Before you get to the numbers aspects, it will be good for you to prepare an itemized list corresponding to each category listed above.

A restaurant, like any service business, needs a population adequate to sustain it.

To calculate your capital investment requirements, you need to obtain the cost of each of these items. For this to be a meaningful exercise, you must obtain actual cost figures; do not use fabricated cost data. This will be the data you will use to calculate your return on investment. After having identified your needs, go to suppliers in order to obtain accurate prices.

Old or New Business?

Before you initiate a feasibility study, you need to decide whether you will enter an existing business or a new business. As an aid in reaching this decision, we suggest that you answer the questions found in Exhibit 4.1.

Established Business

If your conclusion is to enter an existing business, your next move is to locate an existing business that you think you would like to own. After selecting the potential business, answer the questions in Exhibit 6.1 and Exhibit 6.2. (You will want to use the material in Chapter 5 to aid you in arriving at an appropriate price for an existing business.) These exercises should enable you to determine if the proposed business is economically feasible for you.

New Business

If, after completing Exhibit 4.1, your conclusion is to establish a new business, use Exhibit 6.3 to stimulate your thinking in deciding what business is for you.

When you have chosen the type of business you think best, collect the data needed to complete Exhibit 6.4. This exercise should assist you in determining if your business idea is economically feasible.

Sources of Information

To complete the information requested in the various exhibits, you will want to avail yourself of appropriate sources of data. You may find the information in the university or college library or a local public library, from the local chamber of commerce, from the Small Business Development Center (SBDC), your state's industrial development commission or department of industry and trade, trade association publications, and local and regional business and economic publications. For additional information sources, see Exhibit 6.6. Your interpretation of the data from each of these sources may be facilitated by use of the reference mentioned in the footnote to that exhibit.

Summary

In this chapter we have discussed the importance of performing an economic feasibility study. Such a study is needed whether the prospective business is a new business idea or an established business.

We have detailed the mechanics that will enable you to perform such study. In carrying out this study, you can use the exhibits, which have been field tested to guide you through the process.

The economic feasibility study includes an examination of various aspects of your business idea. You must examine the business's external environment and its internal environment. You must also take a careful look at site selection.

Class Assignments

1. Prepare an economic feasibility study for your business idea.
2. Select your favorite business. Analyze the business for the following factors:
   a. Identify the number of competing firms
   b. By using local telephone directories, determine the number of related businesses that have closed their doors during the past five years
   c. Determine if the competing businesses still in existence are growing, stable, or declining
3. Choose a site for your proposed business. Explain the reasons for your choice.

Exhibit 6.1
CHECKLIST TO EVALUATE AN EXISTING BUSINESS

1. Why is the business available for purchase? _____
   _____
   _____

2. What are the intentions of the present owner?
   a. Does the present owner plan another business to compete with you?   Yes _____
      No _____

Exhibit 6.1
CHECKLIST TO EVALUATE AN EXISTING BUSINESS (*continued*)

   b. Is the present owner in good health?   Yes _____   No _____

   c. Does the present owner wish to retire?   Yes _____   No _____

   d. Does the present owner wish to continue to be associated with the business?

      Yes _____   No _____

3. Are demographic factors changing?

   a. Population: Up _____   Stable _____   Down _____

   b. Neighborhood: Better _____   Stable _____   Worse _____

   c. Demand: Up _____   Stable _____   Down _____

   d. Other factors: Better _____   Stable _____   Worse _____

4. Physical facilities

   a. Worn-out or outdated?   Yes _____   No _____

   b. Proper size for demand?   Yes _____   No _____

   c. Laid out properly?   Yes _____   No _____

5. Business operations

   a. How effective are the personnel?

      (1) What is the rate of labor turnover? _____%

      (2) What is the rate of absenteeism? _____%

      (3) Is the workforce unionized?   Yes _____   No _____

      (4) Is productivity high?   Yes _____   No _____

   b. What is the amount of waste?

      (1) Material _____% $_____ per day

      (2) Machine time _____% $_____ per day

      (3) Personnel time _____% $_____ per day

   c. Is the quality of the product or service good?   Yes _____   No _____

      (1) What portion of product is wasted? _____%

      (2) How many complaints about service are received? _____/year

      (3) Are deliveries on time?   Yes _____   No _____

   d. Content and level of inventory

      (1) Does the inventory contain mostly "dead stock"?   Yes _____   No _____

      (2) Is its level appropriate for the firm?   Yes _____   No _____

6. What is the financial condition of the firm?   Good _____   Fair _____

   Poor _____

   a. Have you had a reputable CPA appraise the firm's assets and liabilities?

      Yes _____   No _____

   b. What is the validity of financial statements?   Accurate _____   Overstated _____

      Understated _____

      Warning: Check to see relationship of book value of fixed assets to replacement costs

      Percentage of total accounts receivable over 90 days _____%

      Whether records are kept of age of accounts receivable   Yes _____   No _____
      Dollar amount of bad debts charged off in

      Last 6 months $_____

      12 months $_____

      36 months $_____

  c. Cash position

      (1) Cash on hand $_____

      (2) Cash in bank $_____

  d. Is cash flow adequate to meet obligations?   Yes _____   No _____

  e. Current ratio (Current assets/Current liabilities) _____

  f. Quick ratio [Current assets - Inventories]/Current liabilities: _____

  g. Debt-to-equity ratio (Debt [current liabilities, notes, bonds]/Owner's funds [common stock, preferred stock, capital surplus, and retained earnings]) _____

  h. Ratio of net income to sales (Net income/Net sales) _____

  i. Ratio of net income to equity or investment (Net income/Equity or investment) _____

  j. Amount of debt

      (1) Notes $_____

      (2) Bonds $_____

  k. Terms of debt _____

  l. Can you accurately determine the cost of the product or service?   Yes _____
      No _____

  m. Are there available data to enable you accurately to break down the price of a product or service into costs and profit?   Yes _____   No _____

  n. Is the business solvent?   Yes _____   No _____

7. How much investment is needed? $_____

8. What is the estimated return on your investment? _____%

9. What is your decision? _____

    _____

    _____

Exhibit 6.2
ECONOMIC FEASIBILITY STUDY OF AN EXISTING BUSINESS

One often wonders why people decide to acquire an existing business or join an ongoing family business. In many situations, those making the decision seem to give little thought to the present and future status of the business. There appears to be little evidence of an analysis to determine the economic feasibility of the venture. For example, some students, upon completing college, enter family businesses in geographic areas that are experiencing outbound population migration and an accompanying general shrinkage of economic activity in the local economy. The material that follows is for the use of those considering joining an ongoing business either as an owner or manager.

Exhibit 6.2
ECONOMIC FEASIBILITY STUDY OF AN EXISTING BUSINESS (*continued*)

I. *Economic Analysis*
   A. Nature of the economic environment
      1. Nature of competition
         a. Strong _____   Moderate _____   None known _____
         b. Type of competition
             Large national corporations _____
             Medium-size national corporations _____
             Small corporations serving national market _____
             Regional companies _____   Local companies _____
             Combination of above _____
      2. The business you are considering deals in
         Old products that are well known _____
         A mixture of new and old products _____
         New innovative products _____
         Or, a mixture of old and new services _____
         A new type of services _____
      3. The firm's trade name and products are recognized by customers and competitors for quality
         and reliability   Yes _____   No _____
   B. Nature of the market
      1. Is the market changing?   Growing _____   Stable _____
         Declining _____
      2. Is the population of the market area changing?   Growing _____   Stable _____
         Declining _____
      3. What is the age segment of your market? _____ to _____
      4. What is the population for this age segment? _____
      5. What is the average income of your market segment? $_____
      6. Indicate the population distribution by age in your market area.

Age	Percent of population
_____	_____
_____	_____
_____	_____
_____	_____
_____	_____

Age	*Percent of population*
_____	_____
_____	_____

7. Income of population in your market area
    a. Per capita income $_____
    b. Income of average customer $_____
    c. The income tends to be uniformly distributed among the population.   Yes _____
        No _____
        If *no*, describe how.   _____
        _____
        _____

C. Size of the market
    1. What is the anticipated number of customers?   Individual _____   family ____
        Business _____
    2. What are anticipated dollar sales?
        a. Per customer by: Day $_____   Week $_____   Month $_____
            Year $_____
        b. Total sales by: Day $_____   Week $_____   Month $_____
            Year $_____
D. What is the anticipated share of the market?   _____% of total estimated sales
    of $_____
E. What are the number and size of competitors?
    1. Number: Large size _____   Medium size _____
        Small size _____
    2. Range of capital investment from the small firm to the large firm $_____
        to $_____
F. What is the success rate of existing businesses?
    1. Number of firms that have been in business for   1 year _____   2 years _____
        3 years _____   4 years _____   5 years _____
        6 years _____   7 years _____   8 years _____
        9 years _____   10 years _____   Over 10 years _____
    2. Number of firms that have failed (closed their doors, sold out to a competitor, or merged with
        another business) within
        1 year _____   2 years _____   3 years _____
        4 years _____   5 years _____
G. Indicate any anticipated changes and their impact on the business (examples: construction of a new
    interstate highway that will isolate an area, zoning changes, changes in tax laws or other changes
    in government regulations, or street or road relocations).
    _____

Exhibit 6.2

ECONOMIC FEASIBILITY STUDY OF AN EXISTING BUSINESS (*continued*)

_____

_____

H. Technical aspects
    1. Are there many new processes?   Yes _____   No _____
    2. Are there many new items of equipment?   Yes _____   No _____
    3. Are there many new materials?   Yes _____   No _____
    4. Are there many new products?   Yes _____   No _____
    5. Does technology seem stable?   Yes _____   No _____
    6. Does technology seem stagnant?   Yes _____   No _____
I. Sources of supply
    1. What is the number of suppliers? _____
    2. What is the business's range of distance from suppliers? _____ to _____ miles
    3. List any anticipated changes by suppliers (terms, products, prices, etc.) _____

_____

II. *Replacement Costs of Total Business*
    A. Capital requirements (based on current costs for comparable items for your specific business). Indicate estimated dollar amounts for items applicable to your business.
        1. Land $_____
        2. Building(s) $_____
        3. Parking area $_____
        4. Equipment
            a. Counters $_____
            b. Shelving $_____
            c. Racks $_____
            d. Islands $_____
            e. Tables $_____
            f. Bins $_____
            g. Benches $_____
            h. Platforms $_____
            i. Partitions $_____
            j. Tanks $_____
            k. Piping, valves, etc. $_____
            l. Pumps $_____
            m. Loading docks $_____
        5. Other equipment
            a. Office
                (1) Desks $_____
                (2) Chairs $_____

    (3)   Filing cabinets $_____
    (4)   Typewriters $_____
    (5)   Calculators $_____
    (6)   Computers $_____
    (7)   Copying equipment $_____
    (8)   Communications equipment $_____
  b.   Plant or warehouse: production equipment (list the items and indicate the total dollar amount at end)

  _____

  _____

  _____

                                                                  $_____

  c.   Transportation and materials-handling equipment (indicate whether you plan to purchase or lease this type of equipment)

    Lease _____   Purchase _____

    (1)   Cars: Number _____ $_____
    (2)   Pickup trucks: Number _____ $_____
    (3)   Van/Carryall: Number _____ $_____
    (4)   Stake body truck (1½ ton):   Number _____ $_____
    (5)   Van body truck (1½ ton):   Number _____ $_____
    (6)   Heavy-duty 10-wheel truck: Number _____ $_____
    (7)   Tractor-trailer truck: Number _____ $_____
    (8)   Other automotive equipment

      _____

      _____

                                                                $_____

    (9)   Materials-handling equipment
      (a)   Two-wheel trucks: Number _____ $_____
      (b)   Jack pallets: Number _____ $_____
      (c)   Forklift trucks: Number _____ $_____
      (d)   Air pallets: Number _____ $_____
      (e)   Conveyors: Number _____ $_____
      (f)   Silos, closed piping pumps/blower/screw-feeder system: Number _____
            $_____
      (g)   Other _____

        _____

        _____

      Total estimated cost of all items of equipment included in 4 and 5 $_____
6.   Beginning inventory
  a.   Merchandise $_____
  b.   Raw material $_____
  c.   Supplies $_____

Exhibit 6.2
ECONOMIC FEASIBILITY STUDY OF AN EXISTING BUSINESS (*continued*)

    d. Parts $_____

        Estimated total inventory $_____

7. Beginning working capital

    a. Licenses $_____

    b. Taxes $_____

    c. Permits $_____

    d. Utility deposits $_____

    e. Cash needs for 6 months

        (1) Salaries $_____

        (2) Wages $_____

        (3) Rent $_____

        (4) Phone $_____

        (5) Utilities $_____

        (6) Insurance $_____

        (7) FICA taxes $_____

        (8) Supplies $_____

        (9) Advertising $_____

      (10) Inventory purchases $_____

      (11) Interest $_____

      (12) Miscellaneous $_____

      (13) Other $_____

                Total $_____

III. *Present Book Value of (Name of Company)*

    A. Please obtain the information requested below from company records. (This will give you the present book value of the company. However, you should make a comparative check between book value and the value of the item; that is, determine what percentage of receivables are collectible; what percentage of the inventory is unusable; and which, if any, items of equipment do not function.) From company records prepare a balance sheet.

    B. Investment required to purchase this business $_____

    C. Rate of return on investment: Estimated profits $_____divided by amount invested in business ($_____) equals rate of return on investment (_____%).

    D. Conclusion on purchasing the company. Before reaching a decision on whether you want to purchase the company, review section II above and give special attention to the information in III.A, B, and C. At this point be prepared to conduct your final analysis by comparing your anticipated return on investment with the return on alternative investment opportunities (rate on savings accounts or certificates of deposits or return on treasury bonds, high-rated municipal or corporate bonds, or other business ventures). Is there an adequate return to compensate you for the risk you are assuming in buying this company? Yes _____   No _____

        Therefore, I conclude that I will _____,   I will not _____ purchase this business.

Exhibit 6.3
BUSINESS OPTIONS CLASSIFIED INTO RELATED GROUPS

RETAILING
Food
 · Grocery
 · Fast-prepared
 · Convenience
 · Restaurant
 · Lounge
 · Specialty shops
 · Bakery
 · Donut shop
 · Deli
 · Yogurt
 · Ice cream
Appliance
Hardware and building material
Specialty
Clothing
Office
Retailing pharmacy or drugstore
 with sandwiches and soda foun-
 tain
Computer.
 · Hardware
 · Software
 · Supplies
Telecommunications equipment
Auto parts
Box wrapping
Mail boxes and mailing service

SERVICE
Service station
Auto repair
Appliance repair
Building repair and renovation

Janitorial
Plumber
Electrician
Floor covering
F.B.O. (fixed base operation air-
 craft)
Travel agency
Software information systems

WHOLESALING
Jobber
Broker
Distributor
Manufacturing agent

*RESEARCH AND
DEVELOPMENT*
Materials
Products
Specialized machinery
Manufacturing systems

CONSULTING
Management
Management information systems
Financial
Investment
Marketing
Risk management
Land use and development
Engineering
Economic
Government
Various additional highly special-
 ized areas

MANUFACTURING
Metals
 · Sheet metal
 · Machine shop
  (a) General
  (b) Special equipment
 · Foundry
 · Mini-steel mill
Plastics
 · Extrusion
 · Application
 · Formulation
 · Injection
Food processing
 · Meat
 · Vegetables
 · Specialty items

RECREATION
Tennis club
Racquetball club
Driving range
Miniature golf

MARICULTURE
Public fish pond
Commercial fish pond
 · Catfish
 · Bass
 · Bream
 · Crayfish
Commercial frog production
Freshwater shrimp
Pearl production

Exhibit 6.4
ECONOMIC FEASIBILITY STUDY OF A NEW BUSINESS

Sometimes you may fall into a trap that others before you have encountered—not correlating the economic data, gleaned from various data sources, in a meaningful manner with your business. For example, many businesses only appeal to certain age segments of the population. Therefore, in your economic analysis, it is essential that you identify the size of those age segments suitable to your business and indicate what *realistic* proportion of the group you anticipate to have as customers. This in turn should enable you to project the

Exhibit 6.4
ECONOMIC FEASIBILITY STUDY OF A NEW BUSINESS (*continued*)

sales volume for your new business idea. Please give the appropriate answer below, either by using a check or by writing in the appropriate information.

I. *Economic Analysis*
    A. The nature of the economic environment
        1. Nature of competition   Strong _____   Moderate _____
            Weak _____   None known _____
        2. New product _____   New service _____   New to market _____
            area _____
    B. Nature of the market
        1. Is the market changing?   Growing _____   Stable _____
            Declining _____
        2. Relationship to population
            (a) Age segment _____ to _____
            (b) Population number in this age segment _____
            (c) Average income of your market segment _____
        3. Income of population in your market area
            (a) Per capita income $_____
            (b) Income of average customer $_____
            (c) The income tends to be uniformly distributed among the population   Yes _____
                 No _____
                 If not, describe how. _____
                 _____
                 _____
                 _____

    C. Size of the market
        1. What is the anticipated number of customers?   Individual _____   Family _____
            Business _____
        2. What are anticipated dollar sales?
            (a) Per customer by: day $_____   Week $_____   Month $_____
                 Year _____
            (b) Total sales by: Day $_____   Week $_____   Month $_____
                 Year $_____
    D. What is the anticipated share of the market? _____% of total estimated sales
        of $_____
    E. What are the number and size of competitors?
        1. Number: Large size _____   Medium size _____
            Small size _____
        2. Range of capital investment from the small firm to the large firm $_____ to
            $_____ .

F.   What is the success rate of existing businesses?

    1.   Number of firms that have been in business for   1 year _____

        2 years _____   3 years _____   4 years _____

        5 years _____   6 years _____   7 years _____

        8 years _____   9 years _____   10 years _____

        Over 10 years _____

    2.   Number of firms that have failed (closed their doors, sold out to a competitor, or merged with another business) within

        1 year _____   2 years _____   3 years _____

        4 years _____   5 years _____

G.   Technical aspects

    1.   Are there new processes?   Yes _____   No _____

    2.   Are there many new items of equipment?   Yes _____   No _____

    3.   Are there many new materials?   Yes _____   No _____

    4.   Are there many new products?   Yes _____   No _____

    5.   Does technology seem stable?   Yes _____   No _____

    6.   Does technology seem stagnant?   Yes _____   No _____

H.   Sources of supply

    1.   What is the number of suppliers? _____

    2.   What is the business's range of distance from supplies? _____ to _____ miles

II.   *Sales Projections, Cash Receipts*

A.   Capital requirements (based on competitors and plans for your specific business). Indicate estimated dollar amounts for items applicable to your business.

    1.   Land $_____

    2.   Building(s) $_____

    3.   Parking area $_____

    4.   Equipment

        (a)   Counters $_____

        (b)   Shelving $_____

        (c)   Racks $_____

        (d)   Islands $_____

        (e)   Tables $_____

        (f)   Bins $_____

        (g)   Benches $_____

        (h)   Platforms $_____

        (i)   Partitions $_____

        (j)   Tanks $_____

        (k)   Piping, valves, etc. $_____

        (l)   Pumps $_____

        (m)   Loading docks $_____

Exhibit 6.4
ECONOMIC FEASIBILITY STUDY OF A NEW BUSINESS (*continued*)

5. Other equipment
    (a) Office
        (1) Desks $_____
        (2) Chairs $_____
        (3) Filing cabinets $_____
        (4) Typewriters $_____
        (5) Calculators $_____
        (6) Computers $_____
        (7) Copying equipment $_____
        (8) Communication equipment $_____
    (b) Plant or warehouse: production equipment (list the items and indicate the total dollar amount at end)

    _____

    _____

    _____

                                                                $_____

        Total estimated cost of all items of equipment included in 4 and 5 $_____
6. Beginning inventory
    (a) Merchandise $_____
    (b) Raw material $_____
    (c) Supplies $_____
    (d) Parts $_____
            Estimated total inventory $_____
7. Beginning working capital
    (a) Licenses $_____
    (b) Taxes $_____
    (c) Permits $_____
    (d) Utility deposits $_____
    (e) Cash needs for 6 months
        (1) Salaries $_____
        (2) Wages $_____
        (3) Rent $_____
        (4) Phone $_____
        (5) Utilities $_____
        (6) Insurance $_____
        (7) FICA taxes $_____
        (8) Supplies $_____
        (9) Advertising $_____
        (10) Inventory purchases $_____

(11) Interest $_____

(12) Miscellaneous $_____

(13) Other $_____

      Total $_____

8. Profit and loss statement (date: _____ to _____)

    Gross Sales

      Less

          Freight $_____

          Discounts $_____

          Returns—No fault $_____

          Returns—Defective material $_____

          Allowances—Defective material $_____

          Bad debt variance $_____

                                                          $_____

          Net Sales $_____

    Less Selling Expense

          Salaries $_____

          Overtime—Excess wages $_____

          Rent $_____

          Taxes $_____

          Insurance $_____

          Amortization $_____

          Telephone and telegraph $_____

          Dues and subscriptions $_____

          Professional $_____

          Advertising $_____

          Distributor discount $_____

          Living $_____

          Travel $_____

          Entertainment $_____

          Miscellaneous sales expense $_____

            Total Selling Expense $_____

    Gross Profit less Selling Expense $_____

    Less Administrative Expense

          Salaries—Officers $_____

          Salaries—Clerical $_____

          Overtime—Excess wages $_____

          Rent $_____

          Taxes $_____

          Insurance $_____

Exhibit 6.4
ECONOMIC FEASIBILITY STUDY OF A NEW BUSINESS (continued)

Depreciation	$_____
Amortization	$_____
Office supplies	$_____
Stationery and printing	$_____
Telephone and telegraph	$_____
Dues and subscriptions	$_____
Legal and professional	$_____
Employee relations	$_____
Computer maintenance	$_____
Computer software	$_____
Computer supplies	$_____
Computer rental	$_____
Other office equipment maintenance	$_____
Employee education	$_____
Living	$_____
Travel	$_____
Entertainment	$_____
Interest	$_____
Life insurance	$_____
Donations	$_____
Gifts and gratuities	$_____
Other administrative expense	$_____
Total Administrative Expense	$_____
Gross Profit less Administrative Expense	$_____
Less Manufacturing Expense	
Materials cost	$_____
Freight in	$_____
Salaries—Supervision	$_____
Wages—Production	$_____
Wages—Maintenance	$_____
Wages—Material handling	$_____
Overtime—Excess wages	$_____
Repairs and maintenance	$_____
Plant expense	$_____
Machinery rent	$_____
Utilities	$_____
Building rent	$_____
Taxes	$_____

Insurance $_____

Depreciation $_____

Amortization $_____

Packing $_____

  Total Manufacturing Expense $_____

Net Operating Profit $_____

Other Income $_____

Income Before Income Taxes $_____

  Provision for Income Tax $_____

Net Income $_____

9. Beginning cash contingency fund $_____

10. Total beginning working capital $_____

  Total capital requirements (sum of all items in A): $_____

B. Rate of return on investment: Estimated profits ($_____) divided by estimated $_____
    capital requirements ($_____) equals rate of return on investment (_____%).

C. Conclusion on entering this business. Comparing the return on this investment with return on al-
    ternative investment opportunities (rate on savings accounts or certificates of deposits or return on
    treasury bonds, high-rated municipal or corporate bonds, or other business ventures), is there an
    adequate return to compensate you for the risk you are assuming in the above business?

    Yes _____   No _____

    Therefore, I conclude that I will _____,   I will not _____ enter this business.

Exhibit 6.5
ESTIMATED SOURCE OF FUNDS

ITEM	COST	OWN	CASH	BORROW	SUPPLIER	SALES RECEIPTS
1. Land						
2. Building(s)						
3. Parking area						
4. Equipment						
a. Counters						
b. Shelving						
c. Racks						
d. Islands						
e. Tables						
f. Bins						
g. Benches						
h. Platforms						

Exhibit 6.5
ESTIMATED SOURCE OF FUNDS (*continued*)

    i. Partitions

    j. Tanks

    k. Piping, valves, etc.

    l. Pumps

    m. Loading docks

5. Machines

    a. Office

        (1) Desks

        (2) Chairs

        (3) Filing cabinets

        (4) Typewriters

        (5) Calculators

        (6) Computer

        (7) Copying equipment

        (8) Communication equipment

6. Plant or warehouse—production
    equipment (list items with dollar
    amount for each)

    a.

    b.

    c.

    d.

    e.

    f.

    g.

    h.

    i.

    j.

    k.

    l.

    m.

    n.
    [If space is insufficient use additional sheet(s)]

7. Transportation and materials-
    handling equipment

    a. Automotive

        (1) Car(s)

        (2) Pickup truck(s)

        (3) Vans/carryall

(4) Stake body truck (1-1/2 ton) _____ _____ _____ _____

(5) Van body truck (1-1/2 ton) _____ _____ _____ _____

(6) Heavy-duty 10-wheel truck _____ _____ _____ _____

(7) Tractor-trailer truck _____ _____ _____ _____

(8) Other automotive equipment

    (a) _____ _____ _____ _____ _____

    (b) _____ _____ _____ _____ _____

    (c) _____ _____ _____ _____ _____

    (d) _____ _____ _____ _____ _____

    (e) _____ _____ _____ _____ _____

    (f) _____ _____ _____ _____ _____

    (g) _____ _____ _____ _____ _____

b. Materials-handling equipment

  (1) Two-wheel trucks _____ _____ _____ _____

  (2) Jack pallets _____ _____ _____ _____

  (3) Forklift trucks _____ _____ _____ _____

  (4) Airpallets _____ _____ _____ _____

  (5) Conveyors _____ _____ _____ _____

  (6) Silos, closed piping pumps/ blowers/screw-feeder systems _____ _____ _____ _____

  (7) Other

_____ _____ _____ _____ _____

_____ _____ _____ _____ _____

_____ _____ _____ _____ _____

_____ _____ _____ _____ _____

_____ _____ _____ _____ _____

_____ _____ _____ _____ _____

8. Inventory (beginning)

  a. Merchandise _____ _____ _____ _____

  b. Raw material _____ _____ _____ _____

  c. Supplies _____ _____ _____ _____

  d. Parts _____ _____ _____ _____

9. Working capital (beginning)

  a. License _____ _____ _____ _____

  b. Taxes _____ _____ _____ _____

  c. Permits _____ _____ _____ _____

  d. Utility deposits _____ _____ _____ _____

  e. Six months cash needs _____ _____ _____ _____

    (1) Salaries _____ _____ _____ _____

    (2) Wages _____ _____ _____ _____

Exhibit 6.5
ESTIMATED SOURCE OF FUNDS (*continued*)

(3)	Rent						
(4)	Phone						
(5)	Utilities						
(6)	Insurance						
(7)	FICA taxes						
(8)	Supplies						
(9)	Advertising						
(10)	Inventory purchases						
(11)	Interest						
(12)	Miscellaneous						
(13)	Other						
10.	Cash—Beginning Contingency Fund						
	TOTAL						

Exhibit 6.6
INFORMATION SOURCES FOR FEASIBILITY STUDIES

*1. Consumer attitudes and buying power plans—Conference Board.
*2. Intercity cost of living indicators project—American Chamber of Commerce Researchers Association.
*3. Statistical bulletin—Conference Board.
*4. *Sales and Marketing Management:*
   • July special issue: Survey of buying power, Part I. Featuring metro markets statistics on population, effective buying income, and retail sales.
   • October special issue: Featuring metro markets projections, merchandise line sales, annual survey of newspaper and TV markets and zip code characteristics.
*5. Monthly retail trade: sales and accounts receivable—Department of Commerce.
*6. Monthly wholesale trade: sales and inventories—Department of Commerce.
*7. Surveys, polls, censuses, and forecasts directory—Gale Research.
*8. 1986 (87) Sourcebook of Demographics and Buying Power for every county in the US.
*9. *Sales and Marketing Management:* Survey of Buying Power Data Service.
*10. NPA Data Services: Regional Economic Projections Series.
*11. County business patterns.
*12. Blue chip economic indicators: What top economists are saying about US outlook for the year ahead.
13. Yellow Pages.
14. Manufacturing directories.

* Provide information needed for assembling feasibility study.
A source that you may use to interpret the data found in Exhibit 6.6 is William Layer, *Handbook of Demographics for Marketing and Advertising: Sources and Trends on U.S. Consumer* (Lexington Books, 1987).

C H A P T E R 7

FRANCHISING

One of the most dynamic areas in the American economy is franchising. The number of new franchise ventures continues to have a significant yearly increase, as does the number of franchise units and sales volume.

In this chapter we will cover such topics as the magnitude and diversity of franchises, and recent regulatory changes regarding franchises, notably the requirement of a prospectus. We will explore deciding whether to obtain a franchise or be independent. We will identify and discuss some of the more popular types of franchises, including motels, fast-food restaurants, convenience markets, and auto service. We will examine the risks of a franchise and then analyze the factors involved in deciding whether to obtain a franchise. Finally, we will analyze issues to consider in deciding to franchise your own business. Our purpose in the development of this material is to help you evaluate franchises as an ownership option.

After reading this chapter you will be able to

- Discuss the size and scope of franchising in the economy
- Analyze whether to obtain a franchise
- Discuss some of the more popular types of franchises
- Identify the risks of franchising
- Assess whether your business idea can become a franchise

Franchising in Perspective

The growth in franchising reflects a strong interest among prospective entrepreneurs as well as consumers. As Exhibit 7.1 indicates, franchises were expected to account for 34 percent of retail sales in a recent year. When compared to previous years, this indicates continued growth. As Exhibit 7.2 shows, franchising includes great diversity and a wide range of activity.

Exhibit 7.3 further places in perspective the diversity and magnitude of franchising as a method of doing business. You will note that these franchises

Exhibit 7.1
FRANCHISING AS A PERCENTAGE OF RETAIL SALES

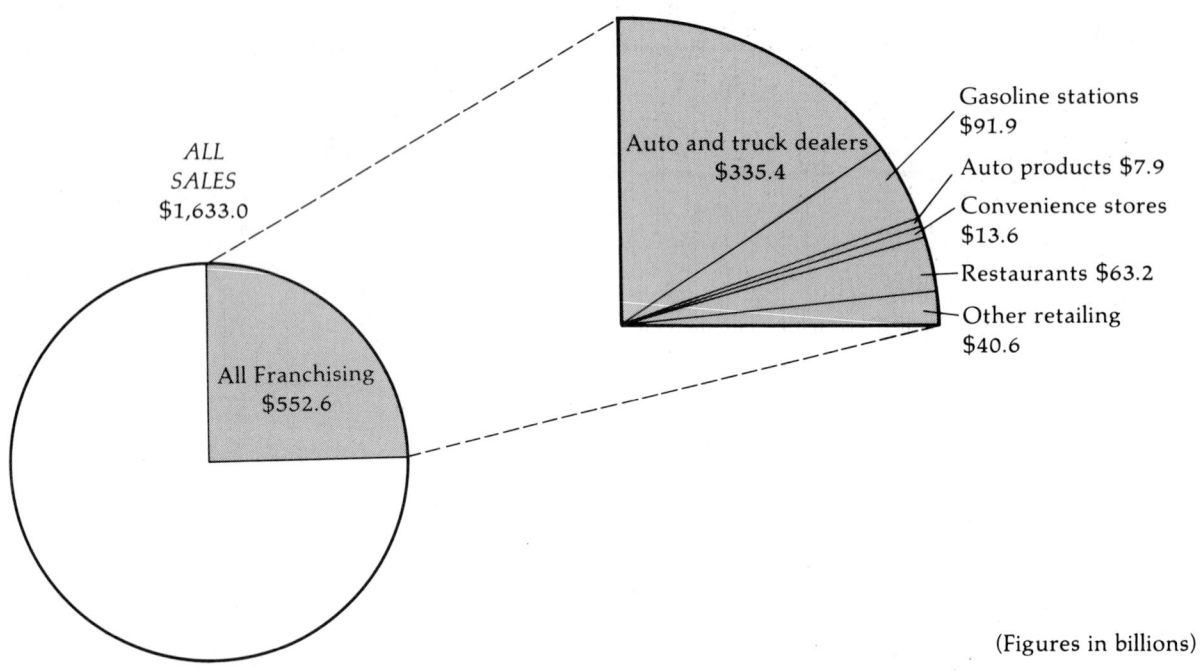

ALL
SALES
$1,633.0

All Franchising
$552.6

Auto and truck dealers
$335.4

Gasoline stations
$91.9

Auto products $7.9

Convenience stores
$13.6

Restaurants $63.2

Other retailing
$40.6

(Figures in billions)

Source: Bureau of Industrial Economics, U.S. Department of Commerce, "Franchising in the Economy 1988," p. 15.

show a range of success. These data are issued annually in the Department of Commerce's publication "Franchising in the Economy."

Exhibit 7.4 identifies the franchises that grew the fastest in a recent year. In this exhibit, growth is measured by the number of units added in a year.

Exhibit 7.5 indicates the franchise types with the best growth by industry. Note that fast food, the largest and one of the most expensive groups, also shows the greatest growth.

Exhibit 7.6 reveals the ten most expensive franchises to acquire. Expense is measured not by franchising fee, but by startup cost. Despite their high cost, the three hamburger companies on this list also made the top ten in the Franchisor 100. Burger King had a two-year waiting list for franchisees.

Exhibit 7.7 lists the ten least expensive franchises to acquire (again, startup cost is the factor used to judge expense). Other franchises may be inexpensive, but they require real estate or an existing business. The ten listed in this exhibit could be started for less than $50,000.

Much data on franchises is developed annually by *Venture* magazine and is published in its November issue. In addition to the material found in these exhibits, a master chart for the top 100 franchises appears. This master chart is

Exhibit 7.2
TYPES AND NUMBERS OF FRANCHISES[a]

TYPE	NUMBER	TYPE	NUMBER
Automotive products and service	93	Insurance	5
Auto and trailer rentals	21	Laundries, drycleaning—services	10
Beauty salons and supplies	21	Lawn and garden supplies and services	7
Business aids and services	131	Maintenance, cleaning, sanitation—	
Campgrounds	4	services and supplies	39
Children's stores, furniture, products	1	Motels and hotels	21
Clothing and shoes	20	Optical products and services	5
Construction and remodeling—materials		Paint and decorating supplies	1
and services	49	Pet centers	3
Cosmetics and toiletries	10	Printing	18
Dental centers	14	Real estate	28
Drug stores	7	Recreation—entertainment, travel—	
Educational products and services	29	services and supplies	30
Employment services	49	Retailing—art supplies and frames	11
Equipment rentals	8	Retailing—computer sales and services	15
Foods—donuts	14	Retailing—florists	5
Foods—grocery, specialty stores	50	Retailing—miscellaneous	77
Foods—ice cream, yogurt, candy, popcorn	52	Security systems	6
Foods—pancake, waffle, pretzel	6	Swimming pools	1
Foods—restaurants, drive-ins, carryouts	280	Tools, hardware	4
General merchandising stores	3	Vending	5
Health aids and services	34	Water conditioning	6
Hearing aids	1	Miscellaneous wholesale and service	
Home furnishings and furniture—retail,		business	32
repair, service	41		

[a]Number reflects number of businesses in the field that offer franchises, not the total number of franchise outlets.

Exhibit 7.3
FRANCHISING IN THE ECONOMY

KINDS OF FRANCHISED BUSINESS	ESTABLISHMENTS (NUMBER)			SALES ($000)		
	Total	Company-Owned	Franchisee-Owned	Total	Company-Owned	Franchisee-Owned
Total: All Franchising	462,123	88,500	373,623	569,078,748	85,371,999	483,706,749
Automobile and truck dealers[a]	27,600	0	27,600	307,256,000	0	307,256,000
Automotive products and services[b]	36,763	4,851	31,912	11,300,863	3,800,495	7,500,368
Business aids and services	52,718	6,676	46,042	13,288,254	2,338,187	10,950,067
Accounting, credit, collection agencies and general business systems	1,914	22	1,892	161,877	5,228	156,649
Employment services	5,605	2,159	3,446	3,219,968	1,478,586	1,741,382

Exhibit 7.3

FRANCHISING IN THE ECONOMY (*continued*)

KINDS OF FRANCHISED BUSINESS	ESTABLISHMENTS (NUMBER)			SALES ($000)		
	Total	Company-Owned	Franchisee-Owned	Total	Company-Owned	Franchisee-Owned
Printing and copying services	4,905	121	4,784	1,028,948	34,486	994,462
Tax preparation services	8,274	3,602	4,672	461,203	248,868	212,335
Real estate[c]	14,016	141	13,875	5,133,471	48,764	5,084,707
Miscellaneous business services	18,004	631	17,373	3,282,787	522,255	2,760,532
Construction, home improvement, maintenance and cleaning services	18,900	748	18,152	4,615,360	1,351,950	3,263,410
Convenience stores	15,524	8,974	6,550	11,278,895	6,732,322	4,546,573
Educational products and services	8,625	537	8,088	935,166	208,037	727,129
Restaurants (all types)	78,203	24,364	53,839	52,273,863	18,803,699	33,470,164
Gasoline service stations[a]	120,510	21,692	98,818	86,618,000	15,591,000	71,027,000
Hotels, motels and campgrounds	8,203	1,147	7,056	15,983,990	5,061,835	10,922,155
Laundry and drycleaning services	2,297	103	2,194	291,802	26,016	265,786
Recreation, entertainment and travel	7,901	419	7,482	3,549,025	727,095	2,821,930
Rental services (auto-truck)	9,528	2,449	7,079	6,155,006	3,523,889	2,631,117
Rental services (equipment)	2,718	665	2,053	716,019	306,096	409,923
Retailing (nonfood)	45,456	11,228	34,228	23,102,779	7,324,902	15,777,877
Retailing (food other than convenience stores)	19,852	3,509	16,343	10,746,011	2,781,204	7,964,807
Soft drink bottlers[a,d]	1,203	662	541	19,662,000	16,516,000	3,146,000
Miscellaneous	6,122	476	5,646	1,305,715	279,272	1,026,443

[a] Estimated by ITA based on Bureau of the Census and trade association data.

[b] Includes some establishments with significant sales of nonautomotive products such as household appliances, garden supplies, and so on.

[c] Gross commisions.

[d] Includes soft drinks; fruit drinks and ades; syrups; flavoring agents; and bases. Data do not include figures for independent private label and contract-filler bottling companies, which account for 22 percent in 1986, 22 percent in 1987, and 22 percent in 1988 of the value of shipments of the total industry.

Source: Bureau of Industrial Economics, U.S. Department of Commerce, "Franchising in the Economy," p. 15.

the most comprehensive single source of information available on the top franchises.

Legal Changes Regarding Franchising

Franchisors are now required by the Federal Trade Commission (FTC) to provide the prospective franchisee with a prospectus. Upon receipt of this document, have it reviewed by a competent attorney as well as a competent CPA.

Recent court decisions indicate that, where franchises are concerned, federal law takes precedence over state franchise laws. Recent decisions also establish that franchisees may join in legal action to seek redress from a franchisor that has contributed economic damage to the franchisee or is in a position to cause economic damage.

Exhibit 7.4
TEN FRANCHISES WITH FASTEST GROWTH

FRANCHISE	GROWTH	UNITS ADDED	FRANCHISOR 100 RANK
Dynamark Security Centers	525%	84	65
Coverall	198	214	17
Security Alliance	163	62	82
"TCBY" (The Country's Best Yogurt)	145	133	28
Jack in the Box	140	94	53
Cost Cutters Family Hair Care	135	81	50
Mail Boxes Etc.	113	187	46
Sylvan Learning Centers	100	102	45
Great Clips	95	56	66
Whirla Whip	85	40	96

a. Growth is measured by greatest percentage of gain in number of units in the last reported fiscal year.

Source: Reprinted by permission from *Venture* (November 1987), p. 38.

Do I Want a Franchise?

When you consider all the advertising done by franchises as well as all of the franchisors that you observe, it can be easy for you to become convinced that franchising is the path that guarantees you success. Prior to your becoming caught up in making a commitment to become a franchisee, you should carefully investigate the franchising field.

You not only need to study the prospectus of the prospective franchisor. You also need to answer a number of additional questions:

1. What can this franchise do for you that you are unable to do for yourself?
2. Does the franchise have a uniform and consistent product or service?
3. Does the franchise have a favorable image regionally and nationally?
4. Are the franchise units uniform in color and architectural design?
5. Does the franchisor's logo have an eye-grabbing appeal?
6. Does the franchise have an efficient layout?
7. Is the franchise production system uniform in character, and does it provide for operational efficiency?
8. Is there a well-formulated, efficient cost-control information system available for the franchisee?
9. Does the franchisor require that the franchisee provide periodic operational reports to the franchisor? After the receipt of the franchisee report, will the franchisor provide the franchisee with a composite feedback statement?
10. Does the franchisor have supply requirements? Are specific vendors on a must-use list? Do you perceive this as advantageous?
11. Does the franchisor conduct frequent unannounced onsite management and operational audits?

Exhibit 7.5
FRANCHISE GROWTH BY INDUSTRY

INDUSTRY	NUMBER OF COMPANIES IN FRANCHISOR 100	AVERAGE ANNUAL INCREASE IN UNITS PER FRANCHISOR[a]
Fast-food restaurants	16	160
Video	3	130
Health and fitness	4	125
Ice cream and yogurt	4	112
Maintenance and cleaning	11	110
Hair cutting	5	92
Auto rental	7	92
Business service	4	91
Construction	1	83
Education	2	70
Retail—miscellaneous	5	67
Real estate	5	67
Auto maintenance	9	61
Rental service	1	61
Travel	5	60
Home decorating	4	60
Printing and copying	9	58
Retail—computers	3	58
Convenience stores	2	42

a. Based on two-year average.

Source: Reprinted by permission from *Venture,* November 1987, p. 42.

12. In the event that a franchisee is observed to not comply with the franchisor's performance standards, what action may the franchisee anticipate?
13. Are existing franchisees interested in selling their franchises?
14. Does the franchisor require new franchisees to participate in company training programs before beginning operations? Are franchisees required to participate in refresher training programs?
15. Are there any advertising requirements?
16. Are there any territorial restrictions?

Exhibit 7.6
THE TEN MOST EXPENSIVE FRANCHISES

FRANCHISE	LOWEST STARTUP COST	LOWEST FRANCHISE FEE	REAL ESTATE OPTION	FRANCHISOR 100 RANK
Days Inns of America	$4,500,000	$25,000	BC	76
Quality Inns	1,890,000	25,000	LB	47
Econo Lodge	1,800,000	20,000	LBC	38
Hardee's	406,600	15,000	LBC	9
Burger King	280,800	40,000	LB	3
Super 8 Motels	300,000	20,000	B	56
McDonald's	270,000	12,500	L	2
Round Table	260,500	20,000	LB	89
Budget Rent A Car	259,800	15,000	LB	27
Taco Bell	209,000	35,000	LBC	29

Source: Reprinted by permission from *Venture*, November 1987, p. 38.

Exhibit 7.7
THE TEN LEAST EXPENSIVE FRANCHISES

FRANCHISE	LOWEST STARTUP COST	LOWEST FRANCHISE FEE	REAL ESTATE OPTION	FRANCHISOR 100 RANK
Sunshine Polishing System	$ 1,700	$ 975	N	61
Coverall	400	3,250	N	17
Caustic-Glo	1,300	8,750	N	91
Chem-Dry Carpet Cleaning	4,400	6,100	N	60
Jani King	8,500	7,500	N	1
Video Data Services	2,500	13,950	N	72
Decorating Den, Bethesda	4,500	15,500	N	42
Rainbow International	5,600	15,000	N	8
ServiceMaster	13,300	11,500	N	16
Stained Glass Overlay	12,600	34,000	N	36

Source: Reprinted by permission from *Venture*, November 1987, p. 38.

To assist you in reaching a decision on whether you prefer to have your own independent business or to acquire a franchise, use Exhibit 7.8. Answering the questions in this exhibit should aid you in reaching a conclusion concerning you and franchising. You should consider two other questions as well:

1. Do you now believe that a franchise business will better serve your needs than an independent business?
2. After applying the previous series of questions to a specific franchise, do you think that it will be appropriate for you?

In the process of analyzing a particular franchise, you should not only carefully study the franchisor's prospectus. In addition, you should research the *Wall Street Journal, Business Week, Forbes,* and the *New York Times* for the past year. Some sources indicate that a particular franchise is a good opportunity when information found in other sources shows that this franchise is experiencing difficulties. Reviewing data in a variety of sources helps you get the most information possible so that your analysis is reliable.

It can be misleading when you view the mass of franchises since all franchise firms do not ensure success. There are many gradations of performance quality among franchises. Some, such as McDonald's, can be the equivalent of an oil well in your backyard. Others (gumball machines, stamp machines, and swimming pool sales, for example) have little or nothing to offer. Some franchisors will take your investment and leave you to fail. Nevertheless, franchises as a whole have a higher rate of survival than independent ventures.

Exhibit 7.8
EVALUATING WHETHER TO BE INDEPENDENT OR
TO OPERATE A FRANCHISE

In today's world, individuals may have the greatest number of choices in history in selecting the kind of entrepreneur they would like to be. These choices fall into two broad categories with a multiplicity of combinations in each. The two categories are to be an independent entrepreneur or to be a franchisee. It is the purpose of this questionnaire to aid you in making this choice.

Please indicate your choice by checking the appropriate space.

1. My objective in life is
   a. To make a lot of money _____
   b. To be my own boss _____
   c. To have a comfortable living _____
   d. To have a business of my own that will allow me leisure time _____
   e. To work for someone else _____
   f. To avoid accepting responsibility
      (1) For providing employment for others _____
      (2) For providing products or services to others _____
   g. To spend whatever time and effort necessary to achieve success _____

2. My present economic status is
   a. Net worth
      (1) Equity value of real estate $ _____
      (2) Cash surrender value of life insurance $ _____
      (3) Marketable securities $ _____
      (4) Savings $ _____
      (5) Other   • $ _____
   b. Annual income
      (1) Salary $ _____
      (2) Special income $ _____
      (3) Investment
          (a) Rental income $ _____
          (b) Stocks $ _____
          (c) Bonds $ _____
              Total investment income $ _____
      (4) Interest $ _____
      (5) Annuities $ _____
      (6) Trust $ _____
      (7) Estate $ _____
      (8) Other $ _____
              Total annual income $ _____
   c. Annual financial responsibilities
      (1) Mortgage payments $ _____
      (2) Home insurance $ _____
      (3) Real and personal property taxes $ _____
      (4) Car payments $ _____
      (5) Life insurance $ _____
      (6) Utility bills $ _____
      (7) Other loans, principal and interest $ _____
      (8) Alimony and child support $ _____
      (9) Children's education expense $ _____
      (10) Medical and dental expense $ _____
      (11) Medical insurance $ _____
      (12) Household expense $ _____
      (13) Home and lawn maintenance $ _____
      (14) Auto expense $ _____
      (15) Food $ _____
      (16) Business and professional expense $ _____
      (17) Other $ _____
              Total annual personal expense $ _____

Exhibit 7.8
EVALUATING WHETHER TO BE INDEPENDENT OR
TO OPERATE A FRANCHISE (*continued*)

3. Marital status

    a. Married _____

    b. Single _____

    c. Divorced _____

    d. Children   Yes _____   No _____

       Ages _____

4. Education

    a. Elementary _____

    b. High school _____

    c. Technical school _____

       Type training _____

    d. College

       1 year _____   2 years _____   3 years _____

       4 years _____

       Kind of degree _____   Major _____   Minor _____

       Master's degree _____

       Kind _____

       Fields _____

       Other _____

5. Experience (list in order from last to earliest)

    a. Last or current job _____

       Employer _____

       Title _____

       Dates of employment _____ to _____

    b. Previous job _____

       Employer _____

       Title _____

       Dates of employment _____ to _____

    c. Previous job _____

       Employer _____

       Title _____   Dates of employment _____ to _____

    d. Identify what ability you gained from each employment situation

       _____

       _____

       _____

6. My strengths are

    a. Directing the activities of another _____

    b. Planning an activity in a manner that takes the least time, effort, and material _____

    c. Serving people in a pleasing manner _____

    d. Helping people resolve their personal differences _____

    e. Managing money _____

    f. Keeping records _____

    g. Organizing people, money, machines, and things to produce products or service _____

    h. Effectively following instructions and directions of others _____

    i. Effectively being my own boss _____

    j. Being a self-starter _____

    k. Taking initiative _____

    l. Making decisions _____

    m. Innovative ability to create new ideas for products and services _____

7. My weaknesses are

    a. I can't make decisions _____

    b. I postpone making decisions _____

    c. I try to get others to make decisions for me _____

    d. I dislike assuming responsibility _____

    e. I avoid responsibilities _____

    f. I do not handle money well _____

    g. I seem unable to keep my checkbook balanced _____

    h. I am generally insecure without someone to guide and support me _____

8. Could you accept working within the rigidity of the organization framework imposed by a franchisor system?   Yes _____   No _____

9. What kind of business would you be most happy operating as an owner-manager? (Please be honest with yourself in answering this question. Be as specific as necessary to provide an adequate description of the business.)

    Answer: _____

    _____

    _____

    _____

10. Please carefully review the answers you have given to questions above. Be honest and frank with yourself. Do you think that you could accomplish your objectives in life and achieve a reasonable level of success and happiness by:

    a. Having my own independent business _____

    b. Owning a franchise _____

    c. Working for someone else _____

Types of Franchises Showing Growth

In recent years, we have observed a rapid growth in certain kinds of franchises (see exhibits 7.2 and 7.3). Let us look at some specific industry categories where growth is occurring.

Motel Franchises

The nature of the franchise motel industry has undergone a number of changes since the energy crunch of 1973–1974. This phenomenon made the motel industry, located at the interstate interchanges and attuned to the family customer, aware of its vulnerability. Once thriving businesses were suddenly lacking customers. The franchisors that survived this dilemma became aware that, in the interest of long-term growth and stability, it was time to redefine the target market. A number of franchisors began to think in terms of urban, metropolitan, airport, and resort locations. This shift resulted in a change in the type of customer to be served. The shift also meant that capital requirements for property development increased dramatically because more expensive land was being sought. Some franchisors began to think of introducing gambling in their properties. Many motel franchises were no longer directing their marketing activities toward the family customer but more toward the upper-middle and higher-priced business and resort market.

Some franchises shifted many of their older properties to position as economy class motels. Others demanded upgrading or facelifts of these properties; failure of the franchisee to respond to these requests resulted in termination of the franchise contract. Some franchisees shifted to other franchises. In some instances, the new name and logo belonged to the previous franchisor. On occasion, the franchisee elected to become an independent operator.

These facts have been presented to help you become aware of the motel industry's changing environment. Do not assume that all good motel opportunities are gone. It has been our intent to provide a word of caution, however, since the motel market has changed, and the capital requirements are different. The caveat regarding the acquisition of a motel franchise or an independent motel property is "let the buyer beware." Do a thorough analysis of the franchisor's prospectus. If an existing property is for sale, carefully analyze its operating status.

Fast-Food Restaurants

The fast-food franchise business continues on a fast track, but not every franchise is reaping the rewards of success. New fast-food franchises continuously enter the field, but many of these newcomers find it difficult to survive. Some of these franchises are closing their doors, others are taking the Chapter 11 bankruptcy route, others are being acquired, and some seem to be struggling for survival in a declining market with little hope for recovery.

As the number of working couples and single-parent families continues to increase, the number of people eating out will continue to grow. The trend in restaurant sales should continue to increase, with the greater growth occurring in the fast-food segment of this industry. This fact has added to the sales increase and has resulted in the growth in the number of franchises, and in the unit sales.

Some fast-food franchises have been experimenting with their menus by adding items. Breakfast items have been added at some chains, as have salad

One of the latest of McDonald's stores.

bars. Some franchises have been successful with these changes while others have not. In one case, the franchisor failed to maintain an acceptable level of quality for the food, resulting in the franchisor's failure.

It is not our intent to tell you to avoid a fast-food franchise. Again, our purpose is to caution you to make a careful investigation and analysis to determine the franchise's quality. There are still good quality fast-food franchise opportunities to be had.

Check what is happening with franchises in your geographic area. Remember that a drive-in service window is a must for fast-food stores. Some franchisors indicate that as much as 40 percent of their unit sales come through the drive-in window. You should beware of new, unproven franchises. Do not forget the franchisor's prospectus—have your CPA, lawyer, and banker review it. McDonald's continues to be a good model for you to use as a comparison with other fast-food franchises.

Auto-Service Franchises

Recently, we have observed a growth in the number of auto-service franchises. These include companies that provide tune-ups, transmission service, mufflers, brakes, engine repair, and oil and lubrication; auto-parts stores; and car washes (including do-it-yourself; hand wash, wax, and polish; and mechanical washers).

In the auto-service category of franchises, capital requirements vary. Certain characteristics seem to prevail among these franchisors. As a group they tend to be owned by males. They prefer that the franchise not be a family affair;

One of the most important auto-service franchises.

they prefer that a male head of household owns and operates the franchise. Many of these businesses do not require that the owner have an education beyond high school. Generally, these businesses emphasize that the franchisee have sufficient capital to purchase the franchise and to provide adequate working capital to cover operating expenses and pay for inventory replacement as needed. In this type of franchise, you will not find a training and support arrangement such as you will find among some fast-food and motel franchises.

As in other types of franchises, we caution you to thoroughly investigate the success rate and profitability of any auto-service franchise that you are considering. Carefully analyze the franchisor's prospectus.

Retail Hardware Stores

One of the more recent growth areas among franchises has been retail hardware stores. Many of these retail hardware franchises are cooperatives, tied to a major hardware wholesaler. Examples are Ace, Armor, True-Value, and Servistar.

The advent of the franchise retail hardware store has placed considerable competitive pressure on the independent hardware retailer. If your interest is in the retail hardware business, we suggest that you carefully study the competitive environment of your proposed site. Should you choose the independent or franchise route?

Convenience Markets

The 1973–1974 energy crisis produced a change in the retail marketing of gasoline and related products. The shift resulted in the closing of many full-service service stations or the conversion of these units to convenience markets that sell gasoline. They joined an already large field of convenience stores. Some of these convenience markets are franchised. These franchises may be local, regional, or national. Some examples are Golden Pantry, Minit Mart, and 7-Eleven.

Not all convenience markets sell food and gasoline. Those that market other items include Craft Shack, Radio Shack, Auto Shack, computer stores, and Kinko Copy Stores, among many others. These stores assemble a specific type of merchandise or provide a special type of service.

Real Estate

Franchising of real estate historically has related to farm real estate. More recently, however, due to urban growth and the high rate of mobility among the population, residential real estate franchises have been established. Some examples of these franchises are RE/MAX, Electronic Realty Association (ERA), Realty World, Better Homes and Garden, Century 21, and Coldwell Banker.

The ability to access a national referral system has been a major selling point for these franchisors. This type of franchise has enabled smaller real estate firms to compete more favorably with larger firms. Under the national referral system, the national real estate franchise firms' fees are split between the franchisees. Even so, for an aggressive operator, the volume of fees may be considerably more than would be possible from a local operation with no franchise connection. This assumes increased volume of sales due to franchisor services. A more recent service provided by some of these franchises is to guarantee the sale of local property at the appraised value within 90 days if the homeowner will purchase a new home from a franchisee of the same firm.

Recognizing the Risks of Franchising

Like the standard corporate stock prospectus, the franchisor prospectus only presents a statement of facts. Therefore, you travel at your own risk.

We have observed, unfortunately, a number of persons invest part or all of their life savings into a franchise venture doomed to fail. The burden of determining the quality of a franchise rests on the prospective franchisee. You should be aware that there are risks in the acquisition of a franchise.

Asking the Right Questions

As you consider a specific franchise, determine what the franchisor's objectives are. Does the franchisor have a long-term objective of growing into an ever-larger firm with ever-increasing sales and an ever-increasing number of franchise units? Or is the franchisor's objective to fleece as many franchisees as quickly as possible? You may find the following questions useful in determining whether you wish to invest your money in a specific franchise.

1. What is in it for you? What return on investment and salary can you expect?
2. Is the franchisor unloading a bad deal on you?
3. What services will the franchisor provide for the franchisee? Are these services offered at a discounted price or are they overpriced for the benefits they offer?
4. What is the attitude of existing franchisees? Are they seeking to unload the franchise, or are they happy with the results they are achieving?
5. What is the attitude of your banker, lawyer, CPA, local Better Business Bureau, Chamber of Commerce, and community in general toward the franchisor and existing franchisees?
6. Does the franchise contract contain a clause that will permit the franchisor, at will, to purchase the franchise back on terms more favorable to the franchisor than the franchisee?

Be aware that even in the best franchise situations, the franchisor tends to hold an advantage. This advantage may relate to operating standards, supply and materials purchase agreements, and franchise repurchase agreements. Even so, many franchises offer you an opportunity to derive an acceptable income and a satisfactory return on your investment.

To make an objective evaluation of a prospective franchise, fill out the form in Exhibit 7.9 for each franchise under consideration.

We offer one final note on this part of the chapter—avoid the franchise that announces that it guarantees your investment.

Franchising Your Business

It is not unusual for us to hear a small business owner observe, "I would like to franchise my business." There are three reasons why this step might have appeal:

1. It shifts the burden of financing the business to others.
2. It facilitates faster growth.
3. It expands the business's earning capacity.

Before you commit yourself to franchising your business, you will need to consider the requisites for franchising.

Exhibit 7.9
EVALUATING AN EXISTING FRANCHISE

Subject company: _____

I. Time
   A. How long before I can obtain a franchise? _____
   B. After obtaining a franchise, how long will it be before I will be open for business? _____

Some of the better franchises have a lengthy waiting period before a franchise is available; that is, the demand for their franchises is so great that the waiting line may be closed in some areas and lengthy in open areas. It should not deter you when you are told that you may have to wait two years. There may be locations that will enable you to jump the waiting order.

II. Requirements for Obtaining Franchise
   A. Economic requirements
      1. Initial cost of franchise license $_____
      2. Minimal facility cost $_____
      3. Working capital requirement $_____
      4. Total investment required $_____
      5. Percent of equity required at outset $_____
      6. Debt amortization period in years   _____
      7. Financial assistance provided by franchisor?   Yes _____   No _____
          Assistance as percentage of total cost_____%
      8. Debt service cost (annual rate)   _____%
      9. Does debt contract provide for a penalty for prepayment?   Yes _____
          No _____   How much? $_____
     10. Will franchisor own building, equipment, and land?   Yes _____   No _____
     11. Does franchisor retain the right to purchase the franchise from franchisee?   Yes _____
        No _____
        If yes, describe the arrangement briefly.

        _____

        _____

   B. Service provided at outset by franchisor
      1. Financial assistance?   Yes _____   No _____
      2. Site location?   Yes _____   No _____
      3. Architectural assistance?   Yes _____   No _____

Exhibit 7.9
EVALUATING AN EXISTING FRANCHISE (*continued*)

4. Real estate procurement? Yes _____ No _____
5. Franchisor-owned facility? Yes _____ No _____
6. Lease-purchase? Yes _____ No _____
7. Turnkey job? Yes _____ No _____
8. Other services _____
   _____

C. Criteria for selecting franchisee
   1. Age
      a. Minimum _____
      b. Preferred age range _____ to _____
      c. Maximum _____
   2. Education
      a. Minimum education required

Grade school _____	College—2 years _____
High school—2 years _____	College—3 years _____
High school—4 years _____	College—4 years _____

      b. Desired education

High school _____	College—2 years _____
Technical school _____	College—4 years _____

         Degree _____
         Comments _____
         _____
         _____

   3. Marital status desired _____
   4. Economic status preferred
      a. Cash, bank deposits, near cash $_____
      b. Other investments $_____
         Total net worth (a + b) $_____
      c. Line of credit available at bank $_____
   5. Indicate type of work experience franchisor prefers of its franchisees.
      _____
      _____

III. Services Provided by Franchisor
   A. Buyer advantage
      1. Sources of supply
         a. In-house (franchisor) Yes _____ No _____
         b. Does the franchisor have contracts with outside suppliers to service needs of
            the franchisee? Yes _____ No _____

c. Does the franchisor become involved with the franchisee's sources of supply?

Yes _____   No _____

d. Explain the justification for depending on the franchisor for supply assistance.

Economic _____

_____

Quality _____

_____

Difficulty in locating reliable sources of supply _____

_____

2. Nature of contracts with supply sources (explain).

_____

_____

What items? _____

_____

_____

3. Company logo   Yes _____   No _____
4. Parent organization managerial style

   a. More centralized   Yes _____   No _____

   b. Less centralized   Yes _____   No _____
5. Franchisee supervision

   a. More centralized control   Yes _____   No _____

   b. Less centralized control   Yes _____   No _____
6. Management information systems

   (1) More centralized   Yes _____   No _____

   (2) Less centralized   Yes _____   No _____
7. Audit and inspection procedures   Yes _____   No _____

   Describe _____

   _____

   _____

8. Change in menu, parts, or service offerings

   a. Expand number of items   Yes _____   No _____

   b. Reduce number of items   Yes _____   No _____

   c. Method in preparation   Yes _____   No _____

   How? _____

   _____

   _____

9. Service system   Yes _____   No _____
10. Quality of product or service   Yes _____   No _____
11. Kind of support service by franchisor _____

Exhibit 7.9
EVALUATING AN EXISTING FRANCHISE (*continued*)

_____

12. Management assistance   Yes _____   No _____
    How? _____

    _____

    What? _____

    _____

13. Buying assistance   Yes _____   No _____

B. Advertising program offered by the franchisor
    1. National   Yes _____   No _____
    2. Regional   Yes _____   No _____
    3. Local   Yes _____   No _____

C. Does the franchise provide a special advantage in the marketplace?   Yes _____
    No _____   What is it? _____

    _____

D. Management assistance
    1. Technical assistance   Yes _____   No _____
       What? _____

       _____

    2. Operation audit   Yes _____   No _____
       How often? _____

    3. Market research   Yes _____   No _____
       Describe _____

       _____

    Frequency
    Continuous _____   6 months _____
    3 months _____   9 months _____
    4 months _____   12 months _____
    Other (specify) _____

    _____

    4. Performance evaluation   Yes _____   No _____
       Frequency

Monthly   _____   6 months   _____

3 months   _____   9 months   _____

4 months   _____   12 months   _____

Other   _____

_____

_____

Summarize what takes place in a performance evaluation   _____

_____

_____

   5.   Nature of feedback from performance evaluation

     a.   Graded response   Yes   _____   No   _____

     b.   Composite performance data comparison   Yes   _____   No   _____

     c.   Suggested changes   Yes   _____   No   _____

     d.   Other comments   _____

_____

_____

   6.   Availability of management consultant service

     a.   By request of franchisee   Yes   _____   No   _____

     b.   By request of franchisor   Yes   _____   No   _____

   7.   Cost of management consultant service

     a.   Covered by the franchise fee   Yes   _____   No   _____

     b.   Shared by franchisor and franchisee   Yes   _____   No   _____

     c.   Charged to franchisee by franchisor   Yes   _____   No   _____

        Flat fee   _____

        Fee based on time spent by consultant   _____

   8.   General statement concerning services provided by franchisor

_____

_____

_____

_____

IV.   Future Plans of Franchisor

  A.   Status of company-owned units

    1.   Increase in ownership

      a.   New units   Yes   _____   No   _____   _____% increase

      b.   Old units   Yes   _____   No   _____   _____% increase

    2.   Decrease in ownership

      a.   New units   Yes   _____   No   _____   _____% decrease

      b.   Old units   Yes   _____   No   _____   _____% decrease

  B.   Status of franchisee-owned units

    1.   Increase in ownership

      a.   New units   Yes   _____   No   _____   _____% increase

      b.   Old units   Yes   _____   No   _____   _____% increase

Exhibit 7.9
EVALUATING AN EXISTING FRANCHISE (*continued*)

    2. Decrease in ownership

        a. New units   Yes _____   No _____   _____% decrease

        b. Old units   Yes _____   No _____   _____% decrease

  C. Change in unit characteristics

    1. Expand size of units   Yes _____   No _____   _____% increase

    2. Eliminate small units   Yes _____   No _____

        Rate per year   _____

    3. Expand services and facilities   Yes _____   No _____

        Explain _____

        _____

        _____

    4. Establish classes of unit structures   Yes _____   No _____

        Nature of structures _____

        _____

        _____

  D. Indicate planned changes

    1. Target markets   Yes _____   No _____

        Identify _____

        _____

        _____

    2. Identifying architectural design   Yes _____   No _____

        Why? _____

        _____

        _____

        _____

V. What Happens If Franchise Is Not Successful?

  A. If this franchise does not prove successful, what will happen to the franchise facility? _____

    _____

    _____

  B. What will happen to my investment? _____

    _____

    _____

  C. What uses have been made of unsuccessful franchise properties? _____

    _____

    _____

  D. Will I have the discretion to use the property as I choose?   Yes _____

    No _____

VI.   In Success, What May I Anticipate?
   A.   What kind of monthly income may I reasonably expect from the franchise in the first year?

Month	Salary	Profit
1	$_____	$_____
2	$_____	$_____
3	$_____	$_____
4	$_____	$_____
5	$_____	$_____
6	$_____	$_____
7	$_____	$_____
8	$_____	$_____
9	$_____	$_____
10	$_____	$_____
11	$_____	$_____
12	$_____	$_____

Average monthly salary after first year $_____
   B.   What kind of net worth projection may I anticipate?
      1.   End of 1st year $_____
      2.   End of 2nd year $_____
      3.   End of 3rd year $_____
      4.   End of 4th year $_____
      5.   End of 5th year $_____

Determining the Franchising Quality of Your Business

Before franchising your business you must first determine if it possesses the attributes found in a successful franchise.

1. Does the business produce a product or service that is consistently uniform?
2. Is the quality of the product or service uniform?
3. Is the product or service simple in form, effective in application, and easily understood?
4. Have you developed an effective and uniform accounting and control system? (This system needs to be something that individual franchisee can successfully use.)
5. Have you developed a system for monitoring and measuring the effectiveness of the franchise?
6. Have you considered the importance of a program to provide management and technical assistance for the franchisee?
7. Have you conducted a feasibility study (see Chapter 6)? Before franchising you might try expanding to a second location to determine if the business idea travels well and if you can manage multiple units.

Planning Your Franchise Package

If, after analyzing and evaluating your business, you decide that it satisfies the qualities of a franchised business, the next step is to plan a franchise package. The quality and adequacy of the package will largely determine the franchise's marketability. Remember that you must develop a prospectus that satisfies the FTC'S regulation. Therefore, you will need the assistance of a competent attorney in preparing the prospectus.

In developing the package, consider the following factors:

1. Define the criteria for location. If your financial resources permit, you, the franchisor, should own the land, building, and parking lot. This ownership will afford you better protection.
2. Design the building with its own unique structural characteristics.
3. Develop a logo with an accompanying sign.
4. Give interior design and layout a uniqueness that will identify the franchise.
5. Develop a uniform equipment package.
6. Formulate or design the product or service.
7. Develop an identifying package or container.
8. Identify a price for each product or service.
9. Write a statement of personnel requirements.
10. Create management and employee training plans for the parent company and for the franchisee.
11. Devise the franchise fee arrangement, consisting of three parts:
    a. *Initial fee.* This fee needs to be substantial in order to attract a better-quality franchisee.
    b. *License fee.*
    c. *Royalty.* This fee should be tied to gross sales. You will want to structure it similarly to the following example: 8 percent on gross sales as a franchise fee plus 3 percent on gross sales as a rental fee.
12. Create a management assistance program.
13. Develop an operation monitoring and audit system.
14. Make arrangements for supplies.
15. Provide sources of financial assistance (which would be optional to franchisees).
16. Write a franchise repurchase agreement.

In the development of a franchising package we recommend the use of specialists: lawyers, accountants, bankers, engineers, architects, and so on. You should also plan to use specialists whose expertise is related to your kind of business. (On occasion, this service may be supplied by interested vendors.) Developing a franchise package may also require bringing in professional management.

After having read the material on franchising your business, do you think that your business can become a franchise?

Summary

Franchising is a growing field that provides business opportunities to many types of businesses, from drycleaning to fast food, from real estate to computer sales. The annual franchisor issue of *Venture* magazine provides an excellent overview of the current status and condition of franchises.

While franchising offers excellent opportunities, not all franchises are promising. Some franchisors are interested only in taking the money of unsuspecting franchisees; they offer neither quality products or services nor management or financial support. Such franchises are not opportunities, but recipes for disaster. A careful analysis of a franchise firm's condition, its treatment of franchisees, and its prospectus is an essential step before embarking on a franchise.

Some entrepreneurs believe that franchising their own business idea would provide an excellent source of growth. Such may be the case, but a careful analysis of the business is needed before this decision can be made. If you do decide to open your business to franchising, you must develop a detailed workable franchising plan.

**Class
Assignments**

1. Using the material in your text, prepare a plan for selecting a franchise.
2. Develop a summary plan to use for franchising your own business.
3. Visit a number of different franchise stores and observe the effectiveness of their operation. List the strong features and weak features of each operation.

CHOOSING YOUR PROFESSIONAL ADVISERS

This chapter concerns choosing those professional advisers who are going to help you with your business. Accountants, bankers, lawyers and insurance agents form the core of your adviser cadre. Selecting your advisers may be one of the more important long-term decisions that you will make; using them wisely may be one of the most important actions you will take. Using the family professional adviser may not be the wise thing to do. Selecting your accountant and lawyer based on the fees they charge can also be a mistake.

Many people enter business without any real appreciation of how to select their advisers, resorting to their use out of necessity or desperation. Unfortunately, many businesses fail—not because the business lacks potential but for other reasons. Two of those reasons can be the failure to get good, practical advice when such advice is needed and the receipt of bad advice. It is clear, then, that seeking advisers who will give you sage counsel when it is needed can help you succeed.

We have chosen to focus on four types of professional advisers. Of course, at times you will need to call on the expertise of other advisers. We have chosen these four because we believe that you will need these professionals irrespective of what business you choose. To this extent your accountant, lawyer, banker, and insurance agent should form the core of your advisers.

After reading this chapter you will be able to

- Discuss the assistance you can get from your banker
- Explain the factors to consider in selecting a lawyer
- Discuss the tasks that an accountant can perform for you
- List the types of insurance you need and explain the factors involved in obtaining each

Your Banker

The banker is generally the first person you will need to consult with to begin or purchase your business. It does you little good to spend money to determine what legal form your prospective business should take or whether it should use the cash or accrual method of accounting if you do not have available the money to begin and operate your business.

Your banker is not merely the person who approves your loans. He or she should be one of your unpaid partners. To be a worthy partner, your banker must have some real expertise in how a successful business is operated. Bankers are now becoming specialized, just as physicians have been for years. You would not think of going to general surgeon concerning a coronary bypass; neither should you choose your banker merely because he or she happens to work for a bank and lends money.

Find a bank that has a commercial loan department. A commercial loan officer with the rank of assistant vice-president or higher will have had specialized training in dealing with businesses. Your banker should be much more than a source of money. Use his or her expertise. In a sense, you pay for his or her services when you pay the bank interest. But you pay interest to any bank; any loan officer can make you a loan. The expertise that you are seeking goes beyond getting the loan and is really at no additional cost to you, so use it.

What kind of expertise can your banker provide? If you have not found the business you wish to buy, your banker may be able to identify several businesses that can be acquired. If one happens to be a business that the banker has been servicing, he or she will be able to give you an opinion of its potential. With the owner's consent, the banker can also provide considerable information that will assist you in evaluating the feasibility of your acquiring the business.

Your banker can help you decide on the capitalization the business will require in order to support its operation. Your banker will have computers and programs to run pro-forma operations and cash-flow analyses. Use them. You may have a preconceived idea of the capital required to support operations; your banker may be able to advise you of the soundness of your evaluation.

What you need is not merely a loan; what happens after you obtain that loan is of equal or greater importance. It sometimes happens that with adequate collateral you can borrow more money than you can repay out of the profits generated. You need to know this information before the loan is closed. You will learn how to develop your financial plan in Chapter 12. Review that plan with your banker; get comments, suggestions, and alternative options. What you are seeking is the best plan, not just a plan that will get the loan. If there is a better plan, you want to know it.

Develop a relationship with your banker—a relationship that benefits both you and the banker. This principle is unfortunately often overlooked, even by experienced business people. There seems to be a tendency to see the banker as an adversary. This tendency is wrong. Your banker should be viewed as an additional resource to help you succeed in your business. Develop a frank and open relationship with your banker. Provide all the information you have available about your business, good and bad. There is a natural tendency to hide from the banker any negative information or information that you think may be detrimental to your getting the loan. This is a mistake. If you view your banker as your adviser, someone who wants to help you succeed, you will provide complete information. Remember that if your business succeeds and grows, you will need help in expanding the business. If your banker has been kept informed with timely and accurate financial information, you will not have to sell your expansion plans to the bank. Many times, in fact, your banker will suggest that you need to expand. Provide quarterly and annual financial statements to your banker without being asked to do so.

Credit is not just a matter of collateral; it is confidence in you and your business. One easy way to obtain the confidence of your banker is to let him or her know that you are on top of your business. The way you do this is to provide financial information and to discuss current information concerning your business with your banker. Failure to keep the banker informed is the source of more problems than you can imagine. If increased business is resulting in cash flow being squeezed, alert your banker well in advance of the time that you will need a line of credit to cover a cash shortage. Bankers do not like surprises. They will think, with some justification, that if you do not know enough about managing your business to anticipate a cash-flow shortage, you may not be able to repay their loan. On the other hand, if you can anticipate a problem on the horizon, inform the bank why the problem is arising, and reassure the banker that it is only temporary, he or she will usually understand and help you. To reiterate, keep your banker informed.

The last reason that your banker must have a good grasp of business is to avoid lending you too much money. Many businesses fail not because they do not have much business but because they have too much. While this statement sounds incredible, it is nevertheless true. If your business takes off and sales exceed expectations, the natural tendency is to expand in order to capitalize on your early successes. The most expedient way to expand is with borrowed capital. In such a situation you and your banker may not be exercising the wisdom and restraint to be patient and build an equity base sufficient to support expansion. You borrow more money in order to expand. You can justify it because your cash flow is adequate to service the loan. More equipment is purchased; other fixed overhead is layered onto your operating statement. Then a downturn hits, as it inevitably will. Your fixed overhead remains, but your cash flow does not. Leverage is great on the way up; it is disaster on the way down. To prevent this problem from occurring, you need a banker with enough business judgment to know what loan level is safe. You may not appreciate your banker putting the brakes on when business is great, but you will thank him or her when the decision helped you survive a recession.

In summary, select a commercial loan officer who understands business, one that will be an additional resource to your business and your plans for the future. Use your banker's expertise in helping you solve problems. You want an adviser, not just someone who will loan you money. An uninformed banker may very well lend you too much money—more than you can repay.

Your Lawyer

In choosing your lawyer, remember that you are seeking advisers to help you begin and operate a business. Today, most lawyers specialize. In selecting your lawyer, you want someone who specializes in areas that will be beneficial to your business. A well-known trial lawyer will not be a good business lawyer; just the opposite is usually true. You should seek someone who specializes in corporate law and in taxation and is known as a good business lawyer. You want someone who has had sufficient experience to be a counselor to you, not an inexperienced lawyer who will be learning from mistakes made with your business. There is no reason for you to invent the wheel; find someone who has a reputation for having good business judgment so that you can avoid the costly mistakes that threaten all businesses.

Tax planning is becoming more and more important to the businessperson. Good tax planning means using the right form of ownership for your business. The right business form may be a sole proprietorship, a traditional corporation that pays tax, or one that has elected S corporation status. (Study Chapter 10 to learn more about the different forms of businesses.) Consult with an experienced lawyer before deciding on the form for your business. Every dollar you can save in taxes can be used to make your business more fiscally sound.

A good lawyer can help you acquire the business. The covenants, representations, and warranties that the seller of the business makes to you are extremely important. A good lawyer can discover the pitfalls that may exist in the business you are acquiring, or he or she may be able to insert a clause in the agreement requiring the seller to indemnify you against unexpected and expensive surprises.

In acquiring a business, it is important that the purchase price be allocated among the assets being purchased so that you can recoup as much of the purchase price as possible through amortization. Perhaps an escrow of some of the purchase price should be created so that you can be assured of recouping part of the purchase price if the warranties made to you by the seller do not prove to be true. Each situation is different. There is no set way to structure an acquisition that will work every time. You need an attorney who will be able to guide you through the land mines with the greatest safety.

If you do not own your own land and building, the lease you acquire can be important. Do you have protection against rent increases? What happens if there is a fire? Do you have adequate options to renew the lease, and on what terms? Do you have the right of first refusal should the landlord decide to sell the property? The list goes on and on. You need to have all options explained to you so that you can make an informed business decision. Your lawyer can help with these issues.

You will usually find that the better lawyers are also the more expensive. Do not let this scare you away. You need the expertise that a good business lawyer can bring to bear in acquiring and helping you start your business. To save money, do not use the lawyer to do things that you or someone else less expensive can do just as well; only use the lawyer to do those things for which his or her expertise is needed. On the other hand, do not try to save money by hiring an inexpensive lawyer. As in virtually everything else, you invariably get only what you pay for. Try to get the best.

Your Accountant   Seek an accountant who can work with your lawyer and you as a team to plan business strategies. Many accountants are very good auditors, but they are not necessarily good advisers. Accountants are conservative by nature, which is a good trait. Using your lawyer and accountant as a team is a good practice because these members of the team usually complement each other. You want to hear all sides of an issue before making up your mind. Using your advisers in this manner is a good technique to obtain as many options as possible.

However, you must be mindful of the cost of these advisers. Hourly fees are not insignificant, and excessive use of their time will be counterproductive and lower your profits. After your business is up and running, consider scheduling a one-hour conference with both of them about twice a year. Holding these conferences about midyear and again at the beginning of the last month of the fiscal year is a good practice. The meeting at midyear can spot problems before it is too late in the year to do anything about them. The second meeting can be used for year-end tax planning and planning for the next year. You will find this practice to be well worth the money. Nothing is more frustrating than to finish your year and to have your advisers say: "If you had only done thus and so, you would have saved thus and so." Such a postmortem analysis is useless for the year just ended. Biannual meetings will help prevent this from occurring.

What other support can you expect from your accountant? One task that the accountant may perform is maintaining your monthly financial reports. As pointed out in Chapter 12, maintaining monthly financial reports is a must for any well-run business. You may find that it is cheaper to have your accountant's office prepare payroll tax reports, W-2's, and financial reports than it is to have your own full-time bookkeeper. You can usually find a less expensive employee to maintain daily records that are adequate to allow your accountant to prepare these reports for you. You should do an analysis to determine which approach to handling payroll is less costly.

You will want your accountant to help you set up adequate controls in your daily operations to help prevent theft or embezzlement. Embezzlement is a fact of life for every business. You cannot completely prevent theft, but you can discourage it by implementing good systems and procedures in your office. These systems should be created at the beginning; then you can be sure that they are adhered to thereafter.

You will want your accountant to set up the best method of accounting for your particular business. You can elect any method of accounting allowed by the Internal Revenue Service (IRS), but once you select a method, you must get the permission of the IRS in order to change it. Obtaining this permission is usually difficult. Whether you will be better off using the cash, accrual, completed contract, percentage-of-completion, or some other method of accounting is very valuable information. The method chosen can affect the timing of your income taxes and your cash flow. Many businesses do not give this decision sufficient thought. If you select an improper method of accounting (one not permitted by the IRS for your type of business) the IRS can require that you change to a proper method. The regulations give the IRS great power to require you to change to a method that it judges to be proper. This change invariably results in an increase to income, producing unexpected income tax and interest payment. Do not fall into this trap. Good advice at the beginning will prevent this result from occurring.

You will probably be better off allowing your accountant to prepare your business and personal income tax returns. In preparing both returns the accountant can be sure that nothing is omitted or duplicated. Tax returns have become so complex and the penalties so severe that having a professional prepare them is good business.

Usually it is not necessary to have your business audited or your annual statement certified by your accountant. An audited statement is expensive and is not warranted—unless your banker requires it. Your banker usually will not require audited statements unless he or she is uncomfortable with your monthly reports. Using the procedure referred to above will usually satisfy your banker.

Your Insurance Adviser

The insurance adviser is the adviser most overlooked by the average business owner. The insurance agent has come to be the adviser that business owners attempt to avoid. Since insurance agents call upon prospective clients, most business owners seldom think of selecting their agents with the same care and attention that they use in choosing their accountant and lawyer. As a result, they usually end up buying insurance from the most persistent salesperson, which may be a costly mistake.

The business owner has four basic insurance needs:

1. Property and casualty
2. Hospitalization, medical, and major medical
3. Life
4. Disability

Depending upon the type of business you own, product liability insurance may also be needed.

Just as lawyers and bankers have become specialized, insurance agents have become more and more specialized. The danger is in dealing with an agent who offers all products. Insurance products are now so diverse and complex that it is difficult to find one agent who has the requisite expertise in all these areas to give you the right product at the best cost. It is not unusual to find an agent who can competently handle both life and disability insurance. This agent can sometimes also competently handle hospitalization, medical, and major medical insurance. In general, however, it is preferable to seek out three different agents: one for property and casualty; one for hospitalization, medical, and major medical; and a third for life and disability insurance.

Seek out, investigate, and retain these agents with the same care and attention that you expend on choosing your other advisers. Stay with your insurance adviser as long as you are getting good service at a competitive price. Just as the lower fee is not necessarily the determining factor in selecting your accountant or lawyer, the cost of the premium may not be an adequate gauge for the quality of the insurance product. Insurance companies have become so competitive that their prices for comparable products are very close. What is left as the basis for a choice is the quality of advice and of service. These important factors should be your guide in selecting your insurance adviser.

Property and casualty insurance is extremely important to your business. This broad term covers fire and casualty damage to your business, workers' compensation, protection from loss due to theft or embezzlement, and liability insurance for negligent acts by you or your employees that causes injury to other people or damage to their property. Choose this adviser with care to be confident that you have adequate coverage. If you are getting competitive quotes from several agents, have them all quote on predetermined written specifications. Otherwise, a low quote may not include some coverage or benefit you need. Few business owners can competently read and understand an insurance policy (indeed few take the time to read policies). For this reason, you should select an insurance adviser who has the expertise to know what to recommend for your business and who has such integrity that you can place confidence in what he or she recommends.

A competent property and casualty agent will make sure that you have necessary coverage for your business. Nothing is so devastating as to suffer a loss that you thought was covered, only to learn that the policy had an exception that excluded coverage for that type of loss. Many property and casualty agents write insurance for several companies, which helps them find the best coverage at the best cost.

With the ever-escalating cost of illness and hospitalization, you cannot afford to be without health insurance. This coverage has become so important that it is a fringe benefit for employees in virtually all places of employment. If you choose to cover your employees as well as yourself, a group policy is preferable because you can spread the cost of the coverage over all those covered. This spreading of the risk will result in a lower cost per person than would be the case were each person covered by an individual policy.

Since medical costs have increased so much, the cost of health insurance has also increased. Yet major medical coverage is almost a necessity due to the risk of catastrophic illness. For these reasons, it is again important that your insurance adviser have the requisite expertise to find adequate coverage at a cost you can afford. Many creative products are being introduced. Your adviser must be knowledgeable about the evolving coverage possibilities so that you have access to all the alternatives before deciding on a product. It is preferable to have an adviser who writes policies for many companies so that you have access to as many options as possible.

Life insurance, particularly for you, can be extremely important. The importance of life insurance increases dramatically if you have a family. You need to be sure that you have considered life insurance to cover the debts of the business and to cover the costs of operating the business until your estate can sell or liquidate it. You will want to have adequate insurance to provide for your surviving spouse and to educate your children. Life insurance, too, is constantly evolving to keep pace with a rapidly changing society. Your adviser should have the competence to know the products, but also the integrity to sell you only the products you can afford and you need. Term insurance is only one of many options for low-cost coverage until you can afford a more permanent solution for your insurance needs.

Disability insurance is often overlooked—despite statistics indicating that you have a greater chance of being disabled before age sixty-five than of dying. If you are disabled and do not have insurance coverage, your business is jeopardized and your personal financial future is at risk. Disability coverage for a young person is not expensive; it can be paid by the business, and it can be written so that the insurance company cannot cancel the coverage before age sixty-five. Some products allow you to increase coverage from time to time, even though you may later become uninsurable. There are many options and products to choose from. You need an adviser who can explain the whole range of options to you so that you can make an informed decision.

Summary

Choosing your advisers is critical. While making good choices will not ensure your business's success, your failure to choose advisers who have expertise and integrity can foretell underachievement and possibly failure. It is important that you spend time in the beginning seeking out who your advisers will be. Check around; ask other business owners. Ask your banker who he or she thinks are the most competent lawyers, accountants and insurance agents. Ask accountants who they think are the top business and tax lawyers in town. If you happen to select your lawyer first, ask his or her opinion about the top accountants and insurance agents. Once you get two or three recommendations in each category, talk with as many business owners as possible about the reputation of these advisers for expertise, honesty, and integrity. These last two virtues, while not related directly to competence, are very important criteria for selection of your advisers.

Class Assignments

1. Which of the four advisers discussed do you think is the one most often overlooked, and why?

NEGOTIATION

Everyone negotiates every day. If you think about it, everything you will ever want is either owned or controlled by someone else. Your objective is to get it. It may be a business you want to buy; it may be an order for sales you want to obtain. If you have employees, you negotiate with them. But though we are all negotiators, very few of us are good negotiators.

Very few business schools include a course in negotiation as part of their curriculum. This chapter is designed to make you a better negotiator; our advice is to supplement this material by undertaking a program to make yourself a better negotiator. Above all, remember that good negotiation is achieved only through practice. Negotiation is an art. There are no born negotiators, just as there are no born airline pilots or born writers. All of these arts are learned. As such, they require education, understanding of the subject matter, and development of the related skills in order to do them well.

As a small business owner, your success will depend to a great extent on your ability to negotiate. The better negotiator you are, the more successful you will become.

We will analyze various styles of negotiating to determine which are more efficient. We will analyze some fundamental mistakes many negotiators make and study how to eliminate them. We will learn how to recognize varying styles of negotiators, and how to deal with them in order to get what we want.

As you will see, good negotiation sometimes means going against instinct. We will explore the tactics and strategies that people use to negotiate that are counterproductive, inefficient, and capable of destroying relationships with other people. Finally, we will explain how succeeding in negotiation means learning to be creative. Try to help the other party get what he or she wants. It is rare that you and the other party will want the same thing.

After reading this chapter you will be able to

- Assess a negotiation and develop strategies for addressing the human-related aspects of a negotiation
- Analyze a negotiation and find ways to focus on the interests involved
- Examine a negotiation and generate a range of alternative solutions

- Assess a negotiation and identify objective criteria that options can be measured against
- Avoid common obstacles to or mistakes in negotiations

Methods of Negotiation

Positional Negotiation

Unfortunately, most negotiations take the following traditional form. One side takes a position: "In order to be your CEO, I must be guaranteed a retirement benefit at age sixty-five of $40,000 per year for ten years." The other side takes a position: "We have only allotted $100,000 to be contributed to your retirement benefit. Unfortunately, that will only buy $20,000 of retirement benefit at age sixty-five. That is the best we can do." The lines are drawn. Each side digs in and defends its position. The negotiation now becomes a contest of wills and egos. The person who blinks first loses.

This kind of negotiation takes place every day. The common thread that runs through the logic of positional negotiation seems to be: take an extreme position, make small concessions, and try to end up somewhere close to where you really want to be. Stonewalling, stalling, threatening to walk out, and similar tactics are common. This is inefficient negotiation.

Being nice is not a viable solution. In soft negotiations the threefold strategy is to make the concessions necessary to keep the negotiations going, to trust the other side, and to avoid confrontations. This approach is efficient in that results are attained quickly. Unfortunately, that result is often bad. The soft negotiator will always be eaten alive by the positional negotiator.

The Alternative: Negotiating on the Merits

Use neither the soft approach nor the positional or hard approach. You need to change the game. This method—called negotiation on the merits—has four basic elements:

1. *People.* Separate the people from the problem.
2. *Interests.* Focus on the interests, not on your position.
3. *Options.* Generate a variety of possibilities before deciding what to do.
4. *Criteria.* Insist that the result be based on some objective standard.

People. People have strong emotions, and it is easy to allow egos to become dominant. The parties should see themselves working side by side to solve the problem and not be attacking each other.

Interests. Positions invariably hide what the parties really want. Settling between positions (the traditional way of negotiating) is unlikely to produce an agreement that will solve the parties' human needs, which is what led the parties to take their positions in the first place.

Options. It is hard to have to develop options in front of your opposition. You need to set aside some time in advance of the negotiation to think up a wide range of possible solutions that aid the shared interests of all parties. You need to learn to invent options for the mutual gain of all parties.

Criteria. Where the interests of each party are opposite, one party may become stubborn and lock into a position. You need to insist that the agreement must be fair, independent of the will of each side. Some standard, such as fair market value, third-party expert opinion, or custom or law should control the outcome. By discussing the criteria rather than what the parties are willing to settle for, neither side has to give in since both can defer to a fair solution.

The negotiating process, from beginning to end, has three stages:

1. Analysis
2. Planning
3. Discussion

In analysis, you need to diagnose the situation and gather information that bears on the problem and organize that information. Consider the people problem; identify your interests and the interests of the other side. You should also note the options that are already on the table. Identify any criteria that have been suggested as a basis of a possible solution.

With planning, you need to deal with the four elements listed above for a second time. Decide how to handle the people problem. You must determine which of your interests are the most important. Set some realistic objectives. Generate more options and the criteria for deciding among them.

As for the discussion stage, you should use the same four elements a third time—as subjects to discuss. You will need to address the differences between the parties in this stage. Each side must be made to understand the interests of the other during this stage. Both sides can then generate options that may be helpful to both sides.

Separating the People from the Problem

Remember that negotiators are people first. People have emotions, deeply held values, and different backgrounds and viewpoints. During the negotiation, ask yourself whether you are paying enough attention to the people problem.

Every negotiator has two kinds of interests: in the substance of the transaction and in the relationship between the parties. The relationship often becomes entangled with the problem. We tend to treat people and the problem as one. Our egos invariably tend to become involved with the real problems. People draw unfounded inferences from comments made by the other side, and they treat these comments as facts about that person's intentions and attitudes toward them.

Positional bargaining sacrifices a good relationship for results related to substance. But caving in on the substance usually does not buy friendship—it just shows that you are easy. The point is, do not try to solve people problems with substantive concessions.

People problems usually fall into three categories:

1. Perception
2. Emotion
3. Communications

Bear in mind that you must deal with your own people problems. Your emotions may block an agreement; your perceptions may be one sided; and you may not be listening or communicating adequately. The techniques described in the following sections apply to you as well as to the other side.

Perception

Differences in how two sides think is the problem. Difference is defined as the difference between your thinking and theirs. People usually quarrel over an object or an event. They differ because a difference exists in their thinking; the object or event is perceived differently. Objective reality may be useful, but the reality as each sees it constitutes the problem in negotiation and opens the door to a solution. The solution can be achieved by using various techniques:

1. *Put yourself in their shoes.* People tend to see what they want to see. The ability to see the situation as the other side sees it is one of the most important skills a negotiator can possess. To influence them, you must understand clearly the power of their point of view and feel the emotional force with which they believe in it.
2. *Do not deduce their intentions from your fears.* People tend to assume that the other side intends to do whatever they fear. The cost of interpreting whatever the other side says or does in its worst light is that fresh ideas in the direction of agreement are spurned and subtle changes of position are usually ignored or disregarded.
3. *Do not blame them for your problem.* Even if blaming the other side is justified, it is usually counterproductive. The other side will become defensive and resist what you have to say. They will cease to listen and strike back. Assigning blame entangles the people with the problem. You must separate the symptoms of the problem from the person with whom you are talking.
4. *Discuss each other's perceptions.* One way to deal with differing perceptions is to get them on the table and discuss them with the other side. Communicating clearly and convincingly the things you are willing to say and the message they would like to hear is one of the best investments you can make.
5. *Look for opportunities to act inconsistently with their perceptions.* The best way to change the other side's perception of you is to send a message different from what they expect.
6. *Give them a stake in the outcome by making sure that they participate in the process.* If not involved in the process, the other side is not likely to approve the result. If you want the other side to accept a conclusion that is at first disagreeable to them, involve them in the process of reaching that conclusion. Agreement becomes much easier if both parties feel

ownership of the ideas. Get the other side involved early. Ask their advice. Giving them generous credit for ideas (even if they are not the author) will give them a personal stake in defending those ideas to others. Resist the temptation to take credit for the ideas yourself. Apart from the merits of the result, the feeling of participation may be the single most important factor in determining whether a negotiator accepts a proposal. In some ways, the *process is the product.*

7. *Face-saving.* Make your proposals consistent with the other side's values. Usually a misunderstanding about face-saving reflects a person's need to reconcile the stand he or she takes in a negotiation or an agreement with his or her principles and past words and acts. Sometimes people hold out simply because they want to avoid the feeling or appearance to backing down to the other side. If the substance can be phrased or conceptualized differently so that it appears to be a fair outcome, the other side will accept it. Face-saving reconciles an agreement with principle and with the self-image of the negotiators. This is a very important point.

Emotion

If the dispute is bitter, you must realize that the parties may be more willing to do battle than to cooperatively work out a solution. Emotions become involved. You must recognize this and deal with the emotions—yours and theirs. You can deal with emotions using the following strategies:

1. *Recognize and understand emotions—theirs and yours.* Are you angry at the other side? Are they angry at you? Ask why you are angry. Why are they angry? Are emotions spilling over from one issue to another?

2. *Make emotions explicit and acknowledge them as legitimate.* Talk with the people on the other side about their emotions. Talk about your own emotions. Freed from the burden of unexpressed emotions, people will be more likely to work on the problem.

3. *Allow the other side to let off steam.* Helping people release their anger and frustration is an effective way to deal with their emotions. The best strategy may be to listen quietly without responding to attacks. While this is hard to do, the approach gives little support to the inflammatory substance, and the speaker is encouraged to speak out himself.

4. *Do no react to emotional outbursts.* Releasing uncontrolled emotions can lead to a violent quarrel. When more than one person at a time gets emotional, an argument is almost inevitable. A good rule for any negotiation is that only one person at a time can get angry.

5. *Use symbolic gestures.* Acts that can produce a favorable emotional impact on the other side often involve little or no cost. For example, a note of sympathy for the loss of a loved one, a small present for a grandchild, eating together, or an apology are excellent opportunities to improve a hostile situation at a small cost.

Communication

Without communication, there is no negotiation. Negotiation is a process of communicating back and forth for the purpose of reaching a joint decision. Whatever you say, and however you say it, expect the other side to hear something different. Clear communication is difficult at best. Some of the more common problems with communication are

1. *Use of third parties.* The negotiators may be talking through third parties. Clear communication is difficult even when the parties are face to face, much less when they are talking through third parties.
2. *Failure to hear the other party.* Even if the parties are talking with each other, one may not be hearing the other.
3. *Misunderstanding.* What one side says, the other side often misinterprets.

These problems do have solutions, however:

1. *Practice active listening and acknowledge what is being said.* "Did I understand correctly that you are saying that . . . ?" Pay close attention to what is said; ask the other side to spell out carefully and exactly what they mean. Resist the temptation, while listening, to phrase a question or a response; otherwise, you are likely to misunderstand what is being said. Try to understand them as they see themselves. Work at understanding their perceptions, their needs and their constraints. Show them that you do understand them by repeating what you understood they said. Phrase it positively from their point of view and make the strength of their case clear. This is important, but hard to do. Remember that understanding is not the same as agreeing, but showing such understanding is essential. Unless you can show them that you understand and grasp their point of view, you will have trouble explaining your viewpoint to them. If you can state their case better than they can and then refute it, you may increase your chances of dealing with the merits of the matter and minimize the chances of their believing that you have misunderstood them.
2. *Speak to be understood.* Talk with them; remember that negotiation is not a debate. Rather, negotiation should be viewed as two judges getting together and trying to decide a case.
3. *Speak about yourself, not them.* It is more persuasive to describe a problem in terms of its impact on yourself than in terms of what they did. "I feel let down" is more effective than "You broke your word and let me down." A statement about how you feel is difficult for them to challenge.
4. *Speak for a purpose.* If you disclose how flexible you are, it may make it more difficult, not easier, to reach agreement. The rule is: before making a significant statement, know what you want to communicate or find out and know what purpose this information will serve.

Prevention is still the best cure. You should structure the negotiation so that the other party's ego will not get involved with the issues. You need to work to build a working relationship. Get to know the other side, their likes and dislikes. Work on getting both sides to focus on the problem, not on each other. If you can get the parties to view themselves as working side by side in search of an agreement that is fair to both sides, then communications will usually be good.

Focusing on Interests

The basic conflict in almost every negotiation is between each side's needs, desires, concerns, and fears. Interests motivate people; they are the silent force behind positions. Your position is what you have decided upon. Your interests are what caused you to choose that position. The important point is that every interest usually has several positions that would satisfy it. When you look behind the position for the motivating interest, you may find an alternative position that meets both your interest and theirs.

It is usually difficult, and sometimes impossible, to reconcile the position of the other side. We tend to assume that because the other side's position is opposed, their interests are opposed to ours. This is an unwise, and often unwarranted, assumption. Behind opposed positions lie shared or compatible interests, as well as conflicting ones.

Identifying and Expressing Interests

A position is concrete and explicit; the interests underlying the position may be unexpressed, intangible, and inconsistent. Two valuable techniques can help you identify interests:

1. *Ask why?* Put yourself in their place and ask why they have taken this position. Ask what basic concerns could lead them to take their position.
2. *Ask why not?* Think about their choice. A useful way to uncover interests is to ask yourself what interest of theirs may be standing in the way of their agreeing to your proposed solution. If you are going to change their minds, you first must understand where their minds are now. This technique involves identifying what is called the currently perceived choice.

In almost every negotiation each side will have many interests, not just one. A common mistake in diagnosing a negotiation is to assume that the person on the other side has the same interests as you. This is almost never the case. An old example is the story of two sisters who were arguing over who was to get the last orange in the family fruit basket. The mother, tired of hearing the argument, cut the orange in two and gave each sister half. One sister peeled her half orange and ate the fruit; the other peeled her half orange, threw away the fruit, and used the peel to make a cake. Had the sisters understood the other's interests, each could have had more of what she wanted. The position of wanting the orange masked their real interest.

The purpose of negotiation is to serve your interests. The best chance of that happening increases when you communicate them. The other side may not know what your interests are, and you may not know theirs. If you want the other side to take your interests into account, you must explain what those interests are.

It is your task to have the other side understand exactly how important and legitimate your interests are. One guideline is to be specific. Concrete details not only make your description credible, they add impact. As long as you do not seem to imply that the other side's interests are unimportant or illegitimate, you can afford to take a strong stand in setting forth the seriousness of your own concerns. Part of your task in impressing the other side with your interests lies in establishing the legitimacy of those interests.

Each of us tends to be so concerned with our own interests that we pay too little attention to the interests of the other side. We seem concerned that to acknowledge the interests of the other side weakens our case. As noted earlier, however, people listen better if they feel that you have understood them. If you want the other side to appreciate your interests, begin by demonstrating that you understand and appreciate their interests.

Another point to remember is to look forward, not backward. It is surprising how often we react to what someone else has said or done. What often occurs is that we disagree with the other side over some issue; though talk goes back and forth as though we were seeking agreement, the argument is in fact being carried on as a ritual, or a pastime. We are engaged in scoring points against the other or gathering evidence to confirm our view about the other side. Neither side is seeking agreement or trying to influence the other.

The question, "Why?" has two different meanings. One looks backward for a cause and treats our behavior as determined by prior events. The other side of the coin faces forward for a purpose and treats our behavior as subject to our free will.

You will satisfy your interest better if you talk about where you would like to go rather than where you have come from. Instead of asking the other side to justify what they did yesterday, discuss who should do what tomorrow.

In a negotiation, you need to know where you are going. People seem not to want to face up to the difficult task of deciding ahead of time what they will accept. They often go into a negotiation with no other plan than to sit down and see what the other side offers or demands and then decide on what they will accept.

How do you move from identifying interests to developing specific options and still remain flexible with regard to those options? Ask, "If the other side agrees to go along with me, what do I want them to go along with?" To preserve flexibility, treat each option as a possibility—always think in terms of more than one option that will meet your interests. If you want to become a successful negotiator, discipline yourself to do this before each negotiation.

An overriding rule to remember is to be hard on the problem and soft on the people. Be tough in talking about your interests but not rigid in maintaining a position. It is not wise to commit to a position; it is wise to commit to your interests. Spend your energy discussing your interests. The other side will tend to have optimistic expectations of the range of possible agreements. Strongly advocating your interests may get you the maximum gain at minimum cost to the other side.

Attack the problem without blaming the people. You can even be personally supportive: listen to them with respect, show them courtesy, express your appreciation for their time and effort, and emphasize your concern about meeting their basic needs. Be as positive in your support of the people on the other side as you are aggressive in advocating your interests. This combination of support and attack is inconsistent, but psychologically this inconsistency helps make it work. This strategy is based on a theory called *cognitive dissonance,* which proposes that people dislike inconsistency and will tend to eliminate it. By attacking the problem but giving positive support, you create cognitive dissonance. To overcome this dissonance, the other side will be tempted to dissociate themselves from the inconsistency; thus, they will help you solve the problem.

Skills to Help Focus on Interests

Focusing on interests in something the average person does not normally do in negotiation. To help you acquire the habit of focusing on interests, we will explore some ways to develop useful skills.

Probing   Probing is the skill of asking questions or making statements in order to

1. Elicit information from the other party
2. Determine the other side's needs, interests and ideas
3. Ensure understanding of the other side's needs, interests, and ideas before responding to them

Often a negotiator will become locked into an inflexible position by making fixed demands rather than by asking questions to uncover the interests behind the other party's position. If this happens, the negotiator will react without any understanding or appreciation of the other party's real needs. By uncovering the needs and interests underlying the other side's position, it is possible to work on mutually acceptable alternatives.

When do you probe? Probing is particularly important when

1. You need to uncover or verify information.
2. You have to make a decision or commitment on the basis of what has been said.
3. Your immediate impulse is to reject, ignore, or disagree with what has been said.

Probing at these points will help avoid miscommunication and unnecessary conflict that can undermine negotiations.

The two kinds of probes are called open and closed. An open probe encourages people to speak freely and respond as they wish. Open probes often begin with words such as *who, how, what, tell me, when, show me, where, explain to me,* and *why.* Closed probes limit the other person's response to yes or no or to a choice among alternatives that you supply. Closed probes usually begin with words such as *is, do or does, are, will, would, either . . . or, can,* or *could.*

Open probes are effective for uncovering the other side's needs, interests, or ideas and for encouraging them to share information with you. For example, to reveal needs, ask "For what purpose will you be using . . . ?" To discover ideas, ask, "How can we resolve this?" To learn information, say, "Tell me how this has been handled in the past." Open probes are effective when you are not sure what the other side is saying or why it is being said. For example, the following phrases can be useful. "I'm not sure I understand." "What, exactly, are you suggesting for the . . . ?" "Why do you feel that way?" "Please explain your thinking on. . . ."

Closed probes are effective for pinning down specific and getting detailed information from the other side. Examples are such questions as "Are you suggesting a final delivery date of July 15 or July 31?" "Have you been working on a cost-plus basis or a fixed-price basis?" "Will you be able to meet the quality standards we have specified on Exhibit A?" Closed probes are effective to confirm your understanding of what the other person is saying and why he is saying it. To confirm understanding, there are two steps:

1. State your understanding of what has been said and why.
2. Use a closed probe to ask for confirmation.

This technique produces such statements as: "Let's see. You're asking for a guaranteed volume so you can do a forecast. Is that it?" or "Are you asking for a guaranteed volume so you can do a forecast?"

Offering Ideas and Information   Another skill that helps focus on interests is to offer ideas and information. There are two steps for offering ideas so they will be heard:

1. Indicate your intent.
2. Present your reasons before your conclusions.

These steps are highly effective in preparing other people to listen to what you have to say. Remember, there are two separate and distinct steps you must go through to effectively offer your ideas or information to the other side.

You should indicate your intent whenever you want to present an idea, support an idea with information, or introduce an idea by asking a question. Indicating intent prepares the other side to hear what you have to say and respond accordingly. It gives you time to prepare what you want to say before you say it. You might use phrases like these to indicate your intent: "If I might make a suggestion," "Let's look at," "There is some information you might find," "Let me ask you about." Do not indicate your intent if you are about to offer criticism or make an opposing statement—this virtually ensures that the other person will not listen to what you have to say.

Most people stop listening once they have heard the bottom line, so present your reasons before your conclusions. Then the other person will be more likely to hear you.

Inventing Options

Skill at inventing options is one of the most useful assets a negotiator can have. Often negotiators fail to reach agreement when they might have or reach an agreement that could have been better for each side. Why? In a dispute, people usually believe they know the answer—their view should prevail.

Obstacles to Inventing Options

In most negotiations four major obstacles limit the number of options:

1. *Premature judgment.* Inventing options does not come easily. Nothing is as harmful to inventing options as a critical person waiting to pounce on the weakness of any new idea. Prejudging ideas hinders imagination.
2. *Searching for the single answer.* If the first hurdle to creative thinking is premature judgment, the second is premature closure. Inventing is not a part of most people's negotiating process. Since the end product of negotiation is a single decision, many fear that a free-wheeling discussion will only delay and confuse the process. This is not the case. In truth, there is almost always more than one satisfactory answer.
3. *The assumption of a fixed pie.* The third and most prevalent reason that there are few options on the table is that each side sees the negotiation as an either-or matter—either I win, or you do. A negotiation often appears to be a fixed-sum game in which one dollar more for you means one dollar less for me. This assumption is rarely true, but this blind spot prevents many negotiators from realizing that the parties often do not want the same thing.
4. *Thinking that solving their problem is their problem.* Each side may be concerned only with its immediate interests. To reach an agreement that meets your self-interest, you need to develop a solution that also appeals to the self-interest of the other side. People are frequently reluctant to accord any legitimacy to the views of the other side. Short sighted self-concern leads the negotiator to develop only positions, partisan arguments, and one-sided solutions.

Ways to Invent Options

To invent creative solutions, you can use four techniques:

1. Separate the act of inventing options from the act of judging them.
2. Broaden the options on the table rather than looking for a single answer.
3. Search for mutual gain.
4. Invent ways of making their decisions easy.

Separating Inventing from Deciding   Since judgment hinders, separate the creative process of thinking up possible decisions from the process of selecting from among them. Invent first; decide later. Consider the desirability of arrang- ing an inventing session with a few colleagues. Such a brainstorming session will generate ideas. The key thing to remember is to postpone all criticism and evaluation of ideas until after the session is over.

Broaden Your Options   Even with the best of intentions, participants in a brainstorming session are likely to operate on the assumption that they are looking for the one best answer. At this stage, you should not be looking for a single best path. You are developing room within which to negotiate. Room can be made only by generating a substantial number of different ideas—ideas on which you and the other side can build upon and among which you can jointly choose. A brainstorming session frees people to think creatively.

Try breaking down your problem into smaller and perhaps more manage- able units. Agreements may be partial, involve fewer parties, cover only se- lected subject matter, apply only to a certain geographical area, or remain in effect for only a limited period of time. It may be helpful, where possible, to ask how the subject matter might be enlarged so as to sweeten the pot and make agreement more attractive.

Look for Mutual Gain   The third major hurdle to creative problem-solving lies in the assumption of a fixed pie in which less for you means more for me. Rarely is this assumption actually true. Both sides can be worse off than at present; conversely, there is almost always the possibility of joint gain. This may take the form of developing a mutually advantageous relationship or of satisfying the interests of each side with a creative solution.

One key ingredient to look for is shared interests—interests that are the same for both sides. Obviously, shared interests help produce agreement. By definition, then, inventing an idea that meets interests shared by both parties is good for you and good for them. As with so many other things, however, in practice this picture seems less clear. In the middle of a negotiation over price, shared interests may not appear obvious or relevant. Shared interests are pres- ent in every negotiation, however; sometimes you simply have to look hard to find them. Ask whether you and the other party have a shared interest in pre- serving the relationship. What would be the costs if negotiations break off?

Shared interests are only opportunities. To be useful, you have to make something out of them. It is helpful if you make a shared interest clear-cut and express it as a shared goal. You will find that if you stress your shared interest with the other side, negotiations will go more smoothly.

In many cases a satisfactory agreement is made possible because each side wants different things. However, differences can lead either to a solution or a problem. The kinds of differences that best lend themselves to dovetailing are differences in interests, in beliefs, in the value placed on time, in forecasts, and in aversion to risks. Suppose if you want more money; the other side may be able to pay more money if they can spread out the payments. If you do not insist on your money right away, this difference may lead to agreement. You may differ with the other side about forecasts. They believe profits will be great;

you believe they will be small. You might agree to pay a reasonable base salary, with incentives based upon results. Since the other side believes profits will be good, they may agree with this approach. If you are right, the reasonable base salary will protect you. If you are wrong, the higher salary based upon incentives will not hurt, but in fact will help you.

Make Their Decision Easy Success in negotiation depends on the other side reaching the decision you want. The object, then, is to do what you can to make the decision of the other side easy. Give them a choice that is as painless as possible. Negotiators usually pay too little attention to how they can advance their case by taking care of the interests of the other side. To overcome your own immediate self-interest, put yourself in their shoes. Without some option that appeals to them, there is likely to be no agreement.

You will understand the other side's decision-making process better if you pick one person—probably the person with whom you are dealing, or his or her boss—and see how the problem looks from his or her point of view. You may then come to see your role as helping your counterpart by giving arguments that can be used to persuade his or her boss to go along. Your task is to give them answers, not problems; to give them easy decisions, not tough ones. It is crucial to focus your attention on the context of the decision.

Many negotiators are uncertain whether they are asking for words or performance. The distinction is crucial. Usually you want words—a promise or an agreement. Try drafting a few possible agreements. Even early in the negotiation, this is an aid to clear thinking. Prepare multiple versions, starting with the simplest one possible. What terms could the other side agree to? Can you reduce the number of people whose decisions will be required? Can you draft an agreement that will be easy for the other side to implement?

When asking for agreement on actions, remember two points. It is easier to refrain from doing something than it is to stop some action already underway. It is easier to cease doing something than it is to undertake an entirely new course of action.

Choosing Criteria

The other side is more likely to accept a solution if it seems the right thing to do—right in terms of being fair, legal, or honorable. Make the options appear to be legitimate solutions.

Few things facilitate a decision as much as precedent. Look for it. Look for a decision or a statement the other side may have made in a similar situation and try to base a proposed agreement on that. This provides an objective standard for your request and makes it easier for them to go along.

We often try to influence others by threats and warnings of what will happen if they do not decide as we would like. Offers are usually more effective than threats. Concentrate on making the other side aware of the consequences from their point of view. How can you make your offers more credible? What can you invent that will be attractive to them but low in cost to you?

A final test of an option is to write it out in the form of a "yesable proposition." Try to draft a proposal to which they can respond with a simple "yes" and such a response would be sufficient, realistic, and operational. When you can do this, you reduce the risk that your own self-interest may have blinded you to the necessity of meeting the concerns of other side.

Irrespective of how well you have done the foregoing, you will eventually face the situation where interests conflict. If you try to settle these differences of interest on the basis of who has the stronger will, you will find that this approach has a high price tag. The solution is to negotiate on some basis independent of the will of either side, that is, on the basis of objective criteria.

The approach is to commit yourself to reaching a solution based on principle, not pressure. Concentrate on the merits of the problem, not the will of the parties. Be open to reason, but closed to threats.

The more you bring standards of fairness, efficiency, or objectivity to bear on a particular problem, the more likely you are to produce a final package that is wise and fair. The more you and the other side refer to precedent and community practice, the greater your chance of benefiting from past experience. A lease that contains standard printed terms has little risk that either side will feel harshly treated.

One coauthor was once negotiating a sale with buyers from the Middle East. Near the end, the sellers brought out a mortgage document that had been drafted. The buyers objected to many of its terms. The terms were standard, but no amount of persuasion would convince the other side of the reasonableness of the document. Finally, it occurred to the sellers that a printed mortgage sold by business supply stores was available. The sellers brought out this mortgage, and the other side agreed to it immediately. Ironically, this printed mortgage was as favorable, if not more so, than the one that had been drafted. The power of the standard, printed form turned the trick.

Problems with Negotiating

People Who Refuse to Be Reasonable

Some people refuse to deal with you in a reasonable manner. Deadlock, stalemate, or giving up is not the solution. You have three approaches to direct their attention to the merits and keep it there. The first approach is for you to concentrate on the merits, not on your position.

The second approach is used if the other side continues with positional bargaining. In this case, you change to a strategy that deals with what they may do. If they criticize your proposal, you will be tempted to defend it. If they criticize you, you will be tempted to defend yourself and counterattack. If you give in to any of these temptations, you are playing the positional bargaining game. Refuse to react. Sidestep these attacks and redirect the attack against the problem. Use the following techniques:

1. When the other side sets forth their position, neither accept nor reject it. Instead, look behind it for the interests that it expresses and the principles it reflects. Then identify ways to improve the position so that it can help meet your interests as well.

2. Instead of resisting criticism, invite it. Ask what is wrong with your proposal or idea. Examine the comments to find their underlying or unstated interests. Rework your ideas based upon what you learn from them. Another technique to redirect their criticism is to turn the situation around and ask for their advice. Ask them what they would do if they were in your position. If you can get them to confront your problem, they might just invent a solution that meets your concerns.

3. When the other side attacks you personally, just listen. When they finish, recast their attack on you as an attack on the problem: "I understand your frustration. The problem is a difficult one. We must find a solution to it. The problem has a solution, if we can just work together to find it." It is amazing how this approach diffuses their attack on you and gets everyone back on track again.

4. Use questions instead of statement. Statements generate resistance; questions generate answers. Questions offer no target to shoot at; they do not criticize, they educate.

5. Silence is one of your best weapons. If you have asked a question to which they have given an insufficient answer, just wait. Do not take them off the hook by going on. Your silence will invariably drive them to go ahead and give a more complete answer.

The third approach to use when confronted by a positional negotiator is the one-text procedure. In this technique, after listening to all arguments, statements, concerns, and interests, you prepare a written proposal that no one has accepted. Ask for comments and criticisms. Then rewrite it and ask for comments and criticisms again. Continue, until you say, "this is the best I can do." It is interesting how often this will get agreement.

Common Mistakes

The mistakes made near the end of a negotiation happen so fast that they are often not recognized until the negotiation is over. When agreement is within your grasp or when you fear that deadlock is about to occur are critical times in the negotiation. The following mistakes can happen to anyone who is under pressure caused by nearing agreement or fearing deadlock:

1. Never assume that an impasse on an issue will result in deadlock in the overall negotiation. If an impasse occurs, go on to the next issue and take up the problematical issue later. If you make progress on the other issues, the troublesome issue has a habit of getting worked out later.

2. Do not be intimidated by the other side's last and final offer. They will probably be back. Be prepared and help them save face when they return.

3. Do not make a last and final offer yourself until you have carefully evaluated how the statement will be made and how discussions will be continued if it is not honored. Never bluff unless you know what you will do if the bluff is called.

4. Never get panicked into a final agreement by a time deadline. It is easy

to fall into the time trap. Be skeptical about deadlines. Most deadlines are negotiable.

5. You will not succeed in winning your objective if you try to be liked in the final phase of negotiation. The crisis stage is a severe test of each party's intentions and motives. It is not a social tea, nor is it necessarily fun. The person who wants to be liked usually gives away quite a lot.

6. Never let an issue be discussed unless you are prepared for it. The temptation to play it by ear must be resisted. No one is smart enough to know what to do unless he or she thinks about it first. Such a situation may come up near the end of the negotiation; you will be tempted to wing it. Resist this temptation.

Summary

Negotiating is a common occurrence in business—and a necessary skill to business success. Unfortunately, this important skill is not taught. The central principle of successful negotiation is to negotiate on the basis of the merits of the problem and to refuse to play the game of positional negotiation.

An important set of negotiating skills to develop is to address the needs of your side and the other side as people. This approach means addressing the importance of perceptions, finding ways of eliminating the potential blockage caused by emotions, and promoting good communication.

Another valuable consideration in negotiations is to focus on the interests of each side and not on the positions taken. Positions are simply expressions of each side's interests. Discovering and addressing those interests is directing your attention to what really matters to each side.

A third technique is to recognize that an abundance of options can help solve a problem. Most problems have more than one solution. Spending time to generate as many solutions as possible enhances your ability to actually solve the problem.

Finally, it can be valuable to identify objective criteria against which the solution can be measured. By appealing to law or custom, previous agreements, or past behavior, you can help convince the other side that the action you are asking them to undertake is reasonable and fair. They are then more likely to accept the need to take that action.

Class Assignments

1. Why is it important in any negotiation to know what your best alternative to a negotiated agreement is?
2. If the object of negotiation is to win, why would anyone be interested in a "win-win" orientation?

GETTING IT ALL TOGETHER

Chapter 10
Business Organizations: What Form to Use?
This chapter describes the four most frequently occurring legal forms of organization: the sole proprietorship, partnership, corporation, and joint venture. The chapter offers guidelines to help you decide which may be best for you based on the advantages and disadvantages of each.

Chapter 11
Raising Your Capital
This chapter points out the problems that business owners face when they underestimate how much money they will need to start their companies. The chapter discusses the types of capital and explores how to obtain the capital that you will need.

Chapter 12
Developing Your Financial Plan
This chapter places a heavy emphasis on managing your cash wisely in order to pay your bills, survive, and prosper. The discussion examines how to assess the business's needs for working capital. The chapter also explores how to manage the business's cash flow.

Chapter 13
Your Business and the Tax Laws
This chapter examines the tax issues that most new and small businesses confront. Tax laws, regulations, and interpretations change frequently, but you need to evaluate their effects on the profitability of your firm. The discussion focuses on the tax implications of the form of business, the operation of the business, and the termination of the business. The chapter examines the status of S corporations.

Chapter 14
Business Agreements You Will Need
This chapter helps you to understand the types of business contracts and agreements that you will probably need to enter into as you start your company. These agreements focus on two issues: operational control of the business and the continuance of the owner's interest in the business in the event of death, retirement or other withdrawal, or disability.

Chapter 15
Formal Business Plan
This final chapter in the part presents guidelines for drafting the formal business plan that sets your course of action. There is more work than most prospective owners realize to being fully prepared to start a business. A comprehensive effort up front will pay off for you later.

BUSINESS ORGANIZATIONS: WHAT FORM TO USE?

In this chapter we assume that you have decided to enter business for yourself and whether to buy an existing business or begin your own business. We assume that you have already evaluated the worth of the business, if you are buying an existing business, that you have selected your advisers, and that you are ready to get started. But what vehicle are you going to start with? What form of business will you use?

It may not have occurred to you that the form of business you choose is a significant decision. Because this decision has many implications, you must be aware of the advantages and disadvantages of each form, so that your choice of one is well founded.

In this chapter you will learn the four basic forms available for the operation of your business: the sole proprietorship, the corporation, the partnership, and the joint venture. These four forms will be analyzed and compared with each other in relation to four main considerations:

1. Formation of the business
2. Operation of the business
3. Tax consequences to the business
4. The consequences of termination or liquidation of the business

Each of these considerations will affect whatever business entity you choose. The selection of one entity may give you a better result in one of these areas but a less favorable result in another. What often results is a balancing of these considerations in order to arrive at a decision.

You will see that each business form is different and that there are few general rules to selecting the best form to use. You will learn how to analyze the various forms available to you and how to relate these to your business in order to decide which form is best for you.

After reading this chapter, you will be able to

- Distinguish among the four forms of business ownership
- Analyze the four types of business ownership based on rules for forming the business, operational concerns, tax consequences, and circumstances that arise when terminating the business
- Explain the special considerations related to S corporation status

Introduction to the Forms of Business

Proprietorship

The proprietorship, sometimes called a *sole proprietorship* does not have any of the formalities required of a partnership or corporation. The term *sole proprietorship* is actually redundant since a proprietorship is by definition the ownership of a business by one person. If you purchase assets in your own name and begin to operate a business, you are the proprietor of that business. If two or more people own a business not in corporate form, they are not proprietors, but either partners or members of a joint venture, depending upon the facts under which they are operating. We shall analyze a little later the effects and consequences to you of operating as a proprietorship.

Partnership

A partnership is ownership of a business by two or more individuals in which the business does not take corporate form. The business should have a formal written partnership agreement that details how the partnership is to be operated, how the profits or losses are to be shared, and many other considerations (see Chapter 14). If no written partnership agreement exists, the laws of most states treat the relationship as a partnership and specify what legal rights, duties, and responsibilities the parties have to each other.

A partnership, by definition, excludes operating in corporate form, although two or more corporations can join together and operate as a partnership. Other than the fact that the partners are corporations, the comments above still apply to the partners and the partnership. Another combination can occur, in which one or more proprietorships join with one or more corporations to form a partnership.

Corporation

A corporation is a legal entity recognized by all fifty states. The corporation is a creation of the law. It is also a legal fiction; that is, the law treats the corporation as if it were a legal person. The corporation (with one exception) is a taxpayer, and it can sue and be sued in its corporate name. Each corporation is required to be formed according to certain legal formalities. These formalities vary from state to state but are fairly uniform among the states. The ownership of the corporation is vested in the hands of shareholders. The formation and operation of a corporation will be treated in greater detail later in this chapter and in Chapter 14.

Joint Venture

The joint venture is not a typical method of operating a business. It usually exists when two or more separate businesses join together to perform a project or several projects on a predetermined negotiated basis. This form is fairly common in construction in which no one business is able to handle alone a large project; in this situation, several businesses who can perform one or more aspects of the project join together to accomplish it. A joint venture may look like a partnership, but because of the legal agreements between or among participants, it may not be treated under the law as a partnership. It is rare that a joint venture will operate over a long period of time; it is more common for the joint venture to last only until the project is completed. Each participant is treated as a separate business. The joint venture may be made up of proprietorships, partnerships, corporations, or a combination of these entities.

We now examine each of these business forms in detail, considering in each instance their formation, operation, tax implications and termination of business.

Proprietorship

Formation

The creation of the proprietorship has few requirements. No formal documents have to be filed in order to become a proprietorship although, if you are going to operate under a trade name or assumed name, state statutes usually require registration of that name with the local clerk of court in the county courthouse. This filing puts the public on notice as to the ownership of the trade name. Usually this trade name is used for advertising, logos, and the telephone book.

Operating Factors

The key to operating as a proprietor is that you are the business. Your personal assets are on the line if your business fails or if you or your employees cause damage to third parties while operating the business.

This aspect of proprietorship becomes very important if your business is the kind that has the potential for causing damage to third parties. Examples are businesses in manufacturing, the food and drug industries, and trucking. You must assess this risk before you begin operating the business. While the risk can be mitigated by insurance coverage, it cannot be eliminated. With the large awards currently being granted in liability suits, insurance adequate to cover all risks will usually prove to be either impossible to obtain or prohibitive in cost.

If your business has very small risk of damaging customers or third parties, the proprietorship has advantages. It offers simplicity of operation. No upfront legal costs are incurred to begin operating as a proprietorship, there is no separate legal entity to be concerned with, and the accounting is simplified. Because the risks are great, however, be sure that you obtain the advice of your lawyer and your insurance agent about operating as a proprietorship. Be sure that they lay out the hazards and that you have a clear understanding of your areas of risk and the magnitude of these risks.

If substantial risk exists or if the risk cannot be adequately insured against, you will be well advised to consider incorporation as a means of limiting your liability.

Tax Implications

Since a proprietorship is really your business alter ego, it follows that you will bear the tax losses and enjoy the taxable profits of your business. The income or loss of the proprietorship is reported as a part of your individual income tax return, usually being recorded on Schedule C of the Form 1040. The proprietorship is not a separate taxpayer, like the corporation. As a result, there is no opportunity to split the income between yourself and another taxpayer.

Termination of Business

The proprietorship is easy to terminate. All that is necessary is to stop doing business, pay all expenses, dispose of all the assets, and (hopefully) put the proceeds in the bank. No formalities have to be observed to terminate such a business.

Winding up the proprietorship has no adverse tax consequences. The sale of the business generates a taxable gain or loss under the usual tax rules. The sale of a capital asset generates a capital gain or loss, modified in some cases to the extent of depreciation previously taken. Before selling business personal property on an installment basis, check with your tax adviser to ascertain the tax consequences. Tax laws have been under almost constant change of late, and you should have a clear understanding of the tax consequences before deciding how to dispose of business assets.

Partnership

Formation

Very few, if any, states require a formal registration procedure for a partnership. The partnership is formed by two or more persons entering into a business relationship for the purpose of sharing profits and losses. Although no formal registration is required, you should never enter into a partnership without first having articles of partnership prepared, approved by all the partners, and signed.

The partnership, like the proprietorship, often operates under a trade name. If you wish to operate under a trade name, you should have that name registered with the appropriate officials. A record of trade names is usually kept by the clerk of the county court. Registration protects the name, but only to a limited extent. It is usually not sufficient to prevent your trade name from being used elsewhere in the state.

While the partnership agreement is being prepared, you need to apply for a federal identification number. Although the partnership is not a taxpayer, it does have to file a federal and state income tax return (in those states that have state income taxes). These returns are only informational, but they must be filed. The partnership also has to file quarterly tax returns for payroll taxes and pay state unemployment taxes. You should either acquire this identification number or have your accountant obtain it for you. It should be obtained as soon as possible because most documents that the partnership prepares will ask for the number.

Operating Factors

You will recall that a partnership is a viable form of operating your business when the business is owned by you and someone else. You and your partner share the profits and losses of a business enterprise.

It is strongly recommended that, before you join the partnership, all parties agree on all the areas discussed in this chapter. The agreement should be in writing and signed by all the partners. Do not fall into the trap of waiting until later to get the agreement written and signed. By that time the economic situation among the partners may have changed, causing their memories to be affected—possibly to your detriment.

The risks associated with a proprietorship also apply to a partnership, except that partners are also exposed to additional risk. This additional risk stems from the power your partner has to bind you to agreements made on behalf of the business. Your risk is also increased due to your being jointly liable with your partner for acts of negligence he or she commits in furtherance of the business. Again, have your lawyer and insurance agent detail for you the risk of operating as a partnership.

The partnership is a useful form of business if the risk of liability to customers or third parties is minimal and can be adequately protected by insurance. A partnership may be appropriate if you and your partner have different talents to lend to the business. Bear in mind, though, that these benefits can also be obtained by forming a corporation, particularly one that has S corporation status. (This corporate form is explored in greater detail in the section dealing with operation of the corporation.)

A partnership may be useful if one of the partners has contributed capital for the business but is not involved in day-to-day operations. In this situation, the partners who are involved in daily operations usually receive compensation in the form of salaries. The net profits and losses of the business are then shared between or among the partners in proportion to their percentage of participation in the profits and losses. This result can also be obtained in a corporation with S corporation status. The service business is one type of business that sometimes lends itself to operation as a partnership because such firms usually require limited amounts of capital, and limited liability may not be of great importance.

In the absence of an agreement to the contrary, each partner has a say in the management and operation of the partnership, and a majority of the partners governs the partnership's routine business affairs. It is advisable to designate one partner as the managing partner or some similar title. If not, chaos may rule—when everyone is in charge, usually no one is in charge.

The partnership is limited as to its choice of an accounting period. The Internal Revenue Code requires that the partnership tax year be the calendar year if any of the partners are individuals. Consult with your advisers as to your options for a tax year.

The method of accounting is another important decision. If inventories are a material income-producing element of your business, then the partnership must be on the accrual method of accounting. However, straight accrual is not the only accrual method. Be sure that your tax adviser looks at all the options and that the partnership chooses the accounting method that is best for your business.

The partnership agreement should also speak to the following issues:

- *Additional capital contributions.* If the partners are going to be required to make additional contributions, the event that triggers those contributions must be agreed upon.
- *Loans to the partnership.* Loans to the partnership usually require the assent of some or all of the partners. The question is, how many and which ones. This issue needs agreement. If the managing partner or some other partner is to be authorized to obtain loans on behalf of the partnership, limits should be placed on the amount, interest rate, collateral pledged to secure the loan, and other terms and conditions deemed necessary.

Tax Implications

The partnership is not a taxpayer separate from its partners; however, it is required to file an informational tax return. The tax consequences of the business flow through the partnership to the individual partners. Each partner reports his or her taxable income or loss on an individual tax return.

Tax considerations do affect the allocation of income or losses among the partners. The allocation of income or loss must bear some relation to the amount of capital or labor contributed by each partner, and your tax adviser should be consulted before you agree how this allocation will be handled.

You can transfer assets into the partnership in return for an interest in the partnership without tax consequences. The transfer to the partnership, if it is tax-free, results in a transfer of the assets at book value; the partnership takes the assets (if they are depreciable) at the depreciated value in the hands of the transferor. If the assets are nondepreciable (like real estate), the transfer is made at the cost basis of the transferor. Keep in mind that this valuation of transferred property is for the transferror's tax purposes only. For the purposes of the partnership's books, the value carried is the depreciated or cost amount. For example, suppose that you have a piece of real estate, which originally cost you $12,000, but is now worth $75,000. If you transfer the property to the partnership, you are credited with a capital contribution of $75,000 even though the property goes on the partnership books at $12,000. You get credit for partnership purposes for the full fair market value of your contribution.

In order for the partnership to obtain an asset at a value equal to the property's fair market value, the property must be sold to the partnership. If a partner sells the property to the partnership for cash and then contributes the cash to the partnership, two tax consequences result. The partnership values the property at an amount equal to the price paid for it, and the partner selling the property has a taxable gain on the difference between his or her adjusted basis of the property and the selling price. Such a transaction would probably only occur if the property were depreciable property and the partnership wanted to get a stepped-up basis for purposes of depreciation. If you should sell personal property to the partnership on an installment sale, keep in mind that under current tax law, you will have to report all the gain in the year of sale, even if you do not receive all the proceeds of the sale in that tax year. Consult with your tax adviser before selling property to the partnership to prevent unexpected tax results that could have been avoided by better planning.

Termination of Business

The partnership has a limited life in that the death or withdrawal of a partner usually dissolves the partnership as a matter of law. This feature is one major disadvantage of operating as a partnership. In addition, any partner may withdraw at any time and thereby dissolve the partnership. A dissolved partnership does not always liquidate, however. Generally, liquidation of a partnership means that the business is terminated, the assets are disposed of, and the debts are paid. This result can be prevented in the event of the death or withdrawal of a partner if the partnership agreement specifies that such actions do not dissolve the partnership. Refer to Chapter 14 for a more detailed discussion of this area of planning and protection.

Liquidation of the partnership can result in substantial losses to the partners. Adequate provisions must be placed in your partnership agreement to ensure continuation of the business. If a partner dies, the deceased partner's estate cannot join as a partner in continuing the business without a written agreement permitting such action. Similarly the surviving partners are usually prohibited from purchasing the interest of the deceased partner from his or her estate without written agreement. In short, careful planning and a good partnership agreement are necessary to guard against the inadvertent dissolution and liquidation of the partnership.

Under the applicable state laws, certain events give rise to a dissolution of the partnership. A winding-up period then follows in which the pending business is completed, accounts receivables are collected, assets are sold, and bills are paid. After this winding-up period, assets are distributed—first to remaining creditors and then to the partners.

One must be careful because a dissolution of the partnership under state law may not be the same as a termination of the partnership for federal tax purposes. In most circumstances, state law and principles do not control the tax consequences of a particular transaction or event. Thus, for example, the liquidation of a partner's interest in the partnership may cause a termination of the partnership under state law, but this liquidation generally does not cause the partnership to terminate for federal tax purposes. On the other hand, an event may result in dissolving the partnership for federal tax purposes but not for state law purposes.

The events giving rise to termination of the partnership for tax purposes under the Internal Revenue Code are as follows:

- Cessation of all business, financial operations, or ventures of the partnership
- The occurrence of an event that results in the partnership ceasing to operate in the partnership form (for example, the purchase by one partner of another partners' interest in a two-person partnership)
- A sale or exchange of interest in 50 percent or more of the profits and capital of the partnership during a twelve-month period

This area of partnership law is very technical. For this reason it is important to keep in mind the differences in terminology used in the Internal Revenue Code and under state law. Without keeping these differences in mind, concepts can become confusing.

All three events (dissolution, winding up, and distribution of assets) must occur for the partnership to be terminated under state law. These three steps are also sometimes referred to as the *liquidation* of a partnership. As pointed out above, federal tax law only recognizes partnership termination, which occurs only if one of the three events set forth above occurs. Otherwise the partnership continues for tax purposes. Confusion is sometimes created for those who are not specialists in partnership tax by the use of the term *liquidation*. The concept of the liquidation of a partnership does not appear under the Internal Revenue Code; however, the Code does contain the concept of the liquidation of a partner's interest in the partnership. This distinction points up the necessity of a good partnership agreement and good advisers in this specialized area.

Corporation

Formation

The laws of each state require that certain legal formalities be observed before the corporation comes into being. Usually the corporation is born when the articles of incorporation (or corporate charter) are issued by the secretary of state (or other designated official) and the minimum capital required by statute is subscribed and paid for. Since the corporation is a creature of state law, it is usually necessary for a lawyer to obtain the corporate charter.

You should consider several matters before you incorporate. The basic consideration is whether to incorporate at all. (We will discuss the issues related to this question in the next section.)

Once you decide to incorporate, the first step is to choose your corporate name. State statutes usually require that the corporate name be reserved and issued by a central office, usually the secretary of state's office. The laws also prohibit confusingly similar names from being used. Choose your name carefully. Your corporate name can be an excellent marketing tool. Since the office that issues name certificates will not issue names that are similar to other corporate names in use, you should decide on several choices and list them in order of preference.

The articles of incorporation usually require you to specify the minimum and maximum capital stock that the corporation is authorized to issue. Check to see if your state taxes you on the maximum authorized shares. If so, keep the maximum as low as possible.

In performing your financial plan (see Chapter 12), determine what capital structure will be necessary to support your business. After you have determined this, consult with your tax lawyer or accountant to determine whether some of the capital needed can be in the form of debt rather than equity. You will want to subscribe for the minimum amount of stock you can because once you have shares issued to you as paid-in capital, you cannot recover those funds without adverse tax consequences unless you sell your stock or liquidate the corporation. If you can safely lend your corporation part of the capital needed and have the corporation issue you its note, it can repay these loans later without tax consequences. You do not wish to tie up your personal funds indefinitely if you can help it.

Another important point is not always addressed when the corporation is formed. If you overcapitalize in the form of paid-in capital, you are, in effect, holding down your return on investment. Keep in mind that one objective in owning your own business is to get as great a return on your invested capital as possible. Thus, you want your extra working capital in the form of loans. When the corporation can afford to repay the loan, your profits are added to retained earnings and your annual after-tax profits indicate your return on invested capital.

Operating Factors

The main feature of a corporation is that, since it is a legal entity and can sue and be sued, you have an extra measure of protection. Corporate obligations are obligations of the legal entity, and unless you have guaranteed or otherwise assumed that corporate obligation individually, the corporation is liable. The corporation and its assets stand behind the obligation, but your personal assets are not at risk if the corporation does not satisfy those obligations. This practice is what is known as *limited liability.* A liability of the corporation is limited to being satisfied by the corporation.

An important point to remember in this regard is that if you want an obligation to be that of the corporation, you must always be sure to obligate the corporation. Always enter into contracts, agreements, and other obligations in the name of the corporation. To enter an obligation on behalf of the corporation, a corporate officer must sign in a representative capacity. If the president of the Acme Company intends to bind the company to an agreement, the name of the corporation must be written on the contract or agreement and the president must sign as a representative of the company. This step is achieved by indicating the office following the signature.

Until your corporation has substantial net worth, your banker is not likely to allow the business to borrow money without you personally guaranteeing the loan. Exert every effort to have all other obligations of the company signed in your representative capacity, on behalf the corporation.

You will need to place a corporate resolution on file with the bank. This document authorizes the bank to honor checks drawn by the individuals designated in the resolution. The same resolution specifies who is authorized to borrow money on behalf of the corporation. It is wise to require two signatures to draw checks. If you are going to allow anyone other than you to sign checks, limit that person's authority in the resolution to, say, amounts not more than $500. Only you should be authorized to borrow money on behalf of the corporation unless there are other shareholders. In that case, all shareholders should be authorized. But if all are authorized, all should be required to sign.

If anyone other than the shareholders is going to be authorized to sign checks for the corporation, have that person bonded by an insurance company. We also recommend that you ask your accountant to recommend adequate controls for those who handle money or are authorized to write checks. Good controls will not prevent a determined individual from stealing, but they may allow you to stop the theft before the damage is too severe.

If there is more than one shareholder, they should have certain written agreements with each other. These are addressed in greater detail in Chapter 14.

The death, retirement, incompetency, or bankruptcy of a shareholder of a corporation does not legally affect the continuity of the corporation. Ownership of the shares in the corporation, in and of itself, does not have anything to do with continuity of the corporation or even with its management. This lack of connection is especially true in large, publicly traded corporations. In small, closely held corporations, however, it is not uncommon to see the shareholders involved in management. In closely held companies, the death, retirement, incompetency, or bankruptcy of one owner may, in fact, have a profound effect on the continuity of business. However, the corporation as a legal entity is not affected by these events.

A corporation that has not elected S corporation status can choose a fiscal year that ties in with its business cycle. Traditionally, businesses want their operating and tax year to end in the month that coincides with their historically slowest business month. The election of a fiscal year-end is available to corporations (except for S corporations), but it is generally unavailable to partnerships and proprietorships, which are generally restricted to the calendar year-end.

Tax Implications

As emphasized earlier, the corporation is a separate legal entity, which means that it is a separate taxpayer. Tax laws change so frequently that it is difficult to make any statement about tax consequences of a corporation without being fearful the statement will be inaccurate at time of publication. Nevertheless, we offer a few general comments.

It is important at the outset of this discussion to review the S corporation. An S corporation is a status that can be elected at specified times by all the shareholders; this status causes the corporation to be treated differently for tax purposes. Generally speaking, the election of S corporation status provides for a pass-through of profits and losses to the shareholders similar to that enjoyed by partners in a partnership. An S corporation generally has no income tax at the corporate level.

It has been common practice to incorporate in order for the owners to limit their liability and then elect subchapter S status in order to obtain tax treatment similar to that of a partnership. An S corporation election is often made in the early years of a corporation's existence, when losses are expected, and then terminated in later years, when the corporation becomes profitable. However, an S corporation election is also beneficial for a profitable corporation because it provides a mechanism for passing through a pro-rata share of the corporation's profits to a shareholder who is not an employee without incurring double taxation.

An exhaustive treatment of the tax status of corporations is beyond the scope of this book. However, some elementary concepts may be helpful and allow a more intelligent choice.

The tax rates for a corporation are progressive, but they differ from those for an individual taxpayer. The corporation pays taxes on the income it retains. Distributions of corporate earnings and profits to shareholders in any form other than salaries, bonuses, or repayment of a debt to a shareholder, is taxed as a dividend. This means that the shareholder pays tax on the distribution at the shareholder's applicable tax rate, but that the corporation does not get to deduct the distribution. As you can see, this is a double tax, once at the corporate level and again at the shareholder level. Salaries and bonuses paid to employees, even those who are also shareholders, are deductible expenses to the corporation provided that the payments are reasonable. The shareholder-employee and the IRS often reach conflict over what is reasonable.

The corporation can also retain its net profits, which are then called *retained earnings.* Earnings can be retained without restriction up to an amount set by the Internal Revenue Code (presently $250,000). Any amounts retained beyond this safe harbor must be justified by good business reasons—another phrase that has been a source of conflict between the IRS and the corporation. Any amount retained in any corporate tax year beyond the reasonable business needs of the corporation is subject to a penalty tax called the *accumulated earnings tax,* which is levied beyond the regular corporate rate.

A corporation may also be subject to a personal holding company tax if five or fewer individuals own more than 50 percent of the value of the corporation's outstanding stock at any time during the last half of the taxable year and at least 60 percent of the corporation's adjusted ordinary gross income is personal holding company income as defined by section 542(a) of the Internal Revenue Code. Personal holding company income consists of passive investment income such as dividend, interest, rent, and royalties. The personal holding company tax is also a penalty tax, levied in addition to the normal corporate income tax.

S corporation status is helpful in that an S corporation is not subject to any corporate income tax, accumulated earnings tax, or personal holding company tax. As you may have surmised, S corporation status also renders moot the issue of the reasonableness of salaries, provided that all shareholders are employees and render comparable services to the corporation. Since under an S corporation, profits and losses are passed through to the shareholders in the same percentage as their stock ownership, salaries are not as important as they are in a corporation of traditional form.

S corporation status is also beneficial even if some shareholders do not render any services to the corporation as employees or independent contractors. In a traditional corporation, any payment to a shareholder who does not render services or who is paid in an amount greater than the amount of service rendered is usually deemed a dividend by the IRS, with the resulting double tax. Such sums would pass through to the shareholder in an S corporation and only be taxed once.

The Internal Revenue Code of 1986 created additional pressure for many small businesses to elect S corporation status. Prior to 1986, a corporation could sell its assets in bulk and then liquidate, distributing the proceeds from the sale and retained earnings, with a few exceptions, in a manner that resulted in income tax being paid only by the shareholders. They paid on any gain from their investment in the corporation's stock. This arrangement was accomplished by having the corporation elect to liquidate under Section 337 of the Internal Revenue Code. This provision was particularly beneficial if assets owned by the corporation had appreciated in value since their acquisition. The general effect was that shareholders of closely held corporations could usually count on being able to liquidate their company without the corporation having to pay any tax on its gain in assets. While there was a tax on any gain realized at the shareholder level, the gain was taxed only once.

Now, in the post–1986 world, a corporation that distributes to its shareholders assets that have appreciated in the hands of the corporation incurs a tax on the gain, even if the distribution is in complete liquidation. The Internal Revenue Code of 1986 made many changes in the tax law, but this change, which taxes appreciation of assets at the corporate level upon their distribution in complete liquidation, will have more impact on corporations than any change in recent time. This provision means that the gain is doubly taxed—at both the corporate and individual levels.

This gain is taxed at the corporate level regardless of whether the assets are sold by the corporation and the proceeds distributed to the shareholders or the corporation distributes the assets themselves to the shareholder. This lurking double tax has affected the way many businesspersons act in the post–1986 world. Many businesspersons are now leasing operating assets to the corporation. The shareholder continues to depreciate those assets that are depreciable and the corporation pays the shareholder-lessor rent on the assets. This practice is particularly appropriate if the assets are likely to appreciate in the future. Since the assets are operated by the corporation under a formal arm's-length lease, the limited liability of the shareholder should not be affected. If the corporation then elects S corporation status, retained earnings do not build up.

Without assets to appreciate and without retained earnings building up, the corporation's exposure to a substantial tax is reduced.

With the new law, owners of closely held corporations who wish to sell are more likely to insist that the buyer purchase their stock in the company rather than the corporate assets. The sale of assets and subsequent liquidation of the company triggers the double tax, whereas the sale of stock produces only the shareholder tax.

Termination of Business

The corporation suffers no inadvertent termination of the business entity, as the partnership may. You will recall that one of the characteristics of a corporation is continuity of existence. Another attribute of the corporation is transferability of interest. The shareholder can transfer his or her interest in the corporation by simply transferring his or her stock in the company. (A contractual restriction may limit transferability.)

Termination of the corporation can only be accomplished by formal liquidation and dissolution. The dissolution of a corporation is accomplished by following the statutory requirements. While these procedures vary from state to state, in general they are very similar.

Upon the death or retirement of a shareholder, a corporation may redeem the shareholder's stock or the remaining shareholders may purchase the shares. A closely held corporation usually has no market for the shareholder's stock. For this reason, the shareholders or the shareholders and the corporation should enter an agreement by which the surviving shareholders or the corporation purchases the decedent shareholder's stock (see Chapter 14).

There are tax consequences associated with the redemption of stock in the corporation. Time and effort in planning for redemption is recommended. This area is fraught with tax traps for the unwary.

The tax consequences of liquidation of a corporation were covered above and must be kept in mind before beginning the liquidation process. In this case, the tax tail wags the dog. The tax consequences of corporate liquidation may be severe if the liquidation is handled inappropriately. Advice from your tax adviser is very important, and it should be obtained before you begin the process. Some tax consequences cannot be undone, and this is one of them.

While it is not technically a termination of the corporate structure, the loss of S corporation status can have unexpected consequences. Because the election of S status has taken on more importance since 1986, we need to take a closer look at how to elect S status and how it can be lost.

The prerequisites to qualifying as an S corporation are aimed at organizing a corporation with a simple capital structure. The following initial requirements must be satisfied:

1. The corporation must be a U.S. domestic corporation.
2. The maximum number of shareholders is thirty-five.
3. All shareholders must be individuals (some limited exceptions exist for

certain types of trusts). A partnership or a corporation cannot be a shareholder.

4. Only one class of stock can be issued and outstanding. There has been some confusion in the past, with some courts calling debt a second class of stock. For tax years after 1982, a safe harbor is established whereby straight debt will not be treated as a second class of stock. (Straight debt is defined as a written unconditional promise to pay on demand or on a specified date a sum certain where the interest rate and interest payment dates are not contingent on profits, the borrower's discretion, or similar factors; there is no convertibility of the debt into stock; and the creditor is an individual, an estate, or one of the qualified trusts alluded to above.)

Failure to meet any requirement for S corporation status results in the disqualification of the entity as an S corporation, effective as of the date that the corporation failed to meet the requirement. S corporation status may also be terminated by voluntary revocation. Revocation occurs when shareholders holding more than half the stock consent to the revocation. A revocation is effective on the first day of the taxable year if made on or before the fifteenth day of the third month of the taxable year. A revocation made after the fifteenth day of the third month of the taxable year is effective on the first day of the following taxable year.

The Joint Venture

Formation

The joint venture is created by two or more individuals or businesses joining together in order to combine their resources and expertise to perform a task or complete a project. A joint venture is created by agreement between or among the parties. A written joint venture agreement is preferred.

Since the joint venture may look like a partnership, it is important for you to make sure that all parties understand that you are operating as a joint venture and not a partnership. If you allow yourself to be held out as a partner, you may end up being treated like a partner by a creditor or some damaged third party. In a partnership, each partner is jointly and severally liable for each partner's business debts and the negligent acts or omissions of the other partners. Joint and several liability means that you can be held liable for the debts and negligent acts of your partners or you can be held liable along with them. In a joint venture, however, each party is responsible only for his or her own obligations, debts, and actions and not for those of the other participants.

Operating Factors

Since the joint venture is born of the need to accomplish a particular project or obtain a desired result, the operation of the joint venture must, of necessity, be agreed to and set forth in the joint venture agreement. There are no hard-and-fast guidelines as to what the agreement should provide. There are, however, three areas that should be addressed in the agreement because they have proven, over time, to have been areas of conflict and trouble:

1. *Areas of responsibility.* The agreement should clearly delineate who is to be responsible for what. Since by definition a joint venture is a joining together of two or more individuals or entities to accomplish a specific task, each participant usually has an area of expertise. It is where these areas overlap and in the coordinating of the project that problems arise. The agreement must deal with these areas.
2. *Division of the money.* If problems in a joint venture arise, they invariably concern money and the division of money. The agreement must be very detailed and specific about how the money is to be divided among the participants in the joint venture.
3. *Warranties or guarantees.* If any contractual warranties and guarantees have been made, the agreement must deal with each participant's responsibility to those warranties and guarantees. When the job is over, each party's interest is in trying to keep its expenditures down and its profits up; such is not the time to deal with these issues.

Tax Implications

The tax consequences of a joint venture follow the kind of entities involved in the venture. The joint venture is not a recognizable legal or taxable entity. Each party to the joint venture will retain its tax attributes as a proprietorship, partnership, or corporation. The discussion of tax implications in the previous sections should be reviewed to determine the tax consequences of each party.

Termination of the Business

Since the joint venture is not a recognizable legal entity, the business of the joint venture is limited by the duration of the project undertaken. The agreement should provide a bright line indicating when the venture is over.

No formal dissolution or liquidation requirements exist for the joint venture, as they do for the corporation. No events can inadvertently dissolve the joint venture, as they can a partnership. The joint venture agreement should specifically deal with termination of the arrangement and how the parties are to disassociate themselves when the project is completed.

Summary

The four basic forms of business ownership are the proprietorship, the partnership, the corporation, and the joint venture. Easiest to form and to terminate, the proprietorship has a single owner whose income is taxed at individual tax rates and whose personal assets are liable to meet the obligations of the business. The partnership, too, involves the liability of owners' assets to meet business obligations, such as debts or amounts due to others as a result of lawsuits.

Partnerships, however, have more than one owner. It is essential that an agreement be developed to govern the rights and responsibilities of different partners and to provide for the continuance of the business after the death or departure of a partner.

The corporation is a legal fiction—the law considers the business to be an entity that, like any individual, can incur obligations. In this form, then, the personal assets of owners are protected from business liabilities. Corporations are the most difficult form of business to create. They have a significant disadvantage as well. The earnings of corporations are taxed twice—once as corporate earnings and once as the earnings of individual owners. Under certain circumstances, a corporation can elect S corporation status, which removes this double taxation.

The last form of business—the joint venture—is actually a combination of any two or more of the other three forms, which join in order to accomplish a specific task or project. As with a partnership, the contributions and obligations of each participant should be spelled out in a detailed agreement. The joint venture expires upon completion of the task or project.

Class Assignments

1. If limiting your liability is an important consideration to your business, what legal form gives the greatest amount of protection to you as an individual?

RAISING YOUR CAPITAL

Experts cite undercapitalization as a major cause of new business failure. Surprisingly, many of these failures occur as the result of or on the verge of success. A restaurant owner is so impressed with her initial sales volume that she opens a second location, only to find it draining off the resources she had accumulated. A construction company acquires a government contract for a project larger than it has ever had before and learns that, although government payments are notoriously slow, creditors will not wait. A laundry owner is the low bidder for servicing a large convention center without realizing that the expense of expanding his operation exceeds the revenues from the new customer.

Often, new enterprises are undercapitalized because the entrepreneur neglected to estimate all the costs that he or she should have reasonably expected to incur or because he or she made an early blunder and does not have an adequate contingency fund to recover. Sometimes the fledgling firm is destroyed when an unforeseeable event occurs that is too expensive. Careful planning is required to be as prepared as possible. Chapters 5, 6, and 12 give you some ideas about what costs you can expect to face and how to prepare for the unexpected.

After reading this chapter, you will be able to

- Distinguish among the types of capital available to entrepreneurs
- Identify five sources of capital
- Explain how to locate and approach the sources

Issues in Raising Capital

We stress the costs of doing business so frequently in this book that you may reach the conclusion that the process of opening a business is impossibly expensive. Obviously, people can and do start businesses on the proverbial shoestring. A third of all businesses start with an initial investment of less than $10,000 (see Exhibit 11.1). Our role is to ensure that you temper your ambitions with reality and that you are aware of costs that a new enterprise incurs.

Exhibit 11.1
CAPITAL INVESTMENT PRIOR TO FIRST SALE

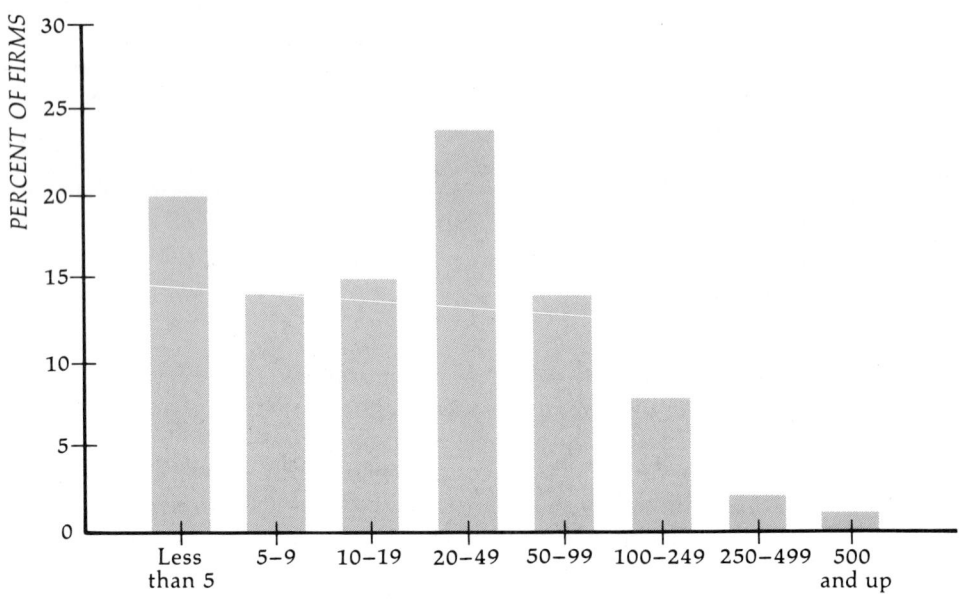

In the broadest sense, the capital that you use to cover your expenses can be categorized as either physical or human. Physical capital includes cash, cash equivalents (bank accounts, investments, and so on), goods, materials, facilities, land, equipment, and supplies. These items appear as current and fixed assets on your balance sheet. Human capital is represented not only by labor and time, but also by the skills, knowledge, and ideas that workers possess. New businesses often find that they cannot make sizable initial investments in physical capital and substitute by being more labor intensive, that is, by spending more hours on the job, performing more hand work than machine production, and taking other steps that replace physical capital with human capital.

There are costs associated with all forms of capital. We can categorize these costs as opportunity, ownership, or interest. If the invested capital comes from your personal resources, you forego alternative returns to that investment (for example, the interest you might have earned in a certificate of deposit). This represents an opportunity cost. If your cousin provides you with $10,000 for a 10-percent share of ownership in your company, your cost is the obligation to provide your cousin with a return on that investment; at a minimum, your cousin would be entitled to 10 percent of the proceeds in the event of your business being liquidated. The third cost is the interest charge you must pay for any borrowed capital.

You can see from these costs the dilemma faced by the typical small business owner. You seek to minimize risking your own capital in the business, yet you want to avoid heavy debt payments to your creditors and also avoid sharing control with other investors. Let us examine the types of capital available for starting or buying a business in order to identify ways to handle this dilemma.

Types of Capital

We first categorized capital as human and physical. On a company's balance sheet, the assets of the firm have been acquired through two types of capital: debt and equity. Debt refers to a financial obligation your firm has to repay a creditor; equity is a capital investment in the firm that results in a share of ownership. Capital can also be classified as long term or short term. Generally, equity capital is long term; that is, the asset is part of the business for more than one year. Debt may be long term (a mortgage) or short term (a loan to purchase inventory).

The need for capital does not automatically create it, however. For example, Mike and his partners had years of experience selling men's clothing and were convinced that the city could support a top-quality custom tailoring business. Mike shopped suppliers in New York and returned with prices and assurances. He wrote a business plan showing the need for a $400,000 loan for material, ready-made suits, accessories, equipment, and other startup expenses. He began calling on banks. Loan officers were not impressed and gave him little time and no interest. The partner pulled out, and Mike looked for other venture opportunities. This example demonstrates a major frustration for budding entrepreneurs: the inability to get people with money to catch your enthusiasm about your business idea.

Prospective lenders often have a fiduciary responsibility to make rational decisions about the money they lend. If it is not clearly evident that the loan will be repaid or the money is protected, do not expect bankers to put themselves in jeopardy by handing it over to you.

You also need to think about why you want the loan, how you will pay it back, and how long you will need the money. Let us examine the types of debt capital that small business owners use and the concerns associated with each.

Debt Capital

Debt capital can be raised in many ways. One method is to obtain trade credit or revolving credit lines, in which you promise deferred payments to suppliers for merchandise, materials, or equipment delivered. The other approach is to borrow cash by obtaining loans, which can be of various durations.

Trade Credit   Rarely recognized for its importance in financing a new business, trade credit actually represents the largest proportion of small business debt. The normal process involves obtaining services, goods, materials, supplies, or equipment from a vendor and deferring payment. Although you do not directly borrow money in this process, you do acquire what you might otherwise have borrowed money to purchase. Often, you need not pay interest on this type of debt if you make timely payments.

Trade credit can sometimes be difficult to obtain initially if you have no track record for repaying debts. If you abuse your trade credit, penalties can include being placed on a COD basis or being cut off from your source of supply. In Chapters 17 and 18 we explain the significance to your marketing strategy of maintaining good relations with your suppliers.

Revolving Credit Lines   When you establish a line of credit, you negotiate a dollar figure that you may borrow up to, a ceiling on the interest rate you will pay, and a term for repayment. This method enables you to borrow to cover what are normally short-term, low-amount demands or opportunities, such as adding to your inventory to take advantage of a seasonal discount. You will probably need collateral, often real estate, to set up your line of credit until the bank has experience dealing with your company. Interest rates can fluctuate with market conditions.

Short-Term Loans   A short-term loan is usually borrowed for a specific purpose, such as the renovation of a store's facade. These loans are expected to be paid back when the project, event, or activity is concluded. Most short-term debt is repaid within one year of when it is borrowed. Small businesses usually pay a premium over the amount charged to larger businesses for short-term money.

Intermediate-Term Loans   Intermediate term loans are normally for one to five years. They are frequently tied to the purchase of some asset, such as furniture, equipment, a vehicle, or the expansion of a plant.

Long-Term Loans   Loans that are repaid over periods of time longer than five years are considered long-term loans. Such loans are usually for the purchase of major assets for which the business will recoup costs over a long time. Real estate purchases and the construction or purchase of a building are typical examples. This type of debt must be carefully considered. In securing a long-term loan, you take on an obligation that influences your cash flow and your ability to borrow additional funds for years.

Equity Capital

Equity financing results in some share of ownership in the business. You need not put money into a business to acquire ownership, but if there are multiple shareholders, anyone not participating in financing the enterprise would be presumed to invest in kind, such as serving as manager of the enterprise. Many small business owners are loathe to share equity in their companies for fear of losing control to other shareholders.

The nature of equity is related to the legal form of the enterprise (see Chapter 10). Equity in proprietorship and partnership comes from direct investment by the owners. In corporations, ownership results from acquiring stock. Equity financing is obtained by initial and subsequent stock issues and by retaining some earnings within the company rather than distributing those earnings to stockholders.

There are many varieties of stock, which differ according to the priority of distribution and voting privileges. Preferred stock gives priority for the distribution of earnings and assets; common stock carries the right to vote on corporate matters, normally the election of officers and directors.

Some financing options combine features of equity and debt. One example is a convertible debenture, which is a debt instrument with certain rights of conversion to equity. Another example is a term loan with an equity kicker. This loan, secured by company assets, carries options to acquire equity during a specified term.

Sources of Financing

In Exhibit 11.2, we see the major sources of financing the purchase of creation of a business. Let us examine some of these sources.

Personal Savings

As shown in Exhibit 11.2, the vast majority of small firms rely on the personal savings of owners, usually invested as equity. You should consider, however,

Exhibit 11.2

SOURCES OF FINANCING TO START OR PURCHASE A BUSINESS

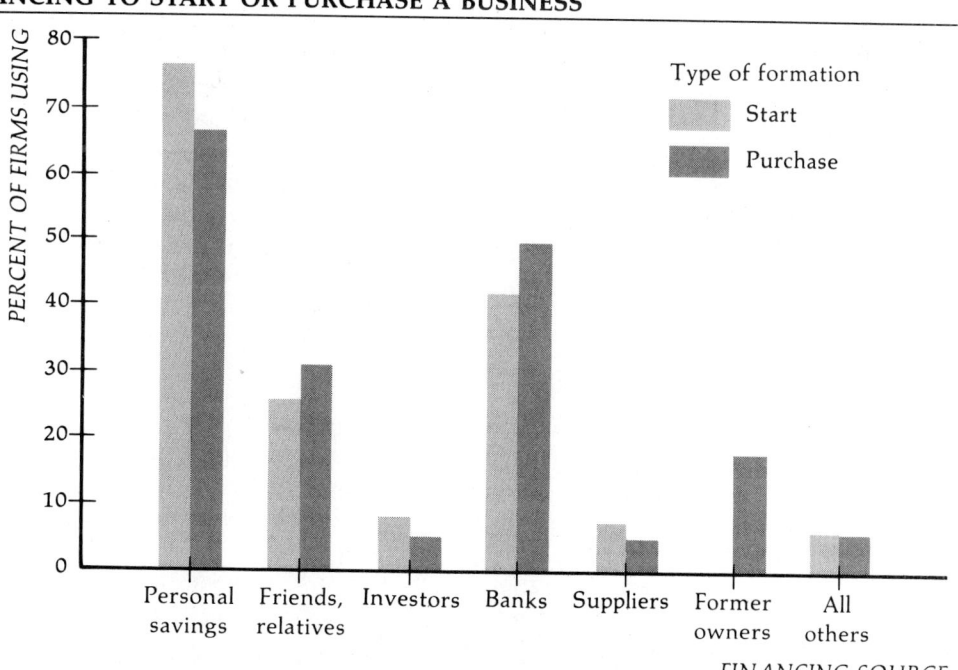

FINANCING SOURCE

that it may be advantageous to loan savings to your company rather than using them as equity. In this way, you draw dollars out as a repayment of your loan rather than as a taxable salary or distribution of earnings. Check with an accountant (see Chapter 8) to determine the best approach for your situation.

It is also worth noting that personal savings includes dollars borrowed by the owners as individuals rather than loans made to the business. Such borrowing might include a second mortgage on a home or even charges made on a personal credit card.

Many prospective business owners try to minimize their investment to protect their personal assets. Before taking such a step, think about this from the perspective of potential investors or lenders. They expect you to work harder to make the company a success if your own assets are on the line.

Banks and Other Financial Institutions

Although nearly 50 percent of business starts and purchases involve bank financing, 80 percent of all bank financing to small business is short term, averaging forty days according to the Small Business Administration. This can result in an early cash crunch for the new owner. Additionally, since a new business has no track record, banks tend not to make early stage loans unless they are secured by assets. Guaranteed loan practices by the SBA influence bank lending (see the appendix).

Friends and Relatives

If your friends and relatives do not think that you or your business have enough merit to warrant their investment, why would strangers buy your products or services? Many of us are hesitant to jeopardize personal relationships by asking for money, but contributions from friends and relatives are a major source of new venture financing, both equity and debt. In securing such financing, however, treat friends and relatives in a professional manner. For the security of all parties, put everything in writing, whether the capital is debt or equity.

Former Owners

You may want to tie a former owner to your company through debt or equity because he or she possesses expertise or knowledge that you want to access. Also, such a loan or investment gives the former owner a vested interest in your success, preempting him or her from becoming a competitor or aiding one.

The willingness of an owner to finance the sale of his or her company is very much contingent on current tax laws and regulations. A qualified accountant should always be consulted when negotiating for the purchase of a business.

Other Private Sources

Venture capital firms sometimes invest in new businesses, but only rarely. Eighty percent of formal venture capital investment occurs in third- and fourth-round financing, when an existing business needs a major capital infusion to expand. On the other hand, a significant amount of informal financing at the seed, or venture creation, stage does take place. Informal investors, called *angels*, can be hard to find and do few deals. Nevertheless, they are critical to the success of many firms. Efforts are being made around the country to establish networks that bring angels and entrepreneurs together.

Public Sources

In addition to the Small Business Administration (see the appendix), many federal, state, and local agencies make funds available to small businesses or assist them in obtaining financing. Some agencies provide loans, some give loan guarantees, and others make outright grants. Still others play the role of intermediary by trying to link small businesses with lenders and investors.

The SBA, Economic Development Agency (EDA), and Farmers Home Administration (FHA) all guarantee loans under various guidelines related to the size, type, and location of the firm. As of this writing, the SBA and FHA make some direct loans, but the amount of money available for such loans is tiny and often targeted for special purposes. In approving guaranteed loans, the agencies examine your application thoroughly and verify your credit worthiness. If your loan request is questionable to a banker, it probably will not be approved by a government agency.

Other federal agencies and departments can make money available to small businesses. The *Federal Register* publishes requests for proposals (RFPs) from federal agencies that your company may qualify for. RFPs are usually requests for contracts to perform a task or provide a service, but they may give you an infusion of funds at a stage when your company needs it. Several departments participate in the Small Business Innovation Research (SBIR) program. They give grants to companies that are conducting research relevant to their respective department's mission.

States offer a variety of financial incentives to small businesses. Examples include setting aside a stipulated percentage of state pension funds for venture capital investment and establishing a pool of money for a revolving loan fund. State initiatives are often tied to local development activities by cities and town. They may be targeted toward business creation and expansion in inner cities or in several communities.

Asking for Money

Sources of capital generally match the life cycle stage of your company. (Refer to the life cycle model in the Introduction.) At the startup stage, only you and people who know you will put money into the company. Any money you borrow will be based on your personal credit, not on the credit of the business.

For most small businesses, capital requirements in the growth phase are not great. These businesses provide supplementary or substitute income, and the need for external capital is minimal. If you do experience rapid growth, it will normally be fueled by the informal venture capital network. Bear in mind that an angel will not passively sit by while you manage your business. He or she makes few investments and wants absolute assurance that each will pay off. You find angels by talking to everyone you can think of who might have money or know someone who does. You can also make presentations to venture capital clubs.

Some owners seek equity funds from suppliers or customers. Exercise caution when soliciting capital from someone you are doing business with. You may later regret what you have tied yourself into.

Third-round financing, the type to boost you to your next plateau and perhaps position you for a public offering, is where formal venture capitalists come in. These investors expect to take a sizable chunk of your business and earn substantial return on the investment. How much are you prepared to give up for what you need? Some studies show that few original entrepreneurs are still running their companies five years after accepting venture capital.

Business newspapers and magazines frequently run lists of or advertisements for venture capitalists. Your professional advisers—your CPA, attorney, and banker—will probably be able to direct you to some. Most venture capitalists specialize by stage of development of the company or product, by size of investment, by industry, by geographic location, or in some other fashion.

Mature businesses tend to use traditional financing sources. In this stage, you are well known to your banker and other creditors. Unless you are planning an unusual expansion, financial transactions are relatively routine. Your concern at this stage is to avoid becoming complacent. Money is like the other commodities on which you base your business: shop around periodically and make sure that you are getting your best deal.

Whatever stage your business is in, do your homework. Do not contact a lender or investor without being prepared. Keep your business plan up to date. Be able to explain how much money you want, how you will use it, what the lender or investor will get back, and when the repayment will occur. You will be approaching sophisticated people, or they would not have compiled the money to put into your business in the first place. Have contingency plans showing how they will be protected if the business does not go as well as you expect. Be able to demonstrate how the business will pay the creditor even if something happens to you. With most small businesses, the investment is made more in the person than the enterprise. You must prove that the lender or investor will not be in jeopardy.

Summary

In this chapter you learned about the main types of capital used by small businesses: debt and equity. Debt capital involves the obligation to repay the debt at a later time. Equity capital involves obtaining a share of ownership. The sources of capital include the owner, friends and relatives of the owner, the former owner, other private sources, and public sources. Most of these sources can provide either of the two types of capital. The source you approach for capital is linked to the stage of your business—the need for capital does not arise only at the beginning of the business, but may occur in later stages as well, as you prepare for growth or expansion. Before soliciting capital you should develop a plan that will reassure the potential investor or creditor that the money will be protected and some return given on the investment.

Class Assignments

1. Thoroughly read a recent issue of the *Wall Street Journal* and list the types and sources of new venture financing that you find.
2. Look up the term *leveraged buyout* (LBO). How is it defined? Find an article in a business magazine about a leveraged buyout and summarize the transactions.
3. Why does a new business owner borrow money? What are the advantages and disadvantages?
4. Why would an entrepreneur be willing to share ownership of his or her firm? Why might he or she avoid giving up equity?

Appendix: How to Raise Money for a Small Business[1]

Successful small business expansions and new formations lead the way in creating new markets, innovations and jobs that fuel economic growth and prosperity.

In recognition of the importance of small business to a strong economy, Dun & Bradstreet Information Resources has joined with the U.S. Small Business Administration (SBA) to help meet the information needs of existing business owners and aspiring entrepreneurs.

We hope *Focus on the Facts* meets your needs and we invite your comments and questions. Your success in business depends on what you know and how well you can apply what you have learned.

Raising Money

One key to a successful business start-up and expansion is your ability to obtain and secure appropriate financing. Raising capital is the most basic of all business activities. But as many entrepreneurs who are just beginning quickly discover, raising capital may not be easy. It can be a complex and frustrating process. But if you are informed, well prepared and have planned effectively, raising money for your business will not be a painstaking experience.

This information summary focuses on the ways a small business can raise money and describes how to prepare a loan proposal.

Where To Find the Money You Need There are several sources to consider when looking for funding. It is important that you explore all of your options before making a decision.

---

1. "Focus on the Facts: How to Raise Money for a Small Business," prepared by the U.S. Small Business Administration and cosponsored by Dun & Bradstreet, Inc.

- *Personal savings:* Most new businesses are started with the primary source of capital coming from personal savings and other forms of personal equity.
- *Friends and relatives:* Many entrepreneurs look to private sources such as friends and family when starting out in a business venture. Oftentimes, money is loaned at no interest, or with low interest, which can be beneficial when getting started.
- *Venture capital firms:* These firms provide start-up and other needed money for new companies in exchange for equity or part ownership.
- *Banks and credit unions:* The most common source of funding, banks and credit unions will provide a loan if you can show that your business is sound.

Borrowing Money   It is often said that small business people have a difficult time borrowing money. This is not necessarily true.

Banks are in the business to make money, and the way they make money is by lending money. However, it is the inexperience of small business owners in financial matters, that prompts many small business loan requests to be turned down. To be successful in obtaining a loan, you must be prepared and organized. You must know exactly how much money you need, why you need it and how you can pay it back. You must be able to convince your lender that you are a good credit risk.

Requesting a loan when you are not properly prepared makes a statement to your lender. That statement is "high risk!"

Types of Business Loans

Short-Term Loans. Loans that are paid back in less than one year. Types of short-term loans include:

- Working capital loan
- Accounts receivable loan
- Line of credit (revolving credit line)

Long-Term Loans. Loans with maturities greater than one year but usually less than seven years. These loans are used for major business expansions, purchases of real property, acquisitions and in some instances start-up costs. Types of long-term loans include:

- Personal loan
- Commercial mortgage
- Term loan

How to Write a Loan Proposal   Approval of your loan request depends on how well you present yourself, your business and your financial needs to a lender. Remember, lenders want to make loans, but they want to make good loans, loans they know will be repaid. The best way to improve your chances of obtaining a loan is to prepare a written loan proposal.

A good loan proposal will contain the following key elements:

General Information

- Business name, name of principals, social security number for each principal and business address.
- *Purpose of the loan.* State exactly what the loan will be used for and why it is needed.
- *Amount required.* Request the exact amount you need to achieve your purpose.

Business Description

- *History and nature of business.* Give details of your business's age, number of employees and current business assets.
- *Ownership structure.* Provide details on your company's legal structure.

Management Profile

- *Management description.* Develop a short statement on each principal staff member in your business; provide background, education, experience, skills and accomplishments.

Market Information

- Clearly define your products and market.
- Identify your competition and explain how your business competes in the marketplace.
- Profile your customers and explain how your business can satisfy their needs.

Financial Information

- *Financial statements.* Provide balance sheets and income statements for the past three years. If you are just starting out, provide a projected balance sheet and income statement.
- *Personal financial statement.* Prepare a personal financial statement on yourself and other principal owners of the business.
- *Collateral.* List all collateral you would be willing to pledge to the bank as security for the loan.

How Your Loan Request Will Be Reviewed   A loan officer's primary concern when reviewing a loan request is whether or not the loan will be repaid. To help answer this question, many loan officers will order a copy of your business credit report from a business credit reporting agency. Therefore, it is helpful if you work with these agencies to help them prepare an accurate picture of your business. Using the credit report, and the information you have provided, the lending officer will consider the following issues:

- Have you invested savings or personal equity in your business totaling at least 25%–50% of the loan you are requesting? Remember a lender or investor will not finance 100% of your business.
- Do you have a sound record of credit worthiness as indicated by your credit report, work history and letters of recommendation? This is very important.
- Do you have sufficient experience and training to operate a successful business?
- Have you prepared a loan proposal and business plan which demonstrates your understanding of the business and your commitment to the success of the business?
- Does the business have sufficient "cash flow" to make the monthly payments on the loan request?

SBA Financial Programs

The SBA offers a variety of financing options for small businesses. However, it rarely makes a direct loan to an individual or company. The Agency is primarily a guarantor—it guarantees loans made by banks and other private lenders to small business clients. SBA guaranteed loans generally do not exceed $500,000, of which the Agency guarantees 85 or 90 percent of the loan balance to the bank. The average size of an SBA guaranteed loan is $175,000 and the average maturity about eight years. SBA guaranteed loans are obtained through private lenders.

How to Get More Information

Information is power! Make it your business to know what business information is available, where to get it and most importantly, how to use it. Sources of information include:

U.S. Small Business Administration

- SBA District Offices
- Small Business Development Centers (SBDCs)
- Service Corps of Retired Executives (SCORE)
- Small Business Institutes (SBIs)

Consult your telephone directory under U.S. Government for your local SBA office or call the Small Business Answer Desk (1–800–368–5855) for information on any of the above resources. In Washington D.C. call 653–7561. Also, you may request a free Directory of Business Development Publications from your local SBA office or the Answer Desk.

Other Sources

- State economic development agencies
- Chambers of commerce
- Local colleges
- The library
- The manufacturers and suppliers of small business technologies and products.

Good luck!

DEVELOPING YOUR
FINANCIAL PLAN

This chapter is divided into two parts. The objective of the first part is to introduce you to net working capital, its significance to your business, and its sources and uses. This part of the chapter will help you estimate your business's net working capital requirements for operation and expansion and understand the various sources of internal and external working capital to your business. The chapter also shows how to prepare a working capital cash flow statement to review the financial activities within your business during the most recent period. With a working knowledge of net working capital and sources of funds, you should have the foundation with which to plan and manage the growth of your business.

The second part of the chapter explains how to prepare and interpret cash flow statements. This section also introduces the net liquid assets approach to funds and the working capital statement. Finally, the chapter presents the essential elements of cash budgeting and cash management. This knowledge will assist you in attaining budgeting skills and appreciating that cash flow management and budgeting is the foundation of long-term success.

After reading this chapter, you will be able to

- Calculate additional net working capital needed to expand operations
- Explain the effect of inventory turnover on cash flow
- Prepare a cash budget

Why Should You Plan?

A financial plan is like a road map—it tells you how to get to where you want to go and lets you know when you get there. Everyone who starts or buys a business knows that you must have a financial plan, but not everyone knows how to develop and use one. Financial plans, however, are much akin to the weather—everyone talks about them, but few do anything about them. The initial inquiry must be what is the purpose of the financial plan—is it to buy a business, to start a business from scratch, or to operate and manage a business? The answer, of course, is all of the above. At some time in your career, you will probably need each of these plans. Seldom will you need more than one at a time.

This chapter is devoted to the subject of working capital needs, cash flow, and cash flow budgets. It is highly unlikely that any business will be successful in the long run without sound planning in these areas. There will always be businesses that will take off like a rocket but fail. There are many reasons for failure, of course, most of which are cautioned against in this book. But if one of the other pitfalls is not the culprit, a safe bet is that planning for working capital and cash flow needs was inadequate or lacking altogether.

Whether you are starting from scratch or have found the perfect business to purchase, the financial plan for your business must command your total commitment to thought, study, and follow through. Everyone talks about capital, but there is seldom enough capital. A sound financial plan will allow you to take off with the capital you have and operate the business successfully.

Working Capital   Need for Additional Net Working Capital

Rob and Jim own and operate R&J Poultry, Inc., a corporation that provides fresh poultry to grocery stores and restaurants. The company buys its poultry directly from poultry processors located near its office; it specializes in fresh poultry and excellent service. After a year of operation the sales volume has stabilized at $300,000 per month.

During the coming year R&J are planning to add two additional trucks in order to increase sales. The company cannot increase sales appreciably with the three trucks and drivers it now operates without the service level falling. Since service is a vital part of the business's success, expansion without additional trucks and drivers is out of the question. Jim, who handles sales, projects that R&J's total sales will increase by 50 percent by the end of the coming year. Rob, in charge of operations and financial management, anticipates that the company will require additional working capital to add the additional trucks and drivers and to support the expected increase in sales.

Rob also wants to pay off an existing $116,000 note payable, which comprises all of the company's present long-term debt. This note, secured by the office building and the three trucks, is due to mature in two years. The bank has indicated that it will be helpful to retire this old debt and clear the way for new long-term financing.

Rob needs to answer the following two questions:

1. How much additional working capital will be required to purchase the new trucks, expand the business, and retire the $116,000 debt?
2. Where should the company acquire this capital?

Estimating Cash to Support Operations

To determine the total cash requirements, Rob wants to forecast the amount of current assets that he feels will be necessary to support R&J's projected level of sales of $450,000 (a 50-percent increase over current sales of $300,000 per month). Rob has found that 70 percent of expected monthly sales ($315,000) is an adequate amount of cash to have on hand. By projecting the need for cash on hand as a percentage of sales, Rob feels that the increased cash to fund the new drivers' salaries and the cost of operation of the trucks will be adequate.

R&J's sales have consistently run 40 percent cash and the balance on account. Forty percent of the credit sales pay in 7 days, and 20 percent pay in 30 days. Customers do not always pay on time, but the average time of payment is 22 days, or 0.75 months after purchase. Therefore, Rob estimates accounts receivable to equal 0.75 months' worth of credit sales, or $202,500 (0.75 × $270,000, the amount of credit sales if they are 60 percent of total sales).

R&J's poultry is sold at an average markup of 11 percent of the cost of the product. This means that poultry costing $0.40 per pound is sold at $0.44 per pound. Rob has found that R&J needs an average inventory on hand equivalent to 8 percent of sales volume. Rob therefore projects an inventory level of $24,000 at the increased volume of sales (cost of one month's sales × 0.08 × 0.89 × 0.75 and rounded). Rob also projects that supplies, which currently run $3,000, may increase to $5,000.

Rob's projected requirements for total current assets are therefore $546,500 (cash $315,000, receivables $202,500, inventory $24,000, and other current assets $5,000). Rob knows that current creditors will finance a part of these assets by allowing R&J to purchase inventory and services on 30-day account. Rob has found that current liabilities have averaged 91 percent of current assets (a 1.1 to 1 ratio), and he sees no reason for this ratio to change. Rob therefore projects $497,315 of current liabilities. Net working capital to sustain the projected increase in sales volume is thus $49,185 ($546,500 minus $497,315).

The entire $49,185 would be required as new funds if R&J were just starting the business. Since the business is established, however, it only needs to obtain an additional amount over the requirements of its present level of operations. Thus Rob first needs to see if R&J has any excess net working capital. This excess net working capital can be used to reduce R&J's demand for new working capital. Rob must determine what R&J's minimum net working capital needs are at its current level of operations. He finds that the company can operate with $32,760 of net working capital. The additional cash requirements for the expansion planned is thus $16,425 ($49,185 minus $32,760).

Estimating Cash to Acquire Equipment

R&J can acquire two new trucks, fully equipped to handle its poultry, at a cost of $60,000. R&J plans to acquire these trucks for cash and obtain long-term bank financing to fund these purchases and refinance its current long-term debt.

Estimating Cash to Retire Long-Term Debt and Fund Owner Bonuses

R&J needs $116,000 to retire its long-term debt. Rob and Jim have each been withdrawing $30,000 per year from the corporation as a bonus. Rob's plan must provide adequate cash so that these bonuses can be continued for the coming year.

R&J's total cash requirements, then, is, $252,425, which includes the following uses and applications:

Acquire new trucks (long-lived assets)	$ 60,000
Retire long-term debt	116,000
Bonuses for Rob and Jim	60,000
Increase balance for net working capital	16,425
Total uses	$252,425

Identifying Sources of Working Capital

Where can R&J obtain the additional $252,425 needed for working capital? A business can look for additional working capital in only two places: inside the business or outside the business. These are usually referred to as internal sources and external sources of funds.

The two internal sources of working capital are the sale of long-lived assets and after-tax net profits, or funds from operations. Because long-lived assets are not a part of current liabilities and their sale will generate additional cash, they become a possible source of working capital. The sale of long-lived assets is not possible for R&J, however, because they have no plans for such a sale. (Usually long-lived assets are a source only when some of these assets are outdated and obsolete or when a particular asset is no longer needed in the business.)

The second internal source of additional working capital is funds from operations, or after-tax net profits. The first place to check for this source is R&J's income statement for the past year. As Exhibit 12.1 shows, funds from the past year's operations are $184,000 (net income after tax of $137,000 plus depreciation of $47,000). Depreciation is added back to after-tax net profit because depreciation is an expense that does not require cash.

In reviewing the income statement for the past year to identify net profits, you must look for income items that will not normally occur in the next operating year. These are called *extraordinary items of income.* In planning for the next year, these items must be subtracted to prevent projected income from being overstated. R&J's income statement for the year just ended has no extraordinary items. Can Rob safely assume that the same amount of income from operations will be generated for the coming year? Such an assumption would be very conservative given the projected 50 percent increase in sales. Neither profits nor expenses generally increase in proportion to the increase in sales, however. Since an income statement is history, Rob needs to look at anticipated

Exhibit 12.1
R & J POULTRY: INCOME STATEMENT FOR YEAR ENDING
DECEMBER 31, 19X2 (in thousands)

Gross sales	$3,600	
Cost of goods sold	3,243	
Gross profit		$357
Operating expenses		
Wages and salaries	$ 58	
Utilities	10	
Insurance	20	
Supplies	3	
Depreciation	47	
Interest	12	
Total operating expenses		150
Income before taxes		207
Provision for income taxes		(70)
Net income		$137

income from operations for the coming year. A pro-forma income statement for the coming year will show the projected income from operations. See Exhibit 12.2 for the pro-forma income statement for the coming year that Rob prepared.

In general, think of funds from operations as net income after tax, plus noncash expenses that have been deducted, and minus any noncash revenues that have been included. While this definition will usually work, it is not technically correct. Gain on the sale of long-lived assets is not included in income

Exhibit 12.2
R & J POULTRY: PRO-FORMA INCOME STATEMENT FOR YEAR ENDING
DECEMBER 31, 19X2 (in thousands)

Gross sales	$5,400	
Cost of goods sold	4,900	
Gross profit		$500
Operating expenses		
Wages and salaries	$120	
Utilities	15	
Insurance	50	
Supplies	5	
Depreciation	60	
Interest	8	
Total operating expenses		258
Income before taxes		242
Provision for income taxes		(87)
Net income		$155

from operations. A workable formula to calculate funds from operations is to begin with net income after taxes, add noncash expenses and losses, and subtract noncash income and gains and any gain on long-lived assets sales.

If you apply this formula to the pro-forma income statement in Exhibit 12.2, you see that R&J can anticipate the coming year's funds from operations to be $215,000:

Net income after taxes	$155,000
Depreciation expenses	60,000
Funds from operations	$215,000

Thus far we have identified the sources of additional net working capital from internal sources as the sale of long-lived assets and funds from operation. R&J can anticipate nothing from the first source and $215,000 from the second. There is actually a third internal source of funds, which is not really an additional source of new net working capital. Surplus net working capital can be drawn down for use by the company. Exhibit 12.3 gives R&J's most recent balance sheet, and it shows the net current working capital to be $41,000 (total current assets less total current liabilities). You recall that Rob determined the net working capital needed to maintain R&J's current level of operations to be only $32,760. R&J thus has $8,240 of excess net working capital, which can be used to fund the company's additional requirements.

R&J has total requirements for $252,425 of net working capital. Rob has determined that $223,240 will be available from internal sources ($215,000 from income from operations and $8,240 from excess net working capital). The balance ($29,185) must be obtained from outside the company.

A business has only two external sources of net working capital: additional long-term debt and additional owner investment. Obtaining cash from short-term creditors is not a source of funds because no net working capital is gener-

---

Exhibit 12.3
R & J POULTRY: BALANCE SHEET AS OF DECEMBER 31, 19X2 (in thousands)

ASSETS		*LIABILITIES AND EQUITY*	
Current Assets		Current Liabilities	
Cash	$210	Accounts payable	$273
Accounts receivable	135	Wages payable	7
Inventory	24	Other current liabilities	48
Total Current Assets	$369	Total Current Liabilities	$328
Long-Term Assets		Long-Term Liabilities	
Land	$ 15	Noncurrent notes payable	$110
Buildings	50	Total Long-Term Liabilities	110
Vehicles	90		
Accumulated depreciation	(47)	Owner's equity	39
Total Long-Term Assets	108	TOTAL LIABILITIES AND	
TOTAL ASSETS	$477	EQUITY	$477

ated. You will recall that net working capital is total current assets minus total current liabilities. Borrowing cash on a short-term basis increases current assets but also increases current liabilities by the same amount. Thus, such a loan does not affect net working capital.

Rob must now determine how much of the $29,185 R&J can raise by long-term debt financing. This decision is affected by the company's long-term debt capacity. You should always talk with your banker to determine the long-term debt capacity of your business. This capacity is usually expressed as a ratio obtained by dividing total long-term debt by the sum of total owner's equity and the long-term debt.

In order to compute R&J's projected ratio for the coming year, take the beginning owner's capital from the balance sheet for the current year ($39,000) and add the projected after-tax net profit for the coming year. If you are taking this from the pro-forma income statement (Exhibit 12.2), you must subtract owner's bonuses. The projected owners' equity at the end of the coming year is thus $134,000. Assume that R&J's bank has set a limit of 25 percent on the company's maximum long-term debt. Under the bank's limitations, R&J will be able to obtain $33,500 of long-term debt. Since the amount of additional outside cash required was $29,185, R&J can fund its additional cash from long-term debt. If the total needs could not have been obtained from long-term debt, the balance would have had to come from owners' investment in the company. The projected sources of net working capital are as follows:

Funds from operations	$215,000
Excess net working capital	8,240
Additional long-term debt	33,500
Total sources	$256,740

Cash Flow and Budgets

The Importance of Cash Flow

In the final analysis, it will probably be cash flow, or the lack of it, that determines whether your business continues to operate. Few businesses fail due to lack of business. Very few fail out of a lack of competent employees to get the job done. Many businesses, however, fail because they have too much business. Business is so good that new equipment has to be purchased. Employees are so overloaded that new workers must be hired. A wall has to be knocked out to add additional space, which is desperately needed to handle increased volume. After these expansions, the bookkeeper asks a telling question, "How are we going to make payroll Friday?" Unless payroll can be met or drastic measures are taken, the business will have to close. Drastic measures should be reserved for unplanned, catastrophic events, outside the control of having enough liquid assets, cash or its equivalent, to meet the day-to-day operating needs of the business.

Cash flow is having the funds on hand to make the payroll, to pay for purchases so that discounts can be taken, to pay quarterly tax payments, and to handle all the other items that require cash. A company with poor cash flow may still run a profit. It is just that the profit is residing in accounts receivable, inventory, equipment, or additional space.

Estimating Cash from Operations

The financial report that shows financial management is the working capital cash flow statement. This statement covers the financing and investing of cash. The statement may be for the most recent period or it may cover a future period as a projection. You should become very familiar with this statement. It is often equivalent to the statement of changes in financial position and can be an adequate indicator of cash flow. Exhibit 12.4 shows a typical format for a working capital cash flow statement. This report is a good management tool, not only to review the sources of cash during the period covered, but to see how that cash was applied. It can also be used as a pro-forma statement for planning purposes.

Calculating Funds from Operations To understand cash flow, we must talk about basics for a minute. Sometimes we make something simple into something complex. By focusing on isolated parts of the problem, the problem becomes manageable. There is nothing in business quite as basic as the operating cycle, which generally works as follows: cash is used to acquire inventory, inventory is sold to customers on account, and cash is then collected on these accounts, completing the cycle. Let us examine these elements of the operating cycle one at a time.

Inventory is an important ingredient in virtually every business. What makes up the inventory varies from business to business: for the manufacturer, it is raw materials; for the retailer, finished goods; and for the service business, the firm's investment in time to serve the customer. They are all inventories. In

Exhibit 12.4
FORMAT FOR WORKING CAPITAL FUNDS FLOW STATEMENT

SOURCES		APPLICATIONS	
Net increase	$_____	Purchase long-lived assets	$_____
Plus depreciation	_____	Retire long-term debt	_____
Less gain on sale of long-lived assets	_____	Distribute to owner	_____
Funds from operations	_____	Increase balance net working	
Sale of long-lived assets	_____	capital	_____
New long-term debt	_____	TOTAL APPLICATIONS	$_____
New owner investment	_____		
TOTAL SOURCES	$_____		

order to generate revenues, inventories must turn over. The more often the inventories turn, the more potential revenues are generated during the period being measured. The goal is for a quick turnover.

You must identify the industry norm in inventory turnover for your business. Once you know that, you must set about to improve your business to better the average. An inventory turn is the time required for the item of inventory to be converted into a receivable and then into cash. From the time the investment is made to acquire the item of inventory until it is converted into cash, your cash is tied up, reducing the amount available to you. The more you invest in inventory or the slower your inventory turns, the more cash you will require to have on hand to cover operating expenses. You must determine what your inventory mix will be: what level of inventory you will have, and how often the inventory must turn. Generally, the tendency is to have too much inventory.

Accounts receivable is significant to cash flow as well. Receivables that are high soak up your cash by requiring you to use reserve cash to pay day-to-day operating expenses. The faster the accounts receivable turn over, the more cash is available to operate the business. So we can say that management of accounts receivable is another key ingredient of cash flow.

To manage receivables you must again identify the industry norm (you should especially be certain to check the credit practices of your competition). Then decide on your policy for credit sales. You must have a written, clearly articulated policy on credit sales, and this must be communicated to your customers at the beginning—before the sale. Your credit policy will affect your business. With limited capital, a tighter rein on accounts receivable—even though it will restrict business—may be a more appealing alternative to having too much business, high receivables, and no cash. Given time and good management, your capital will grow to accommodate the growth that is sure to come.

There is truth to the old adage, "What gets measured, gets done." Many small business owners do not measure their inventory and accounts receivables turns. Suppose that your operating cycle averages three months. If your sales average $200,000 per month and your accounts receivable are averaging $450,000, the reduction of this turn time by one half a month will result in an increase in cash flow of $75,000. This reduction does not mean that you will *earn* more, but it does mean that your cash flow will increase. This fact, simple as it is, must be understood if cash flow is to be adequately managed.

Making Adjustments for Assets   Cash is constantly being used to start operating cycles on new sales of inventory. At any given moment, many different cycles are underway in different stages of completion. If these separate and overlapping cycles were of the same duration and if they started on a regular basis, then cash from operations would be the same as funds from operations.

Overlapping cycles are not usually the same in either length or frequency, however. To obtain exact cash flows for a given period, funds from operation must be adjusted for changes in the balances of net working capital other than cash.

If you can see these adjustments, you can better understand cash flow increases and decreases. If you can understand the logic of these adjustments, it will make it easier for you to plan for your cash needs. Let us go through several examples to see how this concept evolves. In these examples, we will assume that funds from operations from the current year, 19X2, equal the increase in net working capital from the prior year. All funds from operations result in an increase in net working capital.

In the first example, we will assume, for simplicity's sake, that there were no current assets other than cash and no current liabilities. (Remember that we are only examining current assets and liabilities because comparing these items determines net working capital.) Of all 19X2 funds from operations, $100 is cash:

	19X2	19X1
Cash	$200	$100
Total current assets	$200	$100
Current liabilities	(0)	(0)
Net working capital	$200	$100

Now assume one additional current asset besides cash, inventory, valued at $50:

	19X2	19X1
Cash	$150	$ 50
Inventory	50	50
Total current assets	$200	$100
Current liabilities	(0)	(0)
Net working capital	$200	$100

The portion of cost of goods sold representing inventory used was matched by inventory purchased. Total dollars invested in inventory did not change from 19X1 to 19X2. Remember, we are looking for the changes from one period to the next. Therefore, we know the cost of goods sold was equivalent to cash purchases for the year. In this example, the $100 of funds from operations would still equal $100 of cash generated in operations.

Now let us vary the inventory from one period to the next:

	19X2	19X1
Cash	$165	$ 50
Inventory	35	50
Total current assets	$200	$100
Current liabilities	(0)	(0)
Net working capital	$200	$100

In this example, $100 of funds from operations did not equal cash from operations. Inventory for the year decreased by $15. That means that cost of goods sold included items purchased and replaced plus a $15 reduction in inventory, which was not matched by cash outflow. Thus, the $100 of funds from operations included $15 that did not represent a cash outflow. Cash generated by operations would thus be $15 greater than the $100 of funds from operations, or $115.

In determining cash generated in operations, then, you must add any decrease in the balance of noncash current assets. A decrease in accounts receivable would represent extra cash collected over and above all credit sales for the period. Since this is a decrease in noncash current assets, you would add that decrease to funds from operations to obtain cash from operations.

Now we need to consider an increase in inventory as a noncash current asset:

	19X2	19X1
Cash	$135	$ 50
Inventory	65	50
Total current assets	$200	$100
Current liabilities	(0)	(0)
Net working capital	$200	$100

In this example, inventory increased by $15, which means that $15 more cash flowed out from purchases than was represented by cost of goods sold. Net cash generated in operations was $85. Purchases of additional inventory are not part of the current year's operations. The amount of cash spent to purchase inventory was $15 more than cost of goods sold. The cost of goods sold was the inventory used. In determining cash generated in operations, then, you must deduct any increase in the noncash current assets. Thus any increase in accounts receivable represents revenue not yet received as cash.

Making Adjustments for Liabilities   The calculation of funds from operations must also take into account current liabilities. Let us assume that current liabilities from year one to year two have increased by $65:

	19X2	19X1
Cash	$265	$100
Total current assets	$265	$100
Current liabilities	(65)	(0)
Net working capital	$200	$100

When current liabilities increase from one period to the other, the increase is an operating expense that has not yet been paid. Since it has not been paid, there was no cash outflow. Generally, increases in current liabilities are added to funds from operations in order to determine cash generated from operations.

However, if there is a decrease in current liabilities from one period to the other, the amount of the decrease is deducted from cash from operations. The reason is obvious: a decrease in current liabilities means that there has been a cash outflow. If current assets remained the same and if current liabilities decreased from one period to the next by $65 and funds from operations were $100, cash from operations would be $35 ($100 munus $65).

Converting Funds from Operations to Cash from Operations   The formula to convert net working capital funds from operations to cash from operations is as follows:

1. Calculate funds from operations
2. Adjust for changes in noncash current assets related to operations by adding any decrease in noncash current assets or subtracting any increase in noncash current assets
3. Adjust for changes in current liabilities related to operations by adding any increase in current liabilities

The result is the cash generated or lost in operations. For example, assume that your business generated $75,000 cash from operations and that funds from operations were $100,000. Current liabilities increased by $15,000 and current assets increased by $40,000. You can then determine the cash generated from operations as follows:

Funds from operations	$100,000
Increase in current liabilities	15,000
	$115,000
Increase in current assets	(40,000)
Cash from operations	$75,000

Other Sources of Cash   You will recall from earlier in this chapter that there are three sources of working capital: funds from operations, the sale of long-lived assets, or the drawing down of cash on hand. Outside sources of cash are long-term debt or additional owner investment of cash.

There are other sources as well, which do not involve a flow of working capital or cash. Examples include incurring long-term debt in order to purchase a long-lived asset, the exchange of one long-lived asset for another, additional owner investment combined with the purchase of a long-lived asset, and a refunding loan in which old long-term debt is exchanged for new long-term debt with the same balance owned. Where these methods are used in combination, the noncash items have to be eliminated in order to identify the amounts that involve cash flows. Since these items occur in pairs, they offset each other and the result does not affect cash flow.

Preparing a Cash Flow Statement

We now have the knowledge necessary to prepare a cash flow statement. A summary of the possible sources and uses of cash is set forth as Exhibit 12.5.

Exhibit 12.5

CHECKLIST OF POSSIBLE SOURCES AND APPLICATION OF FUNDS

SOURCES	*APPLICATIONS*
Funds from operations	Funds lost in operations
Sale of long-lived assets	Purchase of long-lived assets
Additional long-term debt	Extinguishment of long-term debt
Additional owner investment	Distribution to owner
Reduction of net working capital balance	Increase of net working capital balance

You should use this as a checklist when you prepare your own cash flow statement to be sure that you do not omit a possible source or use of cash.

Generally, you will know where you want to use your cash in your business. The problem is where you are going to get the cash to make those planned expenditures. The value of the cash flow statement is that it shows whether you will have the cash to make the desired expenditures. Another use is to show you the increase or decrease in the cash on hand for a period. If you see that cash is being used to fund losses from operations, you realize that unless the trend is halted you will soon be in a cash flow crunch and possibly be out of business.

You should always prepare these reports on a monthly, quarterly, and annual basis. The profit and loss statement is not the best tool to determine cash availability. Bear in mind that profit from a profit and loss statement may look good, but you may still be short of cash. You want to know about possible cash shortages ahead of time. If you know that you will be short of cash during your slowest two months of the year and can project how great the shortage will be, you can usually plan to overcome it. Your bank wants reassurance that you can manage your business well enough to know that you will be short of cash but only for two months. If you are not managing well enough to anticipate a cash shortage until it occurs, the bank will probably doubt that you are managing your business well enough to consider granting you a loan.

Cash Budgeting

In contrast to financial statements that report history, budgets present plans or expectations for the future. Budgeting in all its ramifications and applications is beyond the scope of this book; however, cash budgeting is so critical to the success of your business that some mention of it must be made here.

We have been discussing net liquid assets. Cash budgeting deals with these liquid assets. You should prepare monthly cash budgets for the next twelve months of operations. Doing so involves predicting cash receipts, cash disbursements, and short-term financing or owner contributions.

Estimating Cash Receipts   Businesses generally obtain cash from four different sources: cash sales, collections of accounts receivable, miscellaneous cash revenues, and borrowing. The first step in preparing a cash budget is to estimate the receipts from these four sources. Your budget sales for the coming period and your anticipated collection of accounts receivable constitute the data for planning cash receipts from the first two sources.

Assume that you have budgeted sales to be $100,000 per month for the coming year. If 10 percent of your sales are for cash and 90 percent are sold on account, then you must determine how your credit customers pay you on average. Let us assume that 45 percent of the credit sales pay you within the first month of sale; 30 percent pay you in the second month after the sale; 10 percent pay you in the third month after the sale; 4 percent pay you in the fourth month after the sale; and 1 percent never pay you. In the fourth month of the year and each month of the year thereafter, then, your budgeted cash should be $99,000. Budgeted cash for the first three months of the coming year will be determined by the level of sales for the last three months of the previous year.

Budgeted cash receipts from credit customers is then combined with cash generated from other sources (interest and so forth) and any planned receipts (loans, sale of long-lived assets, or owner investments) to determine total cash receipts for each month. Sales are seldom the same each month; some months are traditionally better or worse than the others. You will have a better cash budget if you can project your sales for each month rather than using average sales.

Estimating Cash Disbursements   The second step is to project cash disbursements for each month. It is much better to use these disbursements based on new information, such as tax estimates, property taxes, insurance, and so forth. Based upon the sales budget, you then plan your expenses for purchases and other operating expenses, estimated for each month. You then convert this estimate into a projection of cash outflows, taking into account the timing of payroll periods, the credit terms of your suppliers, and so forth. Remember that some months have five pay periods rather than four, which must be taken into account. Operating cash outflow is then combined with any planned cash outlays for the purchase of assets and for debt payments to obtain total projected cash disbursements each month.

Budgeting Short-Term Debt   After you combine the beginning cash balance with expected cash receipts and outlays, a projected cash balance for each month is prepared. This balance will be either positive or negative. Where your projected cash balance is negative, you can plan for temporary short-term loans. A cash balance that becomes negative more than once a year is a good indication that the business needs additional long-term financing or more owner investment. It is good business to take discounts for prompt payment to your suppliers, so not paying a creditor promptly is generally not a wise option. It is also good to always have a required minimum cash balance on hand in order to meet unexpected demands.

Exhibit 12.6 is an example of a cash budget for R&J Poultry Company for the first quarter of the coming year.

Work with your reports on working capital, your cash flow statements, and your cash budgets on a continuing basis to prevent being surprised. Remem-

Exhibit 12.6
R & J POULTRY: CASH BUDGET, FIRST QUARTER 19X2

PRELIMINARY (without FIA[a])	JANUARY	FEBRUARY	MARCH
Cash balance—Beginning of month	$100,000	$ 11,500	$ 23,500
Budgeted cash inflows	375,000	455,000	450,000
Cash available during month	$475,000	$466,500	$473,500
Budgeted cash disbursements	493,500	423,000	423,000
Cash balance—End of month	($ 18,500)	$ 43,500	$ 50,500
FINAL (including FIA)			
Cash balance—Beginning of month	$100,000	$ 11,500	$ 23,500
Net cash change without FIA	(118,500)	32,000	27,000
Short-term borrowing	30,000	—	—
Repayment of short-term borrowing	—	(20,000)	(10,000)
Cash balance—End of month	$ 11,500	$ 23,500	$ 40,500

a. Financing and investing activities
b. Assumptions
    1. The only expected cash receipts during the quarter are from cash sales and accounts receivable collection.
    2. The cash balance as of January 1 was $100,000.
    3. Operating expenses requiring cash are projected to be $16,500 per month.
    4. Budgeted purchases and cash liabilities are usually paid one-half in the month incurred and the other half in the following month.
    5. The accounts receivable as of January 1 were $60,000, but will be increasing due to increased sales.
    6. Accounts payable as of January 1 totalled $273,000 due to some extraordinary expenses, but are budgeted to come back into line.
    7. Forty percent of sales are for cash, and the balance are credit sales, with one-half paying in an average of 10 days and the other half paying in an average of 30 days.
    8. Sales for the past year have averaged $300,000 per month, but are budgeted to rise during the current year to an average of $450,000 per month.
    9. Long-term debt repayment is budgeted to be $1,500 of principal per month.

ber, the business that fails is usually not the one that does not have enough business; it generally is the one that has too little cash. Planning for cash flow will alert you to problems ahead of time so that they can be solved before they become a crisis.

Summary

Your business's financial plan is a key to survival—it is the blueprint for your company's financial health. One feature of the financial plan is to calculate the working capital required. To identify this amount, you need various reports; two (the balance sheet and income statement) describe the business's history. Others (various pro-forma statements) project the future.

A company that needs additional net working capital can turn to internal or external sources. Internal sources include the sale of long-lived assets and net after-tax profits from operations. The external sources are additional equity or debt.

Rapid turnover of inventory is essential to the financial health of a business. The time from the acquisition of inventory to the receipt of cash for sales is time during which cash is not available; the shorter that time, the better.

To make a cash flow projection, you need three sets of figures: monthly cash disbursements, monthly cash receipts, and short-term debt. By regularly preparing cash flow projections, you can anticipate periods of cash shortfall and take steps to obtain needed funds.

Class Assignments

1. In analyzing cash flow, when and how does an expense item become a part of a cash flow?
2. What are the internal sources of net working capital?
3. Why is it preferable not to be forced to look to external sources of working capital?

YOUR BUSINESS AND THE TAX LAWS

Income tax laws are written to raise revenue for the government. The Internal Revenue Code is a compendium of the social and economic policies of this country. Amendments to the Code reflect the current thinking of Congress. Because the Code has been revised with frequency in recent years, it has been difficult to get an accurate reading of the tax law at any point in time. As a result, the businessperson operates in a state of confusion, which results in the deferral of decisions until the law is clearer. Unfortunately, prolonged deferral of such decisions as capital investments can have a depressing effect on production and the rate of employment.

Tax rules and regulations, Internal Revenue Service rulings and pronouncements, and court interpretations of these rules and regulations create a complex environment—one far too complex for the average businessperson to comprehend. This situation makes your selection of tax advisers, an accountant and tax attorney, even more important (see Chapter 8).

While a business owner need not be a tax expert, it is important to have a working knowledge of certain tax laws in order to more prudently manage the business. The subject of taxes and your business could well comprise an entire volume or two; therefore, the treatment of this subject in a single chapter is fraught with problems. First is the problem of what topics to cover. Second is the problem of language. Since tax law is extremely technical, a simplified presentation that is understandable to the layperson may not be sufficiently precise. This chapter, then, simply aims to acquaint you with the concepts, tax traps, and planning opportunities deemed to be the most important.

We have broken this chapter into three categories to correspond with three phases of any business: its beginning, its end, and the time in between. Traps for the unwary, as well as planning opportunities, present themselves at each of these phases of the business.

This chapter should be studied in conjunction with chapters 5, dealing with the valuation of an existing business; 8 concerning your advisers; 10, which discusses the choices of a form of business; and 12, which discusses developing your financial plan.

After reading this chapter, you will be able to

- Explain the tax implications of various arrangements used at the beginning of your business
- Describe the tax implications of operational arrangements for your business
- Outline the tax implications of arrangements for the termination of your business

Tax Laws and the Beginning of Your Business

Buying an Existing Business

Suppose that the business you are buying is presently being operated as a conventional corporation (one that is a separate taxpayer from the shareholders and is called a *C corporation*) and you plan to buy the stock of its present shareholders. Your decision to operate the business in the future as an S corporation or as a partnership may have adverse tax consequences. If you elect to conduct the business as a partnership, you need to liquidate the corporation, which may result in the payment of substantial taxes by the corporation and by you as its shareholder. The exact tax effects on the corporation and on you should be determined by your tax advisers before this decision is made.

As for the S corporation alternative, other factors are involved. A C corporation that has retained prior earnings (called accumulated earnings and profits) and later elects to be taxed as an S corporation is treated less favorably than is a corporation that has never been a C corporation. In addition, the Code contains provisions that could result in taxes being incurred by a corporation that owns appreciated property at the time its shareholders elect to have the corporation taxed as an S corporation. These provisions are beyond the scope of this chapter, but the point is that you must be aware of the potential problems. Ask your tax advisers about your options in converting the corporation to a partnership or an S corporation. These issues should be resolved before you acquire the stock in the C corporation.

It may occur to you to ask the seller to liquidate the corporation first and then sell you the assets to avoid these problems. Although this solution is workable for you, it is seldom acceptable to the seller. The seller choosing this alternative invariably faces double taxation—first at the corporate level and then as an individual when receiving the assets from the corporation. As a result, such a practice usually produces a higher price for the business as the seller tries to cover the tax and still net the desired price for the business. The differences that such an arrangement make to the seller and to the buyer create a tension that will make for some interesting negotiations. It may be worth more to you to buy assets rather than stock in a C corporation that has substantial retained earnings or appreciated assets.

If you buy assets, you can choose to operate the business as either a proprietorship, a partnership, or a corporation. If the assets can be depreciated (virtually everything but land), the cost of the property can be written off (taken as an expense and deducted from taxable income) over its useful life. The write-off period will be determined by the kind of property it is, following guidelines published by the Internal Revenue Service.

Deciding to Incorporate

The creation of a C corporation means that a new taxpayer has been created. There may be nontax reasons why a corporation is selected as the form of doing business (Chapter 10), but you must obtain answers to several questions before deciding how you want to organize and operate the corporation:

- What is the tax rate for income earned by the corporation?
- What is the tax rate for income earned by you as an individual taxpayer?
- Is there likely to be a double tax incurred in order for you to distribute to yourself the money and property earned and accumulated by the corporation?
- What decisions result in the lowest total combined tax being paid by the business and you?
- Are there enough business reasons to justify paying a higher total combined tax than is possible?

There are four ways for you as a shareholder to get money out of a corporation:

1. As a salary or bonus for work performed on behalf of the corporation
2. As a dividend payable to the corporation's shareholders
3. As a loan from the corporation
4. As a distribution in liquidation of your interest as a shareholder in the corporation

The first, second, and fourth methods all generate income that is taxable to you. The second and third choices are always taxable to the corporation. The fourth choice is also taxable to the corporation if the corporation sold its assets at a profit in order to raise the money for the distribution. If instead of distributing money to you in payment for your stock, the corporation distributed appreciated property to you, the corporation is still taxed on the gain on the appreciated property. Therefore, to determine the total taxes payable on these two choices, you would add your effective tax rate to the tax rate of the corporation on its taxable income. There is almost always a better way than paying dividends or liquidating the corporation.

Almost every newly formed corporation needs some of its earnings to remain in the business for operations and growth. When earnings are not distributed in the form of bonuses or salaries, the corporation incurs a tax on the income. What rate the corporation pays on that income is an important consideration. At present the maximum corporate rate is 34 percent, as compared to a maximum rate of 28 percent for a business conducted in an unincorporated form or as an S corporation.

All newly incorporated businesses cannot be carried on as either partnerships or S corporations. As discussed in Chapter 10, strict rules for eligibility must be met in order to elect treatment as an S corporation. Your business's eligibility for S corporation status should be thoroughly investigated before making the decision to incorporate. Also bear in mind (see Chapter 10) that the corporate form has certain nontax advantages over operating as a proprietorship or a partnership, particularly in the areas of estate planning, disposing of the business, and compensation of its owners.

Tax-Free Incorporation   If you buy the assets of a business, you are permitted to put them into your newly formed corporation without any tax consequences if you do so according to the procedures provided by the Internal Revenue Code and the regulations published by the Internal Revenue Service. If you transfer property to a corporation solely for shares of stock in the corporation or for long-term notes (called *securities* by the Code) and if you are in control of the corporation immediately after the transfer, the transfer has no tax consequences. Control for this purpose, means that you possess at least 80 percent of the total combined voting power of all classes of stock entitled to vote and at least 80 percent of the total number of shares of all other classes of stock in the corporation.

Some other requirements must be met for this incorporation to be tax-free. First, your corporation must record the value of the assets on its books in the same amount as you paid for the assets. Even if you think that some of the assets are worth more than you paid, the corporation cannot enter their value on its books at an amount greater than you paid without causing tax consequences. Second, although the corporation can assume certain liabilities of yours associated with the business or with assets being transferred to the corporation, these liabilities cannot exceed the cost to you of the assets. For example, if you use a personal note or a loan to purchase assets for $150,000 and then transfer those assets to a corporation you form, you can only transfer $150,000 of that debt to the corporation—an amount that does not exceed the purchase price of the assets. Any liabilities transferred by you to the corporation that exceed the cost of the assets will be taxable to you to the extent of the excess.

Transfer of Assets to the Corporation   Having made the decision to incorporate and to transfer certain assets to the corporation in return for stock or long-term notes, you must decide what assets to transfer. This decision will be influenced in part by whether you decide to operate as a C or as an S corporation. Irrespective of which form you choose, however, it is generally wise not to transfer real property (land and buildings) into the corporation. If the real estate is to be used in the business, it is almost always subject to a double tax if the corporation should later sell it and you want to get the cash from the sale. As a general rule, lease the real estate to the corporation for an arm's-length amount of rental, thereby keeping the real estate out of the corporation. (An arm's-length rental is that rental that could be obtained if the property were rented to an unrelated third party; it is based on the amount of rental being obtained by others for comparable property.)

With a C corporation, you should be reluctant to transfer to it assets that are likely to appreciate in value—that is, assets likely to be worth more than their cost minus depreciation, using the straight line method. The reason has to do with potential future sale of the business. If the buyer does not want to operate the business as a C corporation, he or she will want to buy the assets of the business and not your shares of stock. The sale of the assets, however, triggers a tax to the corporation if the selling price of the assets is greater than their book value (the corporation's cost less accumulated depreciation). If the corporation sells the assets to a buyer for more than its book value, the corporation incurs a tax on the gain. In addition, the seller incurs tax if he or she takes the proceeds of the sale out of the corporation in liquidation of stock and if the proceeds of the sale are greater than the amount paid for stock.

You might wonder why anyone would want to operate as a C corporation. One reason is that S corporation status may not be possible. Another is that the tax benefits for accumulation of working capital are worth the risks. Corporate rates under present law are 15 percent on the first $50,000 of taxable income, 25 percent on the next $25,000, and 34 percent above $75,000. If this corporate rate is lower than your individual rate, you pay less tax and can accumulate working capital faster in a C corporation. With proper planning, you may be able to avoid the potential double tax on a later sale. The key is planning. Plan for the results you want, rather than being caught unaware in a tax trap.

In a corporation that has always been an S corporation, it is not necessarily disadvantageous from a tax viewpoint to place assets used in the business into the corporation in return for stock or securities. (Bear in mind, however, the earlier admonition against placing real estate used in the trade or business into a corporation regardless of its form.)

S Corporation Status   Assuming that your corporation can qualify as an S corporation, what considerations are involved in making this decision? Several provisions of the Tax Reform Act of 1986 change the considerations that previously favored conducting a business as a conventional corporation. One of the most significant changes—the inversion of the maximum tax rates for individual and corporation taxpayers—has already been discussed. Beginning in 1988, the highest individual tax rate was 28 percent. Beginning in 1989, the income level at which this top rate begins is adjusted for inflation. Further, as previously discussed, current rules make distributions by a C corporation of appreciated property in liquidation subject to a tax at the corporate level.

Not all businesses are profitable from the very beginning. In fact, it is rare for a new business to be profitable in its first year. In the event that your business is not profitable for the first year, you should plan how the losses are to be handled. If you create a new C corporation to operate your business, losses cannot be carried back to a prior year because there is no prior year. Losses can be carried forward, however, for as many as fifteen years; they are then applied against profits in subsequent years. This practice works fine if you have subsequent profitable years.

If you elect S corporation status, any losses incurred by the corporation are passed through the corporation to the shareholders in proportion to the percentage owned by each shareholder. In planning how to capitalize the corporation, it is important to plan to be able to allow any losses to pass through to the shareholders. As a shareholder in an S corporation, you can use the losses of the S corporation to reduce your taxable income only if you have either purchased stock or made loans to the corporation in an amount equal to your prorata share of the losses. If the corporation needs to borrow money, you, as a shareholder, should borrow the money and loan it to the corporation. If you have the corporation borrow the money and you guarantee the loan, you are not qualified to use the losses of the S corporation unless you actually pay the money to the bank under your guarantee. It is permissible for you as a shareholder to borrow money from the bank and loan it to your corporation even if the corporation pledges its assets to the bank to secure your loan. It is not unusual for S corporations owned by knowledgeable businesspersons to experience initial losses without those owners being able to use the losses to offset their personal income merely because they did not know how to structure the loans. In summary, if your S corporation needs any loans, it is best for you to obtain the funds and loan them to the corporation.

One situation in which it is advantageous to elect S corporation status or to operate as a partnership is if you have to borrow the money to invest in the business. Subsequent to the Tax Reform Act of 1986, there are severe restrictions on the deductibility of interest. The law now divides interest into four categories. Personal interest is not deductible, except for limited amounts through the 1990 tax year. Investment interest and portfolio interest are only deductible to the extent that you have matching investment or portfolio income. The fourth category, though, interest incurred in a trade or business, is deductible. Generally, interest incurred to invest in a corporation is investment interest, and therefore deductible only to the extent that you have investment income, which you may not have (a salary from a corporation is ordinary income, not investment income).

While regulations have not been written at the time of this writing, the legislative history of the Tax Reform Act of 1986 and recent IRS announcements indicate that interest on loans incurred to invest in a partnership or an S corporation may be fully deductible as interest incurred in a trade or business. The General Explanation of the Tax Reform Act of 1986 (P.L. 99–514), prepared by the staff of the Joint Committee on Taxation, in footnote 57 on page 265 gives the following explanation:

> As under prior law, interest on indebtedness incurred to purchase an interest in a trade or business partnership as a general partner (that is not treated as an interest in a passive activity) generally is not treated as investment interest for purposes of Section 163(d). . . . Similarly, it is intended that interest on indebtedness to acquire stock in an S corporation whose assets are used solely in conducting a trade or business, where the stock is not an interest in a passive activity because the taxpayer materially participates in the trade or business of the S corporation, is not investment interest, but rather is treated as interest incurred or continued in connection with a trade or business.

Internal Revenue Announcement 87–4, 1987–3 I.R.B. 17, also confirmed this position on the subject. Note that for such interest to qualify as deductible you must materially participate in the business and the assets of the S corporation must be used solely in the conduct of a trade or business. Interest on a loan made to invest in a C corporation, however, is treated as investment interest and therefore is deductible only to the extent that you have investment income. If this situation holds, if you have to borrow the money to buy or begin the business, your ability to deduct the interest on the borrowed money may be reason enough to operate it either as a proprietorship, partnership, or S corporation.

Startup Losses of a New Business

Almost all new businesses operate at a loss for some period of time. This period varies, but it can be as short as a few months or as long as a few years. You need a cash-flow analysis and pro-forma profit projections so that you can predict with some degree of accuracy the time at which your business becomes profitable. After the projected period of losses is identified it is important to identify the form of business that takes the best advantage of the startup losses.

Startup Losses and the C Corporation   If you create a new C corporation, any losses incurred cannot be carried back to a prior year because there is no prior tax year. To carry back a loss means to file an amended tax return for profitable tax year not more than three years earlier. In the amended return the loss offsets an equal amount of taxable income, thereby generating a tax refund. Although losses can be carried back for only three years, they can be carried forward for as many as fifteen years and be used to offset profits in subsequent years.

The C corporation, however, is not a pass-through entity, and the shareholders in such a C corporation do not get any current tax benefit by being able to offset their share of the losses of the corporation against other taxable income. The C corporation itself cannot derive any tax benefit from the losses unless and until it has some profitable years. Then the losses can be applied against the profits to reduce tax.

Startup Losses and the S Corporation   If you elect S corporation status, any losses incurred by the corporation are passed through the corporation to the shareholders. The pass-through to the shareholders is in proportion to the percentage ownership of each shareholder; if you own 75 percent of the stock in the corporation, you will be charged with 75 percent of the taxable income or have 75 percent of the taxable loss. Although there are a few limitations on the ability of S corporation shareholders to use their share of the corporation's losses to offset other income, the S corporation does offer its shareholders the potential to obtain a current tax reduction from losses that the corporation incurs.

Startup Losses and Section 1244 Stock   When the corporation is organized, ask the attorney who is organizing the corporation to be sure to issue the stock in such a manner as to qualify as Section 1244 stock. While several restrictions limit the availability of Section 1244 status, they relate primarily to the amount and type of property received by the corporation for stock as a contribution to capital and as paid-in surplus and to the makeup of the corporation's income. *Section 1244 stock* means stock issued in conformity with Section 1244 of the Internal Revenue Code. If a loss is incurred on such stock, the loss is treated as an ordinary loss by the shareholder and can offset $50,000 of ordinary income ($100,000 in the case of married individuals filing joint returns).

Section 1244 is only available to individuals. If the stock is not qualified under Section 1244, any loss incurred on the stock is merely a capital loss. This means that the loss can only be offset against capital gain. If you have no capital gain, only $3,000 of the loss can be used per year. At such a rate, it might take years to get the full benefit of a loss in stock. If the corporation qualifies, the stock should always be qualified under Section 1244, but it is even more important in a C corporation since that may be the only way that a loss on the disposition or worthlessness of the stock can qualify as an ordinary loss.

Startup Losses and Tax Basis in Your Stock   We have seen how the S corporation may allow you to reduce your tax liability by offsetting losses incurred in a startup of your business against taxable income. However, this result must be planned for. As a shareholder in an S corporation you can use losses of the corporation to reduce your taxable income only to the extent that you have basis in your stock. As explained elsewhere in this chapter, net income increases each shareholder's basis, but net losses decrease that basis. Basis begins as the amount you pay for your stock in the corporation and the amount of any loans you make to the corporation. If the corporation needs to borrow money, consider borrowing the money and loaning it to the corporation (particularly where you have to guarantee the loan to the bank). Doing so increases your basis, enhancing your ability to have startup losses of the corporation pass through to you. If the corporation borrows the money and you guarantee the loan, this will not qualify you to use the losses of the S corporation unless and until you actually pay the money to the bank under your guarantee. In summary, if your S corporation needs to borrow money, consider borrowing the money yourself and loaning it to your corporation.

Startup Losses That Are Not Temporary   In spite of the best-laid plans and in the face of countless pro-forma projections showing substantial profits, many small businesses never turn the corner. What were viewed initially as temporary startup losses turn out to be permanent losses. You need to understand that if the business does not make it, there is a financial difference to you in the results under a C corporation and an S corporation.

The S corporation has an initial advantage in that you are able to use the losses sooner than you can in a C corporation. In an S corporation, losses pass through immediately to lower your other taxable income. Of course, the losses only pass through the corporation in proportion to the basis in your interest in the corporation. Since your basis is reduced by the losses that are passed through to you from the corporation, you must contribute or lend sufficient capital to the corporation to keep your basis at least equal to the amount of losses being thrown off by the corporation. Once the aggregate losses exceed your basis, you cannot use any further losses incurred by the corporation. The only way you can use the losses is to buy more stock or lend the corporation more money. At some point, you may be better off not putting any more money into the corporation, even though you may have some losses you will not be able to use because of insufficient basis. Since a tax bracket of 28 percent will only yield 28 cents per dollar of loss, you can see that losses are not all that great a tax benefit.

Where the business is a high-risk business, you may be better advised to use the C corporation form. Even though you cannot use the losses as quickly as under an S corporation, if you have organized your corporation using Section 1244 stock, you can claim a loss upon the eventual worthlessness of your investment. You may be less tempted to continue to feed new dollars into a losing C corporation than a faltering S corporation. If the risk of failure is low, however, the pass-through of startup losses by an S corporation is still advantageous.

Substantial Startup Losses and New Investors   You need to plan for the possibility that new investors may be needed if the losses are greater than you forecast or the term of unprofitability lasts longer than you anticipated. You may be able to find sufficient investors among your friends, who will invest as individuals. In the typical situation, however, either the nature or the number of investors will destroy the ability to remain qualified as an S corporation. For example, your new investors may insist that their corporations or their grandchildren's trust be the investor. Corporations and most trusts cannot be shareholders in an S corporation. Some new investors may insist upon preferred stock. An S corporation can have only one class of stock. Perhaps you will need more than thirty-five shareholders, exceeding the limit allowed for S corporations.

If an S corporation loses its status as an S corporation, it cannot thereafter elect S corporation status again for a period of five years. Therefore, try to anticipate the need for new investors; it may be preferable for you to begin as a C corporation in order to accommodate such a need. After the corporation becomes profitable and you have liquidated some of these new investors, you will likely prefer S corporation status so that you can avoid the double taxation of the traditional plan.

Startup Losses As Passive Losses   In the complicated tax world that resulted from the Tax Reform Act of 1986, you have to ask what kind of income or losses will be generated. If the income or losses can be classified as passive, then planning has to be done to take this into account. Rental activities are one example of income that the Code treats as passive.

The passive loss rules generally provide that taxpayers can deduct losses from passive activities only against income from passive activities. Passive losses that are disallowed because you have no passive income can be carried forward and used against passive income in the future. If not used in this manner, they may be deductible when you sell your interest in the business. Neither of these arrangements, however, is usually satisfactory.

The classification of passive losses affects the decision to choose S corporation status. Passive losses generated by such a corporation pass through to you as passive losses. If you do not have any other passive income, you cannot deduct these losses.

A personal services corporation is a corporation whose principal business is the performance of personal services, and in which these personal services are substantially performed by the shareholders. A professional medical corporation or dental corporation is an example of a personal services corporation (PSC). A closely held C corporation that is not a PSC is treated differently under the passive activity rules than an S corporation. A corporation qualifies as a closely-held C corporation if at any time during the last half of its tax year more than 50 percent in value of its outstanding stock is owned, directly or indirectly, by or for five or fewer individuals. A closely held C corporation is not restricted to deducting passive activity losses against passive activity income.

Therefore, if your business will be classified as a passive activity, do not elect S corporation status, especially during the startup phase, unless you have enough other passive income to offset your share of the corporation's passive losses. Instead, begin as a C corporation so that the losses can be carried forward and offset against profitable years.

Operation of the Corporation

After the Tax Reform Act of 1986, a C corporation is penalized if it either distributes all its assets to its shareholders in complete liquidation or sells its assets to a third party and then distributes the cash to its shareholders in complete liquidation. In either situation, a double tax applies. One tax is imposed on the corporation when the assets are distributed to the shareholders or when they are sold to a third party. A second tax is imposed on the owners of the corporation when they receive either the assets or the proceeds from the sale.

This double tax is not the case for S corporations. An S corporation that sells its assets and distributes the proceeds of the sale in complete liquidation does not generally incur a corporate tax.

The Built-in Gains Tax

To keep corporations from electing to be taxed as S corporations simply to escape the double tax on the sale of its assets, Congress enacted the built-in gains tax. This tax applies to assets held by a C corporation at the time it elects S status. The tax is imposed on the appreciation of the assets that occurred prior to the S election if the assets are disposed of within ten years of that election. The years are counted beginning on the first day of the first tax year for which the company was an S corporation. In other words, if you buy the stock of a corporation that was operated as a C corporation and then elect to be taxed as an S corporation, any sale of the corporation's assets within ten years will have to be looked at carefully to determine if it produces a corporate tax. One way to avoid this potential liability is to purchase assets rather than stock.

If you buy the stock of a C corporation and then elect S corporation status, you must keep records of the assets owned at the time of your purchase; these records must show the amount of the assets' pre–S election appreciation. You will have the burden of proof; if your proof is not good enough, the IRS can determine for itself the amount of the pre–S election appreciation. This ability of the IRS to look back can cost you some unnecessary tax dollars unless you protect yourself. One of the best ways to protect yourself is to have the assets appraised by a reputable professional appraiser to determine their fair market value. This appraisal should take place at the time of the S election.

To illustrate this situation, assume that you buy a business that has always been operated as a C corporation. The corporation has some real estate that it bought originally for $15,000 but is worth $45,000 at the time you buy the corporation. Suppose further that you elect S corporation treatment upon buying the business and decide five years later to sell the real estate for $100,000. What are the tax consequences? If you had the property appraised at the time you purchased the stock in the company and can show that it was only worth $45,000 at that time, you will be able to limit your liability to the tax on $30,000 ($45,000 minus $15,000). If you cannot show the property's value at the time of the S election, the IRS could take the position that it was worth more at that time. If the IRS placed that value at $75,000, for instance, the corporation would have to pay tax on $60,000 ($75,000 minus $15,000).

The tax on built-in gains only applies to a corporation that was formerly a C corporation, not one that was always an S corporation. The way to avoid the problem is not to buy stock in a C corporation that has appreciated assets. If that cannot be avoided, you can do one of three things. First, mentioned above, is to get a written professional appraisal at the time you make the S election. Second is to see if you can structure an installment sale of the appreciated asset so that the principal payment is not made until the ten year period has expired. The third possibility is to exchange the real estate for other real estate so that it will qualify as a like-kind exchange. A like-kind exchange will also avoid any tax on the exchange. In a like-kind exchange, you can add the total time that you held the original property from the date of the S election to the time you held the exchanged property. If the total is at least ten years, you do not have the problem of the built-in gains tax.

Tax on Passive Income

If your business has income from rents, royalties, dividends, interest, annuities, or gains from the sale or exchange of stock or securities, it has passive investment income. (Interest earned on notes from the sale of inventory does not count as interest for purposes of passive investment income.) If your business earns some of its income from these sources, the form of your business becomes very important.

Corporate tax is imposed at the highest corporate rate on excess net passive income of S corporations that have earnings and profits from years when they were C corporations. Net passive income is passive investment income reduced by all deductions allowed for expenses incurred in the production of that income. Excess net passive income is equal to net passive investment income multiplied by a fraction, the numerator of which is the amount by which passive investment income exceeds 25 percent of all gross receipts of the corporation and the denominator of which is passive investment income for the taxable year.

Note that the tax on passive income only occurs if the business is an S corporation that was formally a C corporation which had retained earnings. If you buy stock in a corporation that has passive investment income, investigate to determine whether or not you want to operate the corporation as a C corporation and whether or not the corporation has earnings and profits. (Retained earnings are not exactly the same as earnings and profits, but they are virtually the same.) If you find yourself in this situation, attempt first to buy the assets rather than the stock of the corporation. If your S corporation has profits retained from years that it was a C corporation and passive investment income is in excess of 25 percent of its gross receipts for three consecutive tax years, the S election is automatically terminated. This loss of status may be important if some of the owners do not work in the business (thus earning no salary), but expect to get a return on their investment. If S status is lost, you must declare dividends, which means double taxation.

The passive income tax and the potential for termination of the S election are two reasons you should carefully monitor the kind and amount of the corporation's income. If you may have a problem, plan to reduce the corporation's exposure. One solution to losing your S corporation status is to distribute all of the earnings and profits from the C corporation years as a taxable dividend to its shareholders. In some situations, it is advantageous to treat distributions as being made first out of accumulated earnings and profits, including earnings and profits from years that the corporation was a C corporation. In order for this election to be made, however, all shareholders must consent.

Tax Effects of Distributions to Shareholders

In the S corporation, the corporation's income deductions, losses, and credits pass through to the shareholders in proportion to their stock ownership. The shareholders are the ones who are affected, from a tax standpoint, by the corporation's income or loss. The corporation is required to file a tax return, but it is only an information return since the corporation is not a taxpayer. The basis in each shareholder's stock is increased by the amount of the shareholder's share of income and decreased by the amount of the shareholder's loss. Initially the basis is the amount each shareholder pays for stock.

To illustrate this result, assume that shareholder X pays $25,000 for one-third of the stock of Profit, Inc., an S corporation. In the first year of operation, Profit has a net loss of $30,000. X's share of the loss is $10,000; her basis in the stock, which was initially $25,000, is now reduced by that amount to $15,000. X gets to take the $10,000 loss into account on her personal tax return. Assume that in year two, Profit shows a net profit of $60,000. X's proportionate share of this profit is $20,000, and her basis in stock is increased by that amount to $35,000. If Profit then distributes $10,000 to X, the distribution reduces X's basis by a like amount to $25,000. X must report her proportionate share of income on her income tax return whether or not she receives the income. The taxable event to X is the earning of the income by the S corporation, not the distribution of that income to the shareholders.

Accumulated Earnings and Profits

If an S corporation has accumulated earnings and profits, the tax rules get more complex. Please note, however, that an S corporation can only have accumulated earnings and profits in three situations: (1) prior history as a C corporation; (2) pre–1983 history as an S corporation; or (3) certain corporate reorganizations that cause transfers of earnings and profits accounts. Otherwise, all earnings pass through to the shareholders.

The tax law requires that S corporations with accumulated earnings and profits set up a special account called an *accumulated adjustments account* (usually called *AAA*). The AAA corresponds generally to the corporation's net income that arose in S corporation years (reduced by net losses from S corporation years) and was taxed to shareholders, less any income actually distributed to shareholders. The tax law requires that distributions to shareholders be made in a particular order. First the distribution has to be made out of the current year's income. When all the current year's income is distributed, further distributions come out of the most recent year's AAA. To the extent that a distribution does not exceed the AAA, it is not taxable to the shareholders. Such distributions are tax-free because the shareholders already paid tax on them when they were earned. Distributions in excess of the AAA are generally taxed as dividends to the extent of the corporation's accumulated earnings and profits. Once accumulated earnings and profits are exhausted, any further distributions are tax-free to the extent of stock basis and thereafter are taxed to the shareholders.

Shareholder's Cash Flow

The shareholders of an S corporation are individually liable for their share of corporate income. For this reason, be particularly careful that the shareholder's agreement provides for sufficient distributions from the corporation to pay your income tax. Otherwise, you may be in a difficult position—if the corporation fails to distribute sufficient cash for you to pay your tax liability, that liability must be taken from other income. Minority shareholders, who cannot require a distribution to be made, are particularly vulnerable. Since all shareholders must file a written consent with the IRS for the corporation to elect S corporation status, minority shareholders have the leverage necessary to require a written agreement that will provide for distributions from the corporation in amounts sufficient to pay the tax liability.

Tax Implications of Buy-Sell Agreements

After you have established your business and operated it profitably, the next most important consideration is to arrange for business continuity after your death, disability, or retirement. The business aspects of this subject are covered in some detail in Chapter 10. However, some significant tax considerations must be dealt with in how the buy-sell agreement is structured. Some tax traps can create unexpected and unhappy results for the unwary. This section of the chapter will deal with some of these more important issues, problems, and tax traps, together with suggestions on how to deal with them.

We assume that you are operating your business as a corporation. The tax considerations that arise in either a C corporation or an S corporation are sufficiently different that they need to be addressed separately. The buy-sell agreement is usually structured as either a stock redemption or a cross-purchase agreement between or among the shareholders.

Stock Redemption Agreement and Related Shareholders

For purposes of the tax laws, a shareholder is considered as also owning the stock owned by or for his or her spouse, children, grandchildren, or parents. For example, if a son owns 100 shares of the corporation and his father also owns 100 shares of the corporation, both are considered for tax purposes as owning 200 shares of the corporation. The same would be true for any of the other family members listed above.

A problem can occur if a shareholder redeems stock and that shareholder is related to the remaining shareholder or shareholders, irrespective of whether the redemption occurs due to a buyout of a retiring shareholder or a deceased shareholder. Assume that the father (whom we will call *Senior*) and his son (*Junior*) each own Corporation X, with Senior owning 75 percent of the stock and Junior 25 percent. Further assume that Senior reaches retirement age and wants to have the corporation redeem his stock so that he can use the money to enjoy his retirement. Since the corporation cannot afford to pay Senior cash for his stock, it gives Senior a note establishing payment of principal and interest in equal monthly amounts over ten years. Assume that the sale price is $250,000, with monthly payments of $3,033 per month for ten years. Senior is not ready to quit completely, however, and Junior wants him to consult with the company from time to time on important issues. Senior also wants himself and his wife to remain covered on X's group medical insurance policy. So Senior remains on the payroll, receiving $100 per month as a consulting fee. Since he paid $25,000 for his stock when the business was started, Senior expects to have each payment under the sales agreement treated as a return of 10 percent on his capital investment, with the rest as interest and capital gains. Therefore, Senior expects to report as income each year for the next ten years only that portion of the payment that represents interest and capital gain. What is the result?

Unfortunately, the IRS will not treat the sale as a sale at all, but will instead view the $250,000 note as a dividend. Also, the entire $250,000 will be treated as a dividend in the tax year in which Senior receives the corporation's promissory note. Senior will also have to pay tax on that part of the note representing his $25,000 capital investment. Why?

For the sale to be treated as a stock redemption instead of a dividend, Senior must not have any remaining interest in X except as a creditor. If Senior continues to have an interest in X, whether as an officer, director, employee, or consultant or in any other capacity except as a creditor, he will not be treated as having terminated his interest in X. He must also file an agreement with his next tax return stating that he will notify the IRS if he acquires any interest in X (except stock received by inheritance) for a period of ten years from the date that he received the note.

Instead of retiring, suppose that Senior dies. A stock redemption agreement requires the corporation to purchase Senior's shares for $250,000 and pay for them over ten years in monthly installments as described above. Such a transaction is treated as a sale if Senior's interest in X is completely terminated by the redemption. But recall that Senior is treated by the tax laws to own not only his shares, but also the shares of his children—in this case, Junior. So Senior's estate is still considered to own Junior's shares, in which case Senior's interest in X has not been completely terminated. As a result, the payment by the corporation to Senior's estate will be treated as a taxable dividend. The estate, like Senior, will not be able to recover Senior's investment in the stock because the entire amount of the payment will be treated as a dividend. If there was a stock redemption, the amount of Senior's investment would have been recovered tax-free.

This problem can be avoided in two ways: (1) change the structure of the buy-sell agreement from a stock redemption to a cross-purchase agreement between Senior and Junior or (2) have the stock left by will to Senior's wife or some other beneficiary and have the stock redeemed from that beneficiary. In the cross-purchase, the problem is avoided because Junior buys the stock and therefore the money does not come from the corporation. Where the stock is left to Senior's spouse or some other beneficiary, that individual may be related to Junior. Even so, that individual can sign the needed agreement with the IRS promising not to become involved in the corporation again for ten years except as a creditor without notifying the IRS. This waiver will keep the redemption from being treated as a dividend.

How to Fund a Buy-Sell Agreement

You can provide the money to fund the transfer of a shareholder's stock in the event of death in several ways. You can save the money in advance of the shareholder's death, borrow the necessary funds at the time of death, or use life insurance. A fourth way is to make an installment purchase of the deceased shareholder's stock, but this is just another form of borrowing. The only problem with this latter way is that the heirs are, in effect, lending the purchase price of the deceased shareholder's stock on terms and conditions that some banks might not find acceptable.

To compare the three usual methods to fund the buyout, we assume that you will need $400,000 in ten years to fund a buyout of a deceased shareholder. We also assume a 9 percent after-tax interest rate. To have such a fund in ten years, you would have to deposit $26,328 after tax each year and allow this fund to compound at 9 percent. Assuming an average marginal tax rate of 25 percent, you will need $35,104 before tax to yield $26,328 after tax. This means that your business would have to earn $351,040 over ten years (an average of

$35,104 per year) to provide the $400,000 needed. You would need to keep this fund separate from other business accounts so that it is available when you need it.

If you borrow the $400,000 and have to pay interest of 10 percent, you will make annual payments of $82,162.20 to pay the loan off in seven years. This means you will have to pay back $575,135.40 ($82,162.20 × 7), but you have to make the principal payments on an after-tax basis. Assuming a tax rate of 25 percent, your business would have to earn $533,333.33 in order to have $400,000 after tax. Therefore, your business would have to earn $708,468.73 in order to pay off the loan—or average earnings of $101,209.82 each year for seven years. Borrowing is obviously an expensive option.

Let us now analyze using life insurance to fund the $400,000 death benefit. Current life insurance policies make it possible to pay only eight or nine premiums, with the remaining premiums paid out of policy earnings. If we assume that the insured is a male aged fifty, we might expect to pay a premium of about $14,000 per year for eight years to fund a $400,000 policy. This would yield a total cost of $112,000, or $149,333.33 after tax. The insurance policy will provide $400,000 to purchase the stock of the deceased shareholder; under current tax law, that $400,000 will be free of income tax.

To summarize, saving the money requires pretax earnings of $351,040; borrowing the money from a bank needs earnings of $708,468.73; and buying an insurance policy calls for earnings of $149,333.33.

To further analyze some tax issues dealing with a buy-sell agreement, assume that A and B each own 50 percent of the corporation and that the agreed value of the business for buying out a deceased shareholder is $800,000, or $400,000 for each shareholder. Let us further assume that A and B each originally put $10,000 into the corporation when they started the business. A and B have a buy-sell arrangement that requires that the buyer pay the estate of the first to die $400,000 for interest in the corporation. The estate must sell to the buyer. In the following discussion, we will assume that B dies first and that the corporation has a life insurance policy on the life of both A and B in the amount of $400,000. The corporation has paid the premiums and is the beneficiary of the policies. (Though the premiums are paid by the corporation, under current tax laws they are not a deductible expense, but have to be paid on an after-tax basis.)

Upon B's death, the insurance company pays $400,000 to the corporation, which is received tax-free. The net worth of the corporation has been increased by $400,000. The corporation pays B's estate $400,000, which transfers the stock to the corporation. Under the tax laws, B's estate pays no income tax on the $400,000, even though B made an initial investment of only $10,000. The tax law treats B as having paid the fair market value (here $400,000) for the stock at the moment of B's death. If B is deemed to have paid $400,000 for the stock, which is then sold for $400,000, there is no taxable gain on the sale. Thus, no income tax is payable on the sale.

If the buy-sell arrangement were a cross-purchase arrangement, B would have owned and been the beneficiary of the policy on A's life, and vice versa. In this arrangement, A would receive $400,000 tax free when B died and then pay B's estate that money in exchange for B's stock. B's estate would still owe no taxes due to the fair market value argument. Since B owned the policy on A's life, B's estate would also own the cash value of A's policy. A can either buy that policy for its cash surrender value, or B's estate can cash it in for the cash surrender value. In this way, B's estate receives more than it would under the stock redemption arrangement.

Another favorable consequence of the cross-purchase arrangement is that A is treated under the tax laws as having paid $400,000 for B's stock. If A wanted another owner, he or she could sell some or all of B's stock to a new shareholder. If A did not sell the shares for more than the price paid to B's estate, A would not have to pay any income tax on the sale. A could then sell the shares for as much as $400,000 tax-free. If he or she sold the shares purchased from B's estate to a new shareholder for $300,000, A would have a taxable loss of $100,000 available to offset capital gains up to that amount.

Another more creative approach to these arrangements is to have an unfunded stock redemption agreement among A, B, and the corporation. In this arrangement, the corporation neither owns life insurance nor saves the money to fund any stock redemption. However, the corporation does have a contractual obligation to purchase A and B's shares for $400,000 in the event of death. The life insurance is cross-owned by A and B, just as in the typical cross-purchase arrangement. By combining the stock redemption arrangement with the cross-purchase of life insurance, you get some advantages over either of the concepts alone. The premiums are usually funded by a so-called split-dollar arrangement with the corporation. In such an arrangement, the corporation pays the premiums on the life insurance policy company for what is, basically, an interest-free loan. Upon the death of the insured, the corporation is repaid an amount equal to the premiums that it paid and the remainder of the death benefit is payable to the beneficiary.

Under this combination arrangement, when B dies, A receives the $400,000 of life insurance death proceeds, again free of income tax. The corporation, which has a contractual obligation to purchase the shares from B's estate, has several options, with varying tax benefits.

First, A can contribute $400,000 in capital to the corporation, which can use the money to purchase B's stock. B's estate receives the $400,000 tax-free. A can acquire the policy on his or her own life from B's estate. Now A owns 100 percent of the stock in the corporation at a basis of $410,000 ($400,000 paid to estate plus the $10,000 A originally paid).

However, suppose that the corporation has $100,000 in cash at the time of B's death, which the corporation does not need in the business. A could make a capital contribution of $300,000 to the corporation and the corporation could add its $100,000 to A's contribution to purchase B's stock. This leaves $100,000 in A's pocket. A has gotten $100,000 out of the corporation, tax-free, but in a legal manner.

A third option is for A to lend $400,000 to the corporation. The corporation could then repay this principal and the interest in annual installments. The principal payments would come from after-tax earnings, and the interest would be deductible by the corporation.

This combination treatment gives much more flexibility than either the traditional redemption or the cross-purchase arrangement. From a tax standpoint, you have several options; you can choose that alternative which best suits your circumstances at the time.

Summary

Tax laws are significant factors in determining what form a business should take and establishing various other business arrangements. These laws affect the business at its formation, in its operations, and at the end of its life.

The way you acquire an existing traditional, or C, corporation has tax implications if you decide later to reform the business as a partnership or as an S corporation. Similarly the decision to incorporate a new business has tax repercussions. The issues to consider are how to transfer assets to the corporation, whether to elect S corporation status, and how startup losses are treated.

During the operational lifetime of an S corporation, various tax issues need to be considered. These include the built-in gains tax, which applies to assets held by a C corporation before the election of S corporation status; the tax on passive income; the tax effects of distributions to shareholders; and the cash flow position of shareholders.

An important feature of any business must be the creation of a buy-sell agreement that will provide for the most efficient transfer of business assets with predictable tax consequences, in the event of the retirement, death, or other departure of an owner. The family status of the owner can affect the best way to structure such an agreement. The money to fund a purchase contract can come from creating a saving fund, borrowing the money at the time it is needed, or purchasing insurance.

Class Assignments

1. If a shareholder of the corporation is only an investor, does not work in the business so as to qualify for a salary or bonus, but wants to receive an income, what tax election would permit him to do it?

BUSINESS AGREEMENTS YOU WILL NEED

This chapter familiarizes you with the formal, written agreements that you should consider as you begin your business. Once you have decided what form your business will take, you need to negotiate various agreements dealing with the operation and continuation of the business in the event of the death or disability of one of the owners of the business. Written agreements are also needed if you own a minority interest in the business to protect your business interest.

Agreements are also useful in another situation. Sometimes, after the business is begun and your idea and dream have turned out to be even better than you imagined, disagreement arises among the owners. This disagreement can be caused by greed, differences in operating philosophy, and a myriad of other causes. Without a formal written agreement that deals with this contingency, the parties are left to their own devices to work out their problems. Invariably one party or the other gets short shrift, and hurt feelings and economic losses result. Do not enter a business with others without first working out agreements to take care of some of the more common problems that arise in operations. What these problems are and some ways to deal with them are the subjects of this chapter.

The agreements discussed in this chapter basically deal with two different aspects of the business. First are agreements that deal with the operation of the business. Second are agreements that deal with your ownership interest in the business and with your relationship with other owners. This second type of agreement deals with the business owner's disability, voluntary retirement or withdrawal from the business, involuntary expulsion from the business, and death.

You will find the material in Chapter 9 on negotiation to be very helpful in structuring these agreements. The material contained in Chapter 8 dealing with your professional advisers is also relevant to this chapter.

After reading this chapter, you will be able to

- Determine how to plan for operational control of a corporation and a partnership

- Explain how to create a buy-sell agreement that provides for continuance of the business in the event of an owner's death
- Describe the provisions that can protect the business in case of the owner's disability

Agreements Regarding Business Operations

The first class of agreements we consider addresses operations of the business. If your business is a corporation, these agreements are sometimes referred to as *pre-incorporation agreements*. If you operate as a partnership, these agreements are usually called *partnership agreements*. The general term that we use to characterize these agreements is *operating agreements*.

The operating agreements should be discussed, prepared, and signed before you actually invest in the business and it begins operations. Basically, operating agreements specify who is to do what in the business, how the business is to be governed, and how the owners are going to be compensated. Usually these are subjects that the owners discuss before investing in the business. More than mere discussion is needed, however. Owners must flesh out their understanding in considerable detail, reduce it to writing, and sign the written document.

The form of the operating agreement depends on the form that the business takes. Although the matters that should be covered are similar in a corporation and a partnership, the differences are sufficient to warrant a separate discussion.

The Corporation

Planning Control   There are three basic types of corporations as far as control of the corporation is concerned:

1. *One-shareholder corporation.* This type is the easiest to provide control for, but, as we will see below, some potential problems exist and should be addressed prior to incorporation.
2. *Veto-power corporation.* In this corporation, each shareholder has a veto power over corporate action and policy.
3. *Group-control corporation.* In this type, one shareholder or a group of shareholders controls corporate policy. The controlling shareholder or group does not necessarily own a majority of the voting stock.

There are, as you might expect, variations on these types of control. For example, in a corporation of any type certain kinds of corporate action might require unanimous consent, while other kinds might require only majority control. For our purposes, however, we treat each of the above types of control provisions as separate and distinct entities.Now let us discuss those provisions that you and your advisers may use to bring into existence each particular type.

One-Shareholder Corporation   In most states, the corporation is permitted to have only one director if there is only one shareholder. Even if more than one director is required, the shareholder can elect directors expected to be responsive to his or her wishes. In this situation, you can ensure that the sole shareholder maintains control by providing that the shareholder can remove a director at any time and for any reason.

If the sole shareholder is married and subsequently divorces, some of his or her stock in the corporation may be awarded to the spouse by the court. To the extent allowed by state law, consider an agreement between yourself and your spouse providing that, in the event that a division of property is required in connection with a divorce, stock in the corporation will be allocated to you and property of equal value allocated to the spouse. If you do not want to give up all rights to other property to maintain 100 percent control of the corporation, you should at least consider an agreement that provides that, in the event of a divorce, you will retain majority control of the corporation. Provisions can then be placed in the corporate charter to establish, to the extent allowed by law, that the vote of a majority of the corporation's stock is sufficient for any corporate action.

Veto-Power Corporation   Creating a veto-power corporation will be particularly important to you if you go into business with other shareholders and you do not have a majority of the issued and outstanding shares. Usually, veto-power provisions are attainable at the beginning of the undertaking, when everyone is in an agreeable mood and before business success raises the greed level of the parties. The policy behind the veto-power corporation is that each shareholder takes an active part in the business and that no important corporate policy is adopted or action taken without all shareholders' consent.

The easiest way to provide that all shareholders be allowed to participate directly in management of the corporation is to provide that the corporation be managed by the shareholders rather than the directors. Couple this provision with provisions that (1) define a quorum as the presence of all voting shares and (2) require the unanimous vote of all shareholders to approve any action. The result is that each shareholder has an effective veto power over corporate policy.

Having a corporation managed by the shareholders saves the trouble of having both shareholders and directors approve certain corporate action (especially where they are the same parties). In some states (for example, Delaware), it would not then be necessary to have directors. If your state does not permit management by shareholders, the same end can be achieved by making all shareholders elected directors, requiring the presence of all directors for a quorum, and requiring the unanimous vote of all directors to approve any action.

The underlying assumption of a veto-power corporation is that the shareholders have similar corporate goals and will be able to agree on policies and actions to serve these goals. If this assumption proves wrong, the corporate charter or bylaws should provide that any shareholder may require the dissolution of the corporation at will. Without this provision, a minority shareholder may feel pressure to go along with the wishes of the majority despite possessing the power to veto a corporate action that he or she objects to.

In a veto-power corporation, the corporate charter or bylaws should include a formula for determining the amount of dividends to be paid to shareholders. It is crucial for S corporations to have a formula for distributing part of the corporation's taxable income to its shareholders because shareholders are taxed on their pro-rata shares of the S corporation's taxable income even if no income is distributed to them. If no distributions were actually made, each shareholder would have to pay the tax on his or her share of the S corporation's taxable income from other sources. Some shareholders might not have sufficient income from other sources to make the tax payments.

The formula for distributing dividends or income might be based on a percentage of net income (after taxes in the case of a regular corporation and before taxes in the case of an S corporation). The shareholders could decide ahead of time on the amount of reserve the corporation would retain each year in order to grow and expand operations.

Group-Control Corporation   Generally, the controlling shareholders have full authority to run the everyday operations of the corporation, to determine new lines of business, to decide whether to open a new business, and to determine whether to borrow additional money. Nevertheless, the controlling shareholders should be prevented from taking some actions without the consent of other shareholders. For example, all shareholders should have preemptive rights. Preemptive rights allow all shareholders the right to subscribe for stock and have stock issued to them in sufficient amounts to maintain their percentage of ownership. This provision prevents dilution of a shareholder's interest.

One approach is to give the controlling shareholders, rather than the board of directors, the power to manage the corporation. In this way the controlling shareholders have whatever powers the board normally has but not the powers normally reserved to the shareholders—including control of amendments to the articles of incorporation, sale of the corporation's assets, mergers, and dissolutions.

The purpose behind a controlling shareholders corporation is to centralize in one shareholder or a group of shareholders the powers of management held by the board of directors of a public corporation, with such adjustments in the powers of the controlling shareholders and the powers reserved to all the shareholders as may be agreed on prior to incorporation.

With more than one controlling shareholder, disagreements will eventually arise. One alternative is to provide that decisions are to be made by majority vote. Another alternative is to provide for greater than majority approval—for example, a vote of four of the five controlling shareholders. The charter could also provide for unanimous consent, as in the veto-power corporation.

It would seem unwise in a controlling shareholders corporation to allow any single shareholder to dissolve the corporation. To do so unduly limits the power of the controlling shareholders to manage the business. The issue of dissolution should be addressed, however. One alternative is to allow the controlling shareholders to dissolve the corporation. Another approach allows the corporation to be dissolved by shareholders holding a certain percentage of the outstanding stock; the percentage should be substantial (say, one-third) but less than a majority. Another sound approach is to allow dissolution only upon the vote of a majority of the outstanding stock.

You may well invest practically all your money and assets in the business enterprise. You probably expect to devote your full time and attention to the business and earn your livelihood largely by working for it. If you are a minority owner, you need assurance that you will be retained in the business's employ. As a minority owner, you can protect yourself to some extent against being fired by insisting on a long-term employment contract.

Another issue for minority owners is compensation. When the corporation grows and becomes prosperous, the salaries of majority shareholders may be increased without a proportionate increase in your compensation. To protect yourself against such an event, consider insisting that your employment contract provide for a salary increase in proportion to that of other owners. This provision should be an agreement not only with the corporation but with the other shareholders. In the contract with the other owners, they agree to take all necessary action to ensure that the corporation honors its contractual responsibility to you.

The Partnership

Planning Control   Control of a partnership is fundamentally different from the control of a corporation. In a partnership, each partner has a vote, and any partner can cause the dissolution of a partnership under most state laws by simply withdrawing from the partnership.

If greater control is desired, the partnership agreement must deal with these issues. You can achieve most of the results discussed in relation to corporations with a carefully drafted partnership agreement.

A limited partnership has many characteristics of a corporation from the standpoint of control. The general partner is the controlling partner; the limited partners do not have any voice in day-to-day operations. Like shareholders, the limited partners have limited liability (although the general partner is exposed to personal liability for partnership obligations).

The partnership agreement for a general partnership should appoint a managing partner. That partner is charged with specific duties and responsibilities stipulated by the partnership agreement.

Under most state laws, any partner can obligate the other partners. If any limitations are to be placed on the power to obligate other partners, these limitations must be spelled out in the partnership agreement and in the bank resolution furnished to the partnership's bank. Such a provision may be seen as leaving unprotected the third party who holds the obligation. Some protection exists, however. An innocent third party is protected by dealing with one of the partners in good faith. The remedy of the partners who have been obligated to a third party by one of their partners should be for indemnification by the partner who created the obligation. This indemnification should be in writing and is usually found in the partnership agreement.

| **Agreements Re-garding Owner-ship Interest** | **Death of the Owner** |

Death of the Owner

In a Sole Proprietorship or Partnership   The death of a sole proprietor may result in the liquidation of the business. Unless the proprietor wills his or her interest in the business to a child or spouse, liquidation may be required. It is the legal duty of the executor or administrator of an estate to wind up the affairs of the decedent, to take possession of all the property and convert it to cash (with the exception of assets specifically bequeathed by will or property that the heirs agree to accept), to pay the expenses of administration and the obligations of the decedent, and to distribute the balance to the heirs or beneficiaries.

On the death of a partner, the partnership is usually dissolved as a matter of law in most states. The surviving former partners become liquidating trustees, whose duty it is to wind up the business. Any equity that remains after payment of the business's liabilities must be distributed to the former partners and the personal representative of the deceased partner. The surviving former partners are strictly accountable to the heirs of the deceased partner and bear the burden of proof that all steps of liquidation were taken in good faith.

The partnership agreement may provide that the partnership is not dissolved but continues with the surviving partners. In this case the agreement provides how the deceased partner's interest is acquired. In the absence of a business continuation agreement, the employees of a proprietorship or partnership may have to find other employment. Additionally, the assets of the business may have to be liquidated rather than being sold as a going business concern. Any attempt by the executor or administrator of the deceased proprietor or partner to continue the business in the absence of authorization in the will or of court approval may make him or her personally liable for any losses incurred by continuing the business.

In a Corporation   Upon the death of a majority shareholder, the shares owned by the deceased shareholder pass through the estate to his or her heirs or legatees, who thereafter control the business. Despite their control of the corporation, however, the recipients of the stock may lack business expertise and may be unable to make any personal contribution toward the continued success of the business.

Upon the death of a minority shareholder, the surviving shareholders will be able to continue management control of the corporation. However, this event introduces a potential source of friction. Because the deceased shareholder owned a minority interest, it is unlikely that the estate will be able to find a market for the purchase of the shares. As a result, if the shareholders have failed to provide for the purchase of the minority stock, they must accept the new shareholder. The new shareholder may be unable or unwilling to contribute to the business; his or her interests may even be contrary to those of the remaining shareholders. This conflict of interest may result in everyone being unhappy.

The Business Continuation Agreement

A business continuation agreement (often referred to as a *buy-sell agreement*) is an arrangement for the disposition of a business interest in the event of the owner's death. One valuable purpose of a business continuation agreement is the prevention of forced liquidation of the business or the loss of profits due to curtailment of the business. The business continuation agreement should also address the disposition of business interest in the event of the owner's disability, retirement, or withdrawal from the business. There should be a formal written agreement among the owners that satisfactorily addresses all of these events.

Business continuation agreements can take several forms:

- An agreement between the business itself and the individual owners (an entity purchase agreement)
- An agreement between or among the individual owners (a cross-purchase agreement)
- An agreement between the individual owners and a third party (a third-party buyout agreement)
- A combination of the three agreements above

The most common types are the entity purchase plan and the cross-purchase plan. The distinguishing feature of the entity purchase agreement is that the partnership or corporation itself agrees to purchase the interest held by the former partner or shareholder. In a cross-purchase plan, the individual owners agree between or among themselves to purchase the interest of a former shareholder.

The owners of any small business should have a purchase agreement in place from the very beginning of the business. This type of agreement is especially important in the following situations:

- When a guaranteed market needs to be created for the sale of the business interest in the event of an owner's death, disability, or retirement
- When it is necessary to establish the value of the business for federal and state death tax purposes
- When a shareholder or partner would be unwilling to continue in the business with the family of a deceased owner
- When the business involves undue financial risk for the family of a deceased owner and it is desirable to convert the business interest into cash
- When it is desirable to prevent part of the business from falling into the hands of outsiders

Requirements of the Purchase Agreement   A written agreement is drawn specifying the purchase price, terms of purchase, and the funding arrangements. The agreement obligates the withdrawing or disabled owner or the owner's estate to sell that owner's interest in the business either to the business itself or to the surviving or remaining owners. In some instances, the agreement combines the two types of obligations, giving individual owners an option to purchase the interest but specifying that the partnership or corporation must purchase the interest if they choose not to do so. The purchase agreement should also specify the events triggering the respective obligations. Generally, these events are the death, disability, retirement, or withdrawal of the owner.

A procedure must be established for the valuation of the interest held by the owner. (Refer to Chapter 5 for a discussion of various methods of valuing a business.) Usually, valuation should be according to book value, a formula value, or some other agreed-upon amount.

The next important provision is how the purchase of the owner's interest will be financed. The two basic methods of payment are a cash lump-sum payment or installment payments over some period of time. An installment plan usually includes an initial down payment and a provision that secures to the unpaid parties the purchase price. Because the tax implications of a buy-sell agreement are profound, these two alternatives and their relative costs and benefits are discussed in detail in Chapter 13.

Related Issues in Community Property States   Several problems can arise in connection with buy-sell agreements as a result of community property rights. If all or part of the business interest is subject to a buy-sell agreement, careful planning is necessary. First, the other owners want protection from the owner's spouse predeceasing the owner and leaving the owner's community property interest in the business to third parties. Second, they want protection from the agreement being attached by the owner's spouse if the spouse survives the owner and seeks to claim his or her community property interest in the business free of the agreement. If all or part of the owner's interest is quasi-community property, you must take care to protect against the surviving spouse's claim that he or she is entitled to a community property interest in the business regardless of the agreement. To prevent this claim, obtain written consent from the spouse to the buy-sell agreement when it is created. The ability of the surviving spouse to sell the entire community interest of the business or to redeem some or all of it within the scope of Section 303 of the Internal Revenue Code (thus avoiding dividend treatment), is often the most important estate-planning step taken by husband and wife business owners in community property states.

It is important to determine the nature of the business interest held by the owner, not only for purposes of determining whether consent is needed and wills must be reviewed, but also to evaluate the tax consequences. If all the business interest is community property, the community property interest of the owner's spouse is included in the spouse's estate if he or she predeceases the owner and is excluded from the owner's estate if the owner dies first. If all the business interest is the separate property of the owner, it is included in the owner's estate only (unless he or she passes the business interest to the spouse and then dies). If all the business is quasi-community property, the owner's spouse has no interest if he or she dies first, and the full value of the business interest is in the owner's estate for federal estate tax purposes.

Problems arise when attempting to determine whether the business interest held by a married person in a community property state is community property. A portion of the business interest can be separate property and a portion community property. Such is the case, for instance, for a person who owns a business prior to marriage.

Most states use some form of an apportionment rule to characterize the increase of value during marriage of closely held business interests that were originally held as a spouse's separate property. Under the apportionment rule, if one spouse invests separate property in a business and conducts that business during the marriage, the resulting increase in value of the business is apportioned or allocated between the community estate and the spouse's separate estate according to the amount attributable first to the spouse's personal efforts (inuring to the benefit of the community) and second to the capital improvement (inuring to the benefit of the spouse's separate estate).

The possibility of creating such a community property interest in a partnership or corporation originally held as the separate property of one spouse can be determined only by a court in the absence of a written business purchase agreement. Thus it is advisable for the spouses to agree in writing on the nature of their interests and the proportion of community and separate property.

There are other possible combinations of interests, such as community property plus quasi-community property, separate property plus quasi-community property, or all three types of property. In any event, the exact nature of business ownership and the respective proportions of each type should be identified and agreed on in writing. It may be advisable to incorporate the property agreement of the respective spouses of the business owners into the business purchase agreement.

Specific Provisions   The business continuation agreement should contain specific provisions regarding the death or disability of an owner. Let us explore the issues related to these provisions.

Death of an Owner.   In almost all cases, it is desirable for the estate of the deceased owner to have his or her interest in the business purchased in the event of death. Surviving owners normally prefer the purchase of the decedent's interest, rather than having to deal with a new and unknown co-owner.

This purchase should not be negotiated after death occurs but planned for early in the business life of the parties. The surviving spouse is never in a good bargaining position, particularly if the decedent held a minority interest in the business. Unplanned purchase also places the surviving owners in a difficult position; they are likely to lean over backwards in an attempt to be fair, but the surviving spouse is likely to feel that they are offering too little. It is a no win situation.

It is desirable for the sale of the owner's interest to be an absolute requirement rather than an option. An option is not satisfactory because it gives too much power and responsibility to the party to whom the option is given.

The price or a method for arriving at the price should be provided in the contract. A good way to deal with this is for the parties to value the business annually and supplement the purchase agreement with the updated valuation.

While this practice is good in theory, the owners of a closely held business will rarely take the time to get together to arrive at an updated figure. If the annual revaluation method is selected, be sure that the agreement has a backup method for determining value if the parties have failed to update the value within, say, two years.

If the purchase price is to be paid in installments, take care to ensure that the unpaid amount is well secured. The note should be signed by the entity or the surviving co-owners, and the payment should be guaranteed by the other owners. Consider having the business obligated to pledge its assets to further secure the unpaid purchase price, if the business is the type that has assets of sufficient value to ensure payment of the note.

If the co-owners are fairly young and insurable, purchasing a life insurance policy in an amount sufficient to either pay the purchase price or a good portion of it is advised. This relieves the pressure on the business and surviving coowners to make the payments, and the cost can be relatively inexpensive.

Disability of an Owner. Most owners realize the value of obligating the business or the surviving co-owners contractually to purchase the interest of a deceased owner. Unfortunately, they do not view disability with the same concern. Insurance company statistics indicate, however, that a person thirty years of age is more likely to become disabled than die before reaching the age of sixty-five.

A disability that lasts as long as six months can be extremely taxing on the surviving owners, and it goes without saying that the disabled party will have had his or her world turned upside down. As with the death of an owner, the time after the disability occurs is not a good time to negotiate the consequences to the respective parties. The interests of the disabled party are vastly different than those of the remaining co-owners. Do not underestimate the strain that can be placed on the business and the other owners. This is especially the case in a closely held business, in which all owners are active in the day-to-day operations.

Consider how long you are willing to have the business continue the salary of the disabled owner. Six months seems about as long as is practical. If disability benefits are to be funded in part with disability insurance, then six months seems to be a good rule of thumb. Designing the policy so that disability benefits do not begin until after six months of disability seems to give the best break on premium payments. Six months is also about as long as the average small business can sustain this expense without the services of a working owner.

Ask your insurance adviser about disability buyout insurance. Many insurance companies offer a product that funds a monthly buyout of a permanently disabled party. The cost is usually reasonable if the parties are in good health. Usually this policy is structured so that the insurance proceeds are paid to the business, which then makes monthly payments toward the purchase of the interest of the disabled co-owner. Such a plan usually requires continuous disability for at least six months before the buyout provisions are triggered.

Some business agreements require that full salary be paid for some period of time, with reductions then occurring for a specified period before the salary stops altogether and the buyout begins. An example is a contract requiring payment of full salary to the disabled owner for three months and half salary for three months. If the disability continues beyond six months, the buyout is automatically triggered.

In the event of disability, as with death, the value of the business interest should be provided for in the business continuation agreement. Related issues, such as terms of payment and collateral to secure the unpaid price, also apply to the disability buyout as they do to death of an owner.

Summary

Anyone who enters a business must take care to establish written agreements related to two issues. First, these agreements must specify who is to control the business. Second, they must provide for the continuance of the business in the event of the owners' death, disability, withdrawal, or retirement.

Operating agreements are required for corporations and partnerships, both of which usually have multiple owners. Control of the corporation with multiple owners can be divided two ways. Either each shareholder can be given veto power over corporate decisions or a single owner or group of owners can be given control of the corporation's daily operations. In the latter case, the other shareholders will want to retain control over certain major corporate decisions. A partnership also requires a specific agreement that stipulates which partner (or partners) will control operations of the business.

The other class of agreement needed before the opening of a business relates to ownership interest. Such agreements must provide for the handling of the owner's interest in the business in the event of death, disability, retirement, or withdrawal. The document that establishes these provisions is called the *buy-sell agreement.* It is crucial that such an agreement be created, agreed to, and signed before the business begins operations. Waiting until after catastrophe befalls one owner is waiting too long.

Special provisions are required in states with community property laws. Spouses should reach agreement between themselves as to the relative value of separate and community property. This agreement should become part of the buy-sell agreement of the business.

Bear in mind that the buy-sell agreement must also provide for retirement of the owner's interest in the event of disability. Usually such a provision allows for an initial period—often six months—during which the owner's interest is maintained; only if the disability is of longer duration will the owner's interest be purchased.

Class Assignments

1. What is one advantage of a cross-purchase type of buy-sell agreement over an entity purchase?

FORMAL BUSINESS PLAN

After completing your economic feasibility study, the next step is to develop a formal business plan. The well-formulated plan will carry you step-by-step from the idea stage of the business to the stage of opening the door. It is, quite simply, the planned procedure for starting a business and managing it successfully in its early, high-risk days.

After reading this chapter, you will be able to

- Describe the goals and importance of a business plan
- Prepare a business plan

The Goal of the Plan

The formal business plan may be thought of as a guide to action for assembling information and resources essential for starting a business. In broad outline, the plan involves

1. Stating your education and experience background for owning and managing this business
2. Defining the nature and size of your business
3. Determining whether to construct a new building, lease-purchase an existing structure, or rent an existing building with parking and other needed facilities (if you decide to rent, make sure that your rental lease contains an option for renewal)
4. Planning for the peripheral equipment that your business operation needs
5. Planning for your operating equipment requirements
6. Determining your initial supply needs
7. Planning for procuring the operating materials you need
8. Determining your personnel requirements and developing a plan for the procurement of personnel
9. Developing a financial plan

10. Preparing a capital budget
11. Preparing a first-year's operating budget
12. Developing your organization structure
13. Preparing a marketing plan

The Importance of a Business Plan

A properly prepared business plan will facilitate getting the business operational within a time frame as short as possible—it is a plan of action. Any delay in getting the business's door open adds to the cost of starting the business. You have your own and any investors' money tied up. An important axiom for you to remember is that money has cost, whether it is yours or someone else's. Therefore, you will want the business to be generating profit as soon as possible (see Exhibit 15.1).

Former students have returned to stress the importance of the business plan. Their words tell the story:

- "It kept me on track when I was starting my business."
- "It kept me on a time schedule that enabled me to open the doors sooner."
- "It aided me in better controlling the expenditure of funds."
- "Don't ever stop using the feasibility study and the business plan—they are too important. [They] save me a lot of time."

A well-prepared plan can impress others. In recent years, one of our students spent six months developing a business plan for a Middle Eastern resort. Imagine his elation when a potential investor told him that, if he was not able start his business, the investor would pay him $100,000 a year to travel the world and do economic feasibility studies and business plans for hotel and resort properties.

Assembling the Business Plan

You may be surprised to learn of the amount of time needed to develop a business plan. Remember that it takes patience and tenacity to accomplish this project. Use Exhibits 15.2, 15.3, 15.4, 15.5 and 15.6 as a guide for collecting the data and structuring your business plan. You will learn early in the undertaking that this project requires a broad array of information sources. Depending on the type of business you are planning, you need to contact suppliers, wholesalers, equipment manufacturers, utility companies, tax and license offices, and competitors. In addition, you may need the assistance of an attorney specializing in business law and an accountant conversant with small businesses.

Remember that a comprehensively formulated business plan, attractively presented, can produce desirable results. As you present the document to prospective investors or customers, it is in your interest that they are favorably impressed. You want positive responses that will commit them to supporting and doing business with you.

This consideration points out the importance of refining the economic feasibility study and the business plan. The time involved in preparing a polished package can be frustrating. However, the rewards make it worth the effort. It is gratifying, after presenting this package to your bank loan officer, to have him or her tell you, "This looks great, I have never seen anything so comprehensively done."

Summary

The importance of the business plan cannot be overemphasized. Between the text and the exhibits, you have guidelines for the development of a business plan. The benefits of having prepared a well-formulated plan are clear: such a plan can help you get started on the road to success.

Class Assignments

1. Research and prepare a comprehensive business plan for your business idea.

Exhibit 15.1
DEVELOPING YOUR TIMETABLE

This questionnaire/form is intended to assist you in developing a plan for establishing your business in an orderly, rational manner, i.e., "What to do," "When to do it," and "Where to do it." This should enable you to move from the inception of the idea to the point at which you begin operation.

1. Definition of the business that seems best for me

   _____

   _____

   _____

2. Dates for starting and completing the economic feasibility study for the business _____ to _____

3. Date for completing the legal organization of the business _____

4. Date for determining the financial requirements for the business _____

5. Date for completing the financial plan for the business _____

6. Date for completing the financial arrangement for the business _____

7. Date for completing the location requirements for the business _____

8. Date for acquiring the location

   a. Rent (lease) facilities _____

   b. Purchase land or land and building _____

   c. Contract for construction of building, driveways, parking, etc. _____

9. Date for completing plans for equipment requirements _____

10. Date for purchasing equipment _____

Exhibit 15.1
DEVELOPING YOUR TIMETABLE (*continued*)

11.   Date for completing plans for organization structure (chart) and personnel requirements   _____

12.   Date when location will be available for occupancy   _____

13.   Date for receiving equipment and beginning installation   _____

14.   Date for completion of equipment installation   _____

15.   Date for completion of plans for inventory requirements (material, parts, supplies, etc.)   _____

16.   Date for acquiring inventory   _____

17.   Date for decision on firm name   _____

18.   Date for hiring personnel   _____

19.   Date for personnel to begin work   _____

20.   Date for receiving and placing inventory   _____

21.   Date for completing plans for advertising campaign   _____

22.   Date for launching advertising programs   _____

23.   Date to begin necessary business licenses and permits   _____

24.   Date to begin business operation   _____

Exhibit 15.2
DECIDING WHAT SIZE BUSINESS YOU WANT

One of the more important aspects of the process of planning the future of your business is the determination of what size you wish your business to be. Recognizing that it is likely that your personal objectives and the objectives of your business will change as you gain experience in the operation of your business and as the economic environment for your business undergoes change, it is our purpose here to guide you through an analysis that should aid you in determining what will be an appropriate size for your business at the outset, and to appropriately plan for whatever growth seems essential for you to achieve your personal objectives. In planning for growth, you should add in an appropriate factor for inflation.

Personal Objectives

1.   My family size is now
     Wife/husband   _____   Boys   _____   Girls   _____

2.   My future family plans are
     Wife/husband   _____   Boys   _____   Girls   _____

3.   My housing plans are
     a.   Small   _____   Medium   _____   Large   _____
          House   _____
     b.   My principal house should have   Spacious grounds   _____   A swimming pool   _____   Tennis courts   _____   A two-car garage   _____
     c.   I want a second home (beach/mountain/lake)   Yes   _____   No   _____
     d.   Other personal amenities that are important to my life-style are   Boat   _____
          Country/city club membership   _____   Service club memberships (Kiwanis, Rotary,

Lions, Civitans, etc.) _____

Other _____

4. Please carefully review the above checklist and prepare a family budget. Based on this information, indicate your income requirements: On a monthly basis $_____   On a yearly basis $_____

Where Do I Start?

The purpose of the above was to put in perspective your life-style and the income that will be necessary to maintain that life-style. Unless you understand this and your objectives in life, you will not be able to determine what size business you should have at the outset and what your business growth plans should be.

5. Based on my education, my work experience, my skills, my areas of interest, my life objectives, my present objectives, and my economic needs present and future, my threshold for entering business should be (check the appropriate one)

A small unit _____   A medium-size unit _____   A large unit _____

A number of small units _____   A number of medium-size units _____

6. Since the type of business you enter will have some influence on the size your business will be, please consider the possible businesses that may be appropriate for you and indicate the one that best serves your interest and needs. _____

7. Among the choices you have made

a. Does there seem to be an optimum-sized unit?   Yes _____   No _____

b. Does the nature of this type of business seem to preclude its becoming a multi-unit business?
Yes _____   No _____

8. Indicate what sales volume may reasonably be expected by your business

a. 1st month $_____

b. 1st 3 months $_____

c. 1st 6 months $_____

d. 1st 9 months $_____

e. 1st 12 months $_____

f. 2d year $_____

g. 3d year $_____

h. 4th year $_____

i. 5th year $_____

9. Based on your sales projections, indicate a schedule of reasonable profit expectation

a. 1st month $_____

b. 2d month $_____

c. 3d month $_____

d. 1st 6 months $_____

e. 1st 9 months $_____

f. 1st 12 months $_____

g. 2d year $_____

h. 3d year $_____

i. 4th year $_____

j. 5th year $_____

Exhibit 15.2

DECIDING WHAT SIZE BUSINESS YOU WANT (*continued*)

10. At this junction, you will want to review the information above. There is always the temptation to be excessively optimistic when planning sales volume and when planning for profit. It is suggested that you recheck the data from which you derived your answers above.

11. Your next step should be to develop a capital budget for this proposed business. Unless you make an actual determination of the capital facilities that your business requires, there is no way to know the amount of capital involved or the physical size of the business.

   a. Land _____.____ acres; cost $_____

   b. Building _____ square feet; cost $_____

   c. Parking lot, paving, curbing, landscaping, lighting, etc.: cost $_____

   d. Production equipment: cost $_____

   e. Plant maintenance and servicing equipment: cost $_____

   f. Office equipment

Number of Units	Type	Unit Price	Total Cost
_____	Executive desk	$_____	$_____
_____	Executive chairs	$_____	$_____
_____	Couches	$_____	$_____
_____	Upholstered chairs	$_____	$_____
_____	Secretarial desk	$_____	$_____
_____	Secretarial chairs	$_____	$_____
_____	Work tables	$_____	$_____
_____	Bookcases	$_____	$_____
_____	Vaults/safes	$_____	$_____
_____	Filing cabinets	$_____	$_____
_____	Typewriters	$_____	$_____
_____	Copying machines	$_____	$_____
_____	Calculators	$_____	$_____
_____	Computer	$_____	$_____
_____	Other items:		
_____	_____	$_____	$_____
_____	_____	$_____	$_____
_____	_____	$_____	$_____
_____	_____	$_____	$_____

   Total cost of office equipment $_____

   g. Transportation equipment

	Number of Units	Cost
(1) Cars	_____	$_____
(2) Pickups	_____	$_____
(3) Trucks (six-wheel)	_____	$_____

    (4) Trucks (tractor-trailer) _____ $_____

    (5) Other _____ $_____

        Total cost of transportation equipment $_____

  h. Inventory cost

    (1) Raw materials $_____

    (2) Packaging supplies $_____

    (3) Supplies $_____

        Total inventory cost $_____

12. How much capital will this business require

  a. To open the doors $_____

  b. During the first year of operation $_____

  c. During the second year of operation $_____

  d. During the third year of operation $_____

  e. During the fourth year of operation $_____

  f. During the fifth year of operation $_____

Exhibit 15.3
LOCATING YOUR FIRM

Picking a good location of a plant or store can be very important to a company. This questionnaire is divided into area and site location analysis. Many of the figures and rankings will need to be your best estimates to avoid excessive time consumption. However, as you proceed through the checklist, be careful so that you select the best site and avoid a poor site.

General

1. Have you made a location analysis for

  a. Your present site Yes _____ No _____

     If no, you might use the simple "Rating Sheet on Sites," Worksheet 1, for your present location.

  b. For moving or expanding to a new site Yes _____ No _____

  c. Your new business Yes _____ No _____

Worksheet 1. Rating Sheet on Sites

Grade each factor: "A" for excellent, "B" for good, "C" for fair, and "D" for poor.

Factors	*Grade*
1. Centrally located to reach my market	_____
2. Raw materials readily available	_____
3. Quantity of available labor	_____
4. Transportation availability and rates	_____
5. Labor rates of pay/estimated productivity	_____
6. Adequacy of utilities (sewer, water, power, gas)	_____
7. Local business climate	_____
8. Provision for future expansion	_____

Exhibit 15.3
LOCATING YOUR FIRM (*continued*)

  9. Taxation burden   _____

10. Topography of the site (slope and foundation)   _____

11. Quality of police and fire protection   _____

12. Housing availability for workers and management   _____

13. Environmental factors (schools, cultural, community atmosphere)   _____

14. Estimate of quality of this site in ten years   _____

15. Estimate of this site in relation to my major competitor   _____

Source: F. I. Weber, Jr., *Locating or Relocating Your Business* (Washington, D.C.: Small Business Administration, 1969), Management Aids, No. 201.

2. If you need more building (expansion), have you considered

    a. Using space more efficiently   Yes _____   No _____

        Renovating Yes _____   No _____

    b. Adding more space

        (1) On the same floor   Yes _____   No _____

        (2) By adding a floor   Yes _____   No _____

    c. Moving selected operations to a new location and leaving others at the old location

        Yes _____   No _____

        For example, have you considered

        (1) Renting warehouse space   Yes _____   No _____

        (2) Moving early operations nearer materials sources   Yes _____   No _____

        (3) Making office space convenient to customers   Yes _____   No _____

    d. Moving the entire company to a new location   Yes _____   No _____

3. Do you have a special feature in mind which will determine your company location, such as having it near your home? Yes _____   No _____

    Have you exaggerated the importance of this feature so that it limits your opportunities?   Yes _____ No _____

4. To obtain a basis for comparing locations, estimate items using the chart shown below.

	YEAR			
ITEM	*First*	*Second*	*Fifth*	*Tenth*
Volume of sales ($)	$_____	_____	_____	_____
Number of employees—Total number with scarce skills	_____	_____	_____	_____
Volume of purchases ($)				
Space needed (square feet) Plant or store	_____	_____	_____	_____
Expansion	_____	_____	_____	_____

	YEAR			
ITEM	*First*	*Second*	*Fifth*	*Tenth*
Parking and drives	_____	_____	_____	_____
Other	_____	_____	_____	_____
Total acreage needed	_____	_____	_____	_____
Type of transportation needed	_____	_____	_____	_____
_____	_____	_____	_____	_____
_____	_____	_____	_____	_____
_____	_____	_____	_____	_____
Special ecological factors	_____	_____	_____	_____
_____	_____	_____	_____	_____
_____	_____	_____	_____	_____
Other	_____	_____	_____	_____
_____	_____	_____	_____	_____

5. Have you talked to people in or received literature from
   a. State industrial development departments   Yes _____   No _____
   b. Chambers of commerce   Yes _____   No _____
   c. Utility companies, banks, etc.   Yes _____   No _____
   d. Location specialist firms   Yes _____   No _____
   e. Friends   Yes _____   No _____

Area Location Analysis

6. Have you
   a. Located your present customers and/or potential customers on a map
      Yes _____   No _____
   b. Located your sources of materials on a map   Yes _____   No _____
   c. Identified transportation facilities on a map   Yes _____   No _____
   d. Located large potential pools of available labor on a map   Yes _____   No _____
   e. Located areas on a map which meet minimum requirements for special needs, such as water, effluent disposal, space, etc.   Yes _____   No _____
      Shown areas not meeting these specifications   Yes _____   No _____
7. List locations which may fit the needs of your company (sources of information include state industrial development departments, chambers of commerce, the location of like companies, location experts, and friends).

Area, City, Community   *Rank*

_____   _____

_____   _____

_____   _____

_____   _____

Exhibit 15.3
LOCATING YOUR FIRM (*continued*)

Area, City, Community	Rank
_____	_____
_____	_____

8. Collect enough information to narrow the choices for a more detailed analysis.

   Select the most promising locations and complete Worksheet 2, using the data for year _____ in item 4 above. (Where costs are equal for all locations, you can omit. You are interested in comparative costs here.)

9. Does one location stand out as better than the others?   Yes _____   No _____
   a. If yes, make the analysis in "Area location" for that location.

10. Eliminate very poor locations and use items 11–15 to determine the site to select.

Worksheet 2. Comparative Analysis of General Area in Which to Locate

Comparisons may be listed below as
   Column 1   No significant difference in locations
   Column 2   Dollar comparisons (annual costs)
   Column 3   Qualitative comparisons (excellent, good, poor, satisfactory, inadequate)

| | | LOCATION | | | | | |
| | | A | | B | | C | |
FACTORS	NOT SIG. (1)	Cost (2)	Qual. Comp. (3)	Cost (2)	Qual. Comp. (3)	Cost (2)	Qual. Comp. (3)
Land and building—Investment	___	___	___	___	___	___	___
Land and building—Depreciation	___	___	___	___	___	___	___
Marketing—Transportation cost	___	___	___	___	___	___	___
Time to deliver	___	___	___	___	___	___	___
Size	___	___	___	___	___	___	___
Character	___	___	___	___	___	___	___
Purchased goods—Cost	___	___	___	___	___	___	___
Transportation cost	___	___	___	___	___	___	___
Time to obtain	___	___	___	___	___	___	___
Availability	___	___	___	___	___	___	___
Work force—Availability	___	___	___	___	___	___	___
Cost	___	___	___	___	___	___	___
Training costs	___	___	___	___	___	___	___
Skills available	___	___	___	___	___	___	___
Worker relations	___	___	___	___	___	___	___
Productivity	___	___	___	___	___	___	___
Government requirement	___	___	___	___	___	___	___
Transportation—Availability	___	___	___	___	___	___	___

| | | LOCATION | | | | | |
| | | A | | B | | C | |
FACTORS	NOT SIG. (1)	Cost (2)	Qual. Comp. (3)	Cost (2)	Qual. Comp. (3)	Cost (2)	Qual. Comp. (3)
Reliability							
Type							
Cost							
Services—Utilities—Availability							
Reliability							
Cost							
Waste disposal							
Location of competition							
Community—Attitude							
Concessions							
Taxes							
Fire and police protection							
Schools, recreation, etc.							
Appearance							
Character of							
Future—Growth pattern							
Expansion area available							
Community attitude							
Transportation changes							
Quality of site							
Traffic patterns							
Total for evaluation							
Location selected							

Specific Location Within Area Selected

(You have selected one or more areas, and now a site must be chosen.)

11. Have you made your selection of a site?   Yes _____   No _____
    a.   If yes, are you sure that this site is a good one?

      Check Worksheet 2 to be sure.   Yes _____   No _____
    b.   If no, go to 12.

12. Is an industrial district available?   Yes _____   No _____
13. List sites zoned for industrial use

Sites Zoned	Sites Available	Proper Size
_____	_____	_____
_____	_____	_____

Exhibit 15.3
LOCATING YOUR FIRM (*continued*)

Sites Zoned	Sites Available	Proper Size
_____	_____	_____
_____	_____	_____

If only one site, check the factors in Worksheet 3 to determine whether there is any reason for not locating on the site.

14. Using information, complete Worksheet 3 for sites which appear to be suitable. (Be sure to include all costs which vary from site to site.)

15. Does one site stand out as better than the others?   Yes _____   No _____

   a. If yes, this appears to be the site to choose. A recheck may be warranted. Have you missed considering a factor?   Yes _____   No _____
   Have you missed considering an area or site?   Yes _____   No _____

   b. If no, recheck to determine whether factors to consider have been left out or values used are your best estimates. If several areas or sites are equal, you can flip a coin.

Worksheet 3. Comparative Analysis of Sites in Area for Location

Comparisons may be listed below as
  Column 1   No significant difference in locations
  Column 2   Dollar comparisons (annual costs)
  Column 3   Qualitative comparisons (excellent, good, poor, satisfactory, inadequate)

FACTORS	NOT SIG. (1)	LOCATION A Cost (2)	LOCATION A Qual. (3)	LOCATION B Cost (2)	LOCATION B Qual. (3)	LOCATION C Cost (2)	LOCATION C Qual. (3)
Building site—Land investment	___	___	___	___	___	___	___
Acreage relative to needs	___	___	___	___	___	___	___
Slope and foundation	___	___	___	___	___	___	___
Available building	___	___	___	___	___	___	___
Building investment	___	___	___	___	___	___	___
Building renovation	___	___	___	___	___	___	___
Building depreciation	___	___	___	___	___	___	___
Zoning	___	___	___	___	___	___	___
Customers—Nearness	___	___	___	___	___	___	___
Traffic patterns	___	___	___	___	___	___	___
Transportation—Materials	___	___	___	___	___	___	___
Type—Rail	___	___	___	___	___	___	___
Truck	___	___	___	___	___	___	___
Air	___	___	___	___	___	___	___
Cost	___	___	___	___	___	___	___

FACTORS	NOT SIG. (1)	A Cost (2)	A Qual. (3)	B Cost (2)	B Qual. (3)	C Cost (2)	C Qual. (3)
Personnel—Roads							
Automobiles							
Common carriers							
Work force—Quantity available							
Skills available							
Trainable							
Cost							
Utilities—Electricity							
Water							
Fuel							
Waste disposal							
Community—Attitude							
Taxes							
Assessments							
Fire and police protection							
Industrial park							
Appearance							
Character of							
Future—Growth pattern							
Expansion area available							
Transportation changes							
Traffic patterns							
Quality of site							
Total for evaluation							
Site selected							

LOCATION spans columns A, B, C.

Exhibit 15.4

PROCEDURE FOR ENTERING AN ONGOING BUSINESS

When you are planning to enter an ongoing business, it is essential that you do a very careful analytical study of the business. The guidelines that are laid out for you should enable you to collect sufficient information to make an objective decision about whether to purchase the business. In addition, it should enable you to know how to proceed if you should acquire the business.

1. Why is the business available for purchase?
    a. Is the owner overloaded by too many commitments?   Yes _____   No _____
        Will the owner remain in competition?   Yes _____   No _____

Exhibit 15.4
PROCEDURE FOR ENTERING AN ONGOING BUSINESS (*continued*)

   b. Has the owner reached retirement?   Yes ——————   No ——————
   c. Is the owner in poor health (be sure that the problem is physical and not economic)?
       Yes ——————   No ——————
   d. Is the plant and equipment worn out?   Yes ——————   No ——————
   e. Does the inventory contain mostly dead stock unusable at any price?
       Yes ——————   No ——————
   f. Is the market declining?   Yes ——————   No ——————
       (1) Because of a changing neighborhood?   Yes ——————   No ——————
       (2) Because of a declining population?   Yes ——————   No ——————
       (3) Other reasons ————————————————————————
            ————————————————————————————
   g. Is the business insolvent?   Yes ——————   No ——————
   h. Other ————————————————————————————
       ————————————————————————————————

2. Analysis of business resources
   a. Make a close analysis of accounting information
       (1) Analysis of statements
       (2) Validity of supporting data
       (3) Age of accounts receivable
       (4) Age of accounts payable
       (5) Cash flow analysis
       (6) Cash on hand
       (7) Adequacy of cost data (many firms are surprisingly ignorant of costs)
       (8) Does pricing formula cover all costs plus an adequate profit?
       (9) Summarize the results of the above analysis
            ————————————————————————————
            ————————————————————————————
            ————————————————————————————
            ————————————————————————————
            ————————————————————————————

   b. Appraisal
       (1) Management
            (a) How effective is it? ————————————————————
                 ————————————————————————————
            (b) What is the level of efficiency of plant, personnel, and percent of waste—material
                 and equipment? ————————————————————
       (2) What is the quality and effectiveness of personnel?
            (a) Productivity ————————————————————
                 ————————————————————————————
            (b) Dependability ————————————————————
                 ————————————————————————————

(c)   Other _____

_____

(3)   What is the physical condition of the plant? _____

_____

_____

(a)   Is the plant adequate in size and design? _____

_____

(b)   Is the plant efficiently laid out? Discuss. _____

_____

(c)   What is the plant's layout?
1)   Impact on inventory in process _____

_____

2)   Impact on materials-handling cost _____

_____

3)   Impact on labor cost _____

_____

4)   Impact on efficiency of machinery _____

_____

c.   Equipment
(1)   Age and up to dateness; discuss _____

_____

(2)   State of repair; discuss _____

_____

(3)   Efficiency; discuss _____

_____

(4)   Production rate; discuss _____

_____

Exhibit 15.5
PROCEDURE FOR ESTABLISHING A NEW BUSINESS

A. Background for business ideas origination
B. Background of prospective owner
    1. Educational experience
    2. Work experience
    3. Management experience and qualifications
    4. Creativity aptitude
    5. People skills
    6. Financial skills
    7. Organization skills
C. Economic feasibility study
D. Schedule for establishing business
E. Site selection and acquisition
F. Building plans
G. Own building, rent, lease, lease-purchase
H. Itemized list of equipment needs and costs
I. Itemized list of inventory requirements and costs
J. Organizational structure

K. Personnel requirements
L. Operational plans
M. Marketing plans
N. Form of legal organization
O. Capital structure
P. Financial plans—source of funds
Q. Capital budget—including cash flow
R. Pro-forma statements
    1. Balance sheet
    2. Profit and loss statement
S. Operating budget
    1. 6 months
    2. 1 year
    3. 2 years
    4. 3 years
    5. 5 years

Exhibit 15.6
ESTABLISHING A NEW BUSINESS

Little formal planning goes into the process followed by numerous new entrepreneurs. The questions that follow have been used for a number of years, both in the classroom and with individual clients. The success achieved by those following this procedure attest to its value. Of course, you will need to adapt this procedure to your particular business.

A. Your preliminary time table (an itemized list of what you are going to do on what date)
    1. Define business objectives   Date _____
    2. Determine form of business   Date _____
        Proprietorship _____   Partnership _____   Corporation _____
        Holding company _____   Trust _____
        Incorporation date _____   Pre-incorporation agreement date _____
    3. Capital structure   Date _____   Amount $_____   Amount of equity
        $_____   Number of classes of stock _____
        Identify classes of stock _____
        Amount of debt $_____   Type of debt _____
    4. Organization's functional structure   Date _____
        a. Construct organization chart
        b. Develop job titles and job descriptions
        c. Determine personnel requirements   Number _____
            Qualification _____

Classes of personnel _____

_____

_____

5. Plant, store, warehouse, or business location   Date _____
   a. Business location will be _____
   b. The property will be   Leased _____   Lease-purchase _____
      Owned _____
6. If structure or structures are to be constructed, modified, or renovated
   a. Plans will be drawn and approved by   Date _____
   b. Contract will be let for construction   Date _____
   c. Contract completion is estimated to be   Date _____
7. Business layout   Date _____
8. Transportation requirements   Date _____
9. Develop marketing plan (creation of image, determine types of advertising, and selection of media)   Date _____
10. Decide on types of products or service to produce (industrial or consumer)   Date _____
11. Channels of distribution selection (direct to final purchases, manufacturer's agent, wholesaler, jobber, warehouse, broker franchise, chain outlets, etc.)   Date _____
12. Development of pricing policies   Date _____

B. Development of budgetary plans
   1. Development of operating budget (including plan for profit)   Date _____
   2. Capital budget   Date _____
   3. Cash-flow chart   Date _____

C. Selecting source of funds   Date _____

D. Beginning implementation of plan
   1. Obtain capital   Date _____
   2. Obtain corporate charter   Date _____
   3. Contracting and purchasing needed items accompanied by delivery schedule detailed above   Date _____
   4. Personnel selection and procurement   Date _____
   5. Personnel training   Date _____ to _____
   6. Start operation   Date _____

MARKETING YOUR PRODUCTS AND SERVICES

Chapter 16
Selecting Your Customers
This chapter presents guidelines for determining what makes your business, produce, or service special in the eyes of the customer. Leading from your strengths, you are encouraged to develop a marketing plan that includes a clear picture of your customer.

Chapter 17
Building Your Marketing Plans
This chapter explores the marketing plan in more detail by addressing the issues that the business owner faces in making decisions about product or service, price, purchasing, and promotion. The chapter includes an extensive discussion of advertising and concludes with an analysis of direct-mail marketing.

Chapter 18
Satisfying Your Customers
This chapter stresses customer satisfaction. It covers personal selling, delivery of the product or service, quality, and the handling of customer complaints. It is impossible to overemphasize service to the customer. Much as you may love the idea of your business, the ultimate measure of your success is having someone buy from you.

SELECTING
YOUR CUSTOMERS

The title of this chapter conveys the idea that you manage your marketing activities. Your small business has a market that can be targeted and influenced. Your fate is not subject to the fickle and unpredictable whims of the customer—unless you choose to surrender control.

A requisite skill for the business owner is the ability to bring the marketing concept to the firm. Everything we propose in this chapter can be summarized in the words *marketing concept*. This concept is an orientation toward customer satisfaction and profit maximization as the two overriding and compatible long-term goals of the enterprise. Applying this orientation demands that you work backward from those two goals to develop a strategy that encompasses not just marketing, but also finance, production, and all other business functions. Putting this orientation in practice calls for all members of your business to be market driven in their actions.

Small business owners are frequently caught up in their specialized areas of expertise or in family and other issues peripheral to business operations that divert their attention from efforts to satisfy the customer. Such an approach is catastrophic, as an example shows. The owner of a company that supplied parts and equipment for van conversions purchased a computer to facilitate inventory control and financial record keeping. He soon became addicted to the immediate feedback he received in response to his programming efforts. He spent more and more time developing and modifying programs and playing computer games. Delivery dates began to slip. He stopped answering phone calls. Customers sought parts and equipment from competitors. The owner acquired superior computer skills, but he lost his business. Few statements contain more truth than the old business cliché, "Nothing happens until there is a customer." Are you offering a product or service that people want to buy at a price they are willing to pay?

After reading this chapter you will be able to

- Describe the inherent market strength possessed by most small companies relative to their larger competitors

- Review the questions that you will need to answer in order to be success-ful in selling your product or service
- Identify the least expensive and most likely sources of information about your market
- Prepare a marketing plan

Marketing Strengths and Weaknesses of the Small Business

Two major blunders that small business managers often make are attempting to be all things to all people and trying to be the low-price supplier in their markets. Two examples demonstrate the pitfalls:

> A pharmacist in a rural community had a standing policy of placing a double order whenever a requested prescription was not on her shelves. She wanted to ensure that she would always be able to satisfy her customers. At the auction following bankruptcy, it was found that she had the largest prescription inventory of any drug store in the state. She had achieved the objective of having merchandise available, but that merchandise had tied up all her assets so much that she could no longer pay her bills.
>
> A young entrepreneur took great pride in the quality of the wood-burning stove he designed and manufactured. There was general agreement that it was su-perior to others on the market. After pricing the stoves of other manufacturers, he priced his $50 to $100 below comparable models. He was able to sell every unit he produced—but they sold below what it cost him to manufacture the unit. He learned the hard way that "You can't make it up in volume."

Small firms do not have the deep pockets, or financial resources, of their large competitors. You cannot satisfy all customer needs. You are unlikely to enjoy the economies of scale that can make you the low-cost producer. If you believe that these strategies are necessary for your survival, you have not adequately identified your customers and their needs.

Small businesses do have competitive advantages, however. If you have read *In Search of Excellence* by Tom Peters and Robert Waterman, you know that their prescriptions for excellent performance are more readily applicable to small, entrepreneurial organizations than to large, bureaucratic ones. You are close to your customers, perhaps being acquainted with each of them and usu-ally living and working in close proximity. The typical small business owner has a bias toward action. This can be a negative characteristic, suggesting a bias against planning, but in the positive sense, it means that you act before op-portunities pass you by. In a small company, you can apply a hands-on, value-driven management style. The marketing concept is a value-laden approach that will be accepted by employees only if they see it in their boss. Your daily interactions with your employees enable you to develop a climate in your organization that emphasizes long-run profits through customer sat-isfaction.

Other advantages of the small firm are the ability to respond quickly to changing environment demands, the opportunity to profit from market niches that are too small for large competitors, and the general skills of your personnel. You may not be able to hire the legal, financial, marketing, and other specialists employed by large corporations, but you can ensure that a customer contacting your company gets assistance from the first person he or she speaks with. It is not difficult to cross-train a small number of employees so that they are all acquainted with the fundamentals of the business in order to meet customer needs. Studies of human motivation show us that this type of work environment has the added benefit of being more meaningful to employees. They gain an appreciation of the value of all aspects of the business and see the importance of their own contributions.

Classifying Your Customers

Who are your customers? Most owners believe that they know the answer to that question. Yet casual observation is not careful analysis and can mislead you about the clientele that you are trying to serve. If you are not certain who makes up your market, how can you know what your customers' needs are? Who are the pools of people who possess some common characteristics toward which you can direct your marketing efforts?

Consider the companies with which you do business: supermarkets, health spas, auto repair shops, and fast-food restaurants. A casual glance will tell you that they each cater to a broad spectrum of the population in terms of income, ethnic group, education level, and many other factors. Conduct a closer examination and you will be able to construct a customer profile. There are pools of similarities in our very diverse society. The task of the business owner is to locate a common need and target the pool, or market segment, that is most likely to have that need, then find the means to satisfy that group.

Ask yourself whether the product or service you propose to offer is needed more by customers who are

- Individuals, other businesses, or tax-exempt organizations
- Rural, suburban, or urban
- Geographically concentrated or dispersed
- Men, women, children, or families
- Elderly, young, or in between
- Upper, middle, or lower income

When you answer these and other questions about your customer pool, you become able to target your most important customer group more efficiently. In Part Five of this book, you will learn about managing the priority items in your inventory. Similarly, business owners find that they have a set of priority customers toward whom they should devote their attention. Without turning away other customers, you can make location, promotion, price, service, and other decisions that will concentrate your efforts to satisfy these customers, who are most crucial to your success.

Identifying Your Competitive Advantages

Although you lack resources, you are not at a complete disadvantage when competing with larger firms. Formulating and implementating strategy is a long, complex process in a large organization. How does RJR-Nabisco merge the interests of its tobacco and snack-food divisions? Various coalitions of managers vie for control and rewards. Your business, on the other hand, has few key decision makers and does not require the integration of widely diverse units. The astute entrepreneur, having defined a target market, can develop a strategy in which marketing plans mesh with finance, production and operations, personnel, and other plans for long-term success.

Despite the need to be flexible, your limited resources force you to concentrate your efforts and find a niche to fill. Finding a niche to penetrate successfully can be a complex process; it requires that you carefully mesh your strategy with your targeted customer pool. In developing a strategy, your job is to determine what your company's advantages are relative to your major competitors.

Consider four market strategy variables: your industry (whether it is growing, stable, or declining), technology (whether you are a leader or a follower), price (high, medium, or low), and quality of product or service (high, medium, or low). You can see from Exhibit 16.1 that you have fifty-four strategic choices available to you resulting from the price and quality choices that you make under various industry and technology conditions. If you were starting a desktop publishing business, you would be entering, at the time this is being written, a growing industry. To hold down initial costs, you may decide to lease equipment and become a technology follower. Your equipment does not permit you to perform the highest quality work possible, but you can produce medium quality and strive to provide service superior to that of your competitors. To

Exhibit 16.1
POTENTIAL MARKETING STRATEGIES

INDUSTRY		Growing						Stable						Declining					
TECHNOLOGY		Leader			Follower			Leader			Follower			Leader			Follower		
QUALITY		H	M	L	H	M	L	H	M	L	H	M	L	H	M	L	H	M	L
PRICE	H																		
	M																		
	L																		

H = High
M = Medium
L = Low

penetrate the market, you begin with a low-price strategy; when you soon find that your prices do not cover expenses, you move to the medium price range.

Even a small firm can select more than one strategy, particularly if the company sells multiple lines of products or services. The manufacturer of high-quality, high-priced handcrafted furniture, for example, acquired another company that made medium-quality, low-priced tables and chairs for restaurants. Both product lines were successfully marketed using separate brand names. Using the same name would have resulted in a conflict of marketing strategies, working especially against the high-priced products.

Obviously, some strategies on the grid in Exhibit 16.1 are inappropriate under any circumstance. It would be foolish for a technology follower in a declining industry to attempt a high-price, low-quality strategy. It is also worth noting that the grid omits variables, such as general economic conditions or the intensity of competition, that may be significant for your company. Nevertheless, it represents a place to start assessing what your competition is doing and evaluating a viable entry strategy for you. The grid must be used in conjunction with knowledge of the customers you are targeting.

Learning About Your Customers

Helen and Barbara purchased a women's clothing store located across the street from a row of high-rise dormitories adjacent to a large university. They upgraded the lines of dresses that the store carried and began an advertising campaign directed toward women of the community aged thirty to forty-five. They hoped to increase their sales during student vacations, when business activity was virtually dormant. Sales declined steadily as they lost their traditional student market and failed to attract permanent members of the community.

Successfully finding and satisfying a customer is rarely casual or accidental. Alternatively, the small company does not have adequate resources to fund sophisticated market research. What can you do to learn about your customers and be sure you are meeting their needs?

Identifying What You Need to Know

You need information that will aid you in selling your products or services. You need to know about

- *Markets.* Where are your customers? What needs of theirs do you satisfy with your product or service? How do they decide to buy the types of products or services you offer? When do they buy these products or services?
- *Products.* What characteristics of the product or service are essential to the customer? What customer needs are not currently being met? What characteristics of the product or service constrain your ability to market (for example, perishability, technical training, service requirements, and so on)? What other products or services substitute for yours?

- *Competition.* Who are the five major competitors in your industry (the market share leaders who dominate price, promotion, and distribution)? How quickly can competitors react to your actions (for example, with price changes, promotional campaigns, and other strategies)? Which market niches do your competitors fill? Which do they avoid? How easy is it to enter and leave your industry?
- *Prices.* How does your pricing strategy compare to that of your competitors? What are your critical cost factors (labor, materials, distribution, promotion, and so on)? Are prices stable or do they fluctuate? How sensitive are customer purchasing habits to price changes for your products or services?
- *Conditions.* What will be the effect on your business of changes in the economy, laws and regulations, technology, or other areas?

You can see that answers to the above questions can affect decisions about what products and services you offer, how you advertise, and even where you locate your business. What does accurate information cost?

The Cost of Information

Cost-benefit analyses become a part of your life when you own your business. You would be amazed at the number of owners that gamble the survival of their firms by not purchasing insurance, not running credit checks on new employees, or not meeting health and safety regulations. You will find that there are costs of operating a business that you never imagined. As a result, the undercapitalized firm, often the new firm, simply must forego some expenses that an objective observer would consider essential. One of the expenses you will be tempted to postpone is information gathering and analysis.

Before you do so, stop and think—how far and how long can you go without information about your customer? Consider the owner of a failed brass-bed store, who did not realize that, although the location he selected had a high traffic count, it was commuter traffic and not shopping traffic. Consider the operator of a failed tourist center, who did not anticipate the drastic reduction in numbers of travelers on the interstate highway system caused by the oil embargo of the mid-1970s. Consider the failed owner of a fifty-year-old restaurant, who bemoaned his customers' lack of appreciation for tradition while he neglected quality, service, and cleanliness.

You must make efforts to learn about customers and about trends in buying patterns relevant to your firm. Fortunately, there are some inexpensive means of obtaining useful information. The operative word is inexpensive, not free. Bear in mind that, even if the source can be obtained without direct charge (say, from a college or community library), there is a cost associated with your time and whatever else may be involved in compiling and analyzing data.

From a research perspective, there are two types of data: primary and secondary. Primary data are gathered directly by you to answer whatever question you are asking, such as counting pedestrians to determine if you should lease space in a downtown shopping district. Secondary data have been gathered by someone else for some other purpose but is useful to you. An example might be a wage and salary survey conducted by the local chamber of commerce (the Administrative Management Society also conducts yearly salary surveys), which you can use to help determine entry-level pay rates for your employees.

Secondary data are generally less expensive and often more accurate than primary data. Government statistics on population demographics, though dated, may more closely correspond to actual conditions than a survey that you conduct to determine why people shop where they do. Thus your first source of information about your customers is most likely to be U.S. Census Bureau reports. A listing of reports frequently used by business owners is shown in Exhibit 16.2. As you can see, the government compiles data that can be used by retail, wholesale, financial, manufacturing, and other types of firms. Census data are useful to you if you can safely assume that past trends will continue. You can learn whether your customer base is aging, if disposable income in your market area is expanding or contracting, or in what direction county employment levels are moving. You may need to temper these trends, however, with other information about conditions and events in your industry or local market.

Secondary data can be obtained from many other government agencies, including the Small Business Administration, the Department of Labor, the Internal Revenue Service, your state's department of revenue, and local city and county units. Some agencies prepare maps that you can use for an overview of local economic conditions or to plot the geographic distribution of your customers.

You will discover that your firm is capable of generating useful information internally. You can produce reports on customer purchases by size, frequency, length of time before payment, and other items that enable you to learn about your customers—who and where they are and how they pay.

You should also keep track of missed sales opportunities. Are customers requesting items you do not stock? Are they purchasing substitute products or services?

Exhibit 16.2

DATA AVAILABLE FROM THE U.S. BUREAU OF THE CENSUS

Retail trade	County business patterns
Wholesale trade	Quarterly financial report
Service industries	Agriculture
Construction industries	Governments
Manufacturers	Foreign trade
Mineral industries	Population
Transportation	Housing
International	Geography

Other economic data:
  Outlying areas   Enterprise statistics
  Minority- and women-owned businesses

Other sources of information are

- *Customers.* Customers can be queried directly, by enclosing a question-naire with a bill or by using a student team as the project of a high school or college class. Customers are particularly important to you in learning about sources of new business. Where did current customers come from? Should you direct your promotion efforts to those sources?
- *Creditors.* Question creditors through normal professional and social con-tacts. They may have secondary data on market conditions that will prove helpful to you.
- *Suppliers.* Suppliers are interested in your ability to sell to your customers and may collect market data that they can pass on to you.
- *Community leaders.* Elected and appointed officials, leaders of civic orga-nizations, and other recognized leaders often have soft information about future events in your community relevant to your market. You can connect with them by becoming involved informal and informal commu-nity service activities and social events.
- *Competitors.* Not all communication among competitors is illegal or unethical. You may participate with your competitors in trade associa-tions, often excellent sources of market data. Someone in your line of business may act as a mentor to you to help you get off the ground if your company is not seen as a direct threat.

We could list many more sources. Your responsibility is to keep your eyes and ears open. It is amazing how many stories published in your local news-paper or broadcast on radio or television announce changes that impact your company and market. Recognize that not all the information you need to know about your customers resides in your head as a result of your education and experience.

Developing Your Marketing Plan

Identifying your customer and gathering information about your market pre-pare you for the development of a marketing plan. Exhibit 16.3 shows how you can specify the market niche or position for your business after evaluating your customer, market, company, and competition. Your target market segment is determined by the customer profiles you developed, your knowledge of the customers' buying behavior, and the dispersion of those potential customers in the market. How many customers are there? How much do they buy? What trends are likely to affect your ability to reach them? By analyzing the strengths and weaknesses of your company and the opportunities and threats posed by your competitors, you can decide how to focus your products and services. The focus represents how you differentiate yourself from you competition. What benefits of your products and services cause customers to buy from you rather than your competition? You combine the focus with your target to position your company in the market. With your niche clearly in mind, you can draft your marketing plan.

Exhibit 16.3
DETERMINING THE MARKET NICHE

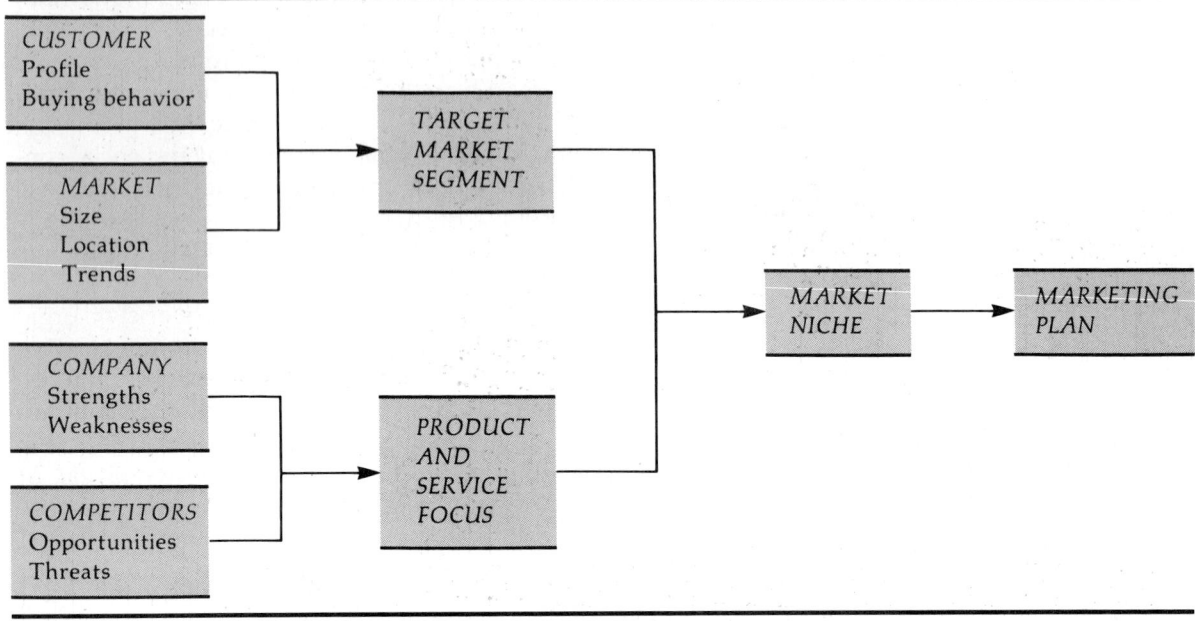

An outline of a typical marketing plan is contained in Exhibit 16.4. The introduction summarizes the plan's purpose, most important marketing objective, and primary strategy (for example, are you going to be the low-cost leader? is your primary advantage your location?)

The situation analysis contains the results of your research, especially from secondary sources. Who are your top five competitors? How would you classify them according to Exhibit 16.1? What trends in your industry, of government action, of technology, or among customers may influence your marketing plans? How does your company stack up? What are your strengths and weaknesses relative to the competition? From scanning the environment, what opportunities have you turned up? What major threats face your firm?

Spell out the marketing goals for your firm. What do you want to accomplish in five years in terms of sales volume, products or services offered, market share, geographic coverage, or other factors? What short-term objective must you achieve in order to reach these long-term goals? Which of these goals are absolutely critical?

The marketing strategies section explains how you will position your firm relative to competition. Precisely what is your niche? What will you be known for regarding products and services? What price image do you want for your business? How will you distribute and promote your products and services? What are your contingency plans if these strategies do not accomplish your objectives?

Exhibit 16.4
OUTLINE OF A MARKETING PLAN

INTRODUCTION
- · Purpose of plan
- · Objectives
- · Business strategy

SITUATION ANALYSIS
- · Competitive environment
  - Major competition
  - Industry trends
  - Other external factors
  - (regulations, technologies, social
  - trends, and so on)
- · Company profile
  - Current competitive position
  - Strengths and weaknesses

OPPORTUNITIES AND THREATS

MARKETING GOALS
- · Long term
- · Short term
- · Priorities

MARKETING STRATEGIES
- · Niche
- · Product or service
- · Price
- · Promotion
- · Distribution
- · Contingency plans

MARKETING TACTICS
- · Tasks and milestones
- · Personnel and responsibilities
- · Budgets

Finally, the marketing plan describes the tactics that you will use to carry out your strategies. These are specific tasks, such as which advertising media to use and when. Milestones provide performance standards to measure effectiveness. Personnel are identified to be accountable for the various responsibilities. Budgets are included for the tasks.

You cannot perfectly predict the future, and your business plan must be changed to adapt to unfolding events. Failure to develop such a plan, however, can only result in wasted resources—resources that are precious in a small company.

Summary   Managing an enterprise successfully begins with the application of the marketing concept, which aims to achieve the dual objectives of profit maximization and customer satisfaction. What are the strengths of your company in achieving these goals? Small businesses, though small, have some significant strengths, such as flexibility and greater customer orientation. Your goal is to define your company's strengths and fashion a compatible strategy built on four dimensions—the industry, technology, quality, and price.

To devise this strategy, you first need to identify your target customers. You must define them in terms of market, product, competition, price, and conditions. To make this definition, you will need information, which you can obtain from primary sources (through your own efforts to compile data) or from secondary sources (using data compiled by others).

The goal of this research is to find your market niche, from which you can devise a marketing plan. This plan outlines your marketing goals, strategies, and tactics. It is the blueprint for your business's success.

**Class
Assignments**

1. Pick out two independent companies in your community—one a manufacturer and one a service firm. Where do they fit on the grid in Exhibit 6.1? Why?
2. What other strengths do small businesses have in competing with large organizations besides those listed in this chapter?
3. What other competitive weaknesses do small companies have?
4. Do tax-exempt organizations (such as universities, United Way-supported agencies, military commissaries, and so on) compete with small business? If so, how? What are the strengths and weaknesses of the small business in this type of competition?
5. Given that census data are often five to ten years old at the time you are assessing your market, what precautionary measures do you need to take in drawing conclusions from those figures about your customers?
6. Pick out a community in your state and choose a retail business that you might open there. Using the census of retailing in your college library, what conclusions can you draw about the market for your store?
7. Contact your local chamber of commerce and find out what market information they provide to industries that they try to recruit into your community.
8. Complete Exhibit 16.5, Exhibit 16.6, and Exhibit 16.7.

Exhibit 16.5
DETERMINING WHETHER YOU ARE USING THE MARKETING CONCEPT PROPERLY

The purpose of this questionnaire is to enable you to determine whether your firm is adhering to the marketing concept.

Meeting Customers' Needs

1. Have you determined what your customers' needs are and how these needs can be satisfied?
   Yes _____   No _____
2. Are your employees guided by the marketing concept?   Yes _____   No _____
3. Have you and your employees learned your customers' likes and made your customers feel that you are interested in them?   Yes _____   No _____
4. Do you give your customers extra service?   Yes _____   No _____
5. Are you an expert on your products, and do you tell the truth about them to your customers?
   Yes _____   No _____
6. Do you sell your customers only as much as they can afford?   Yes _____
   No _____
7. Do you encourage your salespeople to build personal followings among their customers?
   Yes _____   No _____
8. Have you informed your salespeople to give the benefit of the doubt to customers who return merchandise?   Yes _____   No _____
9. By putting yourself in your customers' shoes, do you rate your business at least quarterly and determine what kind of image your firm has?   Yes _____   No _____
   a. Is your firm customer-oriented?   Yes _____   No _____
   b. Can customers find what they want when they want it, and where they want it at an appropriate price?   Yes _____   No _____
   c. Do customers leave with their needs satisfied and with a feeling that they will return?
      Yes _____   No _____

10. Do you and your employees perform little favors for your customers?   Yes _____
    No _____

11. Do any of the following danger signals, which indicate that your store is not following the marketing concept, exist in your business?

    a. Many customers walk out of your store without buying.   Yes _____
       No _____

    b. Many former customers no longer visit the store.   Yes _____   No _____

    c. Customers are not urged to buy additional or more expensive items.   Yes _____
       No _____

    d. Traffic (pedestrian and vehicle) for your store has declined.   Yes _____
       No _____

    e. Merchandise returns are higher than they should be.   Yes _____   No _____

    f. Sales have declined.   Yes _____   No _____

    g. Employees are slow in greeting customers.   Yes _____   No _____

    h. Employees appear indifferent and many customers wait unnecessarily.   Yes _____
       No _____

    i. Employees' personal appearance is not neat.   Yes _____   No _____

    j. Salespeople lack knowledge of the merchandise.   Yes _____   No _____

    k. Employees' mistakes are increasing.   Yes _____   No _____

    l. The mantle of greed is evidenced through raising of prices.   Yes _____
       No _____

    m. Better-qualified employees leave to work for competitors.   Yes _____
       No _____

Market Segmentation

12. Have you specified what market your firm is attempting to serve?   Yes _____
    No _____

13. Does your product or service

    a. Fulfill the needs of a specially defined group of people   Yes _____   No _____

    b. Represent a compromise to suit widely diverse tastes   Yes _____   No _____

14. Have you defined your market segment in terms of these characteristics?

    Economic status _____

    Age _____

    Education _____

    Occupation _____

    Location _____

15. Have you identified a market segment that is now well served by other firms?   Yes _____
    No _____

16. Have you posed these questions?

    a. What is your firm's competitive niche?

    _____

    _____

Exhibit 16.5
DETERMINING WHETHER YOU ARE USING THE MARKETING CONCEPT PROPERLY (*continued*)

    b. Is your firm known for

        (1) Quality   Yes &rule;   No &rule;

        (2) Price   Yes &rule;   No &rule;

    c. If your firm sells industrial products, does it sell to more than one customer?   Yes &rule;

       No &rule;

    d. Your firm has only a limited number of customers. Why?

        &rule;

        &rule;

17. Is your retailing firm straddling the market by attempting to sell both high-quality and low-quality goods?   Yes &rule;   No &rule;

18. Does your firm have a competitive edge—something that is desirable from the customers' viewpoint and gives it an edge over competition?   Yes &rule;   No &rule;

19. What characteristics does your firm stress?

    Quality &rule;

    Reliability and integrity &rule;

    Service &rule;

    Lower prices &rule;

20. Is your competitive edge realistic? Review the characteristics

    a. Is the edge based on facts?   Yes &rule;   No &rule;

    b. Do you know specifically what your customers are seeking?   Yes &rule;

       No &rule;

    c. Does the edge entice the customer away from his present source of supply?   Yes &rule;

       No &rule;

    d. Has market research been used in determining the edge?   Yes &rule;   No &rule;

    e. Is the edge compatible with your firm's capabilities and constraints?   Yes &rule;

       No &rule;

    f. Does your firm have the necessary resources to accomplish the edge?   Yes &rule;

       No &rule;

    g. Is the edge based on conditions that are likely to change rapidly?   Yes &rule;

       No &rule;

21. Does your firm focus on earning profits instead of increasing the volume of sales?   Yes &rule;

    No &rule;

Exhibit 16.6
IDENTIFYING A MARKETING STRATEGY

The purpose of this questionnaire is to enable you and your management to determine the appropriate marketing strategy for your company.

1. Check which marketing strategies your company is following.

    Expand sales into new classes of customers _____

    Increase penetration in market segments corresponding to existing customers _____
    Make no marketing innovations, but copy new marketing techniques and engage in product design and manufacturing innovations _____

2. To reach new markets, have you considered these possibilities?

    a. Develop additional related products or models within your product line   Yes _____
        No _____

    b. Develop completely new products unrelated to your present line   Yes _____
        No _____

    c. Find new applications in new markets for your product   Yes _____
        No _____

    d. Develop customized products or upgrade from low-quality to medium-quality goods
        Yes _____   No _____

3. In introducing new and improved products, do you recognize these factors?

    a. Existing product line and established channels of distribution   Yes _____
        No _____

    b. Cost of development and introduction   Yes _____   No _____

    c. Personnel   Yes _____   No _____

    d. Facilities   Yes _____   No _____

    e. Competition and market acceptance   Yes _____   No _____

4. Is your company trying to compete with

    a. A nonstandard product, either high-priced or an economy model   Yes _____
        No _____

    b. Fast deliveries   Yes _____   No _____

    c. Short production runs of special items   Yes _____
        No _____

    d. High-quality product superior to comparable products of competitors
        Yes _____   No _____

5. Has your company diversified its product lines?   Yes _____   No _____

6. Is your company increasing its penetration of the present market

    a. By expanding its sales to original equipment manufacturers from selling replacement parts
        Yes _____   No _____

    b. By reducing the variety of products and models and realizing operating economies?
        Yes _____   No _____

7. If your company's strength lies in its technical competence, are you adopting current
    marketing practices?   Yes _____   No _____

Exhibit 16.7
EVALUATING YOUR MARKET RESEARCH, SALES FORECASTING, AND SALES PLANNING

The purpose of this questionnaire is to enable your management to determine whether your company's market research, sales forecasting, and sales planning functions are being performed economically and effectively.

Market Research

1. Is the market research function being performed in your company?   Yes _____
    No _____

2. Is your firm using market research to
    a. Identify customers for your products or services and determine their needs
        Yes _____   No _____
    b. Evaluate sales potential for your industry and your firm   Yes _____
        No _____
    c. Select the most appropriate channels of distribution   Yes _____
        No _____
    d. Evaluate your advertising efficiency   Yes _____   No _____

3. Are your market research studies directed toward the measurement of
    a. Population   Yes _____   No _____
    b. Income level   Yes _____   No _____
    c. Purchasing power   Yes _____   No _____
    d. Other indices of sales potential in your trading area   Yes _____
        No _____

4. Are these secondary sources of published data used?
    a. Government publications, such as "Survey of Current Business"   Yes _____
        No _____
    b. Trade association reports   Yes _____   No _____
    c. Chamber of commerce studies   Yes _____   No _____
    d. University research publications   Yes _____   No _____
    e. Trade journals   Yes _____   No _____
    f. Newspapers   Yes _____   No _____

5. Do you use U.S. Bureau of the Census data broken down by county and SMSA and for SIC codes?   Yes _____   No _____

6. Do you use official sources of data, such as census reports?   Yes _____   No _____

7. Do you use your firm's records in performing research?   Yes _____   No _____

8. Do you use external data obtained from your
    a. Dealers   Yes _____   No _____
    b. Customers   Yes _____   No _____
    c. Competitors   Yes _____   No _____

Sales Forecasting

9. Is your company engaged in sales forecasting and measuring your company's potential market in units and dollars?   Yes _____   No _____

10. Are your sales quotas providing targets for your
    a. Individual salespersons   Yes _____   No _____
    b. Departments   Yes _____   No _____
    c. Sales territories   Yes _____   No _____
    d. Firm   Yes _____   No _____

11. In deriving sales quotas, are you using
    a. Market sampling studies and a study of census data   Yes _____   No _____
    b. Salespersons' knowledge obtained through customer contact   Yes _____   No _____
    c. Questionnaires mailed to companies   Yes _____   No _____
    d. Interviews with your customers and distributors   Yes _____   No _____
    e. Direct data concerning competitors   Yes _____   No _____
    f. Estimates of volume of business by
       (1) Relating sales of your merchandise to other merchandise sold in conjunction with your merchandise   Yes _____   No _____
       (2) Relating known national data to known local data   Yes _____   No _____
    g. Statistical analysis and projection based on past sales, as reflected in your firm's records   Yes _____   No _____

12. Has your company obtained
    a. The services of a market research consultant   Yes _____   No _____
    b. Assistance from
       (1) Trade associations   Yes _____   No _____
       (2) Local chambers of commerce   Yes _____   No _____
       (3) Banks   Yes _____   No _____
       (4) Field offices of the U.S. Department of Commerce   Yes _____   No _____
       (5) Field offices of the U.S. Small Business Administration   Yes _____   No _____

13. Has your company engaged in cooperative research with other small companies concerning
    a. Evaluations of traffic flow   Yes _____   No _____
    b. Parking availability   Yes _____   No _____

14. Does your firm follow closely market changes due to shifts in
    a. The composition of your customers   Yes _____   No _____
    b. The values and preferences of your customers   Yes _____   No _____
    c. The locations of your customers   Yes _____   No _____

Exhibit 16.7
EVALUATING YOUR MARKET RESEARCH, SALES FORECASTING,
AND SALES PLANNING (*continued*)

15. Do you specify the objectives of each market research project?   Yes ⎯⎯⎯⎯⎯
     No ⎯⎯⎯⎯⎯

16. Do you make market tests before introducing new products?   Yes ⎯⎯⎯⎯⎯
     No ⎯⎯⎯⎯⎯

Sales Planning

17. Prior to fixing your sales plan, do you check your production capacity?   Yes ⎯⎯⎯⎯⎯
     No ⎯⎯⎯⎯⎯

BUILDING YOUR MARKETING PLANS

Your marketing strategy may be intelligently developed, comprehensive, and innovative, but it will not work unless you implement it properly. As important as it is to spell out your objectives and identify your competitive edge, you can only succeed by attending to day-to-day details. Establish your marketing tactics—those operating plans that specify what actions you and your employees need to take to sell your goods and services. But you must also work harder than your competition.

In this chapter, we present some basic marketing tactics for a small business. You will learn how to reassess your product and service offerings, why and how to establish a pricing policy, purchasing tactics to help make your pricing policy work, tactics for advertising and promoting your products on a limited budget, the use of direct-mail marketing for the small firm, and the importance of layout and merchandising in increasing your sales and profits.

This chapter does not substitute for a course in marketing. Nevertheless, here and in Chapter 18, we introduce you to the traditional four Ps of marketing: product, price, promotion, and place. Our purpose is to get you to think about devising tactics of a new or mature, independent, limited resource firm.

After reading this chapter, you will be able to

- Discuss factors that influence decisions about the benefits of the product or service offered
- Analyze the factors that influence pricing decisions and devise a pricing strategy
- Assess the desirability of a potential supplier before making a purchasing agreement
- Evaluate advertising media and develop an appropriate advertising campaign
- Explain how the appearance of a business can affect sales

Product and Service Choices

In the first section of this book, you learned how people make decisions about whether or not to go into business and what kind of business to start or buy. We explained in Chapter 15 how to prepare a business plan, including describing the product or service on which your business will be based.

Even after beginning the business, you continue to make tactical decisions about your products and services, as the following example shows. Celeste's is a hair- and skin-care business operating three salons in a metropolitan area. Celeste's obtained a line of cosmetics from a local manufacturer, which put Celeste's private brand on the product labels. Although the cosmetics represented less than a third of the company's sales, they generated about half the profits. This contribution resulted from a high markup on the cosmetics. The owners of Celeste's wondered if they should begin manufacturing their own line of cosmetics. Part Five of this book investigates the question of making versus buying products or parts. It also covers such topics as quality, technology, and inventory control. These subjects all relate to marketing tactics. The make-versus-buy decision facing Celeste's involves more than a cost-benefit analysis. The owners must weigh their company's image to their customers. How important is it in attracting and retaining customers to have a distinct brand and product? Customer behavior dictates many product decisions.

Small business owners develop tactical marketing plans for their products and services to determine when to make changes, additions, or deletions to their mix of offerings. Some pointers for small businesses follow:

- Most small businesses are followers rather than leaders in their industry. Determine the niches that the leaders leave open, such as geographic location or market segment, and exploit those niches.
- Do not use all your resources trying to change customer buying habits. Rather, identify what they look for in your product or service and how you can deliver that better than your competition.
- Use a brand or company name that conveys the image you want and helps your customers know who or what you are.
- Figure out secondary uses or benefits for your product or service that your competitor has not exploited.
- Know your product inside and out. Do not diversify in ways that spread your expertise or resources too thin.
- If you are not going to service your products, be ready to help your customers obtain satisfactory service.
- Stay up-to-date. Do not let yourself be surprised by competitive or technological changes that threaten what you are doing. Remember from the Introduction that products have life cycles.
- Consider whether to engage in research and development. Statistics show that small companies get more innovations from their R&D dollars than do large corporations.
- It is virtually impossible to be too concerned about quality.
- Listen to your customers. They will tell you when you have a product or service problem if they think you will act on their suggestions.

Pricing to Sell   It is hard to imagine a more difficult decision for the new business owner than how to price merchandise. Most small business owners use personal judgment more than any other technique. Judgment without experience, however, rarely results in good decisions.

You might have one or two advantages regarding pricing. First, you may, like many business owners, own a business connected with an industry in which you worked before. You may thus be familiar with industry pricing practices. Second, you may have given pricing serious consideration while conducting your feasibility study and preparing your business plan. Indeed you had to make some pricing decisions in order to forecast revenues for your pro-forma financial statements.

Do not be misled into thinking that frequently used formulas for calculating price will solve all your problems. Pricing policy involves making decisions on a complex set of issues, including

- Will you offer discounts or allowances? These discounts could apply to customers who make large quantity purchases, pay cash, buy in your off-season, give assistance in promotion, or fit certain categories (for example, senior citizens or students).
- Will you use sales incentives? These include contests, rebates, premiums, coupons, trading stamps, or push money (advances to the salespersons working for your customers if they push your products).
- Will you accept trade-ins?
- Will you charge for services such as delivery, alterations, or gift wrap, for example?
- Will you offer discounts to your employees?
- Will your prices be firm or will you negotiate with customers?

Many factors enter into formulating your pricing policy. First you must study your market. Find out whether prices are increasing, decreasing, or stable. Learn if the quantity of products or services sold changes when prices change, or is relatively insensitive to price changes. Next you must forecast industry demand. Identify whether demand is growing, declining, or stable. Find out if the number and size of competitors is growing, declining, or stable. To make these projections, you can use information on trends from relevant trade associations.

An important step is to study the competition. Read their ads and compare their prices. See which competitors price above market, at market, and below market and try to identify why. Given your overall competitive strategy, where should you fit? See how competitors react to one another's competitive actions (such as sales, new product introductions, or market expansion). Estimate how they are likely to react to different price levels that you might offer.

Next determine what share of the local, regional, or national market you want to capture. Then select a strategy to achieve your goal. Two possible strategies are skim-the-cream and penetrate the market.

- Skim-the-cream, which means setting prices high and dropping them gradually as dictated by the reaction of competition. This strategy works in four situations: when demand is not price sensitive, you need to recoup development costs, competitors are not likely to respond quickly, or you have a technological edge.
- Penetrate the market, which means setting prices low to preempt competition. This strategy works in three situations: when demand is price sensitive, you can achieve economies of scale (costs per unit drop with increased volume), or competitors are likely to react quickly.

Decide whether to be a price leader or a price follower. Most small businesses are price followers, changing their prices in reaction to industry leaders. Studies show, however, that even among small firms, price leaders outperform price followers.

Finally, considering their fit with your other marketing tactics, set your prices. Most owners base price decisions on either cost factors or market factors. Those that use cost figures generally have more sophisticated accounting systems. Decide whether to use price lining, which is also called price points. A typical example is a clothing store that prices one group of apparel at $29.95, the next quality up at $34.95, and so on. Determine whether to use loss leaders. Such merchandise is characterized by being low cost, being purchased frequently by a cross-section of your customers, and carrying a regular price that they are familiar with. If yours is a retail business, evaluate whether off-price or discount merchandising makes sense for you.

Purchasing Practices

Your ability to offer competitive prices and enjoy adequate profits depends on the efficiency and effectiveness of your purchasing skills. You must seek the best value (quality for the price) you can obtain for your fixed assets, raw materials, parts, inventory, supplies, services, and any other purchases you make. Carelessness in purchasing may not ruin you overnight, but it can ultimately bleed you to death. Two areas require planned negotiation: the prices you pay and the accompanying services you receive. (See Chapter 9 on negotiation; few aspects of running a business will be of any greater importance.) Chapter 18 discusses how to maintain good working relationships with your suppliers.

Buying for your business is not like most of your experience in shopping. You will not walk into a store and pay the prices as listed, looking for the occasional discount or special. Purchasing for a business involves considering multiple vendors and weighing a variety of factors, some which you control and some which you do not control. For instance, you cannot control general business conditions, but you can consider how to take advantage of opportunities that these conditions may create. For example, high interest rates may stimulate some of your suppliers to make concessions on inventory that they are financing. Similarly, the financial health of one of your vendors may create an opportunity for you to negotiate a lower price. Most goods or services have seasonal sales patterns. Although the purchases made by a small business will not change those patterns, you may be able to get a better price by purchasing goods during the vendor's off-season. Even in the face of apparent domination by larger competitors, small businesses can give themselves a marketing edge. In 1988, Nintendo became the biggest selling game of all time. Major chains such as Toys 'R' Us could get enough inventory for the Christmas season, but independent toy stores were left with empty shelves. What can the small business owner do to overcome these uncontrollable fluctuations in demand? Many relied on superior service to the customer. They made a point of being able and ready to answer customer questions, give demonstrations, and show alternative toys and games, particularly items not carried by the chain stores.

Factors affecting the price you pay that you can control include the quality and quantity of products and services. Your inventory levels and those of your suppliers influence the price you offer and what they accept. Promotion, specials, and closeouts—both yours and the vendor's—weigh in negotiation. Who will pay transportation costs and who will pay for services such as advertising or packaging?

Price is only one subject to negotiate in purchasing. You may be willing to pay extra in order to have consistent quality, reliable shipments, beneficial payment terms, product guarantees, service after the sale (such as installation or maintenance), merchandising aids, emergency deliveries, a return policy, and many other significant factors.

Remember that purchasing practices do not end when the sale is negotiated and closed. Develop a procedure—which you can control and evaluate—that identifies who is authorized to receive sales calls, place orders, and process the accompanying paperwork. Determine how merchandise should be received, checked, and marked. Follow up with vendors on quality, price, and service. These aspects of purchasing, as they relate to just-in-time inventory control, are addressed in Chapter 21.

Advertising to Increase Sales

Business executives often talk about advertising costs or expenses. You have probably heard the cliché complaint, "Half the money I spend on advertising is wasted; the problem is, I don't know which half!" Starting now, think of advertising as an investment. Spend advertising dollars with the full intent of getting more in return.

Many small businesses spend little or nothing on advertising beyond the small cost of creating signs or business cards or other incidental activities. These firms expect that location or word-of-mouth or some other feature will attract enough customers to keep them going. Few of these companies enjoy significant growth or provide owners with more income than they could receive working for someone else. Many other businesses budget money for advertising without a clear idea of what that money should accomplish. As a result, they tend to spend according to the best or first media salespeople who come around. Their budgets are often exhausted on ill-conceived campaigns aimed at the wrong audience and run at the wrong times of year.

Advertising Strategies

Successful advertisers have clearly defined objectives with well-developed strategies to achieve them. Simply translated, successful advertisers know what they want their message to accomplish, to whom it is addressed, and whether or not they can expect a large enough increase in sales to exceed the advertising investment. Typical objectives and strategy choices are presented in Exhibit 17.1.

With rare exceptions, every dollar spent on advertising should generate an increase in sales that more than offsets the expense. It is easy to think of advertising approaches that seek short-run, direct responses from prospective customers. Less obvious are the strategies that aim toward long-run, indirect results. You may, for example, design a campaign to assist distributors in selling your product, thus making them more willing to carry your line. The objective may be to encourage any response by potential customers who, even if they do not make a purchase, can then be identified as leads for direct sales contacts.

Small businesses cannot afford the luxury of advertising to any and everyone. As Exhibit 17.1 shows, products and services are normally marketed to either consumers or industrial users. Your market category influences your choice of advertising media. Select a medium that reaches your target market with the frequency and continuity that enable you to achieve your objective.

Advertising Budgets

The small business owner has limited funds and must budget advertising dollars carefully in order to achieve objectives. Advertising dollars can be eaten up quickly. Inexperienced owners do not anticipate all the solicitations that they

Exhibit 17.1
ADVERTISING OBJECTIVES AND STRATEGIES

OBJECTIVE	PRODUCT OR SERVICE[a]	TARGET[b]	MEDIA[c]	TIMING[d]
Introduce new business or ownership	1	C,E,F,S	D,N,R,T,X	O
	2	C,E,F,S	D,N,X	O
Maintain and increase awareness of name	1	C,E	All	Y
and type of business	2	C,E	D,M,X	Y
Increase sales of regular products or	1	All	D,N,R,T,X	O,S
services	2	All	D,M,X	O,S
Introduce a new product or product line	1	C,E,F,S	D,N,R,T,X	O
	2	C,E,F,S	D,M,N,X	O
Open a new location or enter a new market	1,2	C,G	All	O

a. 1 = Consumers; 2 = Commercial or industrial users
b. C = Customers of competitors; E = Existing market; F = Former customers; G = New geographic market; S = New market segment
c. D = Direct mail; M = Magazine; N = Newspaper; O = Outdoor; R = Radio; T = Television; X = Other
d. O = One time only; S = Seasonal; Y = Year round

will receive from friends, relatives, and not-for-profit organizations. Companies and individuals with whom you conduct business expect you to reciprocate if they need to sell ads in, say, trade magazines or yearbooks. Budgets often fail by overlooking funds for actually preparing the advertisement.

Budgets should be planned around a calendar. What events will you promote over a twelve-month period? What will your promotion be designed to accomplish? How much will it cost, and what can you afford? Break this budget down by product season, media, territory, and market segment; you can start off by referring to industry averages. This may sound like a lot of work, but be assured: if you do not budget, you will waste your money.

Try to work within your budget, especially when just starting out. Remember that underspending on advertising can be as costly as overspending: it seldom brings returns. Look for ways to leverage or stretch your dollars. What services will a medium provide in order to obtain your business? Will any of your suppliers or distributors pick up some of your costs through cooperative advertising? Expect to spend more to begin a new advertising campaign than it would cost to maintain an existing campaign. Recognize that certain products or services require a relatively larger advertising budget than others (high-volume, high-margin impulse items, for instance, compared to industrial goods). Anticipate the impact of inflation on your budget.

Finally, include funds to evaluate the effectiveness of your advertisements. These may be used for such techniques as including coupons or special offers in certain advertisements, which are not promoted elsewhere; simultaneously running two different ads in different territories; or allocating personnel costs for tracking the sales of specific items or counting customers. These activities may not involve out-of-pocket advertising costs, but they should be factored in. Each of these techniques helps you determine what return you are receiving on your advertising investment.

Advertising Media

Although Exhibit 17.1 lists six major advertising media, there are several more. Point-of-purchase advertising, specialty advertising (such as calendars or pens), directories (the Yellow Pages or industrial directories), transit advertising, and flyers represent the many alternatives available to you.

Advertisers consider three criteria in making media selections. Reach is the size of the audience that the media can command. A rule of thumb for comparing media is to determine the cost-per-thousand of your advertising exposure. This figure is the amount of money you spend on the advertisement divided by the number of people, in thousands, that the advertisement reaches. Frequency is the number of times a potential customer is exposed to your advertisement during a specified period of time. Continuity is the period of time that your advertisement runs. On a limited budget, you normally have to trade off among these three criteria.

By applying the three criteria to the six media in Exhibit 17.1, we come up with the three continua shown in Exhibit 17.2. The cost-per-thousand calculation for reach should be calculated for each product, firm, and medium. In general, however, a good mailing list allows you to send your advertisement to

Exhibit 17.2
ADVERTISING MEDIA COMPARISONS

				REACH				
Focused	D	M	R	T	N	O		Broad

				FREQUENCY				
Single	R	T	N	O	D	M		Multiple

				CONTINUITY				
Short-lived	R	T	N	O	D	M		Long-lived

Key: D — Direct mail   O — Outdoor
M — Magazine   R — Radio
N — Newspaper   T — Television

a very focused group of potential customers. Alternatively, most outdoor advertising is exposed to the general public, most of whom are probably not potential customers for your business.

Regarding frequency, your decision relates to how many exposures your budget can afford. Since experts believe that it takes five exposures to make an impression, you would not wish to purchase a single radio spot, but rather buy a package of exposures.

Similarly, the continuity of ads is contingent on the package that you buy. In single units, radio ads usually have the least continuity and magazines the most. After all, a single radio commercial can be heard once and is gone whereas magazines are often retained, reread, and passed on to other readers.

Hints for the Small Business

Try to plan your advertising at least a month in advance. Do not be talked into an ill-conceived promotion because you are being offered the deal of a lifetime.

Make sure that there is some point to your message. Is it clear from your advertisement who your market is? Are you telling your audience something that is useful for them to know? Examples of important information are price, your location, what products or services you offer, the quality of those products or services, how to use them, what additional services you provide, guarantees, ingredients, color, or packaging.

Cultivate news media representatives. Advise them of your activities whenever you have something newsworthy. Publicity can be an inexpensive way of making your business known.

Finally, review your advertising with your employees. They should be knowledgeable when the customers call.

Direct-Mail Marketing

Consider the case of Andy Bower. Andy was not satisfied. He had landed the job he wanted with a big corporation after completing his MBA. Andy worked hard and had the pay raises and promotions to show for it. Somehow it was not enough. Andy felt that he was losing control of himself, that the rules and procedures of the company dictated his every move. His only goals seemed to be to minimize errors and minimize delays in getting projects completed.

Andy was unhappy, but he was not crazy. While he believed that the answer to his dilemma might be to go into business for himself, he was not about to risk everything he had built up without looking long and hard at what he might be getting into.

After a lot of self-evaluation, Andy decided that his best course of action might be to start a mail-order business operated from his home. With a small initial investment and the help of his wife, he figured that he could begin without quitting his job until the new business established itself.

The Bowers looked at several opportunities before settling on fishing and hunting equipment. The merchandise was of interest to them, as they were long-time avid outdoors people. They found that most potential mail-order competitors were located in other sections of the country. From hours spent in the library, they saw clear trends toward increases in both mail-order sales and sales of their prospective merchandise lines. Also using library data, they calculated the market potential of their region, estimated a reasonable share that they could attain from that potential, and then forecast the sales that they would strive for on a monthly basis during their first two years.

Next, the Bowers estimated the costs of running a mail-order business. There were variable costs for the merchandise sold and for shipping. Administrative expenses would include transportation, office supplies, advertising, accounting fees, salary, insurance, utilities, a business license, a post office box, debt service, catalogs, mailing lists, and building supplies for converting their basement. With these estimates in hand, Andy worked up a forecast of the proposed firm's cash flow for the first twenty-four months. While he calculated that there would be wild fluctuations, he was able to determine how much credit to request and when he would probably need to borrow.

Direct mail is a marketing strategy that many people use as a relatively inexpensive springboard into their own business. Significant startup costs are for mailing lists, the preparation and printing of a brochure or catalog, and postage. Minimal fixed expenses and low initial personnel costs reduce the entrepreneur's risk.

The heart of direct mail is a qualified list of prospects. A good list is well worth the investment. A large percentage of wrong addresses and unqualified buyers can be extremely costly. Over time, you should compile your own mailing list from your customers. Most firms find that repeat business ensures survival for the long term. If you start a direct-mail business, you will need to purchase a list at first. If you define your target market carefully, there is probably a broker who can supply you with a list based on the demographics you provide. You may also compile your own, using such things as business directories (for example from the chamber of commerce), membership lists of associations (such as religious or fraternal organizations), or government sources (voter registration lists).

Be prepared to spend enough to produce a first-class brochure or catalog. You waste your money on a list and postage if the material describing your product or company makes you look incompetent.

A few pointers regarding direct-mail selling:

1. Use handwritten addresses when you have high-volume mailings.
2. Try envelopes with illustrations that tie into the promotion.
3. Enclose reply envelopes to increase responses and the likelihood that payments will be included with orders.
4. Print in color unless it is cost prohibitive.
5. Include letters with circulars, brochures, or catalogs.
6. Include testimonials.
7. Have a professionally designed letterhead.
8. Place a time limit on the offer.
9. Offer a response incentive or premium.
10. Depending on the unit price, offer payment terms.

When Customers Visit

The physical space and the image projected are important to your business. Do not think that this applies only to a store or restaurant. Clients may stop in your accounting office. Retailers may rush over to pick up an order at your distribution center. Mass merchandisers may check out your production facility. What will they see? Will they get an impression of someone with whom they want to do business or be associated? Do the physical surroundings encourage people to purchase more frequently or in greater quantity or to buy complementary (including impulse) items? Let us examine factors that work for many small businesses.

Layout

Take a long critical look at your facility, inside and out. If you cannot be objective, ask someone else to critique your layout. Your teenage children are great for this; your parents are also good choices. Your customers may have an opinion about your business based on conversations with other people, contact with one of your salespersons, or exposure to your advertising. That opinion will be supported or refuted in a flash by the customer's direct observation. A small Italian restaurant on a busy street in a downtown shopping district could easily be overlooked by passersby. During the noontime rush, one of the co-owners steps out on the sidewalk wearing the restaurant's logo on his apron and T-shirt. Waving menus, he shouts, "Lasagna! Pizza! Stromboli!" The aroma wafting from the open door is unmistakable. Through the window, prospective customers can see an attractive, immaculate interior. They see the owners' family members vivaciously preparing and presenting meals. Guess what colors you see on the sign and exterior of this restaurant? If you know the Italian flag, you know the answer.

Consider the impact that a business's exterior has on customers. Look at the condition of the paint, the roof, doors and windows, the parking lot surface, signs (including whether anything prevents people from seeing them), lighting, and landscaping. Does all this add up to the image that you want to project to your customers?

Do not think that your business must be immaculate. A doctor's office should have an antiseptic odor, but would you want the same smell in the pizza restaurant we just described? Norms exist in most industries that let you know how your business should look. Most should be clean and reasonably organized. Your door should open easily and trigger some noise to let you know that someone has entered. The layout should permit safe and easy access to utilities and service to machinery and equipment. You should be able to move materials and inventory easily. Problem areas (noise, heat, dirt, and so on) should be isolated. Storerooms should be laid out for minimal handling of materials, opportunity for theft of inventory, and product deterioration. There are many recommendations in the preceding sentences, but you will pay a price for going against conventional wisdom.

Merchandise

Your business's interior should be designed to encourage customers to buy or place orders. Colors should be coordinated to highlight merchandise. Combined with lighting, color can influence shopping patterns and employee morale. It can even reduce stock pilferage.

We offer a few pointers to make shopping convenient for customers and stimulate orders:

- Set convenient hours. Does your clientele come in during normal business hours or on their way home from work and on weekends? It is not unusual for a new dentist to build a practice by scheduling appointments a couple of nights a week and on Saturday mornings.
- Inform neighboring businesses that you are there. Recently we wanted to try a new restaurant we had heard about. We stopped in a nightclub at the end of a city block and asked for the location of the restaurant. The host professed never to have heard of it. The restaurant turned out to be at the other end of the block. Invite your neighbors over to get acquainted with you and your merchandise. They can direct business your way.
- Make life easy for your customers. Merchandise should be accessible, although if you have a lot of damage from browsers, you need to change. Restrooms should be clean and convenient. If local laws permit, have an identifiable smoking area.
- Traffic normally flows counterclockwise in retail establishments. Measure sales in different areas of your store to determine where to place merchandise that you want to move.
- Low unit-cost items can be turned over as impulse purchases when they are placed adjacent to the cash register.

Summary

The four Ps of marketing are the factors that you must assemble to implement your marketing plan. In making decisions about the product or service that your company offers, you must consider what your product or service can do for your potential customers and how to get them to perceive its value. Quality and additional service can be valuable attributes for marketing a product or service.

Pricing decisions are often based on cost or market factors. Understanding costs and your market will help you identify the best mix of pricing techniques that will generate sales at a profitable level. Such tactics as coupons, rebates, discounts, loss leaders, and above-market or below-market prices can be manipulated in many different combinations.

Purchasing is a significant factor in the marketing mix—one that requires the art of negotiation. It is important to judge suppliers on the basis of more than just price. Quality, reliability, and service are but three of many dimensions on which you must evaluate suppliers before making a choice.

Getting customers to know about your business and its offerings is essential to your success. A well-planned, well-budgeted, and well-controlled advertising campaign can increase your sales. You need to identify the appropriate objectives, target, media, and timing for your advertisements to make them effective. One valuable technique is direct mail, which can put information about your business in the hands of prospective customers.

The look of your business—the design and condition of its facilities and equipment—can affect your sales by influencing customers' attitudes toward your products and services. Neatness, cleanliness, and good organization are three factors that help make customers feel at ease.

Class Assignments

1. Visit a store where you shop regularly. Draw a floorplan for the business, both interior and exterior. What changes can you recommend for its improvement? Draw a revised floorplan showing the effects of your recommendation.
2. Interview the owner of a manufacturing company, a retail store, and a service business about how they set their prices. Ask what would happen if they raised prices by 5 per cent. What would happen if they cut them by 5 per cent?
3. Pick out a consumer product that you use. Choose one that has been on the market at least twenty years. Go to the library and find magazines in which the product is advertised. How have the ads changed over the past twenty years? What would the charges have meant to you as an independent retailer if you had carried that product?
4. Interview friends of yours in other classes about direct-mail marketing. What products and services do they receive material about in the mail? Have they ever purchased anything through the mail? If so, what did they purchase, and why did they use this method? Can they think of any direct mail advertisements that really offended them? Were there any that impressed them positively?

Exhibit 17.3
CHECKLIST FOR MARKETING TACTICS

Product or Service

1. Have you decided what advantages will give your firm a competitive edge over other firms?   Quality of products _____   Innovative product design _____   Service related to product _____   Price _____   Reliability, integrity _____

2. Check the characteristics that your firm stresses.   Quality _____
    Reliability _____
    Service _____   Price _____

3. Have you compared your company's strengths and weaknesses with competitors' strengths and weaknesses?   Yes _____   No _____

4. Are you
    Concentrating on a narrow product line _____
    Developing a highly specialized product _____
    Providing a product or service package with an emphasis on service _____

Price

1. Did you compare your prices to competitors' prices?   Yes _____   No _____

2. In periods of rapid inflation do you constantly monitor costs and make price changes to provide for continued profit ability?   Yes _____   No _____

3. Does your sales contract contain an accelerator clause as a protection against inflation?
    Yes _____   No _____

4. Do your initial markups cover
    Operations, particularly selling expenses _____
    Operating profit _____
    Subsequent price reductions _____

5. What guidelines do you have for discounting damaged merchandise?
    _____
    _____

6. Do you review the adjustment and damaged merchandise policies frequently with employees?
    Yes _____   No _____

7. Do you regard customers' satisfaction with these policies as being important and influential in establishing guidelines?   Yes _____   No _____

8. Do you think of what the typical customer is willing to pay when pricing items?   Yes _____
    No _____

9. Do you practice the technique of averaging markup rather than aiming at the same markup percentage for all products or services?   Yes _____   No _____

10. Is your price consistent with the quality and image of the product
    or service?   Yes _____   No _____

11. In reducing or raising prices, do you consider your competitors' probable reactions?
    Yes _____   No _____

Purchasing

1. Who has the authority to issue a purchase order? _____

2. Can orders be issued without authorization?   Yes _____   No _____

3. If yes, what is the dollar limit? _____

4. Who initiates purchase requests? _____

5. Does the purchaser work with others in the organization to evaluate possible substitute items?
    Yes _____   No _____

Exhibit 17.3

CHECKLIST FOR MARKETING TACTICS (*continued*)

6. Does the purchaser maintain up-to-date vendor files with current price lists?   Yes _____

    No _____

7. Do vendor files include analyses of vendor performance?   Yes _____   No _____

8. Are many orders marked rush?   Yes _____   No _____

9. Are all available discounts taken (quantity and time)?   Yes _____   No _____

10. Are invoices checked against purchase orders and receiving reports and approved before

    being paid?   Yes _____   No _____

11. Are competitive prices compared?   Yes _____   No _____

12. Do you negotiate with suppliers for the best possible prices?   Yes _____   No _____

13. Do you speculate by buying large quantities of items when the price is low?   Yes _____

    No _____

14. If yes, how many months' supply do you limit this to? _____

15. Are you or have you ever been placed on a waiting list because of a low-volume order or because you

    are not a longstanding customer with the company?   Yes _____   No _____

16. Do suppliers or sales representatives ever pass you by for any other reason?   Yes _____

    No _____

17. How often do sales representatives call or stop by? Do they impose on your daily duties as a manager?

Advertising

1. Have you developed an advertising budget showing the outlay of funds for advertising?

    Yes _____   No _____

2. Do you vary your advertising expenditures seasonally?   Yes _____   No _____

3. Are you attempting to measure the results of your advertising?   Yes _____

    No _____

4. Do you plan your advertising at least four weeks ahead?   Yes _____   No _____

5. Do you familiarize employees with new promotions or information?   Yes _____

    No _____

6. Are your company's advertising and sales promotional programs continually compared to those of its

    competitors? Yes _____   No _____

7. Have you determined what market segment your advertising should be directed towards?

    Yes _____   No _____

8. Have you tried any of the following sales promotion techniques?   Special displays _____

    Premiums _____   Contests _____   Free introductory services _____

9. Has your advertising agency assisted you in any of these areas?

    Sales training _____   Preparation of sales and service literature _____

    Public relations and publicity _____

Layout

1. Are all items displayed in such a manner that facilitates easy examination?   Yes _____

    No _____

2. Are any items ever damaged by browsers?   Yes _____   No _____
3. Do you have a recognizable pattern and coordinated design?   Yes _____   No _____
4. Is maximum floor space utilized to display items without looking cluttered?
    Yes _____   No _____
5. Is someone responsible for maintaining your facilities in a neat and clean manner?
    Yes _____   No _____
6. When problems with physical structures are reported, are they fixed promptly?   Yes _____
    No _____
7. Are follow-ups done on repairs?   Yes _____   No _____
8. Is there a system for reporting needed repairs?   Yes _____   No _____
9. Is the equipment up to date?   Yes _____   No _____
10. Have you inspected the condition of the following?
    Exterior paint surface _____
    Seals in doors and window casements _____
    Condition of doors and windows _____
    Condition of glazing on doors and window glass _____
    Condition of gutters, drains _____
    Roof _____
    Parking lot surface _____
    Carpeting _____
    File _____
    Line markings in parking area _____
    Landscape, shrubs _____
    Handles, pulleys, drawers, hinges _____
    Parking lot lighting _____
    Electric signs, painted signs _____
    Concrete walls _____
    Beams and wood surfaces _____
    Inside lighting _____

SATISFYING
YOUR CUSTOMERS

You may be familiar with business owners who have the attitude, "This is my business, and I'll run it the way I please." How does that attitude make you feel as a customer? To the customer, you, the owner, are the business. For that matter, your employees are the business to the customers with whom they come in contact. How employees approach customers is a function of your behavior. The owner of a pizza restaurant was awakened by a ringing door bell at 3:00 A.M. and found a boxed pizza at her doorstep. A note attached stated, "See how you like cold pizza delivered late!" Messages like this jolt us into recognizing that we may have forgotten our true priorities. More often, the message from customers is more subtle—they quietly begin doing business with someone else.

In Chapter 16, we described the marketing concept as an orientation toward the dual objectives of customer satisfaction and profit maximization. Maximum profits over the long run result from the return business and word-of-mouth advertising of satisfied customers, whether industrial customers or consumers. The keys to customer satisfaction are personal selling, delivery of the product or service, quality, and handling complaints in a positive way.

After reading this chapter, you will be able to

- Describe the role of personal selling in achieving customer satisfaction
- Explain how distribution of the product or service can help achieve customer satisfaction
- Explain how quality affects customers' sense of value
- Describe how to build positive relationships with customers, including how to handle complaints

Personal Selling: More Than Pushing Products

We asked you in Chapter 16 to learn who your customer is. For your marketing strategy to work, you need to have a customer profile to target your efforts. In selling your product or service face-to-face, you take that profile to a personal level. Who is that individual customer? What is he or she looking for?

Success in personal selling for the small business owner stems from having empathy with your customers and relying on natural friendliness.

Since most employees in a small company come in contact with customers at some time or other, all should be taught basic selling skills. Guidelines for personal selling are contained in Exhibit 18.1. We can summarize these easily in one phrase: be a problem solver. Your responsibility is to train your employees to be experts in your products, services, and business. Share with them your attitude of caring about the customer and wanting the customer to come

---

Exhibit 18.1
GUIDELINES FOR PERSONAL SELLING

THE CRITICAL FIRST IMPRESSION

- Appropriate appearance
  Attire
  Health
- Demeanor
  Poise
  Confidence
  Sense of humor
  Mannerisms

- Attitude
  Friendly
  Sincere
- Speech
  Voice
  Vocabulary
  Listening skills

MAKING THE APPROACH

- Observe the prospect
- Observe the prospect's premises

- State how much time you need
- Stick to your time limit

PROFESSIONAL PRESENTATIONS

- What are the buyer's objectives?
- What are the key features of your product or service that meet those objectives?
- Are you open and honest?
- Are you holding the buyer's interest?

- Are you answering questions when you really do not know the answer?
- Are you making it easy for the buyer to understand?
- Can you demonstrate the product or service?
- What lasting impression will you leave?

USING SELLING AIDS

- Choose appropriate types
- Do they appeal to buying motives?
  Are they simple and easy to understand?
  Are they distracting?

  Do they aid in gaining commitment?
- Be prepared in how to use them
- Use them to control the situation

HANDLING OBJECTIONS

- Anticipate
- Forestall

- Evaluate
- Be positive

CLOSING THE SALE

- Satisfy objections
- Satisfy objectives
- Look for signals

- Ask more than once
- Have selling points in reserve

FOLLOW UP

- Reinforce the decision
- Offer new information

- Let buyer know about after-sale service and warranties

back. Be open to your employees' ideas as well. Each employee should consider himself or herself a consultant seeking ways to meet customer needs.

A few pointers for personal selling in the small firm:

- Employees expect to be compensated for making sales. Consider all forms of rewards, and not just income. You can use prizes, awards, recognition, and other techniques to reinforce sales efforts. Salespeople should feel that they have equal access to sales incentives.
- Every customer and every sale have the potential to provide you with useful information. Make some person responsible for communicating information learned from sales to those in the organization who handle production, credit, personnel, or other functions.
- Sales training should include training in public relations. Even if someone is not a customer, he or she should be treated in a way that leaves him or her with the image that you want to project—that person may be a customer some other day.
- The activities of salespeople should be coordinated. Duplicated efforts by salespeople harass customers and frustrate the employees.
- Personal contact with customers is critical for the small business. Coach your employees on remembering customers and calling them by name whenever possible.

Getting the Product to Customers

Students sometimes confuse physical distribution with channels of distribution. Often they are identical, such as when a farmer sells products to consumers from a roadside stand. A channel of distribution refers to the transfer of the title to goods from producer to consumer. A channel may be direct, as in the example of the roadside stand, or it may include entities such as manufacturers' representatives, who never actually handle the goods. By contrast, physical distribution is the movement of the goods themselves. It may include such entities as warehouses, which store the products but do not participate in title transfers.

Moving goods from where they are produced or stored to where they are used is critical to the satisfaction of the customer awaiting those goods. Many of the operations associated with this movement, such as inventory control and materials handling, are addressed in Part Five. The marketing concerns of physical distribution relate to your ability to put the product in the hands of the purchaser with minimal errors and delays.

Physical distribution channels are often beyond the control of the independent business owner. The channels to be used are often dictated by product factors (for example, the perishability of fresh produce) or industry factors (such as regulations for handling prescription medicines) or by large corporations with economic power. National retailers, for example, may shift the burden of inventory storage to their smaller suppliers as a required condition of sale.

What discretion do you, the small business owner, have in product distribution in your attempts to serve your customers? You may be able to exercise control over

- *Packaging.* Do your packages protect the products? Will they aid your client in merchandising the product? Are you packaging appropriate quantities?
- *Inventory.* Are you shipping the right quantities in the right frequency? Can you provide emergency shipments? Are you minimizing your out-of-stock situations?
- *Service.* Is technical assistance required for installing or operating your product? Are you providing the service or ensuring that others (such as the manufacturer) will provide it? Do your customers have technical problems that you can help solve? Do you follow up to verify customer satisfaction after the sale?
- *Transportation.* Do you deliver? Are your facilities accessible to customers for pickup? Do you use reliable delivery services?
- *Storage.* Can you hold merchandise for customers in off seasons? Can you sell on consignment? (In using consignments, you leave your products with a retailer or other intermediary and take payment only if they sell the goods.) Do you offer services such as deferred billing or advance shipping? (Deferred billing means postponing the billing to allow the customer enough time to resell the products; advance shipping means delivering goods before the agreed-upon billing date.)

Your objective in physical distribution should be the timely delivery of the quantities customers want in acceptable condition at a reasonable cost. If you are operating out of your garage or otherwise too poor in resources to provide the distribution services suggested above, remember that the dominant entity in the physical distribution channel is often the wholesale distributor. These companies stockpile large quantities of various goods from multiple sources and then redistribute them to multiple retail outlets. An example shows how wholesalers can be used. Coffee sells at prices set at international commodity exchanges. An independent importer was able to negotiate a series of intermediate-term contracts to purchase Mexican coffee during a period of rapid devaluation of the *peso* relative to the dollar. The contracts, in *pesos,* allowed the importer a cost advantage for a considerable period of time. The importer did not have the size or capacity to negotiate directly with large retailers for shelf space, however. A deal was struck with a large distributor that specialized in selling to convenience stores. The distributor marketed the coffee to these stores not for over-the-counter sale, but to be brewed for sale to consumers. The importer, therefore, was able to sell all the coffee over a limited period of time without having to establish brand recognition, fight for shelf space, or worry about physical delivery to retail outlets.

How might your physical distribution tactics satisfy your customers and assist your marketing efforts? A small company needs a reputation for reliable delivery. As will be explained in the discussion of just-in-time systems in Part

Five, you can help your customers by reducing their order cycle length or out-of-stock frequencies. A willingness to provide emergency shipments can make customers loyal to you. Can you help your customers by shipping smaller quantities or shipping more frequently than your competitors? Another key is to keep your customers informed regarding the status of their orders.

Maintaining Consistent Quality

Superior quality is expensive. So is inferior quality. Surveys of dissatisfied customers have found that 30 percent stop patronizing the business and another 45 percent plan to make fewer purchases. Even more important, unhappy customers communicate their dissatisfaction to an average of ten other persons. You cannot assume that you are holding down costs by omitting quality controls. (In Chapter 20, we discuss standards for quality and productivity.)

There is no evidence to suggest that small businesses are more successful either as the high-quality competitor, the low-quality competitor, or somewhere in between. There are, however, two rules to follow to achieve your goal of customer satisfaction through quality of service and product:

- Provide the best quality for the price.
- Ensure consistency in quality.

Bear in mind that customers doing business with your company or purchasing your product for the first time normally have a basis for comparison. Whatever product or service they have been using in the past is their point of reference for evaluating value for their dollar. Repeat customers are familiar with the value received when they purchase from you; they expect that value to remain consistent. Changes in quality will send them elsewhere. This is particularly true of your business clients. They require reliability in your products so that they can maintain quality for their own customers.

Repeat customers may well be more loyal to your employees than to you, your company, or your product, as an example shows. After several years of working in a salon owned by someone who lived in another state, a hairdresser concluded that business ownership must not be too tough if the owner did not even need to be present. Feeling that his customers were loyal to him and not the salon, he believed that he could carry most of his clientele with him. He opened a shop of his own in the same community and found that he did retain his patrons. He also found that managing other beauticians was not as easy as he had assumed. With a great deal of turnover among his staff, he discovered that personnel changes wreaked havoc with his customers. As in his own case, clients of his hairdressers often moved from salon to salon to keep the same quality of service. If a customer changed from one beautician to another, the owner was likely to hear complaints about service not meeting expectations. He found himself exasperated by the demands of customers for consistency in service. Continuity of personnel is important (strategies for retaining employees appear in Part Six). Customers like doing business with people they know. Few actions by your employees are more valuable than greeting customers by name.

Another consideration in quality and customer service is the request to customize. Many customers seek to have a product or service tailored to their individual desires. These requests can be critical, such as when you are subcontracting from a general contractor on a major project. The small firm is often more flexible than its larger competitors, making it better able to satisfy requests for customization.

Developing Good Relations with Customers	Perhaps the most direct impact on your customers' perceptions of your firm results from their interpersonal contacts with you and your staff. These contacts occur face-to-face, by telephone, and through correspondence. Are you and your employees giving customers the impression that they are valued and that their continued patronage is desired? The owner cannot avoid the role of salesperson and the need for effective sales and interpersonal skills. The owner of a drugstore observed the rude treatment that a pharmacist in training was giving to various customers. If their prescriptions were to be handled by Medicare or Medicaid, the customers were addressed curtly and often made to wait until the transactions of "paying" customers were done. After the store closed, the owner asked the young pharmacist to chat with her in her office. "You know," the trainee began, "those Medicare-Medicaid patients drive me crazy. They ask so many questions, and they're not even paying for the prescriptions." "That may be so," the owner responded gently, "but *we are* being paid, and those people deserve the same courtesy as all of the customers who come in the store. The payments we receive for their prescriptions help keep us in business." She went on to explain the need to treat all customers with dignity, not simply because of the moral responsibility, but also because of the image of the store and because of the need to maintain good relations with the doctors and hospitals who send patients to the store to have their prescriptions filled.

One of your first concerns should be the visual effect of your enterprise on the customer. What will the first impression be? Take a look around and ask yourself:

- Is this a professional place of business?
- Is it neat, orderly, and attractive (this applies to industrial settings as well as retail stores)?
- Does the workplace convey an image of competence without ostentation?
- Are the employees professional in appearance?
- Do employees appear to take pride in themselves, their organization, their products and services?
- Do employees acknowledge the customer immediately, whether in person or by phone? Do they smile and give the customer their complete attention?

These initial impressions are critical to retaining the customer. The importance of good first impressions must constantly be reinforced by the owner.

A few points to consider when dealing with customers on the telephone include:

- Answer in as few rings as possible.
- Do not put the customer on hold without obtaining his or her permission.
- Smile when speaking and speak clearly.
- Do not keep them listening to recorded music for too long.
- Do not refer the customer to someone else without following up to verify that the customer received the requested assistance.

You even convey an image to the customer through the mail. Are your advertising materials, flyers, and company descriptions professional in appearance? Do they accurately represent your business and what it is capable of doing for the customer? What is the quality of the stationery you are using? Does it have your logo, business name, address, and phone number? Do you proofread every letter to ensure that it is error free? Messy letters or correspondence with typographical errors project an image of incompetence that your actions may never overcome.

Doing Business Honestly and Ethically

It is impossible to overemphasize the need for your marketing practices to be honest and ethical. Lapses in this regard come back to haunt you in countless ways: lost customers, tarnished image, dishonest employees (by example or by training), lawsuits, fines, even prison terms. You also have an obligation to your profession or industry. Dishonest behavior reflects on everyone in your line of business. Similarly, although the actions of a dishonest or unethical competitor may open a market opportunity for you, they also make customers more skeptical of all companies in the industry.

Marketing has a negative image among some consumers. Because of personal experiences, they associate marketing with fraud, misrepresentation, and exaggeration. How many times have we seen phony testimonials, misleading labels, emotional claims that have nothing to do with the real usefulness of a product, an approach offensive to good taste, or other excesses? You take on an ethical burden as a business owner because you know more about your goods and services than your buyer does.

What are the consequences of unethical behavior? When the abuse becomes extreme enough, expect more government control, often through taxation or censorship. Think about all the federal agencies with some power to oversee marketing practices: these include, among many others, the Federal Trade Commission, Food and Drug Administration, Federal Communications Commission, Postal Service, Securities and Exchange Commission, Alcohol and Tobacco Tax Unit, Agriculture Department, Commerce Department, Customs Bureau, Justice Department, Farm Credit Administration, Federal Power Commission, Interior Department, Internal Revenue Service, Interstate Commerce Commission, Labor Department, Patent Office, and Treasury Department. State and local governments are also sources of legislation and regulation. They monitor such aspects of business as truth in advertising, advertising restrictions on certain commodities, regulating occupational and professional advertising, and regulating outdoor advertising.

Business owners often express exasperation over the volume of laws and regulations and their occasional contradictions. Again, however, we emphasize that your business integrity is paramount. A reputation for integrity is integral to any marketing strategy.

Handling Complaints

A key feature of customer service is how you handle complaints. You cannot expect to keep customers happy all the time. Serving the customer extends to dealing with the angry customer, whether or not that anger is justified. Getting rid of that anger can help the business, as an example shows. A customer entered a local bank and stood at the end of one of three available lines. As so often seems to be the case, it was the wrong line. People on his left passed through. People on his right passed through. He waited. He grew annoyed. He boiled. When he reached the teller, he expected her to say "May I help you?" in a tone that really said "What do *you* want?" Instead, the teller said "I'm very sorry you've had to wait so long. How may I help you?" The customer's anger was defused. He reported later that he wanted to reach across the counter and give the teller a big hug.

Both you and your employees should consider solving customer complaints to be an obligation. Taking this perspective can be difficult when you know that the business is your business; you may feel that you should be allowed to behave as you choose. It is also difficult to ask employees, with whom you are personally close, to act politely to customers who are being unreasonable. Resolving to handle customer complaints need not mean that you and your employees must lie down and become doormats for angry customers. Keep in mind that the anger is not directed at you as a person. Allow the customer free and full expression of the anger; doing so dissipates the hostility. Identify the problem causing the anger by asking questions that solicit factual, not emotional, answers; address problems, not symptoms. Seek areas of agreement wherever possible. Customers who believe that they have been dealt with fairly will communicate their satisfaction to others.

Summary

Two old sayings sum up the information in this chapter: "You never have a second chance to make a first impression," and "The customer is *always* right!" These sayings have become trite because you hear them so often, but you hear them so often because they contain so much truth. Your business exists as long as someone is willing to pay for your product or service. Customers are willing to pay as long as they believe that they are receiving value for their money. They expect, and reasonably so, that your company will provide a product or service at a time and place convenient to them as customers. They expect to receive quality products and services for their money relative to what they can obtain elsewhere. They expect the quality to remain consistent when they return to buy again. Finally, your customers expect to be treated with courtesy and respect, even if they do not reciprocate. They are paying you hard-earned dollars and do not want to be treated as though you are doing them a favor. Your job is to find ways to help your customers solve their problems.

Class Assignments	1. Walk into five independent businesses and report on what you observe. What first impression does each business make? Do you feel welcome? What, if anything, do the employees say to you? What are your reactions to the physical appearance of each business?

2. Identify a business that always has what you want when you want it. Why do you think it is able to do that? Identify a business that does not have the product or service that you want when you want it or where you want it. Why do you think that this happens?

3. Have you ever been an angry customer? What caused the problem? How could the business have avoided the problem? What did the business do, if anything, to try to satisfy you? How might employees have done a better job of solving the problem?

4. Visit three restaurants. What strategies do they use to assume quality food and service? Do any have questionnaires for customers? Do customers fill them out? Do the questionnaires provide useful information? Why or why not?

5. What are the primary means of transporting goods into your community (rail, air, highway, and so on)? How does the availability of a means of distribution affect the products sold in your area? Do these factors create special problems for independent business owners?

6. Complete the checklist in Exhibit 18.2.

Exhibit 18.2
EVALUATING YOUR CHANNELS OF DISTRIBUTION AND LOGISTICS

The purpose of this questionnaire is to enable you and your management to determine whether your channels of distribution and logistics are economic and effective.

1. Do your channels of distribution meet the needs of your firm?   Yes _____
   No _____

2. Do you use different channels of distribution for your new products than for your well-established products?   Yes _____   No _____

3. Are you aware that changes in buying locations may dictate a change in marketing channels?
   Yes _____   No _____

4. In determining whether changes in marketing channels are necessary, do you examine the following indicators?
   a. Shifts in the types of sources from which consumers buy   Yes _____
      No _____

b. The development of new needs relative to service or parts   Yes _____

No _____

c. Changes in the amount of the distributors' profits   Yes _____

No _____

d. Changes in the policies and activities of outlets   Yes _____   No _____

e. Changes in your organization   Yes _____   No _____

f. New objectives concerning customers and marketing areas   Yes _____

No _____

g. New products   Yes _____   No _____

h. Changes in competitors' distribution plans   Yes _____   No _____

5. Have you established a distribution plan that includes these factors?

a. Geographic markets and consumer types arranged in order of importance

Yes _____   No _____

b. Coverage through

(1) Many outlets   Yes _____   No _____

(2) Selected outlets   Yes _____   No _____

(3) Exclusive distributors   Yes _____   No _____

c. The kind and amount of marketing effort expected of each outlet   Yes _____

No _____

d. Policy statements concerning areas of conflict   Yes _____   No _____

e. Provision for feedback information   Yes _____   No _____

f. Adequate incentives to motivate resellers?   Yes _____   No

6. Have you decided whether to ship directly from the factory or to establish regional warehouses?

Yes _____   No _____

7. Do your outlets cooperate with you on product promotion?   Yes _____

No _____

8. Have you arranged cooperative advertising with your dealers to share promotion costs?

Yes _____   No _____

9. Have you specified criteria for the selection of outlets and applied them?   Yes _____

No _____

10. What are those criteria?

_____

_____

_____

_____

MANAGING YOUR OPERATIONS

In the next five chapters, we cover several topics of interest to the small business owner or manager. Every business, whether large or small, retail, distribution, service, or manufacturing, can profit greatly by understanding the basic concepts of operations management. A dry cleaner, a service station, a beauty salon, a shoe repair shop, a gift store, a videocassette rental store, a doctor's office, a convenience store, a restaurant, an automobile repair shop, and a car wash have an operations function. Few people working or managing these small businesses have been educated in how to manage the operations in these businesses. One set of skills is required to be a beautician or a cook or a mechanic or a clerk in a small business. A completely different set of skills is required to manage the operations function of one of these businesses. If, however, you understand basic operations principles, these principles can be applied to almost any operations activities in any size or kind of business.

Few small business texts treat the operations function in enough depth to provide students the ability to apply what they read to actual small businesses. This text is different. We have provided enough information in these five chapters for you to use most of the techniques without requiring further information. In those cases where further information might be required, we have provided additional references at the end of the chapter. We feel that understanding the operations function of your business is critical to your business success. This indepth approach has been taken in the accounting and finance areas, the operations area and the personnel area of this book. We have identified those topics within each function we felt were critical to the success of a small business and provided enough information so that you would know how to use the technique in your business.

This how-to approach requires a level of detail that may not suit the format of all small business courses. Instructors and course objectives differ, as do opinions concerning the emphasis and importance of one function versus another. Teachers and practitioners are divided over the importance of the various functions, accounting, finance, marketing, policy, operations and personnel in any business. What is critical to the success of a small business? What are the causes of small business failures? Small businesses succeed and fail for many diverse reasons. Not having enough capital to support operations is the primary reason for business failures, but having excess funds does not ensure business success. Success and failure are the result of different factors, as discussed in Chapters 2 and 3.

This overview is written to provide the instructor and the student an introduction to the topics of each chapter in the operations management section of this book. We hope that you have enough time to read the detailed presentation of each topic within these chapters, but we recognize that time is a serious constraint in every course. We recommend then that you read this overview in detail and then select the chapters and topics within each chapter that you feel appropriate for your course, balancing the educational value against the time constraints.

Chapter 19
Defining Operations

This chapter explains that developing an operations strategy to support the business strategy is vital to any business. Companies can compete on product characteristics, process characteristics, low cost, high quality, short lead times, delivery as scheduled, flexibility, and field service. The chapter gives examples of firms that compete on each of these competitive advantages. The five chapters on operations management provide techniques to assist you in designing and managing your operations activities so that you can compete on several of these advantages simultaneously. The chapter includes an example of a small business that is competing effectively.

Defining the facility layout is closely related to how you want your small business to compete. Four basic types of layout are described and the advantages and disadvantages of each type discussed. In this manner, you should be able to match the layout types to the competitive edges of your operations strategy. Layout is as important in service operations as in manufacturing. Do you have enough space for customers to unload their purchases at the register? Do you have adequate room for waiters and waitresses to move among tables? Have you overloaded your appointment schedule again? How much "meet the public" space versus "do the work" space is required? What is the best layout for each of these types of space? Several layout guidelines based on volume of business are provided for small businesses.

Industrial engineering techniques have been used to great advantage by small and large manufacturing firms and by large service firms. These same techniques for evaluating your current operations are useful for any small business, including services. The chapter provides a list and description of several useful, easy-to-use techniques. Additionally, three techniques are discussed and illustrated. You should be able to construct and use the flow process chart, the operation process chart, and the flow diagram based upon studying this chapter. The flow process chart is a graphic representation of all of the operations, transportations, inspections, delays, and storages related to making a product or providing a service. This chart is useful in reducing your operations times and distances. The operation process chart is a graphic aid to studying the operations, inspections, time allowances, and materials used in producing a product or service. Such charts are useful in identifying the locations and relationships of work areas for an ideal layout. The flow diagram is a graphic representation of the flow of activities in producing goods or services drawn on your current or proposed layout or floor space diagram. The flow diagram is another graphic aid invaluable in making your physical facilities as efficient as possible.

The just-in-time philosophy is a major reason behind the Japanese successes in manufacturing in recent years. This philosophy, aimed at eliminating all waste, is applicable to small manufacturers and service firms. In fact, many of the elements of JIT are present in service operations. Do not underestimate the power of these concepts—they will allow you to compete more effectively at lower costs. Twelve elements of JIT are layout, management commitment, focused factory, level schedule, a Kanban system, setup reduction, reduced lot sizes, supplier involvement, multiskilled workers, quality circles, workplace organization, preventive maintenance, and statistical process control. Each element is described and a few applications to small service businesses are provided.

Chapter 20
Managing Operations

The proper management of your scarce resources is essential to meeting the needs of your customers at a reasonable cost. Estimating the demand for your product or service, or forecasting, is vital to planning your resources: manpower, equipment, materials, and capital. Forecasting is the first step in managing operations. Forecasting can be quick and simple to understand. A step-by-step graphic approach to constructing a forecast is given. Additionally, a couple of forecasting methods and ways to check your forecast accuracy are provided. Simple exponential smoothing is illustrated through an example.

Once an estimate of the demand for your products or services has been developed, planning and controlling of priorities and capacities must be undertaken. Priority planning is the process of determining the sequence of working on items. Capacity planning is the process of determining the amount of work to be done and the amount of work that can be done given your resources. Priority control is the process of comparing the planned sequence to the actual sequence of work and taking corrective action. Capacity control is the process of comparing the planned amount of work to the actual amount of work and taking corrective action. A proper understanding of these four functions is important to any service organization. Each of these four functions is described in detail through an example of planning and controlling a simple service operation. How to use a Gantt chart to plan and control priorities and capacities is explained.

Managing operations in a small manufacturing firm adds the need for a fifth planning and control function, master scheduling. Planning the finished products is the first function to be executed. The remaining four functions previously listed are also required in manufacturing but apply to managing the products. This type of management system, called material requirements planning (MRP), allows you to coordinate your material and capacity requirements to customer orders. Its popularity with small manufacturers has increased tremendously over the last five years with the development of powerful inexpensive microcomputers and software.

Like the just-in-time philosophy, the synchronized manufacturing philosophy is a revolutionary approach to managing your business that focuses on scheduling the constraint. The chapter outlines its basic philosophy and principles. Statistical fluctuations and dependent events are defined and methods of preventing Murphy's law from disrupting your operations are listed. These concepts and principles are new and easy to implement in any operation. You should be able to increase your small business skills significantly with an understanding of this new approach to focusing your energies at the control points or constraints to your business.

Chapter 21
Managing Inventory

Inventory management consists of developing, implementing and administering inventory procedures, policies, and systems. In many businesses, material costs are over 60 percent of the product cost. Inventory is an idle resource at best and a liability at worst; inventory levels should be the result of conscious decisions and not poor planning. Inventory is defined as having the right item at the right place at the right time. Anything else is considered a waste and therefore a misuse of your resources. Too much inventory can tie up your money with no financial return and too little inventory can cost you sales and customers.

Several new inventory concepts are presented with respect to developing a strategy for making your small business a fierce competitor. Our major emphasis, however, is to instill in you a proactive attitude to managing your inventory. Operations and inventory are inseparable; you cannot manage one effectively without managing the other effectively. Inventory located in the right place is a strategic weapon that can produce competitive advantages. Inventory in the wrong place is worse than no inventory.

The types of inventory in service and manufacturing organizations are lot size or cycle inventory, fluctuation inventory, pipeline inventory, and anticipation inventory. Costs are associated with each of these types. The more efficiently you manage the inventory, the less the inventory costs. Shortcomings of using the traditional economic order quantity are identified. The use of time buffers is discussed as an alternative inventory ordering policy. A time buffer is an amount of inventory equal to the demand for the item to cover a given time period. A series of questions are provided to assist you in identifying the amount of inventory investment required for each of your inventory items.

The chapter describes ABC analysis, a method of focusing your attention on the planning and controlling of the vital few inventory items that contribute most to your success. Usually 10 percent of your inventory can account for over 50 percent of your inventory investment. These items are classified as A items. Identifying these vital few items is essential to improving your inventory position at little to no cost. How to conduct an ABC analysis and how to plan and control each class of inventory are described and illustrated. Many other important uses of ABC analysis are provided for the small business owner.

Methods of improving your inventory accuracy are described. Cycle counting is an effective alternative to taking physical inventories and provides numerous additional benefits. The logic of using random and control cycle counting groups is explained in addition to steps in implementing each of them. Random group cycle counting improves inventory accuracy, thus allowing you to carry less inventory. In contrast, control group cycle counting is effective at identifying the causes of inventory errors.

The periodic review method, the perpetual inventory methods, the two-bin system, and the time-phased order point method are four important inventory methods. The first two methods (periodic review method and the perpetual inventory method) are commonly used, but may not be the most effective inventory management methods for a small business. The two-bin system and time-phased order point method may be far more appropriate for your small business needs. The two-bin system offers the simplicity of visual identification of inventory needs. The time-phased order point system offers the advantage of consolidating inventory needs from the same vendor to save on shipping and handling costs and provides you the ability to manage seasonal demand inventory items.

Chapter 22
Planning Information Needs

Many people confuse information systems with computer systems, but many good information systems are manual. A measure of the value of the information system is how well it supports the objectives of your business. Prior to purchasing any information system software, you should evaluate the functional activities and supporting policies and procedures to determine whether the activities are necessary, are properly integrated into the overall business activities, and can be improved prior to computerization. In most cases, businesses assume that their problems will be solved by buying a software package and a computer. The results are that the problems are usually only magnified by providing you with incorrect information faster than before.

The rule is to simplify and standardize prior to automating or computerizing.

Applications in each of the functional areas are described. Remember in selecting any specialized information system software that the overall business objective is to have an effective organization. The objective is not to have an effective specialized application unless the overall organization benefits. Simple marketing, accounting, finance, personnel and human resources, and operations information systems are described.

Problems in implementing information systems can be classified as ineffective operations and supporting activities; ineffective policies and procedures to support the operations and supporting activities; lack of top management commitment and involvement; technical problems; and human relations problems. We have provided guidance in solving each type of problem.

The chapter concludes with a brief review of considerations involved in computer purchases. Our advice to you is not hardware or software specific. You should review computer magazines and industry and trade magazines for new applications and commercial software prior to investing in either software or hardware. Experts agree that computer system decisions should be based on software and not hardware capabilities. What applications would be profitable for you to computerize? Computer costs include the hardware, the software, and the personnel education and training to operate the system. Check with several vendors prior to purchasing software and hardware. Compare the advantages and disadvantages of each product, vendor support requirements, and education and training required. Do not underestimate these costs. The computer is only a tool and must be used correctly and in the right applications to provide competitive advantages to your business.

Chapter 23
Controlling Operations

Planning and controlling are as vital to small businesses as to large businesses. Control requires a performance measurement system to ensure that progress is being made toward your business goals. Performance measures for each of your business's competitive advantages are required. It makes no sense to identify competitive advantages unless you are going to track your progress on them and on profit. Identify your competitive advantages, set a target level, and set limits around the target. Measure your actual performance. Compare your performance to the target and limits. If your performance is outside of the limits, identify the cause and take appropriate actions. An example of setting and measuring short- and long-term goals on profit for a small business is discussed. Differences between controlling operations in manufacturing and services are discussed. Generally, services cannot be inventoried, quality is subjective, lead times are short, customer contact is high, facilities are small, labor is intensive, and markets are local. Many of these service characteristics are present in small manufacturers also.

Product, process, low cost, high quality, short lead times, delivery as scheduled, and flexibility are competitive advantages that require performance measurement. To achieve your goals, you should also apply performance measures to the inputs, transformation processes, and outputs of your operations functions. Methods of effectively using and measuring these resources to reach your organization goals are provided. The objective is not to have effective use of one resource, but to combine the use of your resources in meeting customer expectations while making a profit. Guidelines for designing an efficient production system and an effective performance measurement system are provided.

Summary of Operations Management

A good understanding of operations management is required to manage a profitable small business, no matter what the industry. In the past, operations management was taught as a set of techniques and areas. Today, with competition intensifying across all fronts, this approach is inappropriate, particularly in a small business. In a small business, you can see how poor decisions in one area have impact on other areas much more quickly and more dramatically. A small business manager must be able to evaluate the impact of decisions in marketing, sales, personnel, finance, and other areas on operations, and conversely the decisions made in the operations area on the other functions.

C H A P T E R   1 9

DEFINING OPERATIONS

Operations management is the planning and control of the activities required to transform inputs into products or services. Every organization, whether a bakery, drycleaner, department store, appliance repair shop, or dentist's office, has an operations function. Defining operations means formulating an operations strategy and selecting the best methods of combining company resources (facilities, machinery, materials, workers, and managers) to carry out this strategy. In this chapter, we discuss the basic types of layouts and their relationship to the volume of goods or services produced. We also discuss industrial engineering (IE) techniques to help you determine the best layout for your facility. These IE techniques are fundamental to analyzing and improving the flow of materials or customers. You will find these techniques critically important in implementing your operations strategy. We also describe a manufacturing philosophy that provides you, the small business owner, with a perspective on how to define, organize, and manage your operations effectively. The just-in-time (JIT) philosophy provides several useful concepts and techniques for the small business.

After reading this chapter, you will be able to

- Develop an operations strategy that combines two or more competitive advantages
- Describe the basic types of layout and identify when each type should be used
- Identify how to use three basic industrial engineering techniques to analyze and improve operations within your small business
- Explain the basic components of the just-in-time philosophy and how they might be used to make your small business more competitive

Developing Operations Strategies

In the past, companies have selected their business strategy based on one of the following competitive advantages:

- Product
- Process

- Low cost
- High quality
- Short lead time
- Delivery as scheduled
- Flexibility
- Field service

Many companies have developed an operations strategy around one overriding competitive advantage and been very successful. The fast-food industry provides examples of several well-known companies that illustrate the use of these various strategies. Hardee's promotes charbroiled hamburgers (product and process). Krystal sells four of its Krystal burgers for one dollar (low cost). Wendy's advertises high quality and seldom competes on price (quality). McDonald's competes by providing its offerings without waiting (short lead time). Domino's competes by guaranteeing delivery in 30 minutes or less or you get a discount on your pizza (delivery as scheduled). Burger King emphasizes product flexibility with its advertising slogan "Have it your way." Each company emphasizes a different competitive advantage in its business strategy.

This strategy affects more than marketing, however. The strategy also dictates the type of layout, the type of equipment, the worker skills required, the scheduling policy, and the proper location of inventory.

The Grill, a small independent restaurant in Athens, Georgia, illustrates how several competitive advantages can be used simultaneously. The Grill is noted for its large homemade-style hamburgers made from Grade A meat. This hamburger is slightly more expensive than a hamburger at a fast-food restaurant. During the lunch hour, the owner of the Grill stands in front of the restaurant taking patrons' orders and estimating the time until a table will be vacant. The restaurant is very competitive with fast-food restaurants in terms of time spent waiting. Patrons do not feel as if they are wasting time because they can place their orders before entering. Further, when they depart the restaurant, the owner is still standing outside the entrance, thanking them for their patronage. Based on the volume of business normally handled during lunch, the Grill starts cooking hamburgers ahead of the actual receipt of orders to decrease the lead time in preparing your lunch.

The Grill has formulated its operations strategy to capitalize on several competitive edges—product (homemade-style hamburgers), quality (Grade A meat), short lead time (by taking orders immediately and cooking hamburgers continually during lunch hour), delivery as scheduled (the owner's estimate of seating times), and flexibility (hamburgers prepared to order in no extra time). The Grill provides an excellent example of how a small business can compete effectively using several competitive edges.

You, as a small business owner, should examine your operations strategy to identify how you might be able to compete successfully by utilizing your resources more effectively. You can also take advantage of being a small business by getting to know your customers better and being more responsive to their needs.

Taking lunch orders at The Grill.

Defining the Facility Layout

Defining the facility layout is deciding on the physical arrangement of equipment, workers, and materials to make a product or service. Layout decisions are based on your competitive edges and the volume and characteristics of your products or services. The four basic types of layout are illustrated in Exhibit 19.1. The fixed position layout is a physical arrangement in which the object or service is stationary and the workers move to the site to perform their activities. It is used to manufacture large objects. Construction projects such as houses, malls, bridges, and dams are classic examples. A restaurant in which you are seated at a table where a waitress takes your order, serves your meal, delivers your bill, and takes your payment provides a service industry example of a fixed position layout.

The process or functional layout is an arrangement in which similar equipment is located in the same areas or department. Facilities where small quantities of a variety of products or services are produced usually have equipment arranged by function. Using a functional arrangement, a small machine shop would locate lathes in one department, mill machines in another, and drill presses in still another. As shown in this portion of the figure, parts 1 and 2 flow through several departments and are assembled to make product A. The kitchen layout in a restaurant is usually a process layout—dishwashing in one area, cooking in another, salad preparation in another, and so on.

As the volume of a product or service increases, the business must reduce the distances that the product or service must travel and the amount of handling. A product layout is arranged to facilitate the fabrication and assembly of high-volume products by placing the equipment according to the sequence of

Exhibit 19.1
BASIC TYPES OF LAYOUT

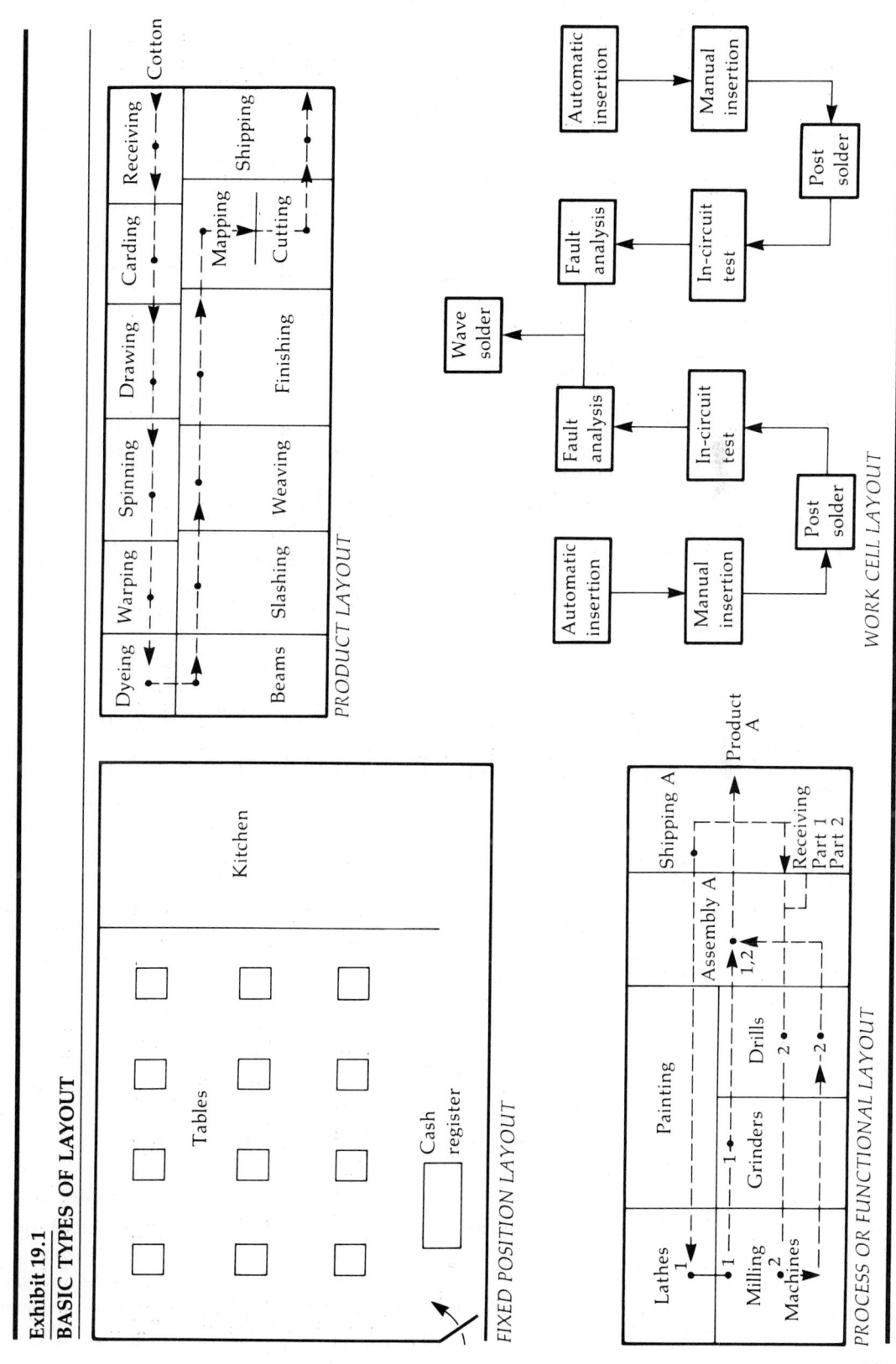

operations required to create the product or service. An automobile assembly line provides the classic example of a product layout. The serving line of a cafeteria represents an example of a product layout in a service environment.

A cellular layout is similar to a product layout. If you make a large number of parts that require the same sequence of operation, you can place equipment to perform these operations next to each other to reduce travel distances, handling, and lead time. This cluster of equipment, called a *cell*, consists of different machines required to process families of parts. Cells may exist with another type of layout to take advantage of grouping machines in a high-volume parts flow arrangement.

Several general relationships exist in designing a layout:

- Different layouts can be used within the same facility depending on the volume and size of parts and the sequence of operations.
- The larger the size of the product or more complex the service, the more desirable a fixed position layout.
- The more varied the sequence of activities, the more desirable a functional layout.
- The higher the volume of a product, the more desirable a product layout.
- The higher the volume of a group of similar parts or a given sequence of operations, the more desirable a cellular layout for these operations.

Industrial Engineering Techniques

Several industrial engineering (IE) techniques are easy to learn and useful to a small business. Exhibit 19.2 provides a list of IE techniques with brief descriptions. The flow process chart, operation process chart, and flow diagram are quite useful in designing or revising a layout. We describe these techniques in detail to assist you in evaluating your layout to improve overall productivity. These charts provide you with a shorthand standardized method to record a brief but detailed description of a process. It is essential that you study the chart and learn to use these techniques to identify and eliminate problems.

The flow process chart is a graphic representation of all the operations, transportations, inspections, delays, and storages occurring during a process or procedure related to one part of a product or service. The symbols and definitions for each of these activities are provided below.

- *Operation:* a circle (three-eighths of an inch in size) indicates a task such as typing a letter, entering a sale on a cash register, tightening a bolt, or wrapping a package.
- *Transportation:* an arrow indicates movement, whether by conveyor, forklift, or worker.
- *Inspection:* a square (three-eighths of an inch in size) indicates an inspection, such as proofreading a letter, reading a gauge or dial, or examining a part for a defect.
- *Delay:* a large capital D indicates a delay, such as a letter waiting to be mailed or filed, a customer order awaiting pickup, or a part waiting to be processed.

Exhibit 19.2
USEFUL IE TOOLS FOR THE SMALL BUSINESS

- *Flow process chart:* lists the sequence of operations, movements, storages, delays, and inspections encountered by a part or item as it goes through the process; shows the details of one item or part
- *Operation process chart:* lists the sequence of operations, time allowances, and materials used in a manufacturing or service process from delivery of raw material to shipment of finished good; shows the flow of parts in making a product
- *Flow diagram:* a pictorial representation of the building layout providing the location of all operations; useful in eliminating backtracking and identifying poor layouts
- *Travel chart:* a table showing the volume of material flowing from one department to another, useful in examining materials handling and layout problems in process layouts
- *Motion economy:* twenty-one guidelines to assist in improving the use of the human body, the layout of the workplace, and the design of equipment and tools in developing work methods
- *Man and machine process chart:* lists the time relationship between the worker and machine, useful in analyzing one worker and one or more machines
- *Gang process chart:* shows the time relationships (idle and operating) of a number of workers to the operation of one machine, useful in reducing the workers' and machine's idle times
- *Line balancing:* an approach to determining the number of workers required to work an assembly line for a given volume of production
- *Operator process chart:* (also called a *left-hand, right-hand process chart*): shows the relationship between the hands and performing work, movements, and delays, useful for analyzing and improving highly repetitive work activities
- *Time study:* an approach to recording the elements of and times for performing an operation, useful in setting a production standard and improving an operation

- *Storage:* an inverted triangle indicates an item in storage such as a letter in a document file, chemicals stored in a tank, or a product in finished goods inventory awaiting a customer order.

The flow process chart is useful to you in helping identify ways to reduce the time taken to make a part by analyzing the time and distance associated with each activity. Exhibit 19.3 shows such a chart for the movement of patients through a doctor's office. From examining the amount of time the patient spends at the office, you probably agree that room for improvement exists. Of the 51 minutes spent in the office, 15 minutes are used in productive activities (signing in, filling out insurance forms, having blood pressure and temperature taken, being examined by the doctor, and paying the bill), 1 minute in inspection, and 35 minutes in waiting. After studying these activities, the doctor could reduce or eliminate the delays, reduce the distances traveled between operations, and combine or eliminate operations.

The operation process chart is a graphic technique that shows the chronological sequence of all operations, inspections, time allowances, and materials

Exhibit 19.3
FLOW PROCESS CHART OF PATIENT PROCESSING IN DOCTOR'S OFFICE

FLOW PROCESS CHART

Present method: _____√_____   Date: 12/5/91

Proposed method: _____   Charted by: JFC

Subject: Patient processing from entering to leaving office

Symbol	Distance or Time	Brief Description
→	20'	Enter office and go to receptionist
O	1 m	Sign in
D	5 m	Wait
O	5 m	Fill out insurance forms
D	15 m	Wait
→	30'	Go to examining room
O	5 m	Blood pressure, temperature, etc.
D	15 m	Wait for doctor
O	3 m	Examination by doctor
→	20'	Go to pay bill
□	1 m	Inspect bill
O	1 m	Pay bill
→	45'	Leave office

m = Minute
' = Feet

used in producing a good or service from the ordering of each raw material to the delivery of the finished good or service to the customer. In constructing the operation process chart, a circle is used to denote an operation and a square to denote an inspection. (The symbols are drawn at three-eighths of an inch in size.) An operation takes place when the part is intentionally transformed. An inspection takes place when the part is examined to determine its conformity to standard. The operation process chart indicates the flow of all components entering into a product. Such charts of the primary products or services are invaluable in identifying the location of work centers for an ideal plant layout. An example of the use of this charting technique by a small manufacturer of jackets is provided in Exhibit 19.4.

In studying the operation sequences of manufacturing the jackets, you might ascertain whether the volume of jackets produced would support dedicating four sewing machines to this product line for a period of time. You could then set a flow line for sewing the zipper, sewing the lining, sewing the sleeves, and sewing the sleeves to the jacket. In laying out your facility in this manner, you can complete an operation on the jacket and pass it to the next worker to perform the next task. By overlapping these sewing processes, you can reduce lead time (the time it takes to make the jacket), decrease work-in-process inventory, and improve quality.

Exhibit 19.4

**OPERATION PROCESS CHART FOR THE MANUFACTURE OF
A WINDBREAKER JACKET**

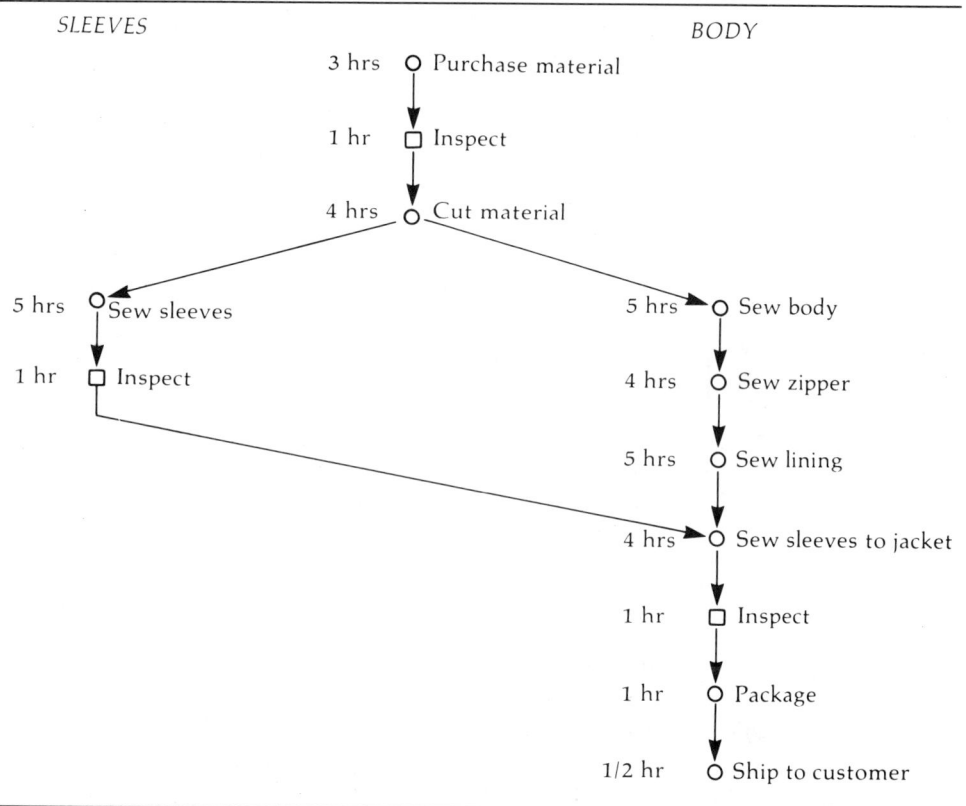

The flow diagram is a pictorial representation of the current or proposed layout of a facility superimposed with the sequence of operations associated with producing a good or service. This tool can assist you in examining the distance that materials must travel between operations to improve the efficiency of a layout. The flow diagram of a mail-order distribution center is provided in Exhibit 19.5. This layout is quite efficient in that material paths do not cross and the distances between consecutive operations are small.

These charting techniques are helpful in deciding how to organize your facilities to make your business more productive. In analyzing your completed charts, question the existence of each activity to ensure that it is essential to producing your good or service. Your objective is to make the total operation more productive. You should eliminate unnecessary operations, reduce others to the smallest amount of time necessary, and combine others to improve the overall production process; you can make these operational refinements whether you run a manufacturing or service firm. This objective will become more apparent when you become familiar with the JIT philosophy.

Exhibit 19.5
FLOW DIAGRAM OF PROPOSED LAYOUT OF A MAIL-ORDER
DISTRIBUTION CENTER

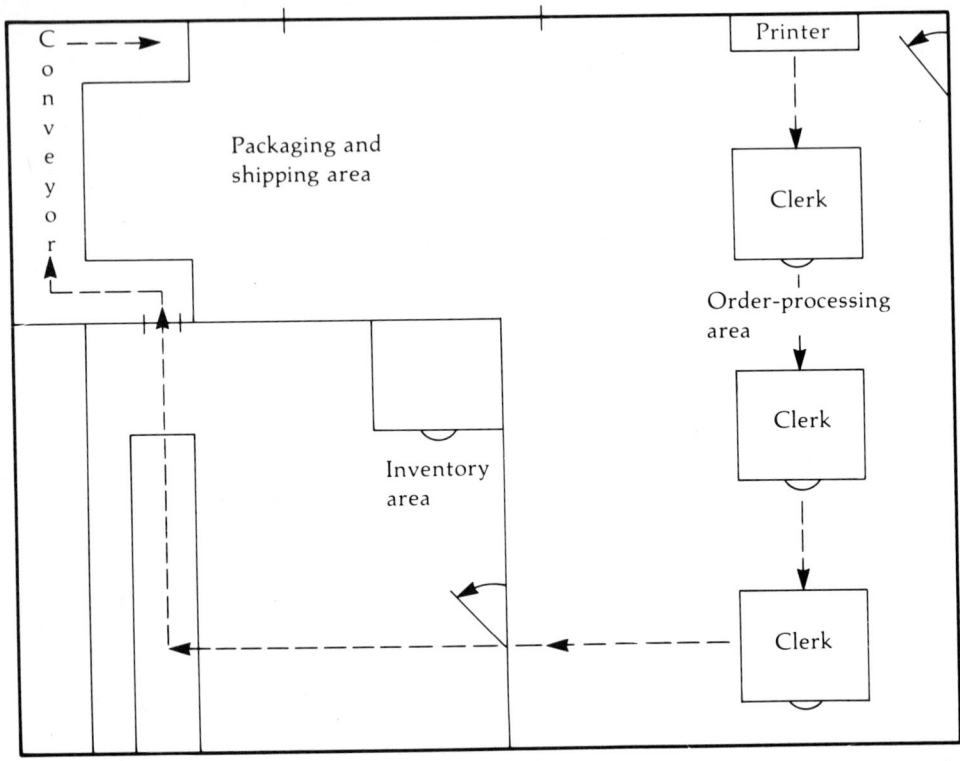

Just-in-Time Philosophy

Just-in-time (JIT) is a comprehensive management philosophy based on the elimination of waste and the continuous improvement of quality, reliability, delivery, products and processes. Waste includes idle inventory. Many U.S. manufacturers, both large and small, are implementing the JIT philosophy to become more competitive. This philosophy can also be implemented in many service operations. The benefits of implementing JIT are reduced lead time, higher quality, more responsiveness to customer needs, less floor space required, lower inventories, and increased worker involvement. Many of the components of the JIT philosophy were originally developed in the United States (in fact, some components were discussed in Henry Ford's book *Today and Tomorrow* in 1926), but the Japanese are credited with combining the components into a comprehensive management philosophy. As practiced today, JIT has thirteen components:

1. Layout
2. Management commitment

   3. Focused factory
   4. Level schedule
   5. Kanban system
   6. Setup reduction
   7. Reduced lot sizes
   8. Supplier involvement
   9. Multiskilled workers
  10. Quality circles
  11. Workplace organization
  12. Preventive maintenance
  13. Statistical process control

Developing an effective layout is essential to promoting product or service flow using the JIT philosophy. The objective of developing the layout is to evolve to using product and cellular formats. As material storage requirements and handling movements are reduced, plant layout revisions are required. The product and cellular layouts reduce the time required for materials handling.

Management commitment is essential for successful implementation of any management system. Commitment means that managers are educated in the nature of the system they want implemented, actively involved in bringing about the implementation, and interested and concerned about the impact the system will have on workers.

A focused factory is a facility that is dedicated to producing a limited product or service line. By definition, a focus on the production of a limited product or service line narrows the set of management goals, therefore promoting overall productivity by eliminating conflicting goals. Many small manufacturers—such as makers of boat cushions, car mats, and so on—are focused factories. Drycleaners and carburetor repair shops are examples of focused service firms.

Level scheduling refers to producing a day's worth of demand each day. Many restaurants, particularly cafeterias, operate in this manner. Both large and small manufacturers, however, make large batches of parts and products to utilize equipment and workers in what they think is an efficient way. Level scheduling is initially impossible in most manufacturing settings and can only be accomplished through reduction of equipment setup times, use of small lot sizes, and improvements to the process. Level scheduling allows the facility to be responsive to market and customer demand without storing large amounts of raw materials, work-in-process, and finished goods inventories. A level schedule generates uniform work loads on the work centers within the facility.

The Kanban system is a method of synchronizing the manufacturing steps and movement of parts through the work centers of a plant to ensure high quality, short lead times, and a minimum of inventory. It is a pull production system based on meeting each day's production schedule by pulling the exact amounts of parts through the various work centers to meet the product schedule. Cards, standardized containers, or even a square painted on the floor may be used to signal to a worker that it is time for him or her to produce one container of parts. This system ensures no excess work-in-process inventory and just enough of each part in the assembly areas to meet the day's schedule. Workers, when not authorized to produce parts, conduct preventive maintenance, practice setting up equipment, help other workers, or move to another work center.

Kanban systems are appropriate for repetitive operations environments. Some small manufacturers have a limited product line; for them, a Kanban system would be beneficial in reducing work-in-process inventory. The flow of materials and Kanbans is illustrated in Exhibit 19.6. Parts flow from WC1 (work center 1) to WC2 once WC2 provides the signal—an empty container and card. No work can be performed at WC1 until this authorization is provided. After a container of parts is completed at WC1, it remains there until the worker at WC2 brings an empty container and card and swaps them for the full container. WC2's output is based on the usage of parts in the final assembly area. When parts are consumed in making the day's production schedule, the empty container and appropriate card are carried to WC2 and swapped for a full container. In this manner, each work center's output is based on the succeeding work center's needs.

Setup time reduction is critical to the smooth flow of parts throughout a facility. Setup time is the time between finishing the last part of one order and starting the first part of the next. In other words, it is the time taken to prepare the equipment for the next order to be produced. Long setup times disrupt the smooth flow of parts through a facility and cause workers at other work centers to wait for an authorization to work (the Kanban signal).

Exhibit 19.6
SINGLE CARD KANBAN SYSTEM

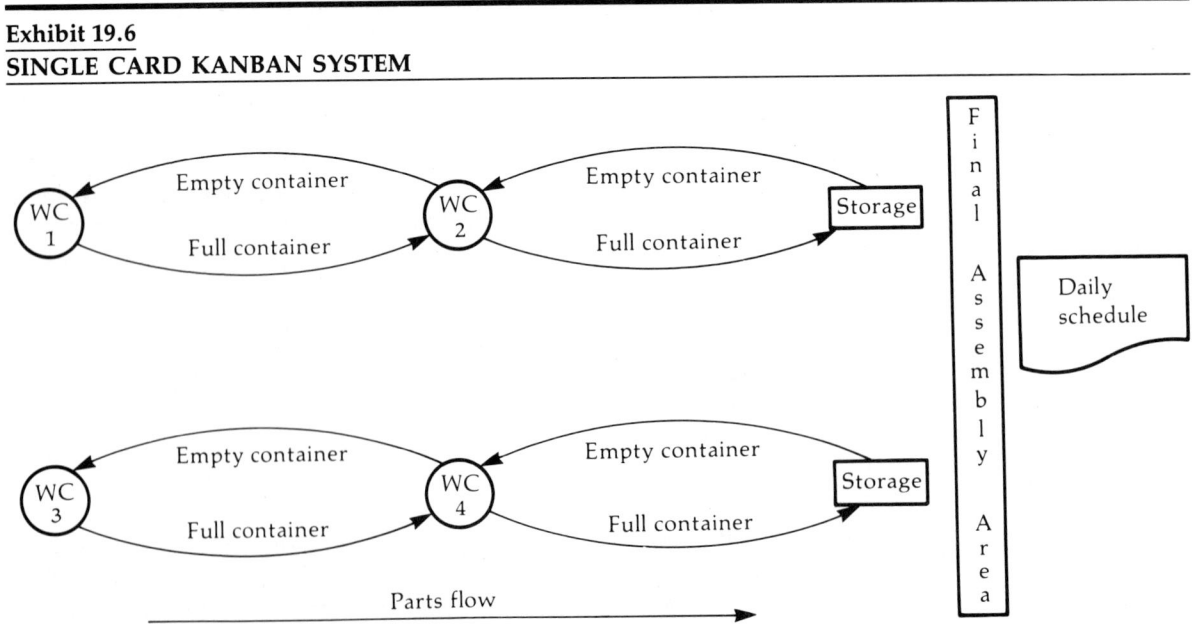

The Japanese use four approaches to reducing setup times. These approaches are based on separating the internal time and the external time associated with equipment setup. Internal time is time devoted to setup while the machine has to be idle; external time is time devoted to setup while the machine could be busy. The first approach to setup reduction is to restructure steps performed during internal time to be performed during external times; this switch is achieved by performing the steps while the machine is operating. The second approach is to convert internal setup time to external time. The third approach is to reduce or completely eliminate the machine adjustment stage. The fourth approach is to standardize parts across and within products and product lines to decrease the number of setups.

The copier operations of a small local copy shop provide an excellent illustration of the four approaches to setup reduction. In operating the copier, a worker performs the following eight steps:

1. Removes the completed order from the copier
2. Carries the order to the table and checks it
3. Gets the next order and carries it to the copier
4. Places the master on the copier and sets the paper size
5. Runs a copy to test the placement of the master on the machine
6. Sets the copier to the appropriate quantity
7. Starts the copier
8. Goes to the table and moves the previous order to the counter

Steps 1 through 7 are currently internal since the copier is idle; step 8 is external since the copier is busy. Using the first approach, a document feeder can be attached to the machine; by allowing automatic feeding of the copier, step 4 is converted from internal to external time. Step 2 can be converted to external time as well by moving it to follow step 8; while the copier runs a second job, the worker can inspect the first. Using the third approach, lines can be drawn on the copier screen to virtually eliminate the adjustment and inspection setup steps (steps 5 and 6). Using the fourth approach, the operator can run only 8-1/2-by-11-inch paper on this copier to eliminate the down time associated with changing the copy size (a partial elimination of step 4). The remaining steps (1, 6, and 7) are performed during internal setup time.

Reduced lot sizes are critical to maintaining parts flow in a JIT environment. They are realistic only after setup reductions have been implemented, however. Small lot sizes encourage workers to identify and eliminate quality problems, are essential to reducing lead times, and provide synchronization of work centers.

Supplier involvement is essential to reducing raw materials inventory levels. Many firms work closely with suppliers to ensure that raw materials deliveries are synchronized with needs at the initial work centers. Suppliers are provided fairly stable manufacturing schedules in advance and are expected to supply parts in short lead times. This is only possible through close cooperation of both parties. In Japan, most companies use only a small number of suppliers and work closely on parts design, product design, and process and quality. Both parties see the relationship as a long-term commitment. A small business can reduce its number of suppliers and consolidate its orders to increase its purchasing power and influence with the remaining suppliers.

Multiskilled workers are a major component of the JIT philosophy. Under JIT, workers are encouraged to cross-train on other jobs throughout the facility so that they become capable of performing adequately at several different operations. Workers are given responsibility for inspecting their work and conducting preventive maintenance on their equipment. A multiskilled workforce provides complete flexibility in assigning workers to maintain parts flow through the facility and prevents disruptions caused by worker absenteeism and turnover or equipment breakdown. Most small manufacturers expect workers to be able to operate several different types of equipment.

Quality circles, sometimes called productivity improvement groups, are groups of six to ten employees from the same work area that meet voluntarily to identify and solve problems related to productivity and quality. Workers, trained in productivity, quality, and problem-solving techniques, meet 1 hour a week to work on a specific problem area. These small group improvement activities allow the worker to contribute to the work environment and provide management with a wealth of knowledge and skill. Small businesses, both manufacturing and service, could benefit greatly by implementing quality circles to capture the knowledge, creativity, and experience that their workers possess. Another advantage of such practice is that participation in job-related decisions can help increase employee commitment to work.

Workplace organization means designing the individual worker methods and arranging tools and machinery to support the worker involvement in producing a good or service. Many of the IE tools listed in Exhibit 19.2 are quite useful in organizing the workplace. The emphasis in the JIT philosophy, however, is on the continuous flow of parts through the production system and not necessarily on the most efficient worker method.

Preventive maintenance is essential to the proper operation of equipment, whether a cash register, computer, typewriter, copy machine, or a drill press. In a JIT environment, machine breakdowns disrupt production because work-in-process inventories are low. When scheduling workers and equipment to manufacture parts or provide a service, you must, therefore, allow time to perform proper equipment maintenance. Workers should be actively involved in and responsible for conducting preventive maintenance on their own equipment. Equipment should be inspected and tested at the end and beginning of each shift. For example, a copier's toner container and paper tray should be refilled, its glass cleaned, and the paper path checked to ensure that there is no paper jam. Workers should be told to report equipment problems immediately to ensure the continuous flow of parts through the facility.

Quality parts and products are critical to operating effectively using the JIT philosophy. Statistical process control is used to ensure that manufacturing processes are producing quality parts. (Some elementary statistical process control techniques are provided in Chapter 23.) Your workers, not inspectors, are responsible for quality and should, therefore, be trained in elementary quality control and problem-solving techniques. Quality has to be built into a product; it cannot be achieved by inspection. Workers should understand their role in making a defect-free part.

Although you may not be able to implement all components of the JIT philosophy, several can easily be implemented in a small business. Each of these components offers considerable benefits.

Summary

Operations management, the planning and control of the activities that a business requires to transform inputs into products or services, is a vital area of concern to small businesses of all types. The best operations managers aim to structure operations so as to support the business's competitive advantages, which can be defined as any combination of eight key factors.

A central feature of operations management is the facility layout, which takes one of four basic types: fixed position layout, process or functional layout, product layout, or cellular layout. Each type has advantages and disadvantages; all can be used for producers of either goods or services.

Industrial engineering (IE) techniques can be used to analyze operations and devise the most efficient methods. Among the key IE techniques are the flow process chart, the operation process chart, and the flow diagram. Each of these techniques can be used to represent an operational flow visually so as to facilitate finding the optimal way to organize production.

A new view of operations, the just-in-time (JIT) philosophy, is being adopted in the United States from Japan. The central focus of JIT is the elimination of waste through an emphasis on quality and reliability. Implementing the JIT system means addressing such issues as layout, the commitment of management to the new program, developing workers to possess many skills, and preventive maintenance. A major focus of the JIT philosophy is to reduce the amount of inventory.

Class Assignments

1. Visit three restaurants such as Pizza Hut, Domino's Pizza, and a local pizza parlor. Compare and contrast their operations strategy and facilities layout. Write a brief report discussing the competitive edges used in their advertisements and how their layout relates to their strategy. How does the local pizza parlor differ from the national chains?

2. Visit three auto repair operations such as Minit Lube, Goodyear Automotive, and a local auto service shop. Compare and contrast their operations strategy and facilities layout. Write a brief report discussing the competitive edges used in their advertisements and how their layout relates to their strategy. In what ways does the local repair shop differ from the national chains?

3. Compare and contrast operations strategies and layouts for a traditional independent and national chain service station with both a self-service operation and a full-service operation.

4. Identify the layout of a barber shop, beauty salon, dentist office, fast-food restaurant, drycleaners, automobile repair shop, supermarket, and hardware store. Discuss the possible operations strategies open to each business.

5. Construct an operation process chart of a student registering for classes at your school. Evaluate the registration process based on reducing student time and distance traveled.
6. Select a small business and interview the owner. What JIT components might be easy and hard to apply to this business? Are any of the components of JIT already present? What is the owner's reaction to the use of various JIT components in that industry?

References

Boeder, S. M. "Large System Benefits for the Small Manufacturing Environment." *American Production and Inventory Control Society 29th Annual International Conference Proceedings.* Falls Church, Va.: 1986, pp. 32–36.

Fagan, M. L. "Logistics: A Key Success Factor for Small Manufacturers." *American Production and Inventory Control Society Fall Seminar Proceedings 1986.* Falls Church, Va.: 1986, pp. 312–317.

Finch, B. J. "Japanese Management Techniques in Small Manufacturing Companies: A Strategy for Implementation." *Production and Inventory Management Journal,* 27, No. 3 (Third Quarter 1986), pp. 30–38.

Finch, B. J., and J. F. Cox. "An Examination of Just-in-Time Management for the Small Manufacturer: With an Illustration." *International Journal of Production Research,* 24, No. 3 (March-April 1986), pp. 329–342.

Hall, R. W. *Zero Inventories.* New York: Dow Jones-Irwin, 1983.

"How JIT Works for a Small Manufacturer." *Modern Material Handling,* 41, No. 12 (October 1986), pp. 101–104.

Hutchinson, R. M., and K. S. Wiesenberg. "JIT Success in a Medium-Size, Highly Seasonal Manufacturing Firm." *American Production and Inventory Control Society 30th Annual International Conference Proceedings.* Falls Church, Va.: 1987, pp. 364–367.

Schonberger, R. J. *Japanese Manufacturing Techniques: Nine Hidden Lessons in Simplicity.* New York: Free Press, 1982.

Schonberger, R. J. *World Class Manufacturing: The Lessons of Simplicity Applied.* New York: Free Press, 1986.

Skinner, W. "The Focused Factory." *Harvard Business Review* (May–June 1974), pp. 113–121.

Staughton, R. V. W., M. A. Knight, and A. Younger. "Assisting Small Manufacturing Companies to Implement Advanced Manufacturing Technology." *International Journal of Operations and Production Management,* 6, No. 5 (1986), pp. 38–43.

Strader, B. "JIT and Small Manufacturing." *American Production and Inventory Control Society 30th Annual International Conference Proceedings.* Falls Church Va.: 1987, pp. 335–337.

Wallace, T. F., and J. R. Dougherty, eds. *APICS Dictionary,* 6th ed. Falls Church, Va.: APICS, 1987.

Wantuck, K. "JIT for the Small Manufacturer." *American Production and Inventory Control Society 28th Annual International Conference Proceedings.* Falls Church, Va.: 1985, pp. 466–470.

C H A P T E R 2 0

MANAGING OPERATIONS

In the previous chapter, we discussed selecting the best methods of combining company resources (facilities, machinery, materials, workers, and managers) to produce goods and services. In this chapter, we describe how to manage your service and manufacturing operations effectively. Several concepts and techniques are useful to managing the operations of your small business.

Forecasting the demand for your goods and services is vital to managing your resources effectively. We identify the basic components of demand and present some simple forecasting methods. Most small businesses—and many large businesses—fail to recognize that managing their priority and capacity functions is vital to the success of their business. Priority and capacity planning and control are defined in this chapter, which also provides a framework to assist you in managing your business. A more complex framework, material requirements planning (MRP), is also provided to assist small manufacturers in planning and controlling their operations. Proper management of these functions ensures return business; poor management, on the other hand, ensures lost customers. Finally, we introduce you to a new philosophy, optimized production technology (OPT) or synchronous manufacturing philosophy. OPT consists of nine scheduling principles that focus on streamlining the complete production system by maximizing the use of the bottleneck resource.

After reading this chapter, you will be able to

- Recognize the basic components of demand for your product or service
- Forecast the random demand component and tell how good your forecasting model is
- Develop a framework to assist you in managing priorities and capacities in a simple service environment
- Develop a framework to assist you in managing priorities and capacities in a manufacturing environment
- Describe optimized production technology (OPT), a new approach to managing operations

Forecasting Product and Service Demand

Forecasting is the process of estimating future demand. It can be accomplished using judgment or mathematical techniques or both. If you use mathematical techniques, always review your forecasts for reasonableness, current knowledge, and accuracy.

One of the simplest approaches to forecasting is to examine the demand for your product or service with respect to time. Has the demand increased or decreased over the past week, month, quarter, or year? Models that use time as the independent variable to help predict demand are called time-series models. In time-series models, there are four components of demand:

1. The random or average component, a level or constant pattern
2. The seasonal component, a repetitive pattern that could be hourly, daily, weekly, monthly, or annually
3. The trend, or the general movement upward or downward over time
4. The cyclical component, reflecting a long-term cycle (3 to 5 years)

Demand patterns illustrating each of the four basic components are shown in Exhibit 20.1.

Exhibit 20.1
FOUR BASIC COMPONENTS OF DEMAND

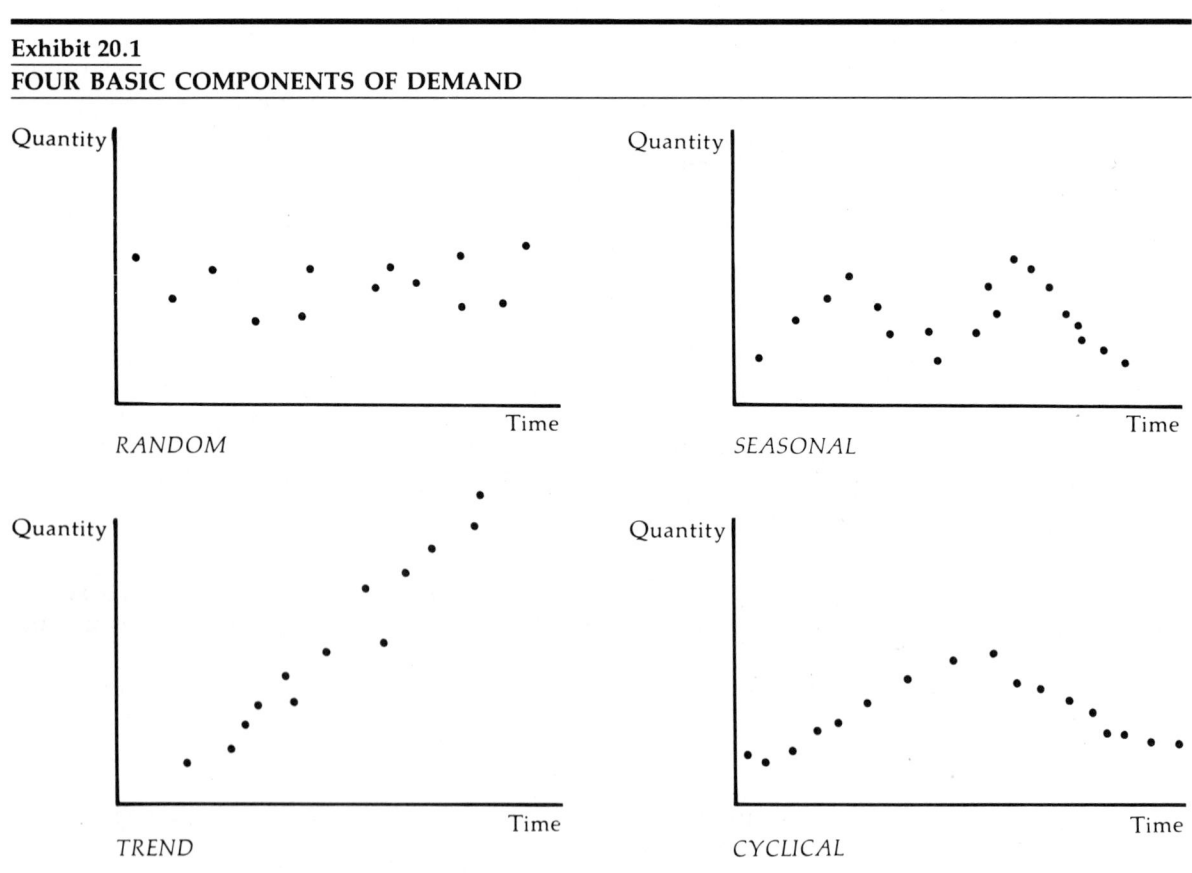

RANDOM   SEASONAL

TREND   CYCLICAL

You do not have to be a mathematician to improve your forecasting ability; you simply need to follow the steps in Exhibit 20.2. The first task is to plot your demand data over a period of time. In step 2, you compare this plot to the patterns in Exhibit 20.1 to identify the components present in your data. In step 3, you select an appropriate model from Exhibit 20.3 to test your data fit. (The exhibit provides a list of forecasting models for each basic demand pattern and some combination patterns.)

While there are literally dozens of different forecasting models, this approach will quickly eliminate most of them from consideration. In step 4, construct a forecasting model using your data. You should add the new data for each period and then forecast demand for the next period. Mathematical complexity does not guarantee good forecasting models. No matter how complex your forecasting model, you should measure its ability to forecast accurately (step 5). Forecasting models should be monitored continuously to ensure their ability to predict future demand. The procedure provided here is simple; sophisticated approaches, of course, identify poor forecasting models more quickly but are beyond the scope of this book.

Let us see an example to illustrate how to identify the type of forecasting model to use on your product. Suppose that you own a small restaurant that emphasizes its luncheon menu. You are having trouble planning purchases and staffing. Following the steps in Exhibit 20.2, you have collected your sales for the past ten week days and plotted them, with the result shown in Exhibit 20.4. You compare your plot to the patterns in Exhibit 20.1 and find that it

---

Exhibit 20.2
STEPS IN CONSTRUCTING A FORECASTING MODEL

1. Plot your demand data with respect to time.
2. Compare your demand pattern to the demand components in Exhibit 20.1 and select the appropriate demand pattern.
3. Using Exhibit 20.3, select an appropriate forecasting method given the pattern you chose.
4. Construct a forecasting model using your data.
5. Compare your forecast to the actual demand to determine how useful the model is. Are you consistently over- or underestimating demand? If so, try another model.

Exhibit 20.3
SELECTED FORECASTING METHODS FOR DEMAND

· *Average:* constant, average, moving average, or single-order exponential smoothing
· *Seasonal:* exponential smoothing with seasonal indices or average with seasonal indices
· *Trend:* time-series regression or exponential smoothing with trend adjustment
· *Trend-seasonal:* time-series regression with seasonal indices or Winter's exponential smoothing model

Exhibit 20.4
PLOT OF LUNCH DEMAND WITH RESPECT TO TIME

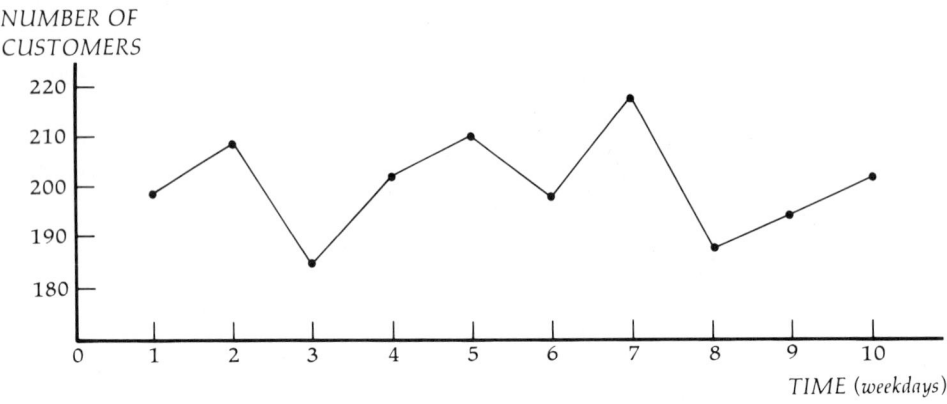

clearly matches the average pattern. For such a model, your choices of a forecasting method are to use:

- A constant
- An average of several previous values
- A moving average (found by adding the newest value, deleting the oldest value, and recomputing the average)
- A single-order exponential model

You choose the last model because it is simple and requires little data. The equation for this model is:

$$\text{New forecast} = \text{Old forecast} + \alpha\,(\text{Actual demand} - \text{Old forecast})$$

In exponential smoothing, you are adjusting the last period's forecast by a portion of the error of that period's forecast. The alpha value (α) or smoothing constant, ranges from zero to one. The smaller the alpha value, the smaller the adjustment caused by the last period's error. The larger the alpha value, the larger the adjustment. If there is little change in demand from one period to the next, a low value (0.05 to 0.1) for alpha is used. If demand changes dramatically from one period to the next, a large value (0.4 or so) should be used for alpha. (More complex exponential smoothing models incorporate seasonal and trend components. See the works by Fogarty, Blackstone, and Hoffmann or by Vollmann, Berry, and Whybark at the end of this chapter for additional information.)

The calculations using exponential smoothing with a smoothing constant of 0.1 are illustrated in Exhibit 20.5. You begin by setting the forecast to the actual demand for period 1; for that period, the difference is 0 and the adjustment is 0. Because demand for period 1 is used as the initial forecast, it is computed at 200 for period 2. Since actual demand for this period was 210, the difference is 10 units. Because the alpha value is 0.1, the adjustment is 1 unit.

Exhibit 20.5

FORECASTING LUNCHES USING SINGLE-ORDER
EXPONENTIAL SMOOTHING[a]

LUNCHES ACTUAL	FORECAST	DIFFERENCE	ADJUSTMENT
200	200	0	0
210	200	10	1
185	201	−16	−2
205	199	6	1
210	200	10	1
200	201	−1	0
220	201	19	2
190	203	−13	−1
195	202	−7	−1
205	201	4	0

[a] $\alpha = 0.1$

The forecast for period 3 then becomes 201. The actual demand for period 3 was 185, and the difference (185 − 201) was −16. The adjustment is rounded to −2, which provides a forecast of 199 for period 4. Other forecasts are calculated in the same way.

To identify whether the forecasting model is still valid, each week you should check the difference between actual demand and forecast for the last several weeks. You should check the differences column to see that:

- There are about as many pluses as minuses.
- The sum is approximately zero.
- There are not seven or more pluses or minuses in a row.

If any of these conditions do not exist, you should consider constructing a new forecasting model by following the steps in Exhibit 20.2. Prior to constructing a new forecasting model, however, ask yourself if there is any reason for changes in your demand pattern. Reasons might include a snowstorm for several days, street repair, special sales by competitors, or a new competitor.

Managing Simple Service Operations

Four basic functions are required in managing the operations of any business:

1. *Priority planning:* the process of determining the sequence of working on items
2. *Capacity planning:* the process of determining the amount of work to be done and the amount of work that can be done given your resources
3. *Priority control:* the process of comparing the planned sequence to the actual sequence of work and taking corrective action
4. *Capacity control:* the process of comparing the planned amount of work to the actual amount of work accomplished and taking corrective action

We will explain these functions in a service environment that all of us are familiar with—an automobile repair operation. Joe, a mechanic-owner, uses a first-in, first-out priority planning policy for repairing cars: the first customer arriving at his shop is the customer whose car is serviced first, the second customer's car is serviced second, and so on. (Other priority planning options are to provide service by appointment only, to do the job with the shortest processing time or the shortest setup time from the current job, to serve the best customer next, or to do the most expensive job next.)

Joe must begin by estimating the capacity available for his shop. If he has no employees and works 40 hours a week on cars, he has 40 hours of capacity available. He estimates that he spends approximately 30 minutes on each customer's car, sometimes less and sometimes more depending on the actual trouble. As a new customer arrives and asks for service, Joe has to estimate whether he can do the job, how much work remains on existing jobs, how long the new customer's job will take, and when he can start and complete the new job. Joe then gives the customer a time estimate for completing the repair. This procedure of estimating the amount of time required for a job and comparing this time requirement to the capacity available is the capacity planning task.

As Joe executes his priority and capacity plans, both problems and opportunities arise that will cause him to change priorities or deviate from capacity estimates. Problems regarding priority might include not having a part for the next customer's car and having to wait for delivery or the arrival of a neighbor and frequent customer named Betty, who drives in and asks for immediate service because she has a crucial appointment across town in an hour. Joe has the capacity to complete the repair, but he has three other cars in front of her job.

The priority control function should at this point compare current priorities to new priorities and allow Joe to judge the problems associated with changing priorities. He should weigh the impact of such a change and determine what action to take. Can he call his existing customer to say that the part will arrive in the afternoon and ask that customer to pick up the car after work instead of at lunch? Can he call his next customer and ask her to pick up her car later because he has an emergency order? Can he inconvenience all of his customers by 30 minutes and not lose any of them? As part of the priority control function, Joe must evaluate his options and either say no to Betty or contact his customers based on his decision.

The capacity control function is the process of comparing what you have actually accomplished to what you planned and making any adjustments to your capacity plan. Suppose Joe was running 45 minutes behind schedule. Joe should identify this condition and notify customers that he is running behind schedule to prevent them from arriving and having to wait for 45 minutes for their cars. Joe also needs to consider the fact that he is 45 minutes behind schedule in promising completion times to new customers. For example, he might decide not to accept any more customers that day if he has promised his available capacity. He could also decide to increase his capacity by working overtime to complete the jobs.

Although most small business owners plan and adjust their capacity commitments in their heads, most would find a Gantt chart to be a useful device in assisting them in planning and controlling priorities and capacities. The steps and symbols used in constructing a Gantt chart are shown in Exhibit 20.6. An example of the Gantt planning chart for Joe's day is provided in the top portion of Exhibit 20.7. The chart for controlling Joe's activities is provided in the lower portion of Exhibit 20.7; this section includes his rescheduling based on the two unexpected activities.

Let us review how to construct Joe's planning chart. Because he is the only resource, he is the only item listed in the first column. A time scale is drawn across the top of the chart. Joe normally starts work at 8:00 A.M. and quits at 4:30 P.M. each day. He takes a 15-minute break at 10:15 and at 2:45 and a half-hour lunch at 12:15; these periods are shown by the symbol for delay. Joe aver-

Exhibit 20.6
PROCEDURE AND SYMBOLS USED IN CONSTRUCTING A GANTT CHART

PROCEDURE

1. List in the first column the departments or individuals responsible for performing work.

2. Draw a time scale across the top of the chart.

3. Use the symbols provided at right to schedule specific tasks related to parts, products, or services to each department or individual.

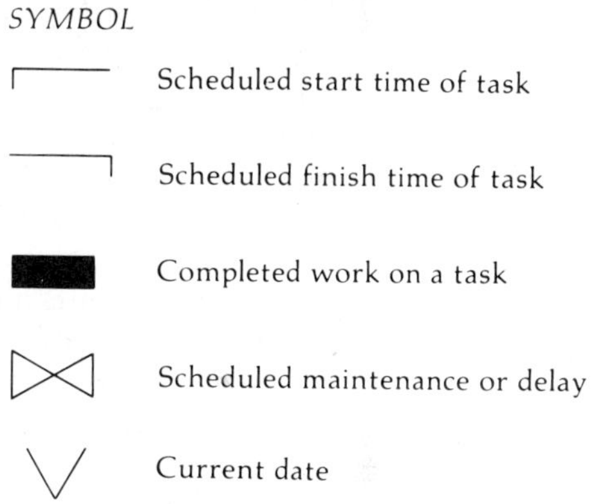

SYMBOL

⌐⎯ Scheduled start time of task

⎯⌐ Scheduled finish time of task

▬ Completed work on a task

⋈ Scheduled maintenance or delay

∨ Current date

Exhibit 20.7
GANTT PLANNING CHART AND GANTT CONTROL CHART WITH ADJUSTMENTS

PLANNING CHART

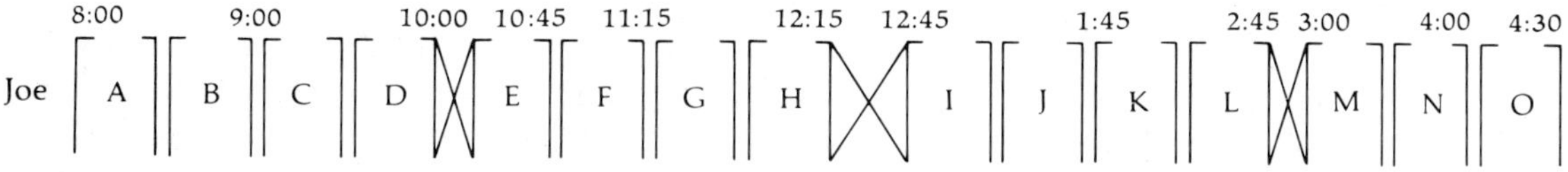

CONTROL CHART

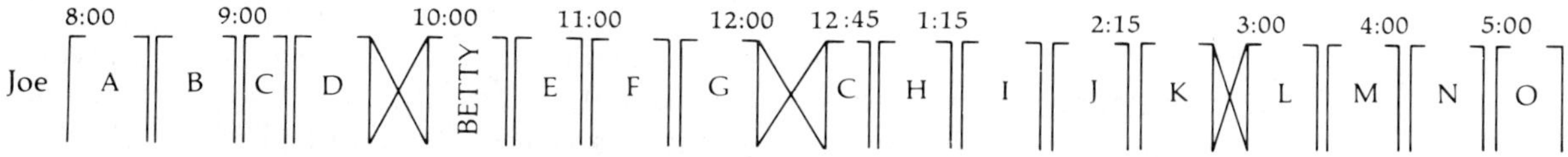

ages 30 minutes per customer and can therefore service 15 customers a day. If Joe had a doctor's appointment or other planned activity to disrupt his workday, he would need to adjust his capacity by reducing the number of customers for that day or plan to start earlier or finish later than his usual schedule. The Gantt chart in Exhibit 20.7 shows the disruption in service to customer C and Betty's emergency. As indicated by the chart, Joe decided to work past 4:30 to catch up on his work.

To control his workload, Joe must compare the actual times for each job to his planned times to ensure that his planning is correct. Additionally, if Joe has a planned job that is to take longer than 30 minutes to complete, he should reduce the number of customers scheduled on that day. These simple techniques assist Joe in planning and controlling his work and priorities. More importantly, he is able to identify a problem ahead of time and contact his customers.

The management of these four functions becomes quite complex even in Joe's garage. Several factors complicate managing these functions. Using several scheduling policies simultaneously, the use of rescheduling rules, planning a process to allow work on two or more customers at one time, and planning for a process that cannot be accomplished without the customer's presence are but a few of the complexities. Most doctors and dentists use a combination of scheduling procedures; the difficulties they can encounter are revealing. The priority planning procedure is usually well defined—patients with appointments are served first, then walk-in patients are seen. Emergency treatment is expected to be given the highest priority and can preempt all other patients. The capacity planning function is frequently missing in doctor's and dentist's offices, however, with the result that both doctor and patients fall behind schedule. The time per patient is underestimated considerably to compensate for patients missing or arriving late for appointments.

Additionally, most doctor's and dentist's offices have little to no priority and capacity control. The various alternatives to rescheduling individual patient priorities are not examined. Decisions are made haphazardly or not made at all; the result is that most patients are frustrated by the long waits and by watching other patients see the doctor or dentist before them. No priority or capacity adjustments are made by calling patients before their appointment to ask if they could reschedule for earlier or later in the day or tomorrow. The result is that customers have to wait for doctors.

There are other complicating factors. Doctors and dentists actually rotate from patient to patient, working for a few minutes with each one as a drug takes affect, X-rays are made, or other services performed. This complicates the scheduling process, but provides a good vehicle for estimating actual capacity by keeping track of previous experience. A Gantt planning chart for a dentist and a hygienist is provided in Exhibit 20.8. The procedure outlined in Exhibit 20.6 was used to construct the chart; of special interest is that the chart is based on the use of three rooms. The dental hygienist rotates between rooms 1 and 2 cleaning teeth. The dentist rotates between filling cavities in room 3 and giving brief consultations with the hygienist's patients in the other two rooms while shots are taking effect on the patient in room 3. The Gantt planning chart is useful in planning how to effectively schedule operations. Should the dentist

Exhibit 20.8

GANTT PLANNING CHART FOR A DENTIST AND HYGIENIST USING THREE EXAMINING ROOMS

ROOM

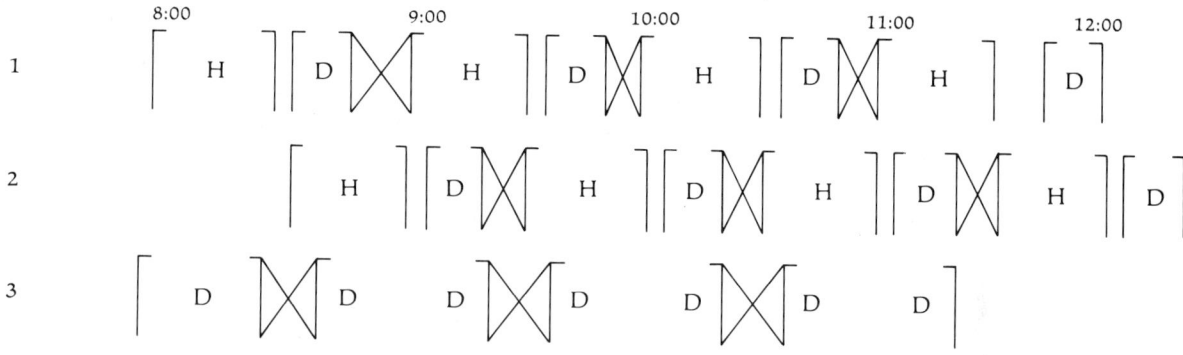

D = Dentist; H = Hygienist

construct a room 4 for teeth cleaning, filling cavities, or both? Should she hire another hygienist and staff both room 1 and 2 simultaneously with hygienists?

Another complicating factor for many service businesses is that the service cannot be stored in inventory. Thus idle time is lost revenue—in fact, it actually incurs expenses. A barber with no customers not only generates no revenue but also incurs cost because utilities are still consumed. If a patient does not show up for a dental appointment, no revenue is earned, but the dentist still has to pay the receptionist, the dental hygienist, and the utilities. Developing an effective capacity plan can help such businesses minimize down time.

Managing Manufacturing Operations

In the last section, we discussed the four operations functions—priority planning, capacity planning, priority control, and capacity control. Most manufacturing operations have to manage one additional function. This function, called *master production scheduling,* links independent and dependent demand items. Independent demand is demand that is unrelated to the demand for other items. This type of demand has to be forecast. Joe, the mechanic, faces independent demand when customers arrive at his shop. Dependent demand is demand that is related to the demand for other items; it can be calculated. The determination of whether four or five functions have to be performed is based on whether independent and dependent demand are present. Most manufacturing organizations face independent demand for the finished product and dependent demand for the parts that make up this finished product. For example, if Jane's Cabinet Shop was scheduled to manufacture 20 bookcases this week, she could calculate the dependent demand requirements based on these orders: she would need 20 back panels, 40 sides, 80 shelves, and so on. The 20 bookcases represent independent demand; demand for back panels, sides, shelves, and hardware represents dependent demand.

Material requirements planning (MRP) is the approach taken to managing the dependent demand items in a manufacturing firm. MRP is a manufacturing planning and control information system and provides you with the ability to coordinate your material requirements with your customer orders. MRP provides you with a time-phased planning approach to managing operations and inventories. A diagram of the traditional MRP system is provided in Exhibit 20.9.

The forecast that begins the process provides an estimate of future demand for products and services over some time span, such as six months or a year. This forecast is used to develop the production plan for the business, which provides a list of what the company plans to make over the next several months or quarters by product line. It is the company's long-range plan for operations. Your short-range plan, the master production schedule, should be in line with your long-range plan, or you will have too few or too many resources to implement the plan. The master production schedule—the driving force of the MRP system—is a list of the independent demand items by time period that you plan to make. A realistic master schedule is a necessity to developing detailed plans for both material and work centers.

Material requirements planning entails using a bill of materials file (a parts list) and the inventory file to calculate the number of parts required for each product in the master production schedule. The parts requirements and their production requirements are used to compute the capacity required at each work center over the time period involved. A schedule of purchasing requirements by time period is produced, as is a schedule of parts production at each work center by time period.

Let us look at an example of the logic of material requirements planning. Suppose you manufacture rulers. A product structure and bill of materials for making a 12-inch ruler are shown in Exhibit 20.10. The master schedule for this ruler and the resulting requirements records are provided in Exhibit 20.11. The product structure tree and the bill of material show that the ruler is assembled from a 12-inch formed piece of wood and a 12-inch metal strip. Six pieces of the wood are cut and shaped from a 1-inch × ⅜-inch × 73-inch wooden plank that is purchased. One hundred 12-inch metal strips are cut from a roll of metal stripping that is purchased. The master production schedule for the ruler shows that 1,000 rulers are due for shipping in week 1; 2,000 in week 2; 4,000 in week 4; and 1,500 in week 6. The component parts requirements are calculated based on this master schedule. The gross requirements for the wood are the same as for the ruler. To arrive at net requirements and to determine when and in what quantities each material should be ordered, on-hand inventory (available now) and scheduled receipts must be subtracted from the gross requirements lines starting in the earliest time period. Similar calculations are performed for each item from finished product to raw materials listed in the bill of materials. This information can then be combined with other product information—for yardsticks, metric rulers, and deluxe rulers—to provide you with an estimate of your materials and capacity needs by time period.

Exhibit 20.9
MATERIAL REQUIREMENTS PLANNING SYSTEM

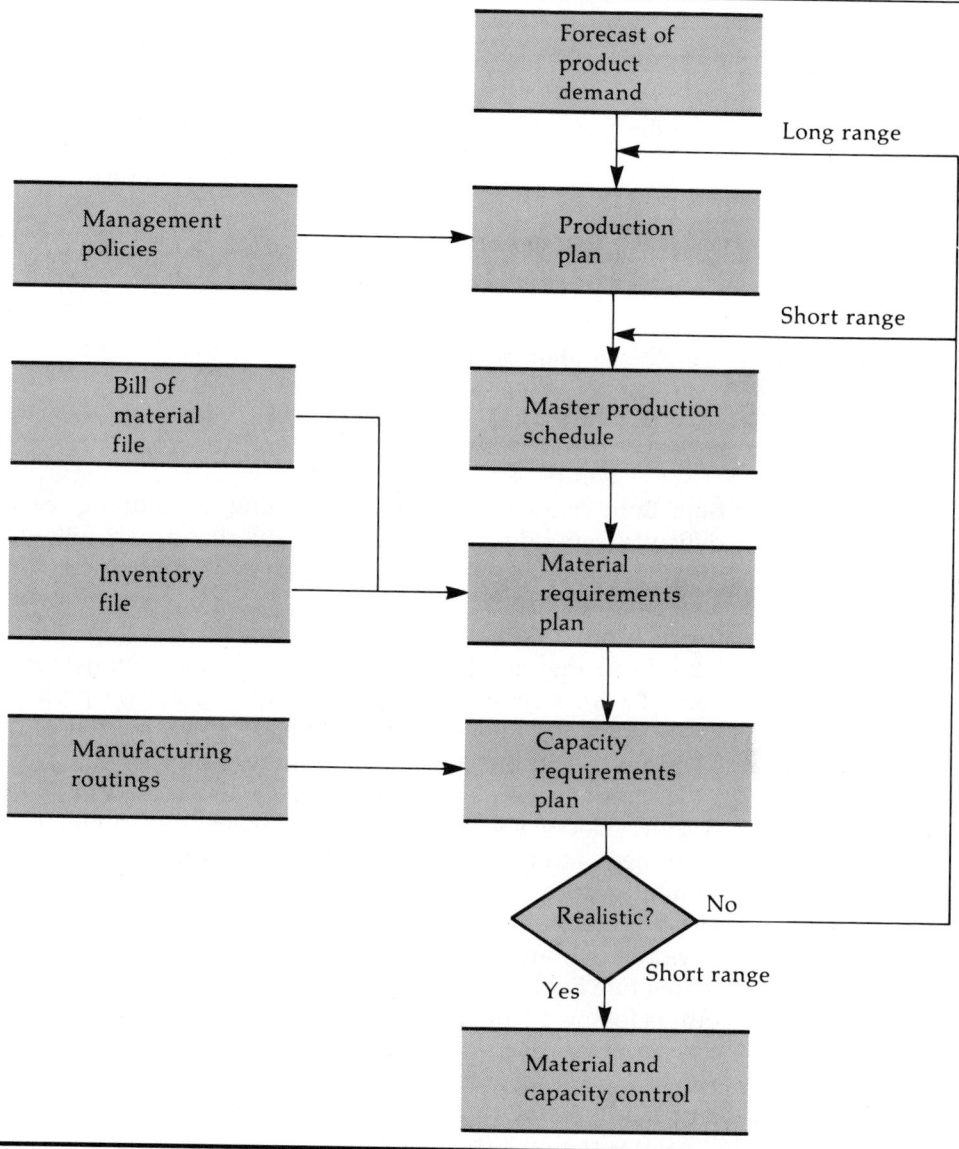

MRP packages are available for use on micro and minicomputers at reasonable costs. (See the Blackstone and Cox reference at the end of the chapter.)

Optimized Production Technology

The philosophy called *optimized production technology* (OPT), developed by Eli Goldratt (*The Goal*, 1986), is based on two characteristics found in both manufacturing and service businesses—dependent sequences and statistical fluctua-

Exhibit 20.10
PRODUCT STRUCTURE TREE AND BILL OF MATERIAL FOR
A 12-INCH RULER

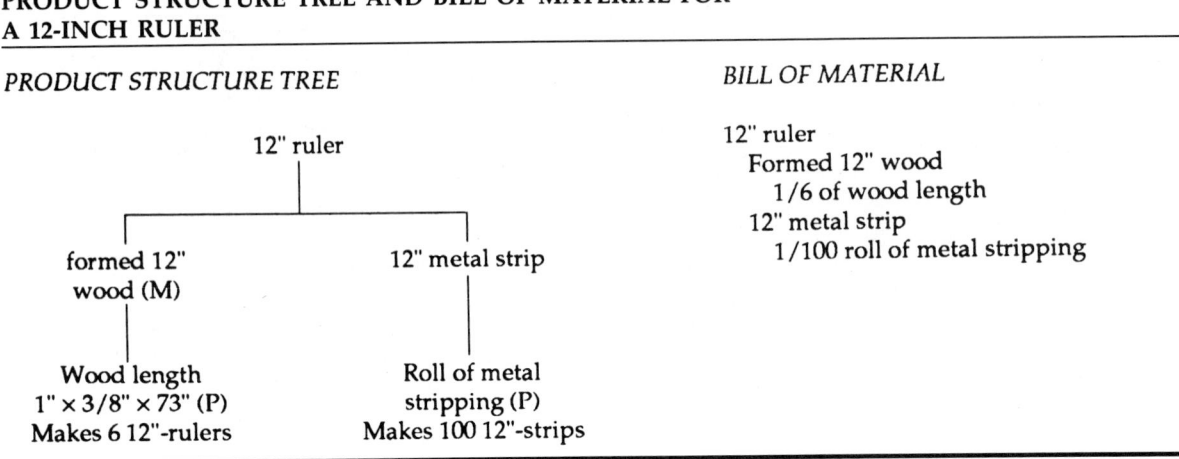

PRODUCT STRUCTURE TREE

12" ruler
- formed 12" wood (M)
  - Wood length 1" × 3/8" × 73" (P) Makes 6 12"-rulers
- 12" metal strip
  - Roll of metal stripping (P) Makes 100 12"-strips

BILL OF MATERIAL

12" ruler
　Formed 12" wood
　　1/6 of wood length
　12" metal strip
　　1/100 roll of metal stripping

tion. Both characteristics make planning, scheduling, execution, and control difficult. Dependent sequencing means that a part follows a fixed path in its manufacturing activities—operation one is performed, then two, then three, and so on—and that each operation is dependent on the completion and timing of another. This operation sequence relationship is expressed in the part's manufacturing routing sheet. Statistical fluctuation means that the time to complete an activity is not the same each time you perform it—one time you might complete the activity in 40 minutes, the next in 35 minutes, the next in 43 minutes, and the last time in 38 minutes.

Dependent sequencing exists in the service sector. The activities conducted within a doctor's office provide an excellent example. A patient with an appointment walks into the waiting room, signs in, waits, fills out a medical information form, waits, follows the nurse to an examining room, waits, has blood pressure and temperature taken, waits, consults with the doctor, waits, pays the bill, and then leaves. The sequence is fixed for most patients. Some follow one fixed path because their appointment is for a physical examination, others follow a different but equally fixed path because they are getting laboratory work. Statistical fluctuation is also present in service operations.

While these characteristics have always been present in manufacturing, large amounts of inventory in the system allowed each work center to act as if it were somewhat independent of other work centers. Inventory buffered the impact of statistical fluctuations at one work center on another. As manufacturers have reduced the amount of work-in-process inventory in their facilities (implementing the JIT philosophy), however, the impact of dependent sequences and statistical fluctuation can be felt on their planning and control systems.

Goldratt and Fox developed the nine principles of OPT, or synchronized production, as it is also called. The OPT philosophy focuses on scheduling the capacity of the bottleneck effectively. The constraint or bottleneck is the slowest

Exhibit 20.11

MASTER SCHEDULE AND COMPONENT RECORDS FOR MANUFACTURING RULERS

MASTER SCHEDULE

	WEEK					
	1	2	3	4	5	6
12" ruler	1000	2000		4000		1500

COMPONENT RECORDS

On Hand	Lead Time		WEEK					
			1	2	3	4	5	6
		12" wood						
		Gross requirements	1000	2000		4000		1500
		Scheduled receipts						
		Available (4000)	3000	1000				
4000	2 weeks	Net requirements				3000		1500
		Planned order receipts				3000		1500
		Planned order releases		3000		1500		
		73" wood						
		Gross requirements		500		250		1500
		Scheduled receipts						
		Available (500)		0				
500	2 weeks	Net requirements				250		
		Planned order receipts				250		
		Planned order releases		250				
		12" metal strip						
		Gross requirements	1000	2000		4000		1500
		Scheduled receipts						
		Available (1500)	500					
1500	1 week	Net requirements		1500		4000		500
		Planned order receipts		1500		4000		
		Planned order releases	1500		4000		1500	
		Roll of metal strip						
		Gross requirements	15		40		15	
		Scheduled receipts	25					
		Available	10	10	10			
0	1 week	Net requirements				30		15
		Planned order receipts				30		15
		Planned order releases		30		15		

resource and dictates the output of the system. A nonbottleneck is a resource that has idle or excess capacity. The nine principles of synchronous production are

1. Balance the flow, not the capacity.
2. Constraints determine nonbottleneck utilization.

3. Activation is not equal to utilization.
4. A lost bottleneck hour is a lost system hour.
5. A saved nonbottleneck hour is a mirage.
6. Bottlenecks govern throughput and inventory.
7. A transfer batch should not always equal a process batch.
8. A process batch should be variable, not fixed.
9. Set the schedule by examining all constraints simultaneously.

Each of these principles will be discussed briefly.

Balance flow, not capacity. This principle is illustrated in Exhibit 20.12 by using pipes of different sizes to represent the capacities of different work centers. Work flow is from left to right, from raw materials to finished goods. The dotted line represents the amount of work that can be processed by the work centers (the WCs). Using the traditional approach (the top portion), a facility is designed to balance the capacity of all work centers, hence all the pipes are the same size. In reality, however, large amounts of work-in-process (WIP) inventory are needed to accommodate such statistical fluctuations as worker absences, poor quality, late deliveries, missing tools, and breakdowns. In its simplest form, the principle of balancing flow (illustrated in the bottom half)

Exhibit 20.12
TRADITIONAL VERSUS SYNCHRONIZED MANUFACTURING PHILOSOPHY

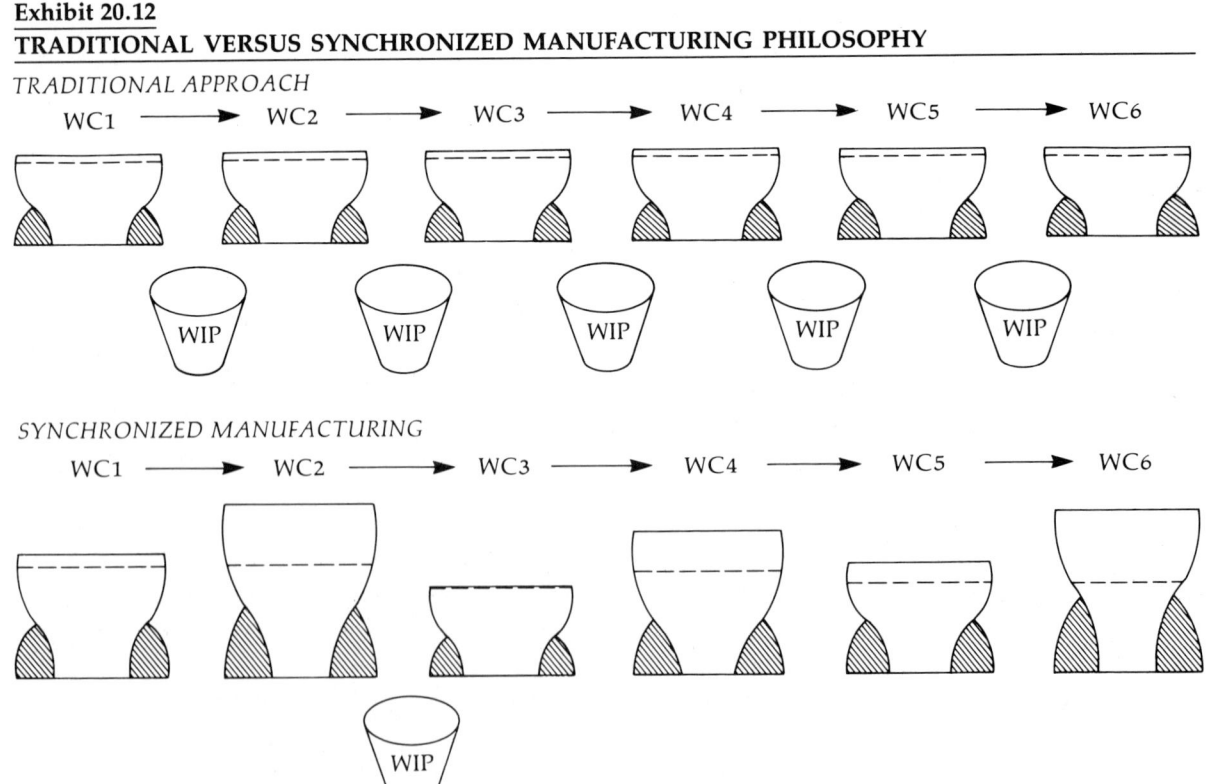

requires management to identify the bottleneck in the system operations (WC3 in our example) and schedule the system based on the capacity of this work center. Raw material will be released to WC1 based upon the actual production at WC3. WIP inventory should be planned to exist only in front of the bottleneck, WC3, to protect against fluctuations at the previous workstations. Excess capacity will exist at all nonbottleneck operations. This excess capacity can be thought of as potential inventory since it gives the firm the capability of catching up to the bottleneck production rate if problems such as breakdowns occur.

Constraints determine nonbottleneck utilization. With large amounts of WIP inventory in a facility, each work center is somewhat independent of or decoupled from other work centers. As firms implement JIT, however, the capacity required by each work center is more clearly determined by the flow through the bottleneck work centers. If nonconstraint work centers work faster than the constraint, then inventory builds up in the system in front of the constraint and little to no inventory accumulates behind the constraint.

Activation is not equal to utilization. " 'Utilizing' a resource means making use of the resource in a way that moves the system toward the goal (your goal is to make money). 'Activating' a resource is like pressing the ON switch of a machine: it runs whether or not there is any benefit to be derived from the work it's doing."[1] Utilization is the effective use of a resource. Activation is the sum of utilization and unnecessary use of the resource. When you schedule nonbottlenecks to produce more than the bottlenecks can use, you are activating that resource.

A lost bottleneck hour is a lost system hour. The bottleneck dictates the amount of goods or services produced by the total productive system. Any increase or decrease in the throughput of this resource increases or decreases throughput of the total system. For example, if a physician generates an average of $100 per hour and decides to reduce her lunch hour by 30 minutes and work the additional 30 minutes, she will increase her office revenues by $50 a day.

A saved nonbottleneck hour is a mirage. Conversely, any time saved at a nonbottleneck work center either represents the creation of idle time for that resource or an increase in inventory that is not needed because the resource continues to produce. Using the physician office again, if a phone system were installed to reduce the receptionist's telephone time, no additional revenue is generated and additional idle time for the receptionist results. Unless the receptionist's idle time can be converted into another competitive edge, the new system does not change the revenue generated by the physician.

Bottlenecks govern throughput and inventory. Bottlenecks have long been recognized as constraining system output. Until recently, however, no relationship between bottlenecks and work-in-process inventory had been established. Now, manufacturers are increasingly recognizing that overloading a master schedule beyond the capabilities of the bottleneck work center results in the production of excess work-in-process inventory. Scheduling to maximize the use of all workers and equipment creates excess idle work-in-process invento-

---

1. E. M. Goldratt and J. Cox, *The Goal*, rev. ed. (Croton-on-Hudson, NY: North River Press, 1986), p. 210.

ries and does not increase output. In our physician's example, the doctor is obviously the bottleneck. If we overschedule her, we have idle patients in the waiting rooms. If we underschedule her, she has reduced throughput (revenue).

A transfer batch should not always equal a process batch. Lot sizing means deciding on the number of units to be ordered or processed at one time. Traditionally, lot sizing, particularly economic order quantity (EOQ), has attempted to balance the cost of ordering and carrying inventory without making a distinction between transfer and processing batches. The process batch is the amount that you would make at one time, the transfer batch is the amount that you would move from one work center to the next at one time. An assembly line draws a clear distinction between process and transfer batches. Ideally, the process batch for an assembly line is infinite in size (therefore eliminating setup costs) and the transfer batch is one (therefore eliminating carrying cost). Reductions in processing and transfer batch sizes decrease lead times and work-in-process inventories by allowing you to work on an order at two or more centers simultaneously. It is best to have large processing batches at the bottleneck in order to maintain system output.

A process batch should be variable not fixed. Traditionally, lot size is calculated based on EOQ or another lot sizing method. This lot size remains basically the same throughout the year regardless of changes in product demand. The lot size, however, should be adjusted for actual customer orders, changes in available and required capacities, product mix, and the load on the bottleneck.

Set the schedule by examining all constraints simultaneously. In many manufacturing firms, the master schedule is constructed haphazardly. Schedules are constructed without regard to capacity constraints; they are dictated more by customer request date than by the manufacturing capabilities to produce the product. In other companies, schedules are based on both material and capacity availability using material and capacity requirements planning methodologies. The appropriate method should be to determine the schedule by looking at time constraints, timing constraints, material constraints, capacity constraints, and worker constraints simultaneously. You should adjust lot sizes within this framework to promote flow through your production system, minimize your work-in-process inventory, reduce your lead time, and—more importantly—fully utilize the bottleneck resource.

Summary

This chapter has provided you with tools to better manage service and manufacturing operations. Forecasting demand begins with identifying which of four components of demand applies: random, or average; season; trend; or cyclical. Demand components have particular forecasting methods associated with them.

The four basic functions of managing operations are priority planning, capacity planning, priority control, and capacity control. These operations apply to both service and manufacturing firms. An additional function, master production scheduling, is valuable in managing manufacturing operations. Material requirements planning, one such technique, focuses on managing dependent demand.

An alternative approach is called optimized production technology, or OPT. Its principles improve system effectiveness and simultaneously reduce lead times. The OPT philosophy states that one or only a few constraints determine operational capacity. Managing operations means identifying these constraints and maximizing the use of these constraints. Processing batch sizes should be large at bottlenecks to maintain high system output and reduce the impact of setups on bottleneck utilization. Processing batch sizes should be small at nonbottleneck operations, thus utilizing the idle time to reduce the lead time of manufacturing the product. Transfer batch sizes should be small and synchronized to ensure a smooth flow of parts to the bottleneck and a reduction in product lead time and work-in-process inventory.

Class Assignments

1. Provided below is the demand history for videotape rentals for Froggy's Video Store for the past 13 days. Analyze the data based on your knowledge of forecasting. What forecasting model did you use? What is your forecast for demand in period 14?

Day	Demand	Day	Demand
1	500	8	590
2	450	9	580
3	650	10	620
4	600	11	610
5	590	12	550
6	620	13	710
7	600	14	?

2. Discuss the four planning and control functions and the appropriate scheduling policies for a
   a. Small CPA firm
   b. Tax preparer's office
   c. Photographic studio
   d. Supermarket with regular and express lines
   e. Car wash

3. Discuss the five planning and control functions and the appropriate scheduling policies for a
   a. Drycleaner
   b. School of business
   c. Pizza parlor
   d. Printer of business cards

4. Describe the bill of materials for a
   a. Large supreme pizza
   b. Box of twelve pencils
   c. Set of darts

5. Describe the use of a material requirements planning system for a small manufacturer of
   a. Pencils
   b. Handkerchiefs
   c. Darts
   d. Boxes of business cards

6. Discuss how OPT principles might be used in an office with three junior accountants, who conduct audits and write reports; two word-processing operators, who type the audit reports; and a senior accountant, who reviews all reports prior to mailing them.

References

Blackstone, John H., Jr., and James F. Cox. "Selecting MRP Software for Small Businesses." *Production and Inventory Management Journal*, 26, No. 4, Fourth Quarter 1985, pp. 42–50.

Chrisman, J. J. "Basic Production Techniques for Small Manufacturers: III. Production Planning, Control, and Scheduling Methods." *Production and Inventory Management Journal*, 26, No. 4 (Fourth Quarter 1985), pp. 14–26.

Convey, R. E. "MRP for Smaller Manufacturing Businesses." *American Production and Inventory Control Society 24th Annual International Conference Proceedings*. Falls Church, Va.: APICS, 1981, pp. 102–104.

Fogarty, D. W., J. H. Blackstone, Jr., and T. R. Hoffmann. *Production and Inventory Management*, 2nd ed. Cincinnati: South-Western Publishing Co., 1991.

Frank, D. N. "Creating and Maintaining Accurate Bills of Materials for Small Business." *American Production and Inventory Control Society Spring Seminar Proceedings 1986*. Falls Church, Va.: APICS, April 1986, pp. 324–328.

Frank, D. N. "A Small Business Strategy for Configuration Management and Control." *American Production and Inventory Control Society Aerospace and Defense Seminar Proceedings*. Falls Church, Va.: APICS, September 1985, pp. 29–38.

Goldratt, E. M., and J. Cox. *The Goal*, rev. ed. Croton-on-Hudson, NY: North River Press, 1986.

Gould, D. E. "How to Implement a Cost-Effective MRP System in a Small Manufacturing Company." *American Production and Inventory Control Society 30th Annual International Conference Proceedings*. Falls Church, Va.: APICS, 1987, pp. 205–207.

Kennedy, L. C. "A Comparison of Forecasting Models for Planning in a Small Business." *American Production and Inventory Control Society Small Manufacturing Reprints*. Falls Church, Va.: APICS, 1985, pp. 10–27.

Malitz, I., and R. Newman. "Simplified MRP." *P & IM Review*. 1, No. 2, February 1981, pp. 20–22.

Savaiano, R. A. "MRP for Small Manufacturers: Keys to Success." *P & IM Review*, 7, No. 12, December 1987.

Steffy, W. *Inventory Controls for the Small and Medium Sized Firm: Computer-Aided Inventory Control and Manual Inventory Control*. Industrial Development Institute of Small Business. Falls Church, Va.: APICS, 1980.

Swanson, F. W. "MRP for Smaller Businesses." *American Production and Inventory Control Society 28th Annual International Conference Proceedings*. Falls Church, Va.: APICS, 1985, pp. 255–259.

Swanson, F. W. "MRP for Smaller Businesses: A Case Study of Successful Implementation." *American Production and Inventory Control Society 29th Annual International Conference Proceedings*. Falls Church, Va.: APICS, 1986, pp. 118–119.

Vollmann, T. E., W. L. Berry, and D. C. Whybark. *Manufacturing Planning and Control Systems*, 2nd ed. Homewood, Ill.: Richard D. Irwin, 1988.

Waliszewski, D. A. "How to Create and Manage a Master Production Schedule in a Small Company Make-to-Stock Environment." *American Production and Inventory Control Society 24th Annual International Conference Proceedings*. Falls Church, Va.: APICS, 1981, pp. 86–87.

Wallace, T. F., and J. R. Dougherty, eds. *APICS Dictionary*, 6th ed. Falls Church, Va.: APICS, 1987.

Westphal, R. "Scheduling and Loading the Small Manufacturing Company." *American Production and Inventory Control Society Proceedings of Seminar on Small Manufacturing and Process Industries*. Falls Church, Va.: APICS, September 1985, pp. 62–68.

Williams, J. R., and P. D. Hitch. "Production and Inventory Control Training in the Smaller, Owner-Managed Business." *American Production and Inventory Control Society Spring Seminar Proceedings 1986*. Falls Church, Va.: APICS, April 1986, pp. 267–277.

MANAGING INVENTORY

Thousands of articles have been written on various aspects of inventory management. This chapter provides an overview of a few of the more important concepts; hopefully it also provides you with an understanding of the importance of inventory in supporting your competitive strategy. Material costs represent the largest part of the product cost; in many companies, this cost comprises more than 60 percent of product cost.

Inventory management includes developing, implementing, and administering inventory procedures, policies, and systems. In both service and manufacturing organizations, proper inventory management is critical to success. Inventory should be the result of conscious decisions and not the result of poor planning and scheduling. Inventory is an idle resource at best and a liability at worst. The Japanese view excess inventory as a waste. In this view, inventory is defined as having the right item in the right quantity in the right place at the right time. Excess inventory, or waste, is having the wrong item, having the wrong quantity, having the right item at the wrong location, or having the right item too soon or too late. These are stringent requirements. Nevertheless, it is essential to manage inventory as if it were your money—it is.

Inventory is both an asset and a liability. On the balance sheet, it is listed as a current asset and is used to generate revenue or income. This perspective has been the traditional way of looking at inventory. Remember, however, that inventory is an idle resource held for future use or resale, earning no interest or revenue. Too much inventory can tie up money with no financial return, but too little inventory can lose sales. In determining your inventory policies, you face two major conflicting objectives. On one hand, you want to maximize customer service by having what your customers want when they want it. On the other hand, you want to minimize your inventory investment by having as little capital as possible tied up in inventory that you will not sell. Manufacturing firms face a third conflicting objective: maximizing plant efficiency. Owners want to keep every worker and every machine busy at all times, or they feel that they are losing money. Each of these conflicting objectives attempts to improve one part of the business at the expense of the other parts. The proper objective to pursue, however, is to maximize the company's long-term profit. The goal then becomes choosing the inventory policy that meets that objective.

How would you like to take inventory here?

Materials management has undergone tremendous changes in the past few years with the development of new management philosophies and information systems. These philosophies and information systems are appropriate, available, and affordable to the small business owner, thus providing the means to make the business a world-class competitor.

This chapter presents some new ideas on inventory and a few of the more traditional approaches that are applicable in a small business. Our major emphasis is to instill a proactive approach to managing the inventory investment effectively. We discuss the relationship between managing an effective operations function and the strategic use of inventory, which can be a tremendous competitive edge. We discuss the traditional functions of inventory and methods of reducing the amount of inventory to support each function. We provide you a method of focusing your attention on planning and controlling the vital few items that contribute the most to your success. This method, called *ABC analysis*, is described in detail. Finally, we discuss methods of physical control and improving your inventory accuracy.

After reading this chapter, you will be able to

- Identify the importance of inventory to implementing your company strategy
- List the functions of inventory in both a service and manufacturing organization
- Identify the types of cost associated with inventory
- Analyze your inventory and determine planning and control techniques appropriate for each item in your inventory

- Improve your inventory accuracy
- Explain when and how to use four independent demand inventory systems

Inventory Strategies

Your business's inventory strategy (where, when, and how much of each type and item of inventory to stock) should be an integrated and complementary part of your operations strategy. The strategic placement and use of inventory can prove to be a powerful competitive advantage. Remember, however, that inventory is both an asset and a liability. Used correctly, it can increase sales tremendously; used incorrectly, it can be a primary cause of bankruptcy. As we discussed in Chapter 20, inventory can be the result of poor scheduling. If lead times for purchasing and manufacturing materials are long, the tendency is to carry large—many times excessive—quantities of inventory.

The first action of a business owner should be to examine the reasons for long lead times. Can these lead times be reduced? Can you order materials more frequently and in smaller quantities? Can you reduce inventory by streamlining operations? Can you reduce cost by eliminating waste, scrap, and rework?

If your lead time in responding to customers' demands for your products and services is long, you can take two actions. First, examine ways to shorten the lead time by streamlining operations. Second, examine your complete production and logistics system to identify the strategic placement of inventory within those systems so as to shorten lead time without carrying excessive inventory.

Functions and Costs of Inventory

Inventory Types and Their Functions

There are four basic types of inventory in most retailing and manufacturing environments; these types are determined by the function of the inventory. They are lot size or cycle inventories, fluctuation inventories, basic pipeline inventories, and anticipation inventories. An understanding of the basic functions is essential to the proper application of inventory planning and control techniques.

- *Lot size or cycle inventories* are "inventories which are maintained whenever quantity price discounts, shipping costs, or set-up costs, etc., make it more economical to purchase or produce in larger lots than are needed for immediate purposes."[1]
- *Fluctuation or buffer inventories* are inventories stocked to protect against unexpected surges in demand. Safety stock, one example of this type, is

---

1. T. F. Wallace and J. R. Dougherty (eds.), *APICS Dictionary,* 6th edition (Falls Church, Va.: American Production and Inventory Control Society, 1987), p. 16.

"a quantity of stock planned to be in inventory to protect against fluctuations in demand and/or supply."[2]

- *Basic pipeline stock* is "inventory to fill the many stocking points in the distribution system. The flow time through the pipeline has a major effect on the amount of inventory required in the pipeline: e.g., if the average time for its passage through all distribution levels to the end user is ninety days, then the basic pipeline inventory must be on the average ninety days supply. Time factors involved include order transmission, factory order processing, shipping, transportation, minimum-maximum inventory system, etc."[3]

- *Anticipation inventory* is "additional inventory above pipeline stock to cover projected trends of increased sales, planned sales promotion programs, seasonal fluctuations, plant shutdowns, and vacations."[4]

Each of these functions includes a tradeoff between the added inventory investment and the cost saved. Inventory-related costs can be grouped into four areas. First is the cost of ordering inventory, which includes clerical, processing, and transportation costs. Second is the cost of carrying inventory, which includes handling, property taxes, insurance, obsolescence, warehousing, and interest costs. Third is the cost of carrying insufficient inventory, which includes poor customer relations, loss of quantity discounts, additional transportation, and expediting costs and lost sales. Fourth is the cost of carrying excessive inventory, which includes obsolescence at the finished goods level, and poor quality and long manufacturing lead times at the work-in-process level.

Analyzing Inventory Costs

The four types of inventory primarily relate to decoupling or disconnecting activities and individual work centers within your business and separating your business activities from those of your vendors and your customers. You should know the costs associated with each type and the methods of reducing both your inventory investment and these costs. Any improvement in operations will effectively reduce the inventory investment and associated costs.

Lot Sizing Inventory   Two groups of costs are associated with lot sizing inventories—ordering and carrying costs. Based on minimizing these costs, the economic order quantity (EOQ) formula can assist you in deciding how much inventory to order of an item:

$$EOQ = \sqrt{\frac{2 \times \text{Annual demand} \times \text{Ordering cost}}{\text{Unit cost} \times \text{Carrying cost percentage}}}$$

2. Ibid., p. 28.
3. Ibid., p. 2.
4. Ibid., p. 1.

The EOQ, developed in 1915 by F. W. Harris, is the most frequently used lot sizing method. One major flaw exists in using the EOQ—it provides the optimum amount of inventory for only one item. EOQ does not minimize the cost of ordering and holding all items in inventory or the total investment in inventory. Yet a company seldom makes only one item or buys only one item from a supplier. A well-known axiom of calculus applies to using the EOQ formula in a business today: "The sum of the local optima is not necessarily the global optima." In other words, while the EOQ provides the best answer for one item in inventory, it does not provide the best answer either to companies with inventories consisting of several items or to companies that have limited working capital, such as small businesses.

A more suitable approach to lot sizing is to lot size by vendor and to use time buffers. A time buffer is an amount of inventory equal to the demand for the item to cover a given time period. The objective is to examine all inventory items ordered from the same vendor and to order each item according to the appropriate time buffer to minimize transportation and associated costs.

A simple example of calculating time buffers is provided in Exhibit 21.1. The annual demand for each item is divided by 50 and rounded to provide an estimate of the amount of inventory used in one week. Annual demand is also divided by 12 and rounded to provide a monthly estimate of the needed inventory. Based on the characteristics of each item (cost, size, weight, and quantity), you identify how frequently you might order the items to economize on inventory investment, transportation costs, and associated costs. For example, items 2, 5, 7, and 10 can be ordered every week and fill approximately three-fourths of a trailer. The remaining items can be ordered once a month: item 1 in the first week, item 4 in the second, items 3 and 6 in the third, and items 8 and 9 in the fourth. These order quantities economize on transportation cost since each order is almost a full trailer load. In this manner, you can plan order sizes from the same vendor to consolidate orders, reduce transportation costs, and reduce inventories. You could also negotiate with the supplier for discounts based on the total annual volume of purchases instead of attempting to purchase large volumes of the same item to receive quantity discounts.

Exhibit 21.1
AN EXAMPLE OF THE USE OF TIME BUFFERS

ITEM	ANNUAL DEMAND	WEEKLY	MONTHLY
1	300	6	25
2	2500	50	2001
3	20	0	2
4	600	12	50
5	1000	20	100
6	6	0	1
7	5000	100	400
8	80	2	7
9	80	2	7
10	60000	1200	5000

Fluctuation Inventories   Fluctuation inventories increase inventory investment and carrying costs. Let us see how this occurs with the example of safety stock. The amount of safety stock is based on the size of your forecast error and your customer service goals. The larger the forecast error, the larger the safety stock needed to support those goals. Conversely, the smaller the forecast error, the smaller the safety stock. The shorter the lead time associated with replenishing the inventory, the smaller the forecast error and therefore the smaller the safety stock needed. Costs related to lost sales should be weighed against increases in inventory investment and carrying costs. Safety stock is also used to protect against inventory record errors. Many business owners believe that it is easier to carry excess inventory than to keep accurate inventory records. Cycle counting, an effective method of increasing the accuracy of records and reducing safety stock, is discussed later in this chapter.

Pipeline Inventories   Pipeline inventories increase inventory investment and carrying costs; these inventories exist because of the time required to move items from one location to another. Pipeline inventories can be reduced by decreasing lead time, by using faster methods of transportation, by improving order processing and transmission of orders, and by implementing more efficient management policies and procedures.

Anticipation Inventories   Anticipation inventories increase inventory investment and carrying and obsolescence costs. Using this type of inventory in manufacturing essentially means storing worker- and machine-hours in inventory to meet future needs. Costs avoided by the use of anticipation inventories are those associated with changing production rates, which includes the hiring and laying off workers. The costs incurred include the increased investment in inventory and related carrying costs. You can reduce both types of costs by cross-training workers to make the flow of materials more level and to provide some capability of increasing output by moving workers to critical areas when the need arises.

Tying Inventory to Strategy

Your decisions on the placement and amount of inventory investment should be made to support the competitive edges in your business strategy. You should classify your inventory items by the function that each performs. Prior to calculating the amount of inventory investment to support each function, ask yourself these questions:

- Can I eliminate the need for this inventory?
- Can I decrease the amount of inventory needed?
- Can I consolidate vendors? Can I order more items from each vendor? Can I order less of each item and order each item more frequently?
- What impact does this inventory investment have on overall inventory investment and long-run return?
- Can I reduce the uncertainty associated with buying and holding this inventory?

- Am I holding this inventory in the right stage of completion and at the right location?

ABC Analysis

A couple of centuries ago, the Italian economist Vilfredo Pareto found that a small percentage (10 percent) of the population of a nation controlled its wealth (70 percent) and that the masses of population (70 to 80 percent) own little or none of the nation's wealth (10 percent). This relationship, known as Pareto's principle, is applicable to several other fields. Inventory investment is one such area; the existence of this relationship provides an excellent opportunity to focus planning and control efforts on a vital few items and thereby control most of the dollar cost. Most companies cannot afford to apply the same degree of inventory planning and control to all items. ABC inventory analysis is a method of separating items into groupings based on the projected annual dollar usage. The larger the amount of money earned by an inventory item, the more important it is to control the investment in that item. Different levels of control are therefore applied to different groupings of inventory items.

ABC inventory analysis is generally based on annual dollar demand, which minimizes seasonal variations. The unit cost of an item is multiplied by its forecast of annual demand to arrive at the projected annual dollar usage. Once all inventory item values have been computed, they are ranked in descending order from the highest dollar value to the lowest. Usually, 10 to 20 percent of the items represent 60 to 70 percent of the projected dollar usage. These items are classified as A items. A second grouping of items can usually be identified. These items, which typically account for approximately 20 percent of the number of items and 20 percent of the annual dollar value, are classified as B items. Lastly, a third group of items is identified. These low-volume items represent 60 to 70 percent of the number of inventory items and only 10 to 20 percent of total annual dollar value. These items are called C items. You may have more or fewer than three groupings; however, the principle is the same: segregate inventory items by class and apply different levels of planning and control to each class. Note that the unit cost is not critical; it is annual dollar usage that is the determining factor. The steps involved in conducting an ABC analysis are summarized in Exhibit 21.2.

Following these steps, you first list your inventory items by part number, unit cost, and forecasted annual usage. An example of such a list is provided in Exhibit 21.3. Next, you should compute the projected annual dollar value for each item and sum these individual values. The sum for the ten items in Exhibit 21.3 is $102,117. Next, rank the items by annual dollar value from largest to smallest (see Exhibit 21.4). Next, compute the cumulative percentage for each item. Item 101 represents 10 percent of the items (it is one of ten items) and 44 percent of the annual usage ($45,000/$102,117). Taken together, items 101 and 106 represent 20 percent of the items (two of ten) and 73 percent of the annual usage. These two items should be classified as A items. You can control 73 percent of your inventory expenditure by closely controlling these two items

Exhibit 21.2

STEPS IN CONDUCTING AN ABC ANALYSIS

1. List all inventory items by part number, unit cost, and total projected annual usage.
2. Compute the annual total projected dollar value for each item by multiplying the unit cost by the total projected annual usage.
3. Rank the inventory items from the largest total projected annual dollar value to the smallest.
4. Recopy the list using the ranking and listing the rank, part number, unit cost, projected usage, and projected dollar value.
5. Compute the cumulative usage and cumulative percentage for each item.
6. Select the divisions for the A, B, and C classes:

   Class A   0–70% annual dollar value
   Class B   70–90% annual dollar value
   Class C   90–100% annual dollar value

Exhibit 21.3

EXAMPLE OF CONDUCTING AN ABC ANALYSIS

PART NUMBER	UNIT COST	PROJECTED ANNUAL USAGE	ANNUAL DOLLAR VALUE	RANK
101	$1.50	30,000	$45,000	1
102	0.06	9,000	540	7
103	0.11	25,000	2,750	6
104	0.05	85,000	4,250	5
105	0.08	125,000	10,000	3
106	0.15	200,000	30,000	2
107	0.03	9,000	270	9
108	0.12	3,000	360	8
109	0.20	44,000	8,800	4
110	0.07	2,100	147	10
			$102,117	

rather than trying to control all ten to the same degree. The other classes are calculated in a similar fashion, as noted at the bottom of the exhibit.

ABC analysis can assist you in deciding whether to use a perpetual or a periodic review inventory system. An A item could be controlled through a perpetual inventory system that includes physical checks and cycle counts scheduled more frequently than for B or C items. If you can focus your attention on reducing your inventory investment in the A items by using better planning and control techniques, you can reduce your inventory investment and associated carrying costs significantly. These techniques include cycle counting more frequently, maintaining perpetual inventory records, having more security, using better forecasting methods, reducing lead times through better scheduling of transportation and production activities, establishing bet-

Exhibit 21.4

RESULTS OF ABC ANALYSIS

RANK	PART NUMBER	COST	ANNUAL PROJECTED USAGE	ANNUAL DOLLAR VALUE	CUMULATIVE DOLLAR VALUE	CUMULATIVE PERCENTAGE
1	101	$1.50	30,000	$45,000	$45,000	44.0%
2	106	0.15	200,000	30,000	75,000	73.0
3	105	0.08	125,000	10,000	85,000	83.0
4	109	0.20	44,000	8,800	93,800	92.0
5	104	0.05	85,000	4,250	98,050	96.0
6	103	0.11	25,000	2,750	100,800	98.7
7	102	0.06	9,000	540	101,340	99.2
8	108	0.12	3,000	360	101,700	99.6
9	107	0.03	9,000	270	101,970	99.9
10	110	0.07	2,100	147	102,117	100.0

Results: Class A is parts 101 and 106
Class B is parts 105 and 109
Class C is parts 104, 103, 102, 108, 107, and 110

ter vendor relations, and streamlining receiving and inspection of A items. You might decide to order a week's to a month's supply for A items. B items might be controlled by using a fixed-period review system, with new orders placed on a joint order. A one- to two-month supply of B items might be ordered. C items, the majority of items, are only a small amount of your total dollar investment. C items might be controlled in a periodic order system or a two-bin system (a simple visual inventory system) and purchased in a three- to six-month supply. Several planning and control techniques for each class of inventory are provided in Exhibit 21.5.

Exhibit 21.5

SUGGESTED INVENTORY PLANNING AND CONTROL TECHNIQUES BASED ON ABC ANALYSIS

TECHNIQUE	INVENTORY CLASS		
	A	B	C
Forecasting	Detailed	Routine	Rough
Cycle counts	Frequently	Routinely	Occasionally
Records	Perpetual	Perpetual	Periodic
Frequency of order review	Continuous	Month	Annual
Safety stock	Small	Medium	Large
Lead time monitored	Continuous	Periodic	Seldom
Issuing method	Issue	Issue	Lot
Quantity ordered	Small	Medium	Large
Order frequency	High	Medium	Low

Improving Accuracy of Inventory Records

Accuracy of inventory records is essential to proper management of inventory. When you are aware of having inaccurate records, you tend to order more units and carry excess inventory to compensate for the record errors. This practice, however, causes unnecessarily high inventories and the waste of money. You may lose a sale for two reasons: your records show that you are stocked out of a requested item when you really have it; or your records show that you have requested an item when you are really stocked out. Both situations are equally bad—and both could have been prevented by applying good inventory control practices.

One method of inventory control is security. The degree of security required for inventory items differs from one firm to another and from one inventory item to another. The degree depends upon the item's size, value, weight, use, and marketability. Establishing and using control procedures are part of good security. Limited access to stock rooms, recording transactions properly, locking stock areas, and instituting a cycle-counting program (discussed later) are appropriate means to providing security.

Good procedures for recording inventory transactions and discipline in following these procedures provide the foundation of accurate inventory records. You must assign the responsibility for developing, implementing, and maintaining accurate records and procedures to specific individuals, and these individuals must be held accountable for meeting your inventory objectives. Inventory accuracy is particularly important in a manufacturing organization. An inaccurate record for one part for a product with hundreds of parts can impact the scheduling of all the other parts and can ultimately prevent the sale of that finished product and even several other products (other products may have used the other parts that you assigned to the product that could not be finished).

Inventory records and the actual physical quantities of inventories on hand must be identical to prevent lost sales and excessive and unknown inventories. Three approaches to reconciling these records are cycle counting, periodic physical inventories, and sampling of inventory items.

Cycle counting involves taking counts of specific items at regular intervals until all items have been counted at least once during the year. The time required to count all inventory items is called the cycle. With an annual cycle, each part number or item is counted at least once a year. On a quarterly cycle, all items are counted at least four times annually; on a monthly cycle, all items are counted at least twelve times a year.

Since the risk and cost of an inventory error are not the same for all items, you might choose to count some items more frequently than others. You can base the frequency of cycle counts on the number of transactions for the inventory item. Another approach is to base the frequency of cycle counts on your ABC analysis. You may want to count A items once a month, B items once a quarter, and C items once a year. This provides more control over your more important items. You can also choose to trigger a count when the reorder point is reached, however; at this point, the quantity to be counted is usually its lowest and the chance for a stockout is at its highest.

Next, you have to determine the annual frequency count. The annual frequency count is the number of times an item is counted each year. These figures are accumulated for all items and divided by the number of working days to determine the number of items to be counted each day. Tolerance levels, the allowable error, are set for each inventory class or item. Each day a count sheet is provided to the individual responsible for the counting. The sheet contains the part number and a brief description of it, along with a description of the location of the inventory if necessary. The counter goes to the location and counts the inventory on hand, identifies any current transactions that may not have been recorded, and makes any transactions required. The counter then compares the inventory balance with the record balance and tolerance levels. If a discrepancy exists, the counter goes back to the inventory location and other locations attempting to reconcile the difference. Manufacturers have long used cycle counting to improve their records accuracy. Wholesalers and retailers are beginning to use this approach.

In cycle-counting programs, a random group and a control group should be set up. The purposes of the random group are to measure accuracy and to correct inventory balances. The purposes of the control group are to identify errors, to determine what caused them, and to eliminate the particular cause of the error. The control group consists of a very few items that are selected because a large number of transactions occur or because each item follows a different paperwork path. These items are counted frequently—possibly each day. The objective is to have the counts frequent enough that the counter can identify the cause of the inventory discrepancy and eliminate it. The hope is that this approach not only eliminates the error in that record, but also removes that cause for other inventory records. If you are unable to implement a complete cycle-counting program because of limited resources, you should consider a control group program that could help eliminate several of the sources of error from your inventory system.

The second approach to correcting inventory errors is taking an annual physical inventory. Preparation for a physical inventory is critical to its success and should include getting the items identified and properly located prior to taking the counting. Additionally, proper instruction and training in counting, recording, tagging, and verifying inventories are essential. Discrepancies between physical counts and inventory records must be reconciled to identify which is in error. Several studies have shown that without proper training and reconciliation, the taking of physical inventories introduces more errors in inventory records than it eliminates.

The third approach to rectifying errors is the sampling of inventory records. A sample of inventory items is selected based upon your ABC classification, frequency of use, or another characteristic. These items are counted to identify and correct errors and provide an estimate of accuracy of inventory records as a whole. This is the least preferred approach since error elimination is almost impossible.

Independent Demand Inventory Methods

Demand for an inventory item can be classified as being either independent or dependent. Independent demand, which is unrelated to the demand for other items, must be forecast. The demand for finished goods or spare parts represents independent demand items. Dependent demand is directly related to or derived from the demand for another item or end product. Parts that go into making a finished product represent dependent demand. Dependent demand can be calculated by multiplying the demand for the finished product by the number of each part that the product requires; such demand should not be forecast.

Proper accounting reporting and physical control of inventory are critical to the well being of any company. There are four major methods for planning and controlling independent demand: the periodic review method, reorder point method, two-bin method, and the time-phased order point (TPOP) method.

Periodic Review Method

Periodic review is a method of accounting for inventory in which the cost and the number of units used are determined by taking a physical inventory at the end of a given or fixed period of time. The accounting and inventory records are updated only at this time (weekly, monthly, or annually).

The periodic review inventory accounting system is generally used with a periodic review inventory method such as a fixed-interval, variable quantity model. In a fixed-interval system, the replenishment of inventory items is triggered by the passage of a fixed amount of time (generally a week or a month) rather than by the level of inventory. The quantity ordered may vary, but it is generally an amount of inventory necessary to replenish the item to a fixed maximum quantity. The lead time offset is the amount of time between the placement of an order and its arrival. This system is portrayed in Exhibit 21.6.

At the end of period 1, the inventory is counted and an order is placed for enough inventory to bring the level up to the maximum. When the order is received, its quantity is recorded and the items are placed in inventory and used. At the end of period 2, the same procedure is followed.

Reorder Point Method

In the reorder point system, an order is placed for a fixed quantity of the item when inventory levels drop to a preestablished level, called the *reorder point*. This system usually employs the perpetual inventory accounting procedure. Perpetual inventory is a method of accounting for inventory at the time that the inventory item is used. A continuous record of inventory transactions with usage and costs is maintained. This method has become more popular with the increased use of point-of-sale equipment and bar coding technology.

The reorder point is based on the demand during lead time and the safety stock required for a given level of customer service. A perpetual record of physical inventory must be maintained to identify when an order should be placed. This system, called a *fixed-order-quantity, variable-interval system,* is presented in Exhibit 21.7. When the inventory level for the item falls to the reorder point, an order is placed, usually for the economic order quantity (EOQ). The inventory is replenished when the item is received. Each time an item is issued from

Exhibit 21.6

PERIODIC REVIEW OR FIXED-INTERVAL INVENTORY SYSTEM

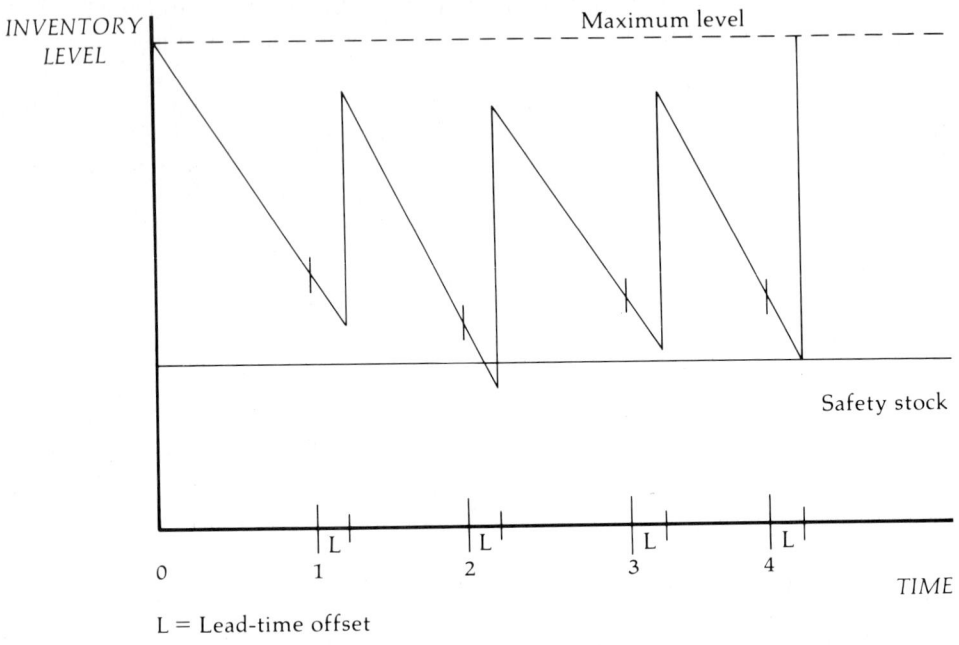

stock, the transaction is recorded on the inventory record. When the item quantity on hand again triggers the reorder point, another order is placed.

Two-Bin System

A two-bin system is a simplified inventory control approach in which inventory is placed in two containers—a use container and a reorder container. Whenever the use container is empty, you place an order for additional material. Until the order is filled, you get material from the reorder container, which has enough stock to last during the required lead time plus additional safety stock. When the order is received, both containers are refilled and you begin again to draw materials from the use container.

The two-bin system allows you to check inventory visually instead of having to continually maintain a perpetual count of an item. It is an extremely effective method of controlling C items.

Time-Phased Order Point Method

The time-phased order point method (TPOP) is similar to the reorder point method. Whereas the reorder point method uses average demand, however,

Exhibit 21.7

REORDER POINT OR FIXED-ORDER-QUANTITY INVENTORY SYSTEM

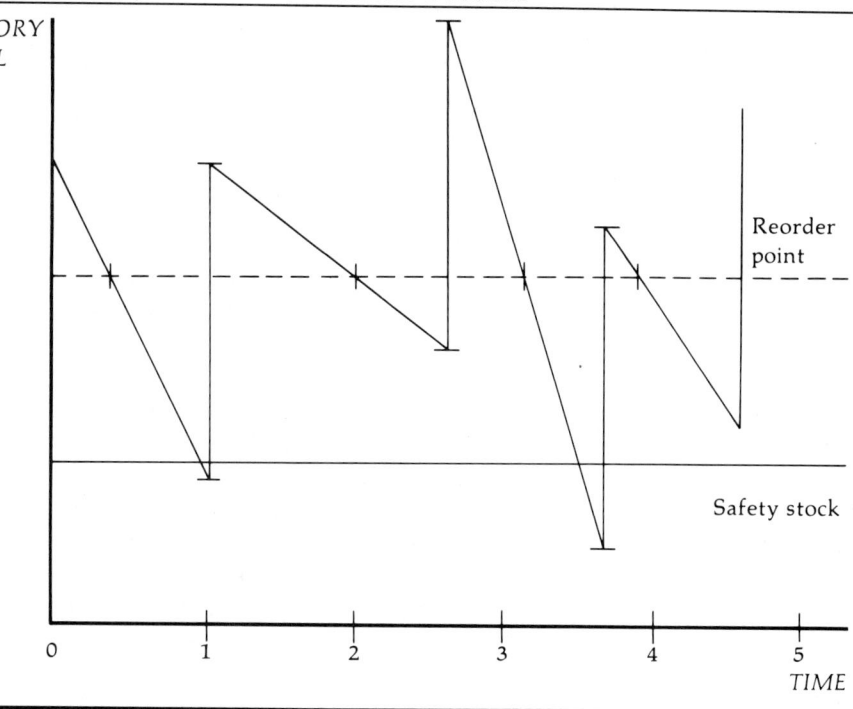

TPOP uses the weekly or monthly forecast to project inventory needs and planned orders by time period. This method is quite useful for lumpy and seasonal demand patterns. TPOP also requires that you maintain a perpetual inventory balance.

An example of the time-phased order point method is provided in Exhibit 21.8. The gross requirements line represents the forecast of demand by time period (week or month). The scheduled receipts line represents the quantity that has already been ordered and shows when the order is expected to arrive. The projected on-hand line indicates the estimated inventory position by time period. The net requirements line is the result of adding scheduled receipts and projected on-hand and subtracting gross requirements. If the result is greater than the safety stock level, an order is not required; if the projected on-hand amount falls below the safety stock level, an order for the item should be placed to arrive within that time period. The amount ordered can be determined in several ways (using EOQ; ordering only what is needed; or ordering a certain number of periods worth of inventory). The timing of order placement is determined by subtracting the lead time from the arrival time and placing the quantity ordered in the appropriate time period of the planned order releases line. The record is updated each week to reflect the actual demand during the period, the receipt of orders, and the placement of orders with estimated arrival dates.

The example in Exhibit 21.8 is simple to follow. Currently, 150 units are on hand, 100 units are required, and 50 units are scheduled to arrive during week 1. At the end of week 1, the projected inventory balance is 100 units. In week 2, the projected requirements (forecast) is 50 units and 50 units are also scheduled to be received from the vendor; therefore, the projected on-hand balance is 100 units. Week 3 has no demand and no scheduled receipts. In week 4, the requirements are 100 units. Safety stock of 100 units are on hand, but an order for 100 units must be received in week 4 so that this safety stock will not be used. If the receipt of the inventory is planned in week 4 and the lead time is 2 weeks, the order must be placed in week 2. The remaining calculations follow this pattern.

This TPOP format provides you the ability to better control critical items by examining your inventory position with respect to actual demand and forecasts. Additionally, order quantities can be calculated to consolidate item orders from the same vendor. In Exhibit 21.9, four inventory records of items purchased from Vendor 1 are presented. For example, you might place an order every week with Vendor 1 for A items, every 2 weeks for B items, and every 5 or 10 weeks for C items. You have the perpetual balance of each item in the time-phased record, therefore you know which items are close to stocking out; you have the next two weeks forecast for each item; and you have an estimate of the inventory position at the next order. You are capable of making much better inventory stocking decisions with this detailed information and you have the ability to respond more quickly to changes in demand.

Comparing Inventory Methods

In comparing the two traditional approaches to managing inventory—the periodic review method and reorder point method—you must examine their impact from the viewpoint of aggregate inventory and not a single item. The periodic inventory method generally requires less labor since records have to be

---

Exhibit 21.8
TIME-PHASED ORDER POINT METHOD

Order policy: Every week

Item: 01
Inventory class: A   Lead time: 2 weeks   Safety stock: 100

					PERIOD					
	0	1	2	3	4	5	6	7	8	9
Gross requirements		100	50	0	100	0	0	50	100	200
Scheduled receipts		50	50							
Projected on-hand	150	100	100	100	100	100	100	100	100	100
Net requirements		0	0	0	100	0	0	50	100	200
Planned receipts					100			50	100	200
Planned releases			100			50	100	200		

adjusted only periodically. The tradeoff is that more inventory is generally carried using this method than using the perpetual method. More orders are generally placed using the perpetual method because the inventory level triggers the reorder of an item. Thus, you might order from the same supplier several days in a row rather than grouping orders to occur every week or month, as under the periodic inventory method.

Exhibit 21.9
TIME-PHASED ORDER POINT RECORDS FROM VENDOR 1

Order policy: Every week

Item: 01
Inventory class: A   Lead time: 1 week   Safety stock: 50

PERIOD

	0	1	2	3	4	5	6	7	8	9
Gross requirements		60	60	60	80	60	60	60	80	60
Scheduled receipts		60								
Projected on-hand	50	50	50	50	50	50	50	50	50	50
Net requirements			60	60	80	60	60	60	80	60
Planned receipts			60	60	80	60	60	60	80	60
Planned releases		60	60	80	60	60	60	80	60	

Order policy: Every 2 weeks

Item :02
Inventory class: B   Lead time: 1 week   Safety stock: 25

PERIOD

	0	1	2	3	4	5	6	7	8	9
Gross requirements		50	50	50	60	50	50	50	60	50
Scheduled receipts		100								
Projected on-hand	25	75	25	85	25	75	25	85	25	75
Net requirements				110		100		110		100
Planned receipts				110		100		110		100
Planned releases			110		100		110		100	

Order policy: Every 10 weeks

Item: 03
Inventory class: C   Lead time: 2 weeks   Safety stock: 20

PERIOD

	0	1	2	3	4	5	6	7	8	9
Gross requirements		20	20	20	20	20	25	25	25	25
Scheduled receipts										
Projected on-hand	200	180	160	140	120	100	75	50	25	
Net requirements										25
Planned receipts										250
Planned releases								250		

Exhibit 21.9

TIME-PHASED ORDER POINT RECORDS FROM VENDOR 1 (*continued*)

Order policy: Every 5 weeks

Item: 04

Inventory class: C   Lead time: 1 week   Safety stock: 20

	0	1	2	3	4	5	6	7	8	9
					PERIOD					
Gross requirements		30	40	40	40	40	40	40	40	40
Scheduled receipts		200								
Projected on-hand	5	175	135	95	55	215	175	135	95	55
Net requirements										
Planned receipts						200				
Planned releases					200					

The TPOP approach is superior to either of these two methods but takes more labor or computer power to operate effectively. Neither of the two previous methods recognizes the possibility of seasonality, sales promotions, known sales, or increasing or decreasing sales. TPOP provides the capability of planning to accommodate nonuniform demand and joint replenishment of different materials from the same vendor. For example, if you were to order from a given supplier every two weeks, your order quantity should be for the next two weeks' demand plus any amount needed to adjust the safety stock to the correct amount. In following this approach, you reduce the number of orders placed and the amount of inventory carried.

In addition to providing the ability to consolidate orders from the same vendor, this time-phased format provides the ability to consolidate orders from customers, warehouses, or distributors to better calculate manufacturing requirements. This use is called distribution requirements planning. Additionally, a service operation that provides preventive maintenance can project material and labor needs by using this format to provide better planning and control of resources.

Summary

In recent years, businesses owners have realized that inventory is both an asset and a liability. As the means to achieve future sales, it is an asset available to generate income; as material that may not be sold, it represents a cost factor that wise business managers learn to control.

Four main types of inventory are common in retail and manufacturing settings: lot size, or cycle, inventory; fluctuation, or buffer, inventory; basic pipeline stock; and anticipation inventory. Each serves a given function, but each must be analyzed in terms of four tradeoffs, which include the cost of ordering the inventory, the cost of carrying it, the cost of carrying insufficient inventory, and the cost of carrying too much inventory.

A method called *ABC analysis* is a useful means of identifying a business's most significant inventory items. This method consists of ranking all inventory according to the annual sales value and classifying items into three priority groupings based on the proportion of total sales value they represent. The idea is to focus efforts on controlling inventory items in class A, which are the items that affect 60 to 70 percent of the year's total dollar value. By closely controlling these items, rather than the lower classes of inventory that are insignificant in terms of annual value, a business can more effectively control inventory costs.

Another key aspect of controlling inventory is to ensure that inventory records are accurate. Cycle counting, periodic physical inventories, and sampling are three techniques of achieving that assurance.

Some businesses, especially manufacturers, must address the question of how to control for independent demand—the demand for inventory that originates outside the company. Four standard methods for achieving this control are the periodic review method, the reorder point method, the two-bin method, and the time-phased order point method. Each of these methods uses forecasts to attempt to identify the amount of inventory that will be required.

Class Assignments

1. Discuss inventory as an asset and a liability for the following businesses:
   1. Produce department of supermarket
   b. New car dealer
   c. Pharmacy
   d. Newsstand
   e. Restaurant
2. Describe the four functions of inventory applied to a
   a. Manufacturer
   b. Restaurant
   c. Mechanic
   d. Supermarket
   e. Dentist
3. Identify which inventory items in the following list are A, B, and C items and describe the types of planning and control procedures you might use for each class.

Part Number	Demand	Price
1	1000	$ 1
2	500	100
3	20000	10
4	6000	5
5	40	200
6	5	1000
7	800	25
8	3000	100
9	100	400
10	600	200

4. You have decided to use ABC analysis to assist you in focusing your attention on your biggest customers. Describe the approach to analyzing your customer data. How would you better focus your attention to each group?

5. You want to set up a cycle-counting program on the 10 items listed in question 3. Describe how you would set up your program and the procedures for each class of items.

References

Bailey, L. J., Jr. "Small Manufacturing: Bringing the Material Control Function Together." *American Production and Inventory Control Society Fall Seminar Proceedings 1986.* Falls Church, Va.: APICS, 1986, pp. 112–116.

Bernheim, R. C. "Tending to Small Business Inventory Control." *P & IM,* 3, No. 4, April 1983, pp. 44–45.

Bowers, J. S. "Materials Management Organization in a Small Manufacturing Environment." *American Production and Inventory Control Society Fall Seminar Proceedings 1986.* Falls Church, Va.: APICS, 1986, pp. 284–291.

Caldwell, C. B. "Material Control and the Small Repetitive Manufacturer." *American Production and Inventory Control Society 29th Annual International Conference Proceedings.* Falls Church, Va.: APICS, 1986, pp. 287–289.

Chrisman, J. J., and D. P. Christy. "The Master Material List: A Useful Complement to Bills of Material for the Small Manufacturer." *Production and Inventory Management Journal,* 26, No. 2, Second Quarter 1985, pp. 36–49.

Frank, D. N. "A Small Manufacturing Approach to Real Inventory Accuracy." *American Production and Inventory Control Society Fall Seminar Proceedings 1986.* Falls Church, Va.: APICS, 1986, pp. 305–311.

Gregory, G., S. Klesniks, and J. A. Piper. "Stock Control in Small Companies." *International Journal of Production Research,* 20, No. 4, July–August 1982, pp. 475–482.

Harris, F. W. *Operations and Costs.* Factory Management Series, Chicago: A. W. Show Co., 1915.

Joyce, J., and R. Buckman. "Materials Management in a Small Manufacturing Company." *American Production and Inventory Control Society Small Manufacturing Reprints.* Falls Church, Va.: APICS, 1985, pp. 39–51.

Wallace, T. F., and J. R. Dougherty, eds. *APICS Dictionary,* 6th ed. Falls Church, Va.: APICS, 1987.

PLANNING
INFORMATION NEEDS

Information systems and computer systems are thought of as synonymous by many people, but they are not necessarily the same. Both areas have undergone tremendous changes in the past few years. Microcomputers, telecommunications, and new software now provide you, the small business owner, the opportunity to use several tools and techniques available only to large firms in the past.

In the first part of this chapter, we discuss the information needs found in most small businesses. We then discuss the problems associated with the successful merging of the elements of a computerized management information system. Next, we describe computer systems and how they relate to a small business. Finally, we briefly discuss word-processing, spreadsheet, and data base software.

After reading this chapter, you will be able to

- Distinguish between information systems and computer systems
- Explain the importance of examining the physical and logical systems and the supporting policies and procedures prior to designing an information system
- Identify the types of information needed when designing information systems for marketing, accounting, finance, personnel, and human resources
- Describe the types of problems encountered in implementing an information system
- Identify ways to help ensure that software and hardware purchases fit your needs.

Information Systems

Many people confuse information systems with computer systems. Many effective information systems are manual systems. A computerized system simply offers the advantages of providing information in a more timely and accurate way.

To measure the effectiveness of an information system, you need to ascertain how effectively it supports the organization in attaining its goals. Proper data management helps to ensure effective support of business functions. Data management includes formulating policies and procedures for consistent identification, definition, processing, use, and control of information within an organization. An overall information system plan should be formulated from the top down to ensure that the system is integrated across functions (marketing, finance, accounting, personnel, and operations) and across time (the short term, the medium term, and the long term). Exhibit 22.1 provides an overview of the functions and levels of decision making in most organizations. Day-to-day activities should be congruent with the tactical and strategic goals of the business. Your information systems should provide assistance in determining the appropriate solutions to both short- and long-term problems and opportunities. At each level of activity, information about trends is essential to decision making.

Designing an Information System

Prior to designing an information system for your small business, you should evaluate the performance of each activity (marketing, finance, and so on) that the system is to support. Your objective is for each activity to be effective. The

Exhibit 22.1
FUNCTIONAL AREAS AND LEVELS OF DECISION MAKING

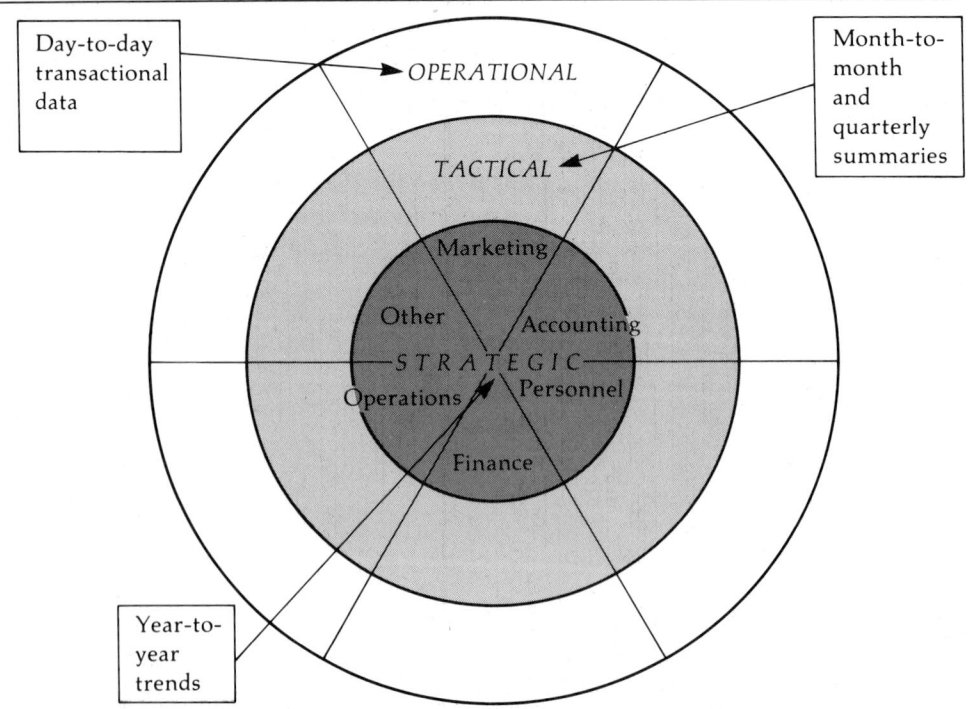

question for the information system becomes, "what information is required to support this activity in contributing to having an effective organization?" The information system is effective only if the policies and procedures for each activity are designed to support the organization. Typically, however, the policies and procedures were implemented over a period of years and have never been evaluated with respect to their impact on the total business. Thus, the assumption that these policies and procedures support the organization is a dangerous one. The objective is not to have an information system that provides an effective functional activity at the expense of total business.

Your evaluation of the functional activity, then, should begin by questioning its relationship to the total business and to other supporting functions and activities. Simplification and standardization of processes should be implemented where appropriate prior to designing the information system. Second, all policies and procedures related to the activity should be identified and studied to ascertain their impact on the firm's competitive strategy. Inconsistent policies and procedures should be eliminated with the objective of retaining only those that contribute to achieving the business's goals. Third, an information system should be designed that provides the essential information to make basic business decisions. Bear in mind that it is much easier to implement and use a simple system than to implement a sophisticated system that defies user understanding.

This approach to designing a management information system follows the Japanese approach to production. In planning and controlling automobile production, Toyota used a two-card Kanban system to signal the movement and production of parts. Thousands of parts are needed to assemble one automobile, and their manufacture and movement are controlled by a simple manual information system understood by all employees. Imagine how much easier this approach would be for a small business. Hundreds of small manufacturers in Japan have adopted Kanban systems to simplify planning and control of their products.

The first step in implementing the Kanban approach is to lay out the production system to promote the flow of parts to products through the facility. Second, policies and procedures (such as using statistical process control, training workers to be multiskilled and instituting preventive maintenance) have to be devised to support the flow of parts, subassemblies, and assemblies to product completion. Last, a simple understandable management information system has to be designed to support production of the product—not of the parts.

In designing an effective system, you should identify exactly what is required to accomplish the activity. An effective method to assist you in identifying your data and information requirements is to examine commercial software packages appropriate for the activity. This review not only helps you determine your information needs but also ensures that you do not reinvent the wheel and spend money unnecessarily by devising your own system when existing systems are available. Your objective is not to buy software but to identify the minimum information needs to accomplish your activity. There is nothing wrong with a manual information system. The easiest information system to computerize is an effective manual information system. If your employees do not use your manual information system, do not expect them to support a computerized information system.

In Chapters 19 and 20 we described approaches to designing and managing operations. Review these chapters carefully prior to designing any information system. Once you are assured that the activity is performed to support the effective operation of the business, the supporting information system requirements have to be identified and defined. We now turn to examples of information systems related to each functional area. Keep in mind that the overall objective is not to have an information system that supports one activity alone. The objective is an effective small business.

Marketing

Most small businesses have forecasting systems, either by design or by evolution. A restaurant owner or manager has to estimate the demand for certain menu offerings and purchase the ingredients. The owner can use a formal or informal information system to perform this forecasting function. Over time he or she can estimate the percentage of each type of meal served and apply this percentage to an estimate of the total meals served—a top-down forecasting approach. Alternatively, the owner can keep detailed counts of each type of meal served and estimate demand based on each specific type of meal—a bottom-up forecasting approach. Point-of-sale terminals (cash registers), which record the data as each sale occurs, can be used to provide data for a forecasting system. Remember that these data represent what was sold and not what was requested.

Another example of a marketing information system is an order-entry system, which is present in most manufacturing and many service operations. In its simplest form, the name and address of the customer are listed on an invoice along with the desired items; goods are picked from finished goods inventory, packed, and shipped to the customer or the customer can get the items desired from the various shelves in the store. If the business is out of stock, the goods must be ordered or manufactured and sent to the customer at a later time. Many automobile and electronic parts retail stores use an invoicing system as the basis of a client data base that is then used for catalog mailings and advertising. In some service operations, the customer is given an appointment or must wait in line for order processing. Hair stylists, doctors, lawyers, and automobile mechanics use simple but effective manual order-entry or appointment systems. At the operational level, such an information system provides such information as who is next, when the appointment takes place, and how much time is allocated for the task. This data base can also be used to support advertising, inventory, and staffing decisions.

An example of a simple and effective operations activity and its supporting information system can be observed in many supermarkets and discount stores. These stores use ABC analysis to segregate sales by cash and number of items purchased; they then provide express lines for purchasers that meet certain limits. Other stores have cash and credit card lines to reduce customer waiting time and streamline the flow of customers. A check or credit card approval process is an information system typically used to streamline operations, increase customer convenience, and reduce bad debts to the firm. Effective means of implementing this function are to provide a customer service desk for check approval or to issue preapproved customer check cards. Either approach maintains the flow of customers through the system.

Accounting

Accounting activities such as payroll, accounts payable and receivable, and the general ledger are usually the first activities computerized. Accounting systems are easy to computerize since they are records of the history of operations and are not required in planning the business's operations activities. They can also be computerized easily because the automated system replaces an effective manual system.

Exhibits 22.2 and 22.3 portray the funds, product, and information flows generally present in a manufacturing and a service firm, respectively. Each activity requires supporting information to ensure that intelligent decisions are made. The revenue cycle may have several isolated or integrated supporting information systems. Order-entry and tracking systems, invoice printing, customer statement printing, accounts receivable, general ledger, and management revenue reports are primary revenue-related information systems. Expense collection systems may include cost accounting, payroll, and accounts payable systems. These systems are based on activities that take place at the operational level and are aggregated to form reports by time period; the reports are used to support tactical and strategic decision making. Each business transaction is posted to the system of accounts, which is closed at the end of the time period. The income statement, balance sheet, and statement of cash flow are constructed to provide information on the company's progress and current status.

Information systems to support accounting activities should be fully integrated to eliminate having to enter the same data two or three times. Additionally, report generation is a vital part of effectively managing a business. Close examination of the type and level of detail (operational, tactical, and strategic) of the reports is essential. The ability to interface with programs that can graph trends and provide histograms and pie charts is quite desirable.

Finance

Financial information on your company's progress and status is useful in deciding future courses of action. Basic ratios, such as the quick ratio and inventory turns, can be computed from accounting information and compared to both past and competitors' performance. Spreadsheets can easily be constructed and manipulated to provide what-if information. This is a relatively new application available to small businesses with the development of inexpensive software for microcomputers. A review of Chapter 11 and its appendix should provide you insight into the potential application for this new technology.

Exhibit 22.2
PRODUCT, CASH, AND INFORMATION FLOWS FOR A MANUFACTURING FIRM

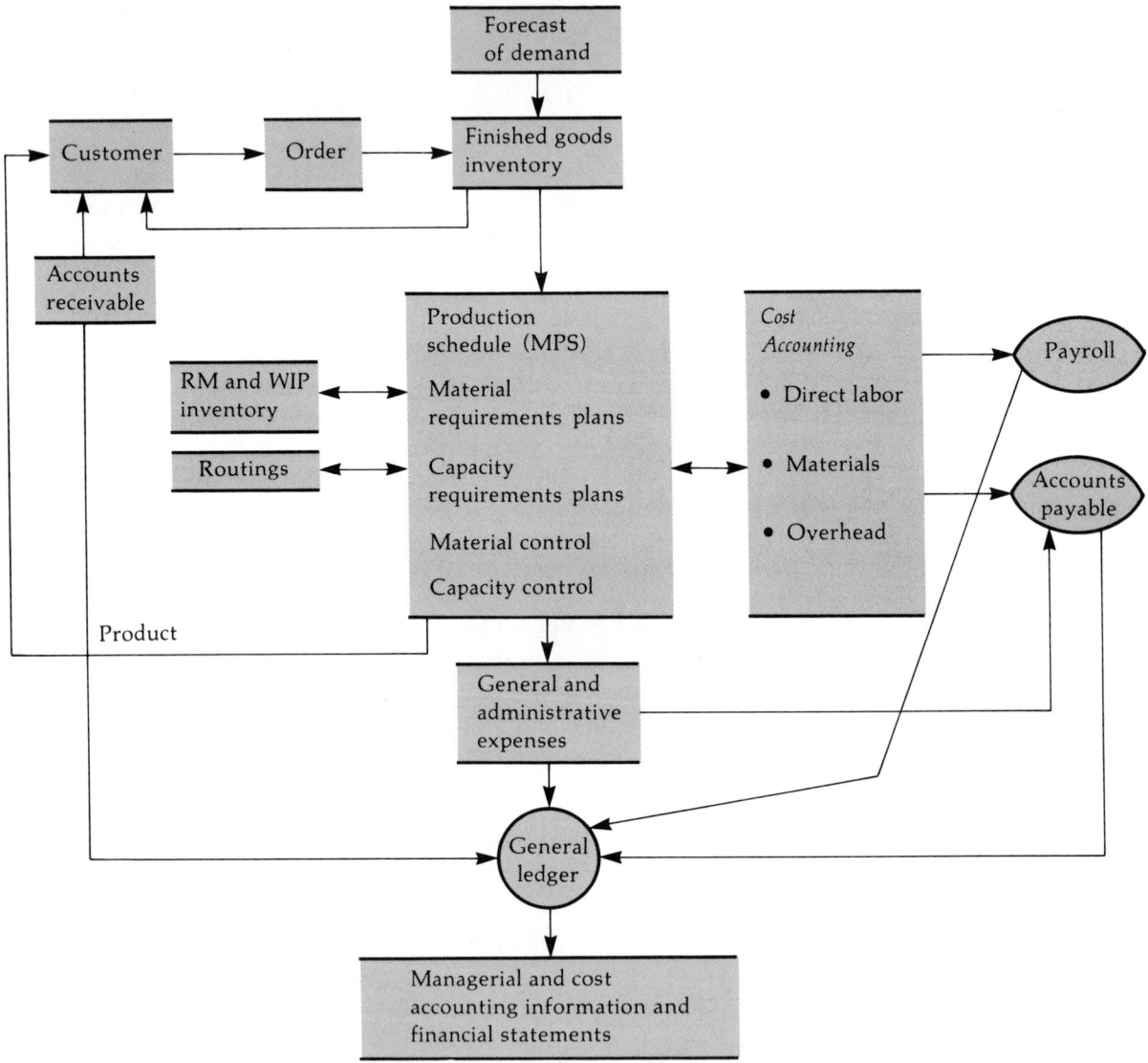

Personnel and Human Resources

Prior to designing a personnel and human resources information system, you should review the personnel and human resources functions described in Part Six of this text. Glenn Bassett (1979) provides seventeen general classifications of data used in personnel and human resources information systems:

Exhibit 22.3
SERVICE, CASH, AND INFORMATION FLOWS FOR A SERVICE FIRM

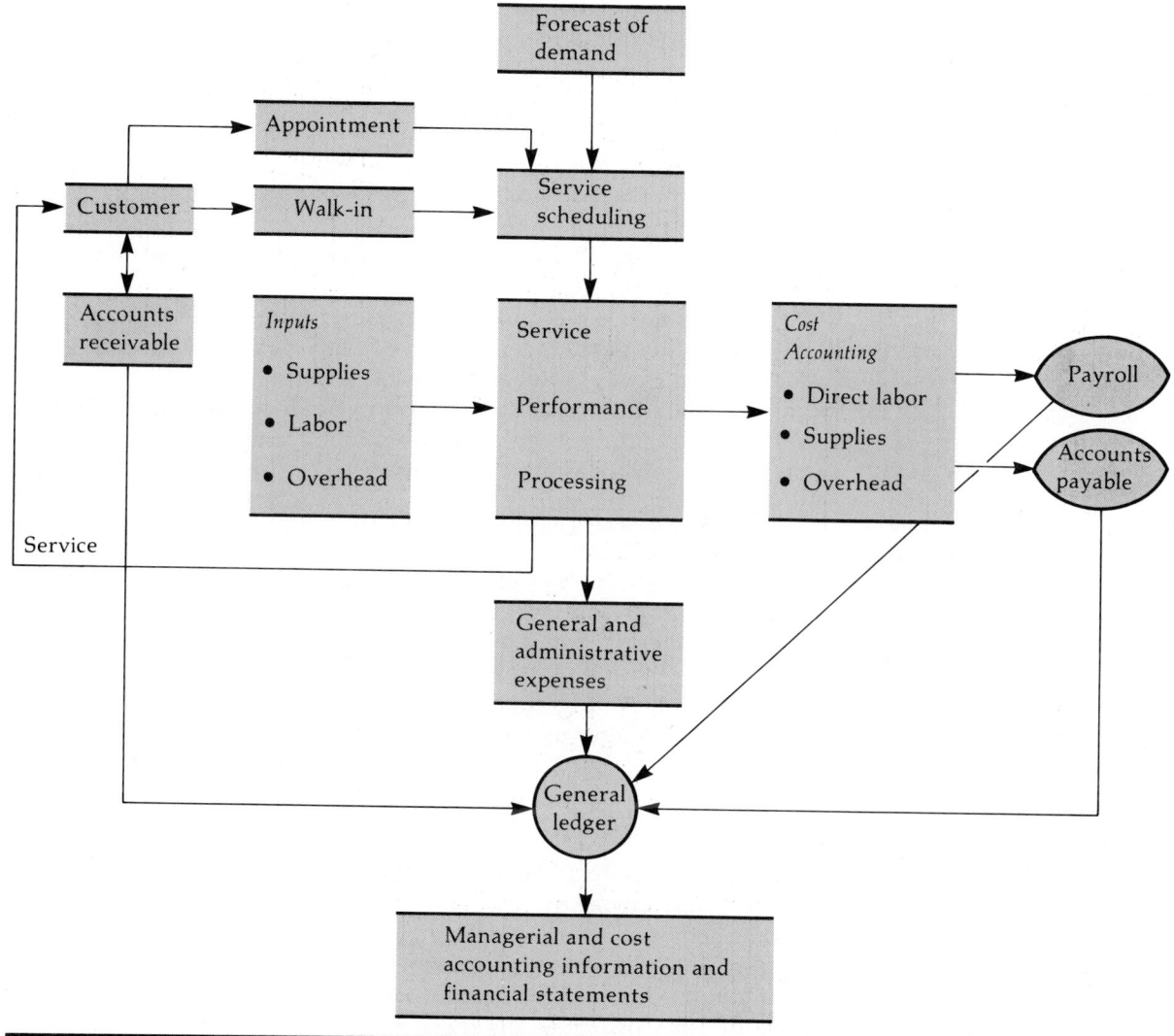

1. Personnel data (name, social security number, address, sex, age, race)
2. Recruiting data (source, data of application, test given, reason for accepting or rejecting, and so on)
3. Work experience (prior employment and skills record)
4. Education (level, degrees, certifications, licenses)
5. Compensation and work assignment (current pay, job class, hours worked, overtime)

6. Performance evaluation (work preferences, appraisal reports, disciplinary actions, and so on)
7. Length of service and layoffs (date hired, laid off, and so on)
8. Employee behavior data (absences, tardiness, grievances, productivity and quality measures, and so on)
9. Union membership data
10. Contact data (who to contact in case of emergency)
11. Benefit plan data (medical or life insurance, pension plan, sick and vacation time, and so on)
12. Separation from company data (date, reason, eligible for rehiring, forwarding address, etc.)
13. Safety data (hazards in work area, injury records, time lost, workers' compensation, and so on)
14. Open position data (job requirements, salary, dates needed, and so on)
15. Work environment data (average pay, education, years with company, accident rate, turnover rate, and so on)
16. Job history data (job number, location in organization, date job was established, past and present employees in job, and so on)
17. Labor market data (prevailing wage rates, labor supply and unemployment by job class, and so on)

Much of this data is historical in nature and requires periodic updating. The data are useful for determining compliance with numerous state and federal laws related to employment. They have a variety of other uses, such as helping in promotion decisions, assessing changes in labor costs, and evaluating the effectiveness of staffing procedures. These information systems are very simple to construct and implement.

Operations

Operations information systems include forecasting, scheduling, quality control, maintenance, and inventory activities, all of which assist planning and controlling. Some activities interface directly with customers and vendors. Retail and manufacturing inventory information systems are more difficult to design, implement, and operate than most information systems since inaccurate data results in lost sales and generally these inaccurate records go undetected until the item is needed. Purchasing is also based on the inventory systems, and errors can be costly. Material requirements planning (MRP) systems are extremely difficult to implement since they introduce a different and formal approach to conducting business.

Exhibit 22.4 lists the benefits of an MRP information system. While the benefits are numerous, this type of information system is extremely difficult to implement even in a small business. An MRP system can provide information useful to marketing, accounting, finance, personnel, and top management. If structured correctly, such a system can provide information useful in making operational, tactical, and strategic decisions across functional areas.

Exhibit 22.4
BENEFITS OF AN MRP SYSTEM

REDUCTION IN INVENTORY
 1. Balanced inventories
 2. Reduction in work-in-process inventories
 3. Reduction in finished goods inventories

BETTER CAPACITY PLANNING
 1. Increased equipment utilization
 2. Identification of bottlenecks in work centers
 3. Better scheduling of maintenance

BETTER PRIORITY PLANNING
 1. Decrease in manufacturing lead time
 2. Rescheduling capabilities

BETTER CUSTOMER SERVICE
 1. Reduction in prices
 2. On-time delivery

 3. Better quality
 4. Reduction in lost sales

BETTER MANAGEMENT
 1. Provides performance measures
 2. Provides insight into the manufacturing process

IMPROVED MORALE
 1. Confidence in system
 2. Better coordination between departments

BETTER LONG-RANGE PLANNING
 1. Marketing
 2. Production
 3. Personnel
 4. Finance
 5. Purchasing
 6. Top management

Problems with Implementing Information Systems

The pitfalls to designing, implementing, and operating an information system, which are numerous, can be classified into five general areas:

 1. Ineffective operations and supporting activities
 2. Ineffective policies and procedures to support the operation and supporting activities
 3. Lack of top management commitment and involvement
 4. Technical problems
 5. Human problems

Problems in these areas generally reduce the effectiveness of any information system. Fortunately, the solutions are general enough to provide assistance to the design, implementation, and operation of any information system.

Ineffective Operations and Supporting Systems

In most companies, an informal system is used to supply the information needs of the operations employees. For example, Joe, who has been with his company for ten years, is the only person who knows how to assemble this product. Joe does not need, understand, or use the formal information system to accomplish his job, but what happens when Joe leaves? A good information system to support product and part manufacturing and assembly could save your business. It is difficult for Joe to lose the role of being the only person who can perform certain tasks, but it is essential to the continued success of your business that a formal information system replace the informal structure currently used. Small businesses, with smaller staffs and with what are frequently undocumented procedures, are especially prone to this problem.

Ineffective Policies and Procedures

Policies and procedures are designed to support operations. Over time, however, the business environment changes; you need to continually evaluate the environment and your operations to keep your policies and procedures useful. As an example of an outdated policy, consider the small manufacturing plant that, four years before, developed a forecasting system to be used by the purchasing agent to buy raw materials. The system was very successful, but in the fourth year the company was forced to expedite several orders from its suppliers at high freight charges and missed customer request dates on an increasing number of orders. The problem was identified. The business initially was a make-to-stock company that manufactured large quantities of each product to be placed in finished goods. In the fourth year, however, customer orders had increased significantly, finished goods inventories had decreased, and the business now had about a three-month backlog of customer orders. The purchasing manager, however, was still ordering raw materials in large batches based on the original forecast of customer demand. This manager should have been examining the actual raw materials requirements for each customer order and ordering exactly what was needed. The environment had changed from a make-to-stock situation based on forecasts to a make-to-order situation based on customer orders, but the firm had not changed its policies and procedures to support the new environment.

Another example of an ineffective policy is using the efficiency of direct labor as a performance measure. This measure is calculated as the standard hours of direct labor for the jobs issued to the shop divided by the actual number of hours of direct labor consumed. Many companies, both small and large, attempt to keep workers busy at all costs. This policy generally results in a tremendous amount of finished parts and products for which there is no customer demand. Additionally, supervisors sometimes circumvent the formal materials release system in order to keep workers busy. Conflicting and inefficient policies and procedures create problems with using the information system as designed and promote the use of informal channels to accomplish the required activities.

Lack of Management Commitment and Involvement

Top management must be committed to and involved in the implementation of any information system that affects how business is conducted. Top management must support the change, reward those that support the implementation, and, if necessary, punish those who inhibit its progress. Particularly in a small business, where the owner or manager is in close contact with the employees, he or she must have a good understanding of the new system and its benefits and the shortcomings of the old system. To be successful, any new system must have a champion to explain and defend its design, implementation, and use. In a smaller business, top management is the natural champion.

Technical Problems

Numerous technical problems related to system design, interface of employees with the system, frequency of updating, size of the data base, and uses of the data base can surface. For example, MRP system design, master scheduling or capacity planning functions, data base structure and file integrity, management of inventory levels, and rescheduling activities all create technical problems that must be resolved prior to the implementation and successful operation of an MRP system. Policies and procedures should be developed in each of these areas to support an effective production and logistics system. Implementing MRP—as with most information systems—requires the reexamination of existing policies and procedures and the implementation of new policies and procedures.

Human Problems

When implementing any new system, you may find that the most serious problems are human problems. People often resist change. This resistance occurs especially when people perceive the change to be unnecessary, have negative consequences for them personally (such as decreased job security, increased job demands, or loss of status or other things they value), or increase ambiguity about what is expected of them. Resistance to change is overcome by thoroughly educating employees in the concepts related to the new information system; having user involvement in the design of the new system; providing proper training; and ensuring top management commitment and support during the design, implementation, and operation of the new information system. You must also alleviate employees' fears of job displacement and loss of status. These actions promote user acceptance of the new system.

Computers

This section is brief for two reasons. First, computer technology is changing so rapidly that almost any discussion of hardware or software will be obsolete prior to the printing of this text. For example, microcomputer systems have decreased dramatically in cost over the past five years. Additionally, computer's speed has increased tenfold over this same period. Second, software applications formerly available only for large mainframe computers are now available to small businesses for use on a microcomputer. You should, therefore, consult several current computer magazines and texts to develop an understanding of current hardware technology and software available to small businesses. Additionally, you should review trade magazines for new applications and commercial software appropriate to your industry.

Experts agree that computer systems should be purchased based on the capabilities of software, not hardware. You should determine whether you need a computer and what applications would be profitable for you. Do you have detailed customer histories to maintain? Do you have a large array of inventory items to track? Do you have a large supplier base? Do you require complex tracking of parts and products for a federal agency? Many of these applications suggest the need for a computer, but questions remain. Is using the computer going to provide a competitive advantage for your business? Is it going to produce a new or expanded capability? Is it going to help you generate more money? Is it going to save you money? Unless these questions can be answered positively, you may, in purchasing a computer, incur the expense without receiving any benefits. The computer is only a tool; it must be used correctly to provide advantages to your business.

When you buy a computer, you are generally buying the central processing unit (CPU), an input device (a keyboard, for example), output devices (a monitor and a printer), and long-term storage devices (floppy disks or hard disks). Several makes and models provide many choices for each of these basic units. Again, software, not hardware, should be the deciding factor in determining what components are needed. The application is what is going to produce the competitive edge, not a bigger or faster computer. Try identifying other small business owners who are in the same industry and who have computerized some operations. Talk with them about their use of the computer and the problems they encountered. Additionally, check with small business software and computer vendors (Radio Shack, IBM, and others) and review their offerings designed for your industry. Ask to speak to customers who have implemented the vendor's systems; reputable vendors are usually willing to provide such lists. Call and visit some of these customers before making any commitment to buying a system.

Do you know how to operate a computer? Do you know the operating system characteristics? Do you know the application that you are implementing? Realize that purchasing hardware and software is only the first step. To make use of the system, you or an employee must become proficient with the hardware and software. This learning process is time consuming and, in many cases, expensive.

Several general purpose application packages are available that can provide you additional capabilities for your computer. Word-processing programs make the typing of complex letters, reports, and figures very easy. These packages also have the capability of merging tables, graphs, and figures into the text. Form letters can be constructed that resemble individualized letters. Data base packages allow you to sort and merge data from various sources rapidly. Electronic spreadsheets allow you to construct templates of complex calculations, tables, and graphs and then explore the possible outcomes of different possibilities by varying the assumptions and recalculating the results.

Several commercial packages for each of these types of software are available, each with different capabilities. Prior to purchasing a package, you should read evaluations of several competing programs to identify the one most appropriate for your needs. These evaluations are generally available in computer magazines. You should also identity available training for the package through such sources as the vendors, community colleges, and trade schools.

Summary

Information systems are not the same as computer systems; automated information systems are merely one type. Before designing an information system, it is essential to analyze the activities that the system is to support to ensure that those activities support an effective organization. Always simplify operations first. Next, ensure that all management policies and procedures support the activity in its organization role. Only then can you identify the information needs of the activity and design the information system. Each operational area has the need for specific types of information.

Designing, implementing, and operating information systems present certain special problems. These problems are ineffective operations, ineffective policies and procedures supporting those operations, lack of management commitment to the new system, technical problems, and human problems.

Computers can be valuable tools for information systems, but the investment in computer hardware and software should only be made after taking the time to determine whether a computerized system offers advantages that outweigh the cost. If your analysis indicates that purchasing a computer is advantageous, it is important to remember to identify first the software you need, and only then begin to shop for the hardware to go with it.

Class Assignments

1. If you were opening a new restaurant that served a limited lunch and dinner menu, what types of information would you want to collect for
   a. Forecasting
   b. Staffing cooks, waiters, and waitresses
   c. Scheduling cooks, waiters, and waitresses
   d. Purchasing food and plates
2. If you were opening a real estate agency, what types of information would you want to collect for
   a. Forecasting volume and dollars of real estate sales
   b. Identifying a specialty for your firm
   c. Identifying travel expenses associated with showing houses
   d. Projecting monthly revenues and expenses
3. Based on an interview with a small business owner, write a brief report on the types of information needed for marketing, accounting, finance, human resources, and operations, and how each type is collected and used to assist in decision making.
4. Visit a computer store and investigate the capabilities of software available to small businesses. Write a few paragraphs on each software application. Compare your findings to those of your classmates.
5. Compare and contrast two different commercial software packages that perform the same small business function (e.g., two general accounting packages).

6. Check out two current periodicals on computers from the library and review two articles on new computer technology.

7. Check the evening courses offered at technical schools and colleges in your area and estimate the cost of becoming computer and software literate.

8. Check your newspaper classified ads for sales on used computers and software. Compare these prices to new equipment prices. How do you explain the differences?

References

Alavi, M. "Microcomputers and Small Manufacturing: A Strategy for Acquisition." *P&IM Review,* 5, No. 1, January 1985, pp. 30–33.

Bailey, L. J., Jr., and C. Caldwell. "P & IC in the Small Manufacturer: Manual or Micro?" *American Production and Inventory Control Society 28th Annual International Conference Proceedings.* Falls Church, Va.: APICS, 1985, pp. 245–247.

Bassett, Glenn A. "Pair Records and Information Systems," in Dale Yonder and N. G. Heneman, tr., *ASPA Handbook of Personnel and Industrial Relations* (1979), pp. 2-57–2-90.

Blackstone, J. H., Jr., and J. F. Cox. "Selecting MRP Software for Small Businesses." *Production and Inventory Management Journal,* 26, No. 4, Fourth Quarter 1985, pp. 42–50.

Boeder, S. M. "Large System Benefits for the Small Manufacturing Environment." *American Production and Inventory Control Society 29th Annual International Conference Proceedings.* Falls Church, Va.: APICS, 1986, pp. 32–36.

Childers, C. N. "Let's Do Production Planning on a Microcomputer." *American Production and Inventory Control Society 30th Annual International Conference Proceedings.* Falls Church, Va.: APICS, 1987, pp. 303–307.

Hamilton, S. "Microcomputer Systems for Small Manufacturers." *American Production and Inventory Control Society 29th Annual International Conference Proceedings.* Falls Church, Va.: APICS, 1986, pp. 7–9.

Hamilton, S. "Evaluating and Selecting the Small System." *American Production and Inventory Control Society Spring Seminar Proceedings, 1896.* Falls Church, Va.: APICS, April 1986, pp. 329–334.

Hoffman, R. E., and S. Hamilton. "Selecting and Justifying the Small System with High Performance." *American Production and Inventory Control Society Proceedings of Seminar on Small Manufacturing and Process Industries.* Falls Church, Va.: APICS, September 1985, pp. 5–14.

Kauth, A. R., and C. L. Case. "Managing for Results in Small Manufacturing." *American Production and Inventory Control Society 28th Annual International Conference Proceedings.* Falls Church, Va.: APICS, 1985, pp. 608–610.

McClellan, C. "Five P & IC Uses for a Microcomputer." *American Production and Inventory Control Society Small Manufacturing Reprints.* Falls Church, Va.: APICS, 1985, pp. 83–97.

Patrick, A. "The Role of the Microcomputer in the Small Manufacturing Business." *American Production and Inventory Control Society 1st World Congress of Production and Inventory Control: Presentations, 1985.* Falls Church, Va.: APICS, 1985, pp. 38–42.

Rubin, M. G. "Managing Materials with a Micro Computer." *P & IM Review,* 7, No. 12, December 1987, pp. 30+.

Schultz, H. K. "Microcomputers and Manufacturing, Distribution, and Service Organizations." *Production and Inventory Management Journal.* 24, No. 4, Fourth Quarter 1983, pp. 87–93.

Volkens, B. J. "Successful Implementation of Small Manufacturing Business Systems." *American Production and Inventory Control Society Proceedings of Seminar on Small Manufacturing and Process Industries.* Falls Church, Va.: APICS, September 1985, pp. 129–136.

CONTROLLING
OPERATIONS

Planning and control are vital business functions. In the past four chapters, we have discussed philosophies, concepts, and techniques that can assist you in defining operations, managing operations, managing inventory, and defining and managing information. Each chapter discusses the traditional approaches and several new concepts. Emphasis was placed on the newer approaches responsible for the increased competitive posture of foreign suppliers.

In this chapter, we discuss the design of control systems for small manufacturing and service operations. We describe how to design control systems for each competitive advantage and for inputs, transformation processes, and outputs. Finally, we discuss evaluating your supporting systems.

After this chapter, you will be able to

- Construct simple performance measurement systems
- Control operations to measure profit
- Design performance measurement systems for your competitive edges
- Apply performance measures to input, transformation processes, and outputs
- Evaluate supporting systems

Performance Measurement

Control requires a performance measurement system. Such a system provides a systematic approach to evaluating the inputs, transformation processes, and outputs of a manufacturing or service operation. A performance measurement system consists of performance criteria, standards, and measures. A criterion is a factor that is to be evaluated. The standard is the acceptable level of performance, and the measure is the actual level of performance. Actual performance is then compared to the standard; if the measure falls short of the standard, it may be necessary to take corrective action.

The performance measurement system should be directly related to the goals or criteria of the organization. The major goal of most companies is to make a profit. Performance criteria for each of your competitive advantages (product, process, cost, quality, lead time, delivery as scheduled, and flexibility) should also be established and monitored to ensure that they help you meet your profit goals. It makes no sense to identify competitive advantages unless you are going to measure your progress on them.

For each criterion, you should

- Establish a standard or target level
- Establish limits or boundaries around this target
- Measure your actual performance
- Compare actual performance to the standard and its limits
- Identify the cause of the deviation if performance falls outside the limits
- Take appropriate action

Controlling Operations to Achieve a Profit

Exhibit 23.1 provides an example of a control technique for monitoring quarterly profits. Suppose you set a profit objective of 10 percent; where should you set the limits or boundaries? Without limits around your goal, you will analyze every deviation, no matter how small. Limits help you identify when you are really in trouble and when you must intervene. You might establish target limits of 2 percent. Doing so translates into a range of 8 to 12 percent profit; as long as profits fall within this range, there is no need to investigate. If profit is either

Exhibit 23.1
CONTROL CHART FOR QUARTERLY PROFITS

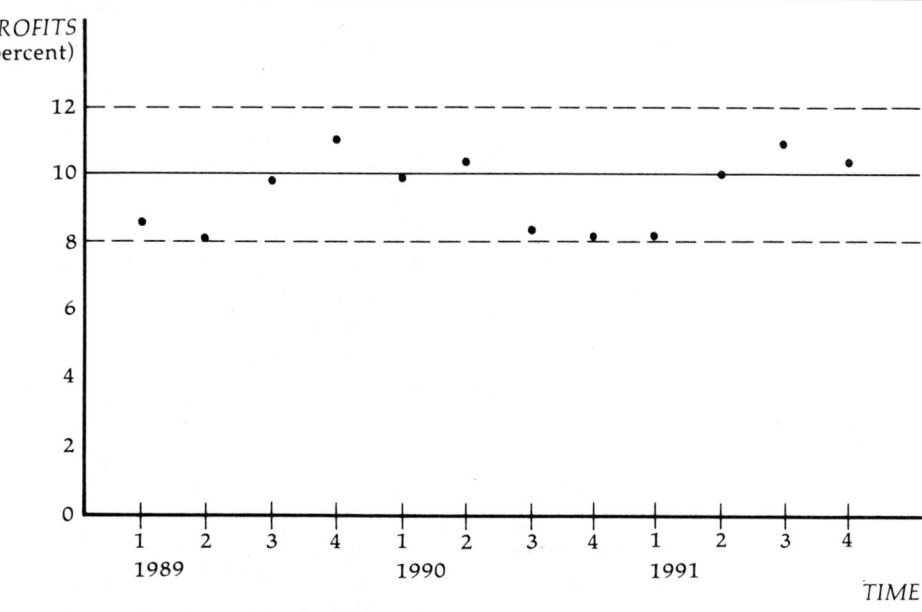

lower than 8 percent or higher than 12 percent, however, the cause should be identified and corrective action taken if required. Should you only realize a 3 percent profit for the quarter, for instance, you should investigate the cause of the deviation.

Even in this example, 3 percent profit may be acceptable. You might have made a large capital investment or undertaken a large expansion for a new service in anticipation of making your 10 percent profit margin or more in the next year or two. Falling outside of the limits is not necessarily bad. The limits simply establish the point at which you want the deviations called to your attention. You might therefore want to establish both short- and long-term performance goals. Setting short-term performance standards and limits allows you the flexibility of considering immediate needs while still reflecting the general direction and level of improvement expected in the long run. This provides more continuity to long-range planning but allows for expected short-term deviations. The point is that if you fall outside of the limits, you need to identify the causes and to be able to take corrective action where necessary.

You also need to study the trends in your performance measures. Information on trends may be much more important than the most recent data point. A few isolated measures outside your limits may not be indicative of poor performance, but it is best to monitor performance and check to identify potential causes of poor performance. Studying trends provides a better estimate of the long-term progress your firm has made toward its objective. In contrast, the most recent measure acts as an immediate status report.

While profit is your ultimate goal, you can very seldom calculate the impact of every decision on your profitability. Therefore you must be able to measure the impact of decisions on other more immediate criteria. The identification of causes of deviations is also much easier at a lower level in the organization than at the global level. As a result, performance measurement systems should be established for product, process, quality, lead time, customer contact, facility utilization, labor and capital utilization, and market penetration. These performance criteria do not replace the profit measure but provide better indicators of what might be causing deviations from short- and long-run profit goals. These performance measurement criteria should be established and coordinated with the competitive advantages that form your business strategy; they should also reflect your overall company goals. Again, you should realize that the sum of the local optima is not the global optima. In other words, you can be performing well on most or all of your local performance measures and still be losing money—or, even worse, going bankrupt.

Differences between manufacturing and services are important in controlling operations. Generally, manufactured products are tangible and durable while services are intangible and perishable. Other characteristics of a manufactured product are that the product can be inventoried; its quality is easily measured; it has long lead times; the company has low customer contact and large facilities; the process is capital intensive; and markets cover large geographical areas. Characteristics of service businesses are that services cannot be inventoried; quality is subjective; lead times are short; the company has high customer contact and small facilities; the process is labor intensive; and markets are local. It is possible, of course, to find examples of both services and manufacturers that seem closer to the general characteristics of the other type. Of primary importance is the impact that each characteristic might have on planning and controlling operations. Let us examine how to control operations for each area on which competitive edge can be based.

Product

In developing a performance measurement system to measure the competitive advantage of your products, you might begin by asking what niche in the market you are targeting. Is your restaurant a fast-food or full-service type? Who are your competitors, and how does your service or product compare with theirs? What time do they open and close? What are their specialties? How does their service compare to yours? What do they do well? Can you learn from them? What actions can you take to compete more effectively? Do you have a fixed market size or are you in a growing or shrinking market? What is your market share?

Performing an ABC analysis of your customers can help you identify your regular customers and your big spenders. Do you take special care to ensure that these customers have first-class service? Do you tell them to contact you if a problem arises? Do they know that you want their business? While everyone strives for impeccable service or zero defects, few if any businesses ever attain this performance level. The better businesses strive for perfection but also ensure that top-priority items get special attention and have more detailed and stringent controls applied to them.

Do you forecast customer demand for your product or service? Do you set limits or boundaries around this forecast? Do you monitor actual customer demand? Do you compare it to your forecast and limits? (A simple procedure for monitoring and controlling forecasting was provided in Chapter 20.)

Answers to these questions will make you aware of your product, your competitors, and your market. Additionally, you should identify what areas need your attention and design a simple control system to measure your progress in these areas.

Process

Product and process are intimately related. The process you use must match your product and market niche for you to compete effectively. Process is, of course, the method of producing the good or service. Are you aware of technological changes in your industry? Do you monitor the process technology by reading trade journals or attending trade shows? Are you a leader or follower in innovations in your industry? For example, if you own a grocery store, are you familiar with point-of-sale cash registers, bar coding, online inventory systems, and related technologies? Are they affordable to you in part or in whole? If you can afford part of them, what should you buy first? If you own a restaurant, are you aware of changes in process technology in that industry, such as the use of drive-through windows, microwave ovens, and a full-time hostess for seating?

Once you implement your process technology, you should continually monitor both advancements and changes in technology. Additionally, controls are needed to ensure that your manufacturing or operations process is functioning as planned. Process control, defined as "the function of maintaining a process within a given range of capability by feedback [or] correction,"[1] is discussed in the quality section of this chapter.

A major competitive advantage is short lead times. Have you measured the processing time for your various products and services? How long does it take to prepare a beef enchilada luncheon special if it is the first order, comes during the busiest period, and is the last order? Do you know what the processing times are for your major services and products? You should continually monitor these times to identify problems. Customers are the first to recognize that what used to take 10 minutes now takes 20 or that a restaurant that is excellent to dine at up to 12:10 provides horrible service at 12:30. If you do not monitor processing time, you may be the last to know why your service has deteriorated. It pays for you to design a performance measurement system to provide early warnings of trouble.

Low Cost

Today's management and cost accounting systems are similar to the systems designed fifty to sixty years ago. The business environment has changed dramatically over this time period, however. Direct labor, once 50 to 60 percent of the cost of the product, is now 6 to 12 percent in many manufacturing firms. In contrast, materials costs approach 60 percent of the cost of the product for many manufacturing firms. In other firms, automation has increased the overhead rate to 5 to 10 times the direct labor costs. These environments create situations where traditional accounting methods are totally inappropriate; in fact, such methods lead managers to make poor decisions.

There is currently no solution to the design of an appropriate operations management and cost accounting system to replace traditional systems. Accountants and operations management researchers are still at the stage of identifying problems and pitfalls with current practices and have not reached the point of proposing new design criteria. We will therefore point out several of the shortcomings of today's systems so that you might at least use your data cautiously.

Economic Order Quantity   The traditional EOQ calculation found in many accounting and management textbooks is inappropriate for several reasons:

- The EOQ provides the local optima and minimizes the costs of one item of inventory. A company stocks more than one item of inventory and generally orders more than one item from one supplier.

---

1. T. F. Wallace and J. R. Dougherty (eds.), *APICS Dictionary*, 6th ed. (Falls Church, Va.: APICS, 1987), p. 24.

- The EOQ does not consider the capacity of bottleneck or other work centers that the part is routed through.
- The EOQ does not consider the order quantity of other parts within the same product (called matched sets).
- The calculation of setup costs is arbitrary to say the least. Which work center are such costs related to: the bottleneck, all work centers along a part's routing, or the assembly operations?
- The EOQ does not consider product mix as parts pass through the various work centers.
- The EOQ does not consider the varying costs associated with sequence dependent setups.
- The incremental cost of placing a purchase or manufacturing order is marginal today with electronic data processing systems.
- The savings associated with consolidating orders from the same vendor more than offset the savings associated with EOQ.
- EOQs do not consider other competitive advantages. Short lead times, delivery as scheduled, high quality levels, flexibility, and responsiveness to market changes are competitive advantages characterized by low inventory levels.
- Setup times have always been assumed fixed. The Japanese have demonstrated that setup times can be driven to less than 10 minutes each and their associated costs substantially reduced.

Lowest Unit Costs   Current cost accounting systems take a myopic view of the vendor-production-distribution-customer system. You buy in large lots to take advantage of volume savings, you produce in large lots to save on setups, and you distribute in large lots, only to see the customer generally buy in small lots, one or two units at a time. What you have created is large amounts of idle inventory waiting just in case someone needs it. The system should be viewed in total with the perspective of selling all items immediately as they are produced. The objective of the production system should be to make what is demanded at the time it is demanded. The production and supporting accounting system should be adjusted to accommodate this philosophy.

Instead, unit costs and labor and departmental efficiencies dominate all scheduling decisions. Parts are made for the sake of keeping workers busy. In some instances, a company may have five years supply of a part sitting in the warehouse. The motivation for producing that quantity was not to meet known sales but simply to keep workers busy. Such a company has committed 60 percent of the cost of the product (material cost) to use up 6 to 12 percent of the product cost (direct labor cost). Interestingly, the company will probably never sell the items—and if they do, they will probably have paid for them several times over in carrying costs.

End-of-Month Syndrome   This is also known as the hockey stick effect. Many companies go through this cycle each month. Orders are rushed through the finishing work centers at the end of the month by using overtime and expediting parts. This attempt to get the order out of the door by month's end is made to allow you to bill customers and met your monthly shipping quota. The impact on the plant and cost structures is devastating. While you have met your shipping quota, you have also drained the last work centers of any work until work from the initial work centers is completed. In effect, efficiencies at the final work centers are extremely low during the beginning of the month because of lack of work and overtime is high at the end of the month to meet the shipping schedule. Can you guess which work centers additional equipment will be purchased for?

The solution to the problem is to plan and control a daily shipping schedule that will balance flow through the complete system. Accounting systems are not designed to function in this manner, however.

Investment Decisions   Investment decisions should be related to the business's competitive edges and not just to cost. Much of the dilemma of foreign competition can be blamed on domestic business's approach to minimizing short-run labor costs by producing products off shore. By moving offshore, a business provides its competitors with technology and trains their maintenance and direct laborers; ten years later, that business is closing its local plants not because it can produce more cheaply overseas but because new foreign competitors can produce the product more cheaply. The textile and apparel industries provide classic examples. Several small businesses have been eliminated by foreign competition in these industries.

Considerable weight should be given to the problem of process technology. The Japanese seldom allow contractors or subcontractors the opportunity to make critical parts for their products. They value the development of process technology highly. Most of their offshore facilities are assembly operations only. Offshore subcontracting is for incidental parts only.

The traditional approach to equipment investment decisions is based solely on minimizing costs and assumes that the equipment operates independently of other equipment in a part's routing and that parts are independent of products. The concepts related to the synchronized manufacturing philosophy should be incorporated into the investment decision. For example, ask yourself whether the equipment is for a bottleneck work center. If so, use the increased profit dollars in evaluating its worth. If not, how are the savings from making the investment generated—through quality, flexibility, or lead time? These are all important factors, but their dollar values are extremely difficult to quantify.

High Quality

Quality is now considered to be the most important competitive advantage by many manufacturers and service managers. They feel that if quality is viewed as the primary manufacturing requirement product costs and lead times will decrease. What is quality and how is it measured? Is quality different for products and services? While product quality has improved tremendously in Japan and in some companies in the United States, service quality seems to have deteriorated. Examples of poor quality in the service sector abound:

- Going through the drive-in window at a fast-food restaurant and later finding that one item was left off the order

- Getting to your appointment on time only to wait 2 hours for the doctor
- Returning your car to the repair shop two or three times to fix the same problem
- Waiting 20 minutes at the express line at the grocery store
- Trying to buy a sale item at a retail store only to be told it is sold out
- Waiting at home for the plumber, who promised to arrive at a given time but never does
- Ordering a medium steak but being served a well-done steak

These examples of poor service quality are among the reasons that businesses lose customers. How frequently do situations like these occur in your business, and what do you do when they do occur? The major problem is that most customers do not complain—they simply do not return. Remember that it is much easier to retain a current customer than to find a new one.

You must be aggressive in providing a quality service. Define what quality service means in your operation. M. B. Brown (1988) provides a comprehensive examination of service quality. Criteria that apply to most businesses include timeliness, speed, courtesy, cleanliness, accuracy, thoroughness, appropriateness, consideration, and friendliness. Each criteria that you select should be tailored to your business. Suppose that you are a restaurant owner and select all of the criteria listed. You may define quality for your restaurant as follows:

- *Timeliness*: the amount of time before a customer is greeted and seated and his or her order is requested
- *Speed*: the amount of time between the order being taken and delivered
- *Courtesy*: the manner and politeness in which employees treat customers
- *Cleanliness*: the appearance of the glassware, silverware, dishes, linens, tables, windows, pictures, floors, and cashier area
- *Accuracy*: the description of the items by employees, the correctness of the bill, and performance to expectations
- *Thoroughness*: the manner in which employees explained the menu items, specials, and procedures
- *Appropriateness*: the correctness of employees' manner, dress, conversation, and actions for various situations and customers
- *Consideration*: the regard, attention, and respect employees show to each other and to customers
- *Friendliness*: the hospitality and warmth displayed by employees

Next, you should decide how you will measure each criteria. For example, the amount of time that passes can be used as the measure of timeliness and speed. A standard of a maximum of 1 minute might be established from the time that a person enters a restaurant and is greeted by the host or hostess. A second standard of 1 minute might be established for the time between the greeting and the seating of the customer unless all available tables are full.

Limits or boundaries should also be set for each standard. An additional 30 second deviation might be allowed for each of the 1 minute standards. In other words, a customer should be greeted no more than 1 minute and 30 seconds after entering the restaurant and seated no later than 1 minute and 30 seconds later.

The person responsible for performing each task should be identified, instructed in the correct performance, instructed in how to handle exceptions, and tested in the performance of the task. Additionally, the person should be observed in the performance of the task to ensure conformity to your standards. This evaluation should occur at irregular intervals on a continuous basis to ensure against the employee taking short-cuts during busy periods.

This monitoring of performance, while common in manufacturing, is uncommon in services. As defined earlier, process control is a matter of monitoring the product or service characteristics *during* the manufacturing or the providing of the service. You are performing the process control function when you measure a steak's doneness by making a slit to examine its color or when you taste chili for seasoning.

Two kinds of control charts can be devised to aid in process control. Control is the key word. The $\bar{X}$ control chart determines whether the average or mean value of the process has changed. The R control chart establishes whether the dispersion or spread has increased or decreased. Answering both of these questions is important to improving your process. The steps in constructing $\bar{X}$ and R process control charts are given in Exhibit 23.2.

The logic of the control charts is simple. First, the average ($\bar{X}$) and range (R) or spread of the process is computed for several random samples, from which a grand average ($\bar{\bar{X}}$) and grand range ($\bar{R}$) is computed. Control limits are then computed for both the average and range using standard formulas. Fourth, graphs for both the average and range and their control limits are constructed. Control limits and process specifications are different. Control limits show the natural variation that exists in the process. The process specification provides your quality standard. You should also enter your process specifications on the chart. Your control charts are now ready to monitor your process. Collect samples and plot the mean and range by time period to continually monitor your operations.

A list of numerical factors useful in constructing $\bar{X}$ and R charts is provided in Exhibit 23.3. The use of these factors eliminates the use of sophisticated mathematical formula. An example of the construction of an $\bar{X}$ and R chart for the time until seating in a restaurant is provided in Exhibit 23.4. The restaurant manager measured the amount of time from the customer entering the restaurant until he or she was seated. Four random observations were made during each hour for ten hours and the average time for each set of four observations was computed. For example, the four times collected between 8:00 and 9:00 in the morning were 30, 25, 35 and 40 seconds. Their average is 32.5 seconds, and the range was 15 seconds.

In step 2, the average of the ten hourly averages and the average of the ten hourly range calculations were computed. For the sample data, the grand average is 33.4 seconds and the average range is 15 seconds. These values are used to construct $\bar{X}$ and R control charts. Next, the appropriate factors were chosen for constructing the control limits. With a sample size of four observations, the A factor used to compute the limits for the $\bar{X}$ chart is 0.73 and the

Exhibit 23.2

STEPS IN CONSTRUCTING $\bar{X}$ AND R CONTROL CHARTS

1. Determine the average ($\bar{X}$) and range (R) for each of ten subgroups of four observations each.

2. Calculate the grand average ($\bar{\bar{X}}$) and average range (R):

$$\bar{\bar{X}} = \frac{\Sigma \bar{X}}{n}$$

$$\bar{R} = \frac{\Sigma R}{n}$$

3. Calculate the upper and lower control limits for $\bar{X}$. (Use the appropriate A value from Exhibit 23.3.)

$$UCL_X = \bar{\bar{X}} + A\bar{R}$$

$$LCL_X = \bar{\bar{X}} - A\bar{R}$$

4. Calculate the control limits for R. (Use the appropriate D value from Exhibit 23.3.)

$$UCL_R = D_4\bar{R}$$

$$LCL_R = D_3\bar{R}$$

5. Construct and plot the control charts for the appropriate sample size. Enter your control limits and process specifications (specs).

factors used to construct the upper and lower control limits on the range chart are 0 and 2.28. For the restaurant example, the process limits are 22.45 and 44.35 seconds for the $\bar{X}$ chart and 0 and 34.2 seconds for the R chart. Enter the specific limit or maximum value allowable on the chart. The standard of 60

Exhibit 23.3

FACTORS FOR COMPUTING $\bar{X}$ AND R CONTROL CHARTS

SAMPLE SIZE (n)	A	D_3	D_4
4	.73	0	2.28
5	.58	0	2.11
6	.48	0	2.00
7	.42	0.08	1.92

Exhibit 23.4

APPLICATION OF $\bar{X}$ AND R CONTROL CHARTS TO SEATING IN A RESTAURANT

1. Determine the average ($\bar{X}$) and range (R) for each of ten subgroups of four observations.

TIME	TIME UNTIL SEATING (SECONDS)				$\bar{X}$	R
8–9:00	30	25	35	40	32.5	15
9–10:00	35	30	40	45	37.5	15
10–11:00	25	15	40	40	30	25
11–12:00	20	25	25	30	25	10
12–1:00	25	35	50	55	41.25	30
1–2:00	30	40	25	30	31.25	15
2–3:00	30	40	30	40	35	10
3–4:00	40	40	30	35	36.25	10
4–5:00	45	40	35	40	40	10
5–6:00	20	25	25	30	25	10

2. Calculate the grand average ($\bar{\bar{X}}$ and average range ($\bar{R}$).

$$\bar{\bar{X}} = \frac{\Sigma \bar{X}}{n} = \frac{32.5 + 37.5 + 30 + 25 + 41.25 + 31.25 + 35 + 36.25 + 40 + 25}{10}$$

$$= 33.4$$

$$\bar{R} = \frac{\Sigma R}{n} = \frac{15 + 15 + 25 + 10 + 30 + 15 + 10 + 10 + 10 + 10}{10}$$

$$= 15$$

3. Calculate the upper and lower control limits for $\bar{X}$.

$$UCL_X = \bar{\bar{X}} + A\bar{R} = 33.4 + (.73)(15) = 44.35$$

$$LCL_X = \bar{\bar{X}} - A\bar{R} = 33.4 - (.73)(15) = 22.45$$

4. Calculate the upper and lower control limits for R.

$$UCL_R = D_4\bar{R} = 2.28(15) = 34.2$$

$$LCL_R = D_3\bar{R} = 0(15) = 0$$

5. Construct and plot the control charts.

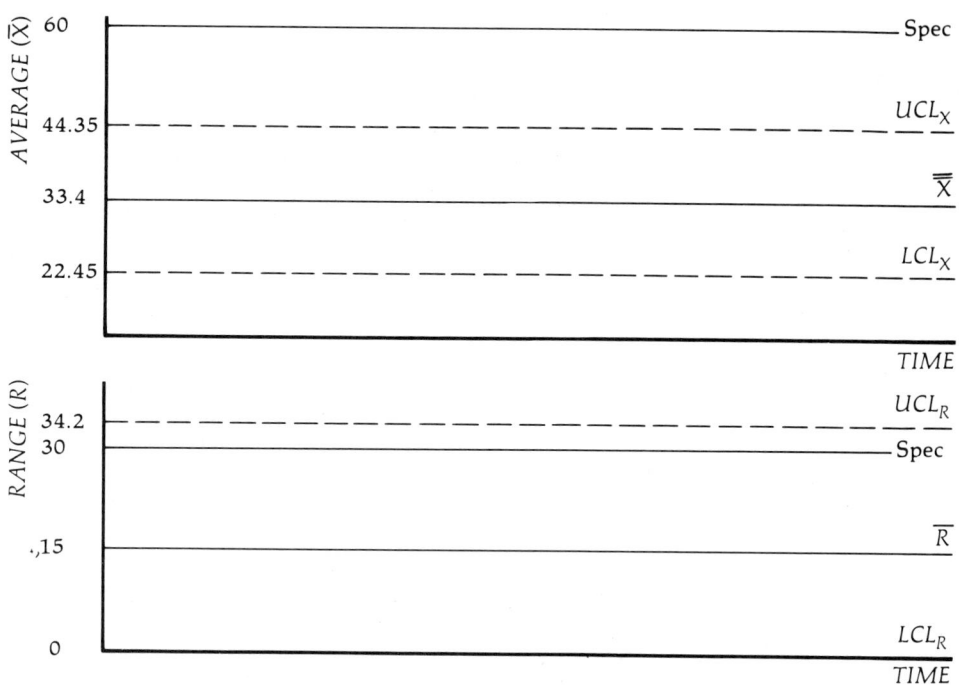

6. Make four observations during each hour and compute the $\bar{X}$ and R for the sample. Enter the values on the charts. (See Exhibit 23.5).

---

seconds for seating with a deviation of 30 seconds was desired. These charts and values are used to monitor hourly and daily activities.

Once you have established your process control and specification limits, you are ready to monitor your operation, as Exhibit 23.5 illustrates. Each hour, a sample of four seating times is taken. The average and range for each hour are then computed and plotted on the charts. As long as the sample readings are within the lower and upper control limits, the process is in control. Other data characteristics can be used to detect problems. If several (seven or more) consecutive sample readings are above (or below) the average values, this suggests that the process is out of control. Additionally, the manager may feel that the process average and range have changed based upon changing methods, materials, and equipment. For example, the standard for seating may have been changed to 45 seconds based on several changes in methods and layout. In such a case, it would be necessary to construct another set of control charts to monitor the new process.

As seen in Exhibit 23.5, the data point for noon (62.5) is outside the upper control limit (44.35) and the specification limit (60). The manager's next step is to investigate the causes for this deviation. The cause might be that customers arrive faster than can be seated by one host or hostess. It may be that the restaurant does not have the seating capacity to satisfy the lunch hour crowd. It may be that tables have not been cleared from previous customers to allow new customers to be seated. The process is out of control, and its cause should be identified and eliminated.

Exhibit 23.5

USE OF AN $\bar{X}$ AND R CHART

TIME	TIME UNTIL SEATING (SECONDS)				$\bar{X}$	R
8–9:00	35	20	30	35	30	15
9–10:00	40	20	25	35	30	20
10–11:00	50	30	35	45	40	20
11–12:00	45	35	45	50	43.75	15
12–1:00	70	65	45	70	62.5	25
1–2:00	40	45	25	30	35	20
2–3:00	20	30	30	20	25	10
3–4:00	30	35	40	35	35	10
4–5:00	25	35	25	20	26.25	15
5–6:00	30	40	50	30	37.5	20

Short Lead Time

Short lead times have given a competitive edge to many firms. Customers do not want to wait for goods or services. How many times have you gone to a restaurant for dinner and been told that it would be an hour before you could be seated? How many times did you wait? Even for large purchases, are you willing to wait four weeks for delivery? Today, most customers want a service or product immediately and are unwilling to wait even a short time. The traditional view of short lead times was that choices are few and relatively expensive. You can make and store inventory ahead of time in anticipation of a sale or can carry excess capacity to respond in case an order is placed. A more contemporary view is that a small business owner must position the business to respond quickly to customer requests. Eliminate the red tape. Streamline the operation to eliminate waiting and material movements by the product. In a manufacturing operation, less than 5 percent of the lead time is actual productive time. Exhibit 23.6 graphs the components of manufacturing lead time. Only two of these components are actually involved in adding values—the set up and the run times.

Identify the components of lead time for your product or service. What percentage of the time is actual productive time? If you are a restaurant owner, you could measure and classify the amount of time from customer arrival to order arrival to customer departure. If you own a drycleaning establishment, how much time transpires and what activities are performed from customer arrival to order completion to customer pickup? Can you reduce the delays? If so, can you use the reduced lead time as a competitive weapon? Can you offer 1- or 2-hour turnaround as the standard drycleaning service? By analyzing your lead time and answering these questions, you should get a good grasp of how to reduce your lead times and become more responsive to customers.

Exhibit 23.6
COMPONENTS OF LEAD TIME

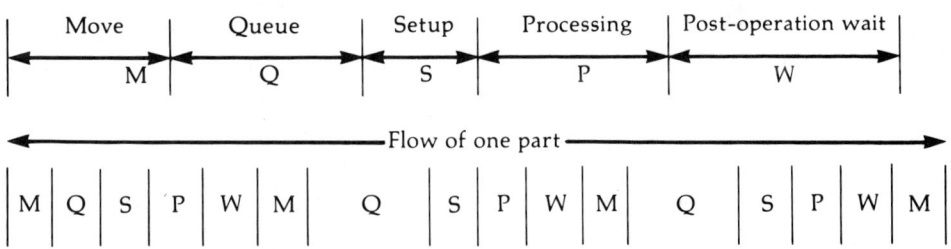

Delivery as Scheduled

How many times have you made an appointment with a doctor, lawyer, accountant, electrician, or hairstylist only to wait? How many times have you been told that you could pick up your car, a package, or your cleaning, only to arrive for the pickup and find that the order is not ready? How many times in your business have you made an appointment with a customer only to make him or her wait? Being able to deliver as promised is as critically important as having a quality product or service.

If you use an appointment system or provide estimates of completion time for customers, you should keep track of your actual delivery as promised rates.

The same appointment book can be used to show appointments and monitor your performance. If you are consistently wrong on meeting your schedule, evaluate and change your procedures to provide delivery as scheduled. If you schedule on 15-minute intervals but take 20 minutes per customer, either reduce your time per customer to 15 minutes by streamlining the process or change your scheduling system to 20-minute intervals. If you have interruptions throughout the day that create your delays, allow a 10 to 15 minute buffer in the mornings to catch up and a 10 to 15 minute buffer at midafternoon to catch up.

Flexibility

Flexibility is the ability to change the quantity, the timing, the product or service, the quality, or the price to meet a particular customer's needs. A critical variable here is knowing your own capabilities and using judgment in making your commitments. Only by measuring previously made, fulfilled, and missed commitments can you provide good estimates of your capabilities to meet customer requests. Ask yourself how flexible your operations function is. Can you respond in a timely manner to the emergency needs of a good customer? Can you get a large order to a customer sooner than initially requested? Can you tailor your product or service to a customer's desires? The ability to work with your customers on the emergency and difficult orders increases your business substantially over the long run. Your willingness to work with customers gets you both their tough requests and their normal business.

Applying the Performance Measures

Your major goals are to have a satisfied customer and to make a long-run profit. To achieve these goals, you should apply performance measures to the inputs, transformation processes, and outputs of your operation. Using intermediate performance measures assists you in reaching these goals.

Inputs

Personnel, materials, and machinery are the primary inputs of most operations functions. The performance of each is required to produce goods and services. Your sole objective should be to produce the good or service in the most effective and efficient manner overall, not to make each of the inputs as efficient as possible. The key to accomplishing this objective is to have flexible resources. Standard materials that can be used in several different products and services eliminate the need to carry small quantities of several different materials. Measure the effectiveness of your materials. How many different products can this material be used in? Measure the efficiency of the material. How many day's worth of this material do you have on hand? How many are actually needed? Idle inventory is idle capital.

Additionally, you should measure the quality, cost, lead times, delivery performance, and flexibility of your vendors and provide the actual measures and your standards to your vendors as feedback as to their performance and your expectations.

Multiskilled workers are essential to successfully competing in today's environment. Workers that are capable of operating several different machines and performing several different operations on each help greatly in keeping materials flowing. A secretary that can type, file, photocopy, take shorthand, compose letters, and operate the switchboard is worth two or three employees. The waiter or waitress that can act as host or hostess, cashier, table clearer, dishwasher, and cook can certainly reduce the number of emergencies that you might face. It might be useful to rotate personnel through different jobs during off-peak times to provide protection against these emergencies. The number of jobs that an employee can perform might be considered a measure of the employee's effectiveness.

A measure of the efficiency of a worker might be the time that it takes for the worker to perform a job. Remember that efficiency becomes critically important at the bottleneck operation and at operations that dictate lead time. For example, a slow dishwasher only becomes critical if you are out of clean dishes or silverware. Workers should always be provided feedback concerning their performance to expectations, given directions on improving, and given incentive to improve. (These topics are discussed in more detail in the next few chapters.)

Machinery or equipment may be the key input. One coauthor once attended a dinner meeting at a restaurant where a large tray was the bottleneck for the serving operation. Forty people waited several minutes while three waiters stood around waiting for the entrees to arrive on the one large serving tray. They served six people and then were forced to wait again while the tray was taken away and refilled in the kitchen. This procedure continued until all forty customers were served. With two trays, the exercise could have been performed in half the time and with three trays, in one third the time. If the waiters had been trained to go into the kitchen and load smaller trays themselves, perhaps the service would have been even more timely.

Measures of equipment effectiveness and efficiency should be established and monitored. How many different operations can a piece of equipment be used for? How efficient is it at performing its primary operations? What is your equipment utilization as it relates to producing throughput (not output)?

Transformation Processes

Each performance criteria should be applied to operations within the transformation process. Remember that the key is not to have each operation as efficient as possible but to make the overall process as efficient as possible. Efficiencies at nonbottleneck operations should be measured against what is needed to get the product produced instead of against a fixed set of criteria. For example, if a work center needs to work only at 40 percent efficiency to feed the bottleneck work center, workers who complete that operation should be moved to another operation to complete the product or be allowed to perform maintenance. Either alternative is better than their producing unwanted parts. Performance to schedule should be measured at each work center and linked to overall performance in relation to customer delivery due date.

Quality of parts affects quality of products. The quality of parts, subassemblies, and assembly should be monitored as they are produced by using process control and by making each worker responsible for doing quality work. The part characteristics to be monitored should be identified with product performance criteria. In other words, process control must relate to product quality.

Outputs

The performance measures of the good or service are ultimately the true measure of getting and retaining a customer. Was the product what the customer requested? Was quality acceptable or exceptional? Was the service or product provided in a timely manner? Was it delivered as promised? Was the firm able to meet an emergency situation? Did the product or service satisfy the customer?

Supporting Systems

In many cases, too much attention is placed on the efficiency of supporting systems and not the effectiveness. Having an efficiently coded computer program is of little value if the information provided is worthless or of little use in planning and controlling operations. Remember: the true objective is to have an efficient and effective process as a whole and not necessarily at each supporting function. Supporting functions should be as simple as possible since sophisticated or complex systems only detract from the true objective of producing a product or service.

Each supporting function should be examined with respect to how well it assists you in performing the operations functions, not with respect to how well the supporting function is accomplished. For example, if a manual accounting system provides excellent assistance to operations, a computerized system should not be implemented unless it provides superior assistance. Accounting is a supporting function and does not contribute directly to generating revenue to the firm. All supporting equipment and materials purchases and personnel hiring should be viewed in this manner.

Summary

Controlling operations to ensure that they support the business's strategic goal is central to operations management. To achieve such control, the business needs a performance measurement system that includes performance criteria, a standard, and a measure to evaluate how performance compares to the standard. An important point of setting standards is identifying the tolerance limits within which deviation is acceptable but beyond which deviation must be investigated and, if necessary, rectified.

Each of the eight main competitive advantages has a set of criteria, standards, and measures that can be used to build a measurement system. The low cost edge currently lacks an adequate control system. A traditional technique, the economic order quantity, has many flaws. The lowest cost units system of relying on bulk purchases to achieve volume discounts ignores the new perspective on the high cost of large inventory. The end-of-month syndrome describes a chronically mismanaged system of overtime at the end of a work period to compensate for downtime at the beginning.

Process control is possible in service firms, although it is not always practiced. Control charts can be devised that use mathematical calculations of the average value of a process and the range of variations for that process. These charts can then be analyzed to determine whether a process is functioning smoothly or needs revision.

In analyzing the efficiency of systems that support operations, it is useful to look past the efficiency of the support system itself in order to focus on how well the operational system contributes to the goals of the organization. The main goal is the effectiveness of the organization as a whole, not simply the smooth working of the support system.

Class Assignments

1. Describe a performance measurement system for a(n)
   a. Barber shop
   b. Automotive parts store
   c. Plumber
   d. Automobile repair shop
   e. Motel
2. Explain how improving quality can reduce cost and lead time.
3. Design a performance measurement system for taking tests in this course.
4. Describe how performance measurement relates to a company's strategy.
5. Identify criteria appropriate for a performance measurement for
   a. The Boy Scouts
   b. A United Fund Drive
   c. A township garbage pickup service
   d. A dentist office
6. Interview the owner or manager of a small service and a small manufacturing operation. Identify
   a. The functional performance measures for marketing, operations, personnel and so on
   b. The company performance measure
   c. The frequency with which each measure is reviewed
   d. Who is responsible for each measure, each functional area, and collecting the data on each measure
   e. Whether performance results are shared with managers and employees

References

Brown, M. B. "Defining Quality in Service Business." *Quality,* January 1988, pp. 56–59.
Crawford, K. M. An Analysis of Performance Measurement Systems in Selected Just-in-Time Operations. Ph.D. Dissertation, Athens, Ga.: University of Georgia, 1988.
Gozzo, M. W. "Small Is Beautiful if Defined, Measured, and Actioned!" *American Pro-*

duction and Inventory Control Society Proceedings of Seminar on Small Manufacturing and Process Industries. Falls Church, Va.: APICS, September 1985, pp. 118–122.

Hartz, O. "Quality Management and Cooperation in Small Firms (Management)." *Quality Progress,* 15, No. 4, April 1982, pp. 18–21.

Wallace, T. F., and J. R. Dougherty, *APICS Dictionary,* 6th ed. Falls Church, Va.: APICS, 1987.

MANAGING YOUR PERSONNEL

Nearly 70 percent of all small businesses have no employees. The remaining range from ma-and-pa operations that employ only members of the family to operations with several hundred employees. These larger operations may or may not be unionized. The following six chapters apply to small businesses that employ people. Moreover, the material in the chapters increases in importance to business success as the small business increases the size of its workforce. In this overview, we summarize the major topics covered in each of the six chapters. Although there may not be enough time in one course to cover all the material presented in Part Six, it would be instructive to read the material, even if briefly. The chapters cannot easily stand alone, since managing people cannot easily be segmented into discrete activities.

Chapter 24
Planning for People to Do the Work
In this chapter we provide background information for planning how to manage a workforce systematically. The chapter provides general information about government regulation of employment practices, how to define the geographic boundaries of your labor market, the evolution of an organizational structure as your business grows, and the means of analyzing and defining jobs. The appendix to the chapter lists the major federal employment laws and the sources from which you can obtain free copies of those laws.

Chapter 25
Compensating Your Employees
In this chapter we discuss two issues that are relevant to all small businesses: compensation laws and the concept of fairness that underlies all compensation decision making. We also describe how formal compensation plans are designed and the characteristics of pay-for-knowledge plans.

As you start your business, make sure you take into account the compensation costs that may be imposed on you by federal and state laws. The major laws that you should be familiar with are the Fair Labor Standards Act, work-ers' compensation laws, unemployment compensation laws, and social secu-rity. Together, these mandated compensation laws can impose a substantial cash-flow burden on your operations.

The Fair Labor Standards Act (FLSA), often called the wage and hour law, has five basic provisions. First, it specifies the rules for employing underage children (this provision is discussed further in Chapter 26). Second, it man-dates certain employers to pay the minimum wage. Third, it details the rules for paying workers overtime for work beyond a standard 40 hour workweek. Fourth, it mandates equal compensation for men and women who perform jobs requiring substantially equal skill, effort, and responsibility and who work under similar working conditions. Fifth, it requires all employers to keep specific records of times each employee works and the pay the em-ployee receives for time worked. You must get a copy of the specific FLSA rules that apply to your business and comply with those rules.

Workers' compensation laws are state laws that provide income to work-ers who cannot work because of illness or injury that arose out of and in the course of employment. Unemployment compensation laws, which are par-tially regulated by the federal government and partially by the states, provide workers with income when they are temporarily unemployed, through no fault of their own, and are searching for suitable employment. States vary considerably in the way they treat employers with respect to these laws. Con-sequently, you should familiarize yourself with your state's plans. With few exceptions, workers' compensation laws require employers to insure against workers' compensation claims. In contrast, unemployment compensation laws impose a federal payroll tax on all employers. The employer who main-tains a stable workforce, however, can get back most of this tax as a credit. In effect, workers' compensation and unemployment compensation programs provide incentives to employers to provide healthy and safe working condi-tions and job security. Employers who are not motivated by these incentives can expect to pay more than 10 percent of their payroll dollars to fund these programs.

Finally, if you employ people, you will also have to contribute a percent-age of each employee's wages to the social security program through the FICA payroll deduction tax. In addition, you will be obligated to withhold the employee's share of the FICA tax through payroll deduction.

The chapter also discusses compensation outlays in the form of employee benefits (e.g., vacation pay, health care insurance, pension plans). Although you may not be able to provide your employees with benefits initially, you may want to offer benefits once you can afford their cost. Some of the reasons for providing benefits are discussed in this chapter. Before you decide to offer benefits, you would be wise to consult with a benefits specialist so that you can take advantage of tax breaks for the benefits that you may provide. Con-sultation with a benefits expert can sometimes help you to provide relatively cost-free incentives as a tool of attracting applicants. For example, you may find that you can hire a lot of motivated young people to work for you part-time if you offer them college tuition reimbursement. Consultation can also prevent you from engaging in action that may prove to be illegal.

The second section of the chapter briefly discusses the meaning of pay fairness. We also point out numerous negative consequences that can result from underpaying people. The bulk of the chapter, however, is devoted to describing the characteristics of a formal compensation plan. When your workforce reaches fifty or so people, you would be wise to start thinking about developing such a plan. A formal compensation plan can help increase your ability to attract, retain, motivate and develop a competent workforce. Perhaps more importantly, it can help control your labor costs by allowing for more efficient use of your compensation dollars.

The development of a formal compensation plan involves a series of decision options and use of highly technical and time-consuming processes and procedures. We discuss these issues and provide you with enough information to enable you to develop your own compensation plan. Even so, you may not want to exert the necessary effort and time on such a project. You may prefer to hire a compensation consultant for this purpose. If you do so, however, you should be able to evaluate the consultant's expertise. Otherwise, you could end up spending a lot of money for a plan that will not meet its objectives. The information provided in this chapter will at least help you to ask the right questions and thus help you evaluate the expertise of the consultant that you may hire.

The last section of the chapter describes the characteristics of pay-for-knowledge pay plans. As these plans are increasingly written about in the popular press, you should become familiar with their positive and negative characteristics so that you can make informed decisions about their use in your operation.

Chapter 26
Staffing Your Business

This chapter will assist you in developing job-related recruiting and selection procedures that increase your chances of hiring good employees. The chapter also describes federal laws that are relevant to staffing decisions. Good hiring decisions will comply with federal and state laws without decreasing your ability to hire the most suitable applicants.

In the first section of the chapter we provide information about three federal laws that directly apply to your staffing practices: FLSA, which regulates employment of underage children; the Immigration Reform and Control Act of 1986, which mandates all employers to verify the citizenship status of all employees hired on or after November 1986; and equal employment opportunity regulation.

In the next section, we alert you to the questions that you may want to ask yourself when you are deciding how to staff your jobs. For example, should you hire full-time or part-time employees? Where can you find the employees you need? Should you transfer or promote current employees, or should you hire from outside your organization? We list a number of advantages and disadvantages to various answers to the above questions, so that you can decide which approaches fit your firm's needs the best.

In the last section of the chapter, we describe five basic selection procedures and recommend ways of making them more useful. These are the application form, reference checking, paper-and-pencil tests, work samples, and the selection interview.

Chapter 27
Training Your Workforce

One way to increase any employee's productivity and commitment to an organization is to help the employee learn how to perform his or her job. So often, the employee learns the job simply through trial and error, sometimes called on-the-job training. On-the-job training is perhaps the most expensive way to train employees. It is expensive in the first place because it forces the person to try a number of different solutions to the problem at hand and in the long run because the solution that works tends to be repeated and other solutions tend to drop out of the person's repertoire. Thus, on-the-job training is a very inefficient way of learning. The quickest and best way to ensure that your new employees learn their jobs well is to implement a *guided* on-the-job training program. This chapter explains the essentials of orientation training, work adjustment training, and job competence training. It also discusses how to determine when skill updating is necessary.

Chapter 28
Managing Your Workforce

Many people think they could be good people managers if they were given the chance. Many small business owners think they are good people managers. Most people, however, are rather poor at managing other people. Consequently, they have difficulties in getting the work done through people.

This chapter focuses on basic issues that you should consider when managing employees. Essential to being a good manager is having accurate perceptions of oneself and of others. Establishing credibility with employees is another key to managerial success. The third section of the chapter lists the major factors that employees think about when they decide whether or not they are satisfied with their supervisor. These factors are not employee quirks. Rather, they define the supervisory behaviors that help instill work commitment and motivate work performance. Finally, the last section of the chapter describes two major ways of controlling employee behaviors and orienting those behaviors toward work goals: performance evaluation and a progressive discipline system.

Chapter 29
Managing a Unionized Workforce

This chapter provides useful information for employers with or without unions. We wrote the chapter from a perspective of managing a unionized workforce. Yet, in many ways, managing a group of employees is analogous to managing a unionized workforce. After all, a union is a group of individuals who have organized together to protect their interests. This definition of a union applies to any cohesive work group. The difference between an informal union group and a formal one is that the latter group consists of workers who decided that they needed a third party—an independent union organization—to represent their interests with their employer. The unionization process is a multistep process. First, the workers within a particular workgroup petition a federal agency, called the National Labor Relations Board (NLRB), stating their wish to be represented by a particular union organization with their employer. If enough workers petition the NLRB, the agency schedules a formal hearing, which is attended by all interested parties (employer, workers, and the union organization seeking to represent the workers). The hearing has three purposes: to determine the degree of employee interest in being represented by a particular union organization; to determine the legal eligibility of certain employees to belong to the proposed union group; and to hear the employee desires regarding which employees should or should not belong to the proposed union group. If the hearing satisfies the NLRB, the agency formally rules on the appropriateness of the union group and schedules a union election. The union that seeks to represent the group of workers must receive 50 percent plus two of the votes cast in the election in order to win the election. If the union wins, it becomes the exclusive and legal representative of the relevant employee group. By this process, the union and the employer enter a legally binding collective bargaining relationship.

As the employee group's representative, the union negotiates with the employer regarding pay, hours of work, and terms and conditions of employment for the group of workers it represents. The union also signs contracts that define employer constraints and the rights and constraints of both the union organization and the workers and shares the responsibility for administering the negotiated contract.

Although there are numerous specific rules that regulate the union-management relationship, we do not focus on these details in the chapter. Instead, we focus on broader issues to help you understand the reasons behind the collective bargaining relationship. Our experience is that many employers have little understanding of the purpose and meaning of a union contract and little understanding of the basis for labor law and its practice. Because they do not understand these issues, they allow their emotions to replace rational decision making. You will find that this chapter contains information that can help you devise fair ways of treating your employees, be they unionized or not. Accordingly, the first section of the chapter discusses the purpose and meaning of a union contract and the basis for labor law in relation to union contract. The chapter then suggests ways of establishing a constructive union-management relationship and of managing day-to-day disputes between employees and their supervisors.

C H A P T E R 2 4

PLANNING FOR PEOPLE
TO DO THE WORK

Many small business owners carefully plan all aspects of their businesses except organizing the work and the people to perform that work. Although some jobs can be performed by machines, most require human effort. If you want to get the desired performance in a consistent manner, you must plan for your human resource needs and implement your plans.

When planning for your human resources, you should give the same degree of thought, time, and effort as you do when planning for your financial resources, capital equipment, and material needs. When you plan for financial resources, for example, you think of how you will use those resources in the most cost efficient way in the long run. When planning for capital equipment, you typically think about the cost and the performance of the equipmnt. When planning for materials, you also try to choose the materials that will provide the best results at the lowest cost. These plans are constrained by government regulation and conditions in your service or product market. In planning human resources, you should also think in terms of long-term performance and cost. You will also find your actions constrained by government regulation of employment practices and by conditions in your labor market.

After reading this chapter, you will be able to

- Describe the major laws that may generally apply to your personnel activities
- Analyze the labor market from which you draw your workforce
- Explain the evolution of an organization and its structure
- Explain the importance of job descriptions to effective and cost efficient management of personnel
- Perform a job analysis to identify the work requirements for your jobs

Government Regulation of Employment Practices

The reason for the government's involvement in employment practices is straightforward. Society has a stake in how employers manage their workforces and the work opportunities that they provide for members of the labor force. Nearly 75 percent of the nation's gross national product comes directly from earned income. Thus our standard of living is highly dependent on maintaining a balance between the competitive needs of employers and the needs of adult workers to earn a decent income. In addition to regulating income, the government regulates the employer's right to hire children and attempts to ensure that citizens who have worked all their lives receive enough income after retirement so as not to depend on government support.

In this section of the chapter, we outline the major federal laws that apply to all personnel activities. (In later chapters of this part, we address laws that relate to specific aspects of personnel policy.) The state in which you operate may have additional laws that you must follow. Space limitations prevent us from discussing unique state laws, but a look at Exhibit 24.1 will give you an idea of the variability among states in their employment laws and the kinds of issues that such laws address.

As you read the material on employment laws, you may become overwhelmed by the number of laws that may apply to your business. There are several ways to deal with this problem. You could decide to employ the services of a labor attorney to help define your responsibility and accountability. You could hire a trained human resource manager to design and manage your business's human resource function and delegate the responsibility for compliance to laws to him or her. Or you could contact the local offices of your state's department of labor and the federal Department of Labor (the Yellow Pages list the telephone numbers and locations of these agencies). You can call each agency for an appointment to talk about the requirements that may apply to your business. Each agency can provide you with copies of the laws and specific regulations applicable to them. As the laws are amended, you have resources available as well. Revised state laws can be obtained directly from your state's department of labor. Amended federal laws can be had by subscribing to the Bureau of National Affairs (BNA) or the Commerce Clearing House (CCH).

Small businesses are subject to somewhat less restrictive regulation than are large businesses. In most cases, your business's yearly dollar sales volume determines whether or not a particular regulation applies to you. Some laws aimed at specific industries require you to comply regardless of the size of your workforce; others apply only when your employee population reaches a certain number. Some laws apply to some of your employees and not to others. Depending on your business, you may be permitted or prohibited from employing minors between fourteen and eighteen. You should also be aware that your definition of an employee category such as supervisor or salesperson may differ from the definition specified by employment law. For example, should you use the services of independent contractors instead of employees, the law may view these people as employees.

Finally, the rules for compliance with employment laws vary for different industries. Although your business may be subject to the federal wage and

Exhibit 24.1
EXAMPLES OF VARIABILITY AMONG STATE EMPLOYMENT LAWS

STATES	Preventing or Hindering Employment of Former Employees	Reference Letters Regarding Separation	Reference Letters for Public Utility Employees	Access to Personnel Files	Applicant Disclosure of Criminal Records or Juvenile Convictions	Lie Detector Tests	Voice Stress Analyzer Tests	Finger-printing	Dismissals for Safety Violations	Dismissals for Whistle-blowing	Requirements for Sterilization	Employment Agreements	Disclosure of Wages Received by the Employee	Smoking in the Workplace
Alabama	*				*									
Alaska						*								*
Arizona	*													
Arkansas	*													
California	*	*	*	*	*	*	*	*		*	*	*	*	
Colorado	*													
Connecticut	*			*							*			*
Delaware				*		*								
Florida	*													*
Georgia	*					*								
Hawaii						*								
Idaho	*			*	*									
Illinois	*													
Indiana	*	*				*								*
Iowa	*													
Kansas	*	*												
Kentucky				*		*				*				*
Louisiana	*													
Maine		*			*	*								
Maryland				*	*	*								
Massachu-setts				*	*	*				*				
Michigan						*				*			*	*
Minnesota	*													

Source: The information in this exhibit was compiled from *Topical Law Reports* (New York: Commerce Clearing House, 1987).

Mississippi
Missouri
Montana
Nebraska
Nevada
New Hampshire
New Jersey
New Mexico
New York
North Carolina
North Dakota
Ohio
Oklahoma
Oregon
Pennsylvania
Rhode Island
South Carolina
South Dakota
Tennessee
Texas
Utah
Vermont
Virginia
Washington
West Virginia
Wisconsin
Wyoming

hour law, for example, the specific rules for your business differ for a motel and for a small manufacturing firm. The appendix to this chapter lists the major federal employment law publications and the sources from which you can obtain them. These publications can help you identify what laws may apply to you.

Laws That Apply to All Personnel Practices

The major laws that apply to all personnel practices are the equal employment opportunity laws (EEO), the Military Selective Service Act (MSSA), the Immigration Reform and Control Act (IRCA), and the Occupational Safety and Health Act (OSHA). We discuss each in sequence.

EEO Laws and Executive Orders   In making decisions about whom to hire, fire, or promote, you have to differentiate or discriminate among people. Basing these decisions on the knowledge, skill, and ability requirements of the job in question is considered in our society to be fair discrimination. In contrast, basing these decisions on factors such as color, race, religion, sex, national origin, age, or the presence of a handicap not relevant to the job is considered unfair discrimination. Because unfair discrimination limits opportunities for large segments of qualified workers, EEO laws and executive orders prohibit such discrimination in the terms and conditions of employment and in compensation for workers historically subjected to such discrimination.

Hundreds of congressional statutes, executive orders, as well as state and local laws govern illegal employment discrimination. The voluminous antidiscrimination regulations, however, are similar in their content. You can gain an understanding of EEO laws by becoming familiar with the basic provisions of the five most important EEO laws.

The United States Constitution. Contrary to common belief, the U.S. Constitution has little relevance to the employment practices of private-sector employers. Along with Title VII of the 1964 Civil Rights Act, the Constitution prohibits religious discrimination. Beyond this prohibition, constitutional protections of employment rights are limited to workers employed by governments. The U.S. Constitution prohibits public sector employers (federal, state, and local governments) from depriving their employees of employment rights without due process of law or to deny any employee the equal protection of the laws. This prohibition mandates government employers to base all personnel decisions on the candidate's merit rather than on his or her political affiliation or any subjective personal characteristic. In contrast, the due process protections of the U.S. Constitution do not apply to private sector employment.

Title VII of the 1964 Civil Rights Act. This law, the major private-sector law, mandates that employers provide equal employment opportunities to employee categories defined by the law as protected classes. All other EEO laws are patterned after this law. Title VII, as amended, prohibits discrimination in employment practices because of race, color, religion, sex, or national origin. Title VII covers almost all employers of more than fifteen employees except for religious organizations, which are allowed to discriminate because of religion;

private clubs, which are not covered; and places of employment connected with an Indian reservation, which are not covered.

Two definitions of illegal discrimination are relevant to Title VII. The first is called *disparate treatment discrimination* and the second is called *disparate impact discrimination.*

Disparate treatment is the common-sense notion of what illegal discrimination means; it is defined as basing an employment decision on any of the five prohibited classifications. For example, if you were not to hire an applicant solely because of race, color, religion, sex, or national origin, you would be guilty of disparate treatment. Usually, sex-based discrimination falls under this definition. Examples include not hiring a woman salesperson because your customers prefer dealing with a man and not promoting a woman with children to a higher-level job but promoting a man with children to that job. Several forms of disparate treatment are unique to sex discrimination:

- *Using sex as a job requirement.* This practice is allowed only if sex is a bona-fide occupational requirement (BFQ). The definition of BFQ is very limited (see Chapter 26).
- *Sex-plus discrimination.* This phrase refers to employment decisions based on the exclusion of a subset of one sex—that is, those that consider sex plus some other attribute. The practice of promoting a man with children but not a woman with children, noted above, would fall into this category. The idea is that men and women in the same circumstances should be treated the same.
- *Generalizations based on sex.* Viewing women as too emotional and men as more rational in their decision making is an example of such prohibited generalizations.
- *Sexual harassment.* Sexual behavior that is unwanted by the person to whom it is directed is prohibited. Title VII makes it unlawful to discriminate with respect to a person's conditions of employment; the word *conditions* includes psychological and emotional conditions that are insulting and degrading to the person. Thus if women are exposed more frequently than men to such working conditions, Title VII is violated and the employer is liable for the actions of supervisors and managers. Examples include calling women *girls* and not calling men *boys* and kissing or pinching women.

Disparate impact discrimination refers to personnel decisions that are not intended to be in violation of Title VII but nevertheless lead to illegal discrimination because the criteria on which they are based are not related to job performance requirements. Examples include requiring a high school diploma for jobs that can be performed by individuals who do not possess a diploma and having a physical strength requirement that is not necessary for performance of the job in question. The former example is illegal because it is likely to disqualify more blacks than whites since proportionately fewer blacks than whites have high school diplomas. The latter requirement is illegal because it is likely to disqualify more women than men since women are not likely to be as strong as men.

Basing personnel decisions on criteria that are not job related is not automatically illegal. Such criteria are illegal only when they exclude a greater proportion of one race, sex, or ethnic group than another from employment opportunities. Disparate impact discrimination concerns the *results* of employment decisions. One rule of thumb used by courts as evidence of disparate impact is the four-fifths rule. This rule states that the employer who hires minority applicants at a rate less than four-fifths of the rate at which he or she hires nonminority applicants may be illegally discriminating against minority applicants. As an example, suppose that the employer's hiring requirement is possession of a high school diploma and that the applicant pool consists of thirty blacks and 160 whites. From this applicant pool, the employer hires six blacks and eighty whites. Thus the rate at which blacks were hired (20 percent) is only two-fifths of the rate at which whites were hired (50 percent). The calculations for the above example are shown in Exhibit 24.2.

Suppose now that a black applicant who was not hired decides to sue the employer for race discrimination. The violation of the four-fifths rule establishes a prima facie case of discrimination for the black plaintiff. The burden of proof—in this case defending the two-fifths hiring rate—is the employer's. The employer has to show that there is a legitimate nondiscriminatory reason for the disparate impact or that the high school diploma hiring requirement is job related, which is very difficult to do. Even if the employer can defend the two-fifths hiring rate, the case may not end there. Now the burden of proof for discrimination shifts to the black plaintiff. The plaintiff can still show illegal

---

Exhibit 24.2
CALCULATIONS FOR THE FOUR-FIFTHS RULE

The four-fifths rule compares the following ratio:

$$\frac{\text{Number of blacks hired}}{\text{Number of black applicants}} \div \frac{\text{Number of whites hired}}{\text{Number of white applicants}}$$

Suppose

Number of black applicants	=	30
Number of blacks hired	=	6
Number of white applicants	=	160
Number of whites hired	=	80

If so, the percentage of whites hired is 80/160 × 1.00, or 50 percent. The percentage of blacks hired is 6/30 × 1.00 or 20 percent. If blacks were hired at the same rate as whites (50 percent), we would expect 15 blacks to be hired (30 black applicants × 50 percent). However, the four-fifths rule specifies that employees are obligated to hire blacks at four-fifths the rate at which they hire whites. Thus employers are not obligated to hire fifteen blacks but twelve. Four-fifths equals 80 percent of the 50 percent hiring rate for whites. Thus 15 blacks × 80 percent equals 12 blacks.
In this example, the employer hired 6 blacks instead of 12 blacks, or two-fifths the proportion of whites hired.

discrimination by establishing that instead of requiring a high school diploma, the employer could have used an equally valid alternative hiring requirement or that the employer's reason for requiring a high school diploma is a pretext for illegal discrimination. Needless to say, it is difficult to defend a Title VII charge of illegal discrimination.

Some employers decide to bypass the potential of being sued for disparate impact discrimination by setting quotas for hiring members of the protected classes in proportion to their representation in the labor market. Employers can defend their employment practices if they can show that the proportion of minorities in their workforce is four-fifths of the proportion of minorities in the relevant labor market. However, under Title VII hiring quotas are illegal. Such quotas may also lead to lawsuits by white male employees for reverse discrimination.

Age Discrimination in Employment Act of 1967. This act prohibits employers with twenty or more workers from basing employment decisions on the employee's age. Workers who are at least forty years old are protected by the Act. This act is more permissive than Title VII, both in allowing actions based on "reasonable factors other than age" (such as physical strength) and in its leniency in accepting age as a bona-fide occupational qualification.

Handicap Discrimination. Two laws cover discrimination against qualified handicapped workers. The Vocational Rehabilitation Act of 1973 protects handicapped workers in businesses that hold government contracts and subcontracts. The Americans with Disabilities Act of 1990 extends handicapped protections to nearly all employers with fifteen or more employees. Both handicap laws are similar. Both define the handicapped individual as any person with a physical or mental impairment that substantially limits one or more of such a person's major life activities. This broad definition includes such disabilities as blindness, loss of limb, epilepsy, alcohol addiction, and communicable diseases. Use of illegal drugs is not considered a handicap, whereas court rulings have declared AIDS to be a protected handicap.

Both handicapped laws also require the covered employers to take affirmative action and to provide reasonable accommodation to the physical and mental limitations of the handicapped individual. Affirmative action refers to favoring the handicapped in employment decisions. The Americans with Disabilities Act, however, details the requirements of reasonable accommodation more than does the Rehabilitation Act. In general, if the employer hires a handicapped individual, the laws consider it reasonable to provide access to the job, to redesign and restructure the job to eliminate noncritical tasks that the employee cannot perform, and to provide professional help for the employee's correctable handicaps, if these accommodations do not impose an undue financial hardship on the conduct of the employer's business. Neither law requires the employer to abandon job-related requirements even if they lead to not hiring or promoting a qualified handicapped individual. Rather, the laws attempt to motivate the employer to recognize the potential of individuals who have been traditionally thought of as unemployable.

Executive Orders. Issued by the president of the United States, executive orders regulate the equal employment opportunity practices of businesses that have contracts or subcontracts with the federal government. Although executive orders do not require congressional approval and can be subsequently altered by the president, they have the force of law. Like Title VII, Executive Order No. 11246, the order currently in force, prohibits discrimination because of race, color, religion, sex, and national origin. The main difference between Title VII and Executive Order No. 11246 is the order's requirement that government contractors and subcontractors "take affirmative action to ensure that applicants and employees are treated without regard to their race, color, religion, sex, or national origin." Affirmative action refers to giving preferential treatment to members of underrepresented groups in making hiring and promotion decisions. Revised Order No. 4 provides employers with a list of steps to take to increase employment of women and minorities. Taking these steps results in designing an affirmative action plan, which has to be approved by the Office of Federal Contract Compliance Programs (OFCCP). Approval by this agency is imperative. Without such approval, the affirmative action plan may be considered a quota system and may be found to illegally discriminate against white males.

Military Selective Service Act (MSSA)   The Military Selective Service Act protects the jobs of American soldiers. The Act outlines the employer's obligations for treating members of military reserve units and for reemploying disabled veterans. In essence, the Act mandates that the employer continue to view the employee who actively participates in military service as a current employee whose job is protected while on military assignment.

Immigration Reform and Control Act of 1986 (IRCA)   IRCA mandates that all employers verify the citizenship status of all employees hired after November 1986 and maintain records of that verification. The Act permits the hiring of legal aliens; it also allows the employer to discriminate against legal aliens in favor of equally qualified U.S. citizens. This act is discussed in greater detail in Chapter 26.

Occupational Safety and Health Act of 1970 (OSHA)   OSHA requires employers to eliminate recognized hazards and to comply with specific safety and health guidelines. On paper, the law also obligates employees, but there are no penalties for employees who violate OSHA's provisions. OSHA inspectors have the right to inspect an organization's operations for safety and health violations, although managers can insist that the inspectors have search warrants before allowing them to enter the premises. This right to require a search warrant does not provide much protection, however; OSHA inspectors are entitled to receive a warrant whenever an inspection is based on a reasonable OSHA policy (such as inspect the worst industries first) or if employees complain directly to OSHA.

Under OSHA, employers have the right to discipline employees for violation of company safety rules. It is advisable to exercise that right because the employer may be held liable if employees do not comply with OSHA's requirements.

Enforcement Agencies

Employment laws are enforced by different government agencies. The Office of Personnel Management enforces all EEO laws applicable to federal government employment. The Equal Employment Opportunity Commission enforces Title VII in the private employment sector and among state and local government employers. The Commission also conducts EEO investigations related to state and local government employers, but the Justice Department brings any lawsuits that result from these investigations. The Age Discrimination Act is enforced by the Department of Labor's Wage and Hour Division. Executive Order No. 11246 is enforced by the OFCCP, a division of the Department of Labor. The Vocational Rehabilitation Act is enforced by the Employment Standards Administration of the Department of Labor. The Military Selective Service Act is enforced by federal district courts. The Immigration Control and Reform Act is enforced by a variety of agencies, the most important of which are the Immigration and Naturalization Service and the Department of Labor.

The responsibilities for the enforcement of OSHA are divided among five entities:

1. The Occupational Safety and Health Administration (OSHA) has the primary responsibilities of establishing safety standards, allowing variances from those standards, conducting inspections, and issuing citations.
2. The Occupational Safety and Health Review Commission (OSHRC) is the court of appeals for employers who disagree with OSHA citations.
3. The U.S. Courts of Appeals hears appeals from OSHRC rulings; the Supreme Court hears any final appeals.
4. The National Institute for Occupational Safety and Health (NIOSH) trains OSHA inspectors and conducts research into job safety and health problems, the solutions to which create new OSHA standards.
5. Individual states. OSHA permits states to take over the responsibility for occupational safety and health, provided that OSHA approves the state's plan.

Common Law

Besides congressional statutes and executive orders, the employment practices are increasingly subject to common law restrictions. Common law (the body of decisions made by judges and juries) has traditionally upheld the doctrine of employment at will. This doctrine is based on the idea that employers and employees enter into a voluntary relationship that can be terminated at will by either party. This means that an employer has the right to fire an employee for any cause, whether just, unjust, or even morally wrong. The major exceptions to this doctrine have been collective bargaining agreements and federal, state, and local laws defining workers who are protected from the employment-at-will doctrine. Now, however, some states are passing laws that limit employer rights to dismiss employees at will. To date, court cases indicate that employers may be prohibited from firing employees for the following reasons:

- Exercising rights granted by other laws. For example, employees who have been injured on the job have the right to submit claims to their state's workers' compensation office. The employer cannot legally fire employees who submit such claims.
- Refusing to commit an illegal act that the employer requests the employee to commit, such as falsifying reports to a government agency.
- Performing a public obligation, such as serving on a jury or supplying information to the police.

In employment-at-will cases, courts have also established that employers cannot fire employees at will if they have given their employees some prior assurance of job security, whether that assurance was written or oral. For example, a personnel manual stating that no employee will be fired without just and sufficient cause would qualify as a binding contract, and thus an exception to the employer's right to terminate at will. Similarly, telling employees that they can stay with the company as long as they do their jobs is also a binding contract. Finally, an employer may be prohibited from exercising his or her right to fire employees at will if that employer is performing a harmful action against his or her employees. An example would be pressuring employees to reveal the name of the employee who has stolen from the employer by firing employees one at a time until the name is revealed.

Labor Markets

Labor market is a generic term that refers to the geographic area from which you obtain your employees. As an employer, you should become familiar with your labor market and its conditions. Those conditions determine how many employees you can hire and how much you may have to pay them. Understanding the basic characteristics of labor markets is important for your staffing and compensation decisions.

Three Labor Markets

As an employer, you compete with other employers for employees. This competition takes place in one of three labor markets: local, regional, and national.

As a small business owner, you can probably staff most of your jobs from the local labor market. This market is typically used to staff clerical, technician, craft, and unskilled jobs. People who can perform these jobs are normally available within a particular community, be it a large metropolitan area, a city, a part of a city, a town, or a county.

You may also find professional and managerial employees within your community. At times, however, you may need to use either the regional or the national labor market for staffing professional and managerial jobs. If you are particularly interested in hiring minority employees, you may have to go to the national labor market to find candidates.

Defining Your Labor Market

Your choice of labor markets and the definition of the local labor market's geographic boundaries should be based on two factors: business interest and compliance with equal employment opportunity regulations.

To hire and retain productive employees, you should be aware of which employers your current employees are likely to view as attractive alternative employers should they decide to change jobs. Professional and managerial employees typically select alternative employers within the same industry. Since most industries are national in scope, you may have to compete for these employees nationally. A national search for such employees has other advantages. Should you wish to hire minorities to fill some jobs, you have a better chance of finding them with a national search. Should you be faced with an equal employment litigation suit, you have a better chance of defending your inability to hire minorities for professional and managerial jobs if you conducted a national search.

Most jobs, however, can be filled with residents of your local community. People in the local community typically select their employers from those available within a desirable driving distance of their homes. Some workers, such as clerical or sales workers, have skills that are needed across industries. Other workers, such as hairstylists, have skills that are normally needed within an industry. Still other workers, such as car mechanics, have skills that may be needed within and across industries. For example, car mechanics are needed by service departments of automobile dealers and they may also be needed by retail auto-parts stores.

As you start your business, think of the employers in your community who may need to hire the same type of skilled workers. These employers are your competitors for labor. Initially, you may not be able to define your precise labor market. The best that you can do is advertise in your local paper and wait to see from what general geographic area you get applicants. As your business stabilizes, you can determine your precise geographic labor market by a relatively easy seven-step process:

1. Make a list of all your employees and their addresses.
2. Get a road map of your standard metropolitan or rural area.
3. Find and mark your company's location on the map.
4. Locate and mark each employees' home on the map.
5. Connect the points from each employee's home to your firm's location to show how far your employees commute from their homes to work.
6. Compute the mileage from your company's location to your employees' homes.
7. Using the computed mileage, extend the mileage driven from the employees' homes in the direction opposite of your location and connect the points in the outer circle.

The connected points identify the boundaries of your local labor market. All companies within those boundaries are your competitors for employees. Your ability to hire the kind of people you want to hire is facilitated if, when recruiting applicants, you advertise job openings in the communities that are within the second furthest connected circle from your company's location.

If you are a federal government contractor, you are required to seek minority applicants actively. You are required to submit to the OFCCP an affirmative action plan based on the steps outlined in Revised Order No. 4. This plan requires you to specify your labor market, but note that the local labor market boundaries required by OFCCP are narrower than those you use to recruit your applicant pool. For affirmative action purposes, you are allowed to use the geographic area defined by the distance from the homes of the majority of your employees to your location (the inner circle boundary drawn in step 5). Exhibit 24.3 shows how to define your local labor market's geographic boundaries for business and affirmative action purposes.

Exhibit 24.3

DEFINING A LOCAL LABOR MARKET'S GEOGRAPHIC BOUNDARIES

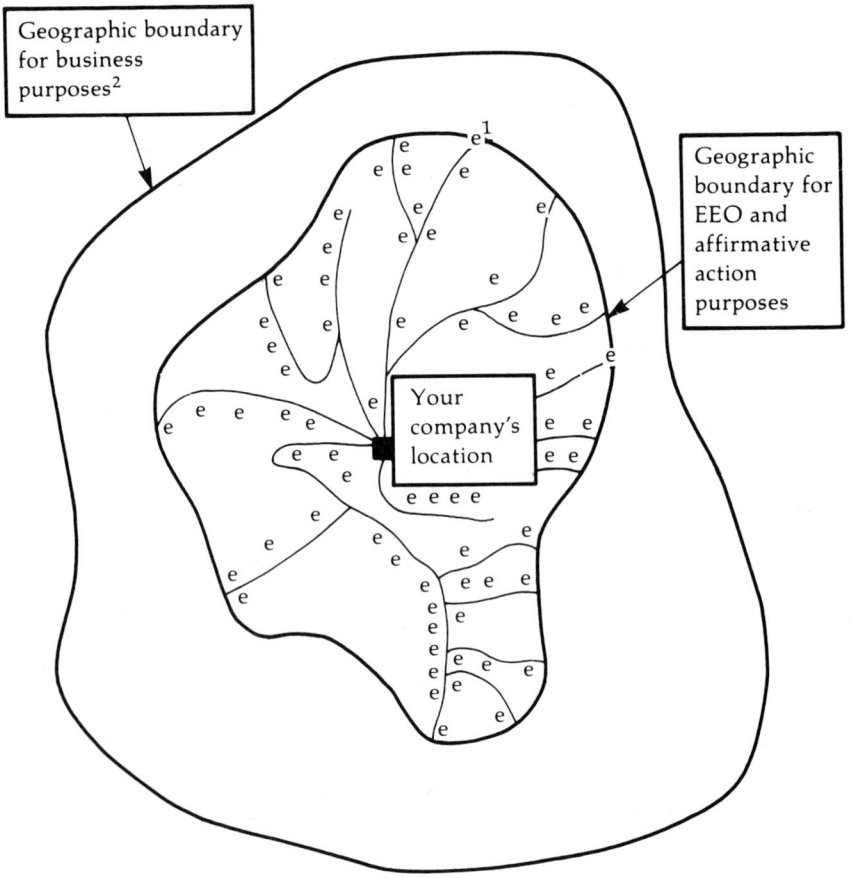

1. Represents the home locations of your workforce.
2. The geographic distance that employees are likely to travel from their homes in the opposite direction from your location in seeking alternative employment.

Conditions in the Labor Market

The number of employers in the same labor market looking for people with the same kinds of skills that you seek determines how many people you can hire at a particular pay rate. At any given time, one of three labor market conditions may exist for any category of skill:

1. *Loose labor market.* In a loose market, more people are looking for work than there are jobs. Under this condition, you can set high hiring standards, offer relatively low wages or salaries, and still hire all the qualified people you need.
2. *Fixed labor market.* In a fixed market, a fixed number of people have the skills you need. If those skills are essential to your operation, you must pay whatever it takes to get the person to work for you.
3. *Tight labor market.* In a tight market, the demand among employers for people with particular skills exceeds the supply of people with those skills. Although these conditions are true for the fixed labor market also, the shortage of workers lasts for a relatively shorter time in a tight labor market. The shortage passes because some people—who might work but do not do so until they think it is worth their while to work—enter the market once you raise the pay for jobs that you have difficulty filling. Thus you can fill those jobs by drawing from a larger pool than you initially could.

Your Organizational Structure

When you start your business and hire employees, you establish an organization. The term *organization* defines the coming together of individuals to achieve a purpose that cannot be achieved by any one individual alone.

The two essential characteristics of an organization are division of work and coordination of activities. To know how to divide work and whom to hire to perform it requires some thought about the functions that have to be performed (marketing, sales, operations, finance), the jobs you need within those functions, and the tasks that have to be performed on a given job. It also requires thought about how to coordinate the work and the criteria you should use to hire the people you need to perform those jobs.

The term *structure* refers to the assignment of responsibilities and decision-making authority to all members of the organization. Structure is usually shown by an organizational chart. Exhibit 24.4 shows three organizational structures that are typically found in small businesses.

The top chart in Exhibit 24.4 depicts a primitive organizational structure, typical in very small organizations such as a ma-and-pa operation. In such a structure, the owner is responsible for both dividing work and coordinating activities. The owner assigns employees to various tasks as needed and coordinates activities personally, overseeing all workers to ensure that the necessary tasks are completed in a timely fashion.

If you have seven or fewer employees you can easily divide work and coordinate activities within a primitive structure. As the demand for your prod-

Exhibit 24.4
THREE ORGANIZATIONAL STRUCTURES

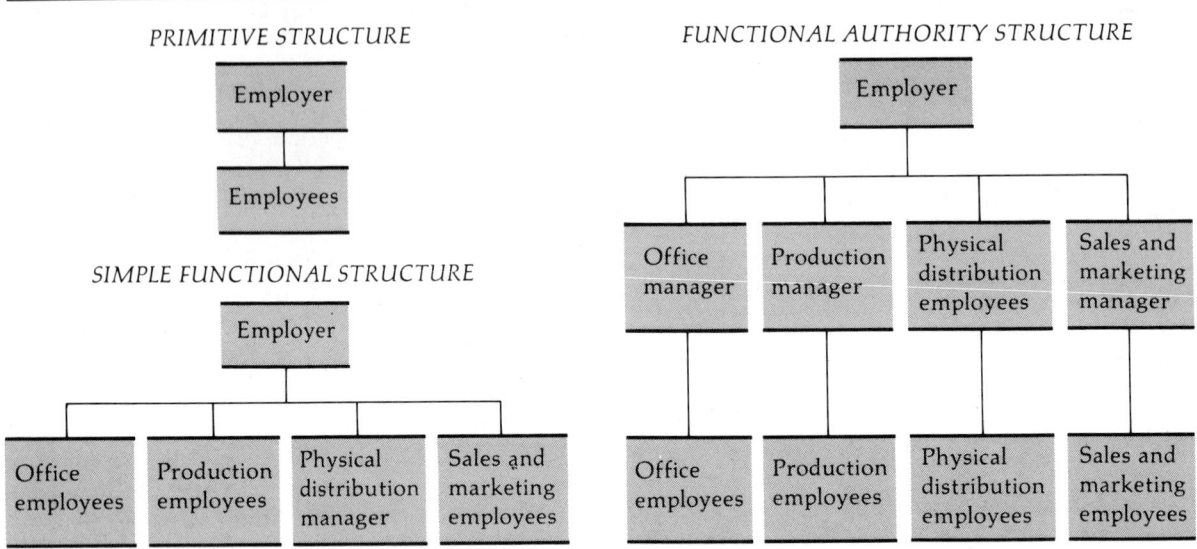

uct or service grows, however, the number and variety of activities that your employees perform increases, as does the workload in each area. To ensure that all tasks are performed by someone, you have to establish a more formal structure for your organization, such as the simple functional structure shown in Exhibit 24.4. The simple functional structure is characterized by a grouping of similar activities into functional departments. All activities necessary to perform all office functions are grouped into an office department, all those necessary to perform the production function are grouped into a production department, and so on.

In a simple functional structure, the owner is still responsible for coordinating the activities performed by each department. However, the owner delegates to a senior employee within each department how those activities are accomplished and coordinated. This employee's role is not only to perform the work but also to oversee other employees in the department to ensure that they perform their work. These employees are typically called *coordinators* or *work directors*.

Under the primitive and the simple functional structures, you may be able to divide the work by simply telling your employees what needs to be done and when the work should be done. In the former case, you personally oversee that all the work gets done. In the latter, you delegate supervisory responsibilities to a senior employee within each functional department. In both cases, when employees encounter unfamiliar situations or problems that are beyond their responsibility and authority to solve, they seek your help.

As your business grows and you add more people to your functional departments, the coordinators or work directors become unable to do their work and also direct and coordinate the work of others. Also, the number of issues that you are asked to deal with becomes impossible to address in a timely manner. At this point, you would be wise to delegate the responsibility for overseeing departmental activities to departmental managers. These managers should be given the responsibility and authority to make decisions regarding the activities performed within their departments. Such a structure frees you to deal with important business issues that you alone can handle and to coordinate your organization's activities through the department managers.

As your organization evolves into a functional organization with a managerial structure, as shown on the right in Exhibit 24.4, you should start thinking about formally managing your employee population. The best way of ensuring that the work gets done is to communicate the responsibilities of each job in a written job description. Procedure manuals should also be written to describe the handling of routine tasks for each job. Such manuals increase efficiency in getting the work done in three ways. First, new employees can learn how to do their tasks by consulting a consistent source. Second, they can also do their jobs without taking the time of senior employees to explain the correct process. Third, the loss of experienced people does not affect your productivity much because written job descriptions inform the new people of what you expect of them and the procedure manuals provide them with basic guidelines for how to perform their jobs.

Unfortunately, the authority structure that evolves as organizations grow is often not very efficient or effective because the jobs within the organization are not very well defined or, if they are defined, those definitions are seldom used or updated. In such a case, new employees are not hired based on the job's performance requirements but because they look like they will fit. Without knowing the job's requirements, employers may also pay some people too much and others too little; they typically hire more people than are actually needed as well. For all of these reasons, you should consider developing written job descriptions that are based on the requirements of the jobs within your organization.

Job Descriptions and Their Importance	A written job description defines the major responsibilities and tasks of a job. Each job in the organization should have a written job description. Three examples are shown in Exhibits 24.5, 24.6, and 24.7.

Notice that all three job descriptions start with identifying the job's title and the department in which the job is performed. Job titles vary among organizations. Consequently, they are not good indicators of a job's content. Notice also the space for job grade on the forms. Job grade refers to the relative ranking of the job compared to others in the organization. This ranking is determined through the process of job evaluation discussed in Chapter 25. The job description also lists the date that the job was added to the organization and the manager who approved that addition. The date is important because job requirements may change as a company grows. The dates that jobs were first implemented may act as indicators that the time has come to reanalyze the job.

Exhibit 24.5
JOB DESCRIPTION FOR CUSTOMER SERVICE REPRESENTATIVE

Title   <u>Customer Service Representative</u>   Job Grade _____

Department   <u>Customer Service</u>

Approved by   <u>VS</u>   Effective Date   <u>9/10/91</u>

PRIMARY FUNCTION
Identifies, processes, and resolves customer inquiries or complaints regarding merchandise orders and product specifications or prices within established guidelines and procedures.

SOURCE OF SUPERVISION
Direct supervision from appropriate customer service area supervisor.

SUPERVISION EXERCISED
None

WORK PERFORMED

1. Operates computer terminal, handfree telephone system, and normal office equipment for up to three consecutive hours.
2. Initiates mail tracers for lost or late merchandise orders.
3. Receives and sends telex correspondence for international accounts.
4. Speaks clearly with customers by telephone or in person to solve problems.
5. Uses persuasive selling techniques in response to customer inquiry.

Exhibit 24.6
JOB DESCRIPTION FOR A PROGRAMMER

Title   <u>Programmer</u>   Job Grade _____

Department <u>MIS</u>

Approved by: <u>VS</u>   Effective Date   <u>6/9/91</u>

PRIMARY FUNCTION
Assists in formulating system applications through assigned research and factfinding to develop or modify a data processing system. Prepares detailed specifications from which programs will be written. Designs, codes, tests, debugs, and documents programs. Maintains and modifies those programs.

SOURCE OF SUPERVISION
Direct supervision from Manager of Information Systems.

SUPERVISION EXERCISED
None

WORK PERFORMED

1. Works independently on several phases of applications systems analysis and programming activities but requires some instruction and guidance in other phases.

2. Programming activities
   a. Writes, codes, tests, debugs, and documents new or modified programs using BASIC language.
   b. Sets up and maintains hardware.
   c. Trains internal end-users in use of programs.
   d. Interacts with internal end users in program development, implementation, and operation.
   e. Trains lower level programming assistants in programming techniques and the BASIC language.

Exhibit 24.7

JOB DESCRIPTION FOR A FINANCIAL SERVICES CLERK

Title ___Financial Services Clerk___   Job Grade _____

Department ___Financial Services_____

Approved by: ___VS_____   Effective Date ___2/12/91_____

PRIMARY FUNCTION
Performs assigned work within established procedures and guidelines. Works in one of three financial areas: accounts payable and payroll, accounts receivable, or credit and collections.

SOURCE OF SUPERVISION
Direct supervision from the financial services supervisor.

SUPERVISION EXERCISED
None

WORK PERFORMED

1. Prepares reports for lenders consisting of sales totals, cash collections, returns, and loans.
2. Processes bad debt collections.
3. Verifies and reports on customer credit information and financial status for credit approval.
4. Processes billing statements, account receivable adjustments, cash transfers, and accounts payable statements.
5. Processes bank deposits.
6. Sets up and maintains appropriate financial files.
7. Assists in bank reconciliations and audits.
8. Matches invoices to receivables for verification of information.

To keep abreast of job changes, many companies reanalyze their jobs every two to three years.

The three job descriptions shown in Exhibits 24.5 through 24.7 are summaries of the job. Sometimes it is useful to write task descriptions. These are still considered to be job descriptions, but are more specific and can assist the employee to know precisely what tasks comprise his or her job responsibilities. Task lists are useful for jobs that contain a large number of incumbents and for jobs that can be filled by low-skilled people. An example of a task list that can be incorporated into a job description is the following:

- Unload containers from transportation.
- Identify and label packages, crates, or boxes.
- Determine items requiring refrigerated storage.
- Forward reports on damaged or improper shipments.
- Rotate items to ensure that oldest stock is issued first.

A well-written job description helps in the following areas of human resource management:

- *Use of personnel.* Knowing what work is done in various jobs helps you eliminate superfluous jobs, avoid assigning duplicate tasks, and ensure that all essential work is done. You can also design career progression paths for your employees by examining the logical movements within your organization.
- *Compensation.* A detailed and unambiguous job description can serve as the basis for ranking your jobs according to their value to your organization and determining how much other employers are paying for similar jobs. (Compensation is discussed in Chapter 25.)
- *Staffing.* By knowing the essential requirements for each job, you can determine the knowledge, skills, and abilities required for new hires. For example, let us look at the job description of the customer service representative shown in Exhibit 24.5. You may decide that operating a computer terminal, one of the task requirements, can be learned quickly on the job. If so, you may not list computer experience as an employee requirement. On the other hand, feeling that "suggestive selling techniques" cannot be easily learned in your organization, you may want to specify the communication skills that an applicant for the job must possess. By going over the entire job description, you can define the precise employee characteristics, called *employee specifications,* that the jobholder must possess to perform the job satisfactorily. Then you can use these specifications as the criteria for hiring. (Staffing is discussed in Chapter 26.)
- *Performance evaluation.* The job description acts as a standard against which you can evaluate your employees' performance. Such evaluation can help you decide how much to increase your employees' pay and whether or not deficiencies in performance are due to a lack of knowledge and skill that can be corrected through training. Performance evaluations based on job requirements also help you to determine objectively which employees are eligible for promotion to higher-level jobs and which employees need broader experience in lateral jobs before their value to your organization can increase. People want to be fairly treated. If you base rewards on job-related contributions measured objectively against a job description, you maintain employee commitment and productivity. Most employees perform their jobs well and are committed to

employers when they think they are being treated fairly and objectively. (Performance evaluation is discussed in Chapter 27.)

Job Analysis

Job analysis is a systematic procedure for obtaining information about a particular job in order to establish a basis for accurately describing it. The care with which the job analysis is conducted results in a more or less accurate description of the job.

As you start your business, you will begin to think about your work requirements. Write down those requirements and then decide how to distribute them among employees. Suppose that you employ family members. You know each person's knowledge, skill, and ability; you also know their nonwork obligations. In such a case, it is relatively easy to match the work requirements to the people who will fulfill them. At this stage of your business, you have the flexibility to adapt to your employees' nonwork requirements. In a real sense, your family needs and your business needs can be easily integrated. Nevertheless, family conflicts can arise out of business conflicts. One way of decreasing such conflicts is to treat your family members as you would treat other employees: let them know specifically what their work requirements are. You can do so by first conducting a job analysis and then communicating the job requirements to each employee.

As your business grows and you start employing nonfamily members, you must rethink your work requirements and reanalyze your jobs. You may also find it useful to write job descriptions for your jobs. When your employee population grows to twenty or so, you should make sure that you have written job descriptions. As noted earlier, job descriptions aid you immensely in making personnel decisions and appropriately rewarding your employees for their contributions to your firm.

In this section of the chapter, we will discuss the characteristics and role of the job analyst, sources of information about jobs, and the job analysis process.

The Characteristics and Role of the Job Analyst

The job analyst must either be familiar with the job to be analyzed or know what to look for in a job without interjecting his or her own opinion about that job. Job analysis is concerned with facts about the job and not about the person who performs it. As a result, the job analyst should avoid analyzing the employee performing the job because one employee's personal characteristics are not relevant to the behavior required on the job.

The job analyst gathers information about a job to determine why the job exists, what the reporting relationships are among related jobs, what tasks comprise a given job, how the work is performed, and under what working conditions the job is performed. The job analyst should also gather information about the knowledge, skills, and abilities required to perform the job. This information is then transferred to a job description and an employee specification, which defines the employee characteristics that are necessary to perform the job.

Sources of Information About Jobs

Some of the more commonly used sources for gathering information about jobs are observations and interviews. Observing employees performing jobs is suitable for repetitive, manual work. For other kinds of work, it is less suitable, since unobserved events that are significant but happen infrequently may be missed by the job analyst. The interview is the most commonly used approach for analyzing jobs. Interviews about a job can be conducted with the immediate supervisor of the job, who knows the purpose of the job, and with the job's incumbents, who know precisely what their job is about.

The Job Analysis Process

A job analysis should start with a review of the organizational chart, which shows the existing relationships and lines of authority among various jobs. Charts for each department should also be prepared to specify the relationships among jobs within and across departments.

A thorough job analysis should answer five questions. As we discuss what issues to address when answering these question, we will use as an example the job of a human resource manager in a small mail-order business that employs eighty people and is a government contractor.

What is the purpose and scope of the job? The owner or the supervisor is the appropriate person to define the job's purpose. The primary purpose of the human resource manager's job is to

> Assist top management in developing human resource policies. Develop human resource systems with the assistance from external consultants. Implement and administer recruiting, selection, compensation, and training programs to meet company objectives and be in compliance with employment laws.

What kind of supervision does the job require and exercise? Typically a job may require one of three kinds of supervision:

1. Close or direct supervision, in which the supervisor directs the job incumbent on how to perform the tasks and oversees the performance of the tasks
2. General supervision, in which the supervisor gives the job incumbent general guidelines on when the tasks should be completed
3. Limited supervision, in which the job incumbent operates relatively independently and consults with the supervisor only if he or she encounters an unfamiliar situation not within the scope of his or her responsibility and authority

Professional and managerial jobs, which require substantial training and experience for performance, normally receive limited supervision. Those jobs that can be staffed by formally trained but inexperienced personnel usually require general supervision. Jobs that do not require much formal training but do require considerable experience may be subject to general or limited supervision. Jobs that can be filled by untrained and inexperienced people typically require close supervision.

Supervision exercised refers to the number of incumbents for which the employee is responsible. The human resource manager reports to the owner. The job also requires supervision of a clerical assistant. The job analysis would thus read as follows:

> Source of supervision: General supervision from owner
> Supervision exercised: Supervises one clerical employee

What tasks have to be performed on this job? A task is a complete activity that is performed; examples are typing a letter, analyzing data, and loading and unloading a truck. To describe the components of each job, the analyst has to identify the major tasks that comprise a given job. To describe fully each task, the analyst must

- Define the use of necessary machines, tools, equipment, and other work aids required to perform the task, such as "uses standard typewriter" or "uses the *WordPerfect* word processing program"
- Identify the process used to accomplish the task
- Choose the appropriate action verb to define the task

Two features of a job are important to defining a task. First is the extent to which the task requires the employee to be involved with data, people, or things. The more complex the involvement the employee has with data, people, and things, the more complex the task is to perform. The second feature is the extent to which the work process is prescribed (routine) or discretionary (nonroutine).

Answers to the three process questions help you identify the complexity of the work process and the necessary knowledge, skill, and ability the employee should possess to be able to accomplish the task.

1. Does the employee have to follow a preset procedure in performing the task? If so, what does the employee have to know and what skill and skill level must the employee possess to follow the procedure?
2. Is the task done at the employee's discretion? If so, what does the employee have to know and what skill and skill level should the employee possess to perform the task?
3. Does the employee interact with other people when performing the task? If so, what is the nature and scope of the interaction? Does the employee simply receive and relate information, or does he or she persuade or negotiate with others when performing the task? Does the employee interact only with other people in the department or in the company, or does he or she have to interact with outsiders, such as customers or suppliers, to get the task done?

In describing each task, the job analyst uses the appropriate action verb as an indicator of task complexity. The word *appropriate* is of great importance. The action verbs used to describe tasks become part of the job evaluation procedure used later to determine the relative value of each job to your organization (see Chapter 25). They can be used for this purpose by following a hierarchy that signifies the complexity of the task. Since more complex tasks are more valuable, the inclusion in each job description of task statements starting with appropriate action verbs is the basis for comparing all jobs within the organization. You can see why so much importance is attached to using action verbs as means of defining each task and then incorporating the precisely defined task statements into a job description. Exhibit 24.8 shows a worker involvement hierarchy of action verbs used by the U.S. Training and Employment Services (USTES) for analyzing jobs.

Notice the action verbs listed from top to bottom under each category in Exhibit 24.8. The verbs at the top of each list signify a high level of complexity; those at the bottom of the list signify a low level. The action verb that starts the task statement can define the complexity of the task. Taken together, the complexity levels for all of a job's tasks define the complexity of the job.

The action verbs that you use to describe each task should come from your job evaluation procedure. Thus before you write task statements, you should review the lists of action verbs contained in your job evaluation to develop a

Exhibit 24.8
HIERARCHY OF WORKER INVOLVEMENT WITH DATA, PEOPLE, AND THINGS

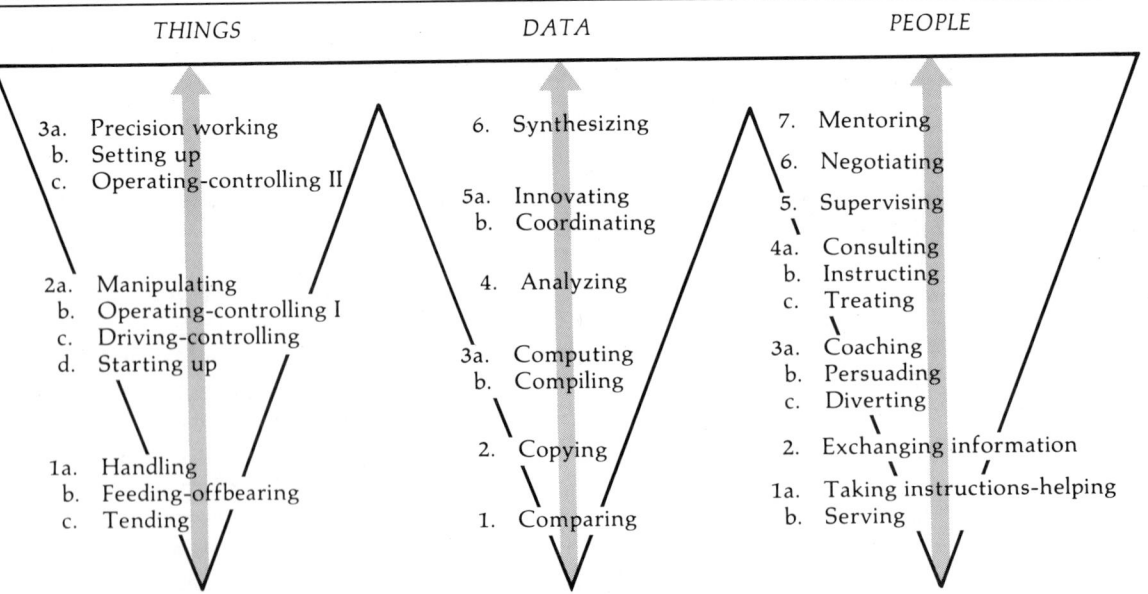

THINGS	*DATA*	*PEOPLE*
3a. Precision working	6. Synthesizing	7. Mentoring
b. Setting up		6. Negotiating
c. Operating-controlling II	5a. Innovating	5. Supervising
	b. Coordinating	4a. Consulting
2a. Manipulating	4. Analyzing	b. Instructing
b. Operating-controlling I		c. Treating
c. Driving-controlling	3a. Computing	3a. Coaching
d. Starting up	b. Compiling	b. Persuading
		c. Diverting
1a. Handling	2. Copying	2. Exchanging information
b. Feeding-offbearing		1a. Taking instructions-helping
c. Tending	1. Comparing	b. Serving

Source: Reprinted with permission from S.A. Fine, "Job Analysis," in Ronald Berk (ed.), *Performance Assessment* (Baltimore: Johns Hopkins University Press, 1986), p. 58.

hierarchy that you can use to describe the complexity of the tasks performed in all jobs in your organization.

Using this hierarchical list of action verbs, the final step in describing each task is to write a task statement. Each task statement should start with the appropriate action verb and mention the tools, equipment, or other work aids necessary for performance of the task. Notice in Exhibit 24.9 that the task state-

---

Exhibit 24.9
TASK STATEMENTS FOR HUMAN RESOURCE MANAGER'S JOB

SUPERVISORY ACTIVITIES

1. Hires, trains, disciplines, evaluates performance, and recommends compensation for one clerical employee.
2. Develops a positive work climate within and across departmental functions.

GENERAL WORK ACTIVITIES

1. Plans and executes a systematic job analysis for all jobs at least every two years or when the job changes.
2. Ensures compliance to FLSA, workers' compensation, unemployment compensation, Title VII, Executive Order No. 11246, Age Discrimination Act, Vocational Rehabilitation Act, Military Selective Service Act, Occupational Health and Safety Act, and other federal and state employment laws.
3. Prepares and administers employee communication programs.
4. Provides individual managers and employees with assistance and job-related counseling and recommends professional counseling.

RECRUITING AND SELECTION ACTIVITIES

1. Develops, implements, and monitors recruiting, selection, and orientation programs that meet company and legal requirements.
   a. Develops and monitors implementation of the affirmative action program.
   b. Selects recruitment sources, implements the recruiting process, and screens job applicants.
   c. Develops and implements employee orientation programs.

COMPENSATION ACTIVITIES

1. Develops, implements, and monitors the compensation program.
   a. Conducts job evaluations for new jobs and changed jobs and when requested by managers or affected employees.
   b. Monitors pay offerings in the external labor market by obtaining and analyzing published wage surveys and conducting cooperative private (written or visit) surveys on a yearly basis.
   c. Develops, implements, and monitors the performance evaluation system.
   d. Develops and implements managerial guidelines and reporting procedures for pay offerings and pay adjustment purposes.
   e. Controls compensation costs by monitoring that pay offerings and pay adjustments for all applicants and employees are within specified guidelines. Approves deviations from guidelines and justifies deviations to top management.

Exhibit 24.9
TASK STATEMENTS FOR HUMAN RESOURCE MANAGER'S JOB (*continued*)

2. Develops, implements, administers, and monitors the benefit program.
   a. Tracks pay for time not worked.
   b. Monitors cost of mandated benefits.
   c. Monitors cost of voluntarily provided benefits.
   d. Assists employees by explaining and processing insurance forms.

TRAINING AND DEVELOPMENT ACTIVITIES

1. Develops and implements in-house and vendor provided training programs.
2. Conducts in-house training programs on a variety of topics such as safety, employee assistance, counseling, discipline, supervisory training, employment laws, employee selection procedures and techniques, orientation programs, and compensation issues and procedures.

---

ments for the human resource manager's job all begin with action verbs. The tasks are also grouped into categories. Such categories are used in describing complex jobs because they organize the job's tasks along the set of broader dimensions.

What are the job's working conditions? Working conditions include the physical demands of the job, such as

- *Physical exertion.* How frequently does the employee lift, stoop, bend, or sit at the computer terminal. How demanding are these motions; for example, how often does the employee have to carry bags whose average weight is 50 pounds?
- *Temperature exposure.* Does the employee perform work in normal settings such as offices, or is the employee exposed to abnormal heat, cold, or humidity conditions?
- *Climbing requirements.* How high does the employee have to climb to perform the job and how frequently does such climbing take place?
- *Unpleasant working conditions.* Does the employee perform work that exposes him or her to unpleasant smell, noise, poor lighting and the like?
- *Work schedules.* Does the employee work day, evening, night, or rotating shifts?
- *Travel.* What kind of travel is required on this job and how frequently does the employee have to travel?

With respect to the human resource manager's job, the working conditions are normal. The job is performed in an office during the day, and travel requirements are minimal.

What knowledge, skill, and ability is required to perform this job? To answer this question, you should review the answers to the first four questions and the task definitions that you have written for the job. If you personally know the job's requirements, it is easy for you to specify the employee characteristics that match them. If you do not know the job, as may be the case for the human resource manager's job, you may consult with other employers or employment agencies to determine the experience or educational characteristics that ensure filling the job with a qualified employee. The tasks listed in Exhibit 24.9 would require a human resource professional to have at least five years of experience. That experience requirement, however, can be substituted by possession of a master's degree in human resource management or industrial relations.

Now that you have answered the five questions, you can write a job description for the job. Simply transfer the information you collected from analyzing the job to a job description format. As we saw in Exhibit 24.5, the job description contains the job's title, department, effective date of approval, primary function, source of supervision, supervision exercised, and work performed.

Summary

Employers are subject to the laws and regulations of the government in applying their personnel practices. State laws vary considerably in scope and provisions, but a number of federal laws are significant. Laws regarding equal employment opportunity (EEO) prohibit unfair discrimination based on color, race, religion, sex, national origin, age, or handicap. Such laws apply both to hiring decisions and to treatment of covered employees during the term of employment. Lawsuits charging illegal discrimination can be brought not only for differential treatment of minority group members, but also for the differential impact on such individuals of policies that appear to be nondiscriminatory. The Military Selective Service Act and the Immigration Reform and Control Act apply to specific groups of people who may be involved in hiring and personnel decisions. The Occupational Safety and Health Act attempts to promote safety in the workplace.

You probably can obtain most of your employees from your local labor market, which means that you will compete with nearby employers from a variety of industries. By defining the boundaries of your labor market, you can identify where to target your search for employees and what businesses you compete against. The amount you pay employees is in part a function of the supply of and demand for workers for a given job.

As an organization grows, managers often feel the need to define more clearly the structure of reporting relationships and responsibility. From a simple relationship of a number of employees reporting to one owner-manager, the business becomes more specialized, with many groups of employees reporting to a number of department managers, who in turn report to the owner.

Preparing formal job descriptions for each job, which specify the reporting relationships, the tasks to be performed, and the employee characteristics required, can facilitate making decisions regarding hiring, compensation, and evaluation. Such a description is derived from a thorough job analysis, which is the process of collecting information about each job and the knowledge, skills, and abilities a worker must have to perform the job. Job analysis is the foundation of all human resource decision making. A key to job analysis is the identification of action verbs that both describe the task to be performed and help rank that task on a hierarchy of all tasks for the organization.

Class Assignments

1. Based on the job analysis of the human resource manager's job, write a job description for that job.
2. Using the three job descriptions contained in the chapter and the human resource manager's job, develop a hierarchy of action verbs. Using this hierarchy, rank order the four jobs from least to most complex. Compare the hierarchy you have developed with those developed by other students; compare your job rankings with those of other students as well.
3. Using the three job descriptions in the chapter, determine the employee specifications (knowledge, skill, and ability) for each job.
4. Determine the appropriate labor market you will use to staff the four jobs described in the chapter.
5. Assuming that you are a government contractor, discuss the laws that influence the kinds of employees you seek to staff these four jobs.

Appendix
SOURCES OF INFORMATION ABOUT MAJOR FEDERAL EMPLOYMENT LAWS

TITLE OF PUBLICATION	*WHERE TO GET PUBLICATION*	*TITLE OF PUBLICATION*	*WHERE TO GET PUBLICATION*
EEO			
Age Discrimination in Employment Act of 1967	WH* Publication 1296, Interpretive Bulletin Revised November 1972 [Title 29, Part 860]	Voluntary Assistance Program	EEOC—Pamphlet Office of Public Affairs 2401 E St. NW, Washington, D.C. 20506 November 1983
Ley Sobre la Discriminacion por Edad en el Empleo	WH Publication 1230, Pamphlet Revised 1975	Equal Pay: Equal Work, Equal Pay, Men and Women	EEOC—Pamphlet Office of Public Affairs 2401 E St. NW, Washington, D.C. 20506 June 1981
Age Discrimination in Employment	WH Publication 1230, Pamphlet Revised September 1974		
The Law Against Age Discrimination in Employment	WH Publication 1303 Revised July 1974		
Age Discrimination in Employment Act	Public Law 90-202 December 15, 1967	Pre-Employment Inquiries and Equal Employment Opportunity Law	EEOC Office of Public Affairs 2401 E St. NW, Washington, D.C. 20506 August 1981
Personas de 40 a 70! Alerta! La Discriminacion por Edad Es Ilegal	EEOC—Pamphlet Office of Public Affairs 2401 E St. NW, Washington, D.C. 20506 November 1982		

WH = U.S. Department of Labor, Employment Standards Administration, Wage and Hour Division, Washington, D.C.

TITLE OF PUBLICATION	WHERE TO GET PUBLICATION	TITLE OF PUBLICATION	WHERE TO GET PUBLICATION
AIDS in the Workplace: Legal Limitations on Employer Actions	John E. Brockhoeft, J.D. Associate Professor, Legal Studies College of Business Administration Loyola University, New Orleans, LA	Regulations, Part 5: Labor Standards Provisions Applicable to Contracts Covering Federally Financed and Assisted Construction	WH Publication 1244-B Revised November 1984 [Title 29, Part 5]
Affirmative Action Guidelines: Technical Amendments to the Procedural Regulations	Federal Register, Vol. 44, No. 14 January 19, 1979 [Title 29, Part 1608]	Small Manufacturing Establishments Under the Fair Labor Standards Act	WH Publication 1360 Revised February 1977
		Federal Wage Garnishment Law	WH Publication 1279 Revised January 1978
The Fair Labor Standards Act of 1938, as Amended	WH Publication 1318 Revised May 1984	The Federal Wage Garnishment Law	WH Publication 1324 Revised February 1978
Records To Be Kept by Employers Under the Fair Labor Standards Act of 1938, as Amended	WH Publication 1261 Reprinted September 1984	Hotels and Motels Under the Fair Labor Standards Act	WH Publication 1306 Revised April 1978
General Statement on the Provisions of Section 12(a) and Section 15(a)(1) of the Fair Labor Standards Act, as Amended Relating to Written Assurances (with respect to "Hot Goods")	WH Publication 1055, Interpretive Bulletin Reprinted January 1966 [Title 29, Part 789]	A Message to Young Workers About the Fair Labor Standards Act, as Amended in 1977	WH Publication 1236, Pamphlet Revised August 1978
		How the Fair Labor Standards Act Applies to Domestic Service Workers	WH Publication 1382, Pamphlet Revised October 1978
		Regulations, Part 1: Procedures for Predetermination of Wage Rates	WH Publication 1242 Revised March 1979 [Title 29, Part 1]
Your Rights As an Employee on a Federal or Federally Financed Construction Job	WH Publication 1241, Pamphlet 1973	The Walsh-Healy Public Contracts Act, as Amended	WH Publication 1001 Reprinted May 1979
Service Contract Act of 1965, as Amended	WH Publication 1146 Revised July 1978	A Guide to the Walsh-Healy Public Contracts Act	WH Publication 1107, Pamphlet Revised January 1978
Contract Work Hours and Safety Standards Act, as Amended	WH Publication 1432 Reissued March 1981	Tipped Employees Under the Fair Labor Standards Act	WH Publication 1433 Reissued July 1979
Regulations, Part 4: Labor Standards for Federal Service Contracts	WH Publication 1267 Revised September 1978 [Title 29, Subtitle A, Part 4]	Regulations, Part 552: Application of the Fair Labor Standards Act to Domestic Service	WH Publication 1409 Revised August 1979 [Title 29, Part 552]

Appendix
SOURCES OF INFORMATION ABOUT MAJOR FEDERAL EMPLOYMENT LAWS (*continued*)

TITLE OF PUBLICATION	WHERE TO GET PUBLICATION	TITLE OF PUBLICATION	WHERE TO GET PUBLICATION
Regulations, Part 541: Defining the Terms "Executive," "Administrative," "Professional" and "Outside Salesman"	WH Publication 1281 Revised June 1983 [Title 29, Part 541]	Child Labor Requirements in Nonagricultural Occupations Under the Fair Labor Standards Act	WH Publication 1330 Revised January 1984
Regulations, Part 529: Employment of Patient Workers in Hospitals and Institutions at Subminimum Wages	WH Publication 1408 Reissued December 1980 [Title 29, Part 529]	Child Labor Requirements in Agriculture Under the Fair Labor Standards Act (Child Labor Bulletin No. 102)	WH Publication 1295 Reprinted December 1984
Regulations, Part 530: Employment of Homeworkers in Certain Industries	WH Publication 1026 Revised March 1980 [Title 29, Part 530]	Employment Relationship Under the Fair Labor Standards Act	WH Publication 1297 Revised 1980 Reprinted December 1984
Regulations, Part 778: Interpretive Bulletin on Overtime Compensation	WH Publication 1262 Revised February 1981 [Title 29, Part 778]	State and Local Government Employees under the Fair Labor Standards Act	WH Publication 1459 May 1985
Handy Reference Guide to the Fair Labor Standards Act	WH Publication 1282 Revised June 1983		
Employer's Guide to Compliance with Federal Wage-Hour Laws	WH Publication 1340 November 1983	*Labor Relations* Text of Labor Management Relations Act, 1947, as Amended by Public Laws 86-257 and 93-360	Superintendent of Documents US Government Printing Office Washington, D.C. 20402 Revised 1982
Wage Payments Under the Fair Labor Standards Act of 1938	WH Publication 1210 Reprinted November 1972 [Title 29, Part 531]	A Guide to Basic Law and Procedures Under the National Labor Relations Act	Superintendent of Documents US Government Printing Office Washington, D.C. 20402
Overtime Compensation Under the Fair Labor Standards Act	WH Publication 1325 Revised April 1985	The National Labor Relations Board: Provides Services for Working Men and Women Employers & Unions	National Labor Relations Board, Pamphlet 1717 Pennsylvania Avenue, NW Washington, D.C. 20570
Executive, Administrative, Professional and Outside Sales Exemptions Under the Fair Labor Standards Act	WH Publication 1363 Reprinted December 1983		

TITLE OF PUBLICATION	WHERE TO GET PUBLICATION	TITLE OF PUBLICATION	WHERE TO GET PUBLICATION
The NLRB . . . What It Is, What It Does	National Labor Relations Board, Pamphlet 1717 Pennsylvania Avenue, NW Washington, D.C. 20570	Your Government Conducts an Election	National Labor Relations Board, Pamphlet 1717 Pennsylvania Avenue, NW Washington, D.C. 20570
The National Labor Relations Board and YOU	National Labor Relations Board, Pamphlet 1717 Pennsylvania Avenue, NW Washington, D.C. 20570	*OSHA* Occupational Safety and Health Act of 1970	Public Law 91–596 December 29, 1970
		Your Rights as an Employee on a Federal or Federally Financed Construction Job	WH Publication 1241 1973

COMPENSATING YOUR EMPLOYEES

Compensation can be classified into two major categories: pay and benefits. Pay refers to wages and salaries plus any adjustments to rate paid an employee at the time of hiring. Pay is the dollar amount that the employee receives on a regular and continuous basis in the form of a paycheck. Benefits refer to all other compensation that provides income. Examples are sick pay, vacation pay, and pay when unable to work because of work-related illness or injury or temporary unemployment. Employer-sponsored programs that enable employees to accumulate capital for the future, such as pension plans, profit-sharing plans, and stock ownership plans are also included in the benefit compensation category, as is employer-funded insurance.

Your compensation costs may amount to a large percentage of business costs, yet you should nevertheless view compensation in terms broader than cost. The compensation you offer is also an inducement for attracting suitable applicants to your business and for retaining valued employees. Compensation is also critical to motivating employees to perform their jobs well and to exhibit other behaviors that have a significant impact on your success.

In this chapter we discuss two issues that are relevant to all small businesses: compensation laws and the concept of fairness that underlies all compensation decision making. We also describe how formal compensation plans are designed and the characteristics of pay-for-knowledge plans. As you start your business, you will informally decide how much to pay employees. As your business grows to about fifty employees performing a variety of work, however, you must implement a more formal compensation plan. Without such a plan, you may spend too much money on compensation and not obtain the productivity and employment stability you need. Because we expect your business to grow, we spend a large part of this chapter discussing the formal compensation plan. This discussion is highly technical and may not be easily grasped by a cursory reading. Bear in mind, however, that understanding the characteristics of a formal compensation plan is vital to your ability to use compensation dollars efficiently and effectively. Such understanding is also necessary for designing a sound pay-for-knowledge plan.

After reading this chapter, you will be able to

- Identify the legal constraints on compensation and compensation practices that are mandated
- Explain the meaning of fairness in the allocation of compensation and the design of formal compensation plans
- Describe the characteristics of a formal compensation plan
- Describe the characteristics of a pay-for-knowledge plan

Legal Constraints on Compensation

As we noted in Chapter 24, nearly 75 percent of this country's gross national product comes from earned income. Thus the compensation that citizens receive for their work determines, to a large extent, the political, social, and economic well being of the United States.

To ensure that members of the labor force are not exploited by their employers and are protected from poverty when they suffer work-related illnesses, injuries, and temporary unemployment, and when they retire, the government has passed laws that mandate certain compensation practices. To further various social and economic interests, the government provides tax incentives for employers who offer various kinds of benefits, provided that those benefits are offered to all employees rather than only to the highly paid employees. Should you decide to offer benefits that are not mandated by law, you will then be required to comply with the laws that regulate such benefits.

Mandated Compensation Practices

The major compensation laws that mandate employer compliance are the Fair Labor Standards Act of 1983 (FLSA), the Walsh-Healy Public Contracts Act of 1936, workers' compensation laws, unemployment compensation laws, and the Social Security Act of 1935.

The Fair Labor Standards Act and the Walsh-Healy Public Contracts Act are intended to prevent workers from exchanging their services for a price that they accept out of desperation rather than in fair exchange for value. Workers' compensation and unemployment compensation laws are state laws passed to help ensure income continuity during periods of unemployment. The Social Security Act is intended to provide continuation of income to ill and disabled workers as well as a basic floor of security from poverty upon retirement.

Fair Labor Standards Act   Also called the wage and hour law, the FLSA establishes requirements for minimum wage, overtime pay, equal pay, and record keeping for employers covered under the Act. The minimum wage provision requires that employers pay the specified minimum wage per hour regardless of whether pay is calculated on an hourly or daily basis or whether salary or incentive pay is involved. The overtime provision requires employers to pay one-and-a-half times the regular hourly rate for each additional hour above 40 hours that is worked during one workweek. The equal pay provision mandates that women and men who perform jobs requiring substantially equal skill, effort, and responsibility and who work under similar working conditions must be compensated at the same rate of pay. The record-keeping provision requires employers to keep specific records of the time worked by each employee and the pay that the employee receives for time worked.

The FLSA specifies which employers and employees are subject to these provisions. Exhibit 25.1 lists the kinds of establishments that are regulated by the FLSA. Exhibit 25.2 describes the kinds of employers and employees that are specifically exempted from the definition of the workweek, minimum wage provisions, and overtime pay provision. Employee exemptions to the FLSA are the basis for the typical classifications of employees as exempt or nonexempt.

Walsh-Healy Public Contracts Act   The Walsh-Healy Act regulates the compensation practices of employers who hold government contracts. Holders of federal contracts of $2,500 or less are required to pay minimum wage. Contractors whose contracts are greater than $2,500 are required to pay the prevailing area wages and benefits specified by the secretary of labor or by the previous contractor's union agreement. Contractors holding federal contracts of $10,000

Exhibit 25.1
ESTABLISHMENTS REGULATED BY THE FLSA

- Federal government.
- All enterprises engaged in interstate commerce.
- All enterprises producing goods for interstate commerce or handling, selling, or otherwise working on goods or materials that have been moved in or produced for such commerce by any person covered by the act.
- All retail or service establishments whose annual gross volume of sales or business exceed a predetermined figure.
- Local transit enterprises having an annual gross volume of sales of at least $1 million.
- Private hospitals, nursing homes, preschools, and other educational institutions.
- Laundry and cleaning establishments.
- State and local government employees who are not employed in settings that are considered to be traditional government activities, such as schools, hospitals, fire prevention, police protection, public health, parks and recreation.
- Employers whose employees are individually engaged in interstate commerce, such as communication and transportation workers; employees who handle, ship, or receive goods moving in interstate commerce; clerical or other workers who regularly use the mails, telephone, or telegraph for interstate communication or who keep records on interstate transactions; employees who perform clerical, custodial, maintenance, or other work for firms engaged in commerce or in the production of goods for commerce.

Source: Vida Scarpello and James Ledvinka, *Personnel/Human Resource Management: Environments and Functions* (Boston: PWS-KENT Publishing, 1988) p. 363. Reprinted by permission of PWS-KENT Publishing Company, a division of Wadsworth, Inc.

Exhibit 25.2

EXAMPLES OF EXEMPTIONS FROM COVERAGE BY THE FLSA

EXEMPTIONS FROM THE DEFINITION OF THE WORKWEEK

Under section 7(j) of the FLSA, hospitals and residential care establishments may, pursuant to a prior agreement or understanding with their employees, use a fixed work period of fourteen consecutive days in lieu of the workweek for the purpose of computing overtime, if they pay time and one-half the regular rate for hours worked over eight in any workday or eighty hours in the fourteen-day period, whichever is the greater number of hours.

EXEMPTIONS FROM THE MINIMUM WAGE PROVISION

Trainees and apprentices may, under certain circumstances, be paid less than the minimum wage. Full-time students in retail or service establishments, agriculture, or institutions of higher education may also be paid less than the minimum wage. Workers who are aged or mentally or physically disabled may also be employed at rates below the minimum wage. For all these exemptions, the employer must obtain special certificates issued by the Wage and Hour Administration of the U.S. Department of Labor.

EXEMPTIONS FROM THE OVERTIME PAY PROVISION

Certain highly paid commission employees of retail or service establishments may be exempt from the overtime pay provision. Auto, truck, trailer, farm implement, boat, or aircraft sales workers, partsmen, and mechanics servicing these vehicles are exempt. Employees of railroads, air carriers, and motion picture theaters are exempt. Taxi drivers, news editors, and farm workers are also exempt.

EXEMPTIONS FROM MINIMUM WAGE AND OVERTIME PAY PROVISIONS

Executive, administrative, and professional employees within the covered enterprises are exempt from both minimum wage and overtime pay provisions. Employees of certain seasonal amusement or recreational establishments, certain small newspapers, switchboard operators of small telephone companies, seamen employed on foreign vessels, certain farm workers, and casual babysitters are also exempt.

Source: Vida Scarpello and James Ledvinka, *Personnel/Human Resource Management: Environments and Functions* (Boston: PWS-KENT Publishing, 1988), p. 364. Reprinted by permission of PWS-KENT Publishing Company, a division of Wadsworth, Inc.

or more are also required to comply to the FLSA's overtime provision. All contractors are required to comply with the FLSA's equal pay provision and record-keeping requirements. If you hold a particular kind of government contract, such as a construction or service contract, you can obtain copies of the regulations specific to your contract type from the Wage and Hour Division of the Department of Labor located in your community.

The Wage and Hour Division enforces the FLSA's minimum wage, overtime pay, and record-keeping requirements in all employment sectors and for all government contractors. It also enforces pay requirements based on prevailing area rates. The Equal Employment Opportunity Commission (EEOC) enforces FLSA's equal pay requirements.

Income Security   Workers' compensation laws provide continuity of income to workers who cannot work because of illness or injury that arose out of and in the course of employment. Exhibit 25.3 outlines provisions of workers' compensation laws that are common across states.

Unemployment compensation laws provide income to workers who are temporarily unemployed and searching for suitable employment. The laws define suitable employment as any employment that is in the worker's customary occupation, located at a reasonable distance from the worker's residence, and free from risk of health and safety. Worker eligibility to collect unemployment compensation varies considerably across states. All states provide that only those workers who are unemployed through no fault of their own are eligible for unemployment compensation. States differ considerably in how they interpret this no-fault requirement.

States assess employers a tax for workers' compensation and unemployment compensation insurance. The tax for each program is based on the employer's past record of claims paid by the state, called the *experience rating.* With respect to workers' compensation, you can decrease your tax obligation by maintaining safe and healthy working conditions, which minimizes the number of workers' compensation claims filed by your employees. Similarly you can minimize your unemployment compensation tax by not firing or laying off employees frequently. If you fire or lay off employees frequently, you may find that you fall into the poor experience rating category and are thus obligated to pay a high unemployment compensation tax.

The Social Security Act established the social security system, which taxes employers and employees equally on wages or salaries paid. The tax obligation is based on the employee's yearly earned income up to a minimum amount. The Federal Insurance Contribution Act (FICA) specifies the tax payments for

---

Exhibit 25.3
COMMON PROVISIONS OF WORKERS' COMPENSATION LAWS

- Replacement of lost income, medical expense payment, some sort of rehabilitation, survivor death benefits, and lump-sum disability payment.
- Worker does not have to sue employer to get workers' compensation. Employers who are covered are exempt from lawsuits.
- Compensation is generally paid through an insurance program financed through employee premiums.
- Employer insurance premiums are based on accident and illness records within the organization.
- The worker's wage or salary loss is usually not covered in full. Most states provide for a maximum payment of two-thirds of wage or salary lost due to accident or illness.
- Medical expenses are usually covered in full.
- All job-related injuries are covered regardless of whose negligence caused them.

Source: James Ledvinka, *Federal Regulation and Human Resource Management* (Boston: KENT Publishing, 1982), p. 144. Reprinted by permission of PWS-KENT Publishing Company, a division of Wadsworth, Inc.

the employer; the employee's contribution to FICA is made through payroll deduction.

Employer compliance to the mandated compensation laws is basically an administrative task. You must ensure that you follow the procedures required by those laws.

Employee Benefits

Employee benefits can be grouped into four categories:

1. Payments for time not worked, such as sick leave, vacation pay, holiday pay, personal leave, funeral leave, jury duty, or military leave
2. Nonmandated hospitalization, disability, and life insurance
3. Private pension plans that supplement social security retirement benefits
4. Capital accumulation plans such as profit-sharing plans that may function as retirement plans or as performance bonuses

Some benefits are mandated by various laws such as FLSA and the Military Selective Service Act, or MSSA (see Chapter 24). Most benefits, however, are voluntarily provided by employers. Employers recognize that benefits serve an important role in the ability to attract and retain productive employees. Most employees today consider benefits to be a part of their compensation. Indeed, benefit packages are often more important than direct pay because benefits provide income security that would be too costly to obtain on an individual basis. Employers also recognize that some benefits, such as profit-sharing and stock-ownership plans, are less costly than other benefits and provide a greater return on investment for the employer than increasing an employee's salary. In new or small companies, employers often have limited cash for the salaries that may be required to attract and retain productive employees. By implementing a profit-sharing or stock-ownership plan, the employer can conserve cash by paying employees less than other employers do in the labor market while still providing a strong incentive to produce and thereby share in the company's profits and growth.

For these reasons, you may decide to provide nonmandated benefits to your employees. If so, you must comply with a wide range of frequently changing regulations. Fear of regulation, however, should not deter you from the positive effects you can gain from providing these benefits. Compliance requirements are less restrictive for small businesses than for large businesses, and the tax breaks you can get for offering some benefits can substantially help your business to grow. Because these tax breaks change frequently, you should consult a benefits specialist to help you develop and modify your benefit offerings.

As a small business owner, you may not be able to afford the pay and benefits that you wish to provide. One way of saving on mandated compensation costs is to limit initial hiring to family members and to full-time employees. Family members have a stake in the business and often work for free until revenue is generated. Full-time employees may save you money because two half-time employees may cost you more in social security payments, unemployment compensation, and workers' compensation claims than one full-time employee. (This cost saving results from the fact that the taxes often have upper limits for the salary on which the tax is due. If the tax is no longer paid after $15,000 of income per worker, an employer may pay less tax on a $20,000 full-time employee than on two $10,000 part-time employees.) Furthermore, if you encounter problems in meeting the payroll, you can provide full-time employees with an incentive to stay with you by giving them the pay you can afford plus a share in your business.

You may also subcontract your work, but before doing so make sure that you check the definitions of subcontractor contained in the FLSA. If you fail to check, you may find that the law defines your subcontractor as an employee and requires you to pay the mandated compensation to that employee. Finally, if you hire inexperienced workers, you may be able to give them lower than mandated pay if extensive training is required for the performance of their jobs. Again, be sure to check the FLSA's provisions for paying trainees.

Fairness in Compensation

As you start your business, your main concern is to maintain cash flow. Fixed costs in the form of employee compensation can have a significant effect on your financial budget. Thus you probably view compensation as a cost you want to minimize. You may view fair pay simply as compliance with compensation laws. Such a view is too narrow. The term *fair* is defined by the ability to balance competitive business interests (through cost control of compensation outlays) with the goals of attracting, retaining, and motivating a competent workforce.

Individuals trade their skills and labor for compensation. Their expectations of pay level and their perceptions of pay fairness are bounded by their occupational and career choices and experiences within the world of work. Considerable research shows that individuals expect to be paid fairly in relation to the external labor market and in relation to their supervisors, subordinates, and peers.

Within budget constraints, employers use compensation to influence applicants' perceptions of the organization's attractiveness for employment and employees' perceptions of fair treatment. The concern is to avoid the perception that your compensation is unfair. Employee perceptions of being underpaid may have serious consequences for your organization, such as:

- Employees slowing down and paying inadequate attention to quality
- Employees not wanting to work the number of hours that you want them to work
- Employees increasing their absenteeism rate and developing a variety of excuses for not coming to work

- Employees believing that they are entitled to some of your products to balance the low pay they receive and thus increasing thefts
- Employees who are good workers deciding to work elsewhere out of a feeling that they are not appreciated
- Employees deciding to unionize in order to receive fairer compensation

For these reasons, your compensation practices should attempt to balance the costs of compensation with inducements for employees to perform.

Characteristics of a Formal Compensation Plan

Design of a formal compensation plan requires that you make three kinds of decisions based on data:

1. *Pay level:* the average wages or salaries that you pay
2. *Pay structure:* the relative pay of jobs within your organization
3. *Individual pay treatment:* the means of rewarding individual employees for their relative contributions

To make these decisions, you must gather data that enable you to assess the likelihood that your employees will perceive these decisions as fair.

The data you need for making the first decision, or pay level, are the going rates of pay and benefits for similar jobs in the labor market. Such data are gathered through pay and benefit surveys. The data you need to decide the relative pay of jobs within your organization—the second decision—are generated within your organization. Before you can make pay structure decisions, you must do three things. First, you must determine the relative value of your jobs by rank ordering those jobs according to their value. Second, you must compare the rank ordering of your jobs to the going rates of pay for those jobs in the labor market. Third, if the market rates do not mirror the value of the jobs within your organization, you must decide which rates to follow. If you are having trouble recruiting and are not concerned about retaining employees, your best bet is to pay the market rates. If there is an oversupply of people in the market who are able to perform your jobs or if you cannot afford market rates, set your pay level as close to the market rates as possible (not lower than 10 percent below market). If you maintain pay rates according to the jobs' internally determined value, your current employees are likely to accept your job pricing decisions.

The data you gather to make these three compensation decisions also provide you with the means to assess fairness and address employee concerns about fairness in a systematic and fair way. Exhibit 25.4 summarizes the decisions, the data needed for the decisions, and the procedures for gathering these data, which are the three aspects to consider in designing a formal compensation plan. Note that compensation laws are also included as an issue that your compensation plan must incorporate. In the following sections, we explore the procedures in more detail.

Exhibit 25.4
ISSUES, DATA NEEDED, AND PROCEDURES TO FOLLOW IN MAKING COMPENSATION DECISIONS

ISSUES	DATA NEEDED	COMPENSATION PROCEDURE
Pay level	Going rate of pay for similar jobs across organizations	Conduct pay and benefit surveys of competitors' compensation practices
Pay structure	Relative value of jobs within the organization	Conduct job evaluations
Individual pay treatment	Relative contributions of employees on a given job	Pay adjustment procedures: • Merit pay programs • Incentive programs • Recognition award programs
Compensation laws	Copies of federal and state laws applicable to your business	Compliance to mandated compensation laws through administrative practices

Pay and Benefit Surveys

Recall from Chapter 24 that, in planning for your human resources, you specified the geographic boundaries of your local labor market, noted that you may have to recruit in the national labor market to obtain minority and nonminority professional and managerial employees, and wrote precise job descriptions for all of your jobs. Those activities affect your ability to conduct a pay and benefit survey. The steps in conducting such a survey are shown in Exhibit 25.5.

Suppose that you own a motel and restaurant that caters to local business and other community organizations. You want to staff the job of a customer service representative. The decisions that you would arrive at, step by step, are as follows:

1. The local labor market is the appropriate labor market for this job. You compete with other employers outside your industry, so you should identify all employers in your labor market who hire customer service representatives. Such employers include other motels and hotels, retail stores, country clubs, banks and other financial concerns, mail-order houses, and manufacturing firms.
2. Given that you have identified a number of different businesses that employ customer service representatives, you must narrow the set of competitor employers to a manageable number. A group of ten to thirty employers from a cross-section of industries enables you to estimate the range of compensation other employers offer for a position.
3. Having identified the employers of interest, you can contact those employers and ask them to enter into an agreement with you to share pay

and benefit information about their jobs on a yearly basis, with the surveying responsibility rotated among the firms each year. You can also obtain pay and benefit information from your area chamber of commerce or various trade associations; you can also contract with firms whose business is to survey compensation practices on a periodic (usually yearly) basis. Examples of such firms are Hay Associates, Cole Surveys, and the American Management Association's (AMACOM) Compensation Service. Using several survey sources will give you more accurate information about the going rate for the jobs of interest.

4. Determine the information to collect. Typical information collected on pay practices is shown in Exhibit 25.6. Besides information about pay, you also want to obtain information about a variety of pay-related issues such as number of hours worked per week, whether or not overtime is paid, and the benefits offered.

5. Collect the desired pay information from the employers that you identified in step 2 as your labor market competitors for customer service representatives.

5. Notice in Exhibit 25.6 that the job description given on the survey is a summary of the job description provided in Exhibit 24.5 (see Chapter 24). The summary reflects the essential requirements of the job. Each employer you choose as a competitor for customer service representatives does not pay these workers exactly the same compensation. Some employers prefer to pay a little more to get better employees; others pay less and still get the quantity and quality of employees that they need. To determine the job's going rate of pay, you must calculate the median pay rate in the labor market. The median is the pay rate at the fiftieth percentile of the pay rates of the surveyed employers. The median pay rate for the job is considered the going rate or market rate. In analyzing the pay survey information, you will first have to determine whether your job's content matches or does not match the content of the surveyed job. This is why so much importance is attached to writing a job description that accurately represents the essential requirements of the job.

The jobs included in a compensation survey are called *benchmark* or *key jobs* because they are stable in content, common in many organizations, and em-

---

Exhibit 25.5

STEPS IN CONDUCTING A PAY AND BENEFIT SURVEY

1. Choose the appropriate labor market for the job of interest
2. Choose the employers within the labor market who are likely to compete for employees who can fill the job of interest
3. Determine how to collect pay and benefit information about the job of interest
4. Determine the information to collect
5. Collect the desired pay information
6. Analyze the survey results

Exhibit 25.6
TYPICAL INFORMATION ABOUT PAY COLLECTED IN COMPENSATION SURVEYS

Job Title: Customer service representative
Job Description: Under direct supervision and within established guidelines and procedures, this worker identifies, resolves, and processes merchandise orders. The employee

1. Operates computer terminal, handfree telephone system, and normal office equipment for up to three consecutive hours
2. Initiates mail tracers for lost or late merchandise orders
3. Receives and sends telex correspondence for international accounts
4. Speaks clearly with customers by telephone or in person to resolve problems
5. Uses persuasive selling techniques in response to customer inquiry

Pay Practices for Above Job

1. Degree of match between the above job and the job in your company (check one)

   We don't have this job. _____

   Our job is larger than above description. _____

   Our job is a close match to above description. _____

   Our job is smaller in scope than above description. _____

2. Title given the above job in your company (please print) _____

   _____

3. Total number of incumbents in this job in your company _____
4. Hourly average rate for this job in your company

   Minimum $_____

   Midpoint $_____

   Maximum $_____

5. Number of hours employees in this job work per week _____
6. Are incumbents paid on an hourly rate or are they salaried?

   Hourly rate _____

   Salaried _____

7. On average, how many hours per month do employees work overtime? _____
8. Are there seasonal variables in overtime required?

   Yes _____   No _____

9. If yes, how many peak work periods are there in one year? _____
10. Typically, how long does a peak work period last (in weeks)? _____
11. How is overtime work paid?

    Straight time _____

    Time and a half _____

    Double time _____

    Not compensated extra _____

12. Percentage of employees in this job who get pay increases every

    3 months _____   9 months _____

    6 months _____   12 months _____

18 months _____   More than 24 months _____

24 months _____

13. Average amount of pay increase _____

14. Basis of pay increase

Across the board _____

Percentage _____

Dollar amount _____

15. Average dollar amount given _____

Average percentage _____

16. Please check the basis used for pay increases

Merit only (based on performance evaluation) _____

Seniority only _____

More merit than seniority _____

More seniority than merit _____

Seniority and merit are equal _____

Incentives (indicate type) _____

_____

_____

Recognition award program (indicate type) _____

_____

_____

ploy a large number of workers. Most jobs in any organization are unique combinations of tasks; they do not correspond to jobs that are priced in the labor market. The way to estimate the prices that should be paid to unique jobs is to compare their content with that of key jobs.

The job descriptions on the survey may be more or less consistent with your job descriptions. The extent of a match between them helps you to identify or estimate the going rates of pay for a given job. For example, the customer service representative's job description in Exhibit 24.5 and the survey job description are essentially identical. This means that your customer service representative job is a key job, and the median price for the job is the market price. Suppose, however, that your job is less complex than the job defined in the survey. If so, you may want to assign a slightly lower rate to your job than the market rate. Alternatively, if your job is more complex than the job listed on the survey, you may want to assign a higher than market rate to your job.

The job descriptions that you have written form the basis for assessing the competitiveness of your pay offerings in your labor market. Some employers use the market rates for benchmark jobs to set the pay for all jobs within their organizations. Such an approach may be useful for organizations that are not concerned about turnover and do not promote from within. By pricing jobs according to market conditions, the employer helps ensure that applicants perceive fairness in pay with respect to the labor market. Bear in mind, however, that market pricing does not guarantee that employees perceive their pay as fair relative to the pay received by other employees in the same organization. Perceptions of unfairness within the organization often lead to dissatisfaction with the organization and reduced commitment to work. Thus, it is equally important to assess the relative value of jobs within your organization and to compare the market rates to your ranking. By so doing, you can allocate the money that you have in ways that help you achieve your compensation goals within budget constraints.

Job Evaluation

As we noted in Chapter 24, the complexity of the job represents the job's value to an organization. Job evaluation is a procedure for assessing relative value of jobs without considering what other employers are paying for those jobs or the performance of employees who are doing those jobs. By conducting a job evaluation, you can construct a hierarchy of each job within your organization.

You might ask, "Why bother doing this? Why not just use the survey and price the jobs according to their pay in the labor market?" You could omit the job evaluation, but doing so may be unwise. Remember that employees assess the fairness of their pay not only in terms of the market but also in comparison to what other employees are paid. Besides market pay fairness, employees also want job fairness. If you just pay according to market rates, you do not know if you are paying fairly for all your jobs. As we noted above, you can only assess the pay rates of benchmark jobs in the labor market. Most of your jobs are unique and therefore do not have a market price.

The most important reason for conducting a job evaluation is that maintaining internal job fairness is usually more important for gaining employee acceptance of your compensation system than is paying market rates. This point is illustrated by the following example.

The manager of a motel and restaurant franchise asked us to help him deal with a pay problem he was having. The manager worked hard to ensure that his employees perceived their pay to be fair. Even though his pay rates were consistent with those of similar jobs in the local labor market, employees were increasingly complaining about their pay. Secretaries complained that their pay was the same as that of the cooks, which they did not think was fair. Cooks complained that their pay was less than that of reservation desk clerks, which they thought was unfair. The secretaries and cooks did not care what other employers were paying. They were concerned about their pay relative to the other employees in the motel. By conducting a job evaluation and ordering the jobs according to value, the manager found that the secretaries' job was indeed more complex than the cooks' job and the cooks' job more complex than the reservation desk clerks' job.

The manager informed the disgruntled employees that he reappraised the complexity of their jobs and would adjust pay rates. All employees accepted the manager's decisions and stopped complaining about their pay. They accepted the new rank ordering of jobs even though the manager explained that, given the realignment of jobs, cooks and reservation clerks could expect slightly lower pay increases next year. Since those jobs were unique in the market, there was no standard against which to price them. Consequently, pay increases the next year would be based on market prices for higher and lower benchmark jobs.

The steps in conducting a job evaluation are listed in Exhibit 25.7. Notice that the first step is to select a job evaluation procedure. Hundreds of such procedures are in existence. Each differs somewhat in the factors it uses to assess the relative value of jobs, called *compensable factors.* Typical compensable factors are experience required to perform the job, education required to perform the job, complexity of job duties, the form of supervision received and exercised, mental demands of the job, physical demands of the job, and working conditions in which the job is performed.

The second step is to conduct a job analysis on each job (explained in Chapter 24). If you hire a consultant to devise your compensation system, the consultant will show you how to write a job description that is based on the compensable factors defined by his or her job evaluation plan. Next the consultant will show you how to use the job description to evaluate and rank order your jobs by value.

As an alternative, you can purchase your own job evaluation procedure. If you choose this approach, we recommend the National Position Evaluation Plan (NPEP). The NPEP plan is one of the most widely used methods of job evaluation. It was developed by MIMA, the Management Association, which is aligned with thirteen similar associations called the NMTA Network. The NPEP consists of four job evaluation procedures, each containing compensable factors that directly apply to a specific group of jobs: production, salaried nonexempt, salaried exempt, and executive. You can buy each of these NPEP procedures by calling or writing MIMA in Westchester, Illinois. Currently, MIMA charges $45 for each procedure and provides assistance to employers in using the procedure and writing job descriptions that will reflect the compensable factors of the NPEP. By using one or more of the NPEP procedures, you can systematically evaluate and rank all of the jobs in your organization.

An example of the NPEP procedure for evaluating salaried nonexempt jobs is shown in Exhibit 25.8. Notice that the NPEP procedure for salaried nonexempt jobs contains eleven compensable factors, each with five degrees of complexity represented by a certain number of points. The sum total of the points on the eleven factors represents the job's point value. Notice also that the procedure gives you a way of rank ordering jobs into levels or grades that corre-

---

Exhibit 25.7
STEPS IN CONDUCTING A JOB EVALUATION

1. Select a job evaluation procedure
2. Conduct a job analysis
3. Write a job description in terms of the compensable factors defined in your job evaluation procedure
4. Conduct a job evaluation by assessing the extent to which the job description contains the compensable factors listed in your job evaluation procedure

Exhibit 25.8
EXAMPLE OF THE NPEP POINT PROCEDURE OF JOB EVALUATION FOR SALARIED NONEXEMPT JOBS

FACTORS AND DEGREES

JOB FACTORS	DEGREES OF COMPLEXITY				
	1st Points	2nd Points	3rd Points	4th Points	5th Points
Training					
1. Knowledge	15	30	45	60	n/a
2. Experience	20	40	60	80	100
Initiative					
3. Complexity of duties	15	30	45	60	n/a
4. Supervision received	5	10	20	40	n/a
Responsibility					
5. Errors	5	10	20	40	n/a
6. Contact with others	5	10	20	40	n/a
7. Confidential data	5	10	15	20	25
Job conditions					
8. Mental or visual demand	5	10	15	20	25
9. Working conditions	5	10	15	20	25
Supervision					
10. Character of supervision	5	10	20	40	60
11. Scope of supervision	5	10	20	40	60

GRADE RANGES

Score Range	Grades
100 and under	1
101–130	2
131–160	3
161–190	4
191–220	5
221–250	6
251–280	7
281–310	8
311–340	9
341–370	10

Example: *Complexity of Duties Factor*
This factor measures the *complexity of the duties* including the degree of independent action, the extent to which the duties are circumscribed by standard practice, the exercise of judgment and the types of decisions, the amount of resourcefulness and planning required.

1st degree. Simple and highly repetitive or routine duties, requiring use of definite procedures and little individual judgment where work involves little or no choice as to method or performance. (15 points)

- 2nd degree. Repetitive or routine duties involving use of various procedures and application thereto of clearly prescribed standard practices, which require the making of minor decisions and use of some judgment. (30 points)
- 3rd degree. Diversified duties involving an intensive knowledge of a restricted field and the use of a wide range of procedures. Requires the use of judgment in the analysis of facts and circumstances surrounding individual problems or transactions and in the determination of actions to be taken within the limits of standard or accepted practice. (45 points)
- 4th degree. A wide variety of duties involving a general knowledge of related organization policies and procedures and their application to cases not previously covered. Duties require considerable judgment to work independently toward general results; to devise new or modify and adapt existing methods, techniques, and procedures to meet new or unusual requirements; and to make related decisions guided by precedent and within limits of established policies. (60 points)

Note: Certain degrees are not applicable to the above jobs and are designated n/a.
Source: The National Position Evaluation Plan (1991). The Management Association of Illinois and the NMTA Network, Unit II of IV, Westchester, Illinois. Reprinted by permission.

spond to a specific range of point values. There are ten possible job grades in this version of the NPEP.

To determine the relative value of jobs and their pay, take each key job's grade and plot that grade against the median hourly pay rate for the job in the labor market. Next draw a line that best fits the placement of the key jobs. Then take each unique job by grade and place the unique job on the line by drawing a point where the grade intersects with the line. By relating the position of each job on the line to the corresponding pay rate for the job, you determine the going rate of pay for your key jobs and the estimated pay rate for your unique jobs.

Now that you have fit your jobs on the market pay line, you know how much your competitors are paying for similar jobs this year. If you assume that the market will be 5 percent higher in the next year, you have to take this change into account now. If you want to pay the market rate, you must adjust the market pay line upward by 5 percent. If you want to pay below the market next year, you can simply use the present market line.

Notice in Exhibit 25.9 that the point that intersects the pay rate with the job grade is the hourly rate of pay for each job. Each job's pay can be expressed either as pay per hour or as a yearly salary range for the job grade. Examples of a pay hierarchy based on pay rates and salary ranges are shown in Exhibit 25.10. Note in Exhibit 25.10 that the two hierarchies are essentially the same. The difference is that the pay rate hierarchy assumes that all employees in a given job contribute equally to job performance, whereas the pay range hierarchy assumes that employees vary in their job contributions.

In the hierarchies in Exhibit 25.10, the points on the line indicate either the actual or estimated market rate for the job. Notice that jobs on the pay range hierarchy vary in pay ranges, with the ranges overlapping to a certain extent. Jobs lower on the hierarchy have narrower ranges than do jobs at the higher levels. These narrower ranges reflect the assumption that employees in the lower grades will be promoted to higher-level jobs in a relatively short time. Because employees in the higher-level grades have fewer opportunities for promotion, they have wider pay ranges to help retain and motivate them.

Exhibit 25.9
GRAPH SHOWING HOW JOBS MAY BE PRICED

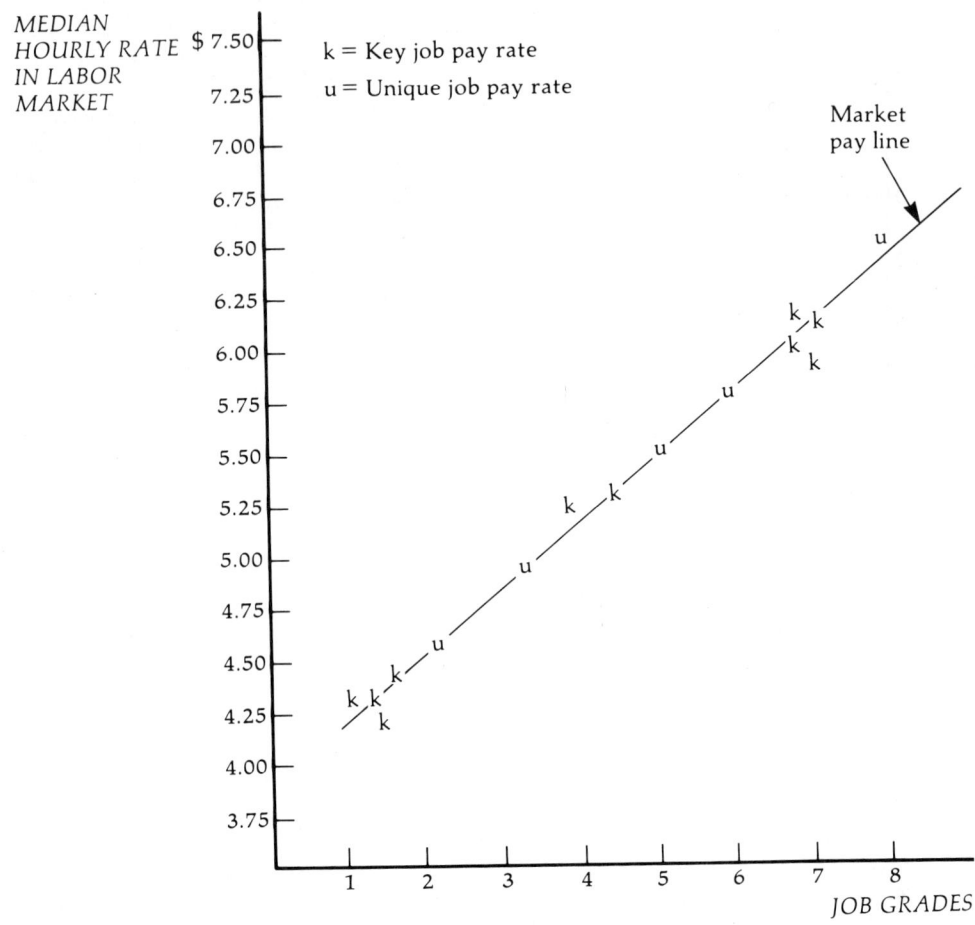

A small amount of overlap in pay ranges is desirable; such overlap allows you to use your compensation budget efficiently. If there were no overlap, you would have to increase the pay of employees whom you promote by a considerable amount even though they are initially unable to perform all of a new job's tasks. Without pay range overlap, you would be overpaying employees with limited qualifications. Similarly, if pay ranges overlap too much, you are not differentiating the value of your jobs adequately and employees would perceive that their pay is unfair compared to that of higher- or lower-level jobs. As a rule of thumb, try to keep the top of each pay range below the midpoint of the next higher pay range and the bottom of each pay range above the midpoint of the lower pay range.

Exhibit 25.10

EXAMPLES OF PAY RATE AND PAY RANGE HIERARCHIES[a]

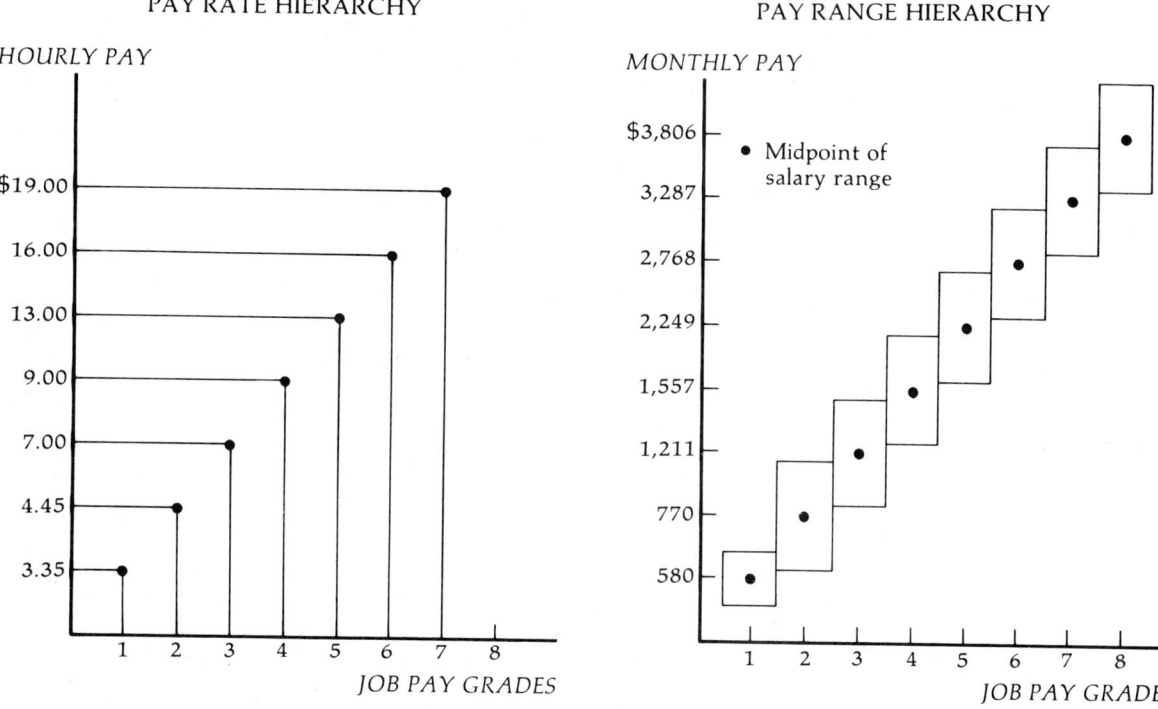

PAY RATE HIERARCHY   PAY RANGE HIERARCHY

a. Dollar amounts in exhibits assume 2,080 work hours during a year.

**Pay Adjust-
ments**

Employees expect to be rewarded for the contributions they make to their jobs. Employers use several methods for recognizing employee contributions in their pay adjustment practices. The most commonly used methods are:

- Merit pay programs, which are used to adjust the pay of salaried employees
- Incentive programs, which are used to adjust the pay of executives, salespersons, and production employees
- Recognition award programs, which are used to reward specific contributions that any employee may make to the organization

We now outline some of the more important features of each method.

Merit Pay Programs

A merit pay program can be more costly than other forms of pay adjustment because one year's adjustment becomes part of the employee's base pay the following year. To control costs and to obtain a return from your pay adjustment practices, it is important that your merit pay system is directly linked to job performance.

Most merit pay systems operate as follows. Through job evaluation, the relative value of the job is established. The going rate for each job is also established by pricing the job in the labor market or by estimating its price based on the market price for benchmark jobs. Each job is assigned a grade and a range of pay. Exhibit 25.11 shows how a typical job grade can be divided into three parts. At the bottom of the range is the minimum salary for the job, which represents the lowest salary necessary to obtain a person with minimum qualifications to fill the job. The midpoint salary represents the market price for the job, the salary paid a person who is fully qualified to perform all the job's tasks and fulfill all the job's requirements at a satisfactory level. The maximum salary for the job grade reflects the maximum dollar value of the job to the organization.

The range between the minimum and the midpoint of the salary range represents the dollar amount that you pay employees who are learning the job. Entry-level trainees with no experience would be paid the minimum salary for the job grade. As these employees learn the job and their performance improves, you can adjust their pay to reflect increased performance. When the employee becomes fully qualified and performs the job satisfactorily, he or she receives the midpoint salary. Provided that the employee continues to perform at that level, subsequent yearly increases should reflect changes in the competitive rate of pay for that job in the labor market. Stated differently, such an employee's pay increase should be the percentage change in your market pay line.

Exhibit 25.11
EXAMPLE OF MAXIMUM, AVERAGE, AND MINIMUM PAY
FOR A WAREHOUSE SUPERVISOR

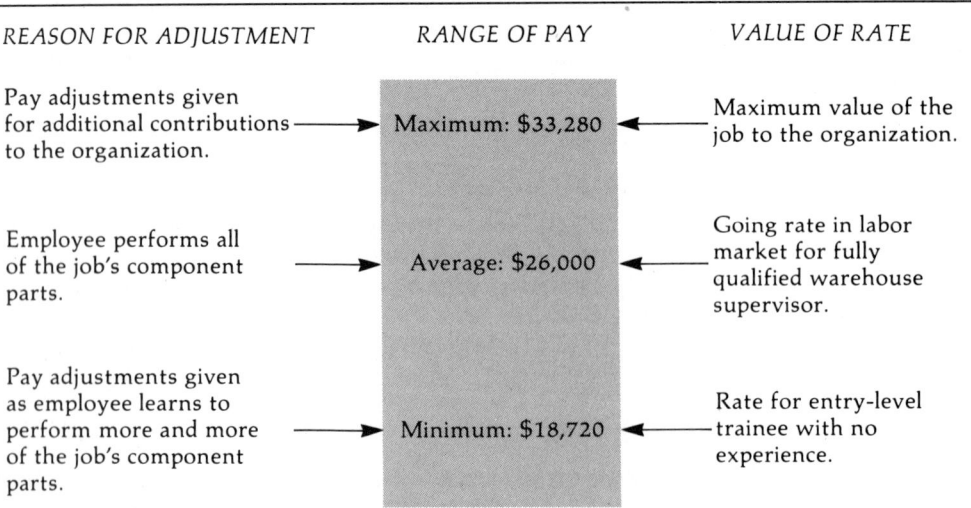

REASON FOR ADJUSTMENT	RANGE OF PAY	VALUE OF RATE
Pay adjustments given for additional contributions to the organization.	Maximum: $33,280	Maximum value of the job to the organization.
Employee performs all of the job's component parts.	Average: $26,000	Going rate in labor market for fully qualified warehouse supervisor.
Pay adjustments given as employee learns to perform more and more of the job's component parts.	Minimum: $18,720	Rate for entry-level trainee with no experience.

The range between the midpoint and the maximum of the salary range represents the money available for rewarding individuals for contributions that go beyond the job's requirements. The two most valued contributions are typically performance and seniority. If you want to pay for performance that exceeds the job's requirements, you increase the pay of top performers by a percentage greater than the percentage by which you increased the market pay line for the year. You can do this until the employee reaches the top of the grade. Once that occurs, you can do two things. You can promote the employee into the next highest grade, which should include a slight pay increase for the promotion. If you cannot promote the employee, you have to freeze the employee's pay, since the job is worth no more than its maximum pay to you. Unfortunately, this step runs the risk of demotivating the employee. Consequently, you should carefully explain the situation to the employee. If you can promote the employee into a higher-level job in the near future, say so. If you cannot, tell the employee that he or she will get a pay increase the next year, when the market price of the job increases.

An alternative to this pay structure is to supplement your merit pay program with other pay adjustment schemes, such as incentives and recognition awards. You can use these techniques to enable your high performers to provide you with value that goes beyond the worth of their specific jobs.

Incentive Programs

Incentive programs pay for job outcomes. The most popular forms of incentive pay are commissions, gain sharing, and profit sharing.

Commissions Sales jobs are often compensated by paying straight commissions. The theory behind paying commissions is that people perform better if they get strong incentives to perform. The major advantages of commission plans are the following: pay is related directly to performance outcomes, salespeople are given the greatest possible incentive to perform, and the pay system is easy to understand and compute.

Usually, however, small companies have a difficult time breaking into a market, and the commissions that salespeople receive are thus inadequate for those salespeople to support themselves in the short run. Because of this, small companies tend to experience high turnover among their salespeople; some even contract with an independent manufacturer's representative to carry their product lines. Doing so can be a risky proposition. Manufacturer's representatives are also owners of small businesses who typically contract with many companies to represent their product lines. When they get a new product line, they make a few calls to their customers to determine the sales potential of the new product. If their customers are not easily sold on the new product, the representatives tend not to push the product. You may believe that the representative is doing everything possible to market your product when in fact he or she is merely keeping the product line just in case a customer shows some interest.

In most cases, the small business owner is better off hiring a salesperson to work for him or her directly. A base pay that enables the salesperson to meet personal obligations should be established for the job. Commissions to supplement this base salary can be useful forms of incentives. You should ensure that those commissions are directly linked to the products that you want sold and that they also motivate the salespeople to establish long-term relationships with customers and not to neglect nonselling aspects of their jobs such as customer service and administrative paperwork.

Gain-Sharing Plans   Gain-sharing plans are incentives to employees to reduce costs. Common to all gain-sharing plans is a bonus divided among employees based on some measure of the work group's ability to reduce costs. The gains realized through cost savings are distributed among employees and management, with employees receiving the major portion. Most gain-sharing plans are variants of three major plans: the Scanlon Plan, the Rucker Share of Production Plan, and the Improved Productivity Sharing Plan (IMPROSHARE). Generally, employees participate in the development and monitoring of gain-sharing plans, with the degree of participation differing from plan to plan. Some of the advantages and disadvantages of gain-sharing incentive plans are shown in Exhibit 25.12.

Exhibit 25.12
ADVANTAGES AND DISADVANTAGES OF GAIN-SHARING PLANS

ADVANTAGES

- Improved efficiency in scheduling and delivery dates.
- Improved profit from improvements in work flow, methods, and equipment maintenance.
- Emphasis placed on product quality and scrap reduction.
- Increased cooperation and teamwork between employees and first-line supervisors.
- Increased employment.
- Decreased absenteeism and turnover.

DISADVANTAGES

- Requires disclosure of financial and operating data to employees, consequently requires establishment and maintenance of trust between management and employees.
- In highly participative plans, decisions may be short range as employees resist changes that may adversely affect the bonus calculation.
- If long-term investments dilute management's portion of cost savings, management is likely to make short-range decisions.
- In an adversarial labor-management relationship, the union may attempt to bargain bonus payments regardless of productivity gains.

Source: Adapted from Alice W. Rova, "Development of an Incentive Pay System for a Small Manufacturing Firm," master's thesis, University of Georgia, Athens, Georgia, 1984.

Profit-Sharing Plans   In profit-sharing plans, a fixed percentage of total company profit is distributed to employees. This distribution may take the form of quarterly cash bonuses or deposits into employee accounts to accumulate funds for retirement. Cash bonus plans motivate performance; retirement plans motivate employees to remain with the employer. Profit-sharing plans are very useful for small businesses and companies just entering new markets. Typically, such employers have limited cash because they need to reinvest earnings in marketing or in the development of production processes. Since the company expects to grow, it can attract, retain, and motivate employees despite lower than market rate salaries by providing higher long-term incentives. One such opportunity is to implement a profit-sharing plan.

Recognition Award Programs

Awards given for specific contributions that employees make to the organization are another useful incentive. The contributions rewarded include performance, good citizenship, and company loyalty. Performance awards include such things as outstanding customer service or suggestions for improving productivity or safety. Good citizenship awards reward such behavior as coming to work on time, not being absent, and working cooperatively. Loyalty refers to tenure or seniority within the organization.

Many employers pay for these contributions through merit pay adjustments. Use of the merit pay plan for such purposes, however, may increase compensation costs (recall that increased costs are a disadvantage of merit pay systems). By developing one-time recognition awards, you can reward your employees without increasing fixed costs.

Recognition award programs can reward a variety of employee behaviors. For such programs to be effective, the behaviors that you wish to reward and the form and timing of rewards should be communicated to employees. If you wish to reward seniority, for example, you may specify that an employee who satisfactorily performs all the job's requirements receives a percentage of current salary as a cash bonus. By setting the percentage at one level for employees with five years of service and at a higher percentage level for ten years of service, you reward seniority. Similarly, suppose that you are an owner of a popular restaurant, in which case the success of your restaurant depends to a large extent on the service provided to your customers. You can develop a recognition award program by having your customers evaluate the service they receive from waiters or waitresses and then, at the end of each month, giving the employee who receives the highest rating a recognition symbol and a cash or product award. You can also include each employee of the month in a drawing for a yearly service award. The recognition symbol may be something as simple as a pin for outstanding service. The product award should be something that employees would value. The size of a monthly cash award should be enough to increase significantly the amount of pay the winning employee receives that month. Employees could also be eligible to win the award multiple times, with their names entering the yearly drawing pool each time they win. The yearly prize should be one that the employee group particularly values, such as an all-expense paid vacation to an exotic place, or a valuable product, such as an entertainment center. The list of possible award programs is limited only by your creativity.

Characteristics of a Pay-for-Knowledge Plan

Most U.S. employers pay for the job that an employee performs. Recently, pay-for-knowledge plans (sometimes called *skill-based pay, multiskill-based pay,* or *pay-for-learning*) have been introduced into U.S. industry. There are two variants to pay-for-knowledge plans. The first links pay to the number of skills an individual masters for doing a variety of unrelated jobs. Another links pay to the increased knowledge and skill the individual acquires for jobs in a specific job category or family of jobs, such as clerical work or a technical grouping.

Pay-for-knowledge plans grew out of quality of work life programs, the underlying philosophy of which is to grant employees significant authority over their work as a means of increasing job involvement. Operationally, such involvement is facilitated by grouping workers into teams. Team members then teach each other the job's tasks and assist in identifying and solving quality and production problems, thereby simultaneously using available resources better and providing members with social and physical support. The expected outcome of team groupings is an improvement in productivity. To support the team concept, the new form of paying employees called *pay-for-knowledge* evolved. Newer manufacturing philosophies such as OPT and JIT (see Part Five) are also firmly grounded in the forming of teams of flexible, multiskilled workers. Consequently pay-for-knowledge systems are often associated with the implementation of these philosophies.

At this stage, there is no one standard or basic pay-for-knowledge plan in use. Development of a pay-for-knowledge plan does not negate the steps followed for the development of a job-based plan. The major difference between the job-based and knowledge-based plan is in the definition of the job. In pay-for-knowledge plans, the word *job* is given a broader definition to include the skills necessary to perform all the work required of a team of workers. Thus the title of the job changes. Instead of being a specific title, the job may be titled *work assignment, workstation, work module* or *skill module.*

Normally, work modules are ordered along a hierarchy of skill complexity (from lowest to highest) and vary in their definitions (skill units, skill blocks, or skill levels). The pay of a given worker is related to the skill modules that the worker is capable of performing, even though he or she may not be performing the skills every day.

Pay-for-knowledge plans, although developed to fit the work situation, appear to have three common features. First, each employee is required to perform a number of assignments requiring different kinds and levels of knowledge or skills. Second, in addition to learning and using specific skills, the employee is involved in planning and scheduling work activities or assignments; establishing standards of quality, quantity, and timeliness; and measuring the results of work. Third, each plan adjusts an employee's pay rate according to demonstrated skills, performed on work assignments over an extended time period.

Given that pay-for-knowledge plans are team-oriented plans, they are more difficult to develop and install than individually oriented job-based plans. The developer of the plan must begin by making the same three basic compensation decisions necessary in designing a formal job-based compensation plan. Although workers' pay is being related to skill modules, the organization must still relate the pay of its employees to that of workers in other organizations. Since most organizations use a job-based plan, this requirement places more pressure on the quality of surveys and the interpretation of survey data. Second, since the pay hierarchy is based on the acquisition of knowledge and demonstration of skill, these factors have to be designed into a multijob evaluation system and recognized in the resulting multijob hierarchy. Third, perhaps the most difficult decision is who determines (and how) when an employee has acquired the knowledge and performed the number of assignments requiring different kinds of levels of knowledge or skill to get a pay increase. This requirement places a heavy burden on administrators for developing an acceptable performance appraisal program. Finally, although similar decisions have to be made for design and implementation of pay-for-knowledge plans as for traditional job-based plans, two other factors have to be carefully monitored. First, at each stage in the pay plan's development, protecting and promoting team effort must be the primary consideration. Second, once the majority of employees reaches the top of the pay plan, the organization must begin to search for and develop additional incentives to maintain the desired levels of productivity and employment stability.

Pay-for-knowledge plans, though intuitively appealing ways of paying employees, require even more sophistication and technical expertise to develop and monitor than do traditional job-based plans. At this stage of their evolution, it would be difficult for you to install such a plan without considerable guidance from a highly paid human resource manager or compensation consultant. Moreover, the monitoring and updating of such a plan involves more work than the traditional job-based plan. For these reasons, we suggest that a job-based plan can serve most employers well, provided that productive employees can be promoted into higher-level jobs with higher pay. Furthermore, rather than using a pay-for-knowledge approach, you can provide team incentives and recognition awards for outstanding team performance, which will supplement the recognition you may provide to individual team members through merit pay.

Summary

Compensation, whether in the form of pay or benefits, is one of the major tools you can use to promote productivity. Viewing compensation simply as a cost is taking too narrow an approach.

Federal law mandates certain practices in regard to compensation. These include payment of a minimum hourly wage; equal pay for equal work, regardless of the sex of the worker involved; and payment of overtime for hours worked beyond 40 hours per week. The minimum wage and overtime provision may not apply to all employees. State and federal law also provide employees with a degree of income protection by establishing funds for workers' compensation, which provides income to workers who have suffered job-related injury or illness; unemployment insurance, which provides income to those who have been laid off; and social security income, which provides some retirement income. Other benefits are not mandated by law, but the law does require that employers voluntarily providing additional benefits do not discriminate in favor of highly paid employees.

Fairness is a significant issue in compensation; employees who perceive themselves as being paid unfairly, either in relation to the market or within the company itself, are likely to lose motivation and even leave. In contrast, employees who perceive the compensation structure as equitable probably will work hard and have incentive to improve performance.

A formal compensation plan consists of three components: the pay level, or average wages you pay; the pay structure, or the relative pay of jobs within your business; and individual pay treatment, or what you pay each worker. To devise such a formal plan, you need to conduct a pay and benefits survey. Such a survey identifies certain key or benchmark jobs, obtains information about pay rates at other businesses for comparable jobs, and attempts to identify the going market rate for those jobs. Other jobs in your organization, unique to your business, then have compensation levels set for them by establishing their value in relation to the benchmark jobs. The job evaluation is the vehicle for the valuation.

Compensation policies include decisions about practices for increasing pay during the time of employment. Increases can be made in light of increases in the market price for a job, but additional pay increases can be given to individuals who have demonstrated superior performance. Such increases exact a cost; they raise the employee's pay for the next year as well. Incentive programs, such as commissions and gain-sharing or profit-sharing plans, can augment pay for the current year only. Recognition awards, whether for job performance or for good behavior, can be used to enhance employee performance as well.

A new approach to compensation is called pay-for-knowledge. In this system, which is suited to work organized in teams, the employee is compensated for a range of skills. Such a program is complex to devise and unlikely to be needed in a small business, where the traditional formal compensation plan can serve well.

Class Assignments

1. Interview selected small businesses and inquire about their compensation practices. Your instructor will assign class members to interview the owners of two businesses in one of the categories listed below and report their findings to the class.
   - Service employer of fewer than ten employees
   - Service employer of more than twenty but less than forty employees
   - Service employer of more than forty but less than eighty employees
   - Manufacturing employer of fewer than fifty employees
   - Manufacturing employer of between 100 and 150 employees
   - Manufacturing employer of between 151 and 200 employees

For the employer category you are assigned to interview, interview one employer who is a government contractor or subcontractor and another employer who is not. In developing your class presentation, you should include:

a. The employer's industry

b. The employer's sales volume

c. The employer's workforce population and skill categories (craft, semiskilled, skilled, professional, managerial)

d. The employer's product or service market

e. The primary labor market from which the employer draws his or her workforce

f. The employer's perception of other employers in the labor market with whom the employer competes for employees

g. Laws that are relevant to the business's compensation practices

h. The employer's view of pay fairness

i. Components of the business's compensation system and why the employer has incorporated those components into the compensation plan

j. The employer's views on workforce productivity and turnover rate over the last two years

k. The employer's future plans regarding changes in compensation offerings and why those changes may benefit the employer's business

STAFFING YOUR BUSINESS

In many small businesses the owner-manager is the person who hires employees. Unfortunately, in small as well as in large organizations, the hiring process is poorly executed. Two kinds of selection errors are common: applicants who would have been good employees are not hired and those hired turn out to be poor employees. Either type of error costs you money.

You should recognize that hiring and firing are the most important human resource decisions that you make. Hiring top performers increases your productivity. Hiring poor performers decreases productivity and increase costs. Top workers in a typical job produce about twice as much as bottom workers.[1] You should also recognize the cost associated with firing poor performers, which include the cost of replacing the fired employee, training a new employee, and, perhaps, paying unemployment compensation to the fired worker until he or she obtains a new job.

In this chapter we show you how to develop a staff process that increases your success in hiring good employees and also minimizes your vulnerability to charges of violating employment law. The elements of this staffing process are shown in Exhibit 26.1.

Notice that the inputs into the staffing process are the job's requirements and the necessary employee characteristics for fulfilling those requirements. The process itself consists of decisions about whether to hire full-time or part-time employees, where to recruit, and what procedures to use for selecting employees. The outcome of the staffing process is hiring a productive and dependable workforce while complying with federal and state employment laws.

This chapter analyzes each of these steps to assist you in developing job-related recruiting and selection procedures that increase your chances of hiring good employees. Developing job-related procedures also allows you to adapt

---

1. See John E. Hunter, "The Economic Benefits of Personnel Selection Using Ability Tests: A State of the Art Review Including a Detailed Analysis of the Dollar Benefit of U.S. Employment Service Placements and a Critique of the Low Cutoff Method of Test Use," Michigan State University (January 15, 1981).

Exhibit 26.1
THE STAFFING PROCESS

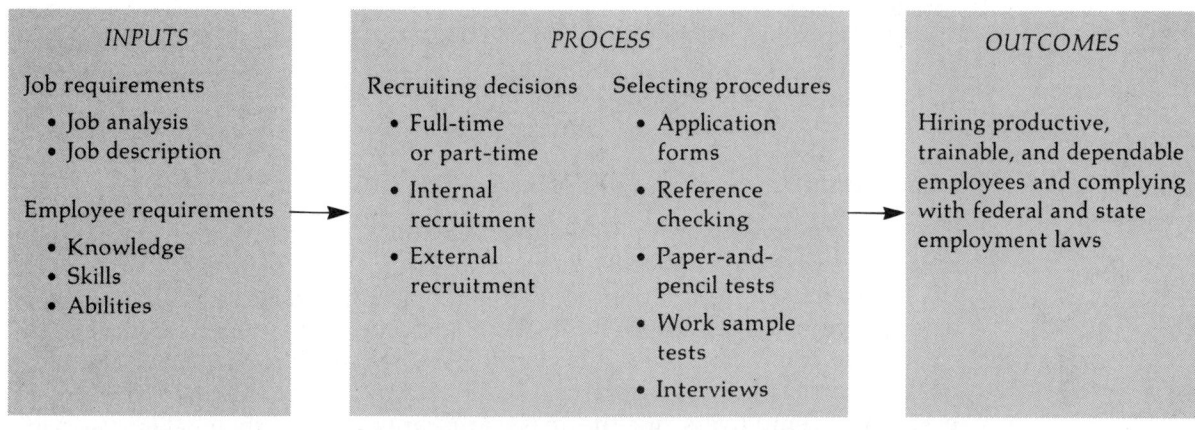

the information collected to assist in making other personnel decisions, such as pay adjustment and promotion decisions.

After reading this chapter, you will be able to

- Describe the major staffing constraints that federal employment laws impose
- Explain how to develop a recruitment plan which incorporates federal employment law requirements
- Describe five commonly used selection procedures and choose the procedure best suited for your situation

Employment Law and Staffing

The most important federal laws that you should consider in developing your staffing process are the Fair Labor Standards Act of 1938, the Immigration Reform and Control Act of 1986, equal employment opportunity regulation, and the Employee Polygraph Protection Act of 1988.

Fair Labor Standards Act (FLSA)

In terms of staffing, the most important provision of the FLSA is the child labor provision. This provision sets forth standards for employing children between the ages of fourteen and eighteen. Under certain conditions, fourteen and fifteen year olds may be employed in all nonmanufacturing and nonhazardous manufacturing jobs. Less stringent restrictions apply to minors between sixteen and eighteen.

The Act's workweek and overtime pay provisions should also be considered when you decide whether you are going to recruit full-time or part-time employees. Similarly, the minimum-wage requirement may limit the number or kind of employees you can afford to hire. Finally, the Act's equal pay provision ensures that you offer the same pay to women as to men whom you hire into essentially similar jobs.

The FLSA also requires that you keep specific records of the time worked by each employee and the pay received for time worked. Compliance with this requirement is a simple clerical process.

Immigration Reform and Control Act of 1986 (IRCA)

The Immigration Reform and Control Act (IRCA) amended the Immigration and Naturalization Act of 1984. The purpose of IRCA is to prevent employment of illegal aliens. It is important to point out that IRCA treats most alien workers as employees. Under other employment laws, a consultant is treated as an independent contractor, but not under IRCA. The reason is past abuses by business owners. To bypass federal regulations regarding the treatment of employees, some employers in the past arbitrarily called their alien workers independent contractors. Recognizing the possibility of such manipulative practices, IRCA treats most alien workers as employees, no matter what employers may call them.

IRCA permits employers to hire legal aliens and also allows them to discriminate against legal aliens in favor of equally qualified U.S. citizens. To ensure its purpose, the Act mandates that all employers verify the citizenship status of all employees hired after November 1986 and maintain records of that verification.

The vast majority of illegal aliens are Hispanic, primarily Mexican.[2] In the past, many employers violated immigration laws and hired illegal aliens. Other employers, afraid of unknowingly hiring illegal aliens, chose not to hire any Hispanics and Mexicans because these groups comprise the majority of illegal aliens. Under IRCA, employers who either hire illegal aliens or refuse to hire Hispanics and Mexicans as a way of minimizing the chance of hiring illegal aliens may receive costly penalties. It is therefore important that you review this regulation.

Provisions of IRCA   The Immigration Reform and Control Act mandates that employers examine documents of all new hires in order to confirm the prospective employee's identity and his or her right to work in the United States. Documents that establish both identity and right-to-work status are any of the following:

- United States passport
- Certificate of United States citizenship
- Certificate of naturalization

---

2. See Jeffrey S. Passel, "Estimating the Number of Undocumented Aliens," *Monthly Labor Review,* 109 (September 1986), p. 33.

- Unexpired foreign passport, if it is endorsed by the U.S. attorney general authorizing employment in the United States
- A resident alien card or other alien registration card, if it contains a photograph of the individual and authorizes the holder to work in the United States

Some applicants do not have any of the above documents in their possession. In such cases, an employer can verify the applicant's right to work by asking the applicant to produce any of the following documents:

- Social security card
- United States birth certificate
- Any other documentation that authorizes employment in the United States as approved by the Attorney General

You can confirm the applicant's identity by examining his or her driver's license or similar documents that contain a photograph and are issued by the state for the purpose of identification.

The record-keeping provision of IRCA requires that, under penalty of perjury, you sign a form stating that you have examined the appropriate documents and verified the applicant's identity and right to work. This form is called a *certification form*. The applicant, under penalty of perjury, also must sign a form attesting that he or she is a citizen of the United States or an alien authorized under IRCA to work in the United States. The law further requires that you keep all certification and attestation forms on all new hires for a period of three years after hire or one year after the termination of employment for that worker. You are also obligated to make the forms available to officials of the Immigration and Naturalization Service and Department of Labor for review. Should you hire applicants referred to you by a state employment service, the service becomes the party required to verify citizenship status and maintain the records for the required period.

In complying with this law, you may be wise to keep duplicate copies of the identity and right-to-work documents and certification and attestation forms on all employees. The law will not penalize you if, acting on good faith, you hire an applicant whose documentation is subsequently determined to be counterfeit. By keeping copies of all relevant documents, you have evidence that you acted on good faith and believed the documents to be authentic. Similarly, by keeping records on all employees, you minimize record-keeping errors that may occur from confusion as to whose records you maintain and whose records are maintained by the state employment agency. Keeping records on all employees does not add to your administrative costs and does minimize the chance of being fined (at a rate of $100 to $1,000 per employee) for failing to comply with the Act's record-keeping requirement.

Risks in Knowingly Hiring Illegal Aliens Penalties for hiring illegal aliens are very high. The penalties under previous immigration laws were low because employers were explicitly exempted from being prosecuted for harboring illegal aliens, but this exemption no longer applies. IRCA eliminated employer immunity and has provided funding to intensify efforts to identify and expel illegal aliens from the United States. Employers found guilty of hiring illegal aliens are subject to the following penalties:

1. *First offense:* $250 to $2,000 for each illegal worker
2. *Second offense:* $2,000 to $5,000 for each illegal worker
3. *Additional offenses:* $3,000 to $10,000 for each illegal worker

Employers found guilty of more than one offense are also subject to imprisonment for up to six months.

Some employers think that one way of hiding the practice of employing illegals is to violate other employment laws. The rationale is that by doing so they decrease the likelihood of being caught for hiring illegal aliens and save on labor costs. This reasoning is faulty. If employed, illegal aliens are entitled to full protection under the Fair Labor Standards Act. Court cases indicate that employers who violate FLSA's minimum wage and overtime pay provisions are liable for back pay awards to the plaintiff.[3] Some states, including California and Texas, also make illegal aliens eligible for workers' compensation (see *Commercial Standard Fire and Marine Co.* v. *Galinda,* 1972). Employers who fire illegal aliens who take part in unionization attempts may be subject to two types of costly penalties: first for violating the National Labor Relations Act of 1935, by attempting to restrain employee participation in a union (see *Sure-Tan, Inc.* v. *NLRB*), and second for knowingly hiring illegal aliens.

Risks in Not Hiring Hispanics and Mexicans   Employers with four to fourteen employees who choose not to hire Hispanics and Mexicans out of fear of hiring illegal aliens may find themselves subject to suits for overt employment discrimination. The Immigration Reform and Control Act prohibits "unfair immigration-related employment practices." Specifically, Section 2748(a) of the Act states:

> It is an unfair immigration-related employment practice for a person or other entity to discriminate against any individual (other than an illegal alien) with respect to the hiring or recruitment or referral for a fee, of the individual for employment or the discharging of the individual from employment because of such individual's national origin, or in the case of a citizen or intending citizen . . . because of such individual citizenship status.

Equal Employment Opportunity (EEO) Laws

The EEO laws listed in Chapter 24 prohibit employment discrimination on the basis of race, sex, religion, national origin, color, age, and handicapped status.

---

3. For court cases see: *NLRB* v. *Apoollo Tire, Inc,* 604 F. 2nd 1180 (CA-9, 1979); *Commercial Standard Fire and Marine Co.* v. *Galinda,* 484 S.W. 2nd 635 (CA, TX, 1972); and *Sure-Tan, Inc.* v. *NLRB,* 104 S. Ct. 2803 (S. Ct., 1984).

EEO laws apply to employers with fifteen or more employees. The law permits you to discriminate against members of these groups in cases of business necessity but the phrase business necessity is very narrowly defined. To qualify as a business necessity, a decision must be shown to have a basis in one of three circumstances:

- The job requires authenticity. You may hire a male model to model men's business suits in a fashion show or a male actor for the role of father in an upcoming movie.
- You were protecting the privacy of customers and coworkers. You may hire women nurses to attend to the personal care of elderly female patients in your nursing home.
- The knowledge, skill, and abilities required by the job are not possessed by all or nearly all members of a race, sex, or ethnic group. This circumstance is difficult to justify. You can always find women who are as strong as men and members of one race or ethnic group who possess the knowledge, skill, and ability possessed by members of another race or ethnic group.

Because of these narrowly defined allowances for business necessity, you should incorporate possible defenses into the staffing process you design. The law considers all selection procedures—including the application form, the interview, or any other performance or written test you use—to be tests of employment suitability and therefore subject to EEO regulation. To minimize your vulnerability to charges of illegal discrimination, you should:

- Make sure that all staffing decisions are based on the requirements of the job in question. This can be done by conducting a thorough analysis of the job and deriving the job and employee requirements from that analysis.
- Attempt to ensure that the proportion of applicants from each race, sex, or ethnic group that you hire is no less than four-fifths of the proportion of the largest race, sex, or ethnic group that you hire.

In the short run, ensuring proportional hiring may be difficult to do because few women or minorities in the labor market may possess the skills you need.

If you hold government contracts or subcontracts, you are required to develop and implement an affirmative action plan, which obligates you to take steps to ensure that women and minority candidates apply to your company for employment and, if qualified, are hired. In such a plan, you establish goals, timetables, and action plans to increase the representation of females and minorities in your workforce. This plan must be reviewed and approved by the Office of Federal Contract Compliance Programs (OFCCP). Without such approval, you may face the charge of setting illegal hiring quotas.

If you do not hold government contracts or subcontracts, you are not obligated to develop an affirmative action plan. Nevertheless, you should try to develop a recruitment plan that helps you to attract qualified minority applicants. If a job applicant charges you with not hiring him or her because of illegal discrimination, the Equal Employment Opportunity Commission looks first at the composition of your workforce. If an obvious imbalance exists between the sex or minority composition of employees in your workforce and the applicant's sex or minority status, EEOC will require you to show that the composition of your workforce is similar to the composition of the labor market. With the exception of managerial and professional employees, the area of the labor market that you use to defend staffing decisions is the geographic distance your current employees travel from their homes to work (see Chapter 24). To make the needed comparison, you must conduct a utilization analysis, which consists of

- A list of all employees by job classification category, sex, race, color, national origin, and religion
- A classification by sex, race, color, national origin, and religion of the workers available in your local labor market for each of your jobs
- A comparison of the composition of your workforce with the composition of workers in your labor market

After conducting a utilization analysis, you may find that the number of women and minorities in your employ are not representative of the proportion of those groups in your labor market. Depending on the degree of imbalance, you may either be allowed to continue using your present recruitment plan or be required to expand the scope of your recruiting efforts to encourage qualified women and minority applicants to apply for openings.

The Employee Polygraph Protection Act of 1988

The passage of the Employee Poloygraph Protection Act was motivated by the widespread complaints that honesty testing methods such as the polygraph or other lie-detector tests were invalid, with high rates of incorrectly labeling people as having lied. Although more than half of the states had already passed legislation to limit the uses of honesty testing in employment, the federal law now prohibits private-sector employers from using lie-detector and other honesty tests in employee selection. The Act allows the use of polygraphs in very restricted cases: drug companies and security service firms can use them to hire security employees, and they can be used in ongoing criminal investigations. The Employee Polygraph Protection Act also provides for penalties against violators and damage awards to victims. In cases of honesty testing, federal law, however, does not preempt the stricter state and local laws. Consequently, you must ensure that you comply to the stricter regulation.

Recruiting Decisions

In Chapter 24 you learned how to define the labor market to use for attracting the largest pool of qualified people to apply for openings. Keep in mind, however, that the availability of the skills you need in the labor market and the extent to which other employers are looking for those same skills greatly influences the number of people you can hire at any given pay rate. Therefore, it is important to review the characteristics of your labor market in order to assess the difficulty or ease with which you may obtain an applicant pool. This assessment may motivate you to seek to fill your positions with part-time employees or with employees who already work for you. In developing a recruiting plan you will have to ask yourself:

- How should the jobs be staffed, full-time or part-time?
- Where should I get the employees to fill the jobs? Should I transfer or promote current employees or should I hire from the labor market?

Full-Time or Part-Time Status

It is often preferable to staff administrative jobs with full-time employees in order to maintain efficiency in operations. Mining and manufacturing firms hire employees full-time for most work. Many small enterprises, however, operate almost exclusively with part-time employees. Among the industries that make the most use of part-time workers are wholesale trade, retail trade, and service industries. For small growing businesses in the service sector of the economy, part-time employment may be an attractive option. There are five main advantages to using part-time employees:

1. Part-time staffing may reduce labor costs by allowing you to better match the size of your workforce to the size of the workload.
2. Part-time staffing increases your flexibility in obtaining the necessary skills when you need them. Among the varieties of part-time work schedules that you may consider are:
   a. Regular part-time, in which the employee is hired to work part-time on a continuous basis. The days and hours to be worked can be standardized or they can vary according to agreement at the time of hire.
   b. Job sharing, in which two part-time employees share the responsibilities of one full-time job. This arrangement is particularly attractive for staffing jobs that require full-time attention by responsible people. Such a schedule may enable you to staff jobs when you encounter difficulties in finding suitable full-time employees.
   c. Temporary full-time or temporary part-time, attractive in situations where the workload varies seasonally.
   d. Contract work, which is similar to the preceding schedule but is typically applied to highly skilled personnel hired to work on special projects. This arrangement allows you to save money normally paid to consulting firms and law firms for their services. Instead, you can hire retired executives, professionals who may be employed elsewhere, or even graduate students who may be going to school in your community. Both you and the worker sign a contract specifying the type of service to be provided, the length of the assignment or hours to be worked, and the compensation to be paid.

3. Part-time staffing enables you to increase the size of the applicant pool and hire workers who may not want to work full-time. Currently, about 14 percent of the civilian labor force works part-time voluntarily. Women, younger workers, and older workers are especially likely to want to work part time.
4. Part-time employees are an excellent source for obtaining future full-time employees needed as your business grows.
5. Part-time employees are likely to minimize your vulnerability to EEO lawsuits. The fair employment opportunity legislation's primary focus is to ensure equal employment opportunities for full-time workers. Moreover, by hiring part-time employees you are likely to employ more women, older workers, and minorities than if you hired full-time employees only.

Using part-time employees has two disadvantages. First, you must plan ahead to ensure that the work gets done in a timely fashion. Second, employment law mandates that the employer contribute to each employee's social security fund and pay unemployment compensation and workers' compensation insurance premiums on all employees. Such contributions made on behalf of part-timers can cost more than the contributions made for full-time workers. These added costs may be offset by more efficient planning, decreased use of overtime pay, increased productivity gained from employing two part-time rather than one full-time employee, and lowered production costs.

Recruiting Decisions

Internal Recruiting   Internal recruiting refers to promotion and transfer of current employees into vacant jobs. Before deciding to recruit externally, you should consider the availability of suitable applicants already within your organization.

Using internal recruiting has several advantages. Commitment to work can increase if employees believe that good performance leads to better jobs. Training costs can decrease because current employees know the workings of the organization and in many instances have actually helped former job incumbents perform some of the job's tasks. Finally, if you provide good working conditions and environment, your labor costs may decrease. You may not need to match competitor pay, for instance, because your employees are less likely to change jobs just to get small pay increases.

For the small business, internal recruiting has no major disadvantages. You may have to use external recruiting in some instances, however, such as when current employees do not possess the skills required and those skills cannot be easily learned on the job. You may also have to use external recruiting when your workload expands or when it is necessary to ensure compliance with equal employment opportunity law.

External Recruiting   When you decide to hire from the external labor market, you must identify recruitment sources that will provide an adequate applicant pool from which to select employees. When trying to identify recruitment sources, ask yourself

- Which sources provided me with the largest applicant pool and the best and worst employees in the past?
- Could further use of those sources lead to problems with EEO regulations?

To check the accuracy of your responses to these questions, ask your current best, worst, female, and minority employees how they heard about the job opening when they first applied to your company. Their answers give you a good start on choosing recruiting sources.

To reach minority applicants who may not live near your business, contact local schools and colleges, minority organizations, and your state's employment service. Exhibit 26.2 lists other sources of information on how to reach minority applicants. These sources may be particularly useful as you expand in managerial and professional employment, where compliance with fair employment regulation increases in importance.

Most people looking for work apply directly to the employer, ask friends and relatives about job openings, and answer local newspaper ads. Exhibits 26.3 and 26.4 provide some insight into people's preferences in job searching activities and how effective they think various job search methods are. Notice that the methods that people think are effective vary somewhat by gender and race. Review of these exhibits should help you decide which sources may be best for attracting the applicants you want to attract.

Exhibit 26.2

SOURCES OF INFORMATION ON RECRUITING WOMEN AND MINORITY GROUP MEMBERS

Directory for Reaching Minority Groups. U.S. Department of Labor, Bureau of Apprenticeship and Training, Office of Information, Employment and Training Administration, Washington, D.C. 20210.

Native American Professional Source Directory. Office of Special Projects, South Western Cooperative Educational Laboratory, 2017 Yale SE, Albuquerque, New Mexico 87106.

Spanish-Speaking Recruitment Sources. Superintendent of Documents, Government Prining Office, Washington, D.C. 20402.

Women's Caucuses, Committees, and Professional Assoications and Supplements. Recruiting Aids #1 and #2. Association of American Colleges, Project on the Status and Education of Women, 1818 R Street, N.W., Washington, D.C. 20009.

Source: M. G. Miner and J. B. Miner. *Employee Selection Within the Law,* Washington, D.C.: Bureau of National Affairs, 1978.

Exhibit 26.3

MOST OFTEN USED JOB-SEEKING METHODS

METHOD	SEX		RACE	
	Men	Women	Nonminority Group Members	Minority Group Members
Applied directly to employer	37.8%	36.4%	37.5%	34.6%
Asked friends				
About jobs where they work	10.2	8.8	9.3	11.7
About jobs elsewhere	4.6	3.9	4.4	3.3
Asked relatives				
About jobs where they work	3.8	3.4	3.4	5.7
About jobs elsewhere	1.8	1.1	1.4	1.7
Answered newspaper ads				
Local	15.9	20.0	18.4	11.3
Nonlocal	1.8	1.4	1.8	.2
Private employment agency	3.9	7.2	5.6	3.2
State employment service	6.3	6.0	5.5	11.8
School placement office	2.9	2.9	3.0	2.1
Civil service test	1.0	1.9	1.2	3.1
Asked teacher or professor	.8	1.2	.9	1.1
Answered ads in professional or trade journals	.8	.4	.6	.2
Union hiring hall	2.8	.1	1.6	1.7
Contacted local organization	.4	.8	.3	2.9
Other	5.0	4.0	4.5	4.8

Source: Vida Scarpello and James Ledvinka, *Personnel/Human Resource Management: Environments and Functions* (Boston: PWS-KENT Publishing Co., 1988), p. 264. Reprinted by permission of PWS-KENT Publishing Company, a division of Wadsworth, Inc.

Exhibit 26.4

EFFECTIVENESS RATES OF JOB-SEEKING METHODS

METHOD	SEX		RACE	
	Men[a]	Women[a]	Nonminority Group Members[a]	Minority Group Members[a]
Applied directly to employer	47.0%	48.5%	48.8%	38.1%
Asked friends				
About jobs where they work	23.2	20.5	21.9	23.4
About jobs elsewhere	12.1	11.7	12.5	7.7
Asked relatives				
About jobs where they work	20.1	18.2	19.0	21.3
About jobs elsewhere	8.0	6.4	7.7	5.1
Answered newspaper ads				
Local	20.9	27.5	25.0	13.6
Nonlocal	9.1	11.9	10.5	5.9
Private employment agency	17.1	31.9	25.3	15.2
State employment service	12.1	16.2	12.6	20.1

School placement office	23.0	19.6	22.5	13.5
Civil service test	9.2	16.6	12.4	13.0
Asked teacher or professor	11.9	12.5	12.1	12.4
Answered ads in professional or trade journals	6.5	9.9	—[b]	—[b]
Union hiring hall	23.7	8.0	22.6	18.9
Contacted local organization	—[b]	—[b]	9.9	17.6
Other	38.5	41.5	—[b]	—[b]

a. Percentage of job applicants using this method who thought the method was best for obtaining employment.
b. Data not available.
Source: Vida Scarpello and James Ledvinka, *Personnel/Human Resource Management: Environments and Functions* (Boston: PWS-KENT Publishing Co., 1988), p. 265. Reprinted by permission of PWS-KENT Publishing Company, a division of Wadsworth, Inc.

Selection Procedures

There are five basic selection procedures: the job application form, reference checking, paper-and-pencil tests, work samples, and the selection interview. These basic procedures are often supplemented by other procedures, such as drug and honesty testing. We omit the latter procedures from this discussion because their use could result in several negative outcomes. First, unless jobs are scarce, good as well as poor applicants may choose not to apply to an employer whom they perceive as not trusting their integrity. Second, unless your company is experiencing severe drug problems, we recommend against such tests because their results are subject to a fair amount of error. For this reason, the use of polygraph tests in selection has been outlawed by federal law. Third, should your drug and honesty tests screen out a disproportionate number of women and minorities, you may find yourself subject to a lawsuit that is difficult to defend against.

Application Forms

An application form is designed to obtain information about the general suitability of applicants for jobs. Most application forms are nearly identical. Questions ask an applicant to state educational background, previous work experience, and other information that the employer thinks is useful as an initial screen of the applicant's suitability for the job. The application form is intended to achieve three goals:

1. Alert the employer as to the number of applicants for the job opening
2. Provide information for quickly assessing each applicant's suitability for the job opening
3. Provide information by which applicants may be compared to each other

The typical generic application form purchased from an office supply store is useful only for determining the size of the applicant pool, however; it is not useful for screening applicants for job suitability. The questions in Exhibit 26.5 are common on generic application forms. These questions are not very useful

Exhibit 26.5
QUESTIONS NOT TO ASK ON APPLICATION FORMS

- What is your sex?
- What is your race?
- What is your age?
- Where were you born?
- What is your marital status?
- What is your maiden name?
- How many children do you have?
- What are the ages of your children?

- What means of transportation will you use to get to work?
- Please submit a photograph for identification purposes.
- How would you describe your general physical health?
- Have you ever been arrested?
- Why did you leave your previous employer?

for matching applicant characteristics to the job's requirements, however. Applicants may interpret the questions as being biased against women, minorities, older or younger workers, and the handicapped. Also, people often lie in answering such questions for fear of being unable to secure employment if they told the truth.

Although you should not ask the questions in Exhibit 26.5 on the application form, you do need to collect demographic data about applicants for EEO purposes. The easiest way to do this is to add an EEO sheet to the application packet; see the example in Exhibit 26.6. Instruct the applicant to place the completed information in an envelope that you provide and seal the envelope. You can open the envelope after you have made the selection decision. Such a practice will protect you from charges of illegal discrimination. For some jobs, an applicant's physical characteristics may be important. Rather than asking the health question, find out if the applicant can perform the job by using a work sample (see below).

To act as a useful screening device, the application form should focus on obtaining information relevant to assessing the applicant's suitability for the job. An example of a useful application form is shown in Exhibit 26.7. Developing such a form takes some time and effort, but the outcome is invaluable. For some jobs, the applicant's responses to the application form may be all the information you need to make a good hiring decision. Notice that the form contains a space for numbering the application. The name, address, and telephone number provide a means of contacting the applicant. The citizenship status and social security questions are the initial screens of the applicant's right to employment in the United States. There is a space allocated for the applicant to check the work schedule the applicant prefers (full-time or part-time).

Some states require licenses for performing certain work. If the job in question requires such a license, the applicants can list the licenses they possess on the form and also whether they would be willing to obtain such a license prior to starting the job.

The form also contains a listing of the job's major duties (this list is derived from a job analysis). The questions that follow ask the applicant to indicate his

Exhibit 26.6
SAMPLE EEO INFORMATION SHEET

We ask all job applicants to answer the questions below. We need this information to help us comply with federal equal employment opportunity laws. We will not use this information to make our hiring decision. Therefore, after you have answered the questions please place this sheet in the attached envelope and seal the envelope. We will open the envelope after we have made our hiring decision.

You have the right not to answer the questions below. In any event, please sign this form to indicate that you have seen it.

Name of applicant _____

Address _____

_____

Job for which applying _____

Sex _____   Age _____   Religion _____

Check appropriate space

I am: White _____   Hispanic _____   Oriental _____   Arabic _____

Black _____   Mexican _____   American Indian _____   Other _____

Military service (indicate type and status here) _____

_____

Handicaps   Yes _____   No _____

If handicapped, please describe your handicap _____

_____

_____

_____

Date   Applicant's signature

Exhibit 26.7
SAMPLE APPLICATION FORM

Application number _____

Name _____

Last   First   Middle

Address _____

_____

_____

Telephone number _____

Are you a U.S. citizen (yes or no)? _____

Are you a legal alien (yes or no)? _____

Social security number _____

Exhibit 26.7
SAMPLE APPLICATION FORM (*continued*)

What job are you applying for? _____

Are you seeking part-time or full-time work? _____

   If part-time, how many hours do you want to work per week? _____
Do you have preferences for working specific hours?

Yes _____   (which) _____   No _____
Some jobs in this company require a driver's license or other state license. Please indicate the following:

1. Do you have a valid driver's license? _____

2. State which issued your current driver's license _____

If you are offered a job that requires a state license, are you willing to obtain such a license prior to starting the job (yes or no)? _____

Please sign the following statement:
If I am hired to perform a job that requires a state license, I understand that I will have to produce the license on the first day that I report for work.

_____
Applicant's signature

Job: Billings and Receivables Coordinator

Job function: The primary function of the Billings and Receivables Coordinator is to manage accounts receivable through planning, credit collection, and maximizing cash collections. Listed below are the major tasks of this job. Please answer as accurately as you can the experience, knowledge, skill, and ability questions regarding each of the tasks listed below.

Task 1: Preparing and explaining monthly
accounts receivable reports

Question 1: What kind of training do you have to have to perform the task?
Please check the appropriate spaces.

   Learned on the job _____   Learned in school _____
If you learned the task on the job, describe what you did.

_____
_____

How much experience do you have performing this task?

_____

List the employers for whom you performed this task and the period of time you were employed.

Employer _____ From _____ To _____

Employer _____ From _____ To _____

Employer _____ From _____ To _____

Question 2: If you have no experience performing this task, what knowledge, skills or abilities do you have that will enable you to perform this task?

Knowledge _____

_____

_____

Skills _____

_____

_____

Abilities _____

_____

_____

Please indicate how you acquired the knowledge and skill to perform this task (formal coursework, self-study). _____

If you acquired the knowledge and skill in school, indicate

Name of school _____

Location _____

or her knowledge, skill, and abilities related to those duties. Answers to these questions can be used to assess how well the applicant's characteristics match the job's requirements. The listing of job duties on the application form also allows the applicant to preview the specific requirements of the job and thereby assess his or her own suitability and interest in further pursuing the employment opportunity.

Notice that the application form excludes certain common-sense questions. No question asks whether the applicant has a high school diploma and no question asks the applicant to list the education institutions attended and degrees obtained. These questions are irrelevant unless the answers can be related specifically to the job in question. Such a connection can be established by asking other questions:

- Indicate how (formally in school or informally on the job) and where (high school, college, employer name) you acquired these skills needed for this job.
- How much experience and what specific experience do you have that you can directly relate to the duties of this job?
- If you do not have work experience, what abilities and skills do you have that are useful to perform the job duties listed above?

By designing an application form for each job, you increase the ability of this screening device to predict the suitability of the candidate for the job and decrease your vulnerability to charges of illegal employment discrimination.

Reference Checking

Many employers try to check the references that an applicant provides before they make a hiring decision. Unless you ask a personal friend for a reference on a former employee, however, reference checking typically provides very little useful information. Federal and state privacy laws limit the kind of information that public sector employers can obtain through reference checking. Although these laws are not yet applicable to private sector employers, it is best to exercise caution. If an employer gives a negative recommendation, he or she may be sued by a former employee for attempting to deprive that employee of the constitutional right to pursue fundamental liberties, one of which is the right to work.

Because of this potential legal liability, many former employers do not reveal performance information or other information that you may want to get through reference checking. The typical information that you receive is simply the length of time the applicant was employed by previous employers. To bypass the legal obstacles of obtaining useful information from prior employers, you may decide to seek personal letters of recommendation. Recognize that these letters are typically from people whom the applicant counts on to write favorably.

Despite the limitations of reference checking, the practice has some benefits. For one, you can verify the applicant's employment record. You can also use the reference information as an additional data point in your selection decision. Letters of recommendation may be useful in assessing the consistency between your interpretation of the applicant's suitability and that indicated by the letter writer. Beware of letters of recommendation that only discuss the candidate's outstanding qualifications, however. Place greater weight on letters that include both positive and negative information and letters that discuss past performance, such as those written by college instructors who indicate the course taken and the letter grade received.

In reviewing letters of recommendation from schools and colleges, pay attention to whether or not the letter comes from an open file or a closed file. An open file permits the student to review the contents of the file. A closed file indicates that the student waived this right. Open-file letters of recommendation introduce two kinds of biases. First, the student may have removed unsatisfactory letters from the file; second, the person writing the letter—knowing that the student may review it—may bias the letter toward making the student look good. Closed-file letters of recommendation have a greater likelihood of containing accurate information.

Paper-and-Pencil Tests

Large organizations often use paper-and-pencil tests such as vocational interest questionnaires, personality tests, and intelligence tests as part of their selection procedures. Such tests are usually expensive to administer. Moreover, unless the employer can show that the tests can actually predict future performance or training success, their use may result in charges of illegal discrimination and costly employment litigation suits. The difficulty and cost involved in showing that these tests measure what they are intended to measure make them impractical for small businesses.

Work Samples

Work samples are tests that require the applicant to demonstrate the ability to execute the job's tasks. These tests are developed from a job analysis. A typing test is a typical work sample, but such tests can be used on any job. For example, suppose that you are trying to hire a bank teller. What tasks must a bank teller perform? Obviously, a teller should be able to count money. One way of finding out how quickly and accurately applicants for a teller's job can count money is to give them some money to count. For jobs requiring physical strength, you may have the applicant lift or carry a bag of material that reflects the typical weight that the jobholder must lift or carry.

Work samples can also be developed to assess various abilities that may be critical to job performance. For example, reading and understanding written material is critical to someone who packages explosive materials. A job analysis can determine how much time the worker's reading deals with packaging safety procedures, with safe work procedures, with company directives, and so on. Then a reading test could be developed that uses the actual materials the employee has to read on the job.

There are three variants of work samples that you may consider developing. The first focuses on the content of the job and the second on critical aspects of the job. A third variant is a combination of these two dimensions.

Job Content and Work Samples   Developing these test is relatively easy and inexpensive. The steps to do so are

1. Conduct a job analysis and from it derive a list of the job's major tasks.
2. Determine the percentage of time that the employee spends on each task per day or per week. For example, a clerical employee may spend 55 percent of a day typing letters from a written draft, 35 percent of the day answering the telephone, 5 percent of the day filing reports, and 5 percent of the day running errands.
3. Decide the time period to allow each applicant for completing the test.
4. Construct a work sample test that reflects both the proportionate content of the job's major task and the complexity of activities that make up the task. Suppose that you allow 1 hour for the clerical work sample test. Within that hour, construct a test with 33 minutes of typing, 21 minutes of answering the telephone, 3 minutes of filing, and 3 minutes to run an errand. The content of the test should match the actual content of the job. If the job consists of typing forms, letters, and reports, all these varieties of typing should be included in the test. If the telephone answering task consists of relaying messages and occasionally dealing with irate customers, the test would include opportunities to do both.
5. Develop procedures to score the performance of each applicant. Think about which aspects of performance the employee controls and which aspects are influenced by outside sources. If the employee has full con-

trol over a task outcome, develop ways of measuring acceptable outcomes. If the employee has only partial control over the outcome, develop ways of assessing acceptable behavior. For example, the employee has control in the typing task. Consequently, you may want to measure the applicant's typing performance with respect to quality and quantity of output. Quality may be measured by such things as number of errors made and words typed within or outside of the lines specified on the form. Quantity may be measured by how many forms were typed in a given period of time. Behavioral measures are appropriate for assessing performance on the telephone answering task. The measures may include such things as frequency of courteous words and composure when dealing with irate customers.

Critical Task Work Samples   Critical tasks are those that, if not performed correctly, lead to substantial human, physical, material, or capital loss. Most jobs do not contain critical tasks, but such tasks are common in such jobs as intensive care nurse and packer of explosive chemicals. In constructing a work sample test, you should try to identify any potentially critical job factors so that you can include them. Moreover, you may want to assign greater weight to performance of these tasks than to frequently performed noncritical tasks.

Selection Interview

Interviewing is the most popular method of selecting employees. It is usually poorly executed, however, and is therefore the most invalid way of selecting employees. Interviews are often invalid because they are not based on job analysis; thus decisions about applicant suitability are based on first impressions. Sometimes those impressions are formed on the basis of such irrelevant factors as the firmness of the handshake, the clothing worn by the applicant, or even the cleanliness of the applicant's car.

Interviews are typically the last step in the selection process. You should design a selection interview in such a way that you can

- Clarify ambiguities or questions that have surfaced upon review of the application blank or the work sample results
- Assess applicant qualities not measured by other means
- Give sufficient information to the applicant about your company and the job so that the applicant has a basis for accepting or rejecting the job offer
- Create a positive impression about your company regardless of the selection outcome

Steps in conducting an effective interview leading to a selection decision are outlined in Exhibit 26.8.

Planning   Planning the interview is a very important and often neglected task. Planning enables you to review the applicant's suitability and identify the

Exhibit 26.8
STEPS IN CONDUCTING AN EFFECTIVE SELECTION INTERVIEW AND MAKING A SELECTION DECISION

1. PLANNING	*2. INTERVIEW*	*3. DECISION*
Review job description	Greet the applicant	Inform applicant and give reason for your decision
Review employee specification	Put applicant at ease	If decision was to hire and the applicant accepts, inform the new hire when to report for work
Review the application blank and results of work sample or other selection tests	Explain purpose of interview	
Write interview questions	Ask prepared questions	
Analyze your impressions and potential biases	Give applicant ample time to answer questions	
Prepare information sheet on your company and your expectations of employee behavior	Take notes on answers	
	Observe applicant's behavior	
	Keep interview on relevant subjects	
Assess and write down positive and negative aspects of the vacant job you are trying to fill	Allow applicant to interview you	
	Provide information on your company	
Reserve private space and uninterrupted time for interview	Explain your expectations of employee behavior	
	Explain your work rules	
	Give the applicant a realistic preview of the job	
	Ask applicant if he or she wants clarification or additional information	
	Thank applicant for interview	
	Tell applicant if unsuitable or tell applicant when you will make your decision	

specific questions to ask. You should engage in a number of activities when planning an interview. First, review the job description and employee specification. Second, review the application form and the results of the work sample. Ask yourself:

- Is the information on the application form clear?
- Does any information on the application form raise questions about the applicant's suitability for the job?
- Is there anything that I should clarify about the results of the other selection procedures?

Third, write down the questions that have surfaced from your review of the job requirements and the applicant information. Because past behavior is usually the best predictor of future behavior, devise some questions to help assess the applicant's work ethic and work motivation. Examples include questions about high school jobs, work while in college, and financial responsibilities. You may also allot five minutes or so for the applicant to explain why he or she is suitable for the job.

Fourth, take some time to think about the impression you have formed about the applicant. Ask yourself if your impression is based on data. Think about your prejudices before the interview. Recognize that people like others who resemble them. Ask yourself:

- Are all people who look like me, dress like I do, and come from similar backgrounds good performers and dependable people?
- Are there things that I like or dislike about myself that could influence how I evaluate the applicant?
- Have I had a particularly positive or negative experience with a few members of the opposite sex, race, or ethnic group? Can this experience bias my judgment?
- What stereotypes do I hold about women, blacks or other minorities? What stereotypes would members of these groups hold about me?

Fifth, prepare an information sheet on your company, your expectations of employee behavior, and positive and negative information about the job that you are trying to fill. Identify the present state and future plans of your company. Indicate factors that affect employees, such as your management philosophy or personnel policies related to promotions, compensation, and the like. Preparing a company statement helps you to communicate the essential information to the applicant in an organized fashion and minimize the time spent giving rather than receiving information.

Think about your expectations for employee behavior. Preparing a statement of expectations helps you communicate clearly to the applicant and helps ensure that the new employee behaves appropriately. Preparing your expectations statement takes some thought. You must think about your company and about how employees can positively or negatively project an image about your company to outsiders. Suppose that you are the president of a small bank. You may want your employees to project an image of being solid members of the local community. Some banks, concerned with such an image require their managers to keep their shoes and cars polished and their lawns mowed. Similarly tellers may be required to wear clothing that reflects the norms of the community; punk clothing and green hair may be viewed as inappropriate dress. Most applicants for such a position would probably not dress in these ways, but you may judge other styles as inappropriate. You have the right to demand that your employees conform to a code of behavior that you establish as long as you require all employees (male, female, young, old, minorities) to conform to the same code of behavior.[4] If you require males to wear conservative clothing, you should also require females to do so.

---

4. You do not have to require males and females to have the same length hair. The requirement may be professionally appropriate grooming.

By defining your expectations, you are better able to communicate them in a consistent way during the interview. You can tell the potential marketing manager, for example, that she will be expected to wear conservative attire, preferably in conservative colors, and that she should keep her car polished at all times. Similarly, you can state that you expect managerial employees to keep their homes in good repair and to keep their grass mowed.

Although your expectations for off-the-job behavior may not stand up if challenged in court, the likelihood of such a challenge is low when you explicitly state those expectations prior to employment. The applicant may decide not to take the job for these reasons. If he or she accepts the job, he or she is likely to conform.

Finally, you should review the work rules in your establishment and how they are enforced. Then you can communicate this information during the interview. If you are hiring a part-time high school student, you can tell the student that except in emergency, you expect him or her to give you three day's notice if he or she is unable to come to work when scheduled. You should stress the importance of being a dependable employee and explicitly state how you define that term.

The third set of issues to consider in your information sheet is the positive and negative aspects of the job. Employers often try to oversell their jobs to applicants. Such practice is inadvisable; it raises expectations that will not be fulfilled once the new hire starts the job. It also has the potential of decreasing the employee's trust in your words, leading to lost credibility. Rather than overselling, you should write down the positive and negative aspects of the job and communicate this information to the applicant. Giving positive and negative information about the job is called providing a realistic job preview. Receiving realistic information enables applicants to have an accurate basis for accepting or rejecting a job, helping them have realistic expectations and adjust positively to the workplace.

As you clarify your expectations for employee behavior, you may want to formalize these expectations and provide each new hire with a copy of your expectations and work rules. Initially, though, you may wish to use your prepared information sheet as a checklist for the issues to discuss during the selection interview.

Conducting the Interview Reserve a private space and uninterrupted time for the interview. Take a few minutes to greet the applicant and put him or her at ease. Be friendly by spending a few minutes on small talk. Explain that the purpose of the interview is to obtain information about the applicant not previously obtained, clarify information already gathered, provide a description of the company, explain the work rules and behaviors required of employees by the company, and give the applicant a realistic preview of the job. Finally, tell the applicant to interview you to clarify any ambiguities that he or she may have.

Spend at least half of the interview asking questions. As you ask the questions you have prepared, take notes. Allow the applicant ample time to answer;

if the answer is not clear, ask how, why, or what happened. Keep the interview on relevant subjects and carefully observe the applicant's reactions and skill in answering your questions. Write your reactions down immediately so as not to forget them.

Close the interview in a friendly and honest manner. If the applicant is unsuited for the job, tell him or her now. Otherwise, tell the applicant what day you will make your decision and call him or her to relay that decision.

Selection Decision   Following the selection process outlined gives you the information you need to make a decision based on the job's requirements. After making that decision, be sure to inform all applicants. Give the applicants the reasons for your decision. If the applicant you decide to hire accepts your offer, inform him or her when to report to work.

Summary

Staffing your business is among the most important activities you undertake. Good hiring decisions provide you with the basis for an efficient, productive staff that can lead your company to profitability.

Federal law affects certain hiring practices. Provisions of the Fair Labor Standards Act establish that women and men must receive equal pay for equal work. The Immigration Reform and Control Act provides strict requirements for obtaining verification of a newly hired employee's status as a citizen or legal alien and maintaining those records. Equal opportunity laws prohibit discrimination on the basis of sex, race, or other factors, but sometimes allow such discrimination if it can meet the standard of business necessity, which is difficult to prove.

In deciding how to recruit employees, the first issue you confront is whether to hire full-time or part-time workers. Part-time workers have many advantages for new businesses. The second issue is whether to recruit from within or without the company. Recruiting from within gives employees the sense that they can advance, which may increase employee commitment; recruiting externally gives you access to a broader range of potential workers.

Five selection procedures are commonly used to aid in making hiring decisions: application forms, reference checks, paper-and-pencil tests, work samples, and interviews. Applications can provide basic information about the applicant, and if properly developed may serve as the primary selection tool for some jobs. Reference checks are of limited value. Paper-and-pencil tests and work samples are valuable ways of assessing an applicant's ability to handle the tasks of a job. Interviews can be a helpful way of resolving any last questions you may have about an applicant, fully describing the business and the specific job, and inquiring whether the applicant has any questions. For an interview to be effective, however, you must plan your questions in advance. Following a planned procedure can help ensure that you make wise hiring decisions.

**Class
Assignments**

1. Contact a local small business owner and request permission to conduct a job analysis on a secretarial job. In conducting the job analysis, determine the percentage of time the secretary spends on each task during a typical day. Construct a work sample test for the secretarial job. The time period for the test is 45 minutes. Explain the work sample test you have developed to your class.

2. Assume that you are the owner of a small mail-order business, which receives $10,000 a year in federal government contracts. Choose one of the three jobs whose job descriptions are given in Chapter 24. Develop an employee specification document for the job you have chosen. Develop a selection interview process that will help you match the job's requirements to the knowledge, skill, and ability of the applicants for the job.

TRAINING YOUR WORKFORCE

As you start your business, much of your own learning will be the result of trial and error. As you begin to staff your organization, your first employees will also learn their jobs in the same way. Some people call such learning on-the-job training and think that it is the best way of learning a job. They are wrong.

Unguided on-the-job training is perhaps the most expensive way to train employees because it forces the learner to try a number of different solutions to the problem at hand. The solution that works tends to be repeated and other solutions drop out of the person's repertoire. Thus it is an inefficient way of learning. If trial and error were the best way of learning, you would not need to read this book. You would simply start your own business and try different things before deciding how something should be done. By reading this book, you are admitting that some knowledge can help you reduce the number of errors that you are likely to make when you start or run your business.

Although you may not be able to totally avoid trial and error learning, you can decrease the amount of such learning by providing your employees with guided on-the-job training. By doing so, you can decrease the time it takes for your employees to learn about your organization and their jobs.

Guided on-the-job training focuses on developing systematic programs for providing new employees with information about your company and their jobs, helping employees adjust to their new work situation, helping employees develop competence on their jobs and maintaining the competencies of your workforce. After reading this chapter, you will be able to

- Describe the principles behind orientation training
- Explain how to conduct work adjustment training
- Describe job competence training
- Analyze whether it is useful to perform skill updating

Orientation Training

Orientation training refers to a formal program for giving new employees information about your company and their jobs. New employees are usually motivated to succeed. Upon entering a new work situation, however, they tend to feel anxiety about what is or is not expected of them. If you want your employees to start their jobs positively, set aside part of the first day on the job for orientation.

The typical orientation program consists of general orientation to the company, specific orientation to the employee's job, and follow-up. Some of the topics and content appropriate in a general orientation to your company are shown in Exhibit 27.1. Some of the topics and content suitable for specific orientation to a job are shown in Exhibit 27.2.

Exhibit 27.1
TOPICS AND CONTENT COVERED IN A GENERAL ORIENTATION

TOPIC	CONTENT	TOPIC	CONTENT	TOPIC	CONTENT
Company overview	Welcoming speech	Review of company policies and procedures (*continued*)	Salary structure	Salary (*continued*)	Tax shelter options
	History of company		Review of terms and conditions of employment	Question and answer session	Communication channels
	Current growth trends, goals, priorities and problems		Promotion and assignments	Employer benefits	Holidays, vacations
	Long-range plans		Performance expectations and probationary period		Insurance Group health Disability Workers' compensation Life Medical-dental
	Operating budget and financial situation		Late arrival or sickness		
	Organization structure and branch relationship		Supervision and performance evaluation		
	Organizational chains of command and facts on key managerial staff		Termination of employment		Leave Illness— personal or family Military or jury duty Bereavement Maternity
			Personnel records		
			Communication channels		
	Service to community	Salary	Pay scale	Employee-employer relations and labor unions	Employee responsibilities and rights
Review of company policies and procedures	Employee classifications		Paychecks Overtime pay Holiday pay Deductions Credit union		Management responsibilities and rights
	Working conditions regulations				

Exhibit 27.1

TOPICS AND CONTENTS COVERED IN A GENERAL ORIENTATION (*continued*)

TOPIC	CONTENT	TOPIC	CONTENT	TOPIC	CONTENT
Employee-employer relations and labor unions (*continued*)	Shop stewards relations Reprimands and discipline Grievance procedures Safety equipment Cleanliness and sanitation	Safety	Handling of rumors First aid stations Fire prevention Accident procedures On-the-job use of alcohol and drugs Working conditions	Physical facilities Introduction to supervisor	Tour of facilities Cafeteria Entrances Parking Restricted areas Restrooms Equipment and supplies Working conditions

Source: "The Complete Employee Orientation Program," by Walter St. John, copyright May 1980, pp. 373–378. Reprinted with the permission of PERSONNEL JOURNAL, Costa Mesa, California; all rights reserved.

Exhibit 27.2

TOPICS AND CONTENT COVERED IN JOB-SPECIFIC ORIENTATION

TOPIC	CONTENT	TOPIC	CONTENT	TOPIC	CONTENT
Department overview	Current goals and priorities Relationship to other departments	Job requirements (*continued*)	Coffee breaks Personal telephone calls and mail Lockers Overtime Extra duty Equipment check out, maintenance Performance evaluation and supervision	Safety (*continued*) Department tour	Security procedures Personal work area Restrooms Lockers Fire alarms and extinguishers Water fountains Smoking area Supervisor's area
Job requirements	Detailed explanation of job content Copy of job description Working conditions: Proper dress Hours of work, time clocks Employee entrances Lunch hours	Safety	Emergency procedures Accident reports Sanitation standards	Question and answer session Introduction to other employees	Depends on employee's questions Social, informational in nature

Source: "The Complete Employee Orientation Program," by Walter St. John, copyright May 1980, pp. 373–378. Reprinted with the permission of PERSONNEL JOURNAL, Costa Mesa, California; all rights reserved.

As you determine the specific content of your orientation program, you should also think about who is going to conduct the orientation. If you have few employees, you will probably conduct both general and specific orientation yourself. As your organization grows, the new employee's immediate supervisor may be more appropriate to conduct the job specific orientation and also to answer any questions the employee may have from the general orientation. Involving the supervisor serves four purposes. First, he or she is probably more knowledgeable about the workings of the employee's department and the requirements of the new employee's job. Second, a new employee may be reluctant to admit to you, the owner, that he or she did not understand something that you said. The supervisor can go over the topics covered in general orientation and thus make sure that the employee understood what was covered. Third, the supervisor can explicitly define the work rules and work expectations in the department. Finally, the supervisor can implement the third part of orientation—follow up.

Following up on the information communicated during orientation is extremely important for ensuring that the employee fully understands the work rules and expectations. If the employee does not fully understand them, he or she is not likely to follow them. To make sure that the employee understands the content of the orientation, have the supervisor schedule a meeting with the employee two weeks after the employee has started working. The best approach is to have the supervisor and the new employee sit down and discuss any problems, difficulties, and misunderstandings that may have occurred during the first two weeks of work. The supervisor should encourage the employee to ask questions and provide the employee with any additional information the employee requires and further clarification of the information supplied during orientation. At the close of the meeting, the supervisor should also encourage the new employee to consult him or her in the future should other questions arise.

Work Adjustment Training

Most organizations have a probationary period of employment for new hires during which the new employee is expected to learn the job and show the organization that he or she understands the work rules and expectations. After the probationary period is over, the new employee is typically granted the right to permanent employment as long as he or she continues to perform and exhibit positive work behaviors. Three months is a reasonable time span for probation.

During the probationary period, you or the employee's supervisor should pay close attention to the employee's behavior. To facilitate positive work adjustment and not confuse the new employee, one person, either you or the supervisor, should take full responsibility for helping the employee adapt to your organization. If you delegate this responsibility to the supervisor, instruct the supervisor to pay close attention to the employee's conduct. If the employee does not behave as expected, the supervisor should notify him or her as to which behaviors meet expectations and which need to be changed.

At the end of the first month, the supervisor should meet with the employee and discuss both the employee's job requirements and how well or poorly he or she is adjusting to the new work situation. Regardless of whether the supervisor's impressions are positive or negative, he or she should give the employee specific feedback about the employee's performance and work behaviors. The supervisor and the new employee should then agree on ways to change any behavior that needs changing during the following month.

At the end of the second month of employment, the supervisor should meet with the employee again to discuss the employee's progress toward meeting work expectations. At this time, further strategies to improve performance and work behaviors can be developed and implemented.

At the end of the third month of employment, you and the supervisor should meet with the employee and either remove the employee's probationary status or terminate employment. Three months of experience with a new employee is usually sufficient time to decide whether or not he or she merits being given a permanent position or should be released. It is highly unlikely that after three months a good employee would suddenly change into a poor one or a poor employee suddenly become a good employee. If you or the supervisor carefully observe the employee's adjustment to the workplace and performance of his or her job, you should have little doubt about whether to keep or terminate the employee at the end of the probationary period.

Job Competency Training

If you are like most business owners, you probably hired inexperienced people to hold jobs that could be quickly learned. Thus it is likely that most of your employees require job competency training.

A job competency training program focuses on ensuring that the trainee is able to perform the job's actual tasks in a competent manner. To ensure job competency, you should develop a training process based on both the requirements of the job (as specified in the job description) and the employee's initial inability to fulfill some or all of those requirements. An equally important ingredient of an effective training program is that someone—either you, a supervisor, or a senior employee—takes full responsibility for implementing the training. In either case, make sure that the training process is conducted in a systematic rather than a haphazard way.

If you delegate the training to experienced employees, you must train them in how to train employees. The best way to train anyone is to show them the appropriate procedure for performing the task and then observe them as they implement the procedure. You should also provide the trainers with incentives to train new employees; the best incentive is monetary. If you delegate training activities to your supervisors or other experienced employees, incorporate training as one of their job requirements and as one standard against which you evaluate their performance. By doing so, you give added importance to the function.

Identifying Training Needs

To identify training needs, you should do two things. First, review the job description and identify the tasks that are performed on the job. Second, review the employee's skills relative to the tasks that have to be performed. A discrepancy between the job's task requirements and the employee's ability to perform those tasks identifies the kind of training that the employee needs.

The detailed examination of each task should include

- Identifying the actual steps involved in performing the task from start to finish
- Identifying the special tools, equipment, and instruments the employee must operate in order to perform the task
- Identifying related knowledge such as math, science, or other background information that the employee needs to have in order to perform the task competently

You can identify these three sets of considerations by either doing the task yourself or observing an experienced worker perform the task.

Identifying the steps necessary for completing each task enables you to teach the task systematically to the new employee. Identifying the tools and equipment and the related knowledge necessary to perform the task may lead you to design the training process in two steps. Depending on the complexity of tools necessary to perform the task, for example, it may be more efficient to teach the employee first how to use the tool or equipment and then how to perform the task using the tool or equipment. Similarly, if the employee lacks the necessary background or math skills, it may be more efficient to provide background training or remedial math training before attempting to train the employee on the task that requires those background skills.

Defining Training Objectives and Evaluation Criteria

If you train people to perform tasks listed on a job description, the objective of each training task is to perform the task so described. This objective needs to be further refined to let the trainee know exactly how well he or she should perform the task and under what conditions the task should be performed. Suppose the task to be learned is sorting mail. The objective is to sort the mail accurately and in a timely fashion. To refine that objective, you would specify that the mail should be sorted within 30 minutes of arrival with no sorting errors and with no help from other employees. You can then use this objective as the criteria against which to evaluate the trainee's performance.

If you look back to Chapter 26 on how to develop work sample tests, you will get more ideas of how to specify objectives and evaluation criteria for assessing competence in task performance. The same logic and approach used to construct work sample tests is used to set training objectives and criteria for evaluating training performance.

Providing Guided On-the-Job Training

The process that you should follow in training employees is outlined in Exhibit 27.3. Following that process facilitates the trainee's learning, ensures that the trainee learns the tasks correctly, and reduces training time. In other words, it provides effective training at low cost. The five components of a guided on-the-job training process are essential for ensuring competent performance of the job. Together, they focus on ways to facilitate learning and ensure performance of new tasks.

Provide an Overview of Training   When faced with new learning requirements, people tend to feel anxiety. High anxiety limits their attention span. To focus attention and reduce anxiety, it is important that you clearly explain the training program in terms of what will be learned, why the learning is important to job performance, how each task will be learned, when each task will be learned, how you will judge the employee's competence in performing the task, and in how much time you expect the employee to be fully competent in performing the task.

When providing the overview of the training process, you should give the employee a copy of his or her job description. This description should indicate the tasks for which the employee will receive training. By doing so, you focus the employee's attention on the training program and the specific tasks that he or she will learn. This focus reduces the trainee's anxiety about the training process by defining its scope. Similarly, you should let the trainee know that mistakes are inevitable in learning. To further reduce anxiety, emphasize that the trainee will be given ample time to practice each task and that you will be available for direction and guidance if the trainee experiences difficulty.

Train in Small Steps   Before you start training, organize the tasks to be taught from simple to complex. Next, break each task down into small steps. As you start training, explain to the trainee that he or she will start by learning the less complex tasks first and will learn each task in small steps. This training format allows quick feedback to the trainee on how well he or she is doing and increases feelings of confidence. Once the trainee has mastered the simple tasks, he or she will be motivated to tackle the harder ones.

Give Clear Instructions   Most people think that the instructions they give are clear. However, the person receiving the instruction usually thinks the oppo-

---

Exhibit 27.3
COMPONENTS OF GUIDED ON-THE-JOB TRAINING

1. Provide an overview of training
2. Train in small steps
3. Give clear instructions
4. Provide opportunities for practice
5. Provide feedback

site. Clear instructions have three essential components: the what, the how, and the why. Suppose that you are instructing the trainee to sort mail. Clear instructions for performing this task include:

- Telling the trainee that the task is to sort mail
- Explaining step by step how to sort the mail
- Telling the trainee why the mail should be sorted in the way that you explained

By incorporating the what, the how, and the why into your instructions, you facilitate the trainee's learning. The employee will know what steps to follow in sorting the mail and why following them is important. By explaining the why, you give the employee a way at looking at the mail-sorting task. Emergencies sometimes arise, and employees have to change their routines to deal with them. If they learn the rules and principles that govern their behavior rather than simply learning to copy that behavior, they learn general principles to use when they encounter emergencies or new situations.

Provide Opportunities for Practice The best way to learn any task is to over-learn it. Recall, for example, how you learned multiplication tables: you practiced endlessly. Now, if someone asks you to multiply 9 × 5, you do not have to think about the answer, you simply say 45. You should allow the trainee to practice the task until it becomes habitual. The slowness or speed with which the trainee learns the new task should act as a guide in deciding when to add a new learning experience to the training program. Remember that your goal is to train the employee to master the job's tasks. Although you should have an idea of how long an average employee takes to learn a job's tasks, recognize that individuals vary in how fast they learn any task. What is simple for one individual may be complex for another. How fast or slow a trainee learns a particular task should not be taken as a reflection of his or her ability to learn all the job's tasks. To ensure correct performance, allow each trainee enough time to master each task fully before moving on to the next.

Provide Feedback The trainee can get two kinds of feedback from performing a task. The first is direct feedback from the task: as the trainee completes the task, he or she has the opportunity to see whether or not the task was done correctly. If the task was done correctly, the immediate feedback motivates further performance. If not, the trainee becomes worried about not being capable of performing the task.

The second type is the verbal feedback you provide, such as saying "you did that exactly right" or "good try, but you didn't get it exactly right that time." If the feedback is negative, explain what the employee can do to improve performance. Encourage the employee to try again by saying "let's try it again and see if you can do it the way I suggested." As you guide the trainee into improving performance, be sure to emphasize the part of the task that was performed right. Doing so will encourage the trainee to try to correct the part that was done wrong.

Guided on-the-job training is based on the idea that the trainer is a facilitator of learning. The learning outcome is mastery of the task. The training process outlined above should help you facilitate your employees' learning of skills. As your employees master the tasks on one job, you can repeat the process so that they can master the tasks on other jobs and become multiskilled workers.

Skill Updating Programs

As your organization grows and jobs change, you must repeat the guided on-the-job training process to maintain the competencies of your workforce. Before you decide to update your employees' skills, review their job descriptions. If the jobs have changed, you should reanalyze the jobs and write new job descriptions. These new descriptions act as the standards against which to develop a training program.

Sometimes an employee's performance declines. You can typically spot such a decline by observing performance and reviewing the employee's performance evaluation. You can also assess the severity of the performance decline by comparing the behaviors of top-performing employees with those of poorly performing employees.

Once you have identified a performance deficiency, do not rush into training. First determine if the deficiency can be remedied by training or is due to other factors. The performance deficiency may be caused by a negative attitude that arose from the employee not receiving feedback on job performance, which demotivates employees and lead to a reduction in the amount of effort they put into their jobs. Poor performance may also be the result of changes in the job if the employee did not have enough information about how to react to those changes. Such other factors as poor working relationships with a supervisor or other employees and personal problems outside of work may also result in performance declines.

In general, training can improve the individual's performance only when the employee does not have the skill to do the job or the poor performance is due to lack of practice.

After evaluating the potential causes of a performance decline, you may decide that the employee's skills are getting rusty. As you start thinking about updating skills, you should also think about the benefits and costs of implementing a new training program. Unless the poor performance is sufficiently hindering to decrease the desired level of productivity, refrain from implementing the training program. The cost of such a program probably outweighs its benefits. Remember that the purpose of skills training is to produce competent job performance and not to train employees for the sake of training.

Summary

An orientation program is a useful mechanism to provide new employees with information about your company and their jobs. The orientation program is also an extremely important method for making sure that new employees understand your work rules and expectations. Most organizations have a probationary period of employment for new hires during which the new employee is expected to learn the job and also exhibit behaviors that match the work rules and expectations. The probationary period also allows the employer and supervisor to observe the employee's adjustment to the work situation and to correct behavioral or performance problems. If you carefully observe the employee's adjustment to work and help the employee make that adjustment, you should have little doubt about whether to keep or terminate the employee at the end of the probationary period.

Since most jobs in any organization are a unique combination of tasks, you will probably have to train most of your employees on how to perform those jobs. Guided on-the-job training is valuable because it focuses on increasing the competency of the trainee. Such a program is based first on an identification of training needs and second on defining training objectives and evaluation criteria.

The process used for training should facilitate the trainee's learning, ensure that the trainee learns the tasks correctly, and reduce training time.

The process used for initial training can be used for periodic training focused on updating skills. However, the latter training should be approached more cautiously. Prior to implementing a skill updating program, you should review and possibly revise job descriptions, identify causes of performance deficiencies, and weigh the costs and benefits of implementing the program. Unless the low performance of your employees is sufficiently hindering to decrease productivity, you should refrain from implementing a training program focused on updating current skills.

Class Assignments

1. Design a training program for a customer service representative or a financial services clerk. (The job descriptions for both jobs are contained in Chapter 24.) Note that both jobs are performed under close supervision. The type of supervision received should alert you to the fact that employees hired into both jobs are inexperienced and untrained. Thus, you must make sure that your training program teaches the new hire all of the job's tasks.

2. Interview selected small businesses and find out how they train employees to competently perform their jobs. Your instructor will assign class members to conduct interviews in two of the following businesses:
   a. A service employer of fewer than ten employees
   b. A service employer of more than ten but fewer than twenty employees
   c. A manufacturing employer of fewer than fifty employees
   d. A manufacturing employer of two hundred or more employees
   You should find out who is responsible for employee training and interview that person. Start the interview by asking if the company has an orientation program, a probationary period, and a way to train employees. Ask the interviewee to describe the orientation program and the training program. Finally, ask the interviewee to define the purpose of the probationary period, describe the process used to evaluate the employee during that period, and the criteria the company uses to change the employee's probationary status to regular employee status or to terminate employment at the end of the probationary period.

Prepare a report for the class that describes the three training programs and your assessment of the similarities and differences between those programs and the suggestions for training discussed in this chapter. Speculate on the reasons for the observed differences and on the significance of those differences for ensuring competent performance and positive work behaviors.

MANAGING YOUR WORKFORCE

Management is the process of getting the work done through people. Although you will have many simultaneous demands on your time, you should be sure to devote adequate time to developing and managing your personnel. The interactions among supervisors and subordinates can enhance or hinder productivity and profits. This chapter focuses on a number of important issues for successfully managing your workforce. After reading this chapter, you will be able to

- Explain the importance of perceiving other people accurately
- Describe how to establish credibility as a supervisor
- List ways to improve employee satisfaction with supervision
- Develop strategies to control performance and other work-related behaviors

Perceiving Other People Accurately

To be an effective supervisor, you have to perceive other people accurately. Accurate perceptions about others stem from your knowledge of yourself.

Knowing Yourself

Our perceptions of other people are largely based on our views about ourselves. If one has a positive characteristic, such as a strong work ethic, one tends to judge other people's work ethic by using oneself as the standard for the appropriate work ethic. Similarly, if one has a negative characteristic, such as a short temper, one tends to evaluate others in terms of this characteristic.

Although our perceptions of other people are largely based on our perceptions of ourselves, we tend not to recognize this fact if we do not know ourselves. Rather, we make the comparisons unconsciously. Observing our own positive or negative characteristics in others, we evaluate others either positively or negatively.

People who know themselves are more aware of their strengths and weaknesses than are people who do not know themselves. Such awareness leads them to accept themselves and others: Because they accept themselves, they feel secure about themselves and confident in their abilities, and secure people are not threatened by other people. Perceiving weaknesses or limitations in themselves, they develop strategies for overcoming those weaknesses or limitations. Similarly, secure people are confident that well-designed and implemented management strategies will overcome the weaknesses or limitations of others. Thus, feeling positive about themselves, secure people hold positive views about other people.[1] Perhaps this is the reason that effective supervisors hold positive assumptions about human nature.[2] Believing that people are motivated to succeed and not inherently lazy, effective supervisors realize that they must devise strategies to develop their employees and use the talents possessed by those employees to achieve organizational goals.

Without self-knowledge and self-acceptance, no amount of work experience or aging results in becoming a good supervisor. To illustrate how self-knowledge motivates effective behavior, consider the experience of one of our former students.

Tom, who has always loved cars, was an experienced mechanic. Upon graduating from the University of Georgia with a bachelor's degree in business administration, Tom got a job with Ford Motor Company as a first-line supervisor in an assembly plant. The employees whom Tom was to supervise were members of the United Auto Workers union.

At age twenty-one, Tom was confident that together with his knowledge about cars, his operations management major, and a course in labor relations he had a good start toward succeeding on his first supervisory job. He also knew that his high school and college jobs prepared him to work effectively with people. In those jobs, Tom experienced some success and learned to overcome failure. His jobs also taught him that people varied in the source of motivation and in the kind of knowledge, skill and ability they possessed. Tom also learned that many managers did not give employees credit for what they knew. Tom's confidence, however, was tempered. After the excitement of obtaining the job wore off, he realized the potential difficulty of managing older and more experienced workers. "I feel so young," said Tom. "Everyone will know that I don't know what I'm doing."

Tom had an accurate perception of his strengths and weaknesses. Instead of pretending that his college education made his knowledge superior to that of his subordinates, he recognized that his subordinates would know that he did not know how to perform the supervisory job.

Upon starting work, Tom was assigned to the body shop department. He knew a lot about the mechanical aspects of cars, but did not know anything

---

1. R. D. Norman, "The Interrelationships Among Acceptance-Rejection, Self-Other, Insight into Self, and Realistic Perception of Others," *Journal of Social Psychology* (1953): *37*, 205–35, see also E. Weingarten, "A Study of Selective Perception in Clinical Judgment," *Journal of Personality* (1949) *17*, pp. 369–400.
2. Douglas McGregor, *The Human Side of Enterprise* (New York: McGraw-Hill, 1960).

about body work. "If only I could have taken a welding class in high school," thought Tom, but that class had not fit into his college preparatory curriculum. Well, thought Tom, "I'll have to learn about welding. In the meantime, I will need help from the welders to spot defects. The best way to start my new job is to admit that I am young and inexperienced and learn all I can about my employees and the jobs that they perform."

To learn about his employees, Tom decided to get to know each one. However, he had forty-eight employees in his section of the department, and the working environment was not conducive to conversation. The machine-paced jobs were very demanding, providing little time for talk. The work performed—molding steel sheets into auto body panels and then welding the panels together—also produced a great deal of noise, further increasing the difficulty of having normal conversations.

Nevertheless, Tom developed a three-part strategy for getting to know his employees. He planned to draw a diagram of the department that included all the workstations and a description of the specific jobs done at each station; listen to the comments that other supervisors made about the employees in the department; and make the effort to talk to two employees during each shift period.

After completing his first week of 12 to 13-hour night shifts, Tom formed the following perceptions. Some of the other supervisors had little respect for their employees. They perceived them to be lazy and requiring constant pushing. Tom, on the other hand, perceived that most of the employees he talked with wanted to do good work. Several of them knew a lot about Ford's market position and even about the newer operation management techniques he had learned about in college. The employee whom other supervisors had identified as a "guy to watch out for" because "he hates college guys" turned out to be a car lover, like Tom. Furthermore, the night after Tom had talked to that employee about sloppy workmanship, this so-called troublemaker told him, "You're going to be a good supervisor; you're an OK guy."

By being aware of his own strengths and weaknesses, Tom developed strategies to overcome those weaknesses. Furthermore, he intuitively focused on getting to know his employees personally. Tom's actions resulted in a predictable outcome—he developed a positive view of his subordinates.

Knowing Others

Tom entered his new job eagerly. Many people enter their jobs willingly, if not eagerly. How this initial commitment to work can be maintained largely depends on their perception of their supervisor's requests as legitimate and their sense that complying with those requests will produce desirable consequences, such as pay increases, good working relationships, and other rewards.

As an owner-supervisor, you probably think that you are a reasonable person. You must recognize that your employees think that *they* are reasonable people. Herein lies a potential problem: what you think is reasonable may not be perceived as reasonable by your employees.

To solve this problem, you must first know what employees think is reasonable. This knowledge can be gained by getting to know your employees personally. Then you must use this knowledge by looking at your demands from their perspective. Once you step into their shoes and view your demands from their perspective, you can evaluate whether or not your demands will be perceived as reasonable. Being perceived as reasonable is basic to establishing trust and a prerequisite for success in getting people to do what you want them to do.

Establishing Credibility as a Supervisor

As a supervisor, you have the primary responsibility for making full use of the knowledge, skills, and abilities possessed by your employees. Although most supervisors are becoming increasingly aware of their role in motivating individual and group behavior, most do not recognize that their influence on the opinions, attitudes, and behaviors of subordinates depends on the impression that those subordinates have about their suitability for managing people. If your employees perceive that you are a reasonable person, your supervisory effectiveness increases.

Good supervisors are perceived as credible by their subordinates. That perception is largely based on their ability to facilitate the development of competence in their employees.[3] If you want your subordinates to be good performers and exhibit commitment to work, you should use the process of establishing credibility outlined in Exhibit 28.1 to help subordinates experience success. That process has four components: serving as a role model, setting specific goals, involving subordinates in goal setting, and providing feedback.

Serve as a Role Model

If you want others to share your work values and behave in certain ways, exhibit those values and behaviors yourself. If you want people to perform their jobs well, be a high performer yourself. If you want people to be honest, be honest in your dealings with them. If you want people to admit mistakes, then you must also admit it when you are not right. By taking these steps, managers gain credibility with employees. Employees and others are perceptive enough to know the wisdom of an old Galician proverb:

> When someone is honestly 55 percent right, that's very good, and there's no use wrangling. And if someone is 60 percent right, it's wonderful, it's great luck, and let him thank God. But, what's to be said about 75 percent right? Wise people say this is suspicious. Well, and what about 100 percent right? Whoever says he's 100 percent right is a fanatic, a thug, and the worst kind of rascal.

---

3. Vandra L. Huber, Gary P. Latham, and Edwin A. Locke, "Management of Impressions Through Goal Setting," in R. A. Giacalone and P. Rosenfeld, eds., *Impression Management in the Organization* (Hillsdale, NJ: Lawrence Erlbaum Associates, in press).

Exhibit 28.1

PROCESS OF ESTABLISHING CREDIBILITY AND HELPING SUBORDINATES EXPERIENCE SUCCESS

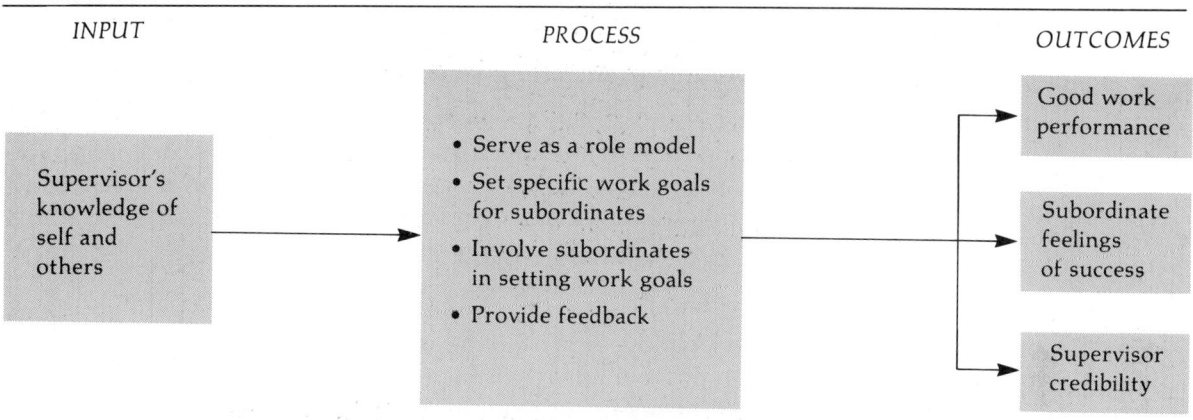

INPUT   *PROCESS*   *OUTCOMES*

Supervisor's knowledge of self and others

- Serve as a role model
- Set specific work goals for subordinates
- Involve subordinates in setting work goals
- Provide feedback

Good work performance

Subordinate feelings of success

Supervisor credibility

Set Specific Work Goals for Employees

To direct employees toward the achievement of organizational goals, you should set specific goals for each employee. Setting goals means that you must clearly communicate the specific results that should be obtained and the time or date when you expect the results. When your employees clearly understand the work that they are to accomplish, you can hold them accountable for the results. Moreover, you will be perceived as fair and impartial when you evaluate the employee's performance because you can use the established work requirements, defined in the employee's job description, as standards. Similarly, your employees will perceive you as fair and logical if they understand the reasoning behind the assigned work.

In assigning tasks, take the time to discuss how the employee may go about accomplishing the task. When the work to be done is complex or the employee inexperienced, such a discussion can help alleviate the anxiety that the employee may feel about how to proceed. When employees know what to do, their performance increases. Even experienced employees perform better if you exchange information on ways to do the work and then allow the employee to proceed on his or her own.

As you discuss work processes, pay special attention to the confidence that the employee displays in his or her ability to do the assigned tasks. Without confidence, employees tend to be easily discouraged if something goes wrong; as a result, performance suffers. If the employee lacks the ability to perform certain tasks, provide training. If the employee has the ability to carry out your assignment but has no confidence in himself or herself, focus your efforts on helping the employee gain confidence. You can build confidence by subdividing the work into smaller segments. When the employee completes the first work segment, check the results and provide feedback on how to continue. By this process, the employee achieves small successes. Over time, the employee perceives that he or she has more ability than previously thought and becomes motivated to test that ability by tackling more difficult assignments.

Involve Your Subordinates in Setting Work Goals

You should always communicate the specific tasks that you want performed and how to perform those tasks to employees who are new, untrained, or inexperienced. When managing experienced and productive employees, however, you should involve those employees as much as possible in goal setting. When you do so, you will be perceived as a manager who wants to hear what employees think.

Involving experienced employees in setting work goals does not mean that you should let the employees choose the work that they want to do. In most situations, you can achieve this result by assigning the work and providing a rationale for why it needs to be done, then asking the employee about his or her ability to complete the work in a desirable time frame. In other words, involving employees in goal setting means asking them about the barriers that they may have in completing the assigned work and then readjusting the work schedule to facilitate the achievement of the most important work goals first. As we indicated in Part Five of this book, delays at any point in a sequence create problems when there is dependent sequencing of work. Such delays may decrease the ability of some workers to complete their assigned work. It is imperative that you identify the barriers to getting the work done and attempt to minimize or eliminate them.

Provide Feedback

Feedback is essential for improving, sustaining, and motivating performance. Whether training an employee to do a new task or evaluating the results of performance, you should always let the employee know how he or she is doing.

In giving feedback, provide the employee with specific behavioral examples of what you consider good or poor performance. It is not enough to say "You did a good job" or "You did a poor job." Similarly, general statements such as "You lack initiative" or "You seem to have a bad attitude" are inadequate. General feedback, whether positive or negative, does not have the motivating force that specific feedback has. Receiving general feedback, high-performing employees may think that you do not really know what they did. Low-performing employees, on the other hand, will not know how to improve their performance.

In the long run, general feedback does not motivate good performance. To motivate performance, tell the employee specifically what he or she did right and wrong. After providing negative feedback, discuss with the employee the kinds of things he or she can do to correct deficiencies.

Employee Satisfaction with Supervision

Our discussion thus far has focused on basic supervisory attitudes and behaviors to motivate employee performance and work commitment. Another key to successful management is employee satisfaction with supervision. This satisfaction depends on a variety of factors in addition to the supervisory attitudes and behaviors described above. The eighteen items listed in Exhibit 28.2 are the major reasons for employee satisfaction or dissatisfaction with immediate supervision. If you incorporate the ideas represented by these items into your supervisory behavior, the majority of your employees will be productive, exhibit good citizenship, and view you as a good supervisor.

Controlling Performance and Behavior

As we have already noted, it is essential that employees perceive that you treat them fairly. Fair treatment relates not just to your behavior as a supervisor but also to the outcomes that employees receive from work. Good employees expect to be rewarded financially, and poor employees expect not to be rewarded when they do not comply with legitimate requests. Simply put, employees expect that rewards and punishments are allocated objectively and, thus, fairly. In order for employees to perceive the allocation of rewards and punishments as fair, you should develop objective systems for evaluating performance and

Exhibit 28.2

FACTORS THAT DETERMINE SUBORDINATES' SATISFACTION WITH SUPERVISION

Subordinates are more satisfied with a supervisor who:

- Displays technical competence
- Sets clear work goals for subordinates
- Gives clear instructions to subordinates
- Clearly defines subordinates' job responsibilities
- Backs subordinates with other managers
- Fairly appraises subordinates' performance
- Allows subordinates adequate time to do the job right
- Allows subordinates adequate time to learn the job's tasks
- Informs subordinates of work changes before they are to take place
- Displays consistent behavior toward subordinates
- Helps subordinates to get the job done
- Gives subordinates credit for their ideas
- Listens to and understands subordinates' job-related problems
- Follows through to get the job's problems solved
- Treats subordinates fairly when they make mistakes
- Shows concern for subordinates' career progress
- Gives subordinates a pat on the back for doing a good job

Source: Adapted with permission from Vida Scarpello and R. J. Vandenberg (1987). "The Satisfaction with My Supervisor Scale: Its Utility for Research and Practical Applications." *Journal of Management* vol. *13,* page 461.

citizenship behavior and disciplining employees who exhibit negative behavior.

Performance Evaluation System

An effective performance evaluation system enables you to ensure fair and consistent treatment of your employees because it helps you:

- Communicate your expectations to employees
- Monitor employee job performance and citizenship behavior
- Document satisfactory and unsatisfactory job performance and citizenship behavior

In designing your performance evaluation system, you should base the performance requirements on the requirements of the employee's job. By using the job description, you can derive performance factors for each job as well as specify the level of performance that exceeds your expectations, meets your expectations, and does not meet your expectations. The steps in designing such a performance evaluation system are outlined in Exhibit 28.3 and described below.

Establish Standards for Performance   The first step is to establish performance standards for each job's major tasks. These standards should explicitly state both the task, which must be under complete control of the employee responsible for performing it, and the level of performance that you expect of the employee performing the task. This level of performance involves both the quantity and quality of work performed.

Even before your business grows, you should write down the performance standards that each employee should meet. As your workforce grows, you may wish to formalize your performance evaluation system by developing a form that can be used. In either case, take the same care in writing performance standards that you did in writing job descriptions. The written standards should specify the behavior and work outcomes that you expect from the employee performing the job. An example of the performance standards for the job of production supervisor is shown in Exhibit 28.4.

Exhibit 28.3

STEPS IN DESIGNING A PERFORMANCE EVALUATION SYSTEM

1. Establish standards for performance
2. Establish standards for citizenship behavior
3. Specify levels of acceptable and unacceptable performance and citizenship behaviors
4. Weight the importance of the standards established in steps 1 and 2
5. Translate the evaluation standards into a rating scale

Exhibit 28.4

PERFORMANCE STANDARDS FOR A PRODUCTION SUPERVISOR

SIGNIFICANT JOB SEGMENTS	*THE JOB OF THE PRODUCTION SUPERVISOR IS WELL DONE WHEN*
Safety	a. Monthly safety meetings are conducted in accordance with company schedules. b. Safe operating procedures are followed by all employees. c. Regular monthly inspections are held in the department in accordance with the approved checklist. d. Action is taken within 5 days to correct any unsafe condition. e. Monthly safety reports are submitted by the fifth of the month.
Controlling costs	a. Waste and scrap are eliminated. b. One cost-saving improvement per month is developed and put into operation. c. Salary controls are exercised in accordance with the salary administration plan. d. At least two team projects a year are undertaken to eliminate causes of significant scrap losses. e. The ratio of productivity to costs is improved by 1 percent every 6 months.
Developing subordinates	a. New employees are inducted and trained in accordance with a definite plan. b. Performance reviews are held with all subordinates on at least an annual basis. c. Discussions are held with subordinates at least quarterly to see that performance improvement takes place according to plan. d. Responsibilities and authority are delegated to subordinates on a planned basis.

Source: Adapted by permission of the publisher from *How to Improve Performance Through Appraisal and Coaching,* by Donald L. Kirkpatrick, p. 39, © 1982 AMACOM, a division of American Management Association, New York. All rights reserved.

If you examine Exhibit 28.4 you will note two essential characteristics of good performance standards. First, the standards are clearly and unambiguously worded. Second, they permit the evaluator either to observe the employee exhibiting the desired behavior or to assess performance by reviewing objective records. For example, performance on the first safety item is easy to assess; the evaluator simply has to observe whether or not the production supervisor conducts monthly safety meetings. Similarly, by checking performance evaluation records, the evaluator can assess whether or not the production supervisor holds performance review sessions with all subordinates on at least an annual basis.

Establish Standards for Behavior   Most employers want employees who show initiative, friendliness, neatness, work commitment, and the like. They consider those factors in evaluating their employees. We strongly advise you not to use such personal characteristics as factors in evaluating employee performance. Such factors may be convenient, in that every employee can be evaluated on the same factors, but they are not appropriate performance standards for several reasons.

First, various personal characteristics may not be important for job performance. For example, some jobs can be performed well without the employee being friendly or neat. Second, telling someone that he or she lacks initiative may be good advice, but it does not tell the person what to do to improve performance. Third, personal characteristics such as neatness are subject to differing definitions. The employee may think that he or she is neat but you may not. Similar discrepancies exist in people's definition of work commitment and many other factors. Moreover, as your organization grows and your employees are evaluated by various managers, those managers will have differing interpretations for the various personal characteristics that they may be asked to evaluate. The result is inconsistent and ultimately unfair evaluations.

For these reasons, you should get into a habit of not using personal characteristics as indicators of employee performance. Instead, you should explicitly define the behavior that you expect your employees to exhibit. For example, if you want neat people, you should specify a dress code and then evaluate compliance with that code. Similarly, if you want work commitment, you should define your expectations with respect to tardiness, breaks, and absenteeism.

Specify Acceptable and Unacceptable Performance and Behavior Levels   The performance standards for each job should specify the level of performance that you consider to be satisfactory. In other words, you must state the level of performance that meets your expectations for performance.

Some employees will exceed your expectations; others will fail to meet them. To evaluate employees fairly, you should also establish the performance level for each performance factor that would exceed or fail to meet your expectations. By doing so, you establish a rating scale or a ruler against which you can objectively measure performance. Taking the performance standards listed in Exhibit 28.4, you would define for each item listed the level of performance that you consider to be outstanding and poor. You should also specify the range of behaviors that you consider as exceeding or not meeting your expectations. Similarly, you can establish a rating scale against which to measure the behavior of all employees.

Weight the Importance of the Standards   In developing your evaluation system, decide whether job performance or citizenship behavior should receive equal weight or one factor receive more weight than the other. Greater weighting of job performance is usually preferable in cases where the employee has discretion over job performance. However, on jobs that do not permit individual discretion, such as machine-paced jobs or jobs whose outcomes depend on group effort, citizenship behavior may receive greater weight.

Translate the Standards into a Rating Scale   In steps two and three, you defined the range of performance and behavior that you consider outstanding, satisfactory, and poor. The final step is to assign a numerical value to each of these levels. For example, you can use three numbers to reflect different levels of performance: outstanding performance is rated 3, satisfactory performance is rated 2, and less than satisfactory performance is rated 1. If you weight performance and behavior standards equally, you can simply add up these numbers to obtain three assessments: overall job performance, overall behavior, and combined overall performance and behavior. If you weight the standards differently, you must incorporate these weights in assigning numerical values to each item and then sum the scores received, as done above.

Implementing the five-step process of performance evaluation serves a number of purposes. First, it enables you to translate subjective assessments into an objective system against which to evaluate employees. Doing so helps you to assess your employees against job- and work-related standards and reward or discipline them accordingly. Review of employee strengths and weaknesses also helps you to decide whether some employees need additional training and others are ready for promotion and more responsibility. Second, defining your expectations of employees enables you to communicate those expectations specifically and explicitly. Employees should know what your expectations are and how they will be evaluated. Such knowledge decreases ambiguity and motivates performance and behavior toward meeting or exceeding your expectations. Thus your organization's productivity and stability is likely to increase. Third, using this process will help employees view the evaluations they receive as fair and objective. As a result, they are more likely to accept the consequences (rewards or punishment) that flow from those evaluations.

Disciplining Negative Behavior

If you stated your work rules explicitly when hiring and orienting your employees, you should experience few discipline problems. However, as employees continue to work for you, some may change their behavior from positive to negative.

A change in an employee's behavior may be due to a variety of causes. Perhaps he or she has difficulty in getting along with new people that you hired. Old employees may also perceive that you treat new employees better than you treat them. Such a change in behavior may also be due to personal problems that are not related to the job. Whatever the cause, behavioral change may decrease commitment to work.

If you know your employees personally, you can easily learn the real reasons for their changed behavior and thus have a better chance of changing that behavior. For example, if the employee has misunderstood your behavior, you can clarify that misunderstanding and confirm the employee's value to your organization. If the employee's work group is experiencing conflict, you can address the conflict and help the work group resolve it. If the behavior change is due to personal reasons, you can help the employee find help from public and private sources to deal with the problem. Knowing the reasons for negative behavior helps you determine how to change that behavior. The behavior itself, however, cannot be ignored. Most people have a sense of justice and know when they deserve to be disciplined.

The major purpose of employee discipline is to change negative behavior. Therefore, you should establish a system of discipline that allows employees to evaluate the consequences of their actions before they act. The characteristics of a good discipline system are shown in Exhibit 28.5.

Employees who choose to violate work rules should be disciplined. The discipline, however, should be based on objective grounds and not on the basis of emotional reactions, such as anger. Before disciplining the employee, you should ascertain the facts, determine the reason for the offense, check into any extenuating circumstances that may have led to the offense, review the discipline you imposed on others in the same or similar situations, and consider the employee's previous record. Only after you have examined all these factors and your anger has cooled are you in the position of objectively deciding what the proper disciplinary action should be.

Progressive discipline systems are typically good discipline systems. With progressive discipline, punishments increase in severity as the number of violations increase. Discipline usually takes a five-step approach:

1. Informal talk
2. Formal oral warning
3. Formal written warning
4. Suspension from work, without pay, for a specified time period (usually from one to five days)
5. Discharge

Exhibit 28.5
CHARACTERISTICS OF A GOOD DISCIPLINE SYSTEM

· *Specific rules,* which leave no doubt about when they have been violated
· *Job-related rules,* which are reasonably related to the employee's work or to some other legitimate organizational objective
· *Clearly stated punishments,* which leave no doubt about the consequences of violating those rules
· *Punishments that fit the crime,* which means that the infraction should be severe enough to warrant the disciplinary action taken
· *Careful investigation,* which ensures that the rules really were violated
· *Prompt* enforcement of rules
· *Consistent* enforcement of rules
· *Documentation* of all observed rule violations and disciplinary actions taken
· *Specific statement of the offense* in communicating with the employee at the oral and written warning steps
· *Discussion confined to the problem at hand* and does not question employee's overall worth
· *Effective communication* of the rules and punishments
· *Advance warning* of any change in the rules
· *An appeals process*

Source: Vida Scarpello and James Ledvinka, *Personnel and Human Resource Management: Environments and Functions* (Boston: PWS-KENT Publishing, 1988), p. 687. Reprinted by permission of PWS-KENT Publishing Company, a Division of Wadsworth, Inc.

To change negative behavior into positive behavior and also to be perceived as fair, you should enforce your discipline rules impartially and consistently. It is essential to treat all employees alike, even though it may be difficult to act the same toward an employee whom you personally like and one whom you dislike.

One shortcoming of discipline systems is that they rely exclusively on punishment. You should not lose sight of the fact that discipline is a method for changing negative behavior into positive behavior. Punishment alone may eliminate the negative behaviors, but it does not lead people to substitute positive behavior. To change negative behavior into positive behavior, you should do the following:

- Focus on the employee's offense and not label the employee as the problem.
- Avoid moralistic judgments; judge your employees only on how well they do their jobs and comply to your work rules.
- Avoid trying to help employees by lowering your expectations concerning their performance, attendance, and the like; such actions are not really helpful.
- Make the employees who violate your expectations set goals for giving up bad habits and for improving their performance or behavior.
- Let the disciplined employee know that he or she is improving by initially giving a pat on the back every time you notice the positive behavior.
- As the employee exhibits the positive behavior more consistently, decrease the number of pats on the back. As the new behavior stabilizes, give these pats only half the time that you observe the behavior. By doing so, you change the negative behavior into positive behavior. Once the employee's new behavior becomes habit, he or she will not revert to the old behavior for which he or she received discipline.

Treat discipline as a method for changing behavior and apply the discipline procedure consistently and impartially to all employees. If you do so, discipline problems will decrease and your employees will exercise self-control over their behavior.

Summary

Good supervision has three essential elements: knowledge of self, knowledge of others, and development of fair and impartial approaches to managing subordinates. Self-knowledge is important for generating positive views about others and for perceiving others accurately. Being perceived as a reasonable person is valuable for a supervisor because it helps promote effectiveness. Holding positive views about people and establishing trust are prerequisites for success in getting people to do what you want them to do.

Supervisors who establish credibility with subordinates are effective supervisors. The four components of the process of establishing credibility are serving as a role model, setting specific goals, allowing the employees to help set goals, and providing feedback.

Controlling performance and other work-related behaviors is an important part of supervision. An objective performance evaluation system is based on communicating expectations to employees, monitoring their performance, and documenting that performance. Such a system focuses on job-related tasks and behavior and establishes an objective means of measuring actual performance against the desired standards. An effective discipline system focuses on replacing negative behavior with positive behavior—reform, not punishment, is the goal.

Class Assignments

1. Interview four people who currently hold full-time nonsupervisory jobs. Choose two people whom you personally know well and two people whom you do not know well. Using the information in the chapter, develop a set of questions to ask the interviewees about their supervisors and how they feel about them. Ask the same questions of the four people. Analyze their responses to determine what is common and what unique. Draw inferences of what the responses would mean to you if you were to supervise the four people whom you interviewed. Report your study and its results to the class.

2. Interview four people who work as full-time supervisors. Using the information in the chapter, develop a set of questions to ask the interviewees about their subordinates and how they attempt to develop them. Ask the four supervisors the same questions. Analyze their responses to determine the similarity and differences from the responses and the material in the chapter. Speculate on the meaning of the differences. Report your study and its results to the class.

MANAGING A UNIONIZED WORKFORCE

Many employers react negatively to unions. By doing so, they allow emotions to replace rational decision making. If you implement the ideas presented in this part of the book, you will treat your employees fairly and impartially. As a result, your employees are less likely to unionize. You may, nevertheless, acquire a firm that is already unionized. If so, you must know many details about laws related to labor relations. You must also learn the details of your union contract. It is also important to be aware of how to work effectively with your unionized employees.

Some sources of information about labor relations are listed in the appendix of this chapter. Our discussion will focus on broader issues that should help you understand the reasons behind the collective bargaining relationship. After reading this chapter, you will be able to

- Explain the purpose and meaning of the union contract
- Describe the basis for labor law and its practice
- List some reasons for developing and ways of establishing a constructive union-management relationship
- Develop ways to manage day-to-day disputes

The Purpose and Meaning of the Union Contract

The union contract is a major exception to the employment-at-will doctrine discussed in Chapter 24. The union contract give employees the legal right to fair and impartial treatment by their employers. Although many nonunionized employers treat their employees fairly and impartially, nonunionized employees do not have a legal right to such treatment. The employer-employee relationship can be viewed as one of power in which the employer is the more powerful party. A union contract is the method whereby the more powerful party (the employer) is legally obligated to treat the less powerful party (the employee) fairly and impartially.

The logic behind the union contract is called *due process of law*. The two basic requirements for due process of law are that the exercise of power should be based on a set of objective rules rather than on the personal preferences of those in power and that the rules should respect the commonly accepted rights of the person against whom the power is exercised.

Following the logic of due process, the union contract consists of two parts. The first, the written agreement, is the outcome of negotiations or bargaining between the employer and the union that represents the employees. The employer's negotiation committee consists of the chief negotiator (the employer, human resource manager, or some other person to whom the employer delegates the responsibility) and selected members of the management team. The union's negotiating committee consists of employees who have been elected by their coworkers to officer positions in the union. The employee elected to be the local union president is the chief negotiator. Additionally, the union committee may include either a representative of the larger union organization or a business agent or both. The representative is an employee of the national or international union with which the local union is affiliated (examples are the United Auto Workers and the Communication Workers of America). The business agent is a person who acts as a franchisor for a national union and is hired by the local union. The role of representatives and business agents is to service their local unions. In negotiations, they act as consultants by providing information and advising the local union officers.

The employer and union committees negotiate wages, hours, and terms and conditions of employment for the group of employees (called the *bargaining unit*) represented by the union. The negotiated agreement is reduced to written form and signed by the employer and by local and international union officials. This agreement spells out the first requirement for due process of law—a set of objective rules that will guide the relationship for the life of the contract period (usually three years). The legal language of the written agreement details constraints on management behavior and specifies union and employee rights and constraints for the length of the contract period. Among the rights and constraints are the means used to resolve disputes.

The second part of the union contract consists of all the oral agreements and all the implicitly or explicitly accepted customary ways of doing things within the workplace. The notion of customary practice reflects the implementation of the second requirement for due process of law—the rules should respect the commonly accepted rights of the person against whom the power is exercised. As one expert termed it:

> A union contract is far more than words on paper. It is also all the oral understandings, interpretations, and mutually accepted habits of action, which have grown up around it over the course of time. Stable and peaceful relationships between the parties depend upon the development of a mutually satisfactory superstructure of understanding which gives operating significance to the purely legal wording of the written contract. Peaceful relations depend, further, upon both parties faithfully living up to their mutual commitments as embodied not only in the actual

[written] contract itself but also in the modes of action which have become an integral part of it.[1]

Under the union contract, the employer retains the right to direct employees; establish working conditions; fire, hire, promote, and demote employees; and suspend, discharge, or otherwise discipline employees. The due process of law constraint, however, restricts the employer from exercising its rights in a capricious and arbitrary fashion. Thus, it prevents management from practicing employment at will.

Nearly all written union contracts contain a clause specifying the procedure to be followed when a grievance arises. The grievance procedure gives all parties the right to challenge the actions of the other parties, but typically challenges are focused on management's actions. This focus is understandable; management makes most of the important decisions to which the union and employees react. The grievance procedure usually consists of several levels of appeals, with the last level being binding arbitration.

Arbitration is a sort of labor court presided over by a neutral outside party called the *arbitrator*. The arbitrator hears management's rationale and evidence for its action and the union's rationale and evidence for why the action was capricious or arbitrary. He or she deliberates on the evidence and renders a decision on the case, either upholding the management action, finding in favor of the union, or choosing some middle ground. This decision is legally binding on both parties unless either party decides to appeal it to a court of law, a relatively rare occurrence.

Union Contracts and Labor Law

The union-management relationship is subject to labor law and a myriad of rules. In the private sector, the primary law regulating the relationship is the National Labor Relations Act of 1935 as amended by the Taft-Hartley Act of 1947. Together, those acts are referred to as the Labor Management Relations Act (LMRA). Besides regulating the union-management relationship, the Taft-Hartley portion of the LMRA also allows states to pass right-to-work laws. These laws give employees the right to work without being required to join a union or pay union dues.

Labor law differs considerably from other law. One distinction is the difference between the law of the land and the law of the shop. Federal, state, and local statutes are the laws of the land, which apply to all citizens subject to their provisions and are enforced through the judicial system. The law of the shop establishes the rules to be followed in the specific union-management relationship provided that the parties in the relationship do not violate the statutory rights of their constituencies, the rights of innocent bystanders (individuals or groups who may inadvertently get involved in a dispute between them), and public policy.

---

1. Arthur T. Jacobs in *Coca-Cola Bottling Co.*, LA 197, 198.

The complexity of labor law comes from its purposes, which are dual and interrelated. On the one hand, labor law attempts to balance the power among employers, unions, and employees. This purpose has the effect of balancing the interests of citizens and thus, maintaining the country's social, political, and economic structure. On the other hand, the purpose of labor law is also to ensure the free flow of commerce by containing and managing the conflicts that may erupt between employers and unions.

The application of labor law to specific and changeable union-management relations and the dual purposes of the law produce a flexible and dynamic system of governance called the *industrial relations system*. This system, which differs considerably from the judicial system, has three distinct characteristics.

First, although labor law is replete with specific rules, literal interpretation of the law or those rules is typically difficult. By design, labor law requirements can be interpreted differently in different situations. Moreover, more than one interpretation in a given situation is possible. When this happens, the appropriate interpretation is one that favors public policy and is consistent with other laws.

Second, federal government involvement in labor relations takes two forms: regulation and assistance. The National Labor Relations Board (NLRB) serves the regulatory function. The NLRB has three purposes:

1. To supervise the election process through which employees choose to be represented by a union (certification election) or choose to cancel such representation (decertification election)
2. To conduct what are called *unit determination hearings* in order to determine the extent to which employees desire to be represented by a particular union and also to determine the appropriateness of the composition of the group (the bargaining unit) that seeks union representation
3. To investigate and prosecute acts by employers and unions that are considered unfair labor practices under the law

The NLRB does not become involved in a situation until it is requested to do so by either the employer, the union, or individual employees. This behavior is consistent with the intent of labor law. As long as the board gets no complaints, it assumes that balance of power and free flow of trade exist.

The NLRB is the regulatory agency, but the Federal Mediation and Conciliation Service (FMCS) serves the assistance function. FMCS acts as a third-party neutral to help employers and unions resolve serious clashes and maintain constructive relationships. This assistance is provided at no cost to either employer or union. The agency becomes involved in the union-management relationship in two ways. First, employers are required by law to notify FMCS when their union contract is about to expire. The purpose of this notification is to alert the FMCS to the possibility of a bargaining impasse. An FMCS agent called a *mediator* contacts the parties and offers assistance in the event that they perceive difficulty in reaching an agreement; either party can also call the mediator for help at a later stage. The mediator has no power to impose solutions on the parties. Rather, he or she uses various persuasive tactics to help the parties solve their own disagreements. The FMCS also responds to requests for assistance during the term of the union contract. Such assistance takes the form of developing and implementing joint union-management training programs to help both parties establish and maintain a constructive relationship.

The third aspect of the labor relations system is that either employer or union can enlist the help of private citizens in settling their disagreements. These citizens, considered third-party neutrals, can come from a wide range of professionals, such as ministers, lawyers, and college professors. The cost of third-party neutrals is typically borne equally by the union and the employer. The FMCS provides mediation services at no cost, but some employers and unions prefer to hire private mediators. One reason is that they may obtain a broader range of services in a shorter time frame. Another is that the parties do not understand the purpose of the FMCS and fear government interference.

The most common form of third-party assistance is grievance arbitration. Exhibit 29.1 shows the seven grievances that are most frequently arbitrated. Analysis of arbitrator decisions for these grievances indicates that the employer's position is upheld about 54 percent of the time and the union's position is upheld about 25 percent of the time. In the remainder of the decisions, arbitrators uphold both positions in part.

Arbitrators have specialized knowledge of labor law and the practice of collective bargaining. Thus, labor lawyers, college professors, and former labor relations professionals (such as retired federal mediators) serve as arbitrators. Both the union and the employer have to select the private arbitrator jointly. If either party objects to the other party's choice, the parties continue the selection process until they both agree.

In some situations, you may want to consult with a labor relations specialist on your own. Because of the wide variety of backgrounds that such consultants possess, we strongly urge you to make sure that the consultant that you

---

Exhibit 29.1
SEVEN MOST COMMONLY ARBITRATED GRIEVANCES

GRIEVANCE	*NUMBER OF CASES IN ONE YEAR*
Discharge	124 cases
Discipline	91 cases
Arbitrability of an issue	53 cases
Wages	52 cases
Promotions and transfers	43 cases
Work assignments and schedules	39 cases
Benefits	33 cases

Source: Perry A. Zirkel, "A Profile of Grievance Arbitration Cases," *The Arbitration Journal* (1983), *38* (1), pp. 35–38.

hire has expertise in the broader field of personnel and human resource management. If you contract the services of a lawyer, make sure that he or she specializes in labor law.

Developing a Constructive Relationship

A union-management relationship starts much like a shotgun marriage; the parties may accept their new relationship and consciously strive to improve it, or they may decide to fight one another. You may think that a stormy relationship will ultimately fail or self-destruct. While some do, most continue to exist—but at high cost to the parties involved. Poor union-management relationships are costly. Perhaps this is one reason that employers develop strategies to rid their organizations of unions.

Such strategies are usually short sighted. Although an employer may succeed in getting rid of the union in the short run, that success may not be worth the cost. First, the employer usually has to hire expensive consultants to help convince employees that they no longer need union representation. This money could be better spent to provide fair pay and benefits to employees. Second, short-run success in ousting the union may result in long-range threats of reestablishment of the union. Unless the employer treats employees fairly and impartially, employees will unionize again, and the subsequent union-management relationship is likely to be more hostile than the previous one.

Some employers recognize that managing a unionized workforce may be easier and more efficient than managing a nonunionized workforce. One reason is that the union contract acts as a guide for appropriate managerial and employee conduct. The contract decreases the need to spend money on management training and reduces the ambiguity that employees may experience about their work requirements and rewards. Another reason is that the responsibility for administering the union contract is shared equally between management and the union. Because it is in the union's interest to ensure that it retains the rights and privileges won through bargaining, the union has strong incentive to make sure that the written contract's provisions are implemented. Consequently, the union shares with management the task of controlling employee behavior.

For these reasons, it may be more profitable to develop a constructive union-management relationship than to attempt to rid yourself of a union. A constructive relationship does not just happen; the burden of its development and maintenance rests with you, the owner. As an employer, you are the more powerful party in the relationship. You make the decisions that affect the profitability of your business and the welfare of your employees. The union is the reactive party. If employees perceive that your decisions may adversely affect them, they will react to those decisions.

To develop a constructive or positive relationship with a unionized workforce and the union, you must do three things:

1. Gain an understanding of unionized workers
2. Learn why employees formed into a union
3. Establish a climate for developing and maintaining a constructive union-management relationship

Understanding Unionized Workers

The two most important factors to understand about unionized workers are the motivations that lead individuals to choose to unionize and the influence that the work group has on its individual members.

Individuals join unions to increase control over important aspects of their working lives. They find unionization to be attractive when they perceive that the existing employment situation is deteriorating and they have little power to change that situation individually. Considerable evidence shows that the major reasons employees attempt to unionize are perceptions of unfair pay and benefits, unfair treatment by their immediate supervisor, and other capricious and arbitrary management actions that threaten their job security. An attempt to unionize is collective action to obtain fair and impartial treatment from employers.

In a small organization, the characteristics of a unionized workforce are similar to those of any work group. A work group is a social group that has a certain amount of influence on its members. That influence is based on the norms or shared values that guide the behaviors and beliefs of the group's members. Norms emerge in all groups. Some, such as performance norms, can increase or decrease productivity. A group whose members share the perception that management does not treat them fairly may develop numerous norms. The group may establish a negative norm based on the notion of an eye for an eye. If the group perceives that some of its members are being victimized by management, it may attempt to right that wrong by endorsing negative norms such as condoning or even sanctioning sabotage and theft.

Group norms are powerful mechanisms for maintaining the group. They are enforced through social pressure that group members exert on individuals who attempt to ignore or rebel against the norms. These individuals act at great personal cost. In most cases, the group maintains strong control over its individual members.

The existence of work group norms results in the following outcomes:

- The work group's behavior is predictable. For example, if the work group is hostile toward management, it will consistently behave in a hostile manner. If the work group also has a high-performance norm, it will be a hostile but high-performing group.
- The work group maintains its norms until they cease to serve a purpose. If the norm is not to trust management, then the work group maintains that norm until it sees a preponderance of evidence that the mistrust is inappropriate.

If you acquire a firm that chose to unionize, you can infer that the work group has strong norms for self-protection and a strong influence over its members. You should also know that over time some group members establish greater influence over the group's functioning than do others. Group leaders, for example, tend to have some discretion to deviate from the group's norms. They also have greater influence on group norms than do other members. Because group leaders have proven their commitment to the group, they have built up credits with the group that allow them some latitude in behavior.

The best approach to managing a unionized workforce, then, is not to try to influence individual group members. Rather, you should develop a good working relationship with the employees whom the group has elected to represent their interests. If you bypass the local union leaders and deal directly with individual employees, you may experience difficulties in managing your unionized workforce. If you work with the leaders, you can, through them, influence individuals. The fact that a work group changes its norms when they cease to serve a purpose alerts you to another principle. By acting consistently and objectively toward the union and its members, you can eventually change perceptions of mistrust. By changing those perceptions, the work group will modify or eliminate its mistrust.

Learning the Reasons for Unionization

To effectively manage a unionized workforce, you need a good understanding of the reasons that your employees formed the union. Just as you have to learn about your individual employees to manage them effectively, you should learn the reasons behind unionization to effectively manage a unionized workforce.

You have two sources from whom you can learn these reasons: managers and the employees who have been selected to union offices. These sources may provide similar and different information. By obtaining information from both sources, you obtain a good idea of past, current, and perhaps future employee problems and concerns.

The best approach to obtain information from your managers is to hold individual meetings with each one. In those meetings, focus on getting the following information:

- The manager's views on unions in general and on the union that represents your workforce in particular. This information establishes the objectivity or biases with which each manager approaches the union.
- The manager's impressions of why the employees chose to form into a union. This information reveals the kinds of problems that motivated your employees to unionize.
- The manager's assessment of issues currently of concern to employees. This information, when compared with that obtained from union officials, helps you understand current employee concerns and the extent to which managers are aware of those concerns.
- The manager's description of key union officials. Particularly important are assessments of leadership skills, performance behavior, credibility

with the manager, and other positive and negative aspects of the union leaders' attitude and behavior. This information shows the power bases of the union leaders, their motivations for seeking leadership positions, and their general orientation toward management.

Do not attempt to meet with each union official individually. Such an approach would meet resistance from the union, and employees may perceive it as a subtle attempt at intimidation. Instead, you should invite the group of union officials to a meeting. In extending the invitation, clearly state that the intent of the meeting is to obtain their views on the nature of the union-management relationship in your firm. During the meeting, let the participants talk and listen carefully to what they say. At the end of the meeting, thank them for their input and let them know that you will get back to them within a specified time period.

After you have evaluated the information from both managers and union officials, schedule a joint meeting with both groups. During this meeting, explain how you intend to manage your operations. You should also explicitly define your expectations of management with respect to their responsibilities and the kind of behavior they should exhibit when interacting with the union. Similarly, you should explicitly define your expectations of the union and of employees. Finally, explain what you think needs to be done to maintain or enhance the working relationship between the union and management.

Establishing a Constructive Climate

Your effort to establish a constructive union-management relationship starts during your discussions with managers and union officials. During those discussions and subsequently, attempt to reduce defensiveness in your managers and in the union representatives. Defensiveness is based on feelings of insecurity. When confronted with new situations, insecure people feel that they may either lose something they value or may be incapable of adapting to new demands. These feelings lead to concern for self-protection and, in turn, to rigidly held positions and the inability to listen to other points of view.

You can help decrease defensiveness by serving as a role model for rational behavior. To do so, you must exhibit an openness to logical solutions to problems, commitment to establishing a constructive union-management relationship, and confidence in the capabilities of the two groups to establish a positive working relationship. You can communicate this openness to logical solutions by showing a genuine concern for finding workable solutions, by asking questions, by clarifying issues, and by not taking sides. You can show your commitment to establishing a constructive relationship by listening to each side without evaluating their input, by showing respect for the speaker's opinion by voicing appreciation for the input, by accepting emotional reactions at face value, and by showing an understanding of the problem at hand and the speaker's position on the issue. You can show confidence in your managers' and union officials' capability of establishing a constructive relationship by taking a relaxed but alert posture regarding disagreements between them. You should also establish regular meetings between the two groups to deal with issues of common concern. Such meetings can help show the parties that there is common ground upon which to build a better relationship. You can also use the same process to develop a productive climate in a nonunion setting.

Managing Day-to-Day Disputes

Most day-to-day disagreements between your employees and their supervisors can be resolved by the supervisor and the employee in question. In cases involving discipline, the union contract gives the employee the right to appeal the supervisor's actions. If union-management relations are poor, union officials often get involved in the very early stages of an employee grievance against the supervisor's decision because the employee seeks help from the official as soon as disciplinary action is taken. If the employee perceives the discipline to be unfair in a business where union-management relations are good, he or she usually complains directly to the supervisor shortly after receiving discipline.

If union-management relations are poor, the union officials always side with the employee complaints. To change perceptions from mistrust to trust, you and your managers must make sure that the discipline procedure is justly administered. Exhibit 29.2 lists the seven basic tests for deciding whether or not a managerial action was based on just or fair cause. If you act within these seven tests, your decisions will be perceived by employees as fair and just. You also increase your chances of defending your position in an arbitration dispute.

Although union contracts provide the grievance procedure as a means of resolving the fairness of management's actions toward employees, the procedure itself is not evidence for an effective system of fair treatment. Sometimes the grievance procedure is used simply as a score card of who wins or loses. To make the procedure work, you have to approach it with the attitude that it serves the mutual interests of management, the employees, and the union. If

---

Exhibit 29.2
SEVEN TESTS FOR JUST CAUSE IN A DISCIPLINARY ACTION

1. Was the worker given advance warning of the probable consequences of his or her conduct?
2. Was the controlling rule or order reasonably related to efficient and safe plant operations?
3. Was the alleged violation of the rule or order fully investigated before discipline?
4. Was the investigation fair and objective?
5. Did the investigation uncover substantial proof of guilt?
6. Was the employer's treatment even-handed and nondiscriminatory?
7. Was the disciplinary action reasonably related to the worker's record and the gravity of his or her offense?

Source: As used by arbiter Carroll Daugherty; Enterprise Wire Company and Enterprise Independent Union, 46 LA 359.

you view the procedure as a mechanism for solving rather than creating problems, you will make it as easy as possible for employees to present complaints, even those that are not specifically defined by the written contract as grievances, while those complaints are fresh in the employees' minds.

Finally, bear in mind that discipline for just cause should be of concern to you whether you are managing a unionized or a nonunionized workforce. Managers now realize the need for managing people fairly and impartially. Moreover, they recognize the need for a procedure that allows employees to appeal supervisors' decisions that the employee considers to be unjust. Thus, to forestall arbitrary acts by management, nonunion companies are increasingly implementing grievance procedures.

Summary

Some employees choose to form together into a union, which then bargains for all employees to establish wages, terms and conditions of employment, and procedures for settling employer and employee disagreements. The provisions of this contract specify how both management and workers must behave. Union contracts come under the jurisdiction of the National Labor Relations Board, the federal agency that regulates labor relations. Assistance to either management or labor can be provided by the Federal Mediation and Conciliation Service, which can help facilitate negotiations when the two sides are unable to reach agreement. Independent third-party neutrals can be hired to provide such assistance as well.

Though managers often feel uncomfortable with a unionized workforce, it is important to devise ways of working constructively with unionized workers. Three steps you can take to develop a constructive relationship are to gain an understanding of the goals and concerns of the workers, to learn why the workers formed a union, and to establish a climate for positive relations between management and workers. A positive climate can be promoted by working closely with the leaders that union members have elected and, through appropriate actions, by showing that workers can trust management to be fair.

Despite the best efforts, disputes between management and labor will sometimes arise. One benefit of a positive climate is that such disputes can be resolved more easily. A fair and consistent approach to disputes helps engender worker trust.

Class Assignments

1. Write a paper describing your views about unions. Discuss how you formed those views. Did you have any personal experiences that led you to form your views. If so, what are they? Are your experiences with unions limited or extensive? Do you usually form your attitudes and beliefs from limited or extensive experience? How often do you reevaluate your attitudes after you form impressions? Should you check the accuracy of your impressions more than you do, or are you satisfied with the accuracy of your impressions in general? After writing your paper, bring it to class for a discussion of attitudes about unions.

2. Go to the library and scan your local newspaper for a month. Collect articles on business issues and on union issues. After collecting those articles, analyze their content to determine the number of times that positive and negative articles were written about business practices and about union practices. Report your findings to the class, indicating the impressions you formed about business and union practices from reading the newspaper.

References

Overview of Labor Relations and Unions

Freeman, Richard B., and Medoff, James L. *What Do Unions Do?* New York: Basic Books, 1984.

Gompers, Samuel. *Seventy Years of Life and Labor.* Ithaca, NY: Industrial Relations Press, New York State School of Industrial and Labor Relations, 1984.

Goulden, J. C. *Meany.* New York: Atheneum, 1972.

Marshall, Ray. *Unheard Voices.* New York: Basic Books, 1987.

Scarpello, Vida, and Ledvinka, James. *Personnel and Human Resource Management: Environments and Functions.* Boston: PWS-KENT, 1988.

Labor Relations Practice

Brand, Norman. *Labor Arbitration: The Strategy of Persuasion.* New York: Practising Law Institute (B1–1310), 1987.

Coulson, Robert. *Labor Arbitration: What You Need to Know.* 3rd edition. New York: American Arbitration Association, 1986.

Daniels, Gene, and Gagala, Kenneth. *Labor Guide to Negotiating Wages and Benefits.* Reston, VA: Reston Publishing, 1985.

Doherty, Robert E. *Labor Relations Primer: An Introduction To Collective Bargaining Through Documents.* Ithaca, NY: Industrial Relations Press, New York State School of Industrial and Labor Relations, Cornell University, 1984.

Feldaker, Bruce. *Labor Guide to Labor Law,* 2nd edition. Reston, VA: Reston Publishing, 1983.

Front Line Supervisor's Labor Relations Handbook. Waterford, CN: National Foremen's Institute, 1981.

Gagala, Ken. *Union Organizing and Staying Organized.* Reston, VA: Reston Publishing, 1983.

Getman, Julius G., Goldbert, Stephen B., and Herman, Jeanne B. *Union Representation Elections: Law and Reality,* NY: Russell Sage Foundation, 1976.

Harrison, Allan J. *Preparing and Presenting Your Arbitration Case,* Washington, DC: Bureau of National Affairs, 1984.

Scheinman, Martin F. *Evidence and Proof in Arbitration.* Ithaca, NY: Industrial Relations Press, New York State School of Industrial and Labor Relations, Cornell University, 1977.

Trotta, Maurice S. *Handling Grievances: A Guide for Management and Labor.* Washington, DC: Bureau of National Affairs, 1976.

Zack, Arnold M., and Bloch, Richard M. *Labor Agreement in Negotiation and Arbitration.* Washington, DC: Bureau of National Affairs, 1983.

Related Material

Foulkes, Fred, K. *Personnel Policies in Large Non-Union Companies.* Englewood Cliffs, NJ: Prentice-Hall, 1980.

THE CRISIS

Chapter 30
When All Else Fails—Bankruptcy
This chapter explores the major provisions of the main laws related to bankruptcy—Chapter 7, Chapter 11, and Chapter 13. The chapter also examines the provisions related to involuntary bankruptcy. In each case, the law is examined from two points of view—the debtor's and the creditor's. If you become involved in a bankruptcy from either position, you will benefit greatly by knowing your rights and responsibilities.

WHEN ALL ELSE FAILS— BANKRUPTCY

We would like to think that each business, when properly managed, is always successful. Unfortunately, this may not be the way things are. Due to a changing economic, political, and social environment, conditions that accounted for the success of a business may no longer prevail. Customers may no longer be able to pay accounts receivable. Population shifts may leave the business without a sufficient customer base to sustain itself. Changing technology or the enactment of new laws may make the business unable to compete effectively. The labor market may shift to the point that labor costs become excessive. Finally, a business may falter due to inept management.

Should any one or more of these events affect your business, your concern will be to salvage whatever resources possible. People tend to avoid the use of bankruptcy as a protective defense, but it may be to your best advantage. Because bankruptcy law is a complex body of law, you require the services of an attorney who specializes in this area. For this reason, we suggest that you seek the counsel of such an attorney if your business reaches the economic crisis state.

An alternative to bankruptcy is the establishment of a composition of creditors. This option is only applicable when the economic crisis is short term in nature and the prospects for the business to recover are good. This device is a contractual arrangement between you, the business owner, and the creditors of the business. The contract stipulates the conditions for your meeting the creditor obligation. In addition, in the event that you fail to satisfy these conditions, the contract will provide redress for the creditors according to the terms of the agreement. Just as in the case of bankruptcy, this arrangement requires the assistance of an attorney.

Whatever the basis of the bankruptcy action, the process is similar. The debts of the business are totaled and itemized for each creditor. Then the assets of the business are sold, and the proceeds are distributed to the creditors in partial payment of the debt owed. This chapter will explore the specifics of the three main bankruptcy laws—Chapter 7, Chapter 11, and Chapter 13 of the Bankruptcy Code.

After reading this chapter, you will be able to

- Explain the main provisions of Chapter 7 bankruptcy proceedings
- Describe the main provisions of Chapter 11 bankruptcy proceedings
- Explain the circumstances of involuntary bankruptcy
- Outline the main features of Chapter 13 bankruptcy

Applicability of the Law

Unless you are a family farmer, who is eligible to file under Chapter 12 of the Family Farmer Act, or a municipal corporation, which is eligible to file under Chapter 9, as a small business owner you should only be concerned with three basic types of bankruptcy. These are the types defined by chapters 7, 11, and 13 of the Bankruptcy Code.

Any person or corporation may file under Chapter 7 except a railroad, a domestic insurance company, or a bank, savings bank, loan association, credit union, industrial bank, or similar institution that is an insured bank. Chapter 7 also applies to foreign corporations operating in the United States. Chapter 11 is available to anyone, individuals and corporations, except a stockholder, a commodity broker, and a railroad.

Chapter 13 would generally not be available to a small business owner. However, it is important to know what a Chapter 13 filing is and how it works because an employee may file for protection under Chapter 13. This chapter is available to an individual with regular income who owes on the date of filing the petition, noncontingent, liquidated, unsecured debts of less than $100,000 and noncontingent, liquidated, secured debts of less than $350,000.

Whether you are a debtor or a creditor, it is important to know how these chapters work and what can be done to plan for the filing of these chapters in advance.

Chapter 7

From the Debtor's Point of View

Chapter 7 is available to any debtor who is insolvent. Insolvency, for bankruptcy purposes, means the inability to pay debts as they occur. Balance sheet insolvency is not required. When the debtor files a petition of bankruptcy in U.S. Bankruptcy Court, the court appoints a trustee to handle the debtor's estate. The trustee reviews the debtor's petition to determine whether or not there is equity in assets for the benefit of creditors. If there is no such equity, the trustee in all likelihood will abandon his interest in the estate and file a report of no distribution with the court. The debtor receives his discharge very shortly thereafter. If there is equity in assets for the benefit of creditors, the trustee will liquidate those assets and pay those sums to creditors in the order of priority as set forth in the Bankruptcy Code. Of course, the first to receive funds in the distribution would be a secured creditor.

Automatic Stay Provisions   Upon the filing of a voluntary Chapter 7, the debtor must cease doing business. One has the right to petition the court for an order to permit finishing production, but such an order will only be allowed if it is for the benefit of the estate.

Immediately upon filing the petition of bankruptcy, the automatic stay takes effect. This stay provision is a temporary injunction that prevents creditors from proceeding to collect monies from the debtor, from property of the debtor, and from lawsuits against the debtor. The stay is comprehensive in nature. Any violation of it subjects the creditor to a contempt action of the bankruptcy court.

Preference Period   Post-petition payments by the debtor are not allowed without written approval from the court. Payments to debtors made within the 90 days immediately preceding the filing of the petition will be looked into very thoroughly by the trustee (90 days is the preference period). If a preference has occurred, the trustee may avoid (or recover) such preferential payments or transfers. The trustee recovers from the creditor to whom the preferential payment was made those preferential payments and places them into a fund for the general distribution to creditors.

Technically, a preference is defined as a payment or transfer made to or for the benefit of a creditor for or on account of a debt owed by the debtor before such transfer was made; made while the debtor was insolvent; and made on or within 90 days before the date of filing of a petition of bankruptcy or between 90 days and one year before the date of filing of the petition if the creditor at the time of the transfer was an insider. An insider would be, of course, an officer of the corporation, a stockholder, or a member of the board of directors. The final requirement of the definition of a preference is that the payment or transfer enables the creditor to receive more than he or she would receive under Chapter 7 if the transfer had not been made, and such creditor received payment for such debt to the extent provided by the provisions of this title.

There are, of course, exceptions to preferential treatment. A trustee may not void a transfer to the extent that the transfer was intended by the debtor and the creditor to be a contemporaneous exchange for new value given to the debtor and in fact was a substantially contemporaneous exchange. The trustee may not recover payment of the debt that was incurred by the debtor in the ordinary course of business or transfers made in the ordinary course of business and according to business terms. The trustee may choose to allow payments that create a security interest in property to the extent that such security interest secures new value.

Reaffirmation and Redemption   After filing for relief, a debtor may wish to reaffirm an outstanding obligation to a creditor. A debtor is only allowed to reaffirm a secured debt. The reaffirmation must be in writing and must contain a provision that allows the debtor 60 days after signing the agreement within which to rescind the reaffirmation. The agreement must be filed with the court prior to the receipt of discharge by the debtor. An example of a reaffirmation is if the debtor owned a piece of real estate that was approximately equal to the value of the amount of debt which it was securing. If there is much equity in the property over and above the amount owed, chances are that the trustee will liquidate. A debtor will wish to reaffirm a debt so that he may keep the collateral securing that debt. A creditor will want a reaffirmation agreement so that the debt will survive a discharge and to be able to seek a deficiency judgment in the event of default.

A debtor cannot force a creditor to allow a reaffirmation of the debt. However, a debtor does have the right to redeem the collateral by making a lump-sum payment to the creditor for the value of the collateral. An example would be a piece of equipment worth $10,000 that was securing a debt of $20,000. If the equipment had a value to the debtor, he or she could offer the secured creditor the redemption amount of $10,000 and obtain the piece of equipment. The other $10,000 owed to the creditor would then become an unsecured debt and would receive distribution, if any, from the trustee along with the other unsecured creditors.

Exceptions to Discharge   A discharge relieves the debtor from any and all indebtedness and obligations listed in the petition. The debtor is no longer liable to the creditor on those debts. There are certain exceptions to discharge. The law does not allow a debtor to discharge the following debts: certain kinds of taxes; money; property; services; or an extension renewal or refinancing of credit, to the extent obtained by false pretenses; false representations; actual fraud obtained by the use of a statement in writing that is materially false, made and published with an intent to deceive; fraud or defalcation while acting in a fiduciary capacity; embezzlement; larceny; child support; and alimony payments. The debtor cannot discharge a debt which was created by willful and malicious injury to another, or to the property of another; educational loans; or debts that arise from a judgment or consent decree entered by a court of record against the debtor wherein the liability incurred by such debtor was a result of the debtor's operation of a motor vehicle while legally intoxicated. Further, the debtor may not discharge debts against creditors that were not properly listed or scheduled.

The bankruptcy court, for all practical purposes, is a court of equity. Therefore, the debtor and creditors must come into the court with clean hands in order to obtain justice. It is important for a small business owner to be aware of the provisions in the code and—immediately upon realizing that he or she is in financial trouble—consult with a bankruptcy attorney, a tax attorney, or a CPA.

From a Creditor's Point of View

Notice and Meeting of Creditors   If someone who owes you money files for an order for relief pursuant to the Bankruptcy Code, what should you do? Pursuant to the automatic stay provision, you must immediately cease and desist in any further attempts to collect money from the debtor or to recover his or her property. The stay goes into effect upon filing, not upon notification. It is extremely important that, once the petition is filed, you do not make any efforts to contact the debtor by phone or letter regarding the debt—all contact related to the debt should be made with the debtor's attorney. Nor should you take any action that would be considered contemptuous by the court.

After the debtor files, you will receive notification, assuming that you are listed as a creditor, of when and where a meeting of creditors will occur. You may be directed to file a proof of claim if assets are available for distribution. At the meeting of creditors, a trustee reviews the debtor's petition and questions the debtor thoroughly as to his or her assets and debts; you, as a creditor, have a right to appear at the meeting and question the debtor as well. You can use the occasion to discover where your collateral is, what condition your collateral is in, whether or not the collateral is insured, and whether or not the debtor wishes to reaffirm the debt.

This line of questioning applies only if you are a secured creditor. If you are an unsecured creditor, the trustee, through his questioning, determines whether or not assets for a distribution are present or not. If there are assets and you are an unsecured creditor, you may receive some distribution of the proceeds of the sale of the debtor's estate at some future time. If there are no assets, you can just write off your debt. The majority of cases filed in Chapter 7 involve no assets. Therefore, it is extremely important to always be a secured creditor if at all possible.

Recovery of Collateral or Payment   If you are a secured creditor and the trustee is not going to liquidate the estate, your interest is to obtain your collateral. This can be done by filing a motion to lift the automatic stay and asking the trustee to abandon his interest in the collateral. Generally, these motions are handled by consent orders with consent of the debtor's attorney and the trustee. However, if it appears that there is equity in the collateral for the benefit of creditors, the trustee, and most likely the debtor's attorney, will oppose your motion. In such an instance, chances are that the court will not lift the stay to allow you to foreclose your interest. The trustee will be allowed to liquidate the estate and pay you from the proceeds.

As a creditor, you must realize that payments received within the 90 days prior to the debtor filing his petition may be viewed as preferential payments and thus be avoided by the trustee. You may receive a letter from the trustee asking that you return funds received during this preference period; if you receive such a letter, you should immediately consult your attorney to see whether or not the payments are in fact preferences. If they are preferences, it is wise to return the funds without the trustee needing to resort to an adversary proceeding to force their return. If your attorney determines that the payments were not preferential, you should oppose the trustee's attempts to recover them. This situation is one reason that it is extremely important to monitor accounts receivable and attempt to keep receivables coming in on a current basis if at all possible.

If you wish to allow the debtor to reaffirm a secured debt, it is wise to have the debtor enter into a reaffirmation agreement as soon as possible after filing the bankruptcy petition. If the reaffirmation agreement is not filed prior to the time the court enters the discharge order, it will not be allowed and you will not be able to proceed against the debtor personally on the underlying obliga-tion. Even in such a case, you will still be in a position to obtain your collateral.

If the debtor wishes to redeem collateral, he or she will, of course, try to show the value to be as low as possible. It is in your interest, however, to have the value as high as possible because the debtor will be allowed to redeem the collateral for what the court determines to be its fair market value. Fair market value is determined as of the date of filing, not the date the debtor tries to redeem the collateral. Most jurisdictions have a provision that if the secured collateral is not insured, you may file a motion with the court to recover your collateral until such time as the debtor can provide insurance. This provision is very important, for example, on motor vehicles where the debtor is driving the car or truck every day, thus subjecting you as a creditor to substantial loss in the event of total damage. If the debtor cannot provide insurance on a building or on the contents thereof, it is highly unlikely that you can take physical pos-session of those assets; in such a case, it is wise to protect your interest by providing insurance yourself.

The chances of recovery from a debtor in bankruptcy can only come from the recovery of collateral or the liquidation of the estate, unless your debt is declared nondischargeable. Therefore, if at all possible, you should try to place yourself in a position of a secured creditor by retaining a lien of some sort on the collateral which you have sold the debtor, either by filing a UCC-1 Financ-ing Statement, by retaining a lien through a motor vehicle title certificate, or by holding a mortgage security deed or deed of trust in real estate. By so doing, you place yourself in a position by being paid off by the trustee upon liquida-tion or having your collateral returned, and you stand a better chance of receiv-ing dollar for dollar rather than some lesser amount.

| Chapter 11 | From the Debtor's Point of View |

When to File a Chapter 11   Chapter 11 is a business reorganization. This reor-ganization can be accomplished by various means, including through contin-ued operations, a partial sale of assets, a sale of the business itself, or the form-ing of a new corporation. A reorganization is extremely hard to accomplish; therefore, much planning must be done prior to filing under this chapter. You should take a realistic approach as to the future potential of your business. Many issues must be considered prior to filing under Chapter 11. You must look first at the economics of the case, because as a debtor in possession with-out a trustee being involved, you will require the assistance of an attorney and a tax planner at every turn. You will, of course, need friendly creditors and an infusion of capital in order to make any plan of reorganization feasible. The majority of Chapter 11 cases simply delay the inevitable, which is a conversion to Chapter 7.

Assuming that you do file a Chapter 11, you will operate as a debtor in possession without a trustee. A trustee may be appointed by the court for cause, including prior fraud, gross mismanagement, or failure to keep accurate books and records. Again, as in a Chapter 7, an automatic stay goes into effect immediately upon the filing of the petition and your creditors must cease and desist from their efforts to collect.

Period for Filing a Plan   As a debtor in possession, you have an exclusive 120-day period within which to file your plan for reorganization. Extensions are generally granted by the court if it appears that you are making good faith efforts to try to reorganize. Extensions cannot be granted unless you petition the court for the extension.

How to Operate Under Chapter 11   As a debtor in possession, you are governed by various code sections, the most important of which is Section 363. This section sets forth what you can and cannot do in the operation of your business. You can continue to buy and sell in the ordinary course of business, but you cannot obtain credit without approval by the court. One of the most important subsections deals with the use of cash collateral (cash, negotiable instruments, documents of title, securities, deposit accounts, or other cash equivalents whenever acquired in which the estate and an equity other than the estate have an interest). This category includes the proceeds, products, offsprings, rents, or profits of property subject to the security interest. The first move you should make after filing your petition is to file a motion to use cash collateral. Creditors will in all likelihood object to the use of this collateral, because it is how they have secured their loans with you. If the creditor is successful in his objection, your business will effectively be shut down and you will have to convert to a Chapter 7. The courts have been fairly lenient in allowing the use of cash collateral, however; they realize that without such cash there would be no need for Chapter 11.

Immediately upon filing, the debtor is required to open three debtor-in-possession bank accounts: general disbursements, payroll, and taxes. As a debtor in possession, your case will be assigned an administrator from the U.S. Trustee's office. This administrator monitors your case and requires that you file monthly operating statements with their office. The administrator is also entitled to an administrative fee, which must paid every quarter. It is extremely important that you keep accurate books and records and have monthly financial statements available for the administrator.

The Plan   Once you have an idea of where your plan of reorganization is headed, you will file a disclosure statement with the court, a copy of which will be mailed to all creditors. This disclosure statement gives a brief outline of the business, classifies the claims of different creditors (as secured, unsecured, administrative expenses, and so forth), and proposes how to pay these claims. If the court determines that the disclosure statement is adequate, you may accept ballots from your creditors for their approval of the plan. Even if you do not receive approval from the requisite number of creditors, the cram-down provision of Chapter 11 may allow you to force the plan on creditors, provided that the provisions of the cram-down are met.

Fiduciary Responsibilities   As a debtor in possession, you are empowered with the same rights and duties as a trustee. Therefore, you would be able to avoid preferential payments made within 90 days prior to filing the petition of reorganization and you would be required to set aside any fraudulent transfers made during the previous year. In other words, you are in a fiduciary relationship with the creditors and must act accordingly. If the court receives a motion from a creditor or party in interest and determines that you have not handled your duties as a debtor in possession responsibly, it is empowered to appoint a trustee to manage your business affairs. It is difficult to operate a business with both a debtor in possession and a trustee in place; therefore, it is urged that as a debtor in possession you act responsibly.

Treatment of Creditors   As can be seen, there are many difficulties in operating under Chapter 11. You need to maintain a friendly relationship with the majority of your creditors, especially your secured creditors. The chances are that you are in Chapter 11 in the first place because your business was cash starved. You need an infusion of cash from a friendly creditor in order to proceed with your business. Without the help of creditors, it is extremely difficult for a debtor in possession to survive or to effectuate a plan. The plan may propose to pay unsecured creditors anywhere from 100¢ to 0¢ on the dollar. All that is required of a Chapter 11 debtor in possession is that the creditors receive as much as they would have received had the case been liquidated under a Chapter 7. You cannot pay some unsecured creditors zero and pay those with whom you wish to continue to do business 100¢ on the dollar—because all classes of claims have to be treated equally.

Most of the provisions that apply to Chapter 7 also apply to Chapter 11 as far as what you can do and what you cannot do with your business. However, operating as a debtor in possession under a Chapter 11 is highly technical; the costs of attorneys, tax professionals, and accountants can be prohibitive over a long period of time. Assuming that the plan is approved by the creditors and confirmed by the court and you agree to operate according to the terms of the plan, you would be discharged of those debts as provided for by the plan.

From a Creditor's Point of View

Notification and Meeting of Creditors   If someone who owes you money files a Chapter 11, assuming you are listed as a creditor, you will receive a notice that will schedule a meeting of creditors. The stay provisions apply to Chapter 11 creditors. The debtor who has filed the plan will be a debtor in possession and a trustee will not be appointed unless the court orders otherwise. Those in attendance at the meeting of creditors will be an administrator from the U.S. Trustee's office, the debtor, the debtor's attorney, the creditors, and their attorneys. The meeting will be general in nature. You are not required to file a proof of claim at this time unless the debtor does not have you listed as a creditor or the value that you put on your claim differs from the value the debtor lists. The debtor is not required to disclose a plan of reorganization at this time. However, as a general rule, the debtor gives some idea of where he or she is headed with the plan.

Unsecured Creditors   If you are one of the debtor's largest unsecured creditors, you will receive a ballot from the trustee's office asking whether or not you wish to serve on a committee of unsecured creditors. Committee members are entitled to monitor the debtor's operations. The committee can vote to elect a chairman, secretary, and so forth. The committee can also ask the court for approval to hire its own attorney and other professional persons as they deem necessary to inquire into the debtor's business affairs and inspect the books and records. If the debtor does not file a plan of reorganization within the 120-day period or obtain an extension, the committee can file a plan of reorganization of its own.

Secured Creditors   If you are a secured creditor, you need to determine whether or not the debtor is using your cash collateral. The debtor must obtain court approval to use this cash collateral. If he or she has not, you may petition the court to have him stop immediately. It does little good to petition the court to lift the stay on your collateral during the 120-day period because the debtor is entitled to the use of the collateral during that time; except for extraordinary circumstances the court will not lift the stay on your collateral.

   If your collateral is oversecured (for example, the value of the collateral is worth as much or more than the debt), the debtor will probably request that the court allow him or her to pledge this equity to another creditor and obtain a super priority lien, which would be in a superior position to your lien. Of course, if there is no equity in the collateral for the benefit of the debtor to use, the court will not grant this lien. As a secured creditor, you can exert a lot of influence over the direction of the debtor's plan. The debtor may request that you extend credit, thereby giving you some control over his or her situation. If the plan is not filed nor confirmed by the court, you should file a motion to lift the stay and recover your collateral or file a motion to convert the case to a Chapter 7 and allow a trustee to liquidate.

Involuntary Bankruptcy

The discussion thus far has assumed that the petitions in Chapter 7 and Chapter 11 were voluntary. There is a provision in the code that allows for involuntary petitions to be filed by creditors, thereby placing the debtor in an involuntary Chapter 7 or Chapter 11.

Who May File

An involuntary petition can be filed by three or more entities that hold claims against a debtor under certain conditions:

- Such claims are not contingent as to liability or subject to a bona fide dispute

- Such claims aggregate at least $5,000 more than the value of any lien on property of the debtor securing such claims held by the holder of such claims, or there are fewer than twelve such holders excluding any employee or insider or such person and any transferee of a transfer that is voidable under various provisions of the bankruptcy code by one or more of such holders, who holds in the aggregate at least $5,000 of such claim

Procedure After Filing

If an involuntary Chapter 7 is filed, a trustee is appointed; if a Chapter 11, the debtor would continue to operate as a debtor in possession. However, the difference in an involuntary and a voluntary petition is that once the petition is filed, even if it is filed as an involuntary Chapter 7, the debtor can continue to operate in the ordinary course of business until such time as the court enters an order for relief or appoints a Chapter 7 trustee. As the debtor, you can of course oppose the petition and either succeed or at least delay the entry of the order for relief.

If you operate a business placed in involuntary bankruptcy, you must be careful not to pay pre-petition debts with post-petition income. Such transfers may in the future, after the order for relief has been entered, be deemed voidable and therefore subject to recovery by a trustee or the debtor in possession. As a creditor dealing with one who is in an involuntary Chapter 7 or Chapter 11, all funds received from the date of filing the petition through the date of the entry of the order for relief should be applied to post-petition invoices. If the funds are applied to pre-petition invoices and account balances, they are subject to avoidance by a trustee or the debtor in possession once the order for relief has been entered. This is true even if you as a creditor are not aware that the debtor has been placed in involuntary bankruptcy.

Chapter 13 and the Small Business

As a small business, you will probably not qualify to file for relief under Chapter 13. However, an employee may file for a Chapter 13 on his own behalf and an order entered requiring you as the employer to pay monies to the trustee out of the payroll account of the employee. In other words, the employee files a Chapter 13 plan that requests of the court that a certain amount of dollars be withheld during a pay period and paid by the employer to the Chapter 13 trustee's office. It is important that you abide by the Chapter 13 payroll deduction order and send the funds in as required. If the order is not obeyed, your business may be held liable for the amount of funds that should have been withheld and paid to the court. Even though the bookkeeping for accounting and paying monies to the Chapter 13 trustee's office can be expensive and time-consuming, employers are not permitted to fire the employee because he or she sought relief under the Chapter 13 provisions. The firing of the employee, if it takes place, must be on some basis that is not contrary to any other law, including Chapter 13. Such firing must be for cause.

Summary

The guidelines described herein are general in nature and are offered only for the purpose of making a small business aware of the some of the major provisions of the Bankruptcy Code. It is important that you consult a bankruptcy expert prior to filing a bankruptcy petition so that proper planning may be done on your behalf by that expert and by tax accountants. If you are a creditor, contact your attorney about proofs of claim, preferences, or the lifting of the automatic stay. If you have any questions at all regarding how to treat a debtor who has filed, contact your attorney immediately. The best advice for any small business owner is

- Know the financial condition of those with whom you are dealing
- Monitor their financial condition
- Try to obtain a lien of some sort on property of the debtor when he incurs an obligation to you
- Monitor accounts receivable; do not let these accounts get stale or behind; if they are behind, do business on a C.O.D. basis only or require payment by a cashier's check
- Be aware of the financial conditions of your own business in the industry and of those with which you are involved

Sometimes an industry undergoes a domino effect resulting from the filing of bankruptcy by a large debtor. When the large debtor business collapses, small suppliers may also be forced into bankruptcy and employees may have to file personal bankruptcy. It is very important to be aware of these matters at all times. As a business owner, be concerned about how you are going to pay back the debt when you incur debt, and be concerned with how you are going to collect funds when you extend credit.

Class Assignments

1. What form (chapter) of the bankruptcy law allows you to remain in business if you can formulate a plan to get all creditors paid?
2. What is meant by a preference, and what are the likely results of a preference?

PART EIGHT

CASES

SNOW WHITE AND THE FIVE EXECUTIVES

W. EDWARD STEAD
East Tennessee State University

JEAN GARNER STEAD
East Tennessee State University

There's a face layin' up on the bed,
But your nose is down on that line.
You just keep on truckin'
And keep on suckin',
Treatin' your brain like an egg.
You just keep on doin' that junk now.

Gene Cotton,
"The Junk Song"

PART A: BREAKFAST
AT THE BREAUX'S

As was the custom, carried out every morning and every night for the last five years, the mirror with the neat white lines of cocaine was passed around the room. Nothing seemed to vary in this scene except for who and how many were present when the ritual took place, and even that had taken on a consistency over the last several months. There they were again—Dr. Paul Breaux, Ph.D., age forty, research scientist, founder and president of Biological Engineering Services, Inc., a small but surviving

supplier for university research laboratories doing genetic and other biomedical research; Cheri Breaux, thirty-eight, ex-wife and still part-time girl-friend of Dr. Paul Breaux; Max Breaux, six-month-old son of Paul and Cheri; Wallace Mathews, thirty-nine, known to his friends as "Weird Wally" since college days, now a highly paid medical supply executive; and Christine Caldwell, Wally's current, nineteen-year-old girlfriend (he calls her his new groupie).

As the mirror was passed to Paul, he put the rolled up $100 bill in his left nostril and snorted. He did the same thing in his right nostril. First came the rush. Next came the euphoria. Then came the deceiving confidence and verbosity. Finally came the guilt. The guilt came like clockwork; it came every time these days. Every time he snorted coke to relieve the tension or to build his confidence, his guilt about what he was doing mounted. Paul stared into the snowy mirror for what seemed to be an eternity. Where did it start? How did it get so bad? Where was it leading him? Could he stop? These were questions that he knew he either had to answer and answer soon or die.

Where did it all start? There could be a variety of answers to that, but all of them had a common theme—youth and innocence. His first beer in high school to celebrate winning the state football championship was one beginning. As he knows now, and wishes he had known then, he was the son of an alcoholic, which made him a prime candidate for addiction. Or maybe it began in college in the late

This case is heavily disguised and dramatized based on fact. The firm actually exists. The financial information, ownership arrangements, structure of the company, and conflicts among the principals are factual. The cocaine addiction of Dr. Paul Breaux and resultant financial problems are also based on fact. This case, written specifically for this book, is printed by permission.

1960s and early 1970s. He was youthful innocence personified, sitting in at the campus administration building protesting the Vietnam War. A policeman chased him across the campus yard with a billy club that day. He got away, and he celebrated his victory over the "pigs" by smoking a couple of joints with his friends. Smoking pot, taking a little LSD, and eating magic mushrooms now and then were a way of life in those days. And he believed that none of this was harmful. How could it be? It was all a part of peace, harmony, and the beginning of a better world where love replaced war as the dominant human pastime. How could such a time lead to this?

And yet there he was, snorting away his money, his marriage, his business and maybe his life. He was spending $1,000 a week on cocaine for himself, and the results were a financial nightmare. He had spent all available cash and had taken out 90-day notes totaling $50,000 for cocaine purchases in the last two years. His wife had left him. Either his friends were deserting him, he was deserting them, or they were deserting each other. And last, but certainly not least, his partner in the business had begun to use his financial problems as a tool to wrest away the business from him. Youth and innocence seemed so far away.

"Hey, Paul, snap out of it. Pass the snow," said Weird Wally. "I've got to go to work, and Christine over here has got to make a small purchase for tonight's celebration. I made it another week without getting called in by the IRS. Since I make $100,000 a year, drive a BMW, and haven't bothered to file a return for two years, I've decided that weekly celebrations are appropriate. Besides, New Orleans is Christine's kind of town. She loves to party, and it's up to me to see that she isn't disappointed. So, pass the snow, Paul . . . and the doughnuts. I've got to go make some money to pay for this party."

"Another snowy breakfast," Paul thought as he readied himself for another day of work. Gray wool slacks, freshly cleaned light pink button-down shirt, shined penny loafers, a quick blow-dry and beard trimming transformed Paul into the scientist-businessman he was during the day. This was the Paul he liked best. This was the internationally recognized scientist Paul. This was the hard-working, creative, entrepreneurial Paul. This was the Paul that cocaine was destroying. Another wave of guilt overcame Paul as he went into the kitchen for some more coffee.

"Well, Paul, Max and I are going to Mother's, but we'll be back tonight," Cheri said. "I'll get my sister to keep Max so that we can go to Wally's party. Who knows, the party may last until Sunday or Monday, and Frances doesn't mind keeping him for the whole weekend. It's 8:30. Mark will be here soon. See you later."

Mark Charles, armed with an M.B.A. from a top northeastern university and a J.D. from the state's top law school, was one of Paul's business partners at Biological Engineering Services. He was on his way to pick Paul up for another day at the office. Days at the office were becoming more and more of a hassle for Paul. They were dominated by accusing, arguing, lying, and back stabbing among the principals of the firm. Mark, vehemently referred to as the "money man" by the other officers of the firm, was the target of most of the accusations. He had been the financial catalyst that transformed the firm from a nights-and-weekends, basement operation to a legitimate competitor in the bio-supply market. But now his financial manipulations were being questioned by the others. Feelings about Mark's financial management ranged from rage over being cheated to fear over being sued or arrested. This was not a pretty sight in a firm of five executives, three lab assistants, and a receptionist-bookkeeper located in a small office in the suburbs of New Orleans. The close quarters meant that everyone must interact with everyone else everyday. Paul often thought of it as a witch's brew—take four immunologists who don't understand business and think they are being cheated or railroaded to jail, add one M.B.A.-J.D. who does not know beans about immunology, mix in rich amounts of mistrust and deceit, season with a coked-out president who is supposed to be the peacemaker between the factions, then stir for eight hours a day in a small pot over a hot fire.

As his dread of another day in the cauldron reached its peak, Mark drove his well-used but spotless Volvo into the driveway, parked, and got out. He was dressed perfectly for his role, as he always was. His conservative, gray pin-striped suit and wing-tip shoes were expensive but obviously not new. He was clean and neat and yet in slight disarray because of what he called his "executive paunch," which usually caused the ends of his tie to separate at the bottom. His image was one of a well-educated, well-bred but humble southern gentleman who was working hard in the spirit of Horatio Alger to transform himself into a success. He liked his image and did everything he could to maintain it, including keeping his personal life and finances as much a secret as possible. Ironically, it had been this image (and his financial contacts of course) that had both initially made him attractive to Paul and the other officers but ultimately had fueled their distrust of him. His honest southern gentleman image was being replaced by the image of a riverboat gambler who wanted to steal the riverboat. Paul believed that Mark had inherited a large sum of money. There was no way that Mark and his family could have afforded their house off St. Charles Street near Audobon Place on what Mark earned unless he had a stash of cash somewhere. His choice of neighborhood was the only clue Mark gave that his rags-to-riches image may not be entirely honest. The belief that he had available cash caused Paul to worry greatly because it put Mark in a position to gain controlling interest in the firm whenever he liked—a luxury Paul certainly did not share since he was spending every available dime, plus some, on cocaine.

"Knock, knock," said Mark in his aristocratic southern drawl. "Anybody home? Rise and shine, its a beautiful day to make a buck, and, speaking of bucks, do I have some news for you."

"Come on in and pour yourself some coffee. There are doughnuts on the counter," yelled Paul from the bathroom. "I'll be out in a minute." Paul gave his hair and beard a final stroke with the brush and went into the bedroom. There he opened his top dresser drawer and pulled out a small plastic bag of cocaine. He scooped out enough for two short lines, chopped it, and smoothed it with the razor blade. Then he snorted it into each nostril. The rush was immediate. The confidence was there. The guilt would come later. He packed the cocaine in his briefcase. "Lunch" he called it. He looked into the mirror one more time and noticed white powder in his mustache. He then rinsed it off and with a macabre sense of humor sang, "Hi ho, hi ho, its off to work I go. I start my day with snow white, and to bed with it I'll go," as he went into the kitchen to meet Mark.

"Man, do I have news for you," said Mark. "We just got another $100,000 advanced purchase order from West Coast Scientific, and they promise more to come. As much as you didn't seem to like it at the time, I think that my increased ownership with the firm swung the deal our way. After all, the first $100,000 purchase order hasn't been completely filled yet. I told my buddies at West Coast, you know the ones I went to business school with, that I had some real plans for expansion, and that this $100,000 would give us the cash flow to make things happen around here. Cash flow, that's the key, man. That's where our survival lies. A firm as small as ours, which has to invest heavily in research and development, has to have the cash flow to keep us alive while you scientists invent genetically engineered widgets for practical consumer use. Speaking of selling things to consumers, how is the Department of Defense project progressing?"

As usual, Mark was throwing all the business at Paul right away, in rapid-fire fashion. Paul suspected that Mark knew he was coked-out and thus was missing many of the finer points of Mark's discourse each morning. This feeling that Mark was slipping things by him didn't exactly improve Paul's trust in Mark, to say the least.

"Great," said Paul. "I think we'll get the grant, but for how much I don't know. They haven't said how many firms will be participating in the final project yet. I'll get my coat and hat. We need to go." He got his leather coat and felt safari hat from the closet, and he and Mark walked to the Volvo for the drive to the office.

PART B: WASTING GAS AND THINKING

As usual, the drive to the office was filled with big city events, especially traffic jams on the interstate. A twenty minute drive becomes an hour drive with much of your time spent sitting still and wasting gas. Mark talked nonstop about the big deal, emphasizing his role in the whole thing. He must have said "cash flow, that's the key, man," a hundred times between the house and the office. One good thing about Mark talking all the time was that he never had time to check to see if Paul was listening. So Paul usually allowed his mind to wander, isolating himself in a psychological, cocaine-induced cocoon. This was his calm before the storm.

Today his thoughts progressed randomly. He thought of Cheri, his beautiful and creative Cheri. She and Max would be gone soon. He knew that. Holding on forever would be impossible now. She no longer loved him. She loved cocaine. He thought of Max. He didn't seem to really even know Max. Strange. He thought of Weird Wally. A man much like himself—intelligent, motivated to succeed, completely engulfed by cocaine addiction. Wally had lost his wife and child because of his habit two years earlier. He thought of Mark. Who was this man? Was he genuine and sincere about their continued partnership? Or did he want to cash in on Paul's genius, leaving him with little to show for his years of hard work?

But he thought mostly about himself. He had fought a lot of tough battles to get where he was. He had struggled with his alcoholic father, a man he loved and despised at the same time. He had held many jobs, often two at a time so that he could support his first wife in the high style to which she was accustomed. He had spent many years in university research getting paid pittance for his ideas because he did not have a Ph.D.

But all of that turned around for a while. He met Cheri, he finally completed his Ph.D., and he took his ideas from the university to Biological Engineering Services, where they had a chance at least to pay off handsomely. He had owned 33 percent of the firm originally, with Jody Smith, the current production vice-president, and Leah Delgado, the current vice-president of quality control, each having 33 percent as well. This had not worked out because Paul, being the genius behind the firm, needed more control. Eventually they settled on 42 percent for Paul and 29 percent each for Jody and Leah. Of course 42 percent of a basement operation meant little, so when Mark came along waving $50,000 of seed money and contacts at West Coast Scientific their way, they jumped for it. The resulting split was 42 percent for Paul; 11.5 percent each for Jody and Leah; 25 percent for the outside investors, which portion could be purchased for $150,000 (at three for one); and 10 percent for Mark. The outside investors became voting members of the board, along with Paul, Jody, Leah, and Mark. The company got its first purchase order from West Coast Scientific, moved into an office, and began production on a full-time basis; with 42 percent of the stock in the promising company, Paul felt in charge for the first time. Everything looked rosy. It was all about to pay off.

But it fell apart as fast as it came together. Paul and Cheri started doing cocaine. A little at first, for special occasions—anniversaries, birthdays, vacation trips, etc. But they began soon to invent special occasions—like Wally's IRS party—and things were out of control. They bought expensive cars and sailboats and took Club Med vacations. They had joined the yuppie generation and they were going to enjoy it. They needed money, lots of money, to support their habit and lifestyle. Ninety-day notes and credit card advances were enough for a while, but the credit began to dry up. Then came Mark with his offer—one that Paul could not refuse. Mark offered to help Paul out in return for an additional 16 percent of the business. Paul accepted, leaving both Mark and Paul with 26 percent. Of course, Mark's 26 percent combined with the 25 percent from his friends, the outside investors, gave Mark the potential to control 51 percent of the vote on any board issue. Further, if Paul's suspicions about Mark's financial condition were correct, then Mark may have the cash to pay the outside investors their $150,000 and take sole controlling interest of the firm.

Now Cheri had left, his friends were all but gone, he owed more money than ever, his credit rating was terrible, Mark seemed on the verge of either taking over the company or destroying it in the process, and Paul was doing $1,000 worth of cocaine a week. The guilt was back—full force.

"Well, we finally made it, man," Mark said in his usual jovial fashion. "Another hour in the New Orleans traffic. How refreshing. Well, let's go make some money." With that they got out and braved the humidity from the car to the office. Sixty seconds outside in Louisiana in the summer is like taking a steam bath.

PART C: A DAY AT THE OFFICE

As he entered the office, Paul felt the sickening feeling which came with the realization that another day of conflict lay ahead. The factions were already lining up for the daily battle between the scientists and administrators. Leah, Jody, and Alan McClellen, the recently hired vice president of product development, on one side and Mark and Wanda Brown, the recently hired receptionist-bookkeeper on the other side. Paul, being involved in both the scientific and business side, was seen as the peacemaker. The problem was that Paul, for all of his 210-pound bulk, was a timid, insecure person who believed in avoiding conflict at all costs. Thus, his method of peacemaking typically involved shutting himself in his office and immersing himself in his grant or article writing. This, and the cocaine, were his only escapes from the conflict that he hated so desperately.

Leah was arguing with Wanda, the third person in her position in the last six months. Mark was responsible for hiring and supervising the receptionist-bookkeeper. He was insistent that the person filling the position be an attractive, educated, well-groomed female who was smart enough to figure better ways to do her job, but who had little ambition and was naive enough to do what Mark asked and defend his actions without question. He had finally found what he wanted in Wanda. She had a B.S. in secretarial administration, she was tall and attractive, and she wore classy designer clothing that she could not afford—"the miracle of plastic," she called it. She was recently divorced; she thought that the $25,000 a year Mark paid her was the equivalent of striking gold; and she seemed willing to passively adopt Mark's values and wishes as her own without question. Shortly after hiring her Mark said, "She's good looking, smart and will do anything I say. She has no values of her own, and her vision of the future goes no deeper than redecorating her room every year. She's perfect for the job."

"Mark told me to tell you that he was too busy to talk to you today about financial matters," said Wanda, in her normal, complacent tone. "He also said for me to tell you that it was his job to worry about the money and your job to worry about the product, and that's the way it should be."

"Well, you tell him," yelled Leah in a voice that hinted she was out of control, "that if he won't meet with me this morning, then he will meet with my attorney this afternoon." With that she marched back into the back of the office where the production facility was, went into her glassed-in partition of an office, and slammed her coat into the chair. She called Jody and Alan into her office. Then she picked up the phone and called her attorney, Marty Brody. As Jody and Alan came into the office, she was explaining to him that she felt that Mark was mismanaging the funds. "His idea of cash flow," she exclaimed, "borders on criminal activity. Jody and Alan and I are afraid that federal agents may be coming to arrest us at any time because of the way Mark spends the grant money we receive to pay current expenditures. Also, we're sure that he isn't supposed to be borrowing money from the firm the way he does without asking anyone. He acts like he's a king who doesn't have to explain his actions

to anyone. We want you to meet with us and Mark this afternoon." The attorney agreed to a 2:00 P.M. meeting, and Leah hung up. "We'll get him this time," Leah said to the others. "He won't be able to pull that 'you scientists just don't understand finance' routine with Marty here."

"Well, I'm going to call my wife and tell her what's happening," said Alan. "Every morning I come in here with the idea that I'll be spending the night in jail instead of at home. What a great place to work. I'm sure glad I turned down the 10 percent ownership in the firm you offered when you hired me. Maybe they'll just arrest the owners."

"I really think both of you are a little paranoid," said Jody, by far the most level-headed of the three. "No one's going to be arrested, and Marty is going to find out if we're being cheated or doing something illegal. Until then, let's get back to work. We've got some antibodies to produce and deliver. If we don't do that, then we won't have anything for Mark to steal."

Typically the only break in the day came at lunch. That was when all the officers except Mark, who neither drank nor took other drugs, engaged in various forms of "drug therapy" in order to withstand the rest of the afternoon. Paul's lunch generally consisted of an appetizer and two or three Bloody Marys at the local fern bar and restaurant. Paul added to this a toot of coke in the office restroom upon returning. "Just a little boost," he called it, "to get my motor running again."

He had a message to call Cheri at her mother's when got back into his office. As he reached for the phone to dial Cheri's number, it rang. He answered it. "Hey, Paul. This is Weird," Wally Mathews said. "The party is on! Christine came through like a champ! She scored an ounce of 95-percent pure snow for $2,000, and she met a guy who may be able to turn us on to some 'ecstasy,' the new drug sweeping college campuses. 'Euphoria to the max' is how this guy describes it. I'll come by for your $500 this afternoon after I make a couple of calls. See you."

Paul hung up and dialed Cheri. "Hi," she said. "What's up? Max and I are watching the soaps. I'm going down to the shop later to help mother. Guess who called? Ricky Fourcade. He's coming back from Nashville this weekend, and he's bringing some uncut coke. I told him to bring us half an ounce."

"I don't know if I can afford it," said Paul in a fleeting moment of rationality.

"He said he'd front it until payday," Cheri said. "I'll get $1,000 from you then."

"A thousand? Why not $500? What about your half?" Paul exclaimed in an almost pleading tone.

"Well, I thought you might pay this time. After all, I don't have a job, and Max has to be fed. I live with my parents. That's a big sacrifice for me. At least you can provide me with some recreation."

"OK," said Paul. "Don't get huffy. Call Fourcade and tell him about Weird's party. I'll see you tonight. We'll do a few toots, and then go to Wally's. Bring a change of clothes and a towel in a bag. From what Wally told me, the party may last a while."

Another $1,500 spent on cocaine. Paul felt overwhelmed by the financial hole he had dug for himself. He was president of his own company, and yet he was so overextended and cash poor because of his addiction that he could not afford even modest luxuries any longer. He had tried several times after he and Cheri split to buy a small condo, but he could not get the bank to extend him the credit for the modestly priced unit. He had sold many of his and Cheri's possessions, like their spa. He was about to lose his company, and with it his ideas, to Mark. Again, he was overwhelmed by guilt. As usual, by this point in the day, Paul was wishing for the safety of his old job as researcher and manager for a major university immunology laboratory. His thoughts were more nostalgia than reality, however. The head of the lab, Dr. Elton Williams, a renowned scientist, had been the closest thing to a father for Paul for several years. He had taken Paul under his wing when Paul had only a B.S. in biology. Paul credits Elton's nurturing and encouraging as the primary influences in his choice of professions and his perseverance in the Ph.D. program. Thinking of working with Elton again always gives Paul a few seconds of relief from his feelings. Unfortunately, the relief is followed by the realization that working somewhere else, even working with Elton, would do him no good. His problem was not his job. His problem was himself.

The commotion outside of Paul's office couldn't help but get his attention. Leah was yelling again, and Alan was perched beside the door looking like he might have to make a break for it at any moment. Marty Brody entered through the front door, and Leah said, "Come on Alan and Jody. And you too, Paul. You can't hide in your office this time. We're going to have it out with Mr. Mark Charles, today. And we just might be suing him and you too in the morning."

With that Leah walked into Mark's office without knocking. She was timidly followed by Paul, Alan, Jody, and Marty. Wanda meekly protested, but then, on Mark's signal, came in behind the others and closed the door. Mark had spread the firm's financial statements for the last four years (see Exhibits 1 and 2) out on his desk for Marty to see. The debate was interesting, to say the least. Marty was no match for the fast-talking Mark. Being both an attorney and an MBA, Mark knew both what he had to do and what he could not do in the process of achieving his goal to be CEO and controlling stockholder in a thriving, high-tech firm. He opened his books to Marty, explaining in his southern gentleman, "we're friends, you can trust me" fashion how he was the only one other than Paul willing to take a risk. He was borrowing money from the firm because he did not draw a $40,000 salary like the rest insisted on doing. He was the one who made the contacts and got the purchase orders. He was the only one both willing and financially able to sign for loans at the bank. And if he did not spend the grant money for current expenditures then the firm would not have any lights on in the office, and the scientists would have to do their research in the dark.

When Mark finished, he had Marty either convinced or confused; it was hard to tell. Marty's lack of business law experience had been expertly exploited by Mark without a hint of disrespect. Marty said to Leah, "Let's go."

When they got back to Leah's office, Marty said. "I'll have to look into this further, but it appears that things are in order from a legal perspective. Mark may want controlling interest in this company, and he may get it the way things look. But he's done it legally. Face it. Ya'll allowed him to do all the legal work in setting up the company. The agreement ya'll made with the outside investors—*his* friends—making them voting board members and allowing anyone who wished to pay them $150,000 to obtain their voting stock certainly favored Mark. He now owns 26 percent thanks to the recent deal he made with Paul, he may have the potential to buy another 25 percent, and I don't think there's anything you can do about it." With that, Marty got up and left the office.

Leah, Jody, and Alan sat there, dejected. Jody, who was approaching 65, commented that she was tired and ready to retire. Her husband was a successful photographer, and they did not need the money or the hassles. Alan, in his usual paranoid manner, mumbled something about not wanting to die in jail. Then they both got up and left Leah's office. All three went home shortly after. It was only

Exhibit 1
BIOTECH: CONSOLIDATED INCOME STATEMENTS

	1983	1984	1985	1986
Net sales	$ 26,157	$ 50,647	$192,829	$453,435
Less cost of goods sold	3,786	2,871	137,951	87,223
Gross profit	22,371	47,776	54,878	366,212
Less operating expenses	7,991	30,417	79,705	349,389
Income (or loss) before taxes	14,380	17,359	(24,827)	16,823
Less income taxes	2,400	2,000	(2,800)	4,000
NET INCOME (OR LOSS)	$ 11,980	$ 15,359	$(22,027)	$ 12,823

Exhibit 2
BIOTECH: CONSOLIDATED BALANCE SHEETS

	1983	1984	1985	1986
ASSETS				
Current Assets				
Cash	$ 2,113	$ 39,428	$ 8,836	$ 3,625
Accounts receivable	1,953	11,062	36,931	86,769
Inventories	9,327	15,743	73,284	118,773
Lab supplies	—	5,951	5,490	—
Prepaid expenses	—	265	704	704
Refundable income taxes	—	—	3,800	687
Deferred interest	—	—	—	8,963
Total Current Assets	$ 13,393	$ 72,449	$129,045	$219,521
Furniture and equipment	$ 4,874	$ 22,551	$ 64,953	$166,415
Less accumulated depreciation	547	1,812	8,170	12,130
Total Furniture and Equipment	4,327	20,739	56,783	154,286
Other Assets	287	306	150	150
TOTAL ASSETS	$ 18,007	$ 93,494	$185,978	$373,957
LIABILITIES AND STOCKHOLDERS' EQUITY				
Current Liabilities				
Accounts payable	$ 224	$ 9,930	$ 57,078	$123,332
Taxes payable	2,400	2,445	4,883	13,402
Notes payable	—	—	17,500	94,645
Current portion of long-term debt and capital lease obligation	—	480	2,362	—
Deposits on undelivered sales	—	—	45,201	45,855
Total Current Liabilities	$ 2,624	$ 12,855	$127,024	$277,234

	1983	1984	1985	1986
Long-Term Debt				
Lease obligation	$ —	$ 1,217	$ 1,959	$ —
Deferred income taxes	—	400	—	—
Notes payable	—	—	—	22,904
Total Long-Term Debt	—	1,617	1,959	22,904
Stockholders' Equity				
Common stock, $1 par value, 100,000 shares authorized, 800 shares issued and out-standing	$ 800	$ 800	$ 800	$ 800
Paid-in capital	2,883	50,883	50,883	50,883
Retained earnings	11,700	27,339	5,312	22,136
Total Stockholders' Equity	15,383	79,022	56,995	73,819
TOTAL LIABILITIES AND STOCKHOLDERS' EQUITY	$18,007	$ 93,494	$185,978	$373,957

3:30 P.M., but they felt like they had put in a sixteen-hour day.

Paul went back to his office after the meeting with the attorney. He stayed and worked until 5:30 P.M. He got a phone call from the Department of Defense informing him that Biological Engineering had been selected to participate in the research for a new biological warfare test kit. The exact amount of the grant going to Biological Engineering would not be known for a while, but they would definitely participate in the project. This was the kind of break the firm needed. To this point they had concentrated on producing small quantities (milliliters) of high-quality antibodies used in scientific research. Though they had been successful in this market, it simply was too limited. The industry was rapidly moving toward products such as test kits for pregnancy, cancer, drug use, and so on, which were expected to have broad consumer appeal in the near future. If the firm succeeded in developing the kit or some critical part of the kit for the Department of Defense, then the firm would have its first chance to develop a product with a broad, consumer market potential.

Paul's depression about the day began to wane. He became excited at the thought of succeeding in developing the kit for the DOD. What entrepreneur does not dream of the big break that propels his small, struggling firm into a large, dynamic enterprise? Besides, it was Friday afternoon. That meant two days to escape the negative feelings that went

with the work at Biological Engineering these days. Yes, it was Friday afternoon. Party time!

PART D: WEIRD'S WILD WEEKEND

Cheri came by Paul's at 6:30 P.M. with the cocaine she got from Ricky Fourcade. They immediately did two lines each, and then Paul went to work on the oysters bienville he was preparing for dinner before they went to Wally's. Being a gourmet cook was one of Paul's many talents, and he loved to show off his culinary skills. As he went through stages of preparing the oysters, opening, washing, making the cheese sauce and baking, he was rewarded by Cheri with a line of cocaine at each stage. As usual, by the time the oysters were done, Paul and Cheri no longer had a appetite for anything but cocaine. They picked at the oysters while they finished off their first gram of coke. Then they got in Paul's car and drove the thirty minutes across town to Wally's. On the way they had another boost. When they got to Wally's their minds were racing faster than their mouths could get the words out. They felt like they were ready to conquer the world. "This stuff we got from Ricky is dynamite. We're really cookin'," said Cheri, as they entered Wally's condo.

"Hey Paul and Cheri, where have you been?" Wally yelled from across the noisy room. "The ecstasy is already gone. There wasn't much to begin with. But don't worry. We've got enough snow to last for two or three days. Beer and wine are in the cooler in the kitchen. Help yourself. Watch out if you go in the bedroom. Christine's in there, and she's really mad. All I did was to give her hit of ecstasy to Big Leroy when he showed up unexpectedly with Ricky Fourcade. I told her that I had to take care of my friends. But, as usual, she didn't see the humor in it. She hit me with her high heel shoe and ran into the bedroom. Rumor has it that she's in there snorting her brains out, crying, and threatening anybody who comes in with bodily harm."

"You're as crazy as always, Weird." Paul remarked. "Pass me that mirror and razor blade next to you, and I'll cut some coke to get this party rolling." With that, Paul cut out at least two grams of cocaine, arranged it in about twenty even lines, snorted one line into each nostril, and passed the mirror around the room. The weekend was off and running, and it obviously was not going to stop until all the coke was gone.

He got home Sunday afternoon. Cheri had wanted to go get Max and come back to Paul's to spend the night, but Paul had vetoed the idea. He wanted to be alone for a few hours before he had to start another week. He turned on the television and began watching a Houston Astros baseball game. He fell asleep in front of the tube for about an hour—probably the first real sleep he had since Thursday. When he woke up, he was in a cold sweat. His mind was racing. He was depressed. His guilt about the weekend came to the surface with a vengeance. He was on the verge of his big break in his business career, and he had celebrated by needlessly spending $1,500 on cocaine and snorting himself into the next century. As he stared at the television, he suddenly realized that he had reached his limit of endurance. He was up against the wall, and he did not know where to turn. He knew he needed help, but from whom? He did not have the money to commit himself to a treatment program. He was sure that would mean losing the business to Mark. His friends, the ones he could talk to, the ones who could help him, had been blown off along the cocaine trail. Now he was not even sure they wanted to see him, much less help him. His depression became despair and loneliness. He put his face in his hands and began to cry.

EPILOGUE

Approximately one year after most of the events in this case occurred, Dr. Paul Breaux finally sought help for his problems. He did so by calling his brother, who lives in Florida. His brother, a born-again Christian, came to New Orleans and took Paul to a Christian retreat in the Ozark Mountains. There Paul spent several days without cocaine, contemplating and reflecting on both his past and his future. He seemed to be positively affected by the experience, and he seems to be serious about quitting cocaine, although it is impossible to tell at this point whether Paul will be able to conquer his problem without professional help.

Biological Engineering Services is still in existence. It is still a small supplier of biomedical products, and the test kit for the DOD is still in the research and development stage. The conflicts among the principals have gone largely unresolved, and the result has been an almost complete suspension of communication between Mark and the other principals.

"Y" OR "Y" NOT?

S. LEE OWENS
Tennessee Technological University

MICHAEL L. MENEFEE
Pembroke State University

INTRODUCTION

Mr. Mike Wall was shocked when he read the Sunday *Lawson Dispatch*, the local newspaper of Lawson, Georgia. He turned to his wife and said, "This will probably destroy our business." His wife, Tina, looked up and said, "What will destroy our business?" Dr. Wall handed her the newspaper and said, "Here, read it for yourself." As Tina read the front-page story of the proposed new greatly expanded YMCA, her face turned pale and she said, "Oh! My goodness!" As she read on she said, "This will probably not only destroy our business but will probably destroy every health club in Lawson."

THE PROPOSAL

According to the *Lawson Dispatch*, the YMCA was making a grand proposal for Lawson. The YMCA had been in Lawson for some ten years. They did not have their own facilities, but instead, borrowed or rented space from the city, county, or private business firms. Now the YMCA was proposing to start a fund drive to build a very modern, beautiful, expanded $2,100,000 YMCA to serve Lawson, a city of some 22,000 people.

The proposed YMCA, according to the *Lawson Dispatch*, is to be completed within two years and is to meet most fitness needs. For example, the new YMCA is to include a full-size gym with equipment and bleachers, a heated indoor 75-foot swimming pool with six lanes, five multi-purpose rooms, a fully equipped Nautilus room, fully equipped fitness-gymnastics room, an aerobic room, two (a men's and a women's) fully equipped fitness centers, two racquetball courts, two steam rooms, two saunas, two whirlpools, an indoor jogging track, four shower rooms, four locker rooms, a furnished meetings-craft-cultural room, and various offices. According to the picture in the *Dispatch*, the facility is to be ultra modern and very beautiful.

COMPETITORS

Several businesses in Lawson feel that they would be in direct competition with the new YMCA. The major competitors are the health clubs, karate clubs, and day-care centers. Others that feel threatened are aerobic centers, diet centers, and gymnastic classes.

The businesses that seem to feel most threatened by the new YMCA are the health clubs and day-care centers. There are four health clubs, one karate studio, and several day-care centers in Lawson. The health clubs are

1. Ladies Long Life Fitness Center, 6,000 square feet, in business sixteen years, and owned by Dr. Mike Wall (a professor at a local university) and Tina Wall
2. Racquetball Fitness Center, 13,000 square feet, in business seven years, owned by John and Tom Howell
3. Lawson Health Club, 4,000 square feet, in business 6 months, owned by Lisa Waters and Bill Waters (also a professor at a local university)

This case, written specifically for this book, is printed by permission.

4. Muscle Shoppe, 6,000 square feet, in business four years, owned by Ed Flowers.
5. The Lawson Karate Club has 8,400 square feet and is said to be the most modern in the south. It has been in business for ten years and is owned by Debra and Will House.

SAME

When the story of the new $2,100,000 YMCA was published, some changes occurred in the Lawson health club industry. Historically there had been a certain degree of animosity between the health club type facilities in Lawson. Almost overnight this animosity vanished.

Almost immediately, the Lawson health clubs and those business units that felt threatened by the new YMCA started forming a unified front against this new threat. During the next few days, after the *Lawson Dispatch* story, threatened business owners were almost constantly on the phone with each other, discussing the pros and cons of the proposed new YMCA. Gone was the animosity—now they discussed in great detail the unfairness they perceived in the situation and raised again and again the question of what could be done about it. One thing they did was to form a local chapter of the Southeast Association for Marketing Equality (SAME).

In the Lawson area, SAME had one immediate overriding objective, which was to try to find ways to have the new YMCA compete by the same competitive rules that apply to the members of SAME.

YMCA ARGUMENTS

Mr. Bill Stone, YMCA director, was delighted when he read the Sunday *Lawson Dispatch*. Finally the fund-raising drive that would take the YMCA out of an old run-down building in a public housing project was under way. For ten years the YMCA had been in rented buildings in various undesirable locations, and now many local citizens had banded together to find the YMCA a new permanent home. Bill could just see the new YMCA building providing the community with recreational and other Christian activities. Mary Stone, his wife, shared his delight. It was like a dream come true for both of them.

Later Bill Stone had learned through several sources in the community that the new YMCA was being opposed by a group of business people in the fitness and day-care fields. This group, called SAME, could hurt the fund-raising efforts of the YMCA as a similar group in the northwest had done in the past.

The Lawson YMCA argued that they compete fairly. The YMCA's major arguments were as follows:

1. The YMCA was in the health fitness business first. The YMCA was first organized in 1854. The modern commercial health clubs did not come along until the early 1970s.
2. The YMCA has been in Lawson for ten years. Why are SAME members waiting until now to complain about unfair competition? Why did they not complain ten years ago, when the YMCA first came to Lawson?
3. The YMCA serves mainly the youth, the needy, and the handicapped. About 70 percent to 90 percent of the YMCA services go to these groups of people.
4. The YMCA will not compete with local businesses. The YMCA will draw its members from a different clientele than will local businesses. Adult members who join the YMCA normally would not join a commercial health club. They feel that the YMCA meets best their needs. In addition, as mentioned above, the YMCA serves mainly the youth, the needy, and the handicapped. Normally, commercial health clubs do not serve these groups.
5. The YMCA will not compete with commercial day-care centers. Instead, the YMCA will serve the low-income population and those that cannot afford to pay commercial rates.
6. The YMCA, instead of competing with commercial health clubs, will be a feeder unit for commercial health clubs. For example, children who learn to play racquetball at the YMCA would, as adults, want to join a more specialized commercial racquetball club where the expertise is greater.
7. The argument that commercial health clubs cannot compete with the YMCA is not valid. In other cities commercial health clubs compete with YMCAs. Why can they not do so in Lawson?
8. The YMCA will complement existing facilities for youth. The county recreation programs do

not reach all youth or provide for all youth activities. The only other nonprofit organization with extensive facilities for youth activities is a large local church, which primarily serves only its congregation. The YMCA program currently fills the void created by these limited programs. Neither the church nor the county have complained about the YMCA activities.

9. SAME members do not provide any recreational activities such as baseball, basketball, gymnastics, or swimming for youth. SAME members currently only provide day care and karate for youth.

10. The YMCA provides most of its youth and adult programs for less than $30 and no youngster is turned away for inability to pay. Many of the workers donate their time to the YMCA as coaches, helpers, referees, and observers.

SAME ARGUMENTS

The members of SAME believe very strongly that society permits the YMCA to compete by a different set of rules than its competitors. SAME believes that this gives the YMCA a very strong advantage over competitors, which in many cases may be a disaster for those competitors of the YMCA. In defense of this position, SAME presents the following arguments:

1. SAME believes the new $2,100,000 YMCA will not be a traditional YMCA that serves mainly the youth, the needy, the handicapped, and the low-income population, but instead, will be a full-blown commercial fitness center catering mainly to the well to do and those able and willing to pay. SAME believes that this new commercial YMCA will seek to serve the same clientele (the same market) served by local mom and pop free enterprise health clubs and day-care centers. If this is true, then the new commercial YMCA will compete head-on with local free enterprise health clubs and day-care centers.

2. The new commercial YMCA will pay little or no taxes, while the small businesses often pay between 20 percent and 40 percent or more to four different taxing units (governments). This should enable the YMCA to underprice competitors by 10 to 20 percent or more.

3. The YMCA receives gifts of money, land, and so on. SAME members (businesses) do not.

These donations should enable the new YMCA to underprice their competitors by about 4 to 10 percent.

4. Often the YMCA saves on interest cost. Mom and pop units must pay their own way and not solicit donations of land, money, and so on. The YMCA not only receives donations, but in Lawson it has hired out-of-town professional fund raisers to help them receive gifts of perhaps as much as $2,100,000. Since it will not have to borrow this money, as would its competitors, this should enable it to underprice their competitors by about 4 to 6 percent.

5. The YMCA receives lots of free advertising through news releases. The YMCA's competitors receive little or no free advertising; they must pay for their advertising. This should enable the YMCA to underprice competitors by about 2 to 4 percent.

6. The YMCA receives lots of free labor. Recently the YMCA, according to the local newspaper, had some 200 Lawson fund raisers out soliciting donations. The YMCA's competitors had none.

7. SAME believes Lawson may not need a new commercial YMCA. According to a survey by SAME, Lawson already has ten gyms, nine outdoor basketball courts, twenty-two baseball and softball fields, eight swimming pools, twenty-two tennis courts, four health clubs, one karate studio, several aerobic centers, several gymnastic classes, and numerous day-care centers. These facilities are almost never fully utilized and often stand unused. In addition to this, Lawson city has an impressive city recreation department. This department has a city-wide youth recreation program.

8. SAME believes that the YMCA has changed its focus. SAME believes that at one time the YMCA focused on and served mainly the needy and the low income but does not do so any more. The new YMCAs seem to be seeking to serve the well to do and those able to pay. For example, Frank Eisenzimmer reported in *The Oregonian* (February 19, 1987, page 18) that the Multnomah County tax assessor, after six months of study, discovered that the average YMCA (there were four in Portland, Oregon) spent only 14 percent of its budget on scholarships; one spent only 2.6 percent. The highest proportion, according to tax assessor Robert Sheffield, was 32 percent, still insufficient in

Sheffield's opinion to warrant a property tax exemption. This suggests that serving the needy is no longer a major focus of the YMCA.

9. The YMCA may give little or none to charity. Many, perhaps most or even all, YMCAs serve the needy through scholarships. The YMCA often recruits an outside private enterprise company or individual to pay for these scholarships. In such cases the YMCA has really donated nothing; instead, they have been paid to serve. The party paying for the scholarship did the giving.

10. The YMCA acts like a business, not a charity. It prices its services like a business. It advertises like a business. It invests like a commercial business. SAME strongly believes the new YMCAs are much more business than charity organizations.

11. Frank Eisenzimmer argues "If they (YMCA) are truly interested in serving the community as a charity, why aren't they willing to pay taxes which go towards serving the public?"[1]

SAME claims that members are not against the traditional YMCA: one that caters to the needy and low income. However, they do protest against the new commercial type YMCA that competes with private enterprise firms.

Southeastern Association for Marketing Equality argues that society has given the new YMCAs so many marketing advantages that it is extremely difficult to compete against them. SAME argues that because of these advantages, the new YMCAs can underprice private enterprise by 20 to 40 percent and that this amounts to unfair competition. SAME argues that all competitors should be able to compete by the same rules.

---

1. IRSA Club Business, February 1986, 82.

OTHER CONSIDERATIONS

Unfair competition, if it is unfair competition, may be a larger problem than just the perceived unfair competition from the YMCA. Nonprofits now generate some $300 billion in annual revenues.[2] *Newsweek* reports that the fastest growing segment of the U.S. economy is the nonprofit sector, which now represents 8 percent of the U.S. GNP.[3] The *Wall Street Journal* reports "Many small business firms find their biggest rivals are often nonprofit."[4]

As Dr. Mike Wall leaned back in his favorite chair, he wondered how to handle the YMCA situation. He knew that many important people in the community supported the YMCA, including the associate dean of his college, who was named as one of the division chairs for the fund raising effort. He knew that it would be difficult to find the right course of action in view of his business, his university job, and his Christian principles.

Bill Stone stared coldly at the bare wall of his current office wondering how anyone could oppose the YMCA. He felt that he was doing the right thing by trying to get a new YMCA for Lawson, but he really did not want to anger the business community or compete against them. He was now in the position of trying to do something about the opposition coming from SAME. To make matters worse for Bill, he was relatively new to Lawson, having been in town for less than three years. His job with the Lawson YMCA and his reputation were squarely on the line.

---

2. *Forbes*, March 23, 1987, 106.
3. *Newsweek*, January 5, 1987, 38.
4. *Wall Street Journal*, June 9, 1986, 23.

NITTANY OUTDOOR PRODUCTS

DAVID N. ALLEN
Pennsylvania State University

EUGENE J. BAZAN
Pennsylvania State University

PHASE ONE: CONCEPT INITIATION

"Well, mate, how are we going to make a lot of money together?" That was it, an invitation to work with Frank on a concept related to his new business. Dave thought that the offer was just the opportunity for which he was waiting. Frank had taken the plunge; his emigration from Australia to set up a business in the United States was clear evidence of his commitment. Frank was trained as a nuclear engineer, but left that field because it provided little independent business opportunity. In Australia he had worked with PVC plastics on various products, substituting the plastic for metal. Wheelchairs were the first focus of his efforts. His firm was in the embryonic stages, and he was looking for support from a few entrepreneurially oriented friends. Dave was on his way to Australia for work and summer vacation and used the two months away to think over a few product ideas.

By the time Dave returned from Australia, Frank had set up his new firm in a local business incubator. Dave, a professor, was teaching a new undergraduate honors course that fall semester, entrepreneurship. As part of the course he had requested students to divide up into teams of two and work with a local entrepreneurer. When class began he offered students the opportunity to work with Frank as one of the projects. Two of the twelve students latched onto the opportunity.

Dave had done a bit more thinking to sort out his interests. He approached Gene, his friend and business partner. Over the previous year Gene and Dave had built a growing business consulting practice. Gene's primary source of income was the consulting practice. They both wanted some hands-on new venture experience to ground them in the world of entrepreneurship. They agreed to take a small portion of the earnings from their consulting business to finance the new firm. They also thought that it would be wise to pursue the business independent of Frank's firm.

Product Development

Gene and Dave are outdoors oriented people, avid bikers and gardeners. Both had yearly gardens and often complained about the knee- and back-breaking work of planting, thinning, and, the worst of all, weeding. Two products in gardening catalogs had caught their eyes. Both products had rubber wheels, were made of metal, and seemed expensive. One, a kind of wheelbarrow carryall cart, was on the market for many years. Many manufacturers produced it, and prices varied from a high of $180 to a low of $80.

The second, a seat mounted on wheels, was a product that appeared to be sold by one retailer and cost about $80. They bought one to examine it. They field tested the product in Dave's garden and found it could be improved, but with a new design. They thought it was too high off the ground, creating instability and back strain; too heavy; and prone to rust.

They took the product to Frank for his assessment and commissioned him to redesign it according to some agreed-upon notions. Frank completed

This case, written specifically for this text, is printed by permission.

the first prototype in about a week, and Dave garden tested it. The design had promise, but it was too boxy, uncomfortable, and expensive. However, it was lighter, stable, sturdy, rustproof, and easier on the back and lower legs than the competitor.

A second prototype was commissioned based on a revised two-piece design. The product's name just popped out at them—the Garden Backsaver. Frank sounded very excited when he called Dave to tell him that it was completed. The design was more continuous and actually had a polished kind of high-tech look to it. The redesigned seat was much more comfortable and even adjustable. The simplified product was less expensive, considerably less than the major competitor's (see Exhibit 1 for a cost breakdown). Upon trying it out, a second seating position became apparent, an unexpected pleasant surprise. Frank made a second smaller version of the prototype. Now, the two fundamental questions of getting their new product off the ground popped into the foreground. Would it grab someone else's attention? Would others find it useful enough to buy?

Preliminary Market Research

During the early fall, while the product was being designed, the two undergraduate students conducted preliminary market research. For the first month they were at a loss because the product was not available and it was difficult to conceptualize it from the image in Dave's, Gene's, and Frank's minds. Nonetheless, they began to examine the strengths and weaknesses of a new firm, at that time tentatively called Appalachian Outdoor Products. In their first milestone report to the class the students were somewhat critical of Dave's and Gene's lack of startup experience. They also questioned the principals' commitment given Gene'e full-time consulting, Dave's professorship and part-time consulting, and their numerous other activities. They wondered about capitalization; neither principal wanted to put much capital into the venture. However, progress was being made and the necessary capital was available. Dave and Gene agreed to keep costs low by doing much of the work themselves, but they realized that $2,000 to $3,000 would need to be spent before they had a clear sense of their product and firm.

Initial marketing ideas centered on catalog and magazine sales. Gardening catalogs were collected and perused for competitive products and product

Exhibit 1
COST BREAKDOWN FOR GARDEN BACKSAVER

MATERIAL TO PURCHASE

Item	Number per Unit	Cost per Unit
PVC tube 1–1/4″ sch 40 AS	8.00 ft.	$2.00
Solvent cement clear for PVC	0.001 gal.	0.10
Acetone priming fluid (clear)	0.001 gal.	0.10
Clips	8	0.80
Butt fittings white, smooth	2	1.20
Mesh	0.25 lin yds.	0.72
Toilet tissue or rag	0.01 rolls	0.05
Armor-All protectant	0.05 ml.	0.02
Label and cover	1	0.10
Cardboard carton: 12–1/2″ × 12–1/2″ × 18″	1	1.00
Packing tape	3 ft.	0.10
Cartage	(various above items)	0.30
Total		$6,49

COSTING

Total time: 45 minutes
(0.75 hours)

Component	Amount
Materials	$ 6.49
Manufacturing cost ($6.00/hr)	4.50
Overheads (25%)	2.74
Total	$13.73

Development (including first model)	$80.00

Production

Quantity	Price (FOB State College)
1	$24.00
5	22.50
10	20.50
100	17.50
1,000	13.50

compatibility. Gardening magazines were examined for the same purpose. The students discovered that about 50 percent of American households have flower or vegetable gardens. Gallup polls indicated that vegetable gardening had appreciably increased during the recession years of the early 1980s, and although the rate of growth decreased, Americans were increasingly involved in gardening.

In late October, Dave called his brother Wayne to discuss the venture. Wayne was a successful entrepreneur. Three years earlier he had started a textile company that bought kitchen and bath goods from manufacturers and repackaged them in product lines, to sell primarily to supermarkets. Wayne's national network of brokers also sold to discount chains, among other low-cost retailers. Many discount chains have lawn and garden departments. Wayne offered to review the product and introduce the team to a broker who might be interested in representing the product. Wayne also informed them that time was running out for a spring product launch. National retailers had already placed spring orders and they would be very reluctant to try an untested product distributed by a new firm.

In mid-November, Gene and Dave made a strategic decision to refocus their marketing direction. The opportunity that Wayne presented with his national contacts was appealing, so much so that they virtually dropped the catalog and magazine approach. Little transpired along that front in October, other than students examining the circulation patterns of a few gardening magazines. By late November Dave and Gene realized that the spring launch window had closed.

Dropping the catalog and magazine approach, however, solved an important marketing risk exposure—copycat products. They believed that pursuing a patent would be expensive and probably not work to protect the product. If the product attained national exposure, it would be a short time before cheaper, offshore lookalikes would appear.

To refocus their marketing strategy, they turned back to their original objectives: gain experience with a startup opportunity with a modest, shoestring budget. Given that they were most interested in a national launch with a large volume discount chain, they asked Wayne about the kind of data buyers needed to make a purchase decision. Wayne talked in terms of margin per square foot, monthly turnover, volume discounting, and other information much more specific than Dave and Gene's current estimate of product and firm capabilities. The decision was made to conduct a controlled product test in the spring to compile the necessary market information.

Getting Feedback from Friends

The first step in the new market strategy was to gauge consumer feedback on the design and a feasible purchase price. They devised a product test protocol for the two sizes of the Backsaver. By mid-December Dave, Gene, and the two students interviewed fifty-four friends, neighbors, students, and office workers. Findings from this exercise provided new insights into the product and market.

- No correlation existed between an individual's comfort and the size of the Backsaver.
- No correlation existed between comfort and height of use; heavy people found it difficult to use the product.
- Individuals liked the comfort and versatility of the product—they were evenly split among the three ways to sit on the product.
- Nearly everyone who gardened was interested in purchasing the product if it were available at a reasonable price.
- Forty percent of the people interested in the product said that they would pay between $20 and $25 for it, an equal percentage responded favorably to the $15 to $20 range, and 20 percent selected under $15 as their purchase price.
- Individuals had many ideas on other uses for the product—most focused on common household chores and sitting outside during recreational events.

PHASE TWO: MARKET TEST

The Women of the Garden Club

The evening of January 7 was a critical milestone for the new firm. Gene arranged to make a presentation of the Mark 2 and 3 prototypes at a local garden club. They felt prepared because they had already tested it among friends and colleagues; but they were also nervous—this was their first crowd of complete strangers.

The women of the garden club received them graciously, listened intently, tried out the Backsaver, and gave very useful feedback. Gene and Dave picked up several key points about their product and customer response, which were to shape their marketing program in the coming months.

First, the women were not willing to pay more than $10 for the product (though they would pay more for the larger size). As Dave and Gene were to find out, there are two kinds of gardeners: those who garden primarily to grow food and reduce their food budget, and those "hobbyist gardeners" for whom gardening is a form of discretionary spending. These gardeners definitely belonged to the first category. Those with back and knee problems, arthritis, and other infirmities improvised with cardboard, old cushions, knee pads and other devices. Unless the product could sell at a low price, they would not be able to market it to the food-producing gardener.

Second, the less athletic, less supple, often heavier, older women had some difficulty using the Backsaver, especially getting down into it, as it sits low to the ground. But once they were there, they found it extremely comfortable. It was during a demonstration that one woman figured out a way, by turning the Backsaver on its end, of using it as a support to help her get up—a feature subsequently incorporated in sales demonstrations. Dave and Gene subsequently produced the Mark 3 prototype, which was midway between the two earlier sizes and a bit more stable.

Third, the group had several suggestions for improving it ("make it adjustable," "add a pouch for tools"), marketing it (the *Victory Garden* television show and gardening magazines), and selling it ("include a pamphlet showing the various positions"). They also suggested other uses (camp stool, foot rest).

Visiting the First Buyer

After the test at the local garden club, Gene and Dave resolved to show the Backsaver to local garden supply centers. The next morning they lined up their first presentation, to take place the following week. They had done some preliminary market research, and figured out roughly how the industry was structured. The typical garden supply store was owner-operated, but a fair number were independently owned chains of two to five stores. Later on, they found out that a very small number of these chains were quite large; a recently formed one already had over 200 outlets.

The larger stores—department-type stores (the garden section in a K-Mart) and large independents—did their buying in the fall; for these, the product was too late. This left Dave and Gene with the locally based independents. These were usually smaller stores, but they were to find out that some of these were quite large.

Gene and Dave put on their suits for the first presentation and drove out to the buyer's office on a chilly January afternoon. It was a bust, but they learned two important things. First, there were garden stores and there were garden stores. The critical criterion in determining interest was whether or not the store carried seeds. In the trade directories, many of the stores claimed to have a garden section, but that descriptor was too broad. In subsequent marketing inquiries—phone calls, cold calls, and random store visits ("Hey Dave, there's a garden store, let's stop in and check it out!"), they used the question, "Do you carry seeds?" as a litmus test for potential suitability. Second, while food producing gardeners were prepared to pay up to $13.95 for the Backsaver, the retailers needed to sell it for $24.95. Experimenting with this discrepancy was to become an important part of the market test.

The First Sale

On the way back from our first presentation, quiet and reflective, they passed a fancy-looking garden center. One of them said, "Nah, too upscale—they'll never go for it." Luckily, the other was driving, and swung his truck into the parking lot. Luckily, the owner was in. He ordered two. They were ecstatic.

Now, they were really up against it. They had no inventory. No promotional material. No display concept. No procedure for boxing or shipping the product. Not even a label for the product (they needed one that would stay stuck to the smooth plastic). It took them a month to pull all that together, and it was only then that they actually filled that first order.

That first sale was a catalytic motivator. Creative juices seemed to flow continuously. The producer, Frank's firm, played a critical role in helping them overcome one obstacle after another. Little things like designing a professional-looking fastener to hold the display placard to the back legs of the Backsaver (a cleverly designed clip) proved very time consuming. Frank also helped on some big things, too—supplying them with shipping boxes one at a time, avoiding having to buy 500 at a crack.

By holding fast to their shoestring philosophy, Dave and Gene saved themselves more than once from spending money foolishly on things where their enthusiasm was bigger than reality. Ultimately, they did not need more than thirteen shipping boxes.

Shoestring did not mean substituting low for high quality. Shoestring meant thinking things through clearly and getting professional help at those precise points where it is needed. For example, they used an attorney to review the warning label after they had roughed it out. They also used a graphics firm to lay out the promotional materials after they had figured out the text and designed the rough draft. They used a high quality camera in a professional greenhouse and an attractive model for promotional photos.

Shoestring also meant crossing bridges only when they got to them—not letting too much planning freeze their ability to take action and get some market feedback. Gene and Dave had too many options at almost every point and had continually to weed many out. A scarce resource in addition to money was time. They could not afford to review every opportunity, follow up on every option, develop each idea. But once they made a decision, they moved quickly to implement it and get feedback. They discovered that putting a product in the buyer's hands forced a kind of honesty that showed up their flights of fancy for what they often were.

The Final Test-Marketing Plan
The second sale came fully six weeks after their first sale. By that time, Dave and Gene had figured out the final test-marketing plan. (Put *final* in quotes, because a test can never be final.) There were numerous other factors that they did not, and could not, anticipate, which demanded mid-course corrections. Consequently, the market test was not clean, from a scientific point of view, but they ended up with a much better sense of the market in the time they had available than they would have, had they stuck to their original test.

Their overall objective was to find out enough about the market for their product that they would be able to convince a large buyer in the fall that it was a product worth considering. They felt that the answers to two questions would be critical in making this case: (1) was the product price sensitive? and (2) in what kind of communities—rural or urban—does the product move best? They reasoned that the food-producing gardener would be found in more rural places, and the discretionary gardener would be found in more urban places. Arraying these two dimensions in a matrix gave them the

framework in Exhibit 2, to which they assigned target market areas.

Gene and Dave limited themselves to firms within their geographic area. First, they wanted to work with a small number of buyers within a reasonable driving distance. Second, they were concerned with overexposure—of having someone else steal their idea.

Their goal was to place the product in five stores in each of four markets in Exhibit 2 (a total of twenty stores) and to sell twenty per store. They realized that they would have to convince buyers to price at their test price levels, and felt they could achieve this by selling to the buyers at a cost that gave the buyers the standard markup.

Exhibit 2
TEST-MARKETING STRATEGY

AREA	SELLING PRICE	
	Low ($19.95)	High ($24.95)
Rural	Huntingdon State College Total sales: 12	State College Altoona Lewistown Total sales: 9
Urban	Exton Devon Harrisburg Mechanicsburg Total sales: 62	Feasterville Total sales: 4

In the end, they placed the product in ten stores, and sold a total of eighty-seven. They ended up having to negotiate the test prices as well. Further, they could not get a balanced loading in each of the four market test areas, but that in and of itself was an important finding.

The Garden Backsaver moved best in the super-large garden supply center in middle-class suburban areas at $19.95. In upper-class areas, homeowners hire out their lawn care and gardening to private firms; consequently, they have no need to buy specialty equipment. In rural areas, where people garden to save on their food budget, the Backsaver did not move well, if at all. Dave and Gene do not have conclusive evidence on this. It might move at $10.95, but the cost of carrying out that test for them was substantial: each Backsaver cost them $20. They were losing on every one they sold, and this brings up a most important point that they had to recall frequently to each other: They were not selling but engaging in test marketing.

PHASE THREE: THE FUTURE

To continue or not to continue . . . that is the question. Do Gene and Dave have a product out of which they (or someone else if not them) can make a business? Where do they go from here?

Acceptability of the Product
Buyers like the product. It has a rugged, yet modern and high-quality look and heft to it. The Backsaver is an easy demo and sale. Dave and Gene have closed all their sales in a matter of minutes, a number of them being cold calls. Buyers liked the self-contained promotional poster, and its limited floor or shelf-space requirements. One store hung several on a pegboard wall surface for great visibility. In the bigger stores, buyers already had a product that purported to do the same thing, but the Backsaver was clearly superior and gave their customers a choice. Additionally, the bigger stores wanted to have a variety of items to attract customers inside. Finally, the investment was small and the markup good—it was worth taking a chance on a new product. Buyers, Gene and Dave found, liked new products.

Acceptability must be assessed for more than the buyer. How many did the stores actually sell? What did the store's customer think of the product in use? These are two critical questions for which Dave and Gene have only rough, indirect answers. They estimate, based on reorders, that stores may have sold in aggregate forty to fifty Backsavers.

Regarding comments on the product itself, Gene and Dave have only anecdotal customer responses from individuals they knew. Two drawbacks are worth mentioning. First, because of the rounded corners on the bottom, the Backsaver rocks a bit in use. Some individuals find this unsettling in that they imagine they could fall off it (all of 10 inches to the ground). In their earlier prototypes, Frank gave

the corners as sharp a radius as he could without dimpling the PVC tubing.

Second, one of the three positions allows the user to sit astride of the Backsaver with his or her legs from the knees down lying on the ground. For some, this is a particularly comfortable position for certain kinds of work (putting in seedlings, intensive weeding around a plant). In this position, however, one's knees (or jeans) are in contact with the soil from the garden, which is regarded as a drawback. The two other positions do not involve this kind of contact with soil.

Cost and Financial Data
In their current vision, Dave and Gene see Nittany Outdoor Products as a marketing firm. They would contract out production. For the limited test market needs, they used Frank, because he is locally-based, to prototype and produce the Backsaver. The costs of production were given in Exhibit 1. Exhibit 1 also shows the discount structure Frank offered them.

Even Frank's lowest possible cost—$13.50—is roughly what Gene and Dave would have to charge buyers so that the buyers could retail it for $19.95 and still make their markup. In short, Dave and Gene would reach breakeven but only on their production costs. While they would capture the high end of the market, they would need to produce the Backsaver at roughly half their current lowest possible cost to hit the larger low end of the market suggested by the women from the garden club, $10.00. A buyer for a large garden chain who had worked earlier for a discount department store confirmed this price. "Your Backsaver," he said, "is a $9.95 item."

Alternative Strategies
Dave and Gene's total investment at this point, including incorporation, prototyping, and test-marketing was $1,800—a bootstrap operation by any standards. What do they do next?

1. Foreign production
2. Job out
3. Make the product in a low-cost environment
4. Sell the product to someone else
5. Market to large department stores

C A S E 4

PILGRIM'S PRIDE: "IT'S MIND BOGGLING"

JAMES HARBIN
East Texas State University

"Sell it or smell it" is the unbending maxim that everyone in the chicken business faces. Because a chicken cannot be stopped from laying or growing, all producers, both literally and figuratively, live or die by the laws of supply and demand.

Pilgrim's Pride is one of fifty survivors out of approximately 4,000-plus firms in existence a few decades ago. Lonnie "Bo" Pilgrim, one of seven children raised during the Great Depression, has taken his concern from a small farm-supply store forty years ago, to one producing over $300 million in 1986 sales. Currently, Pilgrim's is the sixth largest and fastest-growing producer of fresh chickens in America.

This remarkable growth has taken place in a commodity industry about which, every year for the past fifty years, economists have been predicting doom and gloom. Citing industry sales as an indicator, experts have also deduced that the chicken industry has finally matured. The big question facing Pilgrim's today is: can it continue to grow through (1) additional marketing techniques; (2) further cost curtailment; (3) increased integration; and (4) improved genetics and growing techniques while at the same time facing competitors who are larger and just as savvy.

Exhibit 1
LONNIE A. "BO" PILGRIM

Chairman of the Board and Chief Executive Officer of Pilgrim's Pride Corporation (*photo courtesy Pilgrim's Pride Corporation*)

This case, written specifically for this text, is printed by permission.

BO'S BACKGROUND AND PHILOSOPHY

Bo Pilgrim's story is the classic one of deprivation to determination, and then to success. He was born in 1928, a middle child of seven. Bo's father died when he was nine; and he left home at twelve to live with his grandmother.

His entrepreneurial spirit has early roots. One of his first goals in life was "to be able to buy a soda when I wanted it. My father would on occasion give me the money for a cold drink, but only after I had finished some work he wanted done for it," says Bo. He learned early that he could buy his own soft drinks by buying them from his father's general merchandise store and selling them at a profit to the local factory workers.

Bo is a tireless worker at age sixty. Getting up with the chickens would aptly describe Mr. Pilgrim; he starts every morning at 5:15 A.M. He likens business to "a game, even a war." Commenting on how he spends his time, "I spend one third of my working days dealing with the government, one third with lawyers, and the remaining one third of my time is spent constructively."

"Today we don't appreciate how much we have and how easy it is to get things. I'm definitely hooked on the free enterprise system," comments Bo. "In fact, in a recent meeting with President Reagan I reminded him that the chicken and egg industry has never had any kind of subsidy. I also shared my belief that the government should not be in the business of protecting the inefficient."

Educated in a three-room school without electricity, Bo still believes in "old-fashioned Christian values" and the idea that "there is more to life than just making a dollar." He has had three children with his wife of thirty-one years; and for the past thirty years has taught a Sunday School class.

> Entrepreneurship is more than just shooting from the hip. A company has four resources: people, dollars, time, and facilities. Our company's objective is to gain optimum use of these four through planning, building pride, and rewarding your employees.

When asked about his secret of success, Bo responded:

> take your abilities, season them with experience on the job and combine that with drive and motivation and you will be successful. The way to make a difference in your life is to make that mind-boggling decision not to be average.

THE COMPANY

Pilgrim's Pride is engaged in the production, processing, and marketing of fresh chicken and further processed and prepared chicken products. For the 1985 fiscal year, Pilgrim's produced 432 million dressed pounds of chicken, establishing it as the sixth largest producer in the United States. The company's principal product lines are chill-pack chicken, which is packaged in individual trays for sale in the retail grocer's fresh meat counter, and whole or precut ice-pack chicken, which is sized according to the specifications of fast-food customers. In April 1986, the company introduced a new line of further processed and prepared chicken products which includes breast fillets, nuggets, tenders, patties, and deli foods. These products, which undergo one or more further processing steps (including deboning, cutting, forming, battering, breading, and cooking), are packaged in quantities suitable for food service customers and individually packaged for sale through retail grocers.

The company has increasingly emphasized value-added and branded products, including its chill pack and further processed and prepared food lines, because it believes these products generate higher prices per pound, exhibit lower price volatility, and result in higher and more consistent profit margins than non–value-added products such as whole ice-pack chicken. It has devoted considerable resources to developing consumer awareness of its Pilgrim's Pride brand name in its principal metropolitan markets in the southwestern and western United States.

Pilgrim's Marketing

In 1982, the company adopted a consumer-oriented marketing strategy. The implementation of this strategy led to the introduction of the company's first branded chill-pack products and the initiation of support for these products in the form of advertising and promotions. Since 1982, the company's marketing activities and expenditure levels have increased annually as new product and geographic markets have been developed. As a result of its marketing activities, the company has achieved significant consumer awareness for the Pilgrim's Pride

Exhibit 2
PILGRIM'S PRIDE PROMOTIONAL
INFORMATION PACKET

THE HISTORY OF PILGRIM'S PRIDE
A STORY OF SUCCESS THAT JUST KEEPS GROWING

The Beginning

- Started in 1945 as a partnership between Bo Pilgrim and his late brother, Aubrey.
- Began as a farm supply store in Pittsburg, Texas.

Early Growth

- 1950—First Pilgrim's Feed Mill is built.
- 1950–1958—Pilgrim's dominates Texas feed markets with special feed products.
- 1958—First Pilgrim's hatchery erected.
- 1969—Fresh chicken distributed to restaurants.

Rapid Success

- 1982—Pilgrim's enters branded retail chicken market with fresh, chill-pack chicken products.
- 1984—Pilgrim's introduces the world's first fresh, whole boneless chicken.
- 1985—Pilgrim's revolutionizes the poultry industry with first guaranteed lean chicken (less fat, calories, cholesterol).
- 1986—Pilgrim's Pride introduces franks and bologna made from breast frames and containing more protein, less fat and less sodium than beef hot dogs, and a complete line of frozen prepared chicken products featuring tenders made from solid white breast meat.
- 1986—Pilgrim's Pride issues first publicly traded stock, is listed on New York Stock Exchange under ticker symbol "CHX."

Pilgrim's Pride Today

- A totally integrated company producing 800 million pounds of dressed poultry and 45 million dozen table eggs each year.
- The sixth largest broiler producer and nineteenth largest egg producer in America.
- Facilities include modern frozen food plant, five chicken processing plants, five egg processing plants, three feed milling operations and thirty-five company farms.

brand name in certain metropolitan markets in the southwestern and western United States. The company believes this brand awareness is beneficial to the introduction and acceptance of new products, such as its further processed and prepared food lines.

The company presently utilizes extensive television, radio, and newspaper advertising; point-of-sale and coupon promotions; and other marketing techniques to develop consumer awareness and brand loyalty for their products. Bo Pilgrim is the featured spokesman in the company's television and radio commercials, and his likeness in a pilgrim's hat appears on all the company's branded products. Advertising slogans include "Better from the egg to the leg," "It's a mind-boggling thing," and "The honest chicken from real pilgrims."

The company maintains an active program to identify consumer preferences primarily by testing new product ideas, packaging designs, and methods through taste panels and focus groups located in key geographic markets. This program led to the identification and introduction of new products such as the company's whole-boneless chicken in 1983, leaner chicken in 1985, and the entire further processed and prepared foods line in 1986.

Pilgrim's chicken products are sold primarily to food service and retail grocery customers located in Texas and in metropolitan markets in the southwestern and western United States. Currently it sells its products in twenty-eight states. It does not sell in any states east of the Mississippi River.

Food service customers include fast-food restaurants, institutional food-service distributors, schools, hospitals, and military installations. The company's retail customers include national and regional grocery chains and wholesale discount clubs.

The company has regional distribution centers located in Arlington, El Paso, Houston, and Mt. Pleasant, Texas, and Oklahoma City, Oklahoma. Pilgrim utilizes its own sales force of approximately thirty people to market its products directly to retail grocery, fast-food, food distribution, and institutional food service customers. Independent food brokers also are used to market its further processed and prepared food products on a nationwide basis.

Pilgrim's Competition

Pilgrim's competes with other integrated chicken companies and to a lesser extent with local and regional poultry companies that are not fully integrated. Pilgrim's has been competing for retail grocery sales of chill-pack products since 1982 and fast-food product sales of whole and precut chickens since 1965. It currently supplies Church's, Kentucky Fried, Wendy's, Grandy's, and Chili's. It does not supply McDonald's or Burger King.

The primary competitive factors in the chicken industry include price, product line, and customer service. Although its products are competitively priced and generally supported with in-store promotions and discount programs, the company believes that product quality, brand awareness, and customer service are the primary methods through which it competes. In April 1986, the company began production and marketing of further processed and prepared chicken products. Currently, Pilgrim's believes that it has only one competitor (Tyson) with a more complete line of value-added products.

The top five chicken producers, measured by production volume, controlled more than half the market in 1986. They are Tyson Foods Inc., Springdale, Arkansas; ConAgra Inc., Omaha, Nebraska; Holly Farms Corp., Memphis, Tennessee; Perdue Farms Inc., Salisbury, Maryland; and Gold Kist Inc., Atlanta, Georgia. In 1985, the seventh largest poultry processor, Lane Processing, Inc., a fully integrated poultry operation with locations in Arkansas, Oklahoma, and Alabama, filed for bankruptcy. It was acquired by Tyson Food in 1986.

The egg industry is more fragmented than the chicken industry with approximately sixty producers accounting for approximately 56 percent of total sales during 1985. Pilgrim's competes with many larger and smaller egg producers, primarily on the

basis of product quality, reliability, price, and service.

Pilgrim's Employees and Labor Relations

As of August 23, 1986, the company employed approximately 4,600 persons. None of the company's employees have certified bargaining unit representation except the employees at the Lufkin, Texas, processing plant. The company has refused to recognize the bargaining unit at Lufkin, alleging that the union does not have majority representation. The unit has complained to the National Labor Relations Board, and the matter is pending. The company has not experienced any work stoppages and believes that relations with its employees are good.

The Broiler Industry

General

The domestic integrated broiler industry encompasses the breeding, growing, processing, and marketing of chicken products. From 1965 to 1985, the United States per-capita consumption of chicken increased 74 percent while the consumption of beef increased 7 percent.

Prior to World War II, the broiler industry was highly fragmented with numerous small, independent breeders, growers, and processors. The industry has experienced consolidation during the last forty-five years resulting in a relatively small number of larger, more integrated companies. In 1985, the top eight producers of chicken accounted for over 50 percent of total chicken production, compared to approximately 34 percent in 1979. In general, integration of the industry has led to lower profit margins at each independent production stage and enhanced the need for coordination between production stages.

The broiler industry is characterized by intense price competition, resulting in an emphasis on improving genetic, nutritional, and processing technologies in an effort to minimize production costs. These factors, coupled with the feed conversion advantages of chickens, have enabled the industry to enjoy consistently lower production costs per pound than other competing meats. As an example of the adoption of improved methods and technology, certain industry participants have moved toward product packaging at the plant level, including

Exhibit 3
PILGRIM'S PRIDE: COMPANY MISSION AND OBJECTIVES

Mission: To profitably produce and market food products to satisfy the needs of our customers and provide job satisfaction for employees.

Objectives:

1. To be in the top third of our industry in production cost, processing cost, and marketing.
2. ROA not less than 15 percent pre-tax, or ROE not less than 20 percent after tax.
3. Continue to keep our company diversified in poultry, with broilers being our primary volume.
4. Strengthen and expand a food product line in the brand name "Pilgrim's Pride" with quality, economy and proper distribution to consumer.
5. Expand consumer awareness and loyalty in "Pilgrim's Pride" brand value added product.
6. Optimize growth internally and through acquisitions.
7. Market the "Pilgrim's Pride" brand nationally with emphasis on Western and Central U.S.
8. Emphasize internal efficiencies in each department with standards, goals and controls.
9. Continue to develop our management and provide leadership toward the fulfillment of each individual's potential.
10. Provide products and services that cause employees to maintain a high degree of pride and job satisfaction.
11. Continue to develop a favorable company image and support worthy civic affairs.

deep chill processing as an alternative to ice packing whole chickens and shipping in bulk form. Deep chill processing rapidly lowers the temperature of chickens to slightly above freezing, thus extending freshness and shelf life.

Chicken Consumption

Chicken has experienced greater growth in per-capita consumption than most other major meat cate-gories over the last twenty years. Exhibit 4 illustrates per-capita consumption of chicken relative to turkey, fish, beef and pork.

The major factors influencing this growth are consumer awareness of the health and nutritional characteristics of chicken, the price advantage of chicken relative to red meat, and the development of more convenient further processed and prepared chicken products. The principal health and nutritional characteristics include lower levels of fat, cholesterol, and calories per pound for chicken relative to red meat. When compared with other meats, chicken has a significant price advantage, which has increased over time.

Exhibit 5 illustrates the average retail price of chicken compared to turkey, choice grade beef and pork.

Recent growth in the consumption of chicken has been enhanced by new product forms and packaging, which increase convenience and product versatility. These products typically undergo one or more further processing steps, including deboning, forming, battering, breading, and cooking. Production of these further processed products has increased from 1.1 billion dressed pounds in 1980 to 2.4 billion dressed pounds in 1985, establishing this product group as the fastest-growing segment of the broiler industry. The market share of the further processed product group has increased from 10 percent of domestic broiler production in 1980 to 17 percent of such production in 1985.

Industry Profitability

Industry profitability is primarily a function of consumption of chicken and competing meats and the cost of feed grains. Historically, the industry has been characterized by cyclical profitability, where periods of high profitability have led to overproduction and lower finishing product prices. For the most recent 10-year period, the industry experienced relatively favorable margins beginning in 1983. The broiler industry is currently enjoying one of the longer periods of profitability in its recent history.

Industry profitability can be significantly influenced by feed costs, which are influenced by a number of factors unrelated to the broiler industry, including government legislation that provides discretion to the federal government to set price and income supports for grain. Historically, feed costs have averaged approximately 50 percent of total

Exhibit 4
MEAT CONSUMPTION[a]

YEAR	CHICKEN	TURKEY	FISH	BEEF	PORK
1965	33.3	7.4	14.2	73.6	54.7
1975	40.1	8.5	14.4	87.9	50.7
1985	58.0	12.1	16.4	79.1	62.1
Percentage change (1965–1985)	74%	64%	15%	7%	14%

a. In pounds (except percentages)
Sources: Food Consumption, Prices and Expenditures 1964–84, Economic Research Service, U.S. Department of Agriculture, Statistical Bulletin No. 736, December 1985; Livestock and Poultry Outlook and Situation Report, Economic Research Service, U.S. Department of Agriculture, August 1986; per capita consumption of fish during 1985 estimated by the U.S. Department of Agriculture.

Exhibit 5
PRICE OF MEATS[a]

YEAR	CHICKEN	TURKEY	BEEF[b]	PORK
1965	$0.40	$0.48	$0.80	$0.66
1975	0.64	0.78	1.55	1.35
1985	0.76	1.05	2.33	1.62
Percentage change (1965–1985)	90%	119%	191%	145%

a. Dollars per pound (except percentages)
b. Choice grade
Sources: The U.S. Poultry Industry: Changing Economics and Structure, Agricultural Economic Report Number 502, Economic Research Service, U.S. Department of Agriculture, July 1983; Livestock and Poultry Outlook and Situation Report, Economic Research Service, U.S. Department of Agriculture, August 1986.

production costs of non–value-added products and have fluctuated substantially with the price of corn, milo, and soybean meal. Assuming that finished product prices and other factors remain constant, very small movements in feed costs may result in large changes in industry profits from non–value-added chicken products. By comparison, feed costs typically average approximately 25 percent of total production costs of further processed and prepared chicken products such as nuggets, fillets and deli products, and as a result, increased emphasis on sales of such products by chicken producers reduces the sensitivity of earnings to feed cost movements.

Although feed costs may vary dramatically, the cost of producing chicken is not as severely affected by changing feed ingredient prices as are the production costs of beef and pork. Chickens require approximately 2 pounds of dry feed to produce 1 pound of live meat, compared to cattle and hogs, which require approximately 8 to 4 pounds, respectively, of feed.

CHANGING TASTES[1]

In 1987 the U.S. will become a nation of bird eaters. According to the Department of Agriculture, per-capita consumption of poultry will rise to 78.2 pounds. At the same time, per-capita consumption of beef will fall to 75.7 pounds. That will mark the end of more than three decades of dominance by beef (before that, pork was king).

Notwithstanding an occasional salmonella scare, birds are perceived as more healthful than beef. A

1. This section is reprinted by permission of *Wall Street Journal,* © 1987 Dow Jones & Company, Inc. All Rights Reserved Worldwide.

100-gram piece of chicken contains 3.7 grams of saturated fat, compared with 20.7 grams of saturated fat in a piece of T-bone steak weighing the same amount, according to the Agriculture Department.

Chicken is also cheap. Chickens are selling for less than they did in 1923, when Mrs. Wilmer Steele of Ocean View, Del., sold what chicken historians say was the nation's first flock of commercial broilers (she got 62 cents a pound).

And perhaps most significantly, chicken companies have lately increased profit margins by producing scores of what the industry calls value-added items: chicken parts that have been boned or skinned or marinated or otherwise processed for the convenience of consumers. Just as any fool can cook a steak, any fool can now cook a shrink-wrapped chicken breast.

The poultry sector isn't solely chicken; it also includes turkey, duck, goose and quail. But the poultry industry in America is chicken-driven; and, in fact, consumption of chicken alone is expected to bypass beef sometime around 1990 (although beef backers say pounds-per-capita figures aren't strictly fair, because chicken at retail has more bones in it than beef does). Last year chicken nuggets accounted for about 10% of total U.S. broiler output. McNuggets showed chicken companies what could happen if they went beyond selling what are called, in the trade, "feathers-off, guts-out birds".

"Working with McDonald's and others has imposed a new discipline," says Ted Bailey, vice president of Holly Farms Corp. of Memphis, Tenn., the third-biggest broiler producer. "The business has matured. We're looking to marketing now."

Since McNuggets hit the market nationally in 1982, chicken producers have been swamping supermarkets with value-added products—teriyaki tidbits, breaded wings, whole cooked birds with salt and spices injected into their flesh—and consumers have responded. "Demand has expanded for poultry since 1983 in a way that I've never seen demand for any meat take off since World War II," says Patrick Luby, vice president and corporate economist at Oscar Mayer Foods Corp. in Madison, Wis.

Value-added chicken should, of course, properly be called value-subtracted. It is the whole bird, not its processed parts, that offers consumers the greatest value—and that value is considerable when compared with beef and pork.

Why is chicken, pound for pound, cheaper than the competition? The answer has to do with the fact that a chicken is highly efficient at converting feed to flesh. To produce a pound of flesh, a chicken consumes less than two pounds of feed, compared with six or seven for a cow and three for a pig.

Also, a chicken doesn't live long. The shorter a creature's life cycle, the quicker its generations can be manipulated genetically. Chicken breeders have steadily developed birds that grow bigger on less feed in less time. They may be approaching the limits of practicality on this score; modern chickens have "put on so much weight that they have some real problems mating," says Walter Becker, professor emeritus of genetics and cell biology at Washington State University.

Furthermore, chickens don't graze. Raising cattle requires an investment in land; raising chickens doesn't. Chickens used to need to run around in the sun; otherwise, they would develop a vitamin D deficiency and rickets. But in the 1920s, poultry producers solved the vitamin D problem by adding cod-liver oil to chicken feed. Since then they have been able to raise thousands of chickens in confinement, allowing about 0.7 square foot per bird.

Still more efficiency derives from the chicken industry's unusually thorough vertical integration. The biggest producers—ConAgra; Holly Farms; Tyson Foods Inc. of Springdale, Ariz.; Perdue Farms Inc. of Salisbury, Md.; and Gold Kist of Atlanta—generally control everything from the chickens to the feed mill to the trucks to the processing plant. Chicken farmers are merely wardens of the companies' birds, paid to provide housing and labor.

The chicken companies themselves spend much of their energy trying to escape the commodity cycle through marketing. Frank Perdue, with his classic commercials, was the first to demonstrate that a company could charge a premium for a brand-name bird. Today the biggest producers all play the brand-loyalty game—Perdue, Holly Farms and Tyson with their own names, Gold Kist with its Young 'n Tender label and ConAgra with Country Pride. This leaves the chicken producers in an odd situation: they are commodities concerns trying to behave like consumer-products companies.

Under the old rules, the broiler industry operated on a fairly predictable cycle of about three years: a year of good profits, followed by a year of expanded output and declining profits, followed by a year of losses and production cuts. Since the chicken market took off in 1982, however, chicken companies have seen steady earnings increases.

But this year the chicken companies have been rudely reminded that they sell commodities. The industry has increased production by a huge 8 percent, and at that rate it hasn't been able to sustain prices. Last spring, publicity about salmonella sent prices tumbling further. "It's clear that the industry is still susceptible to overproduction, and that is being magnified by the concern over salmonella," says Holly Farms Mr. Bailey. He and others in the industry predict that production increases will drift back to 4 percent or 5 percent annually.

GOING PUBLIC

In January of 1987, Pilgrim arranged for a public offering of seven million shares of common stock, six million of which are to be issued and sold by Pilgrim's Pride Corporation and one million to be sold by a stockholder of the company. The company would not receive any proceeds from the sales of shares by the selling stockholder (the Pilgrim family). It was estimated that the initial public offering price would be in the $13 to $16 per-share range.

The company intends to use $41 million of the net proceeds to retire short-term promisory notes issued to the selling stockholder, $23 million to reduce short-term debt incurred primarily to acquire feed grain inventories, and the balance for general corporate purposes. General corporate purposes may include capacity expansion, additions to working capital, and acquisitions. At the time of the offering the company had no firm plans regarding expansion or acquisitions.

Exhibit 6
EXECUTIVE OFFICERS (as of August 23, 1986)

NAME	AGE	YEARS WITH COMPANY	POSITION
Lonnie A. (Bo) Pilgrim	58	41	Chairman of the Board and Chief Executive Officer
Clifford E. Butler	44	17	Vice Chairman of the Board, Chief Financial Officer, Secretary, and Treasurer
Robert L. Hendrix	50	7	President, Chief Operating Officer, and Director
James J. Miner, Ph.D.	58	20	Senior Vice-President, Farm Production and Director
Lonnie Ken Pilgrim	28	11	Director of Transportation and Director
Thomas J. Garner	36	5	Senior Vice-President, Marketing
John M. Haid, Jr.	50	5	Senior Vice-President, Milling Transportation and Farm Supply
Tommy L. Goodwin, Ph.D.	50	2	Senior Vice-President, Director of Research, Development and Quality Control
Monty K. Henderson	40	5	Senior Vice-President, Complex Manager, DeQueen and Nashville, Arkansas plants
Joseph R. Menefee	37	5	Senior Vice-President, Processing
Robert N. Palm	43	3	Senior Vice-President, Complex Manager, Lufkin and Nacogdoches, Texas plants
Arthur V. Wolfe, Ph.D.	69	7	Senior Vice-President, Industrial Relations

Exhibit 7

PILGRIM'S PRIDE: SELECTED FINANCIAL DATA[a]

	FISCAL YEAR ENDED					ELEVEN MONTHS ENDED	
	June 27, 1981[b]	Oct. 2, 1982[b]	Oct. 1, 1983	Sept. 29, 1984	Sept. 28, 1985	August 24, 1985[b]	August 23, 1986[b]
INCOME STATEMENT DATA							
Net sales	$136,624	$232,578	$254,417	$296,676	$301,548	$268,436	$332,799
Operating income	5,086	3,215	8,131	26,342	18,802	15,848	33,568
Income (loss) before income taxes	3,081	(2,669)	3,522	21,166	15,557	12,934	29,654
Less income tax expense (benefit)	1,022	(832)	1,429	9,201	6,320	5,251	12,336
Net income (loss)	2,059	(1,837)	2,093	11,965	9,237	7,683	17,318
Net income (loss) per common share	$ 0.06	$ (0.05)	$ 0.06	$ 0.34	$ 0.26	$ 0.22	$ 0.49
Pro-forma net income per common share	—	—	—	—	0.44	0.37	0.82
STATISTICAL OPERATING DATA[b]							
Dressed pounds of chicken produced	144,600	336,300	348,300	367,900	431,800	384,000	487,200
Average selling price per dressed pound	$ 0.49	$ 0.45	$ 0.46	$ 0.55	$ 0.50	$ 0.50	$ 0.53
Average feed cost per dressed pound	0.27	0.25	0.25	0.27	0.22	0.22	0.21
Average production cost, excluding feed, per dressed pound	0.20	0.21	0.21	0.22	0.23	0.24	0.23
Total average production cost per dressed pound	0.47	0.46	0.46	0.49	0.45	0.46	0.44
Gross margin per dressed pound	0.02	(0.01)	—	0.06	0.05	0.04	0.09
BALANCE SHEET DATA							
Working capital	$ 709	$ (5,626)	$ 617	$ 5,620	$ 3,932	$ (1,278)	$ 10,760
Total assets	43,804	66,328	74,124	81,591	122,702	119,894	180,379
Short-term debt	10,930	21,698	22,821	8,510	14,537	25,006	27,841
Long-term debt, less current portion	10,136	19,491	23,089	19,446	34,553	25,399	48,080
Total stockholders' equity	9,641	9,076	11,143	22,987	32,044	30,537	49,227

a. In thousands (except per-share and per-pound data)
b. Unaudited

Exhibit 8
TYSON FOODS: SELECTED FINANCIAL DATA[a]

FOR FISCAL YEAR END	1986	1985	1984	1983	1982
Net sales	$1,503,719	$1,135,712	$750,112	$603,537	$559,021
Less cost of sales	1,271,928	954,425	651,901	529,406	495,044
Gross margin	231,791	181,287	98,211	74,131	63,977
Less selling and administrative expenses	116,639	92,264	54,954	44,668	36,475
Less Interest expense	20,648	19,446	11,029	9,585	13,266
Other income	3,410	591	452	599	3,997
Net income before taxes	97,914	70,168	32,680	20,477	18,233
Less income taxes	47,625	35,337	14,516	9,408	8,829
NET INCOME	$ 50,289	$ 34,831	$ 18,164	$ 11,069	$ 9,404
Net income per share	$1.18	$0.88	$0.47	$0.28	$0.24
Cash dividend per share	$0.035	$0.023	$0.016	$0.016	$0.016
AT FISCAL YEAR END					
Total assets	$ 760,675	$ 471,470	$298,172	$254,572	$235,578
Net property, plant and equipment	347,910	226,426	129,619	108,903	101,774
Working capital	66,589	44,370	40,499	30,447	38,125
Long-term debt	211,888	118,564	87,254	81,440	85,319
Shareholders' equity	203,631	154,721	84,299	66,760	55,765
Book value per share	$4.78	$3.64	$2.16	$1.71	$1.44

a. In thousands (except per-share data)
Note: Tyson Foods, Inc., is the number one poultry producer in the industry. It processes thirteen million chickens each week and over two billion pounds each year. It has twenty-one hatcheries, sixteen feed mills, and thirty-one processing plants. The company employs nearly 25,000 people and has grower contracts involving 8,000 farmers.

Exhibit 9
MEAT SALES: ANNUAL PERCENTAGE OF CHANGE

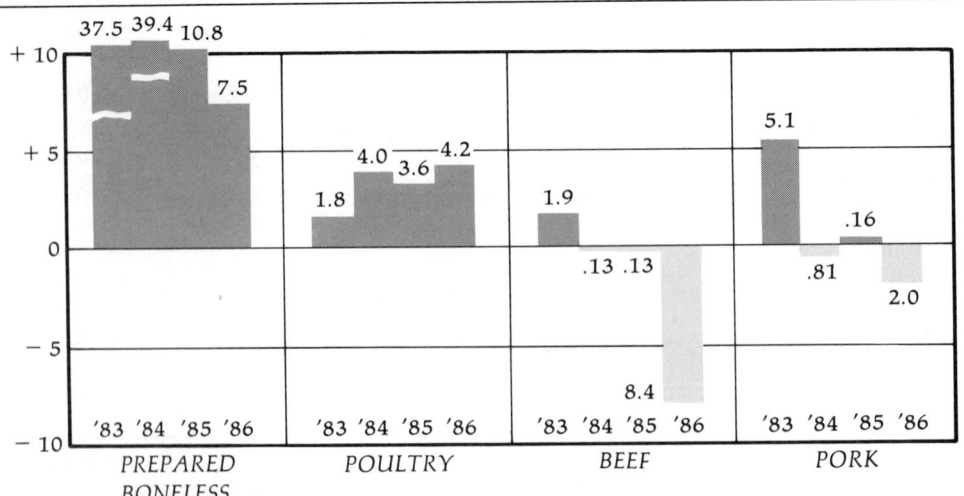

HOW DO YOU GET APPLES FROM AN ELM?

ROBERT P. CROWNER
Eastern Michigan University

How do you get Apples from an ELM? During the 1981 through 1984 period in Michigan, the answer to that question was to see the "Apple Lady," Elaine Moncur. Ms. Moncur was the president and owner of ELM Group, an Ann Arbor–based firm that was the manufacturing representative for Apple computers until September 30, 1984. She became known the "Apple Lady" in Michigan because of the outstanding job she did in representing Apple to dealers in Michigan. As September 1984, approached, she was faced with and necessarily occupied with determining a new strategy for her firm.

THE OWNER

Elaine Moncur did not have the background and training one would expect the president of an aggressive marketing organization to have. She was raised in a poor section of San Jose and was the only woman in her high school class to go on to college. She married and began studying humanities at Michigan State University, where she had her first child. After a move back to California, she decided to study piano and within weeks began teaching piano. She later completed a bachelor of education degree in special education from Eastern Michigan University and a master's degree in learning disabilities from the University of Michigan. She was interested in teaching the emotionally impaired, learning disabled, and blind because she herself had had po-

lio at twelve and as a result had a visual impairment that made it difficult for her to interpret words and numbers. To overcome this disability, she developed a number recognition system that allowed her to learn math, which she had been unable to do in the past.

She taught music to the emotionally impaired in both public and private schools for a number of years, but became unhappy with the violence she had to contend with. She decided it was time to make some money, so she set out to find a new career. She researched the job market extensively in 1980. After some thirty-two job interviews, she determined that her skills best fit into the marketing and sales areas. The job she took was with Barrington International, which represented Texas Instruments computers. Moncur did not have experience in either sales or computers at the time, but she did her homework and within four months was the top salesperson. Unfortunately, Barrington had financial problems and she was soon back looking for a job.

Apple Saleswoman
Ms. Moncur next tried to get a job with Apple Computer, but Apple would not hire her initially because management thought she was not experienced enough nor did she have enough knowledge of computers. She interviewed a number of Apple dealers in Detroit and Toledo to find out about their current sales representatives and what the dealers needed and wanted from their representatives. After thoroughly researching Apple Computers as a company, she was able to get a job as a factory-direct

This case, written specifically for this book, is printed by permission.

salesperson for the state of Michigan. At the final interview she told Apple that her findings showed that what dealers needed was information to help them sell and solve problems and training, which her background uniquely qualified her to provide. She became Apple's first saleswoman in May 1981.

During the year in which she was a saleswoman for Apple, Moncur achieved some remarkable objectives. In spite of Michigan's depressed economy, she sold more Apple III's than any other sales representative in the country, and Apple's sales in the state quadrupled. She did this by attention to details using her organizational skills to handle paperwork, find lost orders, and solve dealers' problems. Although she had never done advertising before, she was able to put together an advertising seminar after being on the job for only two weeks. She did this by talking to advertising agencies, newspapers, radio and television stations, and dealers outside Michigan about advertising. She also researched the local media in the hometown of each person attending the seminar. Needless to say, the seminar was a success. Drawing upon her classroom experience as a teacher, she stressed hands-on participation in her seminar, following up with a test the following week to confirm what had been learned.

Her starting salary was $22,000 per year (compared to $40,000 per year for Apple's salesmen). She received a bonus after achieving 70 percent of her quota and a raise of 35 percent after a spectacular first six months. At Apple's annual sales meeting in Dallas, she was honored for her outstanding performance by receiving a prize cherished by salesmen, a ticket for a "topless shoe shine" at Billy Bob's Bar in Dallas. In order to accomplish all of this, she worked 16-hour days and regularly spent all night on Tuesdays learning new software. During this period as a factory-direct saleswoman, she heard that Apple was planning to change to manufacturer's representatives.

ELM GROWS FROM AN APPLE SEED

Elaine Moncur promptly asked Apple to let her be the manufacturer's representative for Michigan, but was turned down because she lacked experience and Apple's policy prohibited direct reps from becoming manufacturer's reps. She was offered the job of being a trainer for Apple Computer. She was not dissuaded and spent months researching and preparing a proposal with the aid of a professional proposal writer. Apple finally agreed, reluctantly, to her proposal provided that she formed a joint venture with an established manufacturer's rep for the first year, which she agreed to do. Thus ELM Group began in an apartment with her mother as an employee handling the accounting work. Three other employees were added quickly and $10 million in sales were handled from the apartment.

Within six months the company outgrew its facilities and the number of employees rose to eleven. The final facilities move was made to 4,000 square feet of office space on the atrium level of the Burlington Office Building in Ann Arbor. The organization chart for ELM Group is shown in Exhibit 1.

ELM Group grew to include Software Michigan, Inc., and ELM Indiana-Kentucky. All activities for the year ending in September 1984 generated $40 million in sales, on which ELM earned a 3.5-percent commission. The expenses incurred ran about $87,000 per month. A breakdown of these expenses is shown below:

Salaries	$48,000
Entertainment and travel	10,000
Advertising agency fees	10,000
Car allowance ($500/month/person)	5,000
Rent	4,500
Telephone	4,000
Miscellaneous	5,500
Total	$87,000

Marketing

ELM Group's marketing strategy, as set by Elaine Moncur, began where her saleswoman's job left off. ELM's heavy focus was on education. Training was heavily stressed. Although it seemed too complicated at first, it was smoothed out by asking, "Is it logical." ELM trained dealers in how to merchandise, how to do financial reports, and how to inventory merchandise. Elaine was the first to put training classrooms in individual stores, which seemed almost sinful giving the high cost of square footage in the stores. This concept is now accepted nationally. ELM set up distribution so that people were not competing with each other geographically.

ELM approved all Apple dealerships in Michigan and insisted that Apple would look professional.

Exhibit 1
ELM GROUP'S ORGANIZATION CHART

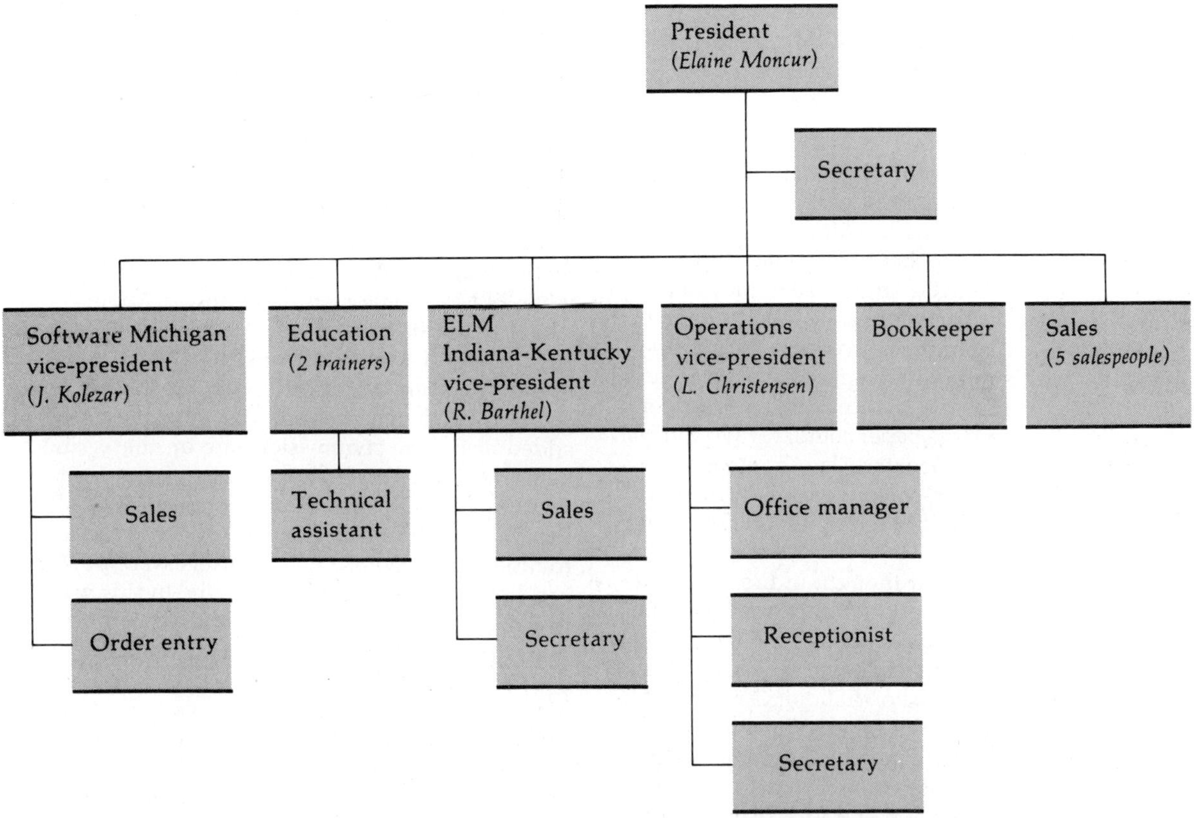

```
                              President
                           (Elaine Moncur)
                                  |
                              Secretary

Software Michigan     Education      ELM              Operations        Bookkeeper    Sales
vice-president        (2 trainers)   Indiana-Kentucky  vice-president                 (5 salespeople)
(J. Kolezar)                         vice-president    (L. Christensen)
                                     (R. Barthel)

     Sales           Technical          Sales         Office manager
                     assistant

  Order entry                          Secretary       Receptionist

                                                         Secretary
```

Anything would be done to help the dealers, including loaning them money, supplying them with product from ELM's own supply, seeing them through divorces, renting a truck to bring in needed stock for Christmas from Chicago, running seminars, and working booths at trade shows. ELM was always there, way beyond the normal expected for a rep firm. It is no wonder that ELM was in Apple's Excell Club for those reps who made more than 150 percent of their quota.

Research was done on compensation programs in order to establish one for ELM. Salespersons were paid a base salary plus a car allowance plus a performance bonus based upon total sales and training efforts carried out. Sales reps made about $25,000 per year base salary and total compensation was $40,000 to $60,000 per year. It was hard for a salesperson to follow in Elaine's footsteps since she had developed so many of the dealer relations originally as an Apple rep. However, she gave her salespeople a great deal of latitude.

In advertising, ELM tried to present what was new for Apple products and software. Promotions were run with slogans such as "Buy an Apple and get an Apple tree." The "Twelve Apples of Christmas" promotion, done for Inacomp, is another example, as is the Apple computer giveaway contest at Detroit Lions games. Advertising agencies were sometimes used, but, since ELM wished to maintain tight control, ads were often developed in-house. The need for clean-looking ads was stressed and all ad material was composed and evaluated very analytically. Moncur used her previous knowledge as a fashion designer to help with layouts.

ELM developed window displays for its dealers. Their use was discretionary. Participation was stressed, with the concept that ELM provided the idea but the dealer was the one who carried it out.

Operations

The operations function for ELM was handled by Leslie Christensen, vice-president of operations. She initially came to work as Moncur's secretary with the understanding that she would learn the business and would have a larger role to play in the future. Her previous background included a degree in political science from the University of California at Berkeley with a minor in business, as well as accounting and auditing experience with a newspaper in New Jersey and a large paper company in California. She also worked in Senator Alan Cranston's San Francisco office handling constituent case problems while she attended the University of California at Berkeley.

She found that Moncur thought in broad strategic terms and realized that one function she could provide was "to get clouds of Elaine's thoughts funneled down and implemented." She thought of herself as "being in the middle of an hourglass filtering ideas down to others." She found Moncur to be a true entrepreneur with incredible stamina, ideas, and motivation. She also found there was little structure in the organization and few records kept. Christensen introduced more discipline and organization into ELM, including the use of forms and records. Changes were often made quickly by Moncur, without sufficient communication made to everyone. Christensen became the organizer and communicator. She made it a practice to debrief Moncur at the end of the day in order to find out what needed to be done administratively.

Operations, marketing, and all areas of ELM worked long grueling hours. A normal day was ten to twelve hours and six-and-a-half-day weeks were the rule. But the atmosphere made it fun and rewarding. ELM prospered, as did all of the employees. Money was not a problem.

Software Michigan, Inc.

Software Michigan, Inc., was established as a separate company because Apple's representation agreement prohibited the representative firm from representing anyone else, even if the other manufacturer was not a competitor. ELM anticipated that Apple would someday do away with its manufacturer's reps because it would become too expensive for Apple to give up the commission to the reps once Apple became large and successful. Software Michigan was set up in May 1983 with John Kolezar in charge. He had known Moncur for several years, having met her when she was a salesperson for Barrington and he was data systems coordinator for Moore Business Forms. His job with ELM was to develop lines of products that were noncompetitive to Apple that would serve as a nucleus for the day when ELM no longer would represent Apple.

Software lines such as Dow Jones, Electronic Arts, State of the Art, Think Tank, and Software Publishing were acquired. Other peripheral items such as Maxell diskettes and disk storage units were added also. The commission rate on these kind of items ran 7 to 10 percent.

Although ELM was limited to the state of Michigan, John Kolezar's strategy was to try to locate distribution firms whose headquarters were in Michigan but who distributed nationally. In this way, he reasoned, ELM could in effect achieve national distribution. He began to work with Michigan firms such as Handleman in Troy, the largest rack jobber in the world. At that time the company was just beginning to handle software in its racks in such stores as Sears and Montgomery-Ward. He also worked with Inacomp and other chains that specialized in computers and computer supplies. The business grew, but in March 1984 Apple found out about Software Michigan and insisted that ELM close it because of the distribution agreement with Apple. Apple insisted that this be done even though Apple knew at that time that it planned to terminate all manufacturer's representatives in May.

THE APPLE STEM TWISTS AGAIN

Apple Computer's selling and distribution strategy had gone through a number of changes since the company's inception. From 1976 through 1978 distributors were used. From 1979 through 1981 factory-direct salespersons were used. Finally, in 1982, manufacturer's reps were used. In 1984, Apple twisted again and announced in May that it was going to return to factory-direct sales. Although many thought the decision for this move had been made as early as December, the manufacturer's reps had been led to believe until a month before the announcement that things would continue. For instance, ELM participated in the public introduction of the Apple IIC in San Francisco within thirty days of the cancellation notice and followed this up with an elaborate local product introduction day at The Fairlane Manor in Dearborn. This single day was very expensive, costing ELM $17,000 to put it on in a very professional manner.

By its contracts Apple was only required to give one month's notice of termination of its manufacturer's reps but it chose to give four month's notice with the termination date being September 30, 1984. Although this seemed fair but devastating for ELM at first, subsequent events called the fairness to question.

During the four-month hiatus period, ELM had to continue servicing its Apple dealers but was prohibited from acquiring any other lines of business. ELM could look for other lines but not begin representing them until after Apple's agreement ended. ELM had to continue to pay employees until September 30, but the employees soon began to relax their efforts since they were guaranteed their money. Apple consistently would not return phone calls from ELM after May. Relations deteriorated to the extent that, when the termination date arrived, Apple company representatives came in to remove anything that said Apple on it, including coffee mugs. They began to remove memorabilia from the walls such as a contrived facsimile newspaper advertisement in a cherry frame that had been presented to Elaine Moncur by her employees. Fortunately her lawyer had his office in the same building and came down to put a stop to the pettiness.

The ending of ELM's relationship was particularly distressing to Elaine Moncur because of her strong ethical values. She was raised as a Mormon. Her special education background showed her compassion. She understood that it was necessary to set up an environment conducive to individuals. Then too she had been the recipient of some bad business practices once she entered the business world. Her working ethical policy had been "what is good for the dealers and manufacturer is best for me." One of her early mentors and advisors, Don Chisholm of Ann Arbor Associates, influenced her with his statement that "A good deal is good for everyone involved." No wonder the ending with Apple was

disappointing when she considered the long hours and tremendous effort she put into the relationship.

She also had wondered about subsequent Apple policies, such as severely discounting its products and selling through schools like the University of Michigan. Selling through the University of Michigan at deep discounts took 45 percent of the total Ann Arbor population and 89 percent of the total buying population away from the dealers. If a dealer were to sell competitively against the University, the salesperson would make $5 versus $120 if a comparable IBM-PC were sold. ELM found out about this move by Apple through a local dealer who in turn found out from a University of Michigan contact. Apple refused to have anyone come to explain things to the dealers. Apple also allowed multiple dealers in some areas, as there was no allowance made for an exclusive location.

THE TASTE OF APPLE

What was Apple like? Apple had the reputation for being creative, wild, and reckless. To ELM Apple was not an easy task master. "Code Red" was the standard operating signal; it meant that decisions made at headquarters on April 15 got to ELM on May 10 and had to be implemented by the dealers on May 15. Apple was not known for tact. For instance, when ELM was phasing out as manufacturer's rep, a meeting was held at the Renaissance Center in Detroit by Bill Campbell, vice-president of sales for Apple, attended by all the Apple dealers in Michigan and by Elaine Moncur and her key people. He proceeded to say that, although ELM had done a good job representing Apple, he and the Apple salesmen would do a much better job. It was hard to be "fired in public." Apple never gave pats on the back to ELM.

Leslie Christensen characterized Apple as "managing by intimidation." They were young, innovative, and arrogant. Apple managers lived in an ivory tower that allowed them to think that there was no need to be IBM compatible. They seemed to never know what their reps were doing and were not aware of the concept called "managing by wandering around." Kolezar characterized Apple's regional sales management as "vanilla and bland, almost pompous."

Once the move to an Apple sales force was announced, a North American Manufacturer's Representatives Association of reps who were dumped by Apple was formed to help the reps get new lines. This group proved to be helpful, but it also made the reps aware of some of the inconsistencies and questionable practices Apple had used. For instance, there were different rates of commission given to various reps and some were paid for educational sales and some not, as was the case with ELM. The rules of the game were not the same for all. Allocation of products that were in short supply, such as the Macintosh when it was introduced, were made at the sole discretion of the area sales manager, which in turn was not done on a logical and fair basis.

Was there sex discrimination against ELM since it was owned by a female and predominantly employed females? Key employees at ELM believed Apple regional sales management took advantage of Moncur because they thought they could get away with it since she was the only female rep. She was advised by the area sales manager not to get married, which would be unusual advice to give to a male rep. According to Moncur, tears were expected when the termination was officially given to her. ELM believed that if women were to be successful they had to be twice as good as men.

Are female managers different? Both Kolezar and Christensen agreed that there were differences. When asked if more intuition would describe the difference, they both thought not. Kolezar saw women as being more sensitive toward employees and giving more attention to detail, so that there were finer edges to a woman's sales presentation, a striving to make it perfect. He thought that decisions were more rational but women were more sensitive, which may be mistaken for intuition. He sees them as being more creative perhaps because they were not caught up in the good old boy syndrome, which could be restricting and hard to break out of. Christensen also believed women were more at-tuned to the reactions of people and could read body language better. She thought there were fewer ego problems and therefore more flexibility and freedom to be creative.

THE FUTURE OF ELM

As September approached, brainstorming sessions were held to develop ideas for future strategy. At first everyone was included in these sessions, but as employees began to make commitments to Apple, it became difficult to know who could be safely included in the sessions. Some of the ideas that surfaced in the sessions were to write a book, become a motivational speaker, become a consulting firm, continue as a manufacturer's rep for other firms (Software Michigan was still intact), become a distributor, or develop a chain of retail computer stores. Still another version of a retail chain was for ELM to organize the independent stores into a chain much like the IGA, Independent Grocers Association, which could achieve favorable buying terms. This concept was investigated in some depth but eventually shelved because independents were in fact too independent and control became the real issue.

Elaine Moncur devoted more time to considering alternative strategies for ELM. The company had been highly successful, and she had weathered many storms. She obviously was not one to give up easily and was highly motivated. Her employees were counting on her. To make matters worse, her fortieth birthday was approaching and she "had to be something more than fat, forty, and divorced." Although divorced, she certainly was not fat. To reward herself for a job well done, she decided to buy a white Corvette and then spent many nights out for a drive thinking about what her future strategy should be.

MAQUILADORAS INDUSTRY NOTE: IS IT A GOLDEN OPPORTUNITY?

WALTER E. GREENE

University of Texas—Pan American

ABSTRACT

Maquiladoras, in-bound plants, twin plants, or off-shore production all mean profits for American business firms willing to relocate part of their operations overseas. To reduce transportation costs, ensure control of operations, and still live in the United States, many companies are locating in the Southwest United States. At this location, their capital intensive operations can be supported by the labor operations just a few miles away in Mexico's *maquiladoras*, manned by cheap semiskilled Mexican workers.

Additional saving in transportation and labor costs offers several advantages to U.S. firms needing to cut costs to remain competitive in the world market.

INTRODUCTION

Most of the major U.S. maufacturers have shifted production abroad in an apparent effort to boost their competitiveness in the U.S. market. Automakers, electronics firms, and many others have been relying heavily on foreign suppliers and building their own plants around the globe. Why this flight of U.S.-owned production capacity abroad? One reason is the domestic impact of foreign competition in U.S. markets. Many manufacturers see a major increase in offshore operations as the only viable choice remaining and as essential to their economic survival. Several executives explained their firm's decision to become more global as a response to the challenge of international competitors. The competitors, with their excess capacity and lower costs, were attracting markets that formerly were served by their firm. Many U.S. firms are faced with price differences of 30 to 50 percent and also face the possibility of being forced out of markets that they had developed over the last forty years. Many CEOs had a choice: either they could compete in the international and domestic market or simply retreat to the United States and beg for governmental protection. Many have chosen to compete by establishing production plants abroad; such operations are commonly known as *offshore production, twin plant operations, in-bound plants,* or *maquiladoras,* depending upon the locations of the plants abroad.

Maquiladoras

During the sixties, the competition created by the prosperous economies of Europe and especially by Japan forced many labor-intensive operations in the United States to look elsewhere for cheaper rates. The U.S. industries chose to establish their produc-

The author acknowledges research done by Nilda C. Betencourt for this article. This case, written specifically for this book, is printed by permission.

tion facilities in Mexico.[1] At that time Mexico was (and still is) one of the best locations to set up off-shore production plants, or *maquiladoras*. The term *maquiladora* derives from *maquila,* a measure of corn a miller takes for himself for the services of grinding it.

The *bracero* program, in which cheap Mexican labor was exported to the United States, had been initiated during World War II. The cancellation of this program in 1964 led to serious unemployment problems in the northern Mexican border. Yet, even though the program had been cancelled, immigrants from the interior of Mexico continued to arrive at the border each day. By 1966, the unemployment rate of several Mexican border cities approached 40 to 50 percent.[2]

The Mexican government under President Diaz Ordaz was confronted with political and economic problems caused by this massive unemployment. To reduce the Mexican unemployment rate, the president established the Border Industrialization Program (BIP), offering the United States cheap labor along the Mexican border. This program allowed foreign corporations to establish assembly plants at roughly 19 kilometers from the U.S. border (see Exhibit 1). The corporation had to pay only a fraction of the U.S. wages and was exempt from paying taxes.[3]

The BIP program, begun in 1965, has grown rapidly. By 1967, 57 *maquiladoras* were operating in the border area; this number increased to 448 plants in 1976 (see Exhibit 2). As documented by Mc-Caughan, 177 plants were established in Baja California (across from California), 54 plants in Sonora (bordering Arizona), 96 plants in Chihuahua (bordering New Mexico and Texas), and 22 and 96 plants, respectively, in Cohauila and Tamaulipas (on the Texas border).[4] By 1985, 772 plants were established in Mexico (see Exhibit 3). Today, the state of Chihuahua has a total of 201 plants and the city of Tijuana has 199 plants. U.S. companies with *maquiladoras* plants in Mexico have located mainly in Texas and California.

REDUCING PRODUCTION COSTS: ALTERNATIVES

By reducing production costs, a manufacturing company can become more competitive in the U.S. market. The *maquiladora* strategy offers several attractive options to U.S. firms seeking to reduce production costs.

First, the firm can set up its own *maquiladora* plant. The corporation can build a plant, hire and train a workforce, and put a management team in place. By establishing its own plant, the U.S. manufacturer will save $12,000 to $15,000 per man each year.[5] However, a company may not be willing to set up a plant in Mexico, for a variety of reasons. The firm may not have enough corporate personnel to cover management positions in Mexico or may distrust a foreign country. (Mexico has a history of seizing "foreign-owned" companies.) The firm may be small, with a low volume of production, and not able financially to build and maintain its own plants in Mexico. The answer, a second option, may be to use a *maquiladora* subcontractor. The use of a subcontractor or a contract with one of the many shelter companies that operates on the United States–Mexican border, is also recommended for the firm that does not know how to do business in Mexico.

In Mexico, reliable *maquiladora* subcontractors operate under the in-bound program. These subcontractors provide factory space, assembly labor, and supervisory personnel to assemble products under contract. They will take the parts or raw materials on the U.S. side of the border—from San Diego, California; Nogales, Arizona; or El Paso, Brownsville, or McAllen, Texas—and return the finished product to the same city. The median price for this type of arrangement in September 1985 was $3 to $4 per worker hour. Many subcontracts also negotiate on a piece-work basis.[6] The CEO may choose either option, as it suits his company.

Also, the CEO can investigate the *maquiladora* process without actually setting up a plant in Mexico. By using a shelter plan—a program run by an industrial park as a means of promoting the park and eventually selling or renting factory space—the firm can test the process. In such an arrangement, the shelter plan operator, usually a subsidiary of the

1. McCaughan and Peter Baird, *Las Maquiladoras en Mexico* (ACLA, 1975), p. 8.
2. Ibid.
3. Mitchell Seligson and Edward T. Williams, *Maquiladoras and Migrant Workers in the Mexico-U.S. B.I.P.* (Austin, 1981), p. 149.
4. McCaughan, p. 16.

5. William A. Orme, "Maquiladoras Thrive on Mexican Border," *Journal of Commerce,* November 1985, pp. 6–11.
6. Richard Wygand, "Opportunities in the *Maquiladora* Industry," *Business Mexico,* November 1985, pp. 54–65.

Exhibit 1
MEXICAN AND UNITED STATES BORDER

industrial park, takes full responsibility for running a pilot operation with the U.S. product. The U.S. company provides the parts and raw materials needed, the equipment required for its assembly or manufacture, and usually a manager or supervisor who understands the process. The shelter plan hires the direct labor, provides all basic installations, handles payroll and administration, supervises the work, and transports the parts or raw materials across the border into the plant and back to the United States, using the necessary customs procedures. The shelter plan charges the client a flat fee per hour on direct daily wage labor. Monthly salaried labor management and expenses are charged at cost. After several months, the cost and productivity of the Mexican operation can be assessed and a decision made on whether or not to establish a full size in-bond operation, fully owned and run by the U.S. company. The average cost for shelter plan services in September 1985 was $2.50 to $2.75 per person hour of direct labor, plus all indirect charges at cost.[7]

OPPORTUNITIES IN THE IN-BOUND INDUSTRY

Mexico's *maquiladora* industry currently ranks as the country's most rapidly expanding industrial sector and is now Mexico's second largest net foreign ex-

---

7. Jose L. Barraza, *Parques Industriales,* Mexico, September 1985, pp. 18–21.

Exhibit 2
NUMBER OF *MAQUILADORAS* PLANTS IN 1976

LOCATION	NUMBER
Total	448
Baja California	177
Ensenada	4
Mexicali	67
Tecate	10
Tijuana	96
Sonora	54
Agua Prieta	10
Nogales	42
San Luis R.C.	2
Chihuahua	—
Ciudad Juarez	96
Palomas	—
Coahuila	22
Ciudad Acuna	7
Piedras Negras	15
Tamaulipas	99
Reynosa	10
Matamoros	55
Nuevo Laredo	32

Source: NACLA.

Exhibit 3
OPERATING IN-BOUND PLANTS IN MEXICO

	TOTAL	BORDER CITIES	INTERIOR CITIES
1975	454	405	49
1976	448	395	53
1977	443	388	55
1978	457	411	46
1979	540	480	60
1980	620	551	69
1981	605	533	72
1982	588	516	72
1983	629	562	67
1984	722	641	81
1985	772	683	89

change earner (after petroleum). The real growth rate should continue to be at least 10 percent a year.[8] Growth is expected to be particularly strong in the automotive sector and in production of television sets and other electronic goods. Manufacturers already established in Mexico, such as General Electric, feel confident about the industry growth prospects. In 1985, GE completed three new in-bound plants in Ciudad Juarez, including a 110,000-square-foot manufacturing facility that was finished in December 1985.[9]

Up to September 1985, value-added re-exports netted Mexico $976.9 million in foreign exchange. This amount represented an increase of 15.3 percent from value-added re-exports, totalling $847.1 million from January to September 1984. From 1970 through 1985, there was an increase of 14.8 percent based on the projected figure of $1.6 billion in 1985.[10] (See Exhibit 4.)

Advantages
Generally, the in-bound plants add approximately $1 of value that incurs duties for each $2.38 worth of U.S. raw materials, parts, or components. Tariff rates vary according to the exact commodity that is entering the United States. Tariff rates on textiles, for instance, can be as little as 8 percent or as much as 35 percent. Under the generalization system of preferences, some items that meet certain criteria and requirements are exempt from duties. Electronic parts for computers, television sets, video casette recorders, and appliances have tariff rates that range from 0 to 10 or 12 percent; these goods must also meet certain criteria and requirements.[11]

Under the *maquiladora* program, U.S. components are shipped duty free to Mexico for assembly, semi-processing, or repair, and subsequently re-exported to the United States. U.S. duty is levied on the returning products only to the extent of the value that is added in Mexico. Mexican duty is levied on the components if they remain in Mexico for sale. Although most of the in-bond production is

8. Steven Rosenberg, "Manufacturing in Mexico," *Business Mexico,* September 1985, pp. 13–14.
9. Wygand, p. 58.
10. Roger Turner, "Mexico Desk Officer, International Trade Administration," *Business America,* November 1984.
11. Interview with J. Trevino, import-export specialist, customs-international bridge, Hidalgo, Texas, April 18, 1986.

Exhibit 4
VALUE ADDED BY THE MEXICAN *MAQUILADORA* INDUSTRY

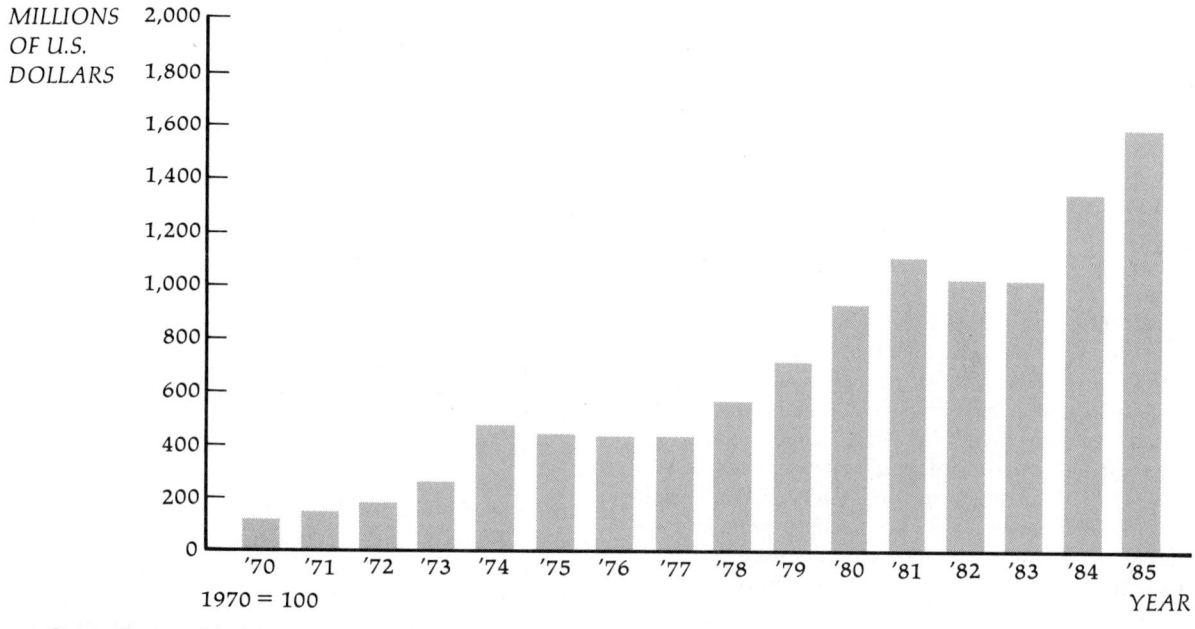

MILLIONS OF U.S. DOLLARS

1970 = 100

YEAR

Source: Business Mexico.

sold in the United States, U.S. firms also benefit from liberal laws regulating *maquiladora* operations. Plants are not confined to the 19-kilometer border area, and under certain restrictions up to 20 percent of the finished products can enter the Mexican market. These firms also have access to the country's raw materials and energy resources, have tax advantages, low freight costs in transferring products across the border, and—because of Mexico's economic agreements with other Latin American countries—easier access to Latin markets. Electricity rates in Mexico average about one-third the U.S. rates, land costs about one-fifth the U.S. cost, and construction rates are about one-half those in the United States. Other advantages are the proximity to the United States, overland door-to-door delivery, speedy access by executives and technicians, and a highly productive workforce. In border locations, the U.S. manager can live with his family on the U.S. side of the border and go to work in Mexico.[12]

---

12. Orme, p. 6.

Disadvantages
In August 1983, the Mexican government authorized sales in Mexico of up to 20 percent of production, under certain conditions. First, the percentage is calculated item by item, not on the total value of production. Second, there can be no similar Mexican production currently satisfying local market demand that could be damaged by the in-bound competition. Third, when there is insufficient Mexican production of an item considered essential to the local market, the proposed in-bond sales must be considered necessary to fulfill local demand. Finally, for sales in Mexico to be authorized, they must also be consistent with government guidelines for development of the industry in question. Authorization for sales in Mexico must be requested annually. Approvals may be reviewed during the year and possibly withdrawn if a Mexican producer proves to be manufacturing a comparable Mexican product in sufficient quantity. Most local sales options that have been approved have been in the electronics sector. Applications for sales of textiles and consumer durable goods usually have been rejected. All applications for local sales are made on Secofin's IM-

5 form. Other 1984 guidelines are: (1) the 20 percent local option should benefit zones I or II where possible (see Exhibit 5); (2) domestic sales cannot be increased at the expense of export sales because firms will still be expected to generate substantial foreign exchange; (3) in-bond companies with Mexican capital will be given priority in local option requests; (4) foreign-source components will require permanent import permits and must pay import duties; and (5) the 20 percent local option may be reduced or expanded as required.[13]

Labor

Because of the Mexican worker's manual dexterity, trainability, and motivation, maquiladora unit output often exceeds U.S. averages.[14] A high percentage of blue-collar workers are females, as can be seen in Exhibit 6. In 1975, 39,000 females and 19,000 males were employed; by 1981, 72,000 females and 38,000 males were employed. From January to August 1985, there were approximately 98,000 female and 74,000 male workers. According to Seligson, the higher percentage of female workers may be traced to their manual dexterity and their ability to adapt to tedium and unskilled jobs.[15] Recently, more skilled jobs have relocated to the *maquiladoras;* hence, the increase in male participation in the *maquiladora* industry.

The cost of Mexican labor is 20 to 25 percent of the cost of comparable labor in the United States. The work week is 25 percent longer, the pace of work is faster, and Mexico's high unemployment rate disciplines the workforce—absenteeism is a mere 2 percent, as compared with 5 to 9 percent in the United States.[16] Direct production labor on the assembly line in Chicago—including all fringe benefits, vacations, holidays, payroll, and tax and social security deductions—costs at least $6.50–$7.00 per hour. The same labor in Mexico equally calculated with full fringe benefits costs $0.80–$1.40 per hour, depending upon location. The cost per hour for an unskilled Mexican employee in U.S. dollars is $0.99

Exhibit 5
CITIES IN ZONES I AND II

BORDER	INTERIOR
Mexicali	Chihuahua City
Reynosa	Hermosillo
Matamoros	Saltillo
Ciudad Juarez	Torreon

COAST	
Veracruz	

along the border, $0.93 in Guadalajara, and $0.82 in Monterrey.[17] This cost includes a 40-percent employee fringe benefit package and the 30 percent increase in the minimum salary which was effective January 1, 1985.

Skilled labor is more expensive, but is still only about $1.35 an hour. All in-bound plants must pay the benefits required under Mexico's Federal Labor Law. Benefits include vacation and Christmas bonuses; seven paid holidays; payroll contributions for social security, education, maternity leave, employee housing, and day-care assistance; and state withholding taxes. Profit sharing of 0.08 percent of total annual plant income is also required. The basic wage rates in the in-bound industry from 1975 through 1985 are shown in Exhibit 7. At the end of 1985, the wage rate paid to the bulk of industry employees was just over $1 per hour with full fringe benefits. From $3,000 to $15,000 per year can be saved per production line worker when compared to U.S. salaries.[18]

Transportation

Mexico also offers the manufacturer the advantage of lower transportation costs, particularly if the Far East is used as a point of comparison. If products are assembled in the Far East, the manufacturer must pay shipping expenses of taking the materials there, bringing the products back, and distributing them worldwide. Most assembly plants in Mexico are about 19 kilometers (less than 12 miles) from the United States–Mexico border, or about 1,000 to

13. Turner, p. 30.
14. Carl A. Nelson, "Manufacturing in Mexico Using a *Maquiladora,*" *American Import Export Management,* April 1985, pp. 66–69.
15. Seligson, pp. 25–27.
16. James W. Russell, "U.S. Sweatshops Across the Rio Grande," *Business and Society Review,* Summer 1984, pp. 17–20.

17. Nelson, p. 69.
18. Ibid.

Exhibit 6
MEXICAN *MAQUILADORA* BLUE-COLLAR WORKERS

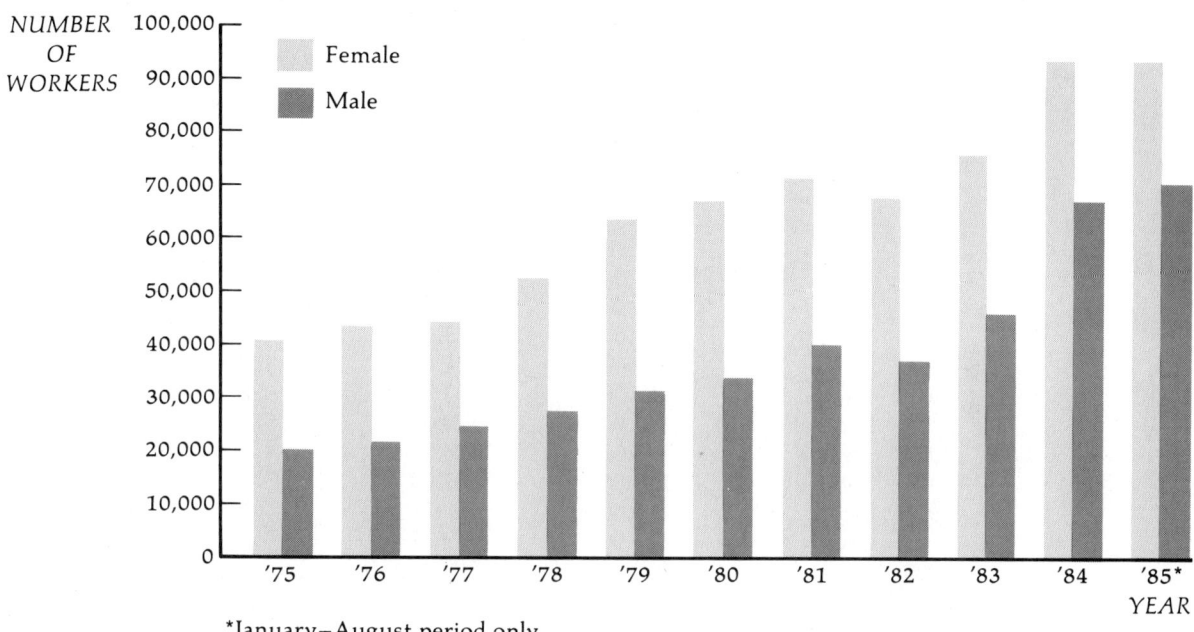

*January–August period only

Source: Business Mexico.

1,500 miles from the central United States. The savings in foreign transportation costs can approach 80 percent.[19]

By establishing near the border, a company could reduce both its shipping costs and delivery time. In the interior there are multiple Mexican consumer checkpoints, which eventually delay product distribution. Mexican law also prohibits foreign nationals from driving their carriers on Mexican highways. Thus Mexican-owned rolling stock must be driven by Mexican nationals, an expensive requirement when Mexican carriers have insufficient rolling stock. The further inland a company is located, the greater the probability that this problem will occur.[20]

19. Carlos Uriarte, "There's a Cheaper Way," *American Import Export Management*, July 1984, p. 30.
20. Turner.

LABOR UNIONS

A union's presence can be a legitimate business consideration for in-bound companies when deciding on the location of their operations. Unionization of in-bond plants is largely a matter of location. With the exception of plants in Tamaulipas, most border plants do not have unions. In Ciudad Juarez at least 35 percent of the *maquiladora* plants are unionized. Most of these unions are affiliated with the Confederation of Mexican Workers (CTM), a union confederation whose aim is to offset the rising costs of living through wage demands. The presence or absence of a union does not predetermine that a plant will or will not have difficulties. A union can be a stabilizing force when workers' demands are at issue. Although many of the workers are members of the unions, strikes are rare because—while the out-of-work employee in the United States receives unemployment benefits—Mexican workers do not. Also, while employees are on strike, the Mexican government closes the plant, keeping supervisory

Exhibit 7
BASIC WAGE RATES IN THE IN-BOUND INDUSTRY

		DAILY MINIMUM WAGE (PESOS)[a]	AVERAGE PESO-TO-DOLLAR EXCHANGE RATE[b]	AVERAGE DAY RATE (U.S. DOLLARS)
1975		84.90	12.50	$6.79
1976		98.80	15.40	6.42
1977		133.90	22.60	5.92
1978		147.00	22.80	6.45
1979		162.00	22.80	7.11
1980		180.00	23.00	7.83
1981		210.00	24.60	8.54
1982:	1st half	280.00	43.18	6.48
	2nd half	364.00	70.00	5.20
1983:	1st half	455.00	108.27	4.20
	2nd half	523.00	132.00	3.96
1984:	1st half	680.00	155.71	4.37
	2nd half	816.00	179.37	4.55
1985:	1st half	1,050.00	209.47	5.06
	2nd half	1,250.00	305.69	4.09
1986:	as of Jan. 1	1,650.00	372.80	4.42

a. Minimum wage for Mexico City as well as such northern border cities as Tijuana, Mexicali, Ciudad Juarez, Reynosa and Matamoros.
b. As of 1982, wages paid are converted at the so-called "controlled" peso-to-dollar rate of exchange.
Source: Business Mexico.

and management personnel out until the strike is settled. The evidence concerning the loss of jobs in the United States to Mexico is conflicting, due to a reallocation of jobs in the United States to support the Mexican *maquiladora* program.

GOVERNMENT SUPPORT

The *maquiladora* industry, like all industries, is influenced a great deal by government and political factors. Firms must comply with regulations dealing with hiring practices, taxes, consumer lending, safety, pricing, advertising, plant location, and pollution. Governmental activity provides both opportunities and threats.

During 1985 President Miguel de la Madrid and his administration provided promotional and structural support for the industry and its growth prospects.

SUMMARY

Mexico's *maquiladora* industry offers considerable advantages to any company that wants to cut its production costs. One of the main savings that the *maquiladora* offers are duty-free imports of raw materials to Mexico for use in production. A firm can cut costs by setting up a *maquiladora* plant, contracting with a *maquiladora* subcontractor, or using a shelter plan. The company will be established in an industry with a real growth rate of 10 percent per year. The tariff rates depend considerably on each commodity. Textile tariff rates can range from 8 percent to 35 percent. Tariff rates for electronic components range from 0 percent to 12 percent. Advantages in the industry are low freight costs in transferring products across the border, low utility rates, cheap labor costs, and a highly productive workforce. Finally, the *maquiladora* industry also has the advantage of having total government support. Thus, a company must look at many factors to decide if the *maquiladora* industry is indeed a golden opportunity.

B&B WOOD STOVE COMPANY

McRAE C. BANKS II
Mississippi State University

Frank Barcus and Bill Blevins, the owners of B&B Wood Stove Company, arrived on time for the appointment with their supplier, the Snow Wolf Wood Stove distributorship. The owners of that company, Jim and Evelyn Strong, were long-time friends of Frank. Jim believed that they would go along, albeit reluctantly, with the details of his plan to purchase 1986 stoves at a discount. Frank, although he had heard each part of the plan explained numerous times, remained skeptical.

The group, which also included Kerry Marvin, Jim and Evelyn's general manager, exchanged pleasantries and sat down at the conference table. Looking around at his partner and his suppliers, Bill began.

"We are interested in purchasing your entire inventory of 1986 model stoves," he said. "Because the 1987 model is available with all of its advanced features, most Snow Wolf dealers are advertising it rather than the 1986 model, which has encountered stiff competition. We don't think you will sell many of the old stoves, but with the right price discount, we think we can move them in our Northern Virginia stores. We are willing to pay $400 per stove."

For a moment, no one spoke. Then, Kerry Marvin, his face distorted with anger, reacted quickly.

"You must be crazy!" he yelled. "You normally pay $573 for those stoves! At $400, we will barely cover our costs. What makes you think you can waltz in here and tell us how much you will pay? It's as if you think you are doing us a favor!"

"How many 1986 stoves do you have?" asked Bill.

"I'm not going to tell you that," Kerry replied.

"OK, suit yourself." said Bill. "If we don't know how many you have, we certainly can't make you an offer." And, turning to Evelyn, he said, "I'm sure you would like to have the money, wouldn't you, Evelyn?"

"Everyone wants money, Bill," she replied. "But I don't think we can afford to sell the stoves for $400. I think we can handle $500. How about it?"

Bill continued, "As I see it, you have two choices. You can sell us the stoves for $400 each, or you can forget about selling them to us. If you sell them to us, you have a nice lump sum of cash which you can take to the bank. If you don't sell them to us, you will lose your business, and we can buy your inventory—perhaps your entire operation—for what we are offering."

Everyone was silent for a minute. Finally, Jim said, "What makes you think we will lose the business?"

"We know that you have a $35,000 note from the bank which is due this afternoon and which has been extended twice already," Bill answered. "We don't think you can pay it and we know the bank won't extend it again."

Kerry countered with, "We can sell the stoves to another dealer at a higher price."

"We don't think so," said Bill. "Look, you have your two retail stores which have not been moving stoves lately. Charlie Dodd has two stores which haven't been moving stoves. He's strapped for cash. In fact, he wanted to borrow money from us. Ron Greenfuss just opened his store last month. In ad-

This case, written specifically for this book, is printed by permission.

dition to being short on capital, he doesn't have an established market.

"We, on the other hand, have been moving thirty to fifty stoves a week. Not only are we the only dealer who has the cash to buy the stoves, but we are the only dealer in a position to buy them because we can move them."

"I don't like it one bit," Kerry said. "How did you get that information?"

"From all of you," Bill answered. "And from observing your operations. Every time we get together you are complaining about how tight cash is, or how expensive your operations are, or how you had to get an extension from the bank on a loan. All we are doing is using that information at an opportune time. But it isn't as if we are gouging you. When we picked up stoves the other day, we estimated that you had 100 of the 1986 models in the warehouse. That's $40,000, more than enough to cover the note, and it relieves you of the old inventory.

"We are offering you a new lease on life. *You* get out from under the bank and have an opportunity to streamline your operations. *We* get stoves at a discount which we can pass on to our customers. *Everyone* wins!"

Jim, Evelyn, and Kerry excused themselves to discuss the offer. When they returned, Kerry asked, "Will you give us a check now for the entire amount and date it yesterday?"

"Let's go to the warehouse and check your inventory," Bill said.

COLLECTION SERVICES, INC.

McRAE C. BANKS II
Mississippi State University

In early January 1987, Raymond Baines received a call from Shana Dupard, president of Collection Services, Inc. Dupard told Baines, a local consultant, that her company was experiencing some problems and she wanted his help in solving them. As she expressed it, "We need some ideas to help us generate more cash. The collections business is very competitive and margins are low. The only way I can see for us to generate more cash is to diversify." They agreed to meet at Dupard's office to discuss Collection Services' problems as Dupard saw them.

When they met, Dupard's story had changed somewhat. Baines learned that Collection Services had lost money the last four years. The cause, Dupard said, was a branch office venture that had been disastrous due to unforeseen and unusual conditions. Later in their conversation Dupard told Baines that "things have been happening so fast it's hard to keep up with them." Still later, she said "I do a lot of good planning but I get a project or program started and the next thing I know some misfortune occurs and I have to change things. I never get to follow things through to the end." When Baines asked about her employees, Dupard shifted uneasily in her seat while stating that her employees were the best and gave their all for the firm.

After more discussion, Baines and Dupard agreed that he would look around, observe, and if necessary, talk with the employees about the business in order to perform a general analysis. From his analysis, Baines could identify the problems of the business and, if Dupard agreed, they could begin working to solve them.

THE COLLECTION SERVICES INDUSTRY

The collection services industry consists of two types of services: commercial debt collection, which handles claims of one company against another, and consumer debt collection, which handles claims of companies against individuals. The industry can be further divided into captive and free accounts. Captive accounts are those that are collected in-house by the maker of the loan. Examples of institutions that use this type of account are banks, credit companies, and many larger organizations such as utilities and hospitals. Free accounts are those that are placed by the loan maker with an external organization. While many collection service companies offer both commercial and consumer collections, most tend to specialize in one or the other, and the vast majority deal with free accounts. Collection Services, while engaging in some commercial collection activity, is essentially a consumer collection agency.

Consumer collection services is a fragmented industry. The top two firms, Payco American Corporation and FCA International Ltd., have less than 3 percent each of the U.S. market. The remaining 94 percent is divided among about 6,500 agencies. Partly because entry is so easy (no particular train-

The material facts presented herein are accurate but the names and some other details have been changed at the request of the client. Some data for this case were collected by Ann Brooks, Denise Martin, and Karen Russell, former students of the author's at Radford University. The author is indebted to Barbara Spencer, Steve Taylor, and Rebecca Porterfield, colleagues at Mississippi State University, for comments on earlier versions of this case. This case, written specifically for this book, is printed by permission.

ing or licensing is required and little capital is needed—in most cases a telephone and an ad in the local paper suffice), collection agencies proliferate. Another reason for the proliferation of collection agencies has been increased demand for services. In 1986 consumer installment debt totaled $595 billion, having grown by 20 percent in 1984, 18 percent in 1985, and 11 percent in 1986. The rule of thumb is that 2 percent of the increase will go to collection.

One important trend, computerization, has emerged in the consumer collections industry. Previously, the high cost of hardware made it difficult for cottage-type industries such as consumer collection agencies to computerize. Additionally, no software was available. However, now that inexpensive personal computers are available, the industry has begun to computerize. Furthermore, several companies now market hardware systems and software designed for the consumer collections industry. Many companies that have computerized indicate that they can now collect small balances productively. Other benefits include an improved work environment and reduced turnover.

HISTORY OF COLLECTION SERVICES

Collection Services was founded in 1951 in Pearisburg, Virginia, a small Giles County community, by Marilyn and Harold Barclay. Marilyn Barclay had worked for a credit and collection company in Atlanta, before moving to Virginia, where her husband had accepted a position on the engineering faculty at Virginia Tech. Ms. Barclay was interested in working but found no credit and collection companies in the area. After considerable discussion, the Barclays decided to start their own company to serve Giles County and parts of neighboring Montgomery County.

Collection Services grew slowly over the next ten years. Population and businesses were growing slowly. Turning a profit was hard because considerable travel was needed in the rural area to visit existing and prospective clients and to collect accounts.

Marilyn was actually relieved when Harold accepted a position at another school outside the area. After meeting with several prospective buyers, the Barclays sold their business to George Beeder, a local businessman who had interests in many different businesses.

Beeder was in the process of moving many of his operations to Vicker's Switch in Montgomery County. His expectation was that nearby Blacksburg would grow substantially as Virginia Tech sought to serve the expanding baby-boom generation. That would mean more students, faculty, staff, and businesses. Additionally, Vicker's Switch was located halfway between Blacksburg and Radford, home of Radford College.

Collection Services, like most mom-and-pop businesses, was small. It had two employees, both of whom remained with the firm when it moved. Beeder personally managed the business for several years before hiring John Miles and Shana Dupard in 1968. Miles was hired to manage the business, although he had no credit or collection experience. Dupard was hired as a telephone collector.

Dupard, a recent high school graduate, quickly established herself as the firm's best collector. Her warm smile belied her aggressive nature, and both qualities helped her to bring in new clients and vigorously pursue collections. When Miles left in 1972, Beeder made Dupard his manager.

As the area prospered, so did Collection Services, due in large part to Dupard's hard work. She hired and trained collectors, met with prospective and existing clients, personally handled the hardest collections, and met with Beeder to discuss ideas for the company. Beeder continued to handle bookkeeping and other financial details, but he always rewarded Dupard handsomely for her efforts.

One of the ideas Dupard and Beeder discussed was computerizing the voluminous records of Collection Services and developing online account access for collectors. This would be a major undertaking because no collection agency in the entire industry had computerized its collection accounts and provided online access to collectors. When five used Digital Equipment Corporation computers were offered for sale by Virginia Tech, however, Beeder saw an opportunity. He purchased the computers, hired a programmer, and began developing programs to handle Collection Services' business.

Beeder's efforts met with immediate success from the industry and from clients. He and Dupard traveled around the nation, speaking to various industry groups about the computerization of Collection Services. Additionally, two major accounts, Mountain Power and Crescent Medical Insurance, were so impressed with the firm's capabilities that they asked Collection Services to handle their collections.

After Collection Services was completely computerized and only minor periodic adjustments were necessary, Beeder realized that his programmer and computers could handle a far greater volume of work than the firm could provide. In an effort to be cost effective, he sought new applications and formed a separate company, Computerized Business Services, to handle all the computer-related work.

By 1981, Beeder was spending more and more time with Computerized Business Services. Realizing that his divided attention was beginning to create problems for Collection Services, Beeder offered Dupard 51 percent ownership at no immediate cost to her. Dupard had to agree, however, to pay Beeder $500 per month for computer maintenance and consulting as long as he lived and as long as the company survived, to use Computerized Business Services for all of Collection Service's computer needs, and to pay any dividends owed him based on his ownership share. Shana agreed, thus becoming Collection Services' chief executive and majority stockholder.

COLLECTION SERVICES UNDER DUPARD

Despite the technological advantage her firm had over competing credit and collection firms, Dupard worried that competitors would grab its big accounts. Certainly, smaller accounts, especially medical offices, had strayed, but they always came back to Collection Services because competitors rarely followed through on their promises. Yet the loss of a major account might damage Collection Services beyond repair.

In order to be closer to the firm's two major accounts, Mountain Power and Crescent Medical Insurance, Dupard opened a branch office in Roanoke, Virginia, home of each company's headquarters. She hired two inexperienced collectors to work in the office and placed one of her top collectors, Carolyn Hayes, in the position of branch manager. Hayes had no previous managerial experience.

Branch operations started slowly. In addition to training the new collectors, Hayes was expected to meet with prospective clients, yet she never had enough time for everything. First she tried working with the trainees in the morning and visiting prospective clients in the afternoon, but the trainees had so many questions and were so unsure of themselves that she never felt comfortable leaving them alone. She also tried having the trainees come in at noon, devoting her morning hours to prospective clients and working with the trainees in the afternoon, but that left the trainees alone after five o'clock when Carolyn went home. Records indicated that, even after the training period, collection productivity was extremely low from 5:00 to 8:00 P.M., when the office closed. The situation worsened when Hayes became ill for an extended period of time. Connie Laurie, Dupard's collections manager, was sent to manage the office on a part-time basis, resulting in even less supervision of collectors and even lower collection productivity in both offices.

Two other problems relating to Roanoke operations deserve mention. First, the branch used modems and conventional telephone lines to access the computers in Vicker's Switch. This was not only slow but expensive. Second, Collection Services was competing directly with the Roanoke Valley Merchants' Association, a membership group that served as a collection agency. Because it was well established and simple and inexpensive to join, the Association had most of the small retail and service accounts in the Roanoke area. Larger companies typically had their own staff for collections.

The Roanoke experience was a disaster. Productivity was low among collectors and not a single new account was acquired. In order to defray part of the loss attributed to Roanoke operations, Dupard sold the credit reporting portion of the business to Computerized Business Services in December 1985. By December 1986, she had given up on the Roanoke branch, fired the collectors, and brought Carolyn Hayes back to the Vicker's Switch office.

AT PRESENT

Collection Services currently has seventeen employees; two are trainees. While the number of employees had remained relatively constant over the past several years, turnover has been a constant problem. Dupard noted that it is not unusual for a person to be hired and start training but quit after less than a week; some even quit the first day. Three employees, Hayes, Laurie, and Brenda Tolley, have been with Collection Services for more than five years. The next longest tenure is twenty-two months, and everyone else has been with the firm less than fifteen months.

Hayes is currently in charge of marketing. Ideally, she coordinates the promotion of Collection Services to prospective and existing clients. As a new task, she has been asked to develop seminars for businesses wishing to improve collection productivity. In fact, Hayes spends most of her time training new collectors, and Dupard calls on some of the larger existing accounts. No one is currently calling on smaller accounts or prospective accounts.

Connie Laurie is collections manager. She is responsible for hiring and firing collectors, training them, and organizing the collection priorities for collectors on a daily basis. Because the computer keeps track of collections, she is able to monitor productivity easily and make adjustments when a collector seems to be having problems. Because Hayes is currently providing training, Laurie feels that she has lost some control over her collectors. Additionally, as the financial fortunes of Collection Services ebb and flow, Dupard alters the collection minimums. Sometimes Laurie must tell her collectors not to worry about collecting any amount less than $50; at other times, the amount is as low as $25 and on occasion, it has been $10. On paper, Laurie has two supervisors assisting her. In practice, they do little because the money they earn is based on the amount they collect, with no monetary consideration for supervising others.

Brenda Tolley, Dupard's assistant, handles a variety of duties, including managing the firm in Dupard's absence. Other duties include minor computer programming chores, answering technical questions by collectors, and bookkeeping. She acquired the latter duty because the bookkeeper quit upon being told the company would be placing all of its financial and bookkeeping records on computer.

Services, Customers, and Procedures

Collection Services collects overdue accounts for a variety of clients. By far the largest clients are Mountain Power and Crescent Medical Insurance. For Mountain Power, Collection Services handles accounts that are overdue by 90 days or more. Accounts are located throughout southwestern Virginia, from Staunton to Bristol and as far east as

Martinsville, and in the southern half of West Virginia. Crescent accounts handled by Collection Services are usually larger and older; most are at least 120 days old and are confined to southwestern Virginia. Other clients are local hospitals and most of the area's medical and dental practices.

Collection Services earns at least one-third of everything collected, though smaller clients may pay as much as one-half the amount collected. At the same time, if Collection Services collects nothing, it earns nothing.

A typical account comes to Collection Services when it is several months overdue. All new accounts are immediately logged onto the computer system and a statement is mailed to the debtor indicating that the account is now with a collection agency and payment is to be made to the agency. In three weeks a follow-up is sent if the account remains unpaid, followed by a certified letter in another week if necessary. After that, collectors start calling.

Collectors must locate a phone number before they can call a debtor. Most information provided by the client is limited to the debtor's name, home address, balance, and account number. Occasionally, a phone number is provided. Dupard does not allow her collectors to call the client and ask for a telephone number fearing that such calls will antagonize the client. Instead, collectors must spend time searching a variety of directories in an effort to locate the debtor.

After a debtor is located, the collector must get a promise that payment will be made. Then the collector flags the file to be reviewed on a certain date to ensure that payment has indeed been made. A complicating factor is that some debtors mail their payments to the original company rather than to Collection Services. If the company does not inform Collection Services that it has received payment, the collector will continue to pursue the debtor, creating additional problems for Collection Services.

If an account remains unpaid and it exceeds $50 in value, it may be turned over to the legal department. The process is to inform the debtor that he or she has 15 days to contact Collection Services and make payment before legal action is taken. If payment is not received within the time period, the appropriate legal documents are prepared and they are turned over to Collection Services's attorney. The attorney is responsible for filing the papers and ensuring that the debtor is served a summons.

Facilities and Equipment

Collection Services occupies half of a small building on Big Lick Road in Vicker's Switch. Space is inadequate for the number of employees. Collectors work side-by-side with only a small amount of space between computer screens and little room to spread out materials. The constant high noise level makes telephone conversations difficult.

Telephone directories and other reference books, the lifeblood of the collector, are in short supply, and several collectors must share each set of books. Because all of the account information is computerized, each collector must have access to a computer in order to contact debtors. Unfortunately, there are not enough terminals for each collector to have access to one and some collectors are invariably idled. In an attempt to solve this problem, Dupard and Laurie have established a ten-hour, four-day work shift. Collectors work from 8:00 A.M. to 7:00 P.M. with an hour for lunch and breaks and have staggered days off. While this arrangement has relieved some of the congestion, it has also lowered employee morale—collectors resent the long hours and the lack of choice of days off. Another problem is that the Digital computers are old and crashes and downtime are common sources of irritation.

People

When Collection Services has openings in its training program, advertisements are placed in the classified section of the local paper, *The News Messenger*, and the New River Valley supplement of *The Roanoke Times*. Applicants are instructed to visit the office and complete an application. The first screening procedure eliminates those who cannot read or write and those with criminal records. All other applicants receive a phone call from the collections manager, who attempts to screen them based on their telephone delivery. Those with acceptable telephone skills are offered employment. Only minimal information is provided about the job.

Training is a two- to three-month process, depending on the trainee's progress. Currently, Carolyn Hayes works with trainees eight hours a day, five days a week. She explains pertinent state and federal regulations, work rules, and the computer system. She also works with trainees in groups on role-playing exercises and sits with them, in groups, as they make live calls.

The proximity of one collector to another, described earlier, often results in short tempers. Employees complain about another person's smoke, spilled coffee, sniffles, loud voice, and countless other things.

Collectors are paid according to the amount they collect, with no guaranteed base wage. The firm is officially closed on holidays, but many collectors work because they know they can catch debtors at home. No insurance (life or health) is provided, nor is there a retirement plan. Occasional contests are run for collectors in which the prize might be an Avon trinket, but the more common competition is against a goal. In such situations, all collectors are contributing toward the accomplishment of a goal which, if reached, results in free pizza.

Sensing an undercurrent of dissatisfaction and unrest, Baines developed a questionnaire (Exhibit 1), which Dupard agreed he could pass out to the

---

Exhibit 1
THE QUESTIONNAIRE

I am seeking your input to help Collection Services become a better company. Please complete this questionnaire and return it in the attached postage-paid envelope. Your responses will remain anonymous and only aggregate information will be provided to the company, not your individual responses. Feel free to use the back of this form or additional paper. Thank you for your assistance.

—Raymond Baines
Consultant

1. The existing training program requires new collectors to be in training for two to three months. Do you have any suggestions which might help shorten the training program while providing a strong program which will prepare new collectors for their jobs? Do you have any other suggestions about the training program?
2. What suggestions can you offer Collection Services on how to increase collection productivity?
3. What can Collection Services change to help you work more efficiently and effectively?
4. What suggestions do you have for making Collection Services a more profitable business?
5. What other comments do you have?

employees. In an employee meeting, he explained the questionnaire and emphasized that responses would be anonymous. They would be returned to him, and only aggregate responses would be passed on to Dupard.

Although Dupard agreed in principle to the questionnaire process, she did not welcome it. She saw no reason to query employees. Initially, she wanted employees to turn their completed questionnaires over to her and she would give them to Baines. In explaining the need for his questionnaire, Baines said that employees sometimes see things about a business that executives cannot see. He said that the survey would be more forthright and more valuable if responses did not go to her.

The responses were informative. Baines's summary for each of the questions is found in Exhibit 2.

With only a few days remaining until he was to meet with Dupard, Baines had to start making sense of all this information in order to determine the problems. Also, he wanted to have some game plan for attacking them if Dupard wanted to move forward.

Exhibit 2
SUMMARY OF RESPONSES

1. The existing training program requires new collectors to be in training for two to three months. Do you have any suggestions which might help shorten the training program while providing a strong program which will prepare new collectors for their jobs? Do you have any other suggestions about the training program?

   Most employees feel that Collection Services needs a better trainer, one who knows how to train collectors. Some suggested that more than one trainer was necessary in order to provide more individual attention.

   New employees should be guided through Collection Services step-by-step rather than having virtually all attention paid to training for telephone collections. They want to see the whole picture.

   Specific suggestions included:
   a. Develop a better training manual with basic collection procedures. The manual should address the firm's method of collecting accounts and discuss other important office duties.
   b. Collectors should be given their own phone directory set, city directories, and a backwards directory for each area.
   c. Use much more role-playing. Show videotapes of different situations and how to handle them

2. What suggestions can you offer Collections Services on how to increase collection productivity?

   Here, employees mentioned the need for more sets of books. Other suggestions were keeping computer records updated, reducing the amount of computer downtime and slowdowns, working out an arrangement with clients where debtor payments are reported to Collection Services, and having a receptionist-secretary who will receive visitors, provide typing, answer the phone, and order supplies.

   Several employees mentioned a need for interpersonal skill development and team building. The feeling expressed was that some employees are making no effort to get along with others. A related suggestion was that more space was needed to reduce stress and confusion.

   Other workers suggested that collectors could perform a variety of tasks to reduce boredom and to increase efficiency. One idea was to have some collectors track down debtors who have disappeared (skip tracing) while others called debtors.

   Finally, most employees indicated an interest in knowing the goals of the firm and the problems and prospects it faces.

3. What can Collection Services change to help you work more efficiently and effectively?

   All but one employee was concerned about the lack of benefits and a feeling of being overworked.

   Several employees feel that a physical rearrangement of the office should be made and better ventilation provided.

   Two employees indicated that a faster computer should be purchased.

4. What suggestions do you have for making Collection Services a more profitable business?

One group of suggestions related to Collection Services's clients. Employees suggested that relations with clients needed to be improved. Better working relationships could result in more debtor information from the clients, more timely receipt of overdue accounts, and better reporting of debtor payments made to clients.

A second suggestion was that clients should be screened better. There is some feeling that certain clients are turning over accounts that have been dunned to the point of being immune and that such accounts are a waste of time.

Finally, employees want to know the goals of the company and its status. They sense that profits are down but they do not know by how much and how critical that is.

5. What other comments do you have?

New collectors should have a lower collection workload than experienced collectors.

Deadbeat accounts should move to the legal department faster or be purged quicker.

True incentives should be offered.

Employees should be evaluated at least annually and preferably more often. Salaries should be increased and increases should be tied to evaluations.

Employees should be treated fairly and given positive reinforcement.

HUFF CHEMICAL, INC.

EUGENE A. NINI
University of Texas
of the Permian Basin

Troy Huff owns a small chemical processing business. Because of his health, Huff has decided to sell Huff Chemical, Inc.

Joseph Jones has a management consulting firm, and Huff has approached him in January 1988 to set a price to use in selling his business.

Huff wants to sell the corporation as a whole, but

This case, written specifically for this text, is printed by permission.

he will entertain any other suggestions that Jones may have.

Jones asked Huff for two sets of data: (1) current financial statements; and (2) the same current financial statements with all personal living expenses of Troy Huff and his family removed. Jones explained to Huff that he knows that all entrepreneurs rob their businesses and that he will keep all the data confidential.

Huff provides the attached data. Jones calculates a selling price for his business.

Exhibit 1
HUFF CHEMICAL: BALANCE SHEET (December 31, 1987)

ASSETS		LIABILITIES AND CAPITAL	
Current Assets		Current Liabilities	
Cash in bank	$ 5,459.16	Withheld tax, federal	$ 604.00
Cash in bank	2,158.68	Withheld tax, FICA	651.22
Petty cash	100.00	TEC payable	203.49
Accounts receivable	81,570.15	FUTA payable	50.89
Expense advance	1,382.47	Sales tax payable	972.04
Expense advance	100.00	Accounts payable	25,383.65
Inventory	17,473.63	Current portion of notes	22,116.74
Office supplies	321.44	Salary payable	3,597.31
Supplies	2,194.43	Commissions payable	300.00
Expense advance, employee	100.00	Patent royalties payable	1,990.59
Note receivable, Universal	2,690.80	Total Current Liabilities	$ 55,869.93
Note receivable, Vogue	3,653.33		
Note receivable, Troy Huff	18,378.88		
Total Current Assets	$135,582.97		

Fixed Assets			Long-Term Liabilities		
Furniture, fixtures, and equipment	$44,159.43		Mortgage, Ryan	$72,707.40	
Computer printers and equipment	3,381.37		Note payable, IBM computers	1,096.60	
Mixer equipment	4,522.63		Note payable, Dodge pickup	184.41	
1988 Audi	26,867.35		Less current part of notes	(22,116.74)	
Building	70,035.00		Note payable, Audi	15,356.60	
Building improvements	41,000.46		Total Long-Term Liabilities		67,228.27
1983 Dodge pickup	6,103.95		Total Liabilities		$123,098.20
Renovation	5,100.95		Capital		
IBM Computer	2,180.00		Common stock issued	$ 1,000.00	
Accumulated depreciation	(72,121.67)		Paid-in surplus	4,006.13	
Total Fixed Assets		131,229.47	Retained earnings	148,208.11	
Other Assets			Total Capital		153,214.24
Land	$ 9,500.00				
Total Other Assets		9,500.00	TOTAL LIABILITIES AND CAPITAL		$276,312.44
TOTAL ASSETS		$276,312.44			

Exhibit 2

HUFF CHEMICAL, INC.: INCOME STATEMENT (period ending December 31, 1987)

Income			$323,476.80
Less cost of sales			
Cost of goods sold		$55,314.53	
Cost of freight		32,671.16	
Total cost of sales			87,985.69
Gross profit			$235,491.11
Less expenses			
Officer's salary		$ 36,229.41	
Salaries and wages		38,168.48	
Advertising and sales promotion		1,617.39	
Auto and truck expense		7,586.92	
Bad debts		29.13	
Business consulting		5,822.59	
Commissions		4,528.68	
Casual labor		970.43	
Consulting fees		930.00	
Charitable contributions		323.48	
Dues, fees, subscriptions		3,881.73	
Employee awards		1,325.00	
Employee medical		4,528.68	
Employee IRA		2,264.34	
Employee training and conventions		233.48	
Insurance		7,063.45	

Exhibit 2
**HUFF CHEMICAL, INC.: INCOME STATEMENT (period ending
December 31, 1987) (*continued*)**

Interest	9,968.65	
Janitorial	3,881.73	
Legal and accounting	3,558.25	
Office expenses	6,146.06	
Research and development	67.42	
Repair and maintenance	1,617.39	
Supplies	5,175.63	
Taxes, payroll	4,812.09	
Taxes, other	1,940.86	
Telephone	6,146.06	
Telephone lease	970.43	
Travel	2,911.30	
Entertainment	4,528.68	
Utilities	2,264.34	
Depreciation expense	39,787.65	
Employee medical insurance	1,293.91	
Waste disposal expense	323.48	
Building improvements	1,293.91	
Patent royalty expense	2,264.34	
Total expenses		214,455.37
Operating income		21,035.74
Other income		
Interest income	$ 1,617.39	
Discounts earned	25.00	
Early retirement of debt	16,820.80	
Gain on sale of asset	4,852.16	
Miscellaneous income	323.48	
Total other income		23,638.83
NET INCOME		$44,674.57

Exhibit 3
**HUFF CHEMICAL, INC.: ADJUSTED INCOME STATEMENT
(period ending December 31, 1987)**

Income		$323,476.80
Less cost of sales		
Cost of goods sold	$55,314.53	
Cost of freight	32,671.16	
Total cost of sales		87,985.69
Gross profit		$235,491.11
Less expenses		
Officer's salary	$38,000.00	
Salaries and wages	30,700.00	
Auto and truck expense	2,000.00	
Commissions	4,200.00	

Casual labor	2,000.00	
Dues, fees, subscriptions	8,300.00	
Employee training and conventions	300.00	
Insurance	4,100.00	
Interest	7,600.00	
Legal and accounting	4,000.00	
Office expenses	2,800.00	
Repair and maintenance	1,000.00	
Supplies	2,400.00	
Taxes, payroll	5,000.00	
Taxes, other	1,500.00	
Telephone	5,800.00	
Travel	1,600.00	
Entertainment	1,500.00	
Utilities	2,200.00	
Depreciation expense	39,111.68	
Employee medical insurance	1,500.00	
Waste disposal expense	400.00	
Building improvements	1,600.00	
Patent royalty expense	2,000.00	
Total expenses		169,611.68
Less operating income		65,879.43
Other income		
Interest income	$ 1,617.39	
Discounts earned	25.00	
Early retirement of debt	16,820.80	
Gain on sale of asset	4,852.16	
Miscellaneous income	323.48	
Total other income		23,638.83
NET INCOME		$89,518.26

Huff Chemical, Inc. is offering an adjusted financial statement in an effort to accurately reflect its profitability to a nonparticipating owner group. A brief summary of the affected portions of the statements is offered herein.

1. *Assets.* Principal asset adjustments constitute removal of a vehicle the corporation provides to owner (1988 Audi) and mobile home utilized as a storage building. Neither item is essential to the operation or profitability of the firm.
2. *Liabilities.* All current notes payable were reconciled to date. Previously mentioned 1988 Audi was deleted as well as Vice President's (owner's wife) annual salary.
3. *Income statement*
   a. *Salaries.* Officer's salary increased to $38,000. Wages decreased to two employees and a bookkeeper: one employee at $14,700, one employee at $10,800, one bookkeeper at $5,200.
   b. *Advertising and sales promotion.* Due to the nature of this business, they are not needed.
   c. *Aubomobile and truck expense.* Decrease to reflect only 1981 Dodge delivery vehicle, which is free and clear.
   d. *Business consulting.* Deleted.
   e. *Casual labor.* Decreased to reflect labor pertaining to operations only.
   f. *Consulting fees.* Deleted.
   g. *Employee awards.* Deleted.
   h. *Employee IRA.* Deleted; only eligible employee was owner.
   i. *Insurance.* Adjusted to reflect insurance required for operations.
   j. *Interest.* Decreased to compensate removal of 1988 Audi.
   k. *Janitorial.* Deleted, payment was to family baby sitter.
   l. *Office expenses.* Decreased to reflect actual costs; a major portion of this was personal living expenses of the owner.

Exhibit 3
HUFF CHEMICAL, INC.: ADJUSTED INCOME STATEMENT
(period ending December 31, 1987) (*continued*)

m. *Repairs and maintenance.* Decreased to reflect anticipated costs.
n. *Lab supplies.* Decreased to reflect actual cost.
o. *Payroll taxes.* Adjusted to projected salaries outlined previously.
p. *Telephone lease.* Paid in full.
q. *Travel expense.* Decreased to reflect anticipated sales travel and related business travel only.
r. *Entertainment.* Decreased to anticipated costs as related to sales only.
s. *Employee medical insurance.* Adjusted to accommodate projected staff as previously outlined.

Exhibit 4
JONES'S LETTER TO HUFF

Mr. Troy Huff
Huff Chemical, Inc.
P.O. Box 11111
Belton, Calif. 11112

Dear Mr. Huff:

Based on the information provided by you to our office we have completed a comprehensive analysis and valuation for your use.

Following is a list of the investigative and analytical procedures we deemed appropriate for our purposes.

1. All operating statements were thoroughly reviewed and each account was defined by its contents and valued separately.
2. Comparative analysis was limited to the most current periods (specifically the last two years) in an effort to maintain consistent application of forecasting techniques.
3. Income statement and balance sheet figures were adjusted to reflect a non-prejudice operating environment and give a true picture of arm's-length operation from an investor's point of view.
4. Market value figures for the pro-forma balance sheet were developed through a combination of desktop techniques including recent appraisals, auction prices, local producer price index figures, and comparisons of similar industry data.
5. Risk assessment techniques included capitalization rate adjustment, term differentiation, and other statistical evaluation of changes in financial position, which were material in the forecasting process.

Given the aforementioned procedures, we have arrived at a range of values indicative of the various risk assessments that might be applied to this operation. Competitive pressures, price elasticity, availability of personnel, and geographic constraints were all considered, to name a few, and the respective weighting of each of these exogenous variables accounted for the range of relevant values.

In addition to valuing Huff Chemical, Inc., as a going concern, we felt it appropriate to estimate a liquidated value as a measure of potential downside risk. A simple discounting of the fair market value of the assets weighted by their relative liquidity generated this value, and we believe that the result fairly appraises the balance sheet in a worst case condition.

A summary of our analysis follows with appropriate reference to the exhibits found at the end of this evaluation. In an effort to maintain a minimum level of complexity, we have omitted some negotiable considerations that may be material in determining the final value, i.e., patent rights, management contracts, and owner financing. Tax considerations that evolve as a function of structure may also have a bearing on the price. While it is not our intent to give advice on such matters (tax counsel and your CPA should be consulted here), it is generally considered more favorable to the seller if the corporation is sold as opposed to the assets alone being sold. Conversely the buyer, in an effort to avoid known or unknown liabilities, will desire a purchase of assets only.

We have raised this nonexhaustive list of issues to highlight the wide range of values that may be applied to the actual sale of the business and to clarify that our analysis should be considered only as an accurate, well-thought-out starting point.

1. Huff Chemical, Inc., sold as a going concern: $288,000.00 (see exhibit 5)
2. Huff Chemical, Inc., sold as liquidation of assets: $215,000.00 (see exhibit 6)

We believe you should be prepared for an offer of between $230,000 and $260,000 with a 20 percent down payment. The amount you receive in excess of this will be determined almost entirely by your bargaining ability.

Thank you for this opportunity to help. If we may further clarify or in any other way assist, do not hesitate to call.

Sincerely,

Joseph Jones
Partner

Exhibit 5
HUFF CHEMICAL, INC.: PRO-FORMA INCOME STATEMENT

	1987	1988	1989	1990
Sales	$324,000	$375,000	$436,000	$495,000
Gross profit	236,000	270,000	313,000	356,000
Less general and administrative expenses	182,000	185,000	190,000	200,000
Net income	$ 54,000	$ 85,000	$123,000	$156,000
Plus depreciation	39,000	39,000	39,000	$ 39,000
Net cash flow	$ 93,000	$124,000	$162,000	$195,000

Present value of net income rounded to nearest $100

	1987	1988	1989	1990
@ 10%	$ 51,000	$ 72,000	$ 94,000	$108,000
@ 15%	49,000	66,000	82,000	91,000
@ 20%	47,000	60,000	73,000	76,000

Estimated range of selling price of business

High	$325,000
Low	256,000
Most probable	288,000

Exhibit 6
HUFF CHEMICAL, INC.: BALANCE SHEET ADJUSTED FOR MARKET VALUE

ASSETS

Current Assets

Cash	$ 7,500	
Accounts receivable	106,000	
Inventory	16,000	
Supplies	2,000	
Note receivable	9,000	
Total Current Assets		$140,500

Fixed Assets

Furniture and fixtures	$ 28,000	
Computer	34,000	
Mixer equipment	2,800	
Building and improvements	93,500	
Dodge pickup	4,500	
Renovation	4,000	
Total Fixed Assets		166,800

Other Assets

Land	$ 11,000		
Total Other Assets		11,000	
Total Assets			$318,300

LIABILITIES

Current Liabilities

Tax withheld, federal	$ 604	
FICA	651	
TEC	203	
FUTA	50	
Sales tax	972	
Accounts payable	25,383	
Current portion	22,116	
Patent royalties payable	1,990	
Total Current Liabilities		$ 51,969

Long-Term Liabilities

Mortgage	72,707		
Notes payable	1,280		
Less current portion	(22,116)		
Total Long-Term Liabilities		51,871	
Total Liabilities			(103,840)
MARKETABLE NET WORTH			$214,460

BLUE AQUA
SPRINKLERS, INC.

GEORGE H. THOMPSON
Trinity University

Think twice before you go into subcontracting. You'll find that somebody else calls the shots. Besides, you'll wait a long time for your money.

—Sam Aqua

The entrepreneurial urge to start one's own business catches some people unprepared. For some, like Sam Aqua, the result can be disastrous.

BACKGROUND

Sam Aqua worked as a pipefitter in Louisiana and Texas oil fields for fourteen years. He lived in a trailer, hauling it behind his pickup truck from job to job. During that time he met and married Sadie Blue Morrow. She kept trailer house for them, reared no children, and nursed his entrepreneurial dream.

Sadie Blue's friends and relatives started calling her Blue after she married Sam—Blue Aqua.

They saved their hard-earned money. The oil-field camps operated far from the cities with their shopping malls and goods meant for impulse purchase. Besides, the fourteen-hour days left Sam too tired to spend much money. So they saved $60,000.

The Entrepreneurial Urge

Together Sam and Blue decided to leave the oil patch and start a business with their $60,000 in sav-

ings. They listed the firm in Blue's name so they could operate as a minority business. The provisions of Public Law 87–305 guaranteed them attention. They chose to install sprinklers.

Company Background

Automatic fire sprinklers burst into public view when Las Vegas' MGM Grand Hotel, which had no sprinklers, burned with a tragic loss of life. Sam and Blue saw it as an opportunity to put Sam's pipefitting skills to good use away from the oil fields. Thus Blue Aqua Sprinklers, Inc., which specialized in designing and installing automatic fire sprinkler systems, came into being.

At once, the firm started receiving requests for quotations. As a small company, it constantly came up short on contracts, bidding as it did against larger firms. Bidding took a considerable skill in negotiation, Sam soon discovered. His main negotiation goal centered on survival, because Sam ran the firm on the edge of insolvency most of the time.

Sam supervised the firm's six employees. His wife Blue ran the office in their mobile home. Her duties consisted of filing the large engineering drawings and thick specifications packets on jobs awaiting bidding by Sam. Blue filed separately jobs bid but awaiting awards. Her third file contained dormant or completed jobs. Her pride and joy focused on the fourth, the revenue file: jobs in progress. Sam had bid these jobs and gained the contracts. He had gathered the materials; moved men, materials, and tools to the job site; and started installing sprinklers.

This case, written specifically for this text, is printed by permission.

DESIGN WORK

Designing automatic fire sprinklers occupied much of Sam's time. He sketched them himself, drafting the large installation drawings each evening in their mobile home. Summer and winter—on hot, muggy days as on cold days with freezing rain or snow—his routine never changed. No matter what kind of day he faced in the field, he worked each night at the drafting table.

His unvarying work routine had its drawbacks. Sam drew at night, whether or not he was tired. He depended on checking in the field to detect his mistakes. However, Sam supervised work in progress, which often took him in opposite directions from the proposed work. Days might pass before he could check the drawings of his prospective jobs. By that time, Sam had often forgotten the special details of customer requirements.

Blue resented the design work and told him so.

"You sometimes don't make sense, Sam, working so hard to bid a good price," she said. "You furnish all these working drawings. Then, maybe we don't get the contract. I don't see why you give away all these layouts."

"Everybody does it this way, honey," Sam replied. "You gotta give away the drawings if you want to get their attention."

THE MARKET

Large firms dominated the highly competitive fire sprinkler market. Their many resources and economies of scale formed barriers against entry by small firms like Blue Aqua Sprinklers, Inc. Still, Sam could hope to gain two types of business: special customers who wanted to deal only with a small company and jobs too small for the large firms to consider.

The market consisted of four segments: governmental, agricultural, commercial, and residential.

Governmental

Many aircraft hangers, supply depots, and military dormitories operated within 200 miles of Blue Aqua Sprinklers' home base. Federal, state, and local governments seemed constantly to alter existing facilities and occasionally to add new buildings. Government jobs offered the advantage of a partial payment at startup and above all the prompt payment of the balance upon job completion. Blue Aqua desperately needed income.

Agricultural

Greenhouses, plant nurseries, and landscape irrigation jobs abounded throughout the region. Apartment buildings, retirement complexes, and golf courses were added at a steady rate, thereby increasing the demand for landscape irrigation. Housing complexes of a certain caliber used a time-controlled sprinkling system for watering their lawns.

The agricultural market provided more revenue potential than did the residential market. Although they were similar to fire sprinklers, irrigation sprinkling systems required a different license and equipment, which Blue Aqua Sprinklers did not have and could not afford.

Commercial

Office buildings, hotels, hospitals, warehouses, shopping centers, and schools made up the commercial segment. The Uniform Fire Code and the Uniform Building Code required public buildings of three or more stories to have fire sprinkling systems. "Most fire ladders don't reach above the second floor," a fire chief explained. Under the newly enforced standards, the number of office buildings where fire sprinkling systems were required increased noticeably.

Sam and Blue found also that the law required fire sprinklers as a safety precaution for any building that stored combustible material. Restaurants and nightclubs used fire sprinklers, not because the law required them, but because the owners wanted to protect their investments.

The American Fire Sprinkler Association attributed 75 percent to 90 percent of sprinkler business to mandatory laws. Blue Aqua Sprinklers therefore made no conventional marketing effort such as advertising, but focused on bidding jobs competitively.

Residential

Local home builders told Sam that most homes did not need fire sprinklers; home buyers would not bear the installation costs. The builders, however, contended that large custom-built homes could absorb the installation costs better. Sam, they said, might consider serving this market. On checking, Sam found that the small percentage of such homes in the industry made that option completely unfeasible.

One day, Blue suggested educating owners of custom homes on the benefits of a home automatic fire sprinkler system, such as reduced home insurance cost. She pointed out that home smoke alarm installers popularized their systems by emphasizing peace of mind, lower insurance costs, and compliance with new laws. Blue reasoned that they could do the same for automatic sprinkler systems at relatively little expense by using printed flyers, mass mailings, or in-home demonstrations. Sam pondered the suggestion.

In sum, Sam realized that commercial and government contracts offered the most profit. He firmly believed that success would depend on the company's ability to bid competitively.

THE PRODUCT

A fire sprinkler system requires components that range from pipe, pipe unions, elbows, stubs, and hangers of different sizes to sprinkler heads and alarm clock valves. The cost of installing a system varies widely, depending on the job description and specifications.

To bid on a particular job, Sam must first understand the job plan, the quantity and quality of the materials to be installed, and the labor hours needed to complete the task. The second step requires an itemized list that covers all materials and expenses, including the connections to the water supply, the labor cost, and any other costs that the job might incur. In order to break even, the job must cover its variable costs—materials, labor, and transport— and contribute something to fixed expenses.

Installing the fire sprinklers during construction consumes a lot of time and requires coordination with different phases of a building's construction. Sam has to coordinate his work with that of other craftworkers, such as carpenters, electricians, and plumbers. Once Sam installs the sprinkler system, acceptance of his job depends on the final completion of other work, something over which Blue Aqua Sprinklers has little control.

MANAGING THE WORK

As company manager, Sam involved himself fully in supervising the operation of the company. Blue furnished a presence in the trailer-office. She had enough knowledge about the business to give Sam time to look after the job sites. Onsite supervision by management provided firsthand insight into work in progress and bottlenecks. Labor's productivity improved. Sam was able to learn of any changes in the agreed-upon plans before they became unmanageable.

THE TERRITORY

The first year of operation brought Blue Aqua Sprinklers very few contracts, eight in all. By year's end, Sam supervised jobs that spread out over several hundred miles and many hours' driving time.

The first five jobs rimmed the home base. They started and ended at different times. Jobs 6, 7, and 8 started at about the same time. Job 6 consisted of a three-store strip shopping center in a town 190 miles from home base, as Exhibit 1 displays. Job 7 called for designing and installing a sprinkler network in a small civilian airport hanger 274 miles in a different direction from home base. While starting these two jobs, Sam won a contract, Job 8, at the state university, 40 miles north. The contract called for designing and installing a sprinkler system for the third and fourth floors of the new science building. A general contractor built the building according to architects' drawings. Subcontractors provided specific services, including foundations, plumbing, electrical, air conditioning and heating, floors, masonry, lighting, sprinklers, painting, and furniture and fixtures.

Exhibit 1
BLUE AQUA SPRINKLERS' TERRITORY

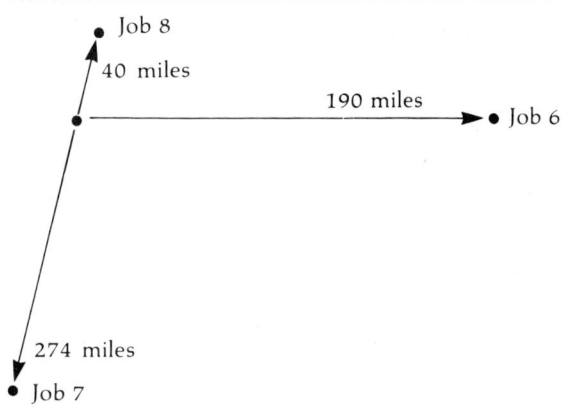

Sam found that he had to schedule his men for Job 8 one day and pull them off the next, because of other subcontractors' activities. Moreover, Sam and the general contractor never discussed changes in plans with him, and he lost all hope of coming out ahead on Job 8 when he discovered that the lighting fixtures hung 18 inches below the ceilings. The installation would have to travel to a light fixture, then dip down below it, and return to ceiling height on the other side. Sam's original design pictured long runs of pipe hung snugly against the ceilings. However much Sam might protest, the light fixtures clearly held priority. Sam had to cut and thread pipe, add elbows, and fashion more hangers to complete the work. Also, the job's completion still depended on the final completion of the ceilings, a circumstance over which Blue Aqua had little control.

THE TRADE ASSOCIATION

Membership in the American Fire Sprinkler Association offers "a greater voice for the Merit Shop Contractor, increased Professionalism, and Financial Gain," according to its membership pamphlet. Like other trade and professional associations, the organization encourages the maintenance of high standards of service to the public and provides lead-ership training and professional development programs. Its newsletter, "Sprinkler Age," promotes training lessons for pipefitters in alarm valves, sprinkler heads, basic hydraulics, storage tanks, fire pumps, and standpipes. However, Sam couldn't afford the membership dues of $500 per year.

FINANCIAL POSITION

The firm's financial condition worsened in 1985, as figures in Exhibits 2 and 3 reflect. Inventories had shrunk, as had receivables, fixed assets, and profit. Payables doubled. Late in 1984, Sam had obtained a $90,000 loan on the basis of Job 8. Without the loan, the firm would have run out of money, because of design confusion, additional costs beyond his estimates, and delayed income from the job. Sam drew shareholder advances to start payment on the loan. The large contract, which once appeared so lucrative, had depleted his firm's resources. Cost overruns, plus the delay in payment for services rendered, spelled financial catastrophe for Sam.

The jarring truths hit Sam hard:

- Not every contract job suits a company.
- A larger contract may appear lucrative, yet deplete the firm's resources.
- It takes much time for the firm to collect payment for services given.

Exhibit 2
BLUE AQUA SPRINKLERS, INC.: BALANCE SHEET
(year ended February 28)

	1985		1984	
ASSETS				
Current Assets				
Cash	$ 324.15		$ (728.07)	
Accounts receivable	39,940.57		52,695.50	
Inventory	12,546.51		26,219.50	
Total Current Assets		$ 52,811.23		$78,186.93
Fixed Assets (net)	$18,521.93		$29,697.79	
Other Assets	725.29		788.00	
Total Fixed and Other Assets		19,247.22		30,485.79
TOTAL ASSETS		$ 72,058.45		$108,672.72
LIABILITIES AND CAPITAL				
Current Liabilities				
Accounts payable	$ 22,841.26		$ 10,990.47	
Provision for income tax	—		7,930.70	

	1985		1984	
Accrued interest payable	470.47		677.67	
Accrued taxes	11,336.50		11,392.05	
Notes payable, current part	23,640.83		19,097.23	
Total Current Liabilities		$ 58,289.06		$ 50,088.12
Deferred Liabilities				
Notes payable	$ 82,971.05		$ 6,793.09	
Shareholder advances	(29,649.33)		1,496.10	
Total Other Liabilities		53,321.72		8,289.19
Total Liabilities		111,610.78		58,377.31
Capital				
Common stock	$ 10,000.00		$ 10,000.00	
Retained earnings (deficit)	(49,552.33)		40,295.41	
Total capital (deficit)		(39,552.33)		50,295.41
TOTAL LIABILITIES AND CAPITAL		$ 72,058.45		$108,672.72

Exhibit 3
BLUE AQUA SPRINKLERS, INC.: INCOME AND RETAINED EARNINGS STATEMENT
(year ended February 28)

	1985		1984	
Revenues	$279,090.97		$230,729.48	
Less cost of revenues	214,838.58		75,562.15	
Gross profit		$ 64,252.39		$155,167.33
Less operating expenses	148,035.55		106,263.55	
Operating profit (or loss)		(83,783.16)		48,903.78
Other income	7,743.53		—	
		(76,039.63)		48,903.78
Less other expenses	14,671.21		677.67	
Net profit (or loss)		(90,710.84)		48,226.11
Provision for income tax	—		7,930.70	
Profit retained (or loss)		(90,710.84)		40,295.41
Beginning retained earnings	41,158.51[a]		—	
Ending retained earnings (or deficit)		$(49,552.33)		$40,295.41

a. Restated to add income tax reduction offset by investment credit taken in 1984.

VALLEY CAB COMPANY, INC.

FIKRU H. BOGHOSSIAN
University of Wisconsin, LaCrosse

HISTORY

Valley Cab Company began providing taxi service to the city of Riverton in 1932. From 1932 to 1967, the company was owned by John Olson, the current owner's uncle. In 1967, John Olson sold the company to his brother Bill Olson, who ran the company with his son William. Upon John Olson's death, William became a part owner and general manager of Valley Cab Company.

Valley Cab Company was incorporated as a small, closely held corporation with William and his mother as the major shareholders. From 1967 to 1974, William and his mother ran the company smoothly with little trouble. As William Olson says, "Overall, during this period the company was profitable, with gross income of approximately $500,000 per year."

Also, during this time the company had no major debt and was able to purchase three new taxicabs per year and retire three old ones. In this manner, Valley Cab Company was able to keep its fleet of taxicabs relatively new and in good condition.

THE MARKET

Riverton is located on the western edge of a large midwestern state. The city has a population of ap-

proximately 65,000, of which 15,000 are students. The population is very diverse, as the city has a broad base of educational, governmental, and industrial institutions. Within the city limits are one university, one college, a two-year technical institute, and a number of nationally and internationally known manufacturers.

Riverton is also a rather old and conservative city. Many residents were born in the city and have lived there through their retirement years. Riverton has a substantial senior citizen population of about 10,000. During the 1960s and early 1970s, senior citizens comprised the major customer base of the company. Because the city had a large population of senior citizens and a number of institutions, homes, and care facilities for seniors, this group was a vital and profitable market for the company.

Second to the senior citizen market were students, especially handicapped students, for whom the company provided transportation to and from school. Other customers included housewives taking shopping trips, businesspeople, and travelers to and from the train station, bus depot, and airport.

PERSONNEL AND EQUIPMENT

At the peak of its prosperity, Valley Cab Company employed sixty part-time drivers. It also employed two part-time office workers, five to six dispatchers for twenty-four hour service, one full-time mechanic, and one part-time mechanic depending on need. The company used a computerized payroll and billing service provided by a local CPA firm.

This case and the accompanying teaching notes were prepared as a basis for class discussion. All rights are reserved by the author and by Case Research Association. This case is printed by permission.

Taxi drivers received a 50-percent commission or a base rate of $3.50 per hour if their commissions did not amount to at least $3.50 per hour. All other employees were paid on an hourly basis. Currently, the drivers do not belong to a union; however, according to Olson, at one point they did join a union, and this was costly for the company. Olson solved this problem by agreeing to a financial compromise with the drivers, and the drivers no longer belong to the union. Presently, Valley Cab employs only twenty-six drivers.

Five years ago, the company operated a fleet of twenty-six taxicabs; now it operates only nine taxicabs. Olson sees a number of reasons for this reduction. A drastic decline in business in one reason. As a result, he can no longer obtain loans to purchase new cabs. Each of the current fleet of taxis has 100,000 miles on its meter, and the condition of each cab is deteriorating. Olson is worried that the poor condition of his cabs is damaging his business. In addition, taxi fares are regulated by the city, and requests for an increase in fares have been turned down twice in the last four years.

Each taxicab is equipped with a two-way radio for communication with the dispatchers and a taximeter for computing mileage and fares. Both of these devices are subject to frequent breakdowns.

COMPETITION

Valley Cab is the only taxicab company in Riverton: a major advantage for the company. Since the company has a virtual monopoly, management did not advertise its services outside the Yellow Pages. An efficient bus service operates from 6:00 A.M. until 10:30 P.M., but the bus route does not extend to the airport.

GOVERNMENT SUBSIDIES

In the mid 1970s, a number of federal and state agencies supplied funds in the form of subsidies to several institutions in Riverton. These subsidies, made available to senior citizen homes and health-care facilities, made it possible for these institutions to purchase their own transportation vehicles.

Olson, fearing the subsidized vehicles would cut into a large portion of his market, submitted a number of proposals (bids) to the government agencies. The proposals stated that his company wanted to work with the government agencies to provide transportation for the elderly and handicapped.

Unfortunately, his proposals were rejected, and subsequently, many of the senior citizen and health-care institutions in the city acquired their own transportation vehicles through the subsidies. Thus, Olson lost a substantial portion of his market.

FINANCE

The financial situation of Valley Cab Company was good until 1977. At this time, the loss of customers and the rising cost of operations started to have an adverse effect on the company. Olson believes that a loss of approximately $200,000 per year in revenues was caused by the subsidies to local institutions. Also, the rapidly increasing costs of the firm's operations began to squeeze revenues (see Exhibits 1 through 3). As Olson reviews his financial statements and his target market, he knows he must make some difficult decisions. Clearly, the very survival of his company is threatened.

Exhibit 1
VALLEY CAB COMPANY, INC.: BALANCE SHEET
(year ended June 30, 1981)

ASSETS		LIABILITIES AND STOCKHOLDERS' EQUITY	
Current Assets		Current Liabilities	
Cash in bank, regular checking	$ 5,669.11	Prepaid fares	$ (121.20)
Petty cash	14.23	Federal withholding	11,761.75
Intercompany account	(319.56)	State withholding	624.43
		Social security withholding	6,246.09

Exhibit 1

VALLEY CAB COMPANY, INC.: BALANCE SHEET

(year ended June 30, 1981) (*continued*)

ASSETS			LIABILITIES AND STOCKHOLDERS' EQUITY		
Accounts receivable,			Accrued expenses	3,528.83	
passengers	9,309.67		Accrued social		
Loans to officers	2,231.06		security	6,360.18	
Miscellaneous			Accrued UC tax	2,259.37	
receivables	281.47		Accrued payroll	3,932.30	
Inventories	957.91		Accrued property tax	219.50	
Total Current			Total Current		
Assets		$18,143.89	Liabilities		$34,811.25
Fixed Assets			Long-Term Liabilities		
Buildings	$10,829.00		Note payable, Metro-		
Accumulated depre-			politan Life	$ 13,531.88	
ciation, buildings	(9,630.46)		Note payable	47,580.26	
Revenue equipment	56,592.74		Total Long-Term		
Accumulated depre-			Liabilities		61,112.14
ciation, revenue			Total Liabilities		95,923.39
equipment	(49,402.88)				
Radio equipment	23,530.60		Stockholders' Equity		
Accumulated depre-			Capital stock	$ 17,500.00	
ciation, radio			Retained earnings,		
equipment	(17,580.22)		prior years	(9,893.82)	
Taximeters	11,017.36		Current year loss	(32,967.62)	
Accumulated depre-			Total Stockholders'		
ciation, taximeters	(2,241.15)		Equity		(25,361.44)
Shop equipment	3,965.67		TOTAL LIABILITIES		
Accumulated depre-			AND EQUITY		$70,561.95
ciation, shop					
equipment	(2,543.29)				
Office equipment	2,071.50				
Accumulated depre-					
ciation, office					
equipment	(1,361.51)				
Franchise, valley cab	1,000.00				
Total Fixed Assets		26,247.36			
Other Assets					
Cash value, corpo-					
rate life insurance	$ 15,312.72				
Unexpired insurance					
premiums	9,350.67				
Prepaid small tools					
and supplies	856.23				
Prepaid license fees	412.00				
Prepaid office					
expense	239.08				
Total Other Assets		26,170.70			
TOTAL ASSETS		$70,561.95			

Exhibit 2

VALLEY CAB COMPANY, INC.: STATEMENT OF EARNINGS OR LOSS
(year ended June 30, 1981)

Income		
Passenger fares	$398,865.18	
Misc income and commissions	981.45	
Total income		$399,846.63
Less cost of sales		
Wages, dispatcher and mechanic	$ 45,403.13	
Commissions, drivers	189,797.71	
Social security expense	15,849.77	
UC expense	7,149.58	
Workers' compensation insurance	5,399.00	
Rent, dispatcher and garage	4,500.00	
Repairs to building	20.00	
Depreciation, building	104.98	
Utilities, dispatcher and garage	2,315.85	
Telephone	3,255.16	
Station supplies and expense	2,161.36	
Water	34.12	
Licenses and permits	1,190.00	
Property taxes	1,352.88	
Insurance	21,108.00	
Grease and oil	1,459.31	
Gasoline	55,859.55	
Tires and batteries	5,156.66	
Small tools	322.26	
Washing taxicabs	412.48	
Repairs to taxicabs	19,556.03	
Repairs, radio equipment	2,682.90	
Repairs, taximeters	53.80	
Repairs, shop equipment	234.21	
Depreciation, shop equipment	341.43	
Depreciation, taxicabs	5,860.17	
Depreciation, radio equipment	1,209.03	
Depreciation, taximeters	1,344.67	
Accident claims, collect	2,072.53	
Total cost of sales		396,206.57
Gross profit		3,640.06
Less expenses		
Officers salaries	$ 15,078.57	
Salaries and wages	12,126.34	
Advertising	871.38	
Travel and entertainment	131.13	
Professional fees	5,290.00	
Bank charges	15.00	
Office supplies and expense	805.14	
Dues and subscriptions	160.00	
Telephone and telegraph	284.01	
Bad debts	3.50	

Exhibit 2

**VALLEY CAB COMPANY, INC.: STATEMENT OF EARNINGS OR LOSS
(year ended June 30, 1981)** (*continued*)

Depreciation, office equipment	170.28	
Christmas expense	380.24	
Corporate life insurance	652.27	
Miscellaneous expenses	215.60	
Total expenses		36,183.46
Net loss		($ 32,543.40)
Other income and expenses		
Interest earned	$ 175.44	
Gain on sale of equipment	175.00	
Interest expense	(541.09)	
Penalties	(158.57)	
Loss on sale of equipment	(75.00)	
Total other income and expenses		(424.22)
NET LOSS		($ 32,967.62)

Exhibit 3

VALLEY CAB COMPANY, INC.: SUMMARY INCOME STATEMENT, 1977–1980

	1977	*1978*	*1979*	*1980*
Passenger fares	$340,663	$398,890	$443,730	$435,848
Gasoline sales	3,877	3,041	—	—
Lease income	2,754	—	—	—
Miscellaneous	2,517	1,710	$ 2,777	1,735
Total income	$349,811	403,641	446,507	437,583
Less cost of sales	309,954	361,041	N/A	N/A
Gross profit	$39,857	42,600	N/A	N/A
Less administrative and other expenses	(41,477)	(40,486)	N/A	N/A
NET PROFIT (OR LOSS)	$(1,620)	$ 2,114	$ 668	$(13,650)

LENCO, INC.

ARTHUR SHARPLIN
McNeese University

In 1975, James Leonard and two brothers decided to open a welding and steel fabrication shop in Joplin, Missouri. The Leonards formed a corporation, Lenco, Inc., bought a parcel of land at the eastern edge of Joplin, and built a small building. Most of the initial equity investment was in the form of welding machines, tools, and other items contributed by the three owners. James worked full time at Lenco while his brothers pursued other interests. The company was profitable from the first year. Sales grew steadily, and the shop was expanded several times during the 1970s. In the early 1980s, James exchanged his interest in some commercial property that the Leonards owned for his brothers' shares of Lenco stock.

Lenco is engaged in four distinct business areas, all related to heavy equipment, especially crawler tractors (often called *bulldozers* or *caterpillars*). First, the company makes and sells a number of welded steel items for heavy equipment. Second, Lenco markets new and used crawler tractor parts. Third, James and his workers provide repair service for heavy equipment owners. Finally, Lenco does high-strength repair welding for heavy equipment. Each of these business area will be discussed further under the heading "Operations."

In January 1988, the business was moved to a new 30,000-square foot facility in what had become a rapidly expanding commercial and industrial area along Interstate Highway 44. Among the more than twenty firms on I-44 near Lenco are heavy equipment dealers representing Deere and Company (makers of John Deere equipment), Case Power and Equipment Company, and Fiat-Allis, Inc. (successor to Allis Chalmers, Inc.). Dealers for the other two major brands of heavy equipment, International Harvester and Caterpillar, are located about 3 miles away.

PERSONNEL AND ORGANIZATION

In recent years, the workforce at Lenco has varied from as many as thirty down to its 1988 level of eleven. As a general rule, Lenco keeps a cadre of experienced workers and fills in with temporary welders and mechanics during busy periods. The company has no formal organization chart. However, the diagram in Exhibit 1 was drawn by James Leonard to represent the organization as it existed in 1988.

The lines of authority at Lenco are not rigidly followed. James routinely bypasses each of his direct subordinates and deals directly with workers. "The managers all work as a team," says James. "Any one of us can make a major or minor decision—or write a $10,000 check." Everyone in the organization is expected to pitch in wherever there is a need for extra help and to accept direction from whoever knows most about the particular job being done. The comments below were made by James Leonard concerning each of the key employees:

> Mike is thirty years old. He is my mother's grandnephew. Mike is dedicated to Lenco. He has a great deal of ability to get the job done. He is a good welder and the best mechanic we

This case, written specifically for this book, is printed by permission.

Exhibit 1
ORGANIZATIONAL CHART OF LENCO

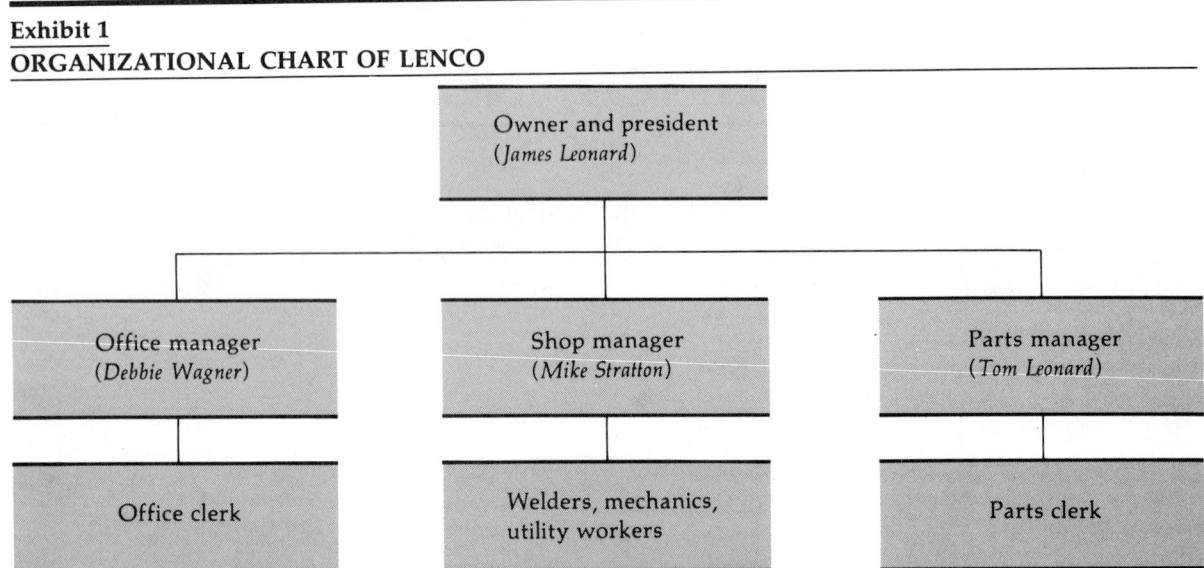

have. The men respect him and that helps make him a good manager. Customers like him; they ask for him. They know they can depend on what he says. During the move, when we were all running just to keep up, Mike sold two excavator buckets. He worked right through a weekend, even though he had the flu, to get the buckets built. He has a good memory, too. He can usually tell a customer if we have a part without even checking the computer. Mike's main recreation is hunting. I try to make sure he has some time off during hunting season. When I decided to furnish him a company pickup, I made sure it was something he has always wanted but never felt that he could afford—a four-wheel-drive "mud hog."

Debbie is in her forties. She has taken a number of college courses. Although Debbie does not have a degree, she knows much more than most college graduates. She is as dedicated as any employee I have. She is the most cost-conscious person in the whole organization, including me. After just a year of working with computers, she knows more about them than the computer "expert" who sold us the machine. Somehow, Debbie and the computer were an instant match. Debbie is a highly reli-

gious lady. I think this accounts to some degree for her diligence, and I know I can trust her with anything I have. There has never been the slightest need for me to check up on her. Everyone here respects her, and her presence helps keep foul language and rowdy behavior at a minimum. Debbie is usually miles ahead of me with any information I need—like sales statistics. She put the used parts on the computer without any guidance. And the information was in a form she knew I could use. If things move too fast she just works nights and Saturdays. She does all the advertising better than any ad agency could. She comes up with the ideas, does the copy, and just runs it by me for approval. Debbie is a perfectionist.

Tom is twenty-five years old. He is my nephew. Tom is strictly work, family, church, and school. He attends the University of Tulsa part-time, studying business. Tom has a good number of outside obligations, including school. But whenever I need him, he is here. He asked me if he should let his school wait while we get over the move and get things back on an even keel. I told him that he might take one course instead of two, only if he thought it best, but I felt he should continue his education without a break. He works hard—wants to do things right. He grew up on a farm, where he often had neither the time nor the equipment to do quality work. Tom is learning fast. In the long term, I think he will be one of our most important people. In fact, he is now. He had to come almost from ground zero—learning welding, learning crawler tractors, learning fabrication. He has done remarkably well in the two years since he came to work here.

There is no formal performance appraisal at Lenco and no written compensation policy. Lenco furnishes medical insurance for James, Mike, and Tom (Debbie is covered under her husband's policy furnished by his employer). The company also pays about one-half the cost of insurance for each worker. The managers are paid on a salary basis. Hourly workers make from $8 to $11 an hour, about average for the area. Every year, James says, he ranks the employees in order of what he considers to be their contribution to the company. Then he adjusts the pay of any whose pay seems inequitable. Practically all hiring and firing is done by James personally, although Mike Stratton has authority to terminate any of his workers.

OPERATIONS

Exhibit 2 shows a typical crawler tractor with the main relevant parts labeled. Practically all of Lenco's mechanical repair work and most of the parts sales are related to tractor undercarriages, final drives, and steering clutches. The undercarriage is that part of the tractor nearest the ground, including the heavy steel tracks along with rollers, sprockets, and structural members designed to pull the tracks and keep them in alignment. The final drive is a large, closed gear box that transmits power to the track. (In Exhibit 2 the final drive is hidden from view behind the sprocket.) The steering clutches are located above the final drives. They allow either the left or right final drive to be disengaged so that the brake can be applied on the respective side, causing the tractor to turn.

The tracks and related components cannot be insulated from the sand, dirt, and gravel in which a tractor usually operates. Consequently, all of the moving surfaces wear away steadily, especially those in contact with one another. The track chain is similar to a large bicycle chain. As the track is pulled

by the sprocket around the idler and rollers, the pins wear mainly on just one side. Each pin fits into a bushing, which also wears in the direction of the stress. A typical undercarriage will require major repair after 3,000 hours of use and overhaul after 1,500 additional hours. Major repair consists of removing the tracks and turning each pin and the respective bushing half around so that the least worn surfaces are in contact. To do this, a portable hydraulic press is used to press out one of the pins. This may require 200 tons of force. Then the tracks, weighing as much as 3,000 pounds each, are moved to the track press, where the remaining pins are pressed out, along with the respective bushings. All parts are then inspected and the tracks reassembled with the pins and bushings in their new positions. While the track is off, all undercarriage components are inspected for cracks, leaking oil seals, excessive wear, and other defects. Of course, any needed repairs are made before the tractor is reassembled.

When major overhaul is due, pins and bushings are replaced, idlers and rollers are exchanged or reconditioned, and new sprockets are installed. About every second major overhaul, worn grousers have to be cut off and new ones welded onto the track pads. The entire track chain may also have to be replaced. Less frequently, final drives and steering clutches require repair.

Among the items Lenco manufactures are rollover protective structures (cabs) such as that shown on the tractor in Exhibit 2. Many of Lenco's customers are involved in land clearing. The tractors they use must have heavy steel screens welded or bolted around the cabs to protect the operator from tree limbs. Lenco also makes and installs these screens. The cabs and screens are made from ordinary steel. However, most of the items the company makes involve the use of high-strength steel, about three times as strong and hard as ordinary steel (and more than twice as costly). Several of these items are shown in Exhibit 3.

The special steel is used for cutting edges and strength members on the blades and buckets. This steel is purchased from major steel distributors and stocked in 8-foot by 20-foot sheets, ranging in thickness from three-eighths of an inch to 2 inches. A portable acetylene cutting torch, which runs on a small track, is used to cut the steel to shape. Pieces that are to become cutting or digging edges are clamped in a vertical position and the edge beveled at a steep angle using the same kind of automatic

Exhibit 2
A TYPICAL CRAWLER TRACTOR

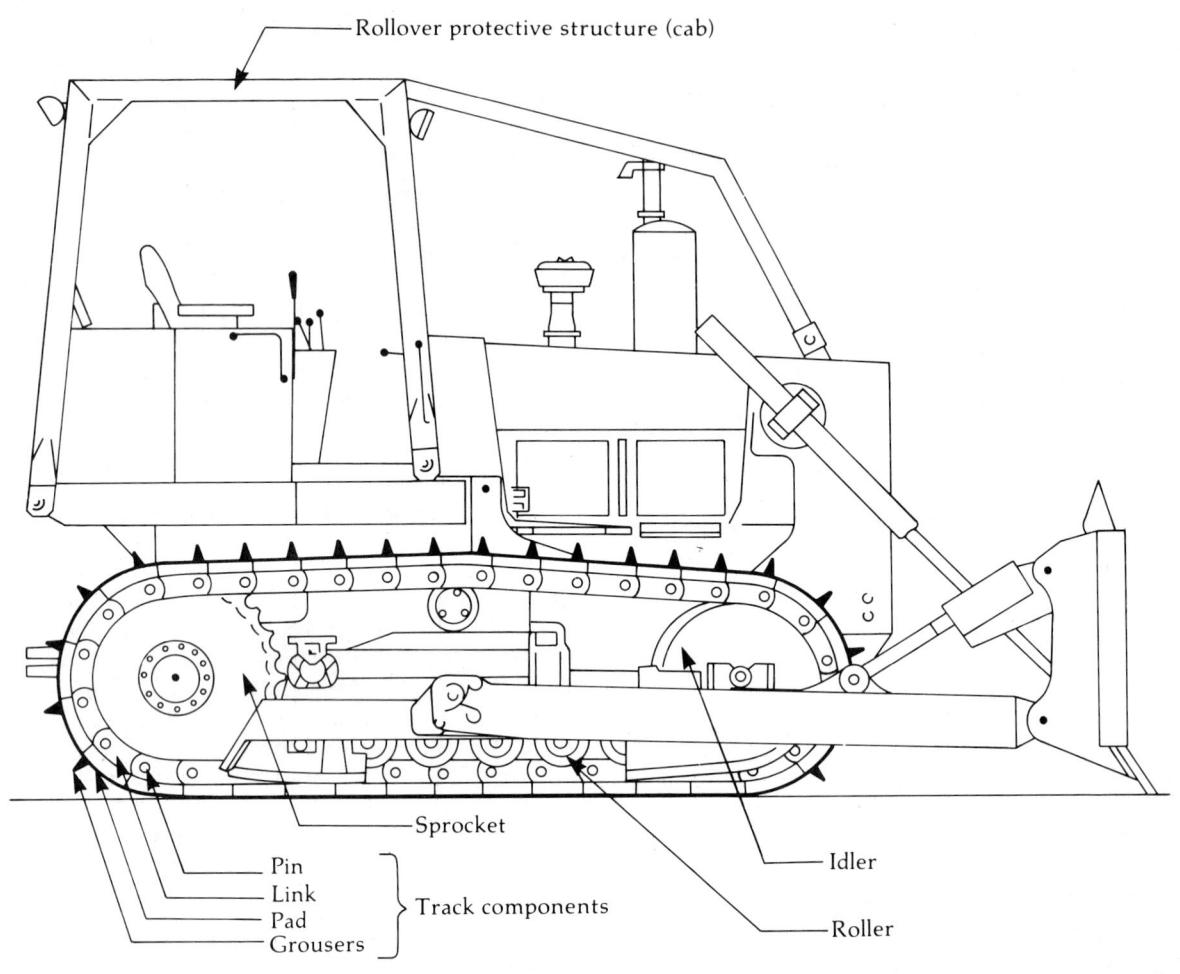

Rollover protective structure (cab)

Sprocket

Pin
Link
Pad
Grousers

Track components

Idler

Roller

torch. Curved pieces of mild steel (used for noncritical parts of digging buckets) and the steel pins and bushings used to attach the buckets to hydraulic excavators and backhoes are furnished by a local machine shop.

After the parts of a digging bucket or land-clearing blade are cut and shaped, they are welded together just enough to hold them. Then they are carefully inspected prior to final welding. To ensure against failure, Lenco workers weld all critical points manually, allowing components to cool between layers of weld material. This process requires special high-strength electrodes (welding rods). Less critical welds can be made with semiautomatic

machines, which are much faster and easier to operate than manual ones and which use large rolls of wire instead of individual welding electrodes. Lenco digging buckets range in size from small standard buckets weighing only 300 pounds to trapezoidal buckets weighing over a ton and measuring 17 feet across. A trapezoidal bucket is designed to dig a complete drainage canal as the hydraulic excavator or backhoe to which it is attached slowly drives along the intended canal path, scooping out as much as 3 feet of new ditch with each stroke and laying the dirt aside. Lenco land-clearing blades and rakes weigh up to 8 tons. The largest Lenco vee blade has two serrated cutting edges, each 20 feet

Exhibit 3
ITEMS LENCO MAKES USING HIGH-STRENGTH STEEL

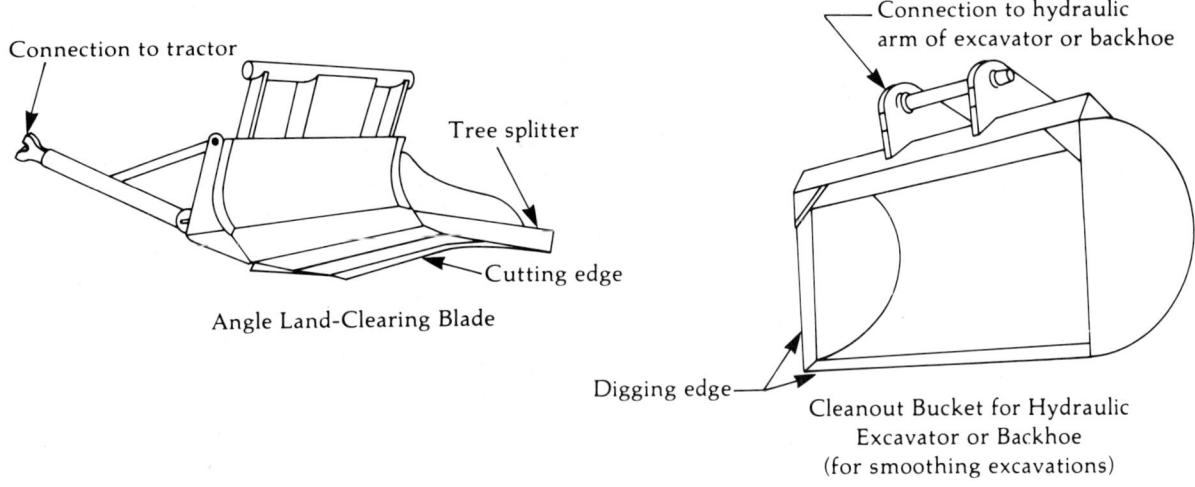

Connection to tractor

Tree splitter

Cutting edge

Angle Land-Clearing Blade

Connection to hydraulic
arm of excavator or backhoe

Digging edge

Cleanout Bucket for Hydraulic
Excavator or Backhoe
(for smoothing excavations)

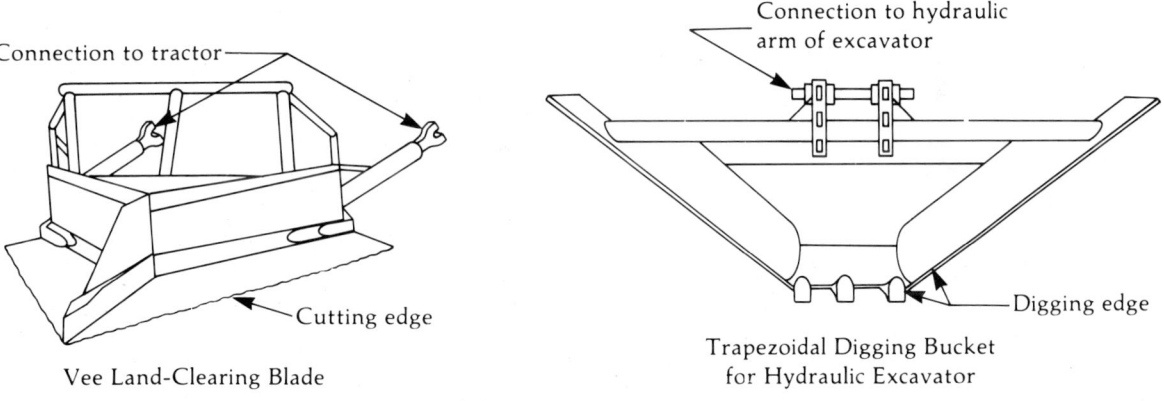

Connection to tractor

Cutting edge

Vee Land-Clearing Blade

Connection to hydraulic
arm of excavator

Digging edge

Trapezoidal Digging Bucket
for Hydraulic Excavator

long. Pushed by the largest production model tractor made by Caterpillar or Fiat-Allis, one of these
blades clears a swath 16 feet wide through timber
that is up to 30 inches in diameter.

Blades and buckets require replacement of cutting edges and other wearing surfaces after extended use. Each item is designed so that the worn
parts can be cut loose and new ones installed

through a procedure similar to the original manufacture.

All of the items Lenco reconditions or manufactures are painted at the Lenco plant. Rollers and
small parts are simply dipped into a paint vat.
Larger items are spray painted. In addition, practically all of the equipment that comes in to be repaired is covered with dirt and mud. Cleaning is ac-

complished in the wash area, using a special high pressure washer. Construction machinery and components to be repaired are usually brought to the Lenco plant on customer trucks, although Lenco does keep several trucks of varying sizes to make pickups and deliveries when necessary. The layout of the new Lenco facility is shown in Exhibit 4.

MARKETING

Lenco's customers include contractors, owners of large farms, and other heavy equipment owners, as well as equipment dealers who purchase Lenco products and services for resale. Several equipment dealers employ Lenco to repair tracks and recondition rollers and idlers for them.

Lenco subscribes to a computerized, used-parts dealer network whereby subscribers exchange information on price and the availability of needed parts. As a result, the company ships an increasing number of parts, especially used ones, to dealers around the country.

Although the customer list totals more than 1,000, only 100 contractors accounted for two-thirds of Lenco's 1986 cash flow. For example, one land-

Exhibit 4
LENCO'S PLANT LAYOUT

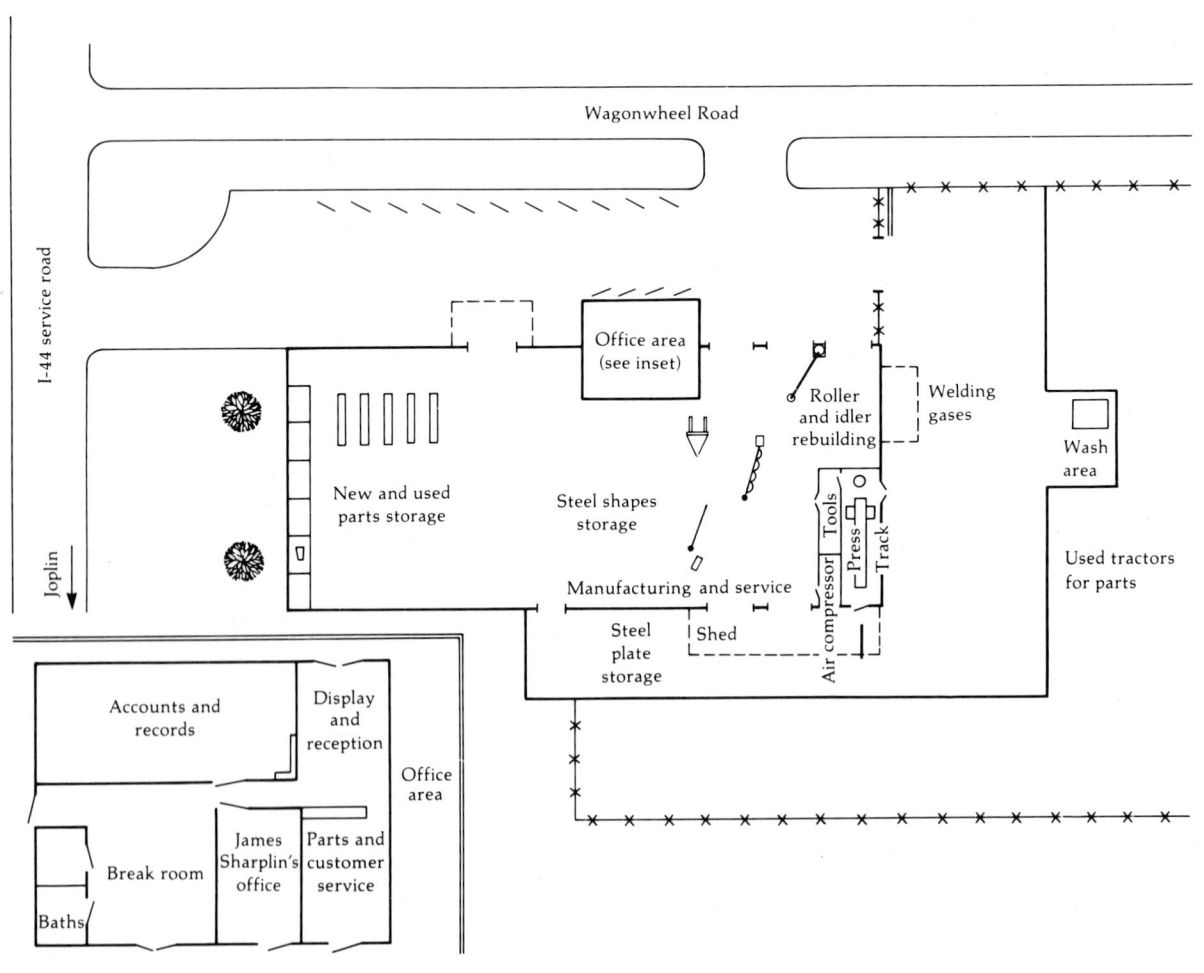

clearing contractor, with just four tractors, was billed $98,900 during 1986. Eighty percent of Lenco's 1986 sales were to customers within a 100-mile radius of Joplin. "That is changing rapidly, though," said Debbie Wagner. "We are getting inquiries from all over the country because of the dealer network." For the months of August, September, and October 1986, ninety equipment owners, mostly contractors, were billed $355,571 out of Lenco's total sales of $432,149. Shown this list of customers, James Leonard identified fifty-seven of them as having been regular customers for at least three years.

Lenco's overall pricing policy, as expressed by James Leonard, is "whatever the traffic will bear." For new tractor parts, he says, this is normally about 80 or 85 percent of dealer retail price. For used parts, it ranges from 25 to 60 percent of retail, depending upon whether the part in question is a frequently needed one or one which seldom fails. Lenco prices its digging buckets at or above dealer list prices. According to James Leonard, this is justified because the Lenco buckets have a significantly lower failure rate than those that equipment dealers furnish. When repair jobs are priced in advance, parts and labor are usually combined. Lenco tries to stay just below usual original equipment dealer prices on such work. This often results in the loss of jobs to smaller independent service shops, which often price well below what major tractor dealers charge. About one-third of Lenco's repair work is done on a time and materials basis. Under this kind of billing procedure, customers usually bargain on major components to be installed. But minor items (such as bolts, steel plate for welding reinforcement, and replacement track pads or links) are priced at 90 percent suggested retail, while labor is billed at standard billing rates, currently $31 per hour (local new tractor dealers charge an average of $35 an hour).

Prices are also used to keep Lenco concentrated in its main businesses. When a customer insists that the company repair a transmission or engine, for example, the price for that work is intentionally elevated. Price changes are also used to control the overall level of work activity. When spurts in demand occur, hourly rates and markups on materials are increased, both for the time and materials work and for work that is priced in advance. When demand slackens, workers are laid off until the crew is down to the ten or twelve person cadre of experienced workers. Only then are prices and markups sacrificed to sustain sales volume.

The primary means of promotion is direct mail. Currently the mailings are sent to all customers once a month. James has made plans, however, to program the company's computer to segment the mailing list along several dimensions and to mail more personalized advertisements to differing customer groups. Lenco also spends about $700 a month on Yellow Pages advertising. This provides for a quarter-page ad under "Contractors: Equipment and Supplies," a quarter-page ad under "Welding," and a business card type advertisement briefly listing Lenco's businesses under "Tractor Equipment and Parts." About once a quarter, Lenco inserts a series of three two-page advertisements in consecutive issues of *The Contractor's Hotline*, a national weekly newspaper offering heavy equipment and parts for sale to about 5,000 equipment owners and dealers. These advertisements cost about $1,400 for each 3-week sequence. James, Mike Stratton, and Tom Leonard make infrequent sales calls within about 50 miles of Joplin.

FINANCE AND ACCOUNTING

Summaries of Lenco's recent financial statements are provided in Exhibits 5 though 8. The short-term borrowings shown on the 1987 balance sheet are represented by 180-day notes held by a small bank in Carthage, Missouri, the Leonard family's hometown. These notes are secured by mortgages on Lenco's inventories and the Lenco plant. As the notes mature, the accrued interest is paid, and the principal is refinanced as needed. James has signed continuing guarantee agreements with regard to all present and future Lenco debt at the bank.

The bank has agreed to convert the short-term debt to a single five-year loan with fifteen-year amortization and interest established annually at the bank's prime rate, normally about 1.5 percent above the prime rate in New York. In addition to the five-year loan, the bank has agreed that it will provide Lenco a $170,000 credit line for any needed additional working capital.

The long-term debt on the 1987 balance sheet includes a $230,000 purchase-money obligation on the new Lenco plant and the land on which it sits. The purchase-money mortgage is subordinated to the bank debt mentioned above. Lenco's old plant with related long-term debt attached was given in part payment to the developer who built the new plant.

Exhibit 5

LENCO, INC.: BALANCE SHEETS

	1984	1985	1986	1987
ASSETS				
Current Assets				
Cash	$ 56,833	$ 10,074	$ 11,736	$ 9,625
Accounts receivable	67,610	65,409	131,468	131,468
Reserve for bad debts	(11,470)	(22,657)	(25,658)	(23,758)
Notes receivable, stockholder	56,841	70,845	91,104	100,783
Inventory	203,920	109,604	175,516	362,374
Total Current Assets	$373,734	$233,275	$384,166	$ 580,492
Fixed Assets				
Building and improvements	$138,881	$138,881	$216,968	$ 338,365
Machinery and equipment	163,182	163,182	130,461	130,461
Office furniture and equipment	18,234	18,234	15,484	32,134
Vehicles	62,596	71,939	119,624	110,280
Total	$382,893	$392,236	$482,537	$ 611,240
Less accumulated depreciation	187,762	226,635	223,569	158,952
Net depreciated assets	$195,131	$165,601	$258,968	$ 452,288
Land	39,112	54,936	63,860	109,250
Total Fixed Assets	$234,243	$220,537	$322,828	$ 561,538
Other Assets				
Utility deposits	575	575	1,093	1,357
TOTAL ASSETS	$608,552	$454,387	$708,087	$1,143,387
LIABILITIES AND STOCKHOLDERS' EQUITY				
Current Liabilities				
Accounts payable	$ 32,727	$ 6,715	$ 25,760	$ 26,593
Accrued expenses	22,792	14,475	15,939	14,492
Withheld and accrued taxes	7,097	6,200	1,687	1,440
Accrued payroll	—	—	—	1,337
Accrued income taxes (overpayment)	13,381	(5,213)	(366)	7,395
Notes payable	197,340	93,473	213,753	308,781
Deposit from customers	10,350	—	—	—
Total Current Liabilities	$283,687	$115,650	$256,773	$ 360,038
Long-term liabilities				
Notes payable	24,487	9,303	68,299	297,860
Total Liabilities	$308,174	$124,958	$325,072	$ 657,890
Stockholders' Equity				
Common stock	38,619	38,619	38,619	38,619
Less treasury stock	(13,013)	(13,013)	(13,013)	(13,013)
Retained earnings	274,772	303,833	357,409	459,883
Total Stockholders' Equity	$300,378	$329,439	$383,015	$ 485,489
TOTAL LIABILITIES AND STOCK-HOLDERS' EQUITY	$608,552	$454,397	$708,087	$1,143,387

Exhibit 6
LENCO, INC.: INCOME STATEMENTS

	1984	1985	1986	1987
Revenue				
Welding shop	$319,816	$ 342,179	$ 252,008	$ 308,621
Undercarriage shop	332,746	653,635	739,002	663,893
Direct parts sales	167,100	166,717	226,663	359,852
Steel	94,432	61,479	48,516	51,663
Miscellaneous	12,442	10,405	9,423	20,064
Total revenue	$926,536	$1,234,415	$1,275,612	$1,404,093
Less direct costs				
Materials	$377,003	$ 650,892	$ 642,962	$ 655,615
Labor	92,135	115,574	129,098	136,487
Subcontractors	6,380	13,040	19,373	15,819
Freight	6,685	6,235	7,771	9,208
Other direct costs	274	89	58	644
Total direct costs	$482,477	$ 785,830	$ 799,262	$ 817,773
Gross profit	$444,059	$ 448,585	$ 476,350	$ 586,320
Less indirect costs	366,596	413,236	415,839	469,344
Profit before taxes	$ 77,463	$ 35,349	$ 60,511	$ 116,976
Less income taxes	13,381	6,287	6,937	14,502
NET PROFIT	$ 64,082	$ 29,062	$ 53,574	$ 102,474

Exhibit 7
LENCO, INC.: INVENTORIES, DECEMBER 31, 1987

Steel	$ 39,888
New parts	187,444
Used parts	115,175
Supplies	630
Finished goods	13,938
Work in process	5,299
Total	$362,374

Exhibit 8
LENCO, INC.: SALES BY MONTH (UNADJUSTED)

	1984	1985	1986	1987
Jan	$64,370	$ 85,632	$ 69,766	$ 59,216
Feb	77,904	105,279	95,445	85,892
Mar	89,702	127,816	79,689	48,047
Apr	84,364	91,437	60,220	80,725
May	98,836	146,001	52,180	174,334
Jun	37,876	88,726	108,549	164,013
Jul	75,783	125,336	158,477	163,881
Aug	79,891	159,499	159,710	134,391
Sep	76,925	110,104	100,764	211,267
Oct	88,612	95,587	171,675	133,385
Nov	88,512	65,234	121,573	56,543
Dec	59,024	28,534	88,184	73,862

By prior agreement with the developer, James Leonard designed the office area and mechanical features (piping and electrical systems, cranes, and so on) of the new plant and constructed them using Lenco workers and several subcontractors. This effort was financed with short-term bank borrowing. Upon completion, the new Lenco facility was appraised at $874,000.

In early 1987, Debbie Wagner computerized the company's accounting records. The computer in use is a Dynabyte with 20 megabytes of hard disk storage, a 16-bit microprocessor, and three interactive terminals. One of the extra terminals is located in James Leonard's office and another is situated on the customer service counter. The new parts inventory of about 1,500 items is carried on a first-in, first-out basis. When a used tractor is purchased for parts, the cost of the tractor, plus all labor required to dis-assemble it, is added to used parts inventory. When a used part is sold, the entire selling price of the part is subtracted from the inventory line item representing the tractor from which it came. A subsidiary file is kept for each tractor, indicating which parts have been sold. So anyone inquiring at one of the terminals can easily determine which used parts are available for sale. James Leonard has been advised that the accounting procedure he is following significantly understates the used parts inventory. Despite a recommendation from the company's CPA, he has not authorized changing the procedure.

Lenco's steel inventory is taken at the end of each year and priced at current costs. The steel consists of plates (rectangular flat pieces 4 or more feet in both width and length) and shapes (long, straight pieces of various cross-sectional configurations— e.g., rounds, angled, beams, and channels). No plate or shape is included in inventory if any part of it has been used. In addition, a large quantity of steel, all entirely usable but of slow-selling shapes and sizes, is not counted because it has been declared obsolete. As a result of these practices, the steel inventory is shown on company books at perhaps one-half its current market value. In addition, Lenco owns many land-clearing blades, digging buckets, and tractor parts that were traded in or abandoned by customers, but for which no actual credit was given. Many of these items were later restored to usable condition during slack periods. Total value of these, as estimated by James Leonard, is $17,000.

A job record is prepared for each customer order requiring shop work. One copy is kept in the office and another in a rack in the shop. Each worker is responsible for entering time worked on respective jobs. Parts and other materials issued to jobs are recorded on the office copies of job records. When a job is finished, the shop copy of the job record is brought to the office, and an invoice is completed.

Several years ago Debbie Wagner compared the time applied to customer jobs to the total time for which employees were paid. She found that fully one-third of employee time was unaccounted for. After telling of that experience, she said, "As soon as I can get the right computer program, I will set up a control system to charge every hour for which we pay employees to a customer job or to cleanup and maintenance."

INTERVIEW WITH JAMES LEONARD

The following are excerpts from an interview conducted on June 10, 1987:

Q: James, what do you think is your most important business area?
A: Well, I'd say used tractor parts are going to be our biggest money maker in the long run. When you can buy a D7E (a mid-size Caterpillar tractor) for $11,000, sell $28,000 worth of parts off it and still have two-thirds of it left, that's got to be a good situation. More and more people are looking at saving that 10 or 15 percent, or whatever it is. They don't really care if the part is used or not, as long as it is not hurt. The major tractor dealers have done a really good job, but their prices have just continued to climb. We're able to offer the customer a good part at 50 or 60 percent off dealer list. Customers are looking for that. They also know they can depend on us to install the parts we sell and to stand behind them. There is no question, also, that we are better at providing parts and under-carriage service for the whole list of crawler tractors—John Deeres, Caterpillars, Cases— than the average dealer is for just one brand of tractor.
Q: What do you think are the major attributes that you or Lenco has that will allow you to be successful—just in a general way?
A: We know a great deal more about any under-carriage than dealers do. Of course, dealers have to know the whole tractor and we limit our mechanic work to the undercarriage. The various undercarriages are quite similar, of course, and we've just had a world of experience in that particular area. Also, there's not a better high-quality welding shop, especially for construction equipment, in Southern Missouri. We know that business. We're good at it.
Q: What do you think about your crew right now, James? How does it stack up?
A: On the whole, they're the best group of workers for this type of business in the Joplin area. We have to pick and choose the jobs that we put individual workers on, but we put them on the jobs they're best at doing. Albert Lance,

for instance, is probably the best layout man and general welder that we've got. We use him just for that. But look at Don Walker, who is our fastest welder. We'll let him weld the project out after Albert has cut out the pieces and tacked them together. David Martin is real good with customers. So we like to send him out on field jobs, where he'll be in direct contact with the customer. Randy Bailey is another excellent man. He's kind of a handyman. He takes care of our tractor-trailer rig like it was his own. He's a good welder and a good mechanic. He just generally has a great attitude about anything Lenco wants him to do.

Q: What about the production things you do, the track press, for example, and the roller and idler shop?

A: We run our track press operation quite differently from the way dealers do. We arranged the track press in a room by itself with all the necessary equipment—the turntable, all the tooling. We have it where one man can run the whole operation. It's a two-man job at most dealers. We've kept a real good account of the number of hours it takes to do a job, and we've steadily improved on that. The track press operator we have now, Robert Nichols, has run the press for six years. He's by far the best I've ever seen. About a year ago, Robert hurt his back, and Mike Stratton and I filled in for him until he recovered enough to work again. He had major surgery. For at least a month or a month and a half after he came back, we wouldn't let him lift anything. Just having him here during that time was a great help because he knew so much about how to set up the machine. We rebuild idlers by building up [with an automatic welder] the wear surfaces and replacing the seals—and they are as good as new. We do not weld on the rollers, though, like some dealers do. To get new quality, we replace the worn outer shells of rollers and reuse the shafts, bushings, and collars if they are not hurt. This costs more, and we lose some sales when customers just look at price. But I can't think of a single failure on one of our reshelled rollers.

Q: Why is the crew so small right now, James?

A: I prefer to keep it small and work just a bit of overtime in order to keep a good steady crew over a long period of time. Besides that, it's so much easier to manage ten people compared to twenty people. I know all these people. I know

their problems. I know what makes them tick. I know what will motivate them. When I had twenty or thirty people, I couldn't say that.

Q: What are your long-term plans now for Lenco, James?

A: Just to continue doing what we're good at and to keep our eyes open for any area where we can do a good job and make money: grow if it will; but the big thing is to stay profitable and get it to where we can take just a little more time off.

Q: Do you mean where *you* can take a little more time off?

A: No. I mean the key people—Debbie, Mike, Tom—and myself, of course.

Q: What problems concern you most?

A: Well, the problem is always the same: How to keep expenses down and jack up revenue. I do not ignore human costs, but I have to focus mainly on dollars. There seems to be a conspiracy out there to keep us from making money. Besides, if we are profitable enough, I can handle most of the other problems that crop up. One thing I'm going to do, as soon as we get over the move, is to spend most of my time for two or three months with the computer and the accounting system, just getting on top of the numbers. I want to know where the sales and profits are coming from—geographically, of course, but also, what kinds of customer; what parts and services. I want to know where the costs are, too. We already know a lot of that. I just need to study it and set up the reporting system a little better. I also want to figure out the best ways to promote sales of parts, especially used ones, and digging buckets. The farm economy is down and land clearing is about dead. But there is always some construction work going on and people are tending to fix their old equipment rather than buy new stuff. We are broadening our market area, too.

Q: James, how do you feel about your customers? Just tell me what your feelings are.

A: Quite often, in dealing with them in the past from the place we had built over the years and which was at best just adequate for the job, I felt a little inferior. From the instant we moved into our new place I have felt better. For one thing, I'm not apologetic about a price, not timid at all about giving a man a price quick. I offered no apology yesterday when Tim Newell said, "You're killing me." I sense a new attitude on the part of customers. They seem to be more favorable towards us.

Q: The question I was asking, James, had more to do with whether you develop any kind of personal relationship with your customers.

A: Absolutely, with every one that I possibly can. Anyway we can get interaction, joking or talking about common interests, we do. These things help me to remember the customer, of course. But it also gives us something to talk about and ask about the next time we see them. We've developed relationships with people that go back to when we first went in business. Take the Nelson brothers. We're able to deal with them and do a great deal of business. Certainly, we give them prices, but I think the work—

most of it anyway—would be ours regardless of the price. We know not to get ridiculous, and they trust that we won't. Other customers, like Jack Chambers, have just become real close friends over the years. Jack came by here last week and said, "I'm gonna send you a picture of Lenco when you first went in business. You had three blades in your only building. You didn't even have a door in the back. The shop was so small those three blades completely filled it." He said, "From there to here, you've come a long way—and during that time all the dealers seem to have gone down hill." And he just looked at me and said, "I wonder why that is?"

The following cautionary note is to be used with exhibits 9 through 15. Reprinted from the source of the exhibits—Robert Morris Associates' *Statement Studies*—this note explains how to use and interpret the figures.

Interpretation of Statement Studies Figures

RMA recommends that Statement Studies data be regarded only as general guidelines and not as absolute industry norms. There are several reasons why the data may not be fully representative of a given industry:

(1) The financial statements used in the *Statement Studies* are not selected by any random or statistically reliable method. RMA member banks voluntarily submit the raw data they have available each year, with these being the only constraints: (a) The fiscal year-ends of the companies reported may not be from April 1 though June 29, and (b) their total assets must be less than $100 million.

(2) Many companies have varied product lines; however, the *Statement Studies* categorize them by their primary product Standard Insutrail Classification (SIC) number only.

(3) Some of our industry samples are rather small in relation to the total number of firms in a given in-

dustry. A relatively small sample can increase the chances that some of our composites do not fully represent an industry.

(4) There is the chance that an extreme statement can be present in a sample, causing a disproportionate influence on the industry composite. This is particularly true in a relatively small sample.

(5) Companies within the same industry may differ in their method of operations which in turn can directly influence their financial statements. Since they are included in our sample, too, these statements can significantly affect our composite calculations.

(6) Other considerations that can result in variations among different companies engaged in the same general line of business are different labor markets; geographical location; different accounting methods; quality of products handled; sources and methods of financing; and terms of sale.

For these reasons, RMA does not recommend the Statement Studies *figures be considered as absolute norms for a given industry. Rather the figures should be used only as general guidelines and in addition to the other methods of financial analysis. RMA makes no claim as to the representativeness of the figures printed in this book.*

Exhibit 9
MANUFACTURERS—CONSTRUCTION AND MINING MACHINERY AND EQUIPMENT

	CURRENT DATA					COMPARATIVE HISTORICAL DATA				
	50(6/30–9/30/85)				77(10/1/85–3/31/86)	6/30/81–3/31/82	6/30/82–3/31/83	6/30/83–3/31/84	6/30/84–3/31/85	6/30/85–3/31/86
TYPE OF STATEMENT										
Unqualified	3	32	29	7	71				55	71
Qualified		3	2		5	*Data not available*			5	5
Reviewed	6	11	1		18				14	18
Compiled	8	7			15				23	15
Other	6	9		3	18				14	18
	0–1MM	1–10MM	10–50MM	50–100MM	ALL	ALL	ALL	ALL	ALL	ALL
Asset size										
Number of statements	23	62	32	10	127	101	117	110	111	127
	%	%	%	%	%	%	%	%	%	%
ASSETS										
Cash and Equivalents	7.3	7.3	7.0	7.6	7.2	6.2	7.8	8.7	5.8	7.2
Trade Receivables (net)	30.4	25.9	21.6	23.5	25.4	20.4	19.0	23.3	25.1	25.4
Inventory	29.6	35.5	37.7	32.0	34.7	41.6	39.7	33.5	32.5	34.7
All other current	3.5	3.2	1.6	2.9	2.8	2.1	2.4	2.7	4.3	2.8
Total current	70.8	71.9	67.8	66.0	70.2	70.4	68.9	68.2	67.7	70.2
Fixed assets (net)	21.8	21.8	22.3	22.0	21.9	22.7	24.8	24.7	22.8	21.9
Intangibles (net)	2.3	.8	2.9	.2	1.5	.8	.6	.4	.7	1.5
All other non-current	5.0	5.6	7.0	11.7	6.3	6.1	5.8	6.7	8.8	6.3
Total	100.0	100.0	100.0	100.0	100.0	100.0	100.0	100.0	100.0	100.0
LIABILITIES										
Notes payable-short term	8.9	10.1	9.6	8.8	9.7	13.2	11.7	11.5	11.5	9.7
Cur. mat.-L/T/D	4.4	3.8	3.5	1.6	3.7	2.6	3.6	4.0	5.1	3.7
Trade payables	16.7	17.4	9.0	16.0	15.1	14.2	12.4	13.9	14.6	15.1
Income taxes payable	1.0	1.7	1.7	.2	1.5	—	—	—	1.6	1.5
All other current	10.5	10.3	15.2	12.4	11.8	11.8	10.5	10.0	10.5	11.8
Total current	41.6	43.4	39.0	39.0	41.6	41.8	38.1	39.5	43.4	41.6
Long term debt	13.6	13.9	19.2	26.7	16.2	14.2	15.9	15.0	16.8	16.2
Deferred taxes	.1	1.0	1.5	2.2	1.1	—	—	—	1.1	1.1
All other non-current	3.8	1.1	3.6	2.9	2.4	1.3	2.5	2.6	3.2	2.4

Reprinted with permission. Copyright Robert Morris Associates 1986.

Exhibit 9

MANUFACTURERS—CONSTRUCTION AND MINING MACHINERY AND EQUIPMENT (continued)

Net worth	40.9	40.5	36.7	29.2	38.7	42.7	43.5	42.9	35.6	38.7
Total liabilities and net worth	100.0	100.0	100.0	100.0	100.0	100.0	100.0	100.0	100.0	100.0
INCOME DATA										
Net sales	100.0	100.0	100.0	100.0	100.0	100.0	100.0	100.0	100.0	100.0
Gross profit	29.6	25.4	29.8	20.5	26.9	29.0	27.5	26.9	27.5	26.9
Operating expenses	24.8	22.7	21.4	16.7	22.3	24.6	26.3	27.2	23.1	22.3
Operating profit	4.8	2.8	8.4	3.8	4.6	4.4	1.2	-.3	4.4	4.6
All other expenses (net)	.1	1.1	2.9	2.9	1.5	1.4	2.0	.8	1.5	1.5
Profit before taxes	4.7	1.7	5.4	.9	3.1	2.9	-.8	-1.1	2.9	3.1
RATIOS										
Current	2.9	2.4	2.5	2.6	2.4	2.9	3.6	2.9	2.4	2.4
	1.5	1.7	2.0	1.8	1.7	1.8	2.0	1.8	1.7	1.7
	1.1	1.3	1.5	1.3	1.3	1.2	1.2	1.2	1.2	1.3
Quick	1.2	1.1	1.2	1.2	1.2	1.3	1.7	1.6	1.0	1.2
	.9	.8	.8	.7	.8	.7	.7	.8	.7	.8
	.7	.5	.5	.6	.5	.4	.4	.5	.5	.5
Sales/Receivables	27 13.4	35 10.5	39 9.4	34 10.8	34 10.8	31 11.8	27 13.6	38 9.6	36 10.1	34 10.8
	42 8.7	50 7.3	55 6.6	57 6.4	49 7.4	44 8.3	44 8.3	51 7.2	52 7.0	49 7.4
	52 7.0	68 5.4	63 5.8	79 4.6	63 5.8	61 6.0	61 6.0	73 5.0	78 4.7	63 5.8
Cost of sales/Inventory	33 10.9	57 6.4	91 4.0	73 5.0	60 6.1	83 4.4	83 4.4	62 5.9	57 6.4	60 6.1
	66 5.5	83 4.4	126 2.9	96 3.8	94 3.9	126 2.9	135 2.7	114 3.2	101 3.6	94 3.9
	101 3.6	152 2.4	174 2.1	183 2.0	152 2.4	215 1.7	215 1.7	192 1.9	152 2.4	152 2.4
Cost of sales/Payables	20 18.1	20 18.1	18 20.5	22 16.5	20 18.2	23 16.1	17 22.0	25 14.6	23 16.0	20 18.2
	28 13.0	34 10.7	32 11.5	62 5.9	34 10.8	38 9.6	35 10.4	40 9.2	35 10.3	34 10.8
	48 7.6	63 5.8	42 8.7	78 4.7	63 5.8	68 5.4	57 6.4	57 6.4	58 6.3	63 5.8
Sales/Working capital	4.9	3.8	3.7	2.6	3.8	2.8	2.6	2.8	3.6	3.8
	9.4	6.5	5.3	6.0	5.9	5.3	4.5	4.9	6.0	5.9
	32.6	17.5	7.3	9.8	15.0	13.9	10.7	11.0	13.8	15.0
EBIT/Interest	12.7	7.8	8.1		7.8	6.5	3.5	3.3	5.7	7.8

Right data block

Metric					
Net profit + depr., dep., amort./Cur. mat. L/T/D (88)	2.1 (104)	1.2 (87)	1.1 (98)	2.1 (114)	2.6
	1.0	-.1	-.8	1.1	1.2
	8.0	5.4	5.4	4.6	6.9
(63)	3.3 (72)	2.0 (64)	1.2 (68)	1.8 (85)	3.3
	1.1	.2	-.1	.4	1.2
Fixed/Worth	.3	.3	.3	.3	.3
	.6	.5	.6	.6	.6
	.9	1.1	1.0	1.3	1.2
Debt/Worth	.8	.5	.5	.9	.7
	1.4	1.5	1.5	1.7	1.5
	3.1	3.5	3.0	4.2	4.7
% profit before taxes/Tangible net worth	23.3	14.1	17.6	27.7	40.3
% profit before taxes/Total assets (97)	14.4 (113)	5.1 (106)	3.2 (102)	15.3 (118)	19.1
	2.3	-13.5	-18.2	2.6	4.9
	12.1	7.5	8.1	11.7	12.2
Sales/Net fixed assets	5.2	1.6	.8	5.0	6.9
	-.0	-5.4	-8.0	.6	1.1
	13.3	13.5	13.1	18.1	18.8
	7.9	6.5	6.4	9.0	8.8
Sales/Total assets	4.9	3.8	3.5	4.5	5.7
	2.1	2.1	2.0	2.1	2.4
% depr., dep., amort./Sales	1.6	1.5	1.4	1.6	1.7
	1.2	1.0	1.0	1.2	1.3
	1.1	1.3	1.4	1.2	1.2
(89)	2.0 (106)	2.2 (100)	2.7 (99)	2.0 (116)	2.0
	3.2	3.9	4.6	3.4	3.4
% officers' comp./Sales	2.1	2.9	2.5	3.4	2.1
(28)	3.1 (21)	5.2 (21)	5.1 (18)	4.0 (27)	3.8
	5.7	7.7	10.0	7.5	7.5
Net sales ($)	1389856M	1629436M	1407180M	1924778M	2489589M
Total assets ($)	1020847M	1249508M	1086205M	1475771M	1735576M

Left data block

Metric					
Net profit + depr., dep., amort./Cur. mat. L/T/D (22)	3.7 (53)	2.4 (30)	3.4	(114)	2.6
	2.4	1.1	1.3		1.2
	6.4	7.1	11.2		6.9
(12)	2.8 (39)	3.6 (27)	3.6	(85)	3.3
	1.5	1.3	1.1		1.2
Fixed/Worth	.2	.2	.4		.3
	.6	.5	.6		.6
	1.4	1.1	1.0		1.2
Debt/Worth	.5	.7	.9		.7
	1.4	1.4	1.8		1.5
	3.7	3.9	3.1		4.7
% profit before taxes/Tangible net worth	74.2	35.0	39.7		40.3
% profit before taxes/Total assets (22)	32.2 (57)	19.0 (29)	24.9	7.8 (118)	19.1
	13.6	4.2	5.0	-28.7	4.9
	15.7	11.0	15.8	7.0	12.2
Sales/Net fixed assets	9.6	6.5	8.3	2.1	6.9
	5.0	.6	1.0	-3.4	1.1
	39.1	29.6	11.8	8.6	18.8
	11.9	9.0	7.9	7.3	8.8
Sales/Total assets	7.5	5.3	5.0	4.6	5.7
	2.8	2.6	1.8	1.5	2.4
% depr., dep., amort./Sales	2.4	1.7	1.5	1.3	1.7
	1.8	1.3	1.2	1.3	1.3
	.8	1.1	1.2		1.2
(20)	1.8 (57)	1.8 (30)	2.1	(116)	2.0
	3.6	3.7	3.0		3.4
% officers' comp./Sales	2.9	1.9			2.1
(12)	6.1 (15)	3.0	3.8	(27)	3.8
	8.6	5.5	7.5		7.5
Net sales ($)	30498M	372921M	1132219M	963950M	2489589M
Total assets ($)	12912M	216318M	780722M	725624M	1735576M

M = $ thousand   MM = $ million

Reprinted with permission. Copyright Robert Morris Associates 1986.

Exhibit 10
MANUFACTURERS—FARM MACHINERY AND EQUIPMENT

CURRENT DATA

TYPE OF STATEMENT	0–1MM	1–10MM	10–50MM	50–100MM	All
Unqualified	7	37	13	3	60
Qualified	1	4	2		7
Reviewed	5	9			14
Compiled	11	10	3		24
Other	5	8	1	3	17
	63(6/30–9/30/85)			59(10/1/85–3/31/86)	
Number of statements	29	68	19	6	122
ASSETS	%	%	%	%	%
Cash and equivalents	3.7	7.9	5.9		6.5
Trade receivables-(net)	21.3	20.4	21.0		20.7
Inventory	40.7	41.5	45.4		42.0
All other current	1.8	2.5	2.3		2.4
Total current	67.4	72.4	74.6		71.6
Fixed assets (net)	22.8	23.2	20.0		22.4
Intangibles (net)	1.0	.2	.1		.4
All other non-current	8.7	4.2	5.3		5.6
Total	100.0	100.0	100.0		100.0
LIABILITIES					
Notes payable-Short term	16.8	15.8	16.1		16.1
Cur. mat.-L/T/D	8.1	5.6	3.9		5.8
Trade payables	13.1	11.9	10.8		12.0
Income taxes payable	.5	.3	.5		.5
All other current	5.7	6.8	9.4		7.0
Total current	44.2	40.4	40.6		41.4
Long term debt	20.1	19.3	17.2		18.8
Deferred taxes	.2	.8	.6		.7
All other non-current	3.7	1.4	.5		1.9

COMPARATIVE HISTORICAL DATA

TYPE OF STATEMENT	6/30/81–3/31/82	6/30/82–3/31/83	6/30/83–3/31/84	6/30/84–3/31/85	6/30/85–3/31/86
Unqualified				57	60
Qualified				8	7
Reviewed	Data not available			16	14
Compiled				23	24
Other				20	17
Asset size	All	All	All	All	All
Number of statements	138	135	125	124	122
ASSETS	%	%	%	%	%
Cash and equivalents	5.9	5.9	5.9	7.3	6.5
Trade receivables-(net)	22.8	20.7	21.2	23.0	20.7
Inventory	42.7	42.0	40.9	40.6	42.0
All other current	2.9	2.9	2.3	2.1	2.4
Total current	74.3	71.5	70.4	73.1	71.6
Fixed assets (net)	19.0	20.9	22.0	19.7	22.4
Intangibles (net)	.7	.7	.8	.5	.4
All other non-current	6.0	7.0	6.8	6.7	5.6
Total	100.0	100.0	100.0	100.0	100.0
LIABILITIES					
Notes payable-Short term	14.6	17.1	15.3	15.2	16.1
Cur. mat.-L/T/D	2.5	2.8	3.3	4.3	5.8
Trade payables	13.2	10.2	11.0	12.4	12.0
Income taxes payable	—	—	—	1.1	.5
All other current	10.0	9.1	10.6	9.4	7.0
Total current	40.2	39.2	40.2	42.4	41.4
Long term debt	13.8	16.1	17.1	15.4	18.8
Deferred taxes	—	—	—	.4	.7
All other non-current	2.6	4.4	2.3	2.1	1.9

	31.7	38.1	41.0	37.3	37.3	39.7	40.4	40.3	43.4
Net worth	31.7	38.1	41.0	37.3	37.3	39.7	40.4	40.3	43.4
Total liabilities and net worth	100.0	100.0	100.0	100.0	100.0	100.0	100.0	100.0	100.0
INCOME DATA									
Net sales	100.0	100.0	100.0	100.0	100.0	100.0	100.0	100.0	100.0
Gross profit	34.6	28.5	26.6	30.0	30.0	29.4	28.9	29.2	29.5
Operating expenses	36.4	24.6	22.1	27.3	27.3	25.4	28.4	26.7	24.2
Operating profit	-1.7	3.9	4.6	2.6	2.6	4.1	.6	2.5	5.4
All other expenses (net)	2.8	2.1	3.8	2.5	2.5	2.1	2.8	3.1	3.2
Profit before taxes	-4.6	1.8	.8	.1	.1	2.0	-2.2	-.6	2.2
RATIOS									
Current	2.6	2.6	4.0	2.5	2.5	2.6	2.8	2.9	2.8
	1.5	1.8	1.7	1.7	1.7	1.7	1.8	1.8	1.9
	1.1	1.4	1.4	1.3	1.3	1.3	1.3	1.4	1.4
Quick	1.1	1.3	1.0	1.2	1.2	1.4	1.2	1.1	1.3
	.6	.6	.6	.6	.6	.7	.7	.6	.8
	.2	.4	.4	.3	.3	.4	.4	.4	.4
Sales/Receivables	20 18.4	24 15.4	30 12.2	24 15.3	24 15.3	30 12.3	31 11.9	28 13.2	29 12.5
	32 11.3	43 8.5	46 8.0	41 8.8	41 8.8	48 7.6	51 7.1	42 8.7	45 8.1
	64 5.7	57 6.4	83 4.4	63 5.8	63 5.8	70 5.2	78 4.7	65 5.6	61 6.0
Cost of sales/Inventory	73 5.0	94 3.9	89 4.1	87 4.2	87 4.2	87 4.2	87 4.2	85 4.3	79 4.6
	126 2.9	122 3.0	159 2.3	130 2.8	130 2.8	135 2.7	159 2.3	140 2.6	130 2.8
	192 1.9	166 2.2	243 1.5	183 2.0	183 2.0	203 1.8	228 1.6	203 1.8	192 1.9
Cost of sales/Payables	13 27.4	16 23.5	15 23.8	15 23.6	15 23.6	15 24.3	19 19.5	13 28.2	15 24.3
	26 14.0	27 13.5	24 15.2	28 13.1	28 13.1	29 12.7	34 10.8	24 15.1	33 11.0
	51 7.2	46 8.0	42 8.7	47 7.8	47 7.8	51 7.1	49 7.4	45 8.2	51 7.1
Sales/Working capital	3.9	3.5	2.7	3.4	3.4	3.3	2.8	3.2	3.0
	8.0	5.1	4.4	5.1	5.1	5.6	4.3	4.9	5.3
	21.5	9.1	9.2	9.9	9.9	11.5	10.0	8.9	9.4
EBIT/Interest	3.3	3.2	2.1	3.1	3.1	3.3	3.0	2.2	3.6
	1.4 (25)	1.5 (66)	1.3	1.4	1.4 (127)	1.6 (115)	1.3 (106)	1.2 (113)	1.8 (120)
	-.8	.7	.3	.4	.4	.7	-.5	.1	1.0
Net profit + depr., dep., amort./Cur. mat. L/T/D	1.3	4.7	4.4	3.5	3.5	7.6	4.2	3.9	6.6
	.5 (14)	2.1 (47)	.8 (15)	1.4	1.4 (94)	2.1 (81)	1.3 (76)	1.7 (87)	2.7 (91)

Reprinted with permission. Copyright Robert Morris Associates 1986.

Exhibit 10
MANUFACTURERS—FARM MACHINERY AND EQUIPMENT (continued)

Ratio	C1	C2	C3	C4	C5	C6	C7	C8	C9
Fixed/Worth	-2.7	.3	-.1	1.0	-1.0	-.1	.3	.3	.1
	.3	.3	.3	.2	.3	.2	.3	.2	.3
	.8	.6	.5	.4	.5	.5	.6	.5	.6
Debt/Worth	1.8	1.2	.7	.8	1.0	1.1	.8	1.0	1.2
	.9	.8	1.0	.7	.8	.8	.7	.7	.9
	2.8	1.7	1.7	1.4	1.6	1.8	1.6	1.7	2.0
% profit before taxes/Tangible Net worth	(25)	12.0 (62)	(112)	12.9 (131)	2.7 (120)	2.6 (116)	(135)	12.2 (115)	(115)
	28.4	3.9	2.3 (18)	24.0	19.5	16.8	22.2	29.0	22.6
	12.0	22.2	15.9	1.1	-18.9	-22.1	1.0	.6	-8.8
% profit before taxes/Total assets	6.8	-50.0	-7.0	10.2	7.5	7.0	10.5	10.0	8.3
	-50.0	10.5	7.6	5.0	.8	.9	1.6	3.6	2.3
	10.5	1.6	2.6	.2	-6.7	-8.9	-13.6	-.8	-3.6
Sales/Net fixed assets	19.3	-13.6	-2.3	17.3	13.2	12.1	19.3	16.5	13.1
	10.6	19.3	12.3	9.4	8.1	6.5	10.6	8.9	7.5
	5.3	10.6	7.5	6.4	5.5	4.3	5.3	5.6	5.2
Sales/Total assets	2.6	5.3	5.2	2.2	2.1	1.8	2.6	2.1	2.1
	1.7	2.6	2.1	1.7	1.5	1.3	1.7	1.6	1.6
	1.3	1.7	1.7	1.2	1.1	1.0	1.3	1.2	1.3
% depr., dep., amort./Sales	1.7	1.3	1.3	1.1	1.3	1.7	1.7	1.3	1.4
	3.1 (62)	1.7	1.4	1.9 (124)	2.4 (112)	2.8 (111)	2.3 (18)	2.2 (112)	2.4 (112)
	4.1	2.3 (18)	3.8	2.7	3.7	3.8	3.8	3.2	3.8
% officers' comp/Sales	(22)	2.0	2.9	1.8	2.0	2.9	1.3	2.9	1.7
	2.0	4.1	2.0	3.4 (44)	3.6 (37)	4.2 (38)	2.0	4.3 (34)	3.3
	4.1	(22)	4.1	5.9	6.4	8.1	4.1	8.5	7.0
Net sales ($)	28398M	399237M	592449M	1552894M	2025302M	1652157M	1614180M	1824962M	1552894M
Total assets ($)	15401M	247773M	388115M	1034757M	1196195M	1201033M	1189338M	1308135M	1034757M

M = $thousand   MM = $million

Reprinted with permission. Copyright Robert Morris Associates 1986.

Exhibit 11

MANUFACTURERS—GENERAL INDUSTRIAL MACHINERY AND EQUIPMENT

	CURRENT DATA					COMPARATIVE HISTORICAL DATA				
TYPE OF STATEMENT	0–1MM	1–10MM	10–50MM	50–100MM	All	6/30/81–3/31/82	6/30/82–3/31/83	6/30/83–3/31/84	6/30/84–3/31/85	6/30/85–3/31/86
Unqualified	7	71	48	12	138				161	138
Qualified		5	1	1	7				11	7
Reviewed	29	56	2		87		Data not available		80	37
Compiled	44	19	11		63				73	63
Other	23	36		1	71				57	71
					167(6/30–9/30/85)					
					199(10/1/85–3/31/86)					
Asset size					All	All	All	All	All	All
Number of statements	103	187	62	14	366	349	411	372	382	366
ASSETS	%	%	%	%	%	%	%	%	%	%
Cash and equivalents	9.2	6.1	6.5	6.8	7.1	8.1	8.8	7.9	7.7	7.1
Trade receivables-(net)	32.4	29.3	23.0	24.9	28.9	28.1	25.8	27.3	29.1	28.9
Inventory	28.1	31.5	28.4	30.3	30.0	29.1	28.0	28.7	28.5	30.0
All other current	1.6	2.9	3.0	1.8	2.5	2.8	3.0	2.8	2.2	2.5
Total current	71.2	69.9	60.8	63.7	68.5	68.2	65.6	66.7	67.6	68.5
Fixed assets (net)	22.5	22.5	31.9	24.9	24.2	24.5	26.4	25.2	24.5	24.2
Intangibles (net)	.9	1.4	1.8	.4	1.3	.7	1.0	1.0	.9	1.3
All other non-current	5.4	6.3	5.6	11.0	6.1	6.7	7.1	7.1	7.0	6.1
Total	100.0	100.0	100.0	100.0	100.0	100.0	100.0	100.0	100.0	100.0
LIABILITIES										
Notes payable-short term	8.3	13.3	8.6	4.9	10.8	8.8	8.6	9.3	10.4	10.8
Cur. mat.-LT/D	5.1	3.6	2.7	2.1	3.8	3.0	3.6	2.9	4.0	3.8
Trade payables	17.9	16.3	9.8	8.2	15.4	14.5	13.2	14.3	15.4	15.4
Income taxes payable	1.2	1.5	.8	1.0	1.3	—	—	—	1.5	1.3
All other current	13.0	11.8	9.1	11.4	11.7	13.3	12.0	12.2	10.6	11.7
Total current	45.5	46.5	30.9	27.7	42.9	39.7	37.4	38.6	41.9	42.9
Long term debt	13.9	15.2	19.7	14.4	15.6	14.6	16.1	16.3	16.1	15.6
Deferred taxes	.9	.9	2.2	1.8	1.1	—	—	—	1.1	1.1
All other non-current	1.6	1.8	1.8	3.2	1.8	2.3	1.9	3.0	2.2	1.8

Reprinted with permission. Copyright Robert Morris Associates 1986.

Case 12   LENCO, INC.

Exhibit 11
MANUFACTURERS—GENERAL AND INDUSTRIAL MACHINERY AND EQUIPMENT (continued)

	38.1	35.7	45.3	52.8	38.7	43.5	44.5	42.0	38.8	38.7
Net worth	38.1	35.7	45.3	52.8	38.7	43.5	44.5	42.0	38.8	38.7
Total liabilities and net worth	100.0	100.0	100.0	100.0	100.0	100.0	100.0	100.0	100.0	100.0
INCOME DATA										
Net sales	100.0	100.0	100.0	100.0	100.0	100.0	100.0	100.0	100.0	100.0
Gross profit	35.9	31.1	31.9	28.0	32.4	30.4	30.8	31.1	32.3	32.4
Operating expenses	30.6	26.4	26.5	22.4	27.4	23.3	26.0	28.0	26.4	27.4
Operating profit	5.2	4.7	5.4	5.5	5.0	7.1	4.9	3.1	5.9	5.0
All other expenses (net)	1.6	1.2	2.0	1.2	1.5	1.7	1.8	1.4	1.5	1.5
Profit before taxes	3.6	3.4	3.4	4.3	3.5	5.4	3.0	1.7	4.4	3.5
RATIOS										
Current	2.3	2.2	3.0	3.0	2.5	2.8	3.0	2.9	2.5	2.5
	1.6	1.5	2.3	2.5	1.6	1.8	1.9	1.8	1.7	1.6
	1.2	1.2	1.6	1.7	1.3	1.3	1.3	1.3	1.3	1.3
Quick	1.3	1.2	1.5	1.7	1.3	1.4	1.6	1.6	1.4	1.3
	.9	.8	1.0	1.3	.9	1.0	1.0	.9	.9	.9
	.6	.5	.6	.8	.6	.7	.6	.6	.6	.6
Sales/Receivables	33 — 11.2	41 — 9.0	46 — 8.8	39 — 7.9	9.3	36 — 9.0	43 — 10.2	41 — 8.4	39 — 9.0	9.3
	43 — 8.4	54 — 6.8	63 — 6.3	51 — 5.8	7.1	49 — 6.8	57 — 7.4	55 — 6.4	51 — 6.6	7.1
	57 — 6.4	65 — 5.6	104 — 5.1	65 — 3.5	5.6	64 — 5.4	72 — 5.7	72 — 5.1	65 — 5.1	5.6
Cost of sales/Inventory	30 — 12.1	53 — 6.9	89 — 5.2	48 — 4.1	7.6	45 — 7.6	56 — 8.1	49 — 6.5	48 — 7.4	7.6
	62 — 5.9	87 — 4.2	122 — 3.3	83 — 3.0	4.4	83 — 4.2	94 — 4.4	83 — 3.9	83 — 4.4	4.4
	96 — 3.8	135 — 2.7	159 — 2.3	130 — 2.3	2.8	130 — 2.9	135 — 2.8	130 — 2.7	130 — 2.8	2.8
Cost of sales/Payables	19 — 19.5	26 — 14.0	20 — 16.4	22 — 18.3	16.7	17 — 16.4	24 — 21.3	23 — 15.3	22 — 15.9	16.7
	31 — 11.6	39 — 9.4	30 — 10.9	35 — 12.1	10.3	29 — 10.0	37 — 12.5	38 — 9.8	35 — 9.7	10.3
	54 — 6.7	60 — 6.1	34 — 8.1	55 — 10.7	6.6	49 — 7.0	59 — 7.4	58 — 6.2	58 — 6.3	6.6
Sales/Working capital	6.3	4.9	2.8	2.8	4.3	3.8	3.7	3.4	4.3	4.3
	11.2	8.0	4.5	3.6	7.8	6.4	6.4	5.8	7.2	7.8
	23.3	16.8	8.0	4.7	16.1	14.1	15.9	11.6	16.6	16.1

	Ratio	C1	C2	C3	C4	C5	C6	C7	C8	C9	C10
(88)	EBIT/Interest (287)	6.4	6.3	6.2	11.3	6.4	8.6	6.0	6.0	8.2	6.4
		3.7 (167)	2.6 (57)	3.0 (13)	2.7 (325)	3.0	3.2 (340)	2.2 (335)	2.5 (339)	3.2 (325)	3.0
		1.7	1.4	.9	1.6	1.4	1.5	1.0	.4	1.4	1.4
(56)	Net profit + depr., dep., Amort./Cur. mat. L/T/D (227)	6.1	5.7	5.6	7.5	6.1	10.0	7.8	7.1	6.5	6.1
		3.2 (129)	2.6 (47)	3.2 (11)	4.9 (243)	3.1	3.8 (247)	3.0 (227)	2.7 (244)	2.8 (243)	3.1
		.9	1.2	.9	1.6	1.2	1.6	1.0	.7	1.4	1.2
	Fixed/Worth	.3	.3	.5	.4	.3	.3	.3	.3	.3	.3
		.5	.6	.7	.4	.6	.5	.6	.6	.6	.6
		1.2	1.3	1.1	.7	1.2	.9	1.1	1.0	1.1	1.2
	Debt/Worth	.8	1.0	.6	.4	.8	.7	.6	.7	.8	.8
		1.7	2.1	1.2	1.0	1.7	1.4	1.3	1.4	1.5	1.7
		4.9	4.3	2.2	1.9	4.0	2.7	2.6	2.9	3.4	4.0
(96)	% profit before taxes/Tangible net worth (343)	44.3	44.2	29.8	21.2	41.2	34.6	29.1	27.7	39.6	41.2
		24.9 (176)	17.1 (61)	15.0	16.0 (347)	17.9	22.6 (402)	13.9 (356)	11.8 (360)	20.9 (347)	17.9
		7.2	4.8	1.3	7.1	5.4	8.1	1.3	-3.9	8.7	5.4
	% profit before taxes/Total assets	16.3	11.9	12.3	11.2	13.6	16.3	12.6	10.9	14.0	13.6
		8.6	5.8	6.7	7.1	6.7	9.0	5.3	5.2	8.5	6.7
		1.7	1.9	.2	3.4	1.8	2.8	.4	-3.0	2.0	1.8
	Sales/Net fixed assets	29.3	18.3	7.1	8.4	19.1	16.9	15.1	14.7	16.4	19.1
		15.7	9.8	4.5	4.6	8.6	8.0	7.4	7.5	8.3	8.6
		7.3	5.1	3.4	3.7	4.5	4.5	4.1	3.9	4.4	4.5
	Sales/Total assets	3.2	2.4	1.8	1.5	2.5	2.3	2.3	2.2	2.5	2.5
		2.6	1.8	1.4	1.3	1.9	1.8	1.8	1.6	1.8	1.9
		1.9	1.4	1.1	1.1	1.3	1.4	1.3	1.2	1.3	1.3
(92)	% depr., dep., amort./Sales (304)	1.2	1.2	2.4	1.7	1.4	1.1	1.3	1.5	1.3	1.4
		1.9 (164)	2.2 (57)	3.1 (12)	2.7 (325)	2.4	1.9 (356)	2.3 (335)	2.5 (338)	2.3 (325)	2.4
		3.5	4.2	4.6	4.7	4.2	3.0	3.6	3.9	3.5	4.2
(44)	% officers' comp/Sales (110)	4.8	2.5			2.9	2.1	2.7	2.9	2.6	2.9
		7.4 (67)	3.8		(113)	4.8	3.8 (140)	4.6 (113)	4.3 (121)	5.4 (113)	4.8
		10.7	6.2			8.2	7.3	8.4	8.6	8.6	8.2
	Net sales ($)	128471M	1135678M	1891461M	1372698M	4528308M	4939549M	4809385M	4277387M	6237080M	4528308M
	Total assets ($)	50508M	629075M	1341470M	1020528M	3041581M	3217082M	3365506M	3197572M	3608929M	3041581M

M = $ thousand   MM = $ million

Reprinted with permission. Copyright Robert Morris Associates 1986.

Exhibit 12
MANUFACTURERS—MACHINE SHOPS, JOBBING AND REPAIR

	CURRENT DATA					COMPARATIVE DATA				
TYPE OF STATEMENT	0-1MM	1-10MM	10-50MM	50-100MM	All	6/30/81–3/31/82	6/30/82–3/31/83	6/30/83–3/31/84	6/30/84–3/31/85	6/30/85–3/31/86
Unqualified	8	56	9		73				80	73
Qualified	2	7	1	1	11		Data not available		10	11
Reviewed	100	77	1		177				151	177
Compiled	164	45	1		210				201	210
Other	50	29	1		80				88	80
	265(6/30–9/30/85)	286(10/1/85–3/31/86)								
Asset size	0-1MM	1-10MM	10-50MM	50-100MM	All	All	All	All	All	All
Number of statements	324	214	12	1	551	523	550	511	530	551
ASSETS	%	%	%	%	%	%	%	%	%	%
Cash and equivalents	8.1	6.7	9.0		7.6	7.8	8.0	8.4	7.3	7.6
Trade receivables-(net)	26.1	23.4	19.7		24.9	24.2	21.8	22.3	26.0	24.9
Inventory	15.1	20.5	26.9		17.5	18.7	17.0	17.2	17.2	17.5
All other current	2.1	1.5	1.4		1.9	1.8	2.0	2.0	2.0	1.9
Total current	51.5	52.0	57.1		51.8	52.6	48.7	49.9	52.6	51.8
Fixed assets (net)	40.7	41.6	28.4		40.8	40.5	43.9	43.2	39.5	40.8
Intangibles (net)	.6	1.0	.7		.7	.4	.6	.6	.5	.7
All other non-current	7.3	5.4	13.9		6.7	6.5	6.8	6.4	7.5	6.7
Total	100.0	100.0	100.0		100.0	100.0	100.0	100.0	100.0	100.0
LIABILITIES										
Notes payable-short term	10.3	7.3	6.2		9.1	6.8	7.3	8.8	8.6	9.1
Cur. mat.-L/T/D	7.8	7.8	3.0		7.7	6.0	7.0	7.0	7.0	7.7
Trade payables	11.6	11.7	6.3		11.5	11.2	9.5	10.6	11.8	11.5
Income taxes payable	1.1	1.2	1.5		1.1	—	—	—	1.2	1.1
All other current	8.6	8.9	13.8		8.8	11.6	9.6	9.5	9.0	8.8
Total current	39.4	36.9	30.9		38.2	35.6	33.3	35.9	37.6	38.2
Long term debt	23.4	22.2	19.1		22.8	20.5	21.9	22.7	22.5	22.8
Deferred taxes	.3	1.4	.7		.8	—	—	—	.6	.8
All other non-current	3.0	2.6	3.5		2.8	1.6	2.3	2.6	2.2	2.8

	1	2	3	4	5	6	7	8	9
Net worth	33.9	37.0	45.8	35.4	42.3	42.4	38.9	37.1	35.4
Total liabilities and net worth	100.0	100.0	100.0	100.0	100.0	100.0	100.0	100.0	100.0
INCOME DATA									
Net sales	100.0	100.0	100.0	100.0	100.0	100.0	100.0	100.0	100.0
Gross profit	36.1	28.7	23.7	33.0	31.9	31.4	30.8	32.9	33.0
Operating expenses	30.9	22.4	16.0	27.2	24.5	27.5	28.5	26.4	27.2
Operating profit	5.3	6.3	7.8	5.7	7.4	3.9	2.4	6.5	5.7
All other expenses (net)	1.7	2.4	.3	2.0	1.8	2.0	2.0	2.1	2.0
Profit before taxes	3.5	3.9	7.5	3.8	5.6	1.9	.4	4.3	3.8
RATIOS									
Current	2.2 / 1.5 / 1.0	2.1 / 1.5 / 1.1	2.8 / 1.9 / 1.2	2.2 / 1.5 / 1.0	2.2 / 1.6 / 1.1	2.4 / 1.5 / 1.1	2.3 / 1.5 / 1.0	2.2 / 1.4 / 1.1	2.2 / 1.5 / 1.0
Quick	1.6 / 1.0 / .6	1.3 / .8 / .6	1.6 / 1.1 / .6	1.5 / .9 / .6	1.5 / .9 / .6	1.5 / .9 / .6	1.6 / .9 / .6	1.4 / .9 / .6	1.5 / .9 / .6
(number of statements)	(323)			(550)	(522)		(529)		(550)
Sales/Receivables	29 12.7 / 42 8.7 / 55 6.6	46 7.9 / 63 5.8 / 79 4.6		32 11.3 / 44 8.3 / 60 6.1	33 11.0 / 47 7.8 / 59 6.2	31 11.8 / 42 8.7 / 54 6.7	34 10.7 / 48 7.6 / 63 5.8	37 10.0 / 48 7.6 / 62 5.9	32 11.3 / 44 8.3 / 60 6.1
Cost of sales/Inventory	11 33.6 / 28 13.0 / 56 6.5	62 5.9 / 91 4.0 / 152 2.4		17 21.1 / 38 9.6 / 76 4.8	20 18.6 / 43 8.4 / 83 4.4	15 24.7 / 36 10.2 / 78 4.7	17 20.6 / 40 9.0 / 83 4.4	17 21.0 / 40 9.1 / 70 5.2	17 21.1 / 38 9.6 / 76 4.8
Cost of sales/Payables	12 31.7 / 24 15.0 / 40 9.1	11 33.3 / 19 19.5 / 33 10.9		13 27.5 / 25 14.4 / 42 8.6	15 23.8 / 26 14.1 / 45 8.1	11 32.8 / 21 17.2 / 37 10.0	16 23.9 / 27 13.3 / 46 8.0	13 22.4 / 25 13.7 / 42 7.8	13 27.5 / 25 14.4 / 42 8.6
Sales/Working capital	7.2 / 13.4 / -184.3	2.5 / 5.3 / 12.3		6.5 / 12.3 / 125.5	5.9 / 10.4 / 56.7	5.7 / 12.1 / 114.2	5.2 / 10.9 / -324.0	5.9 / 12.3 / 119.4	6.5 / 12.3 / 125.5
EBIT/Interest	(291) 4.3 / 2.6 / 1.1	6.1 / 4.1 / 1.9		5.8 / 2.7 / 1.3	(487) 6.5 / 4.3 / 1.4	(446) 4.3 / 1.8 / .3	(487) 4.4 / 1.7 / -.3	(506) 5.7 / 2.8 / 1.3	(506) 5.8 / 2.7 / 1.3
Net profit + depr., dep.,	(202) 1.4 / 3.7	2.9 / 1.4 / 4.0		1.3 / 3.9	2.7 / 1.4 / 4.3	.3 / 3.4	-.3 / 3.4	1.3 / 4.7	1.3 / 3.9

Reprinted with permission. Copyright Robert Morris Associates 1986.

Exhibit 12

MANUFACTURERS—MACHINE SHOPS, JOBBING AND REPAIR (continued)

(Values shown per column as Upper Quartile / Median / Lower Quartile, with (number of statements) shown in parentheses on the line where it appears in the source. M = $ thousand.)

Ratio	1827223M	1386442M	1554098M	1671729M	1713479M	315954M	971043M	353474M
amort./Cur. mat. L/T/D	1.7 (315) / .6	1.5 (327) / .5	2.3 (367) / 1.2	2.3 (353) / 1.2 / .6	2.1 (336) / 1.0	2.0 (166) / 1.0	2.1 (178) / 1.0	—
Fixed/Worth	.6 / 1.1 / 1.9	.6 / 1.1 / 2.3	.5 / 1.0 / 1.7	.6 / 1.1 / 2.0	.7 / 1.1 / 2.6	.7 / 1.2 / 3.1	.7 / 1.1 / 2.1	.4 / .7 / 2.3
Debt/Worth	.7 / 1.4 / 2.9	.7 / 1.5 / 3.7	.7 / 1.3 / 2.7	.8 / 1.6 / 3.6	.8 / 1.8 / 4.3	.8 / 1.9 / 5.5	.8 / 1.8 / 3.5	.4 / 1.2 / 6.4
% profit before taxes/Tangible net worth	28.1 / 12.3 (473) / -5.5	24.8 / 8.6 (490) / -14.2	41.3 / 22.2 (531) / 8.0	44.9 / 19.1 (502) / 5.2	47.1 / 19.4 (504) / 6.7	51.4 / 20.6 (201) / 6.5	45.2 / 19.1 (288) / 7.2	29.6 / 13.0 / 7.4
% profit before taxes/Total assets	11.2 / 4.8 / -3.4	10.7 / 3.4 / -7.0	16.6 / 8.6 / 2.2	15.0 / 7.5 / 1.1	14.8 / 6.8 / 1.8	15.9 / 7.2 / 1.4	13.6 / 6.4 / 2.1	14.3 / 5.9 / 3.2
Sales/Net fixed assets	7.2 / 4.2 / 2.6	6.9 / 3.9 / 2.4	8.0 / 4.7 / 2.9	8.9 / 4.8 / 3.0	8.3 / 4.7 / 3.0	9.7 / 5.4 / 3.5	6.0 / 4.0 / 2.8	5.9 / 4.4 / 3.0
Sales/Total assets	2.2 / 1.7 / 1.4	2.1 / 1.6 / 1.2	2.3 / 1.8 / 1.4	2.4 / 1.9 / 1.4	2.5 / 1.9 / 1.4	2.8 / 2.1 / 1.6	2.1 / 1.7 / 1.3	1.6 / 1.2 / 1.1
% depr., dep., amort./Sales	2.9 / 4.8 (489) / 7.6	3.1 / 5.5 (494) / 9.2	2.2 / 3.9 (522) / 6.5	2.8 / 4.9 (516) / 7.9	2.9 / 5.1 (497) / 8.1	3.1 / 5.4 (203) / 8.5	2.8 / 4.8 (303) / 7.7	—
% officers' comp/Sales	4.3 / 7.0 (265) / 10.5	4.4 / 7.2 (272) / 11.3	3.7 / 6.5 (306) / 10.2	3.7 / 6.3 (269) / 9.9	3.7 / 6.2 (293) / 9.5	4.2 / 6.9 (92) / 10.8	3.1 / 5.4 (177) / 7.4	—
Net sales ($)	1827223M	1386442M	1554098M	1671729M	1713479M	315954M	971043M	353474M
Total assets ($)	1117481M	901136M	904644M	966067M	1051528M	148290M	581334M	271592M

(Additional size column: Net sales 73008M, Total assets 50312M.)

M = $ thousand   MM = $ million

Reprinted with permission. Copyright Robert Morris Associates 1986.

Exhibit 13

MANUFACTURERS—SPECIAL INDUSTRY MACHINERY

	CURRENT DATA					COMPARATIVE HISTORICAL DATA				
TYPE OF STATEMENT	0–1MM	1–10MM	10–50MM	50–100MM	All	6/30/81–3/31/82	6/30/82–3/31/83	6/30/83–3/31/84	6/30/84–3/31/85	6/30/85–6/31/86
Unqualified	9	63	47	11	130	Data not available			154	130
Qualified		8	2		10				19	10
Reviewed	30	54	2		86				86	86
Compiled	46	21	1		68				76	68
Other	20	26	9	2	57				56	57
	162(6/30–9/30/85)		189(10/1/85–3/31/86)			All	All	All	All	All
Number of statements	105	172	61	13	351	302	333	342	391	351
ASSETS	%	%	%	%	%	%	%	%	%	%
Cash and equivalents	8.4	7.5	8.1	9.7	8.0	9.2	9.2	9.8	9.1	8.0
Trade receivables-(net)	29.6	26.3	23.5	24.0	26.7	25.1	23.6	24.6	26.2	26.7
Inventory	26.8	30.4	28.6	23.1	28.8	31.4	30.1	29.4	28.3	28.8
All other current	2.5	2.1	3.4	2.2	2.4	2.7	2.4	2.5	3.3	2.4
Total current	67.3	66.3	63.7	59.1	65.9	68.4	65.4	66.4	66.9	65.9
Fixed assets (net)	22.2	26.3	25.8	30.1	25.1	24.0	26.6	24.9	24.4	25.1
Intangibles (net)	1.4	.7	2.0	1.0	1.2	.7	.8	.9	1.0	1.2
All other non-current	9.1	6.7	8.4	9.8	7.8	6.9	7.1	7.8	7.7	7.8
Total	100.0	100.0	100.0	100.0	100.0	100.0	100.0	100.0	100.0	100.0
LIABILITIES										
Notes payable-short term	11.8	9.0	8.2	2.2	9.4	7.4	7.8	8.5	9.1	9.4
Cur. mat.-L/T/D	4.4	3.5	2.6	1.9	3.6	2.7	3.3	3.6	3.5	3.6
Trade payables	15.4	14.7	9.8	7.7	13.8	13.6	12.5	13.0	13.6	13.8
Income taxes payable	1.0	1.4	1.5	.8	1.3	—	—	—	1.8	1.3
All other current	11.5	14.3	12.6	10.2	13.0	16.2	13.9	13.9	12.8	13.0
Total current	44.1	42.9	34.7	22.7	41.1	40.0	37.4	38.9	40.7	41.1
Long term debt	14.1	16.5	15.8	16.1	15.7	14.4	15.4	15.5	16.0	15.7
Deferred taxes	.4	.8	1.3	3.8	.9	—	—	—	.7	.9
All other non-current	2.6	1.5	1.2	2.7	1.8	2.5	2.7	3.9	1.9	1.8

Reprinted with permission. Copyright Robert Morris Associates 1986.

Exhibit 13
MANUFACTURERS—SPECIAL INDUSTRY MACHINERY (continued)

	38.8	38.3	47.1	54.7	40.6	40.6	40.7	41.6	44.5	43.1
Net worth	38.8	38.3	47.1	54.7	40.6	40.6	40.7	41.6	44.5	43.1
Total liabilities and net worth	100.0	100.0	100.0	100.0	100.0	100.0	100.0	100.0	100.0	100.0
INCOME DATA										
Net sales	100.0	100.0	100.0	100.0	100.0	100.0	100.0	100.0	100.0	100.0
Gross profit	34.3	31.1	29.3	37.7	32.0	32.0	31.4	30.5	30.5	30.0
Operating expenses	32.1	27.0	22.9	29.7	27.9	27.9	25.9	27.6	26.3	23.7
Operating profit	2.2	4.1	6.4	8.0	4.1	4.1	5.6	3.0	4.3	6.3
All other expenses (net)	.7	1.0	.7	1.6	.9	.9	1.1	1.2	1.3	1.4
Profit before taxes	1.5	3.1	5.7	6.4	3.2	3.2	4.4	1.8	2.9	5.0
RATIOS										
Current	2.7	2.3	3.0	3.3	2.6	2.6	2.6	2.8	2.8	2.5
	1.7	1.5	1.8	3.0	1.7	1.7	1.7	1.8	1.9	1.8
	1.1	1.2	1.4	2.2	1.2	1.2	1.2	1.3	1.4	1.3
Quick	1.7	1.2	1.7	2.2	1.4	1.4	1.5	1.4	1.4	1.4
	.9	.8	.9	1.4	.9	.9	.9	.9	.9	.9
	.5	.5	.6	1.1	.6	.6	.6	.6	.6	.6
Sales/Receivables	30 / 12.2	37 / 9.8	47 / 7.8	54 / 6.8	37 / 10.0	37 / 10.0	39 / 9.4	40 / 9.2	35 / 10.4	37 / 9.9
	45 / 8.2	51 / 7.2	61 / 6.0	73 / 5.0	51 / 7.2	51 / 7.2	53 / 6.9	54 / 6.7	45 / 8.1	51 / 7.2
	61 / 6.0	66 / 5.5	74 / 4.9	89 / 4.1	68 / 5.4	68 / 5.4	70 / 5.2	73 / 5.0	61 / 6.0	65 / 5.6
Cost of sales/Inventory	18 / 20.3	53 / 6.9	72 / 5.1	89 / 4.1	46 / 7.9	46 / 7.9	49 / 7.5	53 / 6.9	49 / 7.5	51 / 7.2
	61 / 6.0	89 / 4.1	111 / 3.3	99 / 3.7	87 / 4.2	87 / 4.2	83 / 4.4	99 / 3.7	91 / 4.0	96 / 3.8
	104 / 3.5	135 / 2.7	140 / 2.6	126 / 2.9	126 / 2.9	126 / 2.9	130 / 2.8	146 / 2.5	135 / 2.7	140 / 2.6
Cost of sales/Payables	13 / 28.4	20 / 18.3	19 / 19.5	29 / 12.5	18 / 20.6	18 / 20.6	20 / 17.9	21 / 17.1	17 / 21.5	20 / 18.7
	27 / 13.7	38 / 9.5	31 / 11.7	34 / 10.8	34 / 10.7	34 / 10.7	34 / 10.7	36 / 10.2	31 / 11.7	33 / 11.0
	54 / 6.8	58 / 6.3	50 / 7.3	42 / 8.7	54 / 6.7	54 / 6.7	53 / 6.9	55 / 6.6	47 / 7.7	54 / 6.8
Sales/Working capital	5.0	4.8	3.1	2.8	4.2	4.2	3.7	3.4	3.8	3.6
	9.8	7.9	4.7	3.6	7.4	7.4	6.8	6.0	6.3	6.4
	19.2	23.6	8.9	4.2	19.9	19.9	16.0	12.9	13.5	12.2

	6.1		5.3		6.7		23.1		6.2	EBIT/Interest		10.4		6.5		6.9		7.8		6.2
(88)	2.1	(144)	2.6	(53)	3.2	(12)	2.9	(297)	2.6		(263)	3.3	(289)	2.2	(282)	2.2	(335)	3.1	(297)	2.6
	1.0		1.2		1.7		1.5		1.2			1.3		.7		.5		1.4		1.2
	5.3		6.5		10.6		14.3		8.1	Net profit + depr., dep.,		9.0		6.9		5.4		8.0		8.1
(52)	2.1	(128)	2.7	(44)	4.8	(12)	9.4	(236)	3.0	amort./Cur. mat. L/T/D	(195)	3.3	(212)	2.9	(221)	2.1	(265)	2.9	(236)	3.0
	1.0		1.0		2.4		3.8		1.1			1.1		.8		.7		1.1		1.1
	.2		.3		.4		.4		.3	Fixed/Worth		.3		.3		.3		.3		.3
	.6		.7		.5		.5		.6			.6		.5		.6		.5		.6
	1.5		1.2		1.0		.8		1.2			1.0		1.0		1.1		1.1		1.2
	.7		.9		.5		.4		.8	Debt/Worth		.7		.6		.7		.7		.8
	1.5		1.9		1.2		.9		1.6			1.3		1.2		1.5		1.5		1.6
	4.9		3.6		2.7		1.3		3.6			2.7		2.5		3.2		3.3		3.6
	39.8		36.8		31.2		31.7		37.1	% profit before taxes/		36.7		27.5		24.6		39.1		37.1
										Tangible										
(96)	11.3	(169)	14.7	(60)	15.0		11.2	(338)	13.6	net worth	(291)	19.8	(316)	13.3	(327)	11.0	(365)	16.9	(338)	13.6
	–.3		3.2		5.4		4.5		3.2			7.1		1.4		–4.9		5.0		3.2
	12.8		12.9		13.9		15.8		13.0	% profit before taxes/Total		15.7		13.2		10.2		14.9		13.0
	4.9		5.0		6.8		7.2		5.3	assets		7.8		5.5		4.3		6.9		5.3
	–.2		1.0		2.6		2.3		1.0			1.8		–1.0		–2.6		1.2		1.0
	30.4		16.3		8.1		6.5		17.5	Sales/Net fixed assets		15.6		12.2		15.7		14.9		17.5
	14.0		7.7		5.4		4.1		7.9			8.0		6.8		6.5		7.6		7.9
	6.5		3.7		3.9		2.8		4.1			4.7		4.4		3.9		4.5		4.1
	3.1		2.4		1.6		1.6		2.5	Sales/Total assets		2.2		2.2		2.2		2.2		2.5
	2.4		1.8		1.3		1.3		1.8			1.7		1.7		1.5		1.7		1.8
	1.7		1.3		1.1		.8		1.3			1.3		1.3		1.1		1.2		1.3
	1.2		1.4		1.8		2.2		1.4	% depr., dep., amort./Sales		1.2		1.4		1.6		1.4		1.4
(91)	2.1	(166)	2.4	(52)	2.6	(12)	3.2	(321)	2.4		(281)	2.0	(301)	2.3	(305)	2.5	(369)	2.3	(321)	2.4
	3.8		4.0		4.0		6.8		4.1			3.0		3.4		4.0		3.7		4.1
	4.8		2.3						2.8	% officers' comp/Sales		2.2		2.8		3.3		2.8		2.8
(57)	6.9	(50)	4.0					(112)	5.3		(109)	4.1	(105)	4.7	(106)	5.3	(128)	5.4	(112)	5.3
	10.3		7.1						8.7			6.6		7.6		8.5		7.3		8.7
	144391M		992078M		1852522M		1181967M		4170958M	Net sales ($)		3793209M		3892377M		3959431M		4732633M		4170958M
	58190M		568863M		1362527M		944637M		2934217M	Total assets ($)		2458977M		2603363M		2981155M		3341946M		2934217M

M = $ thousand MM = $ million

Reprinted with permission. Copyright Robert Morris Associates 1986.

Exhibit 14
MANUFACTURERS—HEAVY COMMERCIAL AND INDUSTRIAL MACHINERY AND EQUIPMENT

	CURRENT DATA					COMPARATIVE HISTORICAL DATA				
TYPE OF STATEMENT										
Unqualified	30	186	57	14	287				306	287
Qualified	3	19	3		25		Data not available		29	25
Reviewed	124	177	3	5	306				344	306
Compiled	188	98	8	8	294				319	294
Other	75	74	8	2	159				197	159
	473(6/30–9/30/85)		598(10/1/85–3/31/86)			6/30/81–3/31/82	6/30/82–3/31/83	6/30/83–3/31/84	6/30/84–3/31/85	6/30/85–3/31/86
	0–1MM	1–10MM	10–50MM	50–100MM	All	All	All	All	All	All
Asset size / Number of statements	420	554	81	16	1071	1101	1114	1068	1195	1071
ASSETS	%	%	%	%	%	%	%	%	%	%
Cash and equivalents	7.3	5.7	4.7	3.8	6.2	6.4	6.2	6.5	6.0	6.2
Trade receivables-(net)	35.7	31.9	25.4	19.1	32.7	31.1	29.1	31.2	32.2	32.7
Inventory	36.6	36.9	37.2	38.7	36.8	37.4	38.1	37.0	36.4	36.8
All other current	1.7	1.8	2.2	6.0	1.9	2.1	2.4	2.4	2.3	1.9
Total current	81.3	76.3	69.5	67.6	77.6	76.9	75.9	76.9	76.9	77.6
Fixed assets (net)	12.7	16.8	21.1	19.4	15.6	16.3	16.8	15.9	16.3	15.6
Intangibles (net)	.4	.5	.2	.2	.4	.4	.5	.6	.6	.4
All other non-current	5.5	6.4	9.2	12.8	6.3	6.3	6.9	6.6	6.2	6.3
Total	100.0	100.0	100.0	100.0	100.0	100.0	100.0	100.0	100.0	100.0
LIABILITIES										
Notes payable-short term	14.5	16.4	16.0	21.5	15.7	13.8	14.9	15.4	15.5	15.7
Cur. mat.-L/T/D	4.4	3.8	4.0	4.4	4.1	3.8	4.1	3.9	4.0	4.1
Trade payables	25.2	22.2	16.8	13.4	22.8	23.0	21.5	22.2	22.8	22.8
Income taxes payable	.7	1.0	1.2	.8	.9	—	—	—	1.1	.9
All other current	10.0	8.5	8.7	6.7	9.0	10.6	9.5	8.9	8.6	9.0
Total current	54.8	51.9	46.8	46.7	52.6	51.1	50.0	50.4	52.0	52.6
Long term debt	10.8	11.4	18.3	19.7	11.8	11.8	11.4	11.7	11.6	11.8
Deferred taxes	.3	.5	1.1	.9	.5	—	—	—	.5	.5
All other non-current	1.7	1.5	1.8	1.0	1.6	1.7	1.7	2.3	1.8	1.6

(The following is a Robert Morris Associates comparative financial-ratio table, printed sideways on the page. Each turnover ratio is shown as "days — turnover." Ratio groups show the upper-quartile / median / lower-quartile values. Figures in parentheses following a median indicate the number of statements in that sample.)

	C1	C2	C3	C4	C5	C6	C7	C8	C9	C10
Net worth	32.4	34.7	32.0	31.7	33.6	35.4	36.8	35.7	34.1	33.6
Total liabilities and net worth	100.0	100.0	100.0	100.0	100.0	100.0	100.0	100.0	100.0	100.0
INCOME DATA										
Net sales	100.0	100.0	100.0	100.0	100.0	100.0	100.0	100.0	100.0	100.0
Gross profit	29.4	28.0	29.0	22.4	28.5	28.4	28.9	29.1	28.7	28.5
Operating expenses	27.0	24.9	24.6	18.7	25.6	24.5	26.7	27.4	25.4	25.6
Operating profit	2.4	3.1	4.4	3.8	2.9	3.8	2.2	1.7	3.4	2.9
All other expenses (net)	.6	.6	1.9	1.5	.7	1.0	1.2	.8	.9	.7
Profit before taxes	1.8	2.5	2.5	2.3	2.2	2.8	1.0	.9	2.5	2.2
RATIOS										
Current	2.1	2.0	2.2	2.1	2.0	2.1	2.1	2.3	2.1	2.0
	1.5	1.4	1.4	1.4	1.4	1.5	1.5	1.5	1.5	1.4
	1.1	1.2	1.2	1.2	1.2	1.2	1.2	1.2	1.2	1.2
Quick	1.2	1.0	1.0	.7	1.1	1.1	1.1	1.1	1.1	1.1
	.8	.7	.7	.5	.8	.7	.7	.7 (1194)	.7	.8
	.5	.5	.4	.3	.5	.5	.5	.5	.5	.5
Sales/Receivables	31 — 11.7	37 — 10.0	40 — 9.7	40 — 9.1	35 — 10.5	33 — 10.9	30 — 12.0	35 — 10.2	35 — 10.5	35 — 10.5
	42 — 8.6	46 — 8.0	49 — 7.9	49 — 7.4	45 — 8.2	42 — 8.6	40 — 9.2	45 — 7.7	45 — 8.1	45 — 8.2
	55 — 6.6	57 — 6.4	63 — 6.1	63 — 5.8	57 — 6.4	54 — 6.7	52 — 7.0	59 — 6.1	57 — 6.2	57 — 6.4
Cost of sales/Inventory	34 — 10.8	49 — 7.4	52 — 7.0	91 — 4.0	45 — 8.1	44 — 8.3	42 — 8.6	44 — 7.9	45 — 8.3	45 — 8.1
	60 — 6.1	73 — 5.0	91 — 4.0	146 — 2.5	72 — 5.1	76 — 4.8	76 — 4.8	72 — 4.6	72 — 5.1	72 — 5.1
	101 — 3.6	122 — 3.0	174 — 2.1	192 — 1.9	118 — 3.1	114 — 3.2	122 — 3.0	114 — 2.8	118 — 3.2	118 — 3.1
Cost of sales/Payables	24 — 15.4	23 — 15.7	25 — 14.5	26 — 13.9	24 — 15.4	24 — 15.4	22 — 16.7	25 — 14.4	24 — 15.0	24 — 15.4
	41 — 9.0	39 — 9.3	37 — 9.9	42 — 8.7	40 — 9.1	39 — 9.3	37 — 9.9	42 — 8.6	40 — 9.1	40 — 9.1
	62 — 5.9	64 — 5.7	66 — 5.5	72 — 5.1	63 — 5.8	62 — 5.9	61 — 6.0	68 — 5.4	63 — 5.7	63 — 5.8
Sales/Working capital	6.9	5.8	5.0	3.6	6.1	6.3	6.0	5.1	6.2	6.1
	11.0	10.6	9.4	6.7	10.7	10.1	10.1	9.3	10.5	10.7
	30.2	25.0	20.0	18.0	25.7	21.4	22.1	21.5	24.1	25.7
EBIT/Interest (377) / (960)	5.5	4.2	3.7	2.3	4.5	5.6	3.6	4.0	4.8	4.5
	2.6 (491)	2.2 (74)	1.9	1.8 (958)	2.3	2.4 (985)	1.5 (922)	1.8 (1039)	2.3 (958)	2.3
	1.2	1.3	1.2	1.1	1.3	1.3	.5	.6	1.4	1.3
Net profit + depr., dep., amort./Cur. mat. L/T/D (209) / (632)	4.7	5.5	7.0	5.0	5.4	6.3	4.9	4.4	5.0	5.4
	1.8 (349)	2.3 (50)	2.7 (12)	1.4 (620)	2.1	2.5 (639)	1.7 (611)	1.5 (669)	2.2 (620)	2.1
	.6	1.0	.9	.6	.9	.8	.4	.3	.9	.9

Reprinted with permission. Copyright Robert Morris Associates 1986.

Exhibit 14
MANUFACTURERS—HEAVY COMMERCIAL AND INDUSTRIAL MACHINERY AND EQUIPMENT (*continued*)

	1	2	3	4	5	6	7	8	9	10
Fixed/Worth	.1	.2	.2	.3	.2	.2	.2	.2	.2	.2
	.3	.4	.5	.6	.4	.4	.4	.4	.4	.4
	.9	.9	1.3	.8	.9	.9	1.0	.9	1.0	.9
Debt/Worth	1.0	1.1	1.5	1.6	1.0	1.0	1.0	.9	1.0	1.1
	2.3	2.1	2.4	2.4	2.3	1.9	2.1	1.8	1.9	2.3
	5.2	4.5	5.0	3.5	4.8	4.2	4.6	3.7	4.2	4.8
(384) % profit before taxes/ Tangible net worth (1065)	40.5	26.7	31.6	15.5	31.2	34.2	32.7	22.0	22.2	31.2
	16.0 (535)	14.3	17.0	9.9(1016)	16.2(1016)	17.2(1072)	16.2(1016)	8.7(1018)	9.3(1132)	16.2(1016)
	5.3	4.8	3.1	2.2	6.0	5.5	6.0	-4.7	-2.6	6.0
% profit before taxes/Total assets	10.9	8.3	7.8	5.4	9.2	12.0	9.7	8.2	7.4	9.2
	5.3	4.2	3.8	3.4	4.7	5.6	4.9	2.9	2.8	4.7
	.8	1.2	.8	.5	1.0	1.6	1.7	-2.2	-1.7	1.0
Sales/Net fixed assets	74.7	41.9	28.0	15.6	52.2	50.5	46.8	49.0	48.9	52.2
	34.1	20.1	14.4	6.5	25.4	23.6	21.7	21.9	21.6	25.4
	16.8	8.4	5.2	5.0	9.9	9.9	9.4	8.9	9.0	9.9
Sales/Total assets	3.7	3.0	2.3	1.6	3.3	3.3	3.2	3.3	3.0	3.3
	2.9	2.3	1.7	1.4	2.5	2.5	2.5	2.5	2.3	2.5
	2.2	1.7	1.3	1.2	1.8	1.8	1.8	1.7	1.6	1.8
(361) % depr., dep., amort./Sales (997)	.6	.7	.7	1.8	.7	.6	.7	.6	.7	.7
	1.1 (503)	1.3 (66)	1.4 (13)	2.3 (943)	1.3 (943)	1.0(1018)	1.3 (943)	1.2 (954)	1.3 (1055)	1.3 (943)
	2.0	2.5	3.1	3.4	2.3	1.9	2.3	2.3	2.5	2.3
(191) % officers' comp/Sales (466)	3.0	1.9	.9	2.4	2.4	2.1	2.2	2.1	2.2	2.4
	5.2 (178)	2.9 (11)	1.5 (381)	3.8	3.8 (381)	3.7 (471)	3.9 (381)	3.7 (429)	4.0 (467)	3.8 (381)
	7.2	4.8	3.4	6.5	6.5	6.3	6.6	6.1	6.5	6.5
Net sales ($)	707834M	3948026M	2995329M	1429289M	9078478M	9979722M	8870317M	7810476M	10606980M	9078478M
Total assets ($)	230213M	1736257M	1644465M	1061260M	4672195M	4617761M	4296683M	4385595M	5232761M	4672195M

M = $ thousand   MM = $ million

Reprinted with permission. Copyright Robert Morris Associates 1986.

Exhibit 15
SERVICES—WELDING REPAIR

	CURRENT DATA				COMPARATIVE HISTORICAL DATA			
TYPE OF STATEMENT	0–1MM	1–10MM	10–50MM	All	6/30/82–3/31/83	6/30/83–3/31/84	6/30/84–3/31/85	6/30/85–3/31/86
Unqualified	3	3	1	7			8	7
Qualified	1			1	Data not available			1
Reviewed	9	3	1	13			16	13
Compiled	18	3		21			13	21
Other	7	2	1	10			15	10
Asset size	0–1MM	1–10MM	10–50MM	All	All	All	All	All
Number of statements	38	11	3	52	28	37	52	52
ASSETS	%	%	%	%	%	%	%	%
Cash and equivalents	7.2	6.4		7.1	6.3	6.3	8.4	7.1
Trade receivables-(net)	30.5	26.6		29.1	26.5	27.0	29.9	29.1
Inventory	10.4	12.4		11.9	15.2	14.7	13.1	11.9
All other current	2.7	5.6		3.2	2.5	4.6	5.2	3.2
Total current	50.8	51.0		51.3	50.5	52.6	56.6	51.3
Fixed assets (net)	36.7	43.6		38.3	42.4	41.7	34.1	38.3
Intangibles (net)	2.4	.7		2.0	.8	.1	1.6	2.0
All other non-current	10.0	4.7		8.4	6.4	5.6	7.7	8.4
Total	100.0	100.0		100.0	100.0	100.0	100.0	100.0
LIABILITIES								
Notes payable-short term	14.7	8.5		12.8	5.8	12.1	9.5	12.8
Cur. met.-L/T/D	6.9	5.4		6.2	7.4	6.1	7.7	6.2
Trade payables	15.2	10.2		13.8	16.8	13.6	14.5	13.8
Income taxes payable	.7	.9		.7	—	—	1.5	.7
All other current	6.9	8.0		7.4	8.0	8.3	8.1	7.4
Total current	44.4	33.1		41.0	38.0	40.1	41.2	41.0
Long term debt	17.3	21.7		18.3	25.2	19.1	20.7	18.3
Deferred taxes	.3	.3		.4	—	—	2.2	.4
All other non-current	3.8	3.1		4.0	3.0	1.7	1.2	4.0

Current data "All": 17(6/30–9/30/85) 35(10/1/85–3/31/86)

Reprinted with permission. Copyright Robert Morris Associates 1986.

Exhibit 15
SERVICES—WELDING REPAIR (continued)

	34.2	41.8	36.3	33.8	39.1	34.7	36.3
Net worth	34.2	41.8	36.3	33.8	39.1	34.7	36.3
Total liabilities and net worth	100.0	100.0	100.0	100.0	100.0	100.0	100.0
INCOME DATA							
Net sales	100.0	100.0	100.0	100.0	100.0	100.0	100.0
Gross profit							
Operating expenses	91.1	95.8	92.6	98.5	93.2	93.2	92.0
Operating profit	8.9	4.2	7.4	1.5	6.8	6.8	7.4
All other expenses (net)	1.4	2.7	1.7	1.8	1.9	1.5	1.7
Profit before taxes	7.5	1.5	5.6	-.4	4.9	5.3	5.6
RATIOS							
Current	1.9 / 1.2 / .8	2.1 / 1.7 / 1.0	2.0 / 1.4 / .8	2.3 / 1.4 / .7	2.9 / 1.5 / .9	2.0 / 1.6 / .9	2.0 / 1.4 / .8
Quick	1.5 / .8 / .6	2.0 / 1.1 / .8	1.7 / .8 / .6	1.3 / .9 / .5	1.6 / 1.0 / .5	1.5 / 1.0 / .6	1.7 / .8 / .6
Sales/Receivables	28 13.1	12.6	28 12.9	26 14.2	15 24.5	38 9.7	28 12.9
Cost of sales/Inventory	48 7.6	7.2	50 7.3	41 8.8	47 7.7	53 6.9	50 7.3
Cost of sales/Payables	64 5.7	5.5	64 5.7	64 5.7	72 5.1	64 5.7	64 5.7
Sales/Working capital	10.1 / 21.9 / -25.5	5.2 / 13.3 / 117.5	7.2 / 20.2 / -31.3	5.4 / 14.7 / -16.0	6.3 / 11.7 / ±INF	6.6 / 15.8 / -93.8	7.2 / 20.2 / -31.3
EBIT/Interest	(36) 9.8 / 2.5 / 1.4	8.2 / 2.0 / .6	(50) 7.9 / 2.0 / 1.0	(31) 3.2 / 1.1 / -.3	(42) 5.0 / 2.3 / .6	(50) 7.6 / 3.9 / 1.9	(50) 7.9 / 2.0 / 1.0
Net profit + depr., dep., amort./Cur. mat. L/T/D	(16) 10.2 / 2.2 / 1.2	.6	(27) 9.0 / 1.9 / 1.1	(18) 3.7 / 1.3 / .8	(31) 4.5 / 2.6 / .9	(27) 4.7 / 2.8 / 1.4	(27) 9.0 / 1.9 / 1.1

Comparative financial ratio data (Robert Morris Associates). Number of statements shown in parentheses. Quartile values (upper / median / lower) shown for each ratio.

Ratio	Col 1	Col 2	Col 3	Col 4	Col 5	Col 6	Col 7	Col 8
Fixed/Worth	.5	.6	.5	.5	.4	.5	.4	.5
	1.0	1.5	1.1	1.1	1.2	.9	.9	1.1
	2.2	1.6	2.1	2.1	20.0	2.7	2.2	2.1
Debt/Worth	.8	1.1	.8	.8	.8	.8	1.1	.8
	1.9	1.2	1.8	1.8	1.6	1.9	1.7	1.8
	5.8	3.4	5.0	5.0	29.8	4.6	3.8	5.0
% profit before taxes/Tangible net worth	48.3 (34)	22.5	41.8 (47)	41.8	38.0 (24)	47.5 (34)	81.6 (48)	41.8 (47)
	16.4	5.3	14.0	14.0	11.7	19.9	30.5	14.0
	7.1	-9.0	3.5	3.5	-8.8	1.8	10.3	3.5
% profit before taxes/Total assets	12.7	6.0	10.7	10.7	6.8	12.2	22.4	10.7
	7.3	4.0	5.5	5.5	1.0	5.2	10.2	5.5
	1.4	-1.9	.2	.2	-6.7	-.5	4.9	.2
Sales/Net fixed assets	11.7	7.4	10.3	10.3	10.0	9.6	12.4	10.3
	7.8	5.8	6.5	6.5	5.9	6.8	9.1	6.5
	4.0	2.8	3.4	3.4	3.8	4.1	5.0	3.4
Sales/Total assets	3.1	2.7	2.8	2.8	2.9	3.0	3.0	2.8
	2.3	1.8	2.0	2.0	2.3	2.3	2.2	2.0
	1.3	1.4	1.3	1.3	1.7	1.6	1.5	1.3
% depr., dep., amort./Sales	2.2	1.9 (10)	2.2	2.2	1.6 (27)	2.5 (33)	2.7 (50)	2.2 (49)
	3.6 (37)	3.4	3.6 (49)	3.6	3.3	3.8	3.4	3.6
	6.9	5.7	6.5	6.5	5.6	6.0	5.2	6.5
% officers' comp/Sales	2.9	—	2.1 (22)	2.1	2.8 (18)	3.6 (20)	3.1 (25)	2.1 (25)
	8.2 (16)	—	6.3	6.3	7.8	6.5	5.3	6.3
	12.5	—	12.3	12.3	12.3	10.3	9.3	12.3
Net sales ($)	32497M	56467M	101337M	190301M	47402M	57784M	128375M	190301M
Total assets ($)	15762M	30617M	58514M	104893M	24089M	32839M	73059M	104893M

M = $ thousand   MM = $ million

Reprinted with permission. Copyright Robert Morris Associates 1986.

LIL FILLY ORIGINALS

CURTIS E. TATE, JR.
University of Georgia

In 1964, when Ann House began designing and sewing clothes for her granddaughter, Katherine, and her grandson, Kevin, little did she realize what the consequence would be. She was doing what many grandmothers do for their grandchildren, producing garments with the touch and effort of a grandmother's love.

In Ann's own words, she doesn't think of herself as a seamstress. However, she has confidence in her ability to design a garment and fit the fabric together. The success accorded her by time has proven these facts.

BEGINNING OF SUCCESS

Ann's classic designed and sewn clothes for her grandchildren produced almost an immediate response. First friends and then their friends; "Make me one" was followed by "Make me some." A friend talked her into carrying six dresses to Memphis for the owner of a dress shop to see. This resulted in an order for twenty dresses, the conversion of her laundry room into a sewing room, and the hiring of a few women to help with the sewing. When she delivered the first order of twenty dresses to Memphis, this brought another order for twenty more dresses.

On a trip to Nashville to purchase material, she received an order from a Nashville store for a hundred dresses. Ann said, "With that order I almost dropped dead."

This case was prepared as a basis for class discussion. Cases are not designed to present illustrations of either correct or incorrect handling of administrative problems. This case, written specifically for this text, is printed with permission.

PROBLEMS OF SUCCESS

The success of a business does not occur without its accompanying problems. First, the city of Humbolt wanted Ann to move her operation out of the laundry room, out of her residence. She was able to find a larger house in a low-rent neighborhood. The house was two story, laid out somewhat like a duplex. By taking one-half of this house, Ann was able to expand her operation.

FINANCIAL PROBLEMS

In these early years, with the business's accelerated growth, Ann was frequently strapped for funds. She said, "The banker was my salvation. Many times it was necessary for me to put up all my jewelry to get enough money to operate on."

On three different occasions Ann sold the business. Each time she sold the business something always seemed to happen that she ended up with the business.

ANN REMARRIES

From the beginning, the business had been Ann's responsibility. During these early years, Connie, Ann's daughter and the mother of the children, had been of some assistance. However, the major burden had been Ann's to carry.

In 1972, Ann married Jack. Most of Jack's experience had been in the production of hosiery in Kentucky. Nevertheless he had some conceptual understanding of the apparel industry. In addition, he was willing to purchase stock in Lil Filly.[1]

JACK'S CONTRIBUTION

Jack, from his hosiery background, had an understanding of the apparel industry. This included the marketing process, commercial sewing machines, and the mechanical configuration of the machines.

Jack persuaded Ann to shift from domestic sewing machines to commercial machines and to hire some more operators. It was in this period that the operation made its second move. This time, the move was to a larger more adequate building. The installation of the commercial sewing machines resulted in a reduction in labor cost. This along with Jack's ability to repair the machines and other equipment contributed to an improved operation.

Jack's previous experience had acquainted him with the nature of the apparel marts. He encouraged Ann, in her marketing efforts, to utilize apparel marts like New York and Chicago. In addition, Jack had acquaintances in the trade. These contacts were to prove beneficial to Lil Filly in a variety of ways: improved marketing, more appropriate sources of supply, and so on.

BUYING AND INVENTORY DIFFICULTIES

While Ann lacked business training, her strength had always been in designing and fabrication of classic garments. The manner in which the business evolved had always resulted in production of garments for orders and not for inventory. This pattern of operation had necessitated an inventory of fabric, lace, and other trim items. From the outset, the Lil Filly garments were always top of the line. They were for the Ford and Kennedy children and grandchildren, and John Wayne's grandchildren; an order for Amy Carter was mixed up by the Lil Filly ship-

---

1. Ann's first husband was a devoted horseman. The family spent considerable time training and showing horses at various horse shows in the region. Sam, Ann's son, displayed little interest in horses. However, Connie, prior to her marriage, was a regular riding participant in the horse shows. It is this earlier background that was the origin of the firm's name, "Lil Filly."

ping clerk and shipped to the wrong store. There were other orders from comparable people.

The characteristic of this classic apparel calls for lace and trim items produced overseas. This in itself necessitates the need for forward planning of production and inventory requirements. Careful scheduling plans were needed if production and inventory supplies were to be in balance (i.e., if inventory supplies were not to be short or in excess). This was a continuous problem during the Jack era. There were inventory shortages as well as inventory overages.

JACK SELLS HIS STOCK

Lil Filly was approached by a person potentially interested in buying the business. Since Jack wanted his money out of the business, he was prepared to sell out. However, Ann was not interested in selling out.

Sammy McLemore, Ann's son by her first marriage, had, for the past eighteen years, been working for an engineering construction firm in Nashville, Tennessee. Sammy's educational experience included CMA high school and a bachelor of arts from Union University in Jackson, Tennessee. At the time the business sale issue arose, Sammy, due to the family ownership at the business that employed him, felt that his career had peaked and that it was time for him to move on. Consequently, when the opportunity for him to purchase Jack's stock was presented, he was agreeable for the transaction to be consummated. In retrospect, Sammy feels that years of experience he had with the engineering firm enabled him to develop some good management expertise.

THE AGREEMENT

An agreement was reached by which Sammy would purchase Jack's Lil Filly stock (49 percent) and would, upon becoming familiar with the Lil Filly operation, be the company's general manager. In addition, it was agreed that a $150,000 life insurance policy would be purchased on Ann's life. The policy's named beneficiary would be her daughter Connie. Upon Ann's death, her 51 percent of Lil Filly stock would go to Sammy. At this time, Connie was married to a local physician and involved with her family activities and not Lil Filly.

THE TRANSITION

Upon Sammy's entering the business, Jack carried him to New York to meet the appropriate people. Sammy's concept of management is, in his own words, "management is management." Based on his previous managerial experience, Sammy saw an important need for Lil Filly to have a more effective planning and scheduling operation. As a result, he began to plan operations on a yearly basis, determining the number of garments to produce and the cloth and trim requirements this would entail. This process enabled a better match between materials inventory and production. By the same token, this procedure enabled the more efficient use of capital and a more effective use of inventory.

Approximately two years following Sammy's purchase of Jack's Lil Filly stock, Jack died.

ANN'S 1984 REFLECTIONS

In her reflections, Ann could view the miraculous growth that Lil Filly (see Exhibit 1) had experienced since she made those first garments for her grandchildren. The family had changed. Katherine, the granddaughter, had graduated from Lambeth College in June with a major in fashion merchandising. Her present aspirations were to take a postgraduate course in apparel design. Kevin, the eldest grandson, would be a high school senior in the fall and was a member of the football team. His aspirations were to win a football scholarship at a nearby state

Exhibit 1
SALES TRENDS

YEAR	SALES
1970	$177,266.25
1971	222,305.87
1972	290,331.93
1973	321,999.92
1974	395,957.21
1975	444,838.03
1976	576,244.13
1977	677,857.14
1978	649,297.04
1979	716,433.30
1980	875,084.97

college. Connie was adjusting to a divorce from her doctor husband, and was performing some part-time clerical work at Lil Filly. Sammy continued to prove his managerial ability through the company's achievements, and was deriving personal satisfaction from his Corvette and his new boat.

WHERE IS LIL FILLY?

Lil Filly now has sales rooms in the New York, Chicago, and Los Angeles merchandise marts that are open everyday. Ann seems to take great satisfaction from the fact that she bought out her partner in the Dallas Showroom. The showrooms in the San Francisco, Dallas, and Atlanta marts are only open market week. After that, Ann says, "the buyers are looking for a new line."

CUSTOMERS IN 1984

Ann, in identifying her customer groups, seems to have a strong preference for one, even though she sells to two major groups. Ann says,

> The specialty shops owned and operated by an individual are easier to work with as customers. They get to know you, you get to know them, and they tend to pay their bills on time.
>
> The department store customers represent some of the major firm names; however, there can be problems with this class of customer. They are slow to pay. There are frequent changes among buyer personnel. Consequently, it is more difficult to establish and maintain a good working rapport with this group. Another common practice with this group, that adds to the difficulty, is that there is a buyer for each age group.

Lil Filly's lines for girls range from infants to twelve years and for boys the range is from infants to five years.

LIL FILLY OPERATING CYCLE

Ann explains,

> Lil Filly operates on a six-month cycle. Designing starts right after market week. This is followed by making up samples. When the line

samples are complete: (a) a six-month production schedule is made up; [and] (b) inventory requirements are determined, purchased, and deliveries are scheduled to blend with the production schedule. (Many of the inventory items must be procured from foreign sources. This necessitates careful scheduling.) Normally, Lil Filly does complete lines twice a year—two big shows. There are times when we run Christmas and Easter specials. Spring shows are held in April, while fall shows are held in October.

After the designs are formulated, Ann and a female assistant produce a sample garment for each design. Katherine, the granddaughter, then takes each sample garment and executes a black ink drawing. These drawings are used in making up the Lil Filly line catalog.

Ann, when asked about what she wanted Katherine's future role to be, was very specific, "Whatever she wants it to be. I want it to be her decision, not mine. I don't think that I should influence her decision. She has an interest in designing and would like to attend one of the design specialty schools. Whatever she does, I want it to be her."

ANN'S LIL FILLY APPRAISAL

One of Ann's great joys of achievement is the fact that Sammy has Lil Filly's business well in hand. She takes great pride in the fact that Sammy will be able to carry the business on when she is no longer actively involved.

In mid-1984, Ann felt that she did not wish for Lil Filly "to get too big." The present plant (a prefabricated metal building that was originally built for a skating rink) still had capacity to accommodate an additional sales volume. Ann seemed confident that it would not be difficult to increase Lil Filly's sales volume beyond its present level.

As for personnel, most of the employees had experience in the factory. Ann stressed that it had always been Lil Filly's practice to "train the supervisors to do it our way." Another factor that seemed important to Ann was that she had always found, from experience, that older people seemed to make the best employees. Presently, some of the older workers are retiring. Sometimes, some of these people, after they have been off for two or three weeks, will come back and want to go back to work. Ann explains, "The problem we have with the younger people is that they tend to turnover more than the older personnel. Occasionally, we and the employees will celebrate with a covered dish meal. The company will provide the drinks and some other items. We have a good group."

ANN LOOKS TO THE FUTURE

Following Connie's divorce, Ann began exploring possibilities of things she might do to be of assistance to Connie's future and possibly Katherine's. While Ann was visiting with two of her trade friends from Chattanooga, she had become aware of a new business opportunity. The friends knew of a small plant in Haiti that employed approximately forty women. This plant produced ladies' cotton dresses with lace sections, giving them an attractive appeal. The fact that labor costs were lower would enable the dresses to be marketed at a lower price.

At the outset, the possibility of this as a joint venture had a special appeal. It would provide an opportunity for Connie and Katherine, if she wanted it. There was a ready-ready made marketing mechanism to sell these in Lil Filly's existing mart sales centers. Surely, it would provide Ann and Sammy with fresh challenges.

However, there were obstacles to overcome before this venture could become a reality. There are government regulations that require compliance in a venture of this type. A decision had to be reached on whether the cloth would be cut and bundled at Lil Filly and then shipped to the Haiti plant to be sewn, with the completed garment being returned to Lil Filly. Because of government regulations, there could be an advantage by returning the dresses to the United States, lacking some minor item being complete. As an example, it could be sleeve buttons or buttons at the neck.

In Ann's earlier thinking, she had not thought of mixing the new business with Lil Filly. She thought that there should be two separate corporate businesses. This arrangement would provide for Connie to have a more active involvement in the new firm. (See Exhibits 2 and 3.)

Exhibit 2
LIL FILLY ORIGINALS, INC.: BALANCE SHEET (October 31, 1984)

ASSETS			LIABILITIES AND CAPITAL		
Current Assets			Liabilities		
Petty cash	$ 100.00		Accounts payable	$ 59,535.03	
Cash on deposit	(3,172.63)		Accrued payroll	29,000.00	
Accounts receivable	68,411.36		FICA taxes payable	1,590.53	
Savings, Merchants State Bank	266.40		Federal withholding taxes payable	1,608.82	
Inventory	221,817.90		Sales tax payable	2,526.03	
Total Current Assets		$287,423.03	Unemployment taxes payable	476.27	
Fixed Assets			Notes payable, Building	120,898.53	
Lot #1 building	$ 15,000.00		Notes payable, Auto #2	21,627.29	
Building	131,320.00		Notes payable, Sam T. Mc-Lemore	837.51	
Furniture and fixtures	7,506.32				
Machines and equipment	9,187.87				
Autos	28,171.44		Notes payable, Anne W. House	786.29	
Building improvements	33,734.67		Total Liabilities		$238,886.30
Less accumulated depreciation	(63,751.86)		Capital		
Utility deposit	750.00		Common stock issued	7,000.00	
Total Fixed Assets		161,918.44	Retained earnings (November 1)	205,187.03	
Other Assets			Current year income	11,621.18	
Prepaid federal tax	13,353.04		Total Capital		223,808.21
Total Other Assets		13,353.04	TOTAL LIABILITIES AND		
TOTAL ASSETS		$462,694.51	CAPITAL		$462,694.51

Exhibit 3
LIL FILLY ORIGINALS, INC.: PROFIT AND LOSS STATEMENT
(October 31, 1984)

	CURRENT			YEAR-TO-DATE		
Income						
Sales	$59,378.27			$1,138.729.60		
Less sales discounts	(767.53)			(13,366.40)		
Total Income		$58,610.74	100.0%		$1,125,363.20	100.0%

	CURRENT			YEAR-TO-DATE	
Less Cost of Sales					
Purchases	$15,999.36		27.3	$404,383.56	35.9
Less purchase discounts	(612.30)		(1.0)	(4,287.82)	(0.4)
Inventory change	22,408.55		38.2	(49,730.64)	(4.4)
Labor	16,733.89		28.6	333,665.29	29.6
Supplies	114.30		0.2	5,435.42	0.5
Total Cost of Sales		54,643.80	93.2	689,465.81	61.3
Gross Profit		$ 3,966.94	6.8	$435,897.39	38.7
Less Expenses					
Salaries, officers	$35,432.62		58.7	$111,624.06	9.9
Salaries, office	2,480.20		4.2	33,989.66	3.0
Advertising	3,035.10		5.2	4,504.51	0.4
Commissions	4,374.11		7.5	65,544.33	5.8
Donations	—		—	687.04	0.1
Depreciation	5,956.36		10.2	23,502.46	2.1
Collection expense	137.44		0.2	2,337.80	0.2
Dues and subscriptions	—		—	932.00	0.1
Freight and postage	462.20		0.8	5,656.41	0.5
Insurance	1,050.45		1.8	21,563.45	1.9
Insurance, officers' life	—		—	6,160.30	0.5
Interest	1,468.62		2.5	19,376.42	1.7
Laundry	15.09		0.0	167.04	0.0
Legal and accounting	—		—	1,045.00	0.1
Miscellaneous	6.76		0.0	285.82	0.0
Office supplies	125.86		0.2	2,118.40	0.2
Rent	341.00		0.6	3,610.70	0.3
Repairs and maintenance	100.00		0.2	3,243.53	0.3
Contract services	566.35		1.0	8,477.50	0.8
Payroll taxes	2,902.54		5.0	45,360.42	4.0
Taxes and licenses	29.75		0.1	3,687.27	0.3
Telephone	324.48		0.6	3,398.58	0.3
Travel and entertainment	2,188.42		3.7	18,887.11	1.7
Selling expense	2,697.58		4.6	16,231.32	1.4
Auto expense	571.36		1.0	6,703.41	0.6
Utilities	745.18		1.3	12,059.46	1.1
Bad debts	12,541.61		21.4	3,759.15	0.3
Total Expenses		76,553.08	130.6	424,913.15	37.8
Income (Loss)		(72,586.14)	(123.8)	10,984.24	1.0
Other Income					
Miscellaneous income	—		—	25.00	0.0
Interest income	(24.59)		(0.0)	611.94	0.1
Total Other Income		(24.59)	(0.0)	636.94	0.1
NET INCOME (LOSS)		$(72,610.73)	(123.9)	$11,621.18	1.0

POWDER DOLL

BETSY V. BOZE
University of Alaska at Anchorage

KEN M. BOZE
University of Alaska at Anchorage

David Stewart is a twenty-two-year-old college senior. He was born and raised on a ranch near a small town in Louisiana. He is soft spoken, easy going, and unpretentious. He likes gambling, fast cars, and heavily starched, expensive shirts. He has been supported by his family while he is in school and has worked only part time, usually in gambling-related businesses. He is frequently a loner, although he is also a championship golfer and enjoys going to Louisiana Downs, where he can watch and bet on thoroughbred horses.

David has been involved with the horse business since he was four years old. In 1969 his father purchased one half interest in the thoroughbred mare Swoon Bread. Since then both David and his father have had a growing interest in the thoroughbred industry. David's father, a small-town physician, now owns twenty-six brood mares and has a 768-acre ranch in Coushatta, Louisiana.

POWDER DOLL

In 1978, David Stewart had the opportunity to purchase the thoroughbred mare Sindolly for $4,700 from Joe Davis. Davis told him at the time of the purchase that he was interested in buying one of the mare's foals to race.

Stewart sent Sindolly to Kentucky in 1981 to be bred to the young stallion named Powder Horn. The result of that breeding was the 1982 chestnut filly Powder Doll. Stewart called Davis and told him to come and look at the filly to see if he was interested in purchasing her. Davis came, liked what he saw, and bought Powder Doll for $7,500.

Powder Doll started her racing career with a bang as she won her first start on June 6, 1984, for Davis. She then went on to win two of seven starts during her two-year-old career, earning over $50,000.

As a three year old in 1985, Powder Doll won four of nine starts and earned Davis more than $120,000. At the end of Powder Doll's three-year-old year she was voted the Champion Louisiana Bred Three-Year-Old Filly.

The four-year-old year is a tough year on horses because they run against older, more mature horses. These horses have more strength and experience racing than horses just coming into the four-year-old year. For these reasons Powder Doll was taken off the race track in November 1985 and returned to training in February of 1986 so that she could rest and get her strength back before her tough four-year-old campaign in 1986.

STEWART'S ATTITUDES ABOUT THE POTENTIAL EARNINGS OF A HORSE

"There is no way to measure the amount of money that a horse will win. The horse could get injured and never earn a dime. On the other hand, a horse could stay healthy and earn $1 million." While some horses do earn a million dollars, most do not.

"To succeed in the horse business a person must be very patient" David adds. Fortunately David is a very patient person.

This case, written specifically for this text, is printed by permission.

The horse owner also needs to be able to absorb a loss because the chances are better than 50-50 that any horse will not earn enough money to pay his keep. Less than 2 percent of all horses born in the United States ever win an added money race.

David believes that luck also plays a very important role in the thoroughbred business. "If a person has good luck he might be able to make a profit. If a person has bad luck it will be impossible to make a profit." As a gambler himself, this philosophy is understandable.

The thoroughbred industry is a game of uncertainties, a game of chances and odds. And perhaps it is a game of luck. There are never any guarantees, never any sure things. "If a person is looking at starting in the horse business, he had better know the people in the business and have some knowledge of the value of a horse." David was lucky in this regard because he had been raised in the business and he knew horses. He had owned thoroughbred broodmares but he did not own a racehorse.

THE OFFER

On March 1, 1986, Davis approached Stewart about repurchasing Powder Doll. Davis had encountered some serious financial problems and was forced to liquidate most of his assets. Davis was asking $150,000 for Powder Doll. He had attempted to sell her to numerous other people in the business. Because of the state of the economy, they were either not interested or could not raise that much capital.

Stewart agreed to have dinner with Davis and to discuss the possibility of a purchase and what the purchase price would be. Stewart, then a twenty-one-year-old college student, could not possibly come up with that kind of money. But he decided to go anyway and talk with Davis to see if he could get Davis to drop the price to something that he could afford.

Before the meeting Stewart called his father to discuss the proposition that had been presented to him. Dr. Stewart told him that it sounded like a good deal but that he could not possibly help raise that much money. Dr. Stewart told him to try to get Davis to drop the price to around $50,000. If young Stewart could do this, the doctor would cosign a note with him, but David would be responsible for making the entire payments on the note.

At dinner, Stewart told Davis that there was no possible way he could afford to pay $150,000. He explained that the amount of money was simply too much. Stewart then made him an offer of $50,000, which Davis promptly turned down. Davis explained to Stewart the kind of financial trouble that he was in and that $50,000 would not help him. The dinner ended at that, and Stewart felt that the deal was completely off and forgot about it.

About 7:30 on the morning of March 3, 1986, Stewart was awakened by a phone call from Davis, explaining that he had changed his mind and had decided to accept the offer. Stewart told him to meet him at his attorney's office in Coushatta with the title to the horse and that they would talk. When a clear title was transferred, he would supply Davis with a certified check for $50,000.

REGISTRATION PROBLEMS

When a horse is born, it must be registered with the Jockey Club. The Jockey Club is an organization that oversees all activities in the thoroughbred business. The owner is issued a set of registration papers that accompany the horse wherever it travels. A person can put certain liens or mortgages against the horse. When this is done the liens or mortgages are attached to the horse's registration papers. For a purchase to be legal and acceptable, the papers must be clear of any liens or mortgages attached to them. Since the papers accompany the horse wherever it goes, it is sometimes a difficult task to track them down and make sure that they are clear.

At this time Powder Doll was in training at Oaklawn Park in Hot Springs, Arkansas. There was no way of checking the papers for liens or mortgages against the horse without checking them in person.

The papers could not be checked by phone because phone systems to racetracks are shut down prior to post time. The reason for this is to prevent people from calling and betting on the horses with a bookie. The main reason a person would bet with a bookie is because off-track bets such as that do not effect the horses odds at the race track. The only people who benefit from off-track betting would be the big gamblers who play anywhere from $1,000 to $5,000 on a horse. Betting this much money at the track can lower the odds, and consequently the payoff, dramatically. The approximate payoffs for the minimum $2 bet are as follows:

ODDS	PAYS	ODDS	PAYS
1–5	$ 2.40	6	$ 14.00
2–5	2.80	7	16.00
1–2	3.00	8	18.00
3–5	3.20	9	20.00
4–5	3.69	10	22.00
Even	4.00	12	26.00
6–5	4.40	15	32.00
7–5	4.80	18	38.00
3–2	5.00	20	42.00
8–5	5.20	25	52.00
9–5	5.60	30	62.00
2	6.00	40	82.00
5–2	7.00	50	102.00
3	8.00	60	122.00
7–2	9.00	70	142.00
4	10.00	80	162.00
9–2	11.00	90	182.00
5	12.00	99	200.00

Stewart contacted a private pilot, who agreed to take him to Hot Springs to check the papers if a deal was made.

He met with Davis at noon and told him of the problems of clear title. Stewart explained that he was going to fly to Hot Springs to check them. Davis said that he could not wait for him to fly to Hot Springs and back. Once again, the deal was cancelled.

When Davis realized that Stewart was in possession of the $50,000 certified check and was ready to call off the deal he reopened negotiations.

Stewart boarded the plane for Hot Springs about 1:00 that afternoon. When he arrived there, he discovered that Davis owed the trainer over $8,000 in unpaid training bills. The trainer refused to sign the papers over unless he could get some guarantee that he would receive his money. Stewart thought that Powder Doll was not in the best condition and was not sure that he wanted to get involved with the problems with the trainer.

Davis was still waiting in Stewart's attorney's office while Stewart and the trainer discussed the situation, trying to come up with a solution.

TECHNICAL NOTE: THE LOUISIANA THOROUGHBRED INDUSTRY

For pure excitement it is difficult to beat the sport of Thoroughbred racing. The speed, grace and agility of the Thoroughbred, the courage, strength and lightning reflexes of the jockeys; and the roar of the crowd as the field thunders through the stretch all combine to saturate the senses.[1]

The nation's top thoroughbreds compete for more than $16.3 million in purse money during each racing season at Louisiana Downs. The track is located in Bossier City, Louisiana, and is America's fifth largest racetrack.[2]

The thoroughbred industry is one of the leading agricultural industries in Louisiana. The number of horses in Louisiana has been rising for twelve years and is at its highest level. In 1986 2,500 thoroughbred horses were born in Louisiana, up from only 350 in 1975.

Thoroughbred race horses can be very expensive. Prices start at about $15,000 and can easily reach hundreds of thousands of dollars. The prices of horses peaked in 1984 after increasing for ten years. Since then they have been falling at a dramatic rate. The average drop in price in 1986 sales of yearlings was 38.7 percent.

The main reason for the drop in the value of horses was the drop in the price of a barrel of oil. Investment in thoroughbreds has been observed as lagging the price per barrel of oil. When the oil business prospers, people in the oil business have money to put into horses. However, when oil dipped from $26 to as low as $15 a barrel in 1986–1987, the thoroughbred industry suffered with it. Many of the people involved in the oil business are or were involved in the thoroughbred industry, and as their revenues and profits fell their willingness to spend money on horses fell. The drop in oil prices caused many people to leave the horse business simply because they could not afford to maintain their horses properly.

A Day at the Downs

On a typical ten-race day at Louisiana Downs, the 341 betting windows each handle about $8,300. Mutuel clerks work average daily handles of $1.7 million for crowds averaging 10,867.

But the payoff for fans and players alike is also 10 good squirts of adrenaline and the pageantry of thoroughbred horse racing. The excitement and pageantry are the work of hundreds of owners, trainers, exercisers, jockeys, walkers,

---

1. *Louisiana Downs Handicapper's Handbook*, p. 1.
2. *Newcomer's Guide to Louisiana Downs*, p. 1.

valets, stewards and administrators, some of whom have worked a full day by post time for the first race.[3]

By 5:45 the trainers have their first horses on the track. They are back in the barn by 8:30 before the Louisiana heat takes hold.

Track maintenance director Joe Souza and his staff of ten keep an eye on the weather. Souza works seven days a week, often twelve hours a day, and rain complicates his work. Some horses will not run if the track is wet. "You'll find the weather your most favorite TV program, your most favorite radio program, and your most favorite article in the newspaper," he says.

Jockeys' agents like Jerry Harrison (by concensus the most successful agent at the Downs) are in the racing secretary's office by 11:00 A.M., scratching or adding horses for the next day and helping with the draw for post positions. They are also looking a week or more ahead, lining up horses for their riders.

If a horse has run the last four weeks and he's what I call a live horse, the horse has run 1–2–3–4, I'll look for a race for that horse [races are in categories by age, winnings, and so on]. Then I'll see that trainer myself and get my rider on a live horse.

By 12:15 the Rev. Pete Crisswell, retired jockey turned minister, conducts prayer in the racing office building for jockeys assembled for the first race. He prays for safety and prosperity. "God rewards those who honor him," he says.

Shortly before the start of the first race, Hayward Stewart, an outrider, or track lifeguard, positions himself one furlong (one-eighth mile) from the start. It's Stewart's job to help with accidents or runaway horses, something he may encounter ten times in a day. "We're working in seconds," he says.

By 1:01 P.M. Dave Rodman, track announcer, is in full cry in the big, cluttered announcing booth on the fourth floor. It's Rodman's job to watch the race through binoculars and keep horses' names straight. "I have had a hard time in the past with Littlebitapleasure."

Joe Duckett, photo-finish technician at the tracks, works a race with a razon-thin margin. He captures the finish on film snapped from three cameras at the finish wire. In a matter of seconds, he processes the film and shows the result on an overhead projector for study by a room full of judges waiting a floor below. If needed, he prints a photo to confirm the result. "That's the good thing about my job," Duckett says. "I only work about three minutes a race."

The owners are in their suites or boxes or trackside. John Franks, Louisiana Downs' 1987 top-winning owner, reflects on his success last year (250 victories for purses totaling $4.5 million):

You struggle a lot. You lose a lot. Then you realize that there are a lot of nice people in this business, but they're not any smarter than you are. You realize that if you're as smart as they are and you work harder at it, you can beat them. It's lots of fun. I love the crowd and the excitement, but the real excitement is when I have a horse running.

By the end of the day, cleanup crews begin the job of pushing 3.5 tons (6 tons on a big weekend day) of rubbish out the door.

The 125-day racing season peaks with the track's most prestigious, Grade I stakes race, the Super Derby. At this race, three-year-old colts such as Alysheba (the winner of the Kentucky Derby and Preakness Stakes) chase around the 1.25-mile distance in quest of the million dollar purse. Crowds of 20,000 to 22,000 fill the stands each day of the derby. A record crowd of 25,419 bet $4,371,781 at an eleven-race card on Sunday, September 27, 1987.

Thoroughbred Racing Expenses
The basic expenses involved in owning a thoroughbred race horse have taken many unknowledgeable owners by surprise. The claiming price of the horse is only the beginning. These basic expenses have also forced many people out of the business. The following is a minimal list of expenses that the owner can expect to incur for a healthy, well-cared-for horse.

Training Bill. To be a successful trainer a person must be a combination businessperson, diplomat, social director, lay veterinarian, horse person, and handicapper. He or she must constantly be trying to find ways to improve the performance of every horse in his or her care. The bad horses must become good, the good ones great, and the great ones champions. He or she must experiment with blinkers, shadow rolls, workout patterns, diet, shoes and dozens of other things. The trainer who does these things successfully can have a significant effect on the performance of a horse.

---

3. (Shreveport) *Times*, September 27, 1987, p. 1.

The training bill covers the cost of keeping a horse at the race track and in training. The amount of the training bill ranges anywhere from $24 to $125 per day. The dramatic difference in the prices is caused by the quality of the trainer, his or her reputation, and the trainer's actual expenses.

David's trainer, George Hallock, is sixty-six years old and has been training horses for thirty-two years. He is originally from Colorado and now lives in Benton, Louisiana. Hallock charges David $32 a day plus 10 percent of total winnings. He has had almost 200 career wins at Louisiana Downs alone. In his first 127 starts of 1987 he won nineteen races, placed (came in second) in twenty-five, and showed (came in third) in ten. He earned $164,694 in the first eighty-two starts of 1987. He is also one of the top thoroughbred racehorse owners at Louisiana Downs.

Jockey Fees. The part that a jockey plays in winning or losing a race is one of the hottest topics of debate whenever racing fans gather to enjoy their favorite sport. There may be a lot less difference between the number one jockey and the number twenty jockey than most people think. The rider who wins gets the best mounts; the rider who gets the best mounts wins. It is a vicious circle and one that has frustrated the careers of some potentially fine riders.

Certain jockeys consistently do certain things better than others. The *Handicapper's Handbook* suggests that betters should not overlook a horse if it is being ridden by a top rider, especially if someone else has been riding. The rider's agent and probably the trainer of the horse think the horse is ready to win.

There is a flat fee of $50 for a jockey to ride the horse. The jockey also receives 10 percent of the winner's share of the purse if he or she wins. For finishing second through fifth the jockey also receives an additional fee. This fee is different at all tracks but ranges from $25 to $300.

Stewart's preferred jockey is Donald Howard. He is thirty-one years old and weighs 111 pounds fully dressed. He lives in Benton, Louisiana, is married, and has two young daughters. Stewart chose Howard because he has been among the leading riders at Louisiana Downs for the past several seasons. During the first part of 1987, Howard won 50 of 395 mounts, placed in 35, and showed in 49. His first two months' earnings were $479,241.

Pony Fees. There is a $10 pony fee that the owner incurs each time his horse starts. The pony horse is used to help keep the high-spirited thoroughbred under control while he is being warmed up before a race.

License Fees. In order to become an owner in Louisiana, the buyer must first be licensed by the Louisiana State Racing Commission. The fee is $25 for the license and an additional $25 for colors. "Colors" are the rights to the combination colors used in the jockey silks. The jockey wears the owner's colors, which belong to the individual owner. The actual silks worn cost an additional $100.

If the horse is owned in a partnership, the partnership must be licensed at an additional cost of $50 per partner.

Starting Fees. For most races run there is no fee to enter except for the jockey fee and the pony fee. In certain added money races, called stakes or handicap races, there are additional fees.

- *Nomination fee.* Usually between $25 and $100 per horse. This means that the horse is eligible to run in a particular race if the owner chooses to pay the additional money.
- *Entry fee.* The entry fee is around $300 to $750 per horse. The amount will vary according to the size of the purse for that race. This fee entitles the horse to be listed as a starter for the race, but no final commitment has been made.
- *Starting fee.* The starting fee is only incurred if the horse actually starts in the race. This fee falls somewhere between $500 and $1,000 for most added money races.

Insurance Fees. Most common racehorses are not covered by insurance. Some of the more competitive horses are covered, however. The annual rate for insurance on horses usually runs between 6.5 percent and 8.0 percent of the value of the horse. This expense can prove to be one of the most costly for the horse owner but it may also prove to be one of the most valuable.

Transportation Fees. Shipping horses is an expense that may often be overlooked by the owner. Although most owners probably ship their horses once or twice a year, they incur about a $300 to $400 expense each time they do. Two factors influence the cost of shipping a horse: the distance that the horse is shipped and whether or not a professional van service is used. When choosing a van service, a person needs to consider whether he or she is willing to incur additional risks to save a little money. An independent van service, while charging less, may not be able to afford the same quality equipment and personnel that professional services can afford. The horse must stand for the entire trip and will arrive tired. A day or two must be allowed for the horse to recuperate from any trip. Many owners do not want to risk the chance of injury on top of the stress of the trip.

Veterinary Fees. Veterinarian fees vary from track to track, veterinarian to veterinarian, and horse to horse. There is no way to come up with an average veterinary bill because there is no way of knowing when or how seriously the horse is going to get hurt or sick. The best way to avoid high veterinary bills is to make sure that the horse is cared for properly on a day-to-day basis.

Blacksmith Fees. Racehorses must have their shoes changed at least once a month. The cost for shoeing a horse varies from about $40 to $60 per horse, depending upon the type of shoes. This rate also differs among different blacksmiths.

CHISM'S HARVEST FARM

JUNE M. FREUND
Cottey College

BACKGROUND

It is August 1987, and Chism's Harvest Farm is half-way through its third year in business. Scholars may talk of entrepreneurs; Jay Chism is one. His operation, Chism's Harvest Farm, is truly owner-operated and owner-managed, a business created from an idea, developed with creativity and hard work. Jay and his wife Mindy started planning for their farm in September of 1984. Land was purchased in November and the business opened on January 1, 1985. The farm has shown a steady growth, largely due to the time and dedication of the Chisms, who have provided most of the labor themselves. Sales revenue has grown from $2,198 in 1985 to an estimated $19,159 in 1987.

Before starting his business, the young entrepreneur evaluated his education and career goals. He had a bachelor's degree in horticulture from Southwest Missouri State (1984) with an internship at the university's fruit research center. He knew what he wanted in a job: the opportunity to work outdoors, to experiment with new growing techniques, to work with plants—particularly various hybrid varieties—and to graft plants and improve them. On evaluating his list and the options available to him, Chism concluded that he could accomplish his goals working at any of a number of local nurseries. He was secure in his professional ability, having been offered several positions of head grower. Working for a nursery would provide a steady income and

security for himself and his wife. Still, something intrinsic kept Chism from accepting the job offers. He wanted a different environment than that provided in an established job. He wanted a sense of freedom, the ability to try things differently, a chance for experimentation in a variety of tasks, a challenge.

With the support of his wife and a financial outlay consisting of their entire savings account and a loan from a former professor, Chism became an entrepreneur. His business was started on a shoestring, but it was his own business. Like many young entrepreneurs, he had an idea, the professional expertise in a product or service, and little, if any, business skills. In three years the business has grown, thanks to his professional skills and some self-taught business skills. Mistakes have been made and there have been tight financial times, but in this third year of business Jay was confident that he had made the right decision.

LOCATION OF THE BUSINESS

Location had been a prime consideration when the business started. The area was selected because Jay was acquainted with the growing seasons; he had worked with the soil and knew its nutrient contents; he had an established communications network made up of suppliers, nursery owners, the Department of Agriculture, and extension agents.

The farm is located on a 40-acre tract of land on the northern edge of Joplin, Missouri. Joplin is a community of approximately 57,658 located at the intersection of Interstate 44 (an east-west highway) and US 71 (a north-south highway). It is the largest

This case, written specifically for this text, is printed by permission.

city in the triangle formed by the cities of Springfield, Missouri; Kansas City, Missouri; and Tulsa, Oklahoma. Joplin is the center of this standard metropolitan statistical area. Its economy is basically that of a regional trade center for southwestern Missouri, northern Arkansas, northeastern Oklahoma, and southeastern Kansas. Its location provides a sufficient base for any type of retail or commercial trade.

The farm is 7 miles north of Joplin on state highway 43, a major regional highway, and is easily accessible from all directions. Situated on prairie land, the site is relatively flat. It is located in a river valley, with a spillway bisecting the land and small stream on the northeastern corner providing irrigation. On the farm site are a mobile home, a two-car detached garage, and two greenhouses. Exhibit 1 gives a rough sketch of the land, including the locations of the buildings and planted fields.

THE BUSINESSES

Chism's Harvest Farm actually consists of three segments: a plant rental service, a nursery-greenhouse operation, and a fruit farm. The farm was developed in a three-phase process, with the last phase projected to produce revenue in the spring of 1988. Initial estimates on the operating cost of the business

were based on a fruit farm. (See Exhibit 2 for information.) Although there are three segments of the business, separate accounting books are not maintained on each one. Expense and revenue accounts reflect total operation balances.

In 1984, the Chisms paid little attention to the legal form of their new business—hence the lack of separate accounts. In essence, they purchased the appropriate state licenses, filed IRS forms, and began business operations. By default rather than by plan, the business operates as a sole proprietorship. The Chisms' preconceived notion of this form of business, with regard to taxes, governs their accounting system.

Plant Rental Service

The first segment of the business to be developed was the plant rental service. Chism plans to use this service as a source of revenue until the other two segments become self-supporting—at which time he will sell the plant service. At present, Chism's Harvest Farm supplies the plants, baskets or pots, and bedding (moss, rock, and potting soil) to businesses. The Chisms maintain the plants with routine watering and care (pruning, resodding, shining leaves). Plants are rotated when necessary to ensure that those at each location are always in top-quality condition.

Exhibit 1
LAYOUT OF CHISM'S HARVEST FARM

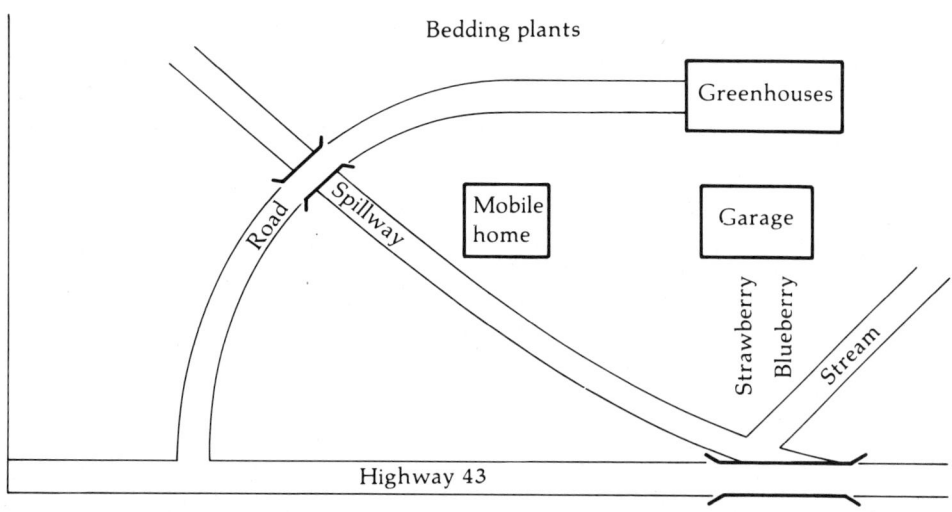

Exhibit 2

COST ESTIMATES FOR CHISM'S HARVEST FARM

	PRO-JECTED	ACTUAL
Land Improvements		
Diversion channel	$ 400.00	$455.18
Entrance drive	500.00	—[b]
Parking lot	500.00	—[b]
Total	$1,400.00	455.18
Crops		
Bedding plants	$1,000.00	259.60[a]
Strawberries	1,300.00	—[b]
Blueberries	4,500.00	2,212.00
Raspberries (fall)	1,200.00	—
Blackberries (thorned)	2,300.00	—
Blackberries (thornless)	2,100.00	—
Total	12,400.00	2,471.60
Equipment		
Belly mower	$1,000.00	$1,095.00
Tractor	1,200.00	860.00
Sprayer	500.00	—
Front end loader	1,500.00	—
Disc	100.00	—
Total	4,300.00	1,955.00
Miscellaneous		
Labor	$4,000.00	$296.50
Changeable letter sign	600.00	—
Liability insurance	660.00	—
Total	5,260.00	296.50
TOTAL	$23,360.00	$5,178.28

a. Denotes only those expenses that specified bedding plants.
b. No specific notation made to funds expended.

Clients are established first through personal contact. Chism simply visits a local business, explains his service, and leaves his business card. If the business owner is interested in proceeding, Chism visits the business again to talk with the owner. He then evaluates the environment in which the plants will live and determines the kind of plants that would be appropriate for the business. At this point he submits a written bid for consideration. If the company accepts the bid, the plant service starts. No formal legal document is drawn up by Chism's Harvest Farm. The only documentation is the original bid and a letter of acceptance from the company.

After the contract has been accepted, the plants are purchased, delivered, and displayed or planted as appropriate. With some contracts, a few rubber plants and hanging baskets of ivy are strategically placed. Other contracts might include indoor and outdoor planters and a minimal amount of landscaping. Once the plants are at their locations, periodic maintenance begins.

In the first year of operation clients of the plant rental service were primarily small local businesses such as a fitness center and a travel agency. No advertising was undertaken. The clients were mostly referrals from the nursery where Chism worked part-time or from current clients. Competition was almost nonexistent. Only a few florists ran plant rental services, and they did not provide the extensive follow-up that the Chisms offered. As the reputation of the service spread, Chism received numerous calls from local businesses concerning his service and asking him to submit bids. One such contact came in December of 1985. A local franchiser for a major fast-food chain asked Jay to submit a bid to supply plants for six locations in three states. When his bid was accepted, Chism felt his plant rental service had come of age. One local nursery wholesaler referred a number of major accounts, including a cafeteria chain with two locations and the newly renovated headquarters of a regional utility firm. Chism also has a federal contract with the George Washington Carver National Memorial to provide the plant rental service and to supply wildflower bedding plants.

Because of the nature of the service, initial expenses are incurred by the company before the revenue is received by the company. Initial expenses include the purchase of plants, baskets, planters, and bedding materials. Often the plants must be in place before payment is made to Chism's. All contracts require a deposit before work begins. Initial expenses amounted to $797 for an account requiring a small number of plants. Maintenance costs include such items as plant food, fertilizers, replacement bedding, cleaning materials, and van mileage to and from each location. Expenses relating to maintenance are not as high as initial cost because of quantity discounts for supplies. Many of the expenses relating to maintenance supplies cannot be tied directly to plant rental, as all segments of the business draw from the same inventory stock. Expenses are kept at a minimum by quality care of plants and rotation of plants to maintain as small a replacement cost to the Chisms as possible. All of these measures are related to the large initial cost.

Due to the high initial expense, the plant rental service often places a cash drain on the business. Chism does not see any way to avoid this problem, since there is no way to predict when this drain will occur until a contract is awarded. When cash drains do occur, a short-term loan is secured to cover the cost of the particular project and is repaid with the generated revenue. Expenses that relate to plant rental service are recorded on the ledgers as either plant rental or items not for resale. Mileage on the van is not separated from other van uses. (See Exhibit 3 for a list of expenses.)

Revenue from the plant rental service is credited with keeping the business afloat that first year. Revenues are generated from the initial fee and monthly service fees. The initial fee is either paid in a lump sum once the plants are in place, or pro-rated over a period not to exceed 12 months and included with the monthly fees. Plant rental provides the only steady stream of income for the business. All revenue in excess of expenses is reinvested in the farm. The income has primarily been used to purchase bedding plants for the nursery. Plant rental provided revenues of $2,124 in 1985 and $4,986 in 1987. The monthly fees charged range from $20 to $200. The revenue generated by the plant rental service has allowed the other two segments to develop faster than was originally anticipated.

Nursery

Sale of various plants accounts for the nursery segment of the business. This segment faces the largest competition. Within the immediate area are eight well-established nurseries. Since Chism opened his business, two nurseries have gone into bankruptcy, while another new nursery has opened. The competition is from family-owned nurseries, most of

Exhibit 3
OPERATING EXPENSES OF CHISM'S HARVEST FARM

ESTIMATED		ACTUAL	
Merchandise and materials	$2,270.16	Legal fees	$ 420.25
Miscellaneous supply	80.41	Rent expense	2,957.78
Advertising	89.27	Seeds	2,647.07
Farm expenses	4,144.04	Freight	144.49
Utilities	667.37	Nuts/bolts	190.34
Tax, licenses	10.00	Repairs	276.55
Equipment expenses	1,492.86	Tractor	451.74
Labor	296.50	Greenhouse	901.13
Tractor	34.96	Taxes	—
Miscellaneous	168.50	Insurance	50.00
Nondeductible	1,183.16	Utilities	1,288.99
Total	$10,437.23	Van expense	1,736.25
		Mowing	359.85
		Truck	900.62
		Advertising	14.97
		Irrigation	299.91
		Conservation	455.18
		Grounds	237.48
		Fertilizer	174.20
		Miscellaneous	3,712.33
		Total	$17,219.13

which are in at least their second generation. Nursery operations began in the spring of 1985 with expanded product offerings in both 1986 and 1987.

Plants are purchased as seeds or seedlings from wholesalers, tended in a greenhouse, and offered for sale. The bedding plants are sold only when their chance of survival outside the greenhouse is ensured, and it is their planting season. Ferns and ivies are sold when they can survive in a natural environment. Plants are not sold in poor condition or out of their growing season. See Exhibit 4 for a sample of products offered in 1987.

Memorial Day 1986 was the nursery's first attempt to enter into holiday sales. Based on the success of the Memorial Day sales, poinsettias were sold at Christmas that year. The supply quickly sold out, and Chism had to find additional supplies. Holiday sales are primarily to commercial customers. Although records are not kept as to particular types of sales, Chism feels that the sales of holiday items have proved profitable.

Minimal advertising is practiced in the form of advertisements placed in the local newspapers. Advertisements are placed during the peak sales periods, normally the months of April to July. During special holiday seasons, Chism advertises holiday plants—chrysanthemums for Memorial Day and poinsettias for Christmas. An additional advertising expense involves printing the sales item sheets that are distributed at various locations.

Initially, the retail customers were friends and referrals from other nurseries. Commercial customers are primarily local feed and grain stores. Chism's Harvest Farm's biggest advertisers are its satisfied customers. The satisfied customers are due, in no small part, to Chism's willingness to talk with the customer concerning watering and care of the plants. When a customer describes a problem that has occurred with a particular plant, Chism offers suggestions as to what might have been the cause and suggests remedies to prevent recurrence of the problems. He takes the time to talk with a customer to find out where the plants will be placed to determine the plant's chance of survival. This service has proved a valuable asset to future sales. Because Chism stresses high quality plants and is particular about their condition, customers seldom report plants dying. Service and quality are important

---

Exhibit 4

PRODUCTS SOLD BY CHISM'S HARVEST FARM

- Vegetable plants
- Broccoli: packman, premium crop
- Cabbage: early flat Dutch, golden acre
- Cauliflower: earlisnowball
- Brussel sprouts: Jade E Cross
- Cucumbers: Parks burpless bush
- Tomatoes: avalanche, better boy, big boy, bragger, Mo Cross surprise, Rutgers improved, patio
- Herbs: dill, sage, chives, thyme, basil (lemon and sweet), spicy globe basil
- Peppers: California wonder bell pepper, jalapeño hot pepper

- Flowering plants: ageratum (blue surf), alyssum (snowcloth), (foliage) coleus (wizard mix), (cockscomb) celosia (jewel box)
- Marigolds: Inca orange, Inca yellow, pineapple crush (yellow), orange boy, yellow boy, harmony boy
- Petunias: color parade (mix), red cloud, blue cloud, orchid cloud, summer madness, red madness, white madness, plum madness, supercascade pink, supermagic white

- Salvia: hotline red, hotline violet
- Vinca: little bright eye (white with pink eye)
- Dianthus: Telstar mix
- Lobelia: cascade mix
- Impatiens: red, pink, blush (light pink with dark center), salmon
- Geraniums: red
- Hanging basket: 10" impatiens, 10" begonias (dbl pink, dark leaf); 8", 10" variegated wandering Jew; 8", 10" red Swedish ivy; 8", 10" Bolivian Jew; 10" Swedish ivy; 8", 10" pothos; 10" ferns

since Chism must compete with discount stores for customers of such items as petunias, marigolds, and ivies. Also, because of his excellent reputation as a horticulturist, Chism has been asked to teach a continuing education class on plant care.

The main nursery expense is the purchase of bedding plants and seeds. To keep costs down, Chism has developed a strong relationship with the local wholesalers. Fertilizers, chemicals, potting soils, and pots are additional expenses. To house and tend the plants requires a greenhouse. Heating and cooling the greenhouse is a major expense of the business. (See Exhibit 3.) Expenses relating to housing and tending the nursery plants are not maintained separately from those of the rental plants. Therefore, it is difficult to determine the cost of goods sold for the nursery. One cost the Chisms had not envisioned, with regard to the nursery, was a need to resurface the road to the greenhouse and construct a bridge across the spillway. The work was required as the result of heavy rain in September 1985, which washed out the existing road. As a preventive measure, the land was contoured in 1986.

See Exhibit 5 for revenue records for 1985 and 1986.

Fruit Farm

The last segment of the business to develop was the fruit farm, a you-pick-it operation. The spring of 1988 will see the first crop offered for sale. The year 1986 was spent in determining the type of crop to plant, cultivating the fields for planting, and setting out the plants. The first year's output (1987) was never offered for sale; thus the initial sales will be in 1988.

The first step had been to determine the crops to plant. Apples and peaches were eliminated due to acreage constraints and competition. In fact, they were never seriously considered. Strawberries were a viable alternative, since the soil was best suited for this crop, but the competition was well established. Blueberries required much the same conditions for growth as strawberries, and they were just beginning to enter the area. Competition was minimal. Before making a final decision, Chism attended a number of seminars on blueberry production conducted by the University of Missouri at Columbia. He also spoke with growers in extreme southern Missouri and northern Arkansas. The closest grower was 60 miles from Joplin, which was not a serious problem in terms of competition. Chism de-

Exhibit 5
REVENUES OF CHISM'S HARVEST FARMS

DATE	CUSTOMER	SALES	DATE	CUSTOMER	SALES
1985			1118	Rainbow payment	35.00
401	OFC monthly payment	$ 50.00	1122	Rainbow payment	35.00
422	Hoden payment	30.00	1201	Gary Degraff: 2 bales	
422	OFC payment, soil	12.95		hay	30.00
501	OFC monthly payment	50.00	1202	Wilma Rice payment	55.00
613	OFC monthly payment	50.00	1203	Gordens payment	19.00
618	NHS payment	191.80	1206	Rainbow payment	35.00
705	Wilma Rice payment	55.00	1219	OFC payment	70.00
715	OFC monthly payment	50.00	1231	CNM payment	66.00
802	Wilma Rice payment	55.00	1231	CNM FOAB contract	800.00
808	Dorothy Ludweig cash	45.00		TOTAL	$2,198.75
816	OFC monthly payment	50.00			
907	Wilma Rice payment	55.00	1986		
908	OFC monthly payment	50.00	108	Rainbow payment	$ 35.00
1015	OFC monthly payment	50.00	117	OFC payment	70.00
1015	Wilma Rice payment	55.00	130	Wilma Rice payment	55.00
1026	Rainbow payment	35.00	210	Rainbow payment	20.00
1116	Carver payment	64.00	210	Carver payment	64.00
1116	Wilma Rice payment	55.00	211	OFC payment	140.00
1116	OFC payment	50.00	214	Wilma Rice payment	55.00

Exhibit 5

REVENUES OF CHISM'S HARVEST FARMS (*continued*)

DATE	CUSTOMER	SALES	DATE	CUSTOMER	SALES
1986			1986		
218	Wilma Rice payment	55.00		payment	9.54
221	Rainbow payment	15.00	414	Deposit: bedding	
313	Wyatt's Cafeteria			plants	7.25
	payment	185.00	418	Ozark Nursery	
315	Wilma Rice payment	55.00		payment	70.00
315	Dorothy Ludweig		418	Carver payment	40.00
	payment	5.00	418	Ozark Nursery	
316	Wyatt's Cafeteria			payment	157.00
	payment	185.00	419	Wyatt's Cafeteria	
317	Deposit: bedding			payment	185.00
	plants	740.31	419	Ozark Nursery	
321	OFC payment	70.00		payment	55.50
322	OFC payment	70.00	424	Wilma Rice payment	60.00
322	Ozark Nursery		424	Wilma Rice payment	60.00
	payment	16.00	425	Ozark Nursery	
322	Joplin G&L payment	12.00		payment	70.50
322	Johnson's Feed		425	Aunt Thel payment	57.25
	payment	4.00	425	Thelma Vannoy	
327	Bedding plant deposit	60.00		payment	38.79
327	Ricket Grain payment	36.00	501	Rainbow payment	70.00
329	Botany Shop payment	24.00	501	Rainbow payment	35.00
329	Albert's Market		502	Ozark Nursery	
	payment	20.00		payment	118.50
329	Johnson Paint payment	24.00	503	Deposit: bedding	
329	Joplin G&L payment	30.00		plants	126.00
329	Ozark Nursery		506	Deposit: bedding	
	payment	30.00		plants	44.00
331	OFC payment	70.00	508	Wilma Rice payment	39.30
331	CNM payment	70.00	508	Wilma Rice payment	39.30
331	Wyatt's Cafeteria		508	Joplin G&L payment	25.50
	payment	185.00	512	Deposit	223.80
402	Johnson Paint payment	28.00	514	Rainbow payment	35.00
403	Ozark Nursery		515	OFC payment	70.00
	payment	8.00	515	Wilma Rice payment	55.00
404	Ozark Nursery		517	Wyatt's Cafeteria	
	payment	18.00		payment	185.00
405	Ozark Nursery		601	McCoy's payment	30.00
	payment	6.00	613	Rainbow payment	70.00
405	Johnson Paint payment	36.00	613	Ozark Nursery	
407	Ozark Nursery			payment	42.00
	payment	22.00	620	Carver payment	35.00
410	Ozark Nursery		623	OFC payment	70.00
	payment	117.00	623	Wyatt's Cafeteria	
410	Johnson Paint payment	24.00		payment	185.00
412	Jewell Elliot payment	18.07	708	Wyatt's-Brass payment	253.44
414	Miriam Morgan		708	Wilma Rice payment	55.00

DATE	CUSTOMER	SALES	DATE	CUSTOMER	SALES
1986			1986		
711	Ozark Nursery payment	100.50	1001	Department of Agriculture	218.00
711	CNM payment	181.00	1010	MCDS payment	45.00
711	Rainbow payment	20.00	1019	not recorded	346.07
718	McDonald's payment	360.70	1017	Wyatt's Cafeteria payment	200.00
718	OFC payment	70.00			
725	Wyatt's Cafeteria payment	200.00	1103	Wilma Rice payment	110.00
725	Carver payment	89.76	1103	OFC payment	70.00
725	Wilma Rice payment	55.00	1103	Ball refund	63.10
802	Thelen Wedding	125.00	1122	MCDS payment	348.78
815	McDonald's payment	141.01	1126	Wyatt's Cafeteria payment	200.00
815	OFC payment	70.00	1126	MCDS payment	45.00
829	Wyatt's Cafeteria payment	200.00	1126	Deposit: bedding plants	3.00
829	Judy payment	21.07	1206	McCoy's payment	30.00
829	Karen payment	42.13	1206	Dorothy Ludweig payment	20.00
829	Lorane Miner payment	21.07			
829	Dan Rodgers payment	21.07	1206	OFC payment	70.00
902	Evens payment	21.07	1208	Wilma Rice payment	110.00
908	Christie payment	21.07	1219	Ozark Nursery payment	199.00
908	Val Williams payment	21.07			
908	MCDS payment	45.00	1222	OFC payment	70.00
929	Wilma Rice payment	344.45	1122	Wyatt's Cafeteria payment	200.00
1001	Ozark Nursery payment	37.00	1222	Best Shot payment	20.00
				TOTAL	$9,941.47

cided to plant blueberries and strawberries as his first crops. He joined the Blueberry Growers Association.

One acre of blueberries and a half acre of strawberries were planted in 1986. An additional half acre of blueberries was planted in 1987. (See Exhibit 1 for the sketch of the farm for location.) Of all the operations of the farm, Chism's favorite activity is growing blueberries. He hopes one day to develop a variety of blueberries especially suited to his soil and climate. Future plans for the fruit farm segment include increasing his acreage of blueberries and strawberries and planting blackberries and raspberries.

The largest outlay of capital occurred in the first year; after the initial expense, costs were minimal. (See Exhibit 2 for blueberry projections.) To eliminate labor costs, the Chisms, with their parents, set out plants by hand—a necessary task. Yearly operating expenses include fertilizers, chemicals, and irrigation.

FINANCES

The business was started with funds from the Chisms' savings account and a personal loan from one of Chism's former professors. The $16,000 loan was used as a down payment on land purchased for $37,000. The remaining balance of $21,000 was owner financed. Owner financing resulted in a monthly payment of $459, with the final payment being made on May 1, 1986. The down-payment loan was a no-interest loan, with a repayment schedule to be determined when the business showed a substantial profit. To date no schedule has been established. A mortgage was taken out on the farm to raise the additional capital needed to begin operations. The mortgage, in the amount of $20,000, was used to make improvement on the land and to purchase necessary equipment. The mortgage was obtained from Chism's home-town bank, Stockton National Bank. The loan was obtained with little documentation of business potential because Chism's mother worked at the bank.

Additional funds were needed for operating expenses. Because of the growing cycle and the seasonal nature of his business, Chism felt that the business would not be self-sufficient during the first year. To supplement income from the business, he took a part-time job at a local nursery. His wife worked full-time as a counselor at the local state college. Jay's income would cover their living expenses, and Mindy's salary would pay off their loans. Any income generated by the farm would be reinvested in the business.

For the first year of business, the established plan worked. Plant rental revenue normally covered the bedding stock cost. On the few occasions when bedding stock payments could not be covered by rental revenue, due to unexpected expenses, a sixty-day, short-term loan was executed with the Stockton National Bank. The loan was repaid from receipts of nursery sales. Short-term notes are still used to cover cash crunches due to the seasonal nature of the business. Each short-term loan is negotiated separately.

In 1986, additional funds were desired to cover blueberry costs. A colleague suggested that Chism apply to the Small Business Administration (SBA) for a loan. To help assist Chism in the process, an accountant was hired at a cost of $300. The accountant was asked to take Chism's blueberry projections, along with financial data available, and complete the loan application. This was submitted to the SBA. After months of deliberation, the loan was rejected. Chism next approached the bank that held his business account; again, after considerable deliberation, the loan was rejected. Chism finally resorted to his home-town bank and received a loan for $10,000. The loan was consolidated with the previous $20,000 loan, resulting in monthly payments of $432.

FINANCIAL RECORDS

From the first, Chism realized that he knew nothing of financial record keeping, nor was he well versed in accounting. Believing that his business could not afford the luxury of an accountant, he purchased a do-it-yourself guide to operating a small business. After reading and studying this book, he contacted the local extension officer and discussed tax considerations. Chism decided for tax purposes to classify his business as a farm. From his how-to book, he knew that ledgers would be required, so he used those provided in the book. No financial records are kept except those necessary for income tax purposes. Taxes are prepared each year by H&R Block. Receipts are placed in a cigar box and recorded to the ledger sheets when time allows on rainy days. During the growing season, books may be as much as four months behind. There is no standardized reporting format.

For the three years Chism has been in business, he has made changes in the way he records his expenses. He has never understood about the headings, or how the items are used in preparing his taxes. Each year he changes the headings to give him a better idea of what type of expenses were incurred that year. For example, labor expenses remain relatively low. Part-time labor is hired during peak periods, mainly to assist with watering. This part-time labor expense is recorded under miscellaneous charges. Jay purchases gas for all his equipment on an as-needed basis from local stations. He has never considered the annual cost of gas. His equipment seems always to be in the repair shop, yet he does not have a total of repair costs for each piece of equipment. Included in the expense ledgers are personal purchases. The couple keeps two checking accounts, one for the business, one as a personal account. Both accounts are on the same bank and are traditional checking accounts. The expense ledgers will show personal purchases written on the business account. The personal purchases are denoted by an entry in a column labeled nondeductible expense. Reimbursement to the account is denoted on the income ledger as a cash receipt. No exact record is available of how much has been withdrawn in this manner, or how much has been repaid. Neither of the Chisms sees any problems with this practice, as neither draws a salary from the business.

On the revenue side, Chism feels more confident. He knows what to expect in revenue each month from all sources. Often his plans for the acquisition of plants are determined by estimating income from plant rental, deducting an average monthly expense balance (derived from a hunch), and using the remainder to purchase additional stock of plants. (See Exhibit 5 for revenue accounts.) No records are maintained for financial planning purposes. Cash flow is determined simply by looking at the balance in the checkbook.

PROSPECTS

The fact that the business has yet to make a profit does not bother Chism. Sales revenue has continued to grow, with projected revenue and operating cost for 1987 of $19,159 and $20,334, respectively. Since 1987 expenses included $2,937 in salaries, Chism figures that if they had not paid themselves, they would have made a profit.

SHOPPERS SERVICE STORE

JEROME A. KATZ
St. Louis University

PHASE 1: BUSINESS ENTRY

By 1977, Shoppers Service Store was a two-site discount department store located in the southeastern regional center of King City. Started in 1956 as a union experiment, a company store owned by the union instead of the employer, Shoppers had lacked experienced management and was quietly offered for sale in 1957.

It was bought in 1958 by three Holocaust survivors who came to King City after World War II. A Pole, Michel Wolfe, then thirty-three, was the driving force among the three. Having left a partnership that ran an exclusive men's store, he brought experience in sales and self-employment. Samuel Flagon, thirty-six, was a Lithuanian who had invested in real estate and laundromats. Kane Jewel, thirty-nine, was another Pole who had been in sales for others.

The years from the store's reopening in 1958 to 1966 were marked by a growing prosperity. Shoppers branched out into pharmacies, eventually running four by 1964. In other operations, they sold discount tires from a large garage down the block and employed two traveling salespeople to sell sporting goods wholesale. They acquired a large warehouse to store wholesale quantities of goods besides the main store's varied lines (major and small appliances, furniture, sporting goods, jewelry, cosmetics, dry goods, shoes, auto parts, hardware, and toys for the Christmas season).

Prosperity peaked in 1966 when three of the pharmacies were sold, giving the partners a substantial windfall, but also decreasing the amount of work that they faced. In deciding what to do with the funds, tensions common to many relationships came to the surface. Soon, Flagon and Jewel were at each other's throats. The three partners had divided the income from the business equally, but each partner's workstyle differed markedly.

Jewel was a classic workaholic. He could pursue a goal in a methodological, consistent, and competent way for any amount of time. He was a good man for details. His strength was in dealing with things and data and less with people. Wolfe was a classic entrepreneur. Capable of totally immersing himself in a project, his attention lasted until he mastered the current goal. With mastery would come his search for new challenges and new opportunities. Wolfe was at his best dealing with the big picture; he quickly tired of details and was at his best using his intuitive skills dealing with people and data. Flagon was the balance for the two other partners. He was more concretely oriented toward the here and now and the social side of business. Like Wolfe, Flagon liked variety, but was not inclined to take risks to achieve it. Like Jewel, he focused on details, but was not as persistent in following through on them. Flagon was also entirely a person-oriented type. As an observer of the business suggested, "If you think of Shoppers Service as a person, Michel would be the brain, Kane the hands and feet, and Samuel would be the heart."

The work had balanced out without major coordinative effort while Shoppers had diversified. However, with the sale of the pharmacies and no new venture on the horizon, the three partners

This case, written specifically for this text, is printed by permission.

found they had too many chiefs and not enough work. Wolfe spent more time outside the store looking for new opportunities and increasing wholesale and tire sales. Jewel revamped and generally tightened up the internal workings of the store and the remaining pharmacy. Flagon was content to wait until he could contribute to some new opportunity.

Flagon's passivity angered Jewel, and to a lesser extent, Wolfe. Although the amount of work each partner was doing was different, they each took home the same wage and profit. Wolfe's work outside the store helped distance him from the issue, but Jewel began to tell Flagon—and eventually other people—how he felt. Flagon did not remain passive about Jewel's jibes, and soon the two were openly feuding. All three knew something had to be done.

The solution worked out by Wolfe and a neutral outsider was for Jewel to go, taking the warehouse and pharmacy, leaving Wolfe and Flagon with the main store and wholesale operation. The cash left over from the pharmacy sale would be divided three ways.

PHASE 2: RIOT, REBUILDING, AND RECOVERY

What followed the owners of Shoppers Service could not have imagined. During the summer of 1968, a riot broke out in King City and Shoppers Service was gutted. Like most small businesses, Shoppers carried only minimal insurance on its inventory, and virtually all the insurance companies were balking on paying out claims due to riots. Wolfe and Flagon knew they would eventually get the money, but it would not be soon.

Their response started as they debated whether they should abandon the original site rather than rebuild. As a precaution to protect their market visibility, they arranged to buy a second location for appliance and furniture sales in a middle-income suburb. However, negotiations with the seller and the financiers dragged on, and it became clear that the new location would not be available until 1970. In the meantime, direct sales were needed to maintain visibility in the marketplace and keep the two families fed.

Despite the unusable store, Shoppers Service had a clientele loyal to Wolfe's and Flagon's personal approach to selling. Either man could be called on to find, deliver, and finance any major purchase a family might need to make. They would visit homes and workplaces to make these large sales. Often they would give the purchaser a gift they thought would be liked by another family member.

As the rebuilt store opened in 1969 and the bought-out suburban store became operational in 1970, the style became firmly entrenched. As is common in stores, a customer coming in to buy a ring for an anniversary gift also makes another major purchase as a gift "for both of us." At Shoppers, the customer would also receive perhaps another $100 for knickknacks (fishing reels, luggage, clothing) given spontaneously to the customer by Wolfe or Flagon so that "nobody in the family feels left out," as both put it. For most customers, going to Shoppers Service was generally a family affair, and the customer base of neighborhood residents, union members from local manufacturing plants, and families from the nearby military base, was fiercely loyal.

This customer base would be important, because the local competition was becoming increasingly capable. Before 1967 the major competition was local independently owned superstores. After 1967, Shoppers also faced strong pressure from the rapidly growing regional and national discount chains such as K-Mart for general merchandise and Scott Appliance or Best Buys for major appliances.

PHASE 3: REFLECTIONS AFTER THE RECOVERY

With a constant presence in the marketplace and a growing and strongly loyal customer base, both stores had consistently posted good earnings. By 1976 financially the business had turned around again. Other factors contributed to this brightening picture. The wholesale operation had grown to include Wolfe's occasional sales of surplus or salvaged canned and frozen food obtained from shoppers and food manufacturers. Certainly, the most important factor was that at last the bills tied to the fire and the breakup of the trio of partners had been completely paid off.

Looked at another way, the partnership breakup, the fire, the rebuilding, and the second store addition amounted to ten years of continuous work. This work included keeping customers during the breakup, doing at-home selling while the store was being rebuilt, changing from two owners at one site to a structure of two owners with two sites, developing a market in a new part of town, and paying off the debt associated with the rebuilding.

The stylistic issues that contributed to the breakup in 1967 had been submerged in the demands of running a business without an adequate number of managers. The need to pay back loans taken out during the rebuilding meant that for years after the fire, Wolfe and Flagon would consider any pending decision and ask themselves, "Will this help us pay off the loans faster?"

PHASE 4: NEW TIMES, OLD PROBLEMS

The loans were now paid off, and with the release of that burden, Wolfe and Flagon found the old tensions emerging. Wolfe started mentioning and investigating (often away from the store) several new projects. These included adding frozen food sales (which he did on his own in late 1975), opening new locations, buying real estate, and developing an innovative route sales approach to selling high-profit items in peoples' homes. Wolfe was making fewer sales than before, but his sales involved larger dollar amounts and more varied types of merchandise, such as the frozen foods sold to institutions.

Meanwhile, Flagon's interest turned to the details of the operation and to his family. During the 1967 to 1976 period, most coordination was done face-to-face by Wolfe and Flagon, and paperwork took a strong second seat to making sales. Now, with some of the pressure lightened, Flagon became more concerned with organizing the paperwork and developing some system of organization in the back office. Meanwhile, his family was demanding more of his time, and for the first time in a decade, he could afford to spend time with them. As a result of these pressures, he was also making fewer sales.

Soon the strain between the two men became obvious. Wolfe saw Flagon as mired in unprofitable details when he was not spending company time on the phone to his family. Flagon saw Wolfe as uncommitted to the store and always searching for a vaguely described "something else." Even to their wives (both of whom were immigrants also), the two seemed like a too-long married couple.

The problem began to impinge on the store's long-term strategy. Wolfe and Flagon realized that they had to make some major decisions about Shoppers, but were unable to do so.

The original store was profitable, but profitability was declining, and further declines appeared likely.

Customers from the nearby Surefoot Tire plant decreased with layoffs and strikes that were increasingly a part of Surefoot's lot. The store's neighborhood had been in decline since the 1968 riots. The neighborhood was losing many of its stable families and the remainder were facing increased poverty, which took its toll at Shoppers in two ways. Not only did local residents have less to spend, but the poverty faced by the poorest made shoplifting an increasingly likely occurrence. Wolfe and Flagon could see that the original store was approaching the point where it would stop being a profit center and become a financial drain.

However, the outlook was not entirely bleak. Black community leaders were interested in attempting a revitalization effort of the neighborhood and had discussed using minority business enterprise funding to help some local residents buy out the store. Even if this did not come to pass, the store could be refocused to sell those things that offered the greatest retail profitability, such as major appliances, jewelry, or food. Wolfe and Flagon agreed that their preference for the next store would be to focus on selling one type of merchandise, to help them focus their energies more efficiently. Using the same reasoning, it was also possible to make the store into a warehouse, closing down the retail operation (or moving more of it to the suburban location), and increasing wholesaling efforts that had only been occasionally pursued with sporting goods and foods.

Faced with these choices, the owners were continually reviewing the options available, unable or occasionally unwilling to make a decision. No one associated with Wolfe and Flagon had wanted to become embroiled, until Abe, the son of a friend and a first-year business student, took the plunge. Coming by often for lunch, Abe listened to their seemingly endless arguments, and he suggested that they meet him after hours to try some of the decision-making techniques he had learned in business school.

PHASE 5: THE FIRST STEPS

When Wolfe and Flagon joined Abe at a hotel that night, he asked them both to write "the most important thing about work." Then he asked them to list their second and third choices.

Wolfe explained his list as follows:

For me to enjoy going to work each day, I have to feel that I am going to be a little surprised— that I can't totally predict what my day will be like. To do the same thing day after day is too much like a jail for me. Next. I've got to feel free to do what I think is right. If that means telling someone to go to hell or if it means deciding to do some of tomorrow's work tonight or whatever; I need that feeling of freedom. I put making money third. It's not that money is a bad thing, but I've found time and time again that I can be just as happy, happier in fact, making $10 profit from a person I enjoy doing business with, than making $1,000 from someone who is a bump on a log. I want to make money for myself and my family, but wherever possible, I want to have fun doing it.

Eyebrows raised, Flagon replied with his list.

You both know my family, and I love them, but they can be a pain, always *nudging* me about this or that. It's bad enough day to day, but if they thought our money wasn't coming in, I'd never hear the end of it. I don't need a lot, but I've got to be sure of always having a reasonable amount, like we've got today. Knowing I'll have that money is the most important thing for me. Like you, Michel, I think to enjoy work I've got to be able to tell someone off, to be able to do things the way I want. Finally, I don't want to be bored. I've seen enough of that in my life.

The three of them assigned shorthand names to the ideas. Wolfe's ranking was variety (ranked first), autonomy, and financial security. Flagon's ranking was financial security (ranked first), autonomy, and variety. Abe asked them, "How long have you had your ranking this way?" Wolfe and Flagon said that the items had been in the top three for as long as they could remember, but the current rank order was the way they had felt for the past year or so.

The next data-gathering step was to identify the profitmaking activities of the store, and assess each in terms of its degree of profitability and its opportunity for expansion. The most profitable was the occasional sale of surplus frozen food (profit margin over 50 percent; average sale of $5,000). Next was jewelry (average profit, 35 percent; average sale, $750). Third were major appliances (profit, 10 percent; sale, $500). The remaining lines at Shoppers Service could not compare in profitability, and the one other profitable line (toys) was highly seasonal,

with over 90 percent of all profits coming in the Christmas shopping season.

Any of the three profitable areas held room for expansion. To maximize profits in frozen food sales would require entering new markets such as institutions that prepared large quantities of food (e.g., schools, prisons, hospitals, and so on). The market was largely unknown, but there was little local competition. However, since institutional sales were national in scope, competition was nationwide, and neither Wolfe or Flagon knew what to expect. The business also required large lines of credit, and substantial overhead in the form of refrigerated warehouse rental space, long-distance costs, and transportation costs. The rebuilt and acquired stores would be largely useless in this business. Finally, Flagon would have to learn much of the business from scratch since Wolfe had handled almost all of the food business since its inception.

Jewelry and major appliances were known markets with well-known and active competitors. Both lines of merchandise, especially jewelry, were subject to the general economy in a way frozen food was not. Expanding sales would require adding salespeople and using more aggressive marketing techniques, but both were possible, given Wolfe's and Flagon's experience in marketing and selling these two lines of merchandise. Either line requires a large inventory cost, and they vary in their overhead costs. The appliance store approach could make use of the rebuilt and acquired stores, although their locations were not known as high-traffic areas for big ticket customers. The best use of the rebuilt store might be as a warehouse and service center for an appliance-focused store, while sales could predominate in the suburban location. For the jewelry store, the rebuilt store would need to be sold, and the suburban store extensively refurbished at a cost of $50,000 to $75,000.

The profit-per-sales contact differed markedly between the three. From experience, Wolfe reported that it took one hour to sell $5,000 worth of frozen food in the institutional market. The time to sell $5,000 in jewelry or appliance was perhaps seven hours on average. They analyzed the selling process for each of these line items of merchandise. Large sums of money were involved, and all three products were important to the buyer and, in turn, important to Wolfe and Flagon.

Wolfe's experience with frozen foods suggested that gathering $5,000 worth of saleable merchandise took about five hours on average. What was required was visiting or calling many frozen food processors, food wholesalers, and warehouses scattered throughout the country, as well as fielding called-in orders of merchandise from these types of firms as well as from transportation lines, supermarkets, and an occasional institution. They both agreed that $5,000 in appliances could be obtained in about ten minutes. Shoppers usually had the products in its inventory, and the time spent in purchasing was minimal. Even when the product was out of stock, calls to the local appliance distributor resulted in definite delivery times in a matter of minutes. Obtaining $5,000 in jewelry might take an hour. One-third of this time was spent commuting to and from a jeweler or jewelry wholesaler; the remainder was spent in selecting the merchandise. Although they could be graded, diamonds and other jewelry were seen by Wolfe and Flagon as more individualistic than appliances, and they trusted only their own judgment in selecting jewelry.

Time costs after the sale also differed. Frozen foods in the institutional market required placing orders for refrigerated transport and then contacting the warehouse holding the merchandise to inform them of its disposition. This sort of work required Wolfe's or Flagon's attention to keep warehousing and transportation costs low, although each thought the tasks could be delegated to a skilled salesperson or secretary once procedures and business relationships were established. For $5,000 worth of products, two hours with follow-up checks might be needed.

Major appliance sales are highly variable. Deliveries were made from Shoppers' own inventory or from the manufactures' warehouses by Shoppers employees. Often, separate calls had to be made by repairpersons to set up major appliances, and it was not uncommon for Wolfe or Flagon to have to drop by someone's home to resolve problems when a washing machine did not make clothes spotlessly white. On average, the after-the-sale time for $5,000 of revenue was roughly two hours.

The good news regarding jewelry was its trivial after-the-sale costs. Diamonds do not break and gold cleans easily, and delivery was handled by customer pick-up. Aside from the time necessary to write-up ring resizing orders for a local jeweler and transporting the rings to and from that jeweler, there was little to do. The after-the-sale time of $5,000 was about one-half hour of Wolfe's or Flagon's time. The transportation was not delegated because both partners worried over jewelry theft and loss.

With the above information, Abe let Wolfe and Flagon leave for the night. On schedule for the next night was Abe's turn to talk, and the top of the agenda would be, "What should we do next with the business?"

The next day Abe obtained from the Shoppers' accountant the dollar sales breakdowns for each of the merchandise lines for each of the stores for the post-fire period. These are listed in Exhibit 1, with a detailed breakdown for 1976 in Exhibit 2.

Armed with the above, he sat down to prepare his analyses and recommendations.

Exhibit 1
POST-FIRE SALES FIGURES: SHOPPERS SERVICE STORE

	PERCENTAGE OF TOTAL SALES FOR THE YEAR							
MERCHANDISE LINE	1968	1969	1970	1971	1972	1973	1974	1975
Appliances, major								
Surefoot store	16	18	13	12	13	14	12	10
Suburban store	n/a	n/a	n/a	n/a	80	72	60	70
Appliances, small								
Surefoot store	7	6	6	5	5	6	5	5
Suburban store	n/a	n/a	n/a	n/a	6	8	10	8
Auto parts and hardware	17	20	18	18	17	15	14	15
Cosmetics	11	10	12	12	10	10	12	9
Dry goods and shoes	21	17	19	18	17	14	14	10
Food, retail	n/a	1	3	3	3	3	2	2

Food, wholesale							
Sales to institutions	n/a	n/a	n/a	2	5	6	10	14
Sales to local firms	n/a	n/a	n/a	0	0	3	5	6
Furniture							
Surefoot store	12	11	10	10	8	8	6	8
Suburban store	n/a	n/a	n/a	n/a	14	20	30	22
Jewelry	5	7	6	7	8	6	4	4
Sporting goods	8	7	10	10	10	11	12	12
Toys	3	3	3	3	4	4	4	5
Total sales (in thousands)							
Surefoot store	$820	$960	$845	$810	$812	$875	$780	$670
Suburban store	n/a	n/a	n/a	n/a	$375	$391	$415	$480

Exhibit 2
SALES AND PROFIT DETAILS: 1976

	TOTAL SALES	DOLLARS PER SALE	PROFIT	SALES TIME PER $1000	SALES ENJOYABILITY[b]
Appliances, major					
Surefoot store	67	500	10%	1.4	5
Suburban store	337	500	10%	1.4	5
Appliances, small					
Surefoot store	33	60	4%[a]	15.5	3
Suburban store	38	60	4%[a]	15.5	3
Auto parts and hardware	101	15	11%[a]	20.0	2
Cosmetics	60	6	2%	10.0	1
Dry goods and shoes	67	25	9%[a]	13.3	2
Food, retail	14	5	30%[a]	10.0	1
Food, wholesale					
Sales to institutions	94	5000	50%	.02	5
Sales to local firms	40	300	12%	2.3	3
Furniture					
Surefoot store	54	1100	9%	2.1	4
Suburban store	105	1100	9%	2.1	4
Jewelry	26	750	35%	1.4	5
Sporting goods	80	30	15%[a]	16.5	3
Toys	34	50	13%[a]	10.0	5
GRAND TOTAL	1,150				

a. Profit levels that had dropped substantially with the decline in the neighborhood.
b. Sales enjoyability reflects how much pleasure Wolfe and Flagon obtained from making sales of this type of merchandise (1 = very low, 5 = very high). Various factors are considered in this factor:
   The likability of the typical customers
   The likelihood of after-the-sale problems
   The profitability of the sale
   The opportunity to "make a deal"
   Satisfaction derived from "selling people something they really need"
There were no major differences between Wolfe and Flagon on these rankings, but the ranking for wholesale food sales to institutions is based on Wolfe's rankings alone, since Flagon did not sell food to institutional customers.

LUCY FOODS

FRANK MARTIN
University of Stirling

This is the case of a small food manufacturing company and its efforts to devise corporate strategies capable of giving the company direction as both it and the business environment changed. By December 1986 that environment had become so competitive that the future of Lucy Foods was in doubt.

> Like all companies, Lucy Foods has a corporate strategy, although many larger companies would hardly recognize it as such. The strategy is not written down, but we know, in our heads, where we are going and what we are trying to do.
>
> —John Mustoe, cofounder

FORMATION

Lucy Foods was formed in 1975 to manufacture snack-food bars for the health-food market. Health foods at this time were very much a minority interest, but there was a dedicated group of consumers in revolt against overprocessed, overwrapped food products full of additives that made up the great majority of the goods on the supermarket shelves.

In reaction against these additives—whether colors, preservatives, sugar, or flavor-enhancers—there was a drive to get back to basics. The new health-conscious consumer wanted natural foods out of burlap bags, and, if it was manufactured food, this consumer wanted it to look as homemade as possible.

This was an important factor in getting Lucy Foods launched because consumers were ready to accept an amateurish product that was new, but made from pure products. Variations in size and color, poor wrapping and plain white display boxes suited the market at that time.

The Product Idea

Lucy Foods was started by Irma Mustoe in 1975. She had worked for American Motors, hospitals, and other organizations as a secretary, so she knew that businesses are run by very ordinary people. She was interested in cooking and baking; that interest, plus this new, growing health-food market seemed a good target. A little market research in the shape of visiting some of the new health-food shops springing up around Manchester, England, was done. In one of them, Country Life (later The Happy Nut House), she found a man who wanted for breakfast a toasted cereal made into a snack bar. She decided to give it a go. After a few tries she developed a new 2-ounce bar made from oats, brown sugar, wheat germ, sesame seeds, and a few other wholesome ingredients free from additives. The bar had a good shelf life, it was tasty, and it was strong enough to be handled and packed.

Into Production

The process was simple. It could be, and was, done in an ordinary kitchen. The ingredients were mixed, baked, cut into 50 mm × 175 mm rectangles, wrapped in clear cellophane film, and then secured by a white paper band. On this band there was a logo, the Ra Bar name, contents, and all the other necessary information. The bars were then packed into boxes of twenty-four, and were ready to sell.

This case, written specifically for this text, is printed by permission.

This was the first cereal health bar sold in Britain, and it may have been the first in the world. While all this development was progressing, Mustoe's husband John, was managing director of a subsidiary of GKN, a large United Kingdom–based industrial holding company. This meant that Lucy Foods did not have to make a living immediately and that money could be plowed back into the business.

Launch Strategy

The strategy was for volume to grow as rapidly as possible in order to reduce production costs. The savings in costs would come from two areas: larger raw materials purchases meant lower unit costs; as output rose, so machinery and equipment utilization would improve.

This was not a sophisticated corporate strategy, but at the time it was felt to be adequate and little else seemed possible. Corporate strategy is based on information about market competitors, consumers and so on, but this information does not exist in a new market. There was only the impression that the health-food market was growing, but hard figures were absent. Between 1975 and 1980 this corporate strategy was followed.

EXPANSION

By early 1977, Lucy Foods had outgrown the kitchen of Irma Mustoe and moved into its first factory, a converted shop in Nantwich, Cheshire. The equipment improved and grew in size, until there were bakery mixers, bakery ovens, a wrapping machine, and full support equipment.

The equipment was all secondhand, but it was serviceable. The workforce rapidly grew to ten part-time women, but for the rest of the life of Lucy Foods this figure hardly changed. As output grew, hand processes were replaced by machine processes. The financial performance for this period is shown as Exhibit 1.

Exhibit 1
LUCY FOODS: PERFORMANCE, 1978–1980

	1978	1979	1980
Sales	£31,400	£43,700	£70,800
Gross Profit	18,400	25,200	43,700
Net Profit	9,500	11,100	15,600
Capital Employed	6,500	11,400	21,000

In 1980 Lucy Foods moved into larger premises: an old, two-story factory building, still in Nantwich. This was justified on the grounds that the increasing stocks and the growing amount of machinery required a better layout than could be obtained in the old shop. John Mustoe was at this time made redundant by GKN, and he joined Lucy Foods full time in 1980.

REAPPRAISAL

The corporate strategy now needed to be rethought. The health-food market was becoming more developed, new competitors had arrived, and market information was fairly easily available. It was clear that Lucy Foods needed a continuous oven fed by an automated mixer and spreader, so that a sheet of raw product went into the oven, and then was cut on exit from the oven, ready for wrapping. This equipment would require larger premises. The cost of this was on the order of £150,000, a figure beyond the internal resources of Lucy Foods.

THE NEW STRATEGY

The new corporate strategy had to take all these changes into account, and it became as follows:

1. To grow as fast as the market (15–25 percent)
2. To align prices to the prices of the market leader (Jordans)
3. To distribute as widely as possible by using any health-food wholesale outlet and to sell to each wholesaler at the same price
4. To manufacture under own name only
5. To introduce closely related new products from time to time
6. To try to get into other markets, such as chemists [pharmacists] and supermarkets

Irma and John Mustoe believed that:

1. Lucy Foods had to maintain growth rates equal to that of the major market in order to keep market share.
2. Because a flour milling company called Jordans had come out with a competitive bar and had quickly established themselves as the market leader, Lucy Foods did not have the advertising power to differentiate the product, so aligning prices became an obvious tactic.

3. The distribution chain that had quickly developed in the health-food industry was such that manufacturers sold to specialist wholesalers who in turn sold to the many small health-food shops. The choice was between using one or two of the large wholesalers or of dealing with a large number of wholesalers of all sizes. The latter course was chosen, because it seemed safer to use many, overlapping distributors.

4. There was a growing demand for own-label products similar to Ra Bars, but the corporate strategy was to keep out of this market. The reasoning was that, if the own-label product sold badly, then Lucy Foods would have short, uneconomic runs, while if it were a success, then the owner of the own-label bar would put in their own facilities to manufacture the bar. The investment was not great and the technology simple.

5. New products, or more accurately, new variations on the old products, would allow for an increased market penetration without changes in equipment. Over time this would lead to the introduction of new bars and of toasted cereals sold in bags and in bulk for wholesalers to bag as their own product.

6. As health foods became established as ordinary products, so the sale of health foods would become common in ordinary food shops, and in a few chemists. Lucy Foods would follow the growing market spread.

The Market Changes

The confidence of the early 1980s did not survive to the middle of the decade, and the corporate strategy became tattered as circumstances overrode plans. This was reflected in the fluctuating financial performance of the company shown in Exhibit 2.

As can be seen, the years 1981 and 1982 were satisfactory and the growth in health foods as a whole appeared to be able to ignore the recession going on in Britain at that time. In fact, the health-food business was simply late in the business cycle. The apparent immunity of health foods had encouraged several large companies into the marketplace with new products. The result was that when the downturn came, it was made more serious by new producers looking for a market share. For Lucy Foods, 1983 became a year of heavy borrowing from the bank that nearly wiped out the capital employed.

Competitive Pressures Increase

In 1983, Quaker Oats brought out Jump Bars and Fox's Biscuits produced their Crunch Bars. In 1984, Applefords introduced their Cluster Bars, made in their new $2 million factory at Wrexham in Wales and launched with $2 million of national advertising. In the same year, Northumberland Fine Foods decided to specialize in own-label manufacture and thus a number of new bars came on the market. Finally in 1986, the Mars company, from its base in Slough, brought out their Tracker Bars. This new product was the result of extensive market research, and was fully backed by advertising. Very clearly, Lucy Foods was not the only health-food snack-bar manufacturer with a corporate plan.

Although sales recovered in 1984 and 1985, the total market was expanding much faster, and so market share was dropping. The large companies coming into the market were advertising and promoting their new bars so successfully that the total market increased, which allowed the small companies, such as Lucy Foods, to grow on the back of their efforts.

The Market Changes Again

After 1985 there was a fundamental change in the market. As far as health-food snack-bars were con-

Exhibit 2
LUCY FOODS: PERFORMANCE, 1981–1985

	1981	1982	1983	1984	1985
Sales	£91,700	£122,300	£92,000	£120,500	£152,100
Gross Profit	51,100	81,300	48,000	64,200	81,500
Net Profit	9,800	27,300	(4,300)	13,100	23,171
Capital Employed	16,900	24,700	1,600	1,100	2,300

cerned, health food shops became a small backwater of the total market. Supermarkets were the growth area, and they took on the well-advertised bars and introduced own-label bars. They would not put on their shelves a bar from a small company not backed by an advertising campaign.

In 1984, Lucy Foods had gotten Ra Bars on the shelves of two small supermarket chains, one in Yorkshire and one in Birmingham. By 1985 the bars were off their shelves because the demand was not there to justify the space they were taking up compared to the advertised brands. This led Lucy Foods to modify its corporate strategy once again. The market was growing, but it was growing in supermarkets. Because it did not have the resources to advertise, Lucy Foods could not sell its own products in the supermarkets. It was therefore obvious that the only way into the supermarkets was by manufacturing for someone who had the financial resources to promote the product.

The first major effort to manufacture own-label products was for a company making a slimming diet. They had a recipe, and they wanted Lucy Foods to make it. Lucy Foods conducted several trials, and established that the bar could be mass produced and at a price that was acceptable.

Failure

Nevertheless, the business went to a competitor because Lucy Foods could not guarantee that a massive increase in demand could be matched by a massive increase in production capacity. Further, the factory was old and did not meet the image standards required by the buyers. Even if Lucy Foods could have moved into a new factory with new equipment and had won own-label orders from a supermarket, the risks of being dependent on one or two orders was felt by John Mustoe to be "too dangerous for a small company." What would be a setback for a larger company in the event of cancellation would have been "fatal" for Lucy Foods.

DEJA VU

By December 1986, Lucy Foods was still in its old factory building, selling its quality products to health-food shops, but health-food shops were selling a smaller and smaller proportion of this type of snack. The market for health-food snack-bars was now on the shelves of the seven big supermarket chains. Irma and John Mustoe faced a difficult situation. Lucy Foods needed a new corporate strategy.

PROFESSIONAL UNIFORMS, LIMITED OR UNLIMITED?

ROBERT GATEWOOD
University of Georgia

E. WALTER WILSON
University of Georgia

Mick and Cathy McGregor sat in the inventory area of their store, Professional Uniforms, and puzzled about the future of the store. They even sketched out some of the options for the division of the physical layout on a notepad. They had had conversations like this one several times in the last month, and this one also ended without a firm decision. "It's a problem," said Cathy, "but not like the bad ones that face some friends of ours who also own small businesses." "Thank heavens," Mick replied, "but that still doesn't mean it can't affect us either positively or negatively."

In some ways, Professional Uniforms had always been kind of a puzzle. Both its start and its growth had been unexpected in many ways. When the McGregors had started their own business eleven years ago, a uniform store was not really in their thinking. They started a maternity and baby clothing store, The Mother and Child Shop, which was still in business. They had gotten the idea for this store when Cathy was pregnant and could not find suitable maternity clothing in their city. She had to drive the 65 miles to Phoenix to find such clothing. The idea was followed by market research and visits to cities similar to theirs to learn more about this type of business. Everything fit into place and, within four months of the birth of their son, they opened the store.

The Mother and Child Shop did well from its start. Within three years it had outgrown its original store and was moved to a larger location in the same shopping center when that became available. The only problem was that the McGregors had signed a five-year lease on the original location. What to do with the remaining two years? Obviously, finding a subleasee was one option. But the McGregors had another idea. In their visits prior to starting The Mother and Child Shop, they had talked with a store owner who had a sideline of nurses' uniforms in his maternity clothing store. This had caught their interest because of its unusualness. Now it became even more interesting. Thinking about the idea, the two realized that some of the same circumstances that aided the growth of The Mother and Child Shop were also present for nurses' and aides' uniforms. There was a fairly large market created by the two regional hospitals and the numerous physicians and dentists the city had attracted. There was a limited number of retail outlets for uniforms. The local department and discount stores carried some items, but this was not considered a main interest. Little attempt was made to carry complete lines or to make sure that inventory was current. In addition, very little marketing was carried out for these items. There were no specialty uniform shops in the surrounding 40 mile area.

Undoubtedly due to the success of their first store, the McGregors decided to take a chance and open the uniform store based on the information they had at that point rather than going through the marketing and visiting research that they had done for their first store. As before, Cathy was responsible for buying the goods and Mick for remodeling the store's layout to suit the new idea. Two months

This case, written specifically for this text, is printed by permission.

after The Mother and Child Shop moved to its larger store, the old store was the home of Professional Uniforms.

The new store, which started with two full-time employees, was a success from the start. As anticipated, nurses, aides, and clerical assistants from hospitals and physician's and dentist's offices started coming in almost immediately. Word of the specialty store traveled quickly within the professions, and the quality and the completeness of the lines were appreciated. The shop even started a monogramming service at the request of customers. For the first year, sales were steady, if not spectacular. There was a combination of enough turnover in existing offices and growth of new facilities in the city to maintain a fairly steady demand. In addition, individuals from the nearby smaller towns learned of the store and became customers. The logistics of this white uniform business were not especially complex. For the most part, there were a limited number of manufacturers and neither style or colors changed very much from year to year. A relatively steady demand facilitated inventory control and ordering schedules. As a matter of fact, inventory was kept to a minimum with almost all articles being on display.

Near the end of that first year, Cathy, who acted as manager of both stores, had a visitor who unexpectedly changed the regular rhythm of Professional Uniforms. It was a lieutenant from the city's police department. The department had a request for the uniform shop, "Could you carry police uniforms?" The lieutenant explained the difficulty the department had. When new officers were hired or existing officers were promoted, they were given an allowance for the purchase of their uniforms. This was a problem for new officers because they were unfamiliar with departmental dress regulations. Therefore, an officer usually accompanied them when they purchased their uniforms. This meant driving to Phoenix, waiting while the individuals were fitted, and then driving back. Obviously, this was not the best way to spend tax income or make use of an officer's time. If a local store would carry the necessary items, it would save the department time and money.

The McGregors thought about it for a short while and decided to try it. If nothing else, it was a useful community service. The first problem that they encountered was obtaining goods from manufacturers. As was the case with the white uniform lines, there were only a few manufacturers of police uniforms and only a few retail outlets. Of the two leading industry manufacturers, each supplied one large retailer in Phoenix. Police departments from up to 125 miles away usually came to one of these two retailers for their uniforms. The problem for the McGregors was that these two major retailers wished to control competition within this area. To do this, each retailer threatened to change all of their business to the other manufacturer if the present one supplied another store in the region with uniforms. Professional Uniforms was, therefore, forced to order from a much smaller, less desirable source.

Within six weeks of agreeing to carry the police uniforms, the first stock was delivered and ready to sell. Because of the exactness of the dress regulations for the local department, only one type of each clothing item was carried. The only variance was in different sizes. Because not much was expected from this line, the uniforms were not even displayed. All goods were kept on shelves in the back of the store, and specific items were brought out when a customer arrived. The local police department was quite happy with the service because it soon became apparent that even new hirees could go to the store by themselves and obtain all the necessary clothing. There was no need to take the time of a current uniformed officer.

This arrangement continued for the next six months with little change. Not very much money was to be made from the small volume of sales; but after the initial startup, there wasn't much extra work either. Customers would be measured for any alterations and a minimum amount of stock would be ordered when inventory ran low. The assistance given to the police department in terms of solving their uniform problem was the biggest return.

It was at this time, however, that the issue became more complex. Two other police departments, one from the local county and the other from a nearby small town came to the store and also asked if Professional Uniforms could carry their uniforms. Mainly because there was still a little more storage room in the back of the store, the McGregors agreed and began to stock the necessary goods. They noticed very quickly, however, that this created more work in terms of inventory control and ordering. Also the small producer they were working with became more irregular in meeting orders.

The addition of these two police departments seemed to start a small chain-reaction. Within a month, three other departments and one security company also requested uniforms. This demand created problems. One was space. Because each department had almost totally different dress regulations, each customer had a separate line. This increased storage demands. Secondly as the orders to the small manufacturer increased, the worse the response became. It was at this time that Mick and Cathy got lucky. They received a telephone call from one of the main uniform manufacturers that they had originally contacted. The working arrangement between this manufacturer and its retailer in Phoenix had become strained, and the manufacturer was willing to work out an arrangement to supply Professional Uniforms with goods. The McGregors quickly changed all business to this company, which also had better quality items. This solved one problem.

The problem of lack of space was also resolved. The five-year lease that was originally taken out for The Mother and Child Shop and which had caused the origin of Professional Uniforms was due to expire shortly. Instead of renewing this, the decision was made to move to a larger store. One with approximately twice the size had opened in the shopping center. The transition went smoothly. The white uniform part of the business had about the same space but some display area and most of the storage went to the police uniform line.

Realizing the sale of police uniforms had a great deal of growth potential, Cathy worked hard at maintaining good quality stock, an up-to-date list of each department's dress regulations, and an adequate inventory. The work paid off, as many departments started sending employees to the store. The success in this line led to further expansion. Within three years, four different lines could be identified. The first was the white uniforms that started the store. This was straight retail trade that featured two well publicized sales (one-third off) each year. The second was police uniforms, which included also sheriff's and other security uniforms. This consisted of both retail sales as well as contract sales. Because police departments are public institutions, contracts with them are usually let through a competitive bidding process. This starts when the department specifies the items it wishes to purchase and the approximate sales volume of the next year. Any retailer can bid by providing a firm price for each item specified by the department. The retailer is expected to sell the item at this price for the length of the contract. In most cases, the contract is awarded to the lowest bidder with no other considerations being given. Because of the small number of manufacturers, all the retail stores that bid have essentially the same cost for the uniforms they sell. Differences in bids are usually very small and are due to desired profit margin and incidental costs.

A third line that became apparent after the police uniforms were well developed was industrial and other career apparel. A wide variety of customers existed for this line (e.g., hotels, restaurants, and various home service companies such as pest control and lawn care). The McGregors did not have as much time to spend on this line as they did with the other two. Even so, it represented a steady business with good growth potential. Business was of the common retail type, with regular discounts being given some of the larger companies. Contracts, such as those with police departments, were not part of this line.

The fourth line was composed of a variety of miscellaneous equipment and clothing items, some of which cut across the other three lines and some of which really fit with only one of the other lines. Examples of some of the specific items in this line were belts, socks, pins, gloves, caps, shoes, polish, and key chains. This was the smallest of the four lines in terms of sales volume. Within the line, shoes accounted for both the majority of sales and inventory.

Growth occurred during the three years after the move to the larger store. Because of the growth, Professional Uniforms eventually got too big for its second location. This time, instead of leasing a larger store, the McGregors took a bigger plunge and bought a store. The facility was approximately 11,000 square feet, was located on a major street within three miles of the original location, and had ample parking. The building had most recently been a supermarket, so quite a bit of remodeling had to be done. The couple's first decision was to divide the facility roughly in half and to refurbish one-half for Professional Uniforms. The other half was to be rented out to help defray the expenses of the building. It took approximately six months to both remodel the store and find a tenant for the other half. This tenant was a general pharmacy, a part of a large, regional chain.

There was no major disruption in business caused by the move, and the next three years, the time to the present, had seen additional growth (sales figures are shown in Exhibit 1). The police

Exhibit 1

PROFESSIONAL UNIFORMS: SALES BY YEAR (in thousands)

	YEAR							
	1	*2*	*3*	*4*	*5*	*6*	*7*	*8*
White	$76	$98	$116	$132	$151	$147	$165	$190
Police	—	38	136	224	234	284	340	403
Industrial and career apparel	—	—	5	26	28	32	83	126
Shoes and miscellaneous	16	21	28	43	46	50	52	67
Total	$92	$157	$285	$425	$459	$513	$640	$786

uniform line was now the largest of the four, with almost twice the sales volume of the white uniform line and clearly more than the other three lines added together. The store had grown to six full-time employees.

There were two activities that were being contemplated to encourage further growth. The first was to add to the job duties of the four full-time sales employees by putting them on the road one day every two to three weeks to maintain personal contact with customers in the region. The sales clerks were positive about this idea after initial discussions. The second was to start advertising the police uniform line to a larger region, perhaps even statewide. If accurate measurements could be obtained for new officers, Mick thought that much of the actual business could be handled through UPS.

These two actions were not the McGregor's chief concern at the moment, however. Instead, the question they had talked about several times already was what to do with the half of the building that had been rented out. Three months ago, the pharmacy had been closed by its parent organization. The lease had now expired. The McGregors had about 5,500 square feet of empty space.

As they saw it there were three options. The first was to find another store to rent the space and continue business as it had been in the recent past. The advantage of this was that it provided a steady income to offset some of the expenses of the building.

The second option was to subdivide the empty area, move The Mother and Child Shop into part of it, and lease out the rest to a small store. This would make managing the two stores somewhat easier for Cathy while still providing some additional income. The downside was the potential risk to the original store. It had been in its present location for eleven years and was well known. Also two competitors had located quite nearby, and this caused customers to frequently compare merchandise in all three stores before making medium-to-large purchases.

The third option had the highest risk. This was to take over the total area for Professional Uniforms. The police line could be separated entirely. Maybe a third store could be developed to carry just that. At the very least, a separate entrance, counter, and dressing area could be built. Mick thought this would be desirable if for no other reason than white uniform customers and police uniform customers were two widely different groups of people. He felt a little uncomfortable about them having to use the same facilities for their shopping. The risk of this option was also larger because the total cost of the building would be borne by Professional Uniforms. In addition, expansion of the police uniform line was not without its costs in terms of remodeling, time, and marketing. If it did not work out, there would be a major impact on total profits. Even if it did work out, there was a question of whether the effort would be worth the return.

The two owners looked down again at the series of sketches before them. These essentially were drawings of their building with different combinations of Professional Uniforms, The Mother and Child Shop, and rented space. All of them looked possible. None of them look certain.

DAKOTAH, INC.

DIANE HOADLEY
University of South Dakota

PHIL C. FISHER
University of South Dakota

In May of 1987, Dakotah, Inc., appeared to be on the brink of a new era of growth and profitability. The South Dakota–based manufacturer of bed coverings and associated textile home furnishings had enjoyed record sales of over $13 million in 1986 and record after-tax profits of nearly $400,000. Its products, marketed from a posh showroom in New York City, were widely recognized by department store buyers and consumers alike as the top of the line in textile home furnishings.

Dakotah was an employee-owned company headquartered in the small town of Webster, South Dakota (population 2,400). It had seven plants located in small towns in three counties in the northeastern corner of South Dakota with a combined population of 24,448 (1980 census).

HISTORY OF DAKOTAH, INC.

In 1970, George Whyte was twenty-one, an age when many of his peers were thinking about finishing college and finding a job. Whyte, however, was worried about rural economic development. As a volunteer with VISTA (Volunteers in Service to America), Whyte had encouraged the farm families of northeastern South Dakota to participate in an economic development program called "Pigs for Pork." Farmers were given bred sows by the federal government to raise and eventually sell at market. When the price of pork plummeted, the program

failed. The pigs cost more to raise than their market value. The program had done nothing to improve the distressed economic condition of farmers in this depressed region.

Undaunted, Whyte hit upon another idea. He had noticed the farm wives making beautiful handcrafted quilts. His grandmother had made quilts, and he knew something of their value. He turned his attention to the talent and skill of the women of the families that were participating in the pig program and saw a new opportunity in quilt making. Whyte convinced the wives and daughters of these farmers that they could successfully produce and sell their handcrafted items. Whyte and Bob Pierce, who headed the Northeast South Dakota Community Action Program, collected hand-sewn quilts, afghans, pillows, shawls, and a variety of other items from the women in a three-county region of northeastern South Dakota. Armed with these samples, Whyte and Pierce flew to the East coast in an attempt to market the products to department store buyers.

They failed miserably. They flew first to Washington, D.C., engaged a hotel suite, got out the telephone book and contacted the department stores listed in the Yellow Pages. "Oh God, it was awful!" exclaimed Whyte, recounting the events. No one even came to look at the products. Whyte and Pierce then flew to New York City and repeated the process, with the same discouraging results. They knew the circumstances required more aggressive tactics, so they put their samples in a trunk and marched unannounced into the office of the quilt buyer for one of New York's leading department stores. They were promptly removed by the store's security guards.

This case was presented at the 1987 workshop of the Midwest Society for Case Research; printed by permission.

On their way back to South Dakota discouraged, but still hopeful, they stopped at Dayton's, a department store chain based in Minneapolis. There they saw the assistant buyer for the drapery and bedspread department. He, too, was not interested in the handicraft products being shown, but he put Whyte in contact with Park B. Smith, a leading independent manufacturer's representative in New York City.

Smith flew to South Dakota in September of 1971, liked what he saw, made some suggestions for design changes, and negotiated a contract with Whyte to produce a line of samples to show in the November home furnishings market in New York. Twice a year, in November and May, buyers gather on Fifth Avenue in New York City to preview new home furnishing merchandise and to place orders for the products that will appear in their stores.

The South Dakota farm women had from Labor Day to November 5 to style and produce their first product line. The women focused on quilts and pillow shams and succeeded in having a line of samples ready for the market. This time the products received a better reception from the department store buyers. A front-page article in *Home Furnishings Daily*, the industry trade journal, stated "Dakotah has the freshest design ideas in the last 100 years in bed covers." Over $50,000 in orders were placed at that first show.

Back in South Dakota, a $54,000 Small Business Administration loan provided the capital to purchase sewing machines and fabric enough to fill the orders, but working capital was still inadequate. The Junior Chamber of Commerce of Webster, South Dakota, raised $1,600 to buy fuel oil; the local Isaac Walton League donated the use of their building; and Whyte and the women worked for six months without pay until they delivered their first shipments of products to the buyers. They organized as the Tract Handicraft Industries Cooperative and the firm was off and sewing.

In 1986 this employees cooperative, reorganized as an employee-owned corporation in 1976, had sales of almost $14 million. It employed more than 400 employees and was considered to be the "Mercedes Benz" of the bed-covering industry.

MARKETING

Dakotah manufactured and wholesaled textile home furnishings products in four major categories.

Bed coverings (bedspreads, comforters, and so on) accounted for 50 percent of sales, and pillows (including decorator pillows) made up 40 percent of sales. The remaining 10 percent of sales was split evenly between window treatments (curtains, draperies, and so on) and miscellaneous items (shower curtains, napkins, placemats, wall hangings, and so on). Approximately 50 percent of these items were sold in department stores, 40 percent in mass and catalog merchants (Spiegels was the largest single customer), 5 percent in bed and bath specialty stores, and 5 percent to the hotel and motel industry. Dakotah also operated its own factory outlet store in Webster. Dakotah products were distributed in all fifty states, and the company had a small amount of export sales.

Dakotah was a very small producer in a large industry. Manufacturer's sales in the textile home furnishings industry were estimated at $3,905 million in 1985. Of this amount, sales of bedspreads and bed sets were $376.7 million (this did not include sheets and pillowcases; sales for those items were estimated at $813.5 million). The largest competitor was Spring Mills with total sales of $1,505 million, 64 percent of which were in textile home furnishings. Another major competitor was Fieldcrest Cannon with sales of $1,083 million. The industry was becoming increasingly concentrated in the face of pressure from foreign competitors. Major developments had been the acquisition of Burlington Industry's sheet and towel division by J. P. Stevens, Fieldcrest's purchase of Cannon, and West Point Pepperell's purchase of Cluett Peabody. Firms chose acquisitions as a means of expanding product lines to avoid the risk and cost of establishing new brand names. Well-established brand names were considered important in succeeding against imports. Another industry response to foreign competition was the increased use of automated production techniques. All large producers used a relatively high degree of automation to produce both fabrics and finished goods. In spite of these developments, the textile industry averaged net profits of only 0.32 percent of sales in 1986.

Competitive pressures forced Dakotah to establish a unique brand identification and a strong product image. As George Whyte explained to the casewriters, "Dakotah sells a lot of sizzle. Once you create the image, the product sells itself. So we have invested a great deal of time and money in creating an image." Dakotah's attempts to create an image began in 1976 when the newly incorporated company contracted with a consulting firm which specialized in the development of corporate identities. The consulting firm's first recommendation was to change the name of the products from Dakotah Handcrafts by Tract, and the name of the organization from Tract Handcraft Industries Cooperative, Inc., to just Dakotah. The company and its products are now identified by the name Dakotah written in distinctive script.

The next step in creating the Dakotah image was to develop a magnificent company showroom in the midst of the home furnishing market in New York City. Much time and money were spent in finding the right location and creating a suitable ambience. Finally a space became available on the ground floor of the textile market building, located on Fifth Avenue between 30th and 31st streets. The building houses offices for several textile and home furnishing manufacturers. Whyte created a spacious and dramatic office that rivals the office of any chief executive officer for a Fortune 500 company.

The New York showroom and offices were owned by a Dakotah subsidiary, Dakotah USA. Employees there were technically employees of the subsidiary. Sales were under the management of Neil Zuber, vice president of sales. Zuber ran the New York showroom and coordinated the selling activities of eleven independent sales representatives, each of whom was assigned an exclusive geographic area. John Panarello, the vice president of national accounts, sold to the large department stores and catalog merchants.

Great care was taken so that the Dakotah name, written in its characteristic script, was the only trademark to appear before the public. Whyte also indicated that the Dakotah name accompany catalog layouts of the products, a practice reserved for a few select designers such as Bill Blass and Ralph Lauren.

Whyte believed that Dakotah's principal strength was its ability to create high-fashion, uniquely designed items. Dakotah focused on designs that created an up-scale contemporary look. The first designs came from Whyte and other staff members. By 1982, Whyte recognized the need to hire a professional designer and asked one of Park Smith's former employees, Belinda Ballash, to join Dakotah. Ballash worked out of her office in Pacific Palisades, California, supplying Dakotah with designs reflecting the most up-to-date trends from the West coast. In May of 1987, Whyte hired another designer housed on the East coast to provide designs reflect-

ing East coast trends. The designers were employees of Dakotah USA. Although Dakotah products were styled to reflect current taste, which, in 1987, was returning to a country look, Whyte believed that Dakotah's emphasis would remain on products with contemporary styling. Whyte's attention to creating a unique look for the Dakotah products had been successful. Dakotah had always had difficulty filling its orders, sometimes running months behind orders and other times not allowing its sales representatives to take new orders for periods of up to two months. In 1987, Whyte negotiated a licensing agreement with The Spring Mills Company, the leading manufacturer of sheets and pillow cases, for use of Dakotah designs for a new line that would feature the Dakotah name. Whyte believed that similar licensing agreements would be negotiated with manufacturers of other home furnishing products.

In 1986, Whyte decided to move Dakotah into the hospitality market. The company had sold furnishings to hotels and motels on a limited scale, furnishing suites for the Hyatt corporation. Whyte was convinced that more appealing interior furnishings would improve occupancy rates. His first major deal was with the Super 8 Motel company. This company, headquartered in Aberdeen, South Dakota, 50 miles from Webster, was a motel franchise chain with over 400 budget motels in the United States and Canada. After testing guest responses to some of the products, Super 8 agreed to purchase bedspreads, wall hangings, and pillow ensembles. Dakotah became the exclusive supplier of bed coverings to the corporate-owned motels, and a recommended supplier for the franchises.

With this success, Whyte planned to pursue the hospitality industry vigorously. In 1987, these sales were being handled by a two-person telemarketing effort located at the Webster headquarters. Initial results had been very encouraging. Company plans were for hospitality sales to be 14 percent of sales by 1988, 30 percent by 1989, 40 percent by 1990, and 50 percent by 1991.

MANUFACTURING

Dakotah bed coverings were unique in that they were made with a technique called appliqué. In appliquéing, decorations are created by cutting pieces of one material and applying them to the surface of another. Manufacturing processes at Dakotah were a mixture of skilled hand work and highly automated processes. The decorative pieces of fabric were bound to the surface of the background material with adhesive, then outlined with zigzag stitching, which was done manually by guiding the fabric through a sewing machine. This process was labor intensive and required considerable skill. Other manufacturing processes, such as the decorative stitching at the edges of the bed coverings, were performed by computer-controlled machines.

Dakotah operated seven plants in six small towns, all in northeastern South Dakota. Two plants were located in Webster. Webster 1 employed 45 people who were engaged in the initial measurement and cutting of all fabric used in the other plants. Webster 1 also produced the batting or fiber filler used to give bulk to the bedspreads. Batting production was highly automated. Batting was made from bales of purchased fiber, which were fed into hoppers. These fibers were then woven into rolls of batting 40 yards long in one continuous automated process, which could be adjusted as to width and thickness of the batting.

Dakotah had recently acquired a computer-controlled laser fabric cutter to cut the pieces of cloth used in appliquéing. Patterns would be fed into the computer, which would lay out the pieces on the fabric so as to minimize waste. Additional benefits from the laser cutter would be reduced labor and increased capacity. The laser cutting would also bind the edges to eliminate ravelling, which sometimes occurred with the current method, which employed a hand-guided, power-driven circular blade.

Webster 2 was located a block away from Webster 1 and included the company's administrative offices. This plant did the finishing and shipping for all products except pillows. In the final step of the manufacturing process, the decorated top of the bedspread and the underside fabric were placed on large frames with the batting in between. Large computer-controlled quilting machines sewed the three layers together. These machines also could be programmed to sew decorative designs on the bedspreads. Some bedspreads without appliqué were decorated entirely with the quilting machines. Appliquéd coverings were then outlined and embellished with stitching, a process in which the coverings were again manually guided through a sewing machine. The operators in this process were the most highly skilled in the plant. The process required manual dexterity on the part of the operators

and the ability to sew the designs from memory. Webster 2 employed 80 people.

Other Dakotah plants were located in Veblen (population 322), where ninety-three people produced and shipped pillows; Wilmot (population 492), which produced shams, or decorative pillow coverings, and employed forty-three people; Eden (population 126), where draperies and bedskirts were made, and thirty-six people were employed; Pierpont (population 165), where appliqués were bound to the coverings, and thirty people were employed; and Sisseton (population 2,717), where thirteen employees made hanging samples used as point of purchase displays. Workers at several of these plants performed skilled handstitching operations to make bedspreads and other products. Approximately 90 percent of the employees in manufacturing were women.

Company executives believed that Dakotah had an important competitive edge in manufacturing skills. While design changes were important in retaining the distinctive look of Dakotah products, protection from copying came largely from the fact that the appliquéd designs were difficult to manufacture and Dakotah had more expertise in the appliquéing processes than anyone else. Only one competitor made appliquéd products. It was also a difficult process to automate or mechanize. As one manager put it, "We have an edge in marketing and design. Survival depends on success in manufacturing."

Manufacturing operations were under the management of Ed Johnson. As a teenager, Johnson had been employed by the Northeast South Dakota Community Action Program and one of his jobs had been to help the newly formed Tract Handcraft Industries Cooperative move from its first quarters to a larger building. At that time, Bob Pierce recommended him for a permanent job with the cooperative. Johnson started as a delivery boy and had grown with manufacturing operations as the company converted from exclusively handicraft to automated processes.

Johnson, thirty-two, was youthful appearing, soft spoken, and articulate. He was able to solve production problems, which had given the company a reputation for not being able to meet promised delivery dates. Previously the company had employed manufacturing managers with experience in textile manufacturing. In Whyte's estimation, the former managers had provided needed technical expertise but lacked the right approach to managing people. "They came from a different school of thought. Theirs was the whip and chain approach." Despite the fact that Dakotah was owned by its employees, there had been a serious attempt to unionize the company in 1984.

Johnson's technical experience had come from his working at many jobs within Dakotah manufacturing, taking home study-courses, attending seminars, but "mostly trial and error learning." He saw his major tasks as maintaining efficiency and meeting delivery commitments.

Improvements in efficiency were sought through continued automation and careful upgrading of equipment. In the case of the laser fabric cutter, once its potential use had been identified, the company had spent a year in evaluating it before making the purchase. Some of the company's equipment was over ten years old, and Johnson believed that improved equipment was important in enabling the company to meet the demand for its products. One company executive estimated that, in 1986, the company had turned away from $2 to $4 million in sales, and company sales representatives were quoting delivery dates of six months. He said, "People can build a house faster than they can get the bedspreads." Continued automation was constrained by capital requirements. For example, the laser cutter had cost $300,000. Dakotah had invested $3 million in plant and equipment during the five years prior to 1987 and planned to invest well over $1 million in 1987.

PERSONNEL

The personnel and human resource manager for Dakotah, Inc., was Jim Nixon. He was responsible for drafting personnel policies and procedures and administering the compensation and benefit plans.

Nixon joined Dakotah in July of 1984 shortly after the unsuccessful union attempt to organize employees at six Dakotah plants. Complaints of favoritism and arbitrary actions had prompted the attempt to unionize. Nixon believed that the union drive failed because workers were reluctant to bring in an outside organization to represent their interests. Nixon's first priority when starting his job was to spend time in the plants, listening to the problems of workers and instituting corrective actions as quickly as possible.

Recruitment was an ongoing source of concern. "The company is under a lot of pressure to fill openings," he explained. "We usually have more job openings than applicants. Sometimes I think we hire every warm body that applies for a job." In fact, Dakotah hired approximately 70 percent of all applicants for work. Nixon was recruited from the entire northeastern region of South Dakota and from a 40-mile radius from the southern edge of North Dakota.

Employees were trained by their supervisors. Nixon provided supervisory training through either in-house training or off-site seminars. He had the most success with the in-house training, as supervisors were reluctant to participate in off-site training.

Nixon formalized job descriptions, posted job openings in the plants, and advertised openings in the local media. Nixon also tested applicants for color perception, manual dexterity, and skills required for the job. Applicants for manufacturing positions were interviewed by Nixon, with the plant supervisor and Ed Johnson making the final decision.

The manufacturing employee turnover for 1984 was 64 percent, compared to an industry average of approximately 10 percent. The 1985 rate was 38 percent, and the 1986 rate was 26 percent. Nixon's goal was to reach the industry turnover rate by 1988. The drop in the turnover rate was attributed to improved hiring and supervisory practices and to reduced seasonal layoffs.

Manufacturing workers at Dakotah were paid an average of $4.52 an hour. Skilled workers, such as fabric cutters or appliqué stitchers, made as much as $4.92. The base wage was 20 percent to 30 percent below the manufacturing wages paid in larger eastern South Dakota cities such as Watertown or Sioux Falls, but well above the $1.50-an-hour labor costs of Korean and Taiwanese textile workers. Wages for clerical workers were comparable to wages for clerical employees in Sioux Falls. Top managers at Dakotah were paid salaries substantially below industry average.

A company document on corporate objectives set a number of goals for employees. Wages should be equal to industry standards by 1988 and above industry standards by 1989. Fringe benefits should be equal to industry standards by 1990 and above industry standards by 1991. Employee turnover and absenteeism rates should be lower than industry averages by 1990. Finally, the number of reportable injuries should be lower than industry averages by 1989. The document called for the establishment of "associate teams" consisting of members from direct labor, office staff, and management. Teams to be established in 1987 were a communication team, a compensation and benefits team, a quality team, and a training, education, and safety team.

EMPLOYEE OWNERSHIP

Employees participated in company ownership in two ways: through an employee stock-purchase plan and through a stock bonus option plan. In the former plan, an employee who completed 1,000 hours of service could purchase up to one hundred shares of Class B stock. After the first 1,000 hours of service, an employee was entitled to purchase one share for each 10 hours of service. This option to buy could be exercised immediately, usually through payroll deductions, or at any time during the year in which the options were earned or during the next calendar year. The purchase price for any year was the book value of the stock as of December 31 of the previous year. During 1986, employees purchased 6,501 shares of Class B stock for $35,430. In 1985 they had purchased 2,040 shares for $10,547. The current stock purchase plan had been revised in 1985 to encourage greater participation. Formerly employees had been required to purchase stock in blocks of 100 shares for cash, a requirement that made participation difficult. While the company had nearly 300 shareholders in 1976, that number had dwindled to 80 by 1980. A total of 112 employees had begun to purchase stock since the revision.

The stock bonus option was a retirement benefit plan. It was first established in 1976 and amended in 1980 to conform to the provisions of the Employee Retirement Income Security Act. The Dakotah board of directors declared stock contributions to the plan in years when company profits were sufficient. Stock dividends were valued at fair market value. For 1986, the directors had paid a dividend of 37,202 shares with an estimated value of $250,000. This represented approximately 9 percent of the aggregated salaries of those employees eligible to participate in the plan. Eligibility in the plan was limited to employees with at least 500 hours in subsequent years could participate in the plan, but vesting rights were earned only in years in which an employee worked at least 1,000 hours.

When employees left Dakotah, they were required to sell their stock acquired through the employee stock purchase plan. The selling price was book value. Other employees had first right of refusal, and if no employee exercised his or her right to purchase, the company would repurchase the stock. Most stock was repurchased by the company. In 1986 the company repurchased 39,886 shares of stock from 24 employees. At the close of 1986, 346,032 shares of Class B stock were outstanding.

FINANCE

Richard Engle, a CPA with an MBA from an eastern business school, was the chief financial officer at Dakotah. Prior to coming with Dakotah he had been employed in New York by Dakotah's public accounting firm, and Dakotah had been one of his accounts. In 1980, he told George Whyte that he planned to leave public accounting. When Whyte suggested that he join Dakotah, his first reaction was "Sure, if you move it to New York." Eventually he agreed to come for two years, and by 1987 had been in Webster, SD for more than six years.

"The concept of this company is to make jobs," Engle said. "We try to control the cost of the product through mechanization, experimentation, and heavy investment." Engle saw the employee ownership concept as being of mixed benefit. It gave employees a sense of commitment, but it severely limited the firm's access to capital. Currently Dakotah had $1,250,000 in outstanding long-term notes. This included approximately $65,000 in a revolving working capital loan financed at 1 percent above the prime rate and the rest in the form of a six-year loan secured by machinery and equipment and at 1.5 percent above the prime rate. At one time the company had paid 4.5 percent over prime. (For financial statements, see Exhibits 1 and 2.)

Engle attributed the company's improved performance in 1986 to several factors. He pointed to the firm's recruitment of more experienced middle managers, significant investments in machinery and equipment, better cost controls, and the development of new markets in the hotel and motel industry. Some of these initiatives began as early as 1983, and the benefits began showing up at the bottom line in 1986.

Dakotah had formal five-year goals for profit and growth. These were: sales growth of 15 percent, net

Exhibit 1

DAKOTAH, INC.: BALANCE SHEETS, 1980–1986

	1986	1985	1984	1983	1982	1981	1980
ASSETS							
Current Assets							
Cash	$ 18,171	$ 16,372	$ 25,558	$ 3,207	$ 81,629	$ 81,447	$ 12,162
Accounts receivable less allowance for doubtable accounts	1,718,731	1,337,006	1,635,032	1,912,920	1,278,584	1,289,537	1,325,765
Merchandise inventory	1,994,279	2,352,272	2,405,746	3,103,208	1,769,199	1,448,964	1,207,482
Prepaid income tax	—	66,441	80,114	115,392	12,880	29,398	35,915
Other current assets	16,094	12,686	7,239	25,142	17,587	3,831	19,413
Total Current Assets	$3,747,275	$3,784,777	$4,153,689	$5,159,869	$3,159,879	$2,853,177	$2,600,737
Property, plant and equipment—Less accumulated depreciation	1,732,239	1,415,983	1,640,582	1,780,827	1,325,579	904,634	775,438
Other assets	9,270	9,190	11,010	11,830	22,770	19,420	19,420
TOTAL ASSETS	$5,488,784	$5,209,950	$5,805,281	$6,952,526	$4,508,228	$3,777,231	$3,395,595
LIABILITIES AND STOCKHOLDERS' EQUITY							
Current Liabilities							
Notes payable—Bank	$ 264,537	$1,124,104	$1,487,241	$1,849,604	$ 11,720	$ 927,856	$ 839,111
Capital lease obligations	20,886	19,140	17,718	16,336	14,868	21,700	21,700
Notes payable—Other	—	—	—	31,153	49,593	92,654	101,385
Accounts payable	828,303	632,589	747,876	1,394,598	853,646	632,225	632,650
Income tax payable	—	—	—	—	—	16,607	8,891
Other current liabilities	408,935	286,303	199,188	277,395	174,971	86,174	122,278
Total Current Liabilities	$1,522,661	$2,062,136	$2,452,023	$3,569,086	$1,604,798	$1,777,216	$1,726,015
Long-Term Debt							
Notes payable—Bank	1,250,000	870,000	1,140,000	1,210,000	880,000	—	—
Capital lease obligations	391,088	412,154	430,821	448,337	465,364	475,398	496,347
Notes payable—Other	—	—	—	—	—	70,541	89,930
Total Long-Term Debt	1,641,088	1,282,154	1,570,821	1,658,337	1,345,364	545,939	586,277

	1986	1985	1984	1983	1982	1981	1980
Stockholders' Equity							
Common stock	1,159,383	936,382	926,434	927,435	927,948	928,999	679,448
Contributed capital	13,207	13,207	13,207	13,207	13,207	13,207	13,207
Retained earnings	1,152,445	916,071	842,796	784,461	616,911	511,870	390,648
Total Stockholders' Equity	2,325,035	1,865,660	1,782,437	1,725,103	1,558,066	1,454,076	1,083,303
TOTAL LIABILITIES AND STOCK- HOLDERS' EQUITY	$5,488,784	$5,209,950	$5,805,281	$6,952,526	$4,508,228	$3,777,231	$3,395,595

Exhibit 2

DAKOTAH, INC.: INCOME STATEMENTS 1980–1986

	1986	1985	1984	1983	1982	1981	1980
Sales	$14,085,870	$11,708,748	$13,729,250	$12,300,726	$9,124,241	$10,721,784	$9,628,706
Less returns and allowances	410,329	645,166	605,621	479,567	344,014	472,897	487,616
Net sales before discounts	—	11,063,582	13,123,629	11,821,159	8,780,227	10,248,887	9,141,090
Less discounts	—	2,659	7,928	7,908	8,647	14,473	17,912
Net Sales	$13,675,541	$11,060,923	$13,115,701	$11,813,251	$8,771,580	$10,234,414	$9,123,178
Less Cost of Goods Sold							
Merchandise inventory	$2,352,272	$2,405,746	$3,103,208	$1,769,199	$1,448,964	$1,207,482	$1,251,553
Purchases	4,721,640	3,642,072	4,551,872	5,326,805	3,532,998	4,227,009	3,576,734
Freight in	141,341	123,026	164,711	238,175	207,934	191,943	195,760
Direct labor	2,350,930	2,206,586	2,478,520	2,769,484	1,591,026	1,820,766	1,615,935
Employee fringe benefits							98,877
Payroll taxes	228,861	197,406	213,148	330,376	140,935	155,466	119,257
Cost of goods available for sale	9,795,044	8,574,8367	10,511,459	10,434,039	6,921,857	7,602,666	6,858,116
Less merchandise inventory–End of year	1,994,279	2,352,272	2,405,746	3,103,208	1,769,199	1,448,964	1,207,482
Total Cost of Goods Sold	7,800,765	6,222,564	8,105,713	7,330,831	5,152,658	6,153,702	5,650,634
Gross Profit	$5,874,776	$4,838,359	$5,009,988	$4,482,420	$3,618,922	$4,080,712	$3,472,544
Less Operating Expenses							
Manufacturing	$1,574,785	$1,349,893	$1,276,410	$1,023,828	$ 729,888	$ 601,535	$ 462,506
Selling	1,844,953	1,656,810	1,831,548	1,788,532	1,393,449	1,772,059	1,254,170
Shipping	371,997	323,299	379,414	336,820	340,730	275,127	312,128
Financial	254,921	326,000	480,412	308,677	218,372	216,027	311,236
General and administrative	1,148,188	1,060,443	937,439	920,559	758,941	722,736	617,110

Exhibit 2

DAKOTAH, INC.: INCOME STATEMENTS 1980–1986 (*continued*)

	1986	1985	1984	1983	1982	1981	1980
Total Operating Expenses	5,194,844	4,716,445	4,905,223	4,378,416	3,441,380	3,587,484	2,957,150
Income from Operations	$679,932	$121,914	$104,765	$104,004	$177,542	$493,228	$515,394
Royalty Income, Net	—	—	—	—	—	—	4,330
Provision for Income Taxes	$40,423	$25,966	$7,328	$(83,951)	$40,949	$52,607	34,299
Contribution to Employee Stock Bonus Plan	250,000	—	—	—	—	250,000	371,213
NET INCOME	$389,509	$95,948	$97,437	$187,955	$136,593	$190,621	$114,212

pretax earnings on sales of 4 percent in 1987 rising to 12 percent by 1991, and an average rate of return on stockholders' equity of 15 percent. "If we want to grow," Engle said, "we have to look to external equity. We can support 10 percent growth but 25 percent will require more. We have reached the limit of debt financing." Engle recognized that going outside the limits of employee ownership for equity capital was a departure from an important company policy. "One thing I have learned is that some things are sacred." Employee ownership was one of those things.

COMMUNITY IMPACT

Since the original purpose of Dakotah, Inc., had been to provide jobs for rural families, the casewriters interviewed community leaders to determine the firm's impact on Webster. Mayor Mike Grosek, also a supermarket owner, said that the company has had a very positive impact on the community. "Over the last three or four years the agricultural economy has been deteriorating. We are all fighting to just survive. Dakotah is an important part of Webster now because it employs so many women from the rural area. It gives them a second income to support the groceries and clothing their families need while their husbands are struggling on the farm. In some cases, it is a primary source of income."

Other community leaders pointed out that employment at Dakotah had enabled people to remain in their home communities when otherwise they would have had to go elsewhere for employment. They believed that the retail businesses in Webster and other communities where Dakotah plants were located had remained healthier than those in other farming communities in the region.

Some perspective on Dakotah's impact on improving the economic situation in northeastern South Dakota can be gained by referring to the following statistics for Day County, where Webster is located: unemployment in Day County was 2.8 percent compared to 3.9 percent for the state of South Dakota as a whole. The labor participation rate, that is, the percentage of individuals aged sixteen and older who were part of the labor force, was 33.3 percent. Individuals not participating in the labor force would include students not employed, housewives, retirees, individuals who have given up looking for work, and people who do not need to work. In 1986, the unemployment rate for Day County was 5 percent compared to 4.6 percent for the state, and the labor force participation was 43.4 percent. In 1970, census figures showed 859 women were employed in Day County. For 1986 the number was estimated to be 1,218. Dakotah employed approximately 230 people in Day County. According to the U.S. Department of Commerce Bureau of Economic Analysis, the multiplier factor for textile manufacturers in South Dakota was 1.42. The 1970 census indicated that the population of Day County was 8,713 people. However, the 1985 estimated census was 7,852 residents; this population decline was typical for rural South Dakota counties over this period.

DAKOTAH'S FUTURE

Dakotah had begun as a manufacturing company established to create jobs in northeastern South Dakota. Over the years the focus of the company had shifted from manufacturing to marketing. "It is our forte," explained Whyte. He believed that marketing opportunities through licensing and franchising could allow the business to grow to a $100 million company over the next ten years.

Licensing possibilities included such products as wall and floor coverings, a more extensive line of window treatments, and other textile products. A franchised chain of Dakotah stores would allow the company greater access to a larger number of consumers. Both of these alternatives would allow the company to increase its revenues with a relatively small capital investment.

Dakotah was beginning to consider other markets. In 1986, Dakotah quietly began selling pillows to Wal-Mart, a large discount chain. Sales were $1.5 million that year, with $2.5 million expected in 1987. The possibilities for sales through discount outlets raised the possibility that overseas manufacturing of Dakotah designs might be considered.

Finally, the capital limitation of confining equity ownership to employees was recognized as an obstacle to growth. Perhaps employee ownership was no longer sacred. However, it was a decision with far-reaching consequences. "The intent is still to create jobs," Whyte said. "The concept of employee ownership has not changed yet."

BENNETT'S MACHINE SHOP, INC.

ARTHUR SHARPLIN
McNeese University

"This won't even be a one-page month," said Pat Bennett. "Worst month we've ever had." Pat is the owner of Bennett's Machine Shop, an automotive engine rebuilder in Lake Charles, Louisiana. He went on to explain what he meant by a "one-page" month: "We write each engine job order on one line of a thirty-two-line yellow legal pad. Last year, we figured out that a breakeven point was about fifty engines a month. If we have three pages in a month, we have really made some money. A single page? We should have gone fishing."

Bennett's engine sales for July 1987 were $57,000, down from $80,000 to $90,000 a year earlier. Pat said, "We install about 40 percent of the engines we rebuild, at about $1,250 a shot. The carry-outs average about $750. So I don't expect sales in August to even reach $30,000."

Pat sees his problem as "too little sales to support the overhead cost." "Because of this, we have a day-to-day cash flow problem." Right after receiving his July financial statement from the accountant, he had laid off the office help (a secretary-bookkeeper and a clerk-parts runner). Earlier in the year, he had released four mechanics and a helper.

Pat himself had been spending most of his time on a tool modification and sharpening contract with Boeing of Louisiana, Inc. (BLI). This work began in February 1987, shortly after Boeing opened its new Louisiana facility, where Air Force KC-135 tankers (a variation of the Boeing 707) were reworked. In July, Boeing had begun returning Bennett's invoices, with a rubber-stamped note that they exceeded the $75,000 contract amount. By mid-August, unpaid billings to Boeing totaled over $60,000. Pat said, "I've cut about everything I can cut and sold about as much as I can sell. I even took out a second mortgage on my condo. If Boeing doesn't pay pretty soon, or a miracle doesn't happen in the machine shop, we're going to be history." Exhibit 1 contains excerpts from an interview with Pat Bennett conducted in mid-September 1987.

COMPANY BACKGROUND

In 1972, Pat Bennett earned a bachelor of science degree in mechanical engineering at McNeese University in Lake Charles. Recalling his senior year, Pat said, "I knew then I would not stick with my engineering career. Besides going through a real burnout, I already had this machine shop idea. There were just three automotive machine shops in Lake Charles. And all the operators were in their late fifties. I knew there would be an excellent opportunity for a new shop in just a few years."

After graduation, Pat took a job with a chemical plant contractor as a designer-draftsman. The contract was completed in six months, and Pat's employer offered him a chance to move to St. Louis. Instead, he quit and hired on at a local Cities Service plant as a field engineer. Since all he actually did at

This case, written specifically for this text, is printed by permission.

Exhibit 1
EXCERPTS FROM INTERVIEW WITH PAT BENNETT

Q: What is your main objective for this year?

A: I guess the goal we're all in business for is to make it profitable, and it hasn't been for the past two years. We've had a real bad downward trend. We might not make a real big profit this year, but I hope we can stop the downward trend and turn it around. That would be a major accomplishment.

Q: What about the longer term?

A: I would like the business to be successful enough so that I could do some of the things I want to do. Travel some, sports in the winter—before I get decrepit.

Q: Can you be a little more specific about what the business would have to do to satisfy you?

A: If we got back to where net profit, including my total compensation, was $70,000 to $100,000 a year—and we've been there—I would think that was okay.

Q: Do you mean in ten years? Twenty years?

A: I'm not really that patient a person. I mean in the next two to three years. That is very obtainable.

Q: Do you think about 25 years from now, when you will be almost 65?

A: No.

Q: Do you feel responsible to make the business support anyone else but you and Cheryl, in the long or short term?

A: Sure, I probably have more loyalty to some of those guys than I should.

Q: Which ones? Do you mean all the workers?

A: I mean as a whole. My dad was a union man his entire life. We grew up with the idea that the company had to provide benefits—medical care, retirement, vacations, days off. Retirement is a big thing Dad always talked about. He always talked about the days before Roosevelt, when there wasn't any Social Security, not much to look forward to.

Q: Do the workers look out for your interests?

A: Sometimes I think they do. But on days like today I wonder.

Q: What happened today?

A: Everybody screwed up. Jack has trouble ordering anybody to do anything. Someday he's got to learn he isn't one of the gang anymore. Dale loaded the wrong engine on a customer truck. Lance spent the whole day chasing his tail, pretending to go get parts. One of my good customers asked for his car at 1:00—and it wasn't out until 4:00. Know what I'm going to do? I'm moving my desk right out to the middle of the shop, right by the boring bars. They'll be nervous with me watching every move. But I'm going to get this mess under control. [Within 3 weeks, Pat had built a 6' × 8' office in the center of the shop near the assembly area. It had one-way windows so that Pat could observe the machinists but could not be seen by them.]

Q: What major changes in the business do you foresee?

A: More diversity. Wait! I mean more diversification. We've had all the diversity we can stand.

Q: What do you mean by diversification?

A: There still are several areas of the engine business that are untouched in Lake Charles. I just did a catalog so we'll be ready to do the parts house business. The closest production shops are in Baton Rouge and Houston, both over 2 hours away. We've got the whole west side of the state. And the crack repair business, cylinder head cracks mainly, is just untapped. I visited a big diesel shop in Houston that does this. The whole system, really nothing more than a big fire-bricked oven, would cost only a couple of thousand dollars. This is an especially good business with today's thin-wall castings on engines. A tremendous number of heads are just thrown away. A plain old six-cylinder Chevrolet head is $400 new, bare. I also think we have a good opportunity in the aircraft industry—the tool work, a heat treating facility. And Boeing is about to certify us for "level II" work, allowing us to make parts which stay on the plant. No more gravy train—we'll have to bid everything. Level II will also let us bid on the work for the big Strategic Petroleum Reserve. They have to send their work 80 miles to New Iberia.

the plant was drafting, he felt that he had been mis-led. He stuck out his one-year contract—all except the last four hours. "On the 365th day when the boss went to lunch, I said 'Goodbye' to the man sit-ting beside me, took just the drafting equipment I could hold in my hand and walked out the back door." Pat's impetuosity cost him the one week of vacation pay he had accumulated.

For the next year (1974–1975), Pat commuted 60 miles to Beaumont, Texas, where he worked for Stubbs-Overbeck, Inc., a petroleum refinery engi-neering firm. According to Pat, this was "my first real engineering job." He explains:

My first day on the job, they fired the civil engi-neer. I was sitting there feeling inadequate, worrying what my assignment would be and if I would remember how to do it. I heard the office manager ask two other guys, "Who are we going to get to run the theodolite (a sophisti-cated surveying instrument) so the design crew can get going?" I got their attention and timidly said, "I know how to run a theodolite." They questioned why a mechanical engineer would know how to do that. I told them I had worked for a civil engineer while in college.

At about the same time, Pat bought a boring bar (a tool used to recondition cylinders in engine blocks) from a farmer for $50. He also sold his wife's washer and dryer for $100 to get the down payment on a valve grinding machine, the other piece of equipment required for the most rudimentary en-gine rebuilder. At night and on weekends, Pat re-built engines in a 6-by-8-foot shack next to the trailer house where he lived with his wife Cheryl. Custom-ers gave Pat money to buy parts, and he charged them only for his labor.

Pat told of his big entrepreneurial decision:

I worked ten hours in Beaumont and drove an hour each way in addition to the time I spent doing engines. The drive just got too danger-ous. I was sleepy most of the time and kept dozing at the wheel. Finally, one morning on the way to work I almost ran off the road. I had to pull over and sleep and didn't get to work until 9:30. When I got home that evening Cheryl and I talked it over and decided I should quit my job and try the machine shop business full time.

Pat rented a small quonset hut as his first shop, paying the owner for the month he used it. Then he moved to a stall in a service station about a block from the trailer park. There, his rent was one-third of all labor charges. The service station owner made additional profit on engine parts. "I could not get any discount parts. I had no business license. We did not even have a name. But the fellow who ran the service station bought parts at jobber prices."

Near the end of 1975, a local garage owner asked Pat if he would split the rent on a larger building the garage owner was considering. Pat would pay $150 of the $400 monthly rent. Pat agreed, and the ar-rangement lasted about two years. During that time Pat hired a helper (a pre-med student) and bought a cylinder head grinder and two other specialized ma-chines (all on credit).

In 1977, Pat incorporated his business as Ben-nett's Machine Shop, Inc., and moved it to a rented building on Prien Lake Road, a busy commercial street. Sales and profits continued to expand through 1979, when his landlord, whom Pat had nicknamed "The Iron Maiden," ordered him to move because of the growing pile of used engines and parts next to the shop building. The shop flooded frequently anyway, and the fire department had complained about the oily rinse water that Ben-nett's discharged into the city storm drains. Pat said, "I told the Iron Maiden that this was about as clean as it was going to get and made plans to move."

"I arranged to borrow $80,000 from Gulf National Bank," said Pat, adding, "I found a 2-acre lot on the old Chennault air base for $57,000. I built a 4,000-square-foot building with the other $23,000, plus $3,000 I had saved." Bennett's Machine Shop moved to the new location in December 1979.

"The first year we really had any extra money was 1981. We bought eleven pieces of property. We put 20 percent down on all of it and borrowed the rest, about $80,000." That year and the next, Pat added 6,000 square feet to the machine shop and built another shop building, all without borrowing. For the first time in 1981, Bennett's began to do over-the-fender work, installing engines and some minor general repair work. At about this time, Pat and Cheryl bought a "real house" in nearby Westlake and moved from their mobile home. By 1985, Pat had bought a new condominium in Lake Charles and a 38-foot cabin cruiser. He had collected twenty-two "muscle cars" and his personal car was a 1984 Jaguar XJS coupe.

"Then we made our big blunder," said Pat "I thought it was time to open a new location, not to rebuild engines, but to install them. We bought the back half of an old Dodge dealership on Ryan Street (about three miles from Bennett's Machine Shop). A Firestone tire store was in the front. Cheryl often reminds me how stupid it was to think I could run the business long-distance."

Pat opened the new shop as Lake Charles Motor Exchange, Inc. He assigned four of his people there. He said, "For fourteen months, I pumped money into the new operation." The Ryan Street location was closed, and the facility was sold at a $25,000 profit in March 1986. "I never realized how personalized the business was." Pat added, "By the way, we proved it again this summer, while I was fooling with Boeing. Things really got out of hand."

OPERATIONS

In late 1987, Bennett's Machine Shop was involved in three types of work: engine rebuilding, over-the-fender work, and tool sharpening and modification (the Boeing contract). Exhibit 2 shows the layout of Bennett's facilities.

Engine Rebuilding

Rebuilding engines is highly technical work. According to Pat, "The heart of it is to start with an empty, bare block. Don't let the customer talk you into skipping the machine work." An actual case will illustrate the steps involved. Exhibit 3 provides an exploded view of a typical engine.

On August 9, 1987, Thomas Winkles, maintenance manager for a local drycleaning firm and per-

Exhibit 2
LAYOUT OF BENNETT'S FACILITIES

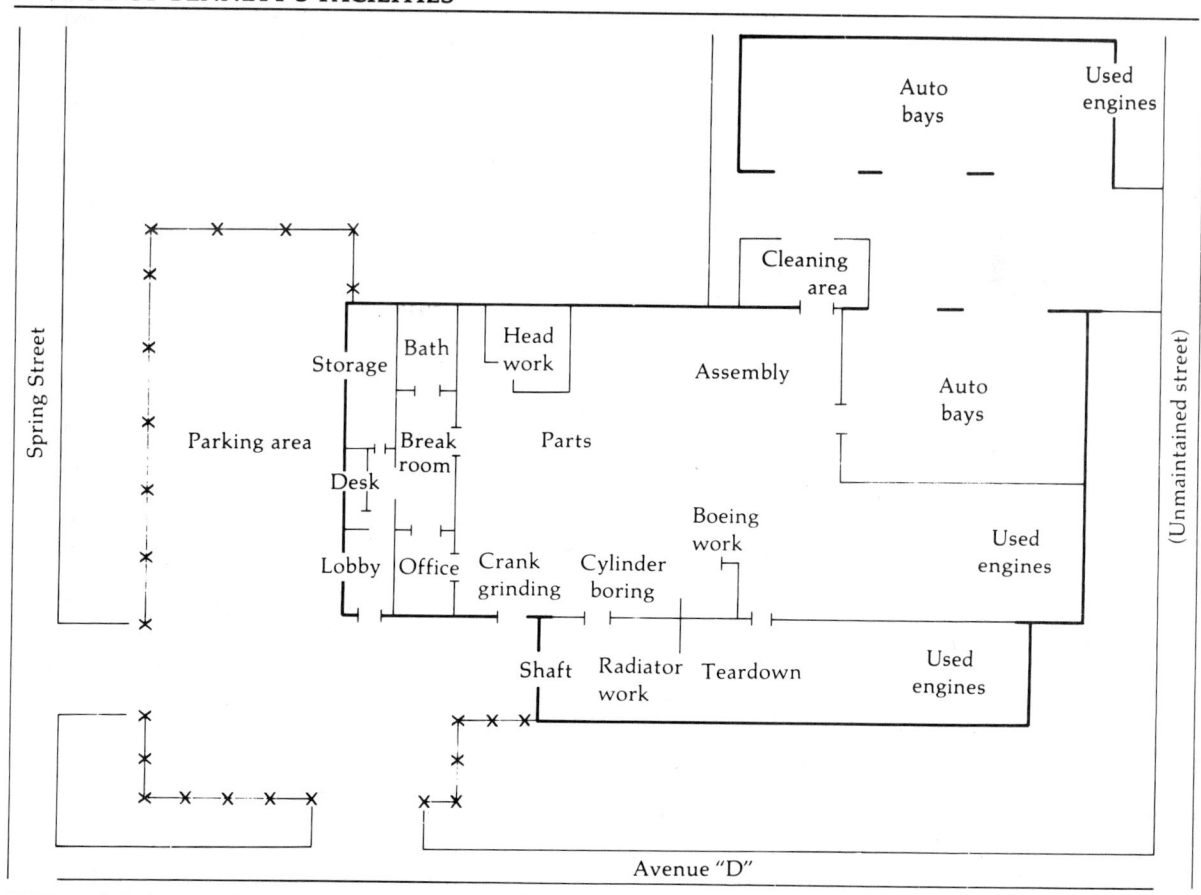

Exhibit 3
EXPLODED VIEW OF GENERAL MOTORS V-6 ENGINE

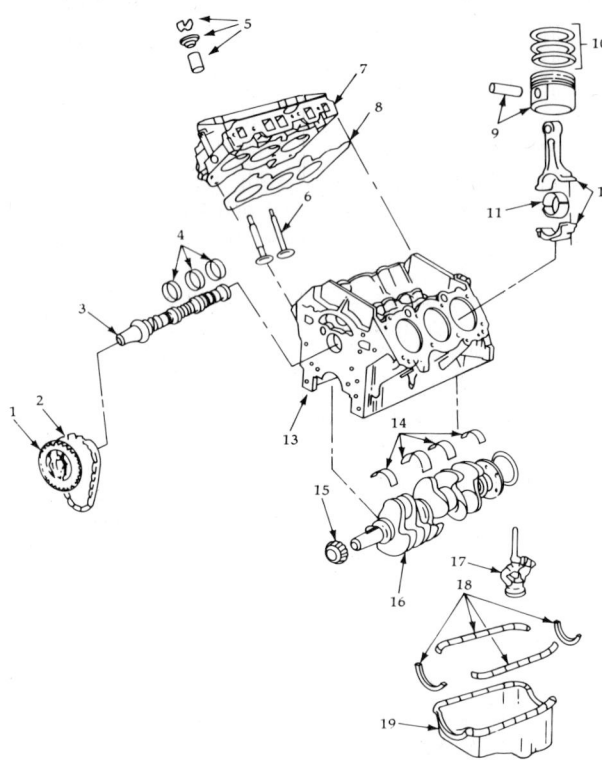

1. Camshaft gear (drives camshaft)
2. Timing chain (connects camshaft gear to crankshaft gear)
3. Camshaft (operates linkage to intake and exhaust valves)
4. Camshaft bearings (steel sleeves with soft metal inner surfaces)
5. Valve spring assembly (two per cylinder—holds intake or exhaust valve closed except when linkage to camshaft opens it)
6. Intake and exhaust valves (two valves per cylinder—open and close to control flow of air-gas mixture into cylinders and burned gases out of cylinders to exhaust system)
7. Cylinder head (two required on this engine—bolted to block to seal off tops of cylinders above pistons; contains intake and exhaust block)
8. Cylinder head gasket (seals joint between cylinder head and cylinder block)
9. Piston and piston pin (six of each required on this engine—pin connects piston to connecting rod)
10. Piston rings (springy metal rings that maintain seal between piston and cylinder as piston moves up and down)
11. Connecting rod bearing (split steel sleeve with soft metal inner surface, separated from crankshaft journal by thin layer of oil)
12. Connecting rod and cap (cap bolted to connecting rod, holding connecting rod bearing tightly)
13. Block (main engine casting—cylinders and certain flat surfaces machined to smoothness)
14. Main crankshaft bearings
15. Crankshaft gear (pulls timing chain so that camshaft turns half as fast as crankshaft)
16. Crankshaft (heavy steel shaft with four main bearing journals concentric with shaft axis and six connecting rod bearing journals off center—the shaft is drilled to allow oil to flow from holes in the block to the main bearings and from there to the connecting rod bearings)
17. Oil pump (gear-type pump that takes a suction from the oil pan and discharges to holes drilled through the block to all points requiring oil under pressure)
18. Oil pan gaskets (cork and rubber pieces that maintain seal between oil pan and bottom of cylinder block)
19. Oil pan (sheet metal pan that collects motor oil returning from the various lubricated points)

sonal friend of Pat, ordered a 1974 250-cubic-inch short block. (A short block is a basic engine core, without the cylinder head, oil pan, oil pump, and several other parts that can be reused. They accounted for about 20 percent of the engines Bennett sold.) Pat felt Winkles was qualified to install the engine. "Otherwise, I would have questioned the customer to make sure the job could be done right. Re-

placing an engine is major surgery. It must not be done by amateurs."

Pat recorded the order on the yellow legal pad mentioned earlier and checked the *Four-Star Engine Catalog* (published by a national engine rebuilder) for casting numbers of the 250-cubic-inch 1974 Chevrolet engines. He found there were two. Notes Pat had made in the catalog revealed that one used a straight and the other an offset starter motor. After having Winkles look to see which he had, Pat wrote the distinguishing feature, "straight starter," above the record on the legal pad.

Pat told the teardown man, Lac Xuan Huyn, that he had added an order to the list. That day, Lac checked the order record and located the appropriate used engine among the several thousand piled here and there around the shop (to augment the supply of exchanged engines from previous jobs, Bennett bought some from a travelling used engine dealer and from individuals who called or came by from time to time). Lac disassembled the engine, then distributed parts to the crankshaft grinding area (crankshaft, pistons, and connecting rods) and the headwork area (cylinder heads). Lac placed the block near the two cleaning machines, which work like large dishwashers but use caustic soda (lye) instead of regular detergent. He put the camshaft in a wood box. The contents of the box were shipped periodically to Cam-Recon, a shop in Houston, Texas, for regrinding. Bolts and valve pushrods were placed in appropriate bins. The oil pan and timing cover were set aside for reuse on this or another engine. And certain parts, mostly sheet metal items such as rocker-arm covers, were discarded.

Bennett's machinists were responsible for checking the legal pad record of orders and making sure parts were available for jobs listed there. There were no written procedures, about this or anything else, and the machinists often failed to verify parts availability. Still, the system worked about as intended for the Winkles engine. Dale LeBlanc, who operated the cylinder boring machines, checked to see that the correct pistons and rings were on hand. He found that the ring set was not in stock. Curtis Manuel, who ground crankshafts and sized connecting rods, located a crankshaft for the engine—as usual, not the one Lac had just delivered. Curtis checked the crankshaft with a micrometer to see how far he would have to grind it and then confirmed that he had all main and connecting rod bearings in the correct undersizes. Byron Woods, the assembler, checked the parts bins for the following items: gasket set, oil pump, matched camshaft and crankshaft gears, camshaft, camshaft bearings, and valve lifters. No gasket was set in stock. Dale and Byron, separately, called a Bennett's supplier in Houston and ordered needed parts, confirming that parts would arrive by bus or UPS the next day.

Dale washed the engine block in one of the cleaning machines. Then, he took the block to the cylinder boring area and "magnafluxed" it. This process involves sprinkling iron fillings over unmachined surfaces and placing a large electromagnet at strategic points. Any crack would have been indicated by a string of concentrated iron fillings. None existed. Dale selected a box of six 0.030-inch oversize 250 Chevrolet pistons. After measuring one of the pistons with a micrometer, he proceeded to bore the cylinders to 0.001 inches larger than the piston size, manually checking cylinder diameters with a hand-held bore gauge after each cut. He visually inspected each cylinder for cracks. Then the block was placed in a honing yank where, in a bath of number 2 jet fuel, the cylinders were honed to 0.002 to 0.003 of an inch beyond the piston size. Dale cleaned the engine again, this time finishing with a steam cleaner. Finally, he sprayed the cylinder walls with light oil and delivered the block to the assembly area.

Still on August 9, Curtis Manuel cleaned the crankshaft he had checked for Winkles's engine. He then positioned it on the crankshaft grinder set up to grind main bearing journals (the shiny surfaces that turn in the main bearings). During grinding, Curtis carefully observed the Arnold gauge, which he had positioned to indicate the undersize dimension in ten-thousandths of an inch. After grinding the main journals to 0.010 of an inch undersize, Curtis moved the shaft to the other grinding machine in an adjacent room and left it set up to do connecting rod journals (Pat said the two machines were located across a wall from each other "to keep from having to rig another electric box"). There, he machined the connecting rod journals to 0.020 of an inch undersize. The whole operation took about one hour. Curtis then cleaned and oiled the crankshaft, as Dale had done for the block, and placed the shaft in a plastic tube. It, too, was taken to the assembly area. Next, Curtis searched the waist-high pile of connecting rods and pistons at his work station for six Chevrolet 250 connecting rods. Unsure of his selection, he called Byron, the assembler, to help verify he had the right ones. Byron confirmed Curtis's choice. Curtis then pressed out each piston pin (the short shaft that joins the piston to the connecting rod). Then, he placed each rod in a rod vise, and using a torque wrench (a wrench that indicates the amount of twisting force being applied), tightened the nuts that secure the rod cap. Next, Curtis measured the inside dimension at the crankshaft end of each rod. Finding all measurements to be within specifications (plus or minus 0.005 inches), he cleaned the rods. Then, he got the box of pistons Dale had used in sizing the cylinders and installed them on the rods. The pistons with rods attached were taken to the assembly area.

If Winkles had ordered a complete engine, instead of just a short block, Scott McConathy or Martin Simmons, the machinists who recondition cylinder heads, would have been involved. Reconditioning a cylinder head mainly consists of resizing the valve guides, grinding valves, and valve seats and regrinding the cylinder head surface. After these operations, the cylinder head is cleaned, reassembled, and painted.

At about 3:00 P.M., Byron finished his previous job and began assembling the Winkles engine. He visually checked each cylinder for cracks. Then, he painted the surfaces of the block that would be exposed to oil with Cast Blast, a grey paint that seals cast iron surfaces and minimizes sludge buildup. Byron also painted the exterior surfaces of the block the appropriate original color. Next, he installed the plugs in the block, which seal holes required for certain casting and machining operations. After that, he manually installed the piston rings on the pistons. Byron then installed the major parts in the block—bearings, camshaft, crankshaft, and pistons—tightening all bolts to specified tightness and checking each part for free movement. Finally, he performed a careful inspection of the entire engine, recording the results on a specially designed form—kiddingly referred to as "the birth certificate."

The finished short block was placed in a bag and banded to a small pallet. The next day, Thomas Winkles picked up his new engine. A few days later, he dropped his old one by Bennett's.

Over-the-Fender Work

Over-the-fender work at Bennett's mainly involved removing and replacing engines. Of course, this often required replacing water hoses, vee belts, and other items that were worn or damaged at the time of the engine job. The engine warranty (12,000 miles or six months) was conditioned upon an exhaust gas analysis, which often revealed the need for carburetor work. Radiator disassembly and cleaning was also required as a condition of warranty, even for carryout engines. In addition to work related to engine replacement, Bennett's accepted general automobile repair work, such as carburetor rebuilding and air conditioning component replacement.

Unlike the machinists discussed above, the mechanics furnished their own hand tools. Bennett's provided testing equipment, hoists, pressurized air systems, floor jacks and stands, hydraulic lifts, and cleaning equipment. Each mechanic has a separate work stall.

"We had a terrible, terrible parts situation. The situation was so out of control, I was actually looking at parts purchases as overhead and not as a profit producer. Items were either not getting on the tickets, or not getting on the cars." To correct this situation, Pat assigned one mechanic, his best, as checker to make sure every part put on each car was on the respective invoice. He also closed all charge accounts with parts suppliers, requiring mechanics to come to Pat or his shop coordinator, Jack Beard, to get a check for any parts purchase. "Now we've got some control over it."

Bennett's kept an inventory of common engine filters, ignition components, vacuum hoses and fittings, and nuts and bolts. Mechanics were required to order and pick up other necessary parts. Pat said, "We don't stock any radiator hoses, belts, or water pumps because there are just too many different ones."

Richard Hardesty, one of the mechanics Pat had laid off in July, leased one of the company's three buildings and the equipment in it to do general automotive repair, engine installations, and exhaust system repairs. Pat explained, "Our whole objective was to get the payroll down. Payroll taxes are a burden. And the $675 lease payment will come in handy. I was able to rent the building to Richard so cheaply because we don't owe anything on it."

Tool Sharpening and Modification

Boeing's operations in Lake Charles involved a great deal of drilling and reaming, especially of rivet holes in the skins of the KC-135s. Many screwed fasteners required countersunk holes to preserve a flush exterior surface. The thousands of drill bits, reamers, and countersinks used by Boeing required frequent modification or sharpening. Also on numerous occasions, specialized tools such as reamer extensions had to be made, modified, or repaired. When Boeing had trouble locating a local supplier for these services, Pat Bennett volunteered to do the work and negotiated a single-source supply contract with Boeing procurement.

Gearing up to do this highly technical work consumed most of Pat's energy and time from February to August 1987. A 1,000-square-foot area of the machine shop building was enclosed and modified to house the tool work. A large horizontal lathe, a cylindrical grinder, two form-relief grinders, two tool and cutter grinders, and a drill bit sharpening machine were purchased and installed in the temperature-controlled enclosure. To find these machines, Pat traveled to Wichita, Cincinnati, Dallas, and Houston.

Boeing was on an extremely tight schedule on its own contract with the Air Force and there were frequent emergencies, often involving innovative solutions to unique problems. For example, Pat stayed up all one night sharpening and resharpening a special cobalt drill bit then being used to drill through a titanium alloy engine mount. Much experimentation was required on this and other jobs, and Pat worked many nights and weekends to solve problems.

Generally, Pat Bennett picked up the tools to be modified at the Boeing plant, a few hundred yards from the machine shop, and returned them there. Because of a Boeing procedure, the tools that only needed sharpening were picked up at a Boeing warehouse at the Lake Charles Port, four miles away. Each batch of tools to be serviced was accompanied by a work order providing instructions for the work to be done. For nonstandard modifications, Pat frequently had to call or visit the supervisor who wrote the order and get clarification of the instructions.

Five machinists, three on days and two on evenings, were hired to do the Boeing work. Two only sharpened drill bits, while the others did the work on countersinks, reamers, and special tools. James Smith, the machinist that Pat charged with quality control for the Boeing contract, did most of the particularly innovative operations. For example, Smith designed and made a number of torque wrench extensions that allowed workers to tighten nuts that were not directly accessible.

Pat personally trained the machinists to do the repetitive operations. "The most difficult operation to perfect was grinding the flutes of a piloted reamer so that they would cut. We were finally able to do it on a German form-relief grinder. Everything on it was written in German. We couldn't read any of the buttons except the one which said 'halt.'" The machine came to be used solely for grinding the cutting

edges on piloted reamers. A large magnifying glass was installed so the machinist could see the tiny flutes. With his left hand, the machinist would orient one of the six flutes on a reamer. Then with his right hand he would move the grinding head into the reamer flute and back, grinding the tiny cutting edge at precisely ten degrees. This was repeated on each of the six flutes. Because of the exactness required, the grinding wheel had to be reshaped daily with a diamond "dresser."

Drill bit sharpening is a fairly standard operation, although the Boeing specification added some complexity. Bennett's drill bit sharpening machine was hardly state of the art, requiring several manual manipulations of each bit sharpened. Still, sharpening each bit took only 45 seconds.

The two-way form-relief grinder used to sharpen countersinks was almost completely automatic. Once the machinist oriented a countersink to the ground, the machine did the rest. The task took about four minutes per countersink.

A great deal of skill was required to set up each of the operations described above and especially to do the custom tool making. But according to Pat, a person of average dexterity could learn any of the repetitive jobs in a day or two.

PERSONNEL

In late 1987, Bennett's employed sixteen people in addition to Pat and Jack Beard, the shop coordinator. There were five machinists and a radiator repairman in the automotive machine shop, five mechanics in the service department, and five machinists in the tool grinding shop.

Jack Beard had been with Bennett's four years. He was about 29 years old. A hard worker, Jack often spent ten hours a day at the shop, including every Saturday—except during hunting season, when Jack and Byron, the assembler, alternated Saturdays. On a weekend in August, Jack rebuilt the engine in a Chevrolet Citation he had bought. The following Monday, he told Pat, "I can see how they have such a hard time getting any motors built. There is only one air hose, tools are scattered everywhere, and the place is filthy dirty."

Pat observed that Jack was right. He had tried several ways to get the workers to keep the shop clean, at one point assigning each person just one little area to clean. "Nothing worked, so that morning I just pulled the main breaker. When everything shut down and the men came to see why, I told them I would restore the power when the shop was clean." Two of the main culprits came in to punch in on the time clock (they were on piece rates) so they would be paid for doing the cleaning. Pat objected to paying them "for cleaning up a mess they had a big part in creating," and they both quit. Asked how he replaced the men, Pat replied, "They weren't worth replacing."

The automotive machinists, Lac, Dale, Curtis, Scott, Martin, and Byron, were mentioned earlier. None had been automotive machinists when Bennett hired them, although Curtis had taken a regular machinist course at a local trade school. Lance Hammack, the radiator repairman, also learned his trade at Bennett's. He had been a welder. Pat said, "It is much easier to teach a person a new trade than to get a person who already knows a trade to change bad work habits."

Lac, a Vietnamese, was hired in 1985. Pat said, "He had to bring an interpreter to apply for the job, he could speak so little English. But his attitude—he just seemed so eager. He learned very rapidly. Meticulous. Pays attention to detail. Terribly dependable. I don't know that he ever missed a day—never even asks for time off."

Dale, Curtis, Martin, and Lance had all been with Bennett's less than six months. Dale was a construction worker before Pat hired him. "Couldn't even read a micrometer," said Pat, "He had some kind of hangup about reading the dial. I got him a micrometer with a digital readout and three days later he was operating the cylinder boring machine." Curtis knew how to run a lathe when he was hired. "So we put him on our crankshaft grinder." (The two machines have similarities but are far from identical.) Martin had been a paint and body technician before Pat hired him. "He turns out the prettiest paint jobs on cylinder heads you ever saw," Pat kidded. Martin worked most Saturdays, in addition to full days during the week. Radiator work was not a full-time job at Bennett's, so Lance helped out in the office, drove the delivery truck, and did other tasks.

Scott and Byron had been hired about four years earlier—Scott right out of high school, Byron off the unemployment line. According to Pat, Scott had a strong interest in cars. "He was easy to train, always thinking. I could just give him a few pointers and he would go with it. He is very thorough. I don't have to check anything he tells me. He doesn't mind stay-ing late during the week, but he likes his Saturdays off." Scott did almost all the "really difficult head jobs—the overhead cams, heads that need new valve seats." Byron, young and unskilled, had started doing engine teardowns. "Most machinists are too proud to do that; they think that is the low-class job in the shop. Byron was so easy-going. There was nothing he wouldn't try to learn, if you needed him to do it."

Next Byron had mastered the cylinder boring machine. Pat told how Byron got his next job: "I was grinding the crankshafts at that time. You should have seen me—an Extendaphone on my belt and a Sony Walkman under my shirt. People thought the Walkman was part of the machine. But I was grooving, listening to fifties music while I watched the cranks go round and round." Pat's wife, Cheryl, was "acting secretary" (the regular secretary had left due to illness) at the time. Cheryl quit after Pat threw a can of blue engine paint at her, so he had to take over the office. Another man, later fired for suspected theft, took over the boring machine, and Byron moved to the crankshaft grinder, relieving Pat. "That was a major accomplishment for Byron," Pat said, "He had never even run a lathe." Byron stayed with that job until March 1987, when he started assembling engines.

The five mechanics were Ronnie Smith, Tim "Tamale" Authemont, Kenneth Thornton, Clyde Brown, and Kevin "Goat" Gauthreaux. Ronnie, in his fourth year at Bennett's, was responsible for inspecting and test driving every vehicle repaired, regardless of who did the work. He also did mechanic work himself—all the carburetor work, certain diesel-to-gasoline conversions, and most of the computer checks. But Ronnie refused to do engine replacements in front-wheel-drive cars. Tim was a helper, supervised and paid by Ronnie. Tim had been with Bennett's over two years, but had worked as Ronnie's helper only about six months.

Kenneth Thornton was the longest-tenured employee Pat had, having been hired eight years earlier, when the shop was on Prien Lake Road. He did most of the engine replacements on front-wheel-drive cars, certain diesel-to-gasoline conversions, and regular repair work.

Clyde and Kevin had only worked at Bennett's a couple of months. Both did all kinds of engine replacements as well as a wide range of other mechanic work. Both were in their early thirties, married, and with children. Pat said, "I am really impressed with their attitudes. Unlike many mechanics, they are not afraid of this new generation of cars—mostly transverse-engined, fuel injected, and computer controlled."

The machinists who did the tool work were James Smith (Ronnie's brother), James McManus, Craig McMichael, John Shearer, and Billy Lambert. James Smith had worked on and off for Bennett's for about five years, doing various construction jobs. He had been hired full time in March 1987. Pat said, "In the early weeks of the Boeing job, I was running that German form-relief grinder while James was building the room around me." As the Boeing work had begun to increase, Pat had taught James to run the grinder. "I would run it on the weekends, he'd do it during the week." James had paid his own way to go with Pat and locate other machines to buy.

James McManus and Billy worked evenings. Craig and John worked days. James and Craig did reamers and countersinks. Billy and John sharpened drill bits. All four were in their early twenties. Pat recruited James and Craig through Sowela Tech, a local voc-tech school, and James continued as a coop student there. John's father, who worked at the Boeing port warehouse, had recommended his unemployed son to Pat one day as Pat picked up an order. John had later recommended Billy.

The automotive machinists, except for Curtis (who operated the crankshaft grinder), were paid on a piece-rate basis, so much for each type of operation and each model of engine. Each has an established hourly rate as well, which is applied to work other than their normal assignments. Curtis was paid on an hourly basis.

The mechanics were paid a combination of piece-rates, commissions, and hourly rates. Piece-rates applied to engine replacements. Most other automotive work was done on a commission basis— each mechanic got one-half of all labor charges that the mechanic generated. Hourly rates were paid for warranty work, like that for the dealerships, and guaranteed the mechanics a weekly minimum.

The machinists who did the tool grinding were all paid by the hour. At first, Pat set the machinists' wages according to the Boeing pay scale. But when Boeing tried to hire some of his people, he hiked the rate by about 40 percent. "I pay James Smith more than the rest, but he and I have an agreement that he doesn't get any overtime pay when he works over forty hours."

Jack Beard, the shop coordinator, and Lance Hammack, the radiator repairman, were also paid by the hour.

Bennett's provided limited fringe benefits. There was a group health plan, paid entirely by the employees. Several chose not to participate. Each employee received six paid holidays each year (after a ninety-day waiting period) and a one-week paid vacation each year after the first. Bennett's paid all costs over one dollar a day of uniform costs, although workers were not required to wear them. "I also let the men work on their personal and family cars in the shop after hours and on weekends."

MARKETING

Exhibit 4 provides demographic and economic data for Bennett's market area.

Spring Street, where Bennett's was located, was "off the beaten path and far from the business district," according to Pat. He said, "The best thing about the location is [that] it's one block outside the city limits. No one bothers us out here, no matter how messy it gets." It was messy. Except for concrete areas, grass and weeds were everywhere. Piles of greasy used engines were here and there—even next to the street behind the facility. Inside the machine shop building, half the space was occupied by piles of engines and useless remnants of others long deceased. Individual blocks, heads, and other parts as well as several derelict cars littered the property, especially around the edges of driveways and other concrete areas. Everywhere there was grease and oil. Two large pitch-coated septic tanks and a stack of rusting metal shelves added to the confusion. A dingy, although lighted, 3-by-4-foot sign near the lobby and office area announced "Bennett's Machine Shop—Engine Rebuilding."

Thirty-second television spots featuring Pat Bennett ran throughout the year at a cost of about $350 per month. A feature article written by Pat appeared in the *American Press*, the local paper, once a month, at a cost of $114 per month. Once a year, when business was slow, a Bennett's supplement would be distributed with the 48,000-circulation newspaper. The cost was $1,600 for each distribution. The supplement offered discounts, good for two months with presentation of the flyer, on reconditioned engines—$50 on carryouts, $100 on installations. "The first time we did this, two years ago," said Pat, "We

Exhibit 4

GEOGRAPHIC AND DEMOGRAPHIC DATA

	LAKE CHARLES	CALCAUSIEU PARISH (COUNTY)	SOUTHWEST LOUISIANA[a]	LOUISIANA	UNITED STATES
Population (July 1980)	77,400	167,223	259,908	4,206,000	226,546,000
Per capita income, 1985	$10,183	$10,224	$8,806	$10,741	$12,772
Change in *real* per capita income, 1980–1985 (percent change for period)	1.2	1.3	1.6	2.3	2.8
Workforce employed in manufacturing, March 1987 (percent)	7.4	17.3	16.2	11.2	18.8
Workforce employed in construction, March 1987 (percent)	8.7	9.4	9.0	6.2	3.0
Land area (square miles)	27	1,082	5,083	44,521	3,539,289

a. Southwest Louisiana parishes include Allen Beaureard, Calcasieu, Cameron, and Jefferson Davis

had to shut down and just answer the phones and take orders for two days. We sold 28 engines, almost a whole page, that time."

A form letter was sent to engine customers, thanking them for the business and asking for referrals to other prospective customers. Once a year, during the local festival called "Contraband Days," Bennett's subscribed to a radio advertising special. A thirty-second spot was run sixty times during a ten-day period at a cost of $450. Pat said, "I've never seen a sale directly related to radio advertising. We did it one time, and they hounded us the next year till I agreed to do it."

Major competitors for engine sales were Dimick Supply company, 100,000 Auto Parts, and Hi-Lo Auto Parts. None of these did installations, and all bought their engines from large remanufacturers. No local automobile service shop other than Bennett's specialized in rebuilt engines, although most bought and installed them from time to time. Periodically, Pat Bennett checked the prices that competitors charged for engines, often simply by calling and asking. He also kept current catalogs and price sheets for the engine remanufacturers who supplied Bennett's competitors. "We get their catalogs because we're a jobber, and sometimes we sell truck engines we buy from others—because the risk is so high if a truck engine fails."

Asked where he set his prices relative to the competition, Pat replied, "We make sure we're a little under everybody except Hi-Lo. They sell almost nothing but short blocks remanufactured in Texas. They are ridiculously low."

Pat said that the quality of all the engines was about the same. "But if you have a problem with a Four-Star or a Roadrunner [the brands sold by Bennett's competitors] you bought from, say, Dimmick, you have to take it out and wait for them to send it back to Texas. And they normally don't help you with labor. By way of contrast, a Bennett's customer can just bring the car in to be taken care of—if it is within warranty and hasn't been overheated or run out of oil." Pat complained, "Carryout customers will go to somebody else if there is just a $20 difference. It bothers me that customers will bring us their car if anything goes wrong, expecting to fix it free. They wouldn't think of doing this at Hi-Lo or Dimmick." He explained that parts-and-labor warranties, in general, only apply to situations where the labor is supplied by the vendor. "Sometimes, a customer will even call me for advice about some trouble with an engine he bought from a parts house. I tell him to call the parts house."

Mechanic labor, priced at $30 per hour, was based on the time estimates in the *Chilton Flat-Rate Manual* (a book that gives estimated times to do all

kinds of repair operations for most automobiles and light trucks). Most good mechanics can beat the flat-rate times significantly. Bennett's priced most parts, other than engines, at locally competitive retail rates. The local parts houses gave Bennett's a 20-percent discount off retail. List prices, usually about 40 percent above retail, are shown on parts house invoices. Pat said, "If we think the list price is fair and the customer is unlikely to check with a parts house, we often use list instead of retail."

For the Boeing work, prices were set according to contract. Drill bit sharpening was so much per item. The other operations were done by the hour. At first, Boeing allowed Bennett's to charge very profitable prices. After the work had totalled about $137,000, Boeing audited Bennett's cost and revised the prices downward by more than 50 percent. The audit was conducted by Boeing's Vendor Cost Analysis (VCA) group and involved many lengthy meetings with four different teams of auditors. In fact, Bennett's initial contract was apparently so renumerative that Boeing assigned a security investigator who asked many questions, implying possible collusion between Pat and various Boeing officials.

Boeing held up payment on past invoices while pressure was exerted on Bennett's to reprice previously submitted invoices at the VCA determined rates. Pat successfully insisted that the invoices be paid as submitted. He did accept the VCA prices during month-to-month renewals of the contract, while Boeing made plans to let the work out for bids. Meanwhile, he was trying to decide how to bid the work. He was making money at the new rates. Profits on the earlier contract had more than paid for all his machines. So he was tempted to bid even a little below the VCA numbers. But he knew that Boeing was having trouble finding other vendors with even minimal competence to do the work, and he had served Boeing faithfully, and at great cost to his other business, for several months.

FINANCE

Exhibits 5 and 6 give financial summaries for Bennett's Machine Shop, Inc. For ten years, Pat Bennett had employed a local accounting firm, Management Services, Inc., to keep financial records, prepare financial statements and sales and income tax returns, submit business license applications, and so forth. During the 1987 tax season, Bennett's was not able to get Management Services to prepare the usual monthly profit and loss statements. Pat explained, "They said they couldn't get to it. So I changed to a real CPA firm in the Lakeside Plaza Building—and that was worse. This guy had less time than Management Services. When he finally, after 60 days, got the first month done, he asked me to come in at 9:00 one day. I got there at 9:15, and nobody except the secretary was at work. I passed him on the sidewalk with his briefcase and his three-piece suit. That's the last time I saw him."

After firing his new accountant, Pat talked with Dorothy McConathy, who had been assigned his work at Management Services, and asked whom he could get to do his bookkeeping. "Dorothy had already told her boss she was going to quit when she got one more account on the side. She already had two, so she agreed to keep my books and gave Management Services notice."

After buying the boring bar when he first started rebuilding engines in 1982, Pat never directly contributed any more equity funds to the business. Equipment vendors furnished financing for most of the machines he bought. When Pat started to buy a used crankshaft grinder, which he had found at a shop in Plaquemine Parish, he approached the bank that handled his checking account. Pat had taken out a few small personal loans at the bank, but the loan officer who had approved them was gone at the time. The bank president refused to loan Pat the $6,400 he needed to buy the machine.

"I got my little file from him and went over to the new American Bank of Commerce," said Pat. Three years later, he needed the $80,000 to buy the Chennault property. "American Bank of Commerce wouldn't make a decision, so I went back to Gulf National. My friend Lloyd Rion, the loan officer who had given the loan three years earlier, was there. He gave me the money, and I moved our checking account back." The loan was a ten-year, fixed-rate loan at 10 percent interest.

From 1980 to 1985, Pat took out several 90-day loans to make additions to the shop facilities. The bank allowed him to roll the loans over once. "Those were super productive years. We never had any money problems."

When Pat bought the Ryan Street shop in 1985, which he sold 14 months later, the seller financed the whole $180,000, for ten years at 10 to 14 percent variable rate. "That's when our trouble started," said Pat, "We loaded up the company with operating

Exhibit 5
BENNETT'S MACHINE SHOP, INC.: INCOME STATEMENTS

	FISCAL YEAR[a]			
	1985	*1986*	*1987*	*1988*[b]
Revenue				
Automotive	$926,243	$1,091,890	$971,950	$140,131
Aircraft tool	—	—	13,318	140,679
	$926,243	$1,091,890	$985,268	$280,810
Less Direct Costs				
Materials	$456,828	$ 570,372	$504,811	$ 64,939
Labor	248,833	316,164	271,858	53,693
Freight	—	—	—	1,031
Total Direct Costs	705,661	886,536	776,669	119,663
Gross Profit	$220,582	$ 205,354	$208,599	$161,147
Less General and Administrative Expenses				
Advertising	$ 10,697	$ 15,831	$ 17,828	$ 1,193
Depreciation	33,550	42,240	29,222	7,269
Equipment leasing	5,680	950	1,657	—
Insurance	23,100	39,298	35,528	11,359
Interest	22,060	24,044	26,504	8,841
Miscellaneous	4,867	7,205	7,020	4,438
Office labor	6,815	11,420	13,300	3,961
Office supplies	5,883	7,015	6,458	2,219
Professional fees	3,696	8,373	6,622	1,175
Taxes	5,623	4,825	5,926	245
Utilities and telephone	15,871	30,767	27,933	8,830
Total General and Administrative Expenses	137,842	191,968	177,996	49,530
Net Income	$ 82,740	$ 13,359	$ 30,603	$111,617
Withdrawals[c]	(61,500)	(53,389)	(70,755)	(17,109)
EARNINGS REINVESTED	$ 21,240	$(40,030)	(40,152)	$ 94,508

a. Fiscal year ends April 30.
b. May to August, 1987.
c. Includes funds to pay income taxes. The corporation is taxed as a partnership/proprietorship under Subchapter S of the Internal Revenue Code

Exhibit 6
BENNETT'S MACHINE SHOP, INC.: BALANCE SHEET[a]

	1985	*1986*	*1987*	*1988*[b]
ASSETS				
Current Assets				
Cash	$ 11,698	$ 1,206	$ 3,475	$ 5,384
Accounts receivable, trade	—	1,225	16,662	65,436

	1985	1986	1987	1988[b]
ASSETS				
Notes receivable,				
stockholder	—	22,568	22,568	22,569
Inventory	37,548	45,436	45,436	45,436
Total Current Assets	$49,246	$70,435	$88,141	$138,825
Fixed assets				
Furniture and				
equipment	$205,292	$165,886	$193,432	$212,209
Buildings	305,657	155,657	155,657	155,657
Total depreciation	510,949	321,543	349,089	367,866
Less accumulated				
depreciation	(133,559)	(134,067)	(143,834)	(155,081)
Net depreciable assets	377,390	187,476	205,255	212,785
Land	126,418	90,000	90,000	90,000
Total Fixed Assets	503,808	277,476	295,255	302,785
Other Assets				
Deposits	492	342	342	342
TOTAL ASSETS	$553,546	$348,253	$383,738	$441,952
LIABILITIES AND CAPITAL				
Current Liabilities				
Accounts payable, trade				
and other	$ 12,727	$ 25,062	$ 29,407	$ 31,242
Notes payable, current	103,160	16,385	60,299	57,775
Accrued payroll taxes,				
interest	—	—	3,223	1,571
Total Current				
Liabilities	$115,887	$ 41,447	$ 92,929	$ 90,588
Long-Term Liabilities				
Notes payable	266,720	175,897	200,052	166,099
Total Liabilities	382,607	217,344	292,981	256,687
Stockholders' Equity				
Common stock	10,000	10,000	10,000	10,000
Retained earnings	160,939	120,909	80,757	175,265
Total Capital	170,939	130,909	90,757	185,265
TOTAL LIABILITIES AND				
CAPITAL	$553,546	$348,253	$383,738	$441,952

a. As of April 30 except for 1988.
b. As of August 31, 1987

loans—a $25,000 three-year loan, a $24,000 five-year loan, and another three-year loan for $12,000, all from Calcasieu Marine Bank. I also let the work force run up to twenty-two people. It was a real runaway situation."

Pat described 1986 as "one helluva bad year." "That's when we could have used some input from the bookkeeper," said Pat. "I didn't realize that payroll and the taxes related to it were having such a devastating effect. We had almost the same sales as in 1984. Just the increase in payroll-based taxes was $70,000. What really ticked me off was that I had to figure this out and show him [the bookkeeper]." Pat had to refinance the ten-year loan on the Chennault property. "I put off laying off the extra people from January to August," said Pat, "That cost me another $40,000 and made me have to redo the loan." Bennett's showed a $12,000 profit in November that year. Pat said, "It was our first three-page month in a long time. I was scared to death. If we had not made a profit with that kind of sales, I didn't know what else to do." On the way to a New Year's Eve party, Pat made himself a promise: "I will not go through another year like that." A friend asked, "What are you going to do to prevent that—as if you have some control over it." "I'm going to work my tail off," Pat replied.

The machinery to do the Boeing work was all financed with $37,000 in 90-day notes at Calcasieu Marine. Another financial crisis came in August, when Boeing held up payment and engine sales collapsed. Pat was able to sell enough assets to meet the payroll and pay operating expenses, but he was unable to pay maturing loans. So Pat mortgaged his condominium and consolidated the three term loans into one $45,000, five-year mortgage. Boeing paid its account up to date in early September, and Pat paid off the $37,000 in 90-day notes.

Until 1987, all the loans mentioned above were in Pat's and Cheryl's personal names, although entered on the company books and sometimes secured by company assets. The $45,000 mortgage loan from Calcasieu Marine was put in the company name, "so we could deduct the interest under the new tax law," according to Pat. But Pat and Cheryl had to endorse the note personally and sign continuing guaranty agreements with the bank.

GORDON BLACK PLC

FRANK MARTIN
University of Stirling

In 1985, Gordon Black, founder and managing director of Gordon Black plc, identified the need to raise £850,000. A proportion of this amount would provide additional working capital for the steady expansion of the existing business and the majority would finance his company's move into giant waterslides. He realized that he was risking the future of the company on the continued popularity of waterslides. But the opportunity seemed too good to miss.

FORMATION

The company was formed in 1981 by Gordon Black under the name of Gordon Black Products. Since its foundation, the company has expanded its operations into three established areas of activity.

1. *The supply of swimming pool equipment.* At the present time this activity accounts for a major proportion of the company's income and essentially involves the supply of equipment to operators of large commercial pools. Basically, this side of the business is a marketing machine, as none of the products sold are actually manufactured by the company. A product range of some 1,500 items is promoted through an effective color brochure and supported by a number of sales representatives. The company's product range is very extensive and provides a swimming pool manager with every product or service he or she might require. In its four years of business, total sales have amounted to £900,000.

2. *The International Swimming Pool Equipment Center.* The center provides a permanent exhibition venue for all those concerned with the design, refurbishment, and management of swimming pools. On view are products from companies who are preeminent in their field of specialization, such as Omega and Biwater Filtration Ltd. Visitors are invited to take part in detailed seminars held by the exhibitors. The center is situated at the company's headquarters in Warwickshire and makes a significant contribution to the company's profits—£50,000 per year (generated from fees paid by exhibitors). It has proved a useful promotional aid for the company's products.

3. *Swimming pool construction and refurbishment.* This side of the business seeks to negotiate contracts for the total supply of swimming pool equipment for new leisures complexes. Having secured the sole distribution rights within the United Kingdom for a new high-quality pool refurbishment material called FRE Coat, which replaces the need for tiles, the company hopes it will be in an excellent position to win such contracts. At present, the company is negotiating a contract worth £226,000, illustrating the lucrative nature of the business although the contract has yet to be delivered.

FOUNDER

Born in 1943, Gordon Black has been involved with swimming for almost all of his adult life. He was the chief coach of the Great Britain swimming team

---

This case, written specifically for this book, is printed by permission.

through two Olympic Games, in Mexico and in Munich. Later he had a career in television as a commentator on swimming events.

In 1981 Gordon Black decided to utilize his talents of selling and managing the media. He formed Gordon Black (Products) Limited to supply swimming pool equipment to operators of large commercial pools.

Much of the success of the company has been dependent upon his personal contribution. He is well known through the swimming world for his appreciation of the various problems facing swimming pool designers, builders, and managers.

COMPANY STRUCTURE

The company employs a total of eighteen full-time and part-time staff, which are distributed throughout the organization as shown in Exhibit 1. The number of employees has increased over recent years, reflecting the expansion of the company. The projected profit and loss account for the year ended December 31, 1986, predicts the staff payroll to be around £100,000.

Gordon Black believes that the present staffing level will be sufficient to cope with the expansion. The projected net profit per employee figure of £11,723, in comparison to a sales per employee figure of £43,980 is in line with other companies of the same size and nature.

Charles Edward qualified with Thornton Baker in 1965 as a chartered accountant and became a partner in the firm in 1976. While at Thornton Baker, the auditors of Gordon Black (Products), he became familiar with the company. In the early part of 1986 he joined Gordon Black plc as its finance director and company secretary.

Brian Scase acts as nonexecutive director for the company. He has been involved in the financial services sector for twenty years, holding a variety of senior posts with different investment companies.

In 1985, the company changed its status to that of a public limited company. With this change of status, Black hoped to streamline administration and to realize his long-term objective of operating a quoted company with interests throughout the leisure and recreation industry. Now the company is formed into a group of four subsidiaries whose activities are coordinated by the holding company, Gordon Black plc. An illustration of the company's structure is provided in Exhibit 2.

GIANT WATERSLIDES

Giant waterslides were first developed in the United States and Canada, where their success has proved unquestionable. Within Europe, waterslides are very much in their introductory stage. In the United Kingdom, they have been growing in popularity since they were first introduced in 1984—over fourteen were installed between 1985 and 1986.

Exhibit 1
MANAGEMENT STRUCTURE OF GORDON BLACK PLC

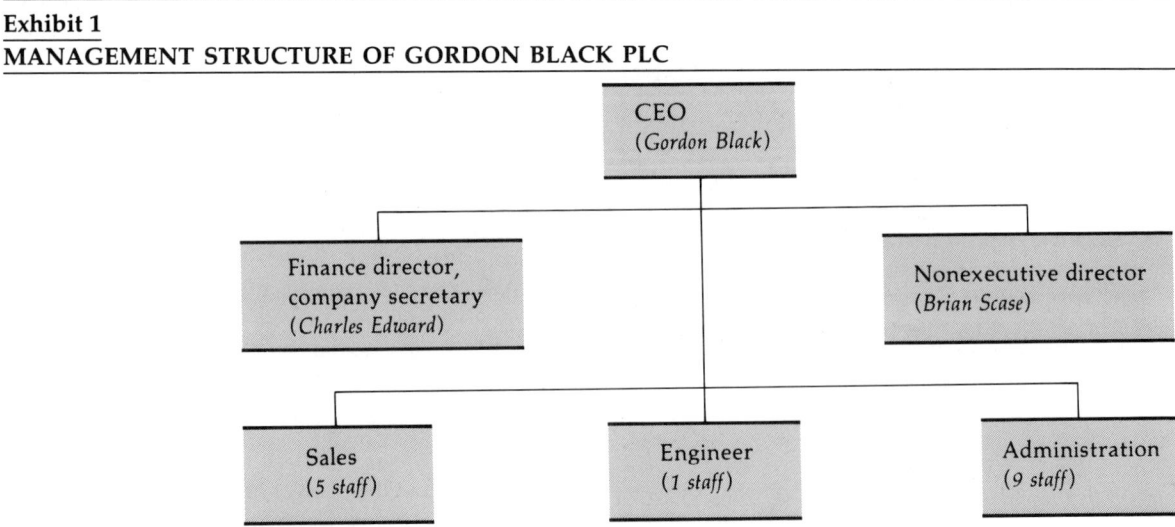

Exhibit 2
CORPORATE STRUCTURE OF GORDON BLACK PLC

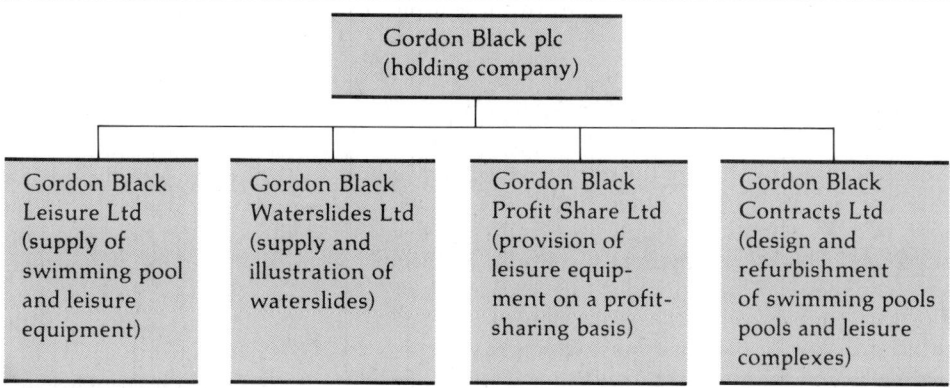

At the present time, it is rather difficult to assess the long-term popularity of giant waterslides. However, limited experience has shown that both adults and children are attracted to the idea of sliding down a water chute at around 15 miles per hour. So far, waterslides in the United Kingdom have varied between 26 meters and 185 meters in length (about 85 feet to 600 feet), with some developments incorporating the use of two separate slides.

During this period, Gordon Black, acting in an advisory capacity, has been involved with the installation of a number of waterslides throughout the United Kingdom. He has been able to devise and test his formula for selling a waterslide package to a local public authority.

THE MARKET

Over recent years the steady expansion of various sectors of the leisure industry has made them a lucrative and an attractive market for investors. Much of this expansion is due to the changing lifestyle of the population, which not only has more money but also more time to spend upon leisure pursuits.

Swimming as a leisure pursuit has always been a popular pastime, which has enjoyed a steady growth in its popularity (around 7 percent per year). This growth has been largely due to a number of reasons:

1. Swimming is a hobby that the whole family can enjoy at a reasonable price.
2. Recent years have seen an increase in the public's general awareness of health and fitness and swimming represents an all-round fitness program.
3. As the unemployed segment of the population has increased, local public authorities have felt obliged to provide adequate leisure pursuits.
4. Some 2,000 pools are managed by local public authorities and an additional 7,000 pools are managed by colleges, hotels, and leisure complexes. Thus, there is a constant demand for pool maintenance and a variety of equipment, including waterslides, to boost attendance rates.

In the new area of supplying and installing waterslides, Gordon Black hopes to monopolize a substantial part of this potential growth market. Specifically, he wants to target the local public authorities; already, his company supplies swimming pool equipment to 70 percent of local public authority pools. He has talked with several authority representatives and estimates that 30 percent of all authorities would be interested in installing giant waterslides in their pools (one per pool). In the provision of waterslides, the company's total potential market is 150 pools. This estimation is based on three assumptions.

1. One slide will satisfy the demand of several geographic areas controlled by an authority.
2. Some pools will be maintained for the serious swimmer.
3. Some pools offer site restrictions.

Yearly demand for giant slides was estimated at about thirty. By retaining the confidence of local public authorities, the company hopes to win contracts totalling 25 percent of the yearly demand—approximately eight waterslides.

Schools or hotels do not appear to offer sales possibilities, as they are unlikely to buy such a high-cost product.

CUSTOMERS

A significant proportion of the company's customer base is made up of local public authorities. However, the company does supply a growing number of private pools owned by hotels, colleges, and leisure complexes. Unfortunately for Gordon Black plc, local public authorities, notoriously bureaucratic, are slow to pay their bills, which has an adverse effect on the company's cash flow. Finance director Charles Edward hopes that cash flow problems will ease as the company widens its customer base. It is worth noting that the annual budget of all local public authorities spent on leisure is £832 million and that about one-tenth of this amount is spend upon the provision and maintenance of swimming pools.

Local public authorities characteristically allocate and spend their entire budget. Expenditures are restricted during the first nine months of the financial year to ensure that there will be adequate funds for the remainder of the year. During the final three months, funds are released more freely. This unusual spending pattern has had a significant impact on the turnover of Gordon Black plc.

Much of the success of this venture depends upon the company's ability to stimulate demand from local public authorities. Accordingly, Gordon Black plc has devised a special arrangement for these authorities in which they do not have to pay. In its simplest form, the arrangement proposed by the company would provide an extra facility that would raise attendance rates at their pools. At the same time, the company would not demand a capital outlay from the authorities—a most attractive provision.

In this package, Gordon Black plc will supply and install the slide, which will remain company property. At the same time, the authority will supply the site and will act as the company's agent in its day-to-day management. In return, the company will receive a major proportion of the net income until it recovers its capital outlay. From then after, the income from the waterslide will be shared equally for a period of up to fifteen years. An example of such a package is given in Exhibit 3.

Exhibit 3
EXAMPLE OF PACKAGE OFFERED TO LOCAL PUBLIC AUTHORITIES

In July 1985, a contract was negotiated with Rugby Borough Council to provide a waterslide for the Ken Mariod Leisure Center, which attracts 120,000 swimmers per year.

The package provided that:

1. Gordon Black plc would finance the construction of the waterslide.
2. Gordon Black plc would also provide for the necessary advertising and media relations.
3. Until the company had retrieved its capital investment plus interest (according to base rate) and a further 2 percent, it would receive:
   - 100 percent of waterslide income
   - 100 percent of increased swimming pool attendance
4. The company would also pay the £30,000 required for the maintenance and running of the slide.
5. Once the company had retrieved its capital outlay (plus extras) then the income generated by the waterslide would be split equally between the local public authority and the company.

COMPETITION

The supply of swimming pool equipment within the United Kingdom is very competitive and consists of around 100 different manufacturers with both specialist and more general product ranges. Approximately 115 different companies are involved in the supply of such equipment. However, these suppliers are generally specialists in outlook and none offer the comprehensive range provided by Gordon Black plc.

SALES

When Gordon Black started the company, he believed that he was entering a market segment that offered a great deal of potential.

Sales in 1985 reached £392,712 but the overall profit position by the end of December 1985 was in deficit to the tune of £42,520 (see Exhibit 4). This was a worrying trend from the position in 1983 and 1984, when the business was profitable (see Exhibit 5).

For some time Gordon Black has been concerned that the company is failing to generate sufficient profit to cover its interest payments. He believes that the situation can be reversed by rapidly devel-

oping the waterslide area of the business. The figure for profit (to December 1986) as given in Exhibit 4 details the possible impact of business in this area on the company's profitability.

The balance sheet given as Exhibit 6 reflects the company's needs for additional financing to support any order for giant waterslides.

Exhibit 4
GORDON BLACK PLC: INCOME STATEMENTS

	DECEMBER 1985	DECEMBER 1986
Product Contributions		
Pool equipment	£281,285	£253,157
Waterslides	43,046	253,000
Construction	—	144,000
Exhibition centre	34,058	30,652
Sundry	34,323	30,891
Gross Sales	£392,712	£711,700
Less Operating Expense	393,121	423,433
Profit before Interest	£ (409)	£279,267
Less Interest Expense	42,111	46,322
NET PROFIT (LOSS) BEFORE TAXES	£(42,520)	£232,945

Exhibit 5
GORDON BLACK PLC: FINANCIAL INFORMATION

SOURCE AND APPLICATION OF FUNDS	MARCH 1983	MARCH 1984	MARCH 1985
Source (Outflow) of Funds from Operations			
Profit (loss) on ordinary activities before taxation	£ 23,428	£26,171	£ 10,271
Extraordinary items	—	—	(10,500)
Total Funds from Operations	£ 23,428	£26,171	£ (229)
Adjustment for Items Not Involving the Movement of Funds			
Goodwill amortization	£ 10,000	£ 8,750	£ 13,500
Depreciation	16,176	18,007	18,595
Amount written off investments	—	—	10,500
Profit (loss) on disposal of fixed assets	(726)	77	(9,327)
Parents written off	—	—	—
Total Adjustment	25,450	26,834	33,268
From Other Sources			
Issue of share capital	£ 2,011	£ —	£ —
Proceeds of disposal of tangible fixed assets	9,000	10,197	38,900

Exhibit 5
GORDON BLACK PLC: FINANCIAL INFORMATION (*continued*)

SOURCE AND APPLICATION OF FUNDS	MARCH 1983	MARCH 1984	MARCH 1985
Long-term loans	125,000	—	—
Loan	—	—	—
Taxation refunded	—	—	—
Total Other Sources	136,011	10,197	38,900
Application of Funds			
Purchase of goodwill	£ 37,500	£ —	£ 6,000
Purchase of tangible fixed assets	206,601	82,536	21,169
Purchase of investment in the subsidiary company	—	8,000	2,500
Loan repayments	4,589	—	—
Total Application of Funds	248,690	90,536	29,669
NET INFLOW (OUTFLOW) OF FUNDS	£(63,801)	£(27,334)	£ 42,270
INCREASE (DECREASE) IN WORKING CAPITAL			
Capital			
Stocks	£ 40,510	£(37,070)	£ 22,560
Debtors	438,639	(166,571)	83,508
Creditors: Amounts falling due within one year	(533,613)	166,513	40,147
Creditors: Amounts falling due after more than one year	—	11,538	16,118
Total Capital	£(54,464)	£(25,474)	£162,333
Net Liquid Funds			
Cash at bank and in hand	10	19	(29)
Bank overdrafts	(7,347)	(1,744)	(120,034)
Total Liquid Funds	(7,337)	(1,725)	(120,063)
NET INCREASE (DECREASE) IN WORKING CAPITAL	£(61,801)	£(27,199)	£ 42,270

FINANCING

Gordon Black and his advisers now had to consider the most appropriate means of financing the company's expansion into giant waterslides.

Three possible ways of securing the necessary funding were identified:

1. *Banking.* The company's headquarters had recently been valued at £525,000, against which short-term finance amounting to £200,000 had previously been provided. This left the company able only to offer security or take out a mortgage to the sum of £325,000. The bankers to the company, The Midland Bank, have a business development loan scheme whereby long-term finance secured against such an asset could be repaid over a period of twenty years.

2. *Venture capital.* As a means of exploring an alternate source of funding, a list of prospective venture capitalists was drawn up. These venture capitalists, who specialize in financing companies of the same size and industry sector as Gordon Black plc, look for a rate of growth of 20 percent per year. Typically, a venture capitalist only looks to secure 10 percent to 40 percent of the equity of a venture that has gone beyond the startup stage. It was felt by the management that, given the existing equity base of the company, the amount of capital being sought would almost certainly have meant relinquishing a far larger stake than this.

3. *Business expansion scheme.* The third possibility examined was the Business Expansion Scheme (BES). This scheme was started in 1983 by the Thatcher government with the declared aim of providing "additional finance to smaller firms where there is a degree of risk involved commensurate with generous tax relief." The scheme encourages personal investors to take a stake in the small firms sector, allowing them to offset their top rate of income tax through investing between £500 and £40,000 per year in the shares of an unquoted company. Since its introduction, over 760 companies have benefited from the scheme.

To qualify under the BES, the company must be unquoted, be based in Britain, and offer an investment in ordinary shares with no preference rights. Excluded from the BES are companies that do more than half their trade in overseas countries and those that have more than half their assets tied up in land or buildings. A company can raise capital through BES in two ways:

a. A fund managed by a merchant bank or venture capitalist in which investors spread their money, and therefore their risk, over a number of firms

b. A direct issue where the company issues a prospectus and invites investors to subscribe for shares in the business

The large amount the company had to raise seemed to rule out the first of the two alternatives. The BES allows an entrepreneur to ask for a higher price for equity than might otherwise be acceptable. Investors are less interested in dividend payments than in securing the tax-free capital gains allowance given if the investors retain their equity stake for a five-year period.

DECISION

In March 1986, the company attempted to raise £850,000 through BES by means of a direct issue. A 32-page prospectus was produced offering 750,000 ordinary shares at a price of 125p each. The projections given to potential investors, showing the impact on the company's profitability of a move into the provision of giant waterslides, is given as Exhibit 7.

The objective was to raise £937,500. Of this amount, £50,000 was allotted for accountant's fees,

Exhibit 6

GORDON BLACK PLC: BALANCE SHEET (December 31, 1985)

ASSETS

Fixed Assets	
Land and buildings	£393,948
Other	6,875
Investments	—
Total Fixed Assets	£400,823
Current Assets	
Stock	£ 20,693
Work in progress	73,000
Debtors	284,603
Group loan	23,568
Directors loan	6,645
Cash in bank	1,095
Total Current Assets	409,604
Current Liabilities	
Loan	£ 76,804
Overdraft	192,000
Creditors	378,410
Total Current Liabilities	647,214
Net Current Assets	(237,610)
Net Assets	£163,213
Creditors (due after one year)	83,122
Provisions for liabilities and change	20,697
NET ASSETS	£ 59,394

CAPITAL

Capital and reserves	£ 2,011
Called up share capital	55,301
Revaluation reserve	2,082
CAPITAL EMPLOYED	£ 59,394

£20,000 for advertising costs, £15,000 for sponsor's fees, and £15,000 for producing the prospectus.

However, the 1986 spring budget introduced a 50 percent assets ruling[1], which had the immediate effect of confusing the eligibility of many companies

---

1. This ruling meant that companies with more than half of their net assets in land or property would not qualify for consideration within the BES. The BES was set up as a source of risk funding. In recent years too many low-rate companies in the property sector had been attracting BES funds and the tax concessions that came with them.

Exhibit 7
GORDON BLACK PLC: PROFIT PROJECTIONS, 1985–1992
(as of December 31)

	1985	1986	1987	1988	1989	1990	1991	1992
Product Contributions								
Pool equipment	£281,285	£309,414	£340,335	£374,390	£ 411,829	£ 453,012	£ 498,314	£ 548,145
Waterslides	43,046	253,000	303,600	364,320	437,184	524,621	629,545	755,454
Construction and re-furbishments	—	144,000	83,000	91,300	100,430	110,473	121,520	133,672
Exhibition centre	34,058	37,464	41,210	45,331	49,864	54,851	60,336	66,369
Sundry	34,323	37,755	41,531	45,684	50,252	55,279	60,805	66,886
Gross Sales	£ 39,712	£781,633	£809,676	£921,025	£1,049,559	£1,198,236	£1,370,520	£1,570,526
Less Operating Expenses	393,121	412,777	433,416	455,087	477,841	501,733	526,820	553,161
Profit before Interest	£ (409)	£368,856	£376,260	£465,938	£ 571,718	£ 696,503	£ 843,700	£1,017,365
Less Interest Expense	42,111	44,217	46,427	48,749	51,186	53,745	56,433	59,254
Net Profit (Loss) Before Taxes	£(42,520)	£324,639	£329,833	£417,189	£ 520,532	£ 642,758	£ 787,267	£ 958,111
Taxation at 35%	—	113,624	115,448	146,017	182,186	224,965	275,544	335,339
NET PROFIT AFTER TAXATION	£(42,520)	£211,015	£214,385	£271,172	£ 338,346	£ 417,793	£ 511,723	£ 622,772

Notes:
1. The figures given for the year ending 31.12.85 were derived by taking 5/12 of the prior year's income and expenses, and adding them to the 7 months accounting period ending 31.12.85 (see: Profit and Loss accounts).
2. In accordance with Note 1, an adjustment was not made to the figure given for the Exhibition Centre (as was the case with other items), as this was already representative of the year's total.
3. The figures given for the income generated from waterslides for 1985 and 1986 were taken from the original profit projections made by Gordon Black plc.
4. For the purposes of this projection, income was increased by 10 percent, except for the income from waterslides, which was increased by 20 percent. Operating expenses and interest charges were increased by 5 percent.

under the scheme. The company was advised by its accountants not to go ahead with the issue and the offer for subscription was duly withdrawn.

This attempt to raise new finance had cost the company £100,000.

CRITICAL SITUATION

Facing a critical financial shortage, Gordon Black authorized the sale of a giant waterslide to one of its local public authority customers at a less than favourable price. This sale raised £120,000.

At this point Brian Scase invested £100,000 in the company to keep it afloat. In return, Gordon Black relinquished his majority equity stake in the company and his position as chief executive officer to Brian Scase.

The situation remained difficult and pressure from creditors was building up.

TOURWAY SAFETY SEAT COMPANY

RICHARD HEAGY
Clemson University

CYNTHIA D. HEAGY
*University of Houston
at Clear Lake*

THE IDEA

Bob started his Kendowing 1000 motorcycle and headed toward Helen, Georgia, for a rally of motorcycle riders. He was meeting a group of friends on the outskirts of Atlanta, and they were motoring to Helen as a group. The rally in Helen would attract several thousand riders for the two-day event. There were rallies all year throughout the country, and some, like "Bike Week" in Daytona, would attract more than 50,000 riders. Bob wanted his wife Sally to go, but she begged off because riding double was tiring on both the driver and the passenger. The passenger rode hanging on to the driver's waist.

The demographics of these motorcycle owners would be a surprise to most non-motorcyclists. Bob was a mechanical engineer and an officer in a successful construction firm. Sally was a CPA with a regional accounting firm. Their combined income was at the $75,000 per year level. Almost all of their rally group were considered "yuppies." While not typical of all motorcycle owners, a very substantial percentage of bike owners was approaching affluence.

The Kendowing 1000 that Bob and Sally owned was a 1987 model that, with saddlebags, windshield, and radio, was dealer priced at just over $8,000. Over 100,000 of the Kendowings were sold each year. Kendo was among the largest of the Japanese motorcycle manufacturers; it sold a total of just over 600,000 units each year in the United States.

While in Helen, Bob noticed that several bike owners had rigged up simple backrests that supported the lower back, offering some relief to the passenger. He also noted that one design, used in several motorcycles, featured a bracket with a padded back that attached to the bike frame. One bike had a backrest with arm supports that had been professionally manufactured. The owner told Bob he had purchased the seat from a custom shop in California for just over $200. Bob examined it closely and saw that it had adjustable arms as well as a back support. He felt that he could improve on the design and decided that he would build his own rather than purchase one.

Over the next few weeks, Bob went to two more rallies and visited a number of motorcycle dealers looking for backrests. He saw several custom-made supports, but these were one of a kind and cost on average about $400. A review of the last two years' issues of the key motorcycle magazines turned up only two references to custom shops, both located on the West coast, that had built backrests as part of a custom job on a bike. Bob decided to write both custom shops and get quotes on backrests.

THE PROTOTYPE

Sketching out his ideas for improving what he had seen to date, Bob drew two 15-inch long, ⅜-inch di-

This case, written specifically for this text, is printed by permission.

ameter steel eyebolts joined with a custom bracket. This frame would support a backrest and two armrests. The unique feature of the new design would be the flexibility of the armrests. In all of the models Bob had seen, the armrests were adjusted to the passenger's size and then fastened with a metal pin that aligned with the correct adjustment of holes in the armrest. In other words, passengers had to adjust the bracket each time they rode. Another drawback was that, once the pin was inserted, the armrest was rigid until the pin was removed. This made getting on and off the bike a hassle. Bob's new design would be spring-loaded so that pressure from the passenger would swing either armrest out to a 90-degree position for getting on or off the bike. Because the armrests would swing open, they would be adjusted for the size of the passenger only one time. This model, Bob felt, would be a major improvement over the others he had seen.

Bob built a prototype of his safety seat at a cost of about $100. The seat was a big hit at the next rally he and Sally attended. A number of people wanted to know where they could buy a unit just like it. When Bob explained that he developed the unit so Sally could travel with him, several people said that Bob and Sally should consider manufacturing the safety seat for sale.

INDUSTRY DATA

The more Bob thought about the reaction to his safety seat, the more intrigued he became about selling it. But first, he had to investigate the potential market for such a product. He found the information on motorcycle sales in the United States shown in Exhibit 1.

KENDO CYCLE COMPANY DATA

The Kendowing 1000 Series was introduced in 1982 and had become an industry leader in sales. Motorcycle Industry Council data indicated that the model had sales of about 144,000 units in 1984 and 165,000 units in 1985. Estimates for 1986 were approximately 175,000 units. Retail sales were handled by about 900 dealers across the United States. Both sales and service were the responsibility of the local dealer with an arrangement that allowed units still under warranty to be serviced at any authorized dealer.

Exhibit 1
MOTORCYCLES SALES IN THE UNITED STATES, 1982–1985

YEAR	TOTAL UNITS	IMPORTS	DOLLAR VALUE
1982	990,000	917,000	$1,110,000,000
1983	1,185,000	540,000	697,000,000
1984	1,305,000	441,000	523,000,000
1985	1,260,000	733,000	783,000,000

Source: Statistical Abstract of the United States, 1986 (Washington, D.C.: U.S. Government Printing Office, 1987).

A new Kendo Cycle plant in the United States was to begin production in late 1987 of the 1000 Series and would have a reported capacity of 200,000 units per year. Industry sources speculated that any excess demand would be met by importing units into the West coast from the plants in Japan.

ADVERTISING DATA

Standard Rate and Data Service lists over twenty magazines oriented to the motorcyclist. Familiarity with cycle magazines helped Bob to narrow the list to four that had serious potential as advertising vehicles. In addition to the four paid-circulation cycle magazines, Bob knew that owners of Kendo motorcycles received *Kendoworld Touring*, a controlled circulation magazine, six times a year from the manufacturer. The other magazines were published monthly. Advertising information for the magazines in shown in Exhibit 2.

PRODUCT RESEARCH

Bob had taken a marketing course when he was a sophomore at the University of Georgia. Although he barely passed the course, Bob learned that research should be undertaken on a product before it is placed on the market. As part of this research, Bob wanted to compare his prototype to similar products available in the market. In a two-year-old issue of *Motorcycle*, Bob found a 1-inch advertisement for a passenger seat. Bob called a number in Los Angeles and talked to the owner of a small custom shop called Jetsos. The owner told Bob his company

Exhibit 2
ADVERTISING RATES FOR MOTORCYCLIST MAGAZINES

NAME	CIRCULATION	1-INCH AD	1/12-PAGE AD
American Touring	124,000	$110	$289
Motorcycle	454,000	360	789
Motorcycle Guide	209,000	315	710
Cycle Universe	328,000	515	998
Kendoworld Touring	288,000	289	795

Sources: Standard Rate and Data Service; Kendoworld Rate Card.

builds seats to order for any of the bigger cycles. The company could build a seat for Bob's Kendowing 1000 for $209 plus $5 shipping and deliver it to Bob in about six weeks. Bob ordered a seat and charged it to his Visa card.

Bob also tested the market for his seat. He produced fifteen seats during the next month. Seven were sold for $169 each at a rally and show in Gatlinburg, Tennessee. Bob and Sally sold out of their motel room and used word-of-mouth to spread the information about the seats. They could have sold about a dozen additional units, but could carry only seven on the bike with them. Three bike owners gave their telephone numbers and asked Bob and Sally to call and confirm seat sales when they got back to Atlanta. They planned to carry as many seats as they could load in their Mazda to the next rally.

Sally had been a much better salesperson than Bob at the rally. Several of the sales had been the direct result of wives talking to Sally and watching her demonstrate the seat.

Back in Atlanta, the remaining five seats were sold locally. Bob made several follow-up calls to customers to see how the seats were functioning and to get suggestions about any improvements that might be made.

PRODUCTION COST DATA

Bob realized that if he and Sally were to produce the seats in large quantities, the cost structure would change considerably. They needed hard data.

One safety seat required 103 steps to complete. Producing the padded back and armrests took 17 steps. The plating operation consisted of 28 separate operations. Metal fabrication and assembly involved 58 distinct steps.

The 17 steps to produce the back and armrests would be farmed out to a custom upholstery shop. Modern Seat Company had done some work on the first few units, and Bob was satisfied they would provide as high a quality as the customer would pay for. The company could produce 200 sets (one backrest and two armrests) per month at a total cost of $21 per set. The company required a minimum order of $400 because of setup time on some equipment. Bob would have to purchase the upholstery fabric each month in advance ($4 per set). The balance would be due 2/10, net 30.

The plating operation also would need to be farmed out. The cost of environmental control and monitoring was beyond the capability of a small operator. Custom Plating, Inc., could perform both production runs and small batch jobs. The company did a lot of production plating for industry but could also work on very small, unique design jobs. While $39 per unit was a major cost, a top quality chrome job added substantial eye appeal to the product. The company required a minimum order of $250. Terms would be a $1,000 deposit with the balance due 2/10, net 30. A contract would be necessary because of the quality aspects of plating thickness and industry standards. Custom Plating, Inc., had a reputation for high-quality workmanship and had a production capacity of 500 units per month.

Industrial Bolt & Screw Company would supply the two special alloy eyebolts plus the other fasteners needed at a cost of $6 per unit. The company would put a special 15-degree bend in the bolts.

Metal fabrication was a problem. The only really unique part was the small metal bracket that tied the eyebolts together just above the rear fender. Bob had been making his metal bracket with the help of a specialty welding shop, but any quantity production would require a metal fabricator working with a custom die and fabrication jigs. Substantial costs could be involved. Rite Tool & Die offered the best proposal on the production of the bracket. They would build a custom die for $2,700 and the necessary jigs for $1,650. The expected useful life of the die and jigs would be five years. Terms would be a cash deposit of $2,000 with the balance due on delivery. Rite would also agree to produce the brackets for $6 per unit with a required minimum order of $300.

The special bracket was both a cost and production problem. A welder had been charging $24 per unit and could produce only about 20 per week. Bob placed an order for 50 to be delivered immediately.

GOING FOR IT

That night at supper, Bob and Sally talked over their plans.

"Sally, I think we should go ahead and jump into the seat business," Bob said. "I plan to keep my job. This will be a night and weekend business. It means that we would need to attend more shows and rallies, but we like that. For the time being we can still work out of the garage," he continued. "We can let the business be demand driven and expand only as we gather new business. We will have to maintain some inventory, but we should be able to keep that to a minimum level."

"Bob, I think we should try a mail-order sales approach," Sally said. "The bulk of our target market receives *Kendoworld Touring* magazine. We need to decide in the next couple of days because the spring issue with the special products supplement has a Friday closing date for advertisers. That is the most widely read issue of the year and has strong pulling power for small mail-order companies, according to the rate card."

"How much will an ad cost?" asked Bob.

"We could do the job with an inch ad for $289 and reach customers who never go to a show or rally. I thought we could say, 'Kendowing 1000 Riders! Take your wife or somebody else's for a ride with the Tourway safety seat with springaway armrests. Only $189 plus $5 shipping. Telephone or mail orders. Visa or MC.' How does that sound?"

"I agree that we should increase the price," Bob replied, "but I'm not sure to what level. That seat I ordered from Jetsos was delivered today. After looking it over, I know that we have a superior product. Our spring-loaded armrests are a major improvement. I also realized that our bracket could be modified to accommodate several angles at the point we tie the eyebolts to the backrest. This will allow us to adapt our seat to several other manufacturers' cycle models and, at the same time, reduce our plating cost by almost 30 percent."

He continued, "I went to Custom Plating today to discuss making the new bracket with the die and jigs. I learned one reason our plating costs are so high—our current bracket has too much rough area that Custom has to clean up. Based on the drawings of our new bracket, our plating cost will drop about $9 per unit!"

After more discussion, Bob and Sally placed a one-inch ad in *Kendoworld Touring* magazine. They arranged for an answering service to take orders when no one was home to answer the telephone. The first week after the magazine's publishing date, they booked orders for fifty-seven seats; the second week, forty-six orders. Payment for these orders was by credit card.

When the first orders hit, Bob and Sally had seven complete seats on hand and forty-four brackets already plated. Modern Seat had just called to say fifty sets were ready for pickup. Orders were placed for additional seats and armrest sets, brackets, and eyebolt sets. Bob and Sally put Custom Plating on notice that they would be bringing in additional brackets for plating. Working evenings and weekends, Bob and Sally could assemble between fifty and sixty sets a week, including packing for pickup by UPS. One person could assemble and box one seat in forty-five minutes.

The cost of the shipping and the linerboard boxes averaged $4 per seat. Sally produced the shipping labels with her Zenith PC.

Sally pulled together a pro-forma income statement and balance sheet (see Exhibit 3). Even though the 103 seats had not been delivered, she prepared the statements as if they had been completed and shipped so the results of these transactions would be included in the statements. The activity to date was surprising. They had sold a total of 87 seats, mostly at rallies, at $169 each. Orders for the additional 103 seats were in hand, and money was in the Tourway Safety Seat Company account for $194 per seat less the 3 percent discount the bank charged Sally for credit card sales. Bob was excited when he looked at the financial statements.

"Sally, we made almost $12,000 doing this part-time," he said. "Perhaps we should go into full-time. We could rent space in that office-warehouse complex near the interstate and hire a couple of people; really do it right. We have fantastic profit margins and are pricing under the competition!"

"Would our margins be this high if we did it full-time?" asked Sally. To find out, Sally prepared pro forma income statements for the next five years (see Exhibit 4).

Exhibit 3

TOURWAY SAFETY SEAT COMPANY: PRO-FORMA FINANCIAL STATEMENTS

INCOME STATEMENT (PERIOD ENDED APRIL 30, 1987)

Sales	$34,685
Less Cost of Goods Sold	19,999
Gross Margin	$14,686
Less Other Expenses	
Advertising	$ 289
Answering service	65
Credit card collection	600
Travel and telephone	2,200
Total Other Expenses	3,154
NET INCOME	$11,532

BALANCE SHEET (AS OF APRIL 30, 1987)

Assets		
Cash	$21,808	
Raw materials inventory	86	
Work in process inventory	103	
Finished goods inventory	100	
TOTAL ASSETS		$22,097
Liabilities and Owners' Equity		
Trade accounts payable	$10,514	
Sales tax payable	51	
Total Liabilities	$20,565	
Bob and Sally, Capital	11,532	
TOTAL LIABILITIES AND OWNERS' EQUITY		$22,097

Exhibit 4

TOURWAY SAFETY SEAT COMPANY: PRO-FORMA INCOME STATEMENTS, 1988–1992

	1988	1989	1990	1991	1992
Sales	$756,600	$833,424	$917,232	$1,008,024	$1,108,128
Less Cost of Goods Sold	300,120	361,277	434,804	522,814	629,074
Gross Margin	$456,480	$472,147	$482,428	$ 485,210	$ 479,054
Less Selling and Administrative Expenses					
Office rent	$ 6,000	$ 6,600	$ 7,260	$ 7,986	$ 8,785
Advertising	60,000	66,000	72,600	79,860	87,846
Credit card collection fee	20,428	22,502	24,765	27,217	29,919
Travel and telephone	15,000	16,500	18,150	19,965	21,962
Insurance	30,000	33,000	36,300	39,930	43,923
Other	15,000	16,500	18,150	19,965	21,962
Total Selling and Administrative Expense	146,428	161,102	177,225	194,923	214,397
Net Income Before Taxes	$310,052	$311,045	$305,203	$290,287	$264,657
Less Income Tax	86,815	87,093	85,457	81,280	74,104
NET INCOME	$223,237	$223,952	$219,746	$209,007	$190,553

PANAMA ART NOVELTIES (PAN) EXPORTS S. A.

CHARLES W. WHITE
Hardin-Simmons University

WILLIAM L. BOYD
Western Carolina University

Roberto Rojo was putting the final touches on a plan to organize a new company to export Panamanian-made art products to the United States. Panama Art Novelties (PAN) Exports s.a. is expected to begin operations within the next year. It will be incorporated and will operate from Panama.

THE PRODUCT

The initial product that PAN Exports is expecting to market is called a *mola*. The *mola* is a piece of unique primitive art made out of layers of fabric. Several layers (panels) of cloth are placed over each other. The top layer is cut and then tacked back to expose the layers underneath and to create an artistic pattern of colors and materials (see Exhibit 1).

Molas are sewn by the Cuna Indians of Panama. The Cuna Indians are a very primitive tribe who inhabit some 365 islands in the San Blas Archipelago off the coast of Panama, in the Atlantic Ocean. Only the women of the tribe are engaged in the making of *molas*. The art is passed from generation to generation with girls as young as seven years of age actually making these pieces. This particular art form is not practiced by any other culture on earth. The Cunas have practiced this craft for over a hundred years. Since the work is by hand, each piece is as unique as the artistry of the worker.

This case, written specifically for this text, is printed by permission.

THE MARKET

The market for *molas* is anyone who is interested in art for decorating a home or office or as a cover for many household and personal items. The majority of the *molas* are framed and used for wall hangings in the place of oil paintings and other interior decorating items. The limitation as to uses is only as narrow as one's vision. People have used *molas* to make lampshades, pillow cases, kitchen appliance covers, eyeglass covers, and tennis racket covers.

It is expected that the market for *molas* will consist of people who are members of young to middle-aged households with a bias toward the upper-middle to upper income groups. Most buyers will tend to be better educated with an appreciation of multiple art forms.

Advertising and Promotion

Due to the nature of the product, Rojo has decided that advertising will focus on print media as the main thrust. Using broadcast media would be too expensive and is not viewed as reaching the primary target market. In fact, the primary advertising is expected to be through magazines and specialty catalogs. The reach of magazines gives much greater coverage to the product; particular titles can be selected to provide the desired demographic profile of potential customers.

Direct mail will be used to reach prospective retailers with information about this product and to elicit sales from potential consumers. Mailing lists can be purchased giving the mailing addresses of

Exhibit 1
CUNA WOMAN WEARING A *MOLA*

Photo courtesy of Society Expeditions

those persons who are within the selected market profile. It is hoped that the reliance on direct mail will attract enough business without having to resort to hiring a salesforce. If there is a lack of response, the company will try to locate an agent middleman who can sell the product for a commission as a complement to other art products.

Retail Operations
PAN Exports does not expect to operate any retail outlets, but rather will act as wholesaler for selected retail outlets throughout the United States. The goal of the company is to recruit 150 retailers in the major metropolitan areas of the United Stats. To encour-

age the retailers to carry the *molas,* thirty-day credit terms will be offered, and PAN Exports will agree to accept the return of any *molas* not sold by the retailer. Under these conditions, the retailer is accepting little or no risk.

PRICING

The smaller *molas* (approximately 12 inches by 16 inches) will be priced to sell from $19.95 to $23.95 at retail. These prices for unframed *molas* will provide a markup of 80 to 115 percent of the cost price (cost to retailers is about $11 while the cost to PAN Exports averages $6). Some *molas* sold through exclusive shops in New York City have retailed for $50 to $300. In fact, the suggested price is less than a tourist would pay for the *mola* at most shops in Panama. Due to special buying arrangements, PAN Exports can deliver at lower costs.

ORGANIZATION AND OPERATIONS

Initially the company will be a closed corporation with Rojo as the majority stockholder and a limited number of minority stockholders. The board of directors will be made up of no fewer than three members, two of whom are not stockholders, as prescribed by Panamian law.
    The initial capital investment is to be $20,000, for which 20,000 shares of $1 par value stock will be issued. If it is later deemed that additional capital is needed, the prospective stockholders have already indicated an ability to double the initial capital investment. Because of the low initial costs associated with this operation, this investment is expected to be sufficient.

Wage and Salary Costs
Only one manager will be used in the startup of PAN Exports. The manager will receive a salary of $2,500 per month plus a percentage of the profits in future years. Rojo will initially hold this position. In addition to the manager, there will be two employees who are paid the equivalent of $1.40 (in U.S. dollars) per hour for a forty-four hour week. These employees will be responsible for packing the *molas* and addressing and mailing the packages. The wages are slightly above the minimum wage level for Panama.

Exhibit 2
PAN EXPORTS: PRO-FORMA INCOME STATEMENT (FIRST YEAR OPERATIONS)

Sales Revenue[a]		$660,000
Less Cost of Goods Sold		360,000
Gross Profit		$300,000
Less Operating Expenses		
Employee salaries	$ 6,160	
Advertising	120,000	
Transportation	10,200	
	$136,360	
Less General and Administrative Expenses		
Consultants	$ 8,000	
Manager's salary	30,000	
Utilities	1,020	
Miscellaneous	6,000	
	$45,020	
Total Expenses		$181,380
NET INCOME		$118,620

a. Sales revenue is based on anticipated sales of 5,000 units per month at $11 selling price.

Consulting Costs

Several consultants will be used in the first year of operation. They include a marketing consultant, a lawyer, and an accountant. The marketing consultant will be expected to set up the marketing program and will be paid $4,000 for that assistance. The lawyer and accountant will be used to prepare the incorporation and set up the accounting system to be used. Each of these will be paid $2,000. The functions performed by these consultants can be assumed by the employees of the firm after the first year of operation.

Advertising Expenses

The advertising expenses are expected to average $10,000 per month or $120,000 for the first year. It is hoped that the advertising will immediately begin to generate revenue so that the current month's advertising can be financed with the preceding month's revenue. Since advertising is so critical to the operation of the business, it will be continued as long as possible, even if revenue is less than expected.

Miscellaneous Expenses

Utilities, transportation, and miscellaneous expenses are expected to average $85, $850, and $500 per month, respectively. There are no rental costs, as one of the prospective stockholders has offered an office with no rent expense until the firm becomes profitable. Likewise, no money will be tied up in inventory since the *molas* will not be purchased until orders are received. Under this procedure the *molas* can be shipped within one to three days after receipt of the order. Since taxes are not levied on earnings from operations and exports outside of the country, it becomes more advantageous to operate in the manner described.

Although Rojo felt that he had touched all bases in the preparation of entering this new business, he was concerned that something had been inadvertantly overlooked. Had he forgotten something? Or is he ready to proceed? Should he seek outside help before proceeding further?

APOCALYPSE DESIGN, INC.

KEN M. BOZE
University of Alaska

MARY LINDAHL
University of Alaska

The March partnership meeting seemed to drag on forever. After a long dark winter, the partners were itching to get outside and take advantage of the sunlight and relative warmth of 30 degrees above 0. The rivers had not yet broken up and one partner could think only of ice fishing. Before the meeting could end, however, important decisions had to be made. The partners had to decide whether or not they would proceed with mail-order marketing nationwide—"the catalogue idea"—as one partner had nicknamed the option. If they decided to go ahead with mail-order marketing, they had to decide how it would be financed. A bank loan was being considered and Richard Flaharty and Sherry Steffens, the operating partners, had a proposal ready for the board to review.

OVERVIEW

Apocalypse Design (AD) is a three-year-old S corporation located in Fairbanks, Alaska. Incorporated in November 1983, the firm manufactures and repairs custom-made outdoor equipment used in arctic and subarctic climates. AD markets its products and services to students, hunters, fishers, military, fish and game personnel, skiers, dog mushers, mountain climbers, photographers, scuba divers, and bikers. It has five shareholders and nine employees, and has experienced rapid growth in the past three years, showing a profit for the first time this year.

This case, written specifically for this text, is printed by permission.

Even before the March partnership meeting, the partners had decided to expand sales on a statewide basis through mail-order marketing. Accordingly, they sent catalogues to 5,000 rural residents who lived north of the Alaska Mountain Range that almost splits the state in half. They were also invited by a separate catalogue publisher to include their products in a dog mushers' catalogue, since the winners of both the Yukon Quest and the Iditarod International Dog Mushing races, along with numerous finishers of that race, use AD equipment. A possible next step, as discussed in the meeting, is to produce an AD catalogue for nationwide circulation. If the partners decide to take this step, they will consider applying to a local bank for an expansion loan. The loan, besides financing the cost of designing, printing, and distributing the catalogue, would enable the firm to acquire more equipment.

AD personnel share a common love of the outdoors and enjoy using the firm's products in the field. The partners, who have tested their products outside, have made many innovative changes in the basic equipment, improving product design and function. They have built a solid clientele based on word-of-mouth referrals and a 0-percent return rate, earning a rapidly growing reputation for high quality durable products.

MANAGEMENT AND ORGANIZATION

AD is legally organized as an S corporation with five shareholders, limiting liability while maintaining partnership tax status.

The two operating partners are Steffens and Flaharty. Steffens runs the cutting room, keeps the books, and handles counter sales. Flaharty operates the sewing room and coordinates all custom work. All other employees alternate between cutting, sewing, and waiting on customers. AD incorporates participatory management into the workplace by holding biweekly meetings where both employee and customer input is encouraged. Employees discuss customer order procedures, pattern adjustments, sales, and new products and designs. Two of the nine employees are part-time, allowing flexibility in scheduling.

Monthly partnership meetings are held to discuss sales, current projects, and future business plans. The other three owners are involved only on a monthly basis at partnership meetings. The two operating partners are paid a small salary from the corporation, and the other shareholders expect no dividends in the near future.

For professional business advice, AD uses a local accountant, an external marketing consultant, a lawyer, and the Small Business Institute Program at the University of Alaska School of Management.

PRODUCTS AND SERVICES

AD products include many complementary items and many container-type items of cloth that are secured by velcro or other fasteners (i.e., custom work). Exhibit 1 lists some of the major product categories. Prices are mid-level.

MARKETING

Until recently, AD's marketing efforts have targeted professional dog racers and the local retail consumer market. The firm has placed advertisements in selected newspapers, used Yellow Pages ads, and posted flyers on bulletin boards. AD has recently expanded into federal, state, and local government contracts and wholesale distribution to a few stores in town. The 5,000 catalogues just issued were sent to people living in small villages in the bush. AD has also been asked to include some of its products in a new dog mushers' specialty catalogue being issued throughout Alaska and the continental United States.

Each August, AD operates a booth at the Tanana Valley Fair; after the fair, sales volume doubles. In December, name exposure, generated by the dog mushing races, increases sales.

Exhibit 1
PRODUCT LIST OF
APOCALYPSE DESIGN

- Day packs
- Gear packs
- Boat bag
- Duffel bag
- Padded video bags
- Padded computer cases
- Field notebook covers
- Diaper bags with zip-out foam pads
- Adult and children's clothing
- Dive bags
- Fanny packs
- Ski jouring belt
- Bicycle bags and panniers
- Motorcycle tank bags
- Dogsled gear
- Ski bags
- Stuff bags
- Dry storage bags with velcro closures
- Klepper carry bags

Because of the small population base in Fairbanks, AD's retail and wholesale market is limited. However, the firm is expanding into Anchorage and Juneau through wholesale distribution to selected stores. The university and local military bases provide a constant population turnover in the community, while government contracts provide AD with a stable sales base. Government contracts are listed in Exhibit 2.

Exhibit 2
GOVERNMENT ACCOUNTS

- Alaska State Troopers
- Department of Fish and Game
- Department of Natural Resources
- Department of the Interior
- State Geological Survey
- U.S. Geological Survey
- University of Alaska: Museum, Geophysical Institute, Bookstore
- Fairbanks North Star Borough ambulance rescue squad
- U.S. Army Northern Warfare Training Center; Fort Greely, Black Rapids

As a public service and as a means of increasing name awareness among teenagers, AD will initiate a sales program with a high school Key Club next fall. Club members will sell packs emblazoned with the high school logo and keep 15 percent of the sales price.

Local competition comes from Clem's Backpacking; Alaska Tent and Tarp, a firm that manufactures and repairs heavy canvas products; and Beaver Sports, a company that offers rentals and retail sales and is expanding into a new building. Other competitors are local dry cleaners (for repairs) and tailor shops. Mail-order competition includes L.L. Bean, REI, Patagonia, Land's End, and Eddie Bauer.

ENVIRONMENT

AD finances its purchases of materials with trade credit. The firm has been operating in a depressed oil-based economy the last two years. Nationally, there has been a rising stock market and long-run decline in interest rates. Oil prices have been rising in the past six months partly due to Middle East hostilities, thus creating increased demand for workers on the North Slope and increased activity in Fairbanks and at the university. The two local military bases have been expanding to accommodate 2,000 new troops with families, so local population is slowly increasing after two years of contraction.

AD has two major risks: a drop in sales or expansion beyond its ability to service customers' orders. Being labor intensive, the firm can expand easily and needs only heated work space with electricity to operate as a factory. A primary concern is training labor quickly enough to maintain quality. Expansion would increase AD's break-even point due to the loan servicing requirements.

LOAN REQUEST

The formal loan request had been distributed to the partners and included the information in Exhibit 3. The majority of the loan proceeds would go to financing the catalogue for nationwide distribution; most of the remainder would finance equipment purchases. One partner pointed out the bank may not approve the loan since there would be little which could be used as collateral.

OPTIONS

Several options were suggested by different partners at the meeting. One was to proceed with the loan request and see how the bank reacted. The bank could either deny or approve the loan, or require additional security, such as personal guarantees. Another alternative was to seek more equity capital, though no one was quite sure how to do

Exhibit 3
LOAN REQUEST PURPOSE AND PROJECTED SALES

ITEM	COST	PURPOSE	PROJECTED SALES
Two sewing machines	$ 4,000	Increase output	
Cutting equipment	1,000	Increase output	
Catalogue: Labor and materials	18,000	Increase sales	$30,000 to 50,000
Labels	500	Product recognition	
Computer	3,500	Increase bookkeeping and inventory efficiency	
Fair booth (rental and display)		Increase visibility and reach new customers	$ 8,000
Total loan requested	$29,000		

this. Still another suggestion was to acquire the computer and some of the production equipment first and see how the rural catalogue and Key Club programs affected sales, focus upon wholesale distribution in Anchorage and Juneau, and then plan the nationwide catalogue for the following year.

Speaking for the group, one partner said, "The primary issues are how does a young expanding firm such as ours find capital and how fast should we expand? How do we coordinate our marketing efforts with our financial and production needs?

How do we obtain the necessary financing for expansion? What happens if we publish the catalogue, purchase the equipment, and the sales do not materialize? Our breakeven point really shifts with the debt. We could seek venture capital, or additional equity capital, or loans from current shareholders. Finally, we could reduce the cost of the catalogue and have a smaller mailing."

The meeting adjourned with a decision to submit the loan proposal to the bank as is.

Exhibit 4
APOCALYPSE DESIGN: INCOME STATEMENTS

	1985	1986
Revenues	$44,807	$102,568
Less Cost of Sales	18,070	29,442
Gross Margin	$26,737	$73,126
Less Operating Expenses		
Wages and salaries	$11,597	$40,626
Rent and utilities	6,703	11,762
Advertising	1,921	1,395
Depreciation	0	1,620
Interest	0	55
Miscellaneous expenses	2,783	7,625
Total Operating Expenses	23,004	$63,083
NET INCOME (LOSS)	$3,733	$10,043

STATEMENT OF OWNER'S EQUITY

	1985	1986
Beginning Retained Earnings	($9,505)	($5,772)
Income	3,733	10,043
ENDING RETAINED EARNINGS	($5,772)	$4,271

Note: Modified accrual method of accounting is used. Production wages and salaries are not counted as part of inventory when GAAP would require this.

Exhibit 5
APOCALYPSE DESIGN: BALANCE SHEET

ASSETS

	1985	1986
Cash	$1,332	$4,785
Accounts receivable	0	1,720
Inventory	6,534	10,235
Equipment and fixtures	1,390	6,865

ASSETS

	1985	1986
Vehicles	2,000	3,750
Less accumulated depreciation	(3,390)	(5,010)
TOTAL ASSETS	$7,866	$22,345

LIABILITIES AND EQUITY

Liabilities

	1985	1986
Accounts payable	$ 0	$ 7,168
Notes payable	2,000	639
Shareholder's loans	4,402	3,031
Total Liabilities	$6,402	$10,838

Equity

	1985	1986
Common stock	$1,000	$ 1,000
Paid in excess of par	6,236	6,236
Retained earnings	(5,772)	4,271
Total Equity	1,464	11,507
TOTAL LIABILITIES AND EQUITY	$7,866	$22,345

Exhibit 6
MONTHLY SALES GRAPH

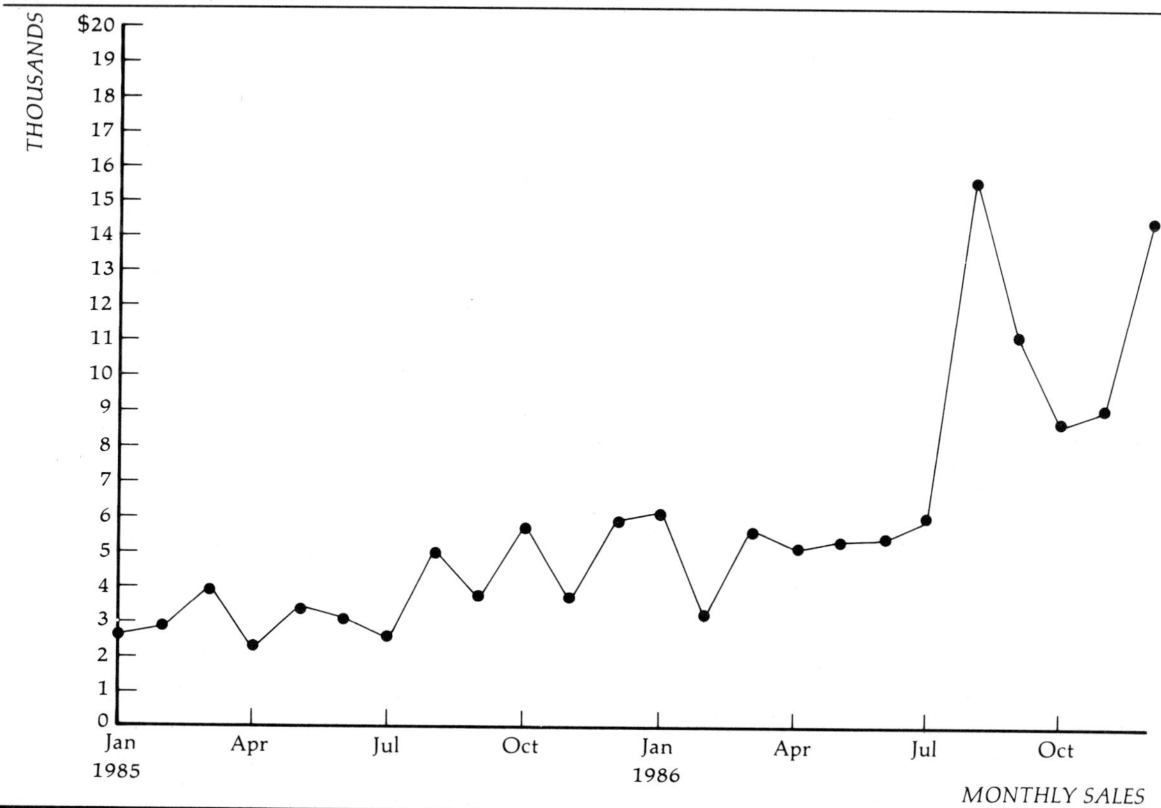

MONTHLY SALES

THE YARN CASTLE

JOYCE M. BEGGS
*University of North Carolina
at Charlotte*

DOROTHY C. DOOLITTLE
*East Tennessee
State University*

After coming inside from getting her morning paper, Anne Crosby shivered from the weather, which had been unseasonably cold for this time of year. Little did she know that the morning newspaper would also contain information to make her continue to shiver. As Crosby read the news, she noticed an ad for a new shop that was opening (see Exhibit 1). From the information given in the ad, the new shop, called Knitting Notions, would sell specialty yarns for knitting. This caused Crosby great concern since she was the sole proprietor of a shop whose primary product line was also specialty yarn. Moreover, the new shop was located only 2 miles from her shop.

Perhaps it was time to reevaluate her present business situation and decide on the future course of action. As she drank her morning coffee, Crosby tried to objectively evaluate the effect of this new business opening in her neighborhood. Crosby was a strong woman who had never asked for any outside help with running her business. However, the news of the competitor shop opening upset her. One of her best customers was a professor of strategic management at the local university, Dr. Little. Crosby decided to give Little a call for some free advice. Dr. Little agreed to come over that afternoon, but asked Crosby to think about both the internal and external environment of her business during the day. Little planned to bring over some information

---

This case, written specifically for this text, is printed by permission. The company's name has been disguised, but all key relationship remain intact.

Exhibit 1
AD FOR KNITTING NOTIONS

GRAND OPENING
Apr. 9 thru Apr. 16
of the
Knitting Notions
2274 N. Stallion
Brewster Center—2nd Level
Johnson City, TN 37601
Hours: Monday–Saturday, 10 A.M.–5 P.M.
Door Prizes
Special Purchases
**Free Sweatshirt Clinic
April 16
10 to 11:30 A.M.**
Call for information
555-8209

tion from the university library to help with the session.

SCOPE OF THE BUSINESS

As Crosby drank her second cup of coffee, she reflected on her present situation. She was the sole proprietor of a specialty yarn shop called The Yarn Castle in Johnson City, Tennessee. The Yarn Castle sold a wide variety of yarns, knitting patterns, and knitting accessories. These yarns were made from natural fibers and were different from those synthetic yarns usually found in discount stores or fabric shops. In addition, the shop carried sidelines of needlework canvas, framing, and handknit sweaters. For a small fee, finishing work was also provided on customers' knitted products.

COMPANY HISTORY

In 1971, Crosby had borrowed $3,500 from her family and opened The Yarn Castle. Although she had no experience in management or running a business, she had experience in sales of retail clothing. In her opinion, this retail sales experience had provided her with the most necessary skill for success in business. That is, she knew how to work with people and how to treat people. As she recalled, very little planning went into her decision to open her shop. As an avid knitter, she thought a specialty yarn shop would prosper. It seemed as though one night she decided to go into business for herself and did so the next morning. Moreover, she had great confidence that she would make a great deal of money with her shop.

LOCATION

The Yarn Castle opened in a small shopping center near Crosby's neighborhood. However, the primary reason for choosing this location was not the proximity to her home but the affordable rent. As the name of the shopping center was King Arthur's Court Shopping Center, she selected a name for her shop that was patterned after the medieval theme—The Yarn Castle. Actually, the shopping center was located on the corner of two small roads, Arthur Drive and Hillcrest Drive (see Exhibit 2). It seemed as though the choice of the name for the center was influenced by the name of the street on which the shopping center was located, Arthur Drive. When The Yarn Castle was first opened, there was little drive-by traffic. However, the two small roads were now four-lane streets, and traffic was quite heavy at this interchange.

Other than The Yarn Castle, the original shopping center housed a barber shop, a uniform shop, a convenience store, a beauty salon, and an automotive supply store. Crosby's shop was located between the convenience store and the beauty salon. She wondered why none of the other stores had chosen names that reflected the theme of the shopping center. The name selection for her shop had been based on customers being able to locate the shop due to their knowledge of the location of the shopping center.

Recently, two additions had been made to the shopping center. In the first addition, a chiropractic center, a temporary employment agency, a tax service, two insurance companies, and a home improvement firm were added. In the second and more recent addition, a children's clothing store, a gift and floral shop, a beauty salon, a home medical equipment store, and a vacant shop were added. A freestanding video rental store was located in the parking lot.

The shopping center was near a housing development, and the appearance of the center was complemented by trees in the back. The parking lot had more than ample accommodations for customers, and access to both Arthur Drive and Hillcrest Road was quite convenient.

Now the location of the store was more of an advantage than it had been in the beginning. As there had been a great deal of growth in the area, the traffic by the center had greatly increased. Unfortunately, the other stores in the shopping center probably did little to attract customers for Crosby's shop. In addition, there was no space in her shop to expand her product offerings.

The shopping center offered no services to the tenants, and the tenants had never run any joint advertising promotions. The Yarn Castle's leasing arrangement was uncertain after the term of the present lease expired. Since the shopping center was sold earlier in the year, Anne did not know what the new owners would charge for the rent. However, all tenants were anticipating a rent increase. The rent for The Yarn Castle has increased from $150 per month in 1971 to $375 per month in 1987. In 1987, the rent expense was 7.5 percent of the net sales.

LOCATION ALTERNATIVES

Crosby had considered moving but was adamant about not having a shop in the mall in Johnson City. There were two reasons for her decision. First, the rent would be too high; second, stores in the mall were open seven days a week. Crosby did not relish the idea of working seven days a week and thought

Exhibit 2
MAP OF KING ARTHUR'S COURT SHOPPING CENTER

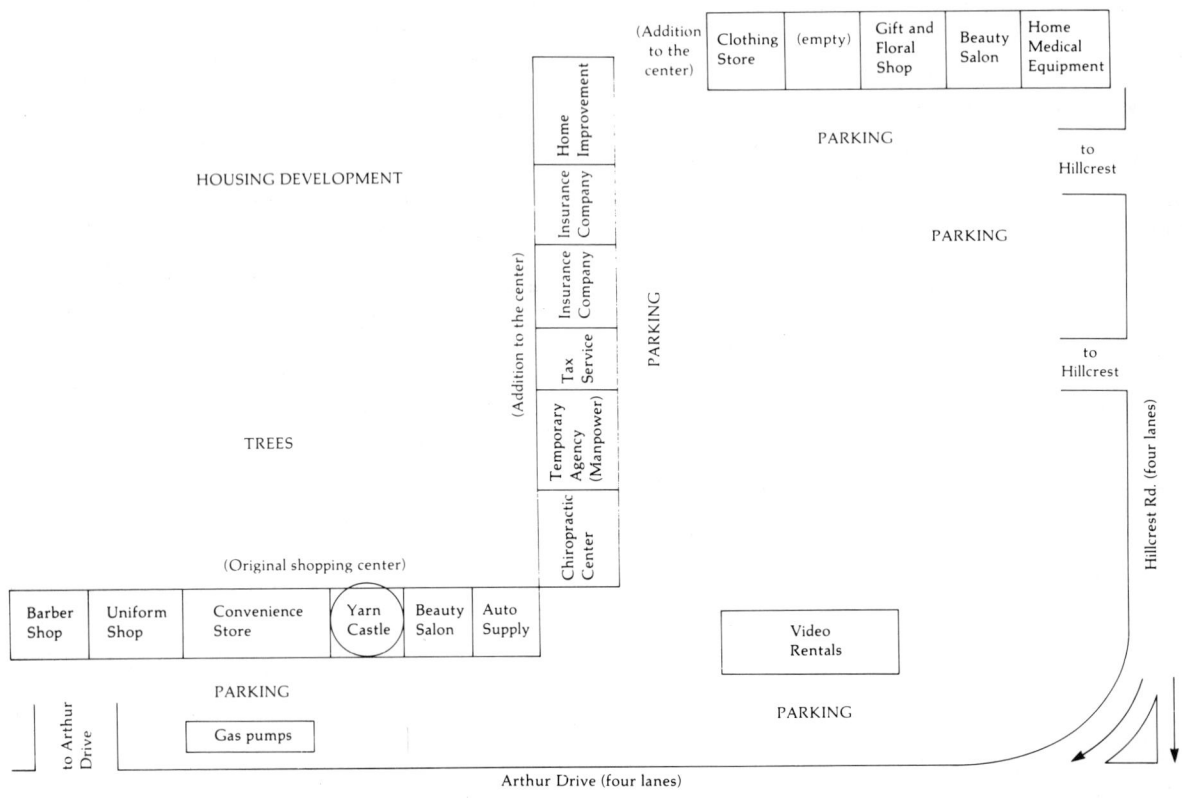

that longer store hours would not result in increased sales.

Crosby would not move to the downtown area. Although there was one extremely nice dress shop downtown, most of the buildings were filled with government offices and secondhand shops. Other shops downtown were stereo shops, furniture stores, a music shop, a union mission, a soup kitchen, an upholstery shop, a blood bank, and several night clubs. The downtown area was not growing as other parts of town were. Moreover, many of the streets were one way, and no parking was allowed on the streets. All those who shop downtown must park in the garage and pay for this service.

Therefore, shopping downtown was rather inconvenient when compared to shopping in a mall or shopping center.

Recently, a new shopping center had opened that had available space. The present tenants were a theater, a Pizza Hut, a Hallmark card shop, a bookstore, a discount store, and a craft shop that specialized in novelty crafts. As Crosby's customers generally were involved in several types of crafts, the craft store could attract customers to her store if she relocated. After having the same location for sixteen years, it was difficult to consider moving. However, the new shopping center certainly was appealing.

THE SHOP

As Crosby entered the shop that morning, she tried to evaluate objectively her present operation. The Yarn Castle was relatively small, with approximately 780 square feet of floor space (see Exhibit 3). Actually, the shop size was similar to that of many other craft shops she had visited. There was one large display window in which Crosby featured colorful hand-knitted sweaters. This display was changed quite frequently to reflect the latest creations. In front of the display was a large round table where Crosby and her customers sat, knitted, and watched the black and white television located in the corner. Since the store had limited space, it appeared a bit cluttered, but was quite inviting.

The castle theme of the shop name was reflected throughout the interior of the store. Decorated in browns and other earthtones, the store was a very comfortable place in which to shop. Yarns were displayed on the upper portion of the two side walls in rows of open plastic containers, which were once five gallon ice cream buckets. This open display allowed customers to see all the vast variety of colors and types of yarns with relative ease. Yarn was also displayed in the center of the store on one side of a rack with needlepoint canvases displayed on the other side. Cabinets along the side walls under the rows of containers held the inventory of yarn. Knitting patterns were on display near the front of the store on a revolving rack, and other supplies such as needlepoint canvases and cross-stitch books were

Exhibit 3
LAYOUT OF THE YARN CASTLE

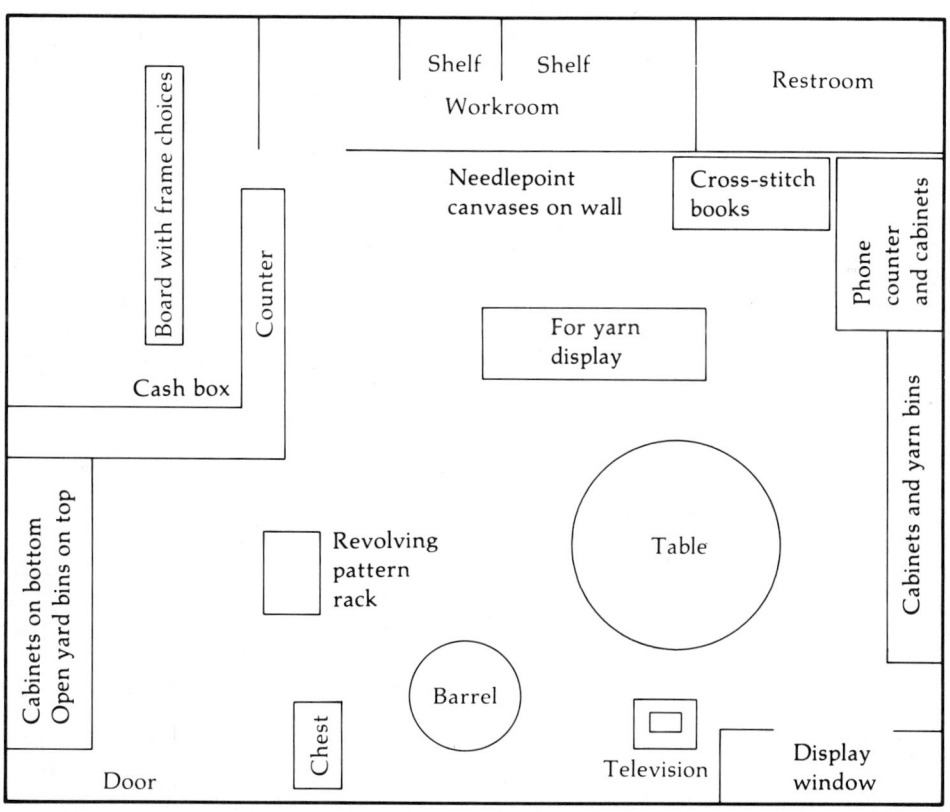

on the rear wall of the store. In addition, framing supplies were on a display board behind the counter for waiting on customers. The framing work was done by a subcontractor and was more or less provided as a service for customers who did cross-stitching.

In the left corner of the shop, behind the counter, was a stand for a cash register. However, Crosby used a cash box rather than a cash register. All sales receipts were handwritten, and money was placed in the box at the time of the sale. In the right corner of the shop was the phone, which rang frequently.

STORE OPERATIONS

In the winter months, the Yarn Castle's store hours are 10:00 A.M. to 5:30 P.M. on Tuesday through Saturday and 10:00 A.M. to 9:00 P.M. on Monday. The store was closed on Sundays. On Monday night, Crosby offered free knitting classes for anyone interested in learning. In the summer months, the hours were cut back to 10:00 A.M. to 5:00 P.M. on Monday through Friday and 10:00 A.M. to 3:00 P.M. on Saturday.

SEASONALITY OF BUSINESS

Crosby thought one of the biggest problems being involved with the craft industry was the seasonality of the business. Business slacks off in April or May, depending on the weather, and picks up again in August. The peaks in business appear to be in October and November and again in February and March. Customers buy supplies in August, September, and October for projects for the Christmas season. During the summer, customers seemed to be less involved in crafts and more involved with outdoor recreation.

Crosby attended two trade shows per year. In the spring, she went to one in Atlanta, and in the fall, to one in Charlotte. At these shows, dealers in knitting, needlepoint, cross-stitch, and frames featured the latest products.

Crosby felt that the craft business was also cyclical. Consequently, she monitored her sales carefully. Through attending these trade shows, she attempted to predict new trends. Currently, interest in yarn seemed to be declining. As her business was

heavily dependent on yarn sales, Crosby optimistically hoped that interest would continue for at least one more year.

Although macramé had been quite popular in the past, it was no longer. Rughooking was now making a comeback in popularity. As a result, Crosby added rughook canvases to the selections in her store. Other crafts, such as cross-stitch, she characterized as more or less dead. As a trend, cross-stitch bottomed out in 1984 when there was a noticeable drop not only in cross-stitch sales, but also framing sales. In general, Crosby was optimistic in her forecasts for the upcoming year and estimated that sales would increase.

FADS

Not only was the craft industry both seasonal and cyclical, it was also subject to fads. A new fad was to put knitted necklines on sweatshirts. The project entailed cutting the original neckline from the sweatshirt and replacing it with one knitted with either contrasting or matching yarns. As this was a good project for beginning knitters, it had attracted many new customers into The Yarn Castle.

Crosby was told about the sweatshirt idea by one of the salesmen that comes by her shop. She showed an eleven year old who had never knitted how to knit the new neckline for a sweatshirt. The child sat in the shop and did three of these sweatshirts in one week. Customers were so impressed that the little girl could do such a good job and do it so quickly that they wanted to try it. In a recent *Knoxville Journal*, an article was run about the popularity of the sweatshirts with college students. This article also helped increase the popularity of the sweatshirt fad.

In response to this fad, Crosby put together a sweatshirt kit for customers. Kits were more popular for those inexperienced in crafts. Including everything necessary to complete the project, even the sweatshirt, the kit was very convenient and sold for $25.

Crosby estimated her costs were as follows. At a cost of $2 per sweatshirt, Crosby had The Uniform Shop located in the King Arthur's Court sew around the sweatshirt neck. She knitted the first row for customers. When purchased in quantity, the sweatshirts cost $6 and supplies were $13, which included a $4 circular knitting needle.

Indeed, the sweatshirt craze had been a positive effect on sales. In fact, the sweatshirts were so popular that Crosby had sold many of them as finished products for $30. However, she recalled the morning news and Knitting Notions, the new shop that was opening. As part of the grand opening festivities, a free sweatshirt clinic was offered. Holding a clinic would have been a good idea at the peak of the fad. However, Crosby thought the fad was waning.

EMPLOYEES

Crosby had one employee, who worked part time. Marie Mills was hired because she was a very good knitter, and many of the sweaters on display were her creations. However, there were other duties required for this position. Mills was to help with sales to customers. Although she had only been working for Crosby about eight months, Mills did not seem to have a natural inclination toward sales.

Mills was in her early forties, which was fairly close to the majority of the customers' ages. Usually she worked three days a week but during busy times she would work more. She was paid $4 per hour. For several years before Mills was hired, Crosby had another part-time worker who was not only a good knitter, but also an aggressive salesperson.

PERSONAL SERVICE

Crosby was proud of the fact that her business allowed her to work one on one with customers. She knew all of her customers by name and took the time to do special things for them. Although the scheduled knitting class was on Monday night, she spent about three additional hours a day teaching in her shop. After store hours, she was willing to make a personal visit to a good customer's home to help straighten out problems with knitting projects. Moreover, customers often stop and proudly show her their finished sweaters.

ADVERTISING AND PROMOTION

Both Crosby and Mills frequently wore their hand-knitted sweaters. This seemed to serve as a source of free advertising, as it generated customer interest. However, Crosby did not feel that other advertising paid for itself in her case. Therefore, her advertising consisted primarily of ads in the Yellow Pages. Her shop was listed under the headings both for needlework and yarn. In the ad, she listed three major lines of supplies, free knitting classes, and the store hours. These two listings cost approximately $80 per month.

One other company was listed under yarns in the Yellow Pages. Although their ad was larger and listed types of yarn sold, the business was located in a town about twenty miles away. Although this shop sold specialty yarns similar to those available at The Yarn Castle, Crosby had never considered this store to be a major threat to her business due to the distance between the two stores.

Crosby did not run ads in the newspapers, on radio, or on television. For the yearly anniversary sale, she put a sign in the display window. Generally, all merchandise was offered at a 15-percent discount during this sale. Odd skeins of yarn (types in which there is not enough to make a sweater) were sold for half of the regular price all year long. These skeins were kept in a large wooden treasure chest and in a barrel in the front of the shop.

Crosby felt that word-of-mouth advertising brought in most of her new customers. Until this morning, she felt that her shop was the only source of specialty yarns for serious knitters locally. Unless customers bought from shops in other towns, she normally got their repeat business. This new shop opening 2 miles away from The Yarn Castle could result in the need for advertising other than word of mouth.

There were two major events in Johnson City in which area businesses set up booths to display their products. The Appalachian Fair and the Appalachian Trade Show drew people from at least a 60-mile radius. Although these shows were quite successful, Crosby had chosen not to participate in either of these.

At one time, she had been a member of the Business Women's Association. She had not found such organizations to benefit her personally. In addition, she had not found them to be worthwhile for business purposes. Giving her time to teach groups such as senior citizens to knit did not result in increased sales. Due to their limited incomes, Crosby believed that they probably bought knitting supplies at discount stores and did not buy specialty yarns. In effect, then, through teaching the classes, she was increasing sales of other businesses. Consequently, she no longer engaged in such community activities.

To announce her free Monday night classes, Crosby put a poster in the shop window. The phone located at the back of the shop rings regularly from those inquiring about new knitting classes times. Actually, these frequent inquiries had been rather distracting when Crosby was servicing customers.

SALES AND PRICING POLICIES

The best-selling products were cotton yarns in the summer and wool yarns in winter. Specialty yarns were marked up 100 percent, and Crosby charged only a nominal fee for finishing work. However, the sweaters on display in the window knitted by Crosby and Mills were sold at very reasonable prices. This not only helped with cash-flow problems but also assured a window display full of new creations. Regular customers used the window as a place to get ideas for new projects, and Crosby used the window to stimulate sales of yarns.

Generally, the sweaters were purchased by someone who was not a strong knitter since they would knit the sweater themselves. Manufactured sweaters made of similar materials would sell for much higher prices in department stores. According to Crosby, no one could afford to pay the knitter for the actual time necessary to knit a sweater. In addition, some sweaters knitted by customers were sold on consignment.

Crosby allowed some of her better customers to charge merchandise. Although she did not openly advertise this service, she would agree to a credit arrangement upon request. Actually, she had had no problems with nonpayment, and the credit balance usually totaled around $400 a month. Overall, about 80 percent of sales were for cash. Yarn sales accounted for 75 percent of the sales, needlepoint sales for 24 percent, and all other lines for one percent.

COMPETITION

Before that morning, Crosby did not consider there to be any major competitors for The Yarn Castle. However, there was one other store in Johnson City that carried a very limited line of specialty yarns. This store was located in an old building with no windows and was primarily thought of as being a fabric store. Moreover, the other store that advertised in the Yellow Pages had not seemed a formidable threat due to distance.

Crosby had never considered discount stores such as K-Mart as being direct competition for yarns sales. The yarns featured in discount stores were a lower product line, which were less expensive and generally made of acrylic, whereas specialty yarns were made of natural fibers such as cotton or silk. The worsted yarns in discount stores sold for less than $1 a skein, but a skein of specialty yarn sold for at least $5 a skein.

Discount stores would not be able to sell specialty yarns in bulk due to the limited market for the product. Normally, specialty yarns were not used for projects requiring a great amount of yarn such as afghans due to the excessive cost. As a result, Crosby had not viewed discount stores entering the specialty yarn market as a plausible threat. However, discount stores did compete directly with The Yarn Castle in other crafts such as cross-stitch and rughooking.

This new competitor located 2 miles from the shop would require a new analysis of the competition. Perhaps Crosby could no longer ignore the competitors.

CUSTOMERS

Crosby's customers had been very loyal. Most knitted seven or more sweaters per year and bought all their supplies from The Yarn Castle. Most of the customers were in their early forties to mid-fifties and worked outside their homes. Crosby thought her customers were from higher income brackets whose average income was over $30,000. She based this assessment on their purchases of specialty yarn. If the customers were from lower incomes, she reasoned, their yarn purchases would be from discount stores.

MEETING WITH LITTLE

Little stopped by the university library to prepare for her meeting with Crosby. She collected information on the demographics of Johnson City and the possible places Crosby might advertise. She left the campus and drove to The Yarn Castle.

Crosby looked up from her knitting and greeted Dr. Little. "This has been one of the longest days of my life. I have been trying to think about the present state of my business and not be overcome with thinking about the past and worrying about the future."

"Calm down and tell me what you think the mission of the Yarn Castle is," replied Little.

"The mission is to make money."

"Are you making any money?"

"Yes, but it is difficult since the craft industry is seasonal, cyclical, and trendy. I have gathered some basic financial information for you, but it is incomplete. I am not an accountant." (See Exhibit 4.)

"If the craft industry is plagued with so many problems, why have you stayed in it?" asked Little.

Crosby responded, "It's my life, I've got so much involved in it. It's just me."

The telephone rang and Little overheard Crosby tell a customer, "I'll be glad to stop by to straighten out that problem with the sweater you're knitting. It would be no trouble at all. I'll come by after five as soon as I close the shop tonight."

Little was surprised that Crosby would make house calls to help customers. Crosby said she would do about anything to help a good customer like the one on the phone. Little was still impressed to see this much personal service and individual attention given to a customer.

Next, a well-dressed customer who appeared rather affluent came into the store. Crosby approached the customer and called her by name. She was looking for yarn to match that being used on a needlework canvas project. Crosby quickly matched

Exhibit 4
THE YARN CASTLE: FINANCIAL INFORMATION

	1987	1986	1985	1984	1983
Assets[a]					
Inventory	$6,500	$6,800	$7,500	$7,600	$8,000
Furniture	150[b]	—	—	—	—
Fixtures	300[c]	—	—	—	—
Liabilities					
Accounts payable	$2,500	$2,750	$3,300	$3,800	$4,000
Buying trips	300	—	—	—	—
	For one month—1987				
Sales	$5,000	—	—	—	—
Credit sales	400	—	—	—	—
Expenses					
Rent	375	—	—	—	—
Wages	434	—	—	—	—
Utilities	70	—	—	—	—
Telephone	30	—	—	—	—
Advertising	80	—	—	—	—
Taxes	30	—	—	—	—
Insurance	34[d]	—	—	—	—
Accounting	100[e]	—	—	—	—

a. Assets have been fully depreciated.
b. The furniture was purchased in 1971.
c. The calculator and cash box are valued at $50; display racks at $50; and other fixtures at $50.
d. $400 per year for $20,000 coverage.
e. $75 for a bookkeeper and $25 for an accountant.

the yarn and showed her a sweatshirt kit. She suggested that the customer's daughter would like the pink sweatshirt with matching yarn. The customer agreed and bought both the yarn for her project and sweatshirt kit.

After the customer left, Little complimented Crosby on her selling style. She replied, "Customers do not come to browse in a specialty store. They come in to buy, and I help them."

While Crosby continued to wait on customers, Little prepared the information from the library. Johnson City was located in Washington County in upper eastern Tennessee. It has a population of 44,600 and was 20 miles from Kingsport, Bluff City, and Blountville; 22 miles from Bristol; and approximately 10 miles from Jonesborough, Erwin, and Elizabethton.

Johnson City had only one daily newspaper, the *Johnson City Press*, with a circulation of 29,900. Ads in the newspaper were priced at $8.50 per column inch. In addition, there was a free weekly newspaper, the *Johnson City Star*, and four other newspapers in the surrounding areas. Little had prepared a list of them with the circulations, addresses, editors, and phone numbers (see Exhibit 5).

There were three television stations affiliated with ABC, NBC, and CBS and an independent station affiliated with Fox Broadcasting (see Exhibit 6).

Exhibit 5
LOCAL NEWSPAPERS

Johnson City Press
204 W. Main Street
Johnson City, TN 37601
Phone: 615–929–3111
Circulation: 29,900
Contact: Roy Carbine, Editor

Kingsport Times-News
701 Lynn Garden Drive
Kingsport, TN 37660
Phone: 615–929–2197
Circulation: 46,000
Contact: Ted Como, Editor

Elizabethton Star
300 Sycamore Street
Elizabethton, TN
Circulation: 10,000
Contact: Rosella Hardin, News Editor

Bristol Newspapers, Inc.
320 Morrison Boulevard
Bristol, VA 24201
Phone: 703–669–2181
Circulation: 41,000
Contact: Ned Bane, Managing Editor

Jonesborough Herald & Tribune
P.O. Box 277
Jonesborough, TN 37653
Phone: 615–753–3136
Circulation: 5,000
Contact: Don Miller, Editor

Exhibit 6
LOCAL TELEVISION

STATIONS
WJHL—TV (CBS)
Channel 11
338 E. Main St.
Johnson City, TN 37601
Phone: 615–926–2151
Contact: Hanes Lancaster, Jr., Station Manager
              Bob Carlton, News Director

WCYB-TV (NBC)
Channel 5
Cumberland-Lee St.
Bristol, VA 24201
Phone: 703–669–4161
Contact: Terry Radnoczi, News Director
              Bob Smith, Gen. Manager

WKPT-TV (ABC)
Channel 19
222 Commerce St.
Kingsport, TN 37660
Phone: 615–246–9578
Contact: George Devault, Jr., Station Manager
              Mark Wright, News Director

TALK SHOWS
First Call
WJHL–TV 11
Contact: Bob Lewis

Mid-day News
WCYB–TV 5
Contact: Teresa Keller

Forum 19
WKPT–TV 19
Contact: Melinda Sightler

Little had contacted the stations for price quotes. Ads for the local stations in the 7:00 to 8:00 P.M. slots were $80–$100 for 30 seconds. To produce the commercial, the station charged $50 per hour and a $50 edit fee. To shoot a commercial on location, the stations charged $65 per hour and a $50 edit fee. There was also the possibility of placing ads on the cable television stations and appearing on the three talk shows.

There were fourteen radio stations in the area. Little had prepared a list of the stations, addresses, and phone numbers (see Exhibit 7). Advertising on the radio would certainly be more economical than advertising on television.

Little had also gathered secondary demographic and economic profile information on Johnson City and Washington County (see Exhibits 8 through 12). This information could be helpful to Crosby for making plans for the future.

When there were no customers in the store, Little asked Crosby about the strengths and weaknesses of The Yarn Castle. She felt that the primary strengths were

1. It was the only specialty yarn shop in Johnson City (prior to that morning's news).
2. The shop had been in the same location for sixteen years.
3. The customers received a great deal of personal attention.

Crosby stated that the main weakness was the lack of money. If there were more money, she would like to paint the shop and buy more merchandise.

Little and Crosby agreed to meet the following week to determine future strategies for The Yarn Castle. Crosby planned to visit the new shop—Knitting Notions—and assess her competition. She might be overreacting to the situation.

Exhibit 7
LOCAL RADIO STATIONS

WETB 79 (AM) Erwin Highway Johnson City, TN 37601 615–928–71731	WKIN 1320 (AM) WZXY 104.9 (AM) 529 E. Market Street Kingsport, TN 37660 615–928–4444	WEBJ 1240 (AM) 626 ½ Elk Avenue Elizabethton, TN 37643 615–542–2184
WFHG 98 (AM) WXBQ 96.9 (FM) Valley Drive Bristol, VA 24201 703–669–8112	WBCV 1550 (AM) 26 ½ 6th Street Bristol, TN 37620 615–698–5221	WJSO 1600 (AM) WJSO 99 (FM) WJSO Road Johnson City, TN 37601 615–926–3121
WJCW 91 (AM) WQUT 101.5 (FM) WJCW Drive Johnson City, TN 37601 615–477–3127	WETS 89.5 (FM) 920 W. Market Street Johnson City, TN 37601 615–926–2184	WKPT 1400 (AM) WTFM 98.5 (FM) 222 Commerce Street Kingsport, TN 37660 615–926–1919

Exhibit 8
DEMOGRAPHIC AND ECONOMIC PROFILE OF JOHNSON CITY/
WASHINGTON COUNTY TENNESSEE

POPULATION CHARACTERISTICS

	Washington County	Johnson City
1980[a]	88,755	39,459
1985[b]	92,900	44,700
1990 (projected)[c]	95,987	
2000 (projected)[c]	102,772	

1980 AGE DISTRIBUTION[a]

Age	Number	Percent
Under 5	5,552	6.3%
5–19	21,690	24.4
20–34	23,561	26.6
35–54	19,546	22.0
55–64	8,560	9.6
65 and up	9,846	11.1

Median age: 30.4

1984 Washington County per capita income: $10,258

1985 Washington County household income: $18,316

a. 1980 Census Bureau
b. 1986 Survey of Buying Power
c. Tennessee State Planning Office

Exhibit 9
JOHNSON CITY/KINGSPORT/BRISTOL, TENNESSEE/VIRGINIA
METROPOLITAN STATISTICAL AREA (MSA)

COUNTY	POPULATION (12/31/86)	HOUSEHOLDS	MEDIAN HOUSEHOLD EFFECTIVE BUYING INCOME	EFFECTIVE BUYING INCOME	RETAIL SALES
Tennessee					
Carter	51,400	19,600	$16,418	$ 421,308,000	$ 138,238,000
Hawkins	46,700	16,900	20,895	435,700,000	129,983,000
Sullivan	147,900	56,900	21,919	1,564,257,000	1,030,678,000
Unicoi	16,900	6,400	18,976	151,701,000	39,316,000
Washington	92,900	34,000	18,316	854,926,000	576,346,000
Virginia					
Bristol (City)	18,500	7,300	18,889	179,760,000	215,424,000
Scott	25,100	8,600	19,801	224,988,000	108,381,000
Washington, VA	49,600	16,500	19,362	428,209,000	134,286,000
MSA	449,000	166,200	$19,687	$4,260,849,000	$2,372,652,000

RETAIL SALES BY STORE GROUP (in thousands)

COUNTY	FOOD STORE SALES	EATING AND DRINKING PLACES	AUTOMOTIVE SALES	FURNITURE/ HOME FURNISHINGS/ APPLIANCES	DRUGS	GENERAL MERCHANDISE
Tennessee						
Carter	$ 39,800	$ 11,235	$ 24,704	$ 6,414	$ 7,889	$ 20,177
Hawkins	43,749	6,993	28,133	2,247	7,702	10,832
Sullivan	182,916	77,719	325,694	41,761	37,385	153,918
Unicoi	10,199	4,933	7,934	1,778	1,563	6,413
Washington	138,510	47,407	135,911	26,229	19,018	89,673
Virginia						
Bristol (City)	32,942	14,955	55,176	9,123	4,217	43,337
Scott	30,393	3,512	38,167	3,265	2,660	1,731
Washington, VA	42,210	12,900	21,719	9,483	3,095	10,417
MSA	$521,719	$179,654	$637,438	$100,300	$83,529	$336,498

Source: Survey of Buying Power, Sales and Marketing, July 28, 1986.

Exhibit 10

EMPLOYMENT BY GROUP IN JOHNSON CITY/WASHINGTON COUNTY

GROUP	EMPLOYMENT	RATE	RATE IN TENNESSEE	RATE IN UNITED STATES
Agriculture and mining	704	1.8%	3.2%	4.6%
Construction	2,230	5.9	6.2	6.2
Manufacturing	10,906	28.6	26.7	22.2
Transportation and communication	2,631	7.0	8.0	6.6
Wholesale	1,764	4.6	4.4	3.9
Retail	6,599	17.3	15.4	16.3
Finance, insurance, and real estate	1,454	3.8	4.9	6.0
Services	10,532	27.6	26.4	28.8
Public administration	1,279	3.4	4.8	5.4
Total	38,099			

Source: 1980 U.S. Census Bureau

Exhibit 11

VARIOUS UNEMPLOYMENT RATES

WASHINGTON COUNTY, 1986		MSA UNEMPLOYMENT RATES, 1986 AND 1987	
Month	Rate	Month	Rate
January	7.7%	1986	
February	8.7	January	7.9%
March	8.5	February	8.4
April	8.0	March	7.8
May	7.5	April	7.3

Exhibit 11
VARIOUS UNEMPLOYMENT RATES

WASHINGTON COUNTY, 1986		*MSA UNEMPLOYMENT RATES, 1986 AND 1987*	
Month	*Rate*	*Month*	*Rate*
June	7.2	**1986**	
July	8.0	May	7.0%
August	6.7	June	7.4
September	6.6	July	7.7
October	6.4	August	6.6
November	6.6	September	6.3
December	6.2	October	6.4
		November	7.0
		December	6.7
		1987	
		January	7.6%
		February	7.8
		March	7.9
		April	7.0

Source: Tennessee Department of Employment Security.

Exhibit 12
FIVE-YEAR ECONOMIC GROWTH

	EMPLOYMENT[a]			
County	*December 1981*	*December 1986*	*Increase*	*% Increase*
Washington County	34,010	41,970	7,960	23.4%
Sullivan County	55,160	66,370	11,210	20.3
Carter County	19,240	23,460	4,220	21.9
Hawkins County	16,670	20,490	3,730	22.3
Unicoi County	6,270	7,670	1,400	22.3
MSA	167,000	202,000	35,000	21.0

	POPULATION			
County	*1980*[b]	*1985*[c]	*Number Change*	*Percentage*
Washington County	88,755	92,600	3,845	4.3%
Sullivan County	143,968	147,500	3,532	2.5
Carter County	50,205	51,300	1,095	2.2
Hawkins County	43,751	46,200	2,449	5.6
Unicoi County	16,362	16,700	338	2.1
MSA	433,638	446,700	13,062	3.0

a. Tennessee Department of Employment Security.
b. 1980 U.S. Census Bureau
c. 1985 Survey of Buying Power

RETAIL SALES (in thousands)[d]

County	1980	1985	Number Change	Percentage
Washington County	$ 343,314	$ 531,096	187,782	54.7%
Sullivan County	661,984	925,329	263,345	39.8
Carter County	106,162	132,247	26,085	24.6
Hawkins County	65,812	119,351	53,539	81.4
Unicoi County	30,112	37,010	6,898	22.9
MSA	$1,571,283	$2,145,582	574,299	36.6

EATING AND DRINKING PLACES (in thousands)[e]

County	1980	1985	Number Change	Percentage
Washington County	$21,693	$ 42,161	20,468	94.4%
Sullivan County	45,782	67,327	21,545	47.1
Carter County	7,673	10,321	2,648	34.5
Hawkins County	3,621	6,166	2,545	70.3
Unicoi County	1,610	4,440	2,830	175.8
MSA	$99,196	$158,317	59,121	59.6

TAXABLE PROPERTY: TOTAL ASSESSED VALUE[f]

County	1980	1985	Number Change	Percentage
Washington County	$229,389,437	$ 544,190,116	314,800,679	137.2%
Sullivan County	655,692,578	1,159,110,826	503,418,248	76.8
Carter County	121,060,493	136,708,287	15,647,794	12.9
Hawkins County	144,432,501	181,532,341	37,099,840	25.7
Unicoi County	53,060,252	58,803,728	5,743,476	10.8

ASSESSED VALUE OF INDUSTRIAL AND COMMERCIAL PROPERTY[f]

County	1980	1985	Number Change	Percentage
Washington County	$ 66,371,262	$175,632,314	109,261,052	164.6%
Sullivan County	186,735,992	315,234,722	128,498,730	68.8
Carter County	27,423,634	30,303,228	2,879,594	10.5
Hawkins County	26,503,680	38,203,044	11,699,364	44.1
Unicoi County	7,187,000	9,969,434	2,782,434	38.7

1985 ACTUAL TAX RATE[fg]

Washington County:	$1.97	Carter County:	$4.27	Unicoi County:	$3.43
Sullivan County:	$3.72	Hawkins County:	$4.28		

d. Survey of Buying Power, 1980 and 1985.
e. Survey of Buying Power, 1980 and 1985.
f. Tennessee Taxpayers' Association: Annual Survey of State and Local Government, 1981 and 1986.
g. Tennessee property tax is calculated by applying the county appraisal ratio to the appraised value of property times the county tax rate.

CHATHAM CANDY COMPANY

JOYCE M. BEGGS

University of North Carolina at Charlotte

"Now, don't forget, Ted, we have to finish up the Father's Day production by Tuesday in order to get our shipments out on time. Oh! And don't forget to have Cindy order more coconut. There's a five-day lead time on that, you know. . . . And be sure to check the number two melter. Jim said it's been acting up lately, and . . ."

"Now, now, Mrs. Chatham. You don't need to worry about a thing. Just relax and have a good time at the trade fair. You deserve a break. We'll take care of everything while you're gone."

"You're right, Ted. I will relax. I know I can count on you to keep things running smoothly."

"Better hurry, Mrs. Chatham. That's the last call for your flight."

Ted was glad Mrs. Chatham was taking a vacation. He knew how hard she had been working lately and was also happy to learn she had faith in him to run the company. Since she had taken over the business, this was the first time that she had trusted Ted enough to take a vacation. However, Ted knew that Mrs. Chatham would never fully relax at the trade fair. After all, these trade fairs were where the Chatham Candy Company got most of their ideas for new products. This particular trade show—Interpack '87 in San Francisco—promised to be the biggest gathering of confectioners ever, and Mrs. Chatham would surely be busy exchanging new product ideas and examining the latest production equipment.

Ted, a trained candymaker, thought about how devoted Mrs. Chatham was to the business. Everyone had been very concerned about the company's survival after Mr. Chatham had passed away, but Mrs. Chatham soon proved that she was a competent, take-charge business owner. When Mrs. Chatham took over in 1980, profits had remained steady and even increased slightly in some years. The employees loved Mrs. Chatham and especially admired her commitment to hard work. She was involved in every aspect of the business, from scheduling production and designing packages to waiting on customers at the front register. In fact, most people felt that Mrs. Chatham *was* the Chatham Candy Company.

HISTORY OF THE COMPANY

In the early 1900s, the Chatham Candy Company was founded by Walter Chatham, Sr., and after his death, Walter Chatham, Jr., took control of the company. In 1980, Walter, Jr., passed away leaving control of the company to his wife, Mrs. Chatham, and their two daughters, Cindy and Marsha. In 1987, Mrs. Chatham was successfully running the company, assisted closely by Marsha. In addition, Cindy planned to help manage the company after earning her business degree from an out-of-state university.

In 1912, at age sixteen, Walter Chatham, Sr., came from Greece to live with his aunt and uncle in Cambridge, Delaware. He got his first job as a crane operator with a local construction firm. After witnessing the death of a close friend in a crane acci-

This case, written specifically for this text, is printed by permission. The company's name has been disguised, but all key relationships remain intact.

dent, he decided to find a safer, easier way to make a living.

Walter purchased several cookbooks and began studying the art of candy making. Shortly thereafter, he purchased a small building in the Cambridge business district and named it "The Sugar Bowl." He sold handmade ice cream and candy, as there was no automation in the industry at the time. At first, Walter was able to run the store on his own, but before long Carol Witt began working closely with him, learning all the ins and outs of the candy-making business. One year later, Walter and Carol were married.

In 1920, the name of the store was changed to "Chatham's" (CCC), and production was relocated to Freedom, Delaware. In 1922, Walter and Carol returned to Cambridge and added a soda fountain to complement their ice cream and chocolates.

By 1951, the soda fountain was gone, and ice cream was no longer being made. The store sold only chocolates; machinery and equipment were being purchased; and the candies were mass produced.

In 1962, following the death of his father, Walter, Jr., took over the business. Three years later, he purchased a building on State Street in Staden, which is the same site where production takes place today. Because of his strong enthusiasm for automation, Chatham's utilized the latest mass-production technologies. Many of the conveyor systems were designed and built by Walter, Jr. Because the systems were so flexible, some of the machinery had been adapted and remained in use.

THE CHATHAM PRODUCT LINE

According to Mrs. Chatham, "Chocolate is Chatham's only business. Hard candies are sold in Chatham's stores, but these are bought from other manufacturers. Hard candy making is a totally different process, and we like to stick to what we do best—chocolate."

Chocolates from CCC were of four varieties: dark, milk, white, and dietetic. However, milk chocolate was by far the biggest seller. The chocolates were either molded into various shapes or were used to cover fruits, nuts, pretzels, creams, peanut butter, and other food products. "We'll chocolate cover anything that will stand still long enough," was a favorite saying of Chatham employees.

Quality was the single most important aspect of the Chatham product line. Walter, Jr., had always insisted that only the highest grade of chocolate available be used. Mrs. Chatham continued that tradition and applied it to the purchase of nuts, creams, fruits, and all other ingredients.

PRODUCTION

As sales of chocolate were extremely slow in the summer months, CCC would limit production to one day per week during this offseason. During the peak season from September 1 and to mid-April, CCC would produce six days a week, eight hours a day. Although the products had a shelf life of fifteen months, CCC preferred that its products leave the factory within a month of manufacture. Because of this policy of freshness, manufacturing was not spread out evenly throughout the year. In addition, candymaking was difficult during the warm summer months. CCC's air-conditioning equipment was not capable of maintaining cool enough temperatures for proper candymaking over extended periods of time.

All production processes began with the placement of 10-pound solid chocolate bars into melters. These melters not only liquified the chocolate in preparation for further processing, but also were used for the storage of excess chocolate. In 1987, CCC utilized seven melters, giving a total capacity of 3,300 pounds of liquid chocolate. One of these melters, a double-decker unit, was especially prized by Mrs. Chatham. It doubled production efficiency, and none of the local competitors had such a melter. Each melter was consistently used for one particular type of chocolate (milk, dark, or white). Therefore, each type of chocolate was always available, and no labor time was wasted switching from one type to another.

There were five distinct production processes: molding, enrobing, handcoating, roasting and cutting, and packing. The first three processes required the chocolate to be tempered, but each process required a different tempering method. (Tempering prepares the melted chocolate for use by cooling it down to the proper temperature—between 86 and 88 degrees.) If the chocolate was not at the right temperature when processed, the products may turn out discolored and may not have the proper "snap."

The enrobing process began with machine-tempered chocolate. From the melters, the chocolate was pumped directly to a machine specially designed for tempering. Once tempered, the chocolate was piped to an enrobing machine, which was connected to a conveyor belt. Food products such as nuts moved down the assembly line passing through the enrober, where they were chocolate coated. The coated candies then moved down the assembly line into a cooling tunnel and were placed into boxes for transport to the packing location. CCC had two enrobing assembly lines, one 10-inch line and one 24-inch line (the lines were measured by width).

Chocolate used in molding was tempered in the double-decker melter. Chocolate was used from the bottom melter while another batch was being tempered by the top melter. Before installing the double-decker, this process had been very time consuming. Operators had had to wait between batches for more chocolate to be tempered.

Although the molds were placed under the dispenser manually, a dispenser machine automatically filled the molds with the correct amount of chocolate. Once filled, the molds were placed in a cooler for the candy to harden. After hardening, the chocolate was removed from the mold; the seams were trimmed; and the candy was decorated accordingly.

Chatham's was unique in that a large assortment of stainless steel molds were used. These molds were leftovers from the company's early years. Today, these stainless steel molds were rarely purchased, due to their extremely high prices. Inexpensive plastic molds were the standard, but these plastic molds often broke and had to be replaced. Because CCC had the stainless steel molds, their mold replacement cost was far below that of the industry.

The production of certain candies required the tempering of chocolate and the mixing of ingredients by hand. Hand tempering was described by Mrs. Chatham as an art, which could only be learned through experience. Candymakers were able to feel when the chocolate was right for coating, and it often took years for employees to develop the skill necessary to get the chocolate consistently properly tempered. All of CCC's candymakers had been trained by Walter, Jr., and the cost of replacing these workers would have been quite high in terms of both dollars and time.

In the hand coating process, candymakers mixed the food products like coconut in large bowls by hand. After the chocolate was determined to be tempered, the mixture was dipped out onto an assembly belt which passed through a cooling tunnel.

Individual pieces, such as the peanut butter meltaways, were packed by a cellophane wrapping machine. Assortment boxes were packed by hand, checked for proper weight, and wrapped with cellophane. Hard candies, which were purchased in bulk elsewhere, were cellophane wrapped individually or in bulk at Chatham's Cambridge facility.

SALES DISTRIBUTION

Chatham Candy Company owned and operated two retail stores. The stores sold the company's own chocolate products as well as hard candies. The first store, in Staden, was in the same facility where manufacturing took place. The store was situated in the front of the building; manufacturing operations and administrative offices were hidden from the view of customers in the back. Thirty customer parking spaces were available at the front of the building.

The Cambridge facility was designed in a similar fashion. Retail sales occurred at the front of the building, while the packaging of hard candies took place behind the scenes. This store was located in a business district, and the only place for customers to park was in the metered spaces along the street.

Both stores measured approximately 930 square feet. The entire Chatham product line was exhibited on shelves, tables, and glass display counters, which looked crowded but neat. Painstaking detail was devoted to the arrangement of every display. The customers said the result was a visual feast that evoked a potpourri feeling of elegance, fun, and indulgence.

Using each facility for multiple purposes helped to minimize overhead costs. Additional benefit was derived in the slow off-season months by having employees in manufacturing serve as counter clerks for the occasional customers.

Forty-seven percent of total sales came from sales to organizations that used the candy for fundraising. An additional 32 percent was contributed from company-owned stores, and sales to other retailers and independent jobbers constituted 8 percent and 13 percent, respectively.

Other retailers (drug stores, candy stores, convenience stores) in scattered areas of the United States carried Chatham candy. If a store desired to carry the products, CCC was contacted. CCC shipped the goods directly to the customer via independent commercial truckers or United Parcel Service, depending on the order size. As CCC had no sales force, these accounts were established only through the initiative of the customers. Most of Chatham's customers were located in Delaware, Pennsylvania, Florida, and New Jersey, but other customers were in California, Texas, Nevada, North Carolina, and South Carolina.

Independent middlemen (two in 1987) purchased candy from CCC at wholesale price and then distributed to their own customers. CCC had little control over goods that moved through this channel, except in the area of price. CCC specified the retail price of its products to both jobbers and retailers. Tactics such as printing the price on packages and threats of termination of the account were used to gain compliance with CCC's pricing.

There were no territorial limitations, geographic or otherwise, on either the jobbers or on CCC. Actually, there was no defined target market. According to Mrs. Chatham, CCC would sell to anyone who wanted to buy. Typical terms of sale to both jobbers and retailers was FOB Staden, net 10.

MARKETING

CCC's products were positioned as high-quality chocolates, with a superior taste that would be appreciated by the knowledgeable customer. Mrs. Chatham felt that these "connoisseur" customers were very loyal to the Chatham brand. However, she was concerned that new consumers were obtained only through word of mouth or chance encounter with the product. Despite this concern, CCC had not implemented any type of marketing program. It seemed that the more immediate concerns of production and administration kept Mrs. Chatham too busy to work on development of a marketing plan.

Marketing strategies were largely left to the distributors and retailers. Occasionally, CCC would provide cardboard displays or offer limited discounts. CCC did not actively seek new retail accounts or new distributors.

Although several media were available in the Staden area (Staden is just 10 miles outside Wilmington), CCC did not use any type of advertising. The rates for local radio stations ranged from $10 per minute to $25 per minute. Mrs. Chatham had been considering using radio advertisement prior to special events such as Christmas, Easter, Mother's Day, and Father's Day. Two local newspapers, as well as two large Wilmington newspapers, were read by residents of the area. As CCC typically served the very local community, Mrs. Chatham felt that newspaper advertisement should be done through local papers only, if at all.

PERSONNEL

Chatham Candy employed nine full-time workers the year round. Three of these workers were candymakers, and the others shared the duties of packing, shelf stocking, candy molding, and clerking. These employees worked eight-hour shifts, five days a week during the slower months, and up to twelve hours a day during the peak season. Full-time employees were paid a fixed salary, received insurance benefits, and would become fully vested in CCC's newly started pension plan after two years. Salaries ranged from $15,000 to $25,000, depending on position and experience. Raises were determined by Mrs. Chatham and were based on seniority and job performance. Bonuses and candy gift boxes were given to the employees at Christmas.

During the peak season, when the workload was heavy, CCC would hire as many as thirty part-time workers. Most of the part-timers were local housewives who knew Mrs. Chatham or one of the employees. These women would submit "standing" applications, and Mrs. Chatham would ask them to come to work when needed. This arrangement benefited both CCC and the employees. CCC benefited by having a steady supply of labor willing to work at short notice. The part-time status meant low payroll costs and little threat of unionization. The women liked the arrangement because the hours were conveniently scheduled (five hours a day) so that they could send their children to school and be home in time for their return.

There were no written employee policies. In addition, there were no requirements that had to be met before hiring, and the company did not give the new employees any tests after hiring. Training was done on the job. The training of candymaker was similar to an apprenticeship. A candymaker trainee was closely supervised and trained by an experienced candymaker until he or she learned the skills of the trade.

The full-time employees had been with Chatham Candy an average of fifteen years. They were very loyal to the company and to Mrs. Chatham. This company spirit was also felt by the part timers. Everyone at the Chatham Candy Company had great pride in the company and was appreciative of the good working conditions.

FINANCIAL PERFORMANCE

Historically, Chatham's had shown a low net income, but the financial statements did not disclose the actual worth of the business. Mrs. Chatham and her daughters received a salary and fringe benefits such as cars and insurance paid for by the company. As these items were expensed, the net income of the company decreased. Therefore, the real value of the business was distorted. In fact, it was an objective of Mrs. Chatham's to keep the bottom line as low as possible. "We take out what we need through salaries and fringe benefits, and any leftovers are put back into business. We don't pay dividends."

Mrs. Chatham was also very reluctant to take on any debt. If possible, all transactions were done on a cash basis. Occasionally, CCC took out short-term loans for cash shortages during peak seasons. The relationship with a local bank enabled them to obtain loans of $100,000 in just a few hours. All the property, plant, and equipment were paid for, and in 1987, CCC did not utilize any debt, either short- or long-term.

COMMUNITY RELATIONS

Throughout the year, many tours of the facilities were conducted for students, scout troops, and other groups. In addition, CCC made donations of money and candy for door prizes to organizations.

RESEARCH AND DEVELOPMENT

In the candy industry, small operators got their new product ideas at trade fairs featuring the displays of larger competitors. Copycat products resulted from visits to these fairs or from imitating a competitor's established product. Over the years, Chatham relied almost exclusively on these methods to add to their product line. However, new ideas from customers, employees, or family members were also given careful consideration.

Since recipes could not be patented, copycat products were common. The result was an open market where any company could easily capitalize on the profitable products of the market leaders. According to Mrs. Chatham, the secret was to make the product taste better than the competitor's product. Mrs. Chatham felt that several of her products were better than the popular name-brand version due to the grade of chocolate used. Although Chatham's used a follower strategy for many products, CCC certainly did not limit themselves to simple duplication.

Although research and development was not performed as a separate function in the company, the monitoring of competitive products has been critical to the company's success. If CCC were to keep pace with its competitors, it would have to maintain continuous monitoring of the environment.

COMPETITION

The chocolate industry was an $8 billion market in the United States that was highly competitive. The larger competitors were M&M/Mars, Hershey, Cadbury-Schweppes, and Nestlé. These four companies made up 87 percent of the U.S. candy market.[1]

M&M/Mars

M&M/Mars was one of the world's largest privately held companies. It was run by Forest Mars and his brother, John, who were grandsons of the founder, Frank Mars. The company was referred to as the "Kremlin" because of its secrecy concerning production, sales, and profits. Controlling 37 percent of the market, the company relied heavily on its proven performers such as M&Ms, Milky Way, Starburst, and Snickers—the number one candy bar in the

---

1. Steve Lawrence, "Bar Wars: Hershey Bites Mars," *Fortune*, July 8, 1985, p. 53.

United States. To compete with Hershey's Big Blocks, the company had begun production of king-size Snickers. Moreover, Royal Chocolates, a higher-quality chocolate produced in bite-size pieces, was being introduced to attract new customers.[2]

M&M/Mars was one of the first candy companies to recognize candy as an impulse item and persuade merchants to place candy displays near the cash registers.[3] M&M/Mars concentrated most of its marketing and advertising efforts on the long-established successful brands. The last market offensive was to create a new image for their candy as a sweet snack and not a fattening, tooth-rotting, pimple-producing, junk food. During the 1984 Olympics, M&M/Mars had paid $5 million to have Snickers and M&M candies named the official snack foods of the 1984 Olympic Games. This gave M&M/Mars a great promotional advantage over its competitors.

Hershey

In 1903, Hershey Chocolate company was founded by Milton Snavely Hershey. In 1909, he and his wife donated a large percentage of their fortune to a school for deprived boys. The school evolved into the coeducational Milton Hershey School, which now owned 50.1 percent of Hershey's stock.[4]

With a 35.5 percent market share, Hershey was competing head-to-head with M&M/Mars for the number one position in U.S. candy sales. In 1985, the candy division generated sales of $1.8 billion, which was 67 percent of the company's total sales and 81 percent of its operating profit. Some of Hershey's top products were Hershey Bars, Kisses, Big Block Bars, Mr. Goodbar, and Krackle. Hershey produced five of the top ten candy bars (M&M/Mars sold the other five) and seventeen of the top sixty bestsellers.

In 1981, Hershey acquired the Friendly Ice Cream Corporation for $166 million. This chain of 714 restaurants and ice-cream shops was purchased to diversify the company.[5] In addition, Hershey recently purchased Luden, Inc., a producer of cough drops and candies such as 5th Avenue Bars, Mellomints, and Peppermint Patties. Hershey's newly introduced products, the Golden Almond/Golden Pecan bars and the Maribou line, were premium lines consisting of a smoother blend of chocolate and whole rather than chopped nuts.

Hershey had targeted eighteen to thirty-four year olds, with special emphasis placed on mothers who frequently made the purchasing decisions not only for themselves but also for their children. Hershey's fifteen-year-old slogan, "the great American chocolate bar," had been replaced with "one of the all-time greats."[6]

Cadbury-Schweppes

Cadbury-Schweppes was the third largest soft-drink producer and the fifth largest candy producer in the world. Although Cadbury-Schweppes was the third largest candy company in the United States, it controlled only 9 percent of the market. In 1978, the company purchased Peter Paul, the producer of Mounds and Almond Joy. In 1985, one half of its $2.43 billion in candy sales was in the United Kingdom, and the other half was in Europe, North America, and Australia.[7]

Sales in the United States had been slow due to poor management and marketing. In 1985, the company turned a $49.3 million profit into a $7.3 million loss in the U.S. market. Management reported sales to candy brokers as being identical with sales to candy consumers, but sales were not. The company's U.S. candy factory was reported as running at half capacity.[8]

Nestlé

Nestlé was the fourth largest candy company in the United States. Controlling 6 percent of the candy market, the company's product line included Crunch bars, Alpine White bars, and 100 Grand bars. Moreover, Nestlé sold Peter's Chocolate to smaller candy companies, including Chatham's, for use in production. Furthermore, Nestlé introduced a new line of individually foil-wrapped fine chocolates under the name of "Henri Nestlé" to appeal to

2. Ibid.
3. Ibid., p. 54.
4. Sally J. Blank, "Hershey: A Company Driven by Values," *Management Review,* November 1986, p. 32.
5. Ibid., p. 31.

6. Patricia Winters, "Chocolate Marketing No Longer Kid's Stuff," *Advertising Age,* May 19, 1986, p. 22.
7. Hesh Kestin, "Lax Britannica," *Forbes,* September 22, 1986, p. 112.
8. Ibid., p. 114.

the superpremium market. This line would consist of four varieties:

1. *Nocturing*—dark sweet chocolate with hazelnuts
2. *Truffon*—chocolate covered truffles
3. *Macaloa*—chocolate-coated macadamia nuts
4. *Cremande*—almond creme and hazelnuts covered with chocolate[9]

Their marketing efforts were focused on adults. The latest advertising slogan, "sweet dreams you can't resist," used soft music and dreamlike sequences.[10]

Campbell's Soup Co.'s Godiva Chocolates

Godiva Chocolatier was known for its premium chocolate with corresponding premium price. The premium chocolate market accounted for 5 percent of the total U.S. candy market. Recently introduced was a new, more Americanized line of chocolates called "Barringers." As this new line was less expensive than the original line, it was advertised as "American Classics Perfected."[11]

Local Competitors

Locally, Chatham's main competitors were Barris Candies, Inc., Sarah's Candy Castle, Geoffrey King Chocolates, Wriston's Candies, and Alice Faye Homemade Candies. These competitors were all privately held companies and located within 40 miles of CCC. Since Barris targeted the same markets as CCC and controlled a larger percentage of the fundraising market, Mrs. Chatham felt that it was the greatest competitive threat. Sarah's Candy Castle sold their candy only at their own outlets and used a less premium grade of chocolate. Alice Faye was considerably smaller than CCC and did not compete in the fundraising market. All the competitors in the local area priced comparably to Chatham's prices.

NOTES ON THE INDUSTRY

A recent study by the Chocolate Manufacturing Association revealed that 97 percent of all Americans eat candy and that 56 percent of these people eat it more than once a week.[12] More people are eating chocolate in the 1980s than in the 1970s, when Americans were very health conscious. There is a growing acceptance of candy as an inexpensive, pleasant, and nutritious snack. In 1986, the per-capita consumption of candy was over 20 pounds in the United States. According to the U.S. Department of Commerce, consumption in the U.S. has gone up one pound per year for the past four years. In 1985, 2.64 billion pounds of chocolate were consumed in the United States.[13]

Today's buyers were more particular about the quality of the chocolate purchased. More sophisticated chocolate buyers were choosing U.S. premium chocolates, which were often handmade by a small producer or single-store boutique, over chocolates from Belgium or France. In 1986, chocolate imports from Europe decreased 14 percent from the previous year. This decrease is attributed to the increase of American premium chocolate producers and the increased price of European candies due to the devalued dollar.[14]

Innovative American chocolate makers have been very daring in experimenting with exotic new flavors, such as bourbon pecan, vanilla malt, and chocolate-coated goat's cheese or chocolate laced with maple syrup and fruit wines.[15] Moreover, many chocolaters have adopted the European technique of shell molding. This building the chocolate from the outside results in a harder, more chocolatey shell that can hold liquor or assume jewel-like shapes. Recent legislation allowing for the interstate transport of liquor-filled chocolate should increase competition in this area.[16]

As baby boom children have grown up, big candy companies have shifted their marketing campaigns to focus more on adults. Studies showed that people over eighteen consume 55 percent of all candy sold. In an effort to appeal to this market, many companies have increased the size of their

9. Winters, p. 22.
10. Ibid.
11. Judann Dagnoli, "Godiva Gets Yank Cousin," *Advertising Age*, October 27, 1986, p. 41.

12. National Confectioners Association, "Sweet Tooth," *Wall Street Journal*, December 2, 1986, p. 35.
13. Winters, p. 22.
14. Meg Sullivan, "U.S. Chocolates Ring Sweet Sales for Small Shops," *Wall Street Journal*, February 13, 1987, p. 27.
15. Ibid.
16. Ibid.

candy 10 to 15 percent in order to be more filling and satisfying.[17]

Advertising had also focused on changing the image of candy as more respectable by showing its place in a well-balanced diet. Companies advertised the nutritional benefits and the "energy boost" of candy, especially chocolate. Trade groups have formulated campaigns to dispel the fears that candy causes acne and rots teeth. Last year, the National Confectionery Association spent $600,000 in public relations efforts touting the nutritional benefits of chocolate.[18]

---

17. Ronald Alsop, "Candy Makers Step Up Fight Over America's Sweet Tooth," *Wall Street Journal,* June 13, 1985, p. 33.
18. Winters, p. 22.

PLANS FOR THE FUTURE

Mrs. Chatham was quite happy with the performance of CCC and was comfortable with her standard of living. "If we grew too much larger," she said, "I wouldn't have any time left to myself." Mrs. Chatham had recently taken up golf and devoted one afternoon a week to her new pastime. The business was going well, and Mrs. Chatham looked forward to the increased leisure time when Cindy and Marsha took a larger role in the company. Indeed, the daughters were eager to take on more responsibility. However, unlike their mother, they felt the company needed more growth and strategic direction.

Exhibit 1
CHATHAM CANDY COMPANY: BALANCE SHEET[a]

	1987	1986
ASSETS		
Current Assets		
Cash	$ 47,005	$ 60,877
Inventory—raw materials, packaging supplies, and finished goods	194,818	122,302
Accounts receivable—trade	14,790	11,609
Prepaid insurance	8,116	6,496
Total Current Assets	$264,729	$201,284
Property, Plant and Equipment—at cost		
Equipment	$178,933	$164,814
Vehicles	21,151	21,151
Leasehold improvements	39,151	39,151
	239,235	225,116
Less accumulated depreciation	164,505	135,007
Total Property, Plant, and Equipment	74,730	90,109
TOTAL ASSETS	$339,459	$291,393
LIABILITIES AND STOCKHOLDERS' EQUITY		
Current Liabilities		
Accrued retirement plan contributions	$16,469	$ 9,677
Accrued expenses	5,646	14,261
Accounts payable	4,400	3,005
Notes payable—Officer	1,261	116,968
Total Current Liabilities	$27,776	$143,911

Exhibit 1
CHATHAM CANDY COMPANY: BALANCE SHEET[a] (*continued*)

	1987	1986
LIABILITIES AND STOCKHOLDERS' EQUITY		
Long-Term Debt		
Note payable stockholder	—	50,000
Total Liabilities	27,776	193,911
Stockholders' Equity		
Common stock—$1.00 par value—		
500,000 shares authorized; 95,000		
shares issued and outstanding	$ 95,000	$ 95,000
Paid in capital in excess of par value	194,473	1,895
Retained earnings	22,210	587
Total Stockholders' Equity	311,683	97,482
TOTAL LIABILITIES AND STOCKHOLD-ERS' EQUITY	$339,459	$291,393

a. See Accountants' Review Report in Exhibit 4.

Exhibit 2
CHATHAM CANDY COMPANY: INCOME STATEMENT[a]

	1987	1986
Sales	$638,673	$568,614
Cost of Sales		
Raw materials	$249,551	$228,313
Packaging supplies	47,923	50,660
Wages	96,725	84,835
Utilities	24,136	22,312
Repairs and maintenance	6,928	10,177
Freight	9,400	6,207
Depreciation	29,498	27,078
Payroll taxes	19,824	17,891
Total Cost of Sales	483,985	447,473
Gross Profit	154,688	121,141
Less General and Administrative Expenses		
Officer's salary	$ 48,000	$ 48,000
Rent	10,800	10,800
Insurance	11,354	9,784
Employee medical benefits	9,739	5,093
Contribution to employees' retirement plan	16,472	9,680
Interest	—	766
Store and office expenses	4,406	5,218
Commissions	10,988	3,262
Dues and subscriptions	643	1,442
Legal and accounting	6,248	6,187
Automobile and truck expense	944	1,104
Taxes	172	548

	1987	1986
Advertising and promotional	13,807	14,887
Miscellaneous expense	456	4,143
Total General and Administrative Expenses	134,029	120,914
Net Income Before Interest Income	$ 20,659	$ 227
Interest income	3,501	4,319
Net Income Before Taxes	$ 24,160	$ 4,546
Income taxes	2,537	—
Net Income	$ 21,623	$ 4,546
Retained Earnings (Deficit) July 1	587	(3,959)
RETAINED EARNINGS JUNE 30	$ 22,210	$ 587

a. See Accountants' Review Report in Exhibit 4.

Exhibit 3
CHATHAM CANDY COMPANY: INCREASE IN CAPITAL[a]

	1987	1986
Financial Resources Provided by		
Net income from operations	$ 21,623	$ 4,546
Add: charges against income not requiring funds—depreciation	29,498	27,078
	$ 51,121	$ 31,624
Other resources: Additional paid in capital in excess of par	192,578	—
Total Financial Resources Provided	243,699	31,624
Financial Resources Used for		
Reduction of long-term debt	$ 50,000	$ —
Additions to equipment and leasehold improvements	14,119	26,740
Total Financial Resources Used	64,119	26,740
INCREASE IN WORKING CAPITAL	$179,580	$ 4,884
Increase (Decrease) in Current Assets		
Cash	$(13,872)	$(23,511)
Accounts receivable	3,181	3,231
Inventory	72,516	14,106
Prepaid insurance	1,620	510
Total Increase (Decrease) in Current Assets	$ 63,445	$ (5,664)
(Increase) Decrease in Current Liabilities		
Accrued salaries—officers	$ —	$ 6,000
Accrued retirement plan contributions	(6,792)	875
Accrued expenses	8,615	5,003
Accounts payable	(1,395)	(765)
Due to officers	115,707	(565)
Total Increase (Decrease) in Current Liabilities	116,135	10,548
INCREASE IN WORKING CAPITAL	$179,580	$ 4,884

a. See Accountants' Review Report in Exhibit 4.

Exhibit 4
ACCOUNTANTS' REVIEW REPORT

NOTE 2:   SUMMARY OF SIGNIFICANT ACCOUNTING POLICIES
- *General Policy.* The company's financial statements are prepared in accordance with generally accepted accounting principles. The company uses the accrual basis of accounting—assets and liabilities are carried at historical cost.
- *Inventories.* Inventories are stated at the lower of cost or market. Cost is determined by the first-in, first-out method.
- *Fixed Assets.* Fixed assets are carried at historical cost. Expenditures for new facilities and major betterments are capitalized. Maintenance, repairs, and minor betterments are charged to expense as incurred.
- *Depreciation.* Depreciation is computed on all assets acquired before January 1, 1981, over their estimated useful lives as follows:

	METHOD	*USEFUL LIFE*
Vehicles	Straight line	2 years
Equipment and fixtures	Declining balance	2–10 years
Leasehold improvements	Straight line	5–15 years

Depreciation (cost recovery) on assets acquired after January 1, 1981, is computed using the accelerated cost recovery system as provided in The Economic Recovery Tax Act of 1981 as follows:

	CLASS OF PROPERTY
Vehicles	3 years
Equipment	5 years
Leasehold improvements	15 years

The total cost of assets depreciated using the accelerated cost recovery system is $101,773.
- *Investment Tax Credit.* The company offsets the investment tax credit against federal income tax expense in the year in which it is utilized for tax purposes.
- *Allowance for Uncollectable Accounts Receivable*—An allowance for uncollectable accounts is established based on management's estimate of uncollectability after a review of all accounts.

NOTE 3:   PENSION AND PROFIT-SHARING PLANS
The company has defined contribution pension and profit-sharing plans covering substantially all full-time employees. Pension costs are accrued and funded currently. Contributions to the profit-sharing plan are determined annually at the discretion of the board of directors and are accrued and funded currently. The board of directors authorized a profit-sharing contribution of $5,000.00 for the year ended June 30, 1986, and $0 for the year ended June 30, 1985.

NOTE 4:   INCOME TAX PROVISION
The provision for income taxes differs from that computed at the statutory 46 percent corporate rate as follows:

	JUNE 30 1986	JUNE 30 1985
Federal statutory rate	46.0%	46.0%
State income taxes	10.5	10.5
Effects of net operating loss carryover	0.0	(10.5)
Allowable credits	(15.0)	(15.0)
Effect of federal surtax exemption	(31.0)	(31.0)
	10.5	0.0

WALTER'S VARIETY STORES, INC.

OTHA L. GRAY
Lander College

BEVERLY LITTLE
Lander College

STRUCTURE OF OPERATIONS

A family enterprise with a fifty-five-year operating history, Walter's Five-and-Ten-Cent Stores originally operated as a proprietorship with fifteen retail stores at the pinnacle of successful operations. The firm currently consists of seven retail variety stores in four corporations with common ownership vested in the three surviving children of the founder, Wallace Walter. There is no common corporate parent-subsidiary relationship. Each corporation operates one or more retail variety stores under a common trade name in one of three contiguous states. Separate corporations were initially organized to benefit from favorable corporate taxation and to segregate interstate operations. Decline of the tax advantage of separate corporate structures and the recurrence of operating losses has led to merging of several corporations. Walter's Five-and-Ten-Cent Stores were traditionally established in small towns and cities with limited populations, serving regional rural areas. They were at one time located in an area some 50 to 100 miles from the central office, but with two exceptions now are no more distant than 35 miles from the general offices. The related corporations operate through the main corporation as a primary financial agent providing service functions of pooled merchandise purchasing, central warehousing, and redistribution to individual retail stores.

PRESENT FINANCIAL SITUATION

Due to a seriously deteriorating financial situation, the current owners of Walter's Variety Stores are facing a major decision. Their alternatives are continuation of business operations, sale to a discount chain, or liquidation. The firm has sustained continuing losses from operations. It is highly leveraged with short-term debt obligations being predominant. Liquidity is severely restricted due to low inventory turnover.

The firm has been unable to take advantage of purchase discounts in recent years. Limited access to capital has reduced the ability to maintain an adequate level of merchandise to meet customer demand even in the staple inventory lines. Retail sales have been declining for several years as a consequence of limited merchandise stock and encroaching competition in the market area from newly established stores such as K-Mart and Wal-Mart. The declining sales revenue has not been offset by a comparable reduction in operating expenses.

Several actions have been taken to reduce operating costs. Termination of the pension plan, which required funding of approximately $30,000 annually, will provide an anticipated recovery of $120,000 in prior year overfunding, which can be applied to reduction of current debt. Management personnel has been reduced. One clerical staff position and one purchasing agent position have been eliminated. A retiring warehouse manager has been replaced by the promotion of an assistant rather than by additional hiring. The resulting cost savings in these actions is already reflected in the financial statements contained in Exhibits 1, 2, 3, and 4.

This case, written especially for this text, is printed by permission.

Exhibit 1
WALTER'S VARIETY STORES, INC.: COMBINED BALANCE SHEET[a]

	1986	1985
ASSETS		
Cash in bank (overdraft on books)	$ (46,900)	$ 37,164
Accounts receivable related corporations[b]	90,000	157,000
Inventories[c]	1,377,900	1,950,000
Store fixtures (at cost)	483,000	483,000
Less accumulated depreciation	(461,800)	(446,000)
Building (at cost)[d]	24,000	24,400
Motor vehicle (at cost)[e]	50,000	50,000
Less accumulated depreciation	(50,000)	(50,000)
TOTAL ASSETS	$1,466,200	$2,205,564
LIABILITIES AND CAPITAL		
Liabilities		
Accounts payable trade [f]	$ 318,800	$ 454,500
Accruals of expenses	50,000	61,500
Accruals (to shareholders for rent and interest)[g]	42,500	30,200
Notes payable to banks (due in 1 year or less)[h]	247,000	347,000
Notes payable to shareholders[i]	227,000	247,000
Total Liabilities	$ 885,300	$1,140,200
Capital		
Capital stock, par value	160,000	160,000
Paid-in capital from mergers[j]	233,000	233,000
Retained earnings	187,900	
Total Capital	580,900	1,065,364
TOTAL LIABILITIES AND CAPITAL	$1,466,200	$2,205,564

a. Accounting policies in general follow accrual methods allowed for tax accounting.
b. Noncombined related corporation accounts receivable for trade merchandise in payment default, $90,000.
c. A retail inventory pricing method was used that uniformly priced inventory on a cost basis determined by applying a standard gross margin reduction of 33.3 percent of retail.
d. An old building not used in operations, at cost.
e. All motor vehicles are fully depreciated.
f. Accounts payable to trade creditors are 45 to 60 days past due date for normal payment and discount.
g. Accruals of interest and rent due to shareholders is separately stated being non-tax deductible until paid, in arrears.
h. Notes payable to banks on renewable 90-day and 180-day notes with personal endorsement by shareholders or officers.
i. Notes payable to shareholders for loans on open notes with rates floating at approximate prime rate with a floor of 10 percent.
j. Several corporations were merged in consolidating operations and utilization of operating losses resulting in paid in capital.

THE FOUNDER AND SUCCESSORS

The founding owner, Wallace Walter, died some twelve years ago. His wife predeceased him, leaving three teenage children, and he did not remarry. Matthew, brother Wally, and sister Sadie inherited equal interests in the estate at the death of their father. Exhibit 5 presents a financial overview of the estate and the cash drain imposed by the payment of estate taxes and interest incurred in seven years of deferred installment payments.

Exhibit 2

WALTER'S VARIETY STORES, INC.: STATEMENT OF COMBINED OPERATIONS

	1986	1985
Sales Revenue	$3,341,362	$4,178,423
Less Cost of Sales	2,296,451	2,657,048
Gross Profit	$1,044,911	$1,521,375
Less Operating Expenses		
Salaries	$ 879,500	$ 895,200
Payroll tax	66,000	71,300
Pension fund	200	26,200
Health insurance	65,000	65,000
Depreciation	15,800	15,200
Auto and truck expense	6,800	10,400
Insurance	25,600	25,800
Travel	6,350	16,200
Rent	153,900	156,100
Utilities	85,900	98,066
Repairs	12,600	13,200
Supplies	29,300	30,900
Housekeeping	4,500	6,600
Advertising	33,100	41,200
Tax and license	66,100	68,600
Postage and office	3,400	3,800
Telephone	12,000	12,000
Legal and professional	3,500	3,400
Miscellaneous unclassified	17,225	11,600
Service charges	12,700	9,800
Bad checks	1,000	700
Donations	400	1,100
Interest	28,500	35,400
Total	1,529,375	$1,617,766
Net Income Before Tax	(484,464)	(96,391)
Income Tax Expense	—	10,330
NET INCOME (LOSS)	($484,464)	($106,721)

Wallace Walter was a shrewd merchandiser with a keen eye for potential profit, but he lacked formal management training and followed no organized plan of control in his business operations. He continually expanded the number of retail stores without a long-term development plan. Over the years Wallace had accumulated investments in securities, assorted real estate, and substantial merchandise value in a growing number of retail stores. These resources provided the collateral to secure critical short-term revolving bank loans or mortgage loans for financing of additional retail store merchandise and fixtures and to meet seasonal needs for working capital. By the time of his death, the firm had become highly leveraged, with much of the permanent capital financed with revolving short-term borrowing from banks and individuals on the strength of Wallace's integrity and his past record of meeting financial obligations in a timely manner.

MANAGEMENT PERSONNEL

No surviving family member had significant experience in the business's operations at the time of Wallace Walter's death. Wally, who was twenty-six years

Exhibit 3
WALTER'S VARIETY STORES, INC.: COMBINED INCOME STATEMENTS[a]

	1986	1985	1984	1983	1982	1981
Gross Retail Sales	$3,341,362	$4,178,423	$4,417,736	$4,447,222	$4,712,141	$4,087,627
Less Cost of Goods Sold	2,296,451	2,657,048	2,707,575	2,641,684	2,703,671	2,394,657
Gross Profit	$1,044,911	$1,521,375	$1,710,161	$1,805,538	$2,008,470	$1,692,970
Less Operating Expenses	1,529,375	1,617,766	1,805,935	1,766,705	1,796,340	1,530,228
Total Costs	$3,825,826	$4,274,814	$4,513,510	$4,408,389	$4,500,011	$3,924,885
Net Income (Loss) Before Tax	(484,464)	(96,391)	(95,774)	38,833	212,130	162,742
Income Tax Expense	—	10,330	4,162	33,941	41,359	1,152
NET INCOME (LOSS) AFTER TAX	($484,464)	($106,721)	($99,936)	$4,892	$170,771	$161,590

a. Four separate corporations with no parent but common ownership. Individual returns and tax losses.

	1986	1985	1984	1983	1982	1981
Average Inventory	$1,500,000	$2,100,000	$2,100,000	$2,300,000	$2,500,000	$2,000,000
Salaries/Sales	26.32	21.42	20.5	20.2	19.5	21.0

Exhibit 4
WALTER'S VARIETY STORES, INC.: MERCHANDISE PURCHASE COMPARISONS

DEPARTMENT	1986	1985	1984
Records and tapes	$ 36,450	$ 52,077	$ 52,192
Health and beauty aids	181,203	258,861	282,022
Photo frames	11,988	17,125	20,814
Jewelry	17,568	25,097	42,574
Flowers	22,728	32,471	43,056
Housewares	134,746	192,495	305,272
Imports	8,347	11,924	84,922
Electronics and appliances	15,393	21,990	57,722
Horticulture	64,366	91,951	128,770
Lawn furniture	3,798	5,425	15,057
Subtotal	$ 496,587	$ 709,416	$1,032,401
Pets	$ 19,391	$ 27,701	$ 31,814
Automotive	1,684	2,405	4,861
Stationery	123,150	175,929	230,115
Notions	87,354	124,789	182,870
Hardware	58,159	83,084	111,951
Subtotal	289,738	413,908	561,611
Ladies	$ 46,183	$ 65,975	$ 73,472
Infants and children	99,740	142,486	209,060
Mens	22,761	32,515	61,090
Hosiery	49,813	71,161	89,714
Lingerie	31,408	44,868	69,290
Accessories	14,721	21,035	44,503
Shoes	15,049	21,499	20,908
Subtotal	279,675	399,539	568,037

Exhibit 4

WALTER'S VARIETY STORES, INC.: MERCHANDISE PURCHASE COMPARISONS (*continued*)

DEPARTMENT	1986	1985	1984
Toys	$ 164,579	$ 235,144	$ 537,911
Domestic	74,470	106,386	159,120
Jennings—Shepherd	30,139	43,049	37,134
Confections	64,939	92,772	132,850
Cameras	16,195	23,136	34,134
Photo development	1,148	1,640	1,876
Sporting goods	5,008	7,155	17,461
Subtotal	356,478	509,252	920,765
Totals	$1,422,478	$2,032,115	$3,082,814
Supplies	15,824	22,600	31,592
Seasonal	138,134	154,192	173,601
Subtotal	$1,576,436	$2,208,907	$3,288,007
Store purchases—Direct	151,753	180,627	228,677
GRAND TOTAL	$1,728,189	$2,389,534	$3,516,684

Exhibit 5

ESTATE TAX DATA FOR WALLACE WALTER

Gross estate composition	
Securities—Stock of Walter's Stores	$ 225,000
—Miscellaneous public stocks and bonds	375,000
Real Estate—Occupied by Walter's Stores	400,000
—Miscellaneous real estate	200,000
Mortgage and notes receivable	150,000
Insurance payable to estate	160,000
Miscellaneous personal property	40,000
Lifetime transfers	10,000
Total	$1,560,000
Allowable deductions—Debts and expenses	
Funeral and last illness	$ 20,000
Personal debts owed	90,000
Mortgages due on property owned	100,000
Total	$ 210,000
Federal tax exemption	$ 60,000
Approximate federal estate tax due	420,000
State death tax credits	50,000
Adjustments in federal estate tax by audit	$ 30,000
Aggregate federal and state death taxes payable	450,000
Additional interest from payment over seven years with interest	175,000
Total cash drain from estate due to death tax	$ 625,000

old, had worked with his father only on a very limited basis. Sadie was a college student, age twenty-three. Matthew, age twenty-one, was serving in the army after having graduated from high school. Neither Matthew or Wally had any formal education beyond secondary school. Both lacked the maturity needed to assume a leading management role in the business.

Frank and Luke Walter, brothers of Wallace, had been associated with the business for some thirty to forty years as merchandise buyers, but they had no overall managerial responsibility or experience. A trusted long-term employee, Jennie, was book-keeper and financial and personal confidant of Walter. He had always been somewhat eccentric in his personal and business affairs, and the financial affairs of the firm were closely guarded private matters divulged only by necessity to Jennie. The firm initially operated as a sole proprietorship and only in recent years had been incorporated. The legal form of organization did not change the informality and lack of structure in management of the business. Walter made all the management decisions, and no opportunity was provided for key personnel and family associates to develop managerial experience.

Walter's will directed the creation of a residual trust with no distribution to be made of the assets until the youngest child reached age thirty, when there was to be equal division among his children. In the interim, responsibility for management of the business was placed on Frank, Luke, and Jeanie, together with individual retail store managers who were allowed to exercise substantial autonomy.

INTERIM FINANCING; ESTATE AND TRUST

In the years since the death of founder Wallace Walter, the family enterprise has survived by some miracle while such retail giants as W. T. Grant, Robert Hall, J. M. Fields, and many less well known regional and national retail merchandising firms had failed. Provision in Walter's will for the residual trust permitted retention of essential financial resources, which were available to assist the financing of the business during the transition years. By drawing on the estate and the trust, the same collateral was available to successor management that had been available to Walter. However, the substantial

shrinkage in assets that resulted from payment of estate taxes severely reduced financial resources formerly available for business needs. Although deferral of estate tax payment over a seven-year period permitted an orderly marshalling of assets, it became necessary to sell or liquidate several of the less profitable retail stores in order to raise cash for tax payments. At the present time only seven of the original fifteen retail stores continue in operation.

When the residual trust was terminated and the assets distributed to the siblings, their personal interests in maintaining a family merchandising business were not compatible. Only Matthew has worked full time in the business since his father's death. Wally participated in the liquidation of the retail operations to raise funds for tax payment, but has not been active in management or merchandising operation. He was undertaking his own business ventures with his share of inheritance. Sadie married and moved away from the area with her family. Her needs for financial support and her personal interests are not strongly supportive of continued participation in business ventures with her share of inheritance. Only Matthew is willing to risk his personal financial resources in continued operation of the family enterprise. Matthew's personal resources are inadequate to provide the financing to support continued business operations, but he would like to borrow the necessary funds to buy out the equity interest of the other owners and continue the business. He believes that concentration of management in a single owner together with a reduced scale of operations will permit a successful continuation of the business. It will be necessary to restructure the existing short-term debt, including personal loans from family members.

BUSINESS SUCCESSION PLAN

The initial plan in the estate provided for purchase of a part of the business by Frank and Luke through the use of proceeds of insurance. Frank and Luke owned insurance policies on the life of Wallace Walter, the premiums having been paid by the business as an additional salary to them. This initial agreement was defective in providing only for mandatory purchase of a business interest with no corresponding mandatory sell agreement. An initial provision in the will directing the executors to sell had been eliminated by changes prior to Walter's death. A subsequent buy-sell agreement with mandatory provisions on both buyer and seller had been drawn by legal counsel and transmitted to Wallace Walter, but was found among his legal papers unexecuted.

Without a mutually binding agreement to buy and sell, Frank and Luke extended personal loans of insurance proceeds to assist the business. Now that Frank and Luke are both at retirement age without any equity interest in Walter's Stores, they wish to recover their personal loans and withdraw from any continued business participation. Loss of these financial resources will further impair the financial viability of the firm.

POTENTIAL FOR SURVIVING; HISTORICAL INFLUENCES

The personal management style of the founder, Wallace Walter, greatly impacted the development of Walter's stores and influenced the survival of the firm.

Matthew Walter reviewed the factors that had shaped the development of Walter's Variety Stores throughout past years and reflected on the changes he would need to make if he succeeded in acquiring sole ownership and control over future operations.

Early Years

Walter's Five-and-Ten-Cent Stores began in the early 1930s following a family tradition of mercantile operations. The initial store was a 5,000-square foot retail unit in the central section of a small town of 2,500 residents. Prosperity in the Depression years developed from good merchandising practices. Expansion of the firm prior to World War II led to establishment of five comparable retail stores in nearby towns of similar size. The five-and-ten-cent store franchise was a popular general merchandising unit of the 1930s era. Good selection of quality merchandise at a fair price was a hallmark of Walter's stores. Strong consumer demand in the post–World War II period provided the impetus to open ten additional retail stores in other nearby towns and small cities, bringing the total number of retail stores to fifteen by the middle 1960s.

Retail Store Units

The first retail stores were located in central business districts of small towns with less than 10,000 population. The development of strip shopping centers in the late 1950s and early 1960s made it necessary to secure more adequate parking space downtown or move retail stores to such shopping centers. Rental costs in the downtown locations were rarely in excess of $500 per month for a 10,000-square foot retail area. Long-term leases ensured the maintenance of low rental costs. The minimum rental cost in a strip center was from $2.50 to $2.95 per square foot in the initial development period. Thus a strip center store would command a $25,000 annual rental compared to a midtown store rental cost of $6,000. The limited local community population base and growing competition from discount stores made it difficult to generate the sales volume necessary to support incremental site costs.

Walter's management faced a dilemma. Remaining in the central business district resulted in declining sales, but a move to the strip center produced significant incremental operating costs. Either decision resulted in sharp reduction in profits without substantial sales volume. Rather than use sales per square foot as a decision criterion, Wallace Walter relied on personal intuition and emotion in decisions regarding store site, relocation, and discontinuance of operations.

Walter's stores were renovated about every ten years to compete with the competitive image of the newer stores. The increasing clerical wage rates forced centralization of checkout of merchandise and a move toward self-service; both these changes led to greater loss of merchandise through theft. The cash registers were never tied to inventory control due to Wallace Walter's apprehension of cost and personal lack of appreciation of the economics that might arise from greater information and control. Physical inventory verification was undertaken only once a year. Retail clerks recorded out-of-stock items from the central warehouse for weekly delivery. Customers developed a loyalty to the Walter's stores due to the personal attention given by personnel and the quality of merchandise available. Every effort was made to secure any out-of-stock item requested by a customer promptly from another retail store location or the warehouse. With the exception of three units, all stores were located within 50 miles of the central warehouse and management offices. Less frequent supervision by central management and more costly merchandise delivery contributed to low profitability and eventual sale or liquidation of the more distant retail operations.

Financial Policies

The initial financing of Walter's stores came from personal loans and reinvestment of earnings. Early profitability provided funding to expand. As the firm grew financially stronger, it was possible to secure mortgage loans on properties being renovated or constructed for store sites. Short-term collateralized bank loans supplemented a limited open line of mercantile credit. The small local banks were not in a position to advance substantial lines of credit without some correspondent banking participation. Significant lines of credit were not negotiated, since that would have required substantial disclosure with audited financial statements. In one instance an effort was made to secure a $250,000 line of short-term revolving credit. The request for audited financial statements led Walter's management to arrange to pay off existing loans with the bank and to use multiple small loans from several bankers who required less financial data. Management was unwilling and unable to provide adequate financial information due to the fragmentary state of the accounting records and financial controls.

Much of the borrowing by Walter from local banks was secured on the basis of his personal character and previous record of satisfactory relationships. In the 1960s Wallace Walter became a founding shareholder in several newly established banks in the towns where he had retail store operations. Typically these banks limited loans to $25,000 to corporate officers and shareholders. With as many as ten different retail store locations having access to $25,000 each in borrowing from individual local banks, as much as $250,000 in open credit was available without the formality of audited financial statements otherwise required for a single credit line of such magnitude. Local bank borrowing was good for business relationships and, coupled with normal trade credit extended by merchandise vendors, provided a substantial source of financing.

There was little evidence of prior financial planning in the expansion of Walter's retail store units, remodeling, or purchase of inventory and fixtures. Walter often entered contractual purchase agreements without prior negotiation of the financing for the project. As a consequence, there was continual financial stress and restricted liquidity as the number of retail store units grew. Mortgage loans and revolving collateralized bank loans were the primary financial instruments used to finance inventory, fixtures, and improvements. The required annual cleanup of open bank loans for at least 30 days per year did not pose an insurmountable problem for Walter since the loans were held by several different banks and staggered maturity dates facilitated the rollover.

Retail Store Personnel and Management

Despite the importance of personal treatment and customer loyalty, the stores' clerical personnel were provided with little practical training and were paid little more than minimum wage. Store managers, responsible for merchandise display, inventory balance maintenance, courteous treatment of customers, and minimization of inventory loss, were considered central to successful operations. Often managers who voluntarily left successful jobs with larger variety chains such as Kress or Woolworth's were hired, and their experience was viewed as a substitute for formal training. Managerial honesty and integrity were viewed as the keys to control of daily receipts and merchandise theft.

Walter gave managers a great deal of autonomy, and store success tended to correspond with the manager's capabilities. Strong managers ran stores as if they were owners, some to the point of not following policies. Slackness in providing paperwork to the central office led to loose control of merchandise and financial resources. A supervisory management system to aid store managers with merchandise management, control, and advertising was conceived but failed due to poor delineation of roles of supervisors and managers and to inconsistent use.

Control System

There was little formal control exercised in the management of the retail stores. The primary control device for operating expenses was percent of salary cost related to sales. This was a key figure watched on a monthly basis, especially as minimum wages began to rise. Inventory control was virtually nonexistent. An annual physical count provided verification of the investment. An annual compilation of shortage or overage on the basis of a retail method was employed, as shown in Exhibit 6. The results of the annual computations were dependent upon the accuracy of records for markups, markdowns, discounts, and other adjustments maintained at the local retail store location. Similarly, the accuracy of the physical count and pricing was a critical factor in

Exhibit 6

WALTER'S VARIETY STORES, INC.: INVENTORY CONTROL PROOF

	RETAIL STORE UNIT							
	S1	S2	S3	E1	E2	C1	C2	W1
Charges								
Beginning inventory—								
Retail	$ 372,594	$303,745	$ 76,660	$130,405	$339,538	$ 613,753	$169,049	$185,348
Markups	894	1,201	480	707	1,216	495	664	979
Shipments at retail	771,219	552,744	372,060	187,214	612,407	1,549,184	251,959	233,205
Total Accountability	$1,044,707	$857,690	$449,200	$318,326	$953,161	$2,163,432	$421,672	$419,532
Credits								
Sales—Retail	$ 708,668	$483,264	$239,670	$174,595	$520,293	$1,394,295	$249,920	$239,034
Adjustments—Retail								
Returns (net/ship)	—	—	—	—	—	—	—	—
Markdowns	30,153	25,970	16,673	6,319	34,243	41,164	11,074	11,237
Damaged	3,690	1,742	2,600	122	5,083	662	331	465
Used	1,560	640	461	177	464	2,005	405	257
Discounts	5,990	3,552	1,934	529	4,530	4,785	645	611
Donated	265	71	273	86	1,850	1,197	—	265
Claims	—	—	—	—	—	—	—	—
Miscellaneous accounts (current charges)	—	—	—	—	—	—	—	—
Ending inventory—								
Retail (per physical count)	396,383	325,669	178,506	141,570	355,052	659,197	161,433	170,151
Total Accounted for	$1,146,709	$840,908	$440,117	$323,398	$921,515	$2,103,305	$423,808	$422,020
(Shortage) overall retail	(96,004)	($16,782)	($9,083)	$5,072[a]	($31,646)	(60,126)	($2,136)	($2,488)
Retail percent of sales	.85	3.47	3.78	2.90	6.08	2.78	.85	.93

a. Overage

credibility of the control reports. Walter's used personnel from various stores to assist in the physical count at each store. Rarely were stores closed for the physical count, and the process was not closely supervised.

A lack of credibility frequently developed when there was some indication of a problem in the computed inventory proof. Rarely would there be any effort to verify the cause of apparent shortage. Reliability of internal records was questioned. A philosophy of "Let's wait until next time and see if the problem is corrected" prevailed and contributed to ineffective control. If the internal record system was not credible, it was difficult to place responsibility for inventory shortages on individual store manag-

ers. In one or two instances, the remuneration of store managers was tied to control of inventory as well as profitability of the retail store. Despite the fact that inventory shortages were less apparent in such instances, this practice of tying managerial pay to results of profits or inventory control was the exception rather than the practice with Walter's Stores. Financial statements for operation of individual retail store units were not prepared as a basis of control. The raw data were available from weekly sales reports by each store unit, but the manual bookkeeping system was too rudimentary to develop verifiable expenses in detail on a timely basis. An informal compilation of store operating results was developed for Walter's annual review, but the results were rarely discussed with individual retail store managers. In fact, the policy was to keep individual store managers uninformed about profitability of their stores. Secrecy was a fetish to Walter. Retail store managers were expected to display merchandise, supervise clerical personnel, and provide security for sales receipts and merchandise. Some managers exercised more initiative, but many did not.

Critical Incidents in Management and Operations

On one occasion it was discovered that retail inventory in ladies' handbags held at one of the retail stores totaled $25,000, despite the fact that annual gross sales at the store had never exceeded $300,000. The inventory of handbags was merely indicative of the excessive inventory holdings in several of the retail store locations. Other items of ladies' and children's clothing were noticeably overstocked and subsequently required sale at significant markdown. Investigation of the overstocking led to suspension of a purchasing agent who had received financial inducements from vendor representatives to order merchandise in excess of rational purchase requirements.

At another time, it was noticed by the tax accountant that the bank balance at one of the smaller retail units exceeded $165,000 in a non–interest bearing checking account and that the balance had been accumulating for some months. Inquiry revealed that the accumulation was planned to enable payment of a cash dividend distribution to minority S corporation shareholders in the separate corporation. Needless to say, discovery of the accumulating balance led to subsequent investment in a certificate at a fair rate of return.

For a substantial period of time, there were over thirty-five active individual bank accounts in the total retail enterprise. Each store conducted business through individual bank accounts for small local payments and transfers to the central management accounts. Service charges, transfer costs, and float time were considerable. The maintenance of the local bank accounts did, however, allow the cultivation of local bankers who were willing to extend loans on an unsecured basis in amounts from $25,000 to $50,000 on three- to six-month terms with renewal at prevailing interest rates. During one time period of tight money, the interest rates reached 21 percent.

WHAT OF THE FUTURE?

Matthew Walter examined the options. He wanted to continue the active operation of the family enterprise. Other family members want to salvage any residual equity and retire from active management. Matthew would like to obtain long-term financing to cover past due trade credit, eliminate the existing short-term bank loans, pay the outstanding shareholder loans, and give himself full equity ownership and managerial control, which he believes would provide an opportunity for profitability and survival of the business.

Matthew's personal financial resources are limited to $40,000 equity in his home, $100,000 interest in jointly owned real estate occupied by the retail store units and central warehousing operations, and $125,000 in securities. Rental payments due on leases of buildings occupied by Walter's Stores are currently in arrears, as are salaries, bonuses, and interest on debt owned shareholders. Matthew's personal income from dividends and interest unrelated to the family enterprise totals about $12,000 annually. Salary from Walter's Stores is currently $25,000 per year. His personal obligations amount to $65,000 in bank loans incurred on behalf of the business, $50,000 mortgage debt on personal residence, and $75,000 mortgage debts on investment real estate.

Consultation with an advisory unit of the Small Business Management Center at a local university led to a recommendation that Matthew undertake a pro-forma analysis of operations. A restructuring plan was proposed whereby the central warehousing and distribution center would be discontinued and replaced by a direct purchase-shipment plan for individual retail stores. The cost to retail merchandise ratio under the proposed plan is estimated at 70 percent. This plan is estimated to reduce overall operating costs of centralized procurement, warehousing, and redistribution by $150,000 annually. The restructuring plan would reduce the number of retail stores to five in a market area within a radius of 30 miles from the central office, offering the potential for more direct supervisory control. The closing of two retail units at remote locations is estimated to reduce gross sales by $1,000,000 annually, but those units are currently operating at break-even level. Competition by K-Mart and Wal-Mart stores in the market area of the retail units targeted for elimination limits the potential for better operating results. Both K-Mart and Wal-Mart have competitive retail operations planned for the remaining market area currently served by Walter's Stores.

If financing is not available, the option of liquidation or bulk sales to potential purchaser remains. There is an offer outstanding to purchase the entire stock of inventory at 40 percent of retail value and to lease the retail store facilities, which are personally and jointly owned by shareholders. The purchase price would be paid at the rate of $25,000 weekly after an initial $100,000 payment. Obligation for payment to outstanding trade creditors, bank loans, and loans to shareholders would remain with the Walter's Store corporation. The corporate structure would be terminated and any residual equity distributed to shareholders. An alternative to the proposed bulk sale is to hold liquidation sales, with the potential of realizing no more than 50 percent of retail value before incurring the labor costs of a minimum liquidation period of one month.

BEAUTY AND THE BALANCE SHEET: A CASE OF VITAL STATISTICS

GRADEN KELLER
University of Houston—Clear Lake

TIMOTHY SINGLETON
North Georgia College

ROBERT McGLASHAN
University of Houston—Clear Lake

5:30 P.M., OCTOBER 29, 1976, DALLAS, TEXAS
EXCERPTS FROM A TELEVISION INTERVIEW BEING TAPED FOR BROADCAST IN EUROPE IN EARLY NOVEMBER

"You returned to your native Texas in 1962 to establish your own agency. What was the modeling business like in Dallas fourteen years ago and what are the differences today?"

"Well, it didn't exist. Not as a real business. Oh, there were a few local girls who worked freelance and a rep here and there, because of the Apparel Mart. But if anyone wanted professional talent, they called New York, period. Even though I had the best of contacts, it was pretty tough getting anyone to believe that Dallas could offer the modeling business anything. It was damn hard just getting models to stay here long enough to establish careers! The only way a model can get work is by having worked. The only way an agency can survive is by getting models work. In this business, you're only as good as your last job.

"The market in Dallas was so small then, I could only support five, maybe six girls full-time. The rest had to make do or leave. The mart was the only thing that kept me going. Occasionally, we would get work in other industry trade shows—oil and gas, autos, boats . . . stuff like that. But it was the mart that gave me my first major contract. By the end of 1967, I was reping thirty models, guys and gals, on an exclusive basis. It didn't hurt either when the Whyte Agency agreed to corep our kids in New York. By 1970, there were eighty-two exclusive contracts in my file cabinet. We rep around 200 now. We get 15 percent from the models and charge our clients 10 percent. Since those days, things have gone pretty smooth."

"Well, not exactly. Isn't it true that in 1971 you were sued by the Saul Agency for $10 million, after it alleged that you stole several of its best models; models who were on exclusive contract to Saul?"

"Anybody can sue you. Getting a judgment is another matter. Look, the only thing bigger than Johnny Saul's ego is Texas. He just got mad when Kim Travis and Lucy Hart decided to sign with me after he tried unsuccessfully to renew their contracts. Both these girls were from Texas. They just wanted to do business with someone from back home. That's all."

"In any event, those two contracts put you on the map."

"There's no question about it. But don't be deceived. The Dallas market—in fact, the entire Southwest—still represents only a fraction of the

This case, written specifically for this text, is printed by permission.

business. Even the smallest of the successful East or West coast firms is a giant against the little bit of work we do down here. That's why we have to be tougher, smarter, and work harder than anybody else to make it. If we want to succeed, we have to be aggressive. Managing a New York agency is hard work, but the market is at your door. Running this agency is another matter. Sometimes, the best business judgment is found in your gut, not in a balance sheet. If you want to make this kind of business work in a place like Texas, you can't sit on your pretty little derriere, and wait for something to happen."

"You were a very successful model, both in America and Europe. The Whyte Agency was your exclusive rep from start to finish, beginning with a stunning Harper's *November cover in 1955, at the age of sixteen. How did you get into modeling, and why?"*

"I remember when I was fourteen, all I dreamed about was being on the cover of a magazine. Momma sent me to Dallas to attend a modelin' school. You know, I thought I had died and gone to heaven, honey! The two old ladies who ran that place put themselves up to be former world class models. In fact, one, Miss Maria, actually had done some modeling in New York, but just for a year, nothing substantial. Anyway, it was enough for her to have some pictures of herself up on the wall. To me, or any young kid from a place like Paris—Paris, Texas darlin'—it was impressive.

"Then one day a beautiful young boy—a local photographer—told me if I would come with him to New York, he would use me as his model. That way he could build a book, and make us both famous. He was nineteen, barely. Six foot, maybe six-one. Blue eyes. The most gorgeous smile you ever saw, and I loved him. Well, as much as you can love someone at fifteen. So we just left. He had a brand new Chevy, wouldn't you know, and I had seventy-five dollars my aunt Molly had given me for my birthday. I told Miss Maria what we were doing, and she cried. I didn't know then if she was crying because she was happy for me, or sad for herself. Anyway, she gave me a list of people to contact, most of whom were dead or gone when I got around to trying to reach them, plus a couple hundred dollars. I hugged and kissed her and told her that I would make it just for her. She looked me straight in the eyes and said, 'Sandy, sweetheart. Do this for yourself, and no one else. There isn't anyone else,

there never will be anyone else, who will love you like you must learn to love yourself.' I can tell you one thing. There have been many times since that day on Miss Maria's front porch that her voice and those words have come to me. I know now what she meant. But then, well, how could I have known. I thought the whole world loved me like my momma did."

"Tomorrow marks the fourteenth anniversary of your triumphant return to Texas. You live in a beautiful home, in an exclusive and fashionable Dallas suburb. Your personal net worth is known to exceed $3 million. What does the future hold for Sandy Pittman, the small-town girl who apparently has reached the pinnacle of success?"

"You make success sound like a place you can go to, and just take it easy. Let me tell you, it isn't like that at all! Success isn't a point you reach or a place you arrive at. It's a never-ending process. And it's always balanced by failure. What does the future hold? I don't know. Do you? Does anyone?"

6:00 P.M., OCTOBER 30, 1976, DALLAS, TEXAS
EXCERPTS FROM A DALLAS EVENING NEWS TELEVISION BROADCAST

"Sandy Pittman, age thirty-seven, was found dead this morning in her home; shot through the head with a single .38 caliber bullet. Police, combing the scene of this apparent burglary turned homicide, say they have found no clues as to the identity nor whereabouts of the assailant or assailants. Pittman was best known as the tough, hard driving, no-nonsense, blond from Paris, Texas who, after five years as the most successful model in New York City, returned to Dallas (fourteen years ago today) where she founded Appeal, now the largest, most successful modeling and talent agency in the Southwest. Rumors have already begun to flourish about the circumstances of her death, but the Dallas County District Attorney issued this statement today at five:

Ms. Sandra Pittman died at approximately 2:33 A.M., today, October 30th, 1976, from a wound caused by a single .38 caliber bullet which entered her head slightly above the left ear resulting in immediate death. Until such time as there is evidence to the contrary, it is the conclusion of this office that Sandra Sue Pittman was murdered during the burglary of her residence. The perpetrators are unknown and at large. Paintings and jewelry are reported missing by Ms. Pittman's niece, Mrs. Jan Stovall, who came to Dallas several weeks ago to visit Ms. Pittman and attend the dedication of the Stovall Cancer Research Wing of the Parklawn General Hospital. In other news today. . . ."

9:20 A.M., MAY 3, 1977, NEW YORK, NEW YORK THE OFFICES OF THE WHYTE AGENCY, NEW YORK'S LEADING MODELING AND TALENT ORGANIZATION, HEADED BY AMY WHYTE, FOUNDER AND PRESIDENT

Glenn Gorman, Whyte's Casting Director, was sitting alone in his office, casually glancing through several fashion publications. Suddenly, he fell back against his chair and sat momentarily stunned. Then he spoke out loud as though someone was in the room listening. "Sue Strong's going to Dallas! God, this is really going to put Johnny Saul into an early grave!" He called to his secretary, "Get Amy on the line!"

The article that had excited Glenn Gorman so much appeared in Women's Wear Daily and referred to the Whyte Agency's chief rival, the Saul Agency. Saul had always been a contender in the New York market, usually ranked as the number four agency, but when Susan Strong appeared as director in 1975, things began to really pick up. The Saul Agency was now ranked number two, only slightly behind Whyte.

WOMEN'S WEAR DAILY
May 3, 1977
"DALLAS' APPEAL IS STRONG-ER THAN EVER!"
J. R. LEVINE

Appeal, the Dallas-based modeling and talent agency formerly owned by Sandy Pittman, has been purchased by Associated Investments (total assets, $71.1 million) of Austin, Texas, for $3.1 million. The agency was owned briefly by Jan Stovall, Pittman's sole heir. Associated Investments is a Texas-based real-estate limited partnership, headed by Jeff M. Strake, thirty-five, from Kansas City, Missouri. Strake earned a BBA at the University of Missouri. He's the son of former Missouri U.S. Representative

and retired Air Force Lt. Colonel, James M. Strake. Strake's business holdings, including his share of Associated Investments, are estimated at $21.9 million (most of which are in Texas real estate). In addition to his interest in Associated (25 percent), Strake has recently become involved in several import/export ventures related to the oil and gas industry.

WWD has learned that before closing the deal for Appeal, Strake flew to New York to meet with his former wife, Kathy DuPont, the French-born beauty, who is the new, rising, young star at Tempo [listed, categorically, number three worldwide in gross revenues, "Modeling & Talent," B&C, 1977, Ed.]. Reportedly, the purpose of the meeting was to convince Ms. DuPont to return to Dallas and manage Appeal. As it turns out Ms. DuPont is not interested in leaving New York or returning to Texas, therefore, Susan Strong, currently with the Saul Agency, will become Managing Director of Appeal, effective July 3rd. Sources say that Strake was leaving the Pierre Hotel when he received an invitation from Amy Whyte to drop by for a chat on his way out of town. Following their meeting, Strake decided to extend his stay and continue the search for someone to run Appeal. Two days later, the announcement was made that Susan Strong would be going to Dallas to head up Appeal.

Strong was born and raised in Massachusetts. Her father, John D. Strong, was special assistant on foreign affairs to Presidents Eisenhower and Kennedy. Strong graduated from Yale in 1967 with a liberal arts degree. Following graduation she modeled for three years in New York. After modeling, Strong became Casting Director for the Whyte Agency. Two years later, she accepted a position with the Saul Agency, where she became Managing Director in 1975. If Strong is as effective at Appeal as she has been at Saul, Strake can begin counting his money right away. It is reported that Strake had to offer Strong a 20 percent interest in Appeal, a buy-sell agreement, in addition to $95,000 annual salary to entice her away from the reported $185,000 annual salary, plus perks she earns at Saul. "We will miss Ms. Strong very much," said Johnny Saul, Saul's founder and president, at the press conference announcing Strong's departure. Strong will take a holiday in Rome, arriving in Dallas on June 15th to settle in before taking over at Appeal in early July.

3:30 P.M., JULY 4, 1981, DALLAS, TEXAS
SUSAN STRONG'S PENTHOUSE CONDOMIN-
IUM, FOUR YEARS AFTER SHE CAME TO DAL-
LAS TO MANAGE APPEAL

The warm Texas sunshine spilled through the large, sparkling glass windows and poured over the plush, white wool carpet. Fresh, long-stem red roses stood stately in a spiraling, hand-cut crystal vase that sat upon a black marble pedestal. On the wall above a slate gray, leather sofa hung a Picasso original; a gift from the Sultan of Runjai. To many, Susan Strong had walked away from a luxurious existence to live in a cultural wasteland. To Susan, she had taken the once-in-a-lifetime chance to accomplish her life's dream; to own her own agency.

"Bill, I don't care what Nancy says. Last quarter's figures don't support the expense. Look, if we take on this kind of commitment, at this time, we could be flat on our face in December. Of course, I know Saul is moving into that market, but he's got megabucks, Bill. I know we need the market to make next year work. Give me two days. I'll be in touch." Susan Strong put the phone down and walked to the balcony. Her tall, lean body tingled from the cool morning shower she had just taken. She slowly began to towel dry her hair (she had never used a dryer). The warm, early morning breeze gently lifted and separated the soft strands as she bent to catch each new rising current of air. She lifted and pulled, then tucked and squeezed each section of hair until only a hint of moisture remained. Then she stood straight, slightly arching her neck backwards, letting the silky, natural blonde hair fall gently upon soft, rounded shoulders.

At the age of thirty-one, Susan Strong had come to Texas full of hope and anticipation. Now, four years later, after a tough, sometimes brutalizing fight to capture the market share needed to sustain the business, the Saul Agency (her former employer) was attempting to cut into Appeal's territory. It didn't make any sense. The Southwest was peanuts compared to the New York market. Susan wondered what was going on. She just didn't have a feel for the situation. Things seemed easier in New York. At least, more predictable. Did she really have what it took to make this thing work? Well, she knew she could count on Jeff. He always seemed to know what to do. She reached for the phone, then decided to wait until she had taken a nap. She spoke to herself as she walked to the bedroom, "I'm so

tired all of the time. I just can't get enough rest. I think I'll call the doctor's office in the morning."

8:45 P.M., July 4, 1981, AUSTIN, TEXAS
THE DRISCOLL HOTEL, AT THE END OF A
SCHEDULED ONE-DAY MEETING OF THE TEN
MAJOR PARTNERS IN ASSOCIATED INVEST-
MENTS

Jeff Strake had been arguing with his partners all day. He had returned to his suite, hoping to retreat from the debate when the call came. It was B.W. Mooney, a wealthy Texas oilman and Associated's largest single investor.

"Look B.W., I still think we're riding the crest of a dangerous wave. This joy ride isn't going to last forever.

"B.W., I know what economists are predicting, but their assumptions aren't realistic. I just spent five days in London. The Arabs are nervous as hell, because they're losing control of the price structure. How long do you think we'll survive if the price of oil drops? You guys don't think I'm right, I know, but as far as I'm concerned, I read the handwriting on the wall last week. I know you're familiar with our Houston Post Oak property. I took that portfolio to the largest estate agent in London. His response was that his clients, who are primarily Arab, have decided to withhold further land investments in Houston at this time. It was their opinion that Houston real estate prices had peaked and would soon bottom out. Don't you think it's strange that when U.S. economists, particularly Texas economists, are predicting long-run price increases in oil, the Arabs are deciding to stop further investment in our real estate markets?

"Look, B.W., I've got my own back to cover. If you guys want to expand, you'll have to do it without me.

"I know you supported me on the Appeal acquisition, but how can you compare that to this. For God's sake, B.W. that company's lived up to everything I said it would. It's served its purpose. There's no way anyone can complain about that deal.

"I figured I'd call in the cows on this one. Well, yes, I'd prefer it that way. Of course, I do. I understand completely. I'll have papers drawn up immediately. Good luck, B.W. I'll see you in Denver next month. So long."

Strake put the phone down and walked to the window of the suite where he had lived since the sale of the house that he and Kathy built. He was, as he recalled his grandpa would sometimes remark, "Bone tired." It had been raining all day and was continuing as night fell. This was a real Texas hill country storm. Great sheaths of rain were battering Austin's famous Sixth Street. Blinding, jagged streaks of lightening bolted across the sky and thunder pounded the clouds like giant sledges against iron anvils. Standing nearly motionless against the glass, Jeff could feel a revivifying current pulse through his veins. Suddenly, without warning, the sky fell dark and quiet; only the soft, gentle patter of tender rain could be heard, as the storm slipped stealthily southward toward San Antonio. Kathy had always been frightened during these storms. He recalled her cries in the middle of the night, remembering how he had often held her until dawn. Something in this storm touched Jeff Strake deeper than words could describe. He slowly turned from the foreboding panorama and sank quietly into bed. But sleep escaped with the storm, and morning found him staring emotionless toward the high cathedral ceiling with its mural of the famous last stand at the Alamo.

9:30 A.M., JULY 5, 1981, HOUSTON, TEXAS
TED L. DENISON & ASSOCIATES, ATTORNEYS AT LAW

That morning, Strake boarded a Southwest Airlines jet to Houston, where he met with his attorney and friend, Ted Denison. Strake placed a sealed envelope on Denison's desk. Denison was told that the envelope contained the bottom line price Strake would accept for his interest in several ventures in which he was presently involved, including Associated Investments.

"I've worked out the preliminaries regarding Associated with Mooney. Call him in San Antonio tomorrow. I'll handle Appeal personally. Ted, I want some R&R. Let's move quickly on this. I want it wrapped up in ninety days.

"That isn't going to be easy, Jeff. I'm not talking about closing a deal. There are plenty of takers on a package like this these days. But I got a call from the accountants yesterday. The land transactions in the Dallas area are almost complete. But it looks like 120 days or so before they can wrap things up. You'll be walking out on big bucks if you sell out before they close. Of course you can structure your deal so as to retain the income from the Dallas land sales, but

anyone who's interested will want a severe reduction in your asking price, even if they don't know what you're getting on the properties."

"I'll think it over, Ted. I know you're right."

"I know it's none of my business, Jeff, but is everything okay?" Denison placed his hand on Strake's shoulder.

"Ted, I'm convinced the price of oil is going to drop severely within two years. If I don't begin to reduce my interests in oil-related investments, I'll go bust. Almost everything I own is related to oil and gas, some way or another. Now, that the Dallas deals are about to close, even Appeal won't be immune. No, I'm committed."

"Well, I hope you're wrong, Jeff. Everything I own is tied up in oil and gas. With Mary's father being head of Cactus. . . . Well, you know how it is."

Jeff Strake nodded his head, shook Ted's hand, and walked out of the office. He knew how it was. He thought of Kathy's father putting the pressure on him to invest in his vineyards. He wondered if his lack of interest in his former father-in-law's business had adversely affected his marriage. After all, Kathy was very close to her family. Maybe she had some neurotic view of his rejection of her father's continual offers as some sort of rejection of her. As he stepped into the taxi he thought about how he was going to handle the situation with Susan tomorrow morning in Dallas.

7:45 A.M., JULY 6, 1981, DALLAS, TEXAS
APPEAL MODELING AND TALENT, INC.

Strake was waiting for Susan Strong when she arrived at Appeal's offices early the next morning. Strake laid the cards on the table. He told Susan he intended to sell Appeal.

"Bryan Cox of London's Media One made a firm offer of $4.8 million two weeks ago. Johnny Saul issued a standing offer several months ago of $4.5 million."

"And, of course, there's my buy-sell?" Susan's mouth was dry. As she spoke she felt her lips quiver slightly.

"If you want to sell, I'll have a cashier's check in your hands tomorrow morning at 9:30. If you want to buy, come up with $3.6 million in thirty days, that's my offer. It's strictly a cash deal. I won't carry anyone on this, Susan. I'll be in Austin. Good luck, kid." Strake turned and walked through the door.

Susan Strong fell back against her chair, facing the Dallas skyline. Her mind was racing. She was trying to calculate her net worth and available sources of capital. She took out a piece of paper and thought to herself as she wrote. "I've got $300,000 in cash, Daddy's trust is $1.6 million, I could sell the condo for $500,000—I owe about $200,000, let's see that's $2,100,000. So, I need $1,500,000." Even if Susan couldn't buy Appeal, her 20 percent would bring her around a million dollars on any other offer Jeff accepted.

Susan reached for the phone to call Bill Cook, Appeal's business manager. "Bill, hi. I need financial statements by this afternoon. Can you run some comparisons? Oh yes, get me our bank statements for the past six months. Thanks. Chow." Susan leaned back, closed her eyes and tried to block out the tension.

9:00 P.M., JULY 6, 1981, DALLAS, TEXAS SUSAN STRONG'S CONDO

Financial statements were strewn across the floor. Susan sat quietly reviewing the information Bill had provided. "Okay, Accounting I and II, now's your big chance." Susan uneasily joked to herself as she pulled the crisp white sheets from their paper jack-

---

Exhibit 1
APPEAL MODELING & TALENT, INC.: COMPARATIVE BALANCE SHEET (in thousands)

	1981	1980	1979	1978	1977	1976
ASSETS						
Current Assets						
Cash	$ 529	$ 409	$ 484	$ 302	$ 305	$ 113
Short-term investments	2,295	2,175	1,505	1,357	857	357
Accounts receivable	240	240	290	253	263	263
Supplies	7	7	7	7	7	7
Prepaid expenses	75	75	75	75	75	75
Total Current Assets	$3,146	$2,906	$2,361	$1,994	$1,507	$ 815
Long-Term Assets						
Long-term investments	$2,084	$1,962	$1,434	$1,034	$ 534	$ —
Buildings and land	51	173	701	1,101	1,601	2,135
Total Long-Term Assets	2,135	2,135	2,135	2,135	2,135	
TOTAL ASSETS	$5,281	$5,041	$4,496	$4,129	$3,642	$2,950
LIABILITIES AND SHAREHOLDERS' EQUITY						
Current Liabilities						
Accounts payable	$ 117	$ 217	$ 299	$ 372	$ 329	$ 259
Commissions, fees and wages payable	72	193	194	185	276	85
Notes payable	275	54	89	112	112	423
Total Current Liabilities	$ 464	$ 464	$ 582	$ 669	$ 717	$ 767
Shareholders' Equity						
Common stock ($1 par)	$ 25	$ 25	$ 25	$ 25	$ 25	$ 25
Retained earnings	4,792	4,552	3,889	3,427	2,900	2,158
Total Shareholders' Equity	4,819	4,577	3,914	3,452	2,925	2,183
TOTAL LIABILITIES AND SHAREHOLDERS' EQUITY	$5,281	$5,041	$4,496	$4,129	$3,642	$2,950

Exhibit 2

APPEAL MODELING & TALENT, INC.: COMPARATIVE INCOME STATEMENT (in thousands)

	1981[a]	1980	1979	1978	1977	1976
Income						
Commissions	$623	$1,357	$1,003	$1,242	$1,476	$1,655
Other	—	538	400	500	534	12
Gross Income	$623	$1,895	$1,403	$1,742	$2,010	$1,667
Less Operating Expenses						
Selling expenses	$186	$ 500	$ 391	$ 569	$ 541	$ 650
Administrative expenses	59	199	160	332	306	345
Other	20	47	51	55	55	50
Total Operating Expenses	265	746	602	956	902	1,045
Income Before Taxes	$358	$1,149	$ 801	$ 786	$1,108	$ 622
Less Taxes	(118)	(376)	(264)	(259)	(366)	(205)
NET INCOME	$240	$ 773	$ 537	$ 527	$ 742	$ 417

a. Through June 30 only.

Exhibit 3

APPEAL MODELING & TALENT, INC.: STATEMENT OF RETAINED EARNINGS (in thousands)

	1980	1979
Balance as of January 1	$3,889	$3,427
Net Income	763	537
Less: Dividends paid	(100)	(75)
Retained earnings balance, December 31	$4,552	$3,889

Exhibit 4

APPEAL MODELING & TALENT, INC.: STATEMENT OF CHANGES IN FINANCIAL POSITION (in thousands)

	1980		1979	
Sources of Working Capital				
Continuing operations				
Net income	$763		$ 537	
Sale of buildings and land[a]	528		400	
Total Sources of Working Capital		$1,291		$937
Application of Working Capital				
Long-term investments[b]	$528		$ 400	
Dividends declared	100		75	
Reduction of long-term debt	—		50	
Improvements to buildings	100		75	
Total Applications of Working Capital		728		600

Exhibit 4
APPEAL MODELING & TALENT, INC.: STATEMENT OF CHANGES IN FINANCIAL POSITION
(in thousands) (*continued*)

	1980	1979
Increase (Decrease) in Working Capital	$ 563	$337
CHANGES IN WORKING CAPITAL ACCOUNTS		
Increase (Decrease) in Current Assets		
Cash	$(75)	$ 182
Short-term investments	670	148
Accounts receivable	(50)	37
Total Increase (Decrease) in Current Assets	$ 545	$367
(Increase) Decrease in Current Liabilities		
Accounts payable	$ 82	$ 10
Commissions, fees, and wages payable	1	12
Dividends payable	(100)	(75)
Notes payable	35	23
Total Increase (Decrease) in Current Liabilities	18	(30)
Increase (Decrease) in Working Capital	$ 563	$337

a. To Associated Investments
b. Real estate and oil/gas limited partnerships, Associated Investments

---

ets. For a moment it seemed as though she held the keys to her dream in her hands.

5:00 A.M., JULY 7, 1981, DALLAS, TEXAS
SUSAN STRONG'S CONDO

Susan sat up abruptly. The loud ringing of the phone had startled her. She glanced at her watch. "My God!" she thought, "it's 5 A.M.!" She reached over and picked up the phone. "Hello?" She wondered who would be calling at this hour.

"Hey, sweetheart! What's cookin'?"

"Johnny! What are you doing calling at this hour?" Susan's mind was cluttered with numbers.

"Hey, I been up two hours. Had a great breakfast. Bacon, eggs, V8, the works! I feel great! What time is it out West anyway?" Before Susan could answer he continued. "Listen, I hear Appeal is gonna be on the block soon. I guess you know I offered your boss more than he should ever hope to get. . . ."

Susan interrupted. She knew it would be the only way she could get into the conversation.

"Johnny, look. I'm tired and I've got to get some rest. I've been up all night."

"It figures. Okay, I'll make it short and sweet, babe. I know this is a big chance for you. What you've always wanted. So here's the straight dope. Fifty-fifty. You run the operation, just like the old days, and I'll push the talent in the big markets. I figure you got about half, maybe two-thirds, of what he wants, what with Daddy's trust and your share of Appeal. So think it over. You know where to find me! Later, sweetheart!"

The phone went dead. Susan rolled over and laid her head against a floor pillow. She had been expecting a call from Johnny sometime, but this was so fast. She closed her eyes and began to drift into sleep. "He's such a schmuck," she thought, "but a lovable schmuck."

10:00 A.M., JULY 16, 1981, DALLAS, TEXAS
APPEAL MODELING & TALENT, INC.

"Susan, I just talked to Texas Republic National. It's going to be tough to get them to come down on the rate. They say there's too much demand for oil and gas loans right now to justify passing cheap money to you to buy Appeal." Bill Cook stood waiting at the door for a reply.

"They want too much. What about First Dallas?"

"Same story, I'm afraid. But at least they're willing to lend the money."

"Yeah, for an arm and a leg." Susan Strong was beginning to feel the heat. Banks in Texas were depleting their reserves as fast as possible, trying to push the Texas oil boom to its limits. Money to finance the $1.5 million she needed was there, but she believed the rate was going to put her in a dangerous position.

"You're being overly cautious, Susan. The company can handle that kind of debt. The way the economists are talking, Texas is on the verge of another series of peaks. I recommend you sign as soon as possible, before the rates go even higher."

"I'll get back with you, Bill. Thanks." Susan turned her back and reached for the phone.

"Daddy."

"Hello, Susan. How's Texas?"

"Hot!"

"Well, New England is, as always, absolutely beautiful. When should we expect you home for a visit? The Kennedys have been asking about you."

"It'll be awhile, Daddy. Things are pretty hectic around here."

"No problem. No one understands the responsibilities of business better than I."

"That's the main reason I'm calling, Daddy. I need advice."

"Okay. Let me start the clock." Susan's father chuckled as he settled back to give his only child his undivided attention.

"Well, here's the complete story [and Susan described the situation]. I'm in a dilemma."

"I'll say. Well, dear, as far as your questions about the economy, it's a toss up, in my opinion. Of course, not everyone is as optimistic as you Texans about the price of oil, but things are looking very promising here along the East coast. You're right about your industry being sensitive to these kinds of fluctuations. If you were operating out of New York, things might appear different. But, in Texas, well, I just don't know enough about the situation down there to advise you, sweetheart. I can say something about OPEC. It's in a very precarious position. Cartels, in my view, are short lived by nature. These crude prices are extremely high. No one really

knows how long these collusionists can sustain their pact. I'm doubtful they can go on much longer. When the price of oil does fall, you can be sure that you folks in Texas will see a statewide depression as a result. If you do move ahead with this venture, you might consider concentrating on building a substantial amount of business on the coasts—if that's possible at all, of course. Regarding the financial papers, I must tell you I'm no wiz in that area. However, Brock Lumack, an old college chum of mine, mentioned to me yesterday that he's going to Dallas on business in a few days. I'll ask him to drop by for a review of the records. You remember Brock, honey. He was special assistant to the undersecretary of the treasury when I was in Washington. Maybe he couldn't straighten out the economy, but he should be able to lend you a hand with those reports."

"Well, I'm going to have to make up my mind soon. Jeff's deadline is coming up fast."

"This Strake fellow. Did he give any indication as to why he has decided to sell?"

"Not really, Daddy. In fact, it came as a bit of a shock to me."

"Well, we all have reasons for what we do. It might be a good idea to look into the matter. Sometimes, knowing why can help clear the vision on these things. If he refuses to discuss his reasons, you may want to reconsider."

"Thanks, Daddy. I love you."

"I love you, too. Keep in touch. Oh, by the way, Gary Stanwick is getting married. He asked me to convey the news to you."

"Well, at least I won't have Mother on my back to marry him anymore."

Susan's father laughed and said good-bye. Susan stood for a long time, holding the phone in her hand, and watching the clouds float carelessly across the expansive Texas sky. "I wonder what Sandy Pittman would do in a situation like this?" she thought, as she pushed the intercom to request lunch be brought up. ". . . and before you call in the order, Marsha, just a few small items. Bring in the headshots on the models for the September shows. Check to see if those comps went out to Neiman's on time. Tell Marie, one more no-show and she'll be booked-out for the rest of the season. What's the status of Mary-Jane's callback on the Pepsi shoot? And tell Billy to bring in the chromes of the Mexico shoot. Oh yeah, call Gorman at the Whyte Agency, and tell him I'll have to get back with him on the new co-rep contract. Just say I've got a very important walk-through coming up, and I'm having to put all my energy into prep time. And say that I've got some very vital statistics to go over."

APPENDIX A: A GLANCE AT THE BUSINESS OF MODELING

A model is an independent contractor. As such, a model works under the terms of a contract. There are two types of contracts: exclusive and nonexclusive. The specific terms of a contract will vary from agency to agency, and are also affected by various other factors such as geography, type of modeling performed, credentials of the model or agency, and many other variables. Some agents do not use written contracts. When a model works without a written contract, the model is considered to be a nonexclusive contractor.

A nonexclusive contract simply means that a model is listed with the contracting agency, but receives no active representation. Under these nonexclusive terms, the model is contracted for work on an availability basis, through the use of a waiting list or on-call system. When a nonexclusive contractual relationship exists, the agency receives commissions only from work which it actually obtains for the model. Agents usually give booking preference to models with whom they have exclusive contracts.

An exclusive contract establishes specific parameters to the model-agent relationship. Exclusivity can cover all phases of a model's work or specify certain areas. For example, a model may have an exclusive contract with an agency that only covers print work. Under the terms of such a contract, the agency will receive commissions on any print work the model performs, even if another agency or source obtains the work. Under some exclusive contracts, the model is liable for damages if another party than the exclusive agent obtains work for the model. Another example of exclusivity relates to products. Many famous models endorse products or have established broad public identification with a product. An exclusive contract may contain a clause that restrains the model from endorsing or identifying with any other product of the same or similar nature. Since many exclusive contracts and clauses restrict a model's work, bonuses are paid to models to compensate them for the opportunity costs involved.

Another important aspect of a model's business relates to ownership of media or related materials developed from a model's work. With few exceptions, models are required to sign release agreements that give permission to the client to own the finished material (print, film, or video). The model relinquishes and forfeits any rights or control over how the material may be used. The pictures become the property of the client, the ad agency, or the photographer.

Commission agreements refer to the amount of money an agent will receive as compensation for obtaining work for a model. This agreement may be separate from or a part of the contract models sign authorizing a particular agency to be their representative. The standard range for such services is 10 to 25 percent. Percentages vary within cities and among agencies. The commission percentage is based on gross earnings. Some agencies pay models upon the conclusion of a job, others wait until the agency is paid by the client. Usually, agencies use a partial method of payment; part upon completion of a job and the balance when the client pays the agency in full. The period during which a model waits to receive full compensation for work may range from the same day to four months.

Rates paid to models vary greatly. Experienced models usually receive higher compensation. The type of work establishes the rate structure. A model's popularity or reputation has an impact upon the rate. Even the city where the model is working or the client affects the nature of rates. Rates are subject to change without notice and can change drastically. Typically, glamour and fashion magazines pay for a day what most other clients pay for an hour. The fees they pay include the consideration that the prestige a model receives as a result of appearing in one of their publications justifies a lower rate. Illustrators pay low rates as well. Traditionally artists have received a break from models, because the income derived from artistic work is more often than not low compared to that earned by media organizations. Other factors influencing rate include the frequency at which materials appear in media form (i.e., commercials or films) and whether such materials are used locally, nationally, or internationally. Beyond standard rates, bonuses are negotiated for extended time, original work, size of target market, and so on. A model's fee structure can become so complex that many highly successful models and agents have attorneys who specialize in such areas handling all negotiations and accountants monitor collection and tax consequences. Unions (SAG and AFTRA) are active in fee structure development and provide members with a variety of information regarding fee structures.

Modeling is among the many businesses that make up the fashion industry. Modeling plays a supportive role to advertising agencies, film companies, publishers, clothing designers, buyers, retailers, and manufacturers. For this reason there are several categories of modeling. Print modeling refers to still photographs, which appear in newspapers, magazines, product ads, product packaging, record albums, book covers, brochures, etc. Runway or fashion modeling takes place in designer showrooms, shopping malls, apparel marts, retail department stores, restaurants, and ballrooms. This type of modeling has the most stringent requirements regarding a model's vital statistics and abilities. Catalog modeling provides the most reliable and regular source of work for models. Basically, this type of modeling involves posing for pictures that will be used to sell clothing in company catalogs. Informal retail modeling takes place in a retail store, shopping mall, or restaurant. Models are expected to know the clothing they model in order to answer questions posed by prospective buyers. Floor or promotional modeling involves the promotion or distribution of products to the public. The promotion usually takes the form of samples of perfume, cosmetics or product demonstration. Fitting modeling requires models to meet rigid dimensions. Models are used exclusively for the design of clothing. Showroom modeling takes place in a manufacturer's showroom and is used to aid buyers in assessing the appeal of various clothes being promoted by the manufacturers sales representative. Television modeling offers the greatest exposure and money to a model. Television modeling provides the greatest amount and variety of work. This form of modeling is closely linked to acting. In fact many models are also actors, and vice versa. Convention and trade show modeling usually involves representing an industry, company, product, or product line. Models may be paid at a daily rate or a fee that covers the total convention or trade show period. The work is usually mundane, but this type of modeling can be a good supplement to other types of modeling. A model usually specializes in one type of modeling, but can work in other areas.

Because the careers of most models are comparatively short (ten to fifteen years for a successful model), models begin to plan for a second or concurrent career soon after they have begun actively working as a model. Models have successfully made the career transition to such jobs as clothing stylist, hairstylist or makeup artist, fashion coordinator, fashion editor, fashion designer, accessory designer, costume designer, actress or actor, broadcast journalist, agent, buyer, manufacturer's sales representative, art director, film producer or director, store manager, and others.

Most modeling work is in the area of print modeling, with national magazines ranking highest. Television follows, then catalog and fashion modeling. Geographically, there are six major cities that provide the bulk of work for models in the United States. New York is the center of the modeling business. It contains the most advertising agencies, photographers, and film production and fashion houses. The most advertising money spent in the country is spent in New York City. The top modeling and talent agencies in theworld locate their main offices in New York. The largest and best known agencies include Ford, Elite, Wilhelmina, and Zoli. Los Angeles provides a tremendous amount of television and film work. Other areas of opportunity include department store and designer or fashion modeling. Detroit provides a great deal of work for convention and trade show models, particularly in regard to the automobile industry. Dallas has a national reputation for its apparel mart and fashion shows. The pinnacle of a successful modeling career is reached when a model expands to international markets. The fashion centers in Europe include Paris, London, Rome, Milan, Munich, and Frankfurt. In Tokyo, American female models are in great demand. Currently, Japan is considered one of the fastest-growing fashion markets in the world.

APPENDIX B: GLOSSARY

Advertising: An organization that creates, produces, and places advertising in print and electronic mediums.

American Federation of Television and Radio Artists (AFTRA):   The union which represents television and radio performers of live or recorded material.

agent: A person who represents models or performers for the purpose of helping them obtain work. An agent receives a commission for services rendered.

Apparel Mart: A location where manufacturers (wholesalers) display their products for sale to retail buyers.

Backstage: A trade newspaper relating to the performing arts. Those interested in television commercials read this. An updated listing of casting directors is published four times a year.

book: To schedule a model for a specific job. May also refer to a model's portfolio of pictures or scripts that demonstrate work history.

booking: A modeling job arranged by a client with an agency.

booker: The person in a model agency who schedules models for specific jobs.

booking editor: Selects models for the assignment.

book-out: To make a model unavailable for a job. For vacation, illness or disciplinary action.

callback: A second audition for a job, usually made when several persons are closely competing for the assignment. When a callback exceeds one hour, models are paid scale.

casting: The process of selecting models or performers.

casting director: The person who interviews applicants for a job. The process usually includes a personal interview or audition or both.

cattle call: An audition where large numbers of applicants (sometimes hundreds) are called to try out.

client: A person or company who hires talent.

commission: The percentage of a model's earnings paid to an agency or agent (usually 15 percent).

composite/comp: A grouping of pictures on a single card (6 x 8 or 8-½ x 11 inches); includes name, agency or agent, and vital statistics.

free-lance: Working without an agent or agency. Involves self-promotion, booking, billing, and so on.

go-see: A model's initial interview with a client.

headsheet: A booklet or poster on which an agency prints a picture collection of its models. Distributed to clients and potential clients for review.

headshot: Photograph of a model's face and head only. Required as calling card.

hold: Reservation made when client wants a specific model for an assignment. A hold is placed on the model's booking time for the client.

location: A modeling assignment out of the studio. Also referred to as on-location.

Madison Avenue Handbook: Reference guide to everyone associated with the business of modeling and television. The comprehensive directory contains lists of casting directors, talent reps, modeling agencies, photographers, illustrators, film producers, and recording or television studios.

manager: One who represents a model in addition to a model agency. Also referred to as a model's representative (Rep) or model's agent.

model agency: An organization that represents models (usually through exclusive contract) to various clients. The agency receives a commission for its services.

model's book: A model's portfolio of pictures. A model's resume. Used primarily for go-sees.

portfolio: A photographic collection of a model's work history or a series of photographs that portray a model's range of capabilities.

preparation (prep) time: Time required for travel, make-up, hair styling, rehearsal, and so on. Models receive full pay for this time.

rates: The pay models receive for work, scaled according to type and place.

Ross Reports: A pocket-sized booklet with information on the television industry. Lists New York advertising agencies, independent casting directors, television producers, and talent agents and is updated monthly.

Screen Actors Guild (SAG): The union that represents television actors and actresses.

rep: Model's agent or manager.

shoot: Denotes taking a series or variety of photographs.

scale: Minimum rate models or performers receive for a job.

talent: Model or performer.

tearsheet: Part of a magazine, newspaper, or catalog advertisement models use to show examples of their work.

vital statistics: Vital statistics of the model are listed on composites and resumes. Regarding female models the list consists of height, weight, clothing size, bust, waist, hips, eyes, hair, shoe size, and talents. For male models: height, weight, jacket size, shirt size, pant length, sleeve length, hair, eyes, waist, shoe size, and talents. (Skin color may be added).

walk-through: An informal rehearsal performed by reading a script so as to gain a sense of what the real scene will be like.

Women's Wear Daily (WWD): The trade newspaper for the fashion industry. Wholesalers, retailers, modeling and advertising agencies, and others read daily. Has been called, "the voice of the fashion industry."

zed card: Alternate reference for a model's composite.

TECHNICAL NOTE: THE TRANSPORTATION INDUSTRY

TAMMIE SHAWN PINKSTON
University of Georgia

THE NATURE, FUNCTIONS, AND STRUCTURE OF THE TRANSPORTATION INDUSTRY

Transportation is defined as "the movement or conveying of persons and goods from one location to another with the least expenditure of time, effort, and cost."[1] The industry is divided into four primary segments—water, rail, truck, and air.

Water Transportation

"Water transport in the U.S. is limited in scope due to the confines of the inland waterway system which generally includes costal routes."[2] This mode is a slow but low-cost transport mode, which has specialized generally in products of low value per pound, such as coal, iron, ore, steel, cement, and gravel.

Water transportation includes deep-sea foreign and domestic transport, Great Lakes–St. Lawrence Seaway carriage, inland waterway movements, and local water-borne cargo shipments. The portion of GNP provided by this segment was $8.1 billion in 1986, an increase from $7.7 billion in 1985 and $7.5 billion in 1983.[3]

Rail Transportation

"Railroads are basically long-haul, slow movers of raw materials and low value manufactured prod- ucts."[4] The majority of rail shipments are termed *carload*, which refers to shipments greater than 10,000 pounds.

Truck Transportation

"The specialties of trucking include fast movement (relative to rail and water), a willingness to handle small shipments ('less-than-truckload,' or LTL), and complete door-to-door service. The motor-carrier industry's geographical coverage is extensive and its frequency of service is extremely high."[5]

Air Transportation

"Air freight shipments are generally categorized as emergency, routine perishable, or routine surface divertible. Emergency services are unplanned with the emphasis on speedy delivery. Routine perishable service is a planned shipment that usually consists of fresh fruit, vegetables, fresh flowers . . . and emphasizes customer's demand and service more than cost. Routine surface divertible is also a planned shipment, but total cost factors are more important than the speed of delivery or demand. In this type of service, the savings in inventory and warehousing costs often offset the incremental increase in the cost of air freight over a competing surface carrier."[6]

1. *Academic American Encyclopedia*, 1988, p. 278.
2. Domestic Airline Industry, 1977, p. xxxiv.
3. *U.S. Industrial Outlook, 1988*, p. 59–14.

4. Domestic Airline Industry, 1977, p. xxxiv.
5. Ibid.
6. Ibid.

Data on historical performance, trends, and forecasts for the latter two segments, truck and air, are provided in Exhibit 1 on the following page.

Industry performance is contingent upon the state of the economy (within which fuel and insurance are two primary cost considerations), the major forces of national tonnage, and the overall demand for transportation derived from production it supports and the distribution it serves. These factors, in turn, impact industry pricing practices and total industry revenues.

Prospects are mixed for those industries providing transportation services. Airline operating revenue is expected to increase 9%. The industry is highly concentrated with nine major passenger carriers accounting for approximately 90% of all revenue passenger miles. Trucking volume is expected to increase 2.3%, but revenues only 1.9%. Rail revenue ton-miles are forecast slightly above 1987 levels, with operating revenues increasing 3.8%. The U.S. flag foreign trade liner sector could show a modest recovery if freight rate improvements during the first half of 1987 can be sustained.[7]

THE TRUCKING SEGMENT OF THE TRANSPORTATION INDUSTRY

Size of the Trucking Segment

The segment's share of the national freight bill rose to 76.3 percent in 1986 from 75.5 percent in 1985 and 72.9 percent in 1980. Out of $201 billion in expenditures (1985), local freight services were $80 billion— three times greater than the combined expenditures for rail, ocean, and air.[8] During 1986, intercity revenues were 4.8 times rail, 7.1 times water, and 17.8 times air. During the period between 1980 and 1985, the number of regulated motor-carriers jumped 85 percent to 33,000.[9] Most of the growth occurred in those carriers with revenues less than $5 million. The structure of the industry is illustrated in Exhibit 2.

Segments of the Trucking Market and How They Are Defined

According to the 1986 *Financial Analysis of the Motor Carrier Industry*, the trucking market is grouped according to revenues. Group A consists of the small general freight carriers with revenues between $1 million and $5 million. There are 293 firms competing in this segment. In Group B, 219 firms maintain revenues between $5 and $25 million. One hundred and five firms comprise the Group C firms, with revenues between $25 and $100 million. Group D is a combination of common and contract carriers of special commodities totalling 1010. These firms are differentiated from the general freight carriers in that they ship goods direct from shipper to destination without stops at terminal facilities on the haul. Composite finances are provided for these groups in Exhibit 3.

The trucking market is also divided into truckload carriers and less-than-truckload carriers. Truckload carriers are those hauling full trailerload shipments, with rates often based on miles hauled. The truckload carriers continue to experience growth with the market share of the industry giants expanding. The giants are taking market share from marginal competitors and are also gaining as shippers consolidate to one carrier.[10] The 1980 Motor Carrier Act and deregulatory policies have allowed numerous entrants into the industry, both fragmenting the market and driving freight charges. Most of the excess capacity has been absorbed as a result.

Less-than-truckload transport (shipments of less than 10,000 pounds) has high capital costs and long startup time requirements in establishing networks, which factors deter potential entrants. Crucial in this area is efficient hauling LTL shipping geared to dock-to-dock activity, with any extra operations costing additional. Often LTL shipping is not structured for rapid response and prefers shipments of less than 500 pounds. For LTL shippers, pricing is accomplished through classifications based on density, value, and claims potential. The higher the classification, the higher the price for shipping.[11]

Since the 1980 Motor Carrier Act, only a small number of short-haul carriers have been estab-

7. *Industrial Outlook*, p. 59–1.
8. Robert V. Delaney, "Managerial and Financial Changes Facing Transportation Leaders," *Transportation Quarterly*, January 1986, p. 35.
9. *Industrial Outlook*, p. R–31.

10. *Value Line*, April 1, 1988, p. 271.
11. "Taking a Piece of the LTL Pie," *Air Cargo World*, April 1987, p. 20.

Exhibit 1

PERFORMANCE, TRENDS, AND FORECASTS IN THE TRANSPORTATION INDUSTRY

HISTORICAL PERFORMANCE: AIRLINES (SIC 451)

Item	*1972*	*1973*	*1974*	*1975*	*1976*	*1977*	*1978*	*1979*	*1980*	*1981*	*1982*	*1983*	*1984*
Operating revenues (billions $)	11.2	12.4	14.7	15.4	17.5	19.9	22.9	27.2	33.7	36.7	36.4	39.0	43.8
Employment (000)	301	311	307	290	303	308	329	341	361	350	330	329	345
Revenue passenger miles (billions)	152	162	163	163	179	193	227	262	255	249	259	282	305

TRENDS AND FORECASTS: TRUCKING, LOCAL AND LONG DISTANCE (SIC 421, 423)

Item	*1984*[a]	*1985*[a]	*1986*[a]	*1987*[b]	*1988*[c]	*Percent Change 1985–86*	*Percent Change 1986–87*	*Percent Change 1987–88*
Revenue ($ billions)	195.4	205.2	213.1	217.1	221.2	3.8	1.9	1.9
Cargo intercity ton-miles (billions)	606	610	627	644	659	2.8	2.7	2.3
Employment (000)	1,071	1,106	1,118	1,149	1,174	1.1	2.8	2.2
Average hourly earnings ($)	10.66	10.71	10.89	10.96	11.07	1.7	0.6	1.0

a. Revised.
b. Estimated.
c. Forecast.
Source: U.S. Industrial Outlook 1988, pp. 59-3, 59-4.

lished. The average length of haul for LTL carriers usually exceeds 1,000 miles while two-thirds of the market involves intraregional movements of less than 400 miles. Traditionally, this two-thirds has been overlooked. With this segment being heavily fragmented and often handled by small, family-owned businesses, the larger firms attempt to utilize their strong financial structures, efficient computerized services, and claims performance to gain market share. The large carriers must promote their quality and efficiency while providing a personal touch and superior service.[12]

The LTL carriers can be further divided into regional and national categories. The regional LTLs operate in a limited geographical area, most often within a 500 mile radius. National LTL carriers perform long-hauls, concentrating on destinations greater than 500 miles from the shipping point. Rate levels will increasingly determine carrier selection in

12. *Value Line*, p. 271.

this section as performance reaches high levels across the spectrum. The smaller companies will be threatened as nationally backed firms focus on price. Those carriers dominating the long-hauls may also become those dominating the short-hauls.

Competitive Structure of the Trucking Market

Competition in the industry stems from both national and regional firms, with many of the larger national firms breaking out divisions to compete on the regional level. Two prime examples are Roadway and Consolidated Freightways. This factor alone results in many of the local carriers being supported by deep pockets. The financial backing that comes from the parent corporation allows this type of firm to operate from a tremendous competitive advantage and provides discounting opportunity not available to the small, independent operators. Brief discussions of the major competitors follow; operating statistics are provided in Exhibit 4.

Exhibit 2
STRUCTURE OF THE MOTOR CARRIER INDUSTRY

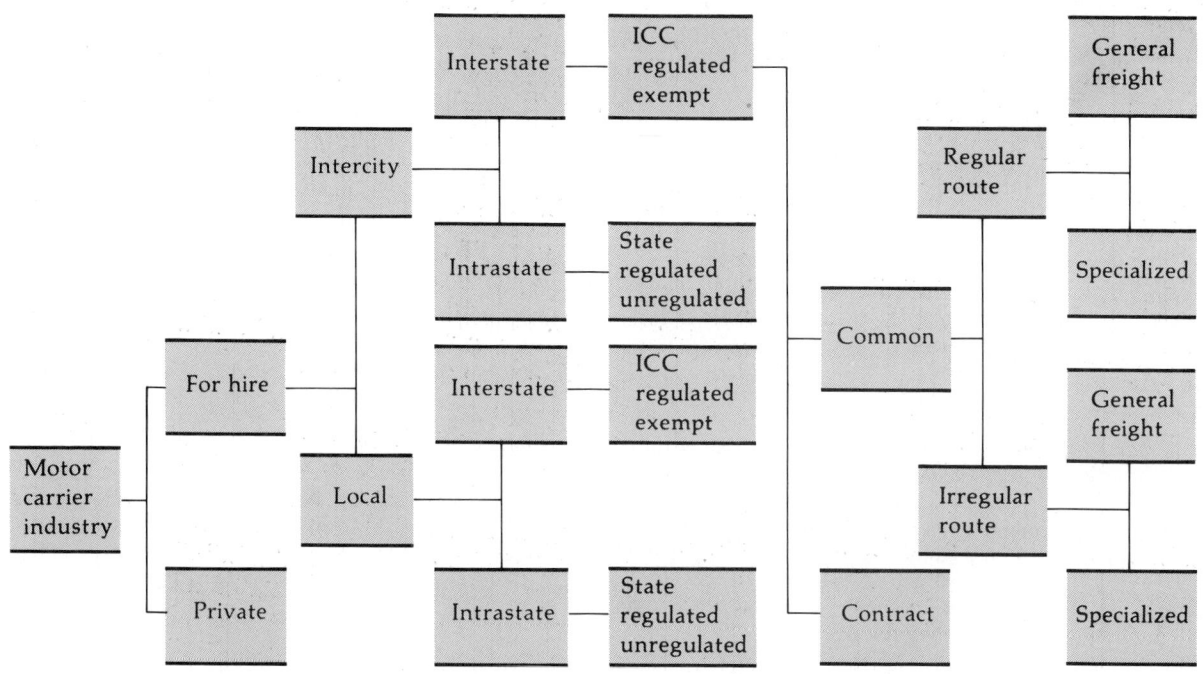

Source: Garland Chow, "The Economics of the Motor Freight Industry," School of Business, Indiana University, 1978, p. 9.

Yellow Freight Systems replaced Roadway Express as the third largest carrier after the two UPS companies. Yellow Freight had revenues of $1.6 billion in 1986.

Roadway Services Inc. is a holding company whose principal subsidiary is Roadway Express. It operates 591 terminals. LTL shipments account for 89 percent of revenues. A small package delivery system was developed in 1985. In 1983 Roadway purchased South Carolina-based Spartan Express, which consists of 50 terminals. With this purchase, Roadways became one of the first major carriers to enter the regional market.

Consolidated Freightways provides air and truck transport primarily through its three regional lines—Conway Western, Conway Central, and Conway Eastern—of 624 terminals. LTL freight ac-

counts for 86 percent of CF Motor Freight revenue. CF Air Freight operates through 115 terminals and contributes 13 percent of total revenues. Under its revenue enhancement program, CF is raising the minimum rate, setting minimum yield levels based on density and correcting misclassified freight.

Big companies such as those competitors described above set pricing and attitudes or customer expectations for the industry. Common carrier rates with discounts today are comparable to 1954 rates without discounts, while costs have risen steadily over those same years. The strategies often revolve around high quality or deep discounter. Deep discounting has removed large carriers from the business. "Around 300 firms have dropped out of the industry over the last five year period, providing tremendous opportunity to the smaller firms as

Exhibit 3

COMPOSITE FINANCES FOR CARRIER GROUPS A–D

	TOTAL GROUP A 293				TOTAL GROUP B 219			
NUMBER OF CARRIERS								
YEAR	1985		1984		1985		1984	
	$ IN MIL	%	$ IN MIL	%	$ IN MIL	%	$ IN MIL	%
Income Statement								
Income and expense data								
Gross revenues	767.92	100.0	809.31	100.0	2,553.39	100.0	2,491.75	100.0
Depreciation	35.17	4.6	33.60	4.2	100.29	3.9	90.07	3.6
Purchased transportation	139.58	18.2	160.15	19.8	700.77	27.4	688.76	27.6
Total operating expenses	759.19	98.9	792.67	97.9	2,493.05	97.6	2,416.96	97.0
Net carrier operating income	8.73	1.1	16.64	2.1	60.34	2.4	74.79	3.0
Interest expense	8.39	1.1	8.50	1.1	28.92	1.1	26.41	1.1
Net income before taxes	12.99	1.7	16.41	2.0	45.50	1.8	59.95	2.4
Income taxes—current	4.38	0.6	5.19	0.6	10.09	0.4	17.35	0.7
Deferred income taxes	0.11	0.0	1.21–	0.1–	4.83	0.2	1.70	0.1
Other adjustments to income	0.32	0.0	1.27–	0.2–	1.22	0.0	0.12–	0.0
Income before extra items	8.82	1.1	11.16	1.4	31.79	1.2	40.78	1.6
Extraordinary items	0.41–	0.1–	9.66	1.2	2.10	0.1	1.00–	0.0
Net income after taxes	8.41	1.1	20.82	2.6	33.89	1.3	39.78	1.6
Balance Sheet								
Assets								
Cash	53.11	13.4	54.42	13.3	106.22	10.5	121.85	12.8
Receivables from affiliates	18.73	4.7	15.84	3.9	47.99	4.7	37.28	3.8
Notes and accounts receivable	100.04	25.3	98.04	23.9	243.96	24.0	235.66	24.3
Prepaid expenses	15.65	4.0	10.99	2.7	38.40	3.8	32.67	3.4
Materials and supplies	3.69	0.9	4.33	1.1	15.67	1.5	15.94	1.6
Other current assets	6.17	1.6	5.63	1.4	2.70	0.3	2.55	0.3
Total current assets	197.39	49.9	189.26	46.2	454.94	44.8	445.95	45.9
Carrier operating property	378.71	95.8	362.14	88.4	967.97	95.3	908.52	93.6
Reserve for depreciation	239.61	60.6	222.19	54.2	536.50	52.8	503.44	51.9
Carrier operating property net	139.10	35.2	139.95	34.2	431.47	42.5	405.09	41.7
Total tangible property	156.32	39.6	157.03	38.3	466.02	45.9	436.34	45.0
Intangibles	8.21	2.1	9.38	2.3	14.24	1.4	10.27	1.1
Other assets	33.31	8.4	53.99	13.2	80.91	8.0	78.04	8.0
Total Assets	395.22	100.0	409.65	100.0	1,016.11	100.0	970.60	100.0

TOTAL GROUP C 105 1985		1984		TOTAL GROUP A B & C 1985		1984		TOTAL GROUP D 1010 1985		1984	
$ IN MIL	%	$ IN MIL	%	$ IN MIL	%	$ IN MIL	%	$ IN MIL	%	$ IN MIL	%
14,151.14	100.0	13,697.77	100.0	17,472.45	100.0	16,998.83	100.0	13,511.51	100.0	13,057.47	100.0
571.99	4.0	501.98	3.7	707.46	4.0	625.65	3.7	560.76	4.2	503.36	3.9
1,698.92	12.0	1,703.93	12.4	2,539.28	14.5	2,552.85	15.0	4,872.62	36.1	4,707.71	36.1
13,568.29	95.9	13,038.68	95.2	16,820.53	96.3	16,248.31	95.6	13,167.06	97.5	12,609.82	96.6
582.85	4.1	659.09	4.8	651.91	3.7	750.52	4.4	344.46	2.5	447.65	3.4
126.65	0.9	110.27	0.8	163.96	0.9	145.18	0.9	188.91	1.4	159.39	1.2
482.07	3.4	572.59	4.2	540.56	3.1	648.95	3.8	293.59	2.2	433.46	3.3
161.03	1.1	161.32	1.2	176.10	1.0	183.85	1.1	79.43	0.6	127.97	1.0
81.42	0.6	70.16	0.5	86.36	0.5	70.65	0.4	18.99	0.1	17.10	0.1
35.94	0.3	32.14	0.2	37.48	0.2	30.74	0.2	13.31	0.1	15.38	0.1
274.97	1.9	373.25	2.7	315.58	1.8	425.19	2.5	208.48	1.5	303.77	2.3
2.70	0.0	2.46	0.0	4.39	0.0	11.12	0.1	0.3-	0.0	5.01	0.0
277.67	2.0	375.71	2.7	319.97	1.8	436.31	2.6	208.45	1.5	308.78	2.4
289.74	4.2	322.61	4.9	449.07	5.4	498.89	6.3	414.90	6.6	423.73	7.6
232.97	3.4	118.61	1.8	299.69	3.6	171.73	2.2	344.87	5.5	298.71	5.4
1,325.12	19.3	1,270.00	19.5	1,669.12	20.2	1,603.70	20.3	1,488.19	23.7	1,282.03	23.0
255.00	3.7	232.70	3.6	309.05	3.7	276.36	3.5	223.85	3.6	189.71	3.4
112.50	1.6	118.07	1.8	131.85	1.6	138.35	1.8	99.04	1.6	103.93	1.9
57.66	0.8	55.04	0.8	66.53	0.8	63.22	0.8	103.90	1.7	77.23	1.4
2,272.99	33.1	2,117.04	32.5	2,925.33	35.3	2,752.24	34.8	2,674.75	42.5	2,375.33	42.7
6,583.78	95.9	6,155.43	94.4	7,930.47	95.8	7,426.10	94.0	5,780.26	91.9	5,176.01	93.0
2,862.39	41.7	2,764.42	42.4	3,638.50	44.0	3,490.05	44.2	3,015.64	47.9	2,767.21	49.7
3,721.39	54.2	3,391.01	52.0	4,291.97	51.8	3,936.05	49.8	2,764.63	43.9	2,408.80	43.3
3,789.89	55.2	3,430.95	52.6	4,412.23	53.3	4,024.32	50.9	2,859.24	45.4	2,511.85	45.2
84.08	1.2	76.43	1.2	106.52	1.3	96.09	1.2	119.85	1.9	92.72	1.7
719.81	10.5	898.50	13.8	834.02	10.1	1,030.52	13.0	638.10	10.1	583.05	10.5
6,866.76	100.0	6,522.92	100.0	8,278.10	100.0	7,903.17	100.0	6,291.94	100.0	5,562.95	100.0

Exhibit 3

COMPOSITE FINANCES FOR CARRIER GROUPS A–D (*continued*)

	TOTAL GROUP A				TOTAL GROUP B			
NUMBER OF CARRIERS	293				219			
YEAR	1985		1984		1985		1984	
	$ IN MIL	%	$ IN MIL	%	$ IN MIL	%	$ IN MIL	%
Liabilities and Equity								
Payables to affiliates	11.88	3.0	13.92	3.4	53.52	5.3	48.33	5.0
Notes payable	14.03	3.5	11.65	2.8	25.42	2.5	17.47	1.8
Accounts payable	57.45	14.5	56.88	13.9	113.51	11.2	107.50	11.1
Miscellaneous payables and accruals	7.64	1.9	7.41	1.8	27.33	2.7	23.00	2.4
Taxes payable	5.56	1.4	6.26	1.5	12.74	1.3	18.42	1.9
Funded debt due within one year	20.79	5.3	18.23	4.5	63.94	6.3	56.26	5.8
Other current liabilities	13.65	3.5	17.76	4.3	55.43	5.5	53.88	5.6
Total current liabilities	131.00	33.1	132.10	32.2	351.90	34.6	324.87	33.5
Advances payable	6.14	1.6	24.69	6.0	35.17	3.5	34.82	3.6
Funded debt due after one year	54.23	13.7	51.90	12.7	168.32	16.6	154.06	15.9
Total long term debt	60.37	15.3	76.59	18.7	203.49	20.0	188.88	19.5
Total funded debt	75.02	19.0	70.13	17.1	232.26	22.9	210.32	21.7
Reserves and estimated liabilities	5.29	1.3	4.91	1.2	10.26	1.0	9.83	1.0
Accumulated deferred tax credits	2.89	0.7	3.14	0.8	25.79	2.5	20.56	2.1
Total liabilities	199.54	50.5	216.75	52.9	591.44	58.2	544.15	56.1
Stockholder's equity	195.68	49.5	192.91	47.1	424.67	41.8	426.45	43.9
Total capital	258.05	64.8	269.49	65.8	628.16	61.8	615.33	63.4
Total Liabilities and Equity	395.22	100.0	409.65	100.0	1,016.11	100.0	970.60	100.0
Analytical Data	RATIOS		RATIOS		RATIOS		RATIOS	
Operating Performance								
Gross revenues to equity		3.92		4.20		6.01		5.84
Gross revenues to total capital		3.00		3.00		4.06		4.05
Gross revenues to net carr oper prop		5.52		5.78		5.92		6.15
Gross revenues to carr oper prop (cost)		2.03		2.23		2.64		2.74
Pretax income to gross revenues %		1.69		2.03		1.78		2.41
Pretax income to total capital, %		5.07		6.09		7.24		9.74
After tax income to gross revenues %		1.15		1.38		1.25		1.64

| TOTAL GROUP C 105 | | 1984 | | TOTAL GROUP A B & C | | 1984 | | TOTAL GROUP D 1010 | | 1984 | |
| 1985 | | | | 1985 | | | | 1985 | | | |
$ IN MIL	%	$ IN MIL	%	$ IN MIL	%	$ IN MIL	%	$ IN MIL	%	$ IN MIL	%
115.98	1.7	106.12	1.6	181.37	2.2	168.37	2.1	308.61	4.9	249.09	4.5
42.27	0.6	29.74	0.5	81.72	1.0	58.87	0.7	162.23	2.6	155.60	2.8
513.33	7.5	511.07	7.8	684.29	8.3	675.44	8.5	673.71	10.7	608.58	10.9
257.95	3.8	182.53	2.8	292.93	3.5	212.94	2.7	102.13	1.6	91.72	1.6
136.96	2.0	115.15	1.8	155.26	1.9	139.83	1.8	74.56	1.2	102.33	1.8
158.95	2.3	132.90	2.0	243.68	2.9	207.40	2.6	403.93	6.4	351.32	6.3
811.79	11.8	707.19	10.8	880.87	10.6	778.83	9.9	337.07	5.4	310.54	5.6
2,037.23	29.7	1,784.70	27.4	2,520.12	30.4	2,241.68	28.4	2,062.24	32.8	1,869.18	33.6
344.66	5.0	461.03	7.1	385.97	4.7	520.54	6.6	354.22	5.6	200.10	3.6
762.27	11.1	679.34	10.4	984.82	11.9	885.30	11.2	1,091.85	17.4	885.76	15.9
1,106.93	16.1	1,140.37	17.5	1,370.79	16.6	1,405.84	17.8	1,446.07	23.0	1,085.87	19.5
921.22	13.4	812.24	12.5	1,228.50	14.8	1,092.70	13.8	1,495.78	23.8	1,237.09	22.2
207.47	3.0	202.37	3.1	223.02	2.7	217.12	2.7	60.20	1.0	49.32	0.9
419.87	6.1	357.94	5.5	448.55	5.4	381.64	4.8	234.15	3.7	207.20	3.7
3,771.49	54.9	3,485.38	53.4	4,562.48	55.1	4,246.27	53.7	3,802.66	60.4	3,211.57	57.7
3,095.27	45.1	3,037.54	46.6	3,715.62	44.9	3,656.90	46.3	2,489.28	39.6	2,351.38	42.3
4,202.20	61.2	4,177.91	64.0	5,086.41	61.4	5,062.73	64.1	3,935.35	62.5	3,437.25	61.8
8,866.76	100.0	6,522.92	100.0	8,278.10	100.0	7,903.17	100.0	6,291.94	100.0	5,562.95	100.0
RATIOS		RATIOS		RATIOS		RATIOS		RATIOS		RATIOS	
	4.57		4.51		4.70		4.65		5.43		5.55
	3.37		3.28		3.44		3.36		3.43		3.80
	3.80		4.04		4.07		4.32		4.89		5.42
	2.15		2.23		2.20		2.29		2.34		2.52
	3.41		4.18		3.09		3.82		2.17		3.32
	11.47		13.71		10.63		12.82		7.46		12.61
	1.94		2.72		1.81		2.50		1.54		2.33

Exhibit 3

COMPOSITE FINANCES FOR CARRIER GROUPS A–D *(continued)*

	TOTAL GROUP A 293 1985		1984		TOTAL GROUP B 219 1985		1984	
NUMBER OF CARRIERS YEAR	$ IN MIL	%	$ IN MIL	%	$ IN MIL	%	$ IN MIL	%
Analytical Data	*RATIOS*		*RATIOS*		*RATIOS*		*RATIOS*	
After tax income to equity, %	4.51		5.79		7.49		9.56	
Return on transportation investment, %	4.25		8.44		11.29		14.21	
Expense ratio %	99.96		98.99		98.77		98.06	
Operating ratio %	98.86		97.94		97.64		97.00	
Average revenue per carrier	2.62		2.76		11.66		11.38	
Net income per carrier	0.03		0.04		0.15		0.19	
Liquidity								
Cash throw off, dollars	43.78		44.82		135.70		132.68	
Working capital, dollars	66.39		57.15		103.05		121.07	
Current ratio	1.51		1.43		1.29		1.37	
Days cash oper exp in work capital	33.34		27.36		15.65		18.92	
Average days collection period	47.55		44.22		34.87		34.52	
Leverage and Debt Service								
Funded debt to equity	0.38		0.36		0.55		0.49	
Net debt to equity	0.06–		0.03–		0.15		0.08	
Funded debt to tangible net worth	0.40		0.38		0.57		0.51	
Cash throw to funded debt due in one year %	210.55		245.82		212.24		235.81	
Cash throw to total funded debt %	58.36		63.91		58.43		63.08	
Interest to total funded debt %	11.18		12.12		12.45		12.56	
Carrier property (Net) to equity	0.71		0.73		1.02		0.95	
Additional Ratios								
Receivables to payables	1.40		1.43		1.76		1.89	
Deprec to debt due in one year	1.69		1.84		1.57		1.60	
Total tang prop to equity	0.80		0.81		1.10		1.02	

TOTAL GROUP C 105 1985		1984		TOTAL GROUP A B & C 1985		1984		TOTAL GROUP D 1010 1985		1984	
$ IN MIL	%	$ IN MIL	%	$ IN MIL	%	$ IN MIL	%	$ IN MIL	%	$ IN MIL %	
RATIOS		RATIOS		RATIOS		RATIOS		RATIOS		RATIOS	
8.88		12.29		8.49		11.63		8.38		12.92	
14.73		17.70		13.88		16.88		10.20		15.36	
96.78		95.99		97.21		96.44		98.85		97.79	
95.88		95.19		96.27		95.58		97.45		96.57	
134.77		130.45		28.32		27.55		13.38		12.93	
2.62		3.55		0.51		0.69		0.21		0.30	
892.44		913.25		1,071.92		1,090.75		774.92		808.85	
235.76		332.34		405.21		510.57		612.51		506.14	
1.12		1.19		1.16		1.23		1.30		1.27	
6.61		9.66		9.16		11.90		17.66		15.19	
34.18		33.84		34.87		34.43		40.20		35.84	
0.30		0.27		0.33		0.30		0.60		0.53	
0.17		0.11		0.16		0.10		0.19		0.16	
0.31		0.27		0.34		0.31		0.63		0.55	
561.45		687.18		439.89		525.93		191.85		230.23	
96.88		112.44		87.25		99.82		51.81		65.38	
13.75		13.58		13.35		13.29		12.63		12.88	
1.20		1.12		1.16		1.08		1.11		1.02	
2.39		2.35		2.18		2.18		1.78		1.68	
3.60		3.78		2.90		3.02		1.39		1.43	
1.22		1.13		1.19		1.10		1.15		1.07	

Exhibit 3

COMPOSITE FINANCES FOR CARRIER GROUPS A–D *(continued)*

	TOTAL GROUP A				TOTAL GROUP B			
NUMBER OF CARRIERS	293				219			
YEAR	1985		1984		1985		1984	
	$ IN MIL	%	$ IN MIL	%	$ IN MIL	%	$ IN MIL	%
Analytical Data	RATIOS		RATIOS		RATIOS		RATIOS	
Income before extra items etc to equity %	4.38		6.70		7.50		9.56	
Gross revenues to total tang prop	4.91		5.15		5.48		5.71	
Productivity Measures (Int-Cty Carr Only)								
Total payroll to revenues %	28.55		28.14		25.57		25.35	
Total payroll (wpt) to revenues %	46.34		47.42		53.01		52.89	
Cargo handler compen to revenues %	2.34		2.27		3.11		3.21	
Linehaul expenses to revenues %	48.42		49.07		52.25		52.51	
Revenue per ton-mile, cents	14.46		15.85		14.59		14.63	
Average load, tons	11.51		10.48		11.92		11.76	
Total tons, thous	16,411.30		17,437.81		42,677.78		42,082.01	
Total miles, thous	319,299.89		332,338.30		1,221,940.22		1,202,563.06	

TOTAL GROUP C 105 1985	1984	TOTAL GROUP A B & C 1985	1984	TOTAL GROUP D 1010 1985	1984
$ IN MIL %	$ IN MIL %	$ IN MIL %	$ IN MIL %	$ IN MIL %	$ IN MIL %
RATIOS	RATIOS	RATIOS	RATIOS	RATIOS	RATIOS
8.91	12.29	8.51	11.68	8.39	12.91
3.73	3.99	3.96	4.22	4.73	5.20
35.09	35.58	33.61	33.95	18.92	18.93
46.67	47.59	47.50	48.29	56.17	56.23
7.51	7.73	6.75	6.93	2.48	3.08
39.64	40.21	41.61	42.17	75.78	75.54
20.59	19.81	19.30	18.78	11.63	11.79
12.80	12.95	12.57	12.61	12.86	12.16
105,289.03	108,039.55	164,378.11	167,559.37	339,380.15	336,125.56
5,121,678.96	5,076,844.72	6,662,919.07	6,611,746.08	7,025,650.48	7,065,039.51

Exhibit 4
INDUSTRY SURVEY EARNINGS

COMPANY	Fiscal Year Year	Quarter	REVENUES Latest Quarter (mil. $)	Change from Prior Year (%)	Rank	Latest 12 Months (mil. $)	Change from Prior Year (%)	Rank	INCOME Latest Quarter (mil. $)	Change from Prior Year (%)	Rank	Latest 12 Months (mil. $)	Change from Prior Year (%)	Rank	PROFITABILITY Latest Quarter Return on Revenue (%)	Rank	12 Months Return on Revenue (%)	Rank	12 Months Return on Equity (%)	Rank
Less-Than-Truckload Motor Carriers																				
American Carriers Inc	87 DEC	DEC	174.27	72.9	1	472.45	17.5	2	-10.56	NM		-15.50	NM		-6.1	9	-3.3	9	-19.3	9
Arkansas Best Corp	87 DEC	DEC	196.66	11.2	7	732.31	6.2	7	3.46	90.6	2	8.76	-51.9	7	1.8	5	1.2	7	7.9	5
Carolina Freight Corp	87 DEC	DEC	191.94	0.4	10	594.91	0.6	9	1.11	-74.0	7	8.62	-48.2	6	0.6	7	1.5	6	7.0	7
Consolidated Freightways Inc	87 DEC	DEC	618.39	12.7	6	2,296.91	8.1	6	20.56	-8.7	4	74.57	-16.3	2	3.3	2	3.2	1	11.0	2
IU International Corp	87 DEC	DEC	415.34F	20.5	3	1,551.18	16.9	3	2.92	-72.1	6	28.56	27.6	1	0.7	1	1.8	6	11.9	1
Preston Corp	87 DEC	DEC	134.53	27.9	2	505.42	20.6	1	-0.70	NM		0.34	-95.4	8	-0.5	8	0.1	8	0.3	8
Roadway Services Inc	87 DEC	DEC	614.51	15.4	5	1,908.75	11.1	5	18.74	-28.1	5	50.51	-33.9	4	3.0	4	2.6	2	7.7	6

Company																					
Transcon Inc-Calif	87	DEC	DEC	86.36	6.1	8	333.41	-2.9	10	-7.03	NM		-19.92	NM		8.1	10	-6.0	10	-35.1	10
Viking Freight Inc87		DEC	DEC	55.33	17.6	4	192.84	12.8	4	1.48	102.6	1	3.90	-17.1	3	2.7	3	2.0	4	8.1	4
Yellow Freight System-Del	87	DEC	DEC	459.32	5.7	9	1,759.99	2.7	8	11.43	10.8	3	41.28	-38.5	5	2.5	4	2.3	3	10.7	3
Truckload Motor Carriers																					
Arnold Industries Inc	87	DEC	DEC	29.41	18.7	3	108.65	14.2	3	2.66	-3.6	2	10.39	4.4	2	9.0	1	9.6	1	21.6	1
Hunt (JB) Transprt Svcs Inc	87	DEC	DEC	80.10	38.7	2	286.42	40.6	2	4.80	-13.7	3	22.42	-9.4	3	6.0	3	7.8	3	21.6	2
Werner Enterprises Inc	87	FEB	FEB	37.77	46.7	1	139.09	47.3	1	2.29	11.6	1	12.07	33.9	1	6.1	2	8.7	2	18.2	3
Air Cargo																					
Airborne Freight Corp	87	DEC	DEC	170.59	18.0	3	632.30	16.7	3	1.72	-70.6	3	5.90	-55.4	2	1.0	3	0.9	3	5.5	2
Emery Air Freight Corp	87	DEC	DEC	357.98F	51.1	1	11,221.63	37.6	1	-18.35	NM		-47.66	NM		-5.1	4	-3.9	4	-30.5	3
Federal Express Corp	87	FEB	MAY	977.17	22.3	2	23,699.85	22.3	2	36.48	1.6	2	176.54	-2.1	1	3.7	2	4.8	1	16.2	1
Purolator Courier Corp	87	SEP	DEC	NA	NA		NA	NA		NA	NA		NA	NA		NA	NA	NA	NA	NA	
Tiger International	87	DEC	DEC	353.13	17.8		41,231.87	10.9	4	21.36	105.4	1	58.68	NM		6.1	1	4.8	2	-244.3	4

Source: *Standard & Poors Industry Surveys* (April 1988), pp. 3, 19.
Reprinted by permission of Standard & Poor's Corporation, Industry Surveys, Railroads and Trucking Basic Analysis.

freight traffic shifts patterns. The interesting thing about this situation is that pricing remains virtually unchanged. The market remains a 'shippers' market,' " comments Mr. Gulbinas.

During economic downturns, many carriers resort to deep rate discounting. In the long run, this strategy may prove detrimental as companies become unable to fund maintenance programs, acquire replacement vehicles, and purchase computer technology to enhance productivity. Alternatives to discounting strategies appear to lie in discounting for volume or repeat business only or for those firms that will perform support functions traditionally done by the carriers.[13]

Operating Practices

Truck transporters have the opportunity to reduce operating costs while improving customer service and efficiency through four means. Firms can enhance driver selection, training, and continuing education as well as embarking on insurance containment programs. The firms can also practice automated route scheduling and fleet sizing programs.[14]

With automated route scheduling, firms can improve vehicle selection, scheduling, and routing by employing computer technology and software packages. With the increasing computer technology available, these mechanisms have become realistic for firms of all sizes.

When examining existing fleet, composition of the fleet, its equipment assignments, and overall cost of the fleet operations, the goal is to match fleet size, composition, and maintenance operations with the present business requirements. This must be done while ensuring long-term flexibility in the program as well.

Market Cost-Price Structure

When the Motor Carrier Act of 1980 was developed, there were 1,700 carriers with ICC operating authority; there are now over 30,000. The market share of the top ten regular route common carriers, in terms of revenues, increased to 54 percent from 40 percent, indicating that shipments were not being distributed evenly in the industry. The same ten made 42.8 percent of total investment in the industry in

1978 while increasing the expenditures to 73.3 percent in 1984. As a result of this calculation alone, industry analysts conclude that "most of those other carriers should not be counted on as active market participants in the coming years." At the same time, the ten top carriers experienced only modest increases in the share of operating income, up to 61 percent in 1984 from 54 percent in 1978.[15]

Since 1979, operating ratios have loomed around 96 percent in all but two years. Essentially, carriers have four cents per dollar of sales with which to pay taxes and interest or otherwise claim as profit. Yellow Freight indicates that its operating ratio increased from 90 to 94 percent in the two final quarters of 1985. Yellow adds, "in addition to higher fuel costs and a decline in operating efficiencies attributable to normal seasonal factors, the operating ratio was also impacted by the increased discounting."[16]

Return on equity for general freight motor carriers decreased to 9.6 percent in 1984 from 12.9 percent in 1976. Other industries were maintaining ROE at relatively stable levels around 13.5 percent.[17]

High insurance costs have eroded operating margins throughout the industry. Because of deregulation, many carriers have been unable to pass on these costs to their customers. In response, after careful analysis, the ICC has allowed some companies to self-insure. Attention to safety performance has increased importance. Those companies operating bare, or without insurance of any kind, will be driven out of the industry.[18]

The Changing Trends in the Trucking Market

The overall transportation industry appears to be in a state of flux as a result of various environmental forces. Deregulation of trucking has made the truckers and interstate carriers become more competitive due to the impending lack of insulation from competitors on their operations. There has been a fundamental shift in the way the businesses are managed. Carriers have previously had protected geographic regions as well as uniform pricing which was relatively high and fixed. Hauls of less than 300 miles are no longer by plane, but are undertaken by

---

13. *Industrial Outlook.*
14. "Any Which Way But Up," *Air Cargo World*, September 1987, p. 26.

15. Borsellino, "The Aftermath of U.S. Deregulation," *Truck Fleet*, April 1986, p. 25.
16. Ibid.
17. Ibid.
18. *Industrial Outlook.*

smaller companies for truck transport. This introduces new competitors and new opportunities into the motor freight market.

Deregulation has shifted patterns of traffic away from organized firms to independent operators. When the larger organizations fail or withdraw from the market, business goes to the small, regional, operator. However, the big companies remaining in the industry are playing bigger. Multimodal transportation companies are expected to continue to grow while acquisitions, mergers, and broker activity increase. As a result, the evolution of the industry structure will speed up and competitive forces will strengthen.[19]

Rapid development of the market and deregulation have encouraged competitors to come into the industry and set prices based on service levels and who could get and maintain the business. This has made the industry a shippers' market. Shippers began to be catered to and realized that numerous discounts were available. Price advantages could be gained by playing competitive carriers against one another. In the effort to gain market share, the big transport companies were discounting up to 65 percent.

The roadrailer, a trailer that operates both on rail and highway, is gaining in popularity. Roadrailer application would allow increased competition by railroads in the trucking sector and vice versa by providing efficient short-haul carriage. Piggyback volume is also increasing, providing the strongest growth sector to the railroads and offering new opportunities and competition to trucking. In 1986, loadings were 10 percent higher than 1985 and account for 15 percent of total rail carloadings.[20] Restructuring the industry segment has reached beyond rails. Rail-truck and rail-water mergers are increasing in numbers, moving competitors towards intermodal transport systems.

"Road feeder service is one of the most prominent air freight-trucking programs of the 1980's which involves intercity truck transport between airline terminal cities for the airlines. Two additional areas of opportunity for trucking are the increased door-to-door pickup and deliveries and the expansion of small package programs. These three activities appear to be more opportunistic to the regional or local trucking firms due to the involved scope of operations," comments an industry expert.[21]

Within organizations themselves, no longer is there simply a traffic manager with a key budget role. Instead, there is a logistics department encompassing production, inventory controls, materials planning, and human resources personnel. The JIT or just-in-time manufacturing orientation is driving many of the organizational changes and the industry's evolutionary forces are accelerating all the time. "The U.S. version of JIT will create opportunities for smart transportation companies that will bundle various companies' stocking requirements and delivery quantities totalling less than trailerload to a number of companies at scheduled times."[22] As a result, industry growth will come from manufacturing companies who trust the carriers to do major dollar business, transporting their goods primarily in the regional sectors.

Time definite trucking is an alternative approach for supporting the JIT systems. With this concept, charges are generally less than those charged by the LTL carriers at the 200-pound minimum cost structure. Time definite trucking offers simplified tariffs, no accessorial charges, and advanced tracking.[23]

The Interstate Commerce Commission (ICC) is extending operating authority to carriers for expanding market reach, balancing operations, improving load factors, reducing unit costs, and tailoring services to shippers' needs. The relaxed environment of the transportation industry has increased entry rates, introduced intense price and service competition, and advanced logistics systems and associated improvements in productivity. Marginal carriers will have difficulty continuing operations. Continued mergers, acquisitions, reorganizations, failures, and bankruptcies can be expected.[24]

THE AIR PACKAGE DELIVERY MARKET

Size of the Market

Though the airline industry carries only about 1 percent of the world's total freight volume, the $6 billion-a-year cargo service is growing in impor-

19. Ibid.
20. Ibid.

21. *Standard & Poor's Industry Surveys*, 1988, p. R–35.
22. The Yankee Group, "Riders Take a Backseat As Cargo Pays the Way," *Air Cargo World*, May 1985, p. 18.
23. "Piece of LTL Pie," p. 20.
24. *Industrial Outlook*, 1988, p. 59–5.

tance. The U.S. Air Transport Association forecasts that freight tonnage will increase 10.3 percent to 11.247 billion overrail. Domestic freight is expected to increase 8.6 percent to 6.134 billion, with small package air freight traffic increasing 15.3 percent and revenues increasing 11.1 percent.[25] Air cargo ton miles totaled 7.3 billion in 1986, an increase of 22 percent from 1985 to 46 percent from 1976. Revenue for this industry segment increased 110 percent during the 1985–1986 period to $5.6 billion.[26]

In the past eight years, the U.S. air transport sector has gone from just over 30 scheduled, certified carriers to about 100. The number of air freight forwarders has expanded from 350 to 2,500, according to industry experts.

Segments of the Air Package Delivery Market

Air transport is classified into four categories: majors, nationals, regionals, and cargo carriers. In 1986, majors carried 26.9 percent of world air freight, with nationals carrying only 1 percent. The majors are experiencing an increasing share of world traffic while their share of revenue is declining.[27] The regionals, broken further into large and small, carried no freight. The cargo carriers were responsible for 10.9 percent of the world air freight.

Competitive Structure of the Air Package Delivery Market

Competition exists among the traditional air freight forwarders, of which many have purchased planes to become carriers themselves; the passenger airlines, which carry freight in the bellies of the craft; the surface transportation companies; and the air couriers. The increasing demand was initiated to a large extent by deregulatory actions, which allowed greater competition by pricing.

The following sections provide data on the major competitors in the air cargo industry. The information has been compiled from the *U.S. Industrial Outlook 1988—Transportation Industry Value Line*, April 1, 1988. Exhibit 5 provides composite financial data for the competitors in the segment.

United Parcel Service is the largest privately-owned package transporter in the United States.

UPS entered the air segment in 1982 by purchasing 28 used aircraft; the bulk of its packages, which total 6 million daily, is still carried by truck. Its entry into the segment caused tremendous turbulence in competitive practice such as pricing and service levels. With UPS air delivery, a 5-pound box shipped anywhere in the U.S. costs $6.50 for 2-day service and $15.50 for overnight service. The same box transported by truck costs $2, with next day delivery expected within 400 miles.[28]

Federal Express provides overnight, door-to-door delivery of small packages to areas in which 95 percent of the United States population lives. It has offices located in 318 cities, and international services are provided to eighty-nine countries. In industry innovation of time, price, and service, Federal Express has been unmatched, having the most extensive electronic communications among all U.S. corporations. Two higher priced delivery services, Priority One and Courier Pak, are growing rapidly.

Emery Air Freight Corporation is one of the nation's largest air freight carriers, with total lift capacity of 3 million pounds. The recent purchase in 1987 of Purolator Courier will expand service operations and lead to greater efficiency gains. Purolator has affected earnings dramatically, placing Emery on a watch list of survivability.

Airborne Freight Corporation provides door-to-door service through its own air-ground transportation system, Airborne Express. Its overnight lift capacity is 900,000 pounds. Airborne secured a major contract from IBM in 1987, which has provided momentum for operations. Airborne is currently in an expansion phase spending $100 million to improve delivery coverage, increase airlift capacity, and enlarge hub facilities. The air courier package-handling capacity has doubled due to a $4-million improvement in its sorting facility.

Market Cost-Price Structure

The most significant trend in 1986 airline finances was the drop in kerosene costs, which resulted in a decrease in fuel costs of about one-third. In the United States, fuel costs decreased from 22 percent to 15 percent of operating expenses in 1986.[29] Industry analysts are quick to point out that the lower fuel costs are expected to be passed directly on to the

25. *Air Transport World*, June 1987, p. 57.
26. *Industrial Outlook*, 1988, p. 59–2.
27. *Air Transport World*, June 1987, p. 57.

28. "Riders Take a Backseat," p. 19.
29. *Air Transport World*, June 1987, p. 55.

Exhibit 5

AIR CARGO CARRIERS FINANCIAL PERFORMANCE DATA, 1985–1986

U. S. CARGO CARRIERS

Airline	Total Operating Revenue (000)	% Change vs. 1985	Total Operating Expense (000)	% Change vs. 1985	Operating Profit or Loss (000) 1986	1985	Net Profit or Loss (000) 1986	1985
Aerial Transit	$ 2,570	3.1	$ 2,602	7.3	$ (32)	$ 66	$ 140	$ 66
Airborne	109,972	21.3	100,197	18.3	9,775	5,954	11,189	6,160
Arrow[a]	41,711	(69.0)	45,466	(66.3)	(3,755)	(135)	(3,755)	230
Emery	887,500	1.3	906,400	6.6	(18,900)	23,800	(5,400)	16,200
Federal Express[a]	2,939,849	—	2,575,117	—	364,732	—	256,232	—
Florida West	9,350	106.6	7,164	90.3	2,186	657	1,281	633
Flying Tigers[a]	1,046,597	(4.0)	991,666	(73.2)	54,931	20,515	(18,645)	(44,232)
Purolator	841,400	5.2	888,480	—	(47,080)	(50,100)	(57,600)	(29,400)
Zantop[a]	113,633	(11.7)	103,456	(5.5)	10,177	19,231	5,520	11,983
Total	$5,992,582		$5,620,548		$372,034	$21,988	$188,962	$(38,360)

a. U.S. DOT data.

U.S. AIRLINES FREIGHT

Rank	Airline	Total System Freight Ton KMs (000)	1986/1985 % Change	Rank	Airline	Total System Freight Ton KMs (000)	1986/1985 % Change
1	Flying Tigers	3,555,085	(4.0)	19	Challenge[d]	62,173	113.0
2	Northwest[a]	1,552,519	13.1	20	Alaska	40,149	7.6
3	Federal Express	1,310,354	37.5	21	Piedmont	34,145	11.6
4	United	1,028,180	27.7	22	Aeron[d]	26,824	24.1
5	Pan Am	807,968	34.2	23	USAir	21,491	(3.2)
6	TWA[b]	539,727	(9.1)	24	Braniff	21,386	122.8
7	American	488,788	13.2	25	Hawaiian	11,299	123.7
8	Eastern	461,861	3.5	26	PSA	11,195	34.2
9	Continental	378,671	39.6	27	AirCal	7,668	104.8
10	Delta	351,696	(3.5)	28	Frontier[c]	7,639	(18.7)
11	Airborne[d]	219,383	18.7	29	Aloha	5,820	84.6
12	Transamerica[c]	183,483	(43.3)	30	Aerial[d]	5,570	10.8
13	Western	154,630	5.3	31	Jet America	3,952	(38.1)
14	People Express	146,492	—	32	America West	3,120	233.39
15	Zantop[d]	136,400	(26.6)	33	Southwest	2,444	(1.1)
16	Arrow[d]	127,300	—	34	TranStar	737	(18.8)
17	World	115,800	0.7	35	Air Wisconsin	283	(10.6)
18	Florida West[d]	76,600	51.4				

a. Includes Republic.
b. Includes Ozark.
c. Partial.
d. Direct airline reports.
Source: Reprinted by permission of *Air Transport World,* June 1987, pp. 126, 127.

consumer. The anticipated result is an increase in volume with no accompanying increases in profit margins.[30]

Analysis indicates that outbound air freight rates from the United States have dropped from $2 per pound to $0.50 per pound, a decrease of 75 percent since 1979. Prices for overnight documents are decreasing by 40 percent and are expected to continue the decrease.[31]

The Changing Trends in the Industry

Domestic growth in the air cargo market is expected in the Northeast, the sunbelt, and on the West coast.[32]

The small package courier express segment has grown rapidly, contributing the major growth in the air segment. The shipments in 1986 grew 15 percent to roughly 220 million.[33] The growing demand for small package door-to-door service has provided opportunity for both new and old carriers to refine services and develop integrated, intermodal door-to-door service. Many of the companies are establishing strong and extensive hub networks. These increased service offerings, coupled with price-cutting, have caused the weaker companies to experience tremendous financial difficulty. At the same time, expansion into international markets has continued to intensify. Observers of the industry expect door-to-door express operations to account for greater than 50 percent of the European market by 1990, in comparison to only 10 percent in 1980.[34]

Through the employment of trucks, airlines are able to provide customers local pickup and delivery in those areas surrounding airports up to a 100-mile radius. Air-truck combinations also allow transport between hubs within a 300-mile travel radius. Intercity services, which involves transport between airports within the same city, is a third means by which

trucks can provide support services for the airlines.[35]

Changing customer demands and needs have brought additional services into the industry. Companies are providing regular volume customers with personal package meters that allow shippers to weigh and rate their own packages. Frequently, personal computers are also being tied from the shippers' systems directly into the carriers to permit customers to monitor the entire distribution process. Drop boxes for packages must be easily accessible for customers. These drop boxes can increase visibility for the shippers, improve customer convenience, and concentrate packages at fewer collection points.[36]

One potential threat to the air cargo market lies in electronic mail. Federal Express has recently placed 6,000 machines in customer offices. This alternative means of letter transport may capture substantial market share from air freight carriers.[37]

Concluding Comments on the Transportation Industry

Those firms able to exploit the synergies across the various transportation sectors are those companies making the industry decisions and the major portion of the revenues. The cottage industry firms or regional, independent operators, which offer their support to the big guys in a fashion similar to the Japanese must either do it better than the major firms or do it for them. Often, the regional firms are more efficient at that level while the customers do not perceive them as having the potential to reach beyond a limited geographical scope. As a result, the smaller companies must develop strong ties with the manufacturers in their areas to transport freight for them in addition to providing local support and hook-up services for the major carriers across all transportation modes. Tremendous potential exists for those regionals that can achieve these relationships.

30. "Overcapacity, Competition Could Hamper Profits in Air Cargo Market," *Aviation Week and Space Technology*, March 10, 1987, p. 217.
31. "Air Cargo Wars Could Spur Mergers," *Journal of Commerce and Commercial*, February 20, 1986, p. 6A.
32. "Overcapacity," p. 217.
33. *Industrial Outlook.*
34. *Value Line*, April 1, 1988.
35. "Catering to the Airlines," *Air Cargo World*, January 1987.
36. "Overcapacity."
37. Ibid.

COUNTRY CONVENIENCE STORES, INC.

KENNETH W. OLM
University of Texas at Austin

ALAN L. CARSRUD
University of Southern California

BACKGROUND

As mom-and-pop grocery stores began to give way to supermarkets and chain stores in the 1930s and 1940s, a countertrend in retailing became evident as convenience stores began to spring up to serve the needs of an increasingly mobile society. The small owner-operated food store continued to serve customers in the older, more settled, and the strongly ethnic-oriented neighborhoods and in rural areas. Regional convenience store chains developed rapidly in the 1950s and 1960s in response to the trend, especially in the rapidly growing sun-belt areas. The most notable of these were the Southland Corporation and later the Circle K stores. A number of local and small regional chains also developed in market areas considered too limited for the major chains.

One of these small regional chains of convenience stores, Country Convenience Stores, Inc., was located in a largely rural area in a large southern state. All stores were located within 50 miles of the company's headquarters. No store was located in a city with a population larger than 25,000 and many were in communities of less than 1,000 inhabitants. By 1984, there were twenty-three stores in the firm,

with total gross revenues of approximately $19 million. All stores sold gasoline and limited automobile supplies in addition to the typical milk, bread, beer, cigarettes, soft drinks, candy, food, and drug products. The second highest volume store, with approximately 1,600 square feet of space and sales of $1.2 million, was located in a community of about 500 population. There were no other competitive convenience chain outlets located within five miles of that store.

Ownership and top management of the company was concentrated in one family. The president of the company was in his early sixties. Store managers were selected by informal methods. About half had some college training, but only two of the twenty-five managers in 1984 held college degrees. In corporate management, four of eight had degrees, plus two of the three family members (not including the president). The new merchandising manager had a college degree from a small college located in the same city as the corporate offices, as did six of the seven other members of management.

Turnover among store managers averaged about 25 percent a year. Managers for new stores came about equally from the ranks of assistant store managers and from outside the company. Pay was not fully competitive with the pay for store managers in the major chains, and fringe benefits were also less. However, living costs in small rural cities where most stores were located were among the lowest in the state. Also, supervision over managers was usually not as tight as was the case with the larger chains, such as 7–11 and Circle K.

This case, written specifically for this text, is printed by permission. The case was prepared by Kenneth W. Olm, Ph.D., University of Texas at Austin, and Alan L. Carsrud, Ph.D., University of Southern California, with the research assistance of K. W. Olm, Jr., BBA.

THE INCIDENT

The former merchandise manager was considered by a number of store managers to be less than fully competent and less than fully dedicated to the job. As troubles in inventory imbalances became apparent and profit margins began to slip, the merchandise manager was kicked upstairs until some other job could be found. The new merchandise manager, a young lady with limited managerial experience but with great energy and self-confidence, was installed in the job.

After making a quick tour of all the stores to meet the managers and to look over their operations, she went back to her corporate office to think about what needed to be done to improve operations under her purview.

Thirty days after her last store visit she drafted a memo and had it delivered to all store managers. The memo in its entirety reads as follows:

To All Managers:

I'm sure by now you have all received a letter from the state regarding your cigarette backstock. The letter tells you that on October 1 at the close of business you have to take a cigarette inventory by the pack and record it on the form they provided. We need that form filled out and sent to the office immediately, not the next week. We have to pay a 1 cent tax on all cigarettes that are in stock on that day. From then on, cigarettes are a taxable item! You ring up cigarettes as 1.15 (or whatever you charge) taxable. So the cost will be 1.21 to the customer. Your cigarette key will be reprogrammed from a nontaxable key to a taxable key. If you forget to do this buildup on October 1, the consequences will be severe!! You will not only have to take the wrath of your supervisor, you will also have to take the wrath of the state.

As some of you may know, we are going into selling cigarettes by the carton at a special price. The day you take your inventory of cigarettes, Oct. 1, will be the first day of carton sales. The carton price will probably be $8.95. Before October 1, I will get with each one of you so we can figure out where to display your cigarette cartons; they will be kept separate from your cigarettes for sale by the pack. When you order prior to October 1, please overorder on your

popular brands that may sell by the carton. On your McLeans invoices, you will have to mark down a certain amount of cartons from the retail on the invoice to $8.95 so your inventory won't be short. These will have to be kept separate at all times. We can go into more detail when I get together with each one of you. If you mess this up, your inventory will get messed up.

Now! I am going to harp on an old subject. It seems that none of you are listening when I talk to you of the preventative measures to take against inventory shortages! I gave my spiel in the last meeting and very few listened. Very few of you are looking at the McLeans tags on each individual item. Did you know that Summit candy bars are not 38 cents? Did you know that Breathsavers are not 33 cents? Did you know that Certs are not 40 cents? Look on the invoice and see how much they are. When you receive your groceries, look at each and every tag and read it!!!! See that what is in the box is what is written on the tag. Those tags serve a very important purpose . . . to inform you of the retail prices on the groceries. These prices are ever-changing and need to be checked every time you receive groceries!! Check every tag on every box of gum, every box of candy, etc. I can't harp on this enough. And while you are checking these prices, take out your marking gun and mark everything . . . gum, candy, etc. These measures will help curb your inventory losses. It doesn't sound like much, but added up together, the losses can be staggering!!

Some of you are still not checking in vendors properly. I had the opportunity to observe a few managers check in vendors and I will tell you about it. I'm not picking on anybody, but if this example sounds like you, straighten up! First I saw a wine shipment come into a store. The manager picked up a box cutter, walked around to the other side of the counter and proceeded to cut open the boxes and see what was in them. If this sounds like you, hooray!!!! I don't give a pooh if the vendor gets mad and doesn't want to wait. Remember, it is their privilege to be there and they can leave at any time. The other one I was disappointed in. A bread vendor came in with two trays, bread on top, cakes on bottom. The manager stayed behind the counter. The bread man counted the loaves himself, and then lifted that tray. He then counted, "10, 20, 30, 2." You could only see the top layer of cakes. The manager then nodded and the vendor proceeded to stock. I followed him and there was truly thirty-two cakes, but what if there wasn't? How much would that manager have been short? If this sounds like you, boooooo!!!!!!! You must open every box and finger count it yourself! How many times have you been told that?

If I witness any check-ins not being finger-counted, I will personally write you up to your supervisor. This in itself will curb a lot of your losses. I know you will say, "But I know this vendor, he's super, he doesn't steal, etc." Bull!!! Look at your inventory shorts and look at how many nice vendors you've got. That says a lot.

Well, I've harped enough. But I will start carrying around employee incident reports, to write up violators.

Also, don't forget to do the cigarette build-ups.

Bobby Sue, Merchandising Manager

REACTION TO THE MEMO

No additional communication was received from either the new merchandise manager or the other corporate officers in the next thirty days. Several of the more secure and literate store managers were appalled with the tone of the memo. Many considered resigning, but none did. Later, one of the managers stated that the older managers considered her incompetent and soon to be fired, so they tended to ignore her. The younger managers were quite concerned that she could give them trouble, so they began to look for other employment.

Less than six months later a rumor surfaced that a Houston-based large oil company was interested in buying the whole company to add the twenty-three stores to its larger regional chain of nearly 500 service stations and convenience stores. A second rumor a month later hinted that almost all of the corporate management would be replaced, including the merchandise manager. In addition, only the better store managers would retain their jobs if the acquisition were to be completed. The rumor was reinforced when a number of inspections were made of the stores in the territory by people who were not CCS employees.

Exhibit 1

COUNTRY CONVENIENCE STORES, INC.: MEDIAN STORE-RURAL, SUMMARY OF FINANCIAL RESULTS (in thousands)

			12 MONTHS	
	MARCH 1985	*PERCENT*	*FISCAL YEAR 1985*	*PERCENT*
Sales				
Merchandise	$ 64.0	51.7%	$ 760.20	52.1%
Gasoline	59.7	48.2	699.46	47.9
Total	$123.7	100.0	$1,459.66	100.0
Less Cost of Sales				
Merchandise	$ 42.0	65.6	$ 493.15	64.9
Gasoline	54.5	91.3	633.31	90.5
Total	96.5		1,126.46	
Gross Profits				
Merchandise	$ 22.0	34.4	$ 264.55	35.1
Gasoline	5.2	8.7	66.15	9.5
Total	27.2		330.70	

Exhibit 1

COUNTRY CONVENIENCE STORES, INC.: MEDIAN STORE-RURAL, SUMMARY OF FINANCIAL RESULTS (in thousands) (*continued*)

| | | | 12 MONTHS | |
| | | | FISCAL YEAR | |
	MARCH 1985	PERCENT	1985	PERCENT
Less Operating Expenses				
Salaries and benefits	$ 12.5	10.1	$ 147.50	10.1
Other	11.5	9.3	135.90	9.3
Total	24.0	19.4	283.40	19.4
Net Before Corporate Expenses	$ 3.1	2.5	$ 53.30	3.7
Corporate Allocation	3.4	2.8	40.12	2.7
NET BEFORE TAXES	$ (0.3)	(0.3)	$ 13.18	1.0

Exhibit 2

CIRCLE K CORPORATION: SUMMARY OF FINANCIAL RESULTS

	1986	1985	1984
Revenue			
Grocery and other	64.8%	64.8%	62.9%
Product sales	35.2	35.2	37.1
Total	100.0	100.0	100.0
Less Cost of Sales	73.4	74.5	75.9
Gross Profit	26.6	25.5	24.1
Less Operating Expense	22.1	21.5	20.00
Operating Profit	4.5	4.0	4.1
Less Corporate Expenses	(1.1)	(.5)	(.2)
Net Before Taxes	3.4	3.5	3.9
Less Taxes	1.5	1.5	1.8
NET INCOME	1.9%	2.0%	2.1%
Revenues	$2.111B	$1.682B	$1.028 B
Operating profit	$93.69M	$66.69M	$42.054M
Number of stores	3372	2669	2185
Net income	$39.8M	$33.4M	$21.7M

Exhibit 3

OPERATING RATIOS OF PUBLICLY HELD CONVENIENCE STORE OPERATORS, 1984

	% OF GROWTH LAST 5 YEARS		NET PROFIT (AS PERCENT OF SALES)	RETURN ON ASSETS	RETURN ON EQUITY
	Sales	*Profit*			
Becker Milk Co.	10.3	8.1	2.18	8.7	14.9
Casey's General	24.7	114.3	0.95	4.9	23.2
Circle K Corp.	17.9	6.3	2.07	7.0	22.9
Conna Corp.	9.4	(69.4)	0.02	0.1	0.4
Dairy Mart	41.8	16.4	1.32	5.1	17.5
Daylight Ind.	(1.0)	(12.0)	0.03	0.0	(.1)
Lil Champ	27.4	16.9	2.77	8.5	16.2
Mini Mart Corp.	8.4	17.8	2.11	7.2	13.2
Munford, Inc.	9.0	34.7	1.91	6.3	15.9
National Convenience	17.2	23.0	2.25	5.3	20.1
Shop & Go, Inc.	22.9	18.9	3.35	12.4	21.2
Silcorp, Ltd.	8.5	(16.3)	0.10	0.4	1.3
Southland Corp.	22.7	12.8	1.55	4.9	13.8
Sunshine Jr.	9.0	(6.7)	1.05	6.2	10.4
Median	17.2	16.4	1.91	6.2	15.9

Exhibit 4

TOP TWENTY CONVENIENCE STORE CHAINS BY NUMBER OF STORES[a]

COMPANY	HEADQUARTERS	NUMBER OF STORES 1983	NUMBER OF STORES 1984	% CHANGE 1983–1984
The Southland Corp.	Dallas, TX	7,299	7,473	+ 2.4%
The Circle K Corp.	Phoenix, AZ	2,167	2,657	+22.6[e]
Cumberland Farms Dairy, Inc.	Canton, MA	1,171	1,175	+ 0.3
Convenient Food Mart. Inc.	Rosemont, IL	1,086	1,134	+ 4.4
National Convenience Stores, Inc.[b]	Houston, TX	1,012	1,101	+ 8.8
Silcorp Ltd.[c]	Scarborough, OT	906	926	+ 2.2
Majik Markets, Div. Munford, Inc.	Atlanta, GA	916	835	− 8.8
AM/PM Mini-Markets, (Division of Arco)	Los Angeles, CA	765	790	+ 3.3
The Lawson Co. (Division of Sara Lee)	Cuyahoga Falls, OH	685	700	+ 2.2
Kampgrounds of America	Billings, MT	695	699	+ 0.6
Becker Milk Co., Ltd.	Scarborough, OT	647	675	+ 4.3
Crown Central Petroleum Corp.[d]	Baltimore, MD	591	612	+ 3.6

Exhibit 4

TOP TWENTY CONVENIENCE STORE CHAINS BY NUMBER OF STORES[a] (*continued*)

		NUMBER OF STORES		% CHANGE
COMPANY	HEADQUARTERS	1983	1984	1983–1984
Sun Co.[e]	Radnor, PA	NA	575	NA
The Pantry, Inc.	Sanford, NC	476	467	− 1.9
Diamond Shamrock	San Antonio, TX	450	441	− 2.0
Shop & Go, Inc.[g]	Mango, FL	431	441	+ 2.3
Dillon Companies, Div. Kroger	Hutchinson, KS	349	440	+26.0
Charter Marketing	Jacksonville, FL	260	434	+66.9
Casey's General Stores, Inc.	Des Moines, IA	406	400	− 1.5
Jr. Food Marts	Jackson, MS	362	372	+ 2.8

a. As of December 31, 1984.
b. Convenient Food Mart's largest regional franchisee is Conna Corp., whose Convenient Industries of America division operates 391 stores.
c. Silcorp Ltd., operates 759 stores in Canada through the Mac's Convenience Stores Division and 163 stores in the U.S. through the Hop-In and FarrView divisions.
d. Crown's wholly owned subsidiary, FZ Corp., operates 547 Fast Fare and Zippy Mart stores. The petroleum company has 65 Express Marts at Crown stations.
e. Sun's convenience store outlets comprise King Kwiks, company-operated Stop-N-Go stores, and Stop-N-Go stores operated by regional franchises.
f. Does not include 449 stores acquired in the July 1985 purchase of Shop & Go, Inc. by Circle K.
g. Purchased by Circle K in July 1985.

OLD TOWN CANOE

DIANE GARSOMBKE
University of Maine

THOMAS W. GARSOMBKE
University of Maine at Presque Isle

INTRODUCTION

Pride in craftsmanship is the foundation on which Old Town Canoe was built. Pride is also what may be used to describe the current mood, as the company has almost tripled its market share and has become one of the largest producers of canoes in the world in just four years time. With this growth in sales has come an increase in profitability, as the company has reversed the trend of successive losses for many years with a record profit for fiscal year 1986.

HISTORY

Old Town Canoe traces its roots back to a small building behind Gray's Hardware Store, in the early 1890s. The store owner, George Gray, simply wanted a canoe for his own use, so he asked one of his employees to build one. Someone noticed the canoe and wanted to buy it, so he started another and it too was sold. That was the start of the Indian Old Town Company (later changed to Old Town Canoe Company). It rapidly outgrew the small building behind Gray's Hardware Store as well as the second and third floors of the hardware store.

The company then moved into the former shoe factory at 58 Middle Street in Old Town, which pres-ently houses the office and factory outlet store. In 1902, the company was incorporated under its present name and in 1905, the Old Town name, which is affixed to all canoes manufactured by the company, was registered. In 1903, the management of the company was turned over to George Gray's son Sam so that George could pursue other ventures. With imaginative advertising focusing on the area's Indian heritage and emphasis on quality, detail, and competitive prices, sales grew rapidly, and the factory expanded. The canoes produced by the company were constructed using modern materials and technology, namely a canvas-covered plant design. In an effort to ensure that their canoes were of the highest quality material, the company purchased large tracts of land, which would provide a ready supply of top quality wood.

With this supply, the company did not limit itself to the manufacture of canoes. It also produced shingles and railroad ties and constructed logger's bateaux and lapstrake boats. Around the turn of the century, there were twenty other canoe manufacturers in the Bangor area. Many of them closed their doors in the years to follow, but Old Town Canoe maintained its strong position in the market.

The first major threat to the company came during the post–World War II era. The aluminum stamping facilities of Grumman Aircraft Company, which were left idle at the end of the war, were retooled to manufacture aluminum boats and canoes. Despite the disadvantages of noise and absorption of temperature extremes, the low material and labor costs involved in producing the virtually indestructible craft brought them the majority of the market share. As a result, annual sales for Old Town Canoe were as low as 200 units in the early 1960s.

This case, written specifically for this text, is printed by permission. This case was developed with the assistance of Tim Reynolds, MBA 1988, Less Shaw, MBA 1988, and Ann Winterhalder, MBA 1988, at the University of Maine.

A second innovation in the industry, the use of fiberglass in boat building, was adopted by the company in the mid-1960s. The company, however, was one of the late entrants into the fiberglass canoe market, as it was slow to drop its dependence on the narrow product line of wood and canvas canoes. When it did change, it also added a variety of kayaks and power boats constructed of fiberglass.

In the early 1970s, the company took its first step toward regaining the position of one of industry leaders. Uniroyal of Indiana was using a material called Royalex, which was molded into canoe hulls and sold to a few manufacturers. The hull was rugged and the foam layer in the material provided extra buoyancy. It was exactly what was needed for whitewater canoeing. In 1972, Old Town Canoe completed design on an oven to mold their own canoes with Royalex sheets. The result was the popular 17-foot Tripper canoe. It was several years before other manufacturers started to catch up to this breakthrough.

In 1974, the company, under the management of the founders' grandson, Deane Gray, was sold to Johnson Wax Company of Racine, Wisconsin. The purchase of Old Town Canoe complimented Johnson's line of camping and fishing manufacturers. The sale of the company provided the catalyst to continue the adoption of new methods and materials into the production of canoes.

In 1984, Old Town Canoe made another organizational change, the acquisition of the oldest manufacturer of canoes in the United States, White Canoe Company, located next door to the plant. The acquisition greatly increased production of the fiberglass and opened additional distribution channels for the company. The company's most current innovation has set yet another industry standard. The development of this process took several years, but the Discovery canoe, constructed with three layers of different polyethylenes, along with the Royalex line catapulted Old Town Canoe to the top of the industry.

JOHN BLASS, GENERAL MANAGER

Blass has always been interested in boats. He built three of them before he owned an automobile. In 1968, he started to work for Browning Arms Boat Division, using metal technology in making aluminum boats as well as building fiberglass watercraft. Before accepting the position of general manager at Old Town Canoe, he was the general manager of Kayot Boat of Minnesota, a manufacturer of pontoon, or party, boats as they are sometimes called.

In 1982, when the current general manager of Old Town Canoe left to pursue other interests, Johnson Worldwide employed a national executive search firm to find a general manager to help turn around the company, which had been incurring losses for several years. Blass did not start with major changes, as some concern was to set the company in a break even position. He hired a new sales and marketing manager but made no other changes in staff. Possibly the most important move that he made was to take the talented Lou Gilman, the research and design manager, away from the daily chores of equipment maintenance to concentrate on the rotomolding process with which he had been experimenting. The idea was that if the process should work resources would be committed to the project to make a determination one way or another. The end result of Lou's work was a technological leap for the company that has not yet been matched by the competition. (See Exhibit 1 for a chart of top management.)

PRODUCT LINES

Old Town Canoe and White Canoe produce various types of canoes that meet the needs of almost all users. They produce a general recreation canoe for family use, which must be stable, easy to control, tough, and available in various sizes. The whitewater canoe is another type, one that is maneuverable and has volume added to the bow and stern to handle whitewater and waves. Yet another is the tripping-recreation canoe for campers and hunters, which must be lightweight for carriers, tough, and able to handle both rough and smooth water conditions with ease. A touring-cruising canoe for weekend racing must be fast, easy to paddle and have an excellent glide. Last of all is the classic wood canoe, which is the highest level of quality and craftsmanship.

PRODUCTION

Production at Old Town Canoe, which includes White Canoe, is limited by both seasonal demand and storage facilities. The maximum number of canoes that can be kept in stock is about 3,500. Only

Exhibit 1
OLD TOWN CANOE COMPANY ORGANIZATIONAL CHART

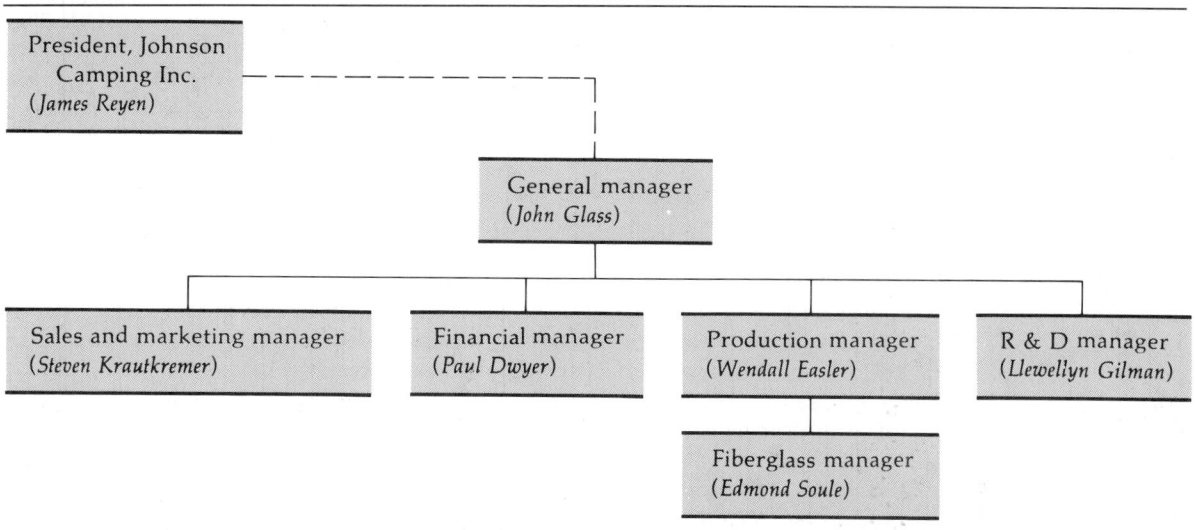

one model of canoes is stackable, so the space requirements for storage are huge. In the production stage the canoes must be stored on racks. When ready for delivery, they are wrapped in three-quarter-inch foam and plastic bags so they can be stacked one on top of the other to save space. Old Town also ships some of its canoes unassembled. In this case the dealer installs the seats and gunwales to save cost. However, the space required is still huge, making off-season production and storage until spring a major problem. The fall dating plan attempts to offset this problem by allowing dealers to take delivery of canoes during the off-season, with no payments due until the middle of the sales season. During the period of April to October, the plant works a mill shift (rotating) schedule, allowing twenty-four hour a day production, seven days a week, during the peak season. This schedule matches the production cycle with demand in order to reduce required inventories from the winter to spring and decrease lost orders.

MATERIALS

Old Town's canoes are manufactured from five materials, the most impressive and most labor intensive of which is wood. The wooden canoe is entirely handcrafted using wood molds with steel strips. The wooden planking is nailed to the wooden ribs and then the completed canoe is covered with either a transparent fiberglass covering or the traditional canvas covering. Old Town is the last large manufacturer that still holds this tradition. The average time to construct a single canoe is about fifty hours, and in 1986 Old Town produced approximately 75. The selling cost for these handmade canoes is in excess of $2,000, which just covers the costs. It is said that many of these canoes never touch the water, but they are used as display models. The wood canoe is more of a tradition than a true product line.

The second most labor-intensive product is the fiberglass canoe. This canoe is hand made by laying-up a fiberglass cloth inside a mold next to a Gelcoat layer. When a resin is applied, the cloth becomes very hard and forms the canoe. The interesting part of this procedure is that the mold is waxed and sprayed with Gelcoat; when the canoe is removed from the mold, the Gelcoat adheres to the fiberglass resin. The finished product has a mirror finish. When the fiberglass has set, the gunwales, seats and flotation are added by hand. A second product, Kevlar, is produced the same way, except the cloth is made of a very tough puncture-resistant fiber that makes the canoe very sturdy. This product is much more expensive and is available for those who want a lightweight premium canoe. Last year Old Town produced about 3,000 canoes in this product line, of which only 250 were made from Kevlar.

The fourth material used to produce canoes is Royalex. This is manufactured by Uniroyal and costs about $225 per sheet. Royalex is made up of many layers of laminated material. Heating the sheets in special ovens makes them very flexible. While still hot, they are placed on a special mold, which uses a vacuum to draw the canoe into the proper shape. When the canoe cools, the form is very hard and is complete except for seats and railings. The sheets may be reheated again if the canoe is not to specifications. Royalex will return to a flat sheet and can be reworked. There is a substantial amount of waste from this process, as much as 30 percent, which makes this product even more expensive.

Although there is no secondary market for this waste, for a period of time, the city of Old Town was grinding it up and using it in their sewage treatment plant to help in the breakdown of the raw sewage. They now have an ample supply, so the waste is now ground up on site to save storage space. The unique aspect about this product is that a Royalex canoe can be completed in about one hour. Last year Old Town produced about 6,000 canoes in this product line.

A material that gives Old Town a competitive edge in the industry is called Crosslink ™, a composition of polyethylene layers with a foam core. It produces tremendous stiffness, thereby eliminating the need for any additional framework. The foam core also produces additional buoyancy. Crosslink ™ is a very inexpensive material that allows a very well built and sturdy canoe at an affordable cost. This process uses rotomolding machines. They are called this because the canoe mold has the material added and is then placed in a huge oven on armlike attachments. While the product is heated, it is rotated and rocked to produce the finished product. This same procedure is used to produce rotomolded seats and decks for Old Town Canoes. Old Town currently has two rotomolding machines for its canoe production. The first was built by Lou Gilman from a variety of parts. The investment required to purchase a rotomolding machine can be as high as $300,000 to $400,000. One of the factors in the variability of cost is the size of the machine needed to produce your product.

Commercially these machines are being used in the production of wharfs, floats, kayaks, and large underground storage tanks for petroleum products. These machines are not what has given Old Town its edge. It is the ingredient, which looks like sand, the cooking and cooling times, and the rocking and rolling motion that keeps the competition from entry. The other uses of the rotomolding machines do not produce the foam center core, which is the extra item that makes the canoes produced by Old Town the top of the line. Other companies are working on development of this material, but so far they have not been able to create the ideal mixture. The cost of material for this canoe hull is about $70, which makes it a low-cost, high-profit product. Last year Old Town produced about 8,000 Crosslink canoes.

MARKETING

According to William Riviere, author of *The Open Canoe* (1985), the canoe industry had the following diversity of manufacturers by type of material used:

- 19 manufacturers of Royalex canoes
- 20 manufacturers of cedar strip canoes
- 5 manufacturers of fiberglass/Kevlar canoes
- 11 manufacturers of aluminum canoes
- 21 manufacturers of lapstrake canoes (a process for applying strips of wood)
- 33 manufacturers of wood and canvas canoes only
- 5 manufacturers of wood and fiberglass canoes only
- 13 manufacturers of proprietary lay-up canoes (confidential combinations of materials)
- 3 manufacturers of polyethylene canoes

(A manufacturer may have several product lines and be included in more than one category.)

Many manufacturers offer a variety of these products, using the material above in different innovative and patented processes. Old Town Canoe, however, remains the largest producer of canoes by far. They offer a product line that has several models for tripping-recreation, whitewater, general recreation, and touring-cruising. Of course Old Town sells 60 percent of the Royalex canoes being made in the world today. Over 90 percent of the canoes they produce today are sold to the family market. Only 5 or 6 percent of their canoe sales are to whitewater enthusiasts. (See Exhibits 2, 3, and 4.)

Old Town Canoe currently sells to markets in the United States, Canada, Switzerland, Japan, and Germany. There is an Old Town Canoe Club in Japan. Canoes are a seasonal business by nature, running from the first whitewater run in the spring to the last duck hunt in the fall. What kind of a customer is a canoeist? To quote William Stearn, an avid canoeist and author of *The Canoeist's Catalog:* "Canoeists are noted for their personal biases [about

Exhibit 2
CANOE INDUSTRY STATISTICS

| | *CANOE INDUSTRY MARKET SHARE BY TYPE* | | | | |
	1987	*1986*	*1985*	*1984*	*1983*
Royalex	10,000	9,000	7,000	8,000	9,000
Aluminum	10,000	14,000	16,000	24,000	24,000
Fiberglass	13,000	13,000	12,000	11,000	11,000
Polyethylene	27,000	22,000	18,000	27,000	28,000
TOTAL	60,000	58,000	53,000	70,000	72,000

| | *OLD TOWN CANOE PERCENT MARKET SHARE BY TYPE* | | | | |
	1987	*1986*	*1985*	*1984*	*1983*
Royalex	60%	56%	63%	57%	60%
Aluminum	—	—	—	—	—
Fiberglass	22	23	25	13	9
Polyethylene	26	17	10	3	—
Total	27%	20%	17%	10%	10%

Exhibit 3
OLD TOWN CANOE MARKET SHARE, 1987

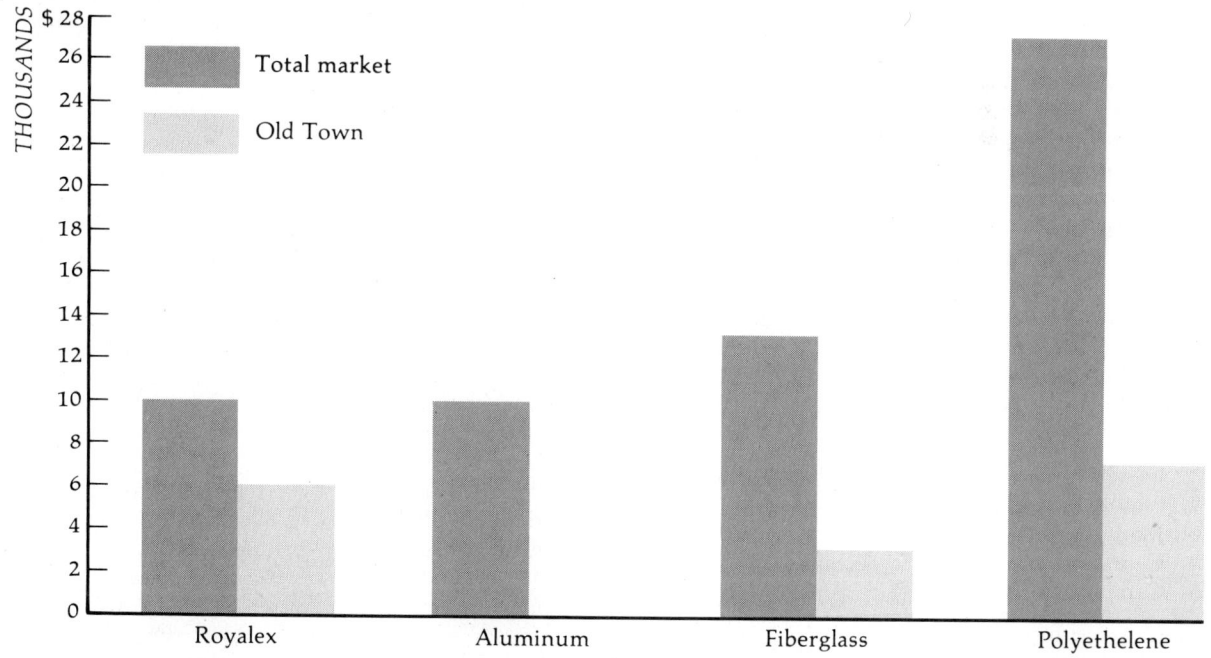

Exhibit 4
TOTAL CANOE MARKET BY TYPE PRODUCT, 1987

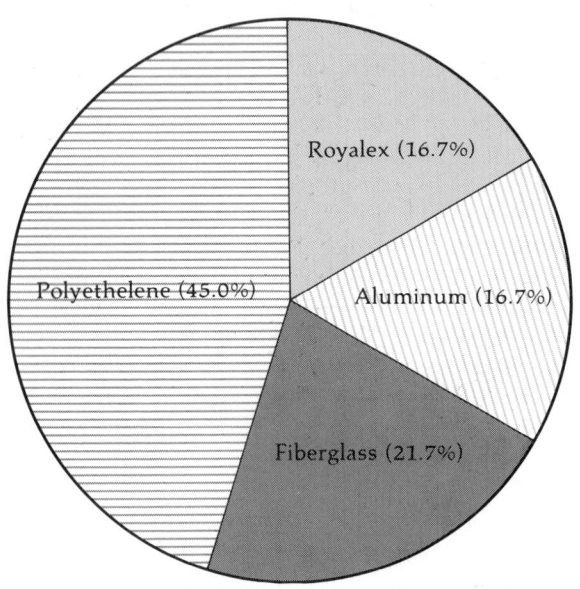

Polyethelene (45.0%)

Royalex (16.7%)

Aluminum (16.7%)

Fiberglass (21.7%)

brand of canoe]. Even if two canoeists are married to each other, they may have different biases and opinions."

Realizing that a canoe that is rented today may garner a loyal brand buyer tomorrow, Old Town Canoe has always favored rental canoes and sells to many camps and institutions. Steve Krautkremer, sales and marketing manager, describes their average customer as a 39-year-old male professional with a college degree, an upper-level income, and a family.

Old Town Canoe delivers canoes to dealers in the United States and Canada using its own fleet of four tractor-trailers. Twenty independent commissioned sales agents also sell Old Town Canoes nationwide.

Dealers fall into five classes:

1. General sporting goods stores (40 percent)
2. Other (28 percent)
3. Marine shops (20 percent)
4. Canoe specialty shops (10 percent)
5. Camps and institutions (2 percent)

These percentages are as of 1984; Old Town Canoe has since added well over 100 dealers. Old Town is

the only canoe company in the industry that offers a 0–8 percent discount to dealers as of August 1st, with payments not due until June 1st of the following year.

Another recent development at Old Town Canoe is the 800-number catalog line. By calling the toll-free number offered in the advertisement, a customer can receive the most recent catalog, which is sent first class and free of charge. To many people, the Old Town name means canoe.

In 1987 Old Town Canoe will attempt to reach 7 million catalog shoppers through another Maine institution, L.L. Bean. L.L. Bean, traditionally selling Mad River canoes under its own label, will come out with a special edition canoe and kayak catalog, featuring canoes from Old Town, Lincoln, Mad River and L.L. Bean. This catalog, expected to reach about 40,000 people, will be billed as "a special offering of the finest boats, accessories, and gear from America's premier manufacturers." Old Town not only was asked to leave their label on the canoe, but also received top billing from L.L. Bean in the summer 1987 Sporting Specialties Catalog (see Exhibit 5).

Innovation has been the key behind Old Town's successes, first with the Oltonar/Royalex tripper canoe, and second with the Crosslink ™ polyethylene Discovery canoe. The man behind the research and development is Lou Gilman, a self-taught engineer who has done things with plastic that textbook engineers say cannot be done. The Discovery canoe revolutionized the market with an inexpensive, durable canoe that has become Old Town's ticket to the family fun market. With this in mind, the marketing resources of the parent company, Johnson Worldwide, were tapped to set up an advertising campaign. The market study conducted revealed that the customer's main concern was durability. The resulting point-of-purchase display depicted a canoe pressed flat between a truck and a tree, followed by a frame showing a canoe that bounced back to its original shape without damage. The accompanying campaign slogan was: "This isn't a problem, it's a Discovery."

Positioned to take over the inexpensive canoe market, the Discovery is advertised as quiet, as it does not clang when the paddle hits it, and slippery, as it glides over rocks. Try to glide over a rock in an aluminum canoe, or attempt to get a Coleman polyethylene canoe back into shape after you have wrapped it around a rock, and you will begin to understand why the Discovery is twice the canoe for approximately the same price.

In a conversation with Blass, the subject of cannibalism arose. What will the Discovery do to Royalex sales? Since Royalex is the company's major line of canoes, will the introduction of a sturdy, lower-priced polyethylene canoe greatly alter the product mix? Old Town Canoe hopes that the lower priced line will attract more dealers, therefore expanding the market for their other product lines.

CORPORATE INVOLVEMENT

The operations of the company are left entirely to the general manager. Corporate headquarters provides several services to the company if they are requested, including legal services, employee benefits, market research, loans and financing, and risk management. Income taxes are prepared at the corporate level.

FINANCE AND ACCOUNTING

Paul Dwyer's background stems from a heavy concentration of cost accounting in a manufacturing environment, which assists him greatly in his current position as financial manager. Dwyer is responsible for the preparation of monthly financial statements, which at the plant level is done by product line. The company must also report, in a standard format, the results to Johnson Worldwide. These statements include a balance sheet, profit and loss statement, cash flow, and a gross profit analysis (see Exhibits 6 and 7 for examples). In addition to the monthly reporting requirements, Dwyer is responsible for preparing the budgets from the strategic plan as well as a forecast of the budget for fall and spring seasons.

The company is able to secure financing for its operations and capital expenditures from the corporation, with the only limit being that approval is required from corporate headquarters for expenditures exceeding $25,000.

Exhibit 5
PAGE FROM L.L. BEAN CATALOG FEATURING OLD TOWN CANOES

Old Town Discovery Canoes

Tough, durable, maintenance-free canoe popular with many guides and outfitters. A superior value. Made of Cross Link 3™, a stiff, durable roto-molded 3-layer polyethylene that withstands abuse without the need for heavy metal framework. Model 158 features flat bottom for stability and easy handling. Model 169 has shallow arch bottom for enhanced speed and better stability in fast water. High bow design cuts through water for efficient paddling. Built-in carry yoke. A good choice for recreational whitewater, general touring and all around use. Made in Old Town, Maine.

Two styles: Maintenance-free, molded, contoured seats with built-in flotation or Traditional cane seats. Two colors: Green. Red. Please specify.

6300LH 158 Discovery Canoe, with Molded Seats, $450.00.
6200LH 158 Discovery Canoe, with Cane Seats, $498.00.
   Length 15'8". 13½" depth at center. 36" width at waterline. Capacity 980 lbs. 22" bow height. Wt. 72 lbs.
B563LH 169 Discovery Canoe, with Molded Seats, $498.00.
B562LH 169 Discovery Canoe, with Cane Seats, $548.00.
   Length 16'9". 14½" depth at center. 35" width at waterline. Capacity 1,080 lbs. 23" bow height. Wt. 80 lbs. See special shipping information.

Reprinted by permission of L. L. Bean.

Exhibit 6
OLD TOWN CANOE COMPANY: BALANCE SHEET, JUNE 1986 (in thousands)

ASSETS			LIABILITIES AND NET WORTH		
Current Assets		$ 86	Current Liabilities		
Cash			Accounts payable—Trade		$ 185
Accounts receivable	$ 764		Administrative fees payable		25
Less allowance for bad debts	(70)		Accrued profit sharing		140
Net accounts receivable		694	Accrued payroll and benefits		60
Note receivable, SCJ/JWA		1,400	Income taxes		223
Inventory		816	Other liabilities		60
Deferred and prepaids		130	Total Current Liabilities		$ 693
Total Current Assets		$3,126			
			Deferred Taxes		46
Other Assets			Total Liabilities		739
Fixed assets	$1,470				
Less Accumulated depreciation	(611)		Net Worth		
Net fixed assets		$ 859	Capital in excess of par		$3,780
Other intangibles		96	Retained earnings		(438)
Total Other Assets		955	Total Net Worth		$3,342
			TOTAL LIABILITIES AND NET		
TOTAL ASSETS		$4,081	WORTH		$4,081

Note: Fiscal year-end changed to September in 1986 to coincide with Johnson Worldwide

PERSONNEL

The company's employment philosophy is to maintain a constant workforce with no layoffs, if at all possible. Old Town Canoe presently employs sixty-five people, of whom forty-nine are in production. The company prides itself on paying competitive wages for the area and periodically does surveys to ensure this. The pay structure is based on skill levels and seniority using hourly or salaried rates. The company also has a full benefits package similar to that provided by the parent Johnson Worldwide. They have a reward system that is based on profitability and longevity. Ten years ago it was estimated that it took seventy-five to one hundred production workers to produce at one third of the present level. The reduction in man-hours was brought about by the technology in producing ABS and polyethylene canoes. The work environment is extremely informal and unstressed, which adds to and helps maintain the quality of the canoes produced. The family atmosphere evident in the company is taken to the extreme in the fiberglass room, as many of the workers are related to each other.

STRATEGIC PLANNING PROCESS

Three months following the September fiscal year end, which corresponds with all Johnson companies, the formal planning process begins. The plan being developed is for a three-year period, with the first year of the plan used as the operating budget.

The process starts with the general manager doing a situation review. Using industry data available from a monthly boating industry survey reporting major manufacturers' production and sales, along with his own observations of the industry, Blass prepares a statement of where the canoe industry is and what future trends are beginning to develop. This industry analysis includes what sales and production capacities the competitors might be expecting as well as what technologies may be implemented or matched by each company in the industry. This review becomes the basis for the next step in the planning process. Also included in this step is the development of a mission statement covering specific goals for the company for the next few years.

The second step is to establish objectives for the company for the plan years. The objective that re-

Exhibit 7

OLD TOWN CANOE COMPANY: PROFIT AND LOSS STATEMENTS (in thousands)

	1986	1985	1984	1983	1982
Sales	$4,308	$3,350	$2,865	$2,586	$2,513
Less Cost of Goods Sold	(2,542)	(2,104)	(1,805)	(1,774)	(1,734)
Gross Profit	$1,766	$1,246	$1,060	$ 812	$ 779
Less Expenses					
Advertising	$ 63	$ 110	$ 83	$ 82	$ 120
Promotions	74	85	89	7	50
Deals	120	0	0	0	0
Sales freight	11	60	83	85	119
Other distribution	124	74	72	75	0
Administrative fees	86	67	57	52	50
Total Direct Expenses	$ 478	$ 396	$ 384	$ 301	$ 339
Less Functional Expenses					
Sales force	$ 180	$ 191	$ 174	$ 118	$ 145
Commissions	205	164	151	146	131
Research and development	86	101	86	83	110
Financial	95	94	88	115	110
Provision for bad debts	12	18	39	25	37
Administrative management	145	151	140	285	260
Total Functional Expenses	$ 723	$ 719	$ 678	$ 772	$ 793
Total Operating Expenses	$1,201	$1,115	$1,062	$1,073	$1,132
OPERATING PROFIT (LOSS)	$ 565	$ 131	($2)	($ 261)	($ 353)

Note: Fiscal year-end changed to September in 1986 to coincide with Johnson Worldwide

ceives the most attention is market share. These are done by product type. Following this, a sales forecast is developed by product line. Also included in the objectives statements are strategic issues for the future, as well as a tentative plan for diversification in the event of planned or unforeseen drops in any of the company's product lines. The last step is the development of a strategy and management action plan. This is done by product line for the Old Town Canoe and White Canoe companies separately.

The initial portion of the planning process takes about two months. At this time, the sales forecasts and action plans developed are converted into numbers. The financial manager prepares operating profit and loss schedules for each product line for the three year period. All direct costs, including advertising and promotion are included in the operating statement as well as overhead allocated on a di-

rect labor basis. In addition to the profit and loss statements, a balance sheet for the period ending September is prepared for the three years as well as several other schedules (see Exhibit 8). The company's performance is gauged not only by meeting profit objectives but by cash flow, ROA, and other objectives outlined in these schedules.

The schedules prepared are compared with the objectives established by the general manager. Changes are made to the plan in the event that the financial budget does not coincide with expectations. This process is completed by March 15. Within the following two weeks, members of the corporate planning staff arrive in Old Town to discuss and review the plan. The fine tuning is done at these meetings and a final plan is decided upon at this time.

One consideration in the planning process is to make sure that a line does not cannibalize the other

Exhibit 8
**SCHEDULES PREPARED FOR THE
STRATEGIC PLANNING PROCESS**

Consolidated profit and loss statement
Operating profit and loss statement by product
  line
Balance sheet
Inventory at standard cost
Return on assets
Cash flow
Capital expenditures
Accounts receivable: days outstanding
Personnel and benefits

lines. There have been no problems up to this point, as Old Town Canoe has been able to sell all of the Discovery canoes it can produce and has had to cut-off orders due to production capacity constraints. The objective is to continue to sell a balanced line of canoes and not necessarily yield the largest profit that can be made in the short term.

FUTURE OUTLOOK

The $20 million canoe industry has remained relatively stable over the past several years, with little indication of substantial growth or decline in the coming years. Within this industry that has little attraction for new major entrants, Old Town Canoe has found growth by increasing market share. But there is a limit to the growth that can be obtained in this manner and the danger of competitors eroding this newly gained market share is always there. Future growth may depend on new businesses capitalizing on the Old Town name and reputation.

PERLIS TRUCKSTOP

DAVID H. MAISTER
Harvard University

In August 1974, Perlis Truckstop, located on Interstate 75, 150 miles south of Atlanta in Cordele, Georgia, had been in operation for three years, providing fuel, food, and other services to truck drivers. The previous year had been a particularly successful one, with pretax profits in excess of $600,000 from revenues of over $5 million. Lamar Perlis was considering a number of growth alternatives for his company, including opening another truckstop and expanding the amenities available at the Cordele truckstop.

THE TRUCKSTOP INDUSTRY

According to the National Association of Truck Stop Operators (NATSO), there were approximately 4,000 truckstops in the United States in 1974, of which some 1,200 were full-facility truckstops, the remainder being fuel stops. The distinction between the two forms of truckstop was one of degree, the former category offering a wider range of services to the long-distance truck driver (see Exhibit 1). However, most truckstops offered the basic twenty-four-hour services of diesel fuel, tire repair, restaurant facilities, and sleeping facilities.

Copyright © 1974 by the President and Fellows of Harvard College
Harvard Business School case 675-077
This case was prepared by David H. Maister under the direction of D. Daryl Wyckoff and W. Earl Sasser, Jr., as the basis for class discussion rather than to illustrate either effective or ineffective handling of an administrative situation. Reprinted by permission of the Harvard Business School.

The industry had grown rapidly since the late 1950s, when there were approximately 800 truckstops, as a result of the construction of the U.S. interstate highway system. As the superhighways were completed, there was a rapid increase in the volume of intercity freight moved by truck and concomitant increase in those industries serving the motor carrier. In addition, the average size of trucks grew, as did the average length of the haul. These developments created a demand for new truckstops offering an increased range of services. By the late 1960s, the industry was generating over $1 billion in annual revenues, and according to a 1971 *Fleet Owner* article, a new facility was opening every 6.5 days. Since many motor carrier industry observers projected a continued rapid rise in truck traffic through the 1970s (a rise of up to 50 percent in tonnage and 25 percent in number of trucks by 1980), the future outlook for the truckstop industry was considered bright.

Although half of the truckstop operators owned their own facility, many truckstops were owned or franchised by major oil companies. Union Oil Company was the industry leader with a chain of over 600 truckstops, approximately 150 of which were on the interstate system. Under the brand name of Union 76, Union Oil had entered the truckstop industry in 1965, with its acquisition of the Pure Oil Company, which had previously developed a chain of truckstops. Union 76, in the early 1970s, was opening full-facility truckstops at the rate of 15 per year. A major source of Union 76's strength in the truckstop industry was its controlled credit card system, which recorded expenses by vehicle and combined them into a single monthly billing to fleet owners.

Exhibit 1

QUALIFICATIONS FOR MEMBERSHIP OF NATIONAL ASSOCIATION OF TRUCK STOP OPERATORS (NATSO)

Minimum Facilities

24-hour service	Overall cleanliness
Diesel fuel	Restaurant[a]
Adequate parking facilities	Sleeping facilities[a]
Tire repair facilities	Showers[a]

Optional Facilities[b]

Ticket printer pumps[c]	Garage or mechanic[c]
Truck washing	Wrecker service[c]
Scales[c]	Western Union
Propane gas[c]	Teletype[c]
Laundry service[c]	Drivers' lounge[c]
Steam cleaning	Brokerage service
Truck lubrication[c]	Warehouse facilities
Wet ice	Tire bank[c]
Dry ice	Merchandise for sale (safety equipment,
Blast chilling	accessories, clothing, etc.)[c]
Barber/beauty salons[c]	

a. Membership requirements allow these facilities to be offered at an adjoining building to the truckstop.
b. Membership requirements included at least five of the services.
c. Facilities offered by Perlis Truckstop.

The second largest oil company participating in the truckstop industry was the Skelly Oil Company, with over 200 truckstops. Like those of most other oil companies, Skelly truckstops were operated in three basic ways: (1) Skelly owned and operated the truckstop; (2) Skelly owned the outlet and leased it to the operator; or (3) Skelly was the supplier and offered financial assistance to the operator to build a stop. In the South, Union 76 supplied 50 percent of the diesel fuel to truckstops, but Skelly, at 6 percent, came in the third behind Texaco, who supplied 13 percent. In a national survey conducted by NATSO, it was revealed that 60 percent of the truckstops were bound by contract to a single oil company for their supplies of gasoline and diesel fuel.

While the oil companies were the main owners and sponsors of truckstop chains, the early 1970s saw other organizations entering the industry. Ryder Truck Rentals, based in Miami, had launched an extensive truckstop acquisition program, commencing with the purchase in 1972 of Truckstops of America, a chain of twenty truckstops. Industry observers believed that Ryder was aiming at a network of one hundred truckstops, with the company's own trucks providing the core business. Other recent entrants into the truckstop business included BTR Corporation (a North Carolina company owned by Holiday Inn) and the Greyhound Corporation, each of which operated a number of Union 76 franchises.

With the increased range of services offered, the average cost of a full-facility truckstop had increased from approximately $800,000 in 1968 to over $2 million by 1972. Average yearly gross revenues had jumped in the same period from $700,000 to $2 million. At the same time, average yearly gallonage had almost doubled from 2.4 million to 4.2 million.

In the NATSO survey of truckstops, the following averages were discovered. Fuel accounted for 62 percent of the revenues of the typical truckstop, which had 9.5 pumps. Owner-operators accounted for 30 percent of customers, with the remainder being fleets. Of the 1 million truck tractors employed in the United States in 1970, approximately 700,000 were operated by 65,000 fleet owners; the remainder were operated by individual owner-operators. Fifty-three percent of truckstops operated printer pumps, which automatically printed sales tickets for fuel sales. These pumps were considered to be an important sales tool, since they provided a guarantee to fleet owners of the accuracy and honesty of transactions between the truck driver and the truckstop operator.

The average truckstop restaurant seated 116 people, 83 percent with waitress service. Sixty-five percent of truckstops operated their own restaurant; the remainder licensed others to do so. Average revenues per restaurant were over $400,000 with a pretax profit as a percentage of sales of 10.4 percent.

Sleeping facilities, with an average of 14.6 rooms, provided 3.3 percent of revenues, with average charges being $7.25 a night for a room with a bath. Garage facilities yielded an average of 11 percent of revenues, and sale of merchandise in the truckstop provided 8.3 percent of revenues. Typical inventory turn for the stores was five. The typical operator had been in business for 9.5 years, although this average fell to less than 6 years in the South.

PERLIS TRUCKSTOP

Lamar Perlis, who was fifty years old in September 1974, had been raised in Cordele, Georgia (population 13,000), and trained as an industrial engineer at Georgia Tech. In 1949, after military service and college, he had entered his father's retail clothing store in Cordele, I. Perlis & Sons. In 1954, Lamar and his two brothers, Louis and Marvin, bought out shares of I. Perlis & Sons, so that the father and each of the brothers owned one-fourth of the company. In 1959 the father and brothers formed Perlis Realty, owned equally between them, to handle the realty transactions involved in opening new stores, as well as other independent realty deals. In 1962, Lamar Perlis, acting for Perlis Realty, built a shopping center, leasing sites to other retail stores. In 1965, another shopping center was established in Tifton, Georgia, 45 miles from Cordele, which was leased and built by Lamar Perlis, and later supervised by Marvin Perlis.

In 1964, Perlis Realty purchased 175 acres of land adjoining I-75 for $125,000. At the time, the brothers did not have a definite purpose for the land. However the location of the site on the highway suggested some facility related to either traveling public or the motor carrier industry. Dissuaded from single-purpose facilities such as a motel, restaurant,

or service station by the seasonality of those businesses, Lamar Perlis began to investigate the potential of the site as a truckstop:

> In late 1964 my wife, Jackie, and I passed the Union 76 truckstop in Wildwood, Florida, and we stopped to take a look. It was the first time I had seen a truckstop, and I was impressed by it, especially when I learned that one could serve both the tourist and truck trade, since these two businesses have complementary seasonality. The idea germinated in my mind that our site would be perfect for a truckstop since Interstate 75 was the only completed interstate highway going into Florida [see Exhibit 2]. Early in 1966 I approached the Gulf Oil Company, since I had grown up with their local distributor. Gulf sponsored a trip for him and me to visit several of their truckstops. I was disappointed with them because they were small operations and did not match with my vision of a truckstop. We continued our trip until we finally discovered a truckstop close to what I had in mind near Richmond, Virginia. It was a Texaco stop, so I contacted Texaco and began negotiations.

Perlis had proposed to develop the real estate and lease it to Texaco. However, Texaco had turned down this proposal and persuaded Perlis to operate the truckstop. The final contract arrangements involved the leasing of the site of 18.5 acres by Perlis & Sons to Texaco for a fifteen-year term. A new company was formed by the three Perlis brothers, called Perlis Truck Terminal, Inc., which leased back the site for fifteen years. The purpose of the lease and leaseback arrangement was to enable the brothers to use Texaco's lease as a basis for obtaining an $850,000 loan at 7.25 percent from the Continental Assurance Company. Perlis Truck Terminal, Inc., also entered into a fuel purchasing contract with Texaco. The contracts were all signed in March 1968. Perlis recalled his feelings at the time:

> However, even after all this, I was a little wary of proceeding. A truckstop was something very new for our family, because we were taking a big risk. We had left our father out of participation in the truckstop, because we didn't want to risk possible bankruptcy for him. Union 76 had just built a truckstop 27 miles north of our site, and I didn't know how to assess traffic potential. I thought the traffic count was very low rel-

Exhibit 2
MAP OF GEORGIA AND SOUTH CAROLINA

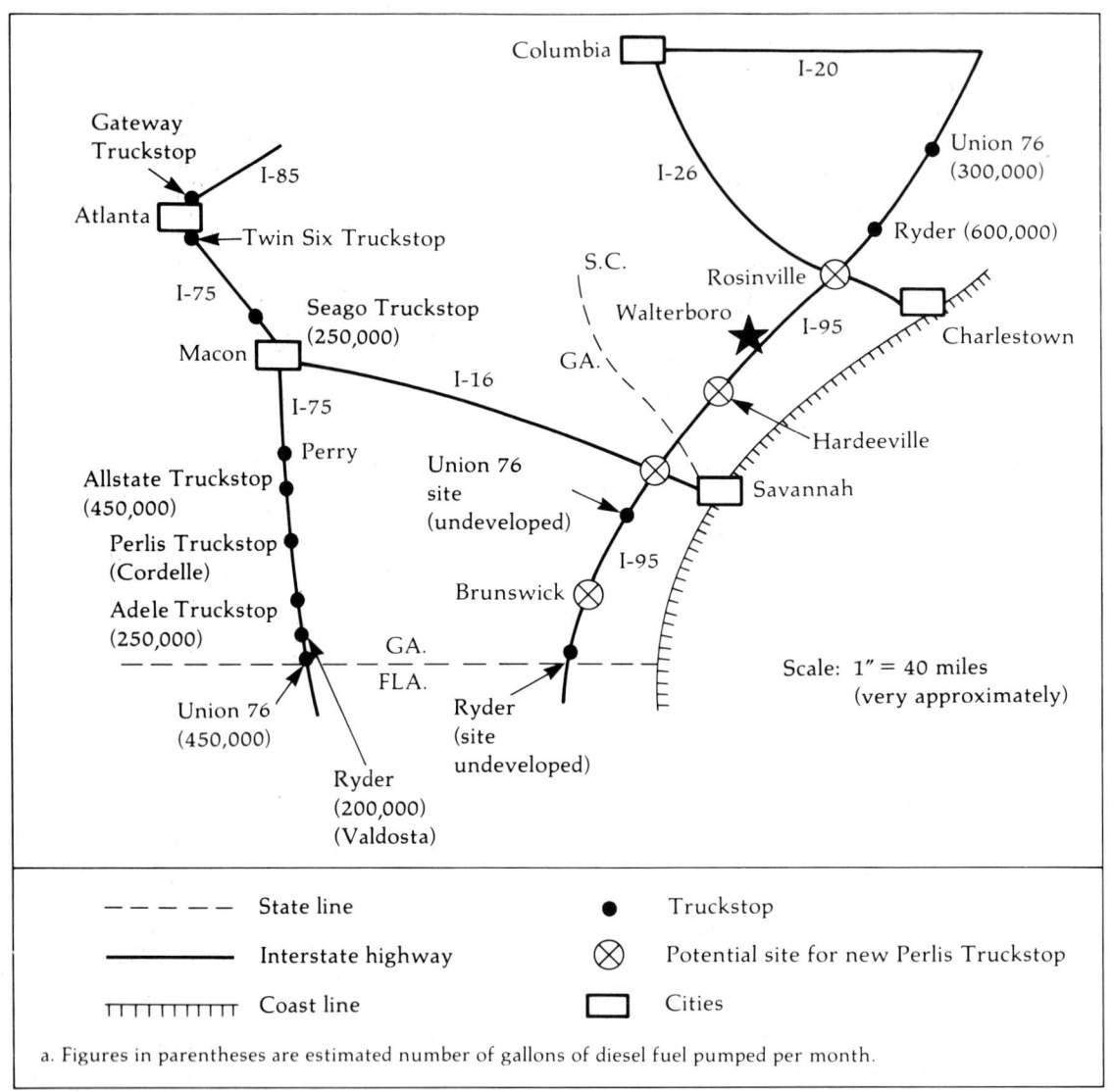

a. Figures in parentheses are estimated number of gallons of diesel fuel pumped per month.

ative to its potential [traffic counts for I-75 are given in Exhibit 3].

Because of his uncertainty about the current levels of the traffic count, and also because of a family cash constraint caused by the opening of a family-owned discount shopping center in Cordele, Perlis delayed commencing the construction of the truckstop by over a year. He was forced to renegotiate the loan arrangement with Continental Assurance, paying a penalty of $33,000 to keep the option open. However, during this period Perlis held discussions with the owner of the Richmond, Virginia, truckstop that had impressed him. He was encouraged

Exhibit 3

TRAFFIC COUNT ON I-75, 1970 AND 1973[a]

	Seasonal Factors	
January	.860	
February	.927	
March	1.141	
April	1.161	
May	.903	
June	1.196	
July	1.242	
August	1.215	
September	.814	
October	.816	
November	.895	
December	.837	
	1970	*1973*
Annual average daily traffic	16,182	22,966
% passenger cars	74.8%	73.0%
% light trucks (gasoline)	6.0%	7.4%
% heavy trucks (diesel)	19.1%	19.2%
% buses	0.1%	0.2%

a. Data are measurements taken by the State Highway Department of Georgia (Division of Highway Planning: Statistical 449–70), at station no. 107, on I-75 just S.W. of the town of Perry.

by the high sales of nonfuel items, such as store merchandise and meals, and so when family finances permitted construction of his truckstop, Perlis decided to go ahead. He entered negotiations with Texaco since he wished to have a building that could be put to another purpose if the truckstop venture should fail. The original construction contract was for $550,000 and another $250,000 was spent on site improvement (detailed asset costs are given in Exhibit 4). Perlis recalled the financial condition of his company at its beginning:

> We projected a loss in our first year and expected to break even in our second year. We were in a cash bind in the first year, because one of my brothers had developed a new shopping center during our planning status that was drawing heavily on the family's funds. We were very much undercapitalized, and the truckstop was expected to be $300,000 short in needed cash in the first year.
>
> We opened in June 1971 and pumped 88,000 gallons of diesel in our first month. Our restaurant had no ceiling or refrigeration, but we opened it anyway, serving soft drinks and donuts.
>
> We started with an employment of 50 people. Both my wife and I put in 20 hours a day in the first year. We had a very amateur organization. I had made earlier efforts to recruit people I knew for the managerial positions. I made it a rule not to recruit from my competitors, because I thought I would need to get along with them.
>
> I had a great deal of trouble finding people with experience, and we didn't have the funds to train a cadre of workers before we opened. Cordele is a small town, and the quality of workers was not high, so we had a lot of problems. Our turnover rate in workers and management has been extremely high. We hired whatever workers were available at the time, hoping to improve as we went along.

OPERATING HISTORY

Although the truckstop operated at a deficit every quarter until June 1972, break-even was reached at that time, and operations had become increasingly profitable (see Exhibit 5). The next operating loss carry-forward from the fiscal years ending September 30, 1972, totaled $94,598 and was used to reduce taxable income in the fiscal year ended September 30, 1973. A statement of income by department is given in Exhibit 6.

Discussing the success of his operation, Perlis commented:

> To do well in this business, you have to do a few simple tasks well. You have to provide fuel, food, and rest to the drivers, consistently and dependably. Other services include message services, check cashing, store merchandise, newspapers, etc. Some truckstops even provide chapels and banks, both of which I am seriously considering for this location.
>
> I am also thinking of additional amenities such as a swimming pool or running track,

Exhibit 4

PERLIS TRUCKSTOP: BALANCE SHEET DATA (in thousands)

	SEPT. 30, 1971	JUNE 30, 1974		SEPT. 30, 1971	JUNE 30, 1974
ASSETS			*LIABILITIES AND OWNER'S EQUITY*		
Current Assets			Current Liabilities		
Cash	$ (58)	$ 2	Accounts payable	$ 154	$ 181
Accounts receivable	23	204	Notes and mortgages	0	162
Inventory	64	345	Other current	19	98
Other current	4	115	Total Current Liabilities	$ 173	$ 441
Total Current Assets	$ 33	$ 666	Long-Term Debt		
Fixed Assets			Mortgage-Continental	$ 817	$ 714
Land	$ 259	$ 259	Assurance Co.[b]		
Building and improvements[e]	806	861[e]	Notes payable-USC[c]	16	9
Fuel service equipment	68	90	Mortgage—1st State		
Autos and trucks[e]	10	121	Bank[d]	239	136
Restaurant and equipment	111	120	Loan—Perlis Realty	93	0
Store equipment	9	13	Loan—I. Perlis & Son	101	98
Motel furniture	9	25	Loan—I. R. Perlis	73	50
Office furniture[e]	9	46	Note payable	0	86
Signs, lights, etc.[e]	306	325	Less current portion	(73)	(162)
Shop and parts department	12	30	Total Long-Term Debt	1,266	931
Total fixed assets	1,599	1,890	Equity		
Accounting depreciation	(51)	433	Capital stock	$ 150	$ 151
Net fixed assets	$1,548	$1,457	Paid-in capital	130	130
Other assets	43	37	Retained earnings	(9)	47
TOTAL ASSETS	$1,624	$2,160	Net income	(86)	555
			Total equity	185	789
			TOTAL LIABILITIES AND EQUITY	$1,624	$2,160

a. September 30, 1971 represented the end of the first quarter of operation.
b. Matures October 1985, guaranteed by stockholders, secured by land.
c. Matures January 1976, secured by phone system.
d. Matures May 1976, guaranteed by stockholders, secured by equipment.
e. The allocation of these assets by department was as follows:

	Buildings and Improvements	Autos and Trucks	Signs, Lights, etc.	Office Furniture
Fueling	19.94%	40%	63%	0
Parts	26.30%	20%	7%	0
Restaurant	15.58%	0	21%	0
Store	9.76%	0	7%	0
Motel	25.57%	0	2%	0
G & A	2.85%	40%	0	100%
	100%	100%	100%	100%

Exhibit 5
PERLIS TRUCKSTOP: QUARTERLY INCOME DATA (in thousands)

PERIOD ENDING	TOTAL SALES	GROSS PROFIT[a]	EXPENSES[b]	INCOME BEFORE TAXES	DEPRECIATION
December 31, 1971	$ 387	$146	$170	$ (24)	$35
March 31, 1972	465	177	187	(10)	36
June 30, 1972	543	208	206	2	36
September 30, 1972	512	240	228	12	35
December 31, 1972	535	195	189	6	36
March 31, 1973	718	262	207	54	28
June 30, 1973	1,017	354	238	116	32
September 30, 1973	1,063	397	307	91	32
December 31, 1973	1,264	423	280	142	33
March 31, 1974	1,727	549	343	207	36
June 30, 1974	1,920	573	367	206	35

a. Gross profit = Total sales − Cost of goods sold.
b. Total expenses shown here includes labor, depreciation, overhead, incidental supplies, and all other expenses.

Exhibit 6
PERLIS TRUCKSTOP: QUARTERLY INCOME DATA, BY DEPARTMENT (in thousands)[a]

	FUELING		PARTS AND SERVICE		RESTAURANT		STORE		MOTEL	
	Sales	Income[b]	Sales	Income[b]	Sales	Income[b]	Sales	Income[b]	Sales	Income[b]
December 31, 1971	$ 224	$ 23	$ 34	$(7.7)	$ 84	$ 1.8	$36	$17.0	$4.5	$(3.9)
March 31, 1972	268	38	60	6.6	95	(7.8)	43	7.0	5.0	(3.9)
June 30, 1972	282	32	67	7.8	107	(1.1)	53	20.0	5.6	(3.5)
September 30, 1972	265	25	73	(17.1)	108	7.7	51	3.5	8.6	(0.6)
December 31, 1972	294	36	72	(1.5)	105	20.0	55	13.8	7.1	(2.0)
March 31, 1973	460	55	68	6.6	125	32.9	54	13.8	7.7	0
June 30, 1973	695	114	97	2.5	126	37.7	70	23.5	7.4	(0.7)
September 30, 1973	715	107	107	7.4	157	42.5	67	23.9	8.4	(0.5)
December 31, 1973	907	154	78	(4.2)	152	35.8	74	24.8	6.8	(0.7)
March 31, 1974	1,273	215	104	18.2	161	39.0	76	19.7	6.4	(0.9)
June 30, 1974	1,421	193	136	22.0	193	42.5	98	42.0	6.8	(1.9)

a. In the period October 1, 1973–December 31, 1973, the transportation department was established. The relevant data (in thousands) are
    December 31, 1973: Sales $39   Income: 12.5
    March 31, 1974:   Sales $88   Income: 20.8
    June 30, 1974:   Sales $136   Income: 30.6
b. All income data includes attributable cost of depreciation but no allocated general and administrative expense.

where the drivers can exercise. Exercise is one of the most easily overlooked needs of the driver because a driver can get very stiff driving all day. However, one must never forget the driver's priorities. First comes fuel, then getting clean, then food, then merchandise, then sleep.

The real keys to success are honesty and cleanliness. This used to be a very rough business. Truckstops were associated with prostitutes and "bennies" (benzedrine tablets used by drivers to keep alert). Those days are gone; both drivers and fleet owners are looking for people they can trust.

Cleanliness is extremely important. The one-stop operator usually keeps a cleaner place than the larger truckstop chains.

These factors have helped us grow and will continue to keep us competitive. Of course, our success was certainly speeded up by the fuel crisis.

THE FUEL CRISIS

During 1972 the demand for petroleum products began to outstrip its supply, and shortages developed in many industries. The gasoline and diesel oil markets felt the pinch later than some other petroleum-based industries, but by early 1973, Perlis was hearing from other truckstop operators that they were encountering difficulty in obtaining oil supplies. However, Texaco continued to supply Perlis Truckstop because it was a new business and a cutback in supplies would have led to severe financial difficulties for Perlis.

In May 1973, a voluntary allocation scheme was urged upon the oil companies by the government. It was recommended that oil companies supply their wholesaling customers with the same amount of fuel as in the corresponding month of the base period (October 1971–September 1972). Then, in September 1973, the Arab oil-producing countries placed an embargo on oil shipments to the United States, and in October 1973, President Nixon signed the Emergency Petroleum Act of 1973, which established the Office of Petroleum Allocation in the Department of Labor. The voluntary allocation scheme outlined above became mandatory. At one point, oil companies were supplying only 90 percent of base-period allocations.

Because a reduced allocation of fuel would have meant financial disaster to him, Perlis prepared a petition to Texaco and the Federal Energy Office, which argued that since 65 percent of Perlis' customers were engaged in the movement of food products, his service was essential and should be exempted in some part from reduced allocations. Perlis explained:

> It was obvious that I had Texaco on my side and that they wanted to supply me. They told me that the Perlis Truckstop was the largest single outlet in an eight-state region. I called upon Sam Nunn, our Senator, and he was very helpful in ensuring that we received sufficient fuel. Our allocation was 1 million gallons of diesel oil a month, which meant that I often had fuel when others didn't. Trucks were often backed up for hundreds of yards. By purchasing outside fuel and obtaining additional state allocations, we were able to sell 1.2 millions of diesel fuel in March 1974.
>
> The fuel shortage did us no harm. We received and sold more fuel than I would have sold if the fuel shortage hadn't hit. We could have made excess profit by charging more at the height of the shortage. But we were happy to make a legitimate profit on a large amount of fuel. Even before price controls were established, I had invited the IRS to audit my books to prove I was charging a fair price. When price controls came in, I did not charge the maximum allowable price and even today I am below my allowable maximum. Between July 1973 and February 1974, Texaco's prices for fuel rose by 51 percent. [The selling price of diesel oil at the Perlis Truckstop is shown in Exhibit 7].

THE SHUTDOWN

As the fuel crisis deepened in late 1973, the owner-operators called a national shutdown of operations and persuaded many fleet drivers to join them. Although the owner-operators, being independent entrepreneurs, were not extensively coordinated, most drivers read *Overdrive* magazine, which played a central role in communication of mutual grievances between drivers.

The owner-operators were frustrated by the lack of fuel. They also argued that raising fuel prices hit them particularly hard since, unlike fleet owners, they could not easily pass on their cost increases to their customers. They also were particularly aggra-

Exhibit 7
SALE PRICE OF DIESEL FUEL,
JUNE 1971–JULY 1974 (cents per gallon)[a]

1971 June	30.9
1973 May 15	31.9
May 24	32.9
June 1	33.9
September 7	32.9
September 29	34.9
October 21	35.9
November 5	36.9
December 8	38.9
1974 January 1	40.9
March 5	43.9
March 20	44.5
April 20	44.9
May 8	46.9
June 6	45.9
June 25	46.9
July 30	48.9
July 31	47.9

a. The data given are all the changes in diesel price at the Perlis Truckstop. Hence, each price was maintained until the next indicated change.

vated by the reduction in the speed limit, which reduced their productivity and threatened their profitability.

In December 1974, Lamar Perlis was awakened from his sleep at 3 A.M. (his home was located directly behind the truckstop) and was told that the truckers had asked the fuel supervisor to shut down the pumps.

I came down to the truckstop immediately, not knowing quite what to expect. I had seen the warnings in *Overdrive* but had never felt that the shutdown would occur. There had been one or two incidents of truckers blocking highways in Ohio in the previous week, and even though there had been some violence there, I didn't think it would really occur here. When I arrived at the truckstop, I was introduced to three leaders of the action and asked them to come to my office to discuss it. As we were ascending the stairs, I was aware that I had never dealt with an organized group and was wondering how I could cool down the situation. So I turned to the leader and asked, "Do you believe in God?"

When he said "Yes," I replied, "Good. Then we'll have something to talk about." We talked until dawn, and I convinced them that I was in sympathy with their objective to obtain a government fuel priority for trucks, since they were spending half their time on the road looking for fuel. After all, a healthy trucking industry is essential to our success. So, I shut down the pumps for a promise that there would be no violence between either striking and nonstriking truckers, or between truckers and law enforcement officers. I was among the first truckstops to be hit in a nationwide shutdown, and the next day all the television networks flew their news teams down to interview me, and I appeared on nationwide television. I repeated my sympathy with the truckers' objective of a higher fuel priority for trucks and stated I could understand their predicament.

My comments also appeared in many newspapers across the country, and I received a great deal of mail from other truckstops and fleet owners. There was only one fleet owner who openly criticized me, but I believe my action was right, especially as deaths had occurred elsewhere during the shutdown. The shutdown ended in four days, when most drivers had left, and I reopened the pumps. Of course, today my truckstop is well known, and when during the February 1974 shutdown, I refused to shut down the pumps, I encountered no trouble. It was a token action on my part because the shutdown was so effective elsewhere that our business was zero for a week.

In retrospect, I am glad that I did not have a general manager involved and was able to handle the situation myself. A man on the scene is very important in this business.

ORGANIZATION

Upon its formation, Lamar Perlis became president of Perlis Truck Terminals, Inc. He had made several attempts to hire a general manager to oversee all the activities at the truckstop but had not found anyone who performed to his satisfaction.

I wanted someone who could do it better than I could. After all, I'm entitled to someone who's capable for the $35,000–$45,000 that I must pay a general manager. None of the people I have tried in the last three years have been satisfactory. When we opened, I hired an assistant general manager for $175 a week, and he was here for a year. But he did not develop into a man I could trust and had certain health problems, so I let him go.

It's a difficult position for me to fill. Even an experienced truckstop operator might not be qualified to take over all my duties. For example, he would not be likely to have the merchandising background that has helped me in making our truckstop successful. And he would be unlikely to be able to make investment decisions as well as perform the duties of sales promotion and public relations with the fleets and drivers.

Although no formal organization chart or structure existed, activities at the truckstop were divided into four operating departments, each with its own department head (see Exhibit 8). These were fueling, restaurant, store, and parts and service (the motel was under the control of the fueling manager). A description of each department follows.

Fueling

The fueling operation, which generated revenues of nearly $1.5 million in the second quarter of 1974 (see Exhibit 6), was the backbone of the truckstop, providing nearly 50 percent of the contribution to overhead. Open 24 hours a day, it pumped approximately 35,000 gallons of diesel fuel per day. An average fill was 65 gallons.

In 1971, Perlis had installed an automatic printer pump, controlled by computer. As he explained:

> Without this, you would always get the occasional driver who would question how much fuel had been pumped. Or else he would ask for a receipt for more fuel than he received so that he could bill his company more. With this device there can be no argument. It's a simple method of ensuring honesty on both sides. With the reputation this business has had in the past years, this is an important consideration. With the printer pump, a trust can be built up between ourselves, the driver, and the fleet owner, since sales are accurately validated.

As well as fueling the trucks, Perlis insisted that his employees always clean the trucks' windshield and bump the tires (hit the tires with a billy club to check their pressure).

Customers at the truckstop could pay in a number of ways: cash, Texaco credit card, Master Card,

Exhibit 8
ORGANIZATION, AUGUST 1974[a]

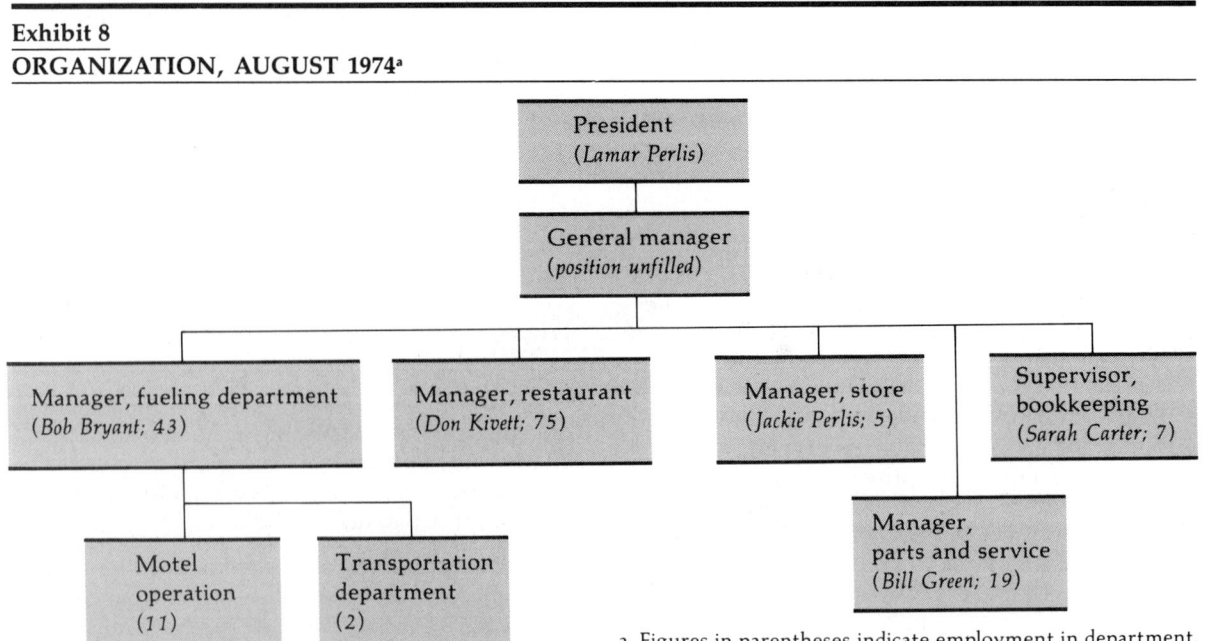

a. Figures in parentheses indicate employment in department.

National Truckers Service card (NTS), Mid Continent card, or charge to the fleet owner's account. The NTS card was a nationwide trucking credit that charged its user 2 percent of the value of the transaction and the truckstop operator the same amount. The Mid Continent card cost the truckstop operator 4 percent of the value of the transaction, with no charge to the customer. Payment to Perlis in both cases was 60 days.

Perlis preferred that the fleet owner maintain an account at the truckstop. "In this way the drivers are dedicated to you, since Perlis Truckstop becomes the scheduled stop and they have to stop here. Otherwise the choice of stop is up to the driver and you must fight harder for his business."

In August 1974, Perlis Truckstop had 900 accounts with operators and fleets. However, 65 percent of fuel revenues came not from fleet trucks, but from owner-operators.

> Even though the majority of our revenues do not come from fleet drivers, they are most accessible. I can design marketing programs and special services for fleets much more easily than for owner-operators. Being so numerous and difficult to reach, I don't know how to attract him to the truckstop, except by running a good operation and relying on word of mouth. I do have seven road signs, of which two are paid for by Texaco.
>
> For fleet owners, on the other hand, I can make a few calls or visits and generate a substantial amount of revenue by establishing an account. I handle the selling myself, although I have employed an outside salesman from time to time.

As Perlis explained, one of the important keys to success in the truckstop business was to "get the driver inside." To this end, a number of special attractions were offered. For example, there was a fuel desk, which, apart from controlling the pump printers, acted as a reception area for the drivers and offered various communications equipment for messages. One of Perlis's innovations was a Wide Area Telephone Service (WATS) line that he had installed, which allowed drivers to call anywhere in the United States free of charge. It was in almost constant use. This facility cost $1,600 a month, but because it was unique, Perlis felt that the expense was justified. Other services offered were free showers to drivers who fueled, a barber shop, and a drivers' lounge with two pool tables and a color television.

In charge of the fueling department was Bob Bryant, who had joined Perlis Truckstop in April 1974, being the fifth man in three years to hold that position.

> Mr. Perlis brought me in because of my six years of experience as operations manager supervising 100 employees. He wanted someone to train and supervise people, not to change things.
>
> My biggest problem is motivation. Pump attendants, who are mainly high school kids, get $2.25 to $2.50 an hour for a continuous eight-hour shift. We have three island attendants to man the twelve pumps in each eight-hour shift and expect them to pump 3,500 to 4,500 gallons each per shift. This means putting through a truck every 10 to 12 minutes. Since they have to clean the windshield and check the oil, headlights, and tires, it can be a very strenuous job. Mr. Perlis can be very demanding and has been known to call down from his office overlooking the pumps to get a resting attendant back to work. I have been told that the truckstop as a whole has gone through 3,000 people in three years.[1]

Bryant controlled the fueling operation by keeping a close watch on the pumping cost per gallon, a figure that he recorded and charted every day. He was also responsible for the motel, the janitors, and the transportation department. In his judgment, the motel had experienced a reasonable occupancy rate since his appointment. He noted that it was often possible to rent the same room twice in the same day since drivers took their rests at different times of the day. The motel charge was $7 a night for any of the seventeen rooms. The transportation department was composed of four tanker trucks which hauled in the fuel from Texaco's storage tanks. Two of the drivers had recently quit, and Bryant stated that they had left for higher pay. (Perlis discovered that Bryant had hired one of the drivers away from the truckstop to operate his own trucks.)

---

1. This fact was not proven by the records. 1,700 U.S. Government W-2 forms were on file in August 1974, covering all classes of regular and part-time workers since opening.

Restaurant

The 160-seat restaurant, the second largest source of revenue to the truckstop operation, had an atmosphere described by Perlis as "convivial."

> It is a good pragmatic place—no place mats or fancy trimmings. Atmosphere and good food are much more important. Running a restaurant is a very specialized task, however, and I have been through half a dozen managers in the past, none of whom really provided the service I required. However, each time we changed we got better, and we are now working towards a really efficient operation.

The current manager of the restaurant was Don Kivett, who had joined Perlis Truckstop in December 1973 after a career in catering. He commented:

> I think we now have a good operation, since morale is very high and the customers seem satisfied. We have almost doubled our revenues since I took over, but unfortunately profits are about the same. The man in this post before me was good at getting profit, but he did it by gouging the staff and gouging the customers. I have changed all that. I added labor to raise volume.
>
> We serve all fresh food, never freezing our chicken and using fresh vegetables. Our prices are competitive, about 25¢ cheaper than our main competition, the Ryder stop in Valdosta, Georgia. We charge $2.25 for a main course with three vegetables. However, with our costs skyrocketing, we will have to raise our prices.

In August 1974 the restaurant had seventy employees, but Kivett indicated that he was in the process of reducing the staff to fifty, both for seasonal reasons and to increase profits. Kivett's bonus was based upon the profitability of the restaurant, under a scheme jointly devised by him and Perlis prior to Kivett's appointment. However, he had become dissatisfied with his total remuneration of $20,000 for the year and was negotiating with Perlis for a change of contract.

> There are really only three things I would like to see changed around here. At the moment there is a carpet in the tourist section of the restaurant, and none in the truckers'. I think this is a mistake, as the truckers must be our first priority. In any event, the carpet needs cleaning so often it is more trouble than it's worth. It should be removed.
>
> The second change I would like to see is the construction of a special room to serve the bus traffic. At the moment the restaurant can seat 160 people and this makes it difficult for me if a bus driver comes to me and asks if I can seat a whole bus load. We could build a room to seat 50 people for $35,000.
>
> A final change I would like is an office, which I do not have at the moment. When I want to speak to an employee, I have to go into the stockroom or some other place.

Store

The store operation was under the general direction of Jackie Perlis. Like her husband, Jackie had come from a merchandising family.

> Although none of us knew anything about truckers when we started, we did not find it difficult to discover what they need, and we now have a stable product line. The store is a big success. Some other truckstops may sell more than we do, but few make as much money. The secret is to avoid the conventional truckstop suppliers and rack jobbers, and to trade direct with the manufacturers.

The biggest selling items were cool cushions (used by the drivers in their cabs), western shirts and boots, and citizen band radios. Mrs. Perlis noted that the truckers like to see well-known brand names, and she had stocked the store with Levi jeans and Thom McAn shoes obtained through the downtown Perlis store. The store employed one salesclerk on each eight-hour shift, as well as a general supervisor to whom Mrs. Perlis had delegated the day-to-day operating decisions.

Parts and Service

The parts and service department at the Perlis Truckstop had three drive-in bays, one for general repairs, one for lubrication, and one for tire repair. No major repair service was offered since Perlis considered that the key maxim for a shop at a truckstop was "can we do it while the driver waits?" He also noted that since Cordele was not near any major truck destination, it was likely that a driver would come there mostly for minor and emergency repairs. It was for this reason, among others, that a brief experiment in performing engine overhauls was abandoned.

As with other departments, Perlis had encountered difficulty in finding a competent manager. The current manager, Bill Green, had originally been hired as a fueling supervisor. Perlis described him as "not a real professional, but he has stabilized and organized the operation."

Perlis was considering an expansion of the parts and service operation. Noting that inventory was excessive in relation to sales (Exhibit 9), he was seeking ways to increase sales. Among these was an attempt to purchase such items as tires at lower prices by being classified as a warehouse distributor. In order to qualify for this classification, Perlis had taken over one of his family's downtown warehouses and was planning to build a 10,000-square foot warehouse at the truckstop at a cost of approximately $75,000. He projected that with an inventory of $400,000 he would be in a position to supply fleets, truck-leasing companies, and other truckstops with their parts and supplies. He was also investigating the possibility of constructing three more bays at a cost of $73,000 to handle the current

---

Exhibit 9

INVENTORIES, BY DEPARTMENT, JUNE 30, 1974

FUELING		
Gasoline	$ 7,530	
Diesel fuel	35,258	
Motor oil	6,580	
Total		$ 49,378
PARTS AND SERVICE		
Batteries, accessories, and parts	$ 73,996	
Tires	100,168	
Supplies and parts	859	
Total		175,023
RESTAURANT		
Food	$ 9,640	
China, glassware, and silver	3,151	
Total		12,791
STORE		
Store merchandise	$106,896	
Vending machine	1,159	
Total		108,055
Total Inventories		$345,246

---

overflow of work. Labor charges in the parts and service department were $15 per hour and labor costs $5 per hour.

Administration and Control

Perlis received three types of reports. Each day he received a computer printout of the previous day's sales, by department. Each week he received a handwritten labor report, which gave total labor costs by department. Each month he received a computer printout of the complete monthly income statement by department.

> I sometimes have some difficulties in assessing these reports. From what I have recently learned at school[2] I know I should be calculating a number of ratios, but except for cost per gallon, I don't know what these should be. So, I just keep a close watch for trends.

Will Kidd, accountant for Perlis Truckstop, agreed that it would be difficult to establish productivity standards because of the rapid change in volume and the inability in some departments, such as parts and service, to decide upon a valid measure of output. He considered that the most significant improvement in control of the truckstop had been the development of meaningful departmental operating statements. However, he did see the need for future development of productivity measures:

> When Lamar decides to leave here to go into other things, we will have to develop a different management control scheme, if only because a new general manager would not be controlling his own money and would therefore not stay quite on top of everything as Lamar does. Lamar thinks everyone is stealing from him and keeps a very close tab on everyone. Of course, you must remember that for twenty years he was in a retailing store where, if anything was wrong, you went straight over and pointed it out to an employee. He hasn't yet learned that you shouldn't do that here.

Perlis later commented:

> I do know that I shouldn't skip my channels of management. After all, that is one of the first rules of management. But I find it difficult not to when I look out onto the concrete and see

---

2. Perlis had been attending a small company management program at Harvard Business School.

something being done wrong. By the time I went through the supervisor, the damage would have been done. I am very aware that my biggest problems are organizational. People management is my weakness. But I don't want to live with a department head that I do not trust. On advice from other operators, I tried general polygraphing of my employees. It was moderately successful, but I am not very proud of having done it. I know it is better to cultivate trust and understanding. I want a man whose character I can build on. So my objective is not to identify an area of improvement but to find ways of solving problems we already know exist.

Perlis had contacted a consultant who specialized in organizational diagnosis and executive search. The consultant had proposed a $20,000 project to design motivation and incentive schemes, written policies, procedures and objectives, and search for a general manager. Perlis was unsure whether he should accept the proposal.

THE FUTURE

Perlis was determined to cease his day-to-day involvement in the truckstop within six months. He felt that with a cash flow of $60,000 to 70,000 a month, the truckstop was now on its feet, and that his first priority was to recruit a general manager. He noted that the prime consideration in appointing a general manager was that he would be responsible for operations twenty-four hours a day, seven days a week; consequently, the individual had to be someone that could be trusted with such a large responsibility.

The big chains do not have these problems. They have the advantages of scale and can train general managers as assistants before giving them control of their own truckstop. But I don't think they would be a good source for me. It goes against my morality to steal staff from a competitor, and I am not sure they will be good enough, because they will be too used to strong guidance and set company procedures.

Perlis has been considering for some time an expansion to a second truckstop. With a cash flow of approximately $1 million per year, the Perlis family did not expect a problem with the availability of loan capital, but Perlis could not commit any of his family's funds to a new truckstop venture, primarily because of the prevailing high interest rate (10 percent in August 1974) and current construction of a shopping center in Dublin, Georgia. He also saw many benefits from a possible joint venture with a company such as Hertz, which leased trucks, because such a company could provide advertising, personnel, and other professional assistance not possessed by the Perlis family. Such a company would also provide a base of guaranteed business and would have an existing fuel allocation. (Government allocation regulations were still in effect until October 1974, and Perlis considered the availability of fuel crucial to any truckstop venture, since the oil companies in August 1974 were not entering into supply contracts with new truckstops.)

Perlis had approached Texaco about another fuel supply contract and Hertz about a joint venture on a new truckstop, but he had not received a positive response from either. However, he was still investigating this approach, because he believed that "one successful venture in this form would carry us further and faster than any other method."

In presenting my plans to Hertz [see Exhibit 10] I was prepared to accept any share of the business between 40 percent and 60 percent. I would have preferred to provide none of the funds and take 40 percent, but I would also accept providing an equal share of the funds and not less than 51 percent of the equity. I wouldn't be concerned about whether the name Perlis was used, but I think it has value now.

In any new truckstop that I did alone, I would begin by overstaffing—getting a really topnotch manager who could help limit the startup costs and do a good job in recruiting and training. I would pay $40,000 to $50,000 for such a person, and if need be would include a share of equity, which I would not do for the present truckstop.

In assessing the site of a new truckstop, Perlis believed there were a large number of factors to take into account, including the physical properties of the land, the proximity to utilities, and the extent of local business. In addition, a site that was at the junction of two interstate highways, which provided a good cross traffic, would obviously be preferable. Perlis believed that the type of labor available was important in that any decision would be

Exhibit 10

PROPOSED FULL-SERVICE TRUCKSTOP VENTURE (in thousands)[a]

	HIGH-CAPITAL PROPOSAL	LOW-CAPITAL PROPOSAL[b]		MOST LIKELY	%	MOST LIKELY	%
Current Assets	$ 450	$ 450	Sales[c]	$10,000	(100)	$10,000	(100)
Fixed Assets			Less Cost of				
Land	450	275	Goods Sold	7,700	(77)	7,700	(77)
Buildings and improvements	1,500	1,030	Gross Profit	$2,300	(23)	2,300	(23)
			Less Operating				
Equipment	925	900	Expenses	950	(10)	1,080	(11)
Loan costs	42	42	Operating Profit	1,350	(13)	1,220	(12)
Total Assets	$3,367	$2,697	Interest and Depreciation	468	(5)	340	(3.4)
Current Liabilities	$ 450	$ 450	Pretax Income	882	(8.8)	880	(8.8)
LTD			Tax @ 50%	441	(4.4)	440	(4.4)
Mortgage	2,100	$1,430		441	(4.4)	440	(4.4)
Venturer's loan	317	317	Cash Flow	$ 675		$ 673	
Venturer's Equity	500	500					
Total Liabilities and Equity	$3,367	$2,697					

a. The data given in this exhibit are taken from Perlis's proposal to Hertz.
b. Low cost construction with reduced facilities. Reaches maturity in four years.
c. All income data are projections for fourth year of operation.

influenced by the level and existence of fuel taxes. He considered that, other things being equal, he would prefer to locate in Georgia, because he had already established contacts with the people he had to deal with on a political level. However, he also saw the advantages of a site on I-95, which did not have a lengthy portion in Georgia. I-95, which was not due to be completed for two to four years, was expected to become the main artery from Florida to the Northeast, with a projected truck count of 5,000 to 6,000 trucks per day.

There are really three sites that I am now seriously considering. My top priority is Pooler, Georgia, just outside Savannah [see Exhibit 2]. It is at the junction of I-16 and I-95 and has the advantage of being near the major port of Savannah. The development of container ships has greatly increased the volume of truck traffic out of this and other ports. Being close to a destination would give you personnel advantages

and allow tie-ins with fleets, whereby one could act as a substitute garage and terminal for them. The opportunity to go in for wholesaling of truck supplies would be great. It does have the disadvantage of being the last portion of I-95 to be complete and would have a much higher cost of acquisition than other sites I am considering. I have already tendered an offer of $300,000 for the land, which was turned down.

A second site I am considering is Brunswick, Georgia. Like the Savannah site, it would develop from scratch, but I can get the land for $250,000. It has good access to the highway and the utilities are good. It would not have the advantage of being near a major city, but it would also avoid the disadvantages of loitering and congestion from retail (local) trade that such a site would have. One big problem is that Ryder will be opening a stop just south of there [see Exhibit 2].

The final site is the Cater's Truckstop in Rosinville, South Carolina. It is a going concern [see Exhibits 11 and 12 for balance sheet and income data], but could do with a great deal of improvement. It has no store, and the restaurant, which is usually halfway decent, seats only sixty-seven people. He leases out his shop work and is pumping about 375,000 gallons of diesel a month. I took my architect to have a look at it, and he threw up his arms in horror, saying there was little he could do with it. Another problem is that most of the business comes from one fleet that is using the stop as a terminal. I would be fighting a very poor reputation and would have to clean up the place, unless I decided to milk the facility. But that is not really my style.

I have a big problem in deciding on the site's value. The figures I have seen are all unaudited, and I have a feeling that the cash flow should be more. He wants $1.4 million for the place, but my CPA says I should not pay more than four to six times earnings for it. The question is, what could the real earnings become?

I don't foresee any problems in controlling two truckstops. I could send in audit teams to each department of each truckstop on a regular basis to be sure all was in order and would plan to make regular visits myself as long as I am in the Georgia-South Carolina region. I can hire a plane for $70 an hour to get me from one stop to the next.

Of course, I could sell the existing stop and would be tempted by a $4.5 million offer, but it is not something I really want to do. We now have a stable organization, and each and every department is making money. I don't want to get out of the truckstop business, although if I do, I will return to real estate work that I enjoy. The key thing is that, at fifty, I am at a turning point in my life and must decide what I am going to do next.

Exhibit 11
CATER'S TRUCKSTOP: BALANCE SHEET, APRIL 30, 1974

ASSETS		LIABILITIES AND EQUITY	
Current Assets		Accounts Payable	$ 40,542
Cash	$ (34,103)	Notes payable and taxes payable	131,104
Accounts receivable	56,273	Total Current Liabilities	171,646
Inventories	50,228	L.T.D.	296,327
Total Current Assets	$ 72,398	Equity	101,023
Fixed Assets	640,536	TOTAL LIABILITIES AND EQUITY	$568,996
Depreciation	(172,843)		
Net fixed assets	467,693		
Land (net)	22,000		
Prepaid Expenses	6,425		
Other Assets	418		
TOTAL ASSETS	$568,996		

Exhibit 12
CATER'S TRUCKSTOP: INCOME STATEMENT, JANUARY 1–APRIL 31, 1974

Sales	
Gas	$112,977
Diesel	629,724
Service	13,393

Oil	18,575
Rooms	8,340
Restaurant	60,129
Other	36,196
Total Sales	$879,334
Less Cost of Sales	645,923
Gross Profit	233,411
Less Expenses	139,722
Net Operating Profit	93,689
Other Income	5,480
Less Interest	11,952
NET PROFIT	$88,217

EVANS PHARMA-CEUTICALS, INC. (A)

JOHN CLAIR THOMPSON
University of Connecticut

On October 17, 1987, John J. Brittain, a consultant in strategy and planning, sat in his office in Eugene, Oregon, pondering what he was going to tell a client of his, Dave S. Evans, the founder and chief executive of Evans Pharmaceuticals, Inc., in a telephone call he was to place shortly.

The situation at Evans had begun unfolding four months earlier when, during Brittain's exploratory first visit to the firm's offices in rural Oregon near the town of Cottage Grove, Evans's bookkeeper came into the CEO's office to ask about the bank overdraft of more than $60,000 in checks which the firm could not cover. As Brittain soon learned, Evans Pharmaceuticals was a very profitable small firm that was growing so fast that its profitability could not keep up with its demands for funds.

The firm's bank, Oregon First National Bank (OFNB), the largest commercial bank in the state and the second largest in the Pacific Northwest, through its local representative, James Baldwin, had supported Dave Evans with reasonable generosity and patience with short-term loans. With the latest developments, however, OFNB had become quite concerned about the status of the firm. In fact, Evans was expecting a visit from Baldwin's immediate supervisor the following Monday, and there was some possibility that his loans could be called by the bank due to his unorthodox financial management.

The tasks that had faced Brittain in June of 1987 therefore had two distinct phases: first, help Dave Evans achieve some rationality in the firm's short-term finances by working with him to set up a cash-flow forecasting system and introduce other methods able to aid the firm to understand and manage its affairs affecting the short term; second, with an eye to the longer—responding to further needs that all three (Evans, Baldwin, and Brittain) agreed were critically important—help Evans formulate and implement a business plan covering the next five years.

Both tasks proceeded apace over the summer of 1987. Evans quickly adopted Brittain's suggestions about making and using careful estimates of the cash impacts of decisions, basing them on calendar weeks, and updating them on the firm's computer by projecting the implications of every significant development. Similarly, regular discussions with Dave Evans began to probe the firm's—and Evan's own—circumstances and thinking about the future: objectives and priorities; problems and priorities; opportunities and alternative paths open to Evans Pharmaceuticals.

In particular, as the short-term threats diminished considerably, the discussion focused on the past, present, and future characteristics of the firm's individual products, product lines, customers, and competitors. Much of this exploration looked forward to the construction in 1988 of a new and larger plant, which would permit not only much greater output but also (when appropriate equipment was installed) additional product forms—liquids and effervescents—that were not possible in the present facility, which was limited to producing swallowable tablets.

Naturally, these discussions had also involved the question of production economies possible in a

This case, written specifically for class use at the University of Connecticut, is printed by permission.

plant designed for Evans's use, rather than the rented, general-purpose facility now in use, which had by the summer of 1987 become so cramped that space had to be leased in other locations and two trailer bodies placed on the grounds for extra storage. Such matters as capacity utilization, vertical integration, physical flow efficiencies, scheduling flexibility and savings, economies of scope and scale, and others were central to the conclusion that the new plant would be beneficial to the firm's profitability, both in dollar and percentage terms.

Needless to say, the prospect of new-plant investment running into seven figures was daunting to a management with just-past difficulties in balancing its checkbook. While Evans believed that the firm's high profitability and his improved cash-flow management would alleviate the short-term pinches, it was clear to him—even before Brittain's remark the first day that the firm badly needed an infusion of outside capital—that substantial new funding was going to be necessary.

Evans's first resort was going to be a State of Oregon program for encouraging development of the rural areas away from Portland and northwest Oregon. A site had been selected in a new industrial park near Cottage Grove in the town of Springfield and three-way discussions undertaken with the park's promoters and representatives of the Oregon Economic Assistance (OEA) program. In fact, one meeting attended by Brittain had gotten so far as to treat tactical matters such as how to complete the paperwork and which OEA officials to contact for further help, all giving the impression that the move could proceed because the financing was assured.

It was all the more important, therefore, to expedite Brittain's work with Evans to produce the two long-term business-plan elements of pro-forma financial projections through 1992 and a substantive business plan covering the firm's outlook and strategy. Meetings between Evans and Brittain continued over the late summer to provide opportunities to explore carefully the background for both elements, until suddenly, on August 14, Brittain arrived at the Cottage Grove offices in the afternoon to find a new face in Evans's office—James Kemper.

Kemper, it turned out, was a former investment banker from San Francisco who now worked on his own as a finder for venture-capital investors. He had contacted Evans on one earlier occasion—before the firm had been interested in outside funding—and in 1987 had again opened discussions

with Dave Evans concerning renewed potentials. The purpose of his visit that afternoon was to fill in details about the firm that would allow him to prepare a prospectus to present to his clients with funds to invest.

Brittain later learned that Kemper's proposal was to raise $500,000 of equity funds from a small group of investors, which would give those outsiders a 10-percent share in the ownership of the firm. What had only been sketched in part were the restrictions that Kemper's backers wanted made part of the package: no other equity financing, no distributions of dividends, minimum requirements for earnings ratios, and limited executive salaries—among others. Still, what Kemper would charge for his finder services seemed exceptionally inexpensive to Brittain compared to the high costs of ordinary equity financing in small offerings: if the arrangements proved satisfactory, Kemper was to receive $25,000, which represented only 5 percent of the total raised. (Should the deal fall through, Kemper was to be paid $5,000. In both cases, a translation of the amounts into equivalents in equity had been suggested.)

For all its attraction—not the least of which was Evans's wife's strong conviction that the half a million dollars would relieve not only the firm but also Dave of much day-to-day anxiety—the equity package was not looked upon very positively by Evans. In particular, he worried about the restrictions on the firm and him that came with the money, even though Brittain pointed out that similar provisions were standard requirements routinely imposed by sophisticated investors or lenders, for example, as conditions of a term loan from a commercial bank or insurance company.

By late August, Brittain had drawn up a projected income statement and balance sheet for the years 1988 through 1992, based on discussions with Dave Evans of the sales prospects for the firm, probable patterns of costs and investments, and other characteristics affecting the pro-forma expression of future finances for the firm. Exhibits 1 and 2 show the unaudited financial statements for Evans Pharmaceuticals, which had been compiled by the firm's outside accountant for 1985 through 1987; Exhibits 3 and 4 show Brittain's estimates (as revised in reviews conducted with Dave Evans) for the years 1988 to 1992.

The upshot of these projections, according to Brittain's interpretation, was that Evans would not really need outside funding beyond the expected

Exhibit 1

EVANS PHARMACEUTICALS, INC.: INCOME STATEMENTS,
YEARS ENDED APRIL 30 (in thousands)[a]

	1985	1986	1987
Sales	$312.7	$628.5	$1,018.9
Less Cost of Goods Sold	282.4	493.0	673.4
Gross Profit	$ 30.3	$135.5	$ 345.5
Less Administrative Expense	91.3	183.2	292.9
Income Before Taxes	($ 61.0)	($ 47.7)	52.6
Less Income Taxes	—	0.1	0.2
NET INCOME	($ 61.0)	($ 47.8)	$52.4

a. Interim income statements for five months ended September 30, in part (figures in thousands):

	1986	1987
Sales	$304.8	$500.1
Less Cost of Sales	229.8	330.7
Gross Profit	$ 75.1	$169.4
Less Administrative Expense	93.8	110.8
NET INCOME	($18.7)	$ 58.6

Exhibit 2

EVANS PHARMACEUTICALS, INC: BALANCE SHEET,
APRIL 30, 1987 (in thousands)

ASSETS

Current Assets

Cash	$ 9.1	
Accounts receivable	146.3	
Inventory	175.3	
Other	175.4	
Current Assets		$346.3
Property and equipment	$379.7	
Less accumulated depreciation	(46.4)	
Net property and equipment		333.3
Other assets		28.4
TOTAL ASSETS		$708.0

LIABILITIIES AND STOCKHOLDERS EQUITY

Current Liabilities

Accounts payable	$174.2	
Accrued items	44.1	
Notes payable	88.6	
Other	59.8	
Total Current Liabilities		$366.7

Long-Term Liabilities
  Notes payable (long-term) $117.6
  Other   21.1
    Total Long-Term Liabilities   138.7
Total Liabilities   504.4

Stockholders' Equity
  Common stock $ 9.2
  Additional paid-in capital   263.2
  Retained earnings   (39.9)
  Treasury stock   (29.9)
    Total Stockholders' Equity   202.6
TOTAL LIABILITIES AND STOCKHOLDERS' EQUITY $708.0

Exhibit 3
**EVANS PHARMACEUTICALS, INC.: PROJECTED INCOME STATEMENTS,
YEARS ENDED APRIL 30 (in thousands)**

	1988	1989	1990	1991	1992
Net Sales	$2,238	$6,176	$8,372	$11,820	$14,775
Less Cost of Goods Sold					
Sales commissions	59	306	469	780	975
Production labor	174	284	494	694	894
Quality-assurance labor	42	72	72	102	102
Insurance and other	35	60	100	140	180
Materials	954	2,602	3,485	4,860	6,000
Other costs of sales	91	251	340	480	600
Less Expenses					
Administrative salaries	120	150	210	300	450
Other administrative	91	251	340	480	600
Rent, building depreciation	16	45	55	80	80
Other property costs	114	314	425	600	750
Other costs	114	314	425	600	750
Total Costs and Expenses	$1,810	$4,649	$6,415	$9,116	$11,381
Net Income Before Taxes	428	1,527	1,957	2,704	3,394
Income Taxes	36	611	783	1,082	1,358
NET INCOME AFTER TAX	$ 392	$ 916	$1,174	$ 1,622	$ 2,036

loan through OEA specifically intended to finance the new plant and start-up there. This meant, of course, that the funds tendered by Kemper need not be obtained. Thus Brittain's intuitive sense was that Evans could maintain greater freedom and autonomy, postpone to a more favorable time the sale of equity to outsiders, and simply enjoy running the firm as he always had run it. Brittain stressed these conclusions during his conversations with Evans, both face-to-face and by telephone.

Moreover, Brittain undertook two further financial analyses: first, he looked into various measures of executive salary compensation that would give him and Evans a means of gauging the adequacy, in

Exhibit 4
EVANS PHARMACEUTICALS, INC.: PROJECTED BALANCE SHEETS,
APRIL 30 (in thousands)

	1988	1989	1990	1991	1992
ASSETS					
Current Asssets					
Cash	$ 50	$ 150	$ 200	$ 270	$ 320
Accounts receivable	300	925	1,288	1,688	2,000
Inventory	120	370	515	675	800
Current Assets	470	1,445	2,003	2,633	3,120
Property—Gross	1,280	1,480	1,980	1,980	1,980
Accumulated depreciation	(63)	(108)	(163)	(243)	(323)
Property—Net	1,217	1,372	1,817	1,737	1,657
TOTAL ASSETS	$1,687	$2,817	$3,820	$4,370	$4,777
LIABILITIES AND STOCKHOLDERS' EQUITY					
Current Liabilities					
Accounts payable	$ 168	$ 512	$ 704	$ 911	$1,067
Accruals	42	129	176	228	267
Current Liabilities	210	641	880	1,139	1,334
Notes payable	200	200	200	200	200
Total Liabilities	410	841	1,080	1,339	1,534
Stockholders' Equity					
Common stock and paid-in capital	272	272	272	272	272
Retained earnings	352	1,268	2,442	4,064	6,100
Treasury stock	(30)	(30)	(30)	(30)	(30)
Total Stockholders' Equity	594	1,510	2,684	4,306	6,342
TOTAL LIABILITIES AND STOCKHOLDERS' EQUITY	1,004	2,351	3,764	5,645	7,876
FUNDS' IMBALANCE (NEED) OR SURPLUS	($ 683)	($ 466)	($ 56)	$1,275	$3,099

the circumstances of the amount Evans was paying himself. The two principal criteria Brittain used were estimates from Robert Morris Associates of executive compensation and Brittain's own matrix of hourly pay (compared loosely with managerial and nonmanagerial rates) multiplied by the long hours devoted by Evans to the firm. Both of these indicated that Evans was much underpaid, especially toward the latter years of the projections, and produced two results—revision of the administrative costs section of the projected income statements and the tentative conclusion that Kemper's backers might resist this augmented pay.

The other calculations involved comparing the half million dollar equity investment to be commit-

ted by the San Francisco group in 1988 with the value of the 19-percent share of the net worth that would accrue to them come 1992. Present-value calculations of the compound return on investment pointed to average annual earnings over the five years of more than 40 percent, a performance that Brittain, at least, regarded as both outstanding and extremely generous to the investor group, more generous than was warranted.

Then there had been no contacts during the entire month of September and the first part of October. When Brittain visited Cottage Grove on October 16 to catch up on events, Evans presented him with Kemper's final document, a confidential memorandum dated October 1, 1987. Evans asked Brittain to study thoroughly this analysis (reproduced in part as Exhibit 5) before reporting back to him. Two aspects were uppermost: first, the suitability of using the document's contents in a formal presentation to OEA of Evans's request for funding for the new plant, and second, the meaning and value of Kemper's analysis (particularly the narrative) for a full business plan that Brittain and Evans would jointly undertake to generate and which would be used strictly inside the firm for strategy formulation and implementation.

Brittain's subsequent evaluation concluded that the narrative sections of Kemper's report were all but ideal for the proposal to OEA in their complete but concise treatment of the character of and prospects for Evans Pharmaceuticals. Study of the calculations provided by Kemper, however, revealed that, although they proceeded from sales totals identical to those used in Brittain's projections, both the income statements and the balance sheets arrived at estimates quite different from Brittain's. Indeed, Brittain came to believe that their divergences meant that a decision had to be made as to which represented the financial future for the firm, since the estimates were really not compatible or resolvable.

Making Brittain's upcoming report to Evans more difficult was a trio of developments. One was that Baldwin still agreed with Brittain that outside equity not only was needed in 1988 but also that later sale of stock would be vastly more favorable in terms of realizable funds for Evans. A second was that Kemper was coming up from San Francisco on October 22 to discuss his proposal with Evans. The third was that, in an unusual twist of events, another prospective financier was also to be present at the meeting—a representative from an SBIC (small business investment company) that was another subsidiary of the parent company of Baldwin's firm. This man was, like Kemper, a potential provider of equity funding.

All these matters were in Brittain's mind as he formulated his presentation to Evans that afternoon. Whatever he ultimately said, Brittain was convinced that matters were rapidly approaching the point where Evans would have to make decisions committing the firm to long-term financing. In turn, these would set significant aspects of the future strategic character of the business as well as Evans's own behavior as an entrepreneur leading an exciting existence at the helm of a burgeoning organization.

Exhibit 5
KEMPER'S PROPOSAL FOR A PRIVATE PLACEMENT

EVANS PHARMACEUTICALS, INC.
$500,000
Proposed Private Placement
Common Stock

This confidential memorandum has been prepared in connection with a proposed private placement by Evans Pharmaceuticals, Inc. (the "Company"). While the information contained herein is believed to be reliable, no representation is made by the Company, or any agent of the Company, as to the accuracy and completeness of such information. It must be recognized that it includes predictions and projections, which are necessarily subject to a high degree of uncertainty. The Company and any agent of the Company expressly disclaim any and all liability for representations, expressed or implied, contained herein, or for omissions from this memorandum or any other written or oral communication transmitted to any interested party in the course of evaluation of this private placement or any other investment in the Company.

SUMMARY
Evans Pharmaceuticals, Inc., was organized in May 1984 to meet the proprietary (over-the-counter) pharmaceutical market's need for quality products—ones that

Exhibit 5
KEMPER'S PROPOSAL FOR A PRIVATE PLACEMENT (continued)

closely emulate the quality of national branded products but can be profitably sold as private (or store) label items at lower retail prices than comparable branded products. For this market, the Company formulates, manufactures, packages, and sells OTC solid dosage products that are best described as copies of national brands such as Tums, Rolaids, Maalox-Plus, Correctol, and Ex-Lax.

Today the Company's growth is limited by the fact that its Cottage Grove, Oregon, plant is stretching its capacity. It now proposes to build a 25,000-square-foot plant in nearby Springfield. In addition to adding capacity, the plant will greatly improve manufacturing efficiency and will expand the product line to include effervescents and liquids, items that cannot be produced in the present plant.

The total cost of the facility (land, building, equipment, moving, etc.) is estimated at $1,030,000. To finance the expansion and an increase in working capital, the Company seeks to raise a total of $1,375,000 as follows: $500,000 through the private placement of common stock and $875,000 through industrial development loan programs of the State of Oregon.

The OTC pharmaceutical market is growing at 4 percent to 4.5 percent a year. Within this market, sales of private label products through chain retail outlets are growing faster than the total OTC market as retailers aggressively promote such health care products for their better profit margins to the retailers. Evans started as a contract manufacturer to quickly build a base of business, but the present thrust and the future growth are in serving the private label OTC market with the Company's own products, a more profitable business than contract manufacturing.

The keys to the Company's success to date and its future growth are: (1) potential of the OTC private label market; (2) benefits to be derived from the new plant; (3) formulation skills which are especially important in duplicating the characteristics of the branded item; (4) ownership of the formulae on all its products; (5) full service from formulating through manufacturing and packaging, which full service is an advantage in its pricing; (6) selection on niche products and avoidance of commodity items; (7) increasing acceptance by chains as a source of quality products; and (8) an experienced, aggressive founder, owner, and chief executive in David ("Dave") J. Evans.

FINANCING PROGRAM; USE OF FUNDS
Operating now at full capacity, the Company is limited in capitalizing on the market potential. Thus Evans proposed to acquire a 4.3-acre site in the Springfield Industrial Park, a development sponsored by the Town of Springfield, Oregon, and to build on that site a 25,000-square-foot facility designed to meet Evans's needs. Purchase of the land and award of a construction contract will not take place unless Evans receives the approval of the Oregon Economic Assistance (OEA) to provide financing. If the OEA commitment is received in the fall of 1987, it is expected construction would start soon after, and the plant would be occupied and operational on or about July 1, 1988.

The cost of the plant and an increase in working capital is estimated at $1,375,000 with funds to be used as follows:

Land	$ 50,000
Building construction	800,000
Machinery and equipment[a]	60,000
Moving present operations	100,000
Fees (engineering, appraisal, legal, OEA, financing, etc.)	50,000
Working capital	315,000
Total Cost	$1,375,000

a. Most of the machinery and equipment in the new plant will be that which is moved from present locations.

As sources of these funds, the Company seeks to raise (1) $500,000 through the private placement of common stock, and (2) $875,000 through the sale of industrial revenue bonds issued by the OEA and possibly, funds from other state programs.

CAPITALIZATION

The April 30, 1987, capitalization of the Company—actual and pro-forma for the proposed financing—is as follows (in thousands):

	APRIL 30, 1987	
	Actual	*Pro Forma*
Current Debt		
Demand notes due Oregon First National	$ 61	$ 61
Current portion, long-term debt	50	50
Total Current Debt	$111	$111
Long-Term Debt		
Outstanding	$138	$ 138
Proposed state loans	0	875
Total Long-Term Debt	138	1,013
Total Debt	$249	$1,124
Common Stock	203	703
TOTAL CAPITALIZATION	$452	$1,827

BACKGROUND ON THE OTC MARKET

The OTC market (at shipments level) has grown from $3.7 billion in 1977 to $6.8 billion in 1986, according to U.S. government figures. The Department of Commerce estimates the market expanded 4 percent in 1986 and will grow 4.5 percent in 1987. Sales of nonprescription drugs are forecast to reach $9 billion by 1991 as more new products are switched from prescription to OTC. Other reasons for growth are the rising cost of professional medical care, the aging of the population, greater public knowledge of their use, and the availability of OTCs.

The importance of proprietaries to the drug chains is shown in a 1986 survey by the trade publication, *Drug Store News*. In that year, OTC proprietaries—with sales at the retail level of $4.5 billion—accounted for 14.8 percent of drug chain sales; this was second to prescriptions (28.1 percent) among fourteen store departments. Gross margins on OTC ran in the 30–35 percent range, less than the 35–40 percent on prescriptions but roughly equal to or better than all other departments but one, which one had only one-third the sales volume of OTC. A nationwide survey of pharmacists by *American Druggist* showed that pharmacists, when asked for recommendations by cus-

Exhibit 5
KEMPER'S PROPOSAL FOR A PRIVATE PLACEMENT (*continued*)

tomers, are increasingly recommending private label or generics in an expanding number of the sixty-one product categories covered by the survey.

Drug chains are increasing their share of the OTC market in drug stores as the number of independents declines. In addition, other outlets such as supermarket chains, combination supermarket-drug chains and mass merchandisers (e.g., K-Mart, Wal-Mart, Zayre's, Ames, Caldor) aggressively retail OTC pharmaceuticals—branded, private labels and generic. A. C. Nielsen studies show that in some product categories of health and beauty aids, food chains have a greater market share than drug chains.

Private (store) label products are increasing in importance as all types of chains aggressively pursue these sales. The retailer's lower purchase price (no heavy advertising and promotion expense) and the lower investment in inventory allow the retailer to take a higher markup and still have his selling price below that of the brand. To the chains, the store label product is preferable to the branded or generic one since it encourages the consumer to return to that particular store for replacement; in contrast, the branded or generic item might be purchased at any one of many outlets.

It is the retail chain of a size that can justify and promote its own store label for OTC pharmaceuticals that is the targeted growth of Evans Pharmaceuticals.

HISTORY AND BUSINESS

Evans Pharmaceuticals, Inc., was incorporated in Oregon in May 1984 to engage in the manufacture, packaging and sale of proprietary pharmaceuticals formulated and owned by the Company. The strategy underlying the Company from inception has been:

1. To meet the growing, nonbranded pharmaceutical market's demand for quality (i.e., duplicating as closely as possible the branded item) products at reasonable prices, enabling Evans and the retailer both to make a fair profit.
2. To focus on business requiring specialized manufacturing techniques for products inherently more difficult to formulate in order to demand a higher price and margin and, at the same time, to distinguish itself from others in the industry.
3. To stress the chain-store, private-label OTC market while at the same time taking advantage of selected opportunities in contract manufacturing and exclusive manufacturing of other companies' branded products.

At the time Dave Evans started the Company with an initial capitalization of $100,000, he had a single customer that guaranteed annual sales of $240,000. (That company continues to this day to be an important customer.) From sales of $313,000 in its first fiscal year, the Company has grown to projected sales of $2.3 million in the year ending April 30, 1988, its fourth year.

PRODUCTS; MANUFACTURING

The Company's product line consists of fifteen products in the categories of antacids, laxatives, decongestants and antihistamines. They are typically copies of brand name items such as Tums, Rolaids, Maalox-Plus, Correctol, Ex-Lax, and Sudafed. Evans manufactures only in solid dosage form including sugar-coated and film-coated tablets, chewable tablets, sustained-release caplets and capsules, and immediate-release caplets. It can package in bottles and rolls, but blister and strip packaging is contracted to others to avoid a major investment in dies.

The new plant will enable expansion of the product line to include liquids (antacids initially and eventually cough and cold remedies) and effervescents (denture cleaners, potassium supplements). This will open important opportunities because of the fact that the liquid antacid market is four times the size of the solid dosage market.

All products have formulae that originate with Evans and remain in its possession and are proprietary to the Company. Customers are given guarantees of analysis and stability along with a list of ingredients, but customers have no rights to the formulae and manufacturing methods.

Evans believes its product and manufacturing strengths are its expertise in interactive compounds, sustained release, and general formulation skills. It seeks to make niche products that capitalize upon its strengths and meet the market's needs. As an example, it was the first company to formulate a rolled antacid for the private label market. It avoids more competitive, commodity-type items such as analgesics and vitamins.

Formulation is much more than just chemical composition. It involves all the elements to make a good product—release of active ingredients within specified time, appearance (especially with tablets), mouth feel and taste in the case of chewables, and extended shelf-life stability. These skills are very important since the marketplace wants a product that resembles the branded item as closely as possible.

Quality control is an important aspect of the manufacturing process. All raw materials are tested before use for purity and identity. Each batch of finished product is tested to be sure it meets the label claims and other parameters of U.S. Pharmacopeia. The first three batches of a new product are tested for stability and shelf life.

MARKETS; SELLING

Evans Pharmaceuticals serves the OTC market in two ways—as a contract manufacturer of the customer's proprietary products and as a manufacturer of the Company's products for the private-label market. The Company started its existence as a contract manufacturer as a matter of necessity. The time between bidding on and manufacturing a product already on the market averages about three months. In contrast, the time it takes to get one's first private-label product into a chain is about a year, most of which time is needed to get chain approval as a vendor. This approval is then good for any product of the vendor. However, the chain will perform its own tests on each of the vendor's products which are of interest to the chain.

As a contract manufacturer, Evans makes the customer's proprietary product, which is sold only to that customer. Product in dosage form is shipped in bulk and the customer does its own packaging. In the case of four contract customers, Evans is the exclusive manufacturer of Evans-formulated products, which are sold as brand names of those customers. There is no active soliciting of contract customers. Most come in through word of mouth, Company reputation, and people who know Dave Evans.

As part of its original plan, in the past twelve months Evans entered the private-label market of sales to the large drug, supermarket, and other mass-market retail chains that sell OTC items under their own labels. These retailers typically like to carry the brand name product and the equivalent store brand, which is priced at retail 30–40 percent below the branded items and which still gives the retailer a better margin than the brand.

Evans introduced itself to the private-label market by displaying its packaged products in a booth at the November 1986 private-label trade show in Chicago. It began shipments to this market in March 1987. Here products are packaged by the Company with the customer's label and are ready for the retail shelf when shipped. In this business, one item may be sold to several customers; only the labels differ. The advantages to Evans of this market are higher profit margins, longer production runs, spread of

Exhibit 5
KEMPER'S PROPOSAL FOR A PRIVATE PLACEMENT (*continued*)

R&D and startup costs over several customers, and avoidance of certain disadvantages of contract work (frequent shutdown to change products, risk of cross-contamination).

To reach the private-label market, it is necessary to have a manufacturers' rep organization since the chains prefer to deal with reps rather than manufacturers. At the November 1986 show, Evans retained a master rep, an individual well established with the chain store buyers, who has put together six rep organizations that cover the nation. When so requested, Dave Evans accompanies reps on calls upon customers or prospects. Because of the success of the reps, the Company expects its fiscal 1988 sales to comfortably exceed the projected $2.3 million.

Customers (both contract and private label) generally do not enter into written agreements. They do give an oral indication of expected volumes and approximate delivery dates which facilitates production and cash flow planning. Such indications may cover a period as long as a year. Customers usually have a back-up source as insurance against any disruption of the Evans operation.

COMPETITION

There are many companies involved in one or more phases of the OTC private-label market. Some perform only one or two of the blending, tabletting, coating and packaging operations. Some have very limited product lines or concentrate on volume commodity items. Major companies in the private label market are Perrigo (part of Grow Groups since February 1986), Pennex Corporations, and Private Formulations Inc. (formerly part of Revco Drug Stores and now part of Pharmacontrol). Evans competes little with the larger ones but does compete on some products with Ford Laboratories and Guardian Drug on antacids and with Generic Sal Inc. on laxatives. On some products the Company believes it has no competition from other private label manufacturers.

The Company believes its competitive position is enhanced by the fact that (1) it is prime in everything starting with formulation through packaging; (2) its pricing is competitive, especially because it is prime; (3) customers have a loyalty to valued suppliers; and (4) it has credibility with the customer as demonstrated by its prior experience with other accounts.

PLANT FACILITIES—PRESENT AND FUTURE

The Company presently leases an 8,500-square-foot facility in Cottage Grove, Oregon (the west-central part of the state, near I-5) under a lease ending in May 1989. The annual rental is $16,800. Recently it has leased an additional 3,500 square feet at two nearby locations for warehousing and some packaging operations.

The proposed new facility will be located in a new industrial park in Springfield, Oregon, a short distance from the present plant. The contemplated 25,000-square-foot building will basically be a general purpose industrial building adapted to the Company's needs. The probable site has a gentle slope, and the two-story building will be placed so that each story has a ground level entrance. The layout calls for the second story to have receiving dock, warehousing, quality control, weighing and blending of raw materials. The blended materials will flow by gravity to the lower floor where there will be the press room (tabletting, coating), inspection, packaging and shipping. As compared with the present plant, the new one will have greater efficiency (better layout, gravity flow of materials, consolidation of three facilities), less waste (elimination of certain hand-performed steps that now result in considerable spillage) and ease of cleaning. The plant will also be equipped to manufacture liquid products.

Management estimates that the present sales level is more than adequate to cover the breakeven point of the new plant. This facility will probably be adequate to allow sales to grow to the $8 million level. To go beyond that level, the Company would expect to expand the building to 40,000 square feet and with that addition it will then add effervescents to the product line; the projections reflect a capital expenditure of $450,000 in fiscal 1990 for this expansion phase.

MANAGEMENT BIOGRAPHIES

David J. Evans, the founder and president, has a B.S. in biochemistry from the University of Idaho and attended graduate school at Idaho in animal science, University of Minnesota in industrial pharmacy, and Drake University in business management. He spent ten years at G. C. Searle—seven years in pharmaceutical research studying cardiopulmonary drugs and three years in the Chemicals Division as a technical consultant to the pharmaceutical industry. In this latter position he worked closely with the Searle salesmen in advising customers on matters such as formulation and manufacturing; customers ran the gamut from small drug companies to the major ethical houses. He and a partner founded Plateau Laboratories, an OTC pharmaceutical manufacturer. Having ambitions greater than the partner's, he sold out to the partner after four years. He then founded the Company, which is owned by his wife and himself.

EMPLOYEES

Evans presently has twenty-one employees—two executive-management, two quality control, three office, and fourteen production hourly. By the end of the first year in the new plant, employment will rise to about forty—two executive-management, two quality control, four office, and thirty to thirty-two production hourly. By the end of the fiscal 1992, total employment is projected at seventy-five people—fourteen management, quality control, and office and sixty-one production.

FINANCIAL

Historical and projected financial data are presented in the following appendices to this memorandum:

DAVIS PHARMACEUTICALS, INC: PROJECTED INCOME STATEMENTS, YEARS ENDING APRIL 30 (in thousands)

	1988	1989	1990	1991	1992
Gross Sales	$2,272	$6,270	$8,500	$12,000	$15,000
Less: returns and allowances	24	94	128	180	225
Net Sales	$2,238	$6,176	$8,372	$11,820	$14,775
Less Cost of Sales	1,442	3,829	5,024	6,856	8,422
Gross Profit	796	2,347	3,348	4,964	6,353
Less Selling, General and Administrative Expenses					
Commissions	$ 59	$ 306	$ 469	$ 780	$ 975
Other	268	494	706	995	1,285
Total	327	800	1,175	1,775	2,260
Operating Profit	$ 469	$1,547	$2,173	$ 3,189	$ 4,093
Less Interest Expense	77	89	81	74	68
Pretax Income	$ 392	$1,458	$2,092	$ 3,115	$ 4,025
Less Income taxes	87	583	837	1,246	1,610
NET INCOME	$ 315	$ 875	$1,255	$ 1,869	$ 2,415

Exhibit 5
KEMPER'S PROPOSAL FOR A PRIVATE PLACEMENT (*continued*)

PROJECTION ASSUMPTIONS
1. OEA financing (or construction loans backed with OEA commitment) taken down on January 1, 1988, and proceeds of the debt and equity financings are expended as planned by April 30, 1988, even though completion of the plant and move-in are expected to be about July 1, 1988.
2. OEA loans: $800,000 for real estate repayable over 200 years ($40,000 per year) and $75,000 for equipment repayable over 10 years ($8,000 per year). Interest at 8.5 percent, which includes ½ of 1 percent for mortgage insurance. Repayments of principal start on April 30, 1989, and each April 30 thereafter.
3. Tax loss carry forwards and available investment tax credits are used up in fiscal 1988; thereafter, federal and state taxes at 40 percent.
4. Capital expenditures: fiscal 1989 includes $100,000 for equipment to manufacture liquid products; fiscal 1990 includes $450,000 for a 15,000-square-foot addition and equipment to manufacture effervescents.
5. Excess cash generated by operations is accumulated, and income statements do not include any return on this cash from its investment in short term securities or accelerated retirement of debt.

DAVIS PHARMACEUTICALS, INC: PROJECTED INCOME
STATEMENTS YEARS ENDING APRIL 30 (in thousands)

	1988	1989	1990	1991	1992
ASSETS					
Current Assets					
Cash	$ 248	$ 258	$ 662	$1,922	$3,821
Accounts receivable	276	761	1,032	1,457	1,822
Inventory	337	892	1,170	1,597	1,961
Prepaid items	8	8	8	8	8
Total Current Assets	$ 869	$1,919	$2,872	$4,984	$7,612
Fixed Assets					
Property, plant and equipment, net	$1,221	$1,257	$1,663	$1,603	$1,540
Moving and financing costs capitalized	150	120	90	60	30
Total Fixed Assets	1,371	1,377	1,753	1,663	1,570
TOTAL ASSETS	$2,240	$3,296	$4,625	$6,647	$9,182
TOTAL LIABILITIES AND NET WORTH					
Current Liabilities					
Accounts payable and accrued expenses	$ 218	$ 472	$ 619	$ 845	$1,038
Current long-term debt					
OEA debt	48	48	48	48	48
Other	25	25	25	25	25
Total Current Liabilities	$ 291	$ 545	$ 692	$ 918	$1,111

Long-Term Debt					
OEA	$ 827	$ 779	$ 731	$ 683	$ 635
Other	114	89	64	39	14
Long-Term Debt	941	868	795	722	649
Total Liabilities	$1,232	$1,413	$1,487	$1,640	$1,760
Net Worth	1,008	1,883	3,138	5,007	7,422
TOTAL LIABILITIES AND NET WORTH	$2,240	$3,296	$4,625	$6,647	$9,182

EVANS PHARMA-CEUTICALS, INC. (B)

JOHN CLAIR THOMPSON
University of Connecticut

As he had often said to himself, Dave Evans badly needed to find breathing room. Being the head of his own firm, Evans Pharmaceuticals, meant that all problems came to him eventually—many for solution by him personally. This involved him in such immediate matters of operating a rapidly-growing business on a daily basis as arranging short-term financing, talking to customers, hiring employees, tracing shipments, and even occasionally filling in at the plant. What always seemed to be sacrificed for those daily problems was pushing ahead on a long-term business plan with its critical analytical and normative content. As his banker, Jim Baldwin, had said: "It's too easy for Dave to get bogged down in tactical decisions and never get time for the strategic ones."

Evans was to meet the next Monday, November 9, 1987, with a consultant in strategy and planning with whom he had been working on and off since June of that year on all manner of concerns to the firm. Although the consultant, John Brittain, had particular skills and experience in long-term, strategic work, his efforts on behalf of Evans had extended to setting up short-term cash-flow systems and projecting five-year financial statements, as well as collaborating with Evans in analyzing, as they arose, many facets of the firm's operations and future plans.

It was not the moment, Dave Evans thought, to press ahead to draw up a true business plan. Oddly enough, he had in hand two documents, each of which could, by some definitions, serve as such a plan. One was an analysis that he himself had written, which laid out, in a general way, the sequence of developments in the firm's markets and products and plant investment. But Brittain had criticized this plan, saying that Evans's approach was inverted because it indicated his intentions and concluded with an examination of the volume of business necessary to support the plant and equipment Dave Evans expected to be utilizing in the late 1980s. Brittain insisted that the plan should instead have derived the market volumes that Evans could command based on market growth and competitive analyses and only then get into the capital investment justified by the business volume that Evans could do.

Another business-plan candidate was the prospectus prepared by James Kemper,[1] a specialist in private equity placements, which described the existing firm and its business, discussed Evans's proposed move to a new plant, and included a set of five-year financial projections. The comments by Brittain on this plan were kinder: appropriate segments would serve well as a mandatory attachment for an application to the Oregon Economic Assistance program for subsidies for the funding of the new plant. Perhaps naturally, Brittain had reservations that even Kemper's shrewd and objective narrative lacked the explicit analyses of the market and competition that would constitute a true strategy-formulation effort, let alone one that incorporated also a workable blueprint dealing with the imple-

---

This case, written specifically for class use at the University of Connecticut, is printed by permission.

1. See Case 33(A) for Kemper's prospectus and an exploration of the issues it involved.

mentation of the strategy contained in the statement.[2]

In the moments that other concerns had permitted them to devote over the summer and fall to questions of conducting a proper and complete development of a business plan, Evans and Brittain had talked back and forth about Brittain's concepts of planning. In fact, Brittain had given him some write-ups of ideas he had worked on over many years.

One summarized a process for analyzing situations evolved by Brittain and termed *PSDM* (for problem solving and decision making). Evans rather thought that this might serve well as an outline for his own reexamination of his firm for purposes of preparing for his meeting with Brittain to decide on the pattern of studying the firm.

The other was a longer document also written by Brittain bearing on the nature of planning. It was Brittain's sense that there were a lot of possibilities when it came to saying what planning was really going to produce in the way of written output. Specifically, Brittain stated that several emphases or even alternatives were often mentioned when planning came up:

1. *Method*—the how-to-do-it, especially environmental scanning
2. *Output*—the documents and paperwork, especially the formats
3. *Content*—the statements of the what, who, where, when, and how of implementation
4. *Process design*—the information flows and decision-making sequences
5. *Systems integration*—the connections with other systems, especially those for motivation, rewarding, and controlling

From this welter of possibilities, Brittain had conveyed his belief that the core relevancies for a business plan intended for the top management's most fundamental understanding and preparation for the future were what he had termed content, together with proper attention to the matters of systems integration. Nevertheless, Evans and Brittain had discussed the necessity to show explicitly as part of the plan just how the conclusions were arrived at.

---

2. For Brittain's own proposals of a fully-analytical program of planning for Evans, see the Evans Pharmaceuticals, Inc. (C) case.

Therefore, the other three alternatives also had something important to contribute, particularly method, with its concern for environmental scanning. The upshot was that Evans was convinced, after long discussion of the manner in which they should proceed, that Brittain's PSDM format—with some tailoring of its final steps to incorporate extra consideration of future implementation and a step-by-step blueprint of upcoming activities in sequence—provided a useful indication of the process of generating the business plan for his firm. Accordingly, Evans determined that he should himself go through Brittain's format in an attempt to review what he could before the two of them started to work.

Evans realized that it would be entirely in keeping with the thrust of Brittain's approach to be certain to accomplish all the essential tasks of the strategy process. Put this way, formulating and implementing strategy consisted of five abstract steps, the first of which was identifying the principal elements of the business—giving an overall description and reducing some of the key items to classifications used by many strategic analysts. Second came analyzing twin frameworks. One had business and economic origins and was concerned with the external environment and the internal resources of the firm. From this set of considerations could come appraisals of the threats and opportunities stemming from the environment, as well as assessments of the relative strengths and weaknesses of the firm when compared to its competitors. It was interesting to Evans to recall that all this fitted neatly into the PSDM format: threats and weaknesses became problems; strengths became competitive advantages, the most pivotal of which was the firm's distinctive competence; and opportunities were not only an element in PSDM themselves, but also constituted the makings of complete alternatives.

The other framework involved in the analysis was that of values and ethics. Brittain argued that the personal values of the management, together with the larger responsibilities of the firm (as seen by its strategic managers) were, respectively, internal and external sources of the objectives that bore so weightily on management's eventual decisions.

The third step—evaluating—continued to grapple with problems and objectives through assigning priorities to both of them. Moreover, the alternatives the firm had discerned for itself were to be evaluated at this stage too. Spilling over into the fourth step—recommending one strategic alternative from among the handful established to provide the firm a true spectrum of choices—the earlier steps all had something to contribute.

Essentially, three criteria were applied to all alternatives: first was the strategic pattern feasible and workable, allowing for the fact that new resources and circumstances had to be allowed for in such long-term thinking; second were the problems, particularly considering their priorities, successfully confronted; and third were the objectives served, also giving proper moment to their priorities.

Finally, came the obvious fifth step in a PSDM effort involving a business plan: implementing the intellectual strategy by moving in two dimensions toward greater specification. First it would be necessary to break down the overall strategy into policies key to furnishing the building blocks of accomplishment. Second it would be necessary to devise a time sequence that worked within the somewhat more detailed, policy-level layout to provide the needed blueprint of activities, each with its time frame indicated.

BACKGROUND OF THE COMPANY

In November of 1987, Evans Pharmaceuticals was in its fourth year of operation, having finally become profitable in its fiscal year ended the previous April 30. It had begun as a supplier of nonprescription drugs to those who would package them and market them at retail under the retailer's name in competition with national brands. This business—the so-called contract business—was relatively simple since it entailed no packaging by Evans except to ship the product in bulk in drums.

Another business, the private-label line, had been started in earnest only early in 1987. In this instance, Evans not only produced the generic product but also packaged it in a form physically identical to that used by the nationally branded product. Often, the generic product even mimicked the branded product's packaging, right down to using the same colors and style of label. (Needless to say, the generic product itself was identical to the branded product in terms of chemical compounding, physical size and form, and such characteristics as color and coating.)

While the private-label business was more profitable for Evans, it was also more complicated since each order had its own packaging requirements. Nevertheless, this was the segment that Evans was counting on to provide most of the significant growth he anticipated for the firm over the next few years. (Sometime in the early 1990s, he wanted to begin his own line of Evans-branded products, but this would require a major front-end advertising effort at the same time it put the firm into new lines such as cosmetics and perfumes.)

At the moment, whether contract or private-brand, products fell into three main categories although there were about fifty specific items manufactured. Antacids were produced to give the retailer an item similar to Tums, Rolaids, Maalox, Gaviscon, or other brand names. Laxatives constituted the second category and Evans mimicked such brands as Dulcolax, Correctol, and Ex-Lax. Finally, there were the cough and cold remedies and allergy medicines and stimulants such as Actifed, Dristan, Contac, and Sudafed to be matched.

The only form of drugs produced in 1987 was dry products—tablets or pills, which could be sugar- or film-coated or uncoated. As for packaging, they could (for the private-label market) be put into plastic blister strips and sold in boxes, rolled in aluminum foil, or put into glass or plastic bottles.

Dave Evans was chafing in a plant that had already reached its efficient capacity and would soon be at its all-out limit. He hoped to construct and occupy a modern plant in less than a year's time, and once settled there intended gradually to add other product forms—liquids, ointments, and effervescents. With these in his offerings, sales for fiscal 1992 had been projected at $15 million. He anticipated this growth would come predominantly from new generics (as well as existing ones), which would gain at the expense of higher-priced branded products, rather than by diverting volume from competitors with already established generics through price shaving.

PRESENT STRATEGIES AND DISTINCTIVE COMPETENCE

Dave Evans knew that Brittain not only had subheadings in the PSDM format but also that he employed a summary shorthand notation to help him characterize the pattern under each. There were two types of present strategies, for instance. One of them, categorical strategy, was concerned with the dynamic nature of the firm's product-market scope. Brittain termed Evans Pharmaceutical's situation diversification because the firm was embarked upon a deliberate program to broaden its offerings in physical form as well as product type. Moreover, these extensions of its initial product line would involve changes also in its manufacturing, marketing, and other policies so that most of the firm's nature would be altered over time by the diversification.

Since Evans's strategy was expansion, two of Brittain's categories plainly did not fit—specialization (narrowing the business lines to a restricted set of products) and liquidation (getting out of the business entirely). On the other hand, three other categories did fit to some extent, even though they were not the main thrust strategically. One was do nothing; in other words, pursue the indicated path of the firm's existing product-market scope. Certainly, Evans was doing this in a major way, for it was not giving up products or markets that it had already established; indeed, it would probably do everything possible to intensify its penetration of these markets to maximize its sales opportunities.

Another strategy category was territorial expansion—whether domestic (to reach beyond regional markets while staying in the United States) or international—to extend the same products into settings in new countries. This was largely inapplicable to Evans Pharmaceuticals since the firm already marketed nationally in the United States, and since international markets for generics were mostly (and literally) unknown territory to Evans in 1987.

The last instance was rather problematic, but did hold some potential of significant strategic shifts which would be advantageous to Evans. It concerned further development of the firm's capacity to supply its needs internally by so-called backward vertical integration such as by manufacturing its own ingredient materials or fabricating packages, or by forward integration, such as in the instances of building its own sales force or even getting into wholesaling or other distribution or logistical activities.

While strategies were defined differently from analyst to analyst, the companion counterpart—the generic strategy—was a matter of wide agreement among analysts, and even was an insight that could be attributed to the work of a single student of strategy, Professor Michael E. Porter of the Harvard Business School. It was Porter's contribution to draw on the industrial-organization stream of thought in microeconomics to derive three possibilities: cost leadership, differentiation, and focus.

Brittain's explanation of the three emphasized that, in accounting for the manner in which the subject firm competed with its rivals, the first relied on the traditional economic advantage of lower price to the customer, the second relied on the product's qualitative dimensions to distinguish it from competing products (in the process obscuring price differences), and the last relied on occupying a niche or limited area in the market, which again avoided price confrontations and comparisons—in fact, all confrontations and comparisons, since the firm was able to carry out its specific production and distribution in an incomparable fashion.

In particular, focus implied that the firm's superior features permitted it to withstand rivals' prices and qualities—or perhaps just to be so small (relatively) that its large rivals did not find the necessary rigorous competition worth the market's potentials, unlike the incumbent. It was a useful supplementary idea of Porter's that the generic strategy of focus was compatible with either of the other two, the reason being that it depended more on size and importance of the firm than on the substantive manner in which it competed.

When all this was applied to Evans Pharmaceuticals, the basic outcome was that the firm was most clearly a cost-leadership competitor because of its approach to the fundamental market for nonprescription drugs. There was also more than a hint of focus because the emphasis in Evans's selling was to reach the large-volume chains and to target only a selected group of over-the-counter medications—antacids, laxatives, and cough-cold remedies and related preparations.

Interestingly enough, two further aspects shed light on the generic strategy, especially in its relationship to the categorical strategy. First, product differentiation did not really account for Evans's past successes or its outstanding prospects. However, in a secondary way, the firm, like any other, did meet (and often exceed) expectations concerning qualitative performance, not only of the product itself, but also of the firm's delivery and other aspects of customer relations—in this instance, the chains and other immediate customers with whom it dealt.

As a matter of fact, Dave Evans said that every supplier had to meet rigorous standards set by the Federal Drug Administration and by the U.S. Pharmacopoeia for content, purity, and other criteria. Thus, product reliability, performance, shelf-life, and the like were not really differences by which customers could distinguish among the generic producers. As Dave Evans put it, "It's not just zero defects; all of the suppliers must do that."

Nevertheless, like firms everywhere, Evans—while relying primarily on the competitive weapon of low price—did all it could to appeal to customers in the qualitative dimensions. Furthermore, although the firm might well someday have to mobilize its ability to beat the competitors on price, it seemed clear that, over time, as it moved toward offerings of products under its own name, Evans would gradually come to greater reliance on advantages of the product-differentiation sort.

The second revealing aspect was that, in light of the plain categorical strategy of the firm to diversify over time, the generic strategy of focus would eventually disappear for all practical purposes. The greater breadth of products and product lines and even possibly further penetration of the group of wholesalers and chains with its products would increasingly make Evans a broad-line competitor. In fact, growth to the extent predicted by Dave Evans and recorded in the projected financial statements would surely place Evans Pharmaceuticals among the handful of the largest firms in its industry. It would therefore no longer be able to hide from view or avoid the attention of competitors—present and potential—due to its small size or its relative insignificance in the market. Instead, it might well become the firm to attack when competitors sought a market opening.

This sort of identification and reflection on strategic characteristics made all the more important one last general identifying description: the distinctive competence of the firm—the specific ability of the firm or its products to outperform the competitive rivals in such a way as to capture the customers' business over those rivals. In the instance of Evans, Dave Evans believed that it was a combination of little things: accommodating delivery, special properties of his drug formulations (like no sodium), and

other extras that were uncommon in a high-spec, low-tech business. Dave Evans may have summarized his advantages when he said that he always strived for "a reasonable production plan and to keep customers happy; I see that as my function as head of the firm."

SUPPORTING POLICIES

Patterns characterizing the functional and nonfunctional activities of the firm that carried out the strategies at the next lower level were thought of as critical to identify in order to understand the way an organization went about its business. The functional policies pertained to activities in the sequence of pushing the output through the stages of production from purchasing through manufacturing to delivery. Nonfunctional activities were those that—in contrast to functional efforts, which were ordinarily confined to a given stage and to a specific department and expertise—involved several departments, stages, or sorts of professional expertise. Pricing, personnel, and accounting were examples of such policies.

These provisions for functional and nonfunctional activities were recognized in most organizations as key arrangements for implementing the overall strategies. In the best-run companies, advice and consultation from those most intimately involved with the making and execution of the individual policies were seen to be invaluable in formulating the strategies which they ultimately were to carry out. Indeed, one reason why well-aimed strategies failed was equally well known to be inefficiency and ineffectiveness at the policy level—inability to carry through the strategic direction.

For these reasons, Dave Evans agreed that careful review of the main policies at Evans Pharmaceuticals would be a useful exercise in devising a thorough business plan that was grounded in how things actually worked in his firm. He knew, too, that it would be important to evaluate how well each of the policy areas seemed to be adapting to the changes coming to the firm as the new product lines and customers were steadily being added. In particular, Brittain had encouraged him to weigh the likely impacts of greater volume, longer production runs, and other possible consequences of growth so that economies of utilization, scale, and scope could be pinned down—and even facilitated—through planning at this second level.

Purchasing

In 1987 Evans was a manufacturer and packager, so for its limited combinations of products and customers it was possible to use worksheets that indicated, for Evan's standard batch size, what the product's ingredients were and what they cost. The worksheets were the responsibility of Dave Evans and his production manager, Christopher Beard; the actual ordering fell to the women in the firm's office, primarily Lynn Simmons, the bookkeeper (and Evans's sister-in-law). As with so many operations in such a small firm, however, arrangements with suppliers were never far from reference back to Dave Evans when there were questions or difficulties.

Delivery from the suppliers was ordinarily quick in spite of Evans Pharmaceuticals' seemingly remote location. The greatest obstacle to establishing a smooth and unruffled purchasing routine recently had been the cash-flow shortages and the resulting delays in paying bills. For a smaller firm like Evans, some suppliers were reluctant to give any credit and demanded COD terms, meaning that there were occasions when Evans could not proceed to manufacture an order because the materials could not be delivered and paid for.

In turn, this had led to an unusual, short-term-oriented decision concerning the trade-off between price and credit terms. Although Dave Evans declared that "mostly, suppliers won't budge on prices," the combination of price and credit evidently provided more room for bargaining. In the summer of 1987, for example, to alleviate the situation of restricted funds, Dave Evans had elected to purchase materials from a national chemical supplier for 80 cents a pound, rather than buy at 60 cents a pound from an alternate supplier because the first firm would give 60 days credit while the second offered short-term credit only.

Production

In the blueprints for his new plant, Evans intended not only to have a logical sequence of product movement through the various steps of manufacturing, but also to utilize such sophisticated means as gravity flow from one floor to the lower one. At one end of the plant would be the receiving area; next, materials would come to the weigh room; then they would be processed through steps involving wet-grinding, granulating, drying, and final-blending—in the instance of producing dry tablets. Finally, the powder would be punched into tablet form and the tablets would be coated either with film or with sugar, inspected, packaged, and shipped.

In 1987, the existing plant, crowded due to growing pressures on capacity and adapted for manufacturing dry tablets, used general-purpose machines to handle batches produced to order. To relieve some of the capacity pinch, Dave Evans frequently scheduled two shifts as well as Saturday work. Still, the nature of batch processing meant that setting up and getting ready for a particular order and later cleaning up (to avoid contaminating products flowing through the same machinery) was anything but smooth and wholly predictable.

Quality assurance was an integral part of production, beginning at the point when materials arrived to be brought together on a packing skid with others intended for the same order. This testing in the firm's own assay laboratory as materials were used was later followed up by two activities: sample-testing the product for label claims and inspecting 100 percent of the finished tablets as well as testing the packaged product for shelf life.

To save space in the main plant, packaging had been moved to a rented floor in an old factory building several miles away. Evans did its own packaging of tablets—in drums (for contract customers) and in glass or plastic bottles and in foil-wrapped rolls for private-label customers—except for encasing the tablets that went in so-called blister packs of plastic. The dies to shape the plastic were unique to each package and were so expensive that Dave Evans had chosen to subcontract the packaging of products in this form to outside specialists.

On the whole then, the increasing pressures on capacity had brought about responses manifest in several jury-rigged solutions to the difficulties. The lack of warehouse space had let to hand-to-mouth ordering and to immediate shipping—although both these were influenced also by the urgencies about cash flow. Similarly, the lack of production space and the inability to schedule production in the most efficient manner meant that individual batches could not be put in the sequences that would optimize the setup and clean-up efforts.

The solutions adopted—including backing two truck bodies up to the plant on a semipermanent basis to add some storage space and using auxiliary space nearby for packaging—really meant that Evans was always scrambling ingeniously for ways to improve its effective utilization of its plant. The conclusion had to be that theoretical estimates of capacity output were doomed to be unmet because of the frictions and inefficiencies in the production system (as well as the marketing methods and the nature of the output itself).

Marketing

Customer development was the key marketing activity. As Dave Evans would point out, getting the firm's products on a customer's accepted list inevitably produced orders for the products. At one time—when all sales were to contract buyers— Dave Evans had handled all marketing himself; since late 1986, however, and the start of Evans Pharmaceuticals' private-label sales, the firm had worked through representatives who received a commission on sales as compensation. (Thinking ahead, Dave Evans stated that he would need his own reps when the firm began selling products under its own label. He also understood that it might become economical—with a relatively small number of large, active accounts and the large sales he confidently expected in the next five years—to have his own exclusive reps, even for the private-label business.)

The reps would make the contacts with the headquarters of the target customer, providing sample products for the buyer to test for specifications, taste, smell, and stability. When and if approved after testing—and if the price from Evans were right—the orders would be expected to come shortly, along with the artwork that the customer and Evans would evolve to put on the package.

Since Evans was really only in the early stages of developing private-label volume, there were retail firms from which the company had obtained approval but from which Evans had not yet received any orders. Still, Dave Evans was proud of the fact that his firm was on the lists of the five largest chains in the United States, including Walgreen, Rite-Aid, CVS, and others—drug retailers that aggregated a total of some 8,000 stores.

The manner in which the drug chains decided to match a brand-name item with a generic product under private label was simple—and it explained why every product and package type was not matched when one inspected retail shelves: the retailer wanted the generic to promise to do at least one-third the volume of the brand-name item. In ab-

solute terms, this translated into a minimum of fifteen dozen sales per store per year. This 180 sales per store totaled 1,440,000 for all 8,000 stores; when converted to dollars using Dave Evans's rule-of-thumb of $0.80 per item, gave a result of $1.152 million in annual revenues for Evans Pharmaceuticals for each product sold across the board to all the major chains.

Pricing

For contract customers, the price charged by Evans was not in a fixed relationship with the ultimate shelf price for the product because of variations in the number of stages of channels the product might have to pass through. Still, Dave Evans made it clear that the price he received for contract output, albeit for products he did not have to package individually but merely sent off in bulk, was much lower than for similar private-label work.

In general, the price to private-label customers was heavily influenced by competitive factors. The brand-name product that a drug chain was selling provided the benchmark for this measurement. The following comparison shows the typical relationships that the customer tried to achieve when it added a generic substitute under its own name:

	BRAND PRODUCT	GENERIC PRODUCT
Retail price	$2.00	$1.20
Cost to retailer from brand manufacturer or from Evans	1.60	.80
Retailer's margin	$0.40	$0.40

The sample calculation contains two critical check points: first the retailer sought to achieve a striking difference between the brand-name and the generic product—not just shave the price a bit. Second, the chain strove to earn the same absolute margin on the two products, a criterion that helped to ensure, in connection with the minimum-volume test, that always scarce shelf space would be productive if turned to generic products.

All these relationships explained why Dave Evans had said to Brittain, early in their acquaintance, "I wonder whether I am making money on everything—is my pricing right?" Using his worksheets for each product, Evans's approach was heavily cost-oriented and principally functioned to let him know whether he was staying safely under the price the chains could accommodate at the same time it ensured him that he was covering his full costs. Again, a sample calculation for a roll of ten antacid tablets packaged in foil is illustrative:

Materials	1.8 cents
Labor	2.0
Foil	0.5
Total out-of-pocket costs	4.3 cents
Gross margin	6.7
Evans's selling price	11.0 cents
Retailer's selling price	30.0 –33.0 cents

Brittain had pressed Dave Evans about the worksheets and the costing and pricing processes because Evans's situation was so unusual: the pricing was ordinarily done once and for all and not revised unless there were cost increments due to inflation or other noticeable boosts by suppliers (although no such adjustments were occurring in 1987). Similarly, the independent pricing by Evans was more a negotiating stance than true price-setting since competition set the ceiling and Evans had little opportunity to price aggressively upward. Emphasis was really on acceptance (or rejection) of the original price; there was relatively little latitude to alter that price subsequently unless the adjustment could be rationalized to the customer.

The worksheet and its cost information—identifying costs, allocating and applying general and administrative expenses, and setting gross margins—Brittain had argued, were not the whole point. He stressed the possibility that the scarce space in the plant could be best utilized by trying to concentrate on the products that returned the most gross margin for the time they required including setup and clean-up in the plant. Of course, this assumed that the product mix could be skewed to take advantage of the nominal margins, and it further assumed that the worksheets were accurate and up-to-date.

So far as the costs on the worksheets were concerned, Evans had a policy of treating labor costs as fixed expenses since people were kept on permanently and there had historically been some slack in the plant. In constructing the worksheet, Evans's practice was to add to the total of materials and labor costs the average of what he called G and A costs for the previous year based on the firm's income-statement ratios. The question naturally arose whether this should be subject to a rolling revision as both plant utilization (in the denominator) and overhead costs (in the numerator) changed over time. In this light, Evans had done nothing to date to arrange for the future by working its hardest to produce and market the items that carried the highest gross margins, instead building volume rather opportunistically.

So while the combination of circumstances and policy bearing on pricing constrained what Dave Evans could do, Brittain's larger argument that cost was not the only basis for pricing that had to be given some attention. Nevertheless, the information from well-maintained and well-focused worksheets had a considerable potential to aid the firm not only with pricing, but also with production priorities, choice of new products, and other decisions and policies.

Accounting and Control

Another set of arrangements worth reviewing, in Dave Evans's mind, were the firm's policies concerning its books. Actually, although Evans Pharmaceuticals had an outside accountant who was a CPA, the man only worked on demand for hourly fees and had not, to date, ever prepared any audited statements for the firm. He did the annual statements routinely but did not actively participate in advising Dave Evans on either specific current problems or on questions of improving or adapting the firm's accounting systems.

For example, it was only at the behest of Baldwin and his bank (when the overdrafts and late payments became frightening) that Evans had first called in Brittain in the summer of 1987 to help get a weekly cash-flow system started. Furthermore, the firm utilized no cost accounting techniques to provide budgets or measures of variances from standard costs, even though its product-by-product worksheets furnished a usable model and contained all the essential data upon which such a system could be based.

The firm used FIFO accounting for its inventories (for whatever it mattered, since mostly it operated on a hand-to-mouth basis on materials), had minimal work-in-process because the production process was relatively short, and did not accumulate finished goods after completion because they were shipped as soon as possible to meet the order which had initiated the production in the first place. These characteristics of a batch-process firm, added to the stability of costs in the products' manufacture, meant that there would be little impact of this inventory-costing policy on financial performance.

Similarly, the firm's depreciation policy in the existing rented plant with the modest amount of owned equipment was the orthodox approach to amortization—straight-line for the permitted life. Over the summer of 1987, events and comments from outsiders, both consultants and financial contacts, had brought Dave Evans around to questioning the bases for his accounting treatments and statements. Although he had said once to Brittain that "he never put together 'la-la land' pro-formas to fool anybody" and that he "never lied to the bank," he was taken by the ideas from Brittain and Baldwin that different statements might be used for different purposes and for different audiences.

The firm had lost money for the first two years of its existence and that tax-loss carry-forward had covered the modest profit in fiscal 1987 and would probably also cancel any taxes owned for fiscal 1988. Nevertheless, Evans Pharmaceuticals faced the prospects of considerable tax liabilities as it grew and prospered. Clearly, for tax purposes, it made sense to structure that set of books to take maximum advantage of depreciation, amortization, and treatments of other deductible costs. On the other hand, for banks and such outside financial interests as the OEA, showing higher profit performance by conservative treatments of costs and write-offs was attractive.

Finally, Brittain had insisted that neither of these sets of books, nor a set for the shareholders (if it differed materially), would be truly suitable for the management's purposes in making short-term and long-term decisions, which required quantitative information. For instance, none could presently provide cost accounting and incremental cost data, particularly if it were desirable to break out this information by product, by product line, by customer, and so on. Specifically, the lack of future-oriented accounting-type information (managerial accounting) probably meant that, over time, the firm would have to develop a much more sophisticated set of statements, better systems for creating them, and innovative formats for presenting data.

Just one example lay in the concerns Dave Evans continually had about refining his pricing. Since he relied on information from the worksheets to analyze prices, his basic approach in 1987 to determining his markup beyond direct costs was to use firm-wide historical costs from the latest annual income statement.

Beyond the obvious (and deceptive) short-cut both Evans and Brittain recognized in this approach, Evans knew too that even absolutely current worksheets were not enough for really tough competitive price setting. Getting measures able to reveal useful estimates of future costs would be one consideration, but demand and competitive factors that cost data could not reveal would surely need much more attention. While none of this diminished the significance of updated and relevant worksheets, it was apparent that a more focused presentation of pricing information—as well as an anticipatory approach—were going to be more important.

Finance

Dave Evans never had a day pass without hard thinking about financial policies.[3] In brief, both equity and debt were used, with bank loans that were essentially short term comprising the debt. Relative to its operating and strategic requirements, the company was pretty clearly undercapitalized. Evans had been told by both Baldwin and Brittain that more long-term capital was needed but that further bank borrowing probably would be adequate—substantial amounts of new equity with their impacts on Evans's control and comfort were not required as the two of them analyzed the financial projections.[4] Nevertheless, these assurances aside, Dave Evans struggled daily with unsettling financial pinches and it was not entirely comforting to be told that the long-term would be easy enough if he could just get past the rough water of the short-term.

---

3. See the Case 33(A), which treats the firm's financial situation, policies, and options thoroughly, tying them to strategic decisions and other matters. Included there are full financial statements for 1985–1987, as well as alternate sets of projected statements for 1988–1992 prepared by Brittain and by Kemper.
4. The pro-forma statements in Case 33(A) reflecting Kemper's judgments of the future disputed Baldwin and Brittain (and the latter's projections) concerning the need for outside equity in the late 1980s.

PRESENT IMPLEMENTATION

In Brittain's approach, present implementation was supposed to reveal how a chief executive like Dave Evans actually went about managing. Its elements were intended to separate the how from the what. Typically three principal dimensions—management systems, structure, and style—were put under the microscope because they cut across such substantive (supporting policy) matters as purchasing, production, marketing, pricing, accounting and control, and finance.

Dave Evans's systems, structure, and style were simple and direct. Systems, specifically, were concerned with information flows back and forth between management and the organization and with mechanisms such as planning and budgeting to utilize this information—through motivation and control, for instance.[5] Systems were informal but, as with structure, everything had to put Evans himself in the loop. Brittain was plainly suggesting that more thorough, more sophisticated information and control were indicated by Evans Pharmaceuticals' size and growing complexity. Evans did use its computer increasingly for recordkeeping and analysis, but it was often Dave Evans who did the work at the computer. Needless to add, Brittain was not satisfied that Evans was doing enough with planning systems.

Structure was essentially the organization chart dimension. At Evans Pharmaceuticals, structure was mostly flat, with everyone reporting to Dave Evans. Day-to-day production decisions and production planning were nominally handled by the production manager, but workers often came into Evans's office with product samples and Brittain had seen Evans haranguing one worker about the need to work overtime so an order deadline could be met. A poignant example of Evans's daily involvement was that on one occasion when Brittain called, Evans was working in the plant and had to wash up before he could come to the telephone.

As Brittain approached it, style constituted the personal manner in which a manager maintained contact with the activities of the organization—literally the way one went about managing. Evans's style would be fairly described as an intervening one: he did not rely on the firm's structure and systems to let him be a hands-off manager; he participated constantly, even in minor decisions.

In discussions, Evans and Brittain had agreed that change had to come in all these dimensions of present implementation if the firm were to grow and prosper. In fact, it was the difficulties that the outdated systems seemed to impose that had brought Brittain in to aid and advise Dave Evans in the first place.

PROBLEMS, OBJECTIVES, AND ALTERNATIVES

Finally, as Evans saw it, Brittain believed that no business plan truly would be complete without getting at the firm's problems, objectives, and alternatives through applying the new planning processes.[6] He and Brittain were soon scheduled to begin studying these aspects of the firm in detail, building up to them carefully. But Evans's views were already, at least to some extent, evident.

In late 1987, Dave Evans actually had listed his problems as follows:

1. Cash flow—needed to purchase materials to meet orders
2. Backlog of orders
3. Lack of space in which to produce shipments and expand volume—Evans said "we can max out every day"
4. Personnel—dependable and permanent employees

On hearing this recitation, Brittain had commented that they should back up and be sure they were both talking about the same thing. Like Baldwin, Brittain contended that problems should be seen in a longer focus, and that they thereby took on strategic weight. Looking to major challenges and threats in the environment and weaknesses in the firm's resources was what Brittain meant, not just immediate difficulties. Brittain, for instance, would have

---

5. Case 33(C) contains Brittain's comprehensive proposals to Dave Evans in November 1987 for systems for the firm.

6. Beyond showing Brittain's proposals for more sophisticated management systems or processes, Case 33(C) indicates fully the nature of the problems and objectives (by way of outlining steps for self-study and analysis) and suggests the role of alternatives in the ultimate long-term strategy formulation.

listed tough competitors and long-term industry demand conditions as prime problems for the firm.

When asked about objectives at this same time, Dave Evans had said that his four objectives in priority order were

1. To achieve $20 million sales within ten years
2. To maintain 17 percent net before taxes
3. To be out of the firm by the time he reached his early fifties
4. To get a new building

When Brittain pressed him a bit about the nature of these objectives and their priorities, again stressing that the list should look to the long-term and to major accomplishments, Evans had altered the lineup to

1. Profit of 17 percent
2. Control personnel (a new objective)
3. Sales of $20 million
4. Retirement by the time he reached his fifties

As for alternatives, just like strategic objectives and problems, Dave Evans recognized that any conversations with Brittain to date had only been to establish a kind of baseline because it was the explicit task of the business plan to expose and consider the three main elements of strategy formulation. Therefore, he did not have deep regrets that his thinking had not utterly exhausted the analysis of the broad options open to the firm.

Still, Evans had some ideas already. Clearly Evans Pharmaceuticals was looking toward expansion, but mostly this was taking the form of orderly development along what Brittain called do-nothing lines. True diversification was in the offing as new and different products—including a line of generics with an Evans name and possibly perfumes and cosmetics under a more romantic brand-name—were developed, manufactured, and marketed. Territorial expansion (internationally) and vertical integration backward had not been explored. Vertical integration forward into plastic-blister packaging and into marketing and distribution were real possibilities, however.

CONCLUSION

As Dave Evans looked back over his afternoon's review, there was much to do at Evans Pharmaceuticals; that he knew well. From his own point of view, the impact of the reflection was to raise two new and difficult questions that he would have to answer before proceeding:

1. Would all the elaborate efforts be necessary? He already knew that Brittain's program would call for hard, complex work.
2. Would he be able to find the time required to work with Brittain? Certainly it would require a lot of his scarcest resource, and he could not delegate it to anyone else.

EVANS PHARMA-CEUTICALS, INC. (C)

JOHN CLAIR THOMPSON
University of Connecticut

By late November of 1987, John J. Brittain believed that the time had come to wrap up his proposal to a client, David Evans, the chief executive of Evans Pharmaceuticals, for establishing both a business plan and an ongoing system of short- and long-term planning. After five months of observations and discussions in the course of his consulting, Brittain felt that he had seen and heard enough to permit him to make confident recommendations to Evans for the firm's efforts to draw up a solid plan for its strategy.[1]

Moreover, in keeping with a twenty-five-year-old conviction of his, Brittain was sure that the firm was capable of absorbing the lessons of planning as a process. That way, it would be able to do most of the analytical work for itself in the future and not have to call in Brittain or another consultant to perform further one-shot feats of analyzing competitive and other strategic circumstances. Instead, it could operate its own ongoing strategic planning system, all the while not only following up the initial patterns and processes but actually refining them to suit its particular needs.

For his presentation to Evans on November 27, Brittain had assembled a number of exhibits that constituted the work effort he believed would be necessary to give Evans a full and usable sense of its strategic circumstances.

This case, written specifically for class use at the University of Connecticut, is printed by permission.

1. See Case 33(A) for an extensive treatment of the decision-making concerning new capital funds for the firm; for Dave Evans's own PSDM-format analysis of the firm's situation, see Case 33(B).

First of all, there was a diagram (Exhibit 1) that attempted to integrate all the systems that Evans and Brittain had worked on, starting in the summer of 1987. It was basically a box of four cells with rows delineated by time frame (short-term versus long-term) and columns by factual status (budgeted versus actual). As a consequence, it could represent, for example, the facts that the cash-flow projections belonged in the short-term–budgeted cell and that strategic intelligence belonged in the long-term–actual cell. Still, the diagram's principal importance stemmed from its capacity to demonstrate the linkages among the various forms, statements, and analyses—particularly the information relationships among them, both as initial formulations and as feedback.

Significant for the background it could provide for this diagram was Exhibit 2, the budgeting and planning agenda, which Brittain had presented to Evans as a basis for discussion in July. Besides dealing with the substance of the efforts that Brittain was advocating that Evans undertake to improve performance, it made explicit two other facets, which Brittain believed were critical. First it indicated the progress made to that stage and then, building on that information, suggested priorities to be assigned to the specific activities, putting them in triage terms.

Triage essentially distinguished steps that were proceeding well and needed no further major attention to accomplish their purpose from steps of two other sorts. One was activities where management and consulting efforts were crucial to success; the other was work that could not yet be undertaken or helpfully influenced by such efforts. The point was that the middle group of activities was clearly where

Exhibit 1
EVANS PHARMACEUTICALS: INTEGRATION OF SYSTEMS

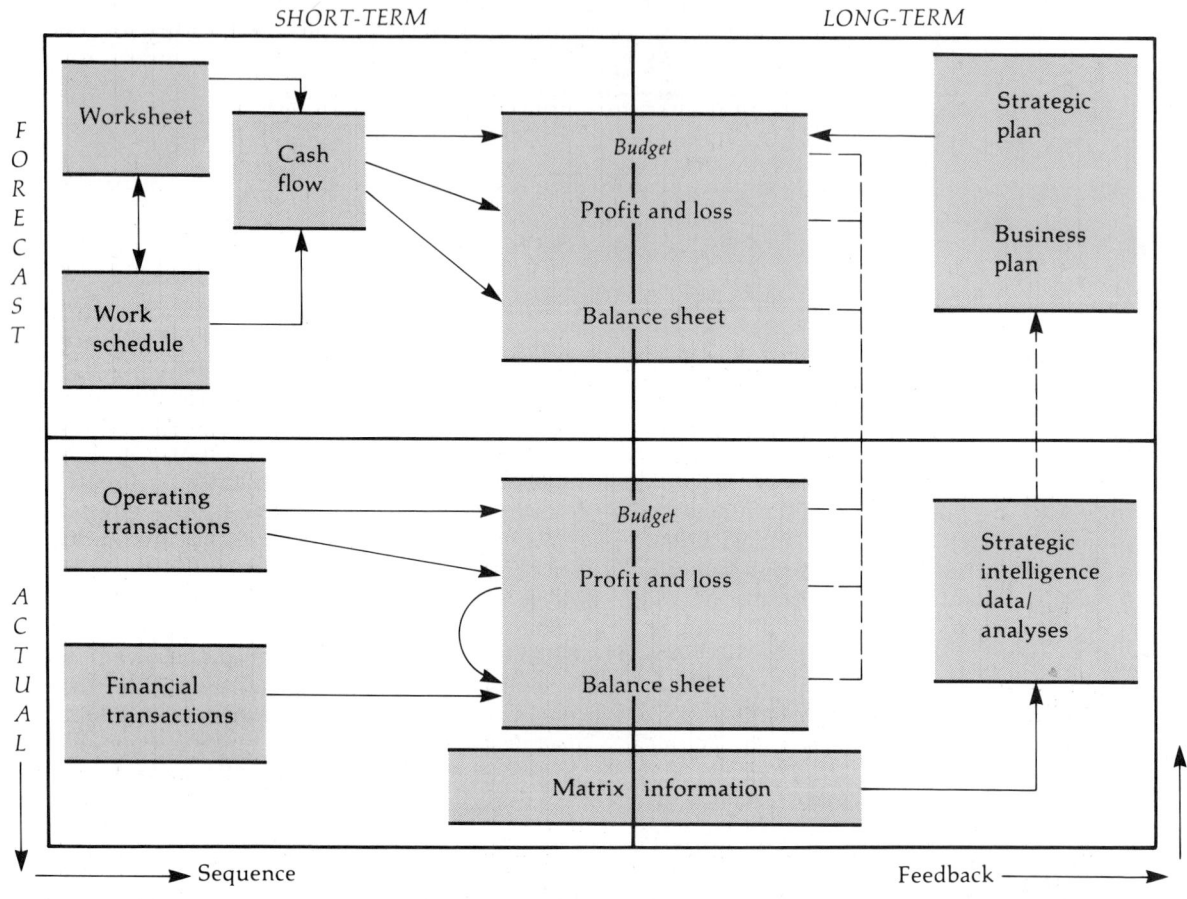

Exhibit 2
EVANS PHARMACEUTICALS: BUDGETING AND PLANNING AGENDA

This scheme is divided roughly into three sections according to the time frame indicated—short term, intermediate term, and long term. Implicitly, priority is given here (as it has been given in work to date) to the needs of the short term first. It is based on some materials already discussed cursorily and includes the following steps:

1. List more or less in sequence the specific activities involved in moving toward a better-organized and provided-for management structure and set of management systems, moving from the needs most imminent in the short-run to the ones sure to be positive and even necessary factors over the longer-run.

2. Clarify both the substance of these activities and their interrelations so that the cumulative effect of gradually introducing and adapting to their discipline can be understood, and ultimately, realized efficiently.

3. Aim toward a further effort (requiring considerable time and work) in which long-term strategy is given appropriate attention, recognizing that the logical step-wise procedure of first formulating strategy and then arranging for its implementation could not be utilized here (the initial short-term and other analyses and installations of approaches being based provisionally on a do-nothing strategy, in the sense of accepting the thrusts of strategies apparent at Evans Pharmaceuticals in June of 1987).

From the list of activities, it should be possible to distinguish (with the aid of some prompters supplied) what completion status each enjoys, as well as what further steps each requires for full effectiveness. As a general rule, most of the consultation to date has emphasized establishing systems into which the management could plug its own data, criteria, and standards in order to solve its problems and achieve its ends.

As attention is turned to examining longer- and long-term strategy—the most evident (and first) manifestation of which will probably be a business plan covering the years 1988–1992—more and more substance not already part of the experience and understanding of the existing management will be crucial. This new substance must come from a combination of outside experience and ad hoc investigation, with the latter (especially) attempting to anticipate the future environmental opportunities and threats as fully as possible and to collate these circumstances wisely with the objectives and priorities of the management. At the same time, anticipating the growth and change in the firm's requirements for resources—labor and managerial ones as well as financial ones—is the critical means to assure accomplishment of the goals along the way. The upshot is that these next steps, which examine the open book of the more distant future, rely increasingly on new and outside information. Both the analysis and the form and procedure will benefit in creating not only a first set of strategic plans but also a basis for an ongoing long-term planning process.

I. Short-Term Activities
   1. Develop the system for short-term planning, beginning with the necessary source forms:
      a. Work schedule (showing start, time in plant, and delivery-ready)
      b. Worksheet for each order (showing materials requirements, labor requirements, packaging requirements, and so on)
      c. Cash-flow format (showing payments in and out dependent on the work schedule)
   2. Set up second-stage information sources, elaborating on and using the basic source forms:
      a. Full sales forecast, displaying recurring orders as well as likely individual orders
      b. Complete cash-flow, including information not tied to individual orders (such as general and administrative expenses, wages and salaries, capital items, and so on)
      c. Operating budget (profit-and-loss) based on periodic cumulations of scheduled work (from worksheets)
      d. General and administrative costs budget (estimating future outlays scheduled for overhead and wages)
      e. Revised worksheets (data based on actual ongoing experience)

Exhibit 2
EVANS PHARMACEUTICALS: BUDGETING AND PLANNING AGENDA (*continued*)

   3. Establish an analytical management information system in its final form with full integration among the elements of the system:

     a. Comprehensive sales forecast and work schedule (cf. 1a, 2a)

     b. Comprehensive (master) worksheet (cf. 1b, 2c)

     c. Comprehensive cash-flow (cf. 2b, 2d, 2e, 3d(3))

     d. Comprehensive budget projections

       (1) Income statement (cf. 2c, 2d, 2e)

       (2) Balance sheet (cf. 3a, prior balance sheet)

       (3) Capital budget

   4. Put into use by management:

     a. Improve initial formats and information—move deliberately to actual, evidence-based, specific case, and thorough estimates and reports from the present more-idealized, expected, average-experience, and approximate-rough picture

     b. Plan expenditures and arrange credit with appropriate lead time—gaining control over amounts and timing

     c. Set up preliminary standard cost estimates

     d. Begin utilizing feedback of actual results for comparison with standards, forecasts, and budgets—exploring variances for potentials to control them or to make plans more realistic

     e. Institute analysis to get at the economics of

       (1) Batch sizes

       (2) Inventory order quantities

       (3) Generous credit trade-offs versus best purchase prices

       (4) Scheduling and sequencing of individual batches

   5. Consider perspectives at this stage: the short-term efforts have stressed firefighting and catch-up through the creation of essential information-system formats, improvement of the data they contain, and their articulation to economize on data collection; steps taken here—data origination and organization, providing for reporting, tying the reports together, and calling for thoughtful revision—all bear on better management; three additional information-system steps need to be added for full effectiveness—selecting criteria for performance and setting performance standards, providing appropriate incentives, and ascertaining that management control does in fact utilize the various feedbacks of information; generally, purposes served by these efforts will be enhanced by subsequent intermediate- and long-term work; these goals include striving to anticipate needs, decide on pricing or repricing, and establishing guidelines (ultimately) for accepting, indeed seeking, business volume; the final result, through better utilization of resources, should be to raise profitability.

II. Intermediate-Term Activities

   1. The purpose of intermediate-term activities explicitly is to force attention to the time frame within which Evans Pharmaceuticals must lengthen its view, projecting systematically from the immediate problems of the short-term activities; improving estimates and analysis aids in dealing with circumstances in which capacity of the existing plant is regularly filled—finding ways to overcome chronic conditions of plant-space shortage.

2. Projections should be extended beyond the monthly frame to the quarterly and yearly frames.
3. Computer methodologies to store formats and data are needed to
    a. Permit reuse of data or its reformation for display in several of the newly refined information applications
    b. Facilitate revision and updating of all reports with a single correction-insertion
4. Sufficient experience must be accumulated and applied to decide what reports and projections are necessary or useful and what the distribution within the management group should be on a routine basis.
5. Further, it should be decided what distributions should be made to others—perhaps including outsiders such as banks and similar stakeholders whose interests do not coincide entirely with management's—as well as whether the variety of distributions justifies creating a variety of bases for the usual income statement and balance sheet within generally accepted accounting principles (such as most-favorable tax treatment, most-favorable income generation, and so on).
6. Analytical use of the information-system products should move into a mode of regularly scheduled sessions examining the intermediate time frame on a predictable basis to supplement the ad hoc analyses directed at short-term matters.
7. Nevertheless, the connections between the details of the short-term frame and the longer view of the annual projections and rolling quarterly projections and reports should be emphasized.
8. Perspectives to consider at this stage: Primarily there are two new thrusts in the intermediate term—enhancing productivity and initiating financial planning; for the former, three sorts of fine-tuning indicate the potentials—offsetting bottlenecks in capacity by adding resources selectively (storage of inventories, overtime, packaging, and so on); managing purchasing aggressively (quantity discounts, vendor selection, bargaining, and so on); and maximizing contribution to profit and overhead by selecting the products and orders which offer the greatest margins per plant space and time required in their processing.

III. Long-Term Activities
    1. The first task—again following the method of starting with initial needs and both refining and extending in time later—is to prepare a business plan looking two to five years out into the future. Its characteristics include
        a. Mostly internal information and extrapolations
        b. Statements of business strategies, distinctive competencies, supporting policies, implementation
            (1) Sense of the pattern
            (2) Opportunities perceived toward which directed
            (3) Success potential anticipated
        c. Notation of problems and priorities
        d. Summary of objectives, performance goals, and checkpoints
        e. Possible presentation of projected brief financial statements
        f. Primarily external audience—for management, this plan mostly represents a formalizing in a statement of existing patterns
    2. The second task—a more protracted and difficult one—is to conduct a rigorous analysis, which releases the implicit assumptions in the business

Exhibit 2
EVANS PHARMACEUTICALS: BUDGETING AND PLANNING AGENDA (*continued*)

plan of a do-nothing strategy (business as usual) and looks ten to twenty years out, employing essentially the same format as the business plan but specifically focusing on alternatives and adaptations possible in the longer time span envisioned

 a. Industry selection—thorough examination of the future of the extended industry in each of the intended business segments, (contract, private-label, Evans-label) in order to set the categorical strategies

 b. Industry positioning—thorough examination of competitive and generic strategies with special attention to marketing-policy imperatives

 c. Formulation and implementation of company strategies—identification, evaluation, and recommendation of

  (1) Categorical and generic strategies and distinctive competence

  (2) Tasks and specialization or complexity keyed to supporting policies

  (3) Arrangements for structure, systems, and style of delegation contributing to present implementation

  (4) Specification of resources' needs (physical, personnel, and financial) and sources and access

  (5) Long-run planning to furnish a program of concrete actions and sequences best able to execute the specified strategies

3. Perspectives to consider at this stage: The business plan is a preliminary effort—a run-through, like a prospectus or red herring, which exposes many of the characteristics of the firm and its future; the longer-term strategic analysis presumes an active firm and therefore undertakes deliberately a full review of the alternative categorical strategies and other matters, making this effort a significant source of background information to incorporate in plans for new physical facilities—especially their flexibility and expandability.

WORK AGENDA IN A TRIAGE FORMAT

TIME FRAME OF ACTIVITIES, APPLICATION, NEED

Long	Short	Intermediate
Self-sustaining	I.1	II.2
Progress by Evans	I.2.b,d,e	II.3
Management with little or no outside consultation, middle priority	I.3.a,d; I.4.1,b,d	II.4; II.5
Close consultation required and fruitful—high priority	I.2.a,c; I.3.a,d; I.4.e; (I.5)	(II.1); III.1,2,3; II.6,7,8
Undertaking efforts presently undesirable or infeasible—low priority	I.4.c	

Evans and Brittain should spend their limited time in order to have the greatest impact.

Exhibit 3 displayed the results of early work done by Brittain to develop a more useful document for the use of Dave Evans and others in his firm, based on a form that they currently employed frequently. This worksheet was already prepared in a less-complete version for each product the firm turned

Exhibit 3
EVANS PHARMACEUTICALS: WORKSHEETS

ACCOUNTING INFORMATION CONTENT (IN PRICE AND QUANTITY FORMAT)
1. Gross revenues (noting breakpoints on quantities)
2. Discounts usually allowed
3. Net revenues
4. Labor for
   a. Setup
   b. Production
   c. Clean-up
   d. Packaging and shipping
5. Raw materials (in detail)
6. Packaging materials
7. Miscellaneous outlays for
   a. Freight
   b. Special quality-assurance
   c. Other direct, incremental costs
8. Contribution (dollar and percentage terms)
9. Alternate G & A allocations—direct labor; gross revenue; plant time; total variable costs

OTHER INFORMATION CONTENT
1. Elapsed time to produce (usual start to finish; planned delays when out of the active workflow—"holds" or "storage")
2. Customer(s) identification(s)
3. Discounts taken (if available)
4. Shipping, delivery time from the factory
5. Collection time
6. Lead time and leeway by customer
7. Number of batches per month and amounts typically produced
8. Yields
9. Product compatibility, contamination potential
10. Labor specialists, mix required
11. Maneuverability on price
12. Inquiries, bids, and possible orders explored with price and quantity data
13. Relation of raw materials' components' requirements for modular batch to typical inventory or purchase order

out. And it already had multiple uses, although the principal ones were limited to furnishing information for handling production, purchasing, and pricing.

It was Brittain's argument that an expanded version would become a key document for a number of the firm's new systems, as shown in Exhibit 2. For instance, in addition to its contributions to operations through specifying data for production and marketing, it could be a starting place for standard costs, cash-flow planning, and profit-and-loss budgeting. Moreover, it would be a critical element in scheduling and in sequencing different batches, to say nothing of its value for analyzing yields, productivity, and other variances.

Finally, the only new specifics that Brittain intended to present to Dave Evans were contained in Exhibit 4, which consisted of eight parts. One was a diagram to assist in visualizing the relationships of the substantive specifics. There followed seven parts, each devoted to a segment of the overall makeup of Evans Pharmaceuticals' relationships with its industry.

Several of these relationships were based on classic competitive strategy approaches proposed by Harvard Business School's Michael E. Porter. In Porter's concept of extended rivalry or extended industry, suppliers and customers were significant parties able to influence and be influenced by a given firm as aspects of its strategy.

Of course, the industry naturally would be seen to include present competitors, but Porter argued persuasively that two quasi-competitor groups should also be embraced in the rigorous study of the extended industry—potential entrants and substitutes. The first allows for future competitors not now represented, and the second makes explicit the possibility that different technologies might be able to accomplish the same purpose for a customer (with the specific product or service momentarily so offbeat as to preclude its being placed with the group of functional competitors).

Building on the familiar concepts from Porter, Brittain had developed the next four segments of Exhibit 4 to grapple with these parties to competitive strategy: products, customers, competitors, and suppliers. While these four certainly contained the core of the work program for constructing the business plan, there were three further segments, each oriented toward a cluster of concerns. Exhibit 4.F, titled "Factory," involves matters of the physical facilities, technology, and the flows of product through the plant. Exhibit 4.G, titled "General," was intended to raise questions about the implementation of the strategy in terms of structural changes and of provisions for strategic planning and for the strategic-intelligence effort for the future. Finally, Exhibit 4.H, "Stakeholders," particularly probed the identities and interests of other parties not involved with owner-management or extended rivalry.

Brittain had arranged Exhibit 4 pretty much in the order of priority as he saw it for understanding Evans Pharmaceuticals' particular situation and for creating a solidly based strategic plan. While he felt sure that the triage concept, which he had borrowed from its original context of battlefield medical care, still had some usefulness for organizing the sequence of approach to the interrelated information focuses, he was equally sure that it would be a mistake in a thorough study of the firm's future prospects and plans to ignore any facet, at least in the initial study processes.

Thus, Brittain saw as possibly deceptive and distorting his provisional working definitions of triage's three divisions in application to setting precedence for the strategic work program: first, "useful—will develop in the course of the firm's progress"; second, "vital and functional—will bear

crucially on strategic decisions"; and, third, "marginal but academic—will not permit the firm to make advantageous changes."

Instead, he had recognized that all the matters should get some attention at least. And while he knew that an iterative process would be ideal because there was naturally much overlapping and reinforcing of the analysis as it moved from segment to segment, he had to admit that expediency forced a more decisive attack. Therefore, he adopted three criteria for the final sequence of Exhibit 4:

1. General importance of the analysis and perspectives in Evans's situation—how easily could failure to comprehend them obscure the firm's vision or weaken its grasp
2. Immediacy of usefulness in allocating activities in the existing facilities—how soon could the insights be used for practical purposes
3. Ultimate significance of the segment to the strategy of the firm—what leverage could be exerted for understanding problems, opportunities, or priorities

As to the sorts of inquiries that each segment posed, Brittain saw two aspects as important. One was to obtain what he had termed in discussions with Evans a matrix of data and other information in which each of the subject components of the segment was treated as an individual. For instance, under products, not only product classes but also specific formulations would get attention as information was developed for separate categories. In a word, the products topic would be disaggregated by specific products in order to reveal the distinctive characteristics of at least the major components of the segment.

Such a cross-matching of information constituted most of the background that Brittain was convinced Evans needed to develop with thoroughness. But there were in each instance some non-matrix aspects that also bore looking into.

The actual information that would be generated was primarily descriptive in character, some of it known or inferred concerning Evans Pharmaceuticals itself and some of it concerning the outside influences in the market or industry—competitors, suppliers, customers, and others.

However, there were some preliminary policy dimensions that Brittain expected to emerge naturally, even though he was prepared to concede that the fullest expression of the business plan was only to be found at the end of the entire investigation represented by Exhibit 4. He believed that strategies and policies would stem from producing a deliberate set of planning documents, but it did seem to him that there were interim normative statements and conclusions that might appropriately be based on the overall sense conveyed by the individual segments' descriptive information. Therefore, he allowed for both "resulting indications for strategy" and "decisive influences" in laying out the requirements for each segment of the exhibit.

As he reflected on what he was going to present to Evans on the 27th, Brittain wanted to be ready to emphasize more than the content he was after in the information-seeking exhibits. Most of all, he was worried that he would be asking Evans to devote a great deal of time to the initial planning efforts being laid out in his questionnaires. On the one hand, he was certain in his own mind that this was a necessary investment, which offered enormous payoffs down the line. On the other hand, he knew also that an entrepreneur like Evans, preoccupied as he invariably was with the pressing day-to-day matters of running a growing business, would be nearly impossible to tie down long enough to get all the serious work attended to.

His real fear was that Evans, because his intuitions about the firm and the industry were so swift and sure, would go through the individual questions and other points at such speed and with so little chance to comprehend them fully that the results directed at the business plan would merely confirm Evans' longstanding insights and conclusions. Lacking true rigor and critical reexamination, especially of the details of the individual segments and matrix elements, there would in the end be only a veneer of strategic intelligence and competitive analysis for the plan.

If this happened, of course, Brittain had every reason to doubt also that any significant ongoing process would be established, leaving serious reservations about the firm's continuing with its own process of strategic planning which it had tailored and thus had come to understand fully. In that instance he further doubted that Evans Pharmaceuticals would be able to continue to deepen and refine the process.

Last of all, Brittain had begun to wonder about the wisdom and workability of including others from the firm in the deliberations over the business plan. In part this was a matter of timing, since sooner or later everyone should be involved by design. But the key argument for their immediate in-

clusion involved more than organizational dynamics. While there was no question that Evans was the firm's foremost expert on the business and its industry—in addition to being the owner and chief executive—getting others to contribute from the early stages offered the potential to gain unique inputs of consequence. Moreover, it held forth the possibility of facilitating the participants' fuller understanding and obtaining their genuine involvement in these critical long-term decisions.

Whatever the outcomes of these intellectual wrestling matches in the presentation he made to Evans, Brittain was determined to fight hard for Evans's attention because of two interrelated perceptions which had come forcefully into his thinking as he had prepared the work scheme. One was his conclusion that the generic, over-the-counter pharmaceuticals industry was currently in a dual environment that Michael Porter had called fragmented on the one hand and emerging on the other. A fragmented environment was characterized by the lack of any firm with significant market share, absence of market leaders with power to shape industry events, and an unconsolidated nature generally. An emerging environment was shown by new business opportunity, a newly formed industry, and a game without rules, with its first-time buyers and high initial costs implying steep cost reductions for the future. These sets of characteristics caused Brittain to be sure that Evans faced unique potentials.

In turn, this led to the other perception. It concerned the premises of a business or strategic plan. The conventional wisdom was that long-term planning permitted the organization to make the most advantageous arrangement of the direction and character of its future moves. This assumed that the firm was playing against immutable circumstances—completely exogenously determined environments, as an economist would put it—so that its efforts were limited to studying the most likely future environments and selecting strategies offering the best prospects for success.

Now this was a tall enough order to keep most organizations—particularly small, inexperienced ones undergoing rapid growth and change—utterly immersed in the strategic processes. But there was a newer view, based on a recent study by Porter and other industrial economists and strategic thinkers. It held an entirely different view of the circumstances: instead of being immutable so far as the subject firm was concerned, the environments were actually malleable, and part of the firm's plan should consequently be devoted to finding ways to make over the future conditions of the industry and other relevant settings.

In other words, Evans was actually in a situation economists would call endogenous in relation to the critical variables since its very behavior would in fact bear on the character of the future environment, thus advantageously influencing the industry's evo-

lution. So Brittain was excited by the opportunity facing Evans Pharmaceuticals—a fragmented, emerging industry where a firm with aggressive, knowledgeable, and thoroughly prepared leadership like Evans could become a pacesetter with the right kind of strategic plan and implementation of it.

Exhibit 4
EVANS PHARMACEUTICALS: BRITTAIN'S PLAN

A. INTEGRATION OF STRATEGIC SYSTEMS

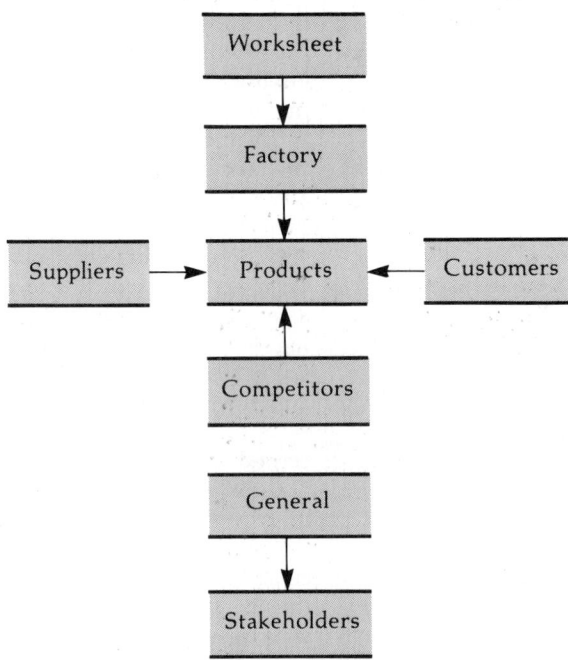

B. PRODUCTS
1. Physical application possibilities and present production
   a. Present and expected volumes
   b. Exports and imports
2. Potential quantities evaluated
   a. Details by main applications
      (1) present lines—laxatives, colds, antacids
      (2) future lines—analgesics, coughs, cosmetics
   b. Details by main classes—contract, private-label, Evans
   c. Details by specific product
   d. Details by size, physical form—dry, liquid, effervescent—and packaging type—foil, glass, blister-box
   e. Potentials for types carried by given outlets—branded product(s), generic, private-label, and Evans

3. Strategies—overall, disaggregated, and time dynamics
    a. Categorical—do nothing, diversification, territorial expansion, vertical integration
    b. Generic—cost leadership, product differentiation, focus
    c. Options and recommendations
    d. Competitive advantages and disadvantages
    e. Barriers to entry—scale, non-scale, differentiation, and so on
    f. Other structural characteristics, especially scale-learning changes in technology or costs
    g. Possible function of an Evans brand
4. Pricing practices, patterns through channels, trends, potentials
    a. Pricing practices and options—absolute character, consistency, and so on
    b. Price patterns at wholesale and retail for brands and for Evans
    c. Price sensitivities, elasticities
    d. Price trends
    e. Price bargaining power with customers
5. Production and contribution
    a. Analysis of contribution and G & A
    b. Economics of batch size, run length in production and packaging
6. Objectives and considerations in product-mix choices
    a. Priorities and tradeoffs with respect to profit
    b. Implications for capacity-use policies
7. Preliminary normative indications for Evans concerning products

C. CUSTOMERS

1. Overall growth and customer potentials
    a. Growth of the market and individual segments
        (1) Contract
        (2) Private-label
        (3) New brands like Evans
    b. Controlling factors in market's and segments' growth
    c. Importance of present individual customers' growth to Evans
    d. Markets beyond the outlets through the largest chains—how large, profitable, reachable, retainable?
    e. What's now on the shelves and what's been preempted
2. Customers at present
3. Strategies and structural characteristics
    a. Categorical and generic strategies
    b. Competitive advantages and disadvantages
    c. Relative bargaining power
    d. Specific barriers
        (1) Product-differentiation in the customers' eyes
        (2) Switching costs
        (3) Other barriers
    e. Other structural considerations—concentration, industry evolution
4. Pricing, margins, and contribution
    a. Patterns and trends in prices
    b. Options for pricing methods
        (1) Direct-cost plus a flat margin
        (2) Direct-cost plus a flexible margin
        (3) Posting, bargaining with a cost floor
        (4) Bargaining without limits preimposed
    c. Analysis of brands and generics—prices and margins

Exhibit 4
EVANS PHARMACEUTICALS: BRITTAIN'S PLAN (*continued*)

     5. Competitors for customers
       a. Present customer-competitor connections
       b. Existence of alternate sources for supplying customers
       c. Number of sources typically maintained by customers
     6. Customer behavior
       a. Spacing, frequency of orders
       b. Long-term contracts' present use and potentials
       c. Possibilities of customers' backward vertical integration
     7. Preliminary normative indications for Evans concerning customers

   D. COMPETITORS
     1. Competitors in the industry, potential entrants, and substitutes
       a. Present and potential firms
       b. Markets in which firms participate—branded, contract, private-label
       c. Structural characteristics—market shares, industry evolution
       d. Strategic groups and mobility barriers
       e. Current technology dimensions and differences
       f. Size of capacity increments
       g. Substitutes' potentials
         (1) Orthodox channels—brand-product manufacturers making a second-tier product for private label
         (2) New distribution channels
       h. Price patterns and trends
     2. Barriers to entry and exit
       a. Bars to new entrants
         (1) General exploration of the standard seven barriers
         (2) Special attention to
           (a) Scale and changes as the industry evolves
           (b) Product-differentiation, especially quality in eight suggested dimensions
           (c) Switching costs and transactions implications
       b. Record of new entrants of significance and viability
         (1) Domestic producers
         (2) Imports
       c. Bars to exit by existing firms—emotional, psychological commitment; specialized assets; spillover to, from other units
       d. Record of exits
     3. Competitive advantages and retaliatory potentials
       a. Competitive advantages Evans enjoys over specific competitors
       b. Competitive disadvantages suffered over specific competitors
       c. Instances, anticipations of retaliatory moves
     4. Industry evolution
       a. Appraisal of the designations of the current environment
         (1) Fragmented
         (2) Emerging
       b. Overall and specific-sector growth of the relevant market
         (1) Measures
         (2) Controlling factors
         (3) Role of exports

    c. Examination of the standard fourteen evolutionary processes as a guide to strategy—changes in growth rate, innovations, new industry boundaries, buyer learning, and so on

  5. Preliminary normative indications for Evans concerning competitors

E. SUPPLIERS

  1. Structural characteristics
    a. General nature
    b. Bargaining power vis-a-vis Evans
    c. Price patterns and trends
    d. Existence of alternate sources for Evans
    e. Vertical integration forward into generic OTC products
      (1) Instances to date
      (2) Likelihood of future attempts
        (a) Attractions
        (b) Feasibility
      (3) Barriers to entry faced
  2. Evolution and dynamics in the industry and in specific firms
  3. Preliminary normative indications for Evans concerning suppliers

F. FACTORY

  1. Capacity and production
    a. Existing capacity in Cottage Grove and Walker
      (1) Pattern of utilization and limits
      (2) Specific bottlenecks at full-capacity
        (a) Locations pinpointed
        (b) Possibilities of alleviation
    b. Capacity in first stage in Springfield
      (1) Expected utilization patterns
      (2) Identification in the planning stage of relief possibilities
  2. Vertical integration
    a. Backward to suppliers
      (1) Own activities to replace suppliers
      (2) Quasi-integration through long-term contracts
      (3) Other possibilities involving just-in-time delivery and similar forms of coordination between parties
    b. Forward to customers
      (1) Own sales force
      (2) Own logistical system
      (3) Own distribution outlets
        (a) Wholesale
        (b) Retail
  3. Orders, worksheets, and scheduling
    a. Analysis of order patterns
      (1) Regular, standing, routine
      (2) Irregular
      (3) Probable
        (a) Implicit only
        (b) Bankable
      (4) Potentials for collaboration with customers to smooth order patterns
    b. More intensive use of worksheets
      (1) Forecasting factory activity
      (2) Scheduling optimal activity levels and patterns

Exhibit 4
EVANS PHARMACEUTICALS: BRITTAIN'S PLAN (*continued*)

        (3) Follow-up analyses
           (a) Revision of worksheets' information
           (b) Examination of productivity, standard costs, etc.
    4. Preliminary normative indications for Evans concerning factory

  G. GENERAL
    1. Development of industry, competitive intelligence efforts
      a. Exploration of existing versus potential approaches
      b. Range of possibilities
        (1) Dave Evans personally
           (a) Trade associations
               i. Pharmaceutical
              ii. ACS group of Small Manufacturing Chemists
           (b) Newsletters
           (c) Journals
        (2) Sales representatives
           (a) Individuals' working contacts
           (b) Scheduled meetings and convention conferences
        (3) Others inside Evans Pharmaceuticals
        (4) Others outside the firm
    2. Exploration of means of updating strategic intelligence
      a. Designation of priorities
        (1) Information and data
        (2) Analyses and assimilation
      b. Assignment to individuals
      c. Provision of time frame and rotation
    3. Creation of scenarios of organization structure
      a. Future organization charts
        (1) Begin with spring 1988
        (2) Space at two-year intervals through 1992
      b. Consideration of implications for recruiting, training, and assignments
      c. Analysis and integration of other implementation aspects
        (1) Management systems
        (2) Leadership and style
      d. Inclusion of consultants and outside providers of expertise
        (1) Examination of changing needs for complementary talent
        (2) Qualification and selection
        (3) Balancing and integration with inside providers
    4. Preliminary normative indications for Evans concerning general

  H. STAKEHOLDERS
    1. Identification of interests, parties
      a. Ownership, management
      b. Outside ownership
      c. Permanent debt financing's providers
      d. Customers
      e. Suppliers
      f. Employees
        (1) Nonownership management
        (2) All others

    g. General community

    h. Others

  2. Examination of relations with each group in strategic context

    a. Nature of existing contacts and communications

    b. Intended, hoped-for, potential future involvements

    c. Implications for developing contacts and communications

       (1) Greater intensity and frequency of mutual involvement

       (2) Possible formats for sharing and interacting, beginning with initiatives from Evans Pharmaceuticals

          (a) Financial statements

          (b) Financial, economic, strategic analyses

          (c) Other

       (3) Tailoring necessary, desirable for different groups

       (4) Definition of reciprocation sought

          (a) Actual and substantive benefits to the firm

          (b) Measure of functioning of heightened programs of contacts and communications

  3. Preliminary normative indications for Evans concerning stakeholders

GLOSSARY

ABC analysis: A method of focusing attention on the few vital items that contribute the most to company's revenues, costs, or profits. For example, 10 percent of inventory parts usually comprise 60 to 70 percent of inventory costs. By focusing planning and control efforts on these items, you can control most of the cost of your inventory.

accounts payable: A current liability representing obligations to creditors for goods and services purchased on account.

accounts receivable: A current asset representing claims against customers for goods or services sold on account.

accrual method: Recognizing income in the year in which all events have occurred that fix the taxpayer's right to receive the income and in which the amount of income can be determined with reasonable accuracy, independent of the timing of cash receipts and payments.

advertising: Method of informing potential customers and promoting the sales of products or services.

affirmative action: Provision in the Executive Order No. 11246 that requires federal government contractors and subcontractors to give preferential treatment to members of underrepresented groups in making hiring and promotion decisions. To be legal, the affirmative action plan must be approved by the Office of Federal Contract Compliance Programs (OFCCP).

Age Discrimination in Employment Act of 1967: States that private sector employers of twenty or more people are prohibited from employment discrimination of people who are at least forty years of age.

alter ego: Literally, the second self. In business terms, a situation in which the shareholders of a corporation have disregarded the entity of the corporation and made the corporation a mere conduit for the accomplishment of their own private business purposes.

amortization: The general process of systematically reducing an account balance to reflect asset expiration or the allocation of premiums and discounts to time periods. Known as depletion for wasting assets, and as depreciation for tangible long-lived assets owned other than land.

application forms: Documents designed to obtain information about the general suitability of applicants for jobs.

appreciated assets: Assets with a fair market value greater than that shown on the balance sheet.

arbitration: A process by which a third party neutral decides the disputed issues. Arbitration is a sort of "labor court" presided over by a neutral outside party, called the arbitrator. The decision made by the arbitrator is legally binding on both management and union unless either party decides to appeal it to a court of law—a relatively rare occurrence. Two basic types of arbitration exist:

interest arbitration—In which the arbitrator is brought into the contract negotiation process to decide the disputed issues.

grievance arbitration—In which the arbitrator is brought in to decide a grievance that arises out of the administration of the union contract.

balance sheet: The financial statement reporting assets and equities as of a specific date. Also known as a *statement of financial position*.

balance sheet insolvency: Situation in which the balance sheet shows a debtor's liabilities are greater than the value of the assets.

basis: A measure or standard to determine how much of the proceeds received on a sale or other disposition represents gain or income. Generally, the cost of property is the basis to be used, increased or decreased, by any adjustments required by the Internal Revenue Code and the regulations.

benefits: Refers to all compensation other than pay, which provides income. Examples are vacation pay, sick pay, pay when unable to work because of work-related illnesses and injuries or temporary employment, pension plans, capital accumulation plans.

bill of materials: A parts list of the raw materials and components required to make a product.

book value: The amount recorded in the business's accounts. For particular assets and liabilities, refers to the item in net terms. For common stock, refers to share of total assets not claimed by creditors and preferred shareholders. For the business as a whole, equals net assets (total assets minus total liabilities).

budgets: *operating budget*—The allocation of resources in dollar amounts among specific items that in combination account for your total operational activity.

cash-flow budget—The accountability of cash inflows in a designated period and the corresponding cash outflow in the same period. Identifying the items related to the inflows and those items that relate to the outflow.

capital budget—The allocation of capital among alternative capital resource opportunity options.

business agent: An employee of the local union who performs the activities performed by international union representatives.

business life cycle: Encompasses a business and its functional activities beginning with the business idea through its various age stages to its termination or until it shifts in a different direction or melds into a different business.

calendar year: A twelve-month reporting period for a business, ending on December 31.

capacity control: The process of comparing the planned work to the actual work accomplished and taking corrective action.

capacity planning: The process of determining the amount of capacity available and the amount of capacity required.

capitalize: To record the effect of an expenditure as an asset rather than as an expense.

cash method: The method of computing income on the basis of cash receipts and disbursements.

charts: *flow process chart*—A graphical technique related to the production of one component of a product or service.

Gantt chart—A graphical technique for planning and controlling the priorities and capacities of activities.

man-machine chart—A graphical technique for showing the activity relationships between one worker and one or more machines.

operation process chart—A graphical technique that shows the chronological sequence of all operations, inspections, time allowances, and materials used in producing a good or service.

operator process chart (right-hand left-hand chart)—A graphical representation of the movements of each hand with respect to each other and the making of a product or service.

R chart—A statistical process control technique used to monitor the range of values in a process to maintain process control.

X chart—A statistical process control chart to measure the average or mean value of a process to maintain process control.

collective bargaining: Sometimes called labor relations or union-management relations, the process through which employers and unions (1) negotiate pay, hours of work, and terms and conditions of employment for the group of workers represented by the union, (2) sign a written contract that defines management constraints and union and employee rights and constraints for the length of the contract period, and (3) share the responsibility for administering the negotiated contract.

common stock: The ownership element of a company that carries the right to vote on corporate matters.

competitive advantage: A characteristic that makes a firm more attractive to customers than its competitors.

conciliation: Attempts by the mediator to get the parties to agree freely to offers made by either side. As a conciliator, the mediator attempts to create a problem-solving climate that will encourage bargainers to seek their own solutions to the issues that are deadlocked.

constraint: The resource that limits the performance of the system.

contempt action: Action taken by the court or someone else subjecting the offending party to sanctions of the court, for violation of the court's orders.

continuity: The period of time an ad runs.

corporation: A legal entity formed under state law, owned by its shareholders, and given certain rights, privileges, and liabilities by law.

C corporations—All corporations except those that qualify and elect to be treated as *S* corporations. It has a tax existence separate and apart from its shareholders and is subject to tax on its net income at rates established by Congress.

S corporations—For income tax determination, a corporation that qualifies and elects to be treated similarly to a partnership for tax purposes.

cost of goods sold: The cost of inventory that has been sold to customers or that has otherwise disappeared, inventory expense.

cram-down: Cram-down provisions provide a vehicle whereby the debtor may force a creditor over the creditor's objections to participate in a plan distribution scheme. A debtor is only required to disburse to creditors what they would receive in a Chapter 7 liquidation. For example, suppose that an unsecured creditor owed $25,000 objects to the proposed payment of 10 percent of the debt. If liquidation under Chapter 7 would provide no more than 10 percent, the debtor is crammed down over his or her objections.

current assets: Cash and any other assets that are expected to be converted into cash, sold, or consumed within a year or within the business's normal operating cycle, whichever is longer. Includes prepaid items or expenses expected to expire within a year from acquisition.

current liabilities: Those liabilities that are payable within one year or the business's normal operating cycle and which will require current assets in settlement.

cycle counting: A method to improve inventory accuracy by counting each item in inventory a given number of times during a time cycle.

data: *primary data*—Data gathered directly to answer a specific question.

secondary data—Data that have been gathered by others for purposes other than the question at hand, but which are useful.

debenture note: A long-term obligation (usually five years or longer) issued by corporation.

debt: The financial obligation of a firm to repay a creditor.

demographics: The statistical study of human population especially with reference to size and density, distribution, and vital statistics.

disparate impact discrimination: Illegal discrimination that refers to personnel decisions which are not intended to be in violation of equal employment opportunity laws but nevertheless lead to underrepresentation of a particular race, color, religion, sex or national origin within the workplace because the criteria used to make personnel decisions are not job related and exclude a greater proportion of one race, sex, or ethnic group than another from employment opportunities.

disparate treatment discrimination: Illegal discrimination that refers to personnel decisions overtly based on any of the five prohibited classifications: race, sex, color, religion or national origin. Examples include paying women less than men for the same work, or refusing to hire or promote blacks.

dissolution: The termination of the existence of a corporation, partnership, or business. The term that is often used interchangeably is *liquidation*, but that is not accurate. Technically a corporation can be liquidated and a partner's interest in the partnership may be liquidated, but a partnership is not liquidated.

due process of law: The basis for the union contract. The two basic requirements for due process of law are that (a) exercise of power should be based on a set of objective rules rather than on the personal preferences of those in power, and (b) the rules should respect the commonly accepted rights of the person against whom the power is exercised. Following the logic of due process of law, the union contract consists of (a) the written agreement that specifies the set of objective rules, and (b) all the oral and written agreements and all the implicitly or explicitly accepted customary ways of doing things within the workplace.

economic order quantity: A lot sizing technique based on minimizing the costs associated with ordering and carrying an individual inventory item.

employee specification: A document that defines the necessary knowledge, skills, and abilities a job applicant must possess to perform the job he or she is applying for.

employment at will: The common law doctrine that gives the employer the right to fire an employee for any cause, whether just, unjust, or even morally wrong.

Equal Employment Opportunity Commission (EEOC): A federal agency whose principal activities are to regulate the enactment of Title VII of the Civil Rights Act. EEO's written regulations give specific meaning to Title VII generalities. Additionally, EEOC is responsible for processing Title VII and Equal Pay Act violation complaints.

equity: A capital investment in a firm that results in a share of ownership.

equity in collateral: There will only be equity in collateral if its fair market value is greater than the amount of the outstanding indebtedness. For example, if a company owes creditors $75,000 and the value of real estate pledged is $100,000, equity equals $25,000.

escrow: The deposit of funds with a trustee (bank, lawyer, and so on) until the terms of the escrow agreement are satisfied.

estate: Everything a debtor owns or has possession of; any receivables or claims against others; interests in property of all kinds, including equitable and possessory interests.

Executive Order No. 11246: A governing statement issued by the president that, like Title VII, prohibits discrimination by federal government contractors and subcontractors because of race, color, religion, sex, and national origin.

exponential smoothing: A forecasting technique where the last period's forecast is adjusted by some weighting factor ranging from 0 to 1 multiplied by the deviation of last period's forecast from the actual demand.

external recruiting: Identifying and attracting a qualified pool of applicants within the external labor market to seek jobs with your company.

extraordinary items: An expense (loss) or revenue (gain) that is unusual in nature for the particular business, not expected to recur in the foreseeable future, and material in amount. Extraordinary items are classified on the income statement following income from operations.

fair compensation: The ability to balance competitive business interests (through cost control of compensation outlays) with the compensation goals of attracting, retaining, and motivating a competent workforce.

Fair Labor Standards Act (FLSA): Also called *wage and hour law*; establishes minimum wage, overtime pay, equal pay, and recordkeeping requirements for employers covered under the Act.

Federal Mediation and Conciliation Service (FMCS): An independent federal agency that acts as a third-party neutral to help employers and unions resolve serious clashes and maintain constructive relationships.

fiscal year: A twelve-month reporting period for a business, which may or may not correspond to the calendar year.

fixed labor market: A situation in which there is a fixed number of people who have the skills needed.

fixed overhead: Includes all costs of doing business, except direct labor and direct materials in manufacturing businesses. It is that part of the overhead costs that are not affected by volume of operations.

fixed position layout: A physical arrangement of equipment and services for performing operations on large products where the item remains in a given location and workers come to the site to perform operations or services.

flow diagram: A pictorial representation of the current or proposed layout of the facility superimposed with the location of each operation associated with producing a good or service.

fraudulent transfer: For bankruptcy purposes, the transfer of assets to an insider (stockholder, officer, family member) or to anyone else for less than fair market value. For example, a debtor, prior to filing, transfers property to his business partner for less than market value in order to keep the debtor's wife from claiming an interest.

frequency: The number of times a potential customer is exposed to an advertisement for a specified period of time.

funds from operations: Working capital generated in operations—the difference between fund revenue (revenue involving an inflow of working capital) and fund expense (expense involving a reduction of net working capital), less any gains on the sale of long-lived assets and before the effect of extraordinary and discontinued items.

Generally Accepted Accounting Principles (GAAP): A standardized system of measurement and reporting.

grievance: An employee complaint or allegation by an employee, union, or employer that a collective bargaining contract has been violated.

grievance procedure: A process for settling employer-employee disputes that gives all parties under the union contract the right to challenge the actions of the other parties.

gross profit: Total profit before the deduction of expenditures.

gross sales: The total dollar amount of sales before deducting returns, credits, and allowances.

guided on-the-job training: A systematic training approach that focuses on developing programs for (a) providing new employees with information about the company and their jobs, (b) helping employees adjust to their new work situation, (c) helping employees develop competence on their jobs, and (d) maintaining the competencies of the company's workforce.

Immigration Reform and Control Act of 1986: Mandates that all employers verify the citizenship status of all employees hired after November 1986 and maintain records of that verification. The Act permits the hiring of legal aliens and allows the employer to discriminate in favor of equally qualified U.S. citizens.

incentive pay plans: Plans that pay for job outcomes. Most popular forms of incentive pay are commissions, gain-sharing and profit-sharing.

commissions—Common incentives for salespeople.

gain sharing plans—Cost-reduction incentives.

profit sharing plans—Distribute a fixed percentage of total company profit to employees on a periodic basis or can be used as retirement plans.

income statement: The final statement reporting all revenues, gains, expenses, and losses for the period.

individual pay treatment: Rewarding individual employees for their relative contributions to a given job.

intermediate-term loan: A debt of one to five years duration.

internal recruiting: Promotion and transfer of current employees to vacant jobs.

international union representative: An employee of the national or international union with whom the local union is affiliated. The responsibilities of the international representative are to organize the unorganized worksites in a specified jurisdictional area, perform service functions for local unions, and represent the international union on committees that bargain labor contracts with employers.

inventory: A current asset representing goods and materials on hand ready for sale or which will be manufactured for sale to customers. *To inventory* means to physically count items in stock or to calculate the cost of items on hand.

job analysis: A systematic procedure for obtaining information about a particular job in order to establish a basis for accurately describing that job. Job analysis answers the questions of who does what, when, why, how, and under what conditions.

job competency training programs: Plans that focus on ensuring that the trainee is able to perform the job's actual tasks in a competent manner.

job description: A written document that defines the major responsibilities and tasks of a job.

job evaluation: A procedure that systematically compares the complexity of the jobs within an organization without taking into consideration the pay for those jobs or the individuals' performance on those jobs.

joint venture: Two or more separate entities or persons joining together to perform a project or projects on a predetermined and negotiated basis.

just-in-time (JIT) philosophy: The Japanese manufacturing philosophy focused on eliminating waste.

Kanban: A Japanese production control information system based on using one or two cards between adjacent manufacturing operations to signal the production and movement of materials between these operations.

key jobs: Sometimes called *benchmark jobs:* jobs that are stable in content, commonly found across organizations, and contain a large number of workers. These key jobs are used to price wages in the external labor market.

labor market: The geographic areas from which employers obtain employees.

labor organization: Sometimes called *union* or *employee associations;* those employee groups who bargain with employers over wages, hours, terms and conditions of employment.

liquidation value: The expected net cash proceeds from sale of an asset other than in the normal course of business.

long-lived assets: A balance sheet classification covering all assets other than those classified as current. Synonymous with *noncurrent assets.*

long term: Noncurrent; extending beyond one year from the balance sheet date.

long-term debt: Obligations that will not require current assets in settlement within one year (period) of the balance sheet date. Synonymous with *noncurrent liabilities.*

long-term loan: A debt to be repaid over a period of time longer than five years.

loose labor market: A situation in which there are more people looking for work than jobs available.

management: The process of getting the work done through people.

marketing: Activities concerned with the sale and distribution of a firm's products or services according to needs of customers.

marketing concept: An orientation toward customer satisfaction and profit maximization as the two overriding and compatible long-term goals of an enterprise.

market niche: A position for a company, product, or service that takes into consideration customers, market, company, and competition.

master production scheduling: The function of planning end item requirements based on the dependent demand requirements for capacity and material availability.

material requirements planning: A production planning and control information system to support manufacturing by planning and controlling material and capacity requirements.

mean absolute deviation: A measure of the error of a forecasting model. The smaller the MAD, the better the forecasting model. The sum of the absolute values of the deviation of forecast from demand divided by the number of observations.

mediation: Attempts by a mediator to introduce solutions to the issues causing the deadlock that have not been put forth by either party.

mediators: Third-party neutrals that perform conciliation and mediation activities for parties in dispute. A mediator contacts the parties and offers assistance in the event that the parties perceive difficulties in reaching a collective bargaining agreement or reach a bargaining impasse. The mediator (as opposed to arbitrator) has no power to impose solutions to the issues causing a bargaining impasse. Rather, using various persuasive techniques, the mediator helps the parties to solve their own disagreements.

"meeting the payroll": Slang for maintaining solvency.

merit pay programs: Programs designed to increase the pay rates of individuals based on their contributions to their jobs. The most common contributions are performance and seniority (or loyalty to the company.)

method of accounting: An acceptable and understood concept of financial accounting for determining when to recognize assets, liabilities, and items of income and expense.

Military Selective Service Act (MSSA): Specifies that members of the U.S. military have a right to get their jobs back or be placed in a job of like seniority, status, and pay when they regain their civilian status.

National Labor Relations Board (NLRB): A federal agency that regulates the enactment of the Labor Management Relations Act. The NLRB has three purposes: (a) to supervise the democratic election process through which employees choose to either be represented by a union of their choice (certification election), or choose to cancel the contract with the union which represents them (decertification election); (b) to conduct hearings called unit determination hearings in order to determine the extent to which employees desire to be represented by a particular union and also to determine the appropriateness of the composition of the group, called the bargaining unit, which seeks union representation; and (c) to investigate and prosecute acts by employers and unions that are considered unfair labor practices under the law.

net income: The difference between the total of all revenue and gains and the total of all expenses and losses for a period. The bottom line of the income statement.

net liquid assets: Includes cash and current marketable securities less current borrowings.

net profit: The profit remaining after the deduction of all expenditures. (It may be expressed as net profit before taxes or net profit after taxes.)

net sales: The residual dollar amount of gross sales after deducting returns, credits and allowances.

net working capital: The amount of working capital in the business representing a necessary long-term investment by creditors and owners. Equals total current assets minus total current liabilities (see also *working capital*).

nonconstraint: Resources for which excess capacity exists.

Occupational Safety and Health Act of 1970 (OSHA): Requires employers to eliminate recognized hazards and to comply with specific safety and health guidelines.

Office of Federal Contract Compliance Programs (OFCCP): Responsible for compliance to Executive Order 11246. This agency is primarily responsible for compliance review—examining the employer's written affirmative action plan and visiting employer locations to determine whether the employer obeys the mandate to "take affirmative action."

operating agreements: Agreements that specify how the entity will be operated, which may modify the normal operating rules.

OPT philosophy: A manufacturing philosophy focused on identifying and managing the constraints to a business.

organization: The coming together of individuals to achieve a purpose that cannot be independently achieved by any one individual.

organization structure: The assignment of responsibilities and decision-making authority to all members of the organization, usually shown by an organizational chart.

orientation training: A formal program for giving new employees information about the company and about their jobs.

paid-in capital: The capital or equity contributed to a corporation by its owners.

partnership: Generally, a voluntary agreement between two or more persons to contribute their money, property, or skill to the operation of a joint business or common enterprise for their common benefit and to divide the profits and bear the losses in certain proportions.

pay: Wages, salaries, and adjustments to the pay rate the employee received when he or she first started the job.

pay-for-knowledge plans: Called *skill-based pay*, *multiskill-based pay*, or *pay for learning*, plans that pay employees for the amount of knowledge they possess or the number of skills that they have acquired.

pay level: Average wages or salaries paid by a company.

pay structure: The array of pay rates for jobs within a company or the relative pay of jobs within the company.

performance evaluation systems: Processes that enable the organization to ensure fair and consistent treatment of employees and help to (a) communicate the organization's expectations to employees; (b) monitor employee job performance and good citizenship behaviors; and (c) document satisfactory and unsatisfactory job performance and citizenship behaviors.

periodic review procedure: A method of accounting for inventory where the cost and the number of units used are determined only through taking a physical inventory at the end of a given time period.

perpetual inventory procedure: A method of accounting for inventory at the time of use of the inventory item.

post-petition payments: Payments or transfers to creditors or other parties after the date of filing the petition.

pre-emptive rights: The rights of the shareholders of a corporation to acquire proportional amounts of the corporation's unissued shares upon the Board of Director's decision to issue them.

preferred stock: A type of equity financing for a company that has priority over common stock for distribution of assets and equity.

preincorporation agreements: Agreements among the shareholders-to-be, signed before the corporation is formed, that deal with the operation and governance of the corporation after formation.

prepetition payments: Payments or transfers to creditors or other parties prior to the date of filing a petition of bankruptcy or reorganization.

priority control: The process of comparing the planned sequence to the actual sequence of work and taking corrective action.

priority planning: The process of determining the sequence of working on items.

process control: The activity of measuring the correctness of the process in making the good or service, which occurs during, not after, the process.

process or functional layout: Machinery is arranged with similar equipment in given departments.

product layout: Machinery is arranged based on product flow, with different machinery sequenced to minimize material flow between operations.

pro forma: Hypothetical or projected statements.

progressive discipline: A discipline program in which punishments increase in severity as the number of violations increase.

proprietorship: A form of business owned and operated by an individual which does not have any of the formalities found in a partnership or a corporation.

quality circles: A worker-involvement program in which groups of six to ten workers from the same work area meet voluntarily to identify and solve problems related to productivity and quality.

reach: The dollar amount spent on an ad divided by the number of people, in thousands, exposed to the ad.

reaffirmation agreement: Agreement whereby the debtor in effect reassumes the debt with the creditor. It can be under the terms of the original note or a new note can be executed. The creditor is treated as if bankruptcy never occurred.

recognition award programs: Programs that give awards for specific contributions employees make to the organizations. Such contributions include performance, good citizenship, and company loyalty.

redeem the collateral: To pay secured creditors the fair market value of the collateral. Payment must be as a lump-sum payment. For example, if the amount of debt is $12,000 and a vehicle's fair market value is $6,000, the debtor may redeem the debt by paying creditor $6,000; balance is an unsecured debt.

retained earnings: Net income not yet distributed to owners. The sum of the income since the start of the corporation, less all dividends declared (cash and stock).

Revised Order No. 4: Provides employers with a list of steps to take to provide affirmative action in employment of members of protected classes.

revolving credit line: A preestablished dollar limit for borrowing that includes a ceiling on the interest rate and a term for repayment.

routing: The sequence of operations to be performed to manufacture a part.

safety stock: Inventory above the forecasted demand, held in case the forecast is wrong.

satellite business: A business whose purpose is to supply goods or services to another business. Generally, the other business is a larger-scale organization.

secured debt: Debt upon which property of all kinds has been pledged. Must be perfected by the filing in the proper office of evidence of said debt, such as a security deed, possession of collateral, motor vehicle certificate of title, UCC-1 (financing statement).

selection procedures: Tests that the company uses to select employees from a qualified pool of applicants.

short-term loan: A debt to be repaid within one year.

sources of funds: The places, activities, individuals, or groups from which a firm may obtain working capital for application elsewhere. Sources include operations, extraordinary gains, sale of long-lived assets, new long-term debt, new owner investment, and reduction of the balance of net working capital already on hand.

spreadsheet: A computer software package that provides you the capability to construct a template of detailed or complex calculations and to vary figures within the spreadsheet to rapidly recompute the complete analysis.

staffing: Filling positions in the organization with suitable employees. Staffing includes recruiting (identifying and attracting a qualified pool of applicants to seek jobs within the organization), selection (choosing employees to hire from the applicant pool), and placement (matching the chosen employees to organization jobs or to training programs that will prepare them to work effectively.)

statement of cash flow: A statement indicating cash generated from operations during the period, together with all other sources and applications of cash during the period. A statement prepared on a cash, as opposed to working capital, basis.

stepped-up basis: A new basis equal to the fair market value of the item of property as of the date of the new basis.

super priority lien: A lien granted in exceptional cases by the bankruptcy court superior to the then existing liens.

taxes: *business taxes*—Those taxes levied by a government jurisdiction as applied to some aspect of the business.

FICA taxes—Federal Insurance Contribution Act (social security).

personal—Taxes levied against your personal income.

sales or excise taxes—Those taxes generally levied against sales to the final customer. However, there are taxes levied against sales of specific items or specific services.

special taxes—Those taxes levied for a specific revenue purpose, generally of short term duration.

unemployment taxes—Those taxes based on the number of employees you have and the stability of their employment.

worker's compensation taxes—Those taxes levied against the employer to compensate for any of your employees that are injured in line of employment.

tight labor market: A situation in which the demand among employers for people with particular skills exceeds the available supply.

time-phase order point system (TPOP): An inventory system that calculates actual inventory requirements based on forecast per week or month and on hand and planned inventory balances.

TPOP is quite useful for seasonal and lumpy demand items.

Title VII of the Civil Rights Act: Federal employment law that mandates that employers provide equal employment opportunities to employee categories defined by the law as protected classes. Title VII covers almost all employers having more than fifteen employees and prohibits discrimination in employment practices because of race, color, religion, sex, or national origin.

tracking signal: A measure of the bias (continuous underestimating or overestimating of demand) of a forecasting model.

trade credit: Deferred payment for services, goods, materials, supplies, or equipment obtained from a vendor.

two-bin system: A simplified inventory control approach in which inventory is placed in two containers—a use and a reorder container. When the use container is empty, an order is placed. When the order is received, both containers are refilled and withdrawal begins again from the use container. The amount of inventory in the reorder container covers demand during lead time and safety stock.

unemployment compensation laws: State laws that provide income to workers who are temporarily unemployed and are searching for suitable employment.

unguided on-the-job training: Trial and error learning on the job.

union contract: Sometimes called *collective bargaining agreement* or *labor-management contract;* a dynamic contract that consists of three elements: (1) compliance with federal, state, and local employment and labor laws, (2) written agreement, and (3) practice and custom established within the workplace. The union contract is a major exception to the employment at will doctrine because it gives employees the legal right to fair and impartial treatment by their employers.

unions: *local union*—An organization of workers confined to a single establishment, employer, or geographic area. The vast majority of local unions are chartered by national unions and can be considered organizational units of the nationals (or internationals) whose rights and responsibilities are determined by the constitution of the national (or international) union.

national or international unions—Organize and represent workers in particular trades, professions, industries or government bodies. The international designation is used by national unions who have organized at least one local union outside the boundaries of the United States, usually in Canada.

utilization analysis: A method that compares the number of equally skilled women and minorities in a company's workforce with their availability in the relevant labor market.

Vocational Rehabilitation Act of 1973: Like Executive Order No. 11264, this act applies to government contractors and subcontractors and requires affirmative action for qualified handicapped individuals.

Walsh-Healy Public Contracts Act: Regulates the compensation practices of employers who hold government contracts.

winding up: The settling of the accounts and liquidation of the assets of a partnership or corporation for the purpose of making distribution and dissolving the concern.

word processing: A computer software package that provides the capability to type and edit (reorganize, delete, add, spell check, format, and so on) documents.

workers' compensation laws: State laws that provide income continuity to workers who cannot work because of illnesses and injuries that arose out of and in the course of employment, defined as *compensable injuries.*

work group: A social group that has a certain amount of influence over its members. The group's influence is based on the norms or shared values that guide the behaviors and beliefs of the group's members.

working capital: In general business use, refers only to total current assets. Total current assets less total current liabilities are defined as net working capital. Possibly because accountants use the term current assets, some texts define working capital as current assets minus current liabilities, and therefore discard net working capital as redundant. Because both definitions are in use, you must be careful to identify the meaning of this term in each situation.

work samples: Selection procedures that require the applicant to demonstrate performance or ability in executing the job's tasks.

INDEX